Oracle Press™

Oracle SOA Suite 11g Handbook

About the Author

Lucas Jellema is CTO at AMIS, an Oracle, Java, and SOA specialist based in Nieuwegein, The Netherlands. He works as a consultant, architect, and instructor in diverse areas such as SQL and PL/SQL, Java, Oracle ADF and WebCenter, and SOA Suite. The running theme through most of his activities is the transfer of knowledge and enthusiasm.

Lucas is an author at the AMIS Technology Blog (http://technology.amis.nl/blog), for Oracle Technology Network, and for international magazines. He is a frequent presenter at international conferences, including Devoxx, JavaOne, Oracle Open World, ODTUG, UKOUG, OBUG, AUSOUG, and Oracle University Celebrity Seminars. He was nominated Oracle ACE in 2005 and ACE Director in 2006.

Before joining AMIS in 2002, Lucas worked for Oracle Consultancy in The Netherlands, where he was a member of the Internet Development Center of Excellence—working on classic products such as Oracle Designer and Forms and the productivity boosters Headstart, CDM RuleFrame, Echo, Repository Object Browser, and JHeadstart.

About the Contributors

Edwin Biemond is an Oracle ACE and solution architect at Whitehorses, specializing in messaging with Oracle SOA Suite and Oracle Service Bus as well as ADF development with Oracle JDeveloper, WebLogic Server, and Security. His Oracle career began in 1997 when he was a database developer and administrator. Since 2001 Edwin changed his focus to integration, security, and Java development. Edwin was awarded with Java Developer of the Year for 2009 by *Oracle Magazine* and has a popular blog called Java / Oracle SOA blog, which can be found at http://biemond.blogspot.com.

Lonneke Dikmans lives in The Netherlands with her husband and two children. She graduated with a degree in cognitive science at the University of Nijmegen, The Netherlands. She started her career as a usability specialist, but went back to school when she lived in California to pursue a more technical career. She started as a J2EE developer on different platforms (Oracle, IBM) and specialized in integration. She now works as an architect, both on projects and as an enterprise architect. She has experience in different industries: government, financial services, and utilities. She advises companies that want to set up or improve a service-oriented architecture, and is responsible for her company's SOA/BPM practice. She speaks regularly at conferences in Europe and the United States, and publishes frequently on the Internet and in magazines. Lonneke became an Oracle ACE Director in 2006.

Ronald van Luttikhuizen is a senior consultant and information and solution architect at Approach, a Netherlands-based ICT consultancy focusing on SOA and Business Intelligence. Ronald has an MSc in computer science from Utrecht University. He has experience in ICT in various roles, such as coach, (lead) architect, (lead) developer, teacher, and team lead. In the last few years, Ronald had focused on architecture and security in BPM and SOA environments. He has in-depth knowledge of Oracle Fusion Middleware. Ronald is a speaker at (international) conferences such as Oracle OpenWorld and regularly publishes articles on Oracle Technology Network (OTN), *Java Magazine*, Optimize, and more. In 2008, Ronald was named Oracle ACE for SOA and Middleware, and in 2010 he became an Oracle ACE Director in that area.

About the Technical Editors

Jeff Davies is a senior principal product manager at Oracle, specializing on the Oracle SOA Suite product. He is the author of *The Definitive Guide to SOA: Oracle Service Bus*. Jeff has over 25 years of experience in the software field and has developed retail applications such as Act! for the Windows and Macintosh platforms and a number of other commercially available applications. He has worked as an architect and developer and ran his own consulting company for some years. Now, at Oracle, Jeff is focused on the practical application of Oracle products to create SOA solutions.

Mike van Alst is an independent architect and Oracle ACE Director. Active within the IT industry since 1984, Mike focuses on the added value that ICT should bring to an organization. Mike has done several successful SOA projects in The Netherlands using Oracle Fusion Middleware. He runs his own blog on SOA at http://soamastery.blogspot.com.

Oracle Press™

Oracle SOA Suite 11g Handbook

Lucas Jellema

New York   Chicago   San Francisco
Lisbon   London   Madrid   Mexico City   Milan
New Delhi   San Juan   Seoul   Singapore   Sydney   Toronto

The *McGraw·Hill* Companies

Cataloging-in-Publication Data is on file with the Library of Congress

McGraw-Hill books are available at special quantity discounts to use as premiums and sales promotions, or for use in corporate training programs. To contact a representative, please e-mail us at bulksales@mcgraw-hill.com.

Oracle SOA Suite 11*g* Handbook

1 2 3 4 5 6 7 8 9 0   DOC DOC   1 0 9 8 7 6 5 4 3 2 1 0

ISBN   978-0-07-160897-8
MHID   0-07-160897-4

Sponsoring Editor
Lisa McClain

Associate Acquisitions Editor
Meghan Riley

Editorial Supervisor
Jody McKenzie

Project Manager
Rajni Pisharody,
Glyph International

Technical Editors
Jeff Davies
Mike van Alst
Ronald van Luttikhuizen

Copy Editor
Bart Reed

Proofreader
Lisa McCoy

Indexer
Jack Lewis

Production Supervisor
James Kussow

Composition
Glyph International

Illustration
Glyph International

Art Director, Cover
Jeff Weeks

Cover Designer
Pattie Lee

Contents at a Glance

PART III

Administration, Security, and Governance

PART IV

Beyond the Basics

Contents

PART II
Developing Composite Applications

PART III
Administration, Security, and Governance

PART IV
Beyond the Basics

Foreword

Oracle Fusion Middleware 11*g* is an extraordinary release in the rich history of Oracle. It provides the foundation for Fusion Applications as well as a complete, open, and integrated platform for the development and integration of modern as well as legacy applications by organizations around the world. FMW provides the tools that enable Service-Oriented Architecture (SOA), Business Process Management (BPM), and Event-Driven Architecture (EDA), based on all the relevant industry standards. Business agility and adaptability is the primary objective, achieved through reuse, encapsulation, interoperability, and loose coupling. Oracle SOA Suite 11*g*, in conjunction with various other key products in the FMW stack, helps organizations design and build, test and deploy, secure, administrate, and govern composite applications according to these architectural guidelines.

This book provides a wealth of information to different types of readers interested in Fusion Middleware and specifically the SOA Suite. Although developers are probably the primary audience for this book, it would seem that IT management staff and business analysts, as well as administrators and testers will find a lot of useful content from the perspective of their respective jobs. The book provides a comprehensive background on the business objectives and potential benefits of introducing Service-Oriented Architecture as well as a concise historical overview of the evolution of both industry standards around services and the Oracle technology that implements those standards, giving great insight in the evolution of the SOA Suite and its role in Oracle's Fusion Middleware stack. It goes into the details of creating BPEL processes and making optimal use of the Mediator, Business Rule, and other service components and adapters. But it also describes how to deploy, secure, administer, and do governance for SOA composite applications. The last part goes beyond the basics, touching on advanced topics and integration between many different parts of Oracle FMW—including ADF and WebCenter—and concluding with a glimpse into the future.

The publication of this book comes at a good moment—at the time when Fusion Applications, as the biggest proof point of Fusion Middleware to date and the best example of applying SOA Suite 11*g*, has started its rollout. And at a time when key components such as BPM 11*g*, OSB 11*g*, OER 11*g*, CEP 11*g*, and Spring Java have all been integrated with SOA Suite 11*g*. The book manages to discuss all these components—and their application to address real business challenges in an imaginary hospital. And although this fictitious St. Matthews Hospital may not be an exact duplicate of your own organization, it possesses many characteristics that will be similar enough as to make the examples in this book useful sources of inspiration for your business environment.

Another aspect of this book is quite close to my heart. Back in 2004, Oracle launched the Oracle ACE and ACE Director program, which formally recognizes Oracle advocates with strong credentials as evangelists and educators in their communities. Since that day, some 200 Oracle ACEs have been nominated as well as close to 100 ACE Directors, across all the various technologies and product lines that are relevant to Oracle and its customers. It is great to see that no fewer than seven ACEs and ACE Directors have collaborated on this book in some form, with many more of them making smaller contributions along the way. It shows how a strong community has evolved among these highly professional individuals and how they participate to share their collective experience and passion for Oracle's products with the rest of the world.

I trust this book will live up to its promise in empowering you to start taking advantage of the full potential of Service-Oriented Architecture through the use of Oracle SOA Suite 11*g*. The information, examples, and pointers should give you the knowledge, enthusiasm, and skills that will prove invaluable when you consider, start, or continue using the product.

Thomas Kurian
Executive Vice President
Oracle Product Development

Acknowledgments

Many people have contributed to this book along the way. And undoubtedly I will not be able to give them all the credit they are due. My heartfelt apologies for anyone I fail to mention.

It all started with Peter Koletzke, who invited me to the Oracle Press author party and introduced me to Lisa McClain, from McGraw-Hill. She liked what she saw—well enough at least to sign me on as an author. Note that this was very early 2008, and to her credit she kept faith where many might have given up on the project, as it was not a smooth ride for the first year and a half.

I would like to thank Lonneke Dikmans, who joined me as co-author in the early days of the project. She helped me shape it, devise the themes and chapters, the case of St. Matthews, and the early drafts of several chapters.

The support I received at AMIS, from the management team and all my colleagues, was simply tremendous. The interest they showed throughout the project, the patience they had with me through some of the more challenging moments, and the encouragement they kept giving me have been very important to me. I have especially treasured the discussions with Peter Ebell, AMIS Expertise Lead for SOA.

Of similar importance was the support I have felt from my fellow members of the Oracle ACE and ACE Director program. Their faith and positive expectations have been very encouraging. I hope this final product meets with their approval.

I would like to thank the technical editors, Mike van Alst, Jeff Davies, and Ronald van Luttikhuizen. Their feedback has helped to polish and refine the book, chuck irrelevant content, and clarify anything I had made unclear. I would like to highlight Ronald's contributions: He has provided countless valuable comments and suggestions, from spelling corrections to structural changes to chapters, and everything in between, both corrective and constructive. He has made a huge and undoubtedly positive impact on the book.

Ronald was not only a diligent technical editor, he also contributed Chapter 15 (on security) as well as part of the appendix (on migration from SOA Suite 10*g*). Edwin Biemond was co-author with Ronald on the appendix, and also made a great contribution. Lonneke, originally co-conspirator on this book, wrote the original drafts for Chapters 1, 2, and 13 and helped in many other ways during the early stages.

It has been a pleasure working with the team at McGraw-Hill: Lisa McClain and Meghan Riley. They kept me on track, forced me along when needed, and kept faith throughout a sometimes bumpy ride. I hope the final result is as satisfactory to them as it is to me.

Many thanks to Rajni Pisharody and Bart Reed, the copyediting team at Glyph International, who turned my fairly crude texts into the book that you have in your hands right now. We worked together in an efficient, smooth, and pleasant way.

At various stages during the creation of this book, I have been helped by several members of various Fusion Middleware Product Management Teams. They provided insights, backgrounds, and inside information, as well as early access to documentation and software. They also reviewed the initial table of contents and provided useful feedback throughout the process. I would like to thank all who have helped, with a special word of thanks to Demed I'Her, Heidi Buelow, Clemens Utschig-Utschig, Dave Berry, and Duncan Mills.

Last and never least, of course, I want to mention the vital support from Madelon and our boys, Tobias and Lex.

Introduction

Service-Oriented Architecture is one of the major trends of our time in enterprise and IT architecture. The promise of business agility, lower costs, and improved quality of operations that SOA presents to business, based on concepts such as loose coupling, reuse, encapsulation, and interoperability, attracts many organizations. Complemented with Business Process Management (BPM) and Event-Driven Architecture (EDA), SOA can add real and sustained business value to enterprises.

Adopting SOA in an organization is a serious challenge that will require major efforts at various levels, from business to IT infrastructure. Crucial to the success of SOA adoption are sometimes intangible elements, including mindset, collaboration across departments and lines of business, communication, process orientation, and business analysis—in terms of interfaces and contracts, with focus on reuse and loose coupling and the implementation of proper governance.

When it comes to the actual implementation of the services and components that have been analyzed and designed, there is a need for an SOA platform—a run-time infrastructure that executes the applications and processes, handles service calls, and provides facilities around security, exception handling, and management. Enter Oracle SOA Suite 11g.

SOA Suite 11g is one of the key components in Oracle Fusion Middleware, a prominent platform to create and run agile and intelligent business applications and to maximize IT efficiency by exploiting modern hardware and software architectures.

This book explains what SOA Suite 11g is, how it can be installed and configured, and how its many components can be used to develop, deploy, and manage service-oriented artifacts. It also discusses how SOA Suite interacts with other products in Oracle FMW.

About This Book

The book is primarily targeted at software developers. Ideally the reader has some knowledge of XML, SQL, and Java and perhaps PL/SQL, but these are not required to benefit from most of the book's content. Readers with administrative responsibilities will find a lot of material supporting them in these tasks. Testers and (technical) architects will also learn a lot from large sections in this book. IT management staff and business analysts will mainly benefit from Part I; if they have a technical background, then Parts II and III will prove worthwhile as well.

The book is organized in five parts. Part I introduces the concepts that make up Service-Oriented Architecture and describes the history of Web Services and SOA-related standards and technology. It concludes with the installation of SOA Suite 11*g* and the creation and deployment of the HelloWorld equivalent in SOA applications.

Part II discusses the development of SOA composite applications using the core service components—BPMN, BPEL, Mediator, Business Rule, Spring Context, and Human Task—and the technology adapters—File System, Database, JMS, and EJB. It also introduces the Oracle Service Bus, the platform to implement the enterprise service bus that connects departments and external partners.

Part III addresses administration and management activities. It focuses on security, deployment, and lifecycle management, management of composites and composite instances, and dealing with changes. Governance is the final large topic in this part of the book.

Part IV is called "Beyond the Basics." It introduces two products that are closely related to the SOA Suite core run time, but provide functionality that is usually considered nonessential and more advanced. These products are Oracle Complex Event Processor and Oracle Business Activity Monitor. This part also discusses the integration between SOA Suite and the Application Development Framework (ADF). The last chapter looks at the application of SOA concepts to user interfaces and also presents the case of SOA in SaaS (Software as a Service)—style applications and cloud-based infrastructures.

Part V contains a number of appendixes with background information on migration, fundamental XML technologies, detailed configuration of the SOA Suite run-time environment, and its APIs and extension points. Note that three of these appendixes are provided online rather than in the printed book.

St. Matthews Hospital Center

Implementing SOA is meaningless without a tangible business context. Services address business requirements, as do composite applications. To illustrate SOA and Oracle SOA Suite, this book uses the case of a made-up hospital, called St. Matthews, that's located in California—although it has a surprising number of Dutch traits as well.

This hospital represents a series of business challenges that are found in organizations across industries and countries. It has interactions with external parties (including customers and business partners), strives to create more efficient business processes across departments that combine automated actions and manual tasks, needs to implement security, continually faces changing requirements with ever shorter times-to-market, and hopes to gain more real-time insight into the current state of affairs.

Many of the solutions discussed in this book for St. Matthews set useful examples for similar requirements in other organizations. And at the very least, St. Matthews provides a context that most readers from many different countries will be able to relate to.

How to Use This Book

The book you are holding is not intended as a reference manual that is easily used to look up specific details on an operation or feature in the SOA Suite.

This book is primarily a guide that invites you to come along and explore the SOA Suite. It introduces concepts and real-life requirements, using the imaginary St. Matthews Hospital as the concrete example. It describes the functionality and features in particular components in the SOA Suite and applies them to actual business challenges. Through step-by-step cases that go beyond the archetypical Hello World and introductory order-processing examples, it demonstrates the application of product features, provides hints and tips for using them, and suggests best practices.

Most is gained from this book by not only browsing and reading it but by also getting your feet wet by following along with the hands-on instructions in the book and the online chapter complements. By having your hands do what your eyes are reading and your brain is processing, you will have a multichannel learning experience that delivers the most thorough and lasting results.

The main case in the book is the patient appointment process in which appointments with doctors and other staff at St. Matthews Hospital are requested, approved by insurance companies, scheduled, cancelled or kept, billed for, and reported on. The case is built up throughout the book, each chapter leveraging the work done in the previous chapters. Even though you can read individual chapters, be aware that they will often refer to decisions made in earlier chapters or implementations created in a previous stage.

There is more to this book than meets the eye. In addition to the printed volume you are currently holding (or reading on your electronic device), there are many online resources that accompany this book: the book's wiki, the online chapter complements, and the online appendices.

Wiki

An area inside the Oracle Wiki has been prepared for this book (see Figure 1). Organized per part and per page, the wiki holds many (references to) resources, such as relevant sections in the Oracle documentation for the SOA Suite and other components in Fusion Middleware, links to the OTN forums and download pages, articles on blogs and websites that further illustrate or complement the subjects discussed in the chapter, downloadable source code for the cases in the chapter, a link to the online chapter complement, and errata. The wiki is expected to be a dynamic environment, with new resources being added as time goes by, including news on software releases, new articles and showcases, information on relevant events, and discussion threads.

The wiki for this book is located at http://wiki.oracle.com/page/Oracle+11g+SOA+Suite+Handbook.

Online Chapter Complements

There is only so much detail you can include in the 800-or-so pages available in this book. I have been struggling at times to find the right balance in the level of detail, the number of screenshots, and the scope of the topics given the physical limits of the book. I finally found the solution via online chapter complements: Most of the chapters in this book are accompanied by an online complement that provides more detailed step-by-step instructions, an abundance of screenshots, additional background information, and practical tips. Some cases are only briefly introduced in the book and worked out in detail in the complement.

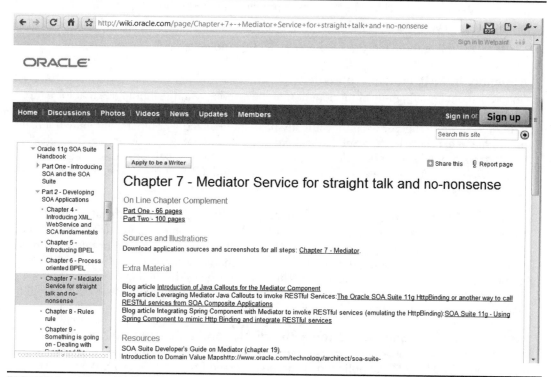

FIGURE 1. *The wiki for SOA Suite 11g Handbook with references to online resources*

You will find the online chapter complements as PDF documents organized per chapter on the website http://groups.google.com/group/the-oracle-soa-suite-11g-handbook-/web.

Online Appendixes

In addition to the 21 chapters and one appendix in the book you have before you right now, there are three more appendices available online. Furthermore, an extended version of the appendix in the book has been published online as well (as Appendix A). The information in these appendices is not considered essential to every reader, but can be useful in specific conditions nevertheless. You will find these online appendices from this URL: http://groups.google.com/group/the-oracle-soa-suite-11g-handbook-/web.

Appendix A: Migration from SOA Suite 10*g* to 11*g*

Appendix A describes the aspects and approaches for migrating from SOA Suite 10*g* to 11*g*. The online complement for this appendix discusses several detailed scenarios for specific components and artifacts that may not be relevant in all situations. Among the topics discussed in this online extension are:

- Domain Value Maps
- Custom XPath and XSLT functions

- Advanced BPEL characteristics, fault policies, unit test suites
- Oracle Web Services Manager (OWSM)
- Technology adapters (WebService, JMS, AQ, and Database)

Appendix B: XML Fundamentals

Chapter 4 contains a high-level introduction of the standards and technologies that form the foundation of the SOA Suite: XML and XSD, WSDL, and SOAP. For many readers, that overview will serve as a refresher for what they already have internalized. For others who may not have had as much exposure to Web Service technologies, it may not nearly be enough to feel comfortable around some of the discussions in the book. Appendix B provides more background and details on the fundamentals of XML, XSD, XPath, and XSLT. Furthermore, it provides links to more extensive resources.

Appendix C: Preparation and Configuration of the SOA Suite Infrastructure

Chapter 3 provides brief instructions on the installation and initial configuration of the SOA Suite. The online chapter complements for this and several other chapters contain or refer to additional instructions for configuration of the SOA Suite, the technology adapters, and some additional components such as a local e-mail server. This appendix gives detailed instructions for the configuration steps required on top of the default installation of the products to carry out all the hands-on examples described in the book.

Appendix D: SOA Suite Run-time APIs, Hooks, and Extension Points

Chapter 12 discusses how Java can be used to implement functionality inside composite applications and how SOA applications can be accessed from within Java programs. This appendix discusses the interaction from Java as well as PL/SQL with the run-time APIs of the SOA Suite itself—for example, for reporting on running and archived instances and performing administrative tasks upon them, for publishing events to the Event Delivery Network, or to leverage APIs in the workflow service and the User Messaging Service. It also describes how we can extend the functionality of the SOA Suite run-time engine by registering custom XPath functions that can add functionality to BPEL, Mediator, and Human Workflow actions.

PART

I

Introducing SOA, St. Matthews, and the Oracle SOA Suite

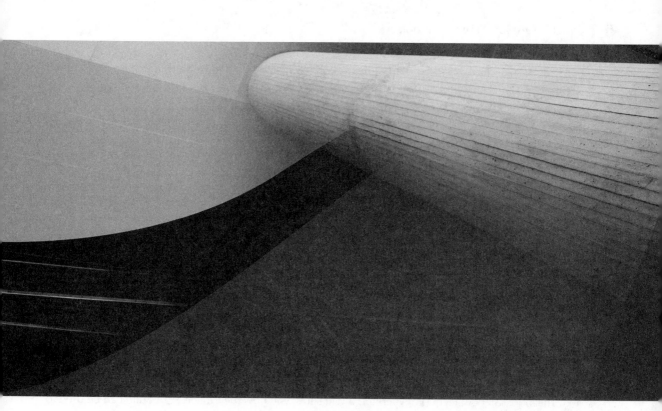

CHAPTER

1

A Typical Case of SOA: Introduction of St. Matthews Hospital Center

OA is BAD! So there, I have it off my chest. It had to be said. It needs to be out in the open. It is really BAD!

Okay, what is SOA again? Service-Oriented Architecture. So clearly it is about architecture (more on that in the next chapter) and about services (more on those throughout the book). But what is this BAD stuff?

It is my way of drawing your attention to the fact that SOA is really about *Business Agility* and not about technical tricks. SOA helps us realize *Business Agility* through *Decoupling*. There you have it: *BAD*. Business agility means the ability of an organization to adapt to new circumstances, opportunities and threats, regulations, and technological advances. IT departments that enable their organizations to flexibly and speedily adjust to new business requirements give these companies a competitive edge, lower costs, and higher quality in the execution of business processes.

SOA gets its significance from the objectives it helps achieve. Some of the most important of these are defined at the business level—not in technical terms, and not directly in the context of the IT department. Business agility is an example of these objectives—others are discussed in the next chapter. Other benefits from SOA *are* achieved in the IT department; of course, these, too, will ultimately contribute to the business results.

SOA is not primarily driven by technology—it is not the latest version of a development framework or a faster edition of a CPU. It is first and foremost driven by business requirements and with business objectives in mind. Having said all that, it should be equally clear that service-oriented computing and the establishment of Service-Oriented Architecture are only possible because of the technology available to us.

This book is about technology alright: It will show you how the Oracle SOA Suite can be used to implement many different aspects of SOA. You will see demonstrations of all the components in the SOA Suite, each playing a slightly different, specialized role in creating services and implementing business processes.

However, all these demonstrations of applying tools and technology can only make sense in the context of an organization that works to achieve business objectives. You do not do SOA stuff just for the technological kick—you do it for business reasons.

This book uses a fictional hospital, St. Matthews Hospital Center, as the business context for the concepts discussed in this book (Service-Oriented Architecture, events and Event-Driven Architecture, and business process modeling) as well as the examples of using Oracle SOA Suite 11*g* and its components. Although we use a hospital, the issues and solutions described here apply to other organizations as well.

This chapter introduces St. Matthews and its business challenges, and provides some of the background that will help you understand the examples discussed later in the book. This chapter might also help you draw parallels to your own organization, especially concerning some of the challenges facing St. Matthews, both at the business level and from an IT perspective. The hospital is fictional, constructed from many examples collected in dozens of organizations around the world, many of them based in The Netherlands.

Note that you can safely skip this chapter (and the next one for that matter) if all you are interested in right now is getting going with the SOA Suite.

Introduction to St. Matthews Hospital Center

St. Matthews is a regional hospital that primarily serves residents in its vicinity. Lately it has attracted some patients from a wider region and even from out of state. The hospital has formulated its mission as follows: "St. Matthews is a modern, flexible, and capable hospital for the residents in the region.

Its goal is to offer high-quality medical care that is easy to access, in an environment where patients feel at home."

It is important to note that both flexibility and quality are in the mission statement. Flexibility is needed because of the ever-changing rules and regulations in healthcare, as well as new treatments and advances in pharmacy, clinical technology, and logistical facilities. Quality is needed because of increasing competition between hospitals, scrutiny from consumer groups and patient platforms, and lurking personal injury lawyers. Quality is not only measured in terms of medical success, but also in terms of patient satisfaction. Even though the mission statement does not explicitly mention it, it goes without saying that a sound financial state of affairs is a necessary condition.

History

St. Matthews has a long history. It was founded in 1850 as a hospital for the poor. Money to build the hospital was raised by local members of the Catholic Church. The nurses were nuns who moved from different cities to help out in the hospital. In 1975, the hospital merged with the hospital in the neighboring town and was named St. Matthews. In the 1990s, government policy was to merge small local hospitals into larger regional hospitals. St. Matthews merged with two smaller local hospitals to form a regional hospital in 1995. Nowadays, funding for new buildings and patient facilities still depends on the local business community: In 2000, a building was donated by local companies to celebrate the 150th birthday of the hospital. Today, the nuns are gone and have been replaced by trained nurses and volunteers. The board of directors is supported by managers of the different departments, and supporting units make sure the hospital can run its day-to-day business. The medical specialists are still there, supported by sophisticated technologies such as electrocardiogram (ECG), laboratories that test tissue and blood samples, and imaging technology.

Trends in Healthcare and Hospitals

As mentioned previously, in the 19th century, most hospitals were built to care for poor people. They depended on gifts from the community. Patient satisfaction was not a major concern; fundraising and public health issues were. At the end of the 20th century, a trend toward larger hospital organizations with professional management resulted in many mergers of small hospitals. Cost reduction and higher quality through scaling were the main drivers for this trend. However, this did not prevent waiting lists from growing. Nor did it reduce the cost of healthcare as it was intended. This was partly because of developments in the field. Technological improvements in, for example, imaging technology, as well as medical breakthroughs in treatment of diseases, led to higher costs for healthcare per patient. Treatments have become more expensive due to advanced equipment, and an increase in patient life expectancy has resulted in more and prolonged treatment per patient, which in turn results in more treatments per patient.

Other trends are increased security demands and the potential worldwide spread of diseases due to globalization. Because of the increased use of the Internet, doctors don't have a monopoly on medical knowledge anymore. Consumer organizations and patient platforms have become important lobbyists. As a result, patients are given more choice: They can decide to go to another hospital if they wish. This makes it more important for hospitals to compete with each other and meet their patients' demands. Government regulations dictate that hospitals report their results in a standardized format to an electronic address. National initiatives have started to encourage collaboration between healthcare providers.

The Hospital from an Architectural Point of View

Technology has become more and more important in the day-to-day operation of St. Matthews. This applies to medical equipment such as magnetic resonance imaging (MRI), but also to the application of Information and Communication Technology (ICT) in all sections of the hospital. Business processes, strategy, and financial management rely on information management. This demands a strong alignment of IT with the business. For that reason, the hospital decided to investigate whether applying enterprise architecture would be beneficial. They have hired an enterprise architect from a local firm to get them started. Mary Johnson has been hired for the project. Her assignment is defined as follows: *Translate the vision and strategy of St. Matthews into an architecture plan and define the steps needed to realize this architecture.*

Showing the board of directors the value of enterprise architecture at an early stage is important to ensure she has the support from the management of the hospital. Enterprise architecture can structure and link business information and propose IT solutions that support business goals. This does not have to take years of thinking and documenting, because a lot of the information is usually already available in some shape or form and can readily be (re)used.

Mary proposes to define three views—or layers—to start with:

- A business architecture view that describes the processes and functions in the hospital. The strategy, organization, and key performance indicators (KPIs) are modeled in this view as well as the primary processes, management processes, and supporting processes. She starts by modeling a high-level overview. Details will be added later, when she has a better idea of the problems and strengths of St. Matthews.

- An information architecture view that describes the structure of the data and the different applications that implement the structure. The data models within the different applications are pretty easy to find. The more interesting part in this context is formed by the data that is exchanged between information domains and between organizations. The structure of this data should be application-independent because it already involves at least two interacting applications. A common approach is to abstract the data formats away from the applications in canonical data models.

  The applications are assigned to business information domains, not to the departments that are currently using the applications.

- A technical architecture view that describes the hardware, middleware, and network topologies of the hospital. Mary herself will not go into the details of this physical layout of the hospital. The information management department has diagrams describing these details. The focus for Mary right now is on the vision, or a statement of direction. Therefore, she will focus on logical components for this view.

Because the hospital has no tool to model the enterprise architecture, Mary decides to introduce the Oracle BPA Suite as a modeling tool because it has support for several diagrams that depict architectural designs.

The following sections elaborate on the three different architectural views to provide an overview of the current situation of St. Matthews.

Business Architecture View

Mary decides to start from the top with the business architecture. She begins by identifying strategy and business needs. She has a lot of information to work with; although the hospital has little or no experience with enterprise architecture, it has started several initiatives that can be used as input for the business architecture. As part of these process improvement efforts, the hospital has already described most of the important processes. Other input for the architecture is the annual report published by the board of supervisors. To identify the business principles, goals, and drivers that the architecture plan needs to support, Mary will describe the following:

- **The organization and its external partners**   This will identify the stakeholders for the architecture in St. Matthews.

- **The strategy that St. Matthews has formulated, with some critical success factors for the goals and strategy**   It is important that design decisions be linked to these goals and critical success factors to make sure the architecture actually supports the business objectives and strategy of St. Matthews.

- **The key performance indicators**   The KPIs will be used to measure the success of St. Matthews in achieving the identified goals.

- **The business processes in the hospital**   The architecture should chart the primary, supporting, and management business processes of St. Matthews.

The Hospital Organization

The region that St. Matthews serves has 250,000 residents. St. Matthews has a capacity of 600 beds. There are 2,000 employees, 125 medical specialists, and over 100 volunteers. The hospital has three locations to make it more accessible to patients and visitors. The hospital treats 150,000 patients per year, both outpatient and inpatient care.

The hospital board of directors is responsible for the strategy. The board of supervisors is responsible for the governance code that is in place. The board of directors consists of both medical staff representatives and patient representatives. Several supporting departments report to the board of directors, including:

- **Marketing and communication**   The marketing and communication department is responsible for both internal and external communication. This means the department needs to communicate with patients, their relatives, and employees. The external communication is directed at people who live in the region, as well as family doctors and other healthcare providers such as pharmacists and physiotherapists. One communication medium the hospital uses is the Internet. The website of the hospital consists of several parts: general information about the hospital, a site where patients and visitors can get information, and an area that is only accessible for registered healthcare providers.

- **Human resources management**   The human resources department is responsible for recruitment of all personnel, assessments, and career planning. The human resources department tries to minimize the number of employee sick days, decrease the number of people who quit their job, and increase the efficiency of the departments. Career planning, selection criteria, and assessments of personnel are all important instruments for the HR department to increase job satisfaction, as are fringe benefits.

- ■ **Information management**   Apart from being responsible for IT in the organization, the information management department is also responsible for the alignment of IT with the business. This means technical employees as well as business-oriented people work for this department to communicate with other departments about changes, requirements for new projects, and opportunities that new technology can offer the hospital. In the technical architecture view of this chapter, we will look at this department in more detail.

- ■ **Quality assurance**   This department is responsible for quality assurance. It monitors the quality and effectiveness of the hospital. Part of the quality system is patient safety and compliance with rules and regulations. This department is responsible for handling patient complaints and reporting key performance indicators to different regulatory organizations.

- ■ **Legal services**   This department takes care of all legal affairs of the hospital and its staff. It deals with patients' rights, hospital liability, legal aid for employees in liability suits, compliance issues when new laws arise, and firing employees who don't perform.

- ■ **Accounting, planning, and control**   This department translates the plans of the board of directors to the budget. This includes cost for patient care (production budget), exploitation costs, personnel costs, education budget, planned investments, and current and planned projects.

The primary processes in the hospital are all about patient care. Two clusters are responsible for patient care:

- ■ **Surgical care cluster**   This cluster is organized around specialties such as plastic surgery and dermatology, but also contains units responsible for operating rooms, admissions, planning, and so on.

- ■ **Internal care cluster**   The internal care cluster has units such as cardiology and lung diseases, as well as units for psychiatry and social services.

Two units support the day-to-day operation of the patient care units:

- ■ **Supporting units**   This department includes groups such as laboratories and radiology. Sophisticated medical technology is applied here by highly technically skilled people.

- ■ **Facilities**   This unit includes hotel services, procurement, housing, technical services, and logistics. These facilities are highly visible to both the patients and employees of the hospital.

External Relations

In general, a hospital deals with three types of relations: other healthcare providers, insurance companies, and patients (see Figure 1-1). The other providers can be hospitals, ambulance services, pharmacies, family doctors, and many other types.

The hospital treats patients and cooperates with other healthcare providers to accomplish this treatment. The patient pays the insurance company for health insurance. Depending on the insurance policy, the hospital is paid by the insurance company or by the patient. When the latter is true, the patient might (try to) claim the money from the insurance company, depending on the coverage specified by the policy. The hospital sometimes reports a planned treatment in advance to make sure it is covered by the patient's insurance policy. With some insurance policies, patients

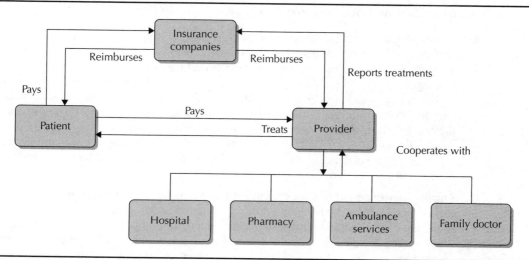

FIGURE 1-1.   *Relationships in healthcare*

are required to go to the hospital designated by the insurance company. Therefore, the insurance companies are important to St. Matthews. They determine to a significant degree how many patients will actually come to St. Matthews for treatment instead of another hospital.

Strategy
St. Matthews has chosen the strategy shown in Figure 1-2. This strategy is centered around the main objective of becoming the preferred hospital for patients.

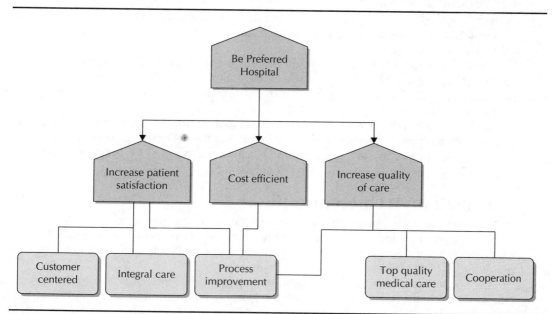

FIGURE 1-2.   *Objectives and critical success factors*

This main objective can be realized through three subobjectives:

- **Increased patient satisfaction** Several critical success factors are associated with this objective. First of all, the hospital needs to be "customer centered." Not the doctor, but the patient should be the starting point in the daily operations of the hospital. Second, the hospital needs to provide for integral care. So rather than having specialized clinics for different diseases, the hospital should be a one-stop shop for patients. The third and final critical success factor to increase patient satisfaction is process improvement. Process improvement can reduce the chance of human error and also increase patient satisfaction because care will be more efficient. Shorter waiting lists and appointments scheduled in accordance with patients' needs—not driven by the doctor's schedule alone—are examples of this.

- **Quality improvement of care via innovation and process improvement** New technologies—both medical and information technology—can improve the quality of patient care. Process improvement can reduce the number of errors and therefore also improve the quality of medical care. Cooperation with other hospitals, insurance companies, family doctors, and pharmacies also increases the quality of care.

- **Cost reduction** Because of advances in medical science and technology, more expensive treatments can—and will—be given in the future. This means that people will live longer and need even more care. Cost reduction is important in this competitive market, especially for insurance companies. The critical success factor for cost reduction is process improvement.

To accomplish all this, St. Matthews will create an environment that is safe and inviting and that stimulates entrepreneurship for its employees.

Key Performance Indicators

All hospitals need to report on specific key performance indicators (KPIs) to make a comparison of hospitals more straightforward for patients, insurance companies, and healthcare providers that refer patients to hospitals.

The key performance indicators that need to be reported can be divided into the following categories: patient satisfaction, safety and quality, patient care and organization of patient care, personnel and organization, financial organization, environment of the hospital, and research and education.

St. Matthews has decided to use these KPIs as input for process improvements. To accomplish this, the KPIs have been associated with one or more of the defined objectives. These objectives should eventually lead to the main goal of St. Matthews: to become the hospital of choice for the region, which itself is measured through the number of patients treated in St. Matthews.

Information Architecture View

St. Matthews has gone through several reorganizations and mergers. To organize the information in the hospital, Mary decides to define functional or business domains (see Figure 1-3), rather than departmental clusters. Every domain is characterized in that it is the owner of both the data it uses and of the associated processing methods.

The hospital uses a number of IT systems to support the different business domains. A common type of system in the healthcare industry is the Hospital Information System (HIS). This usually is

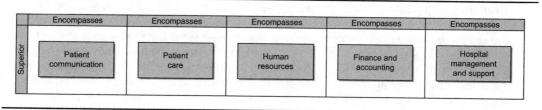

FIGURE 1-3.   *Business domains of St. Matthews*

a commercial off-the-shelf (COTS) application from a large vendor in the field. It is designed to manage all the hospital's medical and administrative information in order to enable health professionals to perform their jobs effectively and efficiently. It often consists of the following modules: clinical information system, financial information system, laboratory information system, nursing information system, pharmacy information system, picture-archiving communication system, and radiology information system.

After the mergers, the department of finance and administration (F&A), as well as the human resources department, managed to consolidate their IT: F&A migrated everything to SAP ERP Financials, and the HR department successfully consolidated on PeopleSoft Enterprise HCM. The consolidation of the other applications has never been finished. There is no single integrated Hospital Information System, but instead a series of applications with overlapping functionality and data. With the exception of the picture-archiving communication system and the radiology information system, all modules are custom built as separate applications *for almost every department.* This means that the processes that span departments are inefficient and there is an abundance of errors. Errors occur because different departments use different definitions for the same concepts or have the same definition for different concepts. There is no such thing as a shared canonical data model. Errors also occur because data that is available in one department is not available in the other department. Another source of errors involves typos and spelling errors.

A representative example is the current process of making appointments between doctors and patients. There are more than ten applications somehow supporting this process currently in use at St. Matthews, varying from custom-made applications to Microsoft Excel spreadsheets. Recently, this has become an even bigger problem because of new laws and regulations. The government demands that reports about KPIs be delivered to a central website every year. Because there are different systems, data is duplicated all over the place. The information about the same patient in real life can be stored in various ways with different attributes and attribute values in different systems. This means that compiling these reports requires manual development of queries, despite all the Business Intelligence (BI) tools at hand. Another challenge is integration and communication with external partners.

External Partners

As mentioned in the discussion of the business view of the hospital, St. Matthews has relationships with other healthcare providers, with patients, and with insurance companies. There is a growing need for information exchange. The intent is to use international and national standards as much as possible for this information exchange, both for interaction between two applications within the hospital as well as for exchanges between St. Matthews and external partners. One such industry standard in the health sector is HL7, which is often used in Hospital Information Systems.

Insurance Companies Currently, point-to-point integration is used by St. Matthews in batch processes to exchange data with insurance companies. Every night, files with records of treatments are sent to the insurance companies for processing. After some time, the results are sent back and checked by the hospital. If a claim record is invalid, it needs to be resent with the next batch.

The files to be submitted to the insurance companies are created using several different modules in the Hospital Information Systems. A custom application that gathers and reconciles all the data from the different Hospital Information Systems has been built by the IT department of St. Matthews. The results returned from the insurance companies are loaded into SAP ERP Financials.

Patients Little electronic communication exists between patients and the hospital at the moment. There is a website with information about the location of the hospital, visiting hours, and telephone numbers, information about the organization of the hospital, and information about disease prevention. "St. Matthews online" is the content management system that is being used by the hospital to facilitate this portal-like site. The marketing and communication departments would like to extend its functionality and create more online interaction with patients—for example, to have patients review and update their appointments and perhaps even request new appointments.

Healthcare Providers Many national and international initiatives have started to facilitate electronic exchange of data between healthcare providers. St. Matthews is part of the following initiatives:

- **Electronic Patient File** A national initiative to facilitate the exchange of patient files between healthcare providers.

- **Regional information exchange** Family doctors in the region and St. Matthews have agreed to use a common system to register referrals.

- **Hospital collaboration** St. Matthews collaborates with several other hospitals to do research on certain topics. Details about the research are exchanged and aggregated to speed up the process and improve the quality of the work.

Technical Architecture View

As was described in the previous section, a lot of different systems are used in the hospital. The hospital has a combination of commercial off-the-shelf (COTS) applications and custom-developed applications. The COTS applications, such as SAP/R3, Planon, and PeopleSoft, are all implemented by external companies. The projects are managed by the project managers of St. Matthews. The custom-built systems are developed using PL/SQL and Oracle Forms by developers in the in-house IT development unit. The Business Intelligence solutions are also implemented by their own development department. A variety of solutions are used for this: Cognos, SQL, and PL/SQL for "on-demand" queries, reports from SAP, and custom reports using Oracle Reports.

The information management department is responsible for the technical architecture. However, the relationship between the other departments and the information department is deteriorating. IT projects are almost always over budget and late, and the users don't get what they need or what they expect. Blame is shifted from the IT development and project management units to the business consultancy group and the application management and support team, but that, of course, does nothing to solve the problem.

Software and Programming Languages

The hospital runs three operating systems: Enterprise Linux for the servers, Windows Vista for the workstations, and Windows 7 for the Microsoft Exchange Server. The company has standardized on Oracle for the DBMS. This is true for all applications: Planon, SAP/R3, PeopleSoft HCM, "St. Matthews online," and the custom applications. Two web servers are currently in use: Apache 2.0 and Microsoft IIS. The middleware installed at the hospital is Oracle Application Server 10*g*. The hospital uses Microsoft Active Directory for authentication and authorization.

The programming languages used in the company are PL/SQL, Oracle Forms, Java and JEE, ABAP for SAP, and PeopleCode for PeopleSoft.

Interfaces and Standards

At the moment it is impossible to tell exactly how many interfaces exist between applications. There are many point-to-point interfaces. Some are part of products that were bought, such as the interface between Planon and SAP. Others are custom-built by developers using a variety of techniques and protocols. These range from database links to HTTP calls and file exchange through FTP. A lot of time and effort is spent in keeping these interfaces up and running.

The hospital has not been able to standardize all the external communication, yet. However, like most hospitals, it does use HL7 version 3.0 for communication about patient data.

Summary

St. Matthews is a fairly well-run regional hospital that strives to be the preferred hospital for patients and insurance companies. To become the preferred hospital, St. Matthews needs to increase patient satisfaction, become more cost-efficient, and increase the quality of care. This has an impact on both the business and the IT sides of St. Matthews. The hospital has decided to use enterprise architecture to trace the business drivers all the way down to the IT systems, and even the infrastructure they run on. This will ensure that the architecture of the hospital is fully aligned with the (business) strategy of St. Matthews. The next step is to design a suitable architecture for St. Matthews, given the business objectives discussed in this chapter and continued in the next.

CHAPTER
2

Introduction to Service-Oriented Architecture

lexibility, or business agility, is an important goal for modern organizations in order to compete in fast-changing markets, keep up with ever-evolving regulations, and satisfy demanding customers. Globalization and the Internet have greatly influenced the rate of change and the range of opportunities for interacting between business partners and reaching out to consumers.

It is the challenge to IT departments the world over to meet the quickly changing requirements from the business—and ideally to provide their organization with innovative capabilities and a competitive edge based on new technological advances. IT needs to be flexible to cater to fast-changing business needs and to realize short times to market—preferably at lower costs and with higher quality. IT can add value to the business in the form of new products and services. Last but not least, IT can improve current operations by reducing (human) errors, reducing the turnaround time of processes, and providing real-time insight in the execution of operations and its possible bottlenecks.

Architecture strives for alignment between business and IT. This chapter introduces Service-Oriented Architecture (SOA) and discuss how it delivers specific capabilities in the overall alignment: SOA aims at providing the agility to quickly respond to changing requirements by rewiring existing and assembling new functionality through the reuse of existing building blocks (services) and providing capabilities in an interoperable, cross-platform, and cross-domain manner; functionality is exposed through services with well-defined interfaces and encapsulated (hidden) implementations.

Associated with SOA are various other topics that warrant our attention. One such topic is Business Process Management (BPM)—a continuous process improvement endeavor that's focused on designing, executing, and monitoring business processes and looking for ways to optimize them; business processes in BPM consist of human tasks and automated operations—the latter implemented through calls to Web Services. BPM promises more control and higher quality, lower costs, and an intrinsic capability to rapidly change the process flow. BPM integrates with and can build on SOA. BPM is discussed in Chapter 11.

Another topic that borders on SOA and that can be seen as an extension or specialization of SOA is Event-Driven Architecture (EDA)—a pattern that promotes a high degree of decoupling between systems and components through event-based, asynchronous communication via a generic mediator from producers to consumers; EDA allows business processes to initiate service execution in response to events without creating direct dependencies that would hamper the ability to change the components. This chapter briefly introduces EDA; it will make reappearances in Chapters 9 and 20.

SOA, BPM, and EDA are related, as you can see in Figure 2-1. The business processes in BPM raise events when certain business conditions occur and call services to perform automated tasks. The services may invoke other services as well as trigger additional events. The event mediator handles the events produced by processes and services, and propagates them to any registered consumer—possibly a service to be initiated or a process to be triggered or updated.

The SOA Suite contains components that help to implement these architectural patterns and also works with other products that provide some of these capabilities. In Part II as well as in Part IV of this book, we will use these components to implement services that provide reusable capabilities and that can be assembled in even more complex and specific business services with higher added value. We will also use them to develop business processes that combine human tasks with the automated functionality from the services. Events produced by services and processes are processed by the event delivery network that hands them to consumers.

Before we start using the SOA Suite product, let's first further define and discuss Service-Oriented Architecture, albeit on a very high level. We will identify some legitimate reasons for

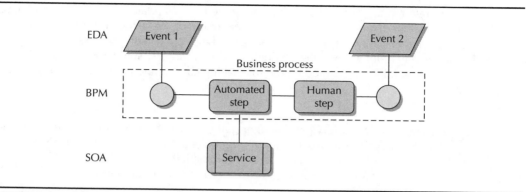

FIGURE 2-1. *SOA, BPM, and EDA*

companies to start with SOA and show why Mary, our architect from Chapter 1, is considering applying these architectural patterns and approaches for St. Matthews as part of the proposed architecture solution. Note that if you just want to get started with the SOA Suite product, you can skip this chapter for now and turn to Chapter 3 for installation and quick-start guidelines.

Service-Oriented Architecture (SOA)

Service-Oriented Architecture is a way of organizing applications and processes in terms of services. Functionality available through automated means is exposed in services that can easily be used and reused. However, services do not need to be automated: An action performed by a human actor can be regarded as a service, too. In fact, one of the key aspects of working with a service is that we do not know how it is implemented or whether it is automated at all.

An important objective and benefit of working with services is decoupling—the ability to have services interact while minimizing their interdependencies. The latter allows us to make local changes with minimal impact on the whole environment, such as modifying the implementation of a service, changing its physical location, or even replacing one service with another. In addition, complex services and processes can easily be composed that offer rich, dedicated functionality by assembling results based on multiple less complex services.

SOA is an architectural concept that has different implications for different people in an organization.

Several important factors that drive the choice for SOA are:

- Increasing competition and changing rules and regulations leading to the need for more frequent and more rapid changes in business processes and IT support for those processes
- A higher degree of integration throughout an organization, across business domains, and across technology platforms
- Increased interaction with external business partners and governmental agencies
- A more process-oriented approach in the way IT supports the organization and a quest for lower costs and higher quality through reuse of existing, proven IT assets

The cornerstone of SOA obviously is the concept of a service. SOA is all about services. And what exactly is a service? For our purposes, we can define a service as a collection of capabilities (sometimes referred to as operations) that are defined in a standardized interface contract and can be invoked by external consumers. The implementation of the service is encapsulated, hidden from the consumers. Services in the context of this book are usually Web Services that have the additional quality of interoperability through the use of industry standards, both for specifying the service contract and for the protocol used for making calls to and receiving responses from the service.

We can discern several types of services:

- **Business services**   Services that offer quite dedicated, often complex functionality defined in business terms and supporting tasks in business processes (called business services or task services); these services are typically exposed to consumers throughout the business domain, the enterprise, or even to a wider audience.

- **Elementary services**   Services with fine-grained functionality with limited scope, often working in the context of a single business object; these services do not offer very high value by themselves, but are good candidates to be reused in the more complex business services. As a result, these so-called entity or elementary services are only locally exposed.

- **Technical services**   Services with no immediate business relevance, supporting other services with cross-domain, technology-oriented capabilities—for example, for logging, transforming, and exception handling. These services are also called utility services.

NOTE
There are many excellent and usually quite voluminous books on the concepts and principles of Service-Oriented Architecture (see this book's wiki for some references). This chapter only aims at giving a pragmatic introduction to some terms and concepts; please refer to one of these extensive resources for detailed discussions and thorough definitions.

We will discuss SOA from several points of view. We will first look at SOA as seen from the business—in terms of business considerations such as cost, risk, opportunity, time-to-market, flexibility, and customer satisfaction in a way that makes sense to nontechnical managers. This discussion includes IT and the IT department—not at the technical level, but in the same business-oriented way.

Next, we discuss SOA from an architecture point of view. We try to get clear on what architecture tries to achieve and what the key architectural principles of SOA are. This discussion introduces a number of terms and definitions that are reused throughout the book. It provides a high-level description of several key infrastructural elements used in an SOA—without going into specifics concerning the components in SOA Suite 11*g* that play the role of those elements (that is for later in the book).

Finally, we come to the technical and implementation level and go into some technical aspects of adopting SOA. We also talk about some of the crucial industry standards and technologies that make SOA happen today.

It is unavoidable to have some overlap between these three points of view. They certainly do not make sense in isolation.

SOA from a Business Point of View

Why would you want to adopt SOA from a business perspective? Service orientation promises business agility. SOA is "BAD," as we saw in the previous chapter: Business Agility through Decoupling. SOA should help us to adapt our business processes and the underlying IT systems much faster, cheaper, and more reliably than we could in the past. Reuse of proven building blocks in new composite services and reworked business processes should allow both for quicker time to market (reuse instead of building from scratch) and higher quality (reuse of services that have been tried and tested). The decoupled design helps to minimize the impact of changes—in terms of effort and risk. There is, of course, a cost benefit in all this as well.

Another trigger for SOA from a business perspective is competitive pressure, demands from a key customer or state regulations. An organization may simply need to have the capability to interact through (Web) Services because important business partners or the government stipulate that. Just the implementation of a Web Service interface exposed to the outside world does not necessarily force the organization to adopt SOA across the board, of course, but it can be the crystallization point.

What does it mean from a business point of view to describe your architecture in terms of services? We have our working definition of a service—capabilities described by a contract and exposed in a way that hides the implementation and allows invocation by various types of consumers, potentially in different business domains, in other technology realms, and even in external organizations. There are different types of services (business, elementary, and utility), but from a business point of view, we only care about services with a clear meaning and value to the business and in business processes—services that the business wants to use in processes and user interfaces or offer to internal consumers in the same or in different business domains or to external clients and partners. Examples of services with business relevance are:

- A service that returns all information about a patient to consumers inside the hospital.

- An ordering service that customers of a manufacturing company can invoke to place their orders (and track the status of those orders).

- An invoicing service for suppliers of a particular company that they can send their bills to.

- The discount calculation service that returns to internal invokers the total discount on an order calculated based on all business logic regarding customers, loyalty programs, order size, and current campaigns. This service is typically invoked as part of a business process around order handling—a process that may very well be initiated by the ordering service mentioned previously.

- Central communication services available to all departments in the organization, such as an e-mailing service or a service for letter printing and mailing.

These business services are usually composed of one or more elementary and utility services. Flexibility is achieved in several ways. Organizations can rapidly create new business services through composition of existing services. In addition business processes are defined as a sequence of human activities, logical flow elements, and calls to business services. As a result, changing a business process, or even creating a new one, is usually a fairly simple task because it largely means rewiring the flow and adding or modifying calls to the services. The hard work was already done—when the services were implemented. Another benefit we get from the layered approach with business services building on elementary services is the adaptability it gains us. It is not just rewiring or recomposing services and processes; it is also the fact that because of reuse, especially of elementary services, a required change (for example, in a calculation or the structure of a database table) typically only needs to be applied once in a single service implementation. Fine-grained, low-level functionality is ideally implemented only once in an elementary service that is frequently reused.

Talking about products and services is not new for organizations or business people. The great thing about SOA is that not just the business is speaking terms of services and products, so is IT. This will make communication between IT and the business easier, both during the initial realization as well as in maintenance. Defining business services won't make the architecture service-oriented, obviously. IT needs to follow through the concept of services all the way down from the business processes and services to the elementary and utility services that do the actual work. Reuse and decoupling need to be engrained in the IT organization.

Existing applications and business logic will have to be exposed as services. Most of the capabilities the services will need to provide are already available, hidden away in legacy applications, ready for reuse. We do not and should not need to throw those away and replace them with code built from scratch. However, we need to win the hearts and minds of the IT staff to adopt the service-oriented way of thinking and acting. This will take training, coaching, and coaxing. As with any new acronym, SOA may be perceived as trying to change the world in a dramatic way—and it should be clear to those involved that while things will change, it is not so much a threat as an opportunity to hang on to many good things and improve what has been holding them back all these years. It is with the IT staff just as it is with the applications themselves: Wrap and reuse, do not rip and replace.

We will have to do some work to service-enable the existing applications, both for exposing their reusable logic—as discussed earlier—as well as to make them reuse services offered to them. We may currently have duplication of business logic in various systems—that situation is undesirable. Ideally, any piece of logic is implemented only once, is exposed as an elementary service, and is invoked from anywhere that logic is currently used. We should identify such code duplication, determine which of the "duplicates" is the one to stay, service-enable that one, and ideally call the service from all other current duplicate locations to reuse and de-duplicate.

When and why should an organization move to SOA? Basically there are three types of motivators—although they are usually related and overlapping:

- Strategic reasons
- IT needs
- Tactical reasons

Strategic Reasons

Organizations that are in fast-changing markets, or in markets with fast-changing laws and regulations or frequent acquisitions and mergers, need to be able to react to these changes in an effective and efficient way. The organizations have to "embrace change" as their mantra. Every single change is usually tactical, but the structural capability of an organization to adapt to changing circumstances is a strategic objective. An organization can decide to use SOA as a way to achieve this strategic business goal to continuously adapt and improve.

SOA can help reduce time to market by making it possible to compose new services out of existing services and redesign business processes in short cycles. SOA can help reduce cost by reusing existing assets (such as mainframes and commercial off-the-shelf software such as ERP systems) in new online services. Some examples of companies in such markets are telecommunication companies (fast-changing markets because of new products and technologies and mergers), insurance companies (fast-changing laws and regulations, mergers, and internationalization issues), and government agencies (changing laws and regulations, cost reduction, and e-government for easier and uniform accessibility).

In the case of St. Matthews, these issues apply as well: The hospital needs to compete with other hospitals, and changes in laws and regulations occur frequently. To the hospital, reusing existing assets is very important. St. Matthews has invested heavily in a number of custom-made systems in the past and is very reluctant to start all over again—because of the time it would take and especially the costs involved. Mary decides to address the need for agility at St. Matthews and to propose SOA as part of the envisaged architecture to the board of directors.

Tactical Considerations

Organizations often suffer from inflexible IT systems. Large monolithic applications tend to mix business logic, user interface logic, and data; there is no clear separation of concerns, and logic is duplicated across applications. These systems often serve multiple functions from different domains. For example, the clinical information system that St. Matthews uses started out as a billing system. To send a bill to a patient or the insurance company, the system needed to include information about the treatment this patient received. There was no system available that offered this information, so it was decided to add this capability to the billing application.

The IT department and the hospital administrators started to use the system as a patient administration system. Soon afterward, it was further expanded with data about laboratory tests. What started out as a lean, easy-to-maintain, single-purpose system grew to a large monolithic system serving several purposes. When somebody requests a change for one purpose, this strongly impacts or even breaks some area of functionality—because it is all manacled together. Every change becomes more difficult to realize, takes more time, and becomes more risky and expensive. The user satisfaction with the system has understandably gone down.

Introduction of more loosely coupled components will reduce the cost of individual changes—because the modifications do not ripple out—and increase the ability to satisfy requests from the users in a timely fashion. Of course, this flexibility comes at a price—or at least so it will be perceived initially: Architecture needs to be thought through, middleware infrastructure is required, and existing applications need to be service-enabled. In the very short term—the scope of a single business requirement—this will not have a great return on investment, obviously.

In the longer run, the IT organization can once more provide the service levels required by the business in terms of time to market, quality, and cost of new requirements as well as the predictability of the software development process. The IT organization could, instead of being the eternal bottleneck, step forward and even suggest business functionality based on technological advances. We will discuss this in more detail in the implementation view.

Loosely coupled components that are autonomous and relatively independent are an example of a more federated approach in the IT environment. Benefits of this federated approach with clearly identifiable, stand-alone components that can be united to work together include the early and more thorough design effort with each individual component, the standardization that is applied, and the resulting ability to deploy these components on various servers—thus allowing the optimal load distribution (and software license cost).

This focus on federation with loosely coupled stand-alone components leans on another important objective: intrinsic interoperability across applications, locations, business domains, project teams, and technology platforms. Interoperability between stand-alone components is the essence of service orientation. Interoperability requires standardized interfaces described by contracts along with up-front trust and acceptable service levels (for example, performance and reliability).

Somewhere in the middle between strategic and tactical considerations is the desire to be vendor-independent and to have the freedom to choose "best of breed" solutions for specific areas of functionality. Instead of being forced to buy all components from a single vendor, many organizations want to be able to shop around for the best possible deal and yet still have all products interact. A service-oriented approach and the underlying open standards enable that interaction. Therefore, all software components—whether bought from commercial vendors, acquired from open-source initiatives, or custom developed—must comply with this approach and these standards.

Sometimes a company starts with SOA because of a specific, urgent need from a specific department in an organization. An example can be a marketing division that wants to introduce short-term campaigns based on popular movies: As soon as a movie hits the top-10 charts, they want to start giving away gadgets with online orders. Those gadgets need to be sent along with the order to keep the extra cost down.

This means that the company needs to combine existing functionality (sending out orders) with new features (ordering and sending gadgets). Using Web Services to open up the legacy systems, as well as creating an ordering process that includes sending gadgets, can solve this problem. A Service-Oriented Architecture makes it possible to use the same functionality in different processes, and thus to be able to change these processes quickly and support specific short-term needs.

Another typical example is an organization with a very important customer that has demanded a Web Service interface for specific interactions, replacing the current manual operations or FTP-based data exchange. This customer needs to be satisfied urgently and, therefore, a small part of existing applications needs to be service-enabled. This can be done in relative isolation, without enterprise architecture dictating a service-oriented approach or SOA strategy.

Tactical—or perhaps we say "opportunistic"—implementation is different from a strategic SOA initiative in several ways: Strategic SOA is more planned and takes into account long-term goals. Tactical SOA solves short-term, localized problems. Strategic SOA has a bigger impact, potentially or eventually impacting the entire organization. Tactical SOA has limited impact; it is far less invasive. The benefit of tactical SOA is immediate and limited; that of strategic SOA can take a little longer. Strategic SOA takes governance into account, whereas tactical SOA tries to manage Web Services along with the traditional application. This poses a risk: If an organization is mid-size to large, it becomes unmanageable after a while.

Tactical SOA makes sense for while, but should mature to a strategic SOA to survive the hype. In fact, one may wonder whether "tactical" and architecture can really go together. Tactical use of SOA principles may solve an urgent, localized problem, but does not touch upon the true meaning and value of SOA. Even though SOA concepts are applied and service-oriented technology is used, there is no real thrust for decoupling, reuse, and enterprise-wide business agility. When tactical SOA-like implementations are not followed up with a strategic SOA initiative, they are hardly any better than traditional point solutions and point-to-point architecture.

Summarizing SOA from the Business Point of View

An organization usually has some combination of reasons to start with SOA. It might start tactical and move to strategic after the first successful projects. Or it starts with a combination of strategic objectives and IT considerations.

From a business perspective, there are both strategic and IT reasons to start with Service-Oriented Architecture for St. Matthews. In Chapter 1, the following strategic objectives were mentioned:

- The hospital needs to cooperate with other healthcare organizations to improve the quality of care.

- The hospital needs to improve patient satisfaction by becoming a customer-centered organization.

- The hospital needs to reduce cost.

Moving to a Service-Oriented Architecture can support these goals. Cost can be controlled by reusing existing assets, cooperation is facilitated by the use of (Web Service) standards, and patient satisfaction can be increased by offering new services to patients faster and ensuring that all departments in the hospital share information about patients.

The main IT reason to move to SOA is the current inability to handle change. As just mentioned, a simple change request from the business takes up too much time due to duplication of business logic and data redundancy, as well as silo-style applications in which process flow, business logic, user interface logic, and data integrity are intertwined and not available for reuse.

Mary has already defined the business services and products of the hospital. She will propose to the board of directors to start a proof of concept with the information management department to evaluate the suitability of the architecture choice based on SOA for St. Matthews.

SOA from an Architectural Point of View

Service-Oriented Architecture is an architectural style. But before we can investigate what this means, let's first define what we mean by architecture. The definition of architecture used in ANSI/IEEE Std 1471-2000 is as follows:

"The fundamental *organization* of a system, embodied in its *components,* their *relationships* to each other and the environment, and the *principles* governing its *design* and *evolution.*"

Components and Their Relationships

The *A* in SOA stands for architecture. So when we are discussing SOA, we are speaking about architecture, and therefore we are talking about the organization of the system. For SOA this means that the organization of the system is described in terms of services. A service itself consists of several parts:

- A service interface that defines the operations, parameters, and result of a service in a common, standardized language.

- A service implementation that "does the actual work."

- A service contract that defines the terms of use: who has been granted access to the service, how often one can use it, and any fees charged for calling the service. Also part of the contract are the service levels offered by the service provider. These specify characteristics such as maximum service response times, availability (opening hours) of the service, and the load the service can handle.

Figure 2-2 shows the two key roles in SOA:

- **Service consumer** The application, business process, or (other) service implementation that uses the service

- **Service provider** The component or application that provides or implements the service

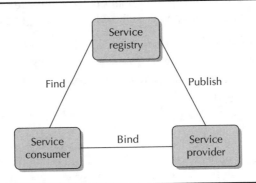

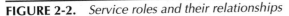

FIGURE 2-2. *Service roles and their relationships*

The third role in this figure (service registry) is discussed later on: It is the intermediary that brings consumers and providers together.

Architectural Principles around Service Orientation

As defined earlier, principles governing the design and evolution of service-oriented systems are part of architecture. Some of these principles are briefly introduced in this section. Note that a thorough discussion is beyond the scope of this book—see, for example, Thomas Erl's *SOA: Principles of Service Design* (2007, Prentice Hall) for such a comprehensive discussion.

Intrinsic Interoperability Service orientation and all the objectives it helps to achieve hinge on interoperability. Functionalities implemented in different applications, technology stacks, business domains, and/or physical locations need to work together. We need to be able to build bridges across traditional divides. A Java-based application must be able to invoke functionality implemented in C# running on a Windows server. And a PL/SQL application running in an Oracle database in the data center in St Matthews' central building needs to be able to interact with the invoice administration in SAP.

Interoperability—largely based on Web Services standards—is one of the key differentiators between Service-Oriented Architecture today and similar concepts and initiatives in past decades.

Loose Coupling Components cannot work together without some form of coupling—either directly on each other or through an intermediary. We need to carefully find the right level of coupling so that the interaction can take place efficiently enough yet the coupling does not inhibit our ability to change the implementation of components or add interactions with other components.

Coupling can exist along various axes. Examples include functional, technical, and temporal. A certain degree of functional coupling is unavoidable: A consumer needs to know the interface of a service in order to invoke it and process the response in a meaningful way. However, the interface should not expose more details than necessary, especially when a consumer may come to rely on such details. Technical coupling refers to the protocol used for communicating with a service as well as the way the messages are constructed (XML, comma-separated, JSON, binary, and so on). The more proprietary the requirements are that a service enforces on its consumers, the higher the degree of coupling. The use of open standards for interaction is an important element in reducing the level of coupling.

Synchronous interactions are pretty common. Yet compared to asynchronous communication, they have additional coupling: They require the service provider to be available when the request is made and to respond in a timely fashion. Asynchronous communication with service providers supplies additional decoupling. The effect the voice mail has on our ability to communicate by telephone is an example of decoupling synchronous interaction through the introduction of an asynchronous mediator.

In general, a higher degree of coupling means less flexibility because it becomes harder to allow components to evolve independently without ripple-down effects on their consumers. Loose coupling makes it easier to modify or replace a component without affecting other components. Loose coupling also makes the reordering of services in business processes more achievable—the service should not depend on the order in which they are invoked, only on the input passed into them.

Encapsulation, Abstraction, and Need-to-Know Basis   Consumers cannot form dependencies on what they do not know about the services they are invoking. That in itself is an argument for strict encapsulation. Anything that a service keeps to itself can be changed without impact on others. Security considerations are another reason for encapsulating the inner workings of services.

Examples of information that should typically be hidden from public view include details about the implementation, both the structure of algorithms and names of private operations, as well as anything about the tools and technology used for creating the implementation. The physical whereabouts of a service is another example of information that should largely remain undisclosed.

Autonomy of Components   The more autonomy a service has, the better it can perform its responsibilities and the easier it can evolve in a flexible manner. Autonomy exists both at run time and design time. Run-time autonomy refers to the degree of control a service has over its processing logic and its environment at run time. Greater autonomy—fewer dependencies on entities that are not controlled—means more freedom for run-time optimizations by administrators, thus leading to consistent, acceptable, and predictable behavior. Such optimizations can include changing the hardware configuration, relocating services, and utilizing hardware appliances to improve run-time performance or attain the required auditing or security levels.

Design-time autonomy refers to the level of freedom service owners and developers have to make changes to a service over its lifetime. When the service is used by few consumers and it is based on its own data model, it has a lot of room for maneuvering. When it is heavily reused and relies on a shared data model, that freedom is limited, depending on how loosely coupled the consumers are and how abstract the service's interface is.

The challenge is to balance our desire for reuse with the freedom to improve services. Loose coupling is obviously important to achieve autonomy (and vice versa), as are encapsulation and abstraction. A service that is not reused by anyone is quite autonomous, but fairly irrelevant as well.

Standardized Service Interface and Contract   In order to facilitate the process of discovering, understanding, and selecting services to reuse, and to automate the creation of interactions with services, it is important that all services be described in a similar way—preferably according to industry standards. The contract for a service consists of various elements, usually at least the following:

- A technical interface description with operations and parameters (input, output, and faults)

- A supporting data definition document that describes the structure of the parameters in detail

- A document specifying Quality of Service aspects of a service—for example, regarding security and reliable messaging

- A service-level agreement (SLA) that describes service characteristics such as response times, availability, and costs involved with invoking the service

- Additional metadata about the service that provides, for example, more elaborate descriptions of the functionality of the service, plans for its immediate future, and information on who is using the service, for what purpose, and what the user satisfaction ratings are

The standard service contract specifies the documents that should be provided in the contract and details the design standards that these documents should adhere to. WSDL (Web Service Definition Language) and XSD (XML Schema Definition) are often used as the underlying standards for the first two documents. Quality of Service aspects can be laid down in a structured document using WS-Policy and more specific standards such as WS-Security Policy and WS-ReliableMessaging. There is no industry standard for SLAs. It would make sense for an organization to design its own SLA template to use for all the service-level agreements it will publish for its services.

Reuse of Existing Assets   One of the important means of achieving agility is the reuse of existing assets when composing new applications and services. St. Matthews can reuse its existing Clinical Information System (CIS) by exposing its functionality through Web Services. This makes it possible to quickly implement composite services and business processes that rely on CIS functionality.

Services must be designed with reuse in mind: The functionality offered by a service should not be determined with a single project, process, or application in mind. Instead, a broader view should be taken, and the place of the service within the business domain or even the enterprise at large should be considered. The interface should not be too specific, tied to a single consumer's purpose. The services need to have the right granularity to invite reuse. More on this aspect a little bit later.

Reuse should be fostered—it typically does not happen overnight, nor does it happen on its own accord. Initially a lot of work may be required on the part of the architects to convince project teams to reuse instead of build from scratch. Management may have to offer some form of reward to get reuse going.

Of course, the infrastructure needs to support reuse: The reused components need to be accessible, available, and scalable. Furthermore, services must allow for concurrent access by various consumers.

Service Discoverability   Reuse can only happen when it is known which assets are available for reuse. Services need to be discoverable. The services need to have metadata associated with them to ensure that service consumers know the purpose of the services and the conditions that apply when invoking them. To facilitate the discovery of services, a third entity frequently joins the party of the service providers and consumers seen in Figure 2-2: an intermediary that helps to bring the other two together. This intermediary is usually called a "service registry," and provides a standardized method for dynamic lookups and/or design-time discovery of services. The service provider can publish its services in the registry, so potential service consumers can find the services they need, with enough information about the functional interface and contract, the service-level agreement, and the current usage of and the longer-term plans for the service, to make a decision on reusing it and how to go about it.

Intrinsic Characteristics of Services   Services should satisfy some general requirements in order to optimally contribute to the service-oriented computing infrastructure:

- **Granularity**   One of the endless debates in service design involves the granularity of the service. Should it be fine-grained, offering functionality that is quite generic, extremely reusable, and with very limited added value? Or should it be coarse-grained, offering tremendous value to very few consumers, with functionality that's very specific and hardly reusable? Services designers must strike a balance, which can be quite a challenge.

  Note that different forms of granularity exist: at the service level (the width of the functional scope of the service), at the level of individual capabilities, applied to data (do we exchange entire object graphs based on the canonical data model or just exchange specialized parameters for capabilities?), and applied to data constraints (how far do we go in defining constraints on the data flowing to and from the services?).

  You will find granularity discussions in the real world too—for example, department stores vs. specialty boutiques, or specialty rosary pliers vs. all-purpose pliers.

- **Atomicity**   A service should execute an atomic operation or transaction in its entirety. If not, an atomic operation would be split over multiple services (and we all know what happens when you split atoms). It would be nonsensical to make it the responsibility of a service consumer to have to invoke all providers of the subatomic parts of an operation. Note that a service may encompass more than one atomic operation, although typically several or all actions executed by the service are still part of a single transaction.

- **Idempotency**   Services should not produce unwanted side effects, especially when a request is submitted multiple times. The background for this capability is that sometimes a request sent to a service does not result in the expected response message. There can be several causes, including a failure to deliver or process the request or a problem with delivering the response. When the response does not arrive, the service may be invoked again. However, because the reason for the absence of the response could be a problem on the return trip of the response message, it may very well be that the service is executed for a second time.

  Ideally, we can prevent this situation from ever occurring by using reliable transports with guaranteed message delivery. However, that may not always be possible, and to cater to such situations the service should be idempotent. This can be achieved by recognizing duplicates of already processed request messages. Alternatively, the capabilities (operations) of a service can be designed not to produce unforeseen side effects. A very fine-grained example could be to design a capability used for raising salary not as raiseSalaryByX but as setSalaryAtX. The effect of invoking the latter service capability is very consistent and clear to the service consumer.

- **Statelessness**   Services should minimize their resource consumption by holding on to as little state information as possible. A successful service is ideally reused and composed many times over. Typically such successful services are invoked very frequently and simultaneously. To not overtax the shared infrastructure and resources—primarily memory—it is important that a service not hang on to large volumes of data. If necessary, especially for a longer-running service, to collect and construct data structures and have those available in later stages of service execution, this state can be transferred to infrastructure components that are optimized for handling state. Examples are a database such as the BPEL Dehydration store and a data grid such as Oracle Coherence. The load on the infrastructure can also be reduced by making a distinction between data that a service needs to process and data that it only needs to pass on; the latter does not need to be handled as state, nor does it need to be deserialized by the service. It could be shipped around as an attachment—or even less intrusive and burdensome as nothing more than a reference or claim check to a bunch of data. Only when the message flow has reached a component that actually requires the data does it have to be retrieved across the infrastructure.

Note that another way to reduce a service's burden on the infrastructure is to offload CPU or other resource-intensive operations to specialized engines such as hardware-accelerated XML parsers or transforming engines.

- **Composability**   Many services have their primary role as a component in composite services. It is therefore important that these services can play their part well. A focus on composability will influence the discussion of the granularity of services and their capabilities. Frequently it will prove beneficial to have a service offer a similar capability at different levels of granularity. For example, the capability to retrieve patient records is ideally available in various forms: get a list of a small subset of attributes for all patients that satisfy certain search conditions; get a full patient record based on a primary key; and more importantly, out of efficiency and composability considerations, get a set of patient records based on a collection of primary keys.

  Execution efficiency is very important, especially for fine-grained services that are candidates for frequent inclusion (and frequent invocation) in composites.

- **Event awareness**   Event-Driven Architecture (EDA) will be introduced later in this chapter to complement service orientation with an even more decoupled means of interaction: Subscribers that are unknown to producers get notified of events that make business sense to them. EDA can only work when any component—application, service, or business process—that comes across occurrences of one of the business events that have been identified as relevant to the business publishes that event to the world—or at least to the event mediation infrastructure (the Event Delivery Network in Oracle SOA Suite 11g). A requirement on all services therefore is that they, too, take on this responsibility of publishing events whenever they encounter or initiate them.

Layering the Enterprise Architecture

When we are describing an enterprise, we often organize the architecture in the layers shown in Figure 2-3. Each layer has specific characteristics, responsibilities, and dependencies, and therefore has different requirements for standardization.

Application Service Components Layer   The application (service) components layer consists of the service implementations. For example, if we have an appointment service, the application component that creates the appointment in our clinical information service is the service implementation.

Services and Events Layer   The services and events layer describes the contracts and the interfaces of the service. The contract of our appointment service could state that it is available during office hours and can be used by authorized personnel only. The interface can be defined

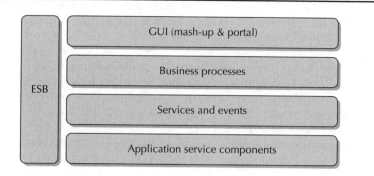

FIGURE 2-3.   *Layering the enterprise architecture*

through operations, inputs, and outputs, as well as the events consumed by the service and published by it. The appointment service, for example, has the following operations: create appointment, cancel appointment, and reschedule appointment. The input parameters for the create appointment operation are patient, date, and doctor; the output parameters are the appointment details. The service publishes the "appointment was cancelled" event and consumes the events with regard to the death of a patient.

Within the services layer, we usually apply a taxonomy—a classification scheme to organize the potentially large number of services. This is useful, because it helps keep track of what services exist in the organization. This is an important precondition for reuse: You can only reuse something if you know that it exists and are able to quickly find it. Even more important: Services with specific classifications have different rules applied with regard to granularity, behavior, security, and more.

Mary creates the taxonomy by defining the following service types for St. Matthews: business services, elementary services, technical services (e-mail, notification service), and enterprise services (the latter are business services exposed outside their business domain).

A service inventory (or service repository) is a collection of services under some form of governance that assists the organization in finding services, defining and maintaining taxonomies, and recording metadata about the services published in an enterprise. Various tools exist that provide an implementation of a service inventory.

The service layers represent different levels of abstraction. Elementary services are specific to a domain. When we use business domains (sometimes called information domains) to organize our applications, we can assign the elementary services to these business domains. Elementary services often offer CRUD-type operations on an entity (CRUD stands for create, update, delete). An example can be an elementary patient service that offers the operation "addPatient." Business services are usually composed of one or more elementary services and perform an atomic operation or task defined in the business domain. An example of a business service is a medication service that has the operation "prescribemedication." This service can use the patient service to look up address information about the patient, and a "MedicalRecord" service can be used to get the prescription needed.

Enterprise services are business services that the organization as a whole offers to consumers throughout the enterprise—across business domains—and sometimes even outside of it, to customers and business partners. A special type of enterprise services in the context of St. Matthews includes services offered to the hospital by its external partners, such as insurance companies, other hospitals, government agencies, and third parties in the cloud. St. Matthews keeps a list of these as well. It is important for the hospital to keep track of all the dependencies on services, including these external services.

Business events are published by services and business processes to a generic event-handling framework. These events carry a (usually small) payload with specifics about the events. Interested consumers—services, business processes, or application components—register their interest in events of specific types with the framework through subscriptions. When an event occurs that they have subscribed to, the framework sends it to them. Thus, events establish a decoupled link between producers and consumers of events. Note that events, too, exist at various levels: business, elementary, and technical. Complex event processing can be used to deal with the finer-grained and more frequently occurring elementary events, as we discuss in Chapter 19.

Business Processes Layer   This layer contains the business processes. Simply put: A business process consists by and large of calls to services for automated operations and human tasks for manual actions—with some flow logic in between. Business Process Management (BPM) is concerned with the management of business processes in an organization. The cycle of Business Process Management consists of the following stages: business process analysis, business process execution, and business process monitoring. BPM is discussed in more detail in Chapter 11.

There are different types of processes. One category is formed by human-centric processes, where most of the work is done by humans and the most important challenge is to assign workloads evenly and to monitor the progress of tasks. This is what is traditionally known as workflow. Another category includes document-centric processes. These are processes that evolve around documents, such as contracts or a press release for a website. Typically, you will see this in document management and content management systems. There will be processes for scanning, editing, approving, and publishing the documents. The third category of processes is system-centric processes. This is what is traditionally called orchestration. One of the biggest improvements in system-centric processes in recent years has been the shift from batch processing to straight-through processing of one item. The last category of processes is called rule-centric processes. A rule-centric process is one that has many alternative paths, depending on existing business rules.

Apart from having different types of processes, we usually define different levels of processes in the process layer (see Chapter 1). Mary decides to use three levels: The first level contains value-added chains that may string several business processes together. We saw an example in Chapter 1. The second level contains the end-to-end processes. This was described for the appointment process in Figure 1-10.

The lowest level is the level that is relevant for developers and end users: This is the process that will actually be implemented and run. It contains implementation details about the types of activities (automated, human step, and so on), and describes in detail the flow logic with loops and parallel flows that can be left out of the model at the second level.

Here are two design patterns that St. Matthews has decided to apply for business processes:

- *Processes should not be too generic.* Designing business services is different from designing a process. In software, you are looking for reuse, whereas in processes you are looking for efficiency and possibilities for improvement—goals that are at odds with generic, all-purpose designs.

- *Use parallel execution flows whenever possible.* One of the ways to speed up a process is to have activities not wait for unrelated events.

Oracle BPM Suite and Oracle SOA Suite 11*g* offer several options for BPM. The components are discussed in detail in the next chapter. To design processes you can use either Oracle BPA Suite or the lighter-weight Oracle BPM Studio, if you don't need the full architecture features and the many dozens of diagram types that BPA Suite offers.

GUI Layer   This layer contains the interface that interacts with end users. Components in this layer, such as back-office applications or customer-facing portlets and mash-ups, use the business processes and services layer to retrieve data and perform actions. For example, St. Matthews could create a portal for all patients. Information about the hospital visiting hours can be displayed there—retrieved from a service that wraps a content management system. Patients could also be offered an entry form to request appointments. This part of the application could use the appointment service we discussed earlier to show free slots and then present the end result: the scheduled appointment itself.

The GUI layer at St. Matthews also contains user interfaces for business partners such as general practitioners and employees at insurance companies. A last, very important group of users of the GUI layer is the staff of St. Matthews itself. Some of these user interfaces may provide the front end of human tasks that are part of the business processes.

Rethinking the Notion of an Application

Not too long ago, many organizations and development teams tended to consider an application to be the combination of the user interface, the business logic, and the database that worked together to provide a specific set of functionality to a group of users. The key applications in organizations typically had (or still have) nicknames or abbreviations that are used with something like "loving frustration." The application may be implemented in Oracle Forms, Visual Basic, Delphi, Oracle Portal & Web/PLSQL, or some other application development tool and technology. Usually, the application and the underlying database go by the same name, are developed by the same team, and are monogamous: They were not designed to interact with other systems.

The data in the database under the application is a valuable enterprise asset that may be needed in other business domains. Frequently and increasingly, the data and business logic in these core applications are also required for other user groups—such as business partners or customers—and through channels other than the current channels, such as self-service web applications or Web Service APIs. Perhaps as a first step on the road to (near) future developments, the mental picture of these archetypical applications should be changed from a single black box containing the database, business logic, and (user interface) application into two logically separate components: database and business logic on the one hand and the application on the other, as shown here:

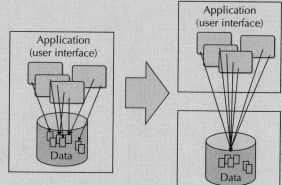

(Continued)

The application is usually quite specific for the group of end users it services, the processes it supports, and the channel that is used—often client/server- or browser applet-based. The application may be complemented by other applications, created using different technologies, and intended for other user groups and offered through different channels, but using the same business logic and database. It is clear, then, that the database has a wider audience and purpose than its original narrow focus on the one application it was used with. There is no exclusive ownership of the database by the application or by the team developing the application. The data(base) is owned by the organizational unit that owns the data (or the domain that the data is part of). That last part can be quite a cultural change in some IT departments—one that needs to be implemented.

The notion of an application is changing. The most tangible manifestation of computer-based processing logic probably still is the user interface, although the Web Services are a similar tip-of-the-iceberg front end for potentially very complex constellations of programs, database components, and other modules. However, a user interface will increasingly be regarded as the front end for a human task at some point in a business process. The workflow engine and to-do list play an important role in dictating when the UI should be presented to the user—not just the user herself browsing through some global menu.

These user interfaces will present data and support operations that are increasingly no longer one-on-one linked to a single database but instead connected to various data sources and other services. This brings us to the next level of architecture where the front end (the user interface or Web Service) is founded upon an amalgamation of services—provided through some form of enterprise service bus, as shown here:

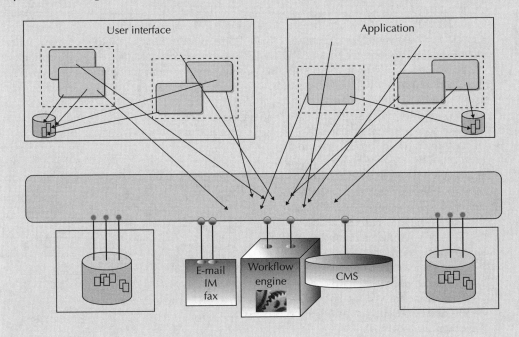

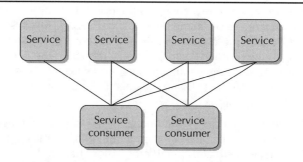

FIGURE 2-4. *Point-to-point interfaces*

Enterprise Service Bus   One of the challenges when considering integration between systems is managing all the connections. If we have point-to-point interfaces (see Figure 2-4) and something changes in a service, all service consumers need to be modified. The service consumer has to be aware of the protocol the invoked service uses, as well as the message format and the location of the service. This tightly couples the consumers to the service providers.

The concept of an enterprise service bus (ESB) has been introduced to help address these challenges. An ESB sits between service consumers and the services they invoke (see Figure 2-5). It typically has a number of features that facilitate the interaction and help decouple consumers from providers:

- **Endpoint virtualization**   When service consumers call a service through the ESB instead of calling the provider directly, location transparency is achieved in the architecture. A service provider can be replaced by another service provider, without the need to change every service consumer to reflect the new address. Only the ESB knows which service provider is invoked exactly; all the consumers leave it to the ESB. This is called virtualization of services.

- **Routing of services**   Sometimes the routing is more specific: Based on the content of the request message from the consumer, the service is selected to forward the request to; this is called content-based routing.

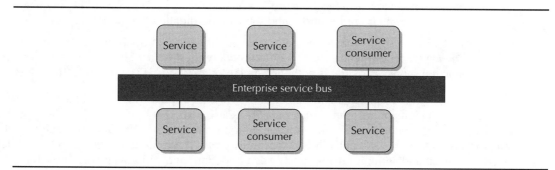

FIGURE 2-5. *Enterprise service bus*

■ **Transformation** Providers and consumers don't always speak the same language: They frequently do not use the same protocols or message formats. The enterprise service bus can transform a request to the format and/or protocol supported by the service and does the inverse to the response before handing it back to the consumer. Messages inside the ESB are based on the canonical data model (CDM); messages are transformed to the CDM upon entering the ESB and may need to transform to application-specific formats when traveling out of the ESB.

A special element in transformation can be message enrichment: The result of the transformation is not just the same data in a different message structure but an enriched message with additional information that has been looked up (for example, an appointment request that has been enriched with the recent medical history for the patient).

■ **Validation** The ESB can validate requests before they are delivered to the service provider as well as the responses coming out of the provider.

■ **Auditing** The ESB can log requests and responses for auditing purposes and send out alerts when special conditions apply.

■ **Messaging** Instead of calling a service, an application can send messages and communicate asynchronously with other applications. The ESB can provide guaranteed delivery and persistence of the message. This is explained in more detail in the section "Events and Event-Driven Architecture (EDA)."

■ **Synchronous/asynchronous adaptation** An enterprise service bus can expose services with either a synchronous or an asynchronous interface—regardless of the nature of the actual service provider(s) it needs to invoke; it can adapt from synchronous to asynchronous, and vice versa. This—together with support for queuing and store-and-forward for services that are temporarily unavailable—provides another very important type of decoupling: The provider does not need to be available at the same time as the consumer, and the consumer does not need to wait for the response from the service it invokes. This has the same impact on service invocations as the answering machine and voicemail had on communication via telephone.

■ **Composition** An ESB may be used to aggregate the results from several services in a single response to a service invocation, effectively publishing a new, composite service; enrichment can also be seen as a special case of composition. Note that other components—such as a business process engine that runs BPMN or BPEL processes—can provide similar composition- and service-coordinating functionality.

An ESB may also be able to mediate between different security protocols: for example, allowing (or requiring) the consumer to send a request with a SAML authentication token while the service provider is authenticated through basic HTTP authentication.

Many of the functions listed are instances of *mediation*—a word with several meanings, including conciliation and matchmaking. The ESB clearly is good at bringing two parties together across various types of divides: communication protocol, location, technology, message format, synchronous/asynchronous, availability, and security protocol. Other functions an ESB may offer include technical and administrative aspects, such as performance improvements through result caching, high availability through clustering, reliability and transaction management, enforcement of authorization rules, throttling of message load, and SLA monitoring.

Canonical Data Model

When we compose applications using services, it is important that the services use a common vocabulary or language. All services base their interface on this data model. Clearly this helps to standardize the service contracts because consumers will encounter the same data structures in all services. It also helps to lower the number of message formats an application has to know about and cater to. The number of resource-intensive—and error-prone—transformations can be reduced.

It feels better to remove the reference altogether.

This Esperanto-like common language for services in the same business domain is called the canonical data model. It has data definitions for the business objects—usually described in XSD (XML Schema Definition). The canonical data model is closely aligned with the business terminology and the business view of information—and is absolutely devoid of technical baggage such as column names, SQL naming conventions, and technical data types. It should be centrally managed by a team that consists of architects, business analysts, and developers.

In addition to the core canonical model with business object definitions, we will make use of utility data definitions. These define special-purpose data structures used for parameters and faults as well as for technical records that, for example, report on the results of data manipulation or other metadata regarding the service execution. These structures usually have references to the business objects. The canonical model can be said to cater to data at rest (the core definitions) and data in motion (supported by this latter category of utility objects and technical definitions that support the operation through metadata or pragmatic data structures).

For example, let's look at a service that provides patient records. This service could offer the capability to retrieve patient records in two ways: "get a list of a small subset of attributes for all patients that satisfy certain search conditions" and "get a set of patient records based on a collection of primary keys." The first capability uses a data structure that defines a collection of records consisting of just a few fields; these records can be defined based on the regular patient element, but are probably better defined using a specialized type. A 360-degree patient type could also be defined with a deeply nested tree structure that brings in everything that possibly could be said about a patient.

Ideally, of course, every service in the world would speak canonical, but they do not (most of them don't anyway). So transformations will occasionally need to take place to translate between noncanonical and canonical message formats. Note that in some industries, standards have been established for data that is exchanged between business partners. The data format described for the data in motion is, of course, a perfect foundation for the data at rest.

In large organizations with multiple business domains, it sometimes proves impossible to establish a single enterprise-wide canonical model. Organizations may have multiple canonical models—for example, per business domain and/or derived from external communities—that are organized into a tree-like structure (using nested namespaces) with various levels of abstraction and specific purposes.

We will see later how the canonical model can be defined as not just a collection of business-based data structure definitions, but also as a library of domain values and even business rules.

Of course, commercial off-the-shelf applications typically do not comply with the organization's canonical data model, although, of course, they may comply with industry standards that can also be used inside the canonical data model. A mediator, such as the ESB, is used then for transforming the data that these applications expose to the canonical data model for the service consumers (see Figure 2-6). Another common pattern is to have all the applications—both consumers and providers—use their own format and then let the mediator transform everything. However, this can be quite expensive in terms of resource usage.

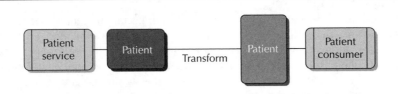

FIGURE 2-6. *Transformation is needed when an application (the patient consumer in this example) can't handle the canonical data definition.*

The data flowing through the service-oriented infrastructure should be canonical as much as possible. This way, if an application does not speak canonical, we should transform from (and to) the application format as close to the application as possible. That usually means that the final step before an application is invoked is the transformation from the canonical to the application-specific format—performed by a mediator. For applications that do not speak canonical and call in to the service-oriented system, we should offer an application-specific interface that feeds into a mediator that transforms to the canonical format as early as possible. In general, transformations should be kept as far down the technology stack as possible—they should be kept out of the higher-level (composite) services if at all possible.

Governance

Traditionally, stand-alone applications—as described earlier—were developed by dedicated teams that remained attached to the application during subsequent stages in the lifecycle. The assets that formed the application were often completely owned, controlled, and exclusively used by this relatively small team.

In Service-Oriented Architecture, most assets end up very much not (exclusively) owned by any team or even department: They are—in theory at least—owned by the enterprise, targeted at widespread reuse, and not naturally controlled by an individual or group. However, every service needs to have an owner who is responsible for the services delivered. Because the service delivers business value, it is a business unit that owns it.

Management of the lifecycle of these assets is important, especially given the extent of reuse we are trying to achieve. To realize reuse, the availability of assets needs to be made public and the assets need to be found and understood. Once reuse has happened, the process of evolving those assets becomes more involved: Multiple parties have a stake in the assets and may have specific requirements with regard to their evolution. SOA governance controls that process.

Other aspects of governance include: How do we ascertain that assets have the required quality and deliver on their (functional) promise? How do we define and record the required service levels and subsequently monitor the actual performance of assets?

Before the management of the assets themselves is in full swing, governance is required to enforce the architectural principles laid down for the organization. What processes must be implemented to ensure that all teams stick to the rules?

Governance must be implemented at every stage of the SOA lifecycle to track ongoing changes to the architecture, design, and implementation—and to define, implement, and execute the processes around designing and implementing changes to assets and the creation of new ones.

Chapter 18 introduces governance in the context of the SOA Suite, but only scratches the surface of that topic (it is mainly outside the scope of this book).

Events and Event-Driven Architecture (EDA)

As described in the beginning of the chapter, SOA and events are closely related. Let's first define events: An event is a signal of a significant change in the state of a business object. Examples are receiving a request, death of a patient, a fire alarm, receipt of a payment, and so on. Employees, partners, customers, and also processes in an organization react to these events.

Some events are triggers that start a process. For example, in the appointment process, we can define the event "Doctor referral received." When this is received by the hospital, the appointment process is triggered and appropriate actions are taken. Some events trigger more than one process: For example, when a patient dies, this can trigger an investigation and at the very least the cancellation of future appointments and any lab tests currently under way for that patient.

Events can be defined in the same layer as the services. Using events decreases dependencies between service providers and service consumers because it provides for asynchronous communication and does not require the publisher to know if and what subscribers exist for a message. The following design principles apply to events:

- Events should contain enough information for the receivers to base decisions on, or to analyze them for business activity–monitoring purposes or complex event processing. A "new patient" event should contain, for example, the date, patient identifier, and department. If a certain process needs more information about this event, the process can fetch it using the patient identifier in the event payload.

- Events should be loosely coupled. An event does not know what process it starts or what activity caused it to be published.

The best-known pattern for events is publish–subscribe (see Figure 2-7): An event is published by a provider, and clients that are interested in the events subscribe to the message based on some characteristics of the message. With some types of subscriptions, message consumers do not need to be available when the message is published by the publisher. We will discuss this in more detail in Chapter 9.

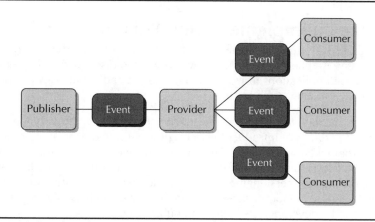

FIGURE 2-7. *Publish-subscribe pattern*

Implementation Considerations   The different types of events can be implemented in several ways: We can have triggers in the database that publish an event to a queue when a record is updated, inserted, or deleted. The same can be implemented using Java and JMS: A call to a Java method could cause a message to be published to a JMS queue or topic. We can publish an event from a BPEL process when we finish a process or a step in the process. We can define sensors (out-of-process wiretaps that emit trace details about the BPEL process and the current activity) in BPEL processes for specific activities, and do the same with ESB routing rules.

The message or event itself can be implemented using different standards: The payload can be XML, text, a Java object, and so on. In an SOA environment, it is easiest to use XML, which is the language for all application components and tools anyway. How a service can be consumed also depends on the implementation that is picked. If we use JMS, we can determine at run time what subscribers exist for a certain topic. But we can also decide at design time what message is propagated to which subscribers, using content-based routing, for example. Last but not least, there is a draft release of a new Web Service specification for events: Web Service Eventing (WS Eventing).

Business Activity Monitoring (BAM)   We can define events that should be published from running processes. These events can be used for business activity monitoring (BAM). The goal of BAM is to provide *real-time* information about the status and results of the processes. When certain events occur, an alarm can be raised. For example, the hospital might want to monitor cancellations in the appointment process. If completion of a cancellation activity takes too long, an alarm can be raised to the supervisor to reassign the task to someone else. We will discuss BAM in more detail in Chapter 19.

Complex Event Processing (CEP)   Sometimes we are not interested in events from a specific process, but we are looking for patterns. Complex event processing deals with the task of processing multiple simple events, with the goal of identifying the meaningful complex events or patterns. This has the advantage that a process does not need to be modeled in advance to be able to detect significant events. Examples are insurance fraud detection, detection of specific predictive patterns in stock trading, and also temperature control in the facilities of St. Matthews. A more detailed introduction and some examples of using CEP are discussed in Chapter 19.

SOA from an Implementation Point of View

We talked about SOA from the business perspective and discussed the architectural meaning of Service-Oriented Architecture. The last view we want to discuss is the implementation view. There are several implications from an implementation and technology perspective when we move to Service-Oriented Architecture:

- *The infrastructure on which services run changes from the traditional "application" infrastructure.* We introduce services, processes, and events into our run-time environment—such as Web Services and business process implementations—that require special infrastructure to run (for example, an enterprise service bus, an SOA or SCA container, a process engine, and tooling to enforce security). Middleware is introduced that needs to be administered; new technologies such as Web Services need to be learned by developers as well as administrators.

■ *The way we deploy and subsequently manage our run-time artifacts changes, too.* Because we introduce sets of loosely coupled components, instead of deploying one big application, we have the option to install well-defined separate components on different servers. We will probably have to do many more but far less complex deployments. Making a small change may result in just a small redeployment effort, instead of a full-blown redeployment. This new approach requires different skills from both our administrators and our developers.

■ *St. Matthews has decided to use the Oracle SOA Suite 11g, after a careful product selection process.* This suite offers all the functionality the hospital needs, and the developers and administrators are already familiar with Oracle products. Apart from that, the suite offers out-of-the-box solutions for PeopleSoft HCM and SAP R/3 through the adapter framework. Last but not least, SOA Suite 11g is component based and standards based. This gives St. Matthews the opportunity to use other tools and middleware for specific areas. The SOA Suite 11g components are discussed at length in Chapter 3.

■ *One of the primary objectives behind SOA is agility, the ability to adapt—the essential attitude to embrace change.* Organizations adopting SOA will typically carry out frequent changes in response to business requirements. These changes can consist of reorganizing business processes, assembling new applications from existing business services or rewiring existing business services or applications, changing the logic of (potentially heavily reused) elementary services, and so on. We need to think about change procedures, automated testing strategies, and efficient deployment.

■ *New programming languages, standards, and frameworks are used.* Because one of the guiding principles of SOA is standardization, adopting SOA in an organization will likely mean some changes in the frameworks, tools, and standards used, shifting the organization to industry standards for Web Services such as XML, SOAP, and WSDL. We will talk about the standards in this section and in more detail in the rest of the book.

■ *The new programming languages, standards, and frameworks introduce a need for new (versions of) tools.* St. Matthews is, as we discussed before, an Oracle shop that has selected the Oracle SOA Suite to develop its SOA artifacts for. Therefore, the hospital will use JDeveloper 11g to create Web Services and other artifacts.

Standards in SOA

One of the important principles of SOA is standardization. It is very hard to communicate with other applications if the protocols and message formats that these other applications use are all different. We saw that in our discussions of canonical data formats and ESB. The same is true for protocols. IT systems in an organization typically use various protocols and programming languages. This makes combining them into new applications difficult, if not impossible. To solve this, services should use standard protocols and message formats. In this section, we will briefly discuss some of the most prominent standards used in SOA. The next chapter introduces many more standards. In the rest of the book, these standards will be discussed in more detail as we encounter them in the examples and cases.

Web Services One of the most important sets of standards is the one concerning Web Services. The World Wide Web Consortium (W3C) describes Web Services as follows (www.w3.org/2002/ws/Activity):

"Web Services provide a standard means of interoperating between different software applications, running on a variety of platforms and/or frameworks. Web Services are characterized by their great interoperability and extensibility, as well as their machine-processable descriptions thanks to the use of XML. They can be combined in a loosely coupled way in order to achieve complex operations. Programs providing simple services can interact with each other in order to deliver sophisticated added-value services."

There are two ways of creating a Web Service: using a formal protocol defining the operations and message format in advance, and using a loose protocol where a hint of the next available set of operations can be derived from the last service response. SOAP Web Services are an example of working according to formal specifications defined in advance, whereas RESTful services are an example of the latter approach.

SOAP and WSDL SOAP Web Services dictate a formal method of communication between applications. Through SOAP and WSDL, an organization can specify the available operations in services and the data that can be exchanged with the services. The specification of these services in such a formal way has several advantages:

■ The interaction is strongly typed: the consumer knows what type of data to expect.

■ Because SOAP is more formal, there is more tool support to create SOAP-based Web Services.

■ Multiple protocols are supported (SOAP over HTTP and SOAP over JMS, for example).

■ Additional features, such as WS-Addressing, WS-Security, and Basic Profile, are used.

The SOAP specification is discussed in more detail in Chapter 4 and in Appendix B.

However, this formal, contract-based, and XML-riddled approach is sometimes perceived as very heavy-handed. The overhead in terms of the infrastructure required for handling SOAP Web Service interaction and the sheer size of the SOAP messages compared to the actual information content of those messages can cause people to shy away from SOAP.

RESTful Services A more lightweight Web Service alternative is available in the form of RESTful services. REST, by the way, is an acronym for Representational State Transfer. Originally introduced by Roy Fielding as a rather formal resource-oriented method of programmatic interaction over the HTTP protocol using the four basic HTTP operations—PUT, POST, GET and DELETE—for CRUD operations, RESTful services have evolved into a plethora of lightweight HTTP-based APIs. RESTful services accept simple HTTP requests and send equally simple responses.

There are no generally accepted standards for RESTful services (for example, the use of contracts of some form of description of the services). Initially, it was almost blasphemy to suggest the need or even the usefulness for such descriptions, whereas in later stages large groups experimented with WADL (Web Application Definition Language), a simpler counterpart to WSDL. REST-style services can return responses in XML, although other formats such as CSV and JSON are popular too.

There is a lot of support for REST on the client side (consuming RESTful services in many programming languages) and some on the server for publishing REST-style services. Some enterprise service bus implementations have some support for REST—although mainly in situations where the payload is XML described by some predefined contract, however lightweight.

REST seems primarily useful for data integration between web clients and servers, not so much for enterprise SOA.

RSS Feeds   Another lightweight approach to programmatic (one-way) exchange of information is through RSS feeds. A simple HTTP GET request (REST-like) suffices to retrieve the information; the format is a predefined XML structure. RSS only supports a very simple interaction pattern, but in some situations may be just what the doctor ordered.

Policies   As we discussed before, a service consists of an interface that can be described in a WSDL, an implementation that can be in virtually any language and contract. The contract describes the quality of aspects of the service. Examples include the number of concurrent calls it can handle, the maximum number of records it returns, its maximum response time, the authorization required for this service, the availability of the service, and the way the service will evolve. Some aspects of the contract can be defined using the WS-Policy standard. For other aspects of what is sometimes laid down in a service-level agreement (SLA), a standard format is currently lacking.

UDDI Directory, Service Registry, and Service Repository   Because we want to reuse our assets and build new applications using existing components by exposing them as Web Services, we need some type of registry to store and publish information about the services in our organization—which services are available and where can they be found. To make it possible for different tools to look up services, a standard has been defined to discover (web) services: UDDI (Universal Description, Discovery, and Integration). UDDI defines a standard method for publishing and discovering network-based software components in SOA. The comparison is frequently made with the Yellow Pages—a directory that you browse through when you are looking for a specific service. It contains an API for publishing and searching for services, and to subscribe to changes to the service metadata.

UDDI was one of the earliest standards in the Web Service arena, along with WSDL and SOAP. However, it has never really caught on for design-time service discovery. Many UDDI implementations or service registries today seem primarily used for *run-time* lookup of the physical location of services, a form of service (endpoint) virtualization.

The originally intended role of the UDDI-based registries has been taken over by a more elaborate service repository—or asset manager—that is primarily used at design time. This serves as a service inventory—a listing of the services available in the organization along with extensive metadata that helps search operations and also provides real insight into the purpose, status, and fit-for-use of the services. Note that the service repository contains many more SOA artifacts than just services (WSDL and XSD); virtually any artifact that can provide insight and facilitate reuse and collaboration, from service-level agreements to canonical data model descriptions, can be recorded. An important role of the service repository is to provide insight into the dependencies between the artifacts, primarily to assess the impact of changes.

Service registries tap into or collaborate with the service repository, using maybe 10 percent of their information for service discovery.

Note that although UDDI is a formal industry standard for service directories, there is no such standard for service repositories. Several vendors offer products that implement the concept of a service repository, but these are not based on some common standard. Oracle offers the Oracle Enterprise Repository.

Industry Standards   Many standards have been developed for structuring messages and services in specific industries and business domains. An example is HL7 in the healthcare domain. HL7 is a framework (and related standards) for the exchange, integration, sharing, and retrieval of electronic health information. Another example is XBRL—a standard for financial reporting.

Service Component Architecture   A relatively new standard is Service Component Architecture (SCA). It is a set of specifications that describes a model for building applications and systems using a Service-Oriented Architecture. It is a widely supported standard, backed by most large vendors of SOA software and tooling. We will discuss SCA in more detail in Chapters 3 and 14, and we work with it throughout the book—SCA underpins Oracle SOA Suite 11g.

Summary

A service-oriented approach will help St. Matthews establish the business services that are required to help automate the business processes. SOA principles will help St. Matthews (and us) design the elementary services with the right level of granularity, based on a common, canonical data model, that are composed to create more complex composite services and business services. The services will work together based on standardized interfaces and contracts that help reach a high level of decoupling (or loose coupling). These interfaces are also essential in order to achieve reuse of the services. Decoupling, service composition, and reuse are some of the factors in achieving more business agility—the ability to flexibly and speedily respond to changing business requirements. They also help to keep the costs down and the quality up: Reuse means less development and testing effort as well as smaller maintenance effort because logic is not duplicated in many components.

Service-Oriented Architecture helps achieve maximum interoperability—potential for interaction across technology stacks and products from different vendors. It thereby reduces the dependency on vendor-specific solutions and allows organizations to use best-of-breed products—provided that these products support interfaces based on open, service-oriented standards.

Event-Driven Architecture (EDA) provides an extra level of decoupling: Through business events that can be produced in any application, business process, or service implementation and that can be consumed by any registered application, business process, or service, we achieve a form of interaction that does not introduce dependencies that might hamper future changes in artifacts because of increased impact. EDA uses asynchronous communication facilitated by process- and service-agnostic infrastructure.

SOA offers flexibility in adapting business processes and underlying implementations as well as cost efficiency by reusing and sharing existing assets and increasing process efficiency.

The eAppointment Pilot Project

Mary proposes to start with a pilot project, called eAppointment, to prove to the board of directors that SOA is the way to go for St. Matthews. This book tells the story of this project and demonstrates how Oracle SOA Suite 11g provides the means to achieve the business, architectural, and technical objectives.

The core business process in the eAppointment project is very visible to the patients: the appointment process. There are several reasons for selecting the first process to take on in such a pilot project: the urgency of existing problems, the visibility throughout the organization, the largest chance of a quick success (the low-hanging fruit), and the toughest nut to crack that would provide the best possible proof for the validity of the approach. In this particular case at St. Matthews, it is

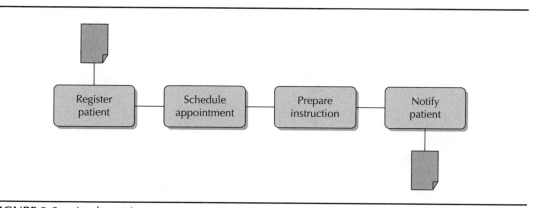

FIGURE 2-8. *Intake patient process—appointments*

actually a combination: The patient appointments process is very visible and is currently a source of frustration among hospital staff and patients alike, and at the same time it's not all that hard to improve and reap some early benefits. Figure 2-8 shows the high-level overview of this process.

The process starts when a referral for a patient is received from a family doctor or another primary healthcare provider. Some system at St. Matthews needs to register the patient data. If the patient is already known in the hospital, the existing record is updated; otherwise, a new patient record is created. If this is the first appointment for the patient, an appointment is scheduled with the first available doctor. Otherwise, an appointment is scheduled with the doctor who had previous appointments with this patient, at least if the doctor is available during the period within which the appointment needs to take place. Then instructions for the patient are prepared, depending on the type of appointment required. The appointment details, along with these instructions, are sent to the patient, either by e-mail or in a traditional letter. The patient does not need to confirm the appointment; it is considered confirmed unless it is canceled. If the patient wants to reschedule, she can call the hospital to change the appointment. If the patient cancels, the appointment is removed from the doctor's schedule. The process ends when the patient arrives at St. Matthews for the appointment. If the appointment date passes and the patient does not show up, the process is terminated as well.

CHAPTER
3

Oracle Fusion Middleware and SOA Suite 11g

t. Matthews is facing several real business challenges, as we have seen in the previous chapter. The hospital has well-defined views as to how to approach these challenges from the business perspective as well as the implementation or technological perspective. Service-Oriented Architecture (SOA) as an overarching design principle is a key element in this approach. To apply the concepts laid down in St. Matthews' architecture blueprints, the hospital needs to put in place a technology stack that supports those architectural concepts. Chapter 2 made the opening moves in this direction.

St. Matthews has evaluated a number of SOA and middleware offerings from various vendors—including open-source products—and has picked Oracle Fusion Middleware (FMW) as its preferred stack. Among the selection criteria, support for open industry standards ranked very highly, along with product functionality, operational (administration) effort, and maturity. Because it is a long-running and rather satisfied user of Oracle technology—RDBMS and various tools, including Oracle Forms—the IT staff at St. Matthews has a natural bias toward the Oracle Fusion Middleware offering. It hopes and expects that FMW will offer additional advantages, such as even better integration with the Oracle technologies already in use (for example, PL/SQL), that alternative products wouldn't provide, in addition to a smoother learning curve based on the current skill set.

This chapter introduces Oracle Fusion Middleware in general and then focuses on the SOA Suite, one of its key components. It first offers an overview of the history of SOA and middleware within Oracle. Then it paints the broader picture of Fusion Middleware before concentrating on the SOA Suite and the products and technologies FMW comprises. The chapter concludes with the installation of the SOA Suite 11*g* and briefly touches upon the migration from previous releases of the Oracle SOA Suite. At the end of the chapter, we'll have the SOA Suite up and running, ready for the development of services.

History of Middleware and SOA in Oracle

Oracle aspires and even claims to be the number-one vendor in the middleware market. Whether or not that claim is justified, and regardless of what being "number one" in middleware exactly means, it is very clear that Oracle has undergone a dramatic makeover from not having a meaningful presence in middleware market at all to being at least one of the dominant players. How did that makeover happen? Why did it happen? And what is middleware anyway?

An exact definition of middleware is almost impossible to give. Historically (from the mid-1980s), middleware was very much associated with messaging and queuing, brokers, transaction monitors, and distributed processing. The essence of middleware is in connecting software components and applications, enabling interoperability between various platforms and different systems, and supporting the automated, structured exchange of data across the IT landscape. As such, middleware became the platform for Enterprise Application Integration (EAI). In more recent years, middleware has become the label for technology for (web) services and SOA. The term *middleware* now encompasses almost all software infrastructure required for implementing SOA. It has come to also be used for areas such as identity management, business intelligence, and content management. Note that although some vendors include databases in their definition of middleware, Oracle does not.

The Mists of Time—Until 2001

It is difficult to point out exactly when Oracle started doing middleware for real and what those initial activities were. It is much easier to see what those early efforts led to.

The Oracle RDBMS has been an interoperability platform from very early on: The RDBMS was released for all major platforms, and many not so major ones as well. Oracle Corporation has always invested a lot of effort in porting the C-based Oracle RDBMS software from Solaris—the primary release platform for many years until Linux (temporarily) usurped that position—to a host of other operating systems running on hardware from PCs to mainframes. Oracle database applications written on one platform will be portable to any of the other platforms that the RDBMS runs on. This means, for example, for PL/SQL programs "write once, run everywhere"—the much-touted Java tagline, was realized before Java even existed! Interoperability with non-Oracle technology was not as hot an issue at that time.

A first stab at messaging (infrastructure) was delivered through Advanced Queuing (AQ) in the Oracle 8.0 RDBMS release (1998). AQ is based on database technology, including tables and PL/SQL. It adds to the database the ability to implement, publish, and subscribe scenarios where applications asynchronously communicate messages. Note that AQ is still the backbone of persistent messaging in WebLogic today.

In the mid-1990s, client/server was all the rage, and in that two-tier architecture there was initially no place for middleware—a third tier. However, the rapid expansion of the Internet as well as several major challenges with the client/server architecture, such as maintenance effort and server-side scalability, resulted in the rise of the three-tier architecture and the introduction of the notion of an application server. An application server can be used to execute common business logic for all clients, thereby decreasing load for both the front end and back end. Also, through the type of functionality offered by this *middle* tier, it is the best place to position and do integration (using *middle*ware).

The need for integration across different systems in the enterprise—and, later, also between enterprises—became more apparent and formed another force that drove the creation of middleware software. The fact that most organizations use technology from different vendors, and that integration therefore also means interoperability across various technology platforms, was one of the drivers for the development of industry standards.

Oracle announced its full support for the Java platform early on, in 1997. In 1998, the Oracle 8*i* RDBMS was released with a Java Virtual Machine (JVM) inside the database. Oracle also released several versions of its ill-fated OAS product, the Oracle Application Server. OAS 4.0, for example, released in 1998, debuted support for CORBA, an early interoperability standard. Based on OAS, Oracle announced the Oracle Integration Server (OIS) at the end of 1999, a platform for … integration! OIS leveraged Advanced Queuing and introduced early versions of technology adapters for integration with packages or views in the database as well as some third-party ERP (SAP, PeopleSoft) systems. Other components new in OIS were Workflow and InterConnect. Until overtaken by the Oracle Enterprise Service Bus (OESB), InterConnect was the primary Enterprise Application Integration product offered by Oracle and it laid the foundation for several pieces of today's SOA Suite.

In 1998, the World Wide Web Consortium (W3C) published the 1.0 release of the XML standard. This turned out to be the foundation for almost every integration and interoperability initiative ever since. Oracle was quick to join the XML crowd. In 1999, the first release (of many) of the XML Development Kit (XDK) appeared. The 9*i*R2 landmark release of the RDBMS had built-in support for SQL/XML and the native XMLType data type. The XML functionality in the RDBMS was collectively labeled "XMLDB," a term that today covers many of the more native database features around XML.

Industry Standards: From 1998 until Now

The evolution of middleware technology within Oracle Corporation took place alongside developments in the industry. Both commercial vendors and open-source products were released, competing with Oracle's offerings. More importantly, most vendors were collaborating in various consortia and standards bodies to create the industry standards that would bring such tremendous change to the world of middleware and the promises of interoperability. The true reason why SOA could bring the success and the results promised by various reuse and integration initiatives since the 1980s lies in the widespread commitment to open standards, among the commercial vendors as well as the open-source projects.

Many of the standards around the Web, Web Services, SOA, and interoperability are created and maintained by standards bodies such as the W3C, OASIS, and JCP, in close collaboration with many of the major industry players. Companies such as IBM, Microsoft, SAP, Sun Microsystems, BEA Systems, Hewlett Packard, Fujitsu, webMethods, Software AG, and, of course, Oracle, frequently join forces to further the evolution and widespread promotion of standards. Implementation of and compliance with these standards has become an important part of marketing efforts, and any product that fails to meet the standards' specifications will have problems competing with similar offerings that do support the standards.

XML (eXtensible Markup Language, inspired by HTML and its predecessor SGML) was the first (and foremost) standard in this area, sponsored by Microsoft and published by the W3C in 1998. XML is today the lingua franca as well as the main lubricant of SOA, Web Services, and other interoperability initiatives, as well as the foundation for many more specialized standards. The XML standard describes a set of rules for creating documents with structured data. XML itself is very generic—something like ASCII or comma-separated files with more structure. Its real value starts to shine in conjunction with standards and tools that describe and perform validation of the structure and content of the documents (XSD), retrieve pieces of information from the documents using structured queries (XPath), and transform documents into different structures (XSL-T). You will see many examples of these core XML technologies throughout this and any other SOA-related book.

Hot on the heels of these standards related to storing information in structured documents and manipulating those documents were standards for exchanging information captured in such documents. The first definition of SOAP (the Simple Object Access Protocol) saw the light of day as early as 1998. SOAP describes a simple envelope-style mechanism for combining payload and metadata in structured packages. In 2000, the Web Service Definition Language (WSDL) introduced the now-omnipresent standard for describing the contract for a Web Service—where the definition of a Web Service by now has been stretched to encompass almost any service and operation that deals with structured information. Fairly well known, though not overly successful, is the Universal Description, Discovery, and Integration (UDDI) standard, also dating from 2000. UDDI is intended to underpin directories of Web Services that tools can browse through in order to discover useful services. Despite its lack of immediate success, UDDI has certainly helped to promote the concept of service registries with listings of useful services that potential consumers such as developers can browse through. UDDI, SOAP, and WSDL can be seen as the first generation of the XML-based standards concerning Web Services. In 2004, the WS-I Basic Profile was published to complement this threesome—a set of guidelines on how exactly to apply these core Web Service standards, to ensure full operability (the original standards allowed for multiple interpretations in certain areas that led to differences between vendors' implementations).

The second wave of standards in the area of Web Services is concerned with more advanced concepts around message exchanges, such as the policies that apply to the message, the security of the messages, sending them in a reliable way to guarantee the reception (in the proper sequence and without duplication) of messages, correlation of multiple messages sent over a longer period, and the specification of return addresses and other concerns. Together these standards are referred to as WS-*: Their names all start with WS, and collectively they constitute a framework for service-oriented message exchanges that make it useful to have a common denominator. The * is usually pronounced *splat* or just *star*. Important members of the WS-* family are WS-Addressing, WS-Reliable Messages, WS-Security, and WS-Policy.

The automation of business processes has always been an important objective for the IT industry. The complexity of many processes and the involvement of multiple IT systems and applications, as well as the required participation of humans, have stood in the way of process automation for a long time.

With the rise of Web Services to overcome the interoperability challenges, fresh opportunities started to open up for business process automation. New ways to describe business processes in a structured way started to appear in 2004. The most prominent examples are Business Process Modeling Notation (BPMN) and Business Process Execution Language (BPEL, defined through BPEL4WS and WS-BPEL). Process definitions include the process routing and decision logic, calls to Web Services, and tasks to be performed by people. As the standards evolved, engines to execute such process definitions were developed by various vendors. BPEL4People and WS-Human Task (2007) have added human task-oriented extensions to BPEL that, by itself, is a rather technical Web Service–oriented language. Table 3-1 provides a chronological overview of some IT industry standards and specifications relevant to middleware and Service-Oriented Architecture.

Service Orchestration and Composite Services

In the previous chapter, we discussed elementary services and business services. The latter are coarser grained, offering more specific and complex functionality, leveraging the elementary services to help provide their functionality. Composing the coarse-grained services takes a combination of flow logic, calls to other services, and logic to process the results of those calls.

The industry had recognized the challenges of service composition or orchestration. In many cases, a number of services need to be invoked to accomplish a certain task, and only when all services have been called and delivered their response is the task done or the composite service complete. If a service call fails—either because of a technical issue or because of a business exception—the task may need to be undone or may need additional steps to overcome the problem. Multiple service calls can be made in parallel. Calls can be made to synchronous services, which send their reply as the return message to the request, and also to asynchronous services, which call back at some later point in time to deliver their response. These clusters of service calls or composites can represent a real business process or implement a composite service. Instances of such composites that perform service orchestration can be long running—up to days or even months when real business processes are implemented. Multiple instances of the same composite can be active at the same time,

Standard	Year of Original Publication	Current Release and Year Published	Standards Body	Purpose
Enterprise Java Bean (EJB)	1997/1999	3.1, 2009	JCP	JEE specification for exposing and accessing remote Java-based business logic
XML	1998	1.1 (2nd edition), 2006	W3C	Flexible yet structured language for creating text documents
SOAP	1998	1.2, 2007	W3C	XML-based protocol specification for exchanging messages with Web Services
XPath	1999	2.0, 2007	W3C	Query language for retrieving information from XML documents
XSLT	1999	2.0, 2007	W3C	Style sheet language for describing transformations for XML documents
WSDL	2000	2.0, 2007	W3C	XML language for describing the Web Services contract
UDDI (Universal Description, Discovery, Integration)	2000	3.0, 2004	OASIS	XML language for publishing a registry of (web) services
XSD	2001	1.0, 2001	W3C	Schema language for defining the valid structure and rules for XML elements (and successor to DTD)
Java Message Service (JMS)	2001	1.1, 2002	JCP	JEE specification that describes a Java API for loosely coupled, asynchronous interactions through Message Oriented Middleware
Java EE Connector Architecture (JCA)	2001	1.5, 2006	JCP	JEE specification for creating adapters to connect Java with Enterprise Information Systems
Security Assertion Markup Language (SAML)	2002	2.0, 2005	OASIS	XML-based standard that describes how security-related information (identification, authorization) can be exchanged
Web Services for Remote Portlets (WSRP)	2003	2.0, 2008	OASIS	Specification for interaction between portals (Portlet consumers) and (remote) Portlets (Web Services with a user interface)
WS-Reliable Messaging	2003	1.1, 2007	OASIS	A wire protocol used in SOAP messages to ensure reliable transport between sender and receiver

TABLE 3-1. *Chronological Overview of Some IT Industry Standards and Specifications Relevant to Middleware and Service-Oriented Architecture*

Standard	Year of Original Publication	Current Release and Year Published	Standards Body	Purpose
Business Process Execution Language (BPEL4WS/ WS-BPEL)	2004	2.0, 2007	OASIS	Executable language for processes that interact with Web Services
Service Data Objects (SDO)	2004	2.0, 2005	OASIS	Data-programming architecture that facilitates working with structured data objects in Service-Oriented Architecture
Business Process Modeling Notation (BPMN)	2004	1.2, 2009	OMG	Standard for ways to graphically describe business processes—and as added bonus simulate or even execute those processes for real
WS-I Basic Profile	2004	1.1, 2006	WS-I	Specification on how to apply standards such as SOAP, WSDL, and UDDI in order to achieve true interoperability across technology stacks
WS-Security	2004	1.1, 2006	OASIS	Specification on how to apply security—for example, through SAML or Kerberos—to Web Services and SOAP messages
WS-Addressing	2006	1.0, 2006	W3C	Standard that provides transport-neutral mechanisms to address and identify Web Service endpoints and to secure end-to-end endpoint identification in messages
XQuery	2007	1.0, 2007	W3C	Programming language for querying collections of XML data (technically a subset of XPath)
BPEL4People and WS-Human Task	2007		OASIS	Extension of BPEL4WS to specify interaction with humans and a human task-definition language
Service Component Architecture (SCA)	2007	1.0, 2007	OSOA	Configuration language for describing composite applications based on service components
WS-Policy	2007	1.0, 2007	W3C	XML language for describing the policies—such as Security and Quality of Service—that apply to a Web Service
WS-I Basic Security Profile	2007	1.1, 2009 (approval draft)	WS-I	Specification on how to apply security standards such as WS-Security in order to achieve true (security) interoperability across technology stacks

TABLE 3-1.   *Chronological Overview of Some IT Industry Standards and Specifications Relevant to Middleware and Service-Oriented Architecture (Continued)*

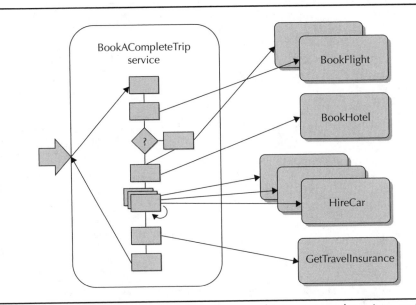

FIGURE 3-1. *An example of service orchestration, combining external services and internal logic and exposing a single coarse-grained business service*

handling different requests from potentially different clients. Figure 3-1 shows an example of service orchestration where the BookACompleteTrip service orchestrates the flight, hotel, car, and insurance-related services.

BPEL was the first language for implementing service orchestration—programs written in BPEL invoke (usually multiple) Web Services, perform process logic, handle faults in service calls, coordinate transactions, and deal with events and timeouts. Programs written in BPEL are known as *BPEL processes*. These processes run in a BPEL container. They are usually started through a call to the Web Services interface published for the BPEL process or initiated by the consumption of an event.

Through BPEL, many organizations successfully created SOA applications: programs or service composites that implemented business logic largely by orchestrating services that do the real work. However, even though BPEL can orchestrate multiple service calls and perform many of the actions required in a service composite, the BPEL container will usually work with other engines to execute all logic in a process and the services it invokes. For example, pieces of computing logic are implemented in Java; a workflow engine is engaged to handle human tasks; adapters are required to interact with databases, message queues, and a file system; and a rule engine implements decision logic that determines the routing through the process at junctions. Service composites usually also involve a fair bit of message transformation, filtering, and routing.

When the BPEL process is really the implementation of a business process, chances are that it will be long running (longer than a few seconds) and will carry some state data—data that it hangs on to for a large part of its lifetime. BPEL processes can also be used to create composite services—the coarser-grained next level from elementary services. In that case, a BPEL process instance will complete much faster and should not be considered stateful.

Note that in many cases the BPEL process could by itself take care of most of the work that can be delegated to other service engines—and before the various dedicated service engines were available, many BPEL processes were developed that actually do all the work themselves. However, for reasons of performance, functionality, and development productivity, it is better to use the best tool for the job. Equally important is the management agility: With all logic programmed into the BPEL process, every little change requires a redeployment of the entire service composite. Especially with long-running processes, such redeployments are not a trivial affair. Better to have the BPEL process collaborate with logic running in other engines that are more easily reconfigured and have different procedures for configuration and deployment. Some engines, for example, support a great deal of run-time configuration.

Recently we have seen a shift away from BPEL: True business processes are increasingly implemented using engines running BPMN. BPEL seems to be primarily an integration engine that combines services to provide the type of coarse-grained service we discussed earlier.

Service Component Architecture (SCA)

With on the one hand the obvious success of BPEL for creating service composites and on the other the ongoing challenges, many vendors working on Service-Oriented Architecture have joined forces to come up with a new standard for creating service-oriented applications.

The objective of this standard was to allow the development of a service-oriented application that could implement every piece of its functionality in the language and run-time engine best suited for it and still have all the pieces integrated in a simple, standardized way, based on the established standards for services. It is assumed—though not required—that the application will invoke several external services. It is also expected that the application will expose a service interface itself. Reuse is an important theme in SOA and is also a key objective for this new standard: Applications developed according to the standard are reusable components that can be included in other applications.

This standard is called Service Component Architecture (SCA), first published in 2007. It is expected to become the dominant guiding principle, according to which vendors build their SOA containers, and thus the framework for development of SOA applications.

The promise of SCA is that developers can use various languages running on different run-time engines to implement various parts of the application—for example, BPEL, Java, another SCA composite application, a rule engine, a workflow engine, and technology adapters to work with databases, queues, and file systems. Each such part of the application is called a (service) component. Each service component publishes a contract that describes its interface through a WSDL document. The developers specify the functional link between these different parts of the application, and it is up to the SCA container or run-time engine to facilitate communication between the components in the most efficient way, usually through a native, binary communication protocol.

The coupling between service components is very loose; they can work together without any knowledge about each other's implementation. This way of creating composite applications is very flexible: It allows replacement of one service component with another that, as long as it fulfills the same contract, could be implemented in an entirely different language running on another service engine.

SCA is not just for easier and more productive development of SOA applications. It also specifies how the behavior of the application can be made configurable to allow administrators to apply changes in the behavior without redeployment of the application. Changes in the location of services called from the application can be changed at run time without impact on the availability of the application. Quality of Service aspects, including security policies and reliability requirements, can be (re)configured during or even after deployment.

SCA helps to simplify the assembly and deployment of composite applications. An SCA composite application can be assembled from a collection of SCA composites and then turned into deployable units.

Not Invented Here (2001–2008)

Around the turn of the century, Oracle had strong support for queuing, Java, and XML in its RDBMS. In addition, it had a number of what one might call "middleware products" that were mildly successful at best. OAS was struggling in a market dominated by IBM WebSphere, BEA WebLogic, Sun IPlanet, and several open-source products. Oracle Integration Server did not get any real traction, and Oracle Corporation seemed to be looking for a product strategy that would make it a serious contender in the now rapidly evolving market for middleware.

During these years, we have seen a slowly but steadily evolving tendency at Oracle HQ to no longer insist on building every technology and product itself. In 1994, Oracle acquired the RDB database from Digital (Equipment Corporation), an acquisition that worked out very well. It demonstrated how Oracle would generally treat products it acquired: continue and frequently even intensify the development of new product releases. Maybe that experience prepared the organization for what was to come in later years.

In 1998, Oracle released JDeveloper 1.0, its first ever Java Development IDE, based on Borland's JBuilder product. This initial release consisted of over 90 percent JBuilder code, and was a rather feature-poor product in the eyes of today's Java developers. However, its significance was huge. Next to the traditional development tools created within Oracle, such as Oracle Designer, Oracle Forms, Oracle Reports, and Discoverer, Oracle offered a tool for Java (web) developers. And it would continue to evolve JDeveloper to become the strategic development platform of Oracle. In 2002, the JDeveloper 9*i* (9.0.3) release meant the end of the last JBuilder remnants in the products. Yet the experience with a product that started out based on a third-party code base probably also contributed to the acceptance of externally developed products at the core of new Oracle initiatives.

In 2001, Oracle radically changed its Application Server tactics. Rather than struggling on with its own OAS product, it struck a deal with a Norwegian company called Orion to license its application server. Orion became the heart of Oracle Containers for J2EE (OC4J) (initially the *J* in OC4J stood for Java), the engine for the Oracle Internet Application Server (iAS). iAS quickly expanded its reach to become the middle-tier platform for such diverse products as Portal, Forms, J2EE Applications, Workflow and InterConnect, Discoverer, Oracle Single Sign On, Oracle Internet Directory, and many more.

Support for Web Services in the Application Server started to appear from 2001 onward, and was complemented by development facilities in JDeveloper almost from the start. Shortly afterward, support for UDDI was added to the Oracle Internet Directory product. The year 2003 saw the announcement of Oracle's implementation of WSRP (WebService for Remote Portlets), a standard that facilitates the integration of Portlets (services with a user interface) across vendor platforms.

In 2004, the cascade of acquisitions started in what was by that time becoming known as the "SOA space." Oracle acquired dozens of companies and products, most of them to be folded into the Enterprise Applications portfolio, but a substantial number in middleware as well. All of these acquisitions quickly helped to put together a suite of products and technologies that covered most of the requirements for implementing Service-Oriented Architecture. The acquisition of Collaxa for its BPEL Process Manager (2004) laid the foundation for the later SOA Suite 10*g* product. Thor, Oblix, and OctetString were acquired in 2005 for their various security, identity and access management (IAM), and services management related offerings. The Oracle WebService Manager (OWSM, frequently pronounced *awesome)* was based on the technology in these products.

As part of the 2005 acquisition of PeopleSoft, the Business Activity Monitor (BAM) was added to the growing range of middleware products. Also in 2005, Oracle gave up its own UDDI implementation and instead decided to license the Systinet Service Registry from Systinet Corporation (bought by Mercury a little later, which itself was acquired by Hewlett-Packard in 2006). In 2006, a partnership was entered into with IDS Scheer, a leading vendor of business process modeling software (acquired by Software AG in 2009), that allowed Oracle to offer a product—Oracle Business Process Analysis (BPA) Suite—based on ARIS.

Another major chunk was swallowed later in 2005, when Siebel Systems was acquired. In terms of middleware, Siebel brought what was to become the BI Enterprise Edition to the table.

Amid all these influxes from the outside, Oracle developed its own Enterprise Service Bus (ESB)—released in 2006. The Oracle ESB leveraged a lot of the work that had gone into developing InterConnect and a wide range of technology adapters, and did this based on standards for XML and Web Services. The first incarnation of the Oracle Rules Engine was published around that same time. With the ESB, Rules Engine, WebService Manager, and BPEL Process Manager components packaged together, Oracle released SOA Suite 10*g* in early 2006, accompanied by JDeveloper 10.1.3 with the design-time environment for these components. Even though the various components were not extremely well integrated, the suite, together with iAS 10*g*, offered a wide range of functionality for developing, deploying, and managing SOA implementations. Table 3-2 lists Oracle's most relevant acquisitions and OEM partnerships around middleware technology (see http://www.oracle.com/us/corporate/acquisitions/index.htm for a complete, up-to-date list of product and vendor acquisitions).

With this first generation of the SOA Suite in place, the next step was to be a much more integrated SOA platform with all the various pieces really integrated together. The outline of SOA Suite 11*g*—the core of the Fusion Middleware platform—was becoming clearer from 2006 onward, with initial technology previews being published starting in late 2007. However, plans were to be changed dramatically in the course of 2008, as Oracle's largest technology takeover until then unfolded. Among its products were the AquaLogic Service Bus (an ESB), BPM Studio (a BPMN-based product for Business Process Modeling), the Enterprise Repository (for governance of services and other IT artifacts), AquaLogic Data Services, Tuxedo (for managing transactions across distributed systems including mainframes), and a number of portal products.

When the Oracle-BEA deal was closed at the end of April 2008, the architects of Fusion Middleware returned to the drawing boards. BEA's products offered valuable opportunities for improving the pending SOA Suite 11*g* that simply had to be taken advantage of—at the cost of a regrettable delay in its original release schedule. The entry of WebLogic into the Oracle stable meant, for example, the early retirement of the OC4J-based Application Server line: All Oracle's middleware were to be delivered on top of the WebLogic platform.

Other acquisitions that had an impact on the middleware product portfolio include Sunopsis (2006, rebranded Oracle Data Integrator), Stellent (2006), and Universal Content Manager and Hyperion in 2007—a solution for corporate performance management. Early 2010 saw the completion of the acquisition of a big (Glass)fish: Sun Microsystems. Sun was a prize for Oracle because of its hardware and its control over Java. As a bonus, Oracle gained control over many Sun products concerning identity and access management, Web Services, BPEL and integration, portals, as well as another JEE application server: GlassFish. None of these products gets the

Year	Type	Vendor	Product	Purpose
2001	OEM	Orion	OC4J	Java/J2EE application server
2004	Acquisition	Collaxa	BPEL Process Manager	Web Service Orchestration
2005	Acquisition	Siebel Systems	BI EE	Business intelligence, OLAP, reporting
2005	Acquisition	PeopleSoft	Business Activity Monitoring	Real-time analysis of business events
2005	OEM	HP (Mercury) Systinet	Service Registry	UDDI service directory
2005	Acquisition	Thor Technologies	Xellerate	Identity and access management
2005	Acquisition	OctetString	Virtual Directory (Engine)	Identity and access management
2005	Acquisition	Oblix	COREid, COREsv	Identity and access management/ Web Service management
2006	Acquisition	Sunopsis	Data Integrator	Data integration (ELT)
2006	OEM	IDS Scheer	ARIS/Oracle BPA	Business process analysis
2006	Acquisition	Stellent	Universal Content Manager	Content management
2007	Acquisition	Hyperion	Hyperion, ESSBase	Corporate performance management
2007	Acquisition	Bharosa	Bharosa Tracker and Authenticator	Security and real-time fraud detection
2007	Acquisition	Bridgestream	Role Manager	Identity and access management
2007	Acquisition	Moniforce	Moniforce	Web user experience monitoring
2008	Acquisition	BEA	WebLogic, AquaLogic Service Bus, Enterprise Repository, BPM Studio, Tuxedo, Portals	JEE Application Server, ESB, SOA governance, BPMN, transaction management
2008	Acquisition	ClearApp	ClearApp	Management of composite SOA applications
2009	Acquisition	Sun Microsystems	Hardware and infrastructure components: GlassFish, OpenESB with IEP, OpenPortal, OpenSSO, Identity Management, Portal, MySQL	Manifold, including middleware for running JEE applications, implementing SOA, processing events, and managing identities/ authentication and authorization
2009	Acquisition	GoldenGate	GoldenGate	Real-time data integration and continuous data (changes) availability
2010	Acquisition	AmberPoint	Governance System, Management System	SOA management and governance, security, business transaction management

TABLE 3-2.   *Oracle's Most Relevant Acquisitions and OEM Partnerships around Middleware Technology*

"strategic" status at Oracle. This means that while some of their capabilities may be added to the existing Fusion Middleware components, none will replace a current FMW product. As such, the impact of the acquisition of Sun on the SOA Suite 11*g* was fairly limited.

More impact—at least on operational management, security, and governance of SOA applications—can be expected from the acquisition of AmberPoint, which was announced in February 2010.

Invented Here after All

Not all new middleware technology was seized from the outside world. Indeed, one of Oracle's current flagship middleware products was built from scratch at Oracle—it simply did not exist anywhere in the world. WebCenter is a product for Enterprise 2.0, the enabler for enterprise-wide collaboration. It delivers the next generation of enterprise portals. WebCenter extends SOA concepts and services with a user interface through its support for WSRP Portlets. It provides the integration point at the user-interface level between many areas of functionality, such as content management, task management and workflow, enterprise-wide search and communication through e-mail, instant messaging (or chat), and VoIP (Voice over IP). It is also a natural fit for user interfaces that expose or leverage the services provided from the SOA.

WebCenter, Oracle Applications, BI Enterprise Edition, BAM Studio, Enterprise Manager, and an increasing number of other Oracle products are developed using the homegrown Application Development Framework (ADF). This framework contains ADF Business Components for smooth interaction with the database and ADF Faces, with a rich Web 2.0 library of user-interface components based on the JavaServer Faces (JSF) industry standard. The rich web applications are agnostic when it comes to their data provider—the ADF Model abstracts the underlying business service—and work equally well with a persistence layer based on JPA and EJB as well as Web Services.

ADF has facilities for very productive, declarative development with several reuse mechanisms and support for advanced data visualization, active (event-driven, server-push) user interfaces, and "design time@run time" (discussed later in this chapter) for application customization and personalization. Development of ADF applications is done with Oracle JDeveloper. The applications run on a J(2)EE application server, typically WebLogic Server.

ADF is used in the SOA Suite to implement the user interface for the human tasks that are part of the SOA applications.

Complete, Open, and Integrated—2009 and Beyond

Around the turn of the century, Larry Ellison stated that enterprises should not go out and select best-of-breed products from a range of different vendors that then would have to be integrated together by "the guys with the glue guns." Much better, he said, to buy a pre-integrated suite—engineered from the beginning to fit together—that does not require such a "glue gun" approach. That pre-integrated suite, by the way, was supposed to be the Oracle 11*i* eBusiness Suite.

Clearly this strategy was not embraced by the marketplace, and organizations continued to acquire best-of-breed products that required integration. Oracle itself started to do the same thing, as was described in the previous section. With PeopleSoft (HRM/HCM), Siebel (CRM), Retek (Retail), Portal (Billing), and many other applications, Oracle bought itself an impressive range of best-of-breed products that required ... integration. At the technology level, by the way, it did something very similar. With Stellent, BEA, Sunopsis, Hyperion, and others, Oracle acquired superior, market-leading alternatives to some of its own products. Of course, these products, too, needed integration.

The continuing and even increased need for integration of business applications provided Oracle with a market opportunity. It could make money in the middleware space to support all the integration efforts going on. In fact, how credible would the position of the Oracle Application Server platform be without support for integration and service orientation? Providing solid and functionally rich middleware was probably not just an opportunity as much as a necessity.

Apart from the external drivers, there was an urgent internal driver that was probably the most pressing one: Customers running a combination of modules from Oracle eBusiness Suite, Siebel, Retek, and PeopleSoft demanded of Oracle that these modules work together smoothly—something they obviously had not been designed for. Although this requirement posed a huge challenge, it was a challenge quite similar to the ones facing most enterprises: how to make legacy, custom, and COTS (commercial off-the-shelf) applications work together. Oracle's middleware had been pushed by the Oracle marketing teams and sales force as *the* solution for such challenges, so now it was time to put their money where their mouths were—or, as is the usual expression within Oracle, it was time to "eat your own dog food."

Based on the Oracle 10*g* SOA Suite, the Application Integration Architecture (AIA) was developed. AIA provides process integration packs (PIPs), collections of BPEL processes that implement business processes across various Oracle Applications products (for example, order processing across modules in EBS and PeopleSoft). Underpinning the PIPs is the AIA Foundation Pack that contains Enterprise Business Objects and Enterprise Business Services, which allow organizations to create their own customized business processes on top of the Oracle SOA Suite, spanning multiple modules from different products in the Oracle Applications portfolio and also legacy applications, including SAP modules and custom-built applications. AIA is crucial to Oracle's strategy with regard to its Enterprise Applications portfolio. AIA's requirements will further drive the development of Oracle's SOA products, and its success will provide clear proof of the value of those products as well as a reference implementation with best practices, reusables, and guidelines for organizations using the SOA Suite for their own SOA implementation.

Fusion

With the acquisition of PeopleSoft, Oracle announced its Fusion vision and roadmap. Later acquisitions had their impact, not so much on the vision itself but certainly on the roadmap and timelines. There has been a lot of confusion as to what Oracle's Project Fusion entailed. At the core, "Fusion" has these aspects:

- The integration of the acquired business entities into Oracle, reorganization as well as staff retention, especially among engineers

- A newly developed next-generation application that is based on industry standards and the latest technology and that takes the best features, flows, and usability traits from the existing application products; this new product is known as Fusion Applications

- Technology for making different products in the Oracle Applications portfolio—such as EBS, PeopleSoft, Siebel, Retek, and JD Edwards—work together, as well as the technology stack for the new Fusion Applications; this technology has been labeled Fusion Middleware

The adage Oracle uses for Fusion Middleware (FMW) is "complete, open, and integrated." This captures the essence of the objectives with and claims for Fusion Middleware.

Complete means that all capabilities in every middleware area you can think of are provided by Fusion Middleware. And to put it even stronger, Oracle claims that every capability in FMW is provided by the best-of-breed offering. So even if an organization wants to pursue a best-of-breed strategy, it would have to select Fusion Middleware components in every area because they are the best of breed in their own right. Oracle further strengthens the completeness claim with Fusion Applications as the living proof. Oracle has a unique ability to maintain the completeness in the future, given its resources, dedication, and internal needs.

Open refers to the fact that Fusion Middleware is hot-pluggable. This means that the FMW components can be replaced by alternative products from other vendors. Oracle recognizes the fact that even though it claims to provide a complete, best-of-breed solution in every area, organizations may have current investments or even deviating views as to which product is the best solution in a certain area of middleware capabilities. Another aspect of openness is the support for open standards. Fusion Middleware complies with every major industry standard in the area of middleware—some 195 standards are supported and adhered to in the FMW 11*g* release. This makes the product open in the sense that it can be interacted with in ways that are common across the industry. FMW is not open source, obviously, but does not tie an organization to Oracle proprietary protocols or hamper interoperability. Custom applications written for use with Fusion Middleware will run with alternative middleware platforms that also support the industry standards.

Now let's consider *integrated*. Not only does Fusion Middleware offer all middleware capabilities (*complete*), it also has all these capabilities nicely integrated and working together. That may sound trivial—if a vendor offers a number of middleware products, you would naturally expect them to work together. However, frequently that is not the case at all—and it wasn't the case for the 10*g* releases of the Oracle SOA Suite. Fusion Middleware provides that integration across different areas of functionality, such as business intelligence, Web Services, content management, enterprise collaboration, identity and access management, governance, event processing, and custom-developed user interfaces. It helps organizations create business processes that integrate with these different technologies across the enterprise.

Fusion Middleware 11*g*: The Innovative Foundation for Enterprise Applications

July 1, 2009, marked a milestone in the history of Oracle Corporation. On that day, the worldwide rollout of Oracle Fusion Middleware 11*g* was initiated, the culmination of many years of helping forge the industry standards, conducting research into interoperability, creating new tools and frameworks, acquiring and absorbing products from external parties, and architecting a complete stack of middleware products. The public unveiling of FMW 11*g* was one of the biggest product launches in Oracle's history.

Fusion Middleware 11*g* consists of many different products that provide solutions in diverse areas, from identity and access management, business intelligence, event processing, content management and data integration to a data grid, web application development, enterprise portal and collaboration, business process management, governance, security, and, of course, Service-Oriented Architecture. Fusion Middleware 11*g* runs on top of WebLogic Server 11*g*. The design time for most products in the stack is JDeveloper 11*g*.

Fusion Middleware is not sold as single product with a simple price tag. Oracle understands that many organizations will, at least initially, only use specific components from the wide range of middleware products. Customers buy licenses for specific product suites, bundles of related products in specific areas of functionality. Among the FMW 11*g* suites offered that are associated with SOA are the BPM Suite, EDA Suite, Governance Suite, and, of course, SOA Suite. Note that these suites have a certain level of overlap. Also note that for most suites, several reduced-cost variations are offered that support usage of only specific products from the suite.

The biggest customer for Fusion Middleware is Oracle itself. The development of Fusion Applications and other products in the Oracle Applications portfolio is all done on top of the Fusion Middleware 11*g* stack. Most organizations will have less stringent requirements for their development and integration efforts than the ones faced by Oracle's internal divisions. Because the exact same technology is available to external customers as is being used internally, Oracle is providing the proof in the FMW 11*g* pudding by eating all of it itself.

SOA Suite 11*g*: The Key Components

SOA Suite 11*g* is first and foremost an SCA container, a run-time engine that can execute composite service applications. Composite (service) applications are SCA-compliant applications that are assembled from various service components that are wired together internally based on WSDL contracts. Composite applications publish a service interface through which they can be invoked by external clients. This interface is frequently a (SOAP) Web Service interface, but other types of bindings are also possible, such as based on EJB/RMI and JMS. SOA Suite 11*g* can run multiple instances of every composite application in parallel. It can handle calls into applications, coordinate messages between components within an application, and facilitate calls from the application to external services.

You invoke a composite application that exposes a Web Service binding by sending an XML message to a URL. That message will be processed—possibly resulting in database manipulation, file creation, human task execution, e-mail sending, and event publishing. At some points during the processing of your message, you may receive return messages that can contain the results of whatever the application has been doing.

The composite applications running on the SOA Suite can make use of the following service languages and engines for executing its components:

- **BPEL Process Manager**   Orchestrates (potentially) long-running service composites with many interactions with external services, both outgoing and incoming.

- **Decision Service or Business Rules engine**   Executes decision logic that can be (re)defined at run time.

- **Human Workflow Service**   For engaging humans in making decisions or providing information.

- **Spring-based Java Beans (as of 11*g*R1 PS 2)**   Custom business logic implemented in Java acting on the messages.

- **Mediator**   For filtering, transforming, adapting, and routing messages.

- **BPMN**   Business process logic defined through BPMN can be executed inside the SOA Suite (by the same engine that also runs BPEL). (This, too, was introduced in 11*g*R1 PS2.)

Composite applications accept incoming request messages and route them through components programmed using these technologies. Note that other SCA containers may support different service engines—for example, running Cobol, C, and C#—and that Oracle may add new service engines to the SOA Suite as well. Each component performs a service that may alter the message, create new messages, have external effects, or influence the onward processing in the application. Composite applications can call out to external Web Services—and receive asynchronous responses or other incoming messages from these external services. Applications can also make use of the Event Delivery Network to publish business events as well as to consume such events.

Ingredients of a Composite Application

When developers create an SOA composite application, what they are actually doing is working on XML files. What gets deployed to the SOA Suite's SCA container typically is a collection of the following files:

- The WSDL and XSD files that describe the interfaces (contracts) of the application as a whole (the services it exposes) as well as the service components running inside the application.

- The files that are the programs to run in the BPEL and Mediator engines or that define the human task to be performed by an end user.

- Files that describe how the SCA components are wired together to exchange XML messages to be processed at run time.

- Definitions for how XML messages are to be transformed en route from one component to the next.

- Some of the XML files provide the configuration details for the adapters that the composite application can use to communicate to external technology platforms, such as database, file system, e-mail server, and message queues.

- Configuration plans that apply environment-specific deployment details.

Most of the XML, by the way, is hidden from view by visual editors that present far prettier and easier-to-understand renditions of those blocks of XML data.

All of the XML files are bundled together in archives—a JAR (Java Archive) or SAR (Service Assembly Archive, aka SOA Archive, a deployment unit that describes the SOA composite application)—that are deployed to the SOA Suite container.

The SOA Suite is shipped with an impressive set of technology adapters. These adapters speak a specific protocol and language to some external technology platform on one end and act like a Web Service on the other. Examples of these protocols, platforms, and languages include the file system, FTP servers, the database, JMS queues, the eBusiness Suite, SAP, and various B2B exchange types, such as RosettaNet, ebXML, HL7, and EDI(FACT). These adapters make it possible for SOA applications to connect to many different components and thereby service-enable existing assets.

Outside of the SCA container—but still part of the SOA Suite license and prepared for integration with the SOA composites—are several other valuable products: the Oracle Service Bus (OSB), Oracle Business Activity Monitoring (BAM), and Oracle Complex Event Processing (CEP).

Adapters

SOA Suite 11*g* is integrated with a large number of adapters that the composite applications can make use of for accessing services across various technologies and protocols. These adapters allow the composite applications to retrieve data from, forward messages to, and leverage functionality in many different places in and even outside the enterprise—from database and file systems to EDI trading partners and legacy applications. Some adapters allow for the activation of composite applications from the outside world. The most important adapters available for use in SOA Suite 11*g* composite applications access the following targets:

- **Database**   For accessing tables and views (query and data manipulation) and calling PL/SQL program units
- **File and FTP**   For reading and writing files from a file system and an FTP server
- **Queues**   For accessing queues through JMS, Oracle Advanced Queuing, and MQ Series
- **Enterprise Java Bean (EJB)**   To communicate with remote Enterprise JavaBeans
- **Sockets**   For reading and writing data over TCP/IP sockets
- **Oracle Applications (aka Oracle eBusiness Suite adapter)**   For retrieving data from and sending data to eBusiness Suite (11*i* and 12)
- **Business Activity Monitoring (BAM)**   For sending data and events to an Oracle BAM server
- **ADF-BC (Business Components)**   For interacting with an ADF BC–based Service Data Object service
- **B2B**   For the exchange of business documents with e-commerce trading partners based on industry standards such as RosettaNet, HL7, and various EDI protocols; also support for interaction with SAP and other ERP applications

Adapters will usually be called by the service components running in a composite application (outbound). Note, however, that most adapters can also initiate a new instance of an application (inbound). The database adapter, for example, can "poll for changed records," and any new or changed record can start a new instance. Likewise, the file and FTP adapters can poll for new files to arrive on the file system or an FTP server, or for new lines in an existing file. This adapter, too, can instantiate a composite application instance when new data is read from a file that has changed.

Other adapters that can act as "service clients" that create new instances of composite applications include the EJB adapter, the JMS adapter, and the AQ adapter. Inbound adapters can connect to existing instances of composite applications (see Chapter 6 for details).

Adapters are discussed throughout the book: For example, the database adapter is discussed in Chapter 5, the file adapter in Chapter 7, the JMS adapter in Chapter 12, and the ADF BC adapter in Chapter 20.

Event Delivery Network

Business events are situations of potential interest. Examples are the reception of an order, cancellation of an appointment by the patient, the failure of a credit check, the crossing of a stock threshold (we are critically low on Band-Aids), and the acceptance of a job offer by a new nurse. These events frequently occur in business processes when certain conditions are met or actions have been performed. Events can also come into existence during the execution of a service component. The business events may trigger the start of new composite application instances or could notify already running instances.

However, the burden of informing any potentially interested party of the event should not be on the service component that happens to encounter the situation. The producer of the event— the application or service component that causes or encounters the situation that is deemed to be of business interest—is not responsible for what happens with the published event, nor does or should it care. This keeps producers and consumers decoupled: Consumers can be added or removed without impact on the producers of events. Likewise, new producers can be introduced without any effect on the consumers. To make this happen, we need a "man in the middle" of sorts, a generic medium that deals with both consumers and producers.

A key part of SOA Suite 11*g* is the Event Delivery Network (EDN), an intermediary that takes on the responsibility of receiving events from producers and delivering them to interested parties.

Business events are defined across services and composite applications as an extension of the canonical data model. The definition of a business event comprises a name, possibly custom headers, and the definition of the payload. These definitions need to be registered with the EDN.

Service components—BPMN, Mediator, and BPEL—can publish events (occurrences of one of the predefined event types) to the Event Delivery Network. Events can also be published to the EDN from ADF applications and through a PL/SQL API.

Service components such as Mediator, BPMN, and BPEL register their interest in one or more of the centrally defined business events with the EDN. Such an interest can indicate all events of a specific type, but also can include more fine-grained selection rules that refer to the custom headers or payload to filter on specific occurrences of an event. When an event has been published, the Event Delivery Network will make sure that all interested parties will receive the event. Note that it is very well possible that an event is not delivered to any interested party at all. In that case, it disappears into the void.

Chapter 9 discusses the Event Delivery Network and presents several examples in detail.

Oracle Service Bus

Composite applications running in the SOA Suite will frequently need to access services made available in an enterprise service bus (ESB), possibly based on services running in other SCA containers, offered by external parties, or running on legacy platforms such as mainframes. In a similar vein, the services exposed by the composite applications within the business domain may need to be made available to a wider audience; this, too, is typically done through an ESB.

SOA Suite 11*g* contains an ESB: the Oracle Service Bus (the successor to BEA's AquaLogic Service Bus, abbreviated OSB).

Chapter 13 describes the OSB and how it can be used along with SOA composite applications.

Business Activity Monitoring (BAM) Server

Oracle BAM provides a framework for creating dashboards that display real-time data as it flows into the BAM server. This is typically data received from physical sensors (security gates, RFID scanners), trace details from computer applications (request logging in web applications, process progress signals from a BPM or workflow engine), or live data feeds with financial data, weather reports, or even sports statistics. Rules can be created in BAM to instruct the framework to highlight deviations and send alerts under specified conditions. BAM is primarily used to monitor aggregates against predefined thresholds for data recently received over relatively short periods (typically minutes to hours, rather than months to years). That, along with the built-in capability to trigger alerts and take actions, is the main distinction between BAM and traditional business intelligence, which tends to be more passive and more historically oriented. BAM tries to facilitate the operational control of business process execution.

Data used by BAM for the actual reports is managed in memory in the Active Data Cache. Data is loaded into this cache in real time via various channels. Probably most important in the context of the SOA Suite is the BAM Adapter—it is not only the fastest option for streaming data into the BAM server; it is also integrated into composite applications like all other adapters. For BPEL there is an additional option through the BAM sensor action that can be enlisted when adding special tracers to activities in the BPEL processes. Alternative routes for data into BAM are Direct JMS, Oracle Data Integrator, and through the Web Services interface exposed by the BAM server.

Chapter 19 introduces Business Activity Monitoring in detail.

Fusion Middleware Infrastructure and WebLogic Server 11*g*

SOA Suite 11*g* runs inside WebLogic Server 11*g*—the SCA container lives inside the JEE container. The underlying run-time infrastructure of Fusion Middleware 11*g* is the WebLogic Server platform, managed through the Administration Console. Several web applications are installed into the WebLogic Server domain as part of SOA Suite 11*g* to support the FMW 11*g* run-time operations. The Oracle Enterprise Manager Fusion Middleware Control Console is the most important one of these—other examples are the SOA Composer, the Worklist application, and several BAM web applications.

The Oracle Enterprise Manager Fusion Middleware Control Console is the integrated console for virtually all run-time monitoring and administration of SOA composite applications and their instances. This console is an ADF 11*g* web application that runs on WebLogic and is accessed from a browser by the SOA Suite administrator to work on tasks in these main categories:

- **Configuring** Adjusting properties from SOA infrastructure and service engines down to components in composite applications.

- **Monitoring** Aggregating metrics, performance figures, and faults across applications, components, and service engines; reporting the current state of running instances; providing an audit trail per composite instance; drilling down to the steps through a component; and inspecting the log files.

- **Managing** Deploying, stopping, and starting composite applications; recovering from faults; terminating application instances; unit testing of composite applications; and attachment of policies to SOA composite applications, service components, and binding components. The Oracle WSM Policy Manager is the integrated facility to attach policies regarding security, reliable messaging, addressing, and logging to Web Services and service composite applications.

The WebLogic Server Administration Console is used alongside the Enterprise Manager Fusion Middleware Control for normal JEE administrative tasks such as the configuration of data sources and JMS objects, administration of the security realm, and management of the technology adapters. Figure 3-2 shows the architecture of WebLogic Server and SOA Suite 11*g* installed on top of it.

User Messaging Service

Another element in the infrastructure is the Oracle User Messaging Service (UMS). UMS provides applications with two-way communication with users across various channels and protocols. Messages can be sent and received through e-mail, IM (XMPP), SMS (SMPP), and voice (VoIP). Most of the time, the message will be initiated by the application, but UMS also caters to

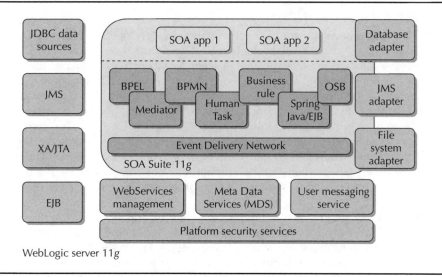

FIGURE 3-2.   *WebLogic Server with the SOA Suite installed on top of it*

scenarios in which the user is the sender of the message and the application is on the receiving end. The arrival of the message is fed into the application by UMS.

Notifications will frequently be sent via UMS from BPEL processes, the Human Workflow engine, and the BAM server. WebCenter, ADF, and other web applications can also make use of UMS. UMS consists of a server that works with a number of drivers to connect with message gateways using specific protocols. These external gateways are not part of WebLogic Server or the SOA Suite. Various e-mail servers, chat (IM) servers, and external providers of SMS and text-to-speech services can be integrated.

Appendix C and the book's wiki provide instructions for configuring the UMS services.

Meta Data Services (MDS)

The Fusion Middleware run-time environment has at least one, and possibly multiple, metadata repositories that contain metadata for Oracle Fusion Middleware system components. A metadata repository contains metadata about the configuration of Oracle Fusion Middleware as well as metadata for different types of enterprise applications. Shared artifacts such as XSD documents describing the canonical data model, data value maps that describe mappings between business vocabularies in different domains, reusable transformations, human task definitions, security policies, business rule definitions, and business event definitions are deployed to and managed in metadata repositories. Artifacts in these metadata repositories can be used during development as well as at run time. Meta Data Services (MDS) provides a single interface across all repositories. MDS provides services to validate, version, tag and categorize, discover, and manage artifacts throughout their lifecycle.

A special facility in MDS is its support for customization. MDS can return specialized versions of artifacts that are created from a base version with context-sensitive deltas applied to it.

Design Time

The IDE (integrated development environment) used by developers to create service composite applications is JDeveloper 11g. JDeveloper is an IDE in more than one way. Most facilities required for developing software are integrated into a single workbench, including editors, debuggers, and support for testing, building, and deploying software artifacts. JDeveloper is integrated with WebLogic Server for easy deployment, execution, and debugging of web applications. JDeveloper also brings together the design time for many different products and technologies—from Complex Event Processor, BPM, UML, Java, and ADF to SQL and PLSQL (SQL Developer), and from WebCenter, Data Integrator, XML, and Web Services to all the technologies and service engines of the SOA Suite. That means JDeveloper is also the *integration* development environment.

Oracle Service Bus currently has two design-time environments: One is a browser-based console and the other is part of the Oracle Enterprise Pack for Eclipse. OSB support in JDeveloper is planned.

The slogan "design time at run time" is becoming fashionable, and describes the ability to change the behavior of already deployed applications at run time. Fusion Middleware supports various forms of this run-time application manipulation. For the SOA Suite, some of the interesting DT@RT bits include editing of business rules; manipulation of domain value maps; configuring properties on service composite applications and adapters; and creating, removing, or changing subscriptions to business events. The Oracle Enterprise Manager Fusion Middleware Control Console, the BPM Process Browser, and the SOA Composer are the tools for most of the SOA Suite's DT@RT, as is the OSB Console.

Related Suites and Products in FMW 11g

Applications running in the SOA Suite or organizations working with the SOA Suite will frequently use other Fusion Middleware products as well. Some of the most likely suspects that you may run into or decide to use alongside the SOA Suite are detailed in this section.

The Application Development Framework (ADF) is a JSF-based framework for developing rich Java web applications. ADF has special integration points with the SOA Suite. To name a few: ADF is used to create the user interface for the human tasks, ADF Business Components (ADF BC) are used to publish SDO services on top of the database (which are used in, for example, BPEL processes), ADF BC is capable of publishing events onto the Event Delivery Network, and ADF applications can consume the Web Services exposed by composite service applications running in the SOA Suite. By the way, ADF was also used by the Oracle development teams to create the Enterprise Manager Fusion Middleware Control Console.

WebCenter has several faces, one of which is its portal capability. Portlets can be seen as a special type of service: a service that has a user interface built into it. WebCenter provides ADF applications with the ability to consume such services, and it also enables ADF developers to expose their applications as Portlet services. WebCenter is also an extension of ADF as a foundation for rich web applications, through a large collection of services that add "integrated collaboration" to ADF applications. This includes support for blogs, wikis, RSS feeds, chat, e-mail, tagging and linking, content integration, management of tasks, activities and events, and enterprise search across all content, services, and application data. WebCenter also adds *design-time at run-time* capability to an ADF application. This enables an application administrator or content editor to change the appearance and content of application components at run time—very much like regular portal products do, but in a more advanced and better integrated-with-ADF way.

Fusion Middleware contains a number of products for governance of SOA artifacts (and other IT assets). At the core of governance is the Enterprise Repository. The Enterprise Repository provides metadata management for technical and software-related SOA assets and sophisticated tools for governing those assets throughout their lifecycle to promote reuse. The Service Registry provides a standards-based (UDDI) reference for the dynamic discovery and use of services and their associated policies at run time. It contains a subset of the metadata managed within Oracle Enterprise Repository that is useful to the run-time infrastructure for dynamic discovery of services and policies.

Oracle BPA is a tool for business analysts and architects to perform process modeling and analysis as well as simulation and publishing of process models. It integrates with both BPM and BPEL: Process models (also called *blueprints)* from BPA serve as the starting point for more detailed, implementation-ready process definitions created in BPM and BPEL.

CEP subscribes to event streams—such as from the SOA Suite Event Delivery Network (although more likely from lower-level and more voluminous sources)—and executes a Continuous Query Language (Oracle CQL) query to search for aggregates, patterns, and exceptions in real-time event streams. The events processed by CEP are usually highly frequent, sometimes physical in nature, and can be quite meaningless by themselves. The results from the continuous queries that reveal a meaningful pattern or an exception are turned into events at a higher, more business-oriented level that can be fed into Oracle BAM or the Event Delivery Network, for example.

Oracle Data Integrator (ODI), together with Oracle GoldenGate, provides a data-integration platform that covers all data-integration requirements—from high-volume, high-performance ELT batches, to real-time, event-driven, trickle-feed integration processes, to SOA-enabled data services. This technology can be used alongside an enterprise service bus to handle large volumes of data that primarily need to be moved from one system to another in not necessarily a service- or XML-oriented way. ODI has support for Web Services as well—both outbound and inbound. In addition, it can be integrated directly with Oracle BAM.

NOTE
ODI intentionally uses the term ELT instead of the more common ETL (Extract, Transform, and Load).

Application Integration Architecture (AIA) is a framework for integrating various products and modules from the Oracle Applications portfolio and for creating cross-module business processes. AIA builds on top of the SOA Suite. Through AIA, JD Edwards, Retek, PeopleSoft, Siebel, EBS, and Fusion Applications—among others—can interact in a loosely coupled way. AIA provides a reference architecture for implementing SOA that can also be used with custom applications and third-party software.

The Oracle Identity and Access Management offering has a substantial number of products that help implement and manage scalable security based on open standards for applications and services. Through Oracle Platform Security Services (OPSS)—an abstraction layer that implements a security and identity and access management API—applications can use a uniform set of services, without having to deal with implementation details of the underlying security infrastructure. OPSS is the platform that provides security to Oracle Fusion Middleware, including products such as WebLogic Server, SOA Suite, WebCenter, ADF, and Oracle Entitlements Server, to name a few. Note that OPSS can run on various JEE application servers, including JBoss and WebSphere, in addition to WebLogic. SOA Suite and WebLogic Server interact with OPSS for securing Web Services and composite applications.

The Universal Content Manager, with supporting tools such as SiteBuilder, is another component of Fusion Middleware. This product will typically not have direct interaction with applications running in the SOA Suite. The same applies to the FMW products for Business Intelligence (BI EE) and Enterprise Corporate Performance (Hyperion).

Oracle has bundled many of its FMW products in suites, such as the SOA Suite. These suites comprise a logically related collection of products sold under a single license. Having said that, most suites can be bought with tailor-made licenses that apply to a subset of the products in a suite. And besides, there is a lot of overlap between the suites that is accounted for when you acquire more than one of them. The most relevant product suites around the SOA Suite are the BPM Suite, EDA Suite, SOA Governance Suite, BPA Suite, and Data Integration Suite.

Getting Started with SOA Suite 11*g*

This book is by no means intended to be only theoretical. Yes, it does tell a story and hopefully explains a great deal about the SOA Suite by showing examples and describing the concepts behind and workings of the service engines, underlying standards, and technologies and supporting tools. However, you—and your fingers—will only start to learn for real once you start practicing what is preached in this book. So now is the time to get into gear. It's time to get yourself a fully operational SOA Suite (version 11*g*) so you can start developing, deploying, and running composite service applications as well as fully appreciate what it is really like to create a service-oriented application.

This section describes the steps to take for installing and configuring SOA Suite 11*g*. It only provides high-level instructions, however, because the details can be found in several excellent installation manuals. The book's wiki provides an online chapter complement with an extensive installation instruction using many screenshots. The complement guides you through the installation of a complete SOA Suite 11*g* environment that goes with the examples in this book.

It is assumed that you will install into a development environment to start dabbling with the SOA Suite—not a full-blown, highly available, clustered production environment.

Installation of SOA Suite 11*g*

The SOA Suite is available for various operating systems, including Windows, Unix, and Linux. You can install and run the SOA Suite on a machine that has at least 2GB of memory, some 10GB of free disk space, and a dual-core 1.5 GHz processor. If you intend to run JDeveloper on the same machine, you should have at least 3GB of memory.

Part of the SOA Suite infrastructure is the metadata repository that needs to be installed in a 10*g* or 11*g* Oracle RDBMS. Note that SQL Server 2005 and 2008 are also supported, as may be other databases at some point. Before you start the installation, you need to make sure you have access to such a database—with 1GB of disk space for the creation of new tablespaces. The database parameters for processes and open_cursors should be set to a value of 500 or above. You need database user credentials with DBA or SYSDBA privileges.

The documentation for the installation (as well as all other details) of the SOA Suite and the other components in Fusion Middleware can be found online at http://www.oracle.com/technology/documentation/middleware.html.

Downloading the Software

Before you can start with the installation, you need to download the required software from Oracle Technology Network. Go to the OTN page for Fusion Middleware Software: http://www.oracle .com/technology/software/products/middleware/index.html. Download the following components:

- **Repository Creation Utility**   300MB
- **WebLogic Server 11*g***   800MB
- **SOA Suite 11*g***   1.5GB
- **JDeveloper 11*g***   1MB
  - JDeveloper extensions for SOA and BPM - 450Mb
  - Oracle Service Bus 11*g* - 900Mb (optional)
- Oracle Complex Event Processing 11*g* (optional)

The design and run-time environment for SOA Suite 11*g* is illustrated in Figure 3-3.

NOTE
This software (the full production versions) can be used for free under the OTN Development License for self-education or for prototyping and development of applications. All you need is a free account on the Oracle Technology Network.

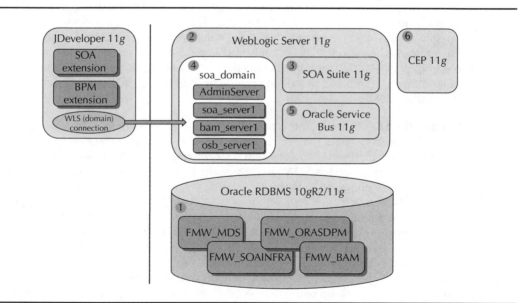

FIGURE 3-3.   *Installation applies to three tiers: the JDeveloper design time, and the run-time setup of the Database and the Middle Tier*

Installation Steps

This section presents the installation steps for the SOA Suite. Further details can be found through references on the the book's wiki.

1. Run the Repository Creation Utility (RCU) to install the metadata repository.   The RCU is started from the rcuHome/bin directory. The RCU creates all tablespaces, schemas, and database objects required in the metadata repository for SOA Suite and BAM. Select at least the SOA Infrastructure and the Business Activity Monitoring component under SOA and BPM infrastructure. The Metadata Services should be selected automatically upon making those choices.

The default (or minimum) tablespace size can be a bit large for a development environment. You can decrease the size of the data file associated with each tablespace to save on disk space.

2. Install WebLogic Server and create the middleware home.   Run the downloaded executable file for WebLogic Server 11*g* (the internal release number is 10.3.x). Select the option Create A New Middleware Home. Accept the option to perform a typical installation and accept other default values by clicking Next until the Finish button is enabled. Then click the Finish button. Now WebLogic Server will be installed. You could start WebLogic Server when the installation is complete to verify the successful installation. However, let's first install SOA Suite 11*g* and create the SOA domain inside WebLogic Server.

3. Install the SOA Suite.   Extract the downloaded ZIP file to a temporary directory. Run the executable runInstaller (Linux and Unix) or setup.exe and pass the parameter -jreLoc, specifying the location of a Java 6 run-time environment (for example, the one installed along with WebLogic Server in MIDDLEWARE_HOME\jdk160_11).

The Installer Wizard appears. It performs a number of checks—available disk space, hardware requirements, and so on. Then it asks for the install location. In the Oracle Middleware Home field, specify the absolute path to your existing Oracle Middleware Home directory; this is the directory created when you installed Oracle WebLogic Server. It presents a summary and allows you to start the actual installation by clicking the Install button. When you click that button, the SOA Suite software is installed in a directory structure starting at SOA_HOME that lives under MIDDLEWARE_HOME.

4. Configure the SOA Suite.   At this point, we have the metadata repository prepared in the database and a clean install of the WebLogic Server. The SOA Suite software has been installed, but not yet configured. There is no SOA container running inside WebLogic Server just yet. The next step entails configuring the SOA Suite inside the WebLogic Server. We do this using the Fusion Middleware Configuration Wizard.

This Configuration Wizard is located in the SOA_ HOME/common/bin directory (for Linux) or the SOA_HOME\common\bin directory (for Windows). Go to this directory; then run the config.sh script (for Linux) or the config.cmd script (for Windows) to start the Configuration Wizard. Unless you have very specific reasons for deviating from the default settings, you should accept them as they are for this development environment.

The wizard will create a new WebLogic domain called soa_domain. You have to provide the credentials for a new user who will have the Administrator role. The default recommended values to accept are *weblogic* for the username and *weblogic1* (the last character is the number one) as password. Note: Another frequently used password is *welcome1*. You may come across it in tutorials and installation instructions or other documentation.)

WebLogic Terminology

The product we just installed is called WebLogic Server 11*g*. However, at this point we cannot run it because it has no instance to start and run.

An installation of WebLogic Server can be used to run one or more domains. For the installation of the SOA Suite and the BAM server in the personal development environment, we will assume for this book that you will work within a single domain. A domain is a logically related group of servers that can share certain resources. A server is a unit that can be started and stopped independently of other servers. Servers host the components and associated resources that constitute your applications—for example, JSF pages and EJBs. Every domain contains a special server: the Administration Server (AdminServer). You use the Administration Server, programmatically or through the Administration Console or WLST, to configure all other server instances and resources in the domain.

All other servers in the domain are called managed servers. When a managed server starts up, it connects to the domain's Administration Server to obtain configuration and deployment settings. However, a managed server can start up independently of the Administration Server if the Administration Server is unavailable. Several managed servers can be linked to form a cluster. Note that a cluster runs within a single domain.

The installation of the SOA Suite that is described next involves an AdminServer, a server for the core SOA Suite components—usually called soa_server1—and a second, managed server that runs the Oracle BAM Server and web applications; this server is called bam_server1 by default.

Specify database connection details for the metadata repository you created using the Repository Creation Utility in step 1. On the Summary page, click Install to start the creation of the new SOA domain with three servers inside: AdminServer, soa_server1, and bam_server1. Note that you can run this Configuration Wizard at a later moment to apply additional configurations to this domain.

The new domain is created in the directory MIDDLEWARE_HOME/user_projects/domains/soa_domain.

5. Install the Oracle Service Bus 11*g*.   (This step can be considered optional at this point, as the OSB is only required for Chapter 13.) Run the setup.exe from the OSB 11*g* download. Provide the JRE location. Install the OSB 11*g* into the same Middleware Home used for the SOA Suite 11*g*. Next, run the configuration wizard to extend the soa_domain created during the installation of the SOA Suite 11*g* with a managed server osb_server1 that contains OSB 11*g*.

6. Install Complex Event Processing 11*g*.   Again, an optional step, Complex Event Processing is only introduced in Chapter 19. The CEP installation process creates a separate lightweight container that runs CEP. Additionally, Eclipse should be installed as the development environment, with the CEP plug-ins to complete the CEP IDE.

7. Start the AdminServer and the managed servers for SOA and BAM.   Before we can start doing anything at all with the SOA Suite, we need to start the servers in the new WebLogic SOA domain. We will use three command-line scripts to get these servers going.

Starting the SOA Server without Entering the Credentials

If you do not want to have to type in the username and password of the administrator account every time you start up the server, you can do the following—after having started the server at least once to have the directory structure created:

1. Create a new directory called "security" under MIDDLEWARE_HOME \user_projects\domains\soa_domain\servers\soa_server1.

2. Create a new text file called boot.properties in this directory.

3. Add two lines to this file with username and password key-value pairs, like this:

   ```
   username=weblogic
   password=weblogic1
   ```

When the server is started, the credentials are read from this file. Note that the file will be changed into a more secure, encrypted pair of values. The same instructions apply to the BAM server and the OSB server.

First, to start the AdminServer, locate the startWebLogic.cmd script (Linux: startWebLogic.sh) in the MIDDLEWARE_HOME \user_projects\domains\soa_domain directory. Run this script from the command line.

When the AdminServer is running, you should start the SOA server and optionally the BAM server and/or the OSB server. Go to the directory MIDDLEWARE_HOME \user_projects\domains\soa_domain\bin, which was created by the SOA Suite Configuration Wizard. Open a command window and enter the following command to execute:

```
startManagedWebLogic.cmd soa_server1
```

(On Linux, use the script startManagedWebLogic.sh.)

To start the BAM server, use this same command for the bam_server1, and for the OSB server replace soa_server1 with osb_server1.

NOTE
You will be prompted for the username (weblogic) and password (weblogic1) of the administrator credentials used to boot the server, so do not go away right after starting the script.

8. Access the Oracle Enterprise Manager Fusion Middleware Control.   With the servers running, now is a good moment to check out the Enterprise Manager. This console is where most of the administration tasks take place with regard to the SOA Suite and the composite applications. The Enterprise Manager Fusion Middleware Control, shown in Figure 3-4, supports various actions, such as deploying, starting and stopping, and testing composite applications, as well as inspecting completed and running instances of the applications, including fine-grained details from individual service engines and every single step in BPEL process execution. The console is available at http://localhost:7001/em. Use the username weblogic and the password weblogic1 to log in to the console.

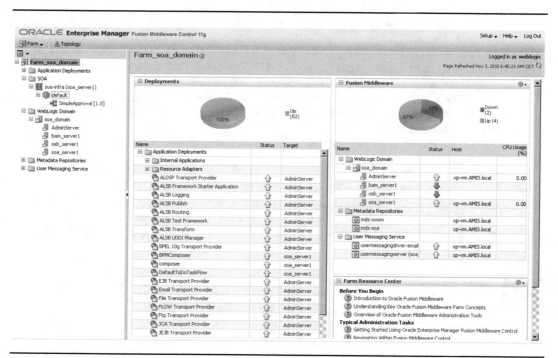

FIGURE 3-4. *The Enterprise Manager Fusion Middleware Control*

The SOA node is the starting point from which you can inspect the list of deployed composite applications—although, of course, initially there are none.

The classic WebLogic Server Administration console is also available and can be accessed at http://localhost:7001/console. You will need this console to create and edit JDBC data sources and JMS queues, as well as to configure various technology adapters and the identity store used by WebLogic Server and SOA Suite.

Other web applications running at this point include the following:

- The BPM Worklist application, which displays the tasks assigned to users by the Human Workflow service. This application can be accessed at http://localhost:8001/integration/worklistapp.

- Running at http://localhost:8001/soa/composer is the SOA Composer, an application that supports live editing of Business Rules and Domain Value Maps.

- BPM Process Composer is the application where business analysts and business process developers meet up to create and edit Business Process Models; it is available at http://localhost:8001/bpm/composer.

- When the OSB server is started, the console—both for development as well as for administration—can be accessed at http://localhost:7001/sbconsole.

- When the BAM server is started, the BAM web applications are available from the start page at http://localhost:9001/OracleBAM.

9. Take further configuration steps. The installation and configuration of the SOA Suite is now done to the point where we can start deploying and running the composite applications. There are some additional configuration tasks you may want to perform, either now or at a later moment. You could, for example, configure JMS queues or JDBC data sources in the WebLogic Server Administration Console.

This may also be a good moment to configure the User Messaging Service (UMS) to allow the composite applications to send and receive notifications via e-mail, IM, SMS, and other communication channels.

Details for the configuration of JMS, JDBC, and UMS can be found online in Appendix C.

Installing JDeveloper

Go to the JDeveloper Downloads page on OTN (http://www.oracle.com/technology/software/products/jdev/htdocs/soft11.html) and download the latest JDeveloper Studio Edition release. After downloading the executable EXE, BIN, or JAR file, run the file to start the installation. Accept the default settings in the Installation Wizard and have both JDeveloper and an integrated WebLogic server installed.

NOTE
We will not use the integrated WebLogic Server for running the SOA composite applications because it does not have the SOA server installed.

Adding JDeveloper extensions When the installation is done, start JDeveloper. Before you can design SOA applications, you need to install the SOA Suite extension—and for BPMN components the BPM Studio extension. Select the option Check For Updates from the Help menu. The Check For Updates Wizard comes up. Make sure that the box for Oracle Fusion Middleware Products is checked on the Source page. The list of available updates will include the latest Oracle SOA Suite Composite Editor 11g plug-in as well as the BPM Studio extension. Check both boxes and click Finish. You will now probably have to provide your OTN credentials. JDeveloper will then start to download the plug-ins (some 450MB in total). After the download completes, you need to restart JDeveloper in order to activate the two plug-ins.

You can also add the SOA Composite Editor and BPM Studio extensions to JDeveloper from local files that you download from the Oracle Fusion Middleware Products Update Center (http://www.oracle.com/technology/products/jdev/101/update/fmw_products.xml). This can be useful when you have to install the same version of the plug-ins on several clients or when the download from JDeveloper fails for some reason (possibly firewall related). Just download the ZIP files for the SOA Composite Editor and the BPM Studio. Then run the Check For Updates Wizard, and on the Source page select the radio button Install From Local File. Select the downloaded ZIP file to install the extension from.

Create a connection to the SOA Suite To deploy SOA applications directly onto the SOA Suite, we need to configure an application server connection in JDeveloper to the WebLogic Server soa_domain.

To create this connection, start JDeveloper and go to the Resource Palette. Click the New icon, select New Connection, and pick the Application Server connection type from the list. Enter **FMW11g_SOASuite11g_local** as the name for the new application server connection and select WebLogic 10.3 as the connection type. Click the Next button. Provide the authentication details:

Again, use the weblogic/weblogic1 username/password combination. Next, you need to indicate the WebLogic hostname (localhost for local installations) and the port for the AdminServer (7001 by default). Also enter the name for the domain you connect to; the name suggested in the on line installation instructions is soa_domain. Click the Next button again. When you test the connection, you should receive a number of success messages, one for each of the different ways of connecting to the domain.

Click the Finish button to close the Create Connection dialog. The new connection is now available on the Resource Palette.

See the on line chapter complement for detailed screenshots.

Sample Application and Fusion Order Demo

Oracle provides a demo application—called the Fusion Order Demo (FOD)—as a showcase for Fusion Middleware applications. This demo application is an end-to-end application example developed by the Fusion Middleware Product Management. It demonstrates common use-cases in Fusion Middleware applications, especially the integration between ADF, SOA composite applications, and WebCenter, as well as the usage of various service engines and adaptors inside SOA applications. The business scenario demonstrated in FOD is a web shop where customers can order products. Every new order triggers various process flows that handle the approval, logistics, and payment details.

You will find the Fusion Order Demo on OTN (http://www.oracle.com/technology/products/jdev/samples/fod/index.html). Installation and configuration instructions are provided on this page.

> **NOTE**
> *To see every aspect of this demo in action, you would have to update JDeveloper with the WebCenter plug-in. However, for inspecting the SOA Composite applications in the demo, this is not required.*

Create and Run the "HelloWorld" of Service Composite Applications

This section walks you through the steps to create, deploy, and test-run (with SOA Suite 11*g*) the world's most basic SOA composite application. At the end of this section—after maybe ten minutes' worth of work—you will have your first application running in the SOA Suite. (Note that detailed, step-by-step screenshots for this section are available in the on line chapter complement on the book's wiki.) The steps are as follows:

1. Fire up the engines.   First, start the database that hosts the metadata repository and then the WebLogic servers in the SOA domain (AdminServer and the managed soa_server1) using the command-line scripts.

Locate the startWebLogic.cmd script (Linux: startWebLogic.sh) in the MIDDLEWARE_HOME \ user_projects\domains\soa_domain directory. Run this script from the command line or terminal.

When the AdminServer is running, you should start the SOA server. Go to the directory MIDDLEWARE_HOME \user_projects\domains\soa_domain\bin, which was created by the SOA Suite Configuration Wizard. Open a command window and enter the following command to execute:

```
startManagedWebLogic.cmd soa_server1
```

(On Linux, use the script startManagedWebLogic.sh.)

2. Start JDeveloper. Be sure to choose Default Role if you are prompted to select a role.

3. Select New from the File menu. From the New Gallery that is presented next, select the SOA Application item in the Applications Category (under the General node). Click the OK button to continue.

You will be prompted to provide a name for the application—for example, HelloWorldSOAComposite. Leave the Application Package Prefix field empty and click the Next button. On the next page, enter **HelloWorld** as the name of the project and click Next again. JDeveloper then asks you what type of composite application this will be; pick Composite with BPEL on the Configure SOA settings step. Click Finish to have the application, project, and service composite created.

4. The Create BPEL Process dialog appears. Specify the name for the new BPEL process (HelloWorld) and the template (Synchronous BPEL Process). Make sure the box Expose As A SOAP Service is checked, and accept the defaults for Namespace, Service Name, and Input and Output (variables). Click OK. The Create BPEL Process dialog is shown in Figure 3-5.

5. The BPEL editor opens up. You will see the basic structure of the BPEL process with a Receive activity and a Reply activity, by default configured to receive a single string and return a single string. You need to add one activity to set the value of that string result: Drag an Assign

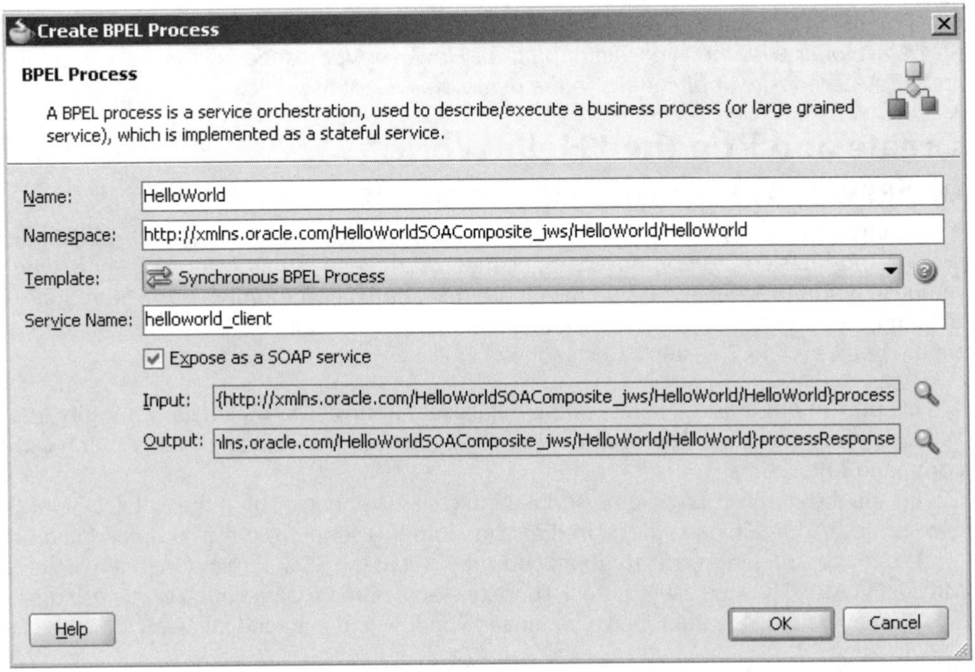

FIGURE 3-5. *Configure the new HelloWorld BPEL process.*

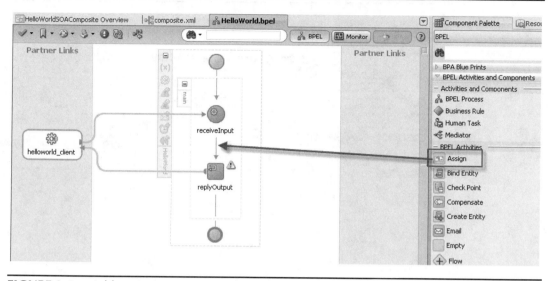

FIGURE 3-6. *Add an Assign activity to the BPEL process.*

activity from the Component Palette and drop it between the Receive and Reply activities already in the process, as shown in Figure 3-6.

Double-click the Assign activity to open the editor. Select the second tab, labeled Copy Operation, if it is not already selected. Click the green plus sign and select Copy Operation from the drop-down list. On the right (or To) side of the window, expand the outputVariable node, the payload child node, and its client:processResponse node, and then select the client:result node. That is the target of the Copy operation.

On the left (or From) side of the window, choose Expression in the drop-down list. Click the calculator icon to open the XPath expression editor. Type the following text in the expression box:

```
Concat('Hello dear',)
```

Position the cursor between the comma and the closing parenthesis. Expand the inputVariable in the BPEL Variables tree, all the way down until you can select the node client:input. Select that node. Click the Insert Into Expression button to add [an expression to extract] the value of the input variable to the expression. Click the OK button to close the expression editor. Click OK again to close the Create Copy Operation dialog and then one more time to close the Assign Editor. Figure 3-7 shows the creation of the copy operation in the Assign activity.

You have now created a valid BPEL process—one that receives a request message that contains a single string and returns a message that will contain the concatenation of "Hello dear" with that same input string. It's not much, but it constitutes a real BPEL process inside the HelloWorldSOAComposite application.

6. To test this application, deploy it first.   Right-click the HelloWorld project. From the context menu, select Deploy and its nested option, HelloWorld.

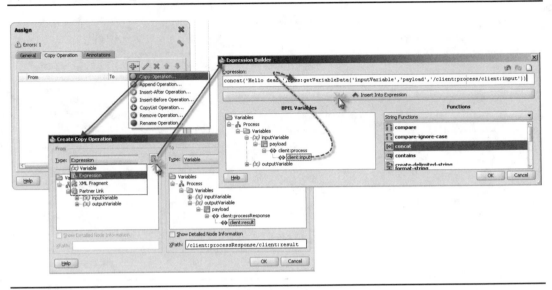

FIGURE 3-7.   *Configuring the Assign activity*

The Deployment Wizard appears, which is a multistep dialog. In the first step, select Deploy To Application Server (instead of deploying to an SAR file). Click Next. Accept all the default settings in the second step, and click Next. On the third page, select the FMW11g_SOASuite11g_ local connection to the WebLogic server with the SOA domain. Click Next. On the next page, select soa_server1 as the target server for deployment. Click Next, and the Summary page appears. Now you can click Finish.

The SOA composite application is built, resulting in an SAR (Service Archive) file. The archive is now handed to soa_server1 in the SOA domain on the WebLogic server. The message "Deployment Finished" should appear in the Deployment sub tab of the console window after several seconds (up to one minute).

7. Deployment is complete.   With the deployment done, we can access the composite application's Web Service interface from tools such as the HttpAnalyzer inside JDeveloper or soapUI (an open-source tool frequently used for testing Web Services). We can also open the Enterprise Manager to first inspect the deployed composite application and then test it.

Open the Enterprise Manager (http://localhost:7001/em). Expand the SOA node and its child, the soa-infra node, under the root node Farm_soa_domain. The node for the HelloWorldSOAComposite application should be listed. Select that node.

The right side of the page is refreshed to present the details for this composite application. Click the Test button to call the service exposed by this composite application. Enter a value for the input field—for example, your own first name—and click the button labeled Test WebService. The Web Service exposed by the HelloWorld application is invoked. This will create a new instance of the composite application. After a few seconds, the result from the service should be displayed, something to the effect of "Hello dear Lucas." Figure 3-8 demonstrates the test run of the HelloWorld application's service.

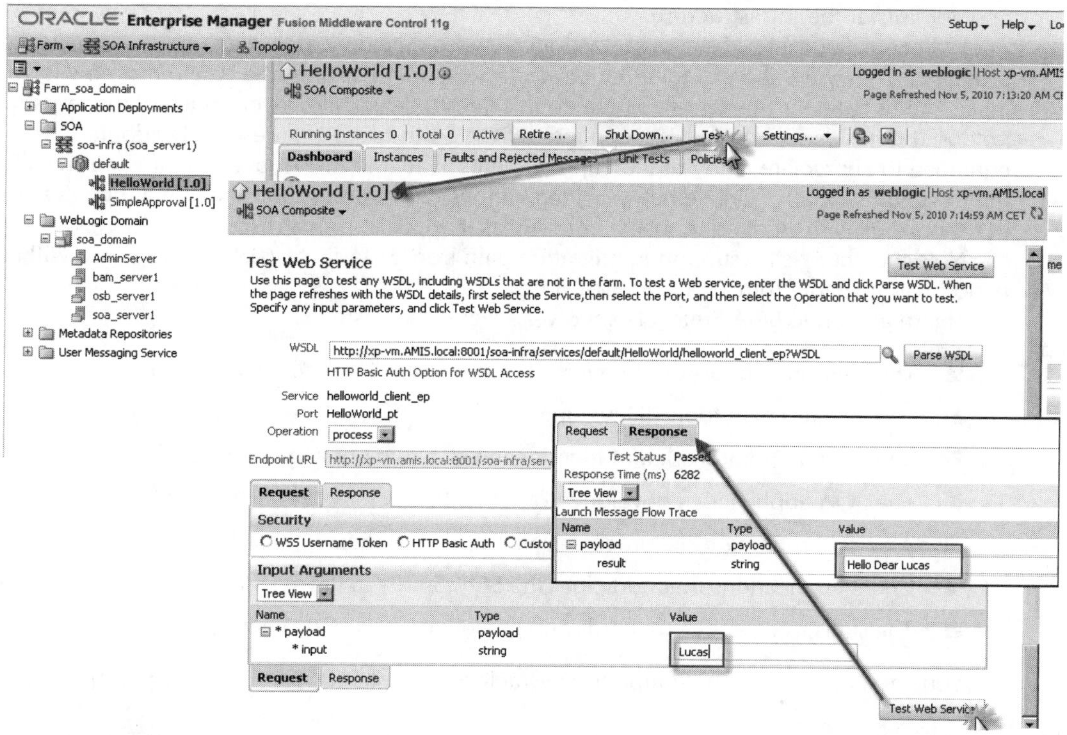

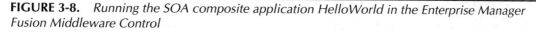

FIGURE 3-8. *Running the SOA composite application HelloWorld in the Enterprise Manager Fusion Middleware Control*

When you click the node for the HelloWorldSOAComposite application, you will see the new instance listed. You can drill down on this instance to find out more about the components in this instance that have executed (how long they took to complete, for example) and all trace details for activity inside those components (such as the activities in the BPEL process). You need to click the instance ID itself to see more information (not just on the row where the instance information is shown).

At this stage, you have achieved quite a bit. The SOA Suite 11*g* run-time environment has been installed and configured. Also, it actually works because it was possible to deploy and run a very simple composite application on it (whatever exactly that may be). The design time (JDeveloper with SOA Suite extension) is also up and running, appropriately configured with a connection to the SOA Suite container.

Migrating from SOA Suite 10.1.3

Many organizations have adopted Oracle SOA Suite 10.1.3 in the recent past, using BPEL Process Manager, the enterprise service bus, and/or Web Services Manager. Some even started with the 10.1.2 release. Such organizations typically have made considerable investments in their environment, the SOA applications, and the skills required to develop the applications and administer the infrastructure.

With SOA Suite 11*g*, these organizations may feel like they are up against the "dialectics of progress": They were the first to adopt Oracle's SOA offerings and as a result they now have to make additional investments to upgrade to this latest release. However, much of the investment is not lost, but instead can simply be applied to SOA Suite 11*g*. And these early adopters are best equipped to appreciate many of the improvements available in 11*g* over the previous releases of the SOA Suite. Finally, Oracle has provided various tools that support the migration. As a result, it may not be as earth-shattering, risky, or costly as it appears from a distance.

Note that there is no supported migration path from SOA Suite 10.1.2 to 11*g*; you will have to perform an upgrade from 10.1.2 to 10.1.3 first.

The migration to SOA Suite 11*g* involves several aspects:

- The environment or run-time infrastructure (from OC4J to WebLogic Server)
- The development tools (JDeveloper)
- The security framework and identity and access management tools
- The SOA applications developed on 10.1.3
- Any long-running BPEL processes with open instances
- Client applications that hook into the SOA Suite via (Java) APIs
- The skills, processes, standards and guidelines, and best practices

You can find more on migration from Oracle SOA Suite 10*g* to release 11*g* in Appendix A.

Summary

Oracle SOA Suite 11*g* did not appear out of thin air. It is the next step in a long evolution in the IT industry at large (and Oracle Corporation in particular).

This chapter gave you a glimpse of the rise of software for integration and later on middleware, in general, within Oracle. We discussed the advent of industry standards, starting with XML and encompassing the Web Services standards, and more recently the standards for business processes and service components. These standards are essential to success of Web Services—the foundation for interoperability—and Service-Oriented Architecture. Oracle plays an important role in the specification process and the promotion of most industry standards.

Oracle itself is an interesting example of integration: The company has acquired and subsequently absorbed several dozens of other companies and their software offerings. Many important parts of today's software portfolio have roots in products from these "scalps." The most striking acquisitions in the area of middleware are Collaxa (2004), BEA (2008), and Sun Microsystems and AmberPoint (both in 2010).

A many-year process of innovation, integration, and interaction with customers, including the important internal Applications Development teams, has finally resulted in Fusion Middleware. On July 1, 2009, Fusion Middleware 11*g* was launched. FMW offers a wide palette of middleware technology, ranging from business intelligence, Web Services, and content management, to enterprise collaboration, identity and access management, governance, event processing, and custom-developed user interfaces. SOA Suite 11*g* is an important element in the FMW 11*g* stack, with interactions with many of the other areas within FMW.

The SOA Suite has at its heart the SCA container that runs SOA composite applications. These applications are built from components that run on specialized engines: BPEL, Mediator, BPMN, Business Rules, (Spring) Java, and Human Task. The components can interact with external Web Services and technology adapters to reach out to the database, file system, messaging infrastructures, and so on. The SOA Suite provides a framework for negotiating events between applications, offering a very decoupled way of making different applications interact. Other products in the SOA Suite are Oracle Service Bus, Business Activity Monitoring (BAM), and Complex Event Processing (CEP).

Organizations that have adopted earlier generations of the SOA Suite will have to go through a migration process when they want to take up the 11*g* release. This migration applies to several aspects, including the infrastructure, applications, other software assets, and the skills of staff such as developers and administrators.

This concludes Part I of the book. The next part introduces the components of the SOA Suite in detail and demonstrates how to create composite applications with them.

PART
II

Developing Composite
Applications

CHAPTER
4

XML and Web Services
Fundamentals

art I of this book introduced St. Matthews (our business case), the key concepts and objectives for Service-Oriented Architecture, the industry standards, and the Oracle product portfolio for implementing SOA. At the end of Chapter 3, we installed the SOA Suite and got our first SOA application running by publishing the obligatory HelloWorld Web Service.

Before we start developing much more complex SOA applications, we need to establish a little foundation, consisting of XML, XSD, and WSDL. Of course, XML is the lingua franca for all messages and most contracts, definitions, configurations, and even programs in our service-oriented world. XSD (XML Schema Definition) is the data-modeling language for describing the structure of XML documents, and WSDL (Web Service Definition Language) is the language for describing service interfaces. This chapter provides only a quick introduction to these three key languages. You may want to check out some of the resources mentioned on the wiki to get a little more background on XML, XSD, and WSDL.

This chapter creates the starting point for the eAppointment project at St. Matthews, a crucial project that must substantially optimize the process for creating and managing appointments. It describes how Margaret Scott and Frank Tiger set out to create the definition of a Web Service that will expose various operations concerning patient data. This service is implemented in the next chapter, based on Frank's existing Patients database.

Kicking the Tires on the eAppointment Project

The board of directors has nominated Margaret Scott, an experienced business-savvy project manager, to lead the eAppointment project. It will be her job to bring together business and IT staff from many different departments and with various roles, and have them share information, responsibility, and ownership of the process of making and managing appointments. A "project start architecture" document has been written, outlining the business objectives and information architecture context of the eAppointment project.

Today, Margaret is meeting with Frank Tiger, team leader for the application management and support team in the information department. He and his team take care of the Clinical Information System, a key application for surgical data whose scope was later expanded to also support the medical laboratories. Frank came to St. Matthews in one of the 1990 mergers. Before that he headed data operations in one of the smaller hospitals that was merged with St. Matthews. Over the past two decades, Frank and his team have been nurturing their database with patient data. Starting out as a small scheduling and billing information system used at the surgical care department, it slowly grew into a patient record system used all over St. Matthews. The team now also tracks simple medical patient data such as blood pressure readings, weight, and height. Today, Frank is sitting on the largest pile of patient records in the hospital—with over 300,000 patient records and many tens of millions of associated table rows. His cooperation is critical for the eAppointment project, and Margaret certainly knows that.

Frank is regarded as an Oracle guru. He started working with Oracle Database version 4 and has seen over a dozen upgrades of the RDBMS. He has even managed to stay abreast of most recent developments in SQL and PL/SQL. He writes Analytical SQL, uses the Model clause, and has traded the DECODE for the CASE operator. However, Java and web applications are *not* his thing, as he is wont to let people know. He has not been involved with any of the SOA initiatives at the hospital so far. In truth, all the buzz and managerial expectations have left him a little anxious.

Margaret and Frank have a little history together. They collaborated on a project for the migration from the VAX/VMS mini computers to the current Unix systems in the early 1990s.

More recently they had some discussions regarding the security of "St. Matthews online," a project managed by Margaret.

Margaret feels that although Frank is very reluctant and a little scared of this SOA thing, she has a good story and sound arguments to win him over.

When the niceties are over and they have established that they are both doing well and it is great to see each other again, Margaret states, "I hear you have a lot of patient data!"

Frank cheers up. That is one of his favorite topics, professionally speaking at least: "That's right! I'm sitting on the largest database with patient records in our hospital!"

"That's just great Frank," replies Margaret. "I was hoping for that. You have probably heard about the new eAppointment system we are creating."

The hospital's board of directors sees a lot of opportunity for improving patient satisfaction through better quality of services, while cutting costs at the same time. Realizing the business benefits promised by SOA are crucial to meeting these objectives. Refocusing the IT department on services rather than on more or less closed, departmental applications and closed data stores will be a challenge. One of the first areas they want to target is the patient appointment process: It is this process that causes much vexation among patients and has a negative impact on patient satisfaction—one of the key performance indicators (KPIs) for St. Matthews. And at the same time, the process is hugely time consuming for hospital staff. The main reasons seem to be the fact that patients are asked to provide the same information over and over again, the inflexibility in changing appointments or scheduling multiple visits next to each other, and the lack of clarity and information about the appointments. The hospital staff responsible for managing the appointments is far from happy with the situation. But now there is hope for improvement, if not revolutionary change—the eAppointment project has been announced.

"I am managing that project," says Margaret, "and we need to be able to retrieve patient records for existing patients or create new ones as part of the process of managing patient appointments."

Frank may not (yet) be into SOA, but he certainly is a service-oriented guy. He immediately offers: "Here, I can give you connect details to our database. Normally there is a formal procedure, but for you I can cut through some red tape. I will give you the full data model, with table and column definitions. You'll be up and running in no time!" He is pleased with himself for being so cooperative. But he slightly miscalculated the situation.

"I am not that kind of girl!" Maggie says girlishly. "I may want your data, but I certainly do not want your dirty tables!" She tries to make it sounded lighthearted, but has to get a very important point across here.

Frank is a bit baffled. Here he was, promising unprecedented access to his data, and he feels utterly rejected. Then, in the rebound, he pulls himself together and suggests, "Let me create a View layer for you! We insulate you from all the complex SQL and provide a business API." He knows the word *business* usually goes down well with project managers.

Margaret stands tall. "To be frank, I do not want to do SQL anymore."

"Hey, I am Frank here!" he makes a feeble attempt at a little humor. But he does not feel lighthearted. With all his good intentions, he is not getting the response he was looking for. What more could she possibly want from him?

Margaret is not oblivious to his confusion. "Frank, look here, we are all into services now. We want to deal with clear interfaces, as technology-free as possible, with no implementation details. I simply do not want to depend on the way you implement your database. I know you are constantly optimizing the data design—and I want you to be free to do so, even if that means moving to a different physical database or even opting for a different kind of data storage—based on in-memory grid technology, for example. What I want from you is a service."

"I suppose that means we will have to do that XML thing," says Frank. He has not been completely unaware of the world around him. The advent of the Internet, widespread use of XML, the introduction of Web Services, liberal use of acronyms such as B2B, OO, SOAP, and more recently SOA, and even talk of business-IT alignment—he has heard it all coming and most of it going as well. Having a tough-enough job as it was, he tried and managed to steer clear of most of the hubbub. And now apparently it has arrived after all.

Margaret replies, "Yes, I would like you to provide Web Services that talk XML. You and your technology talk XML, we and ours do too—even if they are two completely different worlds in terms of platform and architecture."

"How is that better than straightforward SQL?" Frank feels tired. So his database and good-old SQL are not good enough anymore. He wonders whether he is.

Margaret is prepared to explain to Frank what is driving her—and most of the rest of the world. "Using XML-based services means that my team does not need to have SQL skills. We both know that doing SQL properly is specialist's job! And even though SQL is more or less a standard, someone who's an expert in SQL on a MySQL database may royally screw up on Oracle or DB2. So I prefer to leave the heavy SQL lifting to the experts, such as yourself.

"Perhaps even more important than getting rid of my dependency on SQL experts in my team, I will not have a direct dependency on your data model, your upgrades, or even your physical location—like I said before. Loose coupling. That is the magic phrase. Of course, I will still depend on you—or at least on your service—but in a much more subtle way. And if at some point in time your local patient hub is replaced by the new SAP or Oracle Fusion Applications–based standard solution, I will be able to continue running the eAppointment process against the same service, which simply switched from your database to the new solution."

Frank, drinking his coffee, almost chokes on it. Still coughing he enquires of Margaret whether there are plans to replace him. Margaret quickly reassures him: "I was just giving you a longer-term, strictly hypothetical example. As far as I know, there are currently no plans to do anything of the sort."

She continues: "Being able to talk against your Web Service means that we will have a consistent way of communicating with all services we deal with. Yours is certainly not the only one! For us it is great if every service—whether based on a relational database such as your Oracle Database or the facilities department's DB2, or implemented on top of the mainframe or the .NET platform—can be accessed in the same way."

"Yeah, great." Frank is near sarcasm now. "I'm thrilled for you. Would there be something in it for me as well?" He knows he should have seen this coming—and prepared himself. He has had his head in the sand on this one. Silently he is angry with himself.

Margaret, however, really has some good news for him: "Actually, there is quite a bit in it for you too," she tells him. "Well, some of it is good for the hospital in general, and some of it is especially good for you. For starters, you will be the SOA guy—hip and happening all over again! It must have been the introduction of client/server technology and the graphical user interface that was your last chance to shine!"

"Seriously though: I will pay for using your services. I have a pretty substantial budget for realizing this eAppointment system. And since your service will contribute some key functionality, it is obvious that there is plenty of budget to have your team develop the service. Besides, this does not end with the initial development and roll out of the service. We will make an SLA, a contract that states that you will continue to provide the service under certain conditions—like response time, availability, and security—and that the eAppointment's business owner will pay for the service level. So you will continue to have budget for managing and perhaps improving the service.

"As you know better than I do, there are many parties in this hospital who are interested in your data. You have always been helpful in supporting all these parties, but usually in a very informal way. With little or no benefit to your department, apart perhaps from their undying gratitude. The new service approach we are discussing here will allow you to continue to help all those parties, and in a more structured way that is more visible and recognized. They can make use of the same service we are discussing for eAppointment. So you—and the hospital at large—reuse the work you have already done. And you can sign an SLA with each of these parties. That means that everyone will still rely on you—and thank you for it. And they will transfer some of their budget as well as payment for using your service. To you, it may not matter much whether the service is used by one party or by many. But the extra budget from those SLAs will certainly allow you to make the service better and richer.

"Oh, and I shouldn't forget this part: Service-Oriented Architecture is explicitly named in the hospital's strategic outlook for the next three years. The board has named it one of the key elements for the success of the "Happy Client" and "Quality Health Check 2012" programs. To get SOA really going here, they have set up a sponsor committee. This committee is to provide additional funding for implementing services with proven reuse potential. Getting this patient service up and running will most certainly be backed by this committee, resulting in an additional budget as well as pretty high-profile visibility for your team!"

Just as Margaret had hoped, some of the things she has mentioned have piqued Frank's interest. The prestige of his team is important to him—as is being able to continually improve the database and surrounding infrastructure. Having a budget and relative freedom—because of these loosely coupled interfaces—really appeals to him.

"You can improve the implementation" Margaret continues, "without any of you noticing it!"

Frank, starting to see some interesting opportunities, exclaims, "Oh, and I know that George in the lab has a lot of data that may interest my 'service consumers.' He has all kinds of information about the tests ran on their blood and other bodily fluid samples. Today, either they have to ask him for access to data—which he is quite often not able to provide—or they completely overlook him. In both cases, patients are tested for things they have recently been tested for. Together we can really offer a powerful service! And I am sure there are more like him, who have these hidden nuggets of data we can add to the patient service in order to enrich it. Would you like that?"

Margaret would—for two reasons. First of all, the additional data Frank is talking about is very useful. It will save her a trip down to the lab, where she expects a lot more resistance than Frank came up with. And she very much wants to encourage Frank, who, after a hesitant start, is quickly coming round and turning into a very enthusiastic believer.

But then Frank slows down. He calls himself to order it almost seems. He looks at her. He seems to have lost some of his fervor. She is not losing him now, is she? He doesn't seem as sure of himself as he was just a minute ago. What is the matter with this rock-solid database guru?

Frank takes a deep breath. "Margaret, I know a lot about databases and SQL. And you really had me going there, with the service idea and the sponsor committee and the reuse. And the visibility of my team and all. But I know nothing about services—or XML for that matter. Can we do this at all? How do we get going, Margaret?"

Margaret knows it is now time for the next stage. Frank wants to give it a try, and she needs to help him with the first steps.

"Frank, I really appreciate your willingness to help me out with this service. And I am sure you and I will work together just great. Of course, I realize this is going to be a big step for you and your team. I am sure we can do this together."

Margaret continues: "How to get things going, you ask? That is probably not as hard as it may seem to you right now. The first step is that we outline the functionality your service will provide. More specifically, we define the interface for the service. As soon as we have described the service interface, my team can start coding the application that consumes your service, as they will then know exactly how the service will look to them and how they can invoke it. And your team can start thinking about the implementation of the service interface.

"At that point you probably ought to start learning about a few things. You will need some understanding of XML technologies, as the storefront of the service will be XML based. In addition, you need to know about Web Services. At that point, we can discuss several ways for you to implement and publish the Web Service—for example, using either native database facilities, some Java programming, or a service component in the SOA Suite. Note that at this point the hospital's architecture vision plays a role, too, as we are making choices that should be valid into the future.

"The first questions we will address are pretty straightforward. What functionality do we need from your service for eAppointment? We will express the service interface in several elements: What does the service request look like? What input should we send to the service? What are the parameters we could or should include in the service request? And what is the structure—data type, format, allowable values—of the request?

"Next, how is the service response composed? What data will be included in the response, and what will be the structure?

"Finally, will your service throw any exceptions—and if so, what will be the exceptional circumstances? What are the names and types of exceptions?"

Frank interjects, somewhat relieved: "That is really no different from creating a PL/SQL package specification! You describe a function or a procedure with a name, the input parameters, and the return value or the output parameters—which is almost the same as what you are saying. The only real difference I see is that in PL/SQL we may raise exceptions in a program unit, but we do not explicitly say so in the specification—they come as a surprise. I hear Java is somewhat more structured in that area—as hard to believe as it may seem."

Margaret is pleased with Frank's reaction. He really *is* getting the hang of it. And he is right, of course. What she has said about describing the service interface is very similar to the concept of a PL/SQL package specification or an interface in Java programming. One important distinction is the specific format for writing down the interface for a Web Service.

"You are right, Frank. It basically is the same thing. It will look a little bit different, but by and large, describing a Web Service interface is similar to specifying a PL/SQL interface…ahem, package specification."

"Okay. Let's get down to business. You will provide us with a service that we can call, let's say, the patient record service. We can agree, I think, that this service will accept some sort of patient identification message as input—with either the patient ID (for existing patients who remember their ID) or a combination of identifying elements, including birth date, last name, initials, or Social Security Number. Then, of course, the service will return a response message that contains the patient data—the name, contact, and address details, personal information, the medical history, and any recent hospital visits. In addition, the service may return one of several exceptions, such as when the service is called with an invalid or unknown patient ID. We can write down this outline of a contract in a slightly more structured way."

Margaret hands Frank a piece of paper with the following XML:

```
<operation name="getPatientRecord">
  <input message="PatientIdentificationInputMessage"/>
  <output message="PatientDataRecordOutputMessage"/>
  <fault message="UnknownPatientIdFaultMessage" name="UnknownPatientId"/>
  <fault message="NoUniquePatientMatchFaultMessage" name="NoUniquePatientMatch"/>
</operation>
```

Frank recognizes the XML syntax. He realizes this is where it all starts. His SOA and Web Services initiation. And so far, it doesn't seem too hard.

"Is this the standard way for describing services?" he asks Margaret.

She confirms it is, but adds that this is only a part of it. "The service contract is typically laid down in a so-called WSDL document. At the heart of the WSDL contract for a Web Service is the portType element, which contains operation definitions like this one. But more on WSDL later on. You will first need to study some XML basics."

Introduction to XML

Clearly XML is an essential ingredient of Service-Oriented Architecture. Service definitions are expressed via XML documents, the data structure of messages is defined through XML documents, configuration for the run-time infrastructure is, by and large, in XML, the contents of messages sent between services and service consumers is XML based, and the SOAP envelope that wraps the message itself is also—you guessed it—an XML document. In order to delve into doing SOA, there are a few things you should know about XML. For now, let's assume you have dealt with XML in the past. For a basic introduction into XML, as well as a list of other resources with in-depth information on XML, see Appendix B.

Much of the attraction of XML lies in the fact that in all major application-development technologies, tools, and platforms, facilities are available for performing the most frequently needed operations on XML. Whether you develop in JavaScript, PHP, Java, C#, or PL/SQL for the JEE, .NET, or Oracle Database platform, you will have native language facilities help you process XML documents. These operations performed on XML documents are:

- **Parsing**   Reading the XML and turning it into a native data object for the programming language at hand.

- **Data binding**   Going one step beyond parsing and making the data from the XML document available as a custom, strongly typed programming language data structure (or domain model). For example, transforming XML into Java objects, and vice versa.

- **Validating**   Verifying the validity of the XML document against rules specified in a schema such as XSD or Schematron.

- **Querying**   Retrieving specific information from the XML document by applying search questions.

- **Transforming**   Converting the XML document into another XML document (or a different format, such as CSV or HTML) by applying a transformation template or stylesheet.

Although some of the operations listed are handled transparently for us by the tools we will be using for building the SOA, others require attention from the developer and will be discussed in more detail both in this chapter as well as throughout the book. In particular, the use of XML Schema Definitions (XSD) for describing the rules against which XML documents should be validated, the use of XPath for performing queries to retrieve specific information from XML documents, and the application of XSLT stylesheets for transforming XML documents will be fairly familiar to you by the time you are done with this book.

XML Documents

An XML document consists of tagged elements organized in a tree-like structure. An XML document contains various types of nodes:

- Document node (the entire document)
- Element node
- Text node (the literal values contained in element nodes)
- Attribute node
- Comment node
- Declarations and processing instructions such as namespace declarations, character encoding, and XML version

These nodes can be validated and accessed in various ways, as we will see in later chapters. See Appendix B and the references on the wiki for more background on XML.

Creating and Editing XML Documents in JDeveloper 11*g*

Creating XML documents is a task usually performed for us by automated means. Such means include textfile-to-XML converters, use of SQL/XML queries, Java programs that construct XML documents from string data, and text processors that save files in XML format. However, manually creating or editing XML files is still a common task—for example, for testing purposes or for management of configuration files—and, of course, for creating schemas that are not generated by some tool but that are application and technology neutral.

In addition to specialized XML editors, of which there are plenty available, most IDEs including JDeveloper have fairly advanced XML-editing capabilities. JDeveloper 11*g*'s XML Editor has useful features such as checks on well-formedness (does the document comply with the XML syntax rules?) and validity (does the document satisfy the specific rules laid down in the XML Schema Definition?) as well as productivity enhancers such as XML element tag completion, reformat, and code completion.

JDeveloper can also create an XML document based on what is called an XML Schema Definition (XSD), a document that describes the data design of XML elements. JDeveloper creates such an XML document with all required structure (elements and attributes) already in place—though with meaningless, generated content.

Data Design for XML—XML Schema Definitions (XSD)

The provisional service interface definition agreed upon by Margaret and Frank specifies an input and an output parameter. It is implied that these are both XML messages:

```
<operation name="getPatientRecord">
  <input message="PatientIdentificationInputMessage"/>
  <output message="PatientDataRecordOutputMessage"/>
  . . .
</operation>
```

However, it has not yet been determined how these messages are to be constructed. In general, when we deal with XML documents, we know that they will follow the XML grammar rules. Any "well-formed" XML document has a single root element, a tree structure with properly opened and closed element tags, text content, and attributes. But this is still too vague to start exchanging meaningful information or to build software to process the XML documents. We need more specific rules to describe the structure, the data types, and other constraints for the XML document. Without them, we know little more than a database developer who knows that a relational database is used but does not have a database design.

The data model for XML documents is expressed using XML Schema Definitions—or XSDs. An XSD is an XML document—readable to humans *and* software—that describes the vocabulary for XML elements and attributes. Once we have the XSD for the XML documents we will be dealing with, we can determine the validity of XML messages and start building the software that will work with the XML—we know what information to expect and where to find it in the document.

NOTE
XSD has succeeded DTD (Document Type Definition) as the preferred way of describing the structure of XML documents.

XSD documents define the elements that appear in XML documents. For these elements, XSD documents specify the following:

- **Structure**   Child elements, attributes, and their order
- **Types**   Primitive (built-in) and user-defined simple and complex (nested) types
- **Rules or constraints**   Default values, the number of occurrences of child elements, the valid value range or allowable values for attributes, optionality, and updateability

An in-depth introduction to XML Schema Definition is far beyond the scope of this book, even though some examples are provided later on. If you are not yet familiar with XSD, you can take a look at Appendix B for some more detailed examples. Additionally, you may want to check out some of the resources listed on this book's wiki for a more thorough introduction to XSD.

Decoupling in the real world is often hard to achieve with schemas and contracts generated by tools—as is all too easy, for example, with a JAXB utility deriving the XSD from Java classes or with the xsd.exe tool doing the same for .NET classes.

For building loosely coupled systems, it is important that services and underlying schemas are truly owned by the enterprise, not by the applications. The only way to break the hold of applications and technology on your service architecture is to eliminate those generated schemas completely from the services you develop for the enterprise! This means that manual development is almost a requirement for creating schemas (XSD documents) and services (WSDL documents).

Uniquely Identifying XML Elements

Questions that are frequently asked when we (or an automated component) encounter an element in an XML document include, What element definition is this element based on? And what exactly is meant with this element? A <table> element could signify an HTML layout structure or a piece of furniture. An element called <patient> can refer to a person needing a doctor's attention but could also describe a personal trait. And one organization's description of a customer can be quite different in structure and attribute from another organization's (say, when comparing a prison with a hospital). We need to identify those XML elements more accurately than by just using a simple name—otherwise, we will not be able to connect the element and the relevant XSD-based definition of the element and we will not be able to properly programmatically process the element.

Let's take a brief step away from XML and look at your file system. It probably contains several files called readme.txt. However, they are not the same file. When we formulate in a more precise way, these files are not truly called readme.txt—they have something like /etc/directory/otherdirectory/readme.txt for their name. The file is qualified by the entire directory and filename; not by its filename alone.

Let's look at other examples from the worlds of SQL and Java. When we speak about objects in the database, it is easy to see that instructing a database developer to write a SQL query against table CUSTOMERS in a specific database is not a good-enough instruction: There can be dozens of tables called CUSTOMERS. A full identification of the table requires the schema in which it resides. In Java programs, classes are used to construct objects that contain data and execute application logic. Any one class usually calls upon other classes to perform some task. For example, class PageRenderer may call upon class ButtonRenderer to render an instance of a button. Again, using the indication ButtonRenderer is not good enough, because there may be several classes called ButtonRenderer. The fully qualified name for a class includes not just the name of the class, but also the package in which it resides—for example org.superui.renderers. Thus, programmers—and the JVM class loader—can distinguish between org.superui.renderers. ButtonRenderer and my.sandbox.ButtonRenderer.

With XML, we have the same challenge. Without further indication, we could easily misinterpret element names. From the context of the document, we can derive that the "charge" element does not specify electrical information or the Light Brigade storming in, but most likely the bill presented to the patient for this particular visit. However, we should not rely on such subjective, context-based interpretations, but clearly state our intentions. So in XML, too, we use fully qualified names.

A fully qualified name for an XML element is composed of a local name and a namespace. The namespace compares to the package name in Java and the name of the schema in the Oracle database. In XML, the namespace, simply put, is a unique string without any real meaning other than for identification purposes. Slightly less simply put: The namespace identifier is a URI (Uniform Resource Identifier) according to the specifications laid down by the IETF (Internet Engineering Task Force, RFC3986). These are quite simple, for our purpose at least:

> "A URI is a—case sensitive—sequence of characters from a very limited set: the letters of the basic Latin alphabet, digits, and a few special characters."

The IETF also notes that a URI often has to be remembered by people, and it is easier for people to remember a URI when it consists of meaningful or familiar components. A URI does *not* specifically refer to a resource that is accessible at a location that the URI seems to describe. URIs are used for uniquely identifying resources, not for accessing them.

One straightforward way of making the elements you define in your XML documents unique is by using a namespace identifier that contains something unique to your organization or even to yourself. Many namespace identifiers in XML—just like package names in Java—therefore include the URL for the website of the organization. However, any unique string will do. Here are some examples:

```
http://ourhospital.com/patient
http://ourhospital.com/staff
com.ourhospital.patients
PATIENT:UUID673215631265GEE
```

A namespace provides a container in which to collect names that for some reason belong together, as is shown in Figure 4-1. These names frequently share an owning organization, a domain or knowledge area, or an industry. Note that the scope of an XML namespace can have far more impact on your enterprise than a Java package name or database schema identification ever could. A Java package name has a scope that is limited to the application that uses it. An XML namespace can impact the entire enterprise and should be managed with corresponding care.

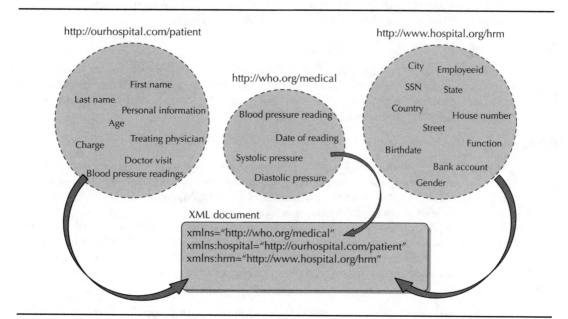

FIGURE 4-1. *Namespaces for elements in different domains*

The URI syntax is commonly organized hierarchically, with components listed in order of decreasing significance from left to right. This does not really mean anything—at least not to software parsing the URI definitions. It is just a convenient method for organizing the URI in a way that is inspired by the structure of the real world. For example, the http://ourhospital.com/patient and http://ourhospital.com/staff namespace identifiers are both defined in "Our Hospital," and describe various subdomains in the hospital—in the eyes of human readers. The fact that their URIs have a partial overlap is meaningless to XML parsers and processors.

We associate an XML element name with a namespace using this syntax:

```
<patient xmlns="http://ourhospital.com/patient">
```

Instead of just "patient," we should now speak about this element as {http://ourhospital.com/patients}patient. This is the qualified name of the element, often referred to as the QName. The name "patient" is the *local name*.

NOTE
XML elements do not have to be in a namespace. The local name of such unqualified elements is equal to their QName. These elements are said to be in the "null" namespace.

Having to qualify every XML name in this way would be dramatic: The document inflates even further, the work involved is almost painful, and the readability is negatively impacted—to put it mildly. So, instead, we can work with simple prefixes and rely on several inheritance rules.

Prefixes allow us to use friendlier ways of associating names with namespaces. Our patient element could be fully qualified with syntax like the following:

```
<hospital:patient … >
```

The prefix can be anything you like. It is up to the XML parser to associate each element via its prefix with the real namespace identifier. The linking pin to make that possible is the *namespace binding,* the declaration somewhere in the XML document that associates the prefix—again, any string you fancy—with the namespace URI:

```
<hospital:patient xmlns:hospital="http://ourhospital.com/patient">
```

Some prefixes are reserved—such as xml and xmlns—and some have become so commonly used for specific namespaces—for example, xsl (http://www.w3.org/1999/XSL/Transform), xsd (for http://www.w3.org/2001/XMLSchema), and xhtml (for http://www.w3.org/1999/xhtml)—that you should refrain from using them for other purposes.

The namespace prefix—unless it is "xml" or "xmlns"—*must* have been declared in a namespace declaration attribute in either the start tag of the element where the prefix is used or in an ancestor element (that is, an element in whose content the prefixed markup occurs). Once a prefix has been associated with a namespace inside some element tag, it can be used in all child elements. Here's an example:

```
<hospital:patient xmlns:hospital="http://ourhospital.com/patient">
   <hospital:personal>
     <hospital:firstName>
```

We can also use the concept of the default namespace: Any element that is not specifically prefixed or associated with a namespace through the xmlns attribute is in the default namespace—if that has been defined. The default namespace is defined through a variation on the declaration we saw before:

```
<patient xmlns="http://ourhospital.com/patient">
```

By simply using xmlns, without the colon and prefix, we state that for this element and all its descendants, the default namespace is set to http://ourhospital.com/patient. Because many XML documents contain only elements from a single namespace, the default namespace further simplifies things considerably. A single namespace declaration in the root element of the document is all we need to associate all elements with the appropriate namespace, as shown here:

```
<patient xmlns ="http://ourhospital.com/patient">
  <personal>
   <firstName>
```

Of course, an XML document may very well contain elements from different namespaces. We can select one as the (global) default namespace—typically the source of the largest portion of elements. The other namespaces can be associated with prefixes or be used as local default namespaces. The declaration of namespace bindings is usually done in the root element, but can be done in any element. See Appendix B for more details and examples.

Creating Real XML Schema Definitions

XSD documents use an XML syntax to define a grammar (or vocabulary) for creating a set of XML documents. XSD uses fixed XML elements such as type, attribute, element, and so on, to define the structure. You will find a basic introduction and more details on XSD in Appendix B.

Let's look at a simple XSD document. It specifies the "address" element in the http://www.hospital.org/hrm namespace. The binding to this namespace is specified through the targetNamespace attribute in the "schema" element. This XSD document states that any occurrence of this {http://www.hospital.org/hrm} address element should conform to the rules laid down in this XSD. The XML elements in this document that are part of the XSD vocabulary itself are all from the namespace http://www.w3.org/2001/XMLSchema, bound to the xsd prefix:

```
<?xml version="1.0" encoding="utf-8" ?>
<xsd:schema xmlns:xsd="http://www.w3.org/2001/XMLSchema"
            xmlns="http://www.hospital.org/hrm"
            targetNamespace="http://www.hospital.org/hrm"
            elementFormDefault="qualified">
  <xsd:element name="address" type="physicalAddress"/>
  <xsd:complexType name="physicalAddress">
    <xsd:sequence>
      <xsd:element name="postalCode" type="xsd:string"/>
      <xsd:element name="city" type="xsd:string"/>
      <xsd:element name="state" type="xsd:string" minOccurs="0"/>
      <xsd:element name="country" type="countryCode"/>
      <xsd:choice>
        <xsd:sequence>
          <xsd:element name="street" type="xsd:string"/>
          <xsd:element name="houseNumber" type="xsd:string"/>
        </xsd:sequence>
```

```
      <xsd:element name="poBox" type="xsd:string" />
    </xsd:choice>
  </xsd:sequence>
  <xsd:attribute name="typeOfAddress" type="xsd:string" />
</xsd:complexType>
<xsd:simpleType name="countryCode">
  <xsd:restriction base="xsd:string">
    <xsd:enumeration value="be"/>
    <xsd:enumeration value="us"/>
    ...
  </xsd:restriction>
</xsd:simpleType>
</xsd:schema>
```

This XSD snippet declares the address element, based on the physicalAddress type. Next comes the definition of this complex type. It contains a number of child elements, such as postalCode, city, state, and country. These must occur in this order. However, the state element is optional. The country element is based on a simpleType, countryCode. The countryCode type is based on the built-in simpleType string. A restriction is defined: The value of countryCode must be one of the values defined in the enumerations.

The physicalAddressType then contains either a poBox element or a street and houseNumber. The xsd:choice element specifies this mutual exclusiveness. Finally, the physicalAddressType also declares an attribute called typeOfAddress, a string that indicates a visiting address or shipping and mail destination.

Figure 4-2 shows the visual representation of this XSD definition and compares it with similar designs in UML and ERD modeling.

An XML instance document with the {http://www.hospital.org/hrm} address element has to comply with the XSD definition to be considered valid by XML processors. Here's an example of a valid document:

```
<?xml version="1.0" encoding="UTF-8" ?>
<address typeOfAddress="emergencyContact" xmlns="http://www.hospital.org/hrm">
  <postalCode>3456</postalCode>
  <city>Luik</city>
  <country>be</country>
  <street>Waffle Avenue</street>
  <houseNumber>123</houseNumber>
</address>
```

NOTE
*Multiple XSD documents can define elements in the same namespace.
And one XSD document can define elements in different namespaces.
There is no mutually exclusive, one-to-one relationship between XSD
documents and namespaces.*

A very special element we can use in an XSD document is the "any" element. We use it to specify the occurrence of a block of well-formed XML—XML content that conforms to the XML syntax rules. No other restrictions apply; it can be anything (as long as it is well-formed XML).

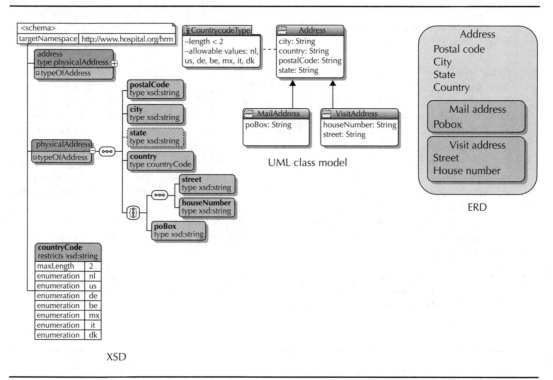

FIGURE 4-2. *XSD compared to other data modeling techniques: UML Class Model and Entity Relationship Diagram*

This "any" element is convenient to allow parties to include additional information in an XML document largely predefined through the XSD definition.

The next snippet specifies that inside the patientType there can be a patientattachment element that contains well-formed XML. The structure or vocabulary for that content is unknown—it can be anything.

```
<xsd:complexType name="patientType">
  <xsd:sequence>
    <xsd:element name="patientAttachment" minOccurs="0">
      <xsd:complexType>
        <xsd:sequence>
          <xsd:any minOccurs="1"/>
        </xsd:sequence>
      </xsd:complexType>
    </xsd:element>
```

In addition to the any element, there is the anyType type, which can be used to specify both elements and attributes. This type does not constrain values in any way—and it can be used, for example, when we have too little information or control to enforce a more specific type.

A complex type can be defined as an extension of an existing complex type, adding new elements to the set already defined in the base type. This extension mechanism is similar to object inheritance in, for example, Java.

Associating XML Documents with XSDs   The XML processor that processes an XML document can be explicitly instructed about the XSDs to apply—either inside the document or through programmatic arguments. When the XML document is a message sent to a Web Service, the relevant XSD is defined indirectly through the WSDL (see later) that contains an XSD reference.

Alternatively, the XML processor may know of one or multiple XSD documents that have been registered with it. These XSDs describe elements in namespaces—with each XSD providing the specification for one or more fully qualified elements. When processing an XML instance document, the QName of the elements in the document is compared with this list of registered schema-based elements. Any element in the XML instance document that can be matched will be validated against the schema definition. Figure 4-3 shows an XML document with elements from multiple namespaces defined in three different XSD documents.

Additionally, the XML instance document can contain an explicit reference to one or more XSD definitions:

```
<address xmlns:xsi="http://www.w3.org/2001/XMLSchema-instance"
         xsi:schemaLocation="http://www.hospital.org/hrm Administration.xsd"
         xmlns="http://www.hospital.org/hrm">
   <postalCode>...
```

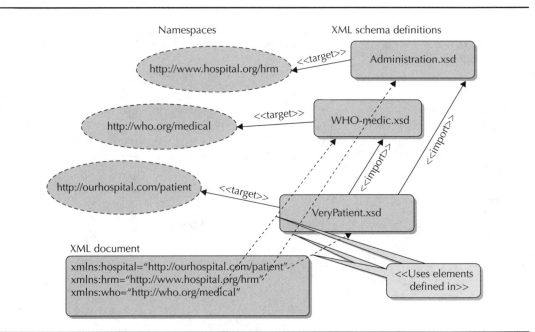

FIGURE 4-3.   *XSD documents describing elements in namespaces—implicitly referenced by XML instance documents*

The hint about the schema location is passed in the form of a schemaLocation attribute that is defined in the http://www.w3.org/2001/XMLSchema-instance namespace. The attribute is included in the root element of the instance document, and has to be preceded by a namespace binding—usually to the prefix xsi.

Managing XSDs and XSD Dependencies

It is considered a best practice to use XSD documents to describe the XML vocabulary we want to use in a specific business domain. Of course, such domains can be quite large with substantial numbers of elements. Fortunately, we do not have to stick to a single XSD document with all those elements in a single file. We can use the "include" and "import" elements in an XSD document, which allow us to organize and manage element and type definitions in multiple documents and help establish reuse of those definitions. For example, we can create an XSD document called VeryPatient.xsd that contains a <patient> element that is used from several other XSDs employed at St. Matthews that all specify XML messages containing patient information:

```
...
<xsd:element name="patient" type="patientType" />
  <xsd:complexType name="patientType">
    <xsd:sequence>
      <xsd:element name="personal" type="personNameType" maxOccurs="1"
                   minOccurs="1"/>
      <xsd:element name="mailAddress" type="hrm:physicalAddress" minOccurs="1"
                   maxOccurs="3"/>
...
```

The patient element is based on the patientType complexType that contains, among others, the mailAddress element, which is based on the hrm:physicalAddress type—from a different namespace and defined in a different XSD document, called Administration.xsd.

The physicalAddress type is bound to the {http://www.hospital.org/hrm} namespace (its prefix hrm is declared at the top of the XSD document):

```
<xsd:schema xmlns:xsd="http://www.w3.org/2001/XMLSchema"
            xmlns="http://ourhospital.com/patient"
            xmlns:hrm="http://www.hospital.org/hrm"
```

The definition for this type is in a separate XSD document that is imported into the VeryPatient.xsd schema:

```
<xsd:import schemaLocation="Administration.xsd"
            namespace="http://www.hospital.org/hrm"/>
```

The import element tells any processor interpreting the XSD document that it should read the contents of the imported XSD document and merge it with the current XSD's definitions. This means that it is transparent to anyone using the VeryPatient.xsd whether the physicalAddress type was in that XSD itself or in some imported XSD.

Similar to the xsd:import, the xsd:include construct also instructs XSD processors to read XSD element and type definitions from the indicated external XSD document. However, include is used for XSDs with the same targetNamespace as the base XSD, whereas import is used with external schema definitions describing elements from a different namespace.

Managing XSD documents is very important, much like the management of the corporate data model. The XSD documents form an important asset for an organization that adopts SOA. Together, the XSDs describe all business data of interest—at the very least the data that is interchanged between systems and published by (web) services.

The ability to link XSDs is essential in building a structure of schema definitions that is manageable. Many organizations use hierarchies of XSD documents. At the root, you will find entities or business objects from specific business domains. It is a common (best) practice to have the namespace associated with the schema definition derive its name from the business domain.

A note or warning here, before you go overboard with an attempt at an enterprise-wide XSD hierarchy. There is some risk involved that theoretical soundness conflicts with the harsh reality of physical components that have neither unlimited memory nor infinitely fast CPUs. An XSD hierarchy, no matter how correct, may become too complex to handle. For example, it cannot be compiled because it imports the entire world into a single XSD that is then used by all Web Services in the organization. In order to compile even the simplest Web Service, over 100MB of XSDs have to be processed.

WSDLs—the service definitions that we will discuss a little later—are often a better place to do the final importing of multiple XSDs. This does not mean that importing XSDs into XSDs is a bad thing; however, the import directive must be used with discretion. The WSDL can choose a subset of XSDs (which may import a small number of dependent XSDs) that it needs to operate, instead of indirectly importing all XSDs in the organization.

Extension, refinement, and composition of elements and types can be done at lower levels in the XSD hierarchy in XSD documents that import the business objects. More specific type and element definitions used for particular applications and services are defined in yet lower levels, again importing from the more generic schema definitions. This approach allows for Object Oriented characteristics such as the reuse and inheritance of business object definitions.

Through the import of the WHO-medic.xsd, we have made the bloodPressureReading element available in the VeryPatient.xsd document. It allows us to specify how instance XML documents can define bloodReading elements inside the bloodReadings child in the patient element.

The Service Contract: Introducing WSDL

With this little bit of XSD under our belt, we can take a closer look at the contract Margaret and Frank should draw up for the service that Frank's team will provide. We have already seen the first draft of this contract:

```
<operation name="getPatientRecord">
   <input message="PatientIdentificationInputMessage"/>
   <output message="PatientDataRecordOutputMessage"/>
   <fault message="UnknownPatientIdFaultMessage" name="UnknownPatientId"/>
   <fault message="NoUniquePatientMatchFaultMessage" name="NoUniquePatientMatch"/>
</operation>
```

This snippet is part of a WSDL document (WSDL stands for Web Service Definition Language, frequently pronounced as *whiz-dul*). WSDL is a W3C standard, originally for defining Web Service interfaces but today used for almost any kind of service—including Java interfaces, database APIs, and RESTful services (with WSDL 2.0). A WSDL document describes the functional interface, including operations, input and output messages, and faults. It also describes the implementation locations of the interface, or rather the physical endpoint (address) where the service can be invoked in combination with the protocol to be used for invoking the service.

An interface can be bound to multiple protocols—such as SOAP, HTTP, and MIME—and each binding can be exposed at one or more endpoints. WSDL has extension points that allow for the definition of other binding types (for example, based on Java, JCA, and JMS). Note that we will focus on the 1.1 release of WSDL supported by the SOA Suite.

Analyzing the Service Interface According to WSDL

The contract for a service has various aspects to it, of course. Some of it is very much like real-world contracts, whereas other parts are quite technical in nature. The WSDL primarily describes the service interface with a number of functional as well as more technical aspects of the contract, in a way that technical infrastructures can understand and that is accessible to human readers at the same time by using strongly typed XML with meaningful element names. We will take a closer look at the essential elements in WSDL documents. Other aspects of a service contract—for example, regarding its response time, availability, and release schedule—are not part of WSDL documents.

Abstract Service Interface: The portType

We have talked about a specific operation Frank's service should provide: getPatientRecord. However, his service may very well offer additional operations as well, just as a Java class may contain (and typically does) multiple public methods and a PL/SQL package specification provides more than one procedure. The WSDL document contains the portType element, a named set of abstract operations, and the abstract messages (input, output, and fault) involved with those operations. Faults (referring to SOAP faults here) are the Web Service equivalent of the exception in languages such as PL/SQL and Java. The portType element is very similar to the Java Interface artifact—it specifies the abstract service interface that is on offer from the Web Service. It is up to the port elements to hook up the implementation of this abstract interface and its operations:

```
<portType name="PatientDataServiceInterface">
    <operation name="getPatientDataRecord">
        <input message="tns:PatientIdentityRequestMessage"/>
        <output message="tns:PatientDataRecord"/>
    </operation>
</portType>
```

Also notice that the input and output messages are now fully qualified and in the namespace denoted by the "tns" prefix. Figure 4-4 provides an overview of the entire structure of WSDL documents. Note the three sections that describe the *what* of the service (what functionality is offered by the service?), the *how* of the service (can this functionality be invoked in terms of protocol and message format?), and the *where* of the service (at which physical endpoint can the service be contacted?).

Message Definition

Frank is nowhere near the point where he wants to start talking about the implementation details such as the endpoint (the URL on which the service can be invoked) for his service. He wants to first further specify the functionality of the getPatientRecord operation, or at least define what the

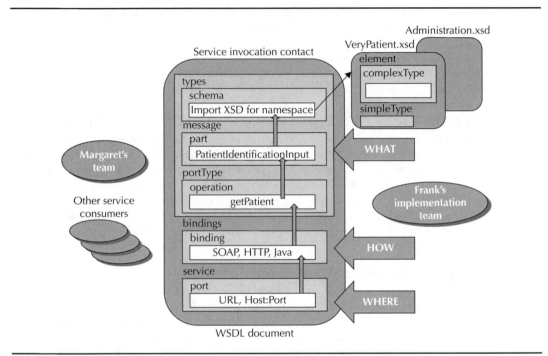

FIGURE 4-4.   *Overview of the structure of WSDL documents*

structure will be for the input and output messages. That is quite a life-altering change from his initial response to Margaret's opening moves, where he almost created the database views on the spot for her. This structured, step-by-step approach sits well with him. It also gives him time to absorb all the new lingo and concepts.

The input and output element each have a message attribute. This attribute refers to a message element defined in the WSDL document or an external XSD:

```
<message name="PatientIdentityRequestMessage">
    <part name="PatientIdentificationPart" element="pat:PatientIdentification"/>
</message>
<message name=" PatientDataRecord">
    <part name="PatientDataRecordPart" element="pat:PatientDataRecord"/>
</message>
```

A message can consist of multiple parts. Each part can be seen to represent a parameter in the operation request or response. Multiple part elements can be used when a message has several unrelated or at least logically separate units.

Two types of styles are used for Web Services: document-style and RPC-style Web Services. For the "document literal (wrapped)" style service (which we will work with most of the time), the WS-I Basic Profile specifies that at most one part is allowed. In general, it seems that unless there is a real need for using multipart messages, sticking with single-part messages is less complex and less likely to have you run into tool limitations. This style works with XML documents that can have a complex, nested structure if needed. The RPC-style service requires individual input and output parameters, which makes the interface definition much less flexible. For the purpose of this book—and almost always in other cases—we will use the document approach. The alternative, RPC, is rapidly going out of fashion. For details, see the almost classic paper "Which style of WSDL should I use?" (www.ibm.com/developerworks/webservices/library/ws-whichwsdl/).

Each part is based on either a type (for Remote Procedure Call or RPC-style services) or an element (for the document literal–style services we will primarily deal with) that is defined in the <types> section of the WSDL document. This section can contain XSD-style element and type definitions, or import one or more external XSD documents. For reasons of loose coupling and reuse of type definitions, as well as keeping the WSDL document readable, working with external XSDs is preferable over including type definitions inside the WSDL document.

The following snippet is an example of a WSDL document that imports message definitions using an external XSD document (VeryPatient.xsd in this case):

```
<types>
    <schema attributeFormDefault="qualified" elementFormDefault="qualified"
            xmlns="http://www.w3.org/2001/XMLSchema">
        <import namespace="http://ourhospital.com/patient"
                schemaLocation="VeryPatient.xsd"/>
    </schema>
</types>
```

Frank and Margaret need to flesh out the structure of the PatientIdentification and PatientDataRecord elements in the Patient.xsd. When they have done so, they have the abstract interface for the getPatientRecord operation in the PatientDataService, because the functionality is defined but no implementation details are specified. At that point, Frank and his team can start working on the implementation—how to fulfill the contract—and Margaret's team can commence with the realization of service clients that will be invoking that service. Well, almost. The two first need to agree on how the service will be called. The precise physical address can be determined later on, but it would be useful to know the protocol via which the service is to be invoked.

Through the operation and message elements, together with any referenced XSDs, we have specified the XML structure for the requests to and responses from the service. What we have not described yet is how the request and the response are communicated. It's like agreeing on the form that we will fill out and send to an agency to make a request. If we do not discuss the address to which we should send the form or the postal service to use—that is what the service and port elements are for there is a chance of that form not arriving in good shape. We should also give consideration to the envelope we should wrap the form in and the fact that we may need to provide a return address if we ever want to receive a reply from this agency.

Many tools, including the Oracle SOA Suite, are able to speak SOAP (formerly known as the Simple Object Access Protocol, but today just referred to as SOAP). Other protocols—such as REST, e-mail, and binary message transmissions—may also be supported.

SOAP: The XML Transmission Language

SOAP describes the meta-details for sending messages between service consumers and providers. It is a W3C standard that describes the structure of an XML document—this time the XML document that contains at its core a message being transmitted, enveloped by metadata pertaining to the transmission itself.

A SOAP message in its simplest form looks like this:

SOAP document

> **NOTE**
> *We discuss SOAP 1.2, as that is the default version used in the Oracle 11g SOA Suite.*

At the core is the payload—that is, the message itself. It's like the letter inside the envelope. The payload is wrapped inside the <body> element. The <header> element optionally contains header elements—elements that provide metadata about the message that is being sent. This is much like the information you may scribble on the envelope in which you send a letter, such as the return address and perhaps a specific indication of the department the letter is intended for or the topic it is about.

The SOAP header can contain various types of metadata, including addressing information—for example, the address to which to send any replies, transaction coordination details, and authorization tokens—used to identify the sender of the message.

Namespaces can be declared at various levels, such as the root Envelope element or the Header and Body elements. The Body element is the container for the actual payload sent in the SOAP message. In the following example, the payload is the {http://ourhospital.com/patient}patientIdentification root element with its contents:

```
<env:Envelope xmlns:env="http://schemas.xmlsoap.org/soap/envelope/"
xmlns:wsa="http://www.w3.org/2005/08/addressing">
   <env:Header>
      <wsa:MessageID>urn:CBCA87702F9311DFBFAEA7F5A2B8D1B8</wsa:MessageID>
      <wsa:ReplyTo>
         <wsa:Address>http://www.w3.org/2005/08/addressing/anonymous</wsa:Address>
      </wsa:ReplyTo>
   </env:Header>   <env:Body>
      <ns1:PatientIdentification>
         <ns1:patientId>3232</ns1:patientId>
      </ns1:PatientIdentification>
   </env:Body>
</env:Envelope>
```

The structure of SOAP messages is the same, regardless of whether the messages contain a request or a reply—just like the basic concept of an envelope is the same, no matter what's in the letter it contains.

The How and Where in the WSDL Contract

The Binding element in the WSDL document is used to describe the fact that the specific operations in the service are callable via a specific protocol binding and data format. Several options are available for bindings, including HTTP, MIME, JCA, and SOAP (the latter being the most prominent among them):

```
<binding name="PatientDataServiceSoapHttp"
             type="tns: PatientDataServiceInterface">
    <soap:binding style="document"
                     transport="http://schemas.xmlsoap.org/soap/http"/>
    <operation name="getPatientDataRecord">
        <soap:operation soapAction="getPatientDataRecord" />
        <input>
            <soap:body use="literal"/>
        </input>
        <output>
            <soap:body use="literal"/>
        </output>
    </operation>
</binding>
```

The type attribute in the binding element refers to a portType element—the element that contains the interface that declares the available operations. The binding element links a portType to a protocol and a style of message formatting. In this case, we have defined the binding of the PatientDataServiceInterface portType to the SOAP protocol using a document-style message format.

The child element of the binding element—in this case, soap:binding or {http://schemas. xmlsoap.org/wsdl/soap/}binding, because the prefix soap is bound to this namespace—indicates the protocol. The soap:binding element specifies the format through the style attribute—which we will always set to document.

For each operation in the referenced portType that we want to support through the binding, we need to include a child "operation" element inside soap:binding. The name attribute on the operation element refers to the name of one of the operations inside the referenced portType.

The input and output elements are finally used to specify whether the SOAP binding has a literal or encoded use for the parameters. We will always use literal—refer to the paper mentioned earlier for details.

The WSDL document will be completed with the Service element that finally assigns physical address details to each of the binding elements in the document. Here is the Service element for the contract Frank and Margaret are drawing up:

```
<service name="PatientDataService">
    <port name="PatientDataRecordServiceSoapHttpPort"
             binding="tns: PatientDataServiceSoapHttp ">
        <soap:address location="URL_To_Be_Defined"/>
    </port>
</service>
```

This element associates a binding element with a physical endpoint. The binding tells us how to invoke the service operations—which protocol and message format—and the port child of the service element contains the details of the whereabouts of the deployed service implementation.

However, note that Frank is at this point far from able to indicate the URL where his service will reside, nor does Margaret need that information at this point. The location is therefore not yet defined in the WSDL.

JDeveloper provides a WSDL editor with both Source and Design views, the latter offering a graphical overview of the WSDL with drag-and-drop support for adding elements to the document. However neat this UI, you will probably find yourself inspecting and editing the source code directly. By the way, most WSDL documents will be generated for you by the SOA Suite design-time environment, based on BPEL process and Mediator service definitions, for example.

Demo: Create the Simplest Web Service Implementation

Once you have the complete WSDL and any referenced XSDs, you can start writing code that calls the Web Service (even if it does not yet exist) and processes its response. Calling a Web Service is supported by libraries and platform infrastructure in many technology environments.

Creating an implementation of a Web Service according to the specification laid down in the WSDL and the XSD is also rather straightforward in various technology stacks. We will discuss this process for Java using JDeveloper.

NOTE
All the source code discussed, screenshots for the important steps, and some bonus material are on the book's wiki.

The Contract for the Simple Web Service

Let's assume a fairly simple WSDL document along the lines of the PatientDataRecordService—but simpler, just to give you the idea. The key parts of the WSDL document are shown here. Let's see how to read it:

```
<definitions
    targetNamespace="ourHospital.PatientData"
    xmlns:tns="ourHospital.PatientData"
    xmlns:hospital="http://ourhospital.com/patient"
    ... >
<types>
    <schema attributeFormDefault="qualified"
            elementFormDefault="qualified"
            targetNamespace="http://ourhospital.com/patient"
        xmlns="http://www.w3.org/2001/XMLSchema">
        <import namespace="http://ourhospital.com/patient"
                schemaLocation="SimplePatient.xsd"/>
    </schema>
</types>
<message name="PatientIdentityRequestMessage">
    <part name="in" element="hospital:patientIdentification"/>
</message>
<message name="PatientDataRecord">
    <part name="return" element="hospital:patient"/>
</message>
<portType name="SimplePatientRecordDataInterface">
```

```
        <operation name="getPatientDataRecord">
            <input message="tns:PatientIdentityRequestMessage"/>
            <output message="tns:PatientDataRecord"/>
        </operation>
    </portType>
    <binding name="SimplePatientDataRecordServiceSoapHttp"
            type="tns:SimplePatientRecordDataInterface">
        <soap:binding style="document"
transport="http://schemas.xmlsoap.org/soap/http"/>
        <operation name="getPatientDataRecord">
            <soap:operation soapAction="getPatientData"/>
            <input><soap:body use="literal"/></input>
            <output><soap:body use="literal"/></output>
        </operation>
    </binding>
    <service name="SimplePatientDataRecordService">
        <port name="GetPatientDataRecordServiceSoapHttpPort"
binding="tns:SimplePatientDataRecordServiceSoapHttp">
            <soap:address location="http://host:port/hospital...
            .../patientservices/GetPatientDataRecordServiceSoapHttpPort"/>
        </port>
    </service>
</definitions>
```

The portType element contains the actual operation on offer in this service. Through the message elements and the schema referenced from the <types> element, we quickly get a feel for the input parameters and the outcome of calling the operation.

We can ask for a PatientRecord by submitting the PatientIdentityRequestMessage (which contains the PatientId, an integer value from the XSD). The service returns to us an XML document—PatientDataRecord—that contains patient details such as name, initials, gender and birth date, recent hospital visits, and some physical characteristics that could include weight, height, and color of eyes. We learn this too from the SimplePatient.xsd document.

The service is (to be) offered through the SOAP protocol—as we can see from the binding element. The endpoint is not yet specified—so we do not know the actual URL where we can call this service.

The (referenced and external) SimplePatient.xsd document looks like this:

```
<xsd:schema xmlns:xsd="http://www.w3.org/2001/XMLSchema"
            xmlns="http://ourhospital.com/patient"
            targetNamespace="http://ourhospital.com/patient"
            elementFormDefault="qualified">
  <xsd:element name="patientIdentification" type="patientIdType"/>
  <xsd:element name="patient" type="patientType"/>
  <xsd:complexType name="patientIdType">
    <xsd:sequence>
      <xsd:element name="patientId" type="xsd:integer"/>
    </xsd:sequence>
  </xsd:complexType>
  <xsd:complexType name="patientType">
    <xsd:sequence>
```

```
        <xsd:element name="name" type="xsd:string"/>
        ...
        <xsd:element name="physicalCharacteristic" type="measurementType"
                     minOccurs="0" maxOccurs="unbounded"/>
        <xsd:element name="hospitalVisit" type="hospitalVisit" minOccurs="0"
                     maxOccurs="unbounded"/>
    </xsd:sequence>
  </xsd:complexType>
  <xsd:complexType name="measurementType">
    <xsd:sequence>
      <xsd:element name="dateOfMeasurement" type="xsd:date"/>
      ...
    </xsd:sequence>
  </xsd:complexType>
  <xsd:complexType name="hospitalVisit">....</xsd:complexType>
  <xsd:simpleType name="genderType">
    <xsd:restriction base="xsd:string">
      <xsd:enumeration value="M"/>
      <xsd:numeration value="F"/>
    </xsd:restriction>
  </xsd:simpleType>
</xsd:schema>
```

In fact, the service does not even exist at this point. Let's first do something about that by creating a simple implementation.

Creating an Implementation of a Web Service

JDeveloper helps with the implementation of a Web Service: You can ask it to generate a service implementation based on a WSDL document. All you have to add yourself is the Java code that does the actual work. All the Web Service deployment details and XML-to-Java data type mapping are taken care of.

When we select the WSDL file in the Application Navigator, we can find the option Create Web Service in the right-click menu. Selecting it brings up a wizard that we can, by and large, accept the default values in. You may want to set a nicer package name in which the Java classes will be generated.

The central class generated by the Create Web Service Wizard is PatientType—based on the XSD element by the same name. Its properties are defined as follows:

```
public class PatientType {
    @XmlElement(required = true)
    protected String name;
    @XmlElement(required = true)
    protected String initials;
    ...
    protected List<MeasurementType> physicalCharacteristic;
    protected List<HospitalVisit> hospitalVisit;
```

The annotations are part of the JAX-WS specification, introduced in JEE 5. They provide additional type-mapping instructions to the container in which the Web Service will be deployed.

It is now up to us to implement the class SimplePatientRecordDataInterfaceImpl—more specifically, the method getPatientDataRecord that accepts a PatientIdType and returns a PatientType:

```
public PatientType getPatientDataRecord(PatientIdType in)
```

We can both deploy and subsequently test the Web Service from the right-click menu once we have implemented this method.

Invoking Web Services from Java and PL/SQL

When they have been implemented and deployed, Web Services can be called from different technology stacks—the main *raison d'être* for Web Services. Invoking the Web Service introduced earlier can be done from, for example, PL/SQL and Java—this is shown in detail on the book's wiki. The wiki also introduces the tool soapUI, which can be used to invoke (and test) the Web Service as well as to provide mock implementations for Web Service contracts.

Summary

The SOA Suite speaks XML. Almost all files we create during the development of composite applications are XML documents. And the vast majority of data processed by those applications when in production is also XML. It is essential for SOA Suite developers—as well as architects and to some extent functional analysts and testers—to be aware of the primary XML concepts and technologies, such as namespaces and XSD as well as XPath and XSLT (see Appendix B for these last two).

The interfaces for services in the SOA Suite are typically specified in yet another XML document, based on WSDL. This chapter introduced the structure of the WSDL document, focusing first on the portType (the interface) that defines the operations and refers to the input and output parameters, whose structure is usually defined in associated XSD documents. The port element in the WSDL document specifies through which protocols (such as SOAP) and on which endpoint the service can be invoked. This element only needs to be defined upon deployment—and it may even be derived as a result of deployment.

The Web Service interface definitions are technology neutral: They can be implemented in and invoked from many different technologies. The chapter briefly discusses the implementation of a WSDL contract using Java. The wiki has examples for other implementations and service consumers.

In the next chapters, we will create SOA composite applications that are the implementation of WSDL contracts. These applications are constructed according to the Service Component Architecture (SCA) specification that was introduced in Chapter 3. The SCA specification goes beyond WSDL. SCA defines a general approach for describing what you could call the deployment contract for services as well as for creating composite services built from individual service building blocks—the service components. Also see Chapter 14 for a more detailed discussion on SCA.

In the next chapter, we will create a service component—using the BPEL Process Manager in conjunction with the Database Adapter—that provides the implementation for the service contract Frank has agreed on with Margaret. This component is embedded in an SCA composite application that offers a single service to the outside world: the PatientRecordService. The SOA Suite runs such composite applications and forwards the Web Service calls directed at the PatientRecordService to the composite that has them executed by the BPEL process.

CHAPTER
5

First Steps with BPEL and
the Database Adapter

hapter 3 introduced the SOA Suite and explained how it implements an SCA container according to the Service-Component Architecture. We develop composite applications in JDeveloper that we can then deploy to and run in the SOA Suite. These applications typically expose public Web Services that clients can invoke. Internally they consist of service components that do the actual work. SOA Suite supports various types of service components, including Mediator, Java (Spring), Human Task, and Business Rule.

Another type of service component is introduced in this chapter: the BPEL Process service component. BPEL (Business Process Execution Language) is a programming language for creating a piece of service logic—logic that exposes a service interface and that typically orchestrates multiple service calls. At the same time, BPEL has many of the traits of general-purpose programming languages, as we will see in this chapter and the next. A BPEL process can be fairly long-running, contains state, and can receive incoming messages in addition to the original request that instantiated the process. This chapter introduces BPEL and the development of BPEL service components. Note that the online chapter complement offers additional screenshots and detailed step-by-step instructions to follow the examples hands-on.

Introducing the Business Process Execution Language (BPEL)

The previous chapter introduced the PatientDataService, which makes data available in a standardized, technology-independent way. Of even more importance to St. Matthews and indeed every organization are its business processes that use the services. The business processes are the concerted actions that an organization performs to achieve its business objectives. For St. Matthews, among its business processes are the "intake patient/treatment patient/discharge patient" processes as well as the "win employee/manage employee/lose employee" and "gather claims/send claims to insurers/process payments" processes.

Continuing our discussion from Chapter 2, we see that when we analyze business processes at the lowest level (where the action is), we can describe them as a series of activities, usually by different actors, in a predefined order that may vary with the results of earlier steps, and with information associated with the processes that is constantly transferred and manipulated between steps and actors. A business process, for example, may have the patient, the reception desk, the departmental office management, a doctor, and the billing department for its actors. The information associated with the process could include the patient's personal details, recent health history, a list of recent hospital visits, the request from the patient to see a specific doctor, as well as the preferred date and time, the best available timeslots for the doctor, and the agreed-upon appointment.

Looking at the business processes from a service-oriented point of view, the actions can be seen as calls to various services. The services are either implemented by software (system-centric) or performed by human actors (human-centric). Executing the business process is largely a matter of orchestrating the services that need to be invoked and managing the state of the process during its lifetime. The business process may run very rapidly—in less than a second, perhaps, if only computers are involved—or it can take hours, days, or even months.

Automating a business process in an SOA environment can be done through BPEL, the Business Process Execution Language. BPEL is a programming language for implementing process flows and composite (or orchestrated) services. BPEL is a standard maintained by OASIS and supported by all major players in the IT industry, including Microsoft, Oracle, IBM, Software AG, Adobe, and SAP. A BPEL program—referred to as a *BPEL process definition*—can be run by a BPEL engine, just like a Java program can be run by a Java Virtual Machine and a PL/SQL program by the Oracle RDBMS. A BPEL process is often published as a Web Service. It then has an associated WSDL document with XSD definitions and one or more operations on a portType that can be called through SOAP messages. Note that we will later discuss other ways to call and communicate with BPEL components.

BPEL Ingredients

A typical BPEL process contains the following items:

- Calls to services. A service in this sense can be a task performed by a human staff member, hiding behind the service interface of a workflow engine, or an automated Web Service, although for the BPEL process, the distinction is not important.

- Specific BPEL activities, including data manipulation (calculation and transformation of variables associated with the process) and flow logic, including decision point (if-then-else and switch/case, iteration, parallelism, wait).

- Event handlers and fault (or exception) handlers.

In SOA Suite 11*g*, BPEL components often work closely together with other service components in a composite application, such as Mediator, and Business Rule service components, to facilitate interaction with other services and provide complex, externalized decision logic.

Human Task components are also frequently wired to BPEL processes for the manual handling of activities in potentially complex workflows. The recent BPEL4People extension to the original WS-BPEL standard adds specifications that define a standardized approach for integrating human interactions more closely with BPEL processes. More on human tasks in Chapters 10 and 11.

Another regular partner for BPEL components is the Notification Service for sending messages to human users via e-mail, SMS, and instant messaging (internally connected to the User Messaging Service, or UMS).

Its good fit with business processes notwithstanding, BPEL also provides a powerful way for implementing composite services that do not necessarily directly relate to an automated business process. Of course, services can be implemented using a variety of technologies, as we have seen in the previous chapter, including Java, PL/SQL, C++, and .NET. However, when a service component has to invoke multiple services—either external to the composite application or provided by other service components inside the composite, and potentially asynchronous and long-running—BPEL is typically a good way to implement the component. This holds especially true when over the course of the component's lifetime some state is built up in variables and process flow logic is involved to loop or conditionally branch.

A BPEL component has the unique capability to receive additional messages, beyond the first invocation that initiated the component instance, and respond to them. This allows clients to interact with the process—for example, to check on its progress, provide additional information, or get a hold of intermediate results.

Synchronous and Asynchronous Services

In the previous chapter, we assumed a pretty simple world, where a call to a service results in a more or less instantaneous response. Or at least, although the response may take some time to arrive, we will just wait for it. Just like synchronous function or method calls in PL/SQL and Java, the process thread blocks until a result is received. However, in the real world, some services do not render responses in a timely enough fashion to justify waiting for them. We may have to ask the service desk, bank manager, or wedding planner to call us back when they have the answer to our query—we just ran out of lunch break and cannot stay on the line any longer. In short, synchronous request/reply cannot include human activities. Well-known examples of asynchronous communication are e-mail and voicemail. We leave a message, do not stick around for an answer—as there is no one to provide that answer—and expect to get a reaction later on.

The same goes for clients that call services in a SOA world. Some services are inherently asynchronous—which means that they will always send their responses by calling us back instead of replying while we are on the line. Asynchronicity is often deliberately used to decouple the service consumer from the provider (or the availability of the provider). In case of an asynchronous call, the caller is not dependent on the immediate availability or fast response time of the provider. Less dependency means more flexibility!

However, whereas the coupling decreases on the one hand—the callee does not need to be available when the call is made, nor does the callee need to respond extremely rapidly—it increases on the other, as the caller needs to implement a callback interface stipulated by the service contract: Only when the consumer implements and exposes the callback interface can the asynchronous response be received and processed. This introduces a new dependency on the definition of the callback interface.

A call to an asynchronous service is handled differently than a synchronous call. The calling party needs to provide a callback address, for example. It also needs to determine what it will do during the time it waits for the callback. Will it be suspended? Will it wait? Can it do other useful things? And how will it know the callback has arrived?

The answers to these questions vary with the technology involved. We will see how BPEL processes deal with calls to asynchronous services—very elegantly, that much I will give away at this point. Many other technologies have more difficulties in dealing with asynchronous service calls natively—usually relying on some form of external message queuing to handle the requests and or the responses.

You can tell asynchronous service interfaces quite easily from the WSDL: The portType has operations without an output element, even though you clearly expect a response. A second portType defines the callback interface with operations that handle the response. The calling party has to implement this portType and let the asynchronous service know what the address or end point is where this "receive asynchronous response" service can be invoked.

A special type of asynchronous service is the fire-and-forget service, a one-way service that never returns the asynchronous response. The client can immediately resume processing after making a call to this type of service and it does not have to anticipate a response in the future.

A BPEL process can be short lived or long running, and it can publish synchronous and asynchronous operations. A BPEL process that has among its activities a human task, a "wait," a "pick," or a call to an asynchronous service will typically publish an asynchronous service—however, that decision is up to the developer.

BPEL is one of the first-class citizens for component implementation included in the SCA standard, along with Java, Spring, PHP, (SOAP) WebServices, and C++. Services implemented using BPEL can easily be configured in SCA components and linked with references provided by other SCA components.

In this chapter, we will get off to a flying start by doing a rapid implementation of an SCA composite application with BPEL-based service components. We will then take a first look at some of the basic programming constructs of the Business Process Execution Language and go on to see how we can leverage other services from a BPEL process (for example, to retrieve information from an Oracle database).

Implementing the Composite PatientDataService

Let's revisit Frank's Patient Data Service—a composite service that we worked on in the previous chapter. It seems that the data that this service will return for a particular patient has to be gathered from various sources. Additionally, the service will have to do some processing and transformation on the data retrieved from those sources to make it fit the requirements of the service consumers as laid down in the WSDL. Even though a request for patient data is not much of a business process all by itself, it *is* a composite service, and because of the service orchestration requirements, BPEL is a good choice for implementing the Patient Data Service.

Now buckle up for a fast BPEL ride with the Oracle 11*g* SOA Suite:

1. Start JDeveloper 11*g*. Create a new application by selecting File | New from the main menu and selecting the node General | Applications in the categories tree. Select SOA Application in the items list shown on the right side. Click OK.

2. You will be prompted to provide a name and a directory for the application. Enter **PatientDataService** as the name for the application. Also enter a directory of your choice (see Figure 5-1).

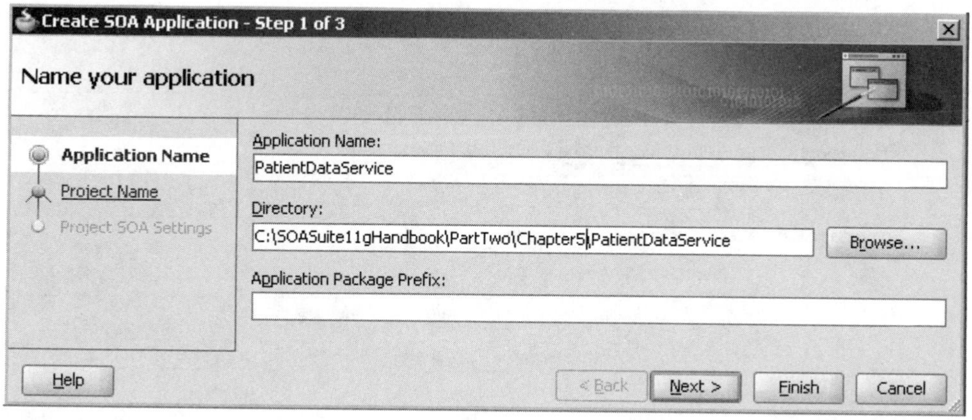

FIGURE 5-1. *The Create SOA Application dialog*

3. Click Next to go to the Project Name page. Enter the project name, **PatientDataService**, and click Next. On the last page, Project SOA Settings, select the composite template "Composite with BPEL" because we will create a composite application with a BPEL service component. Accept PatientDataService as the name for the composite. Click Finish to have the application, project, and service composite application created.

4. The Create BPEL Process dialog appears, as shown in Figure 5-2. Here, we specify the name of the BPEL process, the namespace, and the template we will use. Enter **PatientDataService** as the name of the BPEL process. Enter **http://stmatthews.hospital. com/patient/PatientDataService** for the namespace. Select the Synchronous BPEL Process template because we want to publish the process as a synchronous service—after all, we do not include human activities (yet) in this BPEL process, nor will we invoke any asynchronous services. Enter **PatientDataService** for the service name.

5. Leave the check box Expose As A SOAP Service checked. This will result in the BPEL component being exposed as a Web Service in the composite application. It also leads to an SCA composite with the BPEL process component already wired to an inbound SOAP service binding component. External consumers access the BPEL process through that SOAP service.

6. Accept the default names for the input and output—we will change these into more sensible values later on.

7. Click OK.

At this point, JDeveloper will create a bunch of files, including the BPEL process definition (PatientDataService.bpel) and the SCA composite definition (composite.xml). We talk about all these files and their mutual dependencies in the online chapter complement.

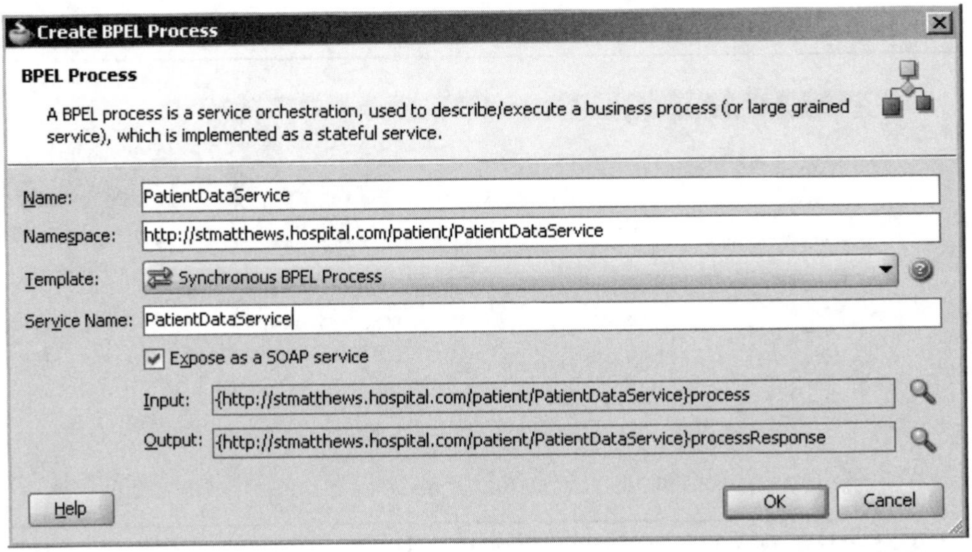

FIGURE 5-2. *The Create BPEL Process dialog for creating a new template-based BPEL process*

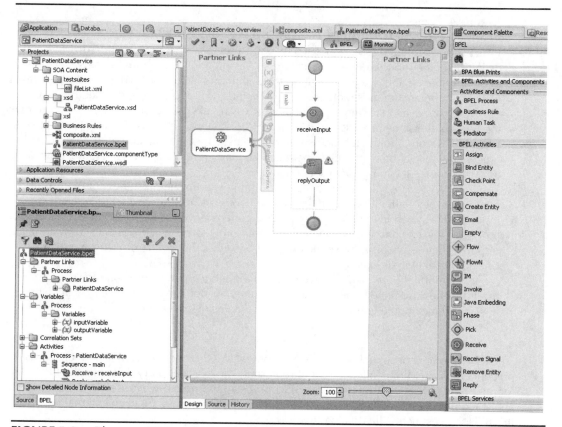

FIGURE 5-3.   *The new SOA project with the PatientDataService BPEL process*

The BPEL process editor opens and presents the Design view of the BPEL process (see Figure 5-3). On the bottom of the editor pane are three tabs: Design, Source, and History. In the Source tab, we can see the underlying XML content of the process definition. The Design and Source tabs provide different views on the same source, so changes can be made in either.

The PatientDataService BPEL process contains two activities at this point: Receive and Reply, as will be the case for all synchronous BPEL processes. The first activity receives the service request from an external partner—a party outside the BPEL process—and causes a new instance of the BPEL process to be created. The Reply activity—usually after some meaningful processing in intermediate BPEL activities that have yet to be added—returns a response to the external partner.

BPEL processes have two types of external partners: the invokers of the service(s) exposed by the BPEL process, and the services that the BPEL process invokes itself. The external partners as seen from BPEL are identified in the BPEL process through *partner links,* which are nothing more than the interaction points between the BPEL component and other components in the same composite.

Business Process (Definition) vs. Business Process Instances

When business analysts speak about a business process, what they are referring to is the definition of the process. When we create a BPEL process, a program to be executed by a BPEL run-time engine, we also work on the definition of the process. However, what takes place in an organization is more than that: The business process can be executed many times per day, even many times simultaneously. And likewise a BPEL engine can run many instances of the same process at the same time. Just like a Java class file is the mold to cast Java objects from, the BPEL process is the mold used by the BPEL container to cast BPEL process instances from—of which there can be many running at the same time, each with its own instance ID and its own set of data.

The SOA console allows us to inspect running and finished instances of our business processes—before finally purging them. It will come as no surprise that BPEL process instances are stored in a database—a process called *dehydration*. This happens when a process is finished and may happen also in mid-processing, when it is paused, waiting for a response to an asynchronous service request or some other event to occur, or when a Checkpoint activity is executed.

It is important to realize that every call to the service published by a BPEL process will result in a new instance to be initiated. Note that it is not just an instance of a BPEL process; it is an instance of the entire composite that contains the BPEL process.

A synchronous or asynchronous BPEL process, like the one we have just created, has one predefined partner link, called Client. It represents the external party that calls the BPEL process (or rather the service published by the BPEL process, and possibly exposed by the composite application). For each service, we will call from the BPEL process; for each external party invoking this BPEL process, we will add a partner link.

JDeveloper has created two BPEL process variables: inputVariable and outputVariable. These are used to capture the input received in the service request and specify the output to be returned as the service response by the Reply activity. Variables in BPEL are based on an XML type or element—either a primitive type or a custom type or element defined in an XSD document associated with the project. The two variables created by default are based on the message types specified in the WSDL for the PatientDataService's "process" operation. This operation is also created by default by JDeveloper.

We can create the absolute minimal BPEL process by adding just a single activity that will set the value of the outputVariable, as we did in Chapter 3 (the BPEL activity used for manipulating the value of variables is called Assign). The steps to create this minimal BPEL process and to deploy and run it on the SOA Suite are described and visualized in the online chapter complement.

The PatientDataService BPEL Process in More Detail

The PatientDataService implemented by our BPEL equivalent of HelloWorld is up and running, assuming you followed the instructions in the online chapter complement. And although it is laughably simple, it already has the core elements that underpin much more complex BPEL processes.

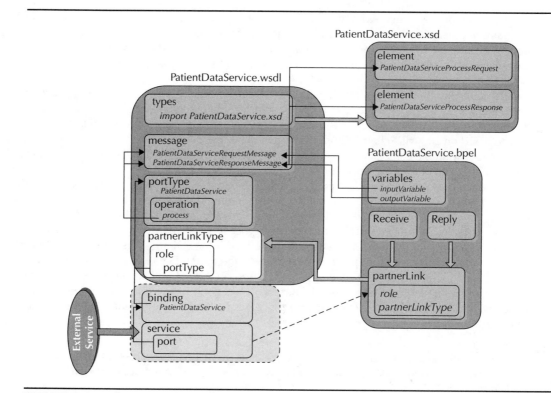

FIGURE 5-4.   *The PatientDataService BPEL process and its associated WSDL and XSD files*

So by analyzing this trivial example, we get a feel for what constitutes this combination of SCA
and BPEL that is exposed as a Web Service. Figure 5-4 shows the files that make up the composite
application, along with their dependencies.

JDeveloper has created the file PatientDataService.wsdl. This file specifies the interface that
our BPEL process exposes and that the composite application will publish externally (because we
left the check box Expose As A SOAP Service checked when we created the composite):

```
<!-- portType implemented by the PatientDataService BPEL process -->
<portType name="PatientDataService">
  <operation name="process"> <!-- the default name that we ought to change -->
   <input message="client:PatientDataServiceRequestMessage"/>
   <output message="client:PatientDataServiceResponseMessage"/>
  </operation>
</portType>
```

The Request and Response message types are based on the elements defined in the XSD
document PatientDataService.xsd that was also created for us. Initially both Request and Response
elements consist of a single string.

The BPEL process—defined in the file PatientDataService.bpel—contains variables, just like programs in other programming languages. Some variables contain the messages received from or to be sent to partners, whereas others contain data required for holding state information or temporary, local data related to the process and are never exchanged between partners. All variables hold data in the form of XML.

The variables are defined in the BPEL process through "variable" elements, which specify the name and the data type or structure of each variable. Variables can be global—accessible throughout the BPEL process—or local to sections of the process (called *scopes* and introduced later). A variable can be based on an XML Schema Simple Type such as string, decimal, or dateTime. Alternatively, a BPEL process variable can be defined in terms of a message type defined in the WSDL document or an element in one of the XSD documents.

A special type of variable is the Entity variable. A variable of this type is bound to an SDO (Service Data Object) published by a Data Access Service (DAS), which could be provided, for example, by an ADF BC data provider. More on this advanced setup in Chapter 20.

The variables in the PatientDataService BPEL process are in reality not simple strings (like they are right now) or integers; their structure is defined by WSDL message types. JDeveloper has created two variables for us: inputVariable, based on the PatientDataServiceRequestMessage message type in the WSDL file, which in turn is based on the PatientDataServiceProcessRequest element in the PatientDataService.xsd document. The second BPEL variable is outputVariable, which is likewise based on the PatientDataServiceProcessResponse element. Figure 5-5 shows the BPEL variable definition.

```
<variables>
  <variable name="inputVariable" messageType="client:PatientDataServiceRequestMessage"/>
  <variable name="outputVariable" messageType="client:PatientDataServiceResponseMessage"/>
</variables>
```

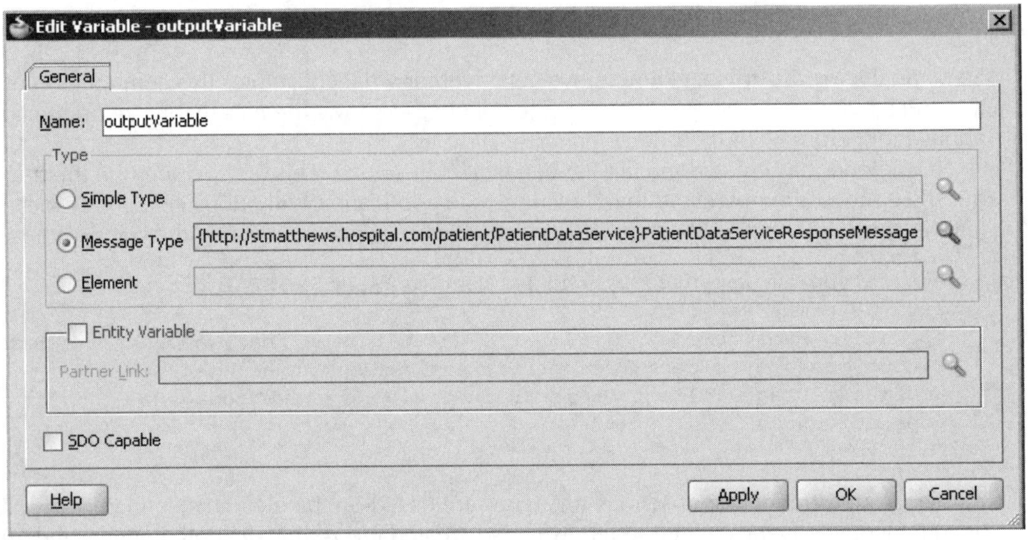

FIGURE 5-5. *The definition of the variable outputVariable based on the message type PatientDataServiceResponseMessage*

Later in this chapter, we will extend the XSD document with a more interesting definition of the PatientDataServiceProcessRequest element. The inputVariable in the BPEL process immediately inherits that more complex structure.

Essential BPEL Activities

BPEL is a programming language with its own XML-based syntax, constructs, and dozens of operations, or activities, as they are called in BPEL. Some will manipulate data, others perform logic (decision, loop), and a number of activities is involved in interacting with external service and event providers and consumers. Here we discuss the essential BPEL elements.

Partner Link Type

A very important element in BPEL processes is the link between the BPEL process and the external world: the services called by the process and the parties external to the BPEL process that access it. Every type of interaction is represented by a PartnerLinkType element, specified in the WSDL file of the BPEL process. Note that we see here a special extension to WSDL that BPEL introduces. The WSDL document created for a BPEL process contains at least one PartnerLinkType element for the partner that invokes the process. A PartnerLinkType specifies "role" elements. Each role element introduces a role that either the BPEL process or the external partner can assume in their mutual interaction: service consumer or service provider. That role is linked to a portType that the partner playing the role should implement. If the BPEL process is asynchronous, the partner link type contains two role elements: The partner is initially the consumer of the service sending a SOAP message to the BPEL process and subsequently the receiver of the response message sent to the callback interface.

In our very simple PatientDataService, we have just one interaction with the outside world: the client calling the service and receiving the immediate response. In the PatientDataService. wsdl file, this interaction is specified through a single partnerLinkType:

```
<plnk:partnerLinkType name="PatientDataService">
  <plnk:role name="PatientDataServiceProvider">
    <plnk:portType name="client:PatientDataService"/>
  </plnk:role>
</plnk:partnerLinkType>
```

The role of PatientDataServiceProvider in this interaction with the external client will be assumed by the BPEL process—the provider of the service. Every party calling this service will be the *client* that uses the PatientDataService portType. It is important to realize that the partner we are referring to is not just a single entity: A service can be (and hopefully will be) invoked by many different partners—BPEL processes, Java applications, enterprise service bus intermediaries, PL/SQL programs, and so on. The point is, of course, that they all play the same role—*client*—in the exchange with the PatientDataService and are therefore all captured under the same partnerLinkType umbrella.

partnerLink

The Partner Link types are defined outside the BPEL process in the associated WSDL file. As stated before, they describe a type of interaction for the process. The BPEL process itself uses Partner Link elements for every specific interaction between the process and the outside world. A Partner Link element is an instance of one of the predefined interaction types. A partnerLink refers to a Partner Link type.

The PatientDataProcess contains just a single partnerLink, associated with the PatientDataService Partner Link type. The attribute myRole is set to PatientDataServiceProvider—this indicates the role played by the BPEL process in this interaction.

```
<partnerLinks>
  <partnerLink name="PatientDataService"
              partnerLinkType="client:PatientDataService"
              myRole="PatientDataServiceProvider"/>
</partnerLinks>
```

Combining this partnerLink with the referenced Partner Link type indicates that the BPEL process will provide the implementation of the PatientDataService portType.

When we deploy the BPEL process, it is up to the container to bind all partnerLinks to physical endpoints. In the case of the Oracle SOA Suite with the SCA run time, the partnerLinks will be exposed as services (for portTypes implemented by the BPEL process) and references (for partnerLinks identifying external services that the BPEL process needs to call). In our current case, the *client* partnerLink in the PatientDataService BPEL process is exposed as a service by the composite application PatientDataService. Whether these services and references are internal within the composite—invoked and satisfied by other service components—or whether they are exposed at the composite level depends on the wiring inside the composite.

Receive and Reply Activities

The Receive activity is present in most BPEL processes, usually at the very beginning. Sometimes it is used to receive in-flight messages or events in already-running BPEL instances. It is the activity that receives a request from a partnerLink and in doing so can start a new BPEL process instance. Receive activities correspond with operations in the portType in the WSDL of the BPEL component.

In our example, the Receive maps to the process operation; a new instance of the PatientDataService process is created whenever the Receive activity starts handling a new request. This is specified through the createInstance attribute on the Receive element. The Receive activity is associated with the partnerLink from which it will receive a request message. Here, that is the client partnerLink. The Receive specifies a BPEL process variable that will be populated with the incoming request message. In this example, the request message is assigned to the inputVariable, which as we have seen before, is based on the PatientDataServiceRequestMessage message.

Although the associated partnerLink should be enough to tie the Receive to a specific portType—and indeed the portType attribute is optional—we still need to specify which operation in the portType is linked to this activity. In this case, it is the process operation for which requests are to be picked up by this Receive activity:

```
<receive name="receiveInput" partnerLink="PatientDataService"
         portType="client:PatientDataService" operation="process"
         variable="inputVariable" createInstance="yes"/>
```

When a BPEL process implements a synchronous operation—one with an output as well as an input, such as the process operation in our example—it needs to contain a Reply activity to complete the synchronous communication that started with the Receive and send the response message to the party calling the service:

```
<reply name="replyOutput" partnerLink="PatientDataService"
       portType="client:PatientDataService" operation="process"
       variable="outputVariable"/>
```

NOTE
This is not an offline callback as with an asynchronous service; instead, it is just the online synchronous reply.

The Assign Activity and BPEL Variables

In between the Receive and Reply activities, the least interesting step takes place: the Assign. Although especially not noteworthy in this example, the Assign activity is one of the most frequently encountered BPEL process steps. Its task, as its name suggests, is to assign values (to variables or partnerLinks). In that sense, you can regard it like the = operator in Java or the := operator in PL/SQL. That should give you an understanding of how important it is.

To extract values from variables, the Assign activity uses XPath expressions. The Assign activity not only uses XPath for retrieving values; it also uses XPath operands and functions to manipulate these values and write them to a specific location in an XML target.

In this example, the literal string value 'John Doe' is assigned to the outputVariable. To be more specific: The outputVariable is based on the PatientDataServiceResponseMessage, which has one part (called payload) that is based on the PatientDataServiceProcessResponse element in the XSD file. This element is based on a complexType with one child element: result.

The variable definition in the BPEL process is as follows:

```
<variable name="outputVariable"
        messageType="client:PatientDataServiceResponseMessage"/>
```

Here's the message definition in the WSDL document:

```
<message name="PatientDataServiceResponseMessage">
    <part name="payload" element="client:processResponse"/>
</message>
```

And, finally, here's the underlying element definition in the XSD document:

```
<element name="processResponse">
  <complexType>
  <sequence>
  <element name="result" type="string"/>
  </sequence>
  </complexType>
</element>
```

The "to" element in the following Assign activity specifies that the value 'John Doe' is assigned to the "result" child element under the PatientDataServiceProcessResponse root element in the "payload" part of the outputVariable:

```
<assign name="Assign_1">
  <copy>
    <from expression="'John Doe'"/>
    <to variable="outputVariable" part="payload"
        query="/client:PatientDataServiceProcessResponse/client:result"/>
  </copy>
</assign>
```

In general, the "from" element in an Assign activity can contain a BPEL variable or a partnerLink (a special type of variable), an XML fragment, or an XPath expression. Inside the XPath expression there can be references to multiple BPEL variables as well as literals and XPath functions, of which there are dozens. The "to" expression can contain a BPEL variable or partnerLink. Note that when either the to or from element refers to a variable, the element can also contain a "part" attribute to refer to the message part as well as a "query" attribute that contains an XPath query into the XSD type on which the message part is based.

To make our life easier, Oracle has defined a number of extensions to the Assign activity as it is specified in the BPEL standard. These extensions are implemented using the built-in BPEL extension framework that *is* part of the standard. The added "append" operation, for example, can be used to append the contents of a variable or XML fragment—which can be a list of nodes or a complex XML fragment—to another variable. Other extensions are copyList, insertBefore, insertAfter, and rename.

The logic that is now implemented in the BPEL process is very simple—and very much like any old programming language. For example, in PL/SQL, the functionality of this program would be represented by code like this:

```
package PatientDataService
function process ( p_input in varchar2)
return varchar2
  l_result varchar2(2000);
begin
  l_output:= 'John Doe';
  return l_output;
end;
```

The Assign Activity and the Use of XPath in BPEL

In the PatientDataService process, we have used the Assign activity to copy data to the output variable using a very simple XPath expression. XPath is a query language used for retrieving data from XML documents. XPath is a key element in XSLT, the transformation language used for converting a certain XML input into a differently structured XML output. Appendix B provides a little background on XPath.

To illustrate the use of XPath in BPEL processes, as well as to show a little more of what we can do with the Assign activity, we will first make our BPEL process somewhat more interesting by enriching the data structures we use.

Extending the Structure of the BPEL Variables

In the PatientDataService.xsd, we create the definitions for the elements PatientDataService ProcessRequest and PatientDataServiceProcessResponse (see the wiki for the complete sources):

```
<schema targetNamespace="http://stmatthews.hospital.com/patient/PatientDataService"
        xmlns:hospital="http://stmatthews.hospital.com/patient/PatientDataService"
        xmlns="http://www.w3.org/2001/XMLSchema">
  <element name="PatientDataServiceProcessRequest"
           type="hospital:patientIdType" />
  <element name="PatientDataServiceProcessResponse"
           type="hospital:patientType"/>
```

```
<complexType name="patientIdType">
  <choice>
    <element name="patientId" type="integer" minOccurs="0"/>
    <sequence>
      <element name="firstName" type="string" minOccurs="0"/>
      <element name="lastName" type="string" minOccurs="0"/>
    </sequence>
  </choice>
</complexType>
<complexType name="patientType">
  <sequence>
    <element name="name" type="string"/>
    . . .
    <element ref="hospital:physicalCharacteristic" maxOccurs="unbounded"/>
  </sequence>
</complexType>
<element name="physicalCharacteristic">
  <complexType>
    <sequence>
      <element name="dateOfMeasurement" type="date"/>
      . . .
    </sequence>
  </complexType>
</element>
</schema>
```

Next, we make a change in the PatientDataService.wsdl document—we base the payload parts of the input and output messages on these new element definitions (instead of process and processResponse):

```
<wsdl:message name="PatientDataServiceRequestMessage">
  <wsdl:part name="payload" element="client:PatientDataServiceProcessRequest"/>
</wsdl:message>
<wsdl:message name="PatientDataServiceResponseMessage">
  <wsdl:part name="payload" element="client:PatientDataServiceProcessResponse"/>
</wsdl:message>
```

Now both the inputVariable as well as the outputVariable in our BPEL process have a more complex structure, and can be used for more meaningful things. The inputVariable can contain a patientId, firstName, and lastName. The latter two are used when the patientId is not known. The outputVariable contains details about the patient and his or her physical characteristics.

Next, we add a variable called temperatureReading to the BPEL process, based on the physicalCharacteristic element in the XSD document. We can do this in Source view, in the <variables> element:

```
<variable name="temperatureReading"
          element="client:physicalCharacteristic"/>
```

Alternatively, open the Structure window (from the View menu or using the shortcut key combination CTRL-SHIFT-S) and then open the node Variables under Process, which is in turn under Variables (see Figure 5-6). Click the green plus sign to open the Create Variable dialog.

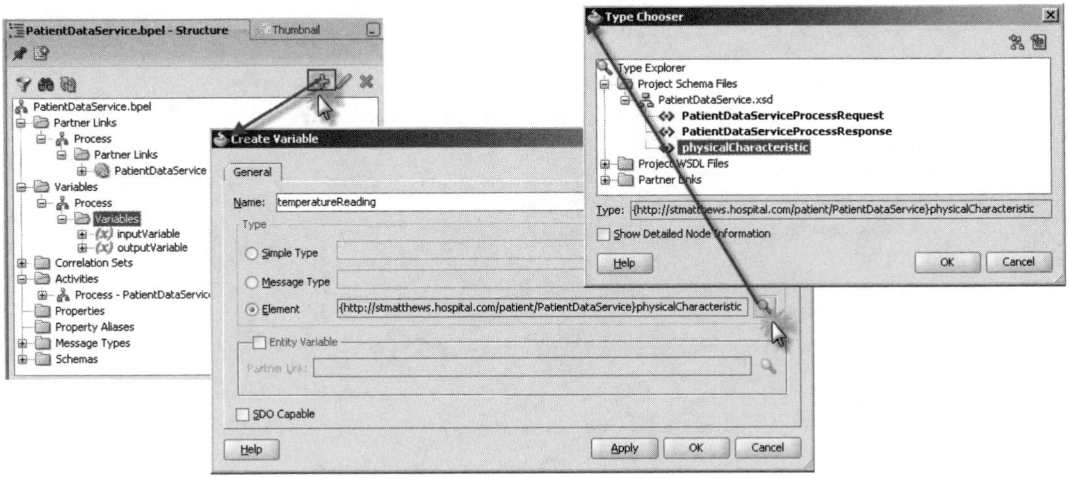

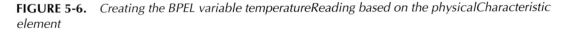

FIGURE 5-6. *Creating the BPEL variable temperatureReading based on the physicalCharacteristic element*

Specify **temperatureReading** as the name and select the Element radio button. Click the browse icon to open the Type Chooser dialog. Open the Project Schema Files node and select the physicalCharacteristic element from the PatientDataService.xsd file. Click OK in the Type Chooser dialog and OK again in the Create Variable dialog.

Using XPath in the Assign Activity with More Complex Variables

Go back to the Assign step and remove the existing copy operation. Then create a new copy operation to assign a value to the new variable. Figure 5-7 shows these steps. On the left side, choose XML Fragment in the Type drop-down. Add a fragment of XML that describes the body temperature characteristic and enter the following snippet:

```
<client:physicalCharacteristic xmlns:client="http://stmatthews.hospital.com/
patient/PatientDataService">
  <client:dateOfMeasurement>2010-12-28</client:dateOfMeasurement>
  <client:whatWasMeasured>body temperature</client:whatWasMeasured>
  <client:measuredValue>38.5</client:measuredValue>
  <client:unitOfMeasurement>Degrees Celsius</client:unitOfMeasurement>
</client:physicalCharacteristic>
```

Note how we need to include the namespace in order to correctly identify the elements in this fragment. Without the namespace, the measuredValue element, for example, could be something entirely different from the measuredValue element as specified in the PatientDataService XSD document.

On the right side, specify temperatureReading as the target variable.

Add a second copy operation that will set the /PatientDataServiceProcessResponse/name element in the payload part of the outputVariable. The value is derived from the firstName and

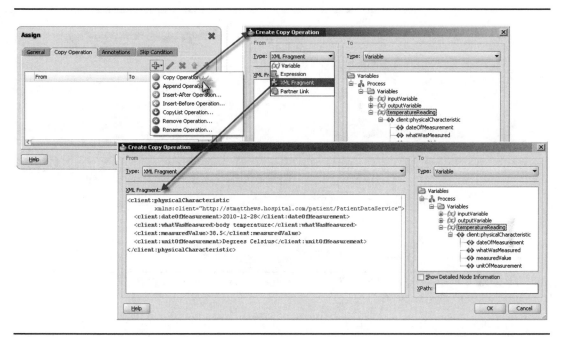

FIGURE 5-7.   *Copying an XML fragment to a BPEL variable using an Assign/Copy operation*

lastName elements in the inputVariable. We will use the XPath concat function to join these two together.

Select Expression on the "from" end of the Assign/Copy and click the icon for the (XPath) Expression Builder. This Expression Builder supports constructing XPath expressions from literals, (nodes in) BPEL variables, and XPath functions, including the Oracle BPEL XPath extensions. Select the concat function from the functions list after first selecting the String Functions category. Then click Insert Into Expression. Position the cursor inside the parentheses and select the PatientDataServiceProcessRequest/firstName element in the payload part of the inputVariable. Click the Insert button again.

The following function is added to the expression:

```
bpws:getVariableData(BPEL variable [,part name [,location path]])
```

This is one of the most important XPath extension functions you will use in BPEL processes. Its task is to extract a value from a BPEL variable. When using this function, you specify the variable from which you want to extract a value and, optionally, depending on the structure of the variable, a part and (possibly) a location path to a specific node in that part.

In this case, we want to extract the firstName element under the PatientDataServiceProcessRequest root in the payload part of the inputVariable by using getVariableData(), like this:

```
bpws:getVariableData('inputVariable'
 ,'payload','/client:PatientDataServiceProcessRequest/client:firstName)
```

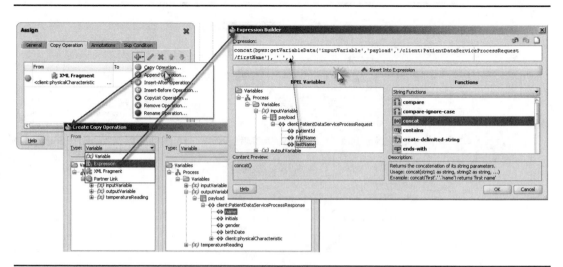

FIGURE 5-8. *Using the XPath Expression Builder to construct the XPath expression for a Copy operation in an Assign step*

Type **,' ',** in the expression editor to add a space between the first and last name. Then insert the lastName element into the expression, as shown in Figure 5-8.

The complete XPath expression now reads as follows:

```
concat
( bpws:getVariableData('inputVariable'
    ,'payload','/client:PatientDataServiceProcessRequest/firstName')
,' '
,bpws:getVariableData('inputVariable'
    ,'  payload','/client:PatientDataServiceProcessRequest/lastName')
)
```

On the right side, specify the name element in the PatientDataServiceProcessResponse in the payload part of the outputVariable as the target for the Copy operation.

Finally, create a new append operation in the same Assign activity, which takes the physicalCharacteristic element in the temperatureReading variable and appends it to the child node list in the PatientDataServiceProcessResponse element in the outputVariable's payload part (see Figure 5-9).

NOTE
Through "append" we can inject XML nodes into variables that already contain XML data; the Copy operation does not allow this. Other fine-grained XML manipulation in Assign activities can be done with operations such as insertBefore, insertAfter, remove, rename, and copyList.

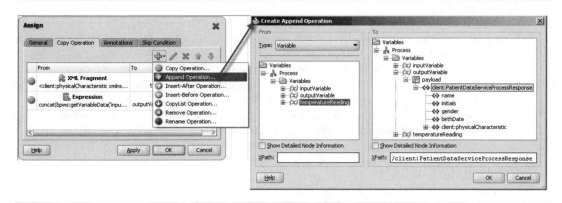

FIGURE 5-9.   *In the Assign activity, appending the contents of one BPEL variable to a node in another variable*

Here it is in plain BPEL code:

```
<bpelx:append>
  <bpelx:from variable="temperatureReading"
              query="/client:physicalCharacteristic"/>
  <bpelx:to variable="outputVariable" part="payload"
              query="/client:PatientDataServiceProcessResponse"/>
</bpelx:append>
```

Deploying and Running the SOA Composite Application

When we deploy the modified composite application in the same way as described in Chapter 3 and in this chapter's online complement and invoke it in the Test Web Service page, the answer we receive for a request with the firstName and lastName set contains the PatientDataServiceProcessResponse with a physicalCharacteristic (bodyTemperature) included.

We see the effect of the various operations in the Assign activity that created the temperatureReading variable based on the XML snippet, appended the entire variable content to the PatientDataServiceProcessResponse in the outputVariable, and copied the concatenation of the firstName, a space separator, and the lastName from the inputVariable to the name element in the outputVariable. This gives us some idea what XPath and the Append activity can accomplish in manipulating BPEL variables—a combination we will often rely on.

However, it also shows the verbosity and complexity of using the Assign activity. Apparently simple operations may not be all that simple through an Assign. When we want to initialize a complex variable, it may be easier to use the Transform activity. This activity uses an XSLT stylesheet—see Appendix B for some background on XSLT—to produce the XML content of the target variable based on a source.

XPath in BPEL

In addition to the XPath functions concat and getVariableData, which we just used, we have a huge library of functions at our disposal for constructing XPath expressions in BPEL and other components of the SOA Suite. These include functions for string and date/time conversion and manipulation (including making the current date and time available), XML manipulation (including transformation with XSLT or XQuery), and parsing of a string value to a DOM node. Other XPath functions support interaction with files, LDAP directories, and even a database directly—although you may wonder whether it would be such a good idea in terms of decoupling to directly access such external systems. If all that is not enough, you can extend the XPath functionality of your SOA Suite instance with custom functions that you implement in Java.

Breaking the Contract

What you may have noticed in the preceding steps is that we changed the interface of the service quite substantially: Both the input message and the output message are very different from the previous incarnation of the service. Yet, we did not need to change the most explicit part of the service contract—the WSDL document. All the changes were in the XSD that describes the structures of all messages exchanged with the PatientDataService. By changing the XSD, we can easily invalidate all current clients of the service—clearly not an action that will make us many friends. It is important to realize that changing an XSD may break clients using our functions.

In such conditions, it is usually a better approach to publish a new version of the service and leave the old version running during a certain grace period in which clients can move to the new version. More on this in Chapter 17.

The PatientDataService as SCA Composite Application

The SOA Suite is about much more than just BPEL processes and the BPEL service engine. It is about composite applications that expose services and possibly references—dependencies on external services that are to be provided to the composite—and that can easily be composed into more complex and functionally richer composites. In this section we may have focused on the BPEL process, but what we have developed is in fact an SCA composite application, albeit a simple one. The composite application contains a single service component—the BPEL process—that exposes a single service.

From the outside, the service interface of this composite is the Web Service that is wired to the BPEL component in the SCA composite. Clients do not interact directly with the BPEL process—in fact, they have no knowledge about the implementation of the service offered by the composite application, nor do they need that knowledge. It would not impact any consumers of the application's service if we exchange the BPEL component for a service component that implements the same service in a different implementation language—Mediator, Java, and so on—running in another service engine.

The content of the composite.xml file describes how the composite application PatientDataService exposes a SOAP Web Service called "client" with a port called PatientDataService_pt that is described by the PatientDataService portType in the PatientDataService.wsdl. Every SOA composite has one, and only one, composite.xml file describing the general structure of the composite. Chapter 14 explains SCA and the structure of the composite.xml file in more detail. The chapter complement on the wiki discusses the details of the PatientDataService composite application.

Implementing PatientDataService as an Asynchronous Service

The BPEL process PatientDataService is implemented as a synchronous process. Given the current functionality in the process, that is a logical choice. However, many processes will be asynchronous, for example, because they include potentially long-running actions, calls to asynchronous services, or human tasks. We will now briefly discuss what would change in the BPEL process itself, the WSDL, and the SCA configuration if PatientDataService were to go asynchronous.

In order to receive the response from an asynchronous service, the partner that calls the service must provide a callback interface: a service implemented by the partner that the BPEL process can send the response to. This is reflected in the partnerLinkType definition in the WSDL document:

```
<plnk:partnerLinkType name="PatientDataService">
  <plnk:role name="PatientDataServiceProvider">
   <plnk:portType name="client:PatientDataService"/>
  </plnk:role>
  <plnk:role name="PatientDataServiceRequester">
   <plnk:portType name="client:PatientDataServiceCallback"/>
  </plnk:role>
</plnk:partnerLinkType>
```

In addition to the role PatientDataServiceProvider—which we already had in the synchronous case—we now have the role PatientDataServiceRequester that refers to the partner calling to the asynchronous service. This role is associated with a new portType in the WSDL—an abstract functional interface that is also added now that the service has become asynchronous. This portType describes the interface to be provided by the partner in order to receive the service response:

```
<portType name="PatientDataServiceCallback">
  <operation name="onResult">
    <input message="client:PatientDataServiceResponseMessage"/>
  </operation>
</portType>
```

Note that there has also been a change in the original portType PatientDataService. Before in the synchronous situation, it had both an input and an output; in the asynchronous case, it no longer has an output. The output is now returned via the callback to the PatientDataServiceCallback portType.

For the BPEL process, not much changes. Synchronously, the process concludes with an "online" Reply to the partnerLink that started the "conversation" with the initial request picked up by the Receive step. In an asynchronous process, we cannot reply because the partner is no longer online. Instead, we have to make a call to the callback service that the partner has made available. Making a call to a partnerLink—when it is not a synchronous Reply—is done through the Invoke activity, just like any other normal service call:

```
<invoke name="callbackClient" partnerLink="PatientDataService"
        portType="client:PatientDataServiceCallback"
        operation="onResult" inputVariable="outputVariable"/>
```

(Continued)

The Invoke step specifies the partnerLink—which is the same PatientDataService that we used for the Reply because we are still conducting communications with the same partner in the same context as before—and therefore we use the same Partner Link type. Only this time the portType is different from the Reply in the synchronous case: We call the operation onResult on the callback portType PatientDataServiceCallback, published by the partner. Note that it is up to the BPEL and SCA run time to determine where the physical location (endpoint) is for that callback service. Usually they leverage the WS-Addressing information found in the service request as sent by the partner.

Accessing the Database from a BPEL Process

Even though we have implemented a perfectly valid BPEL process, it will not necessarily make anybody happy. At St. Matthews, the PatientDataService is supposed to facilitate people such as Margaret by making real patient data available—data that is currently stored somewhere deep down in the database Frank's team controls. In order for this BPEL process to implement the service for real, it will need access to that database. In this section, we will first see how we can use the database adapter to configure a service that accesses Frank's database. Then we will have the BPEL process call this database service to retrieve real patient data.

The database adapter in SOA Suite 11*g* helps to expose data and operations from relational databases in a service-compliant fashion. The database adapter connects to any relational database using JDBC. Other adapters are available for nonrelational databases and mainframe systems. The database adapter uses Oracle TopLink 11*g* for database interactions, itself based on the Oracle-sponsored open-source project EclipseLink, an advanced Java Persistence framework for relational-to-object mapping.

The database adapter allows us to declaratively configure services to interact with a database for virtually any operation you may need: data manipulation (Insert, Update, Delete, Merge), data retrieval (Select, Query by Example, Poll for new or changed records), and stored procedure calls with simple and complex parameters (possibly based on user-defined database types). These services are published as Web Services with their own WSDL and XSD files, and are treated by the BPEL process like any other external service or partner link that is invoked.

We will create two database adapter services for use in the PatientDataService process. One is to select the patient ID from the PATIENTS table, based on the first name and last name in the request for a situation where the patient ID is not known. The second service will call the Patient_Data_Service API—a PL/SQL package created by Frank and his team—to retrieve different types of patient records. We will invoke a function in this package that takes the patient identifier as input and returns a complex database object type with information on the patient, his physical characteristics, and hospital visits.

A Simple Select Service to Retrieve the Patient Identifier

Let's start our introduction of the database adapter with a simple select against a single table. (Obviously in the real world, Frank would never allow this direct prying into his database. We only want to show how a Select service is created in the SOA Suite. To that same effect, we naively pretend that patients are uniquely identified by the combination of their first name and last name.) Suppose the database with all the patient data we are interested in has a table called PATIENTS. This table has, among many others, the columns ID, FIRST_NAME, and LAST_NAME (the wiki contains the SQL script to create this table). We need a service to find us the value of the ID of the patient for whom we have the first name and last name.

In the composite editor for PatientDataService, we drag a Database Service Adapter from the SOA Component Palette and drop it in the External References swimlane, as shown in Figure 5-10.

The Database Adapter Configuration Wizard appears so we can configure this service (see Figure 5-11). Enter **RetrievePatientIdentifier** as the service name. On the next page, select the database connection to use in the development environment. When we deploy the service, we will configure an instance resource adapter connection factory and a data source on the application server to use instead of these hard-coded connection details. By providing a value for the location field, we determine the JNDI name of the database adapter connection factory on the application server this service will hook up with: eis/DB/FranksPatientDatabase.

NOTE
We assume here a database connection called PatientsDatabase has already been created to Frank's database schema with the PATIENTS table and the API. See Appendix C for details on creating a database connection in JDeveloper, as well as configuring the database resource adapter, a connection factory, and the associated data source on the WebLogic Server.

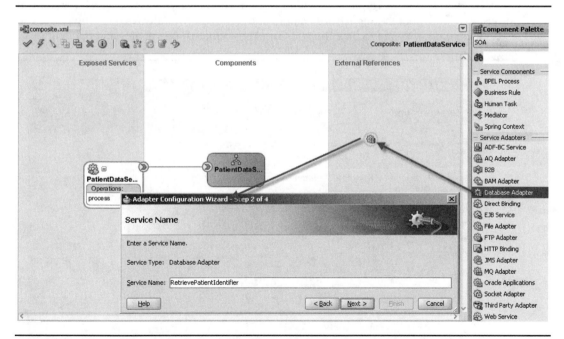

FIGURE 5-10. *Adding a Database Adapter Service in the composite application*

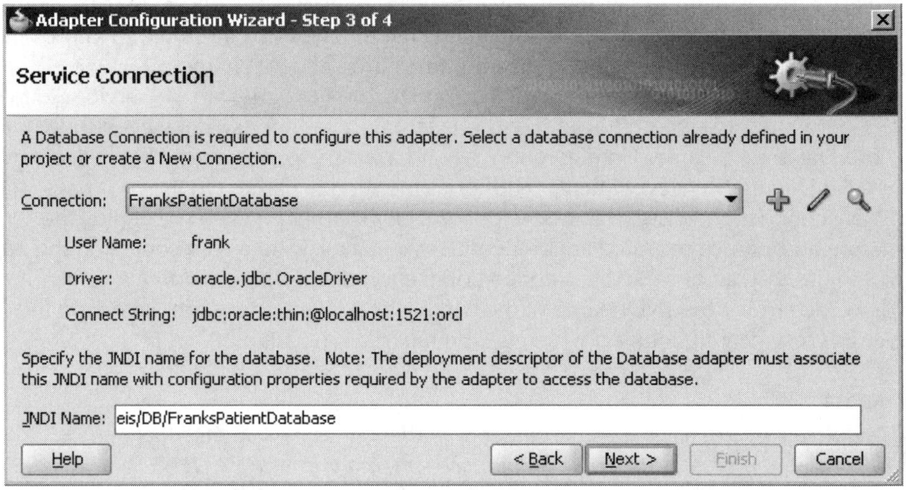

FIGURE 5-11. *Specifying the connection details for the Database Adapter Service*

Next, we specify the database operation this service will provide. We need to perform a query against a table, so we choose the Select operation (see Figure 5-12). We could have picked Query by Example; however, that operation is used when a varying set of search criteria is used. Because we know that the service we want to add right now will always query by first name and last name, we do not want to bear the additional performance penalty for that flexibility.

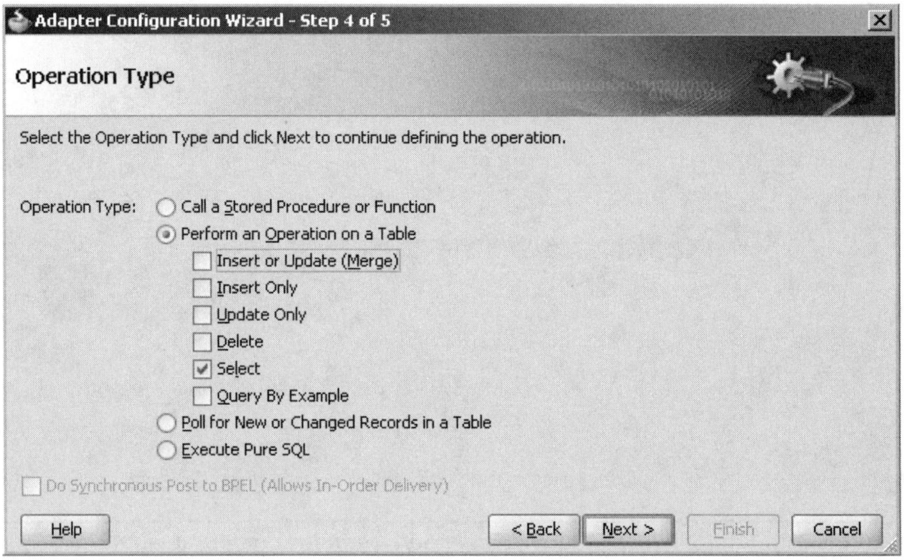

FIGURE 5-12. *Selecting the operation type in the Database Adapter Service Configuration Wizard*

In the next step—Select Table—we select the PATIENTS table. We can then specify Relationships—for the case when we have multiple tables we want to join together, or a table with self-referencing relationships. We ignore this step for now. In the Attribute Filtering step we can deselect the attributes we do not need queried from the database. By excluding information we do not need, we lower the load on both the database, network, and the SOA Suite run time. In this case, we are only interested in the ID, so we deselect the other attributes, except for the first_name and last_name attributes that are needed in the where clause for this query.

On the Define Selection Criteria page, shown in Figure 5-13, we create two parameters: firstName and lastName. These parameters will determine the structure of the request message type that is the input for this service.

Using the Query Expression Builder we create the where clause for the query against the PATIENTS table:

```
WHERE  ((UPPER(FIRST_NAME) = UPPER(#firstName))
AND    (UPPER(LAST_NAME) = UPPER(#lastName)))
```

Note that the parameters are identified using the # character in the where clause.

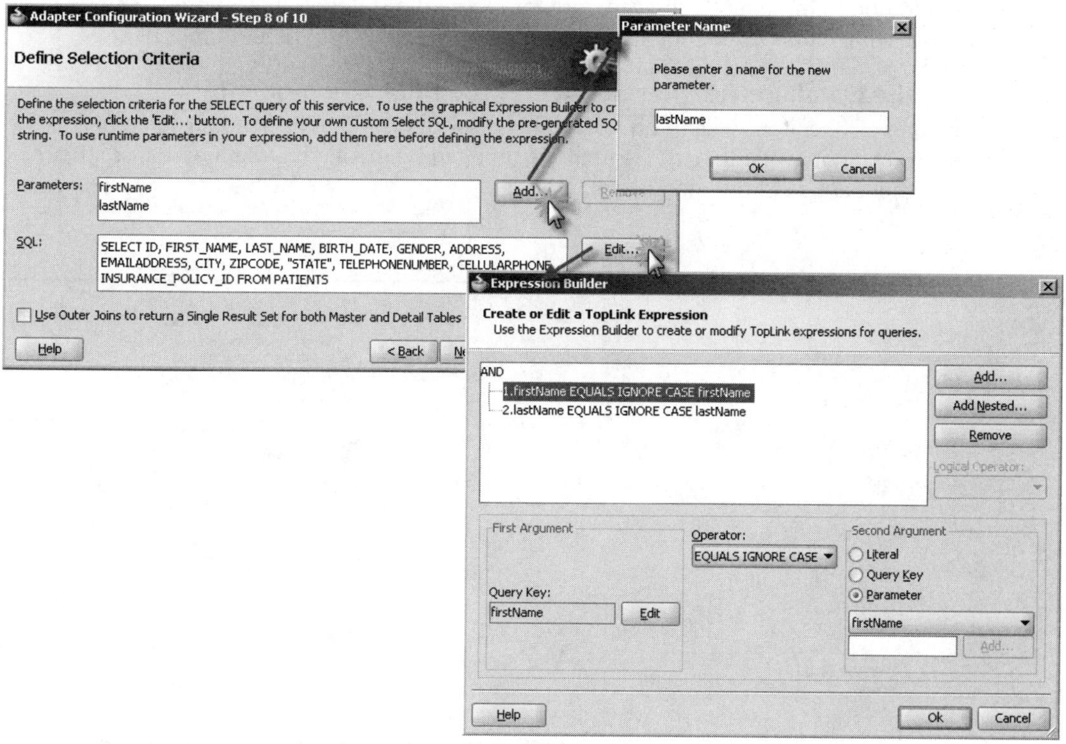

FIGURE 5-13.   *The TopLink Expression Builder for specifying the query selection criteria*

We can skip the Advanced Options page and leave the defaults for now. On the last page, click the Finish button. The Database Adapter Service is now created. This means that a number of artifacts is generated by JDeveloper:

- **RetrievePatientIdentifier.wsdl**   Contains the functional interface for the Database Adapter Service with a portType that includes a RetrievePatientIdentifierSelect operation, message definitions, and an import of the XSD.

- **RetrievePatientIdentifier_table.xsd**   Contains the element definitions for the request and response messages. Note that we will have to deal with these structures in the BPEL process that invokes this service.

- **RetrievePatientIdentifier-or-mappings.xml and RetrievePatientIdentifier-ox-mappings. xml**   The TopLink mapping files that specify how relational tables are mapped to Java objects and those, in turn, to XML types. The records read from the database tables have to be turned into XML data structures that the service consumers such as the BPEL process expect, according to the XSD. TopLink is used to query the database; TopLink maps relational data to Java objects using the mapping instructions in the or-mappings. xml file. These Java objects are then converted to XML structures following the Object-to-XML (ox) mapping definition specified in the ox-mappings.xml file.

In addition to these new files, the composite.xml file is updated: A reference element is added—a service that can be injected (wired) as a reference into other components.

Wiring the Database Adapter Service to the BPEL Component

In the composite editor, we can now wire this new RetrievePatientIdentifier reference to the BPEL process to make it available as a partnerLink that can be invoked. Drag a wire from the reference to the component, as shown in Figure 5-14.

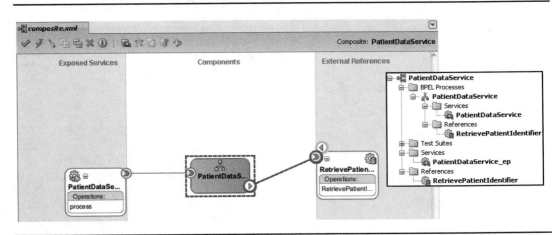

FIGURE 5-14.   *Wiring the RetrievePatientIdentifier reference to the PatientDataService component*

That in turn makes the RetrievePatientIdentifier partnerLink available in the BPEL process:

```
<partnerLink name="RetrievePatientIdentifier"
             partnerRole="RetrievePatientIdentifier_role"
             partnerLinkType="ns1:RetrievePatientIdentifier_plt"/>
```

The partnerLinkType in this case is specified in the RetrievePatientIdentifier.wsdl:

```
<plt:partnerLinkType name="RetrievePatientIdentifier_plt">
    <plt:role name="RetrievePatientIdentifier_role">
        <plt:portType name="tns:RetrievePatientIdentifier_ptt"/>
    </plt:role>
</plt:partnerLinkType>
```

In order to call the RetrievePatientIdentifier service, we only need to add an Invoke activity in the BPEL process that accesses the RetrievePatientIdentifier partnerLink.

Extending the PatientDataService BPEL Process Using the RetrievePatientIdentifier Service

We are now all set to leverage this new RetrievePatientIdentifier service in the BPEL process. However, the process does not always need to call the service: Sometimes the PatientDataServiceProcessRequest will already contain the patient identifier. Only when it does not should we invoke RetrievePatientIdentifier. Time to add a little process logic! That gives us a good opportunity to introduce another important BPEL activity: Switch.

The Switch activity—not surprisingly somewhat akin to the Java switch statement and also similar to the PL/SQL case statement—is used for making choices in the flow of the process. Which of the paths should be taken? The switch contains one or (usually) more mutually exclusive branches, only one of which can be executed. Each branch (except the otherwise branch) has a case condition associated with it, and only when the Boolean XPath expression in the condition evaluates to true is the branch executed. Only one branch can be executed—the first branch in the switch whose condition is satisfied.

In our case, we want to invoke the RetrievePatientIdentifier service when the inputVariable does not contain a patient identifier. To achieve that, we add a Switch activity and set the condition for the first branch to test for the presence of the patient identifier:

```
count(ora:getNodes
        ('inputVariable'
        ,'payload'
        ,'/client:PatientDataServiceProcessRequest/patientId'
        )
      )=0
or
bpws:getVariableData('inputVariable','payload'
        ,'/client:PatientDataServiceProcessRequest/patientId') = ''
```

Add an Invoke activity in the first branch (the branch that is executed when the request does not contain the patient identifier). We connect this Invoke with the RetrievePatient Identifier partnerLink. In the Invoke dialog that appears, we can specify the name for the

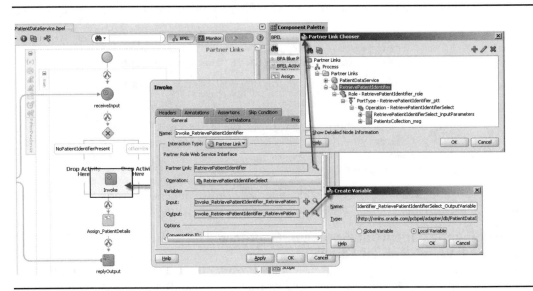

FIGURE 5-15. *Adding an Invoke activity to the first branch of the Switch*

Invoke—Invoke_RetrievePatientIdentifier—and the variables to use for input and output. By clicking the green plus icon, we have JDeveloper conveniently create new variables of the correct message types as specified in the RetrievePatientIdentifier WSDL. Choose local rather than global as the scope for these variables (see Figure 5-15).

The configuration of the input variables and the call to the partner link have now been taken care of. What to do with the outcome of the call? JDeveloper has created the BPEL variable Invoke_RetrievePatientIdentifier_RetrievePatientIdentifierSelect_OutputVariable based on the PatientsCollection_msg message type defined in the RetrievePatientIdentifier.wsdl. This variable is populated during the Invoke activity with the query results. However, we want to have the value of the patient identifier available in a global variable throughout the BPEL process—one with a proper name at that. Therefore, create a new BPEL variable called patientIdentifier of type xsd:integer. Then add another Assign activity, immediately following the Invoke activity, to copy the value of the patient identifier from this generated variable to the global BPEL process variable patientIdentifier. Remember, the condition for this branch checked that the patientId element was initially empty. Figure 5-16 demonstrates how the Assign activity is added and how it is configured with a single copy operation.

The PatientsCollection element in the generated XSD file RetrievePatientIdentifier_table.xsd on which the PatientsCollection_msg is based is defined as a collection of one or more Patients elements. We assume for simplicity's sake that the query will either return a single record or none at all, so the collection will never have more than one element. In the XPath expression we use to extract the value of the id element from the Patients element, we do not need to include the array index because we will get the first element in the array even if we leave it out. However, I do consider it good practice to explicitly include the index in the array:

```
/ns5:PatientsCollection/ns5:Patients[1]/ns5:id
```

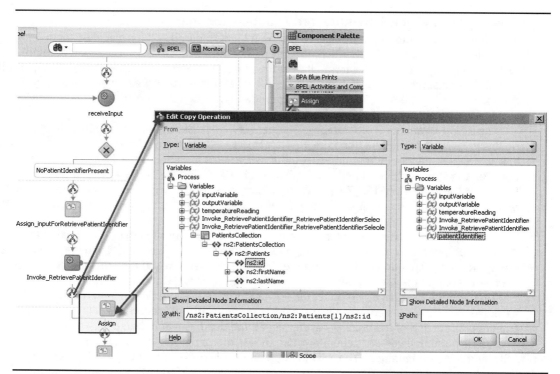

FIGURE 5-16. *Copying the patient identifier returned from the service call*

The square brackets with the index have to be typed in manually in the Copy operation editor because there is no visual declarative support for it.

NOTE
An even better practice would be to explicitly communicate the number of elements required (consumer) or returned (provider) in the service interface. Alternatively, the BPEL process should explicitly check for the number of elements returned before starting to access them—because now we may run into exceptions for accessing nonexisting nodes.

In the "otherwise" branch of the Switch activity, we need to include an Assign activity that sets the patientIdentifier variable based on the value in the inputVariable. Add an Assign activity to the otherwise branch. Specify a Copy operation that takes the value from the patientId element in the PatientDataServiceProcessRequest node in the inputVariable and copies it to the variable patientIdentifier.

At this point in the BPEL process, we know we have a patient identifier—either from the RetrievePatientIdentifier service or received in the original request message. It is time to call upon the database to make the patient data available to us. We will first need to create another Database Adapter Service and then invoke it from the BPEL process.

Creating the RetrievePatientRecord Database Service

Several years ago, Frank's team started work on a PL/SQL-based API for making patient records available. Before that time, other departments came into the database through database links, ODBC, and JDBC connections from all over the place, and performed queries directly against the tables. This became an undesirable situation, for several reasons. For example, data-authorization rules were hard to enforce, but even more importantly, changes to the table layout were virtually impossible because of all the direct dependencies.

The RetrievePatientRecord database adapter service Frank is about to publish will be based on this PL/SQL API. The function GET_PATIENT_RECORD in the package PATIENT_DATA_SERVICES takes patient id (a number) as input and returns an object type: PATIENT_T. This is a complex type that includes a table of PHYSICALCHARACTERISTIC objects, based on the PHYSICALCHARACTERISTIC_T type. The database adapter can work quite well with such types; in fact, it is probably the easiest way of returning nested data structures with data from multiple records and several tables in a single roundtrip.

To create the Database Adapter Service, we go to the composite editor and drag a Database Adapter component from the palette to the External References swimlane. Then we specify the name—RetrievePatientRecord—and set the database connection and the JNDI location of the Database Adapter instance in the same way as for the previous Database Adapter Service.

Then, on the next page, we select the Call a Stored Procedure or Function operation type. Click Next. In the next step, we select the get_patient_record procedure (see Figure 5-17). Continue to the end of the wizard—accepting all the defaults—and then click Finish.

At this point, JDeveloper generates more or less the same bunch of files as before: WSDL, XSD, and JCA configuration. The XSD file contains the representation of the PATIENT_T type.

In the composite editor, we need to wire the new RetrievePatientRecord service to the PatientDataService component, as shown in Figure 5-18.

Just like we have seen before, the wire adds this partnerLink in the BPEL process that now allows us to add an Invoke step in the BPEL process to the RetrievePatientRecord service. Create an Invoke activity immediately after the Switch activity. Have the variables generated for this Invoke, just like before. Add an Assign step just before the Invoke activity to copy the value of the variable patientIdentifier to the input variable used in the Invoke step.

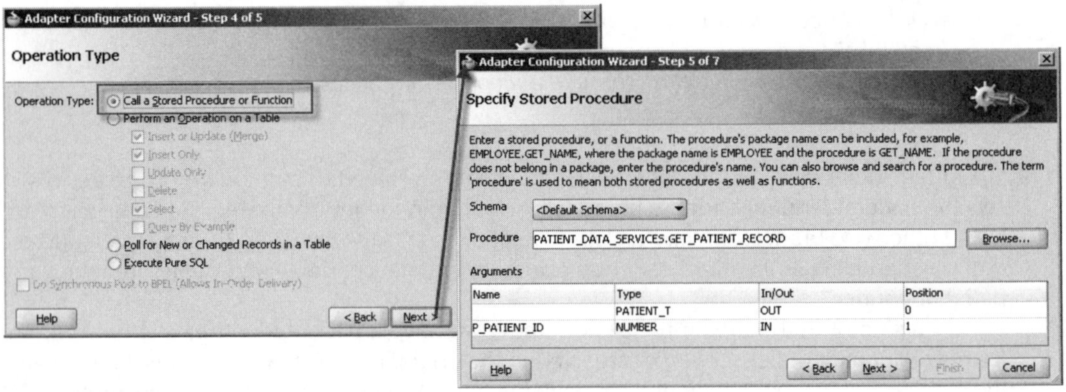

FIGURE 5-17. *Selecting the get_patient_record function in the Patient_Data_Service package*

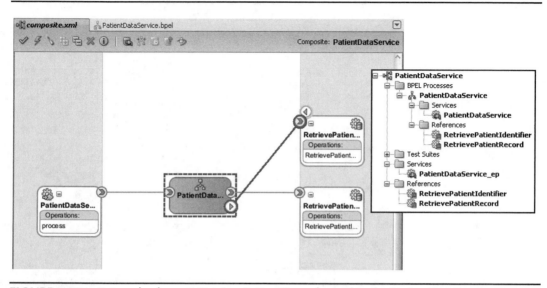

FIGURE 5-18.   *External reference RetrievePatientRecord wired to the PatientDataService component*

Invoking the RetrievePatientRecord service returns a fairly complex XML document. The data from this document should be copied into the outputVariable that populates the response message. We can do so using the Assign activity. However, that would require a substantial number of operations and a lot of work to put together. As an alternative to such a complex Assign step, we can use a Transform activity that leverages XSLT to map one XML document to another, processing many nodes at once rather than assigning them individually.

Drag the Transform activity to the composite editor and drop it after the Invoke of the RetrievePatientRecord partnerLink, as shown in Figure 5-19. Then enter **RetrievePatientData RecordOutput2OutputVariable.xsl** as the name for the Mapper file. Select the OutputParameters part of the Invoke_RetrievePatientRecord_RetrievePatientRecord_OutputVariable as the source for the transformation. Set the payload part of the outputVariable as the target. Click the Apply button to save the changes and bring up the Mapper file editor.

The Mapper editor provides a visual way of editing an XSLT stylesheet that transforms one XML document into another. See Appendix B for some background on XSLT, an XML language for transformations of XML.

On the left (source) side, you see the structure of the patient data record that is returned by the RetrievePatientDataRecord service. On the right is the XSD structure of the outputVariable. The mapping (and therefore the XSLT transformation) is created by connecting nodes from the source with the corresponding nodes in the target. Connect the nodes for initials, gender, and birth date.

The target has a name node, whereas the source offers a first name and a last name node. We will use a function to combine the two input nodes to a single destination node, as illustrated in Figure 5-20. Drag the concat function from the String Functions section on the Component Palette to the center section of the mapping editor. Connect its output to the name node in the target. Connect both the first name and last name node in the source to the input of the concat function. Double-click the concat function to edit its parameters. Click the Add button and add a parameter with the static value ' ' (a space between single quotation marks). Click OK to close the concat editor.

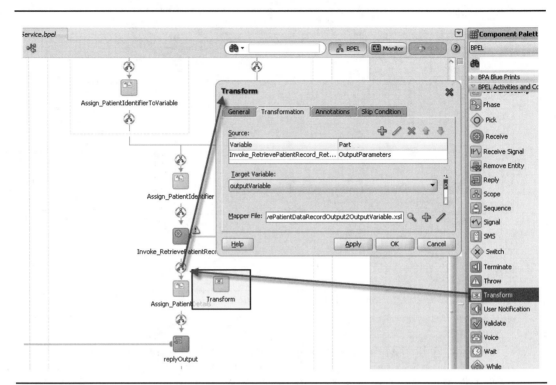

FIGURE 5-19. *Adding a Transform activity to the BPEL process to populate the outputVariable with the patient data record*

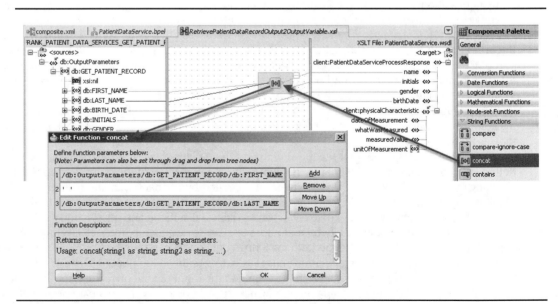

FIGURE 5-20. *Mapping the PatientDataRecord to the outputVariable*

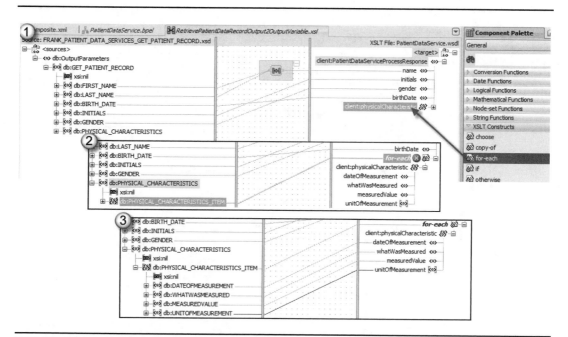

FIGURE 5-21. *Configuring the mapping of the collection of physical characteristic items*

In order to properly transform all physical characteristic items, we have to drag the for-each construct from the XSLT Constructs section in the Component Palette to the physicalCharacteristic node in the target. Next, we connect the db:PHYSICAL_CHARACTERISTIC_ITEM node in the source to the for-each node that was just added to the target. Finally, we connect the child nodes under db:PHYSICAL_CHARACTERISTIC_ITEM to the corresponding nodes in the target tree under client:physicalCharacteristic. These steps are illustrated in Figure 5-21.

This completes the mapping as well as the BPEL process (see Figure 5-22), and even the entire composite application. We are now ready to see it in action.

NOTE
If you still have the Assign activity that we created in the previous section to assign some dummy data to the outputVariable, you should now delete that activity from the BPEL process.

Deploying and Running the Composite Application

Deploy the composite application to the SOA Suite run-time infrastructure in the same way as in the first section of this chapter. Now invoke the PatientDataService from the SOA Console's Test Web Service page. It may take a little bit longer than before, because we now have a process that does some real work: It communicates with the database—once or twice—and has some XPath querying and XSLT manipulation to perform.

As Figure 5-23 shows, it is interesting to take a look at the information about the composite instance we can learn from the SOA console.

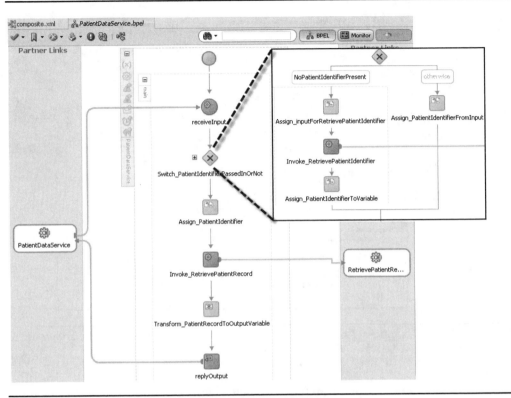

FIGURE 5-22. *The complete PatientDataService BPEL process*

We can get a visual presentation of the flow in this process instance, very similar to the BPEL process design in JDeveloper; however, this one is the visualization of a real process instance, not just the design or mold the instances are created from (see Figure 5-24). By clicking the various steps in the instance, we can learn about the variables involved at each step. It is very much like debugging a program—after it has already run. Chapter 16 delves deeper into the console and the trace information it can provide us with.

For more background on the database adapter, see Chapter 9 of the *Oracle Fusion Middleware User's Guide for Technology Adapters* in the online FMW documentation library.

FIGURE 5-23. *Fusion Middleware Control—SOA console's overview of the flow of messages resulting from a single service call*

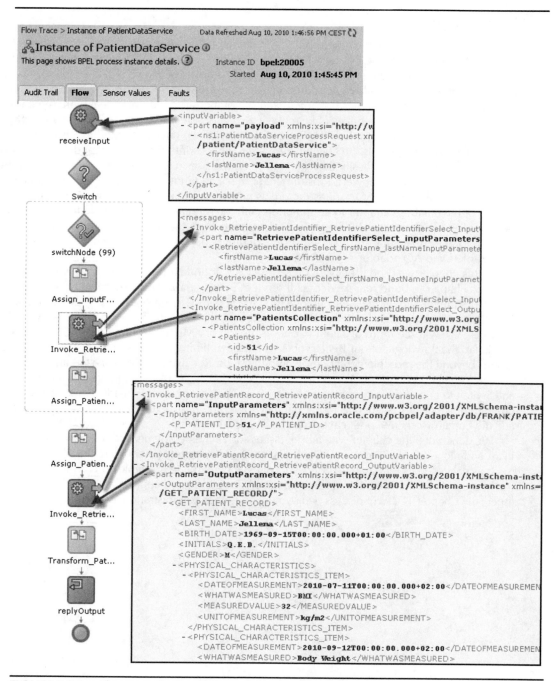

FIGURE 5-24. *Flow trace in the SOA console of a BPEL process instance*

Summary

This chapter introduced one of the important implementation languages for service composition and orchestration: BPEL, the Business Process Execution Language. As the name suggests, BPEL can be used for the implementation of business process flow logic—we will see more of that in the next chapter. BPEL's ability to coordinate calls to external services, process and manipulate the XML messages and variables flowing in and out of these services, and deal with asynchronous services and synchronous services alike make it also very suitable for the implementation of composite services. An example is the PatientDataService we have discussed in this chapter.

External services such as the Database Adapter Services into Frank's patient database that we created in this chapter can easily be wired to BPEL processes using the SCA composite definition. The database adapter is a powerful instrument to make all kinds of operations into relational databases available in our SOA infrastructure as normal Web Services. Chapter 7 will illustrate the use of the database adapter in conjunction with the Mediator component to further decouple BPEL processes and other database services consumers from the database. Besides the database adapter, Oracle SOA Suite ships with a variety of other adapters, such as the EJB/RMI adapter, File adapter, and AQ adapter.

In this chapter we used the XML, XSD, and WSDL foundation that was laid down in the previous chapter to build real services. All services in this chapter are described through the WSDL document and all messages involved by the accompanying XSD files. The XPath language is used to both retrieve and manipulate XML nodes, and is especially important in Assign activities. We will see more of XPath in our discussion of XML transformations in Chapter 7.

So far, the flow logic of our BPEL processes has been limited. The activities discussed do not take us beyond the most elementary programming steps: Receive and Reply to start and end a process instance's execution, Assign to manipulate variables, Invoke to call out to external services, and Switch to choose between execution branches. The next chapter will add some interesting programming constructs, such as loops, parallel flows, and basic event handling. Chapter 10 will add the human workflow, notifications, and exception handling.

We concluded the chapter with a brief discussion of the deployment of composite applications in a stand-alone SOA environment. Deployment is only complete when the required resources (such as data sources for database connections) have been made available and run-time parameters (such as the endpoints for external services) have been configured appropriately. Part III—and especially Chapter 17—will discuss deployment and other administration aspects.

CHAPTER
6

Process-Oriented BPEL

he previous chapter introduced BPEL as one of the prominent implementation languages for service components in the SOA Suite. BPEL is good for creating components that call upon multiple Web Services, that may be asynchronous in nature, and whose combined results are used to achieve some business purpose. A BPEL process can resemble both a short-running composite service that combines several automated elementary services as well as a business process, especially when it is configured to have parallel activities, has a state that runs for longer than a subsecond, and also involves notifications to and tasks performed by human participants. This chapter introduces some of the more advanced BPEL concepts—especially the parallel activities, calling asynchronous services, and handling events and exceptions. Chapter 10 will go into the integration with human tasks, and Chapter 11 discusses workflows and links BPEL to BPMN as another service component language that allows us to model and program business processes in service components.

Note that three terms used more or less interchangeably in this chapter are associated with BPEL: *process, service,* and *component.* In an attempt to make things a little clearer, you can think of a BPEL process as a unit of compilation and encapsulation. As developers, we create or program BPEL processes. These processes expose a Web Service interface through which they can be instantiated. A BPEL process can be one of the (service) components in a composite application.

This chapter works toward the implementation of the parts of the patient appointment process (see Figure 6-1). Chapter 2 introduced this process at St. Matthews.

Each step in this business process can be further drilled down into in order to describe the actual operational steps and their implementation. Several BPEL processes with many BPEL activities, including a number of service calls, are required to put the Appointment process into motion. In this chapter, we will take a closer look at a number of additional pieces of BPEL functionality that are valuable in further specifying and implementing the parts of the Appointment process.

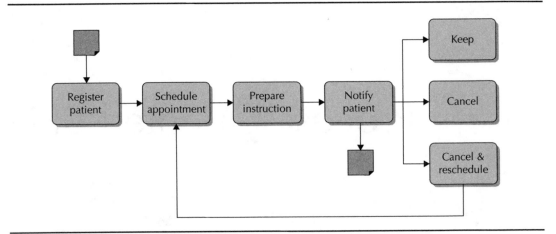

FIGURE 6-1. *The patient appointment process, where patients miss, keep, or cancel (and perhaps reschedule) appointments*

We will see how we can structure a BPEL process—similar to how we can structure a Java method into multiple methods and even multiple classes, or split a single PL/SQL procedure into multiple program units and packages. We also discuss the concept of parallel (strings of) activities in BPEL processes through the Flow activity. An important concept, introduced in the previous chapter, is asynchronous services. We will see how BPEL can deal with calling asynchronous services—and receiving their responses. And we have our BPEL process publish an asynchronous service interface itself.

In this chapter we will see how a single BPEL process instance can receive multiple messages during its lifetime. The initial request typically initiates the instance. However, as the BPEL process instance continues running—potentially for hours, days, or even months—it not only can call out to many services, it can also be called by partners that want to feed additional data into the process or request information from the running instance. Correlation is the mechanism used for routing such calls to the correct process instance. This chapter describes the correlation mechanism and demonstrates what you need to do in order to make use of it. We will discuss this notion of receiving additional requests in a running instance to allow inquiries into the state of the appointment by external parties.

Another facet of BPEL is event handling: capturing events published external to the BPEL process instance and processing them in a meaningful way. Note that events can arrive and be handled parallel to normal process execution. We will deal with "cancel appointment" events that need to reach the correct BPEL process instance to properly terminate it after releasing the resources it has reserved. BPEL components can receive events through incoming WebService calls—discussed in this chapter—and also in a more decoupled fashion from the Event Delivery Network (EDN) in the SOA Suite. This EDN is discussed in Chapter 9. BPEL uses the Pick activity—to explicitly wait at some point in line, in the normal process execution for an incoming message to arrive—and eventHandlers that run parallel to normal processing, to capture messages that arrive at random moments.

NOTE
The online complement to this chapter contains more fine-grained step-by-step instructions, additional screenshots, and detailed code examples for the steps discussed in this chapter; this will be helpful if you want to work through the examples yourself, which I strongly recommend because learning through your fingers is probably the best way of thoroughly absorbing the material in this and the coming chapters.

The Start of the Appointment Process

The appointment process is started when the patient's referral to the hospital is received—directly entered into the system by the general practitioner or more usually in the form of a handwritten document. It contains the patient's identification, potentially some insurance plan details, a priority code that indicates the urgency, a summary of the doctor's diagnosis of the patient's condition, and the type of appointment that is required: which type of medical specialist, which lab tests, and a consult with an extended duration. Based on the referral, a new instance of the Appointment application is started (see Figure 6-2).

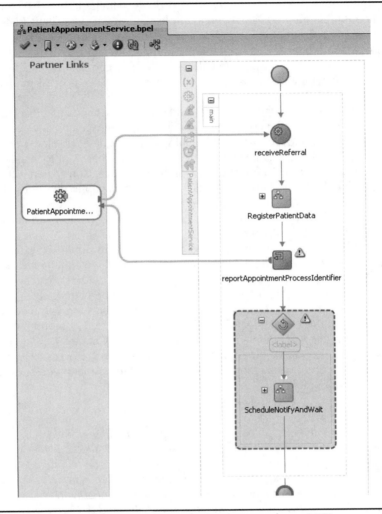

FIGURE 6-2. *The first part of the appointment as implemented as a BPEL process (note the scopes used for RegisterPatientData and ScheduleNotifyAndWait).*

The first step—register patient data—consists of verifying whether the patient is already known at St. Matthews. If the patient is already known, his or her record (in Frank's patients database) is updated; otherwise, a new patient record is created.

In a later iteration of this process design, we may determine that if the patient is already known, there can be circumstances that prevent the creation of an appointment, such as serious debt owed to the hospital by the patient, past bad behavior by the patient, or litigation by the patient versus the hospital.

When the patient is registered and the required information is available, we can send the synchronous reply to whoever invoked the Appointment Service. This reply acts as the confirmation that the appointment will be scheduled, and it also includes the appointmentIdentifier. This identifier can later on be used to retrieve additional information or cancel the appointment.

Scope and Sequence

Figure 6-2 illustrates the use of scopes in BPEL process definitions. A *scope* is a named container inside a BPEL process that can be used to structure the process, similar to the way methods are used in Java classes or procedures are used in PL/SQL package bodies.

At the level of a scope, we can define local variables that are only used and are visible within the scope itself. We will see later in this chapter how we can create a compensation handler and a termination handler in the context of a scope. These handlers are executed either to undo all changes made in a scope that has successfully been completed—when, for example, a subsequent phase in the process failed and all previous steps need to be rolled back—or to handle the forced termination of an executing scope.

A scope is created in the BPEL editor by dragging a Scope activity from the Component Palette into the BPEL process. Existing activities or new ones can be dragged inside the scope and dropped in it to become part of the scope. Conversely, activities can be moved out of a scope, for example, to another scope. Variables can be defined at the scope level in the same way as at the process level, as we did in the previous chapter.

We have seen in the previous chapter how we use specially typed input and output variables for calls to partnerLinks. These variables are usually only meaningful in the context of the Invoke activity that uses them and in the Assign steps just before and after the invoke. An Invoke along with these Assign steps and the required variables are suitable candidates for a scope.

Despite its similarity to Java methods or PL/SQL procedures, scopes cannot be called directly. A scope is—or rather the activities inside a scope are—executed when the flow of the BPEL process hits the scope. It makes no difference for the execution whether the activities are inside a scope or not. Only for accessing local, scope-level elements such as variables or partnerLinks, or for handling exceptions, does it matter whether or not an activity is inside a scope.

Scopes are quite useful when developing large BPEL processes in a structured fashion. Scopes can be nested to any level. They allow clustering of related activities with meaningful labels, making the BPEL process diagram much easier to understand. You can open or collapse scopes in the visual BPEL editor, which allows you to focus on details where you need to and stick to a high-level overview where that is more appropriate. Scopes also help with a top-down design of the BPEL process, as we see in Figure 6-2. At this point, none of the scopes have been defined in detail, yet we have the abstract outline of the process in place. Finally, when multiple developers are working on a BPEL process, allocation of development tasks and merging of changes is typically done at the scope level.

Another structured BPEL activity is the Sequence activity. A sequence contains one or (usually) multiple BPEL activities that are executed sequentially. A sequence can be named and it can be expanded or collapsed in the visual editor, just like a scope. Unlike a scope, a sequence does not have its own variables or handlers—all it has are the sequentially executed activities. Sequences are frequently used for grouping activities inside containers, such as Scope and Flow, that do not allow multiple direct child activities.

When the scope RegisterPatientData is done—which includes a call to the PatientDataService— and all data about the patient is available, the process will send the synchronous response to the client by returning the processIdentifierId. The complement to this chapter shows how the scope is to be implemented to call the PatientDataService service that we have developed in the previous chapter.

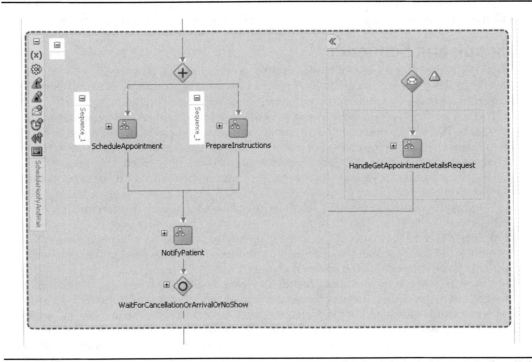

FIGURE 6-3. *Using a flow to process PrepareInstructions and ScheduleAppointment in parallel*

The reply tells the client that the patient's referral is now accepted by the appointment process for further processing. The value for the processIdentifierId is the client's key to further interaction with the process—for example, a request for the appointment details or an indication of the appointment's cancellation. The value of this identifier can be derived from some unique number generator. Options to derive this value include a database sequence or one of the XPath functions generateGUID(), getInstanceId(), or getConversationId().

At any time—from the synchronous reply until the completion of the process instance—the appointment details can be requested. Such a request is responded to in the HandleGetAppointment DetailsRequest scope and is processed parallel to the ScheduleNotifyAndWait scope by an onMessage event handler. You can see this event handler on the right side of Figure 6-3 (the envelope icon attached to the entire ScheduleNotifyAndWait scope). The event handler is discussed later in this chapter.

Flow for Parallel Execution of BPEL Activities

The BPEL process will continue after the reply has been sent to the client. At this point, two actions are performed in parallel. Based on the type of appointment and some patient details, the preparation instructions for the patient are compiled. At the same time, the AppointmentScheduler is invoked with some key details on the patient, the type of appointment, the desired doctor (if the patient is already undergoing treatment), and the scheduling preferences.

The original process design—as discussed in Chapter 2—does not have this parallel step because it was not considered necessary. However, with the two steps processed in parallel, the patient receives her response faster—sometimes considerably faster, depending primarily on the response time from the Scheduler service. Furthermore, the hospital wants to prepare for the situation where the instructions may need some human intervention in special cases before being sent to the patient. Even though that is currently not part of the process, the very real possibility of that coming to pass is another reason for introducing the parallel steps in the process.

Parallel activities are realized in BPEL processes through the Flow activity. A Flow contains two or more Sequence activities that are executed concurrently (see Figure 6-3). This means, for example, that in two branches in the Flow activity an asynchronous call to an external service can be made with both branches waiting for a reply at the same time. Obviously this is more efficient than having to wait for the first response to come in before the second request can be sent out. With a flow, the time it takes for the slowest service to respond determines the processing time of the overall flow, not the times of all calls added together.

The current thinking at St. Matthews is that the instructions for the patient with regard to the preparation for the appointment do not need to include the details of the appointment itself—such as the date and time and the name of the doctor. The preparation can be created from the information available from the referral and the RegisterPatientData step. The service that will prepare the instruction does not have to wait for the ScheduleAppointment service—or the other way round. Therefore, these two service calls are performed in parallel, using the Flow activity. When the instructions should be more tailor-made—for example, instead of stating "Do not eat anything solid 12 hours prior to the appointment," the instructions might be "Do not eat anything solid from 8.30 P.M. on August 30th until the appointment"—the PrepareInstructions step would have to wait for the ScheduleAppointment step to complete and we would not use a Flow activity.

When both the instructions and the appointment schedule itself are in, the flow completes and the next step—NotifyPatient—is executed. This will inform the patient of the scheduled appointment by whatever means apply to the patient (e-mail, mail, telephone, and so on).

BPEL in SOA Suite 11*g* comes with various activities for sending notifications: Email, SMS, VoiceMail, and IM (instant messaging or chat). These activities are Oracle-specific extensions to BPEL—in the BPEL source code these are recognizable from their "bpelx": namespace identifier. SOA Suite 11*g* leverages the User Messaging Service (UMS) that was installed into the SOA domain. UMS is configured through the Enterprise Manager Fusion Middleware Control to work with the e-mail server, chat server, and SMS provider of your choice. Appendix C describes the configuration of UMS for e-mail and chat; the complementary chapter provides instructions for adding a call to the notification service to the process to send word of the appointment to the GP.

In practice you may want to (also) send notifications through a printed letter—a real one, on paper—or have a telephone call conducted by a human staff member. In the latter case, this would be done via a human workflow—more details in Chapter 10.

After sending the notification, the PatientAppointmentService process instance can sit back and relax: Unless the appointment is cancelled, the process instance will wait for the patient to arrive, shortly prior to the appointed time. For a no-show event, the patient does not arrive at all for the appointment, as shown in Figure 6-4. We will consider the appointment a "no show" if the appointment is four hours overdue and neither a cancellation nor a patient arrival has been fed into the process instance.

NOTE
It may be better design to not have our PatientAppointmentService process wait for days or weeks for the arrival of the patient, but instead create a separate SOA application that handles the process that starts with either the patient arrival or a request for cancellation or rescheduling. Resource usage and administrative flexibility are among the design considerations. We will leave that very meaningful discussion for another time.

If the patient wants to reschedule the appointment, she can call or e-mail the hospital to change the appointment. This is treated as a "cancellation with reschedule" request. If an appointment is cancelled—by the patient, the doctor, the insurer, or the hospital staff—the appointment should be removed from the doctor's schedule. In other words, the effect caused by scheduling the appointment through the call to the scheduler service needs to be undone. In BPEL terminology, this is called "compensating," and BPEL has dedicated compensation handlers that can be invoked to undo the effect of scopes that were earlier completed in a BPEL process instance. These are discussed later in this chapter. Note that compensation is not achieved automatically. Developers need to define and implement the compensation using the various BPEL activities available.

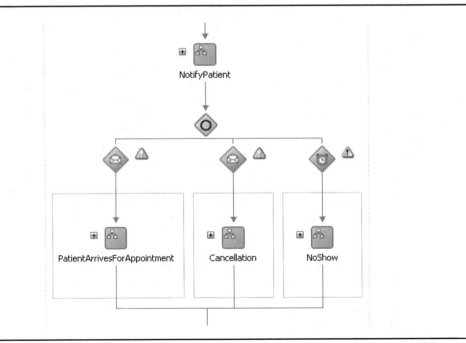

FIGURE 6-4. *After notifying the patient of the appointment, the process waits for one of three events using a Pick activity.*

Invoking a Synchronous Web Service: Prepare Instructions

The first of the two parallel activities in the ScheduleNotifyAndWait scope (refer to Figure 6-2) is a call to the ConsultPreparationInstruction service.

Depending on the type of appointment, scans that could be performed, and the lab tests that may be run, a patient may need to prepare in a special way for an appointment. He or she may be required to refrain from eating during the 24-hour period preceding the appointment. Or the patient may need to bring a stool or urine sample. The patient could also be asked to fill out a questionnaire or bring specific documents (for example, with regard to inoculations or findings in external examinations). In the past a lot of time has been wasted—and a lot of aggravation caused—by not providing patients with the correct instructions for this preparation. Mary and her staff have been very careful in explicitly defining this step in the Appointment process.

The instructions are prepared based on the referral that starts the process and some additional patient details. The fairly simple ConsultPreparationInstruction Web Service can be used for gathering these instructions. It is invoked with a request message that specifies the type of appointment, several patient details (when available, such as age, [most recent measurement of] weight, and gender), and the urgency label. The service returns a response with the instructions for the patient, retrieved from St. Matthews' content management system, which also provides documents for "St. Matthews-online." Some images may be included as Base64-encoded content.

The call to this (or any) Web Service is added to the BPEL process through a few simple steps (assuming we have the WSDL for the service).

1. Open the BPEL process editor.

2. Drag a WebService Adapter to the external reference lane in the BPEL editor. In the pop-up, configure the WebService binding by setting the name to **ConsultPreparationInstructionService** and browsing for the WSDL file (from the file system, the deployed Web Service on the SOA Suite, or the WSDL resource in the MDS Repository—more on MDS in Chapter 18).

3. Open the PrepareInstructions scope in the Flow activity inside ScheduleNotifyAndWait.

4. Drag an Invoke activity from the palette to the PrepareInstructions scope. Link this activity to the ConsultPreparationInstructionService partnerLink.

5. Configure the Invoke activity in the dialog that appears when you create the link to the reference. Have local variables created by clicking the green plus icon for both variables and checking the Local Variable radio button.

6. Add an Assign activity prior to the Invoke activity. Configure it to set the local variable used as input for the call to the ConsultPreparationInstructionService.

7. Add an Assign activity following the Invoke activity. In this activity, we should take the relevant parts in the result from the call to ConsultPreparationInstructionService, which is stored in the local variable, and copy it into a global variable.

See the online chapter complement for more detailed instructions and screenshots of the steps described here.

Invoking an Asynchronous Service: Calling the Appointment Scheduler

One of the crucial steps in the Appointment process obviously is picking a specific date, time, room, and doctor for the patient's appointment. The hospital has defined a service interface for this action—an asynchronous service that can be invoked by any party in the hospital, including the new Appointment process that we implement in the context of the eAppointment project.

It is not necessarily clear to Margaret and her staff whether there is an automated facility—some fancy, smart scheduling tool—that implements this service or if there are some staff members tasked with scheduling appointments, and they do not need to know either—that is encapsulation and decoupling for you.

Whatever the case, the Appointment process leverages this Scheduler service and is thereby relieved from the responsibility of updating the central resource schedule where doctors' agendas, as well as schedules for rooms and equipment, are maintained. It is also the scheduler's responsibility to try to schedule multiple appointments for a patient adjacently during the day, thus saving the patient additional trips to the hospital as well as too-long episodes in waiting rooms.

The Scheduler service is called with the appointment identifier, the patient identifier, an indication of the appointment type, the identifier for the doctor if this is a follow-up appointment, an urgency specification, and possibly preferred date/time combinations.

The Scheduler service is an asynchronous service. After the request is made, it can be anywhere between several minutes up to more than a day before the service makes the return call with its results, although it is fair to say that most requests are responded to within the hour. The essence of an asynchronous service, as we discussed previously in Chapter 5, is that the service and its caller perform a little handshake where they both have to play the role of caller and callee. The SchedulerService publishes an inbound and an outbound portType. The first one is implemented by the Scheduler itself, whereas the latter is actually implemented by the caller because that is where the SchedulerService will call to deliver its response. So in summary, in a synchronous call, the service client invokes the service that returns the response to the client in the same call; in the meantime the client is blocked. In an asynchronous call, the service client invokes the service, resumes its flow (is not blocked), and at some point waits for the service to call the service client with the result.

Implementing the (Mock) Asynchronous SchedulerService

Let's take a closer look at how to deal with asynchronous services. We will employ a simple "mock" implementation of the SchedulerService. It takes an appointmentId, a patientId, and a type of appointment as input. Based on that information, it comes up with a date and time for the appointment, as well as a free-format text element with the name of the doctor and the location where the appointment takes place.

An asynchronous BPEL process is easily created with these steps:

1. Create a new SOA project, called **SchedulerService**.

2. Select the option Composite With BPEL.

3. Choose the Asynchronous BPEL Process template.

The BPEL process is now created with the necessary setup in the WSDL, with two portTypes and two PartnerLinkTypes:

```
<!-- portType implemented by the SchedulerService BPEL process -->
<portType name="SchedulerService">
 <operation name="initiate">
  <input message="client:SchedulerServiceRequestMessage"/>
 </operation>
</portType>
<!-- portType implemented by the requester of SchedulerService BPEL process
     for asynchronous callback purposes  -->
<portType name="SchedulerServiceCallback">
 <operation name="onResult">
  <input message="client:SchedulerServiceResponseMessage"/>
 </operation>
</portType>
```

The SchedulerServiceCallback portType is the special one. It basically describes the service interface that any client of the SchedulerService should implement in order to be asynchronously called back with the response from the SchedulerService.

The partnerLinkType definition in the WSDL document is also special: Instead of a single role element, we now have two. The SchedulerService interacts in two ways with external partners. One way—the familiar one—is via the SchedulerService portType; this interaction is associated with the role of SchedulerServiceProvider. At this point we do not explicitly state who will assume this role, although it is likely in this case to be the SchedulerService itself.

The other interaction—the special one that is introduced because of the asynchronous nature of the service—is via the callback portType SchedulerServiceCallback. This portType has to be implemented by the external partner. This interaction is associated with the role Scheduler ServiceRequester. The asynchronous callback to the requester is handled by the SOA Suite using WS-Addressing to help determine the callback address.

The SchedulerService BPEL process has a partnerLink based on that special PartnerLinkType, for the role SchedulerServiceProvider, that is used in the Invoke activity that returns the asynchronous response. Later on, in the consuming AppointmentProcess BPEL process, we will again create a partnerLink based on these PartnerLinkTypes; however, this time with myRole set to Scheduler ServiceRequester because that partnerLink will then be used to the SchedulerService from the AppointmentProcess.

Figure 6-5 shows the visual presentation of the BPEL process definition.

We can deploy the SchedulerService process to the SOA Suite and test it in the Fusion Middleware Control. However, even though the tester will call the service, it will not handle, receive, or show the asynchronous response. We will only be able to inspect the response by taking a closer look at the message flow trace for the tested instance of the SOA composite application.

Calling the Asynchronous SchedulerService

Now that we have deployed and tested the SchedulerService, we need to call it from the AppointmentService. Calling an asynchronous service is not at all straightforward from most

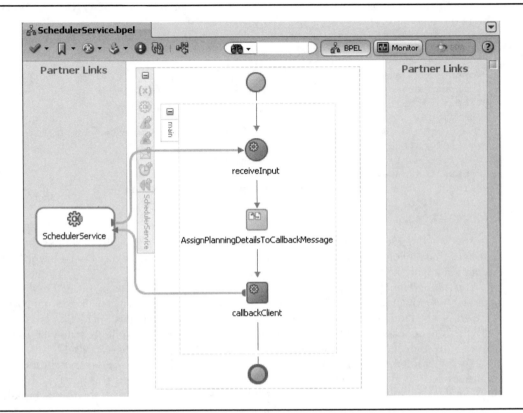

FIGURE 6-5. *The asynchronous SchedulerService*

programming languages and environments. Making the call is not the challenge, but receiving the response is, however. The difficulties include:

- Where can the response be sent to?
- What will the program do while it is waiting for the response?
- How is a certain response fed to the proper process thread (Java) or session (PL/SQL)?
- When do we conclude that no response will be coming and what should be done in that case?

BPEL, in comparison, makes it almost trivial to call an asynchronous Web Service and subsequently receive the response. We will see this in action when we add a call to the SchedulerService in the PatientAppointmentService.

With the PatientAppointmentService SOA application open in JDeveloper, we drag a WebService Adapter to the External References lane in the composite editor. Type **SchedulerService** as the name, browse for and select the WSDL for the SchedulerService (for now, just from the file system), and select the SchedulerService and SchedulerServiceCallback, respectively, for the port types. Next, wire the SchedulerService reference to the PatientAppointmentService BPEL component, as shown in Figure 6-6.

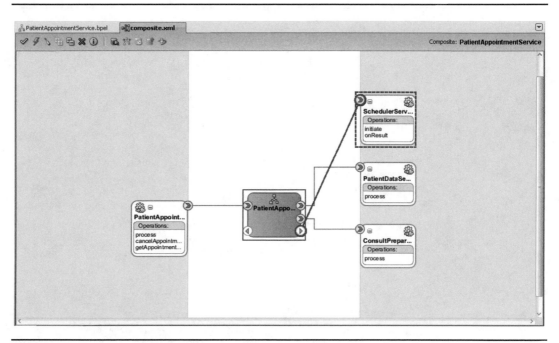

FIGURE 6-6. *Associating the SchedulerService reference with the PatientAppointmentService BPEL component*

Now open the BPEL editor for the PatientAppointmentService and create a new variable at the level of the ScheduleNotifyAndWait scope. This variable is called AppointmentSchedule and is based on the SchedulerServiceResponseMessage.

Drag an Invoke activity from the Component Palette and drop it in the ScheduleAppointment scope inside the Flow activity. Connect this Invoke activity to the SchedulerService PartnerLink.

Have the input variable created as a local variable—that is, inside the current scope. The output variable field is disabled, and that is about the only clue as to the asynchronous nature of the partner link: There is no—synchronous or immediate—output from this call.

In order to receive the asynchronous response from the SchedulerService, we need to add a Receive activity to the scope ScheduleAppointment following the Invoke activity (see Figure 6-7). The Receive is associated with the processResponse operation in the SchedulerService—the operation in the special SchedulerServiceCallback portType we discussed earlier. If we wanted, we could add activities between the Invoke and Receive activities to execute logic that could be done in parallel to the scheduling.

This is the first time we have seen two Receive activities in a BPEL process. Until now, Receive was always the first BPEL activity, the starting point for the process. And now we see a second purpose for Receive: handling the asynchronous response to an earlier Invoke activity, without creating a new instance of the BPEL process. The check box Create Instance controls whether upon execution of the Receive activity a new BPEL process instance should be created. In this case, the check box should be unchecked: No new BPEL instance and no new composite instance are created.

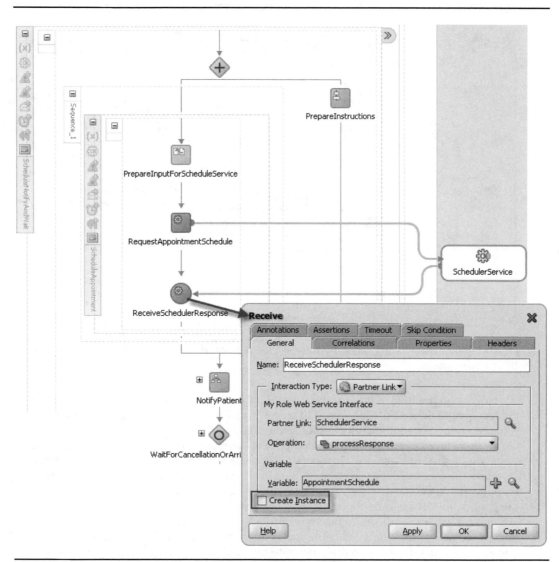

FIGURE 6-7. *Invoke and Receive activities to complete the handshake with the asynchronous SchedulerService*

Sending Notifications from the BPEL Process

By the time the Flow activity is complete and the NotifyPatient activity is executed, the AppointmentSchedule variable contains the result from the ScheduleService and the variable PrepareInstructions holds the instructions for the patient on preparing for the appointment. That means we have all the information required to send an e-mail or some other form of notification to the patient to inform her about the appointment.

The online chapter complement demonstrates how the BPEL process can use the Email activity to send such notifications.

Receiving Request Messages in Running BPEL Instances

BPEL has a unique capability among all the service engines and languages in the SOA Suite: a BPEL process can receive even after it has started running—and this goes beyond processing synchronous or even asynchronous responses to service invocations. Most computer programs are initiated by an original invocation and return a result once they are complete—they cannot easily or at all be accessed from the outside while they are running. A BPEL process can expose multiple operations—one of which will initiate the instance while others feed messages into a running instance.

We have already seen how BPEL processes can continue to run after they have returned a response message. To this special behavior we now add the capability of receiving subsequent messages—either by explicitly waiting for them to arrive or by handling them as unsolicited events. In both instances, the key ingredient to this functionality is a BPEL mechanism called *correlation*—the ability to match an incoming message with one of potentially many running instances.

Receiving messages into a running instance can be done using a Receive activity—as we saw for the reception of the asynchronous response from the SchedulerService. Another method is through an onMessage event handler that we can attach to a scope in the BPEL process. An event handler specifies an asynchronous agent that runs for as long as the scope is running and can do one of two things: wait for a specific moment in time and then act, or receive an incoming message of a specific type and act on it. We will use this latter capability to handle requests for information about the appointment.

A third method for a running BPEL process instance to deal with incoming messages is inside the Pick activity. A BPEL Pick activity is included in a sequence like any other BPEL activity. It, too, deals with events: It instructs the BPEL engine to pause the BPEL process instance until one of potentially many events occurs. The events, as in the case of the event handlers, are either the elapsing of a certain time duration or the reception of a specific message. Unlike the event handlers that sit idle in the background for the entire lifespan of the scope, impacting the BPEL process only when the event they are listening for occurs, the Pick activity stalls the process—or at least the branch in which it lives, because there can be other branches in a common Flow parent—until one of the events for which it is configured takes place. No activity that follows the Pick activity is executed unless one of the Pick events occurs. Figure 6-4, earlier in this chapter, shows how a Pick activity controls the flow in our process after the appointment has been scheduled.

It contains three alternative continuations of the process—of which only one will actually take place in any process instance. Each alternative is either associated with a time event (onAlarm) or with the arrival of a message—or more specifically, in the invocation of an operation on a parterLink's portType.

The onAlarm event handler has been specified in this example. It will trigger—if neither of the two onMessage event handlers has been triggered—four hours after the start time of the appointment. The add-dayTimeDuration-to-dateTime XPath function has been used; it first retrieves the start time of the appointment and adds a dateTime duration that is specified in the string P0Y0M0DT4H0M0S, which means four hours.

One of the other candidate paths is the cancellation of the appointment—associated with the cancelAppointment operation in the PatientAppointmentService portType on the PatientAppointmentService partnerLink. This path should be executed when a cancellation message is received for the appointment.

Consuming an Asynchronous Event: Handling a Cancellation

A cancellation of a scheduled appointment can arrive at St. Matthews in a variety of ways. It can come in through the regular mail, by fax, or through e-mail; or it is communicated by telephone. A cancellation can arrive in a batch from an insurer or can be entered directly in a web application by a family doctor. Finally, an appointment should be cancelled when the "death of the patient" event is received. A cancellation can be accompanied by a request to (re)schedule—although obviously not in the last case. An appointment can be cancelled by various parties for several reasons. The patient can cancel because the physical symptoms have disappeared, the schedule time does not fit the patient's agenda, the patient has found another healthcare provider, or the patient's financial situation does not allow for the hospital visit. The appointment can also be canceled by the insurer because it is not covered by the policy or by the hospital because either the required facilities or the doctor is not available.

The cancellation can arrive at any time, from the moment the appointment was scheduled until the time it takes place. It enters our SOA infrastructure as a Web Service request that should be fed into the BPEL process instance that was created and is still running for that particular appointment. The BPEL process instance receives the request in the relevant event handler within the Pick activity and should then either complete the instance entirely or return to the "schedule appointment" step in case a request to reschedule was part of the cancellation request. In both cases, the reason for cancelling the initial appointment should be recorded because it may provide clues as to how to improve the appointment process and/or optimize the use of resources at St. Matthews. The cancellation should also be reported to the automated Appointment Manager Service, which will notify the doctor and update the resource schedules.

The cancellation Web Service request needs to specify exactly *which* appointment has to be cancelled—just like we would have to do when we cancel the appointment by telephone or e-mail. The appointment is identified by the identifier that was determined early on in the BPEL process and returned in the synchronous response sent from the reportAppointmentProcess Identifier activity. This same identifier is used by the SOA Suite run time to associate the incoming cancellation request with the correct running SOA composite application instance. A precondition for this is that the used identifier should be unique across all process instances. The mechanism that makes this match between an inbound request and an existing instance is called *correlation*.

Correlation for the PatientAppointmentService

Correlation in general deals with the following scenario: A request message arrives at the SOA Suite. It is not intended to start a new composite application instance. Instead, it needs to be routed to an already running instance. It is up to the engine to find the correct instance to hand the message to. In this case, the request to cancel an appointment needs to be handed to the instance that was created for that particular appointment. Refer to Figure 6-8 for an illustration of this.

Of course, the engine needs to be able to extract some sort of identifier from the request message to correlate that message with a running instance. In our example, the PatientAppointmentService was initially invoked on behalf of a patient who needed an appointment. The service responded with a message containing the appointmentIdentifier. Requests for additional information with regard to that particular appointment request should contain this identifier, and each running instance of the

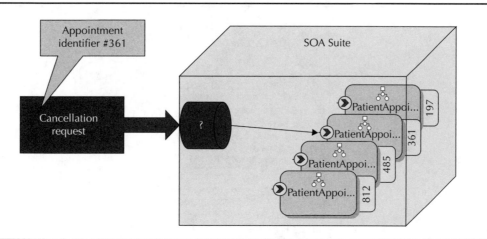

FIGURE 6-8.   *Correlation between an incoming message and running composite application instances*

PatientAppointmentService, too, should be identifiable through that identifier. It is the linking pin to correlate new request messages with running instances.

Correlation of instances of composite applications is built on the correlation of BPEL process instances; a composite application without a BPEL service component does not support correlation. The message that needs to be correlated to a running composite application instance needs to be sent into the BPEL component—and therefore be sent to a service exposed by the application that is wired to the BPEL component.

In order to make the correlation mechanism work, we have to configure the BPEL process to recognize the appointmentIdentifier as that correlation key.

An instance of a BPEL process can be identified for correlation using a *correlation set*. Such a correlation set is a combination of one or more properties, in a way that is very much like a composite primary or unique key database constraint. Properties are defined at the process level, are of a certain type, and are mapped to values in the messages sent from or received by the process. A BPEL process can have multiple correlation sets—just like a database table can have multiple unique keys.

The PatientAppointmentService has a single correlation set that consists of a single property. Let's call this set the appointmentIdentifierSet. We can create a correlation set from the structure window by clicking the green plus icon with the Correlation Sets node selected, as shown in Figure 6-9.

The single property we require in this correlation set is called appointmentIdentifier and is of type String. The property, too, is created in the structure window.

Next, we can add the property to the correlation set and thereby specify that instances of the PatientAppointmentService BPEL process can be uniquely identified by the value of this property (see Figure 6-10).

However, what *is* the value of that property? When and how is that determined? How does the property relate to the variables in the BPEL process or the messages sent to or from the process?

Correlation always takes place in the context of a message exchange. Either when the BPEL process is receiving a message (onMessage and Receive activities) or when it is sending a message (Invoke and Reply) does correlation come into play. And only at such times does the engine need to establish the values of the properties in the correlation set that is attached to the message exchange.

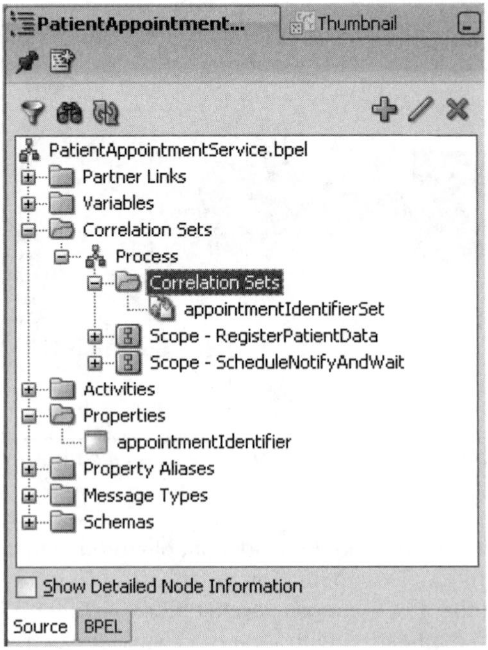

FIGURE 6-9. *The correlation set appointmentIdentifierSet and the appointmentIdentifier property for the PatientAppointmentService*

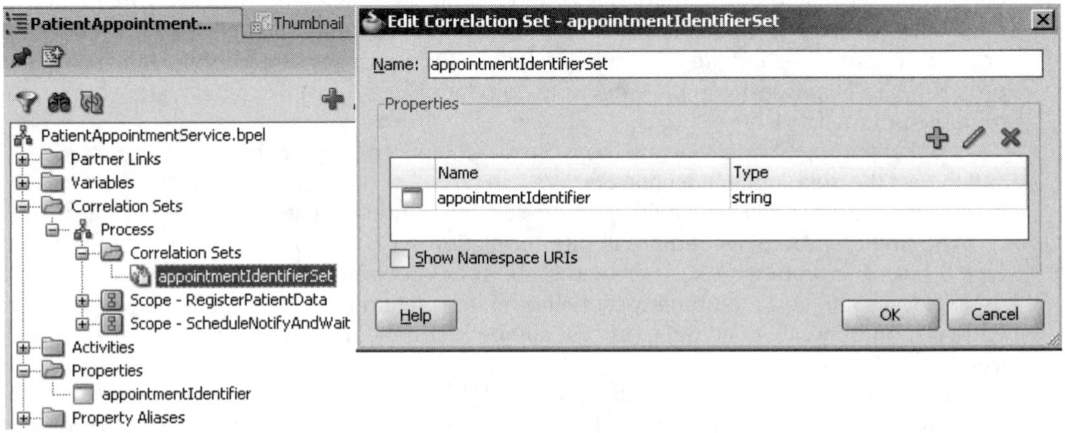

FIGURE 6-10. *Editing the correlation set—specify which properties together uniquely identify an instance of the BPEL process*

The value of a property is associated with the content of the messages sent to or from the process at such exchange moments. For example, the appointmentIdentifier property gets its value from the outgoing PatientAppointmentServiceResponseMessage that is returned from the process in the first, synchronous Reply activity. When the cancellation message exchange takes place, the property will get its value from the incoming AppointmentCancellationRequestMessage.

These associations between the property and a particular message exchange are specified using *property alias* definitions. A BPEL process can contain one or more property aliases that map a property to a specific message part—and to be precise, a specific XPath expression to extract a value from within that message part. This message part is used in the exchange through one of the partnerLinks in the process.

In the case of the PatientAppointmentService, we will eventually have four property aliases, because the appointmentIdentifier is associated with four message exchanges (initial appointment request, cancellation, status request, and patient arrival). This is shown in Figure 6-11.

The identity of the process instance (the values in the correlation set) is established only once—obviously, because that cannot change later on. Establishing the identity takes place through initialization of the correlation set and capturing the values of the properties in the set at that moment in time. In our case, this happens when the PatientAppointmentServiceResponseMessage is sent by the synchronous reply operation labeled reportAppointmentProcessIdentifier. The value of

FIGURE 6-11. *The correlation definitions for the PatientAppointmentService: the correlation set, the property, and the four property aliases*

the appointmentIdentifier element in the AppointmentServiceProcessResponse element in the response message is read and set as *the* value for the appointmentIdentifierSet—a value that will never change for the instance of the BPEL process.

On each subsequent message exchange, the identification of the process instance, as determined in the correlation set, can be compared to the value as extracted from incoming messages. That allows the engine to link the incoming message to the instance with the same value for the correlation set.

Figure 6-12 illustrates the steps in the correlation processes that are described as follows:

1. The synchronous Reply activity initiates the correlation set, and the value is extracted from the response message and used to set the instance identifier.

2. The value for the appointmentIdentifierSet correlation set is extracted from the incoming Status Request message based on the property alias defined for that message and compared with the identifiers for all running instances to find the matching instance.

3. When the PatientArrival message comes in, the property alias definition is used to extract the correlation set value that is then used to find the matching instance of the PatientAppointment service.

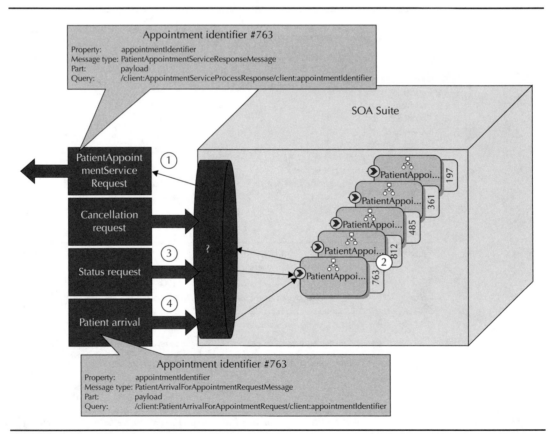

FIGURE 6-12. *The steps in the correlation process*

We have to specify the four property aliases and indicate for each one—for each message exchange that will work with the correlation set—how the value is derived from the incoming or outgoing message.

To create a property alias (refer to Figure 6-13), select the node property aliases in the structure window. Click the green plus icon to add a new property alias. A pop-up window appears in which we first of all need to select the property for which we want to define a property alias: appointmentIdentifier. Next, we have to select the message type and part for which we want to define the property alias. Select the payload part in the PatientAppointmentServiceResponseMessage.

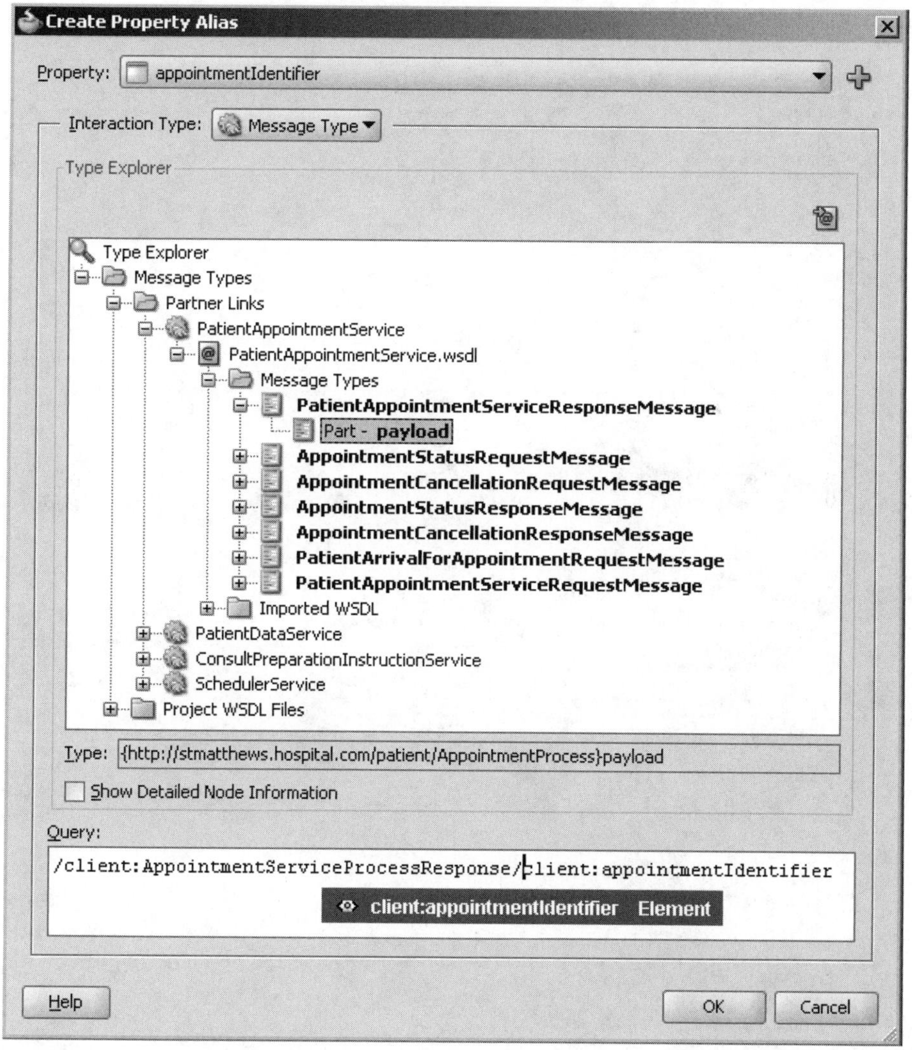

FIGURE 6-13. *Configuring the property alias for the appointmentIdentifier property mapped to the PatientAppointmentServiceResponseMessage payload part*

In the Query field, we must specify the XPath expression to retrieve the value for the property. Hint: Pressing CTRL-SPACEBAR brings up a list of available XML elements to add to the XPath expression.

The final step in making correlation work is to configure the activities that send (Reply) and receive (onMessage handler) the messages that need to be correlated.

First of all, the Reply activity. This activity is special because it needs to instantiate the correlation set. Open the editor by double-clicking the Reply activity. Go to the Correlations tab. Click the green plus icon to add a correlation set that is associated with this message exchange. Select the appointmentIdentifierSet. JDeveloper will populate the properties column for us. You need to set Initiate to Yes to indicate that this Reply step is the moment when this correlation set is instantiated and the identifier for this process instance is set. Figure 6-14 illustrates these steps.

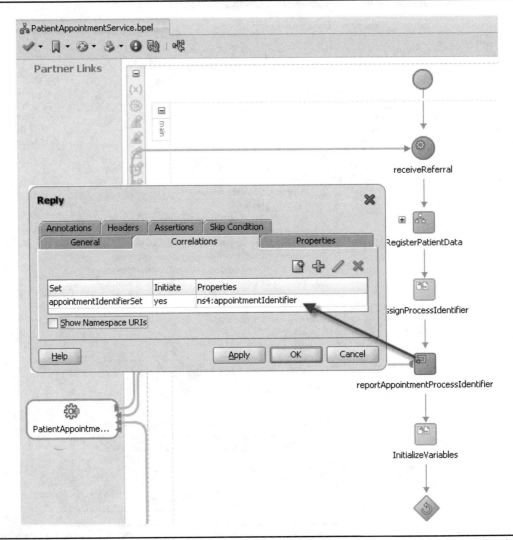

FIGURE 6-14. *Configuring the correlation set appointmentIdentifierSet and its initiation for the Reply activity*

Through this definition, we have ensured that when this Reply activity is executed, an instance of this BPEL process is assigned an identity that can be used for correlation purposes.

As an aside, a BPEL process can have multiple identities through multiple correlation sets that have different properties and different values, and can be established at different points in time. The PatientAppointmentService, for example, could have a second correlation set that also identifies the appointment through a combination of the patientIdentifier and the date and time of the appointment.

Correlation for the Appointment Cancellations

We have laid the foundation for the capability to receive a cancellation request for a scheduled appointment. We have configured a correlation set and ensured that the instance identity is determined when the synchronous reply takes place.

Next, we have to add an onMessage event handler in the Pick activity to handle reception of an AppointmentCancellationRequestMessage when the cancelAppointment operation is called on the PatientAppointmentService. Then we need to configure this onMessage handler to support correlation for this message exchange.

In the BPEL design editor, find the Pick activity and click the Envelope icon to add an onMessage branch. A new branch is added to the pick. Drag a scope from the Component Palette and drop it on this branch. Call the scope **Cancellation**. Double-click the onMessage icon to configure the message exchange it will implement. Figure 6-15 illustrates these steps.

The partner link involved in the onMessage activity is the PatientAppointmentService. The relevant operation in the port type associated with this partner link is the cancelAppointment operation. Specify the input variable as locally created.

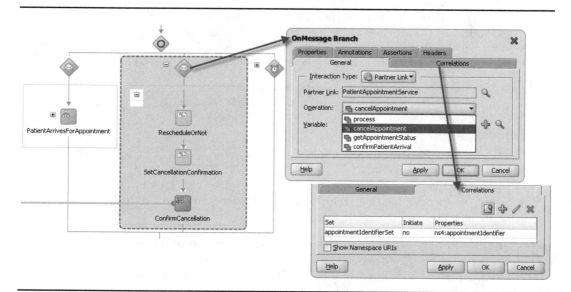

FIGURE 6-15. *Configuring the message exchange and correlation for the onMessage branch that will handle the cancellation requests*

Next, click the Correlations tab. The only correlation set that is involved with this onMessage activity is the appointmentIdentifierSet. It should not be initiated, because that already happened through the outgoing message sent from the Reply activity. For cancellations, we will use the value assigned to the property in the correlation set at that time to correlate with the incoming cancellation message's property value.

If you have not already done so, now would be a good time to create a property alias for the appointmentIdentifier property, mapping it to the incoming AppointmentCancellationRequestMessage. Select the property and click the edit icon. This will take you to another editor window where you can create the alias with its XPath expression against the message. The XPath expression for this property alias should query the appointmentIdentifier element in the AppointmentCancellationRequest.

Cancelling the Appointment: Introducing the While Loop

When the appointment is cancelled, it can be with a request to reschedule. Otherwise, the appointment should just be removed from the hospital's schedules and the doctor's agenda, and the PatientAppointService instance will stop. When the appointment should be rescheduled, the instance should live on and return to the beginning of the ScheduleNotifyAndWait scope.

BPEL does not have the concept of method calls or goto activities—one area where BPMN allows for more flexibility in the process design than BPEL (see Chapter 11 for an introduction of BPMN). However, BPEL has a While loop that we can use in this case to introduce some level of iteration into the BPEL process. BPEL 2.0—which is supported by SOA Suite 11*g*—has added the loop constructs For Each and Repeat Until.

The PatientAppointmentService has a fairly large chunk that can be reiterated when the appointment gets canceled with a reschedule request: everything from gathering preparation instructions, scheduling the request, and notifying the patient, to waiting for the patient's arrival needs to be repeated after the reschedule request—and is therefore inside the While activity (see Figure 6-16). The While activity is configured with a Boolean expression. As long as that expression evaluates to true, the activities inside the While will be executed. The PatientAppointmentService contains a global Boolean variable called needToSchedule. The value of this variable is tested in the While activity and determines whether or not another iteration should be made in the While loop:

```
<while name="ScheduleAndIfNecessaryScheduleAgain"
       condition="bpws:getVariableData('needToSchedule')">
  <scope name="ScheduleNotifyAndWait">...</scope>
</while>
```

The variable needToSchedule is initialized as "true" to ensure that the ScheduleNotifyAndWait scope is executed at least once.

When the Cancellation message is received, it is inspected to see whether it contains a request to reschedule. If it does, the variable needToSchedule is left at true; otherwise, it is set to false. In the latter case, the While loop is terminated.

Using the Replay Fault to Return to the Beginning of a Scope

Instead of using the While activity (or another iterator construct), we can use a special BPEL fault to replay a scope: When the fault is thrown, for example, under certain conditions at the end of a scope, then that entire scope is executed again. The online chapter complement describes this fault and shows how we can redesign the PatientAppointmentService, without the While, using this replay fault.

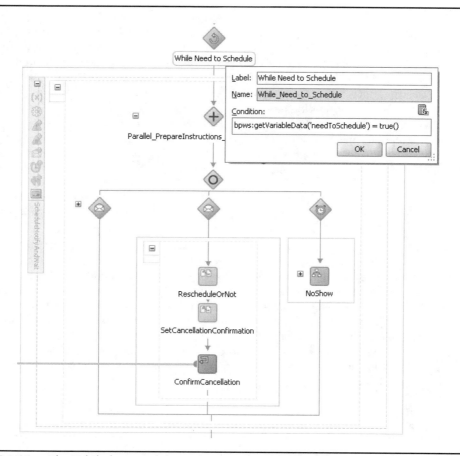

FIGURE 6-16. *The While loop and the onMessage branch handling the cancellation request*

Correlation and Asynchronous Service Calls

Correlation is the primary mechanism used by the SOA Suite run time to match up incoming messages with existing instances of composite applications. Yet we did not discuss correlation when we introduced the implementation of our calls to asynchronous services, even though the response from an asynchronous service such as the SchedulerService is returned in the form of a service call to the callback portType in the PatientAppointmentService.

The reason for this is that the BPEL engine handles this automatically under the covers using the WS-Addressing standards. In other scenarios we have to implement/configure this ourselves because the components we interact with are not BPEL components. We do not need to make any changes to the BPEL process, the composite definition, or the WSDL file in order to leverage the WS-Addressing method for correlation between BPEL process

(Continued)

instances and the asynchronous services they invoke. The BPEL engine run-time framework will add headers to the SOAP message that is sent when an asynchronous Web Service is invoked. These headers—based on the WS-Addressing specification—contain the *endpoint location* (reply-to address) that specifies the location at which a BPEL client is listening for a callback message and the Conversation ID, which is a unique identifier for the BPEL process instance that sent the request.

When the asynchronous service sends the response by invoking the callback service, it can use the information from the WS-Addressing headers to target the response at the right client. When the asynchronous service is itself a BPEL process, like our SchedulerService, the headers are leveraged automatically by the BPEL engine, completely transparently to us as developers.

There are several situations where the built-in, default WS-Addressing correlation mechanism does not suffice when we invoke an asynchronous service. One of those is the case where the asynchronous Web Service provider does not support WS-Addressing and correlation is required to map the response message to the process instance. Another case is a more complex conversation pattern that involves more than two communication partners and a final response that is not returned by the partner that received the original call that started the conversation, as illustrated by Figure 6-17. In this case, the BPEL process should initiate a correlation set and make sure that its value is passed along all services participating in the conversation and returned in the eventual response that is sent to the callback port of the BPEL process.

See the FMW documentation for more information about WS-Addressing, the way it is used in the BPEL engine, and ways to inspect the contents of the SOAP message (and the WS-Addressing headers) using an OWSM logging policy or TCP Listener.

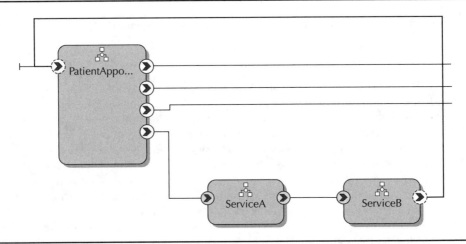

FIGURE 6-17. *Complex conversation pattern that requires custom correlation. The initial request is sent to ServiceA and the final response is sent by ServiceB to the callback port.*

Request Appointment Details from the PatientAppointmentService Instance

BPEL process instances can use another asynchronous way of accepting incoming messages next to Receive activities and the onMessage branches of Pick activities. We can attach event handlers to any scope in the BPEL process as well as the main process itself. These handlers are active during the entire lifetime of the scope they are attached to—listening all the while for either the onAlarm event to happen or messages to arrive. An event handler does not impact the scope it is associated with—it runs in a parallel thread while the scope is executing. When an event handler is triggered, it can, however, decide to halt the execution of the scope.

In the PatientAppointmentService process, we make use of the event handler mechanism to listen for status request messages—an example of a common-use case where a BPEL process allows clients to inquire after its current status, progress, and variables. Such requests are typically handled by event handlers attached to a fairly high-level scope or even the main process. These handlers frequently use several global variables to retrieve status values from several global variables to return to the caller.

To configure the getAppointmentStatus event handler, locate the scope ScheduleNotifyAndWait. Click the Add onMessage Branch icon in the scope's menu bar; refer to Figure 6-18. A new onMessage event handler is added in the diagram. Now drag a sequence from the Component Palette and drop it in the onMessage branch. Call the new sequence **HandleGetAppointmentDetailsRequest**.

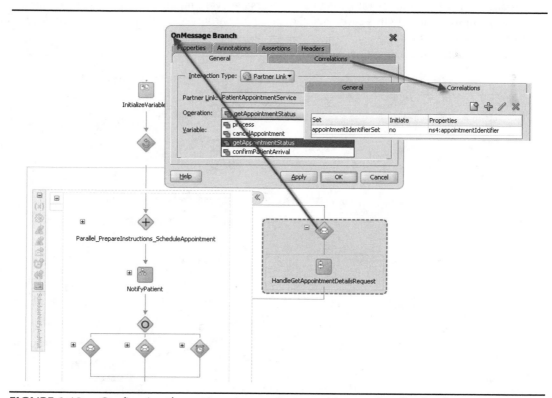

FIGURE 6-18.   *Configuring the getAppointmentStatus onMessage handler for the ScheduleNotifyAndWait scope*

Double-click the envelope icon to bring up the onMessage editor. Select the partnerLink (PatientAppointmentService) and operation (getAppointmentStatus) in this editor and have the input variable created as a local variable. Next, go to the Correlations tab and select the appointmentIdentifierSet correlation set. If you have not already done so, create a propertyAlias that maps the AppointmentStatusRequestMessage to the appointmentIdentifier property.

Next, we should flesh out the sequence in which the work takes place that should be performed when a request for the appointment status is received. Add a Reply activity to this sequence, linked to the getAppointmentStatus operation in the PatientAppointmentService partner link. No correlation settings are required for this outgoing message exchange because it involves a synchronous invocation. Have the output variable created as a local variable because we only use it in the scope of the event handler. Then add an Assign activity to the sequence, right before the Reply step. Copy the relevant values to the ReturnAppointmentStatus_getAppointmentStatus_OutputVariable that is returned to the client asking for the appointment status. These steps are illustrated in Figure 6-19.

Note that event handlers can perform actions on behalf of the scope they are attached to, in reaction to messages or the reaching of specific moments in time. The handlers can send responses, make service calls of their own, and both read and write the values of variables local to the scope or defined in higher-level scopes. Their most far-reaching prerogative is the termination of the scope—using the Terminate activity. However, while the event handler is still running, the scope also continues to execute activities.

By the way, in the case of the PatientAppointmentProcess, we have used an onMessage branch in the Pick activity rather than an onMessage event handler to process an incoming cancellation request. In this case, that choice is fairly arbitrary—both approaches would be able to achieve the same effect.

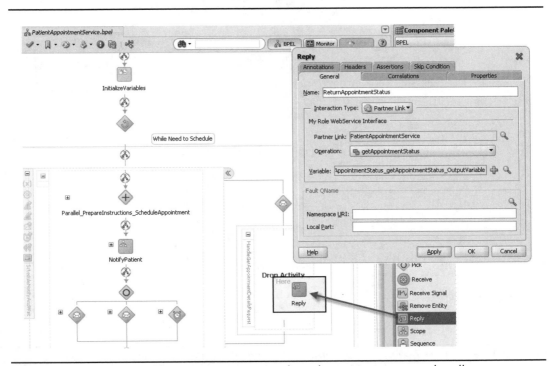

FIGURE 6-19. *Returning the Appointment status from the onMessage event handler*

Other BPEL Activities

This chapter and the previous one have introduced and applied the most common BPEL activities. However, there are several more that can be used in BPEL processes. These are shown in Figure 6-20 and briefly discussed here. Some activities listed here are Oracle's extensions to BPEL that you will not find in other BPEL engines. The BPEL language has a standard way for vendors to add nonstandard extensions to the language. Oracle has used this extension mechanism to add a number of useful activities that developers can embed in their BPEL processes to run on Oracle's BPEL engine. Other engines would simply ignore those unknown extensions—however, they would consider the process definitions valid. Needless to say, such extensions on the one hand add possibly valuable functionality while limiting the cross-container portability on the other.

Terminate is a powerful activity: It immediately ends execution of the process instance, performs no fault handling or compensation, returns no replies to consumers, and completely concludes the instance. The Exit activity—introduced in BPEL 2.0—replaces Terminate.

Empty is not powerful at all—it does what its name suggests, which is nothing at all. Empty is a no-operation instruction (like null; in PL/SQL) and can be used when you want nothing to be done but need an activity, for example, as a temporary placeholder for activities that will be added later on or as the contents of a fault handler.

Wait instructs the BPEL engine to halt processing for a certain specified period or until a certain deadline is reached. Note that the wait only applies to the branch it is in; processing can continue in parallel branches.

BPEL 2.0 has added many new elements to the BPEL language, including RepeatUntil, ForEach, If, Exit, Validate, ExtensionActivity, and Rethrow. It also introduces a very useful repeatEvery feature to onAlarm event handlers and a TerminationHandler.

FlowN is an Oracle extension to BPEL that allows a dynamically determined number of parallel branches to be executed on all elements in a collection. FlowN is similar to the BPEL 2.0 ForEach activity that can also execute a dynamically calculated number of steps, either sequentially or in parallel. ForEach is functionally richer—it not only can do either sequential or parallel processing, but also can end as soon as an indicated minimum number of parallel branches has completed. The latter would be useful, for example, if we want to solicit quotes from a number of vendors and as soon as we have at least three quotes in, we can continue with the process.

Validate explicitly validates the contents of one or more variables in the BPEL process against their XSD definitions. When a violation is detected, the BPEL engine will throw a bpelx:invalidVariables run-time fault. Note that Validate was added as a standard activity to the BPEL 2.0 specification.

Java Embedding allows us to add Java code to a BPEL process—typically small snippets of Java that may call out to more complex objects living in the same JVM as the SOA Suite or through remote EJB calls, even to objects external to the JVM. The Java code has access to the variables of the BPEL process. Exceptions thrown in the Java code are translated to BPEL faults and can be handled using the BPEL fault-handling mechanism. Java Embedding seems especially useful for nonreusable complex calculations, special validations, or additional logging. The ADF-BC and EJB Service Adapters also allow interaction between BPEL processes and SDO-enabled Java objects, whereas the Spring Java component supports simple interaction with POJOs (Plain Old Java Objects). Chapter 12 in this book discusses the interaction between SOA composite applications and Java in more detail.

(Continued)

Signal and *ReceiveSignal* are Oracle-specific extensions to BPEL for the coordination between Master and Detail processes. This coordination is much like a lightweight alternative for correlated asynchronous services. The book's wiki describes how these activities can be used.

Create Entity, *Bind Entity,* and *Remove Entity* are activities that provide support for entity variables in SDO (Service Data Objects) format that are bound to an underlying data service provider—for example, an ADF-BC SDO-enabled Web Service or an EJB. An entity variable acts as a data handle to access and plug in different data provider service technologies behind the scenes. During compilation and run time, the BPEL engine delegates data operations to the underlying data provider service. When dehydrating the BPEL process instance, only the unique key that is needed to link up with the data service is stored, not the current values in the variable. See Chapter 21 for more details on SDO.

Phase is not really a BPEL activity—it is the representation of a BPEL design pattern using two layers of process design and implementation: the first layer is the abstract description of a certain step in the process, including the scopes, and the second layer is the specific implementation of that step.

Transformation is not really a BPEL activity either, even though it looks that way in the Component Palette. It is a specially configured Assign activity with a developer-friendly editor that helps us specify XML transformations (XSLT) for variables in the BPEL process, as we saw in the previous chapter. A transform assigns null values to target parts of the variables that aren't included in the transformation. Assign doesn't have this behavior.

FIGURE 6-20. *Miscellaneous BPEL activities*

Dealing with and Compensating for Exceptional Circumstances

Although, of course, we would like to think that everything in our BPEL processes always happens according to our plan for a happy flow, in actual practice that is unlikely to happen. Several types of faults and exceptions are bound to occur and should be catered to. Sometimes we can recover from exceptions—by retrying an operation after a little waiting time or through an alternative execution path. However, some exceptions we have to accept as irrecoverable. For a process instance that runs into such an exception, we may need to roll back some of the work that was already done by the process before it failed with the exception. In BPEL terminology that is called *compensation*.

Handling Exceptions in BPEL Processes

We can discern a number of exception categories—from fairly technical to more functional and business process-oriented.

At a rather technical level, we have to prepare for the unavailability of infrastructure components or other technical problems with services invoked from the BPEL process.

The external references may also return (predefined) business exceptions in response to the calls from our process, in the form of SOAP faults as specified in the WSDL for the service. Business exceptions are normal situations in business processes, ranging from "the product on order is sold out" and "credit card payment is not validated by the card issuer" to "the type of appointment requested is not available at St. Matthews."

Between these categories is the type of fault that is returned due to validation errors ("the XML request message does not comply with the XSD definition") and security issues ("the authentication failed" and "you are not authorized to invoke this service"). Our BPEL process can also cause faults because of programming errors (for example, by performing erroneous XPath operations).

Finally, the last category of exceptions is the type of exception we willingly throw to cause the current scope to be immediately terminated—almost a programmer's trick for want of a break activity in BPEL.

If one of the exceptions described previously occurs in a BPEL process—and we do not catch it—the process instance ends up in a faulted state. If the instance is synchronously invoked by a partner, the partner will receive a SOAP fault as a reply. If the instance is part of an asynchronous conversation, its invoker will continue to wait for the response message because there won't be one.

Let's see how we catch faults in a BPEL process—to prevent faults from causing a process to fault out.

Catching Faults

The main process activity, as well as every scope in a BPEL process, can have a faultHandler associated with it that contains one or more Catch activities that can each handle a specific type of fault (or all faults) when it occurs in the scope they are defined against—or in one of that scope's descendants or nested scopes. Each fault type in a BPEL process is identified through its name. Catch activities specify the fault type they want to catch through that name. Here's an example of a Catch for the standard fault selectionFailure (defined in the namespace http://schemas.xmlsoap.org/ws/2003/03/business-process/, represented here by the prefix bpws), which is thrown, for example, when an XPath expression has returned an empty result:

```
<faultHandlers>
  <catch faultName="bpws:selectionFailure">
    <sequence>
      <empty name="HandleSelectionFailure_gracefully"/>
      <terminate name="Terminate_process_isNOTgraceful"/>
    </sequence>
  </catch>
</faultHandlers>
```

The BPEL 1.1 standard specifies 11 standard faults, all in the same namespace: selectionFailure, conflictingReceive, conflictingRequest, mismatchedAssignmentFailure, joinFailure, forcedTermination, correlationViolation, uninitializedVariable, repeatedCompensation, and invalidReply. All these faults are typeless, meaning they don't have associated messageTypes and a Catch activity for these faults should not specify a fault variable.

Other faults have data associated with them—for example, the run-time faults thrown by the BPEL run-time engine as the result of problems with the running of the BPEL service component or the Web Services it invokes. A number of such run-time faults is predefined: bindingFault, remoteFault, and replayFault. These faults are included in the http://schemas.oracle.com/bpel/ extension namespace. They are associated with the messageType RuntimeFaultMessage, which contains three parts—each of type string—called code, summary, and detail, respectively.

A Catch activity for a fault that has associated data can specify a faultVariable that will be initialized with the fault's data when the Catch is activated. Figure 6-21 shows the RegisterPatientData scope with a number of fault handlers defined against it. One of them is the following Catch that is defined to intercept a remoteFault. The RemoteFaultMessage variable used here needs to be defined based on the message type associated with the fault. In this case, we need to add the RuntimeFault. wsdl with the required messageType to our project:

```
<scope name="RegisterPatientData">
  <variables>
    <variable name="RemoteFaultMessage"
              messageType="bpelx:RuntimeFaultMessage"/>
  </variables>
  <faultHandlers>
    <catch faultName="bpelx:remoteFault"
           faultVariable="RemoteFaultMessage">
      <empty name="HandleRemoteFault_butHow"/>
      ... additional BPEL activities that handle the
      ... they can access the fault's details in RemoteFaultMessage
    </catch>
  </faultHandlers>
```

In addition to fault-specific Catch elements, we can make use of the catchAll—similar to "when others" in PL/SQL and "catch(Throwable e)" in Java. When no fault-specific Catch is around to take care of the current fault, this all-purpose safety net steps in to handle it. We can find out the name of the fault our catchAll is dealing with using the Oracle BPEL-specific XPath function bpelx:getFaultAsString(), which we can use, for example, to assign the name of the fault to a local variable.

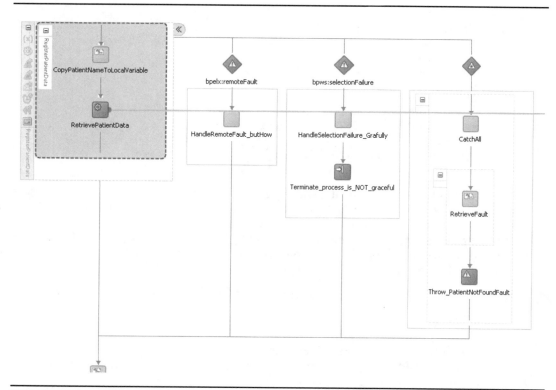

FIGURE 6-21. *BPEL scope RegisterPatientData with FaultHandlers*

So far we have discussed faults that originate in our external partners or in the BPEL run-time engine. There is another category of faults: The faults defined in our own process and thrown in our own logic. These faults are used to control the flow in the BPEL process. By throwing a fault, we interrupt the execution of a scope and hand control to a fault handler for that type of fault. Thus, we can make out-of-line jumps across the process that can be very useful. So in reality, it is more of a control (or flow) type of activity than an exception in the meaning we discussed before.

We use the BPEL Throw activity to instantiate a fault of a specific type. The type of the fault thrown does not need to be predefined in the WSDL or BPEL process—we can just throw any fault (name) we like. We can associate data with the fault by specifying the faultVariable attribute:

```
<scope name="RegisterPatientData">
  <variables>
    <variable name="localFaultNameString"
            messageType="client:PatientAppointmentServiceFaultMessage"/>
  </variables>
<faultHandlers>
  <catchAll>
    <sequence>
      <assign name="RetrieveFault">
```

```
         <copy>
            <from expression="concat('the original fault', ora:getFaultName())"/>
            <to variable="localFaultNameString" part="faultPayload"/>
         </copy>
      </assign>
   </sequence>
   <throw name="Throw_PatientNotFoundFault"
          faultName="client:PatientNotFoundFault"
          faultVariable="localFaultNameString"/>
   </sequence>
  </catchAll>
</faultHandlers>
```

The variable used as the fault variable needs to have been defined earlier in the scope or on some higher level. It needs to be based on a message type—not a simple or complex XML element—in one of the WSDL documents associated with the application.

Faults that are thrown like this can be caught by higher-level faultHandlers. In this example, the PatientNotFoundFault fault is thrown in the catchall handler of the RegisterPatientData scope. The fault is handled by a Catch action at the process level:

```
<process name="PatientAppointmentService"
...
  <variables>
    ...
    <variable name="faultNameString"
             messageType="client:PatientAppointmentServiceFaultMessage"/>
  </variables>
  ...
  <faultHandlers>
    <catch faultName="client:PatientNotFoundFault"
           faultVariable="faultNameString">
      <empty name="CatchFaultThenNothing"/>
    </catch>
  </faultHandlers>
```

When we run the PatientDataService and feed unknown patient data in, the PatientNotFound fault will be thrown because of the RemoteFault that occurs when the PatientDataService returns a fault. That fault is then caught at the process level. Figure 6-22 shows the results in the run-time console.

Sometimes we can recover from the faults—by retrying an operation after a little waiting time or through an alternative execution path. However, some exceptions we have to accept as irrecoverable. The best we can do for such faults is ensure that we turn them into meaningful faults as specified in the WSDL, with relevant associated data, and inform the consumer of the BPEL process. The latter is done in one of two ways, depending on whether the BPEL process was invoked synchronously or asynchronously. In the synchronous case, the fault is returned via the Reply activity:

```
<faultHandlers>
   <catch faultName="client:PatientNotFoundFault"
          faultVariable="faultNameString">
```

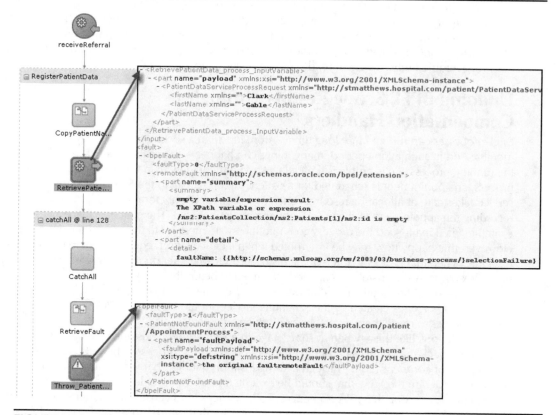

FIGURE 6-22.   *Throwing and catching a business fault, defined inside the BPEL process*

```
  <reply name="reportAppointmentFault"
         partnerLink="PatientAppointmentService"
         portType="client:PatientAppointmentService" operation="process"
         faultName="client:PatientNotFoundFault"
         variable="faultNameString"/>
  </catch>
</faultHandlers>
```

In the case of asynchronous conversation, the BPEL process sends a response to the consumer by calling an operation on the callback portType. If the process wants to communicate about faults with asynchronous consumers, it should specify the callback portType to include an operation that deals with such messages. Note that a third way to communicate a fault in a service is through a notification—an e-mail or chat message to a human operator or an event on the Event Delivery Network.

SOA Suite Fault Management Framework

Outside BPEL processes and SOA composite applications, at the level of the Fusion Middleware Control, we can use the Fault Management Framework to also catch faults that occurred in BPEL processes or other service components. This framework allows us to define fault policy bindings that prescribe automatic actions to be taken when a certain fault occurs. Such automated actions include retrying the faulted operation, executing Java logic that may provide an alternative workaround, and engaging a human administrator to handle the exception. The Fusion Middleware Control provides insight into all exceptions and allows the administrator to recover from recoverable faults. You will read more on this functionality in Chapter 16.

Undoing BPEL Scope Results Through Compensation Handlers

BPEL processes can run for fairly long times—from less than a second to hours, days, or even months. And in such a long period, many things can happen—things that may have an impact on the running process. An example is the PatientAppointmentService: In the early stages of the BPEL process, an appointment is scheduled for a patient through a call to the SchedulerService. That service takes care of allocating resources such as a room and a doctor for the appointment and recording the appointment in the agendas of all people involved. The patient is then notified—for example, via e-mail—and the process goes into hibernate mode until the time of the appointment. However, that happy flow may be interrupted when a cancellation request is sent to the process instance. When that happens, some of the results produced earlier on in the process by scopes that have already been successfully completed may need to be undone. In this case, we cannot—nor do we need to—undo the notification that was sent to the patient. However, the allocation of resources and the agenda entries created by the SchedulerService should be undone. We need to free up those resources to make them available for other engagements.

For situations like this—when at some stage in a BPEL process instance we find out that we need to roll back the changes caused by earlier actions in the process—the BPEL specification has the concept of *compensation*. Through a compensation handler that we create for a certain scope, we program the logic that should be executed to undo the side effects produced by that scope. For every scope that makes changes, calls services, and causes transactions to occur, we should consider implementing a compensation handler that undoes those changes or at least takes the appropriate action. Note that an appropriate action to execute when a scope needs to be compensated could consist of sending an e-mail to an administrator instructing her to make certain manual service calls or even database changes in those cases where the services that were called do not expose a compensate or rollback operation.

It is important to realize that a compensation handler is only ever executed for a scope that has been completed successfully. Compensation handlers are executed automatically for scopes that have been completed successfully and are nested in a parent scope that contains another nested scope that caused the compensation itself (for example, by means of an exception). Scopes that already have completed may have committed transactions themselves or invoked services that completed transactions. Compensating for those local or remote transactions is not a simple technical rollback but usually a functional challenge that requires from external services that they publish compensation operations (unhire car, unallocate doctor, and so on).

We can also explicitly invoke compensation handlers through the compensateScope activity, which we can execute for a specific scope from a faultHandler or compensationHandler on the parent scope.

In the case of the PatientAppointmentService, we want to compensate for the appointment that has been scheduled when that appointment is cancelled (see Figure 6-23). The appointment needs to be unscheduled—the scheduler service needs to know that the appointment is cancelled and the allocated resources are freed up. The actions that need to be performed for the compensation are defined in the compensation handler that is defined against the scope that schedules the appointment:

```
<scope name="ScheduleAppointment">
    <variables>...</variables>
    <compensationHandler>
        <sequence name="UnscheduleAppointment">
            <assign name="AssignValuesForCallToUnschedule">...</assign>
            <invoke name="InvokeUnscheduleService" .../>
        </sequence>
    </compensationHandler>
</compensationHandler>
```

The parent scope contains a fault handler that catches the appointmentCancellation fault. When that fault is caught, the ScheduleAppointment scope is explicitly compensated. That results in that scope's compensation handler being invoked by the BPEL engine.

The onMessage branch in the Pick activity that listens for cancellation messages will throw the appointmentCancellation fault that indirectly results in the appointment being scheduled (see Figure 6-24).

Note that a compensateScope activity will only execute the compensation handler for the scope it explicitly targets. The compensation handlers for the nested scopes are not automatically called as well—these should be called by the compensation handler in the parent scope.

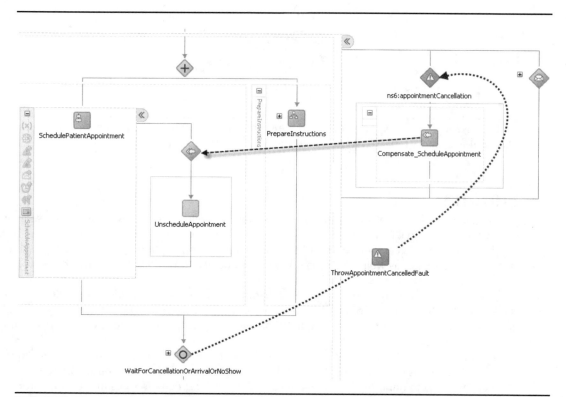

FIGURE 6-23. *The compensation handler defined on the ScheduleAppointment scope and invoked from the fault handler for the appointmentCancellation fault on the ScheduleNotifyAndWait scope*

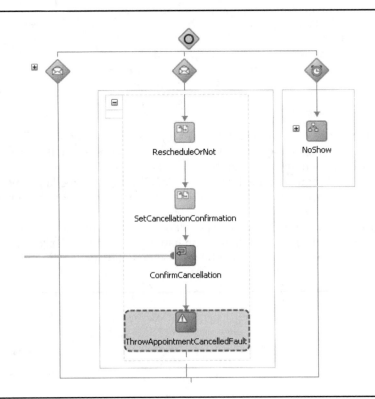

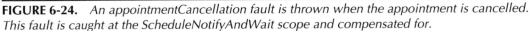

FIGURE 6-24. *An appointmentCancellation fault is thrown when the appointment is cancelled. This fault is caught at the ScheduleNotifyAndWait scope and compensated for.*

Summary

In this chapter we looked at some more advanced BPEL activities that help us to create coarse-grained composite services that invoke various finer-grained synchronous and asynchronous services. These activities are also helpful when we use BPEL to implement a longer-running business process that involves human actors as well as automated services. Chapter 10 will discuss the integration of human tasks in BPEL processes.

Correlation is an important BPEL mechanism that we discussed in this chapter. Correlation is used by the BPEL engine to direct incoming messages to already-running instances of BPEL processes. This allows consumers to update or interrupt existing instances or retrieve specific information about them.

The last part of the chapter introduced fault handling in BPEL processes and discussed the concept of compensation handlers that can be triggered upon business exceptions. These handlers are used to undo the business effects produced by specific scopes in the BPEL process instance that have already been executed.

The online chapter complement demonstrates in great detail and through step-by-step instructions how the BPEL processes outlined in this chapter are to be created, deployed, and executed.

CHAPTER
7

Mediator Service
for Straight Talk and
No Nonsense

ow that we have introduced BPEL as a service component type, we will move on to another SCA component type that often works together with BPEL components: the Mediator. This is an important component in the SOA Suite that takes on some of the core responsibilities described in Part I for the enterprise service bus.

Under close scrutiny, one could argue that all that is happening in SOA composite applications is a more or less constant flow of XML messages—for example, the incoming request message that flows to a service component, one or more messages from that service component that flow to adapter services or other service components, and eventually a response message that flows back to the invoker. Mediator components facilitate these XML message flows in composite applications—by performing validations, transformations, both content- and header-based routing and filtering on messages, as well as adaptation from synchronous to asynchronous, and vice versa, and various other operations.

In this chapter, we will see how to use the Mediator in composite applications. The Mediator will help us connect mutually incompatible components and services. We will also see how the Mediator component is the perfect way to introduce entry points as well as exits to our composite applications through the use of adapter services, without creating dependencies between the adapter services and the service components in our application.

The file adapter is one of the technology adapters that is typically used in conjunction with a Mediator component. It can read incoming files as well as initiate new instances of composite applications to process the contents from these files. It can also write message out to files. This chapter introduces the file adapter and demonstrates how it can be used together with the Mediator.

Note that the online chapter complement available on the book's wiki contains detailed instructions and more screenshots illustrating individual steps in the examples outlined in this chapter.

The Mediator: From the Real World to the World Inside the SOA Suite

St. Matthews interacts with the outside world (patients, suppliers, healthcare providers, and so on) using hundreds of requests and events every day—people calling, e-mailing, writing letters, faxing, or visiting in person with specific questions, commercial offers, or complaints. They want to speak to doctors, managers, lab staff, IT specialists, or other hospital staff. The hospital has a pool with secretarial staff trained in handling these requests. They perform a number of very important functions, for both the callers and the professionals that will eventually deal with the request. These functions include:

- Screening crank calls and rejecting requests that are irrelevant, disallowed, incomplete, or impossible to deal with; they will make a log entry of each call.

- Dealing with callers from many different backgrounds, different terminologies (doctors, chiropractors, dentists, ambulance drivers, teenage mothers), and various languages; the switchboard acts as the first point of contact for external parties as well as between staff from different departments inside the hospital.

- Ensuring that all required information is assembled before the request is passed on, to enable the professional who will have to process the request to do this as efficiently and effectively as possible.

- Routing the request to the right professional at St. Matthews in the internally agreed-upon way. Depending on the type of request and the professional it is forwarded to, that might mean using a certain paper form, entering the request into an internal application, or e-mailing a free-format message.

- Possibly following up on the request. The caller may have held the line, waiting for an answer. Alternatively, the requester can be called, mailed, e-mailed, or faxed back with a response to the request. Note that the response is sent in the format prescribed by the communication protocol of St. Matthews; this frequently means substantially rewording the reply from the hospital professional.

The pool is staffed at least from 7 A.M. until 8 P.M., thus making the hospital much more available than any individual professional could ever be. Outside these hours, a voice response system is active that allows recording of requests. Multiple requests that end up with the same professional can be handled simultaneously by different members of the pool.

One important consequence of the pool is the insulation it provides between external parties requesting services from the hospital and the professionals in the hospital ultimately rendering those services. The internal workings of the hospital can remain invisible to the caller—he does not need to know or understand them, and when they change, it will have no effect on his next call. Besides, the specialists will have more time left to do what they do best: treat patients instead of making appointments and so on. This insulation makes life so easy that many professionals working in the hospital also use the pool to request services, rather than approaching their colleagues themselves.

The Mediator Inside the SOA Suite

A Mediator performs a similar role in the SOA Suite as this hospital switchboard: It is the ultimate messenger boy. Incoming requests to the services published in the hospital's business domains can be dealt with in very much the same way as the requests are processed by the pool of secretarial staff.

Mediators can help provide a friendly interface for consumers: They can transform incoming XML messages in a consumer-friendly format to the usually more specific, formal, strict format mandated by some internal service that the messages are routed to. The responses can also be transformed by the Mediator to a format that is easier for the client to understand before being sent back—very much like the hospital switchboard rephrasing patients' requests and doctors' replies.

Frequently we have little or no control over the XSD of one side of message exchanges (that is, of the *external* services we call). For example, when adapter services such as the database adapter, file adapter, or AQ adapter either initiate the exchange or are at the receiving end, the XSD representation of the message structure is typically generated for us. The same is the case with messages sent from the composite application to external services: We do not always control the XSD for the messages accepted by those referenced services. An important function of the Mediator is to provide a mapping between the (canonical) model used within the composite applications (or even within the enterprise) and the various event and message structures delivered or required by services outside the composites.

The Mediator can receive XML messages, validate them, and route them based on their contents to the appropriate target service at the current endpoint for that service. The Mediator can also call one or more other services using as input a combination of the original request message and the responses received from earlier service calls. It implements the so-called VETRO (Validate, Enrich, Transform, Route, and Operate) pattern.

The Mediator can call both synchronous/asynchronous and fire-and-forget services and provide a bridge between these two. It provides its own operations either synchronously/asynchronously or as fire-and-forget, as desired. A Mediator component can also process business events in addition to receiving service invocations—more on events in Chapter 9—and route the event payload to the appropriate service provider. Instead of routing messages to other services, it can also broadcast business events.

Mediators work well with adapter services that support alternative means of initiating service execution than from formal invocation alone. Adapter services can feed data into the composite application picked up from external sources such as files on the file system or an FTP server, from e-mails, from new or changed database records, from queues or topics in MQ Series, Oracle Advanced Queuing, or Java Messaging Service (JMS). Execution of the Mediator is not started in this case because of externally originated service calls but by the adapter service that was triggered to process some data from an external source. For example, the arrival of a file in a designated directory may trigger the execution of a composite application. In a similar way, Mediators work with adapter services to feed data to external targets, such as a file, database, e-mail, or queue.

Mediator components can be used to implement a variety of integration patterns, such as service virtualization, service aggregation, publish and subscribe, fan-in, and fan-out. The Mediator plays an essential role in achieving decoupling and flexibility as well as reuse—the essential ingredients for a successful SOA implementation.

Enterprise Service Bus: Mediator vs. Oracle Service Bus

Oracle SOA Suite contains two components that implement many characteristics of what the industry has dubbed the *enterprise service bus* (pattern). An enterprise service bus (ESB) provides decoupling between senders of service requests and the service providers. Among the operations that we typically associate with an ESB are reliable messaging (receive and send onward—do not hang on to a message any longer than you need to ensure it is delivered), VETRO (Validate, Enrich, Transform, Route, Operate), service virtualization, split and merge messages, queuing to handle unavailability of the service provider or throttle peak loads, error handling, support for various message exchange patterns, and providing some adaptation, for example, from an asynchronous provider to a synchronous requester.

The ESB pattern can be applied at various levels in the organization. We can discern, for example, between the application level (for the message flow between components of the same application), the domain level, the enterprise level, and the external level (for message exchanges with parties outside the corporation).

Oracle SOA Suite 11*g* contains the Oracle Service Bus (OSB), the next incarnation of BEA's AquaLogic Service Bus (ALSB), as well as the Mediator component, the next generation of the Oracle Enterprise Service Bus (OESB) that was introduced in the 10.1.3 release of the SOA Suite.

The Mediator is tightly integrated into the SOA Suite. It is primarily an intracomposite mediation component that is deployed within a composite. OSB is often used to connect multiple domains within the enterprise as well as to provide a service interface with external parties.

This chapter discusses the Mediator component. In Chapter 13, we will take a close look at the Oracle Service Bus.

Note that the execution of a Mediator (instance) is typically very lightweight when compared, for example, with a (stateful) BPEL process instance.

In short, the Mediator service engine provides a lightweight framework to mediate both at the data and protocol levels between various producers and consumers of services and events within the SCA service fabric and on its boundaries. It is the "man in the middle" between adapter services, service components such as BPEL and Human Task, and external parties.

Note that the use of Mediator as man in the middle is not required per se by SOA Suite. However, it is a best practice and provides several benefits that are discussed in this chapter.

Processing Files with Appointment Requests

Some family doctors will send the requests for appointments for their patients once per day in a single file with comma-separated records. This file can be uploaded via a website or sent as an e-mail attachment to a central e-mail address at St. Matthews. These files are collected in a shared directory and need to be processed. The individual appointment requests that possibly arrive in batch files need to be turned into calls to the Patient Appointment Service we discussed in the previous chapter.

Introducing the Mediator and the File Adapter: Routing and Transformation

Using the file adapter, we can create services with the capability to read incoming files and turn the records in these files into XML messages—or that write files in various formats based on inbound XML messages. The File Adapter Service we will create reads from files. It is wired to a Mediator component that routes incoming messages fed in by the file adapter to consuming services. The File Adapter Service could also start BPEL process instances; however, consider it a best practice to link adapter services to Mediators that perform forwarding and transformation of the XML messages produced by the adapter services.

The Mediator, in this case, routes the appointment requests retrieved from the files to the Patient Appointment Service. It will have to perform some message transformation because the structure and some of the data elements in the files are not perfectly matched with the Patient Appointment Service interface.

The file format was specified many years ago and is used by several hundreds of doctors. The format is a given, and is nonnegotiable. The service interface for the Patient Appointment Service was specified in the previous chapter. It was not specifically designed with these doctors and their files in mind, but we will work with it "as is." The Mediator will help us bridge this gap.

For our discussion here, we will assume a much simplified format for both the CSV file and the input message for the Patient Appointment Service.

NOTE
On the book's wiki, you will find the screenshots for all steps described in this section. The most important ones are included here as well.

File Adapter Service for Reading the Files with Appointment Requests

Creating the File Adapter Service is a simple wizard-driven process. Let's first run JDeveloper and create a new SOA application with an empty composite. Next, drag and drop File Adapter in the SOA Component Palette to the Exposed Services lane on the left side of the Composite Editor.

The Adapter Service Configuration Wizard opens, as shown in Figure 7-1. It lets us configure a service based on the file adapter, described by a WSDL and supported by an XSD.

Obviously, the CSV files uploaded by the doctors do not adhere to an XSD specification. Fortunately, the file adapter can be configured to take files in CSV format and produce XML messages from the records in the files that can then be picked up by a Mediator for further processing. Note that in this case the Mediator is not invoked by an external party but rather triggered by the File Adapter Service that itself is kicked off whenever polling reveals a new file present to be processed. Also note that a single file can trigger the instantiation by the File Adapter Service of multiple instances of the composite application in the case of a file that contains multiple records, where each record results in an XML message that triggers a composite instance. This pattern—one file is dissected to trigger multiple instances—is called *debatching*.

The specific file format of the incoming file does not need to dictate the request message structure specified for the BPEL process that the contents of the file eventually are fed into, because the Mediator will do the mapping or transformation between the two structures. If the file structure changes, or if it turns out that the BPEL process can only handle selected records from the files,

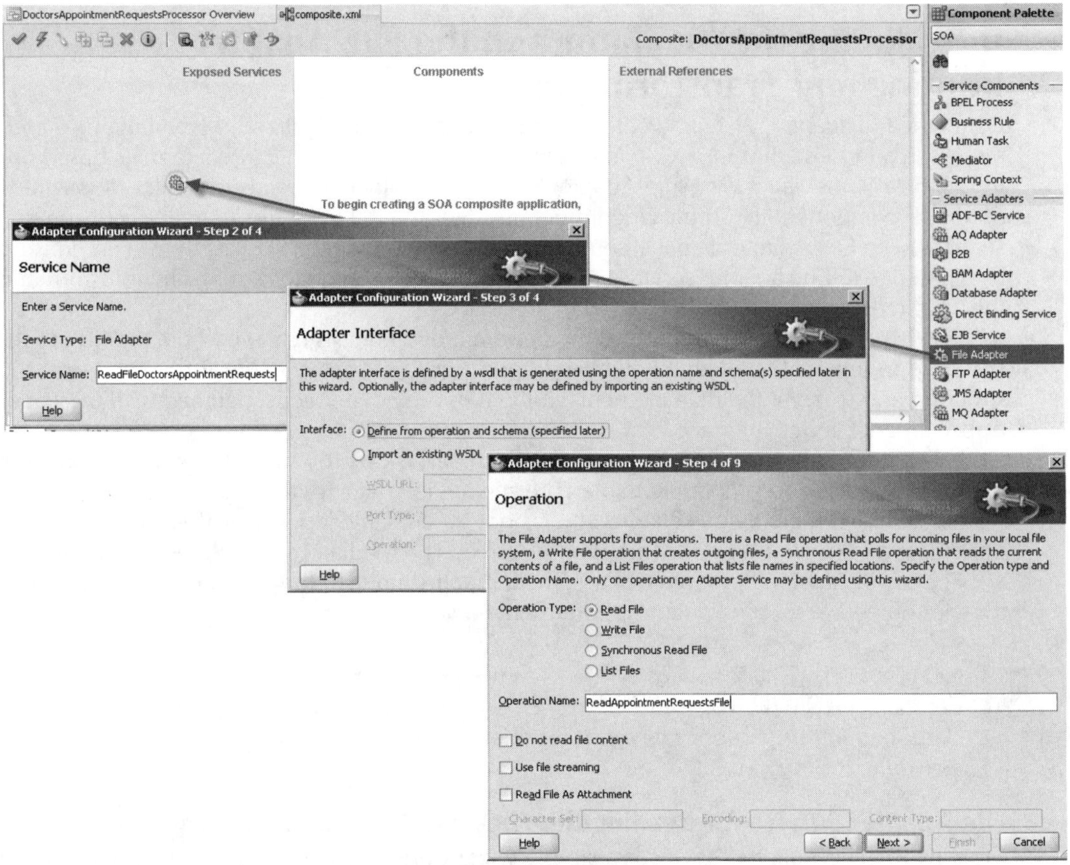

FIGURE 7-1. *Adding an inbound file adapter service to the composite application*

or if we decide that we want to audit or log the records that we process from the file, we can add those capabilities to the Mediator without having to modify the BPEL process. In general, anything we can do with a Mediator is probably best done in a Mediator, rather than in, for example, a BPEL process. A Mediator is faster and lighter weight in terms of resource usage.

The File Adapter Service is configured through the wizard (see Figure 7-2). We have to specify the structure and format of the file—single message or multiple messages (debatch or not), single record type or multiple record types. In this case, the file contains multiple messages (records) of a single record type. Next up are the location (directory) from where the service should read the files as well as the name pattern for the files to process. This name pattern is used as a filter that determines which of the files in the directory should be processed by the File Adapter Servicer. Both "." (single character) and "*" (any number of characters) can be used as wildcards in the name pattern. We can also use regular expression operators to create more complex filename filter expressions.

We should specify a logical directory name, rather than a physical directory path, as to not couple the service definition to a deployment characteristic. In the composite.xml file or through the environment-specific configuration plan (or even at run time through the Fusion Middleware Control), we can specify the physical directory with which the logical directory is associated. More on this in Chapter 17. We can indicate that files in subdirectories should be processed as well—by marking the check box Process Files Recursively.

We typically do not want the file adapter to start processing immediately when the file first appears: It may take some time before the file is completely transferred, especially when it is large. By setting a wait interval, we instruct the file adapter to postpone the processing of the file until that interval has passed.

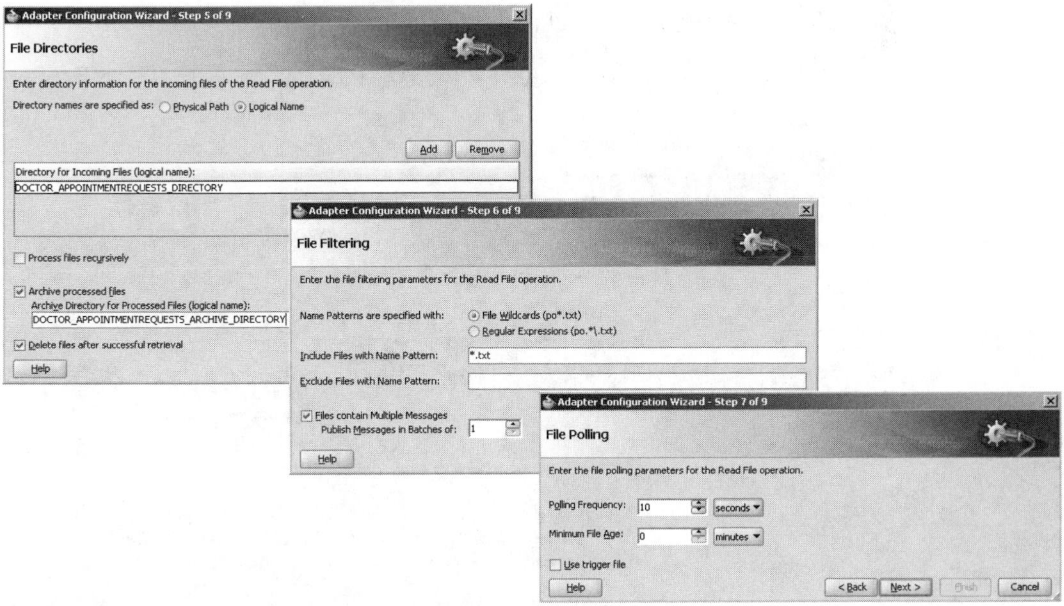

FIGURE 7-2.   *Configuring the File Adapter Service*

Files that have been processed by the File Adapter Service are usually removed from the directory where they were uploaded; this behavior is configured through the check box labeled "Delete Files?" If desired, we can have all files that have been processed archived to another directory for which we can again specify both the physical or the logical directory. Be careful not to archive into a subdirectory of the receiving directory *and* configure the adapter to recursively process files in subdirectories. That would be a snake eating its own tail and choking on it.

Then we can use the Native Format Builder to create a specially annotated XSD schema that describes the field and record delimiters and the structure of the record(s), as shown in Figure 7-3. This step does not need to be performed if the file contents are already in XML format. The easiest way to collect this information is by scanning a sample file that has the same structure as the files that this File Adapter Service will process when deployed. When we browse for such a sample file and locate it, the Native Format Builder will do a best effort so as to prepopulate the field definitions.

We can further refine this structure, for example, by providing field names that will be used for XML element names (see Figure 7-4). Based on this information, the builder creates the XSD that describes the XML message created from the records in the file.

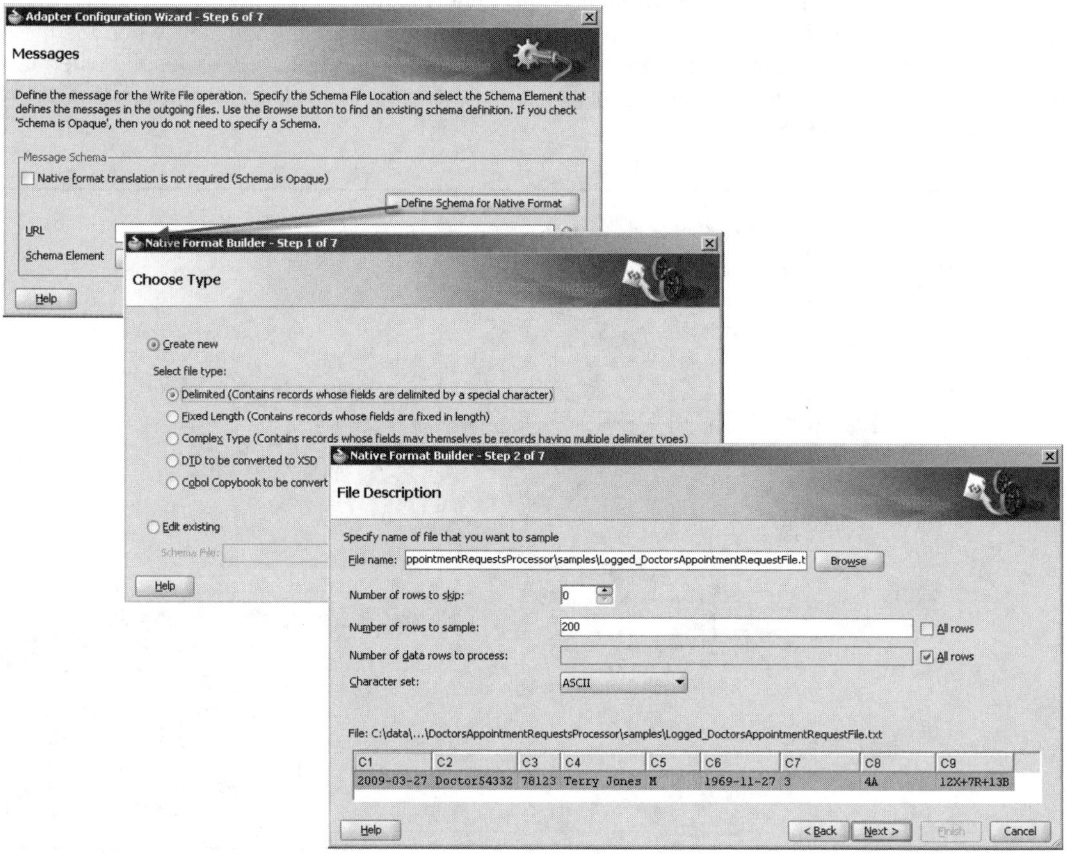

FIGURE 7-3. *Using the Native Format Builder to create an XSD for the CSV file format*

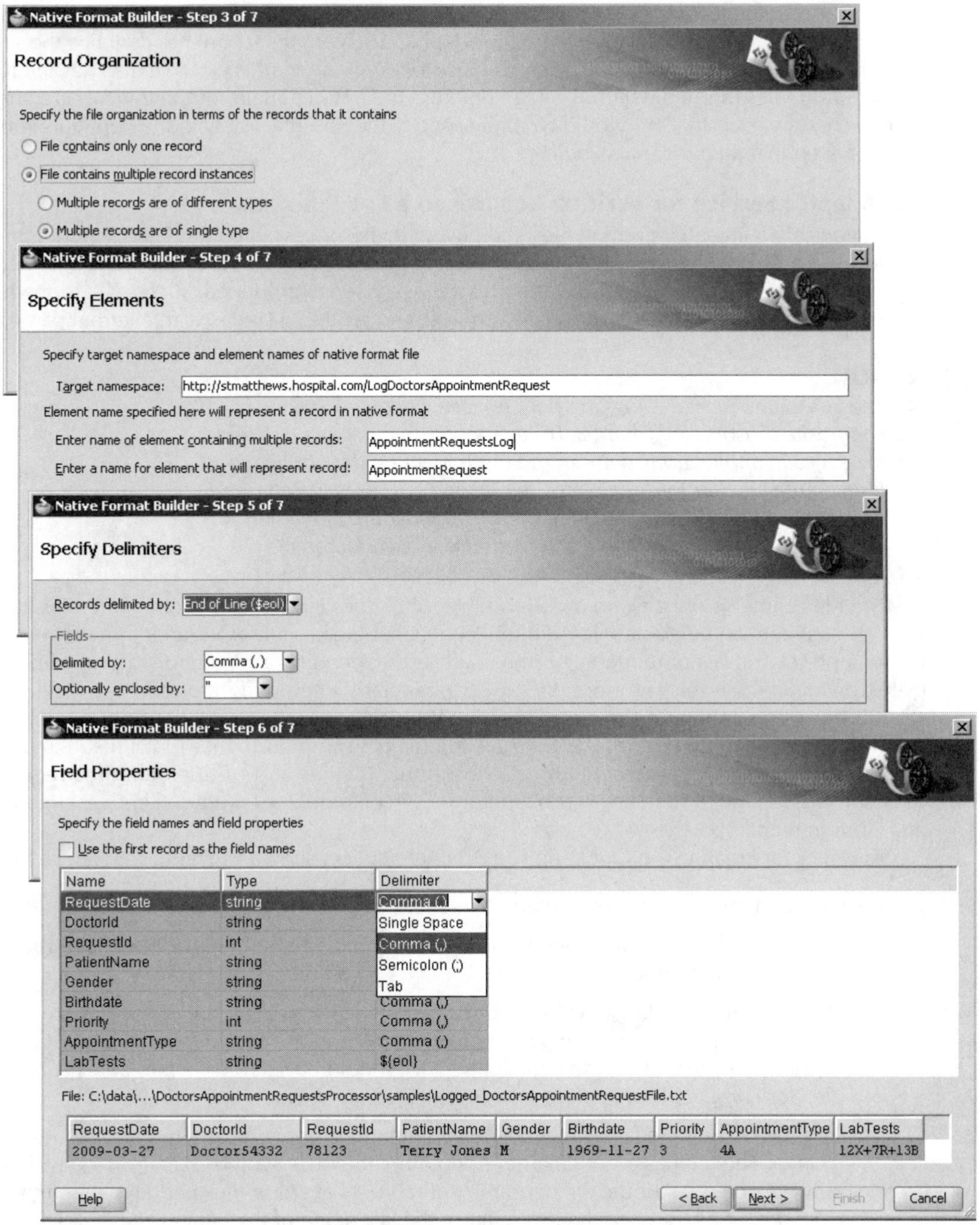

Native Format Builder - Step 3 of 7   ⊠

Record Organization

Specify the file organization in terms of the records that it contains

○ File contains only one record
◉ File contains multiple record instances
  ○ Multiple records are of different types
  ◉ Multiple records are of single type

Native Format Builder - Step 4 of 7   ⊠

Specify Elements

Specify target namespace and element names of native format file

Target namespace: `http://stmatthews.hospital.com/LogDoctorsAppointmentRequest`

Element name specified here will represent a record in native format

Enter name of element containing multiple records: `AppointmentRequestsLog`

Enter a name for element that will represent record: `AppointmentRequest`

Native Format Builder - Step 5 of 7   ⊠

Specify Delimiters

Records delimited by: `End of Line ($eol)` ▼

┌─Fields──────────────────────────────────
Delimited by: `Comma (,)` ▼
Optionally enclosed by: `"` ▼

Native Format Builder - Step 6 of 7   ⊠

Field Properties

Specify the field names and field properties

☐ Use the first record as the field names

Name	Type	Delimiter		
RequestDate	string	Comma (,) ▼		
DoctorId	string	Single Space		
RequestId	int	Comma (,)		
PatientName	string	Semicolon (;)		
Gender	string	Tab		
Birthdate	string	Comma (,)		
Priority	int	Comma (,)		
AppointmentType	string	Comma (,)		
LabTests	string	${eol}		

File: C:\data\...\DoctorsAppointmentRequestsProcessor\samples\Logged_DoctorsAppointmentRequestFile.txt

RequestDate	DoctorId	RequestId	PatientName	Gender	Birthdate	Priority	AppointmentType	LabTests
2009-03-27	Doctor54332	78123	Terry Jones	M	1969-11-27	3	4A	12X+7R+13B

Help   < Back   Next >   Finish   Cancel

FIGURE 7-4.   *Further fine-tuning the Native Schema Builder*

When we close the wizard, the service is displayed in the Composite Editor. The WSDL and XSD files are generated as well as the ReadFileDoctorsAppointmentRequests_file.jca file that contains the configuration details for the file adapter. The composite.xml file contains the service element for the File Adapter Service ReadFileDoctorsAppointmentRequests. It also has the JCA binding properties through which we can configure the physical path for the logical directory used. Note, however, that we would typically specify the physical paths in the configuration plans or even maintain them at run time.

File Adapter Service for Writing Records to a Log File

In addition to reading all incoming files and having them processed by the Patient Appointment Service, the hospital wants to track all appointment requests that are received in this manner in a log file. Especially in the early stages after this new service is introduced, such a file is deemed necessary for clearing up cases of missing requests and settling disputes with external parties.

> **NOTE**
> *The SOA Suite provides logging policies (see Chapter 15) and composite sensors (see Chapter 16) to support tracking actions and messages in applications without (much) impact on the application. Using a file adapter for logging for debugging purposes is not a best practice because it is too intrusive on the application. However, it is a good technical demonstration of how to use a file adapter.*

The file adapter is once again our friend: Not only does it *read* files, it can write files as well. We can configure an outgoing File Adapter Service that creates a file-per-appointment request, a file for a preset number of requests, or one that keeps appending a record for each request to an ever-growing file. It is this latter option we are particularly interested in for now.

It is easiest to configure the Native Format Builder using a sample file of the output format we desire. The first thing to do, therefore, is to create a sample file that looks just like the log file we want this service to create for us. Our sample file has end-of-line delimited records with comma-separated fields of Date, Doctor Id, First Name, Last Name, Gender, Urgency, and AppointmentType.

The steps for creating the Outgoing File Adapter Service, shown in Figure 7-5, are as follows:

1. Drag and drop File Adapter to the References lane in the Composite Editor.

2. Configure the File Adapter Service using the sample file for creating the XSD through the Native Format Builder.

3. Make sure to use a Logical Directory name when specifying the directory where the log file is to be created. At some point between now and the deployment of the application the property created for the logical directory should be set, referring to an existing directory *on the file system on which the SOA Suite is running*.

   For now we will create a single log file with entries for every appointment request we receive. The file has a static name: AppointmentRequestsLog.txt. Later on we will see how we could distribute the appointment requests over log files per day, appointment type, doctor ID, or even the first letter of the last name of the patient.

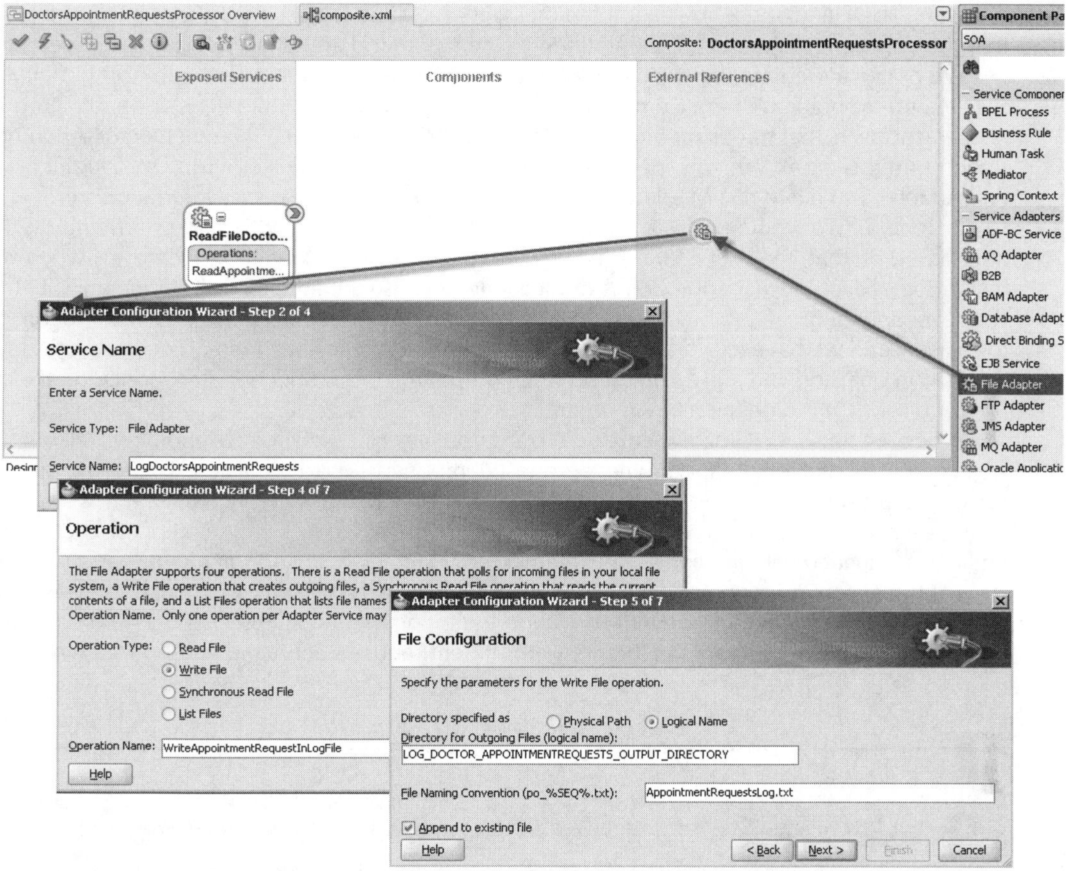

FIGURE 7-5.   *Creating the outbound File Adapter Service*

4. To indicate that the service should add a record to an existing file, we need to check the check box labeled Append To Existing File.

5. Specify the format of the log file by sampling a file with the desired comma-delimited or alternative format and have the XSD generated by the Native Format Builder.

The composite.xml file is updated with a new reference for the outbound File Adapter Service. Other components can create wires to this reference and thus call the File Adapter Service.

Using a Mediator to Process the Doctor's Incoming Appointment Request Files

At this point, we have an incoming File Adapter Service that sends XML messages based on the files it reads—but that go nowhere—and an outgoing File Adapter Service that is ready to process XML messages and send them into a file. However, nothing is connected, so nothing will happen when we deploy the composite application as is.

It is time to bring a Mediator onto the stage that will link the Incoming File (Service) with the Outgoing Log File (Service) by taking the messages from the former and, after transforming them into the appropriate structure, routing them to the latter (and any other relevant target services).

We create a Mediator by dragging a Mediator service component from the Component Palette and dropping it in the Components lane in the Composite Editor—as done in Figure 7-6. A dialog appears that has us provide a name for the Mediator service (HandleDoctorsAppointment Request, in this case). We will specify the interface later—by means of wiring the output from the File Adapter Service to this Mediator, so we choose the template Specify Interface Later.

In general, we would prefer a "contract first design" approach, where we start with the XSD and, based on that, the WSDL that specifies the interface of the Mediator. However, when we use technology adapters, that approach is not feasible because the adapter will derive an XSD from whatever source or target it accesses—the XML structure derived from the CSV file structure in this case—and we have to work with it. When the Mediator sits between a Technology Adapter Service on one side and a predefined service component or another adapter service on the other, it has no room left to define its own contract.

When we finish the Create Mediator Wizard, the files HandleDoctorsAppointmentRequest. mplan and HandleDoctorsAppointmentRequest.componentType are created. The former file contains the definition of the Mediator's internal operations, and is nearly empty at this stage. The latter describes the Mediator as an SCA component, with its services and references. The composite. xml file is extended with the component element for HandleDoctorsAppointmentRequest. Note that we will not expose this component at the composite level, so no Service element is created for it.

In the Composite Editor, we will now wire the incoming file adapter service to the Mediator by simply dragging the ReadFileDoctorsAppointmentRequests Service diamond to the Mediator

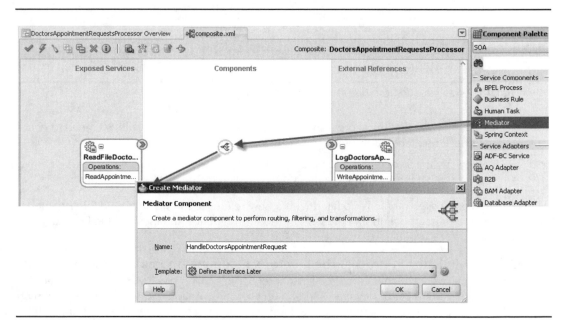

FIGURE 7-6. *Add Mediator HandleDoctorsAppointmentRequest to the composite application*

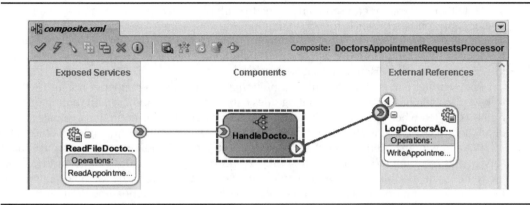

FIGURE 7-7. *Wire the Mediator to both inbound and outbound File Adapter Services*

(see Figure 7-7). Thus, we indicate that the service will send a request for every record (file) it processes to the Mediator. This request will have the structure prescribed in the XSD file created by the Native Format Builder.

At this point, we have specified that the File Adapter Service that reads doctor appointment request files from a central directory feeds the XML messages it creates from the records in those files into the Mediator. The input data structure for the Mediator is now known because it is based on the XSD produced by the File Adapter Service. We now need to specify what the Mediator should do with those XML messages. Where do we want each doctor's appointment request to go?

In this case, we want records of the appointment requests to be collected in one large log file. And, more importantly, we want each request to be sent to the Patient Appointment Service for processing, leading to a real appointment for a real patient.

We instruct the Mediator on where to send messages by configuring routing rules. The main parts of a routing rule are as follows:

- **Target service** The destination of the XML message, which is an operation on a component in the composite application or an external reference hooked into the composite application. Instead of a target service, we can also specify an event to be published or an echo operation to be performed; the latter would just return the transformed request.

- **Mapping** How should the input XML message be transformed into an XML format understood by the target service?

- **Filter Condition** (optional) What condition should the payload (content) or headers of the message satisfy in order for the message to be sent to this target service (content-based routing)?

Other optional elements of a routing rule are validation using a Schematron file, manipulation of message header properties, and a Java callout—a custom Java class that can be used for logging, auditing, message preparation and manipulation, and anything else before, during, or after the transformation and routing of the message.

Note that a Mediator can send a message to multiple target services, with a specific mapping and possibly a filter condition for each target service. These target services can all be called at the same time (in parallel) or sequentially—where the next call is only made when the previous call is complete. The reply from one target service can be forwarded to another. More on this later in this chapter when we discuss message enrichment.

Routing rules can each have a filter condition that determines whether or not they will be followed. Additionally, one of the routing rules can be marked as the "default routing rule." This rule is activated when all other rules have a filter condition and this condition evaluates to false for all of them. The default routing rule is the "otherwise" case. It will step in when no other rule does.

We can wire the Mediator component to the LogDoctorsAppointmentRequests file adapter service and by doing so create a routing rule, as shown earlier in Figure 7-7. To further configure the routing rule, double-click the Mediator in the Composite Editor. The Mediator Editor opens. It lists a single operation—ReadAppointmentRequestsFile—under the heading Routing Rules. There is one routing rule within this operation—it targets the LogDoctorsAppointmentRequest. WriteAppointmentRequestInLogFile operation. New routing rules can be added by clicking the green plus icon.

The basics for the routing rule are defined. The link between input message and target service has been established. At this point, we can specify additional validation to be performed on the input message, over and above the XSD used to describe the message (which can but does not need to be explicitly validated), for example, because a target service has specific requirements that can only be met when the input message adheres to special validation rules. This validation is based on a Schematron XML validation document that can be associated with a specific part in the input message. For more information on Schematron, see www.schematron.com.

We do not have any special validation requirements. However, what we *do* need is a mapping from the input message—produced by the File Adapter Service according to the XSD created by the Native Format Builder—to the XML format prescribed by the XSD for the input message for the Log File Writer (and later on for the appointment service). Click the mapping icon to specify this mapping, as shown in Figure 7-8. The pop-up that appears allows us to select an existing Mapper file or create a new one. In this case, we will create a new one.

Make sure to provide a meaningful name for the Mapper file, one that clearly indicates what is being mapped to what. When the number of artifacts in the composite application starts to grow and the size of the team working on these artifacts increases, the use of meaningful, easy-to-interpret names is invaluable and saves a lot of time and frustration. In this case, a workable name could be doctorAppointmentRequestFromFileRoot_To_AppointmentRequestLog. xsl. The extension of this file indicates what a Mapper file really is: an XSLT stylesheet for transforming XML messages. You can both use the visual mapping editor as well as edit the raw XSLT source. XSLT stands for XML Stylesheet Language for Transformations, one of the core W3C standards for XML technology. Instead of using the visual mapping editor, you can switch to the Source view and program the mapping directly in XSLT. Some advanced transformation steps are not supported by the mapping editor and have to be written directly in the source. More on this later in the chapter and in Appendix B.

Note that XSLT Mapper files are, by default, placed in the XSL directory whereas generated XSD files are placed in the XSD directory of the composite. It is a good design practice to also use these directories for storing your own XSD and XSLT files.

The mapping editor opens (see Figure 7-9). When you create a Mapper file, you basically specify the XML conversion path from the source or input XSD to the target service's XSD. The left side of the mapping editor shows a tree structure representing the input XSD, and the right side shows a tree for the target XSD. You can create a mapping from elements and attributes in the

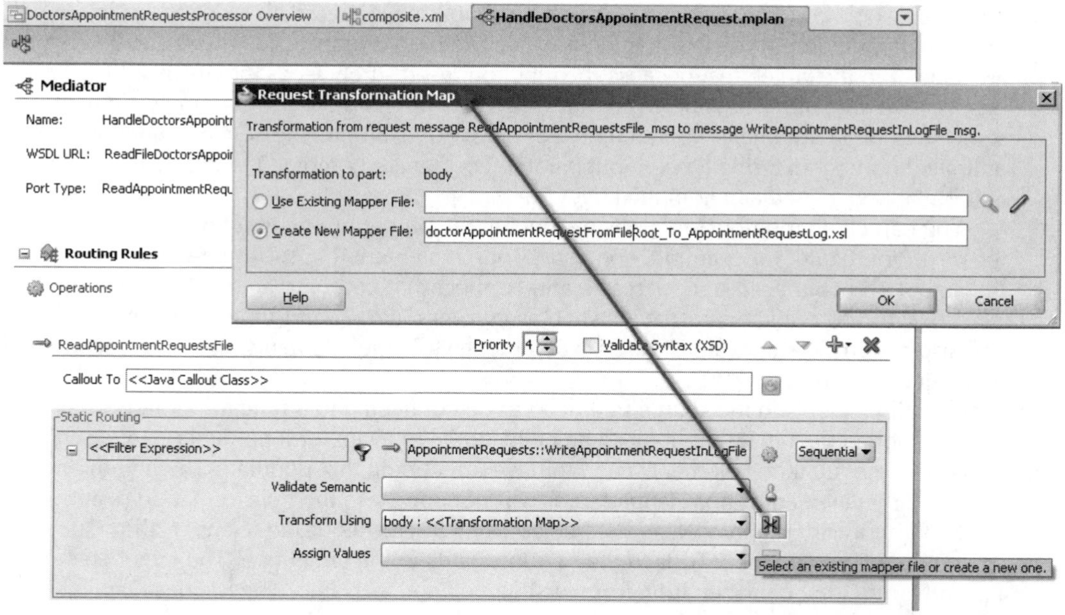

FIGURE 7-8. *Inspect the routing rule and create the message mapping*

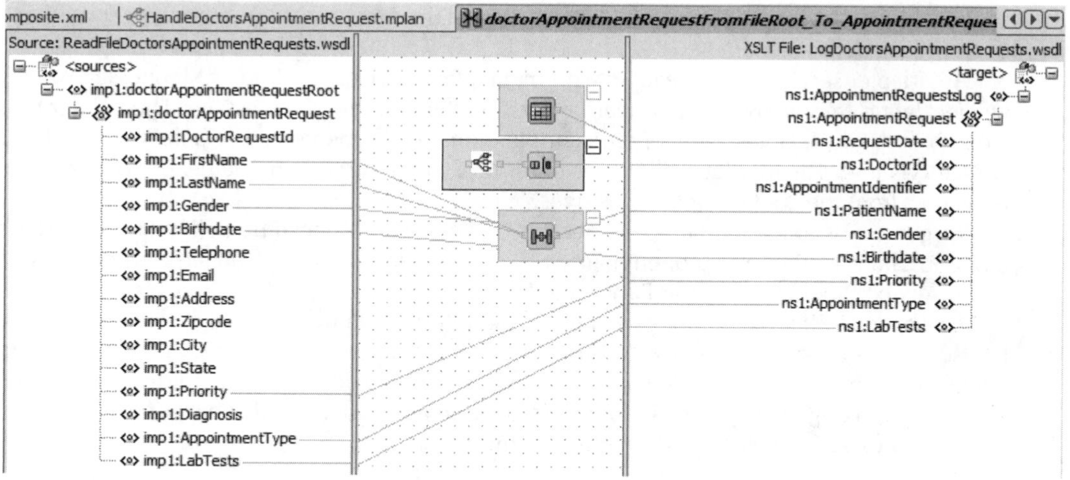

FIGURE 7-9. *The mapping editor for creating the transformation from the source message format to the target service's input message format*

source tree to elements and attributes in the target tree by dragging a source element and dropping it on the associated target element. Alternatively, you may drag XPath functions from the palette on the far right and drop those in the middle zone. The output of these functions can be connected to an element in the target tree, because the function result surely feeds into the resulting XML message we are putting together. The input for a function can consist of a single element from the source tree or a combination of multiple elements. For example, the concat() function can take an unlimited number of String-typed input parameters that are combined to produce a single result that is mapped to an element in the target tree.

You can chain multiple functions by making the output of one function one of the inputs for the next. You could, for example, connect a source element to a substring-before function, take the output and connect it to uppercase, and connect that output to a concat. Note that some functions do not need an input at all, such as current-date, current-time, and generate-guid. We can also assign constant values (XSL Text elements) to target elements, not requiring a function or an input element.

Not all elements in the source tree need to be connected to a function or target element, because not all data in an input message needs to be relevant for a particular target service. At the same time, not all target elements need to have a mapping that populates them with a value; when a target element is not mapped to, it will not appear in the transformation result.

Straightforward mappings can be created from DoctorRequestId, Gender, Birthdate, Priority, AppointmentType, and LabTests to their counterparts in the target tree. The target element PatientName is the concatenation from FirstName and LastName. The RequestDate is set using the XPath function current-date.

Extracting the Doctor Identifier from the Filename

An interesting element in the target tree is DoctorId: The doctor ID is not available inside the XML messages based on records in the file that is processed. However, the name of the file contains both the doctor identification and the date on which the requests were generated. Filenames are specified like <doctor_id>_<requestDate>_additionalnaming.txt. So we need to get hold of the doctor ID from the filename.

All adapter services send headers with metadata associated with the XML messages. This header data is frequently useful to learn more about the origin of a message. The header passed along by the File Adapter Service, for example, contains elements such as FileName and DirectoryName. The Mediator allows us to retrieve information from the header of XML messages as well as from the content of the messages.

To get access to the filename, we need to make use of a special predefined Oracle XPath function: mhdr:getProperty(propertyname). It can be found on the Advanced Components Palette in the section labeled "Mediator Functions."

This special XPath function is used to extract information from message headers (and can also be used in BPEL Assign activities). In this case, we need to extract the filename, which is retrieved under the property name jca.file.FileName. Because the doctor ID can be retrieved from the filename by taking the substring before the first appearance of an underscore character, the complete expression value for DoctorId becomes:

```
substring-before(mhdr:getProperty("in.property.jca.file.FileName"),"_")
```

Testing the Mapping

The mapping editor offers a testing facility. The context menu for the middle section contains the Test option, as shown in Figure 7-10.

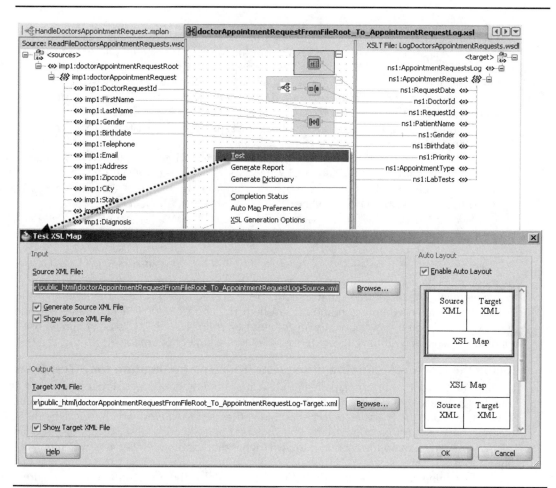

FIGURE 7-10.   *Testing the XSL map*

By selecting that option, we can specify an existing source XML file—one that adheres to the XSD—or have the tool generate one for us. We can also set the target XML file that should be created when running the mapping. When we click OK, the mapping is performed on the source XML file. The result is displayed and enables us to verify whether the mapping runs at all (that is, is correct) and whether its result is to our liking and what we expected.

NOTE
*The mhdr:getProperty() function will not work well in this XSL map
test, so comment it out before running the test.*

Complex Mapping: Constructions and XSLT

The mapping editor supports more complex situations, such as source XSD documents with choice constructs and elements that have multiple occurrences. We can create a for-each node in

XSLT: The XML Stylesheet Language for Transformations

XSLT (or XML Stylesheet Language for Transformations) is an essential part of the XML standards defined by the World Wide Web consortium (W3C). XSLT prescribes the transformation of a source XML document into a target document (often XML, but can also be HTML, plain text, or another text-based document). XSL is template based instead of being very procedural. An XSL processor interprets the XSLT document, applies its rules to a source XML document, and produces a target document. Version 1.0 was released in 1999, and its successor—XSLT 2.0—was born in 2007.

XSLT documents are XML documents with elements from the special www.w3.org/1999/XSL/Transform namespace (usually with xsl: as prefix). These elements use XPath expressions to specify which data elements should be extracted from the source XML document, how they should be transformed, and where they are to be placed in the target document.

More on XSLT can be found in Appendix B and on the W3C site: www.w3.org/TR/xslt.

the target tree that can be connected with such a multiple-occurrence element. Thus, we instruct the mapping engine to create the elements under the for-each node for every occurrence of the source element. The target tree can also contain "if" and "choose" nodes. The if node instructs inclusion of contents when a condition is satisfied. The choose node is accompanied by one or more "when" children and optionally an "otherwise" child. The first "choose" child whose condition is satisfied will have its contents added to the target document.

Taking the DoctorsAppointmentRequestsProcessor Application for a Test Drive

The first stage of our composite application DoctorsAppointmentRequestsProcessor is now almost complete and ready for deployment. The ReadFileDoctorsAppointmentRequests File Adapter Service is wired to the HandleDoctorsAppointmentRequest Mediator, which routes the messages, after appropriate transformation, to the LogDoctorsAppointmentRequest File Adapter Service. Later on, we will expand the Mediator to also trigger the AppointmentService by sending a request to it.

The one thing we may need to do before we can deploy the application is to configure values for the properties DOCTOR_APPOINTMENTREQUESTS_DIRECTORY and LOG_DOCTOR_APPOINTMENTREQUESTS_OUTPUT_DIRECTORY, which specify the directories from where files are read and into which files are written. One approach is the use of configuration plans (see Chapter 17). We create a plan for each environment that the application will be deployed to, and we can set the values of such properties as physical directories in these plans to different values per target run time.

The next steps to try out the composite application are simple.

1. Make sure the SOA Suite is running.

2. Compile and deploy the project using the context menu option. Right-click the composite.xml file and select Deploy.

3. When deployment is complete, copy one or more files with appointment requests to the poll directory—the physical directory specified in the composite.xml file for the property DOCTOR_APPOINTMENTREQUESTS_DIRECTORY. Make sure these files follow the naming convention <doctorId>_<requestDate>_somefreetextofanyformat.txt and that the contents are lines with comma-separated fields just like the sample file.

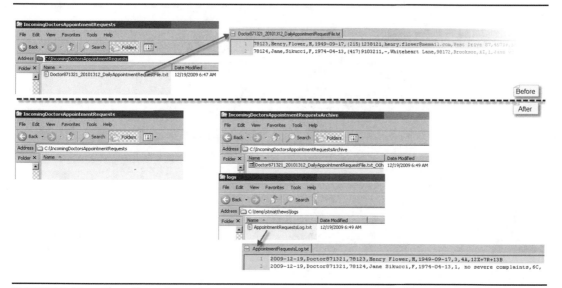

FIGURE 7-11. *The effect of running the composite application on the file system*

4. The composite application should remove the files from the directory you copied them to, process them, and archive them in the archive directory. This processing should result in records being appended to the file AppointmentRequestsLog.txt.

Figure 7-11 shows what we expect to happen as described in steps 3 and 4: file Doctor871321_20101112_DailyAppointmentRequestFile.txt in directory C:\IncomingDoctorsAppointmentRequests is picked up, processed, and archived. The result is in the C:\temp\stmatthews\logs directory.

We can inspect the processing of the files through the SOA console (see Figure 7-12). Every record in every file results in a Mediator instance that writes a single record to the log file.

Sending the Appointment Requests to the Patient Appointment Service

What we have created up to this point is encouraging: The files uploaded by the general practitioners are picked up and processed. Every appointment request from those files is turned into an XML message that can be handled, as demonstrated by the log file created. However, the true value, of course, lies in feeding these requests to the Patient Appointment Service, because that is the service that really needs to handle the requests.

We can achieve this with three straightforward modifications to the DoctorsAppointment RequestsProcessor composite: Add a Web Service reference to the composite for the PatientAppointmentService that is already deployed on the SOA Suite, add a routing rule to the Mediator and link it to this reference, and then create the mapping from the message sent by the File Adapter Service to the request message format required by the PatientAppointmentService.

Go to the Composite Editor. Drag and drop the WebService adapter to the References swimlane. Configure the PatientAppointmentService WebService reference. Open the WSDL browser, select Resource Palette in the drop-down, and select the deployed PatientAppointmentService under the SOA node in the SOA Resource Browser. Note that in "real life," we would not want such a direct

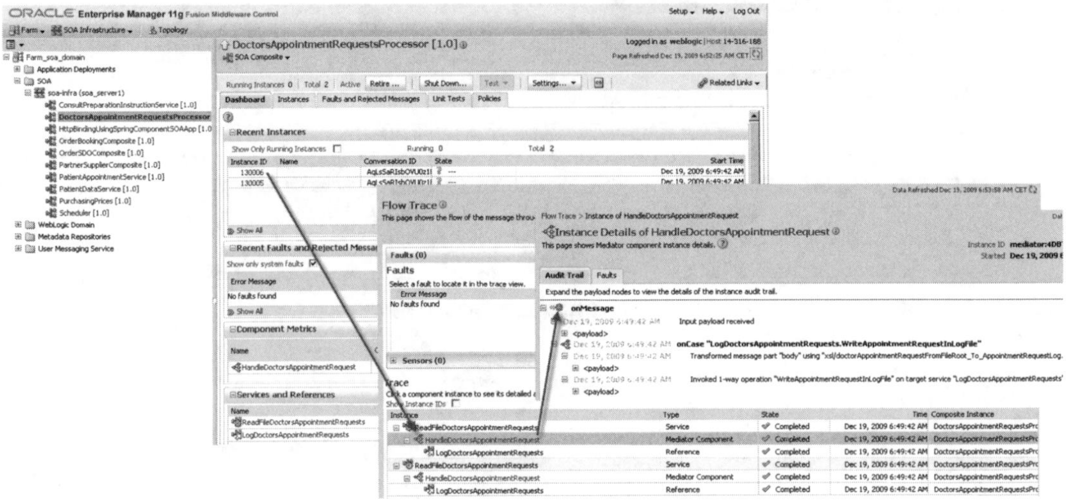

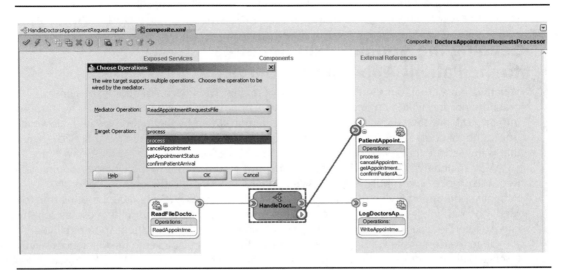

FIGURE 7-12. *Inspecting the SOA console to trace individual instances of the Doctors AppointmentRequestsProcessor application*

dependency on a deployed service and WSDL location. We would use a Service Registry or other service virtualization layer of sorts or apply configuration plans to dynamically set the environment-specific endpoint for the service.

Next, wire the Mediator component to the PatientAppointmentService WebService reference. Select the "process" operation as the target for this wire, as shown in Figure 7-13.

FIGURE 7-13. *Wire the HandleDoctorsAppointmentRequest Mediator to reference PatientAppointmentService*

Go to the edit page for the Mediator. A new routing rule for the ReadAppointmentRequests File operation has been added, with the PatientAppointmentService as the target. We need to create the mapping for the request message passed in by the File Adapter Service to the message format required by the PatientAppointmentService. This mapping is fairly straightforward—with the same approach to extracting the DoctorId from the filename using the getProperty() XPath function.

The composite application now has the Mediator accepting input from a single service and routing messages to two references—the (external) PatientAppointmentService and the (local) logging service.

When we redeploy the composite application, the Mediator will now route each incoming AppointmentRequest message from the File Adapter Service to the logging service and now to the PatientAppointmentService as well, which in turn will take care of scheduling the appointment, informing the patient, and enlightening other internal applications. Figure 7-14 shows the Fusion Middleware Control with the instances that processed a file with two DoctorAppointmentRequests. Note how we can track the flow of the messages through both composites, along every component, service, and reference binding that it passes.

Small-time Enrichment: Adding an Appointment Identifier to Logging

The PatientAppointmentService returns a reply that acts as the confirmation that the appointment will be scheduled. It includes the appointmentIdentifier. This identifier can later be used to retrieve additional information or to cancel the appointment. A question presents itself: What should we do with this reply in the DoctorsAppointmentRequestsProcessor? Obviously the invoker of the Mediator—the essentially one-way file adapter service that reads the file containing the appointment request—is not interested in this identifier. We could just forget about it, or alternatively we could include this appointmentIdentifier in the log file that is being written.

To achieve this last objective—which is a simple form of message enrichment—we will take the response from the PatientAppointmentService and redirect it to the LogDoctorsAppointment RequestsService. We add the response from the PatientAppointmentService to the information from the original message from the File Adapter Service. We need to add the AppointmentIdentifier

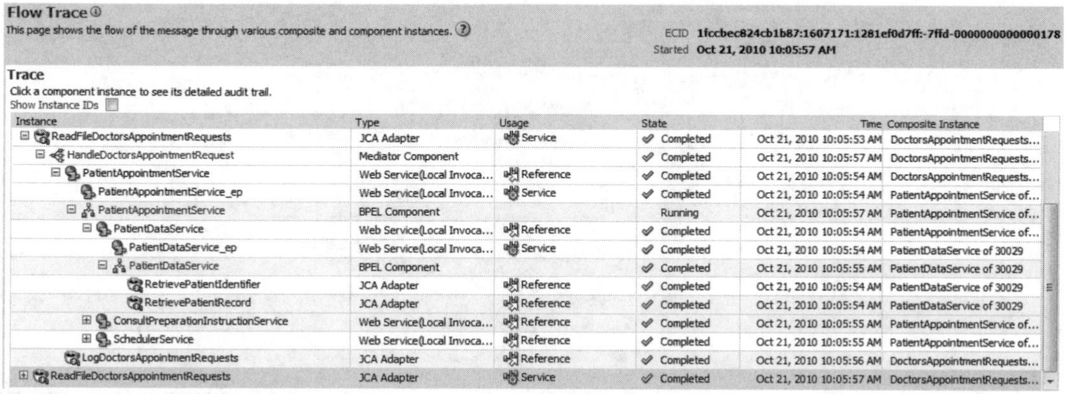

FIGURE 7-14. *Fusion Middleware Control showing the integrated flow through Handle DoctorsAppointmentRequest and PatientAppointmentService*

to the XML schema definition for the logging service. Edit the LoggedDoctorsAppointmentRequest
File.xsd file and add the following element under the RequestId element:

```
<xsd:element name="AppointmentIdentifier" type="xsd:string"
    nxsd:style="terminated" nxsd:terminatedBy="," nxsd:quotedBy="&quot;" />
```

The routing rule that routes the message from the ReadFileDoctorsAppointmentRequests to
the PatientAppointmentService has a part for configuring the routing for the synchronous reply.
The reply needs to be forwarded to the WriteAppointmentRequestInLogFile operation on the
LogDoctorsAppointmentRequestsService service. Figure 7-15 shows how to configure the routing
rule.

Next, click the Mapping icon to create the transformation map. In the dialog that pops up,
choose to create a new Mapper file. Then mark the check box labeled Include Request In The
Reply Payload. This crucial setting makes the contents of the message that went into this routing
rule—that is, the message sent by the ReadFileDoctorsAppointmentRequests service—available
during the transformation to the message that is the input for the LogDoctorsAppointmentRequests
Service. The original request is available from an XSLT variable called $initial. Figure 7-16 shows
these steps and the resulting Mapper file.

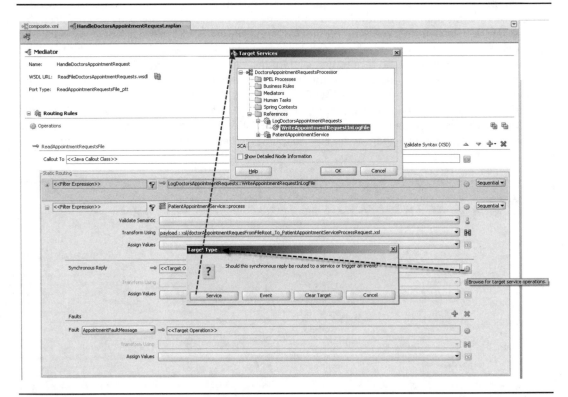

FIGURE 7-15. *Update the routing rule to PatientAppointmentService by forwarding the reply to
LogDoctorsAppointmentRequestsService*

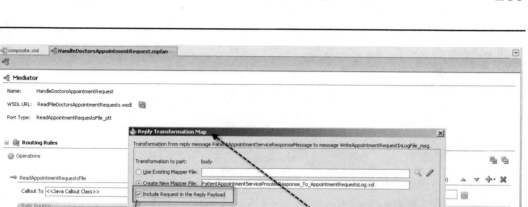

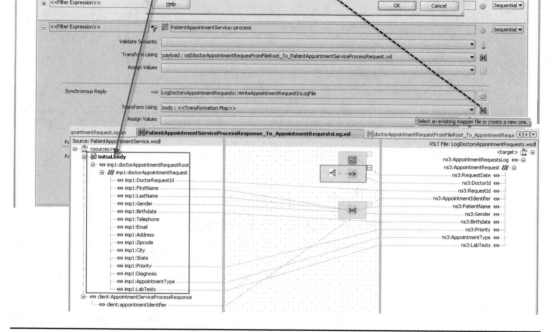

FIGURE 7-16. *Map the combination of the reply from PatientAppointmentService and the original message to the LogDoctorsAppointmentRequestsService*

The mapping is similar to the one in doctorAppointmentRequestRoot_To_Appointment Request.xsl. However, this time the $initial variable is the provider of most of the data. The appointmentIdentifier that gets contributed by the AppointmentService is mapped to the new AppointmentIdentifier element in the log file.

The original routing rule to LogDoctorsAppointmentRequestsService can now be deleted from the Mediator's set of routing rules; otherwise, we would send each AppointmentRequest message to the log file twice.

Figure 7-17 shows what path messages read from the file will follow through our application.

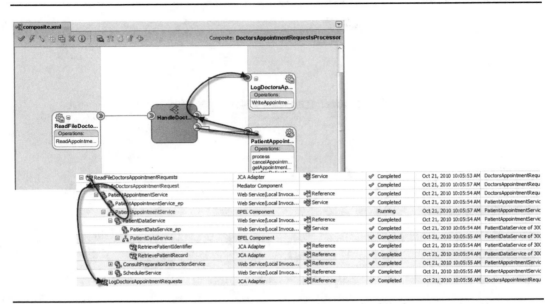

FIGURE 7-17. *AppointmentRequests arriving in a file are enriched in the PatientAppointment Service and then forwarded to the logger*

Adding Flexibility Using Filtering and Transformation of Messages

To ease the burden on all the family doctors in the wider area, St. Matthews has allowed doctors to simply include all requests for all types of appointments in the files they upload to the hospital. This includes appointments for healthcare not provided by St. Matthews itself, such as dental care and appointments with chiropractors. St. Matthews has arrangements with several regional centers and organizations for such external appointments: St. Matthews will collect and forward such requests from a large number of general practitioners. Family doctors pay St. Matthews a small fee for this additional service.

The Mediator we have introduced in the previous section will be extended to filter the appointment request messages: Any request for an externally provided type of healthcare should not go to the Patient Appointment Service. The Mediator should cater for special message routing for various categories of external healthcare, initially for the regional dentists, association and the chiropractors, society. Later on we may introduce other external partners as well.

Content-based Routing for External Appointment Requests

Both the dentists, association and the chiropractors, society make a Web Service available, with similar though slightly distinct operations for submitting an appointment request. These services are specified in our composite application as references. These references can then be wired as a target service in a routing rule in a Mediator.

We can choose between two strategies:

■ Use a single Mediator that takes the XML messages from the File Adapter Service and create multiple mappings between the XSD based on the file format and each of the target services.

■ Use one Mediator to map the XML message from the File Adapter Service to a more generic message (canonical) format and a second Mediator to route and map that generic message to each of the target services.

Even though the second approach, shown in Figure 7-18, requires the definition of an additional Mediator component, it decouples the overall application from the format of the incoming files. Whenever the incoming file format changes, chances are that we need to change the XSD that specifies the input to the first Mediator and therefore the mapping (XSLT) for each of the routing rules in this Mediator. If we have the first Mediator map to a generic, semipermanent AppointmentRequest message structure, then this message format is the robust input for the second Mediator that maps the message and sends it on its merry way to the target services. The second Mediator and all its routing rules and mappings are insulated from changes in the File Adapter Service. Even additional or alternative entry points into our composite—such as a Database Adapter Service—providing appointment requests will not have an impact on this second Mediator.

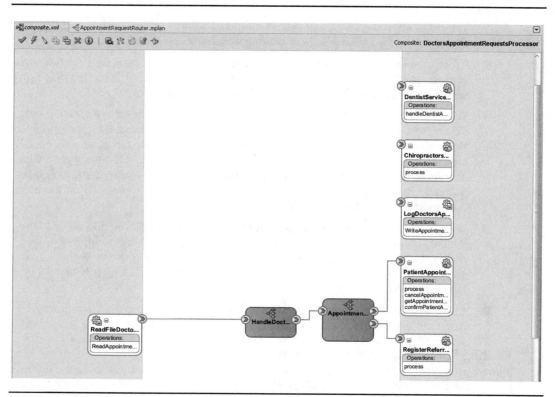

FIGURE 7-18. *The double Mediator approach—decoupling from the external medical service providers*

Decoupling, hiding implementation details, and insulating from the impact of change are our main objectives with SOA in general. It is hopefully obvious that we should adopt—and therefore will adopt—the second approach based on a canonical model.

The steps, therefore, are as follows:

■ Create the AppointmentRequest data structure—the canonical data model—in the form of a new XSD file. The canonical model should be able to hold all data that is required or optional for the services involved. Figure 7-19 shows a visual representation of the XSD file.

We should be very careful with specifying elements as mandatory; note that the canonical model we devise is not only to be used for the current services, but hopefully for future services as well. Applying too strict constraints may limit the reuse potential of the canonical data structure. Too few or too lenient constraints, on the other hand, may pose security risks or place too much burden on downstream components.

The naming of elements should not be geared toward specific services but rather be as enterprise-wide as possible, following naming conventions that apply across the board (canonical data model). We are, for example, likely to encounter elements for first name and last name in many canonical data structures. Ideally, we would always reuse the same generic definition of a Person element, inheriting from the central XSDs describing the canonical data model.

The structure of the canonical model should be easy to understand. Spending a lot of time on creating a sound, logical canonical definition is time well spent!

■ Create a new Mediator called AppointmentRequestRouter. The WSDL for this Mediator is generated based on the canonical AppointmentRequest XSD; it has a single portType with a one-way operation ProcessAppointmentRequest.

■ Wire the Mediator HandleDoctorsAppointmentRequest to the new AppointmentRequest Router; this will create a new routing rule in the Mediator HandleDoctorsAppointment Request with the Mediator AppointmentRequestRouter as the target service. Next, create a mapping from the message structure specified by the File Adapter Service to the canonical AppointmentRequest structure that the AppointmentRequestRouter takes as its input. The DoctorId is derived once again from the header property on the incoming message from the File Adapter Service.

■ Remove the existing routing rules from HandleDoctorsAppointmentRequest to the PatientAppointmentService reference and to the LogDoctorsAppointmentRequests reference. JDeveloper warns us that we will now have a routing rule without a target. The routing rule has become obsolete, so let's remove that routing rule because it is no longer needed.

■ Create WebService references to the DentistServiceCenter and the Chiropractors AppointmentProcessorService.

Routing Rules with Filter Expressions

Shortly we will be creating routing rules from the AppointmentRequestRouter to the internal PatientAppointmentService as well as each of the external services, starting with the dentists and

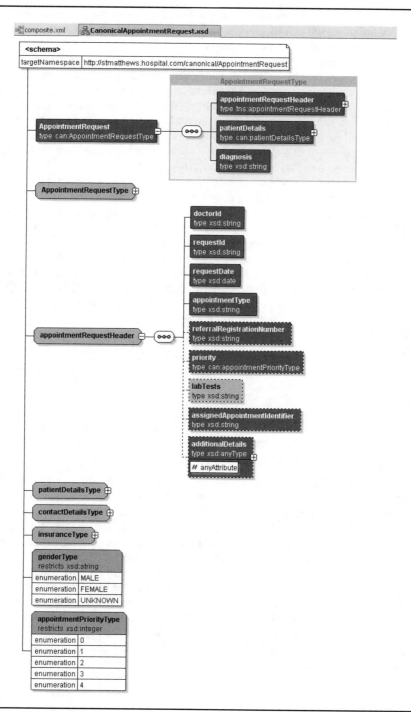

FIGURE 7-19.   *Visual representation of part of the Canonical Appointment Request format*

the chiropractors. Each routing rule should forward only selected appointment request messages. The type of appointment is indicated in the appointment request records and exposed in the XSD through the AppointmentType element.

In this chapter, we assume a very simplistic, hard-coded approach to recognize the type of the appointment; this will be refined in later chapters. For now, appointments for dental care are to be identified from the values Q1, Q2, and Q4 for the AppointmentType. When the AppointmentType starts with W, the appointment is for an external chiropractor. At this moment, all other appointment requests are for the internal appointment service at St. Matthews itself.

We discussed earlier that the Mediator can perform *content-based routing*. What that means is that messages are sent to a target service if and only if their contents (or header details) satisfy the filter expression specified for the routing rule.

When editing routing rules, we can click the filter expression field—the field with the funnel icon. A filter expression is an XPath expression that evaluates to true or false, indicating whether or not the target service will be invoked. The expression may use all XPath functions available in the SOA Suite, including potential user-defined XPath extensions. The expression can refer to the content of the source XML message as well as the values of message header properties.

We first wire AppointmentRequestRouter to the internal PatientAppointmentService, thus creating a new routing rule for the Mediator. Next, we specify the filter condition for this routing rule, which specifies that if the Appointment Type is not equal to Q1, Q2, or Q4 and also does not start with a capital W, then this routing rule takes effect (Figure 7-20):

```
orcl:index-within-string
( ';Q1;Q2:Q4;'
, concat(';',$in.request/inp1:AppointmentRequest...
            .../inp1:appointmentRequestHeader/inp1:appointmentType,';')
) = -1
and not
( starts-with
  ( $in.request/inp1:AppointmentRequest/inp1:appointmentRequestHeader...
    .../inp1:appointmentType,'W')
)
```

Note that although this demonstrates the content-based filtering and routing that the Mediator can do for us, it is not the best way of implementing this particular requirement. The current rules for routing the requests are quite likely to change—for example, as new appointment types are introduced or the hospital starts providing dental services. Each change would require a developer to change this routing rule and the application to be redeployed. In the next chapter, we will discuss the Decision Service (aka business rule component), which we can use to implement dynamic routing rules. Such rules can be changed quite easily at run time by nontechnical staff in roles such as business analyst, application administrator, and process owner.

Back to the routing rule: We need to create the mapping from the canonical appointment request to the message structure required by the PatientAppointmentService. Creating this mapping to the AppointmentService is a lot easier now, because the canonical structure is clear, without peculiarities such as the message header properties that should be retrieved and processed by various XPath functions.

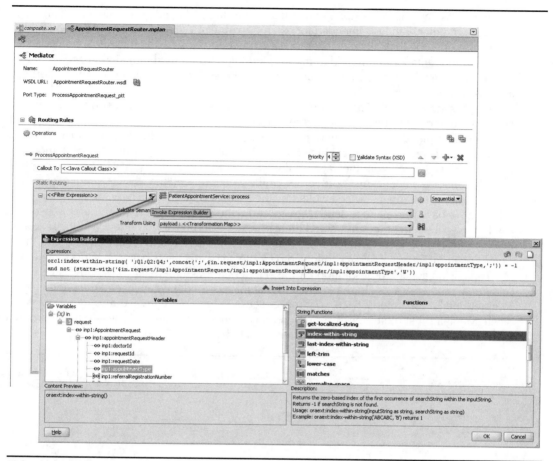

FIGURE 7-20. *Specifying the filter condition for appointment requests that are not intended for external medical services*

Enriching Messages with the Referral Identifier

St. Matthews wants to keep track of all referrals it has forwarded to each of the external partners:
After all, the hospital charges the partners a small fee for each forwarded referral. Every forwarded
referral is recorded by a RegisterReferralToPartner service that stores the referral and returns a
unique registration number that must be included in the message sent to the external healthcare
partner, because that same number will be part of the invoice sent later on to the partner.

Enriching a message can be done by a Mediator: The message is routed to a two-way—
usually synchronous—service that provides the enrichment data, and the reply from that
enrichment provider is routed to the next Mediator or the (external) target service.

NOTE
*The Mediator cannot return the enriched message back to the original
requester—it can only be forwarded to a downstream target.*

In this case, we have the AppointmentRequestRouter call the RegisterReferralToPartner service for all appointment requests intended for external partners. We use a filter expression to select those messages, the logically reverse from the expression used for the internal appointments.

The same remarks with regard to hard-coded logic that is hard to maintain and the better practice of using a business rule component apply here. The next chapter revisits this project to address that point.

The RegisterReferralToPartner service requires a request message that contains a partnerLabel element that indicates the external partner for which the appointment referral is intended—and that should be billed for it. The supported values at present are CHIR, DENT, and STMA. We need to include an XSLT snippet in the Source view of the mapping editor in which the value of this element is derived from the value of the AppointmentType, using XSLT's choose construct.

We cannot use filter expressions to determine where to send the reply that we receive from the RegisterReferralToPartner service invoked by the Mediator. We need a new Mediator for this. So in this case we have the option to send messages from the appointment request router to two different Mediators—one each for dentists and chiropractors—and have both these Mediators do the enrichment via the RegisterReferralToPartner service, or have only one Mediator call that RegisterReferralToPartner service followed by a Mediator that filters between various target services.

There is no generic best solution for this. Here I have assumed that St. Matthews will support additional partner services in the future and that for all of them we will need the enrichment by the RegisterReferralToPartner service, so it makes sense to have the enriched message processed by a single Mediator that routes messages based on content—AppointmentType—to the appropriate partner target service. This approach is demonstrated in Figure 7-21.

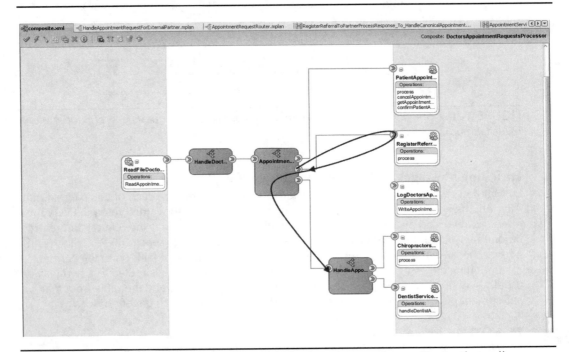

FIGURE 7-21. *The composite application with the AppointmentRequestRouter that calls RegisterReferralToPartner and forwards the reply to HandleAppointmentRequestFor ExternalPartner*

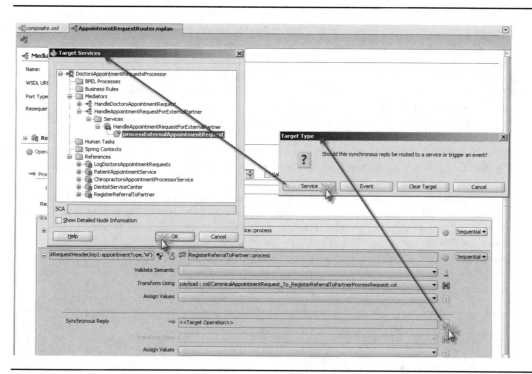

FIGURE 7-22.   *A Mediator's routing rule to a synchronous target service allows configuration of how to deal with the synchronous reply: where to send it and how to map it*

The path that some of our messages will follow is now distinctly curved: First they travel to the RegisterReferralToPartner service and the response from that service is used to enrich the original AppointmentRequest that is then forwarded to the appropriate external target service.

The reply from the RegisterReferralToPartner service is routed to a new Mediator—called HandleAppointmentRequestForExternalPartner—that routes the message to either the dentists or the chiropractors. This Mediator is created based on the WSDL document HandleAppointmentRequestForExternalPartner.wsdl, which defines a single operation, processExternalAppointmentRequest, in the one-way portType processExternalAppointmentRequest_ptt, taking an input message based on the canonical appointment request.

The routing rule in AppointmentRequestRouter that routes the messages to the RegisterReferralToPartner service can be configured to forward the synchronous reply from the RegisterReferralToPartner service to some target, as shown in Figure 7-22. We select the processExternalAppointmentRequest operation on the HandleAppointmentRequestForExternalPartner service as the target for this reply.

NOTE
No filter conditions can be specified for content-based routing of the reply.

Next, we click the Mapping icon to create the transformation map for mapping the synchronous reply to the HandleAppointmentRequestForExternalPartner service. In the dialog that pops up, we elect to create a new Mapper file. And we mark the check box labeled Include Request in the Reply Payload (see Figure 7-23). This crucial setting makes the contents of the message that went into this routing rule—that is, the message sent to the AppointmentRequest Router service—available during the transformation to the message that is the input for the HandleAppointmentRequestForExternalPartner.

The original request is available from an XSLT variable called $initial. This variable is shown in the source tree on the left side of the mapping editor. We can drag nodes from this variable—representing the canonical appointment request message that was sent to this Mediator—to the message flowing out of the Mediator in the same way as we wire nodes from the reply from the RegisterReferralToPartner service.

Note that we can now make good use of the auto-map capabilities in the mapping editor: We can drag the inp1:AppointmentRequest node under initial.request to the AppointmentRequest node under target in the target tree. The mapping editor presents us with the Auto Map dialog, where we can set some preferences as to how the tool can recognize source and target nodes it can connect. In this case, we can accept all the default settings because we are mapping between the same canonical appointment request structure, so all nodes with the same name can be auto-mapped. The result is shown in Figure 7-24.

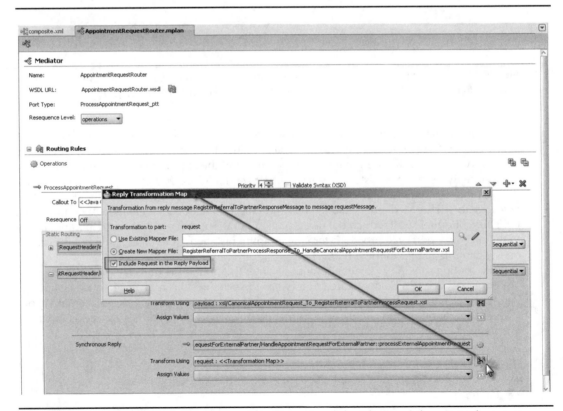

FIGURE 7-23. *Create a mapping of the reply (the referralIdentifier) and the original request message to HandleAppointmentRequestForExternalPartner*

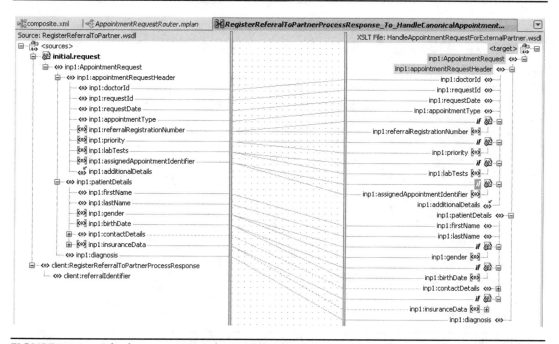

FIGURE 7-24. *Edit the mapping to the HandleAppointmentRequestForExternalPartner in the XSLT Mapper*

The HandleAppointmentRequestForExternalPartner Mediator should be wired to both the ChiropractorsAppointmentProcessorService and the DentistServiceCenter. Associated with each wire is a parallel routing rule with a filter expression based on the appointment type.

The final step now is to add a (parallel) routing rule to the AppointmentRequestRouter that sends details on each appointment request to the LogDoctorsAppointmentRequest service to have the request logged in the designated file. This logging does not contain the referral identifier or the appointment identifier—it is just a record of what the application has processed. Wire AppointmentRequestRouter to the outbound File Adapter Service LogDoctorsAppointment Requests. Set the routing rule to parallel and create the mapping from the canonical appointment request to the logger. No filter expression is required for this routing rule.

Note that in Chapter 15, we will investigate the use of logging policies to achieve the same result without needing to add SOA components such as Mediators. In case of OWSM, this is done through configuration and the capabilities of the underlying infrastructure.

After we deploy the composite application to the SOA runtime—and under the assumption that all references are already available—we can activate the DoctorsAppointmentRequests Processor by copying one or more files with appointment requests to the directory specified in the composite.xml file. Such a file is picked up and processed by the File Adapter Service component, several Mediators, and the logging service. Depending on the appointment type, it may also activate the enrichment service—RegisterReferralToPartner—as well as one of the three appointment services—for St. Matthews itself, the dentists, or the chiropractors.

Figure 7-25 shows the flow trace in the Fusion Middleware Control after processing a single file with four appointment requests, two of which are for external partners.

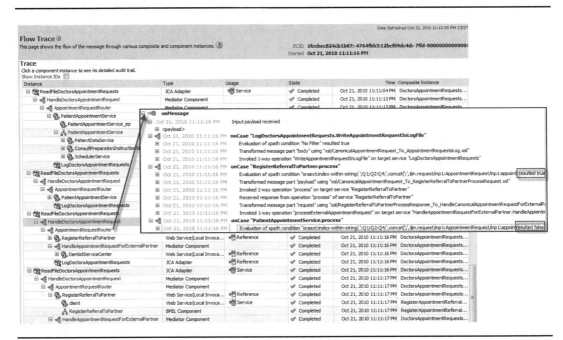

FIGURE 7-25. *Message flow trace in FMW Control after processing a single file with four appointment requests*

Mediator and Message Exchange Patterns

You may have noticed that so far we have only discussed one-way fire-and-forget-type patterns for the Mediator: A message is received, forwarded, and forgotten. No reply is returned from the Mediator, neither synchronously nor asynchronously. This made our discussion somewhat simpler, but it is important to realize that the Mediator is not limited to the one-way fire-and-forget message exchange pattern. The Mediator can engage in a synchronous message exchange with its invoker as well as enter an asynchronous conversation, and it can invoke both synchronous and asynchronous services. It can even convert from synchronous to asynchronous, and vice versa.

This last capability means, for example, that if your client does not support asynchronous service interaction yet and it wants to invoke an asynchronous service, you can interject a Mediator that calls the asynchronous service yet exposes a synchronous service interface to its clients. Note that such an adaptation can only be meaningful if the asynchronous service is relatively quick with its responses; otherwise, the synchronous client may be blocked for a long time. Also, a timeout (exception) may occur. In the same way, a Mediator can in turn expose a synchronous service—that may sometimes take fairly long to complete—as an asynchronous one. For example, most Database Adapter Services involving SQL and PL/SQL are intrinsically synchronous. However, there may be good reasons for exposing these services with an asynchronous interface—and the Mediator can be used for that.

So the Mediator does data transformation, protocol transformation, and exchange pattern transformation as well as supports event publication and consumption (see Chapter 9).

Dynamically Distributing the Appointment Requests over Log Files

The AppointmentRequestRouter routes every appointment request to the LogDoctorsAppointment Request File Adapter Service to have a log entry written to the file. Until now, all entries were appended to the same file, whose name was set as a configurable deployment-time (and run-time) property. As we discussed earlier in this chapter, it is possible to send log entries to specific (and specifically named) log files within the same file adapter. We do this by specifying the filename message header property when routing the message to the outgoing File Adapter Service.

To configure this more specialized naming convention for the log files, go to the composite editor and click the AppointmentRequestRouter. The Mediator differentiates between a message body transformation and message header transformation, so instead of extending the mapping, click the Assign Values icon for the routing rule that forwards the message to the File Adapter Service. Select the appropriate property—jca.file.FileName—and specify the XPath expression used for deriving the name of the file. In this case, we will create log files for every letter of the alphabet—each one will contain records for all appointment requests for patients whose last name starts with that letter. The expression used for the filename property looks like this:

```
concat('AppointmentRequestsForPatientsStartingWith_'
       , substring( $in.request/inp1:AppointmentRequest/inp1:patientDetails...
                 .../inp1:lastName,1,1)
       ,'.log')
```

Moving to Canonical Messages Using Domain Value Maps

There now turns out to be one additional complication with regard to the forwarded Appointment Request messages: St. Matthews and the family doctors in the region have agreed on a set of codes that indicate types of appointments. From the code in the referral, St. Matthews can determine which specialist a patient should see—such as the Q1, Q2, and Q4 we saw earlier. However, these codes are neither used by nor known to the external healthcare providers. For each provider, St. Matthews needs to translate the code received in the original referral from the family doctor to the description used by that healthcare provider. Some of these translations are listed in the following table.

The Mediator will use the Domain Value Map facility to perform this conversion instead of embedded hard-coded values in XSLTs. Domain Value Maps can be changed at run time without needing to change and redeploy composites.

Code Used by Family Doctors and St. Matthews	Code Used by Regional Dentists Association
Q1	SURG10
Q2	CLEAN33
Q4	XRAY9

Until now, when we discussed mappings between source and target messages, we only focused on mapping the message *structure* with fairly mechanical, predefined manipulation of the data values, using XPath functions such as concat and substring. However, we also may need to map or convert the values themselves when going from source to target in more intricate ways than through regular XPath functions. Domain Value Maps help the Mediator bridge between different terminologies, abbreviations, or languages used by partners in a message exchange—in a way that is easier to configure, reuse, and especially much easier to maintain, even at run time, than hard-coding such mappings in XPath expressions would be.

For example, Frank uses M and F in some of his database services to indicate gender. However, the hospital's canonical data model strives for more explicit values to enhance clarity and mandates use of MALE and FEMALE in the XSD. When the Mediator now transforms a message received according to the canonical data model for invoking Frank's data services, it will have to map the values MALE and FEMALE to M and F (or sometimes even M and W).

Such value mapping is performed using the Domain Value Map (DVM) facility in the SOA Suite.

Value Mapping with Domain Value Maps

The Domain Value Maps are created in XML files and can be centrally stored in MDS—Meta Data Services—or added locally to the composite application. XPath functions can access a DVM at run time to translate values in the source message into their counterparts. A value mapping in a Domain Value Map consists of a data value, optionally one or more qualifiers, and one or more associated lookup values. For example, the domain used to translate country names contains entries that consist of a country name in English, a language as a qualifier, and the capital and full name for that country in the specified target language, as shown here:

Country Name	Target Language (Qualifier)	Short Name (Lookup)	Name (Lookup)
USA	Fr	EU	Les Etats-Unis
USA	Nl	VS	Verenigde Staten van Amerika
United Kingdom	Fr	RU	Royaume-Uni
The Netherlands	Nl	NL	Nederland

When we look up the target value of one or more lookup columns, we use the name of the Domain Value Map, the name(s) of the lookup columns we want the value from, and the source value we need to convert as well as each of its qualifiers when applicable. For example, to retrieve the short name of the USA in French, we use *Countries* (name of the DVM), *USA* (the source value), *Fr* (the target language qualifier), and *ShortName* (the name of the lookup for which we need the value).

If the domain needs to be used for translation from other languages besides English, the source language should also be in the domain as an additional qualifier. This would allow the mapping of (Frankrijk,nl,en) to (FR,France) because Frankrijk is the country name for France in Dutch.

Creating and Using the Appointment Type Domain Value Map

Here are the steps for creating a DVM for appointment types:

1. Go to the New Gallery and under SOA Tier | Transformations select the Domain Value Map to create a new DVM. The dialog shown in Figure 7-26 appears.

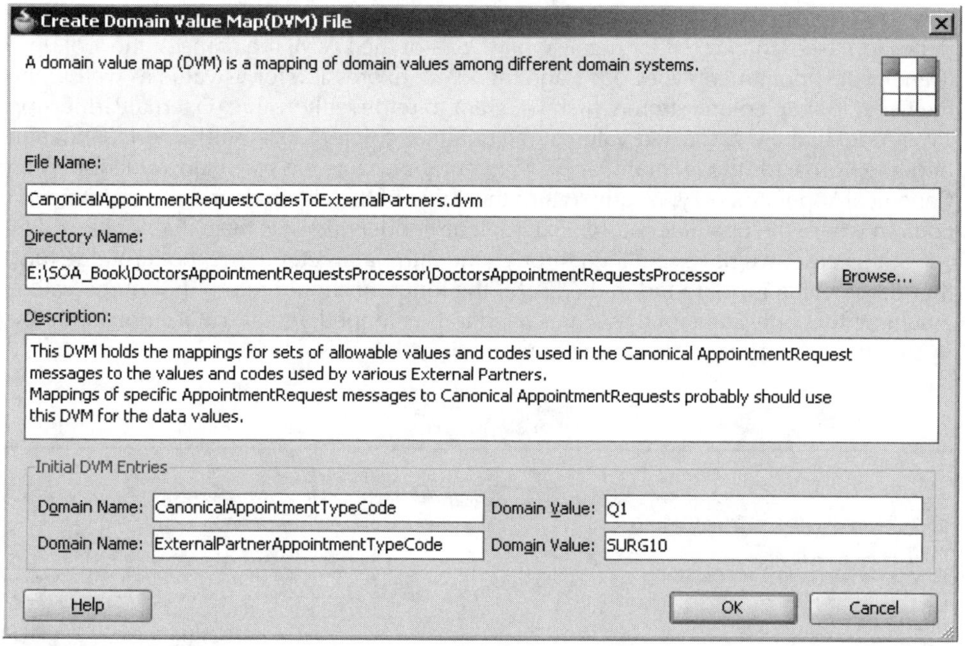

FIGURE 7-26. *Creating the Domain Value Map*

2. Specify the name of the DVM filename—Domain Name (CanonicalAppointmentRequest CodesToExternalPartners.dvm)—as well as the names for one lookup column (the first Domain Name field—CanonicalAppointmentTypeCode) with the first associated value (Q1) and a second (target) lookup column (the second Domain Name field—ExternalPart nerAppointmentTypeCode) and its first associated value (SURG10).

3. Click OK. The DVM editor opens, where you can define the ExternalPartnerIdentifier qualifier (which indicates for which ExternalPartner a row provides the domain value mapping) and more lookup columns as well as more rows.

Here is the XML definition of this qualifier:

```
<column name="ExternalPartnerIdentifier" qualifier="true" order="1"/>
```

We can make use of a DVM in mappings using the lookupValue function. In the mapping from the CanonicalAppointmentRequest in the routing rule to the ChiropractorsAppointment ProcessorService, we want to replace the canonical AppointmentType code with the code used by the chiropractors as defined in the DVM.

Edit the Mediator HandleAppointmentRequestForExternalPartners, find the routing rule to the ChiropractorsAppointmentProcessorService, and open the editor for the mapper file (see Figure 7-27).

Drag the lookupValue function to the center mapping region. In the Edit Function dialog that appears, we specify the filename—either with a local reference or one that points to the MDS Repository (see Chapter 18 for details on MDS)—of the DVM, the name of the lookup column (CanonicalAppointmentTypeCode), and the XPath expression for its value as well as the name of the target lookup column from which we want to retrieve the value (ExternalPartnerAppointment TypeCode) and the name and value of the qualifier column: ExternalPartnerIdentifier and CHIRO. In other words, for the Domain Value Map entry that has the specified value for column CanonicalAppointmentTypeCode, return the value of the ExternalPartnerAppointmentTypeCode column where the qualifier column ExternalPartnerIdentifier has the value 'CHIRO'.

In this case, we have specified through the fifth parameter to the lookupValue function that if the source value is not found in the DVM, the function should return the source value itself, assuming that only some of the values need to be mapped and all values not explicitly converted in the DVM can be sent onward without modification.

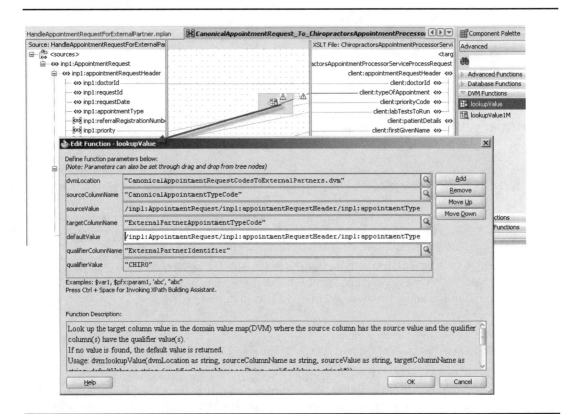

FIGURE 7-27. *Looking up the chiropractor's version of the AppointmentType code using the Domain Value Map*

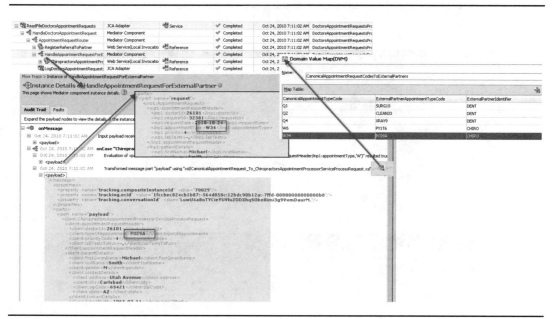

FIGURE 7-28.   *The Domain Value Map in action—converting from W34 to POI9A*

After redeploying the application, we can see the DVM lookup in action (see Figure 7-28). The same file with appointment requests is processed as before. This time, the code W34 specified by a general practitioner is converted to the value POI9A, which is understood by the chiropractor's AppointmentProcessor.

Of course, we could hard-code simple, static value transformations into the XSLT used for the transformation. However, as soon as the same data value mapping is used multiple times, the set of values is not tiny. Also, the mapping values may change over time. Therefore, using the DVM is preferable because it promotes reuse and simplifies maintenance.

Run-time editing of DVMs   Domain Value Maps can be published to the MDS and are then available for use across composites. Using and periodically maintaining the values in the DVMs is an important aspect of having various partners communicate successfully within the organization. The contents of the DVM can be edited at run time using the SOA Composer application—readily accessible for maintenance to application administrators and content editors via the browser. See Chapter 17 for details and Figure 7-29 for a visual impression.

Alternative Means for Value Translation

When the value mapping concerns a hundred or more values, requires some form of calculation or processing of values, and/or is very dynamic in nature, DVM will fall short. In such cases, we can resort to the XPath extension function lookup table or query database to access a database view or table (possibly including stored function calls) to perform more advanced value mapping

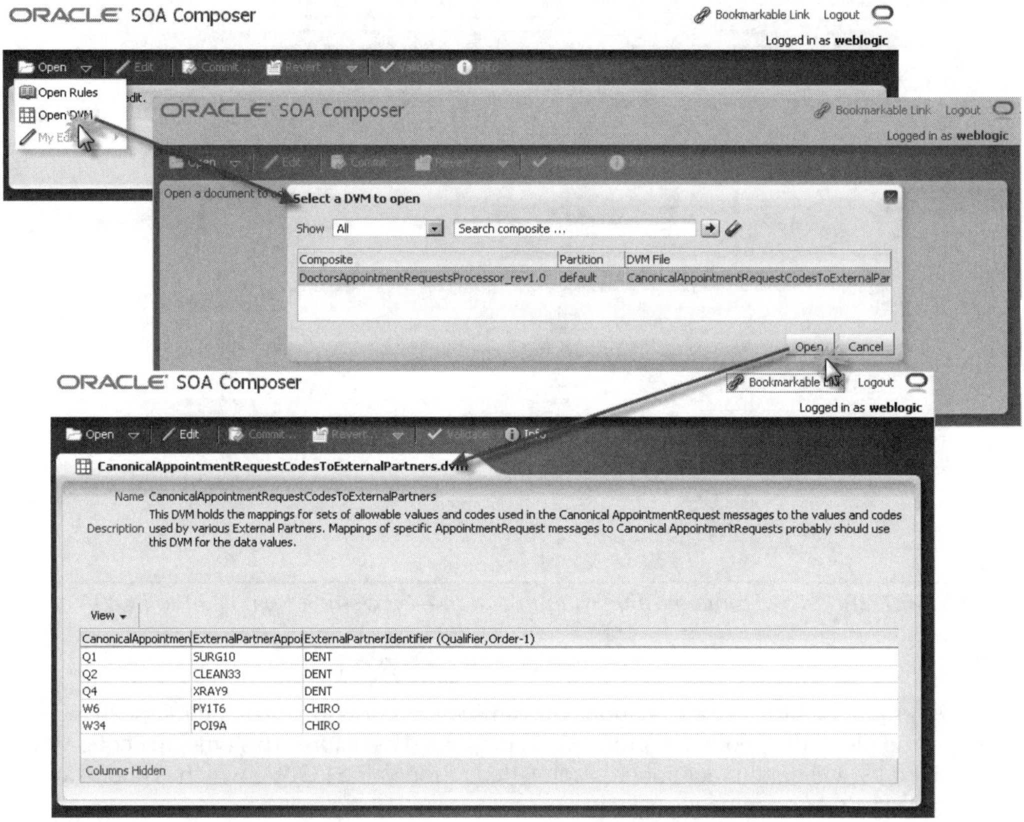

FIGURE 7-29. *Editing the Domain Value Map at run time using the SOA Composer*

Canonical Value Dictionaries

Domain Value Maps could be used to complement the canonical data model with canonical value domains. The canonical data model is used to prevent us from creating bidirectional mappings between all related data formats in the enterprise by having each specific format map to the canonical format. The same would work for domain values.

The example of translation between various languages helps to clarify the concept: We could create dictionaries for translating each pair of languages, requiring n*(n–1) dictionaries (with n being the number of languages); instead, through the use of a lingua franca—which could be English, Esperanto, or your language of choice—we only need to translate from each language to this lingua franca, which means n instead of n*(n–1) dictionaries. The same analogy holds when using an ESB to replace point-to-point interfaces. For Domain Value Maps, instead of languages to translate between, we have to cater for SOA partners speaking in different terminology and code values that we have to bring together. A designated canonical set of values can act as the lingua franca for that challenge.

or conversion. However, these functions create a fairly tight and not entirely desirable coupling, as well as pose a possible threat to the performance of the Mediator service, and should not be introduced without proper consideration.

We can extend the set of XPath functions with our own custom developed functions that can execute any logic we want them to. These functions can be used in mappings just like other XPath functions. Appendix D provides some pointers for this.

Alternatively, the transformation may have to be preceded or followed by a call to a service that performs message enrichment. Examples of such enrichment could include finding geographical coordinates for addresses, translating free text comments from French into English, and converting monetary values from Canadian to U.S. dollars.

We have seen how to implement enrichment earlier in this chapter when we called RegisterReferralToPartner to return a ReferralIdentifier that we used to enrich the Appointment Request message. A service that takes in the identification of the value type, the source value, its qualifiers, and the desired target context could do enrichment of messages in a similar way. Because we control the implementation of such an enrichment service, we have much more flexibility than the DVM feature gives us. Business rules, introduced in the next chapter, are one attractive way to implement such lookup services. However, using such services comes at the price of additional work and extra performance overhead—service calls are likely to be much more expensive than simple DVM lookup actions.

The online chapter complement introduces a special kind of lookup functionality that is used to map identities across applications and domains. This cross-reference feature helps to establish the relation between business objects in, for example, the Financial, HR, and Appointment Planning systems that represent the same natural person.

Appointment Requests via a Web Application

The batch-wise daily uploading of appointment requests will gradually be replaced: As more doctors are permanently online, they will start using a module in the St. Matthew's Online portal—a web application that provides, among others, functionality for entering appointment requests. These requests are recorded in a database by the web application.

From this database, they should be picked up and fed to the Patient Appointment Service. There are plans to have the web application send requests directly into the service rather than insert them into the database. However, they are still that—just plans for a revision of this two-year-old application.

We will now be rewarded for the way we have designed the composite application with the canonical appointment data structure and the AppointmentRequestRouter into which currently only the inbound File Adapter Service feeds. This design now makes it very easy to hook up new appointment request message producers such as a Database Adapter Service that polls the records created by the web application.

Opening Up the Composite to a New Message Producer

To support this new channel for appointment requests, we will extend the composite application with a combination of a Mediator and a Database Adapter Service that performs a polling operation. Every new appointment request record is processed by the RetrieveDatabaseDoctors AppointmentRequests Polling Database Adapter Service and leads to a new request message to the HandleDoctorsAppointmentRequestFromDB Mediator. The Database Adapter Service will be a companion to the File Adapter Service ReadFileDoctorsAppointmentRequests: Both invoke their associated Mediator with an appointment request message retrieved from an external source (either a file or a database table) and route that message in the canonical format to the AppointmentRequestRouter.

Configuring the Inbound Database Adapter Service

The Database Adapter Service is configured through the wizard (see the online chapter complement for detailed instructions). The appointment requests created through the web application are inserted into a table called MDP_DOC_APT_REQUESTS, which has columns for more or less the same fields as are in the CSV files with appointment requests.

We have to indicate the source table on which we want polling performed, specify the primary key columns, and determine how to recognize new records and what to do with records when they have been processed. For this we use the column PROCESS_YN in the table. A value for Y in this column indicates records that have been processed, whereas the initial (default) value of N signals new records. The database adapter will update the column value to X for the records it is currently processing.

NOTE
The process_yn column has been added to accommodate our database adapter. However, frequently we will not be able to change the data model to that extent. The database adapter supports the use of a sequence table (or file) in which it keeps track of the highest ID value or the most recent created/modified date processed so far—and a poll on new records to process will only return records that come after the one indicated in the sequence table.

An alternative solution for a database operation to trigger an SOA composite application is by using a combination of a database trigger and advanced queuing. This is preferable when a higher degree of loose coupling is required and/or more than one components are interested in new records (publish/subscribe pattern using multiconsumer queues).

Creating the Mediator HandleDoctorsAppointmentRequestFromDB

When the RetrieveDatabaseDoctorsAppointmentRequests are configured, we create a new HandleDoctorsAppointmentRequestFromDB Mediator and wire the Database Adapter Service to this Mediator. This automatically specifies the WSDL for the Mediator, including an operation called *receive*. Create a wire from the new Mediator to the AppointmentRequestRouter. The mapping for the routing rule created for this wire turns the message based on the XSD created by the database adapter into the canonical format.

When we now create records in the MDP_DOC_APT_REQUESTS table, they will be polled by the inbound Database Adapter Service and sent to the HandleDoctorsAppointmentRequestFromDB as XML messages, to be processed in much the same way as appointment requests that arrive in the CSV files uploaded to St. Matthew's FTP server. Figure 7-30 illustrates this.

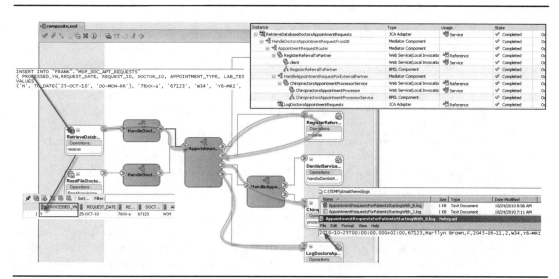

FIGURE 7-30. *Processing appointment requests that the web application created in the database*

Decoupling the Database Adapter Service

In the previous section, we saw how the Mediator has decoupled the PatientAppointmentService from the File Adapter Service. AppointmentRequests that are received by the File Adapter Service are still passed to the PatientAppointmentService. However, changes in the filenaming convention or the record structure do not have any impact on the PatientAppointmentService and the BPEL process that implements it. It does not even matter to the service if we introduce alternative channels for receiving appointment requests, such as a database to have them created from a web application, an FTP server, or a JMS queue: The Mediator insulates the PatientAppointmentService from such new developments. Of course, this may lead to changes in the Mediator—the routing rules or mappings—but such changes are fairly easy to apply.

We would like to achieve the same level of decoupling for the outgoing calls to the Database Adapter Services from the PatientDataService BPEL process.

Decoupling the PatientAppointmentService BPEL Process

In Chapter 5, we created a BPEL process with calls to the Database Adapter Services RetrievePatientIdentifier and RetrievePatientRecord. These Database Adapter Services were contained inside the composite application. They are not exposed externally, outside of the composite, so we currently have no reuse of the services. The XSD and WSDL created for the Database Adapter Services are tied directly into the BPEL process, which means tight coupling rather than the decoupling we seek. Just like Margaret in the past needed to know far too many details about ordering flowers, the BPEL process needs to know too much about these (technical) services.

By using a Mediator to do for the BPEL process what Martin is doing for Margaret, we will remedy these shortcomings and achieve better decoupling.

Decoupling Is the Name of the Game

Margaret is a busy woman. Chairing meetings, writing reports, conducting negotiations with vendors, and kicking butt around the hospital. Irving, her significant other, sometimes gets fed up with her. Every other day, around 6 P.M., he gets that same phone call that something urgent has come up and she will be just a little late—which can mean really anything between 8 P.M. and 10 P.M. He has sort of learned to live with it, because she is otherwise a wonderful person.

Their anniversary is around the corner, and that is a big thing for Irving. He kind of feels neglected from time to time, and Margaret should definitely not miss this occasion for showing her devotion. Her electronic agenda has warned her in time of this upcoming deadline, which gives her ample opportunity to ask her secretary to order a flower bouquet and have it delivered to Irving.

In the past, she tried to deal with florists herself. However, she found it hard to remember which were the good shops, she did not speak the language of flowers and could only order in colors and number, and she had a tendency to call them after their business hours. When she did reach them, she more often than not was kept on the line for long periods of time and sometimes the line was dropped during some internal connect-through. On several occasions the shops she called were out of stock of those yellow flowers her husband likes so much, or they turned out to have moved, changed telephone numbers, or went of business altogether.

In later years, some shops switched to ordering via a website or e-mail—which seemed convenient at first, but became a nuisance as only the next business day they informed her whether they could/would process the order. It was a yearly nightmare for her that took up way too much of her time.

Martin, her secretary, now takes care of all the gritty details. And that works very well. She asks him to have those same flowers Irving liked so much last year delivered on the day of their anniversary. Martin will go away, do his magic, and report back to her after a while that everything has been taken care of. She neither knows nor cares whence he got those flowers and what communications he had to go through to get them. She was, however, very grateful to him as Irving beamed at her from behind his huge yellow bouquet.

Margaret has become decoupled from the flower-ordering process, thanks to Martin ("The Mediator"). Changes in suppliers, their contact details, the communication channel, whether or not they react immediately or call back at some later time, and the procedure for ordering flowers do not affect her at all. Only when Martin leaves will she have a problem.

A strict point of view would be: BPEL processes should never call to adapter services directly. There should always be a Mediator in between, like a Martin of sorts.

In our everyday world, there are plenty of situations where for pragmatic reasons this statement may need to be overruled. However, you probably should adopt it as a starting point.

The Mediator has several functions that all help promote decoupling and agility. The Mediator maps from the canonical data structure to the potentially very specific schema for the adapter service, possibly including any value conversions that may be required. When the Database

Adapter Service is replaced by a different service implementation—with new WSDL and XSD definitions—the BPEL process is unaffected because the Mediator shields it from these changes.

When the data is for some reason distributed over multiple databases, and based on some patient property we have to determine which of those databases to access, the Mediator will take care of this content-based routing.

The Mediator can handle problems with availability of the database service, retrying calls or taking alternative steps. And the Mediator may present what is a synchronous service through an asynchronous interface, which allows a client such as a BPEL process to continue with other, parallel activities or to be dehydrated altogether to free up resources after the call is made, instead of blocking the thread waiting for the reply—which could take fairly long.

The online chapter describes in detail how we can decouple the PatientDataService BPEL process from the Database Adapter Services it currently references using Mediator components.

Summary

Oracle Mediator technology is extensive and complex. It differs from BPEL in the sense that it's faster and more lightweight, does not carry state, and is very message oriented. It implements a number of message exchange patterns, validates and transforms messages, and has (limited) capabilities to enrich the message payload. Mediators are not suitable for orchestration or to implement composite services.

SOA composite applications will usually contain a combination of components, implemented using different technologies such as BPEL, Java, Human Task, and Business Rule. Mediators will almost always be used to decouple from and to the outside world, and to mediate between components and adapter services within the composite through transformation and content-based routing.

One chapter cannot do the Mediator full justice, and although we have discussed the most important aspects of the Mediator, there is much more to learn. Other chapters will show more of the Mediator—dynamic routing rules in the next chapter; the event-handling functionality in Chapter 9; Java callouts in Chapter 12; logging, tracing, and exception handling in Chapter 16; and custom XPath functions in Appendix D.

The last section of the online chapter complement briefly touches on a number of Mediator topics that you may want or need to look at, such as resequencing messages. For additional details, visit this book's wiki, the Fusion Middleware documentation, the Online Help, or one of the many other online resources.

CHAPTER
8

Rules Rule—on
Decision Services

OA composite applications contain various forms of logic. These have some overlap, but they also have their own specific actors, implementation technologies, and maintenance cycles. There is, of course, implementation logic written by programmers in programming languages such as BPEL, XPath and XSLT, Java, and even PL/SQL. There is also process logic, designed perhaps using the Business Process Analysis Suite, modeled in BPMN or BPEL by business analysts.

Another type of logic is business logic—describing and implementing derivations, validations, calculations, and other business rules. Frequently this last type of logic is described by the analysts—in free format text—and then implemented by developers as part of the programs they write. It is fairly common to find the implementation of business logic done in several places in the application using hard-coded values and references. The business logic cannot easily be told apart from the implementation logic of the computer program, cannot be modified without the help of the programmers, and cannot be deployed without redeploying the entire application.

This chapter introduces the Decision Service component in SOA Suite 11*g*, also known as the Business Rule service component. We will use the name Business Rule from now on. This type of component implements business logic and exposes it as an SCA component that can easily be integrated into other components such as BPEL processes, Human Workflows, and Mediators. This business logic can also be invoked through a Java API. Implementing business logic in a central, encapsulated, reusable component makes it much easier to manage and maintain and actually reuse such logic.

Oracle Business Rules is very good at evaluating the business logic expressed in the special RL (Rule Language) language—with high performance and good scalability, especially compared to alternative implementations of the same logic in, for example, XPath. Business rules created within SOA composite applications usually work with the RL language, which allows definition of rules in a very declarative way that is even accessible to nonprogramming business analysts. The run-time infrastructure allows editing the business logic after the application has been deployed, contributing tremendously to business agility, because the frequency with which this type of logic changes is typically different from—and usually higher than—the frequency in which the other types of logic change. It is a huge boon to be able to modify business rules at run time without redeploying your process.

We will meet the Business Rule component in this chapter and see how business rules can be implemented and integrated in composite applications. We will also see how business logic can be changed at run time using the SOA Composer (which we first saw in the previous chapter for the Domain Value Maps), thus allowing for a more agile application.

For St. Matthews, we will first tackle the routing of appointment requests intended for external partners such as chiropractors and dentists, which we handled in the previous chapter using hard-coded filter conditions in Mediator components. Next, we will look at the implementation of system-wide parameters and formulas. Finally, we will see the decision table in action, a straightforward way to implement fairly complex, multidimensional business rules for establishing the priority of an appointment.

The online chapter complement has a more detailed overview of the steps you have to go through in the implementation and integration of business rules. It uses the traditional game of Rock-Paper-Scissors to introduce the decision table in a very simple and tangible manner.

Deriving the Type of the Appointment

In the previous chapter on the Mediator component, you saw how we had to route the appointment request to either the internal patient appointment service or one of the external providers, such as dentists and chiropractors, based on the content of the appointment request. We implemented filters with long, ugly, hard-to-interpret, and hard-coded XPath expressions:

```
orcl:index-within-string
( ';Q1;Q2:Q4;'
, concat(';',$in.request/inp1:AppointmentRequest...
            .../inp1:appointmentRequestHeader/inp1:appointmentType,';')
) > -1
```

We concluded this was not a great solution. Such expressions are tricky to write, hard to read, and a pain to maintain. Changes in the derivation of the appointment type would require development effort as well as a redeployment of the entire application. Furthermore, this same expression was used in several locations in the application because the appointment type was needed in multiple routing rules (and the Mediator does not allow us to create temporary variables that can be reused).

It would be convenient to have a component that returns the type of appointment—dentist, chiropractor, or "in the hospital"—based on the (canonical) AppointmentRequest. The logic of deriving the type of appointment from the appointment request would be in that component only. When this logic needs to be changed, we can do that from the outside, at run time, without changing other parts of the composite application and without redeployment. No involvement from developers or administrators is required.

Furthermore, defining the logic to derive the type of appointment ideally would be written in a more intuitive way than through the XPath expressions we used in Chapter 7—in a way that is easier to understand and more productive to develop.

SOA Suite 11*g* has the Business Rules service engine, which exposes business logic through Business Rule (service) components that live up to that job description.

Creating a Business Rule Service Component

We will now create a Business Rule component to decide on the type of appointment. To keep our example simple, we will create the component inside the DoctorsAppointmentRequests Processor composite application. Alternatively, we could implement the business rule in a separate composite application that would be available for reuse from other composites and would allow for low-impact redeployment when the run-time rule-editing facilities fall short of the need at hand.

We will feed the AppointmentTypeCode in the CanonicalAppointmentRequest message into the Business Rule component, and we will make it return a reply according to a new message type based on the new TypeOfAppointmentType XSD element that makes explicit what type of appointment (external or internal; if external, which party) it concerns. Subsequently, we will add a Mediator to the composite—before the AppointmentRequestRouter—to enrich the CanonicalAppointmentRequest with the appointment type data derived by this business rule. Then we will update the filter expressions in the downstream Mediators to benefit from this new structured information in the appointment request. All business logic currently implemented in the XPath of several filter conditions is pushed to the single business rule.

Implementing the DeriveAppointmentType Decision Service Component

Here are the steps for the creation of the DeriveAppointmentType business rule and Decision Service component:

1. Open the file CanonicalAppointmentRequest.xsd. Add a new complexType TypeOfAppointment and a new complexType AppointmentCode:

```
<xsd:complexType name="AppointmentCode">
  <xsd:sequence>
    <xsd:element name="appointmentTypeCode" type="xsd:string"/>
  </xsd:sequence>
</xsd:complexType>
<xsd:complexType name="TypeOfAppointment">
  <xsd:sequence>
    <xsd:element name="appointmentTypeCode" type="xsd:string"/>
    <xsd:element name="appointmentTypePartnerLabel" type="xsd:string"/>
    <xsd:element name="internalAppointment" type="xsd:boolean"/>
  </xsd:sequence>
</xsd:complexType>
```

2. Add an element called **TypeOfAppointment**, based on TypeOfAppointmentType, to the complexType appointmentRequestHeader.

3. Add a Business Rule component from the Service Components palette to the composite; call it **DeriveAppointmentType** (see Figure 8-1). The input schema type is AppointmentTypeCode. The output type is the new TypeOfAppointmentType.

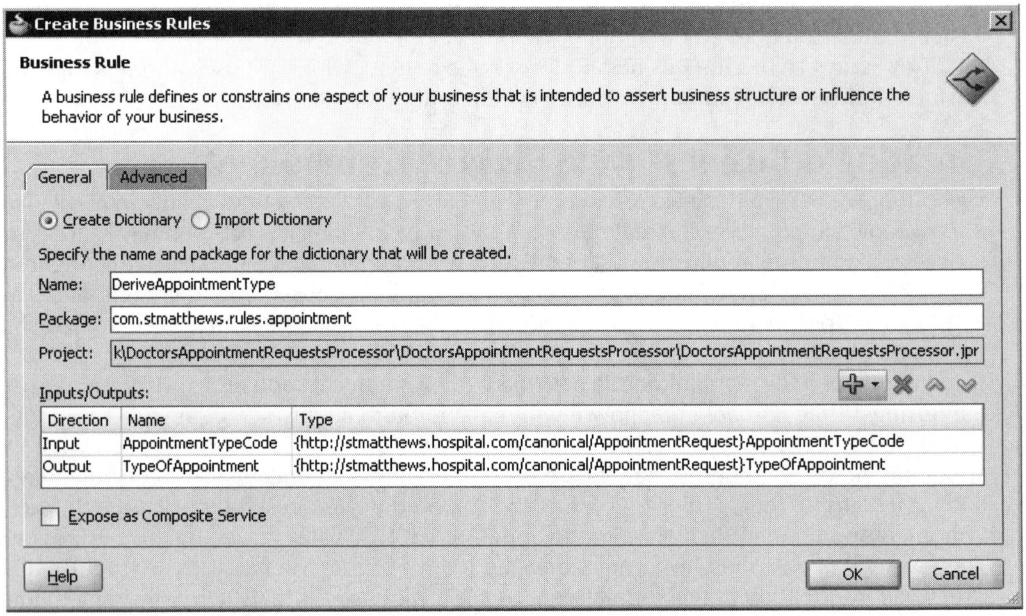

FIGURE 8-1. *Adding the Decision Service component DeriveAppointmentType to the composite application DoctorsAppointmentRequestsProcessor*

We have now specified that the Business Rule component will tell us the type of appointment requested, based on the contents of appointmentTypeCode. It will tell us the label of the partner that should handle the appointment and, through a Boolean flag, whether the appointment is external or internal.

We can invoke the decision service wrapped around this business rule from a BPEL process or Mediator components—and even expose it as a composite service that external partners can call.

First, of course, we need to implement the business logic for the rule. To do so, follow these steps:

1. Double-click the Business Rule component to open the editor.

2. Change the name of the rule set to AppointmentTypeDerivation. Click the current name to edit the title. You could enter a description of the rule set, and indicate whether it is active or not—or exactly when the rule set applies (by specifying effective dates or times of day).

3. Add a business rule of type "IF/THEN rule" by clicking the button (see Figure 8-2). Call the new business rule **Match Chiropractor Appointment Requests**.

A rule set either contains a decision table—which is a special constellation of IF/THEN rules—or plain IF/THEN rules. More on the decision table in the second half of this chapter.

An IF/THEN rule consists of two parts: the *test* and the *action*. The test tries to match the asserted facts in the rule engine's working memory—in our case, derived from the Appointment TypeCode input to the decision service. One or more Boolean expressions combined using AND and OR operators evaluate either to true or false. When the result is true, a match has been made

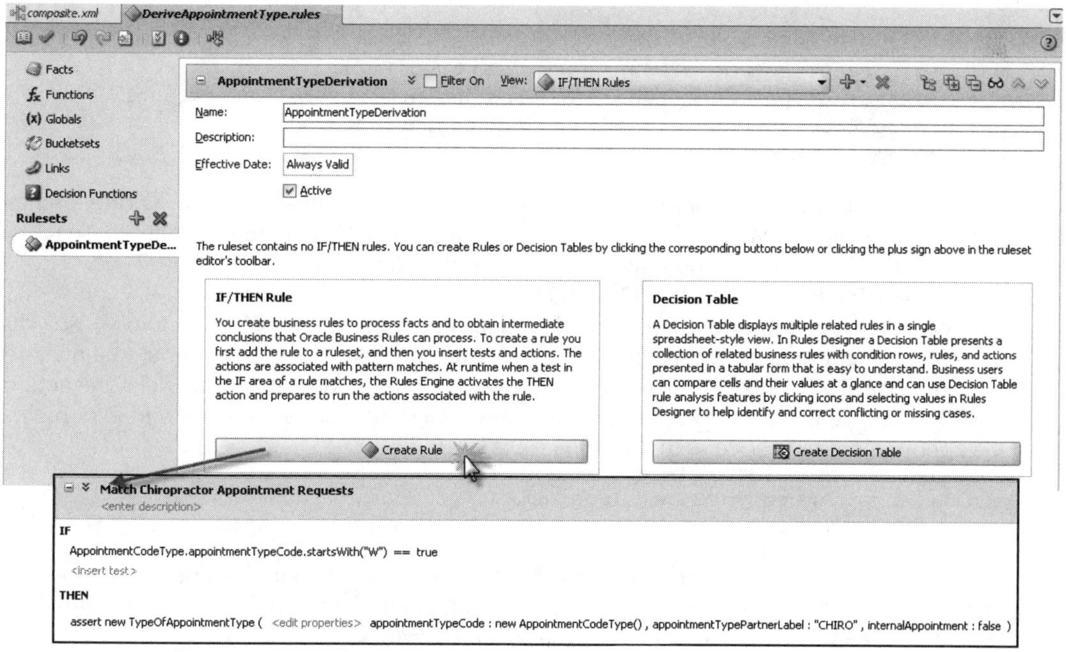

FIGURE 8-2. *Add the first IF/THEN rule to the rule set*

and the *action* part of the business rule is activated. When the result is false, nothing will happen for this rule.

The *test* for our first business rule tries to match the AppointmentTypeCode input fact through the following expression:

```
AppointmentCodeType.appointmentTypeCode startsWith ("W")
```

This means that whenever the input contains an appointmentTypeCode that has *W* as its first letter, a match has been made. When the test results in a match for a business rule, its *action* is triggered or executed.

A business rule action can contain a number of statements in the RL language. The action takes care of creating the output from the decision service by asserting a new fact of the output type—TypeOfAppointmentType in this case. Other possible operations in a business rule action include manipulation of input values or temporary facts, printing of debug statements, and invocation of business rule functions. The action for the chiropractors' business rule asserts a new (output) TypeOfAppointmentType fact that has CHIRO for its appointmentTypePartnerLabel property and false for the flag indicating the internal nature of the appointment:

```
assert new TypeOfAppointmentType( appointmentTypeCode:
AppointmentCodeType.appointmentTypeCode.toUpperCase(),
appointmentTypePartnerLabel:"CHIRO", internalAppointment : false)
```

When the decision service is invoked with an appointment request that has an appointment type code of "W7162," this business rule is matched and the output of the service is an XML element based on TypeOfAppointmentType with child elements of appointmentTypeCode, appointmentTypePartnerLabel, and internalAppointment:

```
<TypeOfAppointment >
    <appointmentTypeCode>W7162</appointmentTypeCode>
    <appointmentTypePartnerLabel>CHIRO</appointmentTypePartnerLabel>
    <internalAppointment>false</internalAppointment>
</TypeOfAppointment>
```

We need business rules for dental appointments and, of course, the vast majority of internal appointments that St. Matthews handles itself. Figure 8-3 shows the rule set after these rules have been created. The dental appointments are easily identified: AppointmentCodeType. appointmentTypeCode in "Q1", "Q2", "Q4".

The internal appointments are really found as the leftovers, the "else" or "otherwise" case— any appointment request not matched by one of the earlier business rules should be matched by this third one. To find these otherwise appointment requests, we use a little trick: The action branch of the dentist and chiropractor rules does a modification of the input variable, prefixing the appointment type code with the string "XXX":

```
modify AppointmentTypeCode( appointmentTypeCode: "XXX"
                      + AppointmentTypeCode .appointmentTypeCode)
```

The rule for the internal appointments matches all appointment type code values, except the ones starting with XXX. It is an easy way of deriving internal appointments as the complement of the external appointments identified by the specific business rules.

⊟ ≫ **Match Chiropractor Appointment Requests**
      `<enter description>`

IF

   AppointmentCodeType.appointmentTypeCode.startsWith("W") == true
   `<insert test>`

THEN

   assert new TypeOfAppointmentType (`<edit properties>` appointmentTypeCode : new AppointmentCodeType() , appointmentTypePartnerLabel : "CHIRO" , internalAppointment : false)

   modify AppointmentCodeType (`<edit properties>` appointmentTypeCode : "XXX"+AppointmentCodeType.appointmentTypeCode)

   `<insert action>`

⊟ ≫ **MatchDentistAppointmentRequests**
      `<enter description>`

IF

   AppointmentCodeType.appointmentTypeCode in "Q1" , "Q2" , "Q4"   `<insert>`
   `<insert test>`

THEN

   assert new TypeOfAppointmentType (`<edit properties>` appointmentTypeCode : AppointmentCodeType , appointmentTypePartnerLabel : "DENT" , internalAppointment : false)

   modify AppointmentCodeType (`<edit properties>` appointmentTypeCode : "XXX"+AppointmentCodeType.appointmentTypeCode)

   `<insert action>`

⊟ ≫ **MatchInternalApppointmentRequests**
      `<enter description>`

IF

   AppointmentCodeType.appointmentTypeCode != null and
   (AppointmentCodeType.appointmentTypeCode.length() < 3 or AppointmentCodeType.appointmentTypeCode.substring(0,3) != "XXX"   `<insert test>`)
   `<insert test>`

THEN

   assert new TypeOfAppointmentType (`<edit properties>` appointmentTypeCode : AppointmentCodeType , appointmentTypePartnerLabel : "STMA" , internalAppointment : true)

FIGURE 8-3.   *Creating the business rules for dental appointments and internal appointments*

Test the Business Rules

There is an easy way, available from within the JDeveloper IDE, to test the business rule set we have been editing. We do not have to deploy the composite application and somehow create test messages. We can simply create a new function in the Business Rule dictionary, have this function call the decision function that exposes the business rule set AppointmentTypeDerivation, and print the results to the console.

To make use of this facility, go to the Functions tab and create a new function called Test_DeriveAppointmentType_DecisionFunction. It has Boolean for its return type and no input arguments. The body of the function will instruct debug information to be published, initialize a new instance of AppointmentTypeCode, set it to Q1, and call the decision function DeriveAppointmentType_DecisionService_1. This function returns a list of results—and we happen to know that the first result in that list is of type TypeOfAppointmentType. A new variable is instantiated based on a cast of the first result, and the partner label is printed to the console. Finally, the Boolean flag internalAppointment is returned. Now the test will seem to fail for external appointments because the function returns false (see Figure 8-4).

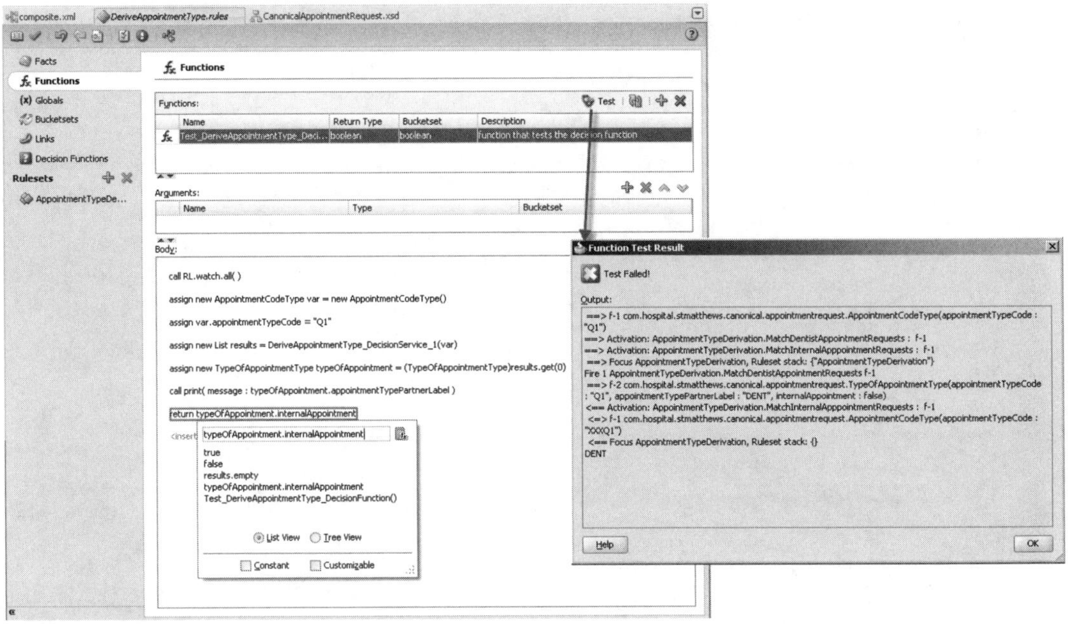

FIGURE 8-4. *Testing business rule DeriveAppointmentType for a dental appointment*

Integrating the DeriveAppointmentType Business Rule in the Composite

Now that the business rule is created and tested, we can wire it up in the composite. To do so, follow these steps:

1. Open the Composite Editor and add a new Mediator, called EnrichAppointmentType, with a one-way interface and an input based on the CanonicalAppoinmentRequest (see Figure 8-5).

2. Wire this Mediator to the business rule. Link the Mediator's execute operation to the callFunctionStateless operation on the business rule's decision service.

3. Double-click the Mediator to edit it. We need to forward the synchronous reply from the business rule to the AppointmentRequestRouter (see Figure 8-6). Click the Browse For Services icon for the reply, and select the ProcessAppointmentRequest operation on the AppointmentRequestRouter as the target destination.

4. Create the mapping from the CanonicalAppointmentRequest that is the input for the EnrichAppointmentType mediator to the AppointmentTypeCode parameter required by the decision service (see Figure 8-7).

   Next comes the mapping for forwarding the reply from the DeriveAppointmentType decision service to the AppointmentRequestRouter. The mapping needs to include the request in the reply payload. Note that we can make excellent use of the auto-mapping facilities in the mapping editor.

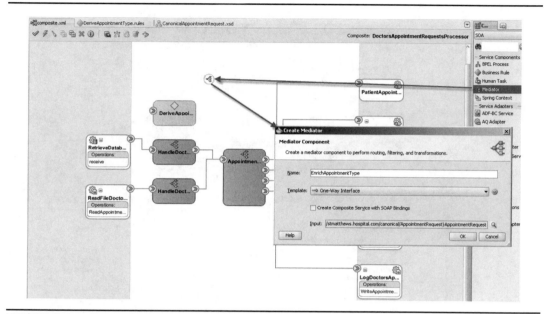

FIGURE 8-5.   *Create the Mediator EnrichAppointmentType*

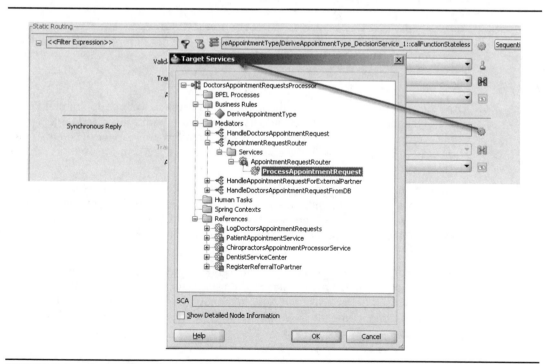

FIGURE 8-6.   *Forwarding the synchronous reply from DeriveAppointmentType to the*
AppointmentRequestRouter

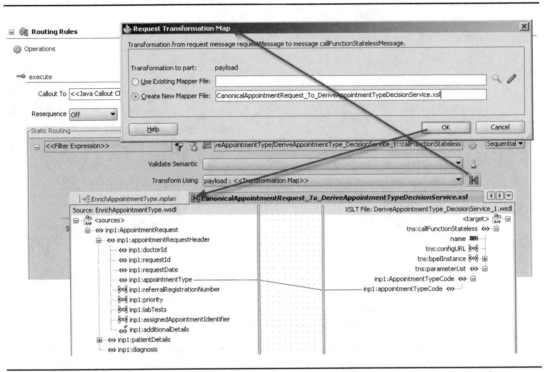

FIGURE 8-7. *Mapping the CanonicalAppointmentRequest to the AppointmentTypeCode parameter required by the decision service*

5. Drag the appointmentRequest in the initial.request source to the AppointmentRequest node in the target. Have auto-map do its job. Because both source and target are the same CanonicalAppointmentRequest type, all elements are mapped. Then map the TypeOfAppointment node in the callFunctionStatelessDecision source to its counterpart in the target document (see Figure 8-8).

   Now is the time to reroute the Mediators HandleDoctorsAppointmentRequest and HandleDoctorsAppointmentRequestFromDB that handle appointment requests from files and database, respectively, and have them route their CanonicalAppointmentRequest message to the EnrichAppointmentType Mediator rather than the AppointmentRequest Router. We'll choose the easiest way to do this.

6. Open the editor, browse for a (new) target service, and select the execute operation on the EnrichAppointmentType Mediator. Then select the same XSL mapping file that the routing rule used before—as both AppointmentRequestRouter (the former target) and EnrichAppointmentType (the new target) have the CanonicalAppointmentRequest for their input.

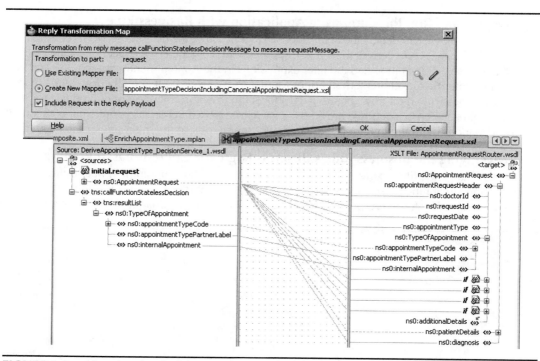

FIGURE 8-8. *Mapping the decision service's reply combined with canonical appointment request to the AppointmentRequestRouter input*

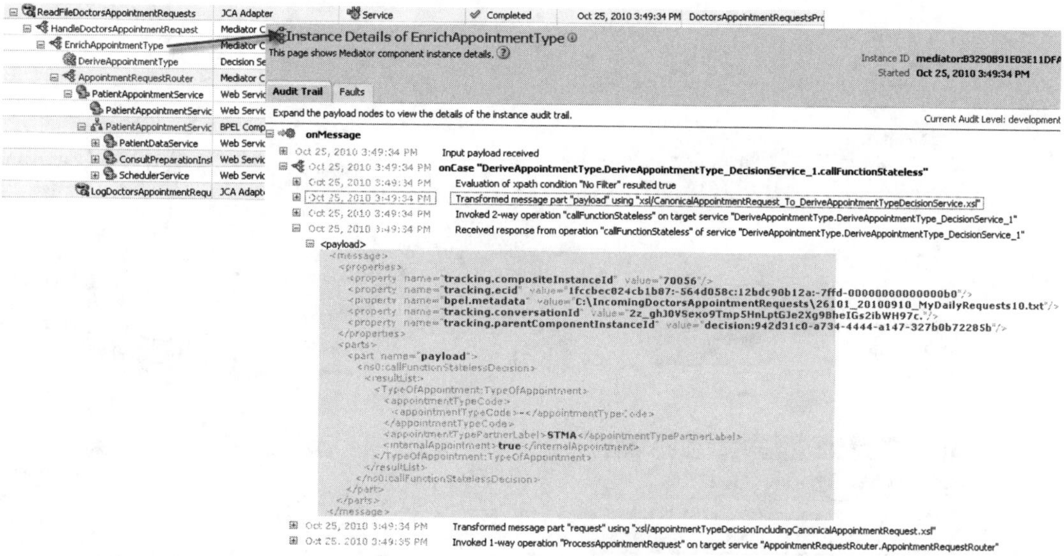

FIGURE 8-9. *The audit trail shows how the business rule DeriveAppointmentType derives STMA as the appointment type partner label*

Deploy and Run the Composite Application with Business Rule

At this point, we can deploy the application and see whether the decision service is correctly invoked and the business rule derives the TypeOfAppointment element as we expect (see Figure 8-9). Note that we have not yet modified the filter expressions in the AppointmentRequestRouter and Handle AppointmentRequestForExternalPartner Mediators, so we do not actually use the result from the business rule right now. Figure 8-10 shows the flow for an appointment request for a dental appointment. The business rule provides the value that is used in Mediators AppointmentRequestRouter and HandleAppointmentRequestForExternalPartner to determine the route for the message.

Leveraging the Business Rule's Business Logic for Content-based Routing

Let's change the filter expressions on the routing rules in the AppointmentRequestRouter—in order to streamline those expressions and untangle the hard-coded business logic dependencies. Open the editor for the AppointmentRequestRouter Mediator. Change the filter expression for the

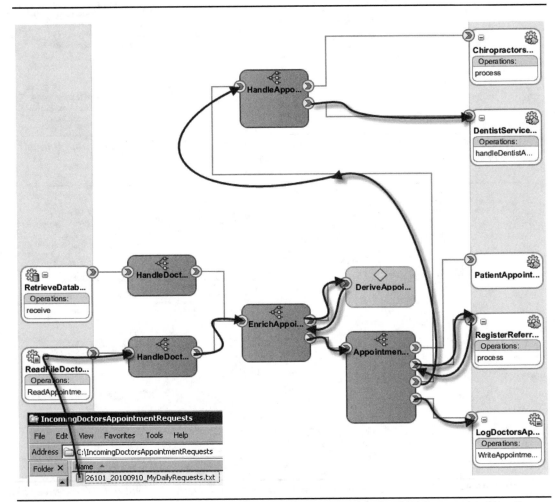

FIGURE 8-10. *The DoctorsAppointmentRequestsProcessor with the decision service in action*

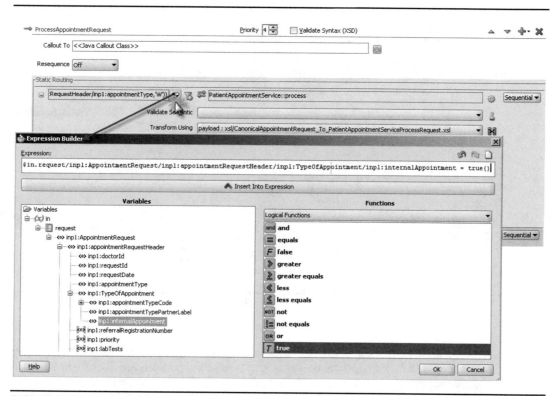

FIGURE 8-11.   *Edit the filter expressions for the Mediator AppointmentRequestRouter*

routing rule for internal appointment requests to the PatientAppointmentService to the following (see Figure 8-11):

```
$in.request/inp1:AppointmentRequest/inp1:appointmentRequestHeader...
                  .../inp1:TypeOfAppointment/inp1:internalAppointment = true()
```

This expression uses the internalAppointment flag that was set by the decision service. The logic behind the derivation of whether or not a request refers to an external appointment has been removed from the filter expression—no more references to W or Q1, Q2, and Q4.

The filter expression for the routing rule to RegisterReferralToPartner is the reverse from the one for PatientAppointmentService.

Next, we need to edit the routing rules for the HandleAppointmentRequestForExternalPartner Mediator. Again, we can remove business logic—all references to W and Q1, Q2, and Q4—and make use of the appointmentTypePartnerLabel value set by the business rule.

The filter expression for the routing rule to ChiropractorsAppointmentProcessorService becomes the following (see Figure 8-12):

```
$in.request/inp1:AppointmentRequest/inp1:appointmentRequestHeader...
       .../inp1:TypeOfAppointment/inp1:appointmentTypePartnerLabel = 'CHIRO'
```

The filter expression for the rule for DentistServiceCenter is similar—replace CHIRO with DENT.

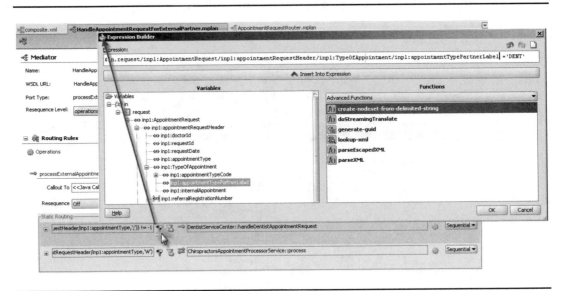

FIGURE 8-12. *Editing the filter expressions for the Mediator HandleAppointmentRequest ForExternalPartner*

With the logic for deciding between internal and external appointments and picking the right external partner externalized in the business rule (and removed from the filter expressions in the two Mediators), this is a good moment to redeploy the application and have it process some appointment requests, arriving in the database table or in a file, to verify its proper functioning.

Handling New AppointmentType Codes

What we had some reason to fear in Chapter 7, and prepared for earlier in this chapter, has come to pass: The dentists have adopted two new codes for their appointments. In addition to Q1, Q2, and Q4 (which we already catered for in our application), they now will use Q9 and Q11 as well.

In the not-too-distant past—before this chapter—we would have had to modify the composite application in several places, a job only a programmer can perform. Then we would have had to retest and redeploy the application. Not a pretty task for such a small, nontechnical change. However, with the business rule in place, we can cheerfully take on such challenges. All we need to do is go into the SOA Composer—a browser-based run-time application that allows us to edit business rules. In fact, using this application is so simple, it hardly requires a programmer—a trained business analyst or application administrator could just as easily make the required change.

Open the SOA Composer at http://*host*:port/soa/composer, where *host* is the server that runs your SOA Suite. Log in to the composer, typically as weblogic. Open the Business Rule dictionary for DeriveAppointmentType (see Figure 8-13).

The rule set is shown. You may note that the rules are displayed in an even (analyst) friendlier terminology than in JDeveloper, with the string "isn't" instead of the operator "!=" and "begins with" instead of "startsWith." Enter edit mode through the Edit button in the top menu bar. Edit the right-side operand of the rule Match Dentist Appointment Requests. Add the values Q9 and Q10 and then commit the changes (see Figure 8-14). This will immediately activate the changed business logic, meaning that any call—including from composite instances that have already started—to the business rule will from now on execute according to this new logic.

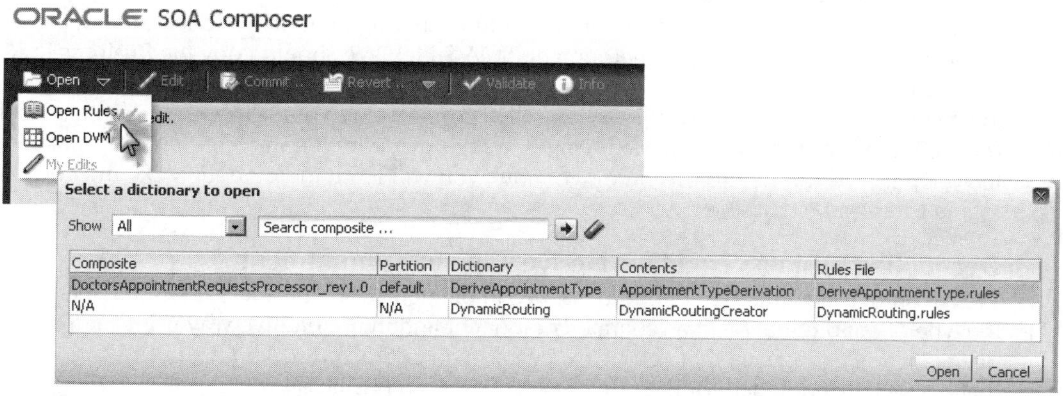

FIGURE 8-13. *Opening the Business Rule dictionary DeriveAppointmentType.rules in the SOA Composer*

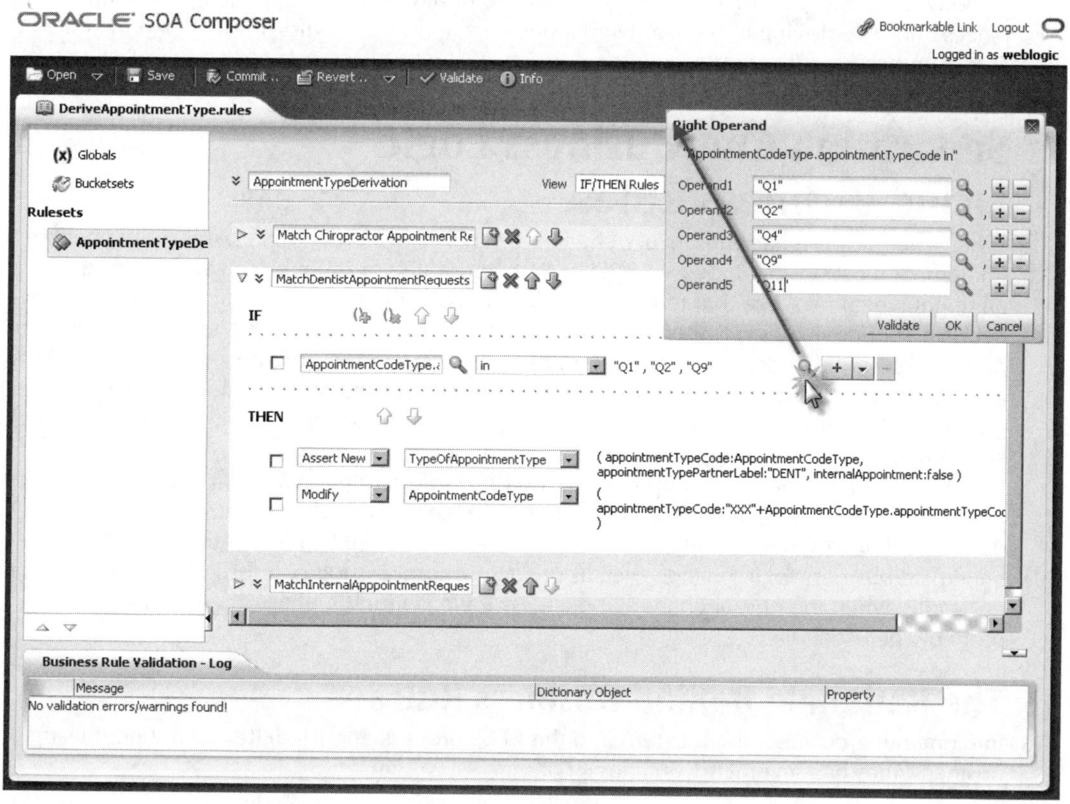

FIGURE 8-14. *Editing the business rule for matching dental appointment requests—adding the two new codes Q9 and Q11 that must be supported*

Run Time Ahead of Design Time

At this point, the rule definitions in our design-time environment (JDeveloper) are out of sync with the definitions on the run-time environment (SOA Suite). We should copy the Business Rule dictionary to the design time before resuming work on it in JDeveloper. An easy way to access the changed rules dictionary is through an MDS connection in JDeveloper. We can inspect the rule definitions and copy and paste changes to the rule definition in the composite application in JDeveloper. We will not do this here right now; you will learn more about MDS and connecting to it in Chapter 18.

Decoupling Business Logic for Derive Type of Appointment

We accomplished what we set out to do. We implemented the business logic—the derivation of the type of appointment—in a separate component and in an intuitive way using an almost declarative rule language that can be executed in an optimized way in the business rule engine that is specially equipped for the task of executing such business logic.

The business rule set that performs the logic is exposed as a decision service that we have integrated with the composite application. Instead of five duplicates of the same logic in hard-to-read and tough-to-write XPath, we have a single invocation of the decision service and straightforward filter expressions that are decoupled from the logic. The real proof of the pudding came when the logic had to be changed. Instead of having to change the application in multiple places and redeploying it, we—or even a business analyst!—could simply make the change in the SOA Composer application.

Separating Out Business Logic Using Business Rules

When your tool is a hammer, every challenge can be considered a nail. It is quite possible to implement most business logic in BPEL, XPath and XSLT, or in Java. You will not frequently get an unequivocal message that tells you that you have really crossed the line and should engage a decision service. However, there are some tell-tale signs that should make you wonder whether perhaps you are overdoing the amount of business logic in the programs you create. Among them are abundant usage of if/then branches, frequent occurrences of hard-coded values, business-oriented calculations and conversions, logic that you need to consult with business analysts on, and duplication of code snippets between components.

Note that the reverse—inappropriate use of business rules—can also occur. Creating and using business rules for logic that doesn't change that frequently can introduce complexity and overhead that serves no good purpose. A good rule of thumb is the frequency with which you anticipate business logic changes versus changes in process logic. If these frequencies differ—and especially when the rate of change in business logic is much higher—then business rules should probably be used.

The Rationale Behind Business Rules

Implementing business logic external to the BPEL process and Mediator component using business rules has several advantages:

- **Separation of concerns.** By separating the business rules from the process flow, both the process flow and the business rules become easier to understand, to change, and to test.

- **Reuse.** The same rules implementing a specific piece of business logic can be used in many different processes and SOA composite applications as well as in Java (web) applications. Note that separating out business logic into reusable components does not mandate the use of business rules—a simple BPEL process or even Mediators with the echo pattern could be used to accomplish something similar in a less flexible, more hard-coded way.

- **Flexibility.** Rules can be changed separately from the flow, even when the process is already deployed. This makes it easier to achieve agility and deal with changing circumstances, business requirements, laws, and regulations.

- **Optimal use of project resources.** Having the business logic implemented in a business rule, the programmer can focus on the implementation logic while business analysts can focus on developing the business rules; business rules are constructed in a way that is not very technical and fairly accessible to nonprogramming staff (although, in reality, creating business rules usually is still quite challenging to analysts).

- **Optimal use of system resources.** The Business Rule engine is created with the execution of—potentially very complex—business rules in mind. Leveraging this engine for running the business logic frees the other service engines from a task they are less well suited for.

Business logic comes in several disguises. It can be logic that specifies validation rules that go beyond the validations defined in the XSD and possibly the Schematron document. Formulas for calculating values according to specific logic and rules or converting values between domains are another category of business logic we can implement using business rules.

Rules can be used to categorize values—applying labels to identify values based on the range they are in. Business rules typically tell us whether a patient is too heavy; a temperature is high or low; an order gets auto-approval or requires manual stamping; an appointment is in the morning, the afternoon, or the evening. A specific type of categorization is validating values against business thresholds. Action may be required when values go over such thresholds. Business rules help settle decisions—using various if/then steps to determine which discount applies or what diagnosis can be concluded. Business logic can steer dynamic routing—where depending on certain conditions and values, a message should be routed to one or another service provider.

Business Rule Architecture

An overview of all artifacts related to Business Rules is shown in Figure 8-15. Business rule definitions are managed in rule dictionaries that, in turn, are stored in the Metadata Services (MDS) repository (see Chapter 18). A dictionary contains *rule sets*—collections of business rules that are executed as a single unit. A business rule consists of two parts—the test (IF) and the action (THEN). The test is a Boolean expression that typically tries to match the input data against predefined conditions. When the test evaluates to true—for example, a match has been found— the action part is triggered. Actions usually create result data—the output of the business rule. However, the actions can do much more, including printing debug information, calling functions, and creating new, intermediary facts.

The data that gets inspected, aggregated, created, or manipulated in business rules is handled as *facts,* the business rule equivalent of variables. A fact is an instance of a Fact type, an object definition based on an XML type in an XSD document, a Java type in class definitions, or an RL fact that is similar to Java Beans or even Map objects. The facts (or Fact types) defined in the dictionary can be processed in various ways in the business rules and in custom functions.

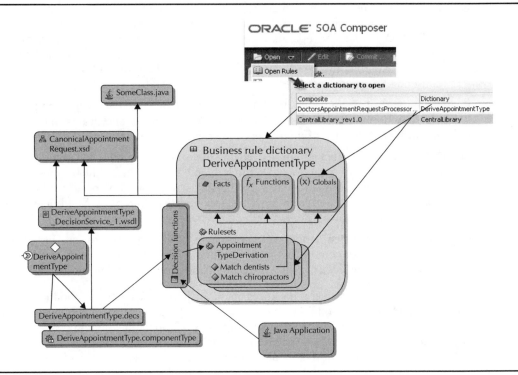

FIGURE 8-15. *The architecture of business rules*

The output of a business rule is prepared through an "assert fact" action—which creates and adds the fact of the specified type to the business rule engine's working memory.

The execution of a business rule set is an iterative process: In the first iteration, the input from the rule invoker is matched against the tests of the business rules. In subsequent iterations, the facts created or modified by the actions of the business rules in the previous iteration are matched against those same tests. The iterations halt when no new or modified facts are matched—the end result is determined at that moment.

The business rules we have created earlier in this chapter to determine the type of appointment are quite simple: The input—the original appointment type—is matched against rules for Chiropractor, Dentist, and "everything else." The actions taken by these rules do not create or change the fact used in the IF-match conditions of these rules, so after the first iteration, processing will cease.

The iterative approach to processing the initial input and the intermediary results produced by the rules themselves are based on the Rete algorithm, which was developed in the late 1970s by artificial intelligence researchers. Oracle Business Rules uses this algorithm to optimize the pattern-matching process for rules and facts. Partially matched results are stored in a single network of nodes in working memory. The Rete algorithm avoids unnecessary rechecking when facts are deleted, added, or modified.

Functions

Rule dictionaries can also contain user-defined functions—next to many standard, built-in functions. User-defined functions are written in the same Java-like RL language used for the business rules. The functions can take one or more input arguments and typically return a result. They can be called from each other and from within both the test and the action part of a business rule. Through functions, business rules can be much simpler, more readable, and better maintainable. Functions are also frequently used to test the business rules defined in a dictionary.

Both functions and business rules can make direct use of *globals,* which are variables that are centrally defined in the dictionary and can be accessed from all over the place—like Java static class members or PL/SQL global package variables (which have the same value across all database sessions). Globals, like business rules but unlike functions, can be maintained at run time through the SOA Composer application.

A specific type of function is the decision function. Decision functions define the way rule sets are exposed to external consumers. Neither business rules nor rule sets are accessible from the outside all by themselves—the only gateway into the business logic held in business rules is through decision functions. A decision function determines input facts (the data against which the initial rule matches are performed) as well as the output facts (the data that is to be returned, created by the actions in the triggered rules, and associated with one or more rule sets that will be used for matching the input data). A rule dictionary can have several decision functions that each operate with a different rule set.

System Parameters and Global Formulas

Hard-coded values in programming code as well as hard-coded business logic should be approached with a lot of suspicion. It is hardly ever a good idea to have hard-coded numerical or string values embedded in the code. Examples of hard-coded values include the name of the hospital, the exchange rate between the U.S. dollar and Euro, the age from which a person can have surgery without parental consent, the conversion rate between pounds and kilograms, the time required for a particular medical procedure such as an X-ray scan of a broken arm, and the start time of the night shift.

Such values may be needed more than once—and to ensure that every time the exact same value is used, a logical reference to a single, globally defined value is to be preferred over hard coding. Apart from nature's constants, most values are susceptible to change at some point. Business logic may change, the hospital may be renamed, currencies may be replaced, regulations may be altered—values that may be regarded as constants frequently turn out over time to not be constant after all. Changing all hard-coded instances of the value is expensive and risky; much easier, of course, would be to change the single, central occurrence of the value.

What is said here about simple values also applies to formulas and calculations. Formatting an address or converting a Fahrenheit temperature to its Celsius counterpart, deriving current age from birth date, determining the Body Mass Index (BMI), calculating a medicine dosage given the age and mass of a patient, or creating a properly laid-out string for a given date and time—these are all candidates for inclusion in global libraries at St. Matthews, allowing for central maintenance and widespread reuse.

We will discuss how we can use the Business Rule service components to help us to get rid of hard-coded values and formulas.

Setting Up the Central Library of System Parameters

The objective here is to create a decision service that we can leverage in multiple composite applications. This service returns the value of the system parameter whose name is passed in. The steps we have to go through are similar to those in the previous section.

Because we want this decision service to be accessible from all composite applications, it should be not deployed as part of a specific application but rather as a stand-alone composite. So we'll create a new SOA composite application, called CentralLibrary.

Initial Creation of the CentralLibrary Application

The first step in this new application is the creation of an XSD document called CentralLibrary Management.xsd, with types ParameterRequestType and ParameterResponseType:

```
<xsd:complexType name="ParameterRequestType">
        <xsd:sequence>
            <xsd:element name="parameterName" type="xsd:string"/>
        </xsd:sequence>
    </xsd:complexType>
<xsd:complexType name="ParameterResponseType">
    <xsd:sequence>
        <xsd:element name="parameterName" type="xsd:string"/>
        <xsd:choice>
            <xsd:element name="parameterStringValue" type="xsd:string"/>
            <xsd:element name="parameterNumberValue" type="xsd:double"/>
            <xsd:element name="parameterDateTimeValue" type="xsd:dateTime"/>
        </xsd:choice>
        <xsd:element name="parameterExpirationDateTime"
                    type="xsd:dateTime"/>
    </xsd:sequence>
</xsd:complexType>
```

Next, we create a new business rule—from the New Gallery. The Business Rule dictionary is called CentralLibrary, the package is com.stmatthews.rules.centrallibrary, and the decision service is CentralLibrary_SystemParametersDecisionService (see Figure 8-16). The input parameter is ParameterRequest (based on the ParameterRequestType) and the output parameter is ParameterResponse (based on ParameterResponseType).

We will use globals to configure the hard-coded values used in the business rule to derive the values of system parameters. These globals can easily be maintained, even by business analysts at run time. Here we create two globals—HospitalName and MaximumNormalBodyWeight—to provide values to be exposed as system parameters (see Figure 8-17).

Next, we need to create a new rule set called System Parameters (see Figure 8-18). In this rule set will be one business rule for every system parameter we need to support. The rules will all have the same structure: a test on the name of the requested parameter and an assertion of the parameter response with the value set as a global and an indication of the expiry date of the value. The business rule for the HospitalName is specified as follows:

```
IF ParameterRequestType.parameterName=="hospitalName"
THEN
Assert new ParameterResponseType ( parameterExpirationTime : XMLDateAfterNow(7),
parameterName: ParameterRequestType.parameterName , parameterStringValue:
HospitalName)
```

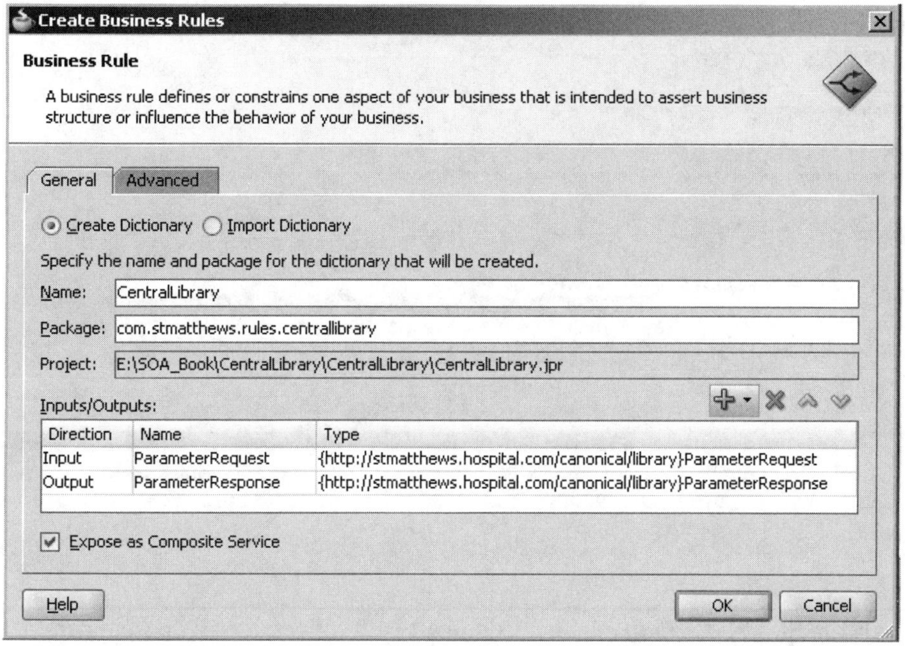

FIGURE 8-16. *Creating a new business rule and decision service called CentralLibrary_SystemParametersDecisionService*

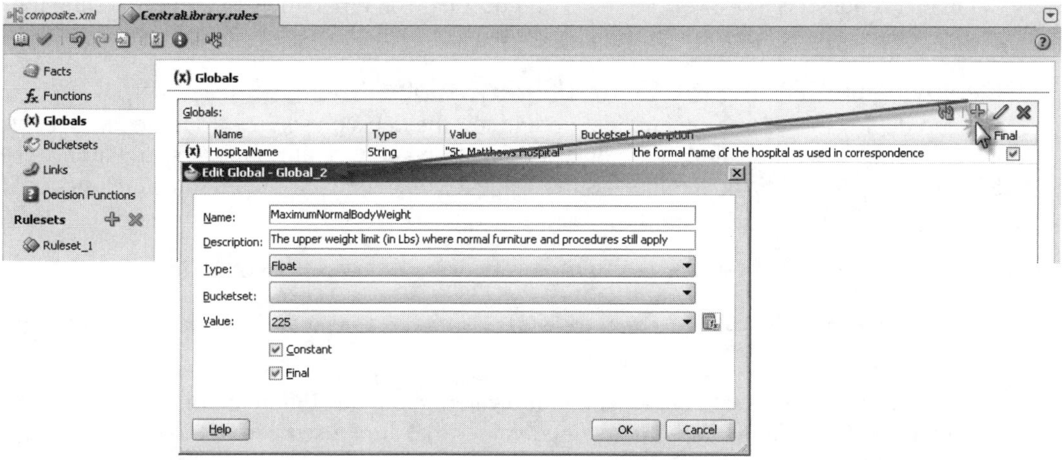

FIGURE 8-17. *Defining globals with the values for the system parameters*

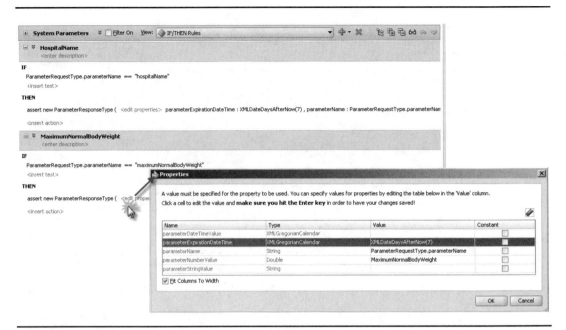

FIGURE 8-18. *The System Parameters rule set with support for two system parameters*

Note that XMLDateAfterNow(numberOfDays) is a custom function that returns an XMLDate that is offset by the indicated number of days from today's date.

We can create a test function to try out our rule set for system parameters, just like we did in the previous section. The test function calls the decision function, passing in the required ParameterRequestType—for example, for the hospitalName parameter—and inspecting the returned ParameterResponseType (see Figure 8-19).

Deploying and Testing the CentralLibrary Application

We can deploy the composite application and test the decision service from the FMW control. It is important to pass the value of the decision function's service attribute—CentralLibrary_SystemParametersDecisionService—as the value for the name attribute in the callFunctionStateful element:

```
<soap:Body xmlns:ns1="http://xmlns.oracle.com/CentralLibrary...
                .../CentralLibrary_SystemParametersDecisionService">
   <ns1:callFunctionStateful name="CentralLibrary_SystemParametersDecisionService">
....
```

The System Parameter service can be integrated into many different composite applications, providing centrally defined and maintained values that are reused across the board. And when the hospital decides to change its name—for example, because of an acquisition or some sort of

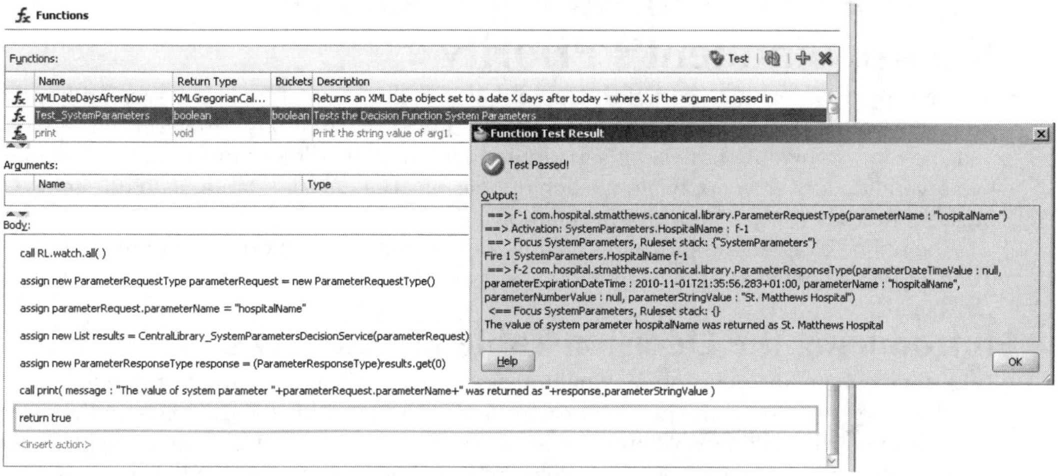

FIGURE 8-19. *Testing the decision function exposing the system parameters*

strategic realignment—all we need to do in order to propagate that name change is open the SOA Composer, change the global's value, and commit the change, as demonstrated in Figure 5-20.

Adding Formulas to the Central Library

It is a small step to extend the central library with formulas for conversion, derivation, and calculation. SOA composite applications can leverage such formulas to have generic, reusable snippets of business logic applied. The online chapter complement on the book's wiki has the source code as well as the screenshots for these steps, demonstrating the Fahrenheit/Celsius temperature conversion formula.

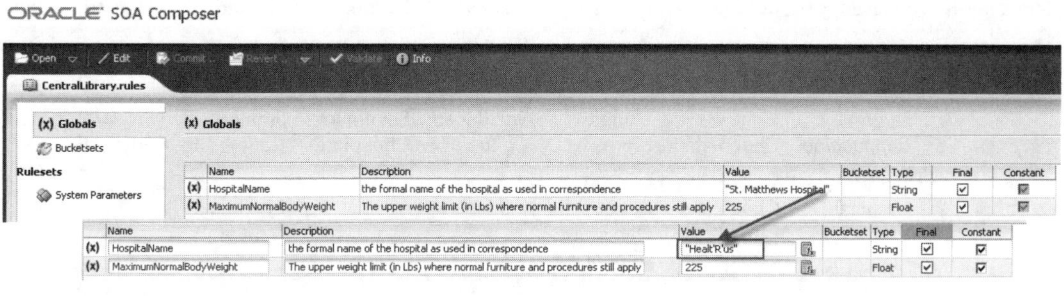

FIGURE 8-20. *Changing the global HospitalName in the SOA Composer*

Using a Decision Table to Establish the Appointment's Priority

Business logic can be quite complex. Up until now in this chapter, we have seen fairly simple, straightforward IF/THEN rule sets with a limited number of variations. However, it is not hard to imagine more convoluted rules, for situations where multiple dimensions influence the outcome and several options may apply along each dimension. The decision table–style rule set in Oracle Business Rules helps to manage such situations.

The online chapter complement contains a more elaborate introduction of the decision table using an implementation of the game Rock-Scissors-Paper.

Introducing the Decision Table at Starbucks

Take, for example, the decision-making process Margaret has to go through at the Starbuck's counter. Several factors influence the process and help determine the outcome. In the morning, coffee is the obvious choice. Afternoons usually are for tea, and coffee again at night. However, in the winter she may opt for hot chocolate drinks in the afternoon and in the spring she typically picks soy milk in the evening. When she has plenty of time and is not stressed at all, she may take the largest drink on offer, except when it is raining. When she has very little time, she may take a cold drink—although never in the fall. And on and on and on.

We see at least four dimensions in the decision-making process—time of day, weather conditions, stress level, and season—and along each dimension, one of several cases may be true. This decision-making process can be turned into a long list of IF/THEN rules, with the likes of *if season = "SUMMER" and stresslevel = "relaxed" and time_of_day = "MORNING" and weather="HOT" THEN assert new Order (drink: "grande latte")*. Such a list would be a pain to create and even more so to maintain. A decision table does more or less the same, but is much easier to read and maintain. For this Margaret@Starbuck's example, it works like this (with only a subset of the 3*3*2*4 = 72 columns):

Conditions	Rule R1	Rule R2	Rule R3	Rule R4	Rule R5	Rule R6	Rule R7	Rule R8
Time of day	Morning	Afternoon	Evening	Morning	Afternoon	Morning	Evening	Afternoon
Weather	Cold	Cold	Cold	Hot	Cold	Cold	Normal	Hot
Stress level	Relaxed	Relaxed	Relaxed	Harried	Harried	Harried	Harried	Relaxed
Season	Winter	Winter	Winter	Winter	Fall	Fall	Spring	Summer
Actions								
	Large Cappuccino	Large Hot Chocolate	Double Espresso	Small Iced Coffee	Small Hot Chocolate	Small Black Coffee	Small Soy Milk	Large Hot Tea (Earl Grey)
	Oatmeal Cookie	Chocolate Chip Cookie	Bar of Dark Chocolate	—	—	Blueberry Muffin	-	Biscuit

Every column can be read like a single IF/THEN rule. For example, the first column: if time of day="morning" and weather ="cold" and stress level = "relaxed" and season="winter" then assert new Order (drink: large cappuccino; snack: oatmeal cookie).

Every row contains a condition—all possible states that may apply to a certain property. A column (rule) is matched for the input record when each row in that column matches the data. Note that the input does not necessarily contain the exact values used in this matrix. In this coffee counter example, it might very well be that the input record contains the current date and time, a temperature, and an indication of Margaret's stress level. The first three values do not directly match the options in the matrix. We need to convert time, date, and temperature to the terminology used in the decision table:

```
(10AM, 4th July, 86F, relaxed) => (morning, Summer, Hot, relaxed)
```

We make use of bucket sets for this. Every property is associated with a bucket set—a set of allowable values or allowable ranges. Well-known bucket sets include Boolean, Gender, and Color of Traffic Light. Instead of a single allowable value, each entry in a bucket set can be an allowable range. When the value for the property falls within the allowable range entry in the bucket set, the associated label or alias can be assigned. For example, the Season bucket set has four entries, each an allowable date range that will convert the date to the season. In a similar way, three time ranges in the Time of Day bucket set help choose between morning, afternoon, and evening.

Logic for Determining the Appointment's Priority

A very raw example of a decision table is field hospital triage, where medical staff decide in a matter of seconds which victim is to be treated at all and, if so, when, how, and by whom. Staff members at St. Matthews have somewhat less dramatic decisions to make—although to individual patients sometimes the consequences can be serious enough. An important decision-making process is establishing the priority of an appointment.

The hospital has limited resources, both in terms of qualified staff and up-to-date equipment. Unfortunately, there is a waiting time for many treatments. The time patients have to wait until they can first visit a doctor depends on the priority assigned to the appointment request. The appointment-scheduling process will jump patients up the waiting queue when the assigned priority is high. When the priority is low, the appointment will be scheduled much later.

Determining the priority is a tricky business. It can take a long time when done by humans. But it may be far too complex and subtle to trust to computers. Still, Margaret and her team are going to take a shot at it. The Business Rule engine and especially the decision table show some promise of being able to take on the priority challenge.

The first attempt Margaret's staff will make takes a small number of factors into consideration: the age of the patient, the state of residence (the hospital is partially state funded and has to assign higher priority to residents), the patient's BMI, and the priority indicated by the family doctor in her referral. We will see how the decision table is created that derives the priority for an appointment request based on the scores for these four conditions.

The business rule is then to be invoked from the BPEL process PatientAppointmentService, just prior to the call to the SchedulerService. It is important that the correct value for the appointment's priority be passed along in that call to the SchedulerService.

Creating the Business Rule AppointmentPriorityRuling

The steps for the initial creation of the business rule are as follows:

1. Open the application PatientAppointmentService.

2. Prepare the XSD elements we will be using for the business rules that establish the priority. For this, create a new XSD document—AppointmentPriorityType.xsd. Create two

complexTypes (priorityRulingRequestType and priorityRulingResponseType) with elements priorityRulingRequest and priorityRulingResponse based on these types. We will use these elements shortly to also base two BPEL variables on.

```
<xsd:element name="priorityRulingRequest"
             type="rules:priorityRulingRequestType"></xsd:element>
<xsd:element name="priorityRulingResponse"
             type="rules:priorityRulingResponseType"></xsd:element>
<xsd:complexType name="priorityRulingRequestType">
  <xsd:sequence>
    <xsd:element name="state" type="xsd:string"/>
    <xsd:element name="bmi" type="xsd:float"/>
    <xsd:element name="birthdate" type="xsd:date"/>
    <xsd:element name="originalPriority" type="xsd:int"/>
  </xsd:sequence>
</xsd:complexType>
<xsd:complexType name="priorityRulingResponseType">
  <xsd:sequence>
    <xsd:element name="originalPriority" type="xsd:int" minOccurs="0"
                 maxOccurs="1"/>
    <xsd:element name="derivedAppointmentPriority" type="xsd:string"
                 minOccurs="0" maxOccurs="1"/>
    <xsd:element name="comment" type="xsd:string" minOccurs="0"
                 maxOccurs="1"/>
  </xsd:sequence>
</xsd:complexType>
```

3. Create a new Business Rule service component in the Composite Editor from the Component Palette. Call the dictionary AppointmentPriorityRuling and set the package to com.stmatthews.rules.appointments. Then specify the input and output for the decision service based on the priorityRulingRequest and priorityRulingResponse elements that we have just created in the AppointmentPriorityType.xsd. Figure 8-21 illustrates these steps.

Preparing the Bucket Sets

The rule dictionary is opened, ready for creating the business logic we need it to perform in order to determine the appointment's priority.

We need to create no fewer than four bucket sets in addition to the one that was predefined based on the derivedAppointmentPriorityType, one for each of the four input values that will be assessed in the decision table.

First, create a bucket set for age. Select the Bucketsets tab, then click the green plus icon, and select List of Ranges from the drop-down list. Create three ranges, with end points of 78, 3, and minus infinity (the last one is a default, predefined endpoint). The aliases for these ranges are Elderly, Medium, and Young, respectively (see Figure 8-22). We will use the birth date of our patients to derive their age and subsequently match the age to this bucket set to determine the category that will then contribute in the derivation of the priority type.

Next is a bucket set for the Body Mass Index, also using a list of ranges (see Figure 8-23). The following labeling of BMI values is one that closely follows the definition on Wikipedia: http://en.wikipedia.org/wiki/Body_mass_index. It suggests five labels, ranging from underweight to

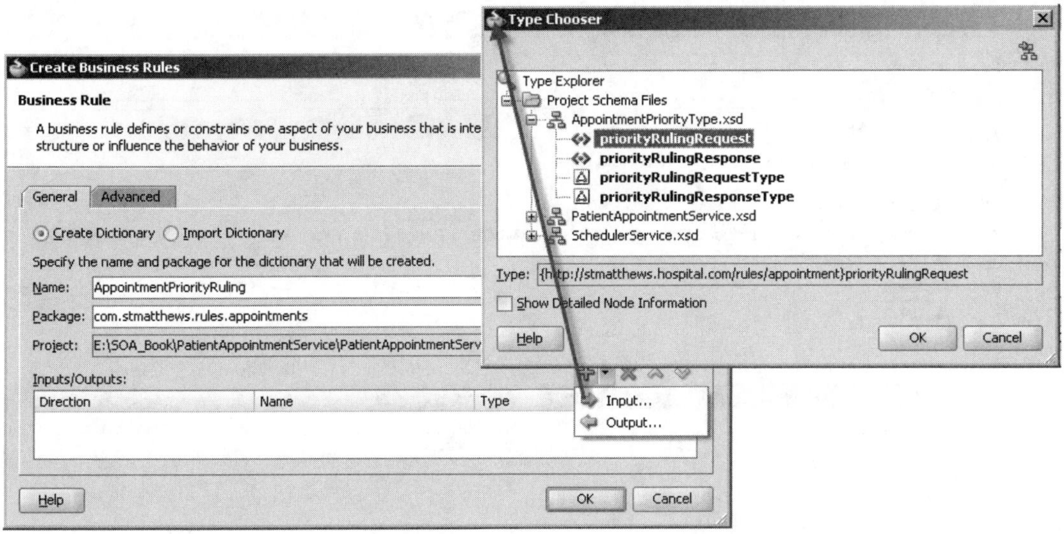

FIGURE 8-21. *Creating the business rule AppointmentPriorityRuling in the composite*

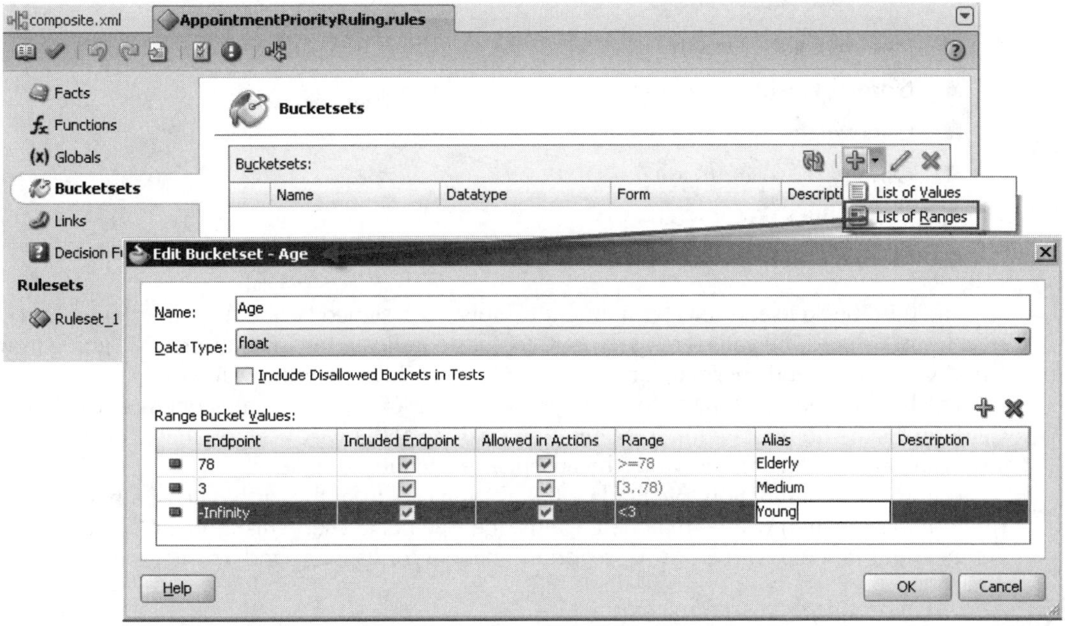

FIGURE 8-22. *Creating the Age bucket set with three value ranges*

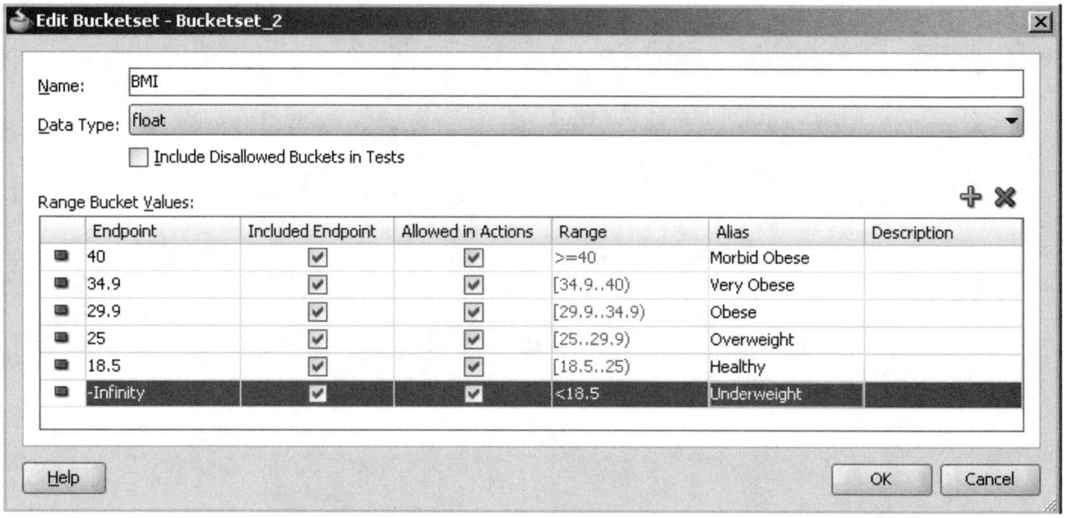

	Endpoint	Included Endpoint	Allowed in Actions	Range	Alias	Description
	40	✓	✓	>=40	Morbid Obese	
	34.9	✓	✓	[34.9..40)	Very Obese	
	29.9	✓	✓	[29.9..34.9)	Obese	
	25	✓	✓	[25..29.9)	Overweight	
	18.5	✓	✓	[18.5..25)	Healthy	
	-Infinity	✓	✓	<18.5	Underweight	

FIGURE 8-23.   *Editing the bucket set BMI for Body Mass Index*

morbidly and dangerously obese. Next, iterations of the business rules may include a higher number of categories, perhaps with some stronger focus on the underweight category.

- **Underweight**   Less than 18.5
- **Normal/Healthy**   18.5–24.9
- **Overweight**   25.0–29.9
- **Obese**   30.0–34.9
- **Very Obese**   34.9–40.0
- **Morbid Obese**   Over 40.0

The third bucket set is for appointment priority, as assigned by the referring doctor and based on a list of values. The values range from 0 to 4, and indicate the level of priority, going from "low" via "lower" and "normal," to "higher" and "very high," for the value of 4.

The last bucket set we need to create is called HomeState. It contains one real value—CA; California is the home state for St. Matthews—and the "otherwise" option that applies to all other state values, including *unknown* or the absence of a value for state.

We will need a function to calculate the age in years from the birth date of a patient. The result of this function will be matched against the Age bucket set. This function is created as getAgeFromBirthdate with an XMLGregorianCalendar for its input and an integer for its output:

```
assign new Integer ageInYears =
    Duration.years between(birthDate,Calendar.getInstance())
return ageInYears
```

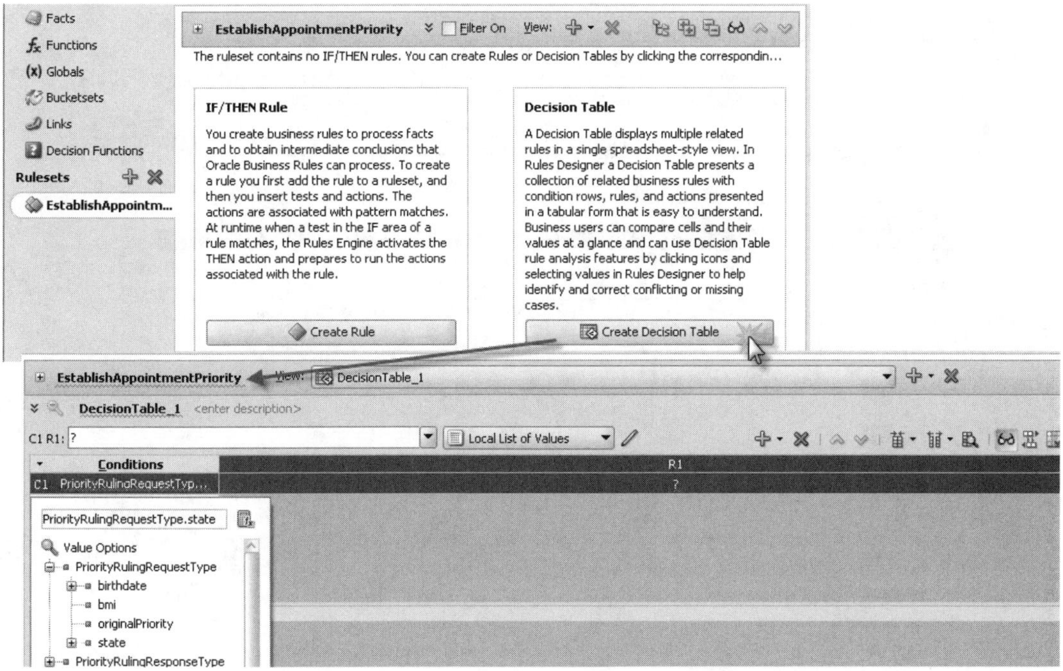

FIGURE 8-24.   *Creating a decision table in the renamed EstablishAppointmentPriority rule set*

Creating the Decision Table

With the groundwork in place, we can now edit the rule set. Let's rename it EstablishAppointment Priority, as shown in Figure 8-24. Click the button Create Decision Table.

The table has three areas: the conditions and the actions (rows) and the rules (columns). A condition is a value that is the result of an expression, usually based on one or more input values (or the current date or time), such as in our example PriorityRulingRequestType.state, Priority RulingRequestType.bmi, and slightly more interesting getAgeFromBirthdate(PriorityRulingRequest Type.birthDate). The decision table for establishing the priority will have one condition for each of the four factors contributing to that priority. Each condition is associated with a bucket set.

The actions in the bottom half of the decision table are activated when a rule matches and the action is enabled for that rule. Click the Action cell to bring up the Action Editor shown in Figure 8-25. The action is usually defined using one or more parameters—whose values depend on the specific rule (or column) that matches the conditions. Our decision table for deriving the priority type has a generic action:

```
assert new PriorityRulingResponseType (derivedAppointmentPriority:Integer)
```

The actual value assigned to the derivedAppointmentPriority is parameterized and will be defined in each rule (or column).

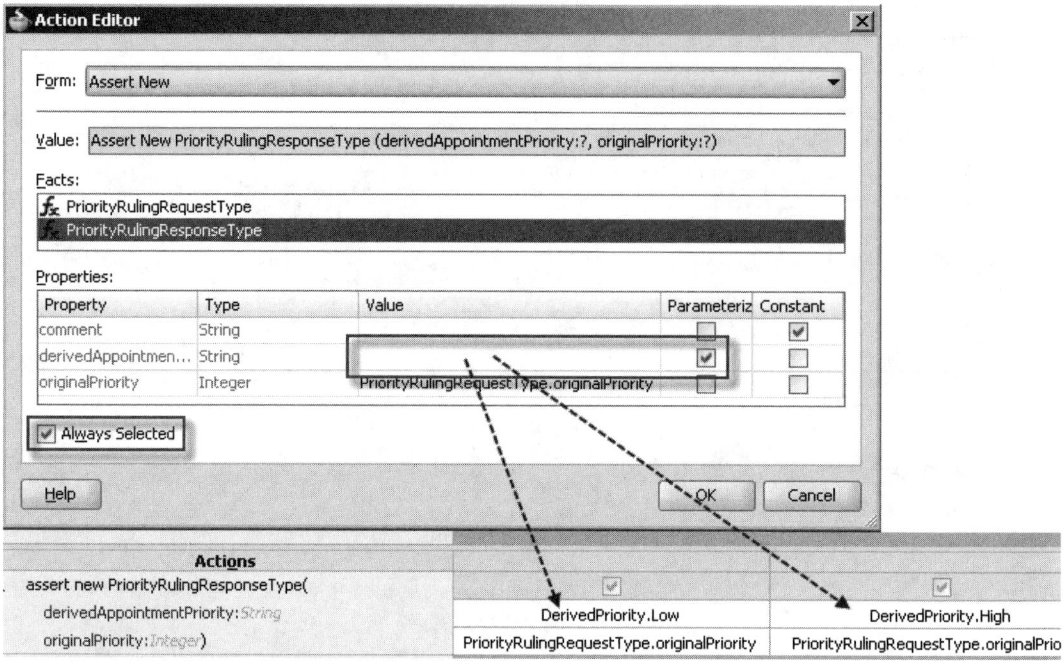

FIGURE 8-25. *Editing the parameterized action "assert new PriorityRulingResponseType"*

The check box "Always Enabled?" indicates whether the action is triggered by a match for all rules or whether it is associated with only a subset of the rules. We can enable actions on a per-rule basis.

The columns in the decision table contain the rules—with every column or rule a combination of matching patterns for each of the conditions. A column will result in a match when each of the conditions corresponds with the matching pattern in the same row of the column. A matching pattern consists of one or several values in the bucket set that are associated with the condition. When a rule has no value in a specific row (for a condition), it means the rule will match for every value the condition may have (in other words, the rule does not care about that particular condition). This may be the case when the referring doctor has indicated a very high priority and we do not need to check the other conditions before simply assigning the High priority outcome.

The Obesity Rule   The hospital—as are state authorities—is anxious to handle problems associated with obesity, and patients with morbid or high obesity, whatever their other circumstances, are always to be treated with high priority. Our first rule will implement that logic.

We need to set the first condition to PriorityRulingRequestType.bmi, associated with the bucket set BMI. The condition cell in the rule column is set to the values Very Obese and Morbid Obese. The derivedAppointmentPriority action parameter should be set to High for this rule (see Figure 8-26).

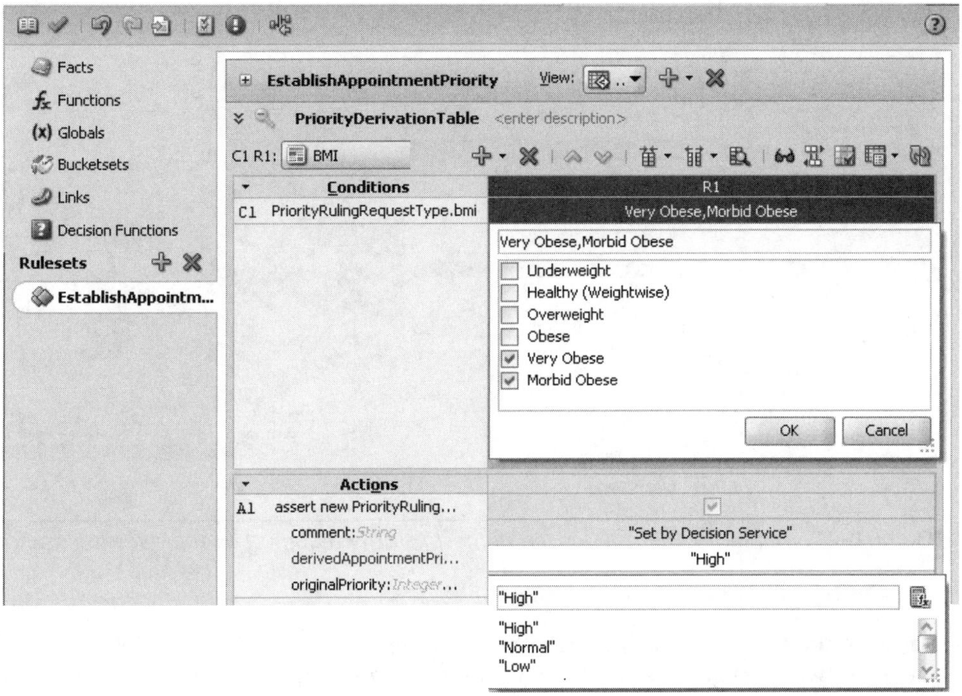

FIGURE 8-26. *Creating a "High" priority rule for BMI values that indicate severe obesity*

Factoring in the Original Referral Priority The second rule will only look for the highest priority value that the referring doctor can specify. When that value has been set, regardless of any of the other conditions, we will have a High priority result returned from the decision table. We need to add a condition for the original priority associated with the ReferralPriority bucket set. Then we add the new rule, which matches on the highest value for the original priority (see Figure 8-27).

The Low Priority Case At the other end of the scale will be a rule that describes the situation of an out-of-stater of medium age, no apparent body weight issues, and without a highest priority referral. The derived priority for this rule will be Low. To create this rule, click the green plus icon and select the option Add Rule. Also add the two missing conditions, on State (linked to bucket set HomeState) and on Age (which is derived using the function getAgeFromBirthdate, linked to the bucket set).

In each "condition cell" in the column, select the values from the bucket set associated with the condition for which the rule should match.

This rule will match the values Healthy (weight-wise), Overweight, and Obese for the condition on the bmi condition. On the second condition on originalPriority, all values will match—except the value "Very High (urgent!)". The third condition, on state, matches on "otherwise" (because we are looking for out-of-state patients). Finally, the rule matches on Medium for age. The derivedAppointmentPriority is set to "Low" for this rule.

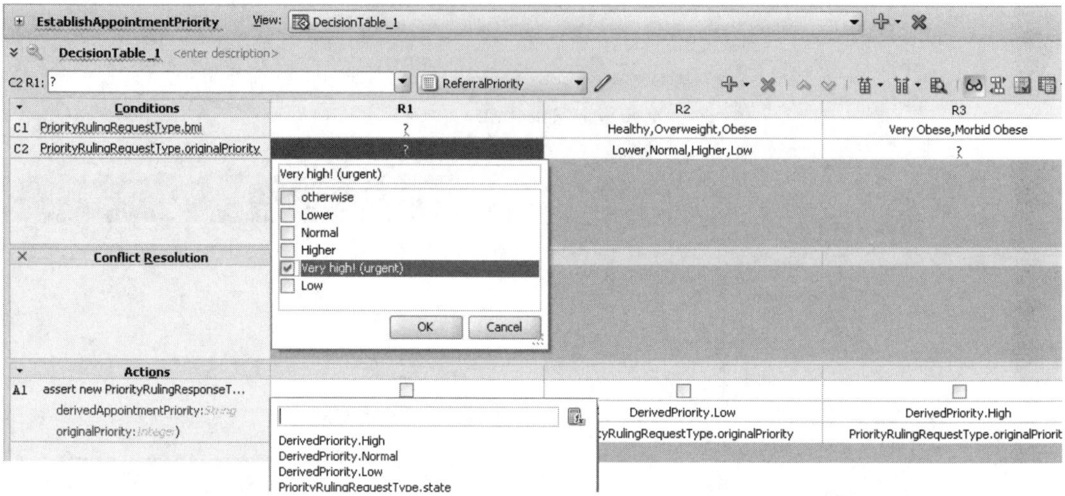

FIGURE 8-27. *Creating the rule for the highest priority assigned by the referring doctor*

Analyzing the Decision Table   Note that the order of the rules is not important. The decision table editor will sometimes move the rule columns around to combine cells where it can do so in order to present a more compact, easier-to-interpret picture.

The decision table editor in JDeveloper has several interesting features. One is the Gap Analysis. This helps us inspect the rules we have specified to see whether we have forgotten rules, given the combinations of condition values that may occur (see Figure 8-28).

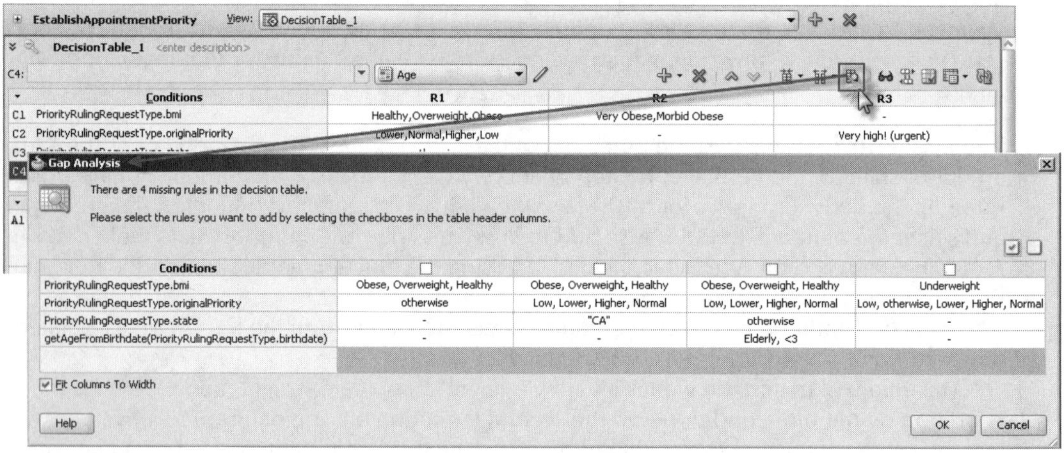

FIGURE 8-28. *Performing a Gap Analysis on the decision table*

The Gap Analysis is presented in the form of suggested rules that could be added to the table to cover all situations described by the bucket sets, complementing the rules already in the table. We can select the rules to be added by marking the check boxes in the column headers. Figure 8-28 shows that by adding four rules, covering a large number of different value combinations, we have a complete set of rules that can derive the priority for all possible requests. Note that we can decide to allow gaps, for example, when we know for certain that certain combinations of bucket values from different bucket sets will never occur—such as morbidly obese children under 3—and therefore need not have rules to cater for them. If that situation should occur after all, no rules will match and no value is assigned as an outcome of the business rule.

Another valuable feature is conflict resolution. The decision table editor can find rules that may trigger for the same set of conditions—and that may try to assign different, conflicting result values. It may be intentional or by mistake. In the latter case, this check allows us to correct the oversight. When the rule conflict is intentional, we have to indicate how the conflict should be resolved. Various methods of conflict resolution are available to us, for each conflict detected by the tool. Through Override and OverriddenBy, we can indicate that one rule overrules the other one (the overridden rule is ignored altogether). With RunBefore and RunAfter, both rules may be activated—in the order specified—and both actions may be executed. Finally, using NoConflict we can instruct the business rule engine to ignore what it thinks is a conflict.

We have a potential conflict in our decision table: We want to implement a fallback option as a final resort that should trigger when no other rules have triggered. This fallback rule will assign the priority value Normal. The fallback rule accepts all values for all conditions—and therefore has a conflict with every other rule.

When we double-click the cell that shows the conflicts, the Conflict Resolution window pops up, as shown in Figure 8-29. We can select the resolution for every conflict for this rule. In this

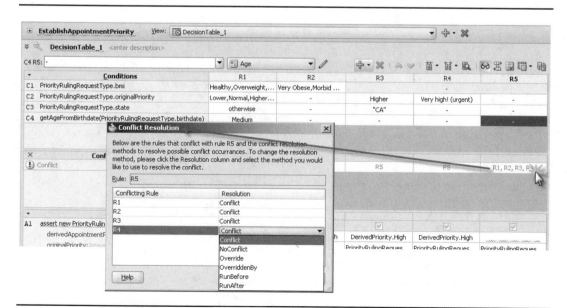

FIGURE 8-29. *Rule R5—the fallback rule that matches always with all conditions—causes conflicts that need to be resolved*

way, all other rules will override this fallback rule—when any other rule has fired, this rule is overridden, which means ignored. Only when no other rule was activated will this rule come in action to assign a Normal priority.

Operations on the Decision Table Other advanced operations on the decision table include split cell and split table, merge cells, and compact table.

Compacting the table can reduce the number of rules we have created by eliminating the rules that are redundant while preserving the no gap, no conflict properties for the decision table. The split operations create additional rules, one for each of the values in the cell that is split. Splitting a cell that currently matches on [Young, Elderly] produces two cells, and therefore columns, one for each of the two values. If a cell has the "do not care" value, splitting the cell produces a cell for every value in the bucket set. This is demonstrated in the next figure.

The merge operations do the opposite from what split does: They combine various condition values into a single cell.

With the decision table complete, we can now test the rule set using a test function. Function test_EstablishAppointmentPriority creates a new variable request based on PriorityRulingRequest Type, invokes the Decision Function that leverages the decision table to produce a result, and prints the result to the output. Using this test function, we can quickly check what the effects are of changes we make in the decision table (see Figure 8-30).

Integrating the Business Rule Service Component in the BPEL Process

From this test, we conclude that the decision table produces apparently meaningful results. This seems like a good moment to integrate the decision service in the BPEL component PatientAppointmentService. Open the BPEL editor for this component.

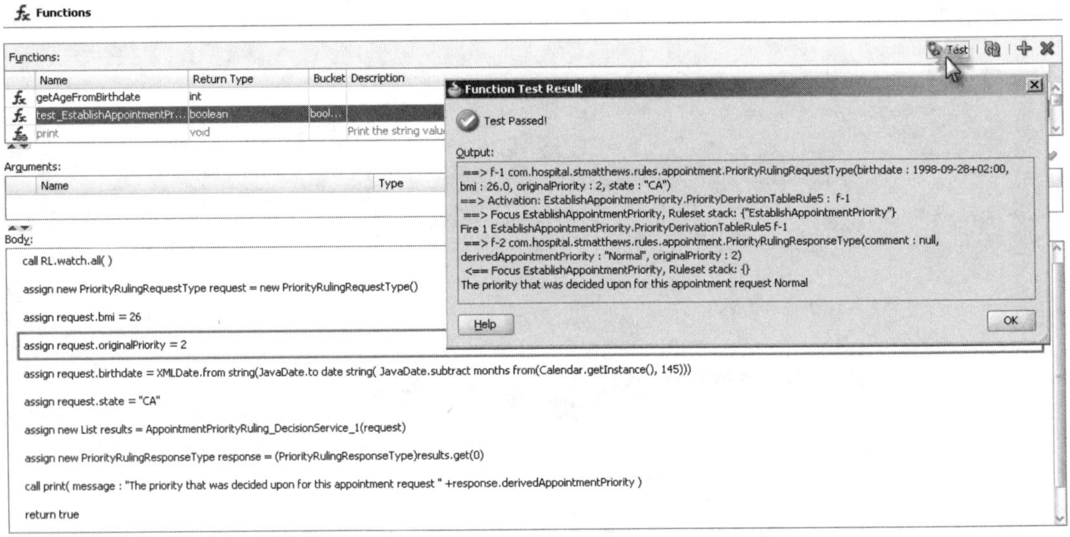

FIGURE 8-30. *Testing the decision table through a custom function*

Mediator with Dynamic Routing Rules

One special application of business rules is in Mediators with dynamic routing rules. Most Mediators have static routing rules, which means that the target for the routing rule is determined at design time. However, routing rules can also be dynamic, determining the target service dynamically at run time. All candidate target services for such a dynamic routing rule need to have the same (abstract) WSDL.

When we create a dynamic routing rule in a Mediator, an associated Business Rule service component is created along with the wiring from the Mediator (see Figure 8-31). The Business Rule dictionary is populated with XML facts based on the type definitions in the XSD used for the input of the Mediator. It also has a decision table set up for us, with predefined actions. All we need to do is add conditions and rules, and then specify for each rule which service binding data it will return. In the conditions in the decision table, we can make use of all data that was sent into the Mediator.

Very appealing is the fact that business analysts can use the SOA Composer to maintain this decision table for dynamic routing and thereby determine through easily editable business logic what target services a Mediator should address.

For example, medical supplies that are very urgently needed might be bought from the local, more expensive vendor, whereas the normal orders up to a certain order total should be sent to the order service of the supplier upstate, and the really large orders with normal or low delivery requirements should be sent to the web service of a vendor in Milwaukee. A Mediator with dynamic routing rules would have an associated decision table where analysts can edit the rules for when an order is urgent and when the order total is large, and then change the web service locations of these vendors or even add new ones.

Drag a business rule from the Component Palette and drop it right after the InitializeVariables assign step. Call the activity EstablishAppointmentPriority. Select the AppointmentPriorityRuling Business Rule dictionary. Figure 8-32 illustrates these steps.

Specify the fact mapping for the Input fact, by copying values from BPEL variables to the four fields in the priorityRulingRequest, and the Output fact, by copying the derivedAppointmentPriority to the priorityCode element in the inputVariable. Some special attention for the XPath used to copy the BMI (Body Mass Index) value for the patient to the Input Business rule fact is required—as we are somewhat optimistically assuming here that the response from the PatientDataService stored in the Patient variable will always have a physicalCharacteristic element for the BMI:

```
bpws:getVariableData('Patient','payload','/ns1:PatientDataServiceProcessResponse...
.../ns1:physicalCharacteristic[whatWasMeasured="BMI"]/measuredValue')
```

The configuration of the mapping business rule facts is all it takes to enlist the services of a business rules component in a BPEL process. JDeveloper adds the required Invoke activity to the decision component, along with the associated variable manipulations.

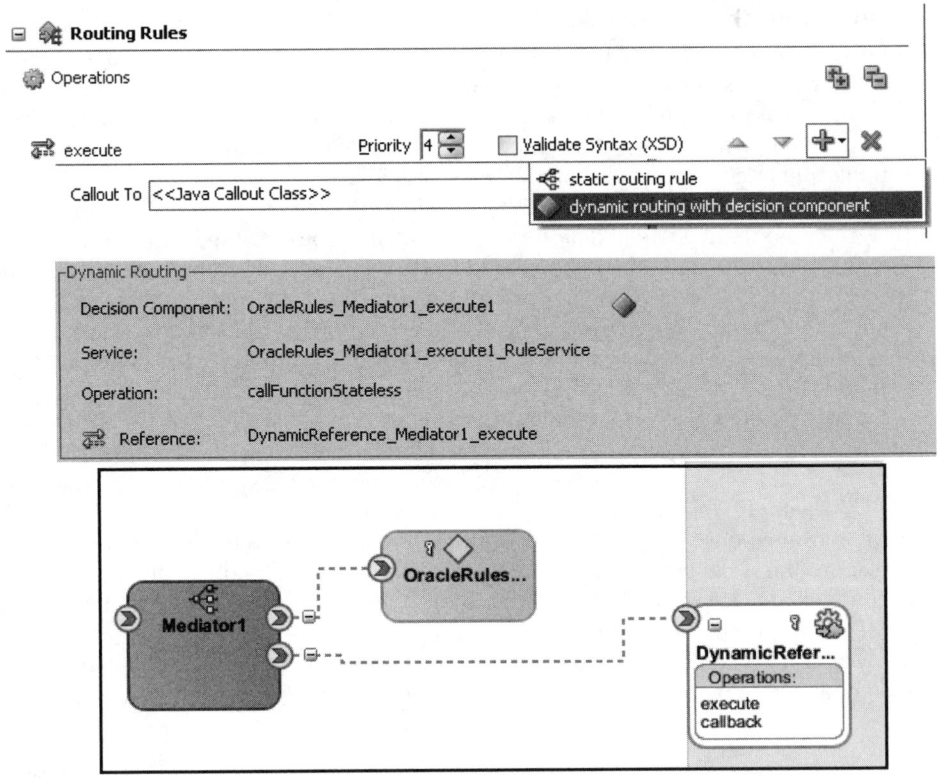

FIGURE 8-31. *Creating a dynamic routing rule in a Mediator automatically brings in a new Decision Service component*

Deploying and Testing the PatientAppointmentService Composite

We can redeploy the PatientAppointmentService to the SOA Suite and test-run the service. Figure 8-33 shows how the new decision service is engaged to determine the priority awarded to the appointment request.

Editing the Decision Table at Run Time Through the SOA Composer

When the business logic for deriving the appointment priority needs to follow changes in the hospital's policies or state regulations, that can be done at run time through the SOA Composer web application we used earlier in this chapter for extending a business rule. The decision table is available in the SOA Composer and can be edited in the same way as in JDeveloper.

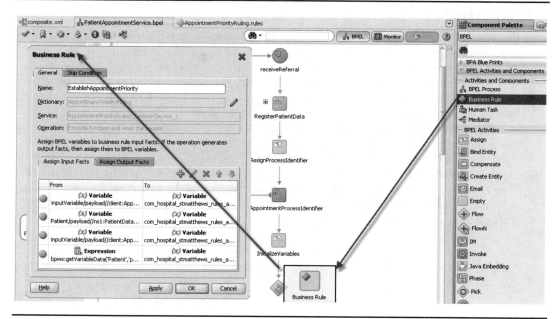

FIGURE 8-32. *Integrating the EstablishAppointmentPriority into the PatientAppointmentService BPEL process*

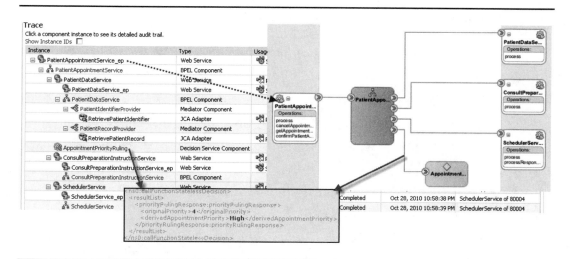

FIGURE 8-33. *Flow trace of the PatientAppointmentService in action, with an embedded decision service for deriving the appointment priority*

Summary

Business rules are reusable service components that encapsulate business logic. Based on a request message, they work their magic and return the decision or calculated result in a response message. Business rules are part of and deployed inside composite applications. Among their special treats is their ability to be edited at run time. Through the SOA Composer, developers or business analysts can refine the definition of a business rule. Such modifications take immediate effect and do not require a redeployment of the application.

Composite applications can leverage business rules to provide adjustable system parameters (as an alternative to hard-coded values); perform potentially complex, reusable calculations; do validations of data; and make decisions given a certain input based on advanced business logic. Business rules help to decouple the logic and their implementation from the Mediator and BPEL components, and allow those to focus on process, routing, and transformation logic. Business rules can also be invoked from external applications as a Web Service and from Java applications through a Java-based API.

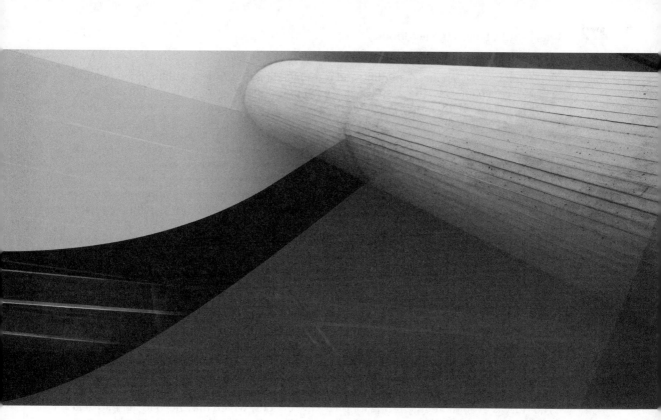

CHAPTER
9

Event-Driven Architecture
for Super Decoupling

OA is about decoupling and reuse, leading to business agility. In the previous chapters we have seen many examples of decoupling, both within and between our SOA composite applications, as well as between these composites and external services and systems.

The use of XML and Web Service standards is good for decoupled interoperability across heterogeneous technology stacks—for example, file systems, databases, Java applications, packaged applications, and SOA Suite. The integration between service components based on the WSDL contracts and the SCA infrastructure allows us to use the best tool for the job—Business Rules for business logic, Mediator for routing and transformation, BPEL for stateful processes, and technology adapters to leverage functionality in other platforms.

The asynchronous capabilities that queues such JMS and AQ, as well as the events introduced in this chapter, provide us with also allow for temporal decoupling where consumer and provider can communicate without having to be available at the same time.

In terms of decoupling, we have at least one other challenge left: How do we make sure that services are called at the right time? Some services provide clear value to their invoker, such as the patient data or the result of a calculation. Such two-way services will be called whenever their functionality is desired by an application. The application is functionally decoupled from the service—the canonical model and reusable Web Service contract in combination, possibly with service endpoint virtualization through the Oracle Service Bus (see Chapter 13) or a service registry, take care of that. However, the application still needs to explicitly invoke the service, needs to know some endpoint location, and work according to the service contract.

The story is even more interesting for one-way services, which may need to get into gear for processing the newly received appointment request, for absorbing the change of address for a patient, for dealing with the sudden unavailability of an operating room as a result of equipment failure, or for handling the patients now 30 days late in paying their bills. Who is responsible for calling these services? No one will call them to get something out of them—because they do not return a response. Other services and applications may have or even generate the information that the one-way services need to get. But whose responsibility is it to get it to them? How should these information owners know which one-way services are interested in their data? And should the onus be on them to explicitly call these services? Surely we do not want to modify and redeploy applications whenever a new consumer of their information comes along—or an existing one loses interest. That would not be decoupling at all!

This chapter introduces the Event Delivery Network (EDN) in SOA Suite—a facility that provides advanced decoupling by mediating events between producers and consumers that are unaware of each other. Composite applications can subscribe to one or more of the centrally defined business event types and are notified by the EDN whenever an instance is published of one of those types. More specifically, both Mediator and BPEL components can produce and consume events. Events can also be correlated into running composite instances through BPEL components.

The online chapter complement contains some of the XML snippets and other sources for this chapter, as well as screenshots and detailed step-by-step instructions to follow through the examples described in the chapter.

Event-Driven Architecture for Super Decoupling

Event-Driven Architecture (with the obvious acronym of EDA) made a lot of heads turn. Seen as the successor to SOA by some and as a welcome complement to SOA by others, EDA is clearly on to something. Extremely Decoupled Architecture would be a perfect secondary meaning of the acronym—because extreme decoupling is one of the things that EDA adds to "traditional" SOA. In the world of EDA, events are the messages, replacing direct service calls. Events are not targeted to a specific service provider. Events are published with some logical name on some central, generic infrastructure that the event producers use in a fire-and-forget mode. After publishing their event, these producers have no more responsibility for it. They have done their job by handing the event to the central event-coordinating facility and no longer have strings attached to the event. In fact, they may later on even consume their own event just like any other consumer—because their origin is unknown to event consumers. Events typically have a header and a payload. The header contains metadata such as the event type and a timestamp. The body or payload contains the details that describe the facts of the event instance that business logic in the consumer will process.

Anyone interested in occurrences of a specific type of event can subscribe to it, registering their interest in that event type with a central facility that coordinates events. This coordinating facility receives all events that get published, relieving the event publisher of the responsibility for the event. After receiving an event, it will traverse all subscriptions for the particular event type, taking into account any filters that may have been defined on such subscriptions to see whether the specific event occurrence should actually be forwarded to the subscription's consumer, and propagate the event to all qualifying consumers. The event coordinator may support mechanisms to retry delivery of an event upon initial failure or deferred delivery for currently unavailable consumers. Figure 9-1 shows an example of an EDA environment with two types of events: The light and dark cubes are published to the event coordinator and propagated to consumers that have subscribed (dashed lines) to the event type(s) of their choice.

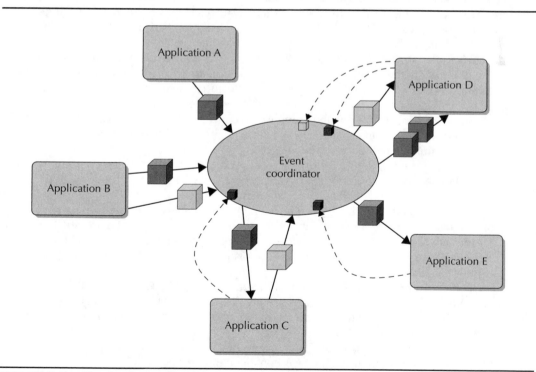

FIGURE 9-1. *The fundamentals of Event-Driven Architecture*

NOTE
None of the producers of events are aware of these registrations. They should continue to publish their events even if no subscriptions exist at all. They should neither know nor care.

The terms *SOA 2.0* and *Event-Driven SOA* have made some inroads into the SOA community. They both indicate a service-oriented architecture where event mechanisms are used to further decouple applications and services from each other. Instead of coupling applications and services that are sources of business events to the (often one-way) services that have a need for the information, events are used to convey the data through a generic facilitating medium: an event coordinator. In the SOA Suite, the role of event coordinator is implemented by the Event Delivery Network.

Introducing the Event Delivery Network

Oracle SOA Suite 11g comes with the Event Delivery Network (EDN), an infrastructure that provides a declarative way of defining, publishing, and registering for consumption of business events. The EDN enables implementation of the EDA patterns in the SOA Suite.

The Event Delivery Network is a man-in-the-middle, a central coordinator that interacts with three types of entities: publishers of events, consumers of events, and the events themselves. The publishers—composite SOA applications or external parties such as Java applications or PL/SQL code running in the database—create an event and publish it by telling the man-in-the-middle about it.

However, before events can be published, their meta-definition needs to be in place, consisting of a (fully qualified) name and an XSD definition of their payload. The payload of an event is the data associated with it, provided by the publisher and available to the consumer. The meta-definitions of the business events are defined in EDL—the Event Definition Language. EDLs are deployed inside composites or stored in MDS. These event-definition files typically import one or more XSD documents that provide the element definitions on which the event payload is based.

EDL is just another XML language—based itself on an XSD (edl.xsd in the JAR file bpm-ide-common.jar) that is registered with JDeveloper. Note that there are no explicit references to EDL files, not from composite.xml or from any of the components' definitions files. All EDL files in a project help provide events that the components can subscribe to or publish, and all EDL files deployed to an SOA Suite instance are available to all composites in that SOA Suite. One EDL file can contain multiple definitions of event types.

The Event Delivery Network works across and beyond the SOA Suite, coordinating events from and to all composites running in the SCA container. The event definitions should therefore ideally be generic, based on canonical data model definitions.

Once event definitions have been registered with the EDN, subscriptions can be created on those events. Composite applications register their interest in events of a specific type with the EDN through Mediator or BPEL components that consume such events. BPMN components—which will be introduced in Chapter 11—can also subscribe to EDN events that are consumed as BPMN signal events.

Upon deployment of an application with event-consuming components, the subscriptions are automatically detected by the EDN and used to distribute the published instances of those events. Publishers of events do not have to be registered beforehand; anyone can publish an event of a type that is defined through EDL.

As you probably already understand, events of a specific type can be published by many different publishers, both inside the SCA container and outside of it. Primary publishers of events to the Event Delivery Network are Mediator, BPMN, and BPEL service components. The SOA

From E-mail to Twitter—Decoupling Through Publishing

Jenny is not necessarily a nosy person. She just happens to know a lot about what is going on in her corner of St. Matthews. New nurses and doctors, staff calling in sick, rare new cases, VIP patients, extra-special operations, and dates between staff members—Jenny knows it all. And her colleagues know that she does.

One day, Victor, one of the interns, asked Jenny to let him know whenever an emergency operation would be scheduled. And Jenny was happy to oblige; whenever the schedule was overhauled because an emergency operation had to be performed, Jenny would page the intern.

Word got around, and after a few weeks, other interns came to her with the same request. And Jenny was a good sport and added their names to her list of people to inform upon interjected operations. Then things started to get a little trickier when she was asked by one or two desperate single nurses to keep them informed of newly admitted, apparently single male patients—via e-mail this time, because paging would be somewhat ridiculous.

Victor came back to her and—eager to participate in more operations than he was lined up for—talked her into letting him know whenever one of his colleagues called in sick and was scheduled to scrub in. And if she could, please page him as well as leave a voicemail on his telephone—because he might be at home or en route.

Jenny could not cope anymore. Keeping track of all the people, the information they wanted, and the channel through which they requested to get it just became too much. She had her own job to do as well!

Then she found a perfect solution: Instead of maintaining lists of people's interests and calling, paging, or e-mailing them whenever a nugget of information fitting with their particular request had become available, she started to use the corporate Twitter. Every tidbit of information that came across her desk she turned into a tweet. And she told everyone who wanted information from her to just "read the feed!"

Life became so much easier. She tweeted her news flashes, not knowing nor caring by this time whether anyone would read them. New readers could join in, and old ones could vanish from the crowd—temporarily or permanently. It no longer affected her.

At some point there was a request to somehow filter her tweets—in order to distinguish between operation warnings, sickness notifications, and hunk alerts. She started to add hash tags (#opr, #sck, #hnk) to her tweets and thus made everybody happy.

Her counterparts in other departments joined in and started to tweet their news as well, in a similar vein. Victor at some point happily scrubbed in on an operation in a remote part of the hospital, thanks to the alert some other "Jenny" had twittered.

Unknowingly, Jenny migrated from a distinctly coupled communication pattern to a much more efficient, decoupled approach based on publishing news and messages in general (to the ether) rather than sending them to individual recipients. With a much lighter responsibility and workload, she can make even more people happy than she realizes.

Suite also exposes APIs in Java and PL/SQL for publishing events. ADF Business Components can be configured to publish events to the EDN when data manipulations on entity objects occur (see Chapter 20). The FMW Control has a facility for publishing events for test purposes—we will be using that feature later in this chapter.

Many different composite applications can subscribe to an event. Each of these applications will receive notification of the events from the Event Delivery Network. Figure 9-2 shows the Event

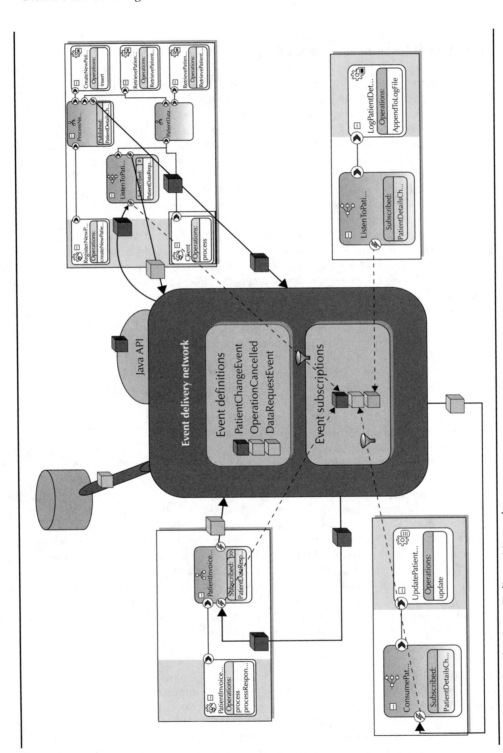

FIGURE 9-2. *The Event Delivery Network*

Delivery Network working with three business event types and four composite applications that each have one event subscription (red dashed lines). Two of those subscriptions have an explicit filter that sifts the relevant instances of the red and yellow events. Two publishers broadcast the red event (PatientChangeEvent) and three broadcast the yellow (OperationCancelled) event. The thin blue lines show red and yellow events being passed to consumers based on their subscriptions.

First Round with EDN: Consuming Events

St. Matthews is moving toward the Event-Driven Architecture utopia. Everyone involved with the SOA initiatives agrees that events are a perfect means of propagating information through the entire organization, making it available to everyone yet forcing it on no one.

A successful adoption of the Event-Driven Architecture can be achieved in steps. The hospital can start with defining one or a few business events and ensure that all communication around those events is implemented in an event-driven way. This requires the right mindset *and* discipline. All owners of processes and applications where these events are generated must be identified and convinced to explicitly publish those events on the Event Delivery Network. All services and processes that need to be triggered by those events must be adopted to consume them through a subscription with the EDN—rather than waiting to be invoked by someone with the information. Mindset and discipline—the latter to take on the responsibilities that come with EDA. There is a responsibility to push events by the instigators or first points of contact in the organization (for example, the applications that register cancellations, registrations, orders, and modifications). And applications, processes, or services that run on information available through events have a responsibility to pull the information from the EDN via subscriptions on the events.

We will dive into the implementation of EDA using the SOA Suite Event Delivery Network and the case of the patient's address changing as our first example.

Synchronizing Patient Data Using the Event Delivery Network

One of the major complaints from patients about St. Matthews is the poor handling of changes in their personal data. The number of times bills and other mail has been sent to the old address of a patient—leading to late payments or even actions by collection agencies that turned out to be rather unjustified—is way too high. Or simply the failure to change the surname after a divorce or marriage or the title after sex-reassignment surgery—even when performed at St. Matthews itself. Patients frequently are overheard sighing. "I *did* inform the hospital! I notified *them* weeks in advance! Why can't *they* understand a simple thing like a family moving!"

Patients have no clue—and should not need to know—that behind the façade with the big sign "St. Matthews Hospital" is a plethora of departments, computer systems, processes, administrations, and procedures that do not necessarily form a unified entity where all speak with one voice and listen with a single ear. "Informing 'the hospital' of some fact and expecting that everyone in the hospital thereby becomes aware of it is plain naïve!" seems the general opinion of the hospital staff, although it is not something one would say out loud to a patient, of course.

Consuming Patient Change Events

Because of the annoyance felt by the patients, and the staff to some extent, as well as for efficiency reasons—the time spent on correcting the errors just described is substantial—it has been decided that changes in the patients' contact details are among the first to be tackled through events. We will see how Frank implements a simple composite application that subscribes to the Patient Details Change event and uses the payload to synchronize his patients database. He uses a Mediator to consume the events and forward them to a database adapter that updates the patients table based on the event payload. Later on he will expand the composite so that the customer change is propagated to all systems within St. Matthews that store and use patient information.

Enforcing a regime where any change in patient details is turned into an event on the EDN, wherever that change first enters the hospital, is beyond the scope of this chapter, as are a discussion on how the correctness of the information is verified, when exactly the new data first becomes valid, and any other security issues that need to be dealt with when using events. However, note that events are not subject to authorization mechanisms: Any composite can register for any event type on the EDN and every instance of events is delivered to every consumer—when allowed by the optional filter expression on the subscription. No authorization can be specified or enforced.

We will also avoid a discussion on whether a missing element should be interpreted as a value that was not changed or one that was nullified. We will focus only on the implementation in the SOA Suite of the simplest interpretation of the event.

The steps are fairly simple then:

1. Create a new SOA composite application called SynchronizePatientsInformation, with a project carrying that same name. The application will initially consist of an empty composite.

2. To keep things simple in this example, just create a new XSD document called PatientDetailsChangeEvent.xsd with its target namespace set to http://stmatthews. hospital.com/events. Create a PatientDetailsChangeEvent and a complexType called PatientDetailsChangeEventType that defines the payload for the event—a timestamp and a patientDetails element based on the patientDetailsType in the imported schema document CanonicalPatient.xsd that contains a simple representation of a patient with her contact details (the same that was used in previous chapters; see Figure 9-3).

    The PatientDetailsChangeEvent is defined in an EDL file—as a hospital-wide event type with a canonical payload—not specific to any application or service and based on elements defined in the canonical data model. Note that the EDL file has to be created and deployed as part of an SOA composite application, even though it does not really belong to any one application—it is applicable throughout the SOA Suite container and is more or less "community property." In Chapter 18, we will see how MDS can be used to centrally store, share, and manage EDL definitions.

3. Open the composite.xml file in the editor. We will now create the EDL file, as shown in Figure 9-4. Bring up the Create Event Definition File window by clicking the event icon in the upper-left corner. Enter **PatientEvents** as name for the EDL file. Accept the default derived namespace. Click the green plus icon to add the first event definition. Select the element PatientDetailsChangeEvent from the XSD with that name in the Type Chooser pop-up window. Enter **PatientDetailsChangeEvent** as the name for the event.

4. Create a Mediator called **ConsumePatientDetailsChangeEvents** that subscribes to the PatientDetailsChangeEvent (see Figure 9-5). Drag the Mediator component from the palette to the composite. Specify the name and select the template Subscribe To Events. In the Event Chooser, select the PatientDetailsChangeEvent from the event definition file created in the previous step. We have now specified that when the event is published

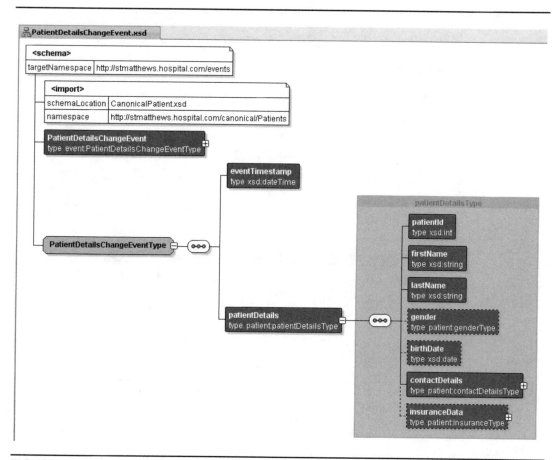

FIGURE 9-3. *The PatientDetailsChangeEvent definition in PatientDetailsChangeEvent.xsd*

on the EDN, the Mediator consumes it and can process it just like any incoming request message—except, of course, it cannot send a response. The column "Consistency" indicates whether the delivery of the event is part of the Mediator's transaction is response to the event (one and only one) or whether the delivery is in separate transaction (guaranteed). The former (and default) setting means that the event delivery is rolled back when errors occur in the Mediator (and the event can be delivered again), whereas the latter causes the event to be lost for this subscription when the Mediator transaction is rolled back. The third value—immediate—specifies that events are delivered to the subscriber in the same global transaction and same thread as the publisher, effectively (and usually very undesirably) coupling the publisher to the consumer. Stay away from that option, unless you have a very good reason for using it.

The column "Run as publisher" is set to yes to have the Mediator executed with the same security context (identity) as the composite that published the event. According to the documentation, alternatively an Enterprise Role can be set to execute the Mediator with. However, the IDE does not appropriately support this.

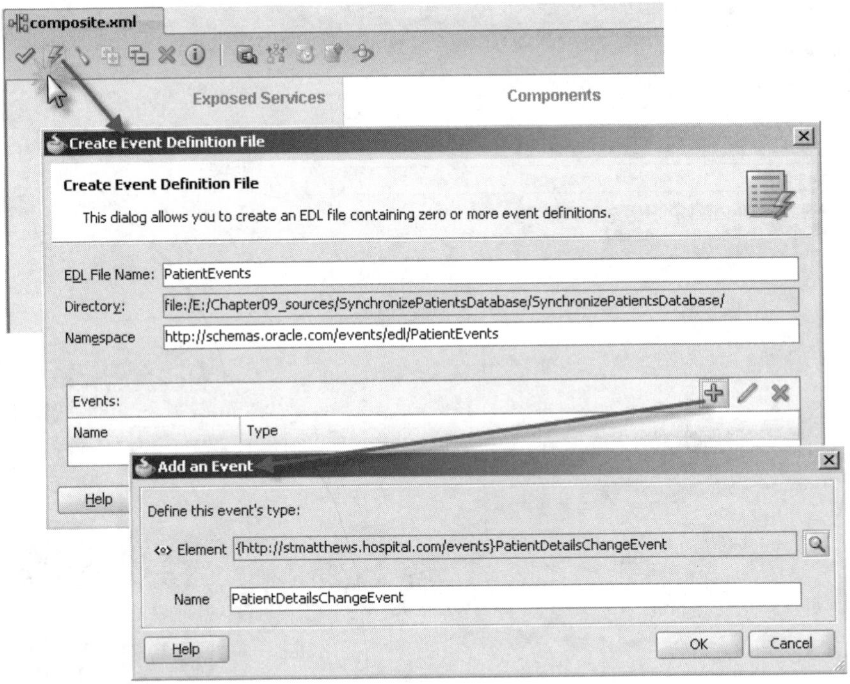

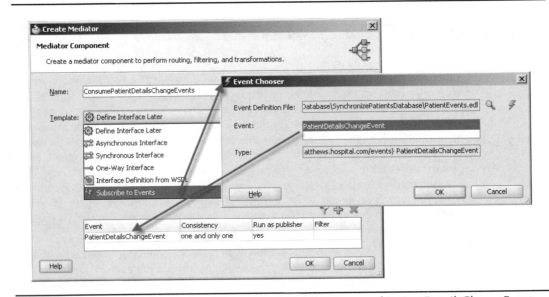

FIGURE 9-4. *Opening the Create Event Definition File window and creating the PatientDetailsChangeEvent*

FIGURE 9-5. *Creating the Mediator that consumes occurrences of PatientDetailsChangeEvent*

5. Create the database adapter service that will update the patients table. A normal best practice would be to go through a database package instead of directly coupling to the table, as was discussed and demonstrated in Chapter 5. However, to see the database adapter do straight updates for once, we will adopt that approach in this situation. The database adapter service locates records based on the patient identifier and can update various details, including surname, address, and contact data.

6. Drag a database adapter service from the Component Palette to the External References lane. Call the service **UpdatePatientsTableWithChanges**. Select the database connection to Frank's patients database. Choose the Update Only operation to perform and import Table Patients. Accept all attributes for inclusion. Click Finish.

7. Wire the Mediator to the database adapter service in the Composite Editor, as shown in Figure 9-6.

8. Double-click the Mediator to edit the routing rule from event to adapter service. Create the mapping from the event payload structure to the input format dictated by the database adapter service (see Figure 9-7).

The composite is ready for deployment. Deploy it to the SOA Suite. The EDL file with the event definition is deployed along with the composite. It is added to the dictionary of business events supported by the container. When you go to the FMW Control, you can inspect the list of all events that the Event Delivery Network knows about, as well as the subscriptions to events. First select the soa-infra node in the tree navigator. Then from the context menu, select the option Business Events (see Figure 9-8). The Business Events page opens. It shows a list of all registered business events—parsed from all deployed EDL files. The Subscriptions tab lists all subscriptions from composites on events, and indicates per subscription the precise consuming component in the composite as well as the delivery method and the filter, if there is one.

We can publish instances of the events from this page, primarily to test the subscriptions. With the PatientDetailsChangeEvent selected, click the Test button to publish a "test patient details change" event and see if the SynchronizePatientsInformation composite picks it up and processes it as expected. Note that there is no other way to test this composite because it does not expose a Web Service interface.

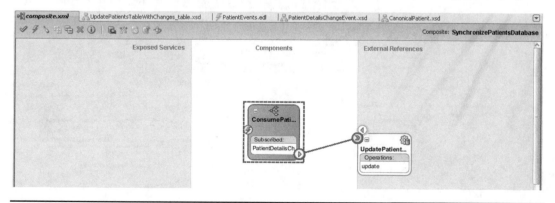

FIGURE 9-6. *Wiring the Mediator to the database adapter service*

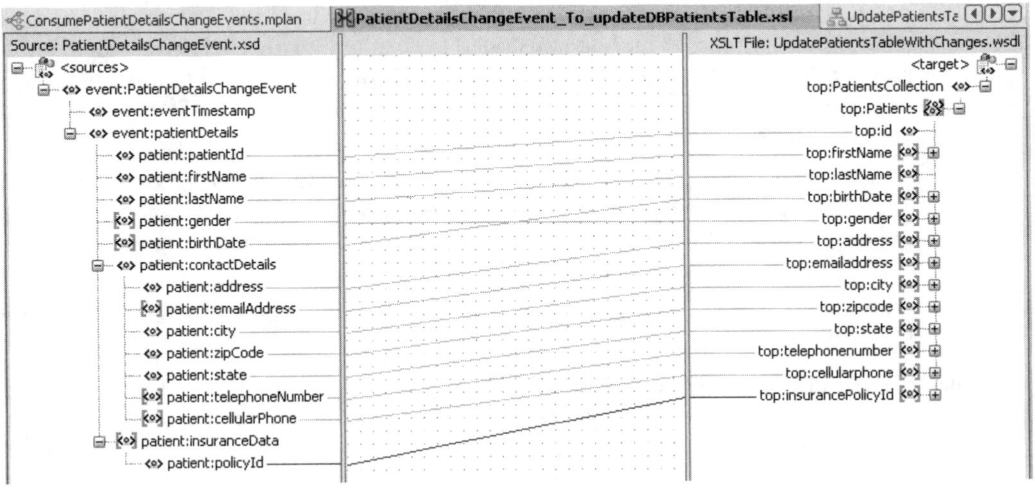

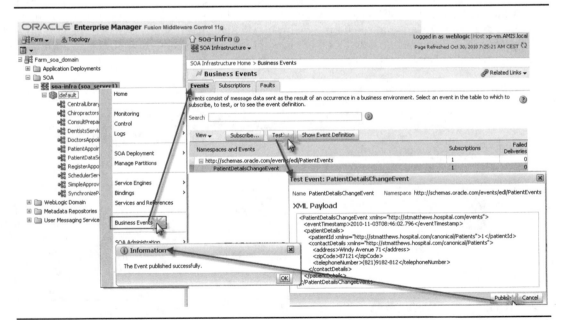

FIGURE 9-7. *Mapping the event payload to the input for the database update service*

The test instance of the PatientDetailsChangeEvent indicates that the patient with identifier 1 has moved to a new address with a new ZIP code and a new landline. He has not changed his name, undergone gender-influencing surgery, or altered other relevant details.

The publication of this event should have triggered an instance of the SynchronizePatients Information composite that has updated the patients table in the database through the database adapter service.

FIGURE 9-8. *Publication of a test instance of the PatientDetailsChangeEvent from the FMW control*

When we check the dashboard for the SynchronizePatientsInformation composite, we will find a new instance. Its message flow trace makes clear that it was triggered by the PatientDetails ChangeEvent—the only way it *can* be instantiated—and called the database adapter service. The message flowing into this service contains the payload from the event in a structure suited to the update service. We do not see the actual update SQL statement in the message flow. However, when we inspect the patients table contents and find the new address, we may conclude that the synchronization of the database has taken place, just as Frank envisioned (see Figure 9-9).

Frank's application does not know the origin of the event. The event appears on the EDN; the application is notified and processes the event's payload. Because the entity at St. Matthews who was first aware of the changed patient data took responsibility to publish the event, Frank's database has been synchronized—in near real time it would seem.

Other Consumers Listening In

One of the essential features of the Event Delivery Network is that the producer of the event is unaware of the consumers of the event. And, of course, that one consumer is completely independent of any other consumer. To perhaps state the obvious: Any event on the EDN can be consumed by one, multiple, or even no consumers at all. In the latter case, even if publishing the event turns out pointless in hindsight, that never relieves the producer from the responsibility to publish it anyway. When we know an event will (or even may) become important, we should publish it.

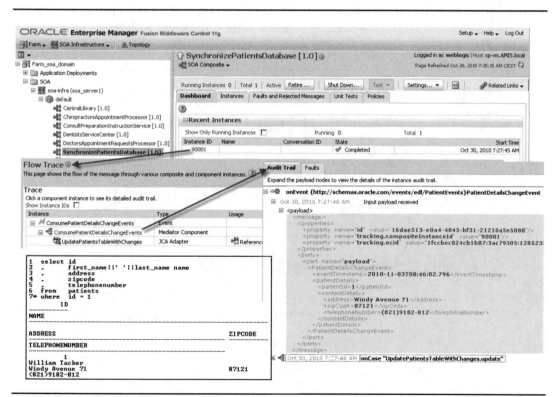

FIGURE 9-9. *The instance of the SynchronizePatientsInformation composite that has updated the patients table in response to the event*

We could create a new composite application called FeedPatientChangesToDWH that consumes the PatientDetailsChangeEvent on behalf of a data warehouse that the hospital has set up, for example, to investigate demographic trends among the patient population, including moving to richer or poorer neighborhoods, marrying and divorcing, and undergoing other changes. This composite would have a Mediator that also consumes the event and propagates it to the data warehouse—through an adapter service that could talk database, JMS, AQ, or file-speak.

When we create the Mediator and indicate the Subscribe To Event template, we have to browse for the PatientDetailsChangeEvent. The most "pure" way of doing so is through the SOA-MDS connection in the Resource Palette. Through this connection, you can browse the resources in any of the composites currently deployed on the SOA Suite. Figure 9-10 shows how to subscribe the Mediator ListenToPatientDetailChangeEventOnBehalfOfDWH to the event by browsing for it in the EDL file that is deployed in the SynchronizePatientsInformation composite.

Creating Picky Subscriptions Using Filter Expressions

Even though a composite registers its interest in a certain event through an EDN subscription, this does not necessarily mean it will have to process every occurrence of the event. It is possible to define a filter expression as part of the subscription (just like we do for content-based routing in Mediators). This filter consists of a Boolean XPath expression that evaluates the event's payload, resulting in "true" for events that should be delivered to and processed by the composite and "false" for events that the composite chooses to decline.

To see the filter mechanism in action, we will help Frank decline a specific subset of occurrences of the patient details change event. It may sound unlikely, but Frank is not interested in a particular category of patients—they are simply outside the scope of his database. All patients with an identifier

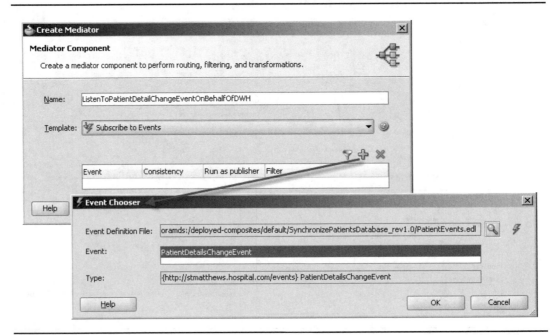

FIGURE 9-10. *Browsing for an event to consume in the SOA Suite's deployed composites using the SOA-MDS connection*

between 100,000 and 200,000 are not his cup of tea (they are managed in the patient administration in the former Ophthalmology Clinic that was merged into St. Matthews several years ago). Rather than have the SynchronizePatientsInformation composite attempt updates that will have zero effect (or even result in errors) because the target record is not available, it is better to stop the event's consumption altogether. We will specify the filter that will only allow patient details change events in the meaningful range.

To begin, open the composite and then open the context menu for the event subscription icon on the Mediator. This brings up the list of event subscriptions for the Mediator, which contains only one subscription. Select the subscription and click the filter icon. This brings up the Expression Builder that helps with the creation of the XPath expression for the filter. It shows the payload structure for the event, making it easy to include the elements we need in our filter expression (see Figure 9-11).

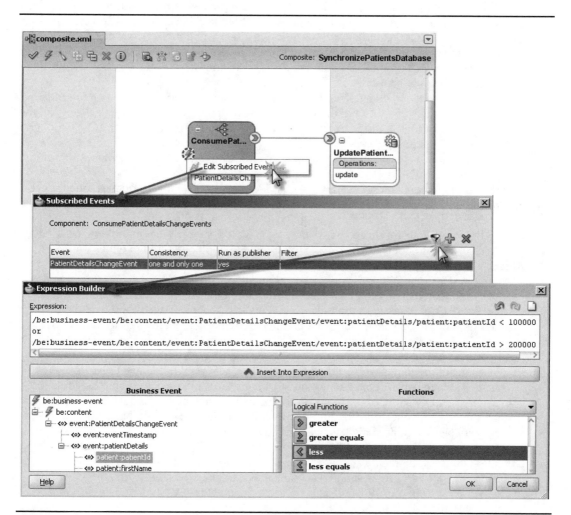

FIGURE 9-11. *Specifying a filter expression for the PatientDetailsChangeEvent subscription*

Create the following filter expression:

```
/be:business-event/be:content/event:PatientDetailsChangeEvent...
                     .../event:patientDetails/patient:patientId < 100000
or
/be:business-event/be:content/event:PatientDetailsChangeEvent...
                     .../event:patientDetails/patient:patientId > 200000
```

Basic Queuing vs. Business Queuing, or JMS and AQ vs. EDN

Publishing messages that are forwarded by a framework to registered consumers in order to achieve a highly decoupled exchange: That, in short, is what EDN adds to the SOA Suite. But that could also serve as a brief definition of both JMS (Java Message Service) and AQ (Oracle Advanced Queuing). And because we already had those two at our disposal without the SOA Suite, as well as technology adapters for both JMS and AQ to make them available from within the SOA Suite, one might wonder what exactly is the added value of the Event Delivery Network.

The fundamental concepts of EDN on the one hand and JMS and AQ on the other are pretty much the same. Most of the things we do with the Event Delivery Network and the supporting facilities in the SOA Suite can also be done with plain JMS or AQ—although it would require a lot more work.

JMS and AQ are not specially geared toward XML payloads or integration into the world of SOA, SCA, and Web Services. In order to work with vanilla JMS or AQ, we would have to implement technology adapter services that are listening to queues, one for every consumer of an event arriving on that queue. These adapter services would work with Mediators that play a similar role as they would when dealing with EDN events.

Before we can get started with our JMS or AQ operations, the underlying JMS queues or topics or the AQ queues would have to be created and configured in either WebLogic Server or the database.

The SOA Suite provides additional value with the EDN style of events. Event definitions are consolidated across the SOA container, defined in EDL files and available from MDS. The FMW Control presents the Business Events in a separate page that shows the events and their definitions, all subscriptions and faulted deliveries, and allows us to publish test events onto the Event Delivery Network. Events have become first-class citizens in the SOA Suite thanks to the EDN.

Many of the things we could do using JMS or AQ and would have to configure ourselves have been prebaked into the SOA Suite EDN infrastructure, making life a lot easier. The EDN allows us to focus on the contents of the events and the logic of event handling, abstracting away the finer technical details of JMS or AQ. However, the Event Delivery Network internally has been implemented on top of these standard messaging technologies. EDN has two different implementations—namely, EDN-DB and EDN-JMS. EDN-DB uses an Oracle Database as a back-end store and depends on Oracle-specific features. EDN-JMS uses a vanilla JMS queue as a back-end store. By default, when the dehydration store runs on an Oracle database, you get the AQ-based EDN-DB, and otherwise the JMS one.

Close the Expression Builder and the Subscribed Events window. Now the composite can be redeployed and we can publish test events to see whether the filter blocks out the events regarding patients in the 100,000–200,000 range.

If we were to deploy the composite as a new revision, we would see something that might seem odd at first. PatientDetailsChangeEvents for identifiers between 100,000 and 200,000 are still consumed and processed, despite the filter expression that should block them out. Events with identifiers outside that range are processed twice by the SynchronizePatientsInformation composite—or rather by the two revisions of the composite.

Events are picked up by all revisions of a composite application—not just the last or the one marked as default! (See Chapter 17 on versions of composite applications.) To receive the event with the latest revision of the composite only, it is recommended that you retire all previous revisions of the composite.

Publishing Patient Details Change Events

Mediators can easily be configured to consume events, as we have seen in the previous section. But they are just as capable of publishing events. A routing rule can be created that forwards a message in the form of an event's payload to the Event Delivery Network, instead of to a target service. Alternatively, you can open the context menu on a Mediator in the Composite Editor and open the Event Chooser by clicking the option Add Published Events (see Figure 9-12). The routing rules are created automatically.

A component such as a Mediator does not need a registration or configuration with the EDN before being able to publish events to the EDN. The Mediator can just send one to the EDN. You will not find a list of event publishers in the FMW Control.

Frank not only consumes patient details change events, he also publishes them to the EDN in situations where updates to patient records first appear in his database. Of course, we need to make sure that no events are published from an update to the database when that update is indirectly the result of another patient change event on the EDN—or that Frank consumes his own events, thus ending up in an infinite loop.

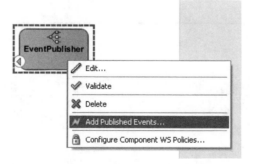

FIGURE 9-12. *Adding published events to a Mediator*

Publishing Database Events via Advanced Queuing

Ultimately, all changes to Frank's patient database end up in the database itself. All data changes can therefore be captured at the core level using a database trigger against the patients table. We would then have to somehow upgrade that database-level DML (data manipulation) event to an event that the EDN can handle. A good, decoupled approach would be to use Advanced Queuing (AQ) to publish the DML event from a database trigger—as shown in Figure 9-13. The database application has the responsibility for publishing the event, but it does not get coupled to the specific ways of the SOA Suite and its proprietary EDN requirements. The trigger uses a concept from its own realm—the Advanced Queue—and what happens next with the published event is out of its hands and mind. However, anyone listening in on the Advanced Queue can process the event in any appropriate way.

From the SOA Suite end, we would use the AQ Technology Adapter to listen to these events that get published on the queue (or multiconsumer topic). This adapter service would forward the event's payload to a Mediator that will then publish the event as described in the EDL on the Event Delivery Network.

Alternatively, the database trigger could also make use of the EDN's PL/SQL API to publish a real EDN event straightaway. That is probably easier than doing the AQ thing. However, it couples the database application to the SOA Suite in a way that could be seen as too restrictive: The availability of the SOA Suite would become a requirement to run and even compile the PL/SQL code.

Java applications can adopt a similar setup with JMS as the pub/sub queuing mechanism instead of Advanced Queuing. In this case, the JMS technology adapter consumes messages from the JMS queue and propagates them to a Mediator that publishes to the EDN. Java applications could alternatively use the EDN's SendEvent Java API.

Another approach is one where database applications and Java applications both could call a very generic, one-way Web Service exposed by a Mediator that turns various request messages into different types of EDN events.

The wiki contains a complete example of a database trigger that feeds DML events into an Advanced Queue and an AQ adapter service listening to these events and forwarding them to a Mediator that publishes events on the EDN. Another example demonstrates the same approach from a Java application using JMS and the JMS technology adapter.

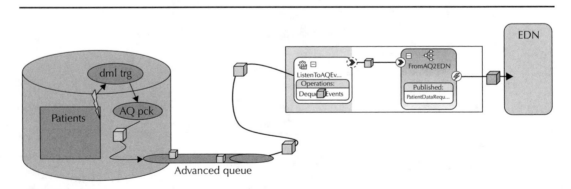

FIGURE 9-13. *Publishing events from the database to the EDN via Advanced Queuing*

Advanced Queuing and JMS are, of course, perfect ways to share events that appear on the Event Delivery Network with consumers outside the SOA fabric—either Java (JMS) consumers or PL/SQL (AQ) consumers. In these cases, a Mediator consumes the EDN event and forwards it to a technology adapter for either JMS or AQ that puts it on the respective queue or topic.

Chapter 20 demonstrates ADF Business Components that can publish EDN events, either in the same or a different container from the one running the SOA Suite.

Publishing EDN Events from BPEL Components

The PatientDataService composite developed in Chapter 5 only supported operations to retrieve a patient record. That application has been extended and now exposes a service for creating a new patient record. This service can be invoked, for example, from the PatientAppointmentService composite that sometimes receives appointment requests for unknown patients, for whom a new record should be created (see Figure 9-14). The operation to create a new record expects a request message that contains all data for the new patient. It will respond with a message that contains the newly assigned patient identifier. Internally it uses a new database adapter service that inserts a record into the patients table and the existing service that retrieves the patient's ID based on the combination of first name and last name.

After the BPEL component ProcessNewPatient has called the database adapter services, first to create the new patient record and then to retrieve the patient identifier that was assigned during the insert from a database sequence, it would be a good moment to publish a PatientDetails ChangeEvent to inform potential consumers of this new patient record. Publishing an event from a BPEL process is a bit special, because BPEL is an open standard and the EDN is not. Oracle has extended BPEL—which is supported by the standard—to support additional activities such as

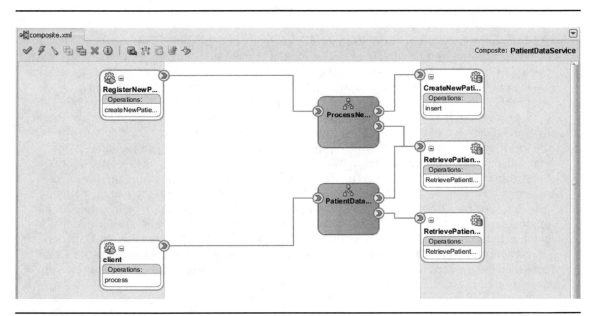

FIGURE 9-14. *PatientDataService composite with support for the "create new patient" operation*

special versions of Receive and onMessage for consuming events as well as special versions of Invoke to publish an event. Also see the next section for some details on these extensions and the evolution of the SCA standard with regard to events. In general, it seems best to use a mediator to either receive or publish events, unless those events are required for correlation purposes: When an event must be consumed by a specific running instance of a composite application, the event consumer should be the BPEL process component.

If we want the BPEL process to publish an event, we have to add an Invoke activity, dropping it after the scope RetrieveNewlyAssignedIdentifier (see Figure 9-15). Call the activity Publish_PatientDetailsChangeEvent. Select the appropriate interaction type of event. The editor changes and now allows us to browse for the event that we want to publish—using the Event Chooser dialog we have used before. In this case, select the PatientDetailsChangeEvent from the PatientEvents.edl found in the SOA-MDS connection in the deployed composite SynchronizePatients Information. After selecting the event, click the green plus icon to have a local variable created that we will set up with the event's payload.

We need to have the XSD document available in our project that contains the definition of {http://stmatthews.hospital.com/events}PatientDetailsChangeEvent. Otherwise, JDeveloper's editors will not know the structure of the variable. We can copy that file (or refer to it), either from MDS or from the SynchronizePatientsInformation application on the file system, to the xsd directory. After creating the BPEL process using the design-time editors, we could remove that file again.

We will now add an activity that will initialize the variable PatientDetailChangeEvent_payloadVariable. We could use an Assign activity with a dozen Copy steps, but it's preferable to use the Transform activity to map the contents from the inputVariable to the variable for the event payload. We then need an additional Assign activity with a single Copy operation to set the patientIdentifier.

With the transform, assign, and invoke (or publish) added to the process, we are ready to deploy the revamped PatientDataService—and find out whether it will publish events to the Event Delivery Network.

Testing the publication of events to the EDN is really only possible when there are consumers of the event. There is no way to track publication of individual events, either through the FMW Control or in any other way, except for the audit trail on the end of the consumers of the event. On the publishing side, there is only an audit trail for events that have faulted delivery.

In this case, we have a consumer of the event—or even two—so we can test whether the BPEL process publishes events as it is supposed to (see Figure 9-16). When we invoke the PatientDataService to have it create a new patient, after making the database adapter perform the insert of the new record, the BPEL process publishes the PatientDetailsChangeEvent that subsequently gets consumed by two composites: FeedPatientChangesToDWH and SynchronizePatientsInformation. The former writes an entry in the log file, and the latter performs an update of the database record that was just created—with the values it already has. Pointless but harmless. In this case, we should add an indication to the event about its origin as well as a filter to the event subscription in the SynchronizePatientsInformation composite to not consume instances that were published by Frank's own Patient Data Service.

Note how the FMW Control message flow trace includes both the composite instance that published the event as well as the two instances for the consuming composites—even though there is no direct relationship between these three composites.

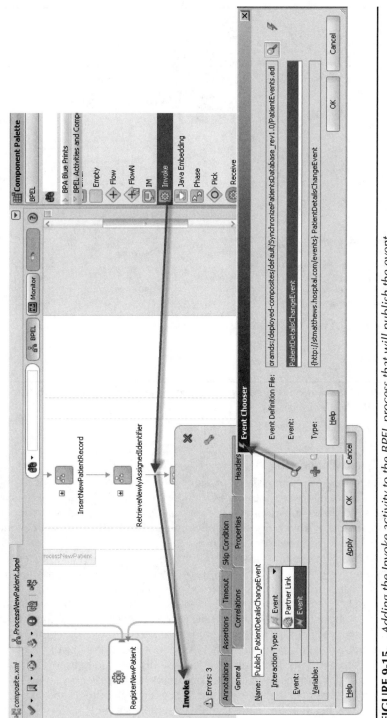

FIGURE 9-15. *Adding the Invoke activity to the BPEL process that will publish the event*

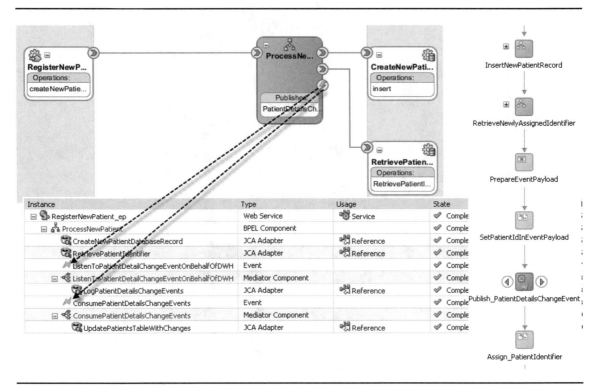

Instance	Type	Usage	State
RegisterNewPatient_ep	Web Service	Service	Comple
ProcessNewPatient	BPEL Component		Comple
CreateNewPatientDatabaseRecord	JCA Adapter	Reference	Comple
RetrievePatientIdentifier	JCA Adapter	Reference	Comple
ListenToPatientDetailChangeEventOnBehalfOfDWH	Event		Comple
ListenToPatientDetailChangeEventOnBehalfOfDWH	Mediator Component		Comple
LogPatientDetailsChangeEvents	JCA Adapter	Reference	Comple
ConsumePatientDetailsChangeEvents	Event		Comple
ConsumePatientDetailsChangeEvents	Mediator Component		Comple
UpdatePatientsTableWithChanges	JCA Adapter	Reference	Comple

FIGURE 9-16. *Testing the creation of a new patient record and subsequent publication of Patient DetailsChangeEvent by the BPEL process*

Complex Event Processing

The SOA Suite license encompasses a product called Complex Event Processing (CEP); however, this is not integrated into the SOA Suite run time (it runs in its own stand-alone, lightweight, specialized container). CEP is not a service engine, and we cannot embed CEP service components in our composite applications. CEP clearly deals with events—so how does it relate to the Event Delivery Network?

Complex Event Processing—discussed in more detail in Chapter 19—deals with high volumes of often very small events (in terms of payload), which are possibly by themselves meaningless. Events processed by CEP can be as frequent and small as RFID sensor detections, stock ticker changes, hits on a page on a website, temperature or humidity readings from a physical sensor, DML events in the database, luggage passing detectors on the airport's conveyor belts, or products being scanned on the cash register. CEP tries to find patterns, derive aggregates, and detect deviations in the streams of events that it processes. The conclusions it may arrive at are usually forwarded as a real business event to a specific consumer or to a queue that consumers may register to. To be sure, the "Complex" in CEP refers to the nature of the processing (algorithms and logic), not to the events themselves, because those are usually extremely simple!

Consider a volleyball match as an example of the difference between the simple events CEP processes and the derived or promoted business events. In this match, every point scored amounts to a simple event (or even every individual ball contact, when gathering match statistics), and only the conclusion of a set or even of the entire match warrants a business event.

The events travelling on the Event Delivery Network usually are business events—with more meaning and larger payloads than the typical event processed by CEP. Events on EDN occur with typically much lower frequencies, orders of magnitude below those of the CEP event streams. However, the results produced from Complex Event Processing may very well be promoted to or published as events on the EDN, propagated via a JMS queue or the EDN's Java API to the SOA Suite.

Event Delivery Network in SCA and BPEL

The definition of events and the publication of and subscription to these events are recorded in a number of files that are read, parsed, and interpreted by the SOA Suite and more specifically by the Event Delivery Network.

The events are defined in one or more EDL (Event Definition Language) files, which are deployed inside composites or stored in MDS.

The subscription to an event, visualized in the Composite Editor through the little lightning icon, is recorded in the composite.xml file. In this file, components can have the child element "business-events." This element, in turn, can contain one or more occurrences of the "publishes event" element as well as one or more instances of the subscribe element.

Analyzing the SCA Configuration Around EDN and Events

The entry in the composite.xml file for the BPEL component ProcessNewPatient is as follows:

```
<component name="ProcessNewPatient">
  <implementation.bpel src="ProcessNewPatient.bpel"/>
  <business-events>
    <publishes xmlns:pub1="http://schemas.oracle.com/events/edl/PatientEvents"
               name="pub1:PatientDetailsChangeEvent"/>
  </business-events>
</component>
```

It is clear to see how this component is configured to publish instances of the PatientDetails ChangeEvent. In a similar way, we find from the entry of the Mediator ConsumePatientDetails ChangeEvents in the composite.xml file for the SynchronizePatientsInformation application that it subscribes to the PatientDetailsChangeEvent, but it filters on a specific condition.

The composite.xml contains the high-level associations between the composite and the events that get consumed or published. The details that specify exactly when and with which payload an event is published are not defined at that level, but rather at either the Mediator or the BPEL process level.

The SOA Suite run time knows how to interpret the event definition in the EDL document. It also parses the event subscriptions from the deployed composite applications, both Mediator and BPEL components, so it knows where to send events of specific types when they occur. The next paragraphs describe the extensions to BPEL and Mediator configurations with regard to events.

BPEL Extensions for Consuming and Publishing Events

Oracle has extended BPEL—in a way that is prescribed in the BPEL standard specification—to implement a special type of Invoke activity that does not call out to a partner link, but instead publishes an event to the EDN.

The code in the BPEL process ProcessNewPatient that publishes the event is extremely simple—an Invoke element with a special attribute called eventName in the http://schemas. oracle.com/bpel/extension namespace that is interpreted by the JDeveloper design-time tools as well as the SOA Suite run-time engine for BPEL to refer to an event defined in one of the EDL files, rather than a partnerLink defined in a WSDL:

```
<invoke name="Publish_PatientDetailsChangeEvent"
bpelx:eventName="ns6:PatientDetailsChangeEvent"
        inputVariable="PatientDetailChangeEvent_payloadVariable"/>
```

A similar extension is used in the Receive and onMessage activities when they are to consume an event instead of an incoming request message.

Consuming and Publishing Events in Mediator mplan Configuration

The Mediator configuration file (mplan) has a proprietary format—there is no industry standard underpinning the mediator's operations (or the Mediator concept itself in relation to SCA). The mplan file has an eventHandler element for Mediators that subscribe to an event (instead of a request message):

```
<Mediator name="ListenToPatientDataRequestEvent"
xmlns:xsi="http://www.w3.org/2001/XMLSchema-instance"
xmlns="http://xmlns.oracle.com/sca/1.0/mediator">
  <eventHandler xmlns:sub1="http://schemas.oracle.com/events/edl/PatientDataEvents"
        event="sub1:PatientDataRequestEvent"
        deliveryPolicy="AllOrNothing" priority="4">
```

It uses a raise element in routing rules that publish an event to the EDN instead of forwarding a message to a target service:

```
<raise xmlns:pub1="http://schemas.oracle.com/events/edl/PatientDataEvents"
        event="pub1:PatientDataResponseEvent"/>
```

Events and Publish/Subscribe in the SCA Specifications

The events and the publish/subscription model we have just seen in action in the Oracle SOA Suite are not part of the original SCA specifications. Only fairly recently did discussions take place in the OASIS SCA committee regarding events, partly instigated by Oracle's representatives. This has led to a specification—published in April 2009—that the OSOA community considers final. For more information on this specification, see the link on the book's wiki to the SCA Assembly Model Specification Extensions for Event Processing and Pub/Sub.

This extension to the SCA specifications details the description of consumers and producers of events in the composite.xml file, very much like the business-events element Oracle currently uses in the composite.xml document for specifying which events are consumed and published by a component.

The definition of events in SCA is similar to the EDL format used in the Oracle SOA Suite. Events have a qualified name and a reference to an XSD element that describes the shape of the event data. The specification also speaks about optional additional metadata associated with event types, such as creation time. The SOA Suite documentation mentions custom headers—which seem similar beasts to these optional metadata elements. However, the custom headers do not seem to currently have a working implementation. The SCA definition also defines filters as a way for consumers to fine-tune their interest in events. A filter inspects the event type, event metadata, and event business data (the payload) and uses expressions—which could be XPath, although other languages are allowed in the specification—that evaluate to true when an event should be accepted by the consumer.

The main distinction between the SOA Suite Event Delivery Network and this SCA extension specification is the concept of a channel in the SCA specification. A *channel* is an intermediary between producers and consumers of events. Channels can be used inside composite applications or at the domain level. Channels can be used for a subset of the full set of event types flowing through the SCA container. Note that filters can be applied to channels as well as to consumers. Channels are primarily a means of organizing and administering the event infrastructure of the SCA container, without adding business functionality. The EDN itself is similar to the *default channel,* and currently the SOA Suite does not support alternative channels.

It seems likely that the Oracle Event Delivery Network will morph into an implementation of this SCA extension for events. That will mean only a slight change in the metadata files (composite. xml and the EDL files) because the logic of events, publication, and subscription remains the same.

Alternative Ways for Publishing Events to the EDN

The most obvious way to publish an event to the EDN is from a Mediator or BPEL service component. For testing purposes, the FMW Control also provides a "publish test event" facility. You can also publish an event from an Ant target, like this:

```
<target name="publishPatientDataRequest">
    <java classname="oracle.integration.platform.blocks.event.SendEvent"
        fork="true" failonerror="true">
        <classpath>
            <pathelement path="${soaEDN.classpath}"/>
        </classpath>
        <arg line="-dbconn localhost:1521:orcl
                   -dbuser FMW_SOAINFRA
                   -dbpass oracle
                   -event patientDataRequestEvent.xml"/>
    </java>
</target>
```

Details for this call, including the setting for the soaEDN.classpath property and the contents of the patientDataRequestEvent.xml file, can be found on this book's wiki.

The SendEvent class used from Ant can also be leveraged programmatically from a Java application to publish an event to the Event Delivery Network. An example is shown on the wiki.

Chapter 20 on ADF explains how ADF Business Components can be configured in a declarative way to publish events associated with data manipulations on Entity objects. Finally, there is a PL/SQL procedure—in the FMW SOA Infrastructure schema—called edn_publish_event with four input parameters: local_name (of the event; for example, PatientDataRequestEvent), namespace (in which the event is defined, such as http://schemas. oracle.com/events/edl/PatientDataEvents), payload (the XML fragment that should go inside the <content> element), and priority (an integer that does not yet seem to have any effect).

Of course, there are many indirect ways to publish events: A Mediator can publish EDN events—and it can be triggered by database, file system, FTP, AQ, and JMS adapters alike or be invoked through the SOA Suite Java API, SOAP, or REST binding.

Decoupling Two-way Services Using the Discussion Forum Approach

In the previous pages, we have used the Event Delivery Network to decouple producers of business events from all interested consumers. The only responsibility we assign to applications that know about or even create new information is to have them publish business events to the central Event Delivery Network of the SOA Suite. These events should have a payload with enough information to make them meaningful to potential consumers. However, the publisher does not concern itself with who might be interested in the event and what those interested parties will do with it. The publisher never has to look back after publishing the event—and certainly not wait for a response! What's more, we can add or remove publishers and consumers without any impact on them.

That, by and large, resolves the decoupling challenge for the one-way services. Then there is still the situation where composite applications call two-way Web Services, because they need a response from those services. This situation introduces some coupling: The calling application depends on the service contract—the message types, portType, and operation names—and needs to know where to find the service. In this case, because the calling application has its own reasons for making the call, this moderate level of coupling is usually acceptable. However, the Event Delivery Network makes it possible to eliminate these direct dependencies in many situations by using the Discussion Forum pattern.

Introducing the Discussion Forum Pattern

To completely decouple service providers from service consumers, we have to rethink the concept of soliciting a response from the service provider. Instead of making a direct call to a specific service to have a specific question answered, we can publish an event that contains the service request to the EDN like a generally broadcasted cry for help. The event publisher does not know who will be able to handle the request and formulate the response. It does not know where the service is located that is capable of handling the request, what its contract is, and whether it is synchronous or asynchronous, if it is available (and if not, whether there is a fallback alternative). It assumes—and that is probably the big challenge with this approach—that some entity consumes the event, processes the request that is contained in it, and publishes the response in the form of a new event.

The original request event contains a special question identifier that is used in the response event and allows the requesting application to pick up the response to its original question.

This approach seems a bit similar to one of the many discussion forums on the Internet—for example, the OTN Discussion Forums. Such forums can produce a response to any question you may ask, sometimes extremely rapidly. And most forums have a mechanism that will send an e-mail to the original requester when a response has been provided. However, sometimes a question is answered only after a fairly long period—or never at all. A forum moderator could monitor questions that do not get answered and take appropriate action. Our composite applications will probably not suffer a lack of response very well, so we may need to ensure that all question events are followed up with response events, if necessary, through an SOA Suite counterpart to the forum moderator.

A First Stab at the Decoupling from a Two-way Service Using the Discussion Forum Approach

Let's see what we need to do to implement the discussion forum approach for getting hold of patient data. At this moment, applications that want to have details on a specific patient can invoke the synchronous PatientDataService that Frank developed in Chapter 5 using BPEL and a database adapter service. We see the coupling aspects that we described earlier: Anyone interested in patient data needs to know about the existence of the PatientDataService, the details of its contract, and the physical location of its endpoint. We are now going to extend the PatientDataService application to make it participate in the more decoupled, discussion forum style of serving up patient details.

The Discussion Forums Pattern in Action

Let's assume a BPEL process that has a need for some patient data. It already knows the patient identifier, but it does not know of any specific service that can provide the patient data. However, it has heard that when one publishes a PatientDataRequestEvent to the EDN, there will be helpful souls out there that may respond to the call for help and publish an event of their own: Patient DataResponseEvent. This response event can be correlated on the eventGUID that was injected into the request message and—presto—there's the data being looked for. This pattern is illustrated by Figure 9-17.

We will work with the PatientInvoiceProcessing composite application. It is intended for creating billing statements for individual patients. This application publishes instances of PatientDataRequestEvent. The PatientDataService composite is extended with a Mediator that subscribes to this type of event and that will publish the PatientDataResponseEvent with the required information.

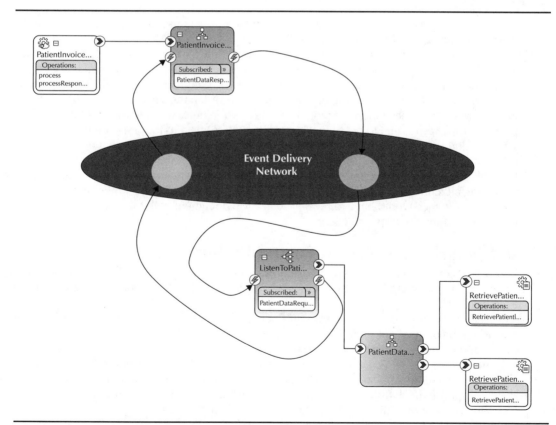

FIGURE 9-17. *The Discussion Forum pattern: soliciting a response from an unknown provider by publishing an event*

The online chapter complement contains the detailed, step-by-step implementation of this.

To then see the discussion forum in action, go to the FMW Control, locate the PatientInvoice Processing composite, and test it, providing some patientIdentifier value. The BPEL process is invoked and will publish a PatientDataRequestEvent to solicit more details on the patient.

The event is consumed by the PatientDataService composite, which processes it and publishes a PatientDataResponseEvent that contains the requested patient data as well as the eventGUID that was sent in the original request. The BPEL component is waiting to receive this response event, and will correlate it on the eventGUID to ensure that the event is consumed by the same instance that sent out the original request event. Note that other consumers could consume the same event—although it probably would not make sense to them.

Extending the Event-based Patient Data Service

We could make things even more interesting by extending the functionality we have implemented so far. We can, for example, introduce a second composite application willing to process request events—only for patient identifiers over 50,000. This composite would have a filter in the event subscription to only accept the over-50,000 identifiers. It would be interesting to see what happens when both consumers handle the request and produce a response event. The first response event would probably correlate with the requesting BPEL process, and the second one simply fades out on the EDN.

We can also add a moderator of sorts—a Mediator that consumes request events and stores them in a database table, along with the date and time. Another Mediator would then consume response events and use them to update the request event records in the database. Request records that have not yet been updated are the unanswered ones that may need moderation.

Responses to "cries for help" can be fairly large. In general, we would like to keep the size of the event payload as small as possible, as to not overburden the service fabric. Instead of sending the full response in the response event, as we have done here, we can use the claim-check pattern for the response: Do not actually send the patient data in the response message; rather, send a unique identifier (claim-tag) that can be used to retrieve the XML document with patient data at some generic, central service that hands out XML documents based on unique identifiers (a bit like the YouSendIt Internet service for handling large attachments by sending a URL from which the attachment can be downloaded rather than sending the attachment itself); the PatientDataService would have to register their XML document with this central document service before publishing the response event.

Judging the Discussion Forum Pattern

This discussion forum, like the event-based reply-response pattern, is clearly not suitable for every situation. First of all, it is an asynchronous pattern that requires the requestor to consume events from the EDN.

Second, the event carrying the response needs to be correlated with the application instance that asked the original question. In the SOA Suite today, only BPEL components can consume events and correlate them to running instances.

The decoupling achieved through this event-based mechanism comes at the price of performance and implementation overhead. A direct, synchronous call to a known service will yield a response much faster than this asynchronous approach that requires the Event Delivery Network as the intermediary for both the request and the response.

These should be serious considerations before adopting this pattern. The primary reason for discussing this pattern—which is really a corner case—is to demonstrate what level of decoupling is attainable through events.

Having Non-Events Published on the EDN

An event indicates that something happens—or so you would think. However, it is quite possible to have a meaningful event when something *does not* happen. When the expected does not occur, that can be quite an event indeed. If the sun or the tide forgot to rise, we would have major events indeed.

On a slightly smaller scale, we, too, have the situation where the fact that something we expected did not actually happen in itself is a meaningful event. The invoice was sent but the payment never materialized; the suitcase went into the baggage-handling system but never came out; the complaint was filed but a response was never sent. Such an event is often called a *non-event*. The absence of an event is an event in its own right.

Non-events are frequently associated with real events: The (real) event takes place and normally has a partner event. The suitcase entering the system is the real event, and the same piece of luggage ending up in an airplane could be its partner event. The absence of this partner event (after a set period) triggers the non-event. A person entering a secure zone is the real event that should partner with the event of that same person leaving the secure zone at some point. The non-event originates when the person does not reappear from the secure zone after some predefined period. Complex Event Processing (CEP) deals with analyzing enormous volumes of events, and one of the goals of CEP is the detection of non-events. Sensors not sending the signal they were supposed to send, the container not appearing at the next RFID sensor station, the car not exiting the tunnel. (More on CEP appears in Chapter 19.) Note that BAM (Business Activity Monitoring), also discussed in Chapter 19, can identify non-events, too.

St. Matthews tries to find the balance between providing emergency care to everyone and safe-guarding the financial budget. Everyone who needs immediate medical attention can be checked into the hospital. There is a special budget—co-funded by state authorities—that will cover costs for up to ten days of hospital care. However, when patients who have no medical insurance are not discharged after this ten-day period, the hospital starts to run possibly substantial financial risks. Therefore, the non-event of patients not being discharged after ten days is an important business event that the financial department of the hospital wants to be informed about.

There is an interesting challenge for the Event Delivery Network. It handles events, delivering them to subscribers. But how can it deliver a non-existing event? Where does the non-event come from? Who is responsible for raising the event?

Unlike CEP, the EDN does not detect non-events. We have to implement some logic to find the non-events and turn them into real EDN business events. Here is one way of approaching this challenge: When the patient is admitted to the hospital, an event is published to the Event Delivery Network (say, the PatientAdmittanceEvent) with the patient identifier or a unique key for the admittance record as payload. A composite application is subscribed to this event and a new instance is initiated upon consumption. This composite contains a BPEL component that consumes the PatientAdmittanceEvent. It enters a Pick activity with two branches: One is a Wait activity that will wait for ten days. The other

(Continued)

branch is an onMessage that will wait for a PatientDischargedEvent. The onMessage will correlate this discharge event on the patient or admittance record identifier. When a patient is discharged, the PatientDischargedEvent should be published. When it is, the BPEL component will consume it, conclude the Pick activity, and terminate the instance altogether. However, if after ten days this event is still not received, the wait branch of the Pick activity is activated and it will publish the non-event PatientNotDischargedWithin TenDaysEvent. The BPEL component turns the absence of the business event—after the specified period—into another business event.

The book's wiki has this example described in more detail, including source code.

Summary

Service-Oriented Architecture has been declared dead a couple of times in recent years, partly because it would not bring the level of decoupling organizations are striving for. Some of the criticism of SOA was probably justified. The conclusions, however, were quite over the top. Event-Driven Architecture (EDA), heralded as the successor to SOA, is actually a perfect complement to SOA.

For example, events are a much better way in many cases to "invoke" one-way services. Applications are not burdened with the responsibility to invoke specific services that need to be notified, creating clearly undesirable dependencies, but only need to take on the responsibility to broadcast the occurrence of events to a generic entity.

Thinking about business events and about the business processes, and from there the applications and services that produce them, is a very useful exercise that provides a lot of insight into the workings of the organization. Analyzing those events and specifying canonical definitions for their payloads are the next steps toward implementation of a more decoupled interaction pattern. Once the event definitions have been agreed upon, consumers can start registering—the easy part—and all points of origin of the business events need to be made to publish those events when they occur—the very hard part! Fortunately, we can start small, with a small number of business events and a moderate initial number of event producers. We can add producers as we go—as well as consumers, by the way. An evolutionary introduction of the event-driven way of interacting is quite possible.

The Event Delivery Network in the SOA Suite is the central facilitator that coordinates event definitions and subscriptions on events and also processes the events when they occur—absorbing them and propagating them to all registered subscribers. Mediator, BPMN, and BPEL components can subscribe to events defined in the EDN. Through the EDN, many aspects of Event-Driven Architecture can be implemented in SOA composite applications.

CHAPTER 10

The Missing Link: The Human Service Provider

hat we still may be lacking in our composite applications—to have them really face the business challenges we know will be thrown at us— is something we could call the "ghost in the machine." After all is said and done by the service components discussed so far—and that is quite a lot, let's make no mistake about that—there is still a category of activities that we do not have the solution for yet. Some things simply cannot be done by Mediators, BPEL processes, adapters, or even Business Rule components. We need something more when it comes to one of the following areas:

- Business logic that involves strategic insight, negotiation skills, creativity, intuition, an understanding of abstract paintings, or capacity to improvise—for example, the final selection from the candidates for a job opening, the slogan for the marketing campaign, or the final bid on an auctioned item

- Recovering from unexpected fault situations

- Processing (and deciding upon) unstructured information such as pictures, PDF attachments, or cryptic content or weighing subtleties lost on (non-AI) computer systems

- Gathering additional information via human channels and from unstructured sources and providing data to the system

- Informing other humans—verbally, in specific terminology or in terminology other than one of the supported languages; in person or via telephone, chat, or sign language; with proper regard for cultural habits and personal sensitivities

- Performing manual operations—wrapping a package, physical verification (signature), measurement

- Conferring with one or more humans to reach consensus and broad support for a decision

- Decisions and choices that we consider too important or far reaching to (already) trust to an automated facility

For these specific areas and situations, we need humans participating in the processing of composite application instances. And just like all other service engines, humans in a composite should come with a WSDL interface and communication specified in XSD too. And that is what the SOA Suite's Human Task Service provides: the interface between the services world of the composite application and the people performing activities in the context of the application (see Figure 10-1).

Human tasks typically implement stand-alone tasks around a single set of data—even though potentially with complex escalation, voting, and routing logic. These tasks typically implement activities in a workflow or business process that may contain other tasks as well as service calls. The next chapter discusses how both BPEL and BPM are used to define and implement those workflows. The human task we discuss in this chapter will reappear in those workflows.

The examples discussed in this chapter are demonstrated and explained in much more detail in the online chapter complement to this chapter on the book's wiki.

Introducing the Human Task Service

The Human Task Service accepts service request messages, just like other service engines do. Service calls to the task service are based on a generic WSDL that defines a number of standard

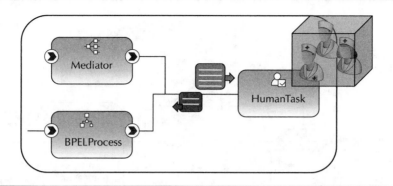

FIGURE 10-1. *The Human Task Service (Engine) integrates people into composite applications*

operations to be performed on a task, such as initiate, update, and cancel a task. When the task is completed, the task outcome is forwarded to the initial task service invoker through a callback from the task service. The interaction with the Human Task Service is inherently asynchronous because humans react distinctly asynchronously. The overall result of executing the task is only reported back to the task invoker at some later moment—and given the involvement of people and potentially complex task-routing flows, this callback may be hours, days, or even longer after the task initiation.

Architecture of the Human Task Service

When a BPEL or (much less common) a Mediator component requires a task to be performed by a human agent, it calls the generic Task Service and specifies which preconfigured task should be performed. All the various human tasks that the Task Service can make people execute are defined in task definition files. The definition of a task describes many details, including the possible outcomes of the task, the users or roles involved in handling the task, the deadline associated with the task, the data passed into the task, and the parameters that can be updated and returned as part of the task result. More advanced settings in the task definition determine the notification, allocation, collaboration, delegation, and escalation of tasks. The Task Service is the central coordinator that takes responsibility for the execution of the specific task instance. The task instance is created as a result of the initiate task request from a composite application instance and based on the task definition. It decouples the machine from the man or woman.

The Task Service works with other services provided by the SOA Suite infrastructure to perform allocation and routing, handle notifications to task participants, and deal with the authorization and storage of digitally signed tasks. Note that the Task Service and other Workflow Services are not only available as service component in SOA composite applications, but can be interacted with through a SOAP/WS and Java API by other applications that are unrelated to the SOA Suite (see Figure 10-2). A frequent use case is the retrieval of task instances for a particular user from a custom-developed user interface.

The task definition files specify parameters—based on elements defined in XSD files. These parameters carry the data specific to the task instance and make it available to the user performing the task. Parameters can be editable. If so, the user can change the data in these parameters, and

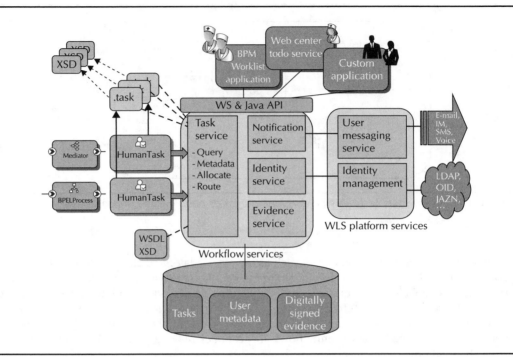

FIGURE 10-2. *Architecture of Human Task Services in the SOA Suite*

these changes are returned to the component that invoked the Task Service together with the outcome of the task instance.

The Task Service needs a way to make people aware of the tasks they should execute, and it must offer those people a way to read the task details, update the task's payload, delegate or escalate a task when necessary, and determine the final task outcome. People, of course, need a user interface to interact with a computer system—you cannot simply send SOAP messages to them. The Task Service can use the User Messaging Service (UMS) to send notifications via various channels, such as e-mail, IM (chat), voice, and SMS. The SOA Suite ships with the BPM Worklist application, a prebuilt web application that provides a user interface for all task participants. It presents the tasks on the current user's to-do list, shows the details for a selected task, and allows the user to perform the actions on the task that may be required.

As a special feature, simple tasks with a limited number of predefined outcomes and no output parameters (or editable payload, which is the better way of putting it for human tasks) can entirely be dealt with from an e-mail. Such an "actionable e-mail" contains hyperlinks for each of the potential task outcomes, and the user can complete the task by simply clicking the desired outcome. A reply e-mail will be sent in which the user can even provide some comments or add attachments. The UMS receives the incoming message and hands it to the Workflow Services that are configured to listen on a specific mailbox for such messages. The e-mail contains an identifier that is used to map the received e-mail to the task. The outcome specified in the e-mail is applied to the task.

Oracle WebCenter ships with ready-built services that ADF web applications can integrate. One of these services—the Worklist Service—revolves around the SOA Suite Task Service. It presents the tasks assigned to the user, along with links to navigate to the task form to perform the task. This WebCenter Worklist Service uses the Java API exposed by the Workflow Services in the SOA Suite, just like the BPM Worklist application. That same API can be used to develop custom applications that query tasks, fetch task details, and manipulate tasks in various ways.

Exploring the Task Service in Detail

We will take an in-depth look at how Human Task service components enable us to engage human agents in our composite applications. In three steps, we will discover some of the intricacies of the Task Service, including integration into BPEL components, notification, payload manipulation, callbacks, and task routing. We will also discuss the integration with identity stores regarding to whom—roles or individuals—a task is assigned or escalated.

First, we will design a simple task that asks a human decision maker to pick one of two possible outcomes (yes or no). Input parameters are passed into the task to provide the user with context for the decision. The only output from this task is the chosen outcome. This task is initially designed to be assigned to a specific user, but it will turn out to be much better to assign the task to a group of users—or more specifically to a role—because individual users may come and go while the task requirements stay the same. Later in this chapter, we will take on this more robust approach of allocating tasks to roles. Also, more on this in Chapter 15 when we discuss security.

The task is to be integrated into a BPEL process that invokes it when a decision is needed from the human agents and will then wait for its asynchronous response. We will see how the default (out-of-the-box) Worklist application presents the task to the user and allows the user to act on it.

We will then add notification functionality and have the task assignees receive an e-mail that informs them of this new task and invites them to inspect and handle the task using the Worklist application. Because this task only supports two predefined outcomes and has no other output parameters, it could be handled entirely from an actionable e-mail—and that is what we will do next. This introduces an alternative to the Worklist application as an interface for dealing with tasks.

Handling the second type of task requires more from the human participant than just choosing a predefined outcome. This task requires the actor to provide some information that cannot be predefined. This data is entered by the user in the generated task form that will be embedded in the default Worklist application. That same form presents the user with the input parameters for the task. In Chapter 20, we will take a look at how to customize the task form or create an entirely custom task form in JDeveloper using ADF.

In the third task discussed in this chapter, we look at the advanced task-routing capabilities offered by the Human Workflow Services. We will see how we can define a task that requires multiple participants to make a contribution. We will specify deadlines for the task, create an escalation scheme, and even look at handling leaves of absence for designated task participants. Note that even though multiple actors are involved, they still collaborate on the same task. Real business processes, where multiple tasks are lined up in logical flows, mixed together with service calls, are discussed in the next chapter. We will see how such task-and-service-spanning flows can be created using BPEL processes or BPMN service components.

Setting Up Notifications

All notifications in the examples for this chapter can be handled through a locally running e-mail server, such as Java Mail Server or Apache James. However, any POP3/IMAP-compliant mail server can be configured with SOA Suite—including Google Mail or your own organization's existing e-mail server. Configuration details can be found in Appendix C of this book and through various references on the book's wiki. The wiki also shows the configuration and usage of instant messaging as a notification channel—for example, using Google Talk as a chat platform.

Defining the First Human Task—Approve Highest Priority

The decision service for determining the appointment priority that we created in Chapter 8 has led to some controversy. It is felt that too many patients jump the queue with High priority because of the stress on obesity. Also, High priority may be too easily assigned by the general practitioners that referred those patients to St. Matthews. Although the consensus is that the business rule component adds a lot of value and speeds up the triage process, the jury is still out on whether the service can entirely be left to its own devices when it comes to establishing the priority. Upper management has decided, following Margaret's suggestion, to add a service component with better understanding of fuzzy logic and political subtleties (though undoubtedly with a knack for illogical and inconsistent decisions as well): human decision makers.

The automated decision service will still do most of the work. However, a Human Task Service will be introduced to make the final decision about appointments that have been assigned the highest priority. To prevent "false positives"—appointments that are undeservedly given highest priority—a final call is to be made by human staff members. The logic of the task is quite simple: The human actor either approves the priority assignment or rejects it. In the latter case, the appointment's priority is set to Normal. The obvious downside, of course, is that due to the introduction of the human factor, this process is both slowed down and made more expensive. Given the consequences of assigning the highest priority, this is deemed justifiable.

Steps for Implementing the Human Task ArbitrateHighPriority

To begin, open the PatientAppointmentService composite application in JDeveloper and then drag a Human Task component from the palette and drop it on the Composite Editor. Call the task **ArbitrateHighPriority** and set the namespace to http://stmatthews.hospital.com/patient/Appointment Process. The Human Task component shows up in the composite application—not yet wired from any other component and as yet without a task definition (see Figure 10-3).

Double-click the human task to start editing it. The human task editor opens the newly created task definition file ArbitrateHighPriority.task.

We need to specify several aspects for a human task, including the input, output, assignee, workflow, and title. We will start with the input parameter for this task. This parameter contains the appointment request details that are needed for the user to interpret and make a decision. We can leverage some of the groundwork we did in previous chapters by reusing the AppointmentService ProcessRequest element in the PatientAppointmentService as the basis for the task input parameter (see Figure 10-4).

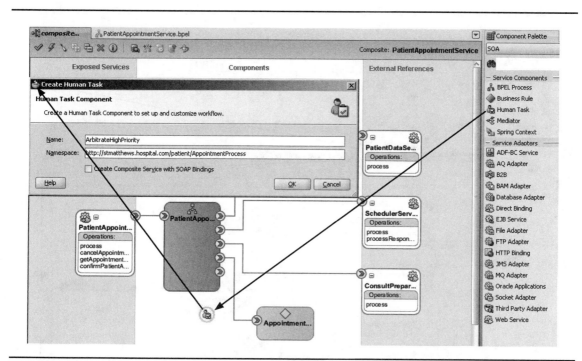

FIGURE 10-3. *Adding the human task ArbitrateHighPriority to the composite application*

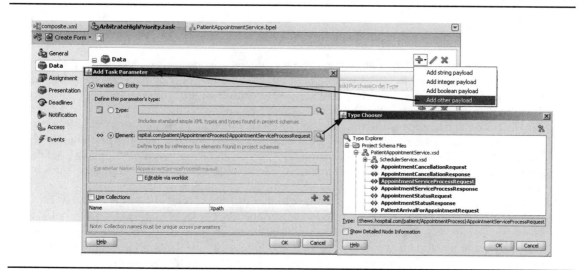

FIGURE 10-4. *Defining the task parameter AppointmentServiceProcessRequest*

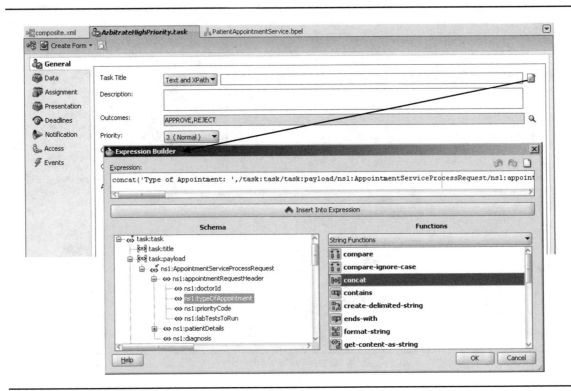

FIGURE 10-5. *Specifying an XPath expression to pass information in the task title*

With this input parameter defined, we can specify the title for the task. Normally, the title will be fairly short. However, for this moment, to save us the trouble of creating a task form, we will pass a lot of information in the title. Create an XPath expression that passes various details such as the birth date, gender, state, and BMI of the patient (see Figure 10-5).

Next, we need to specify the possible outcomes of the human task definition. Based on the outcome of the task, the composite can resume its flow. We can work with the predefined outcomes available out of the box (for example, Approve and Reject) that have been associated with this task by default. It is easy to define other outcomes by clicking the magnifying glass icon right behind the Outcomes field.

If we do not want to simply assign the task to the user "weblogic"—the only user that is configured out of the box—we need to add users to the identity store that comes preinstalled with WebLogic Server. We can manage the default security realm "myrealm" from the console—a management application that can be accessed at http://<host>:7001/console—where the host is likely to be localhost. The Human Workflow Services work out of the box with the users defined in this default identity store. However, you can, of course, plug in a production-quality LDAP server. See Chapter 15 for more information on this.

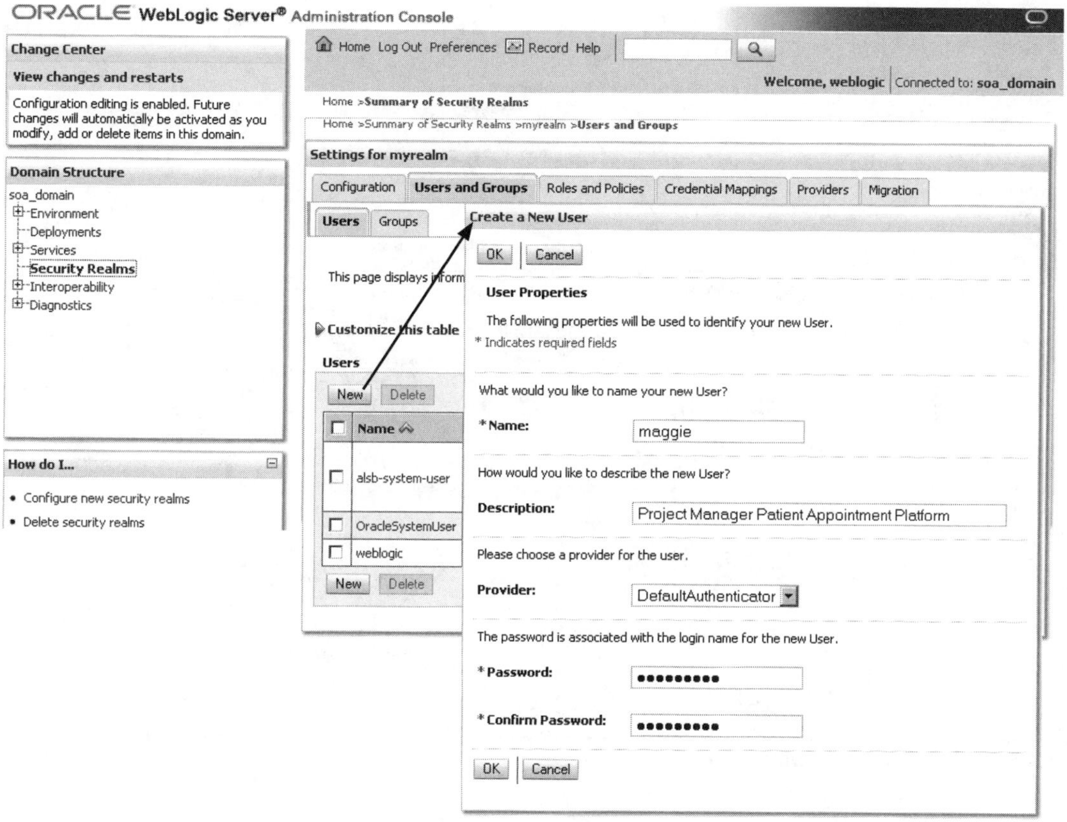

FIGURE 10-6.   *Using the WebLogic Server console to create user Maggie in myrealm*

For now, let's create user Maggie as the person to take on all high-priority appointment assessments for the time being. Open the WebLogic console, click Security Realms in the Domain Structure tree, and then click myrealm in the Summary window. The list of current users—which should at least contain the weblogic user—is presented. Click the New button in order to add a new user. Enter details for Maggie—at least her username and password (see Figure 10-6). Note that we can set additional details, including her e-mail address, later on.

Having created user Maggie, we can assign the task. Return to the Task Editor in JDeveloper. Select the Assignment tab, click the Stage 1 participant, and accept the default participant type of Single (alternatives include Group Vote, Management Chain, and Sequential List Of Approvers). Enter a better-looking label for this participant. Then click the green plus icon and select the option Add User—we are going to add the user by name. In the Identity Lookup window, make sure you have a valid connection to the WebLogic Server soa_domain. Then search for the user you want to assign the task to (see Figure 10-7). Note that you can also use expressions to determine the assign-to user.

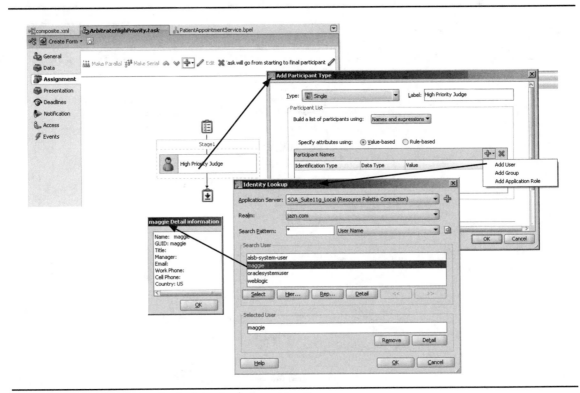

FIGURE 10-7. *Assigning the task to single user Maggie*

This task is simple and straightforward with just a single user; no routing, escalation, or delegation; no notifications; and no task update or fancy task form. The definition of the task is therefore complete. We can focus on integrating the task in the composite—in this case, in the BPEL process.

Integrate the Human Task ArbitrateHighPriority into a BPEL Process

We will integrate the human task ArbitrateHighPriority into the process defined by the BPEL component PatientAppointmentService. Note that to the BPEL process this human task is similar to a business rule, Mediator service, or any other referenced service—there is no special relationship between BPEL and human tasks.

To begin, open the BPEL process editor. The human task should only be instantiated when the EstablishAppointmentPriority Business Rule component returns a High priority value. Therefore, we first need to add a switch with two branches: one branch for priority equals High, which will contain the Human Task activity, and an otherwise branch that can be empty. Drag a Human Task service component from the Component Palette and drop it in the High priority branch (see Figure 10-8).

When you inspect the Human Task activity that was added to the BPEL process, it turns out to be a scope with a special marker that helps JDeveloper identify it as a special Human Task scope. As shown in Figure 10-9, it contains a combination of an Assign, an Invoke, and a Receive

WS-Human Task and BPEL4People Standard Initiatives

The OASIS organization—which maintains standards such as SDO, SCA, and BPEL through its many member organizations, including Adobe, IBM, Oracle, and SAP—has commenced work on an initiative to come up with a standard for specifying human tasks, including aspects such as notifications and the operations that can be performed on a task. This standard-in-progress is called WS-Human Task.

Closely associated with the WS-Human Task initiative is an extension to the BPEL specification called the WS-BPEL extension for People (BPEL4People). This is also an OASIS standard. This extension to BPEL describes how Human Task activities can be made part of BPEL. It describes how the BPEL process provides input to the task instance that is started—including role or user-assignment details, input parameters, and attachments—and how the interaction can take place after the task is started (return the final outcome and also callbacks that may return intermediate results or report task status changes). The implementation of such people activities would be a task definition created according to the WS-Human Task standard.

These two complementary industry specifications mentioned here are not yet finalized. Work is still in progress. Therefore, no current SOA offering—including Oracle SOA Suite 11g—has an implementation for human tasks and their integration with BPEL based on these standards. SOA Suite uses a proprietary format for the task definition files, as it precedes this initiative on the standards. The integration between BPEL and human tasks is achieved through a number of out-of-the-box activities generated when a human task is added to a BPEL process.

The overall approach in SOA Suite is quite similar to the one described by WS-Human Task and BPEL4People; however, the detailed syntax is quite different. When these OASIS specifications are formally published, it is to be expected that the SOA Suite will move to them at some point. When that happens, expect automated conversion from existing task definitions and BPEL/task integrations as well as minimal impact for developers of tasks.

The wiki contains references to resources on WS-Human Task and the WS-BPEL extension for People.

activity (it's essentially nothing more than an asynchronous Invoke from the BPEL component to a partner link). These three activities prepare the data to be passed to the task, invoke the Task Service to create an instance of the ArbitrateHighPriority task, and receive its asynchronous result. In addition to this scope, a Switch activity was added—with branches for each of the outcomes configured for the selected task definition as well as a branch for the otherwise case (terminated tasks, expired tasks, and so on). Note that the outcomes are not updated when you change the possible outcomes of the human task definition. For this task, the outcomes are REJECT and APPROVE, and therefore the switch has three branches.

The generated CopyPayloadFromTask activities in the Task Switch branches—copy the task payload (back) to the BPEL variable. Because this human task does not allow the user to update the payload, these activities are redundant and can be removed. The only thing we need is an Assign activity in the REJECT branch that changes the appointment request's priority from High to Normal (see Figure 10-10).

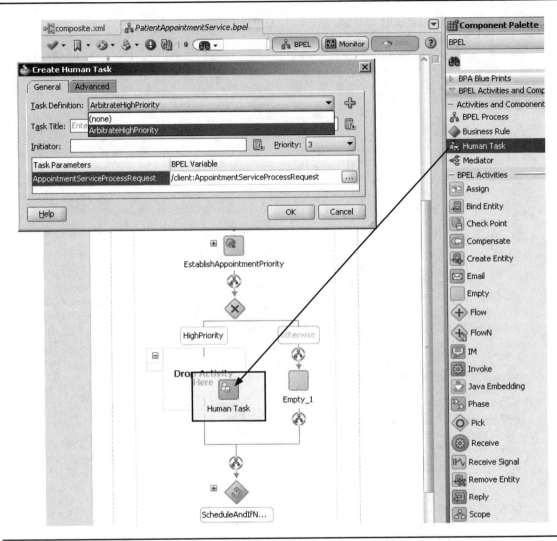

FIGURE 10-8. *Integrating the human task ArbitrateHighPriority into BPEL process PatientAppointmentService*

We have achieved our objective: The BPEL process invokes the human task for any appointment request with a priority of High. A human agent is engaged to determine whether the High priority is really justified. The composite application is now ready for deployment. This deployment can be done in the same way as before—at this point the presence of the Human Task component does not impact the deployment procedure.

The Human Task ArbitrateHighPriority in Action

With the PatientAppointmentService deployed, along with the Human Task service component, we can test the composite with an appointment request that has the highest priority set by the

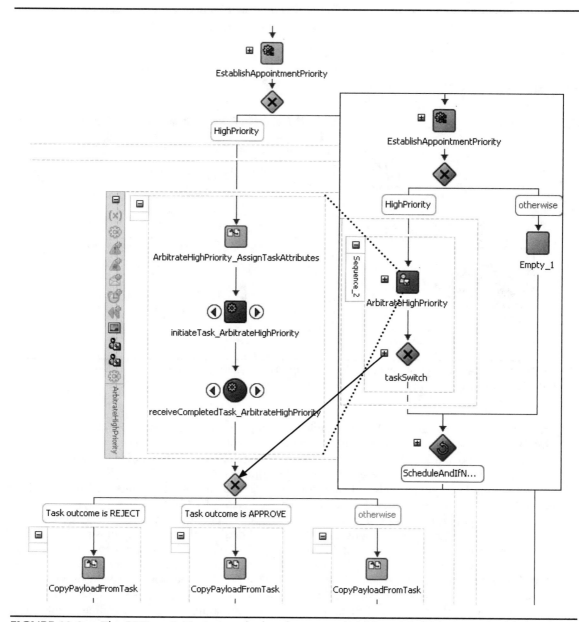

FIGURE 10-9.   *The BPEL activities created when human task ArbitrateHighPriority was added to the BPEL process*

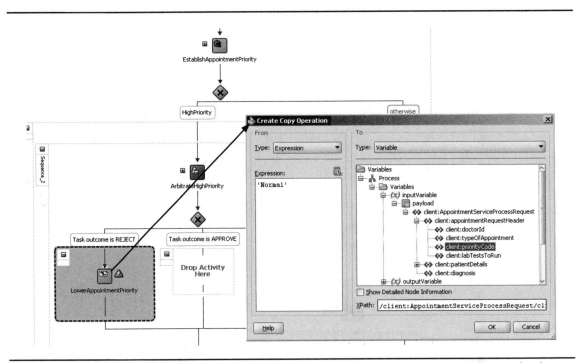

FIGURE 10-10. *Maggie uses the actionable notifications mechanism to execute an instance of task ArbitrateHighPriority by clicking the Approve link in an email*

referring general practitioner. We expect this to instantiate a task for Maggie—who has to judge the High priority assigned by the Business Rule component.

To begin, open the FMW Control. Locate and select the PatientAppointmentService composite. Test the Web Service published by the composite, making sure to enter a value of 4 for the priority—the highest value the referring doctor can assign and the surest way to get a High priority assigned by the Business Rule component (see Figure 10-11).

The test of the Web Service should result in a response fairly quickly—a synchronous reply containing the assigned appointment identifier. The schedule of the appointment is not yet available for this appointment request. When we look at the message flow trace for this test run of the composite application, we can clearly see the steps already completed—call to the PatientDataService, report the appointment identifier, and call to the AppointmentPriorityRuling Business Rule component. After this last call, the switch in the BPEL process entered the High priority branch and invoked the Task Service with a request to instantiate the ArbitrateHighPriority task. And that is the situation right now: We are waiting for Maggie to come into action (see Figure 10-12).

Maggie can go into the BPM Worklist application via her browser, using the default URL http://<host>:8001/integration/worklistapp. She must log in with the credentials created for her in the WLS Console when we created her as a user in the myrealm security realm. Maggie's Inbox contains the task instance that was created and assigned to her by the PatientAppointmentService (see Figure 10-13). In our simplistic approach—a first step without a task form—we stuffed all the

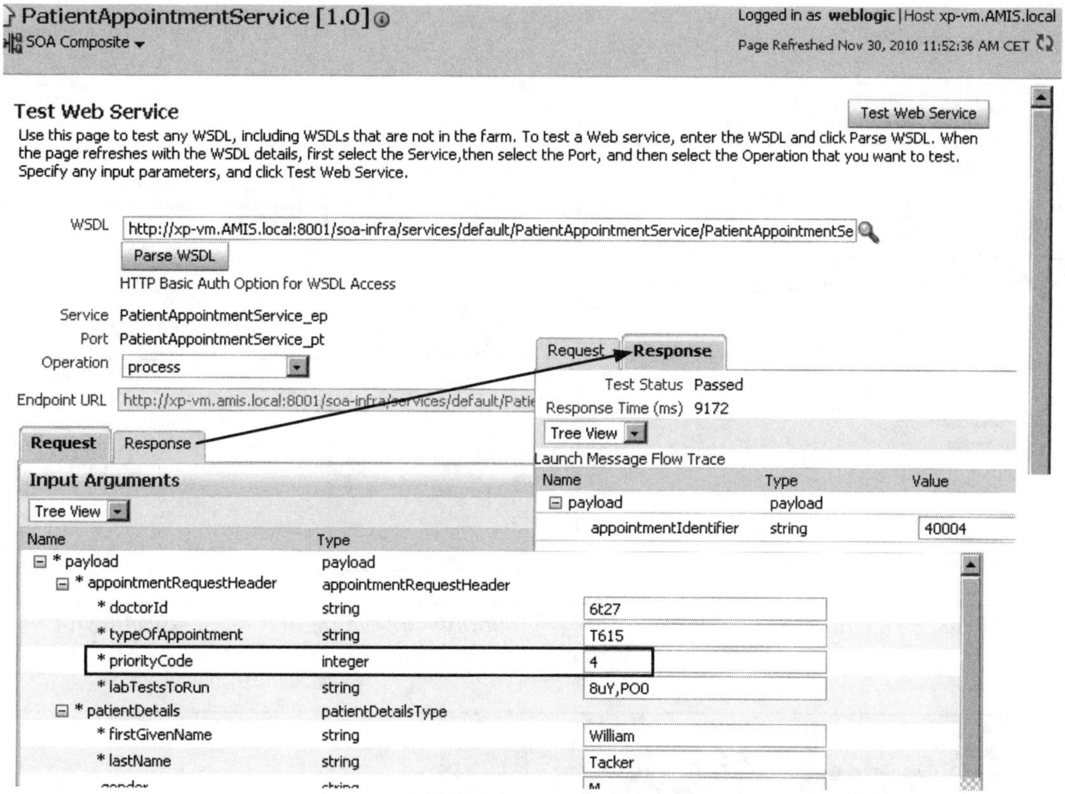

FIGURE 10-11. *Testing the PatientAppointmentService with a High priority request*

task information in the task title. Maggie should use the Actions menu to select the two predefined outcomes with which the task can be concluded. Let's have her select the most interesting one of the two: Reject.

Reject as a task outcome signals to the PatientDataService BPEL process that the appointment request priority should be lowered from High to Normal. An Assign activity in the Reject branch of the task switch takes care of this. The process will then continue. Figure 10-14 shows the run-time message flow trace for the PatientAppointmentService with this Human Task inside.

Extend the Task ArbitrateHighPriority with Notification and Group Assignment

The implementation of the composite application PatientAppointmentService suffers from at least two serious flaws. How on earth is Maggie to know that a task is waiting for her? Should she log in to the Worklist application several times per day—or even more frequently depending on what her service level agreement is for this task? Should she have it open permanently and refresh regularly? We will extend the example by adding notification to the task definition—making the SOA Suite prompt Maggie whenever a new task has been assigned to her.

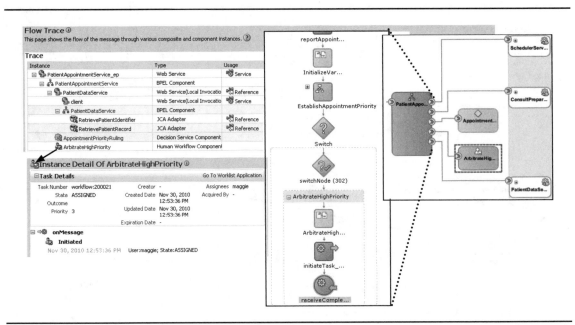

FIGURE 10-12. *The message flow trace for the High priority appointment request—waiting for Maggie to act*

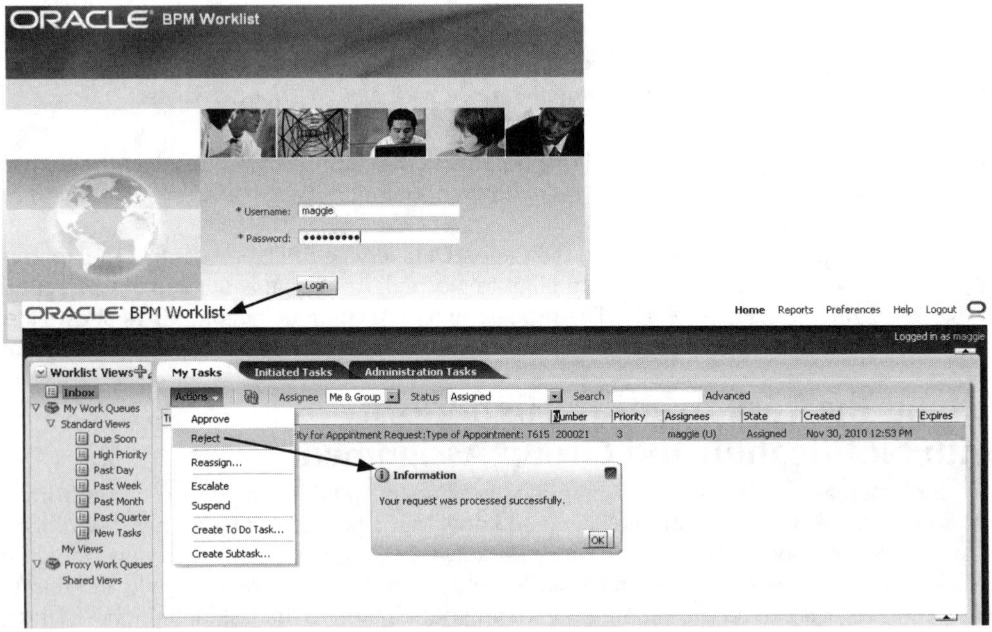

FIGURE 10-13. *The Worklist application with the task created for Maggie*

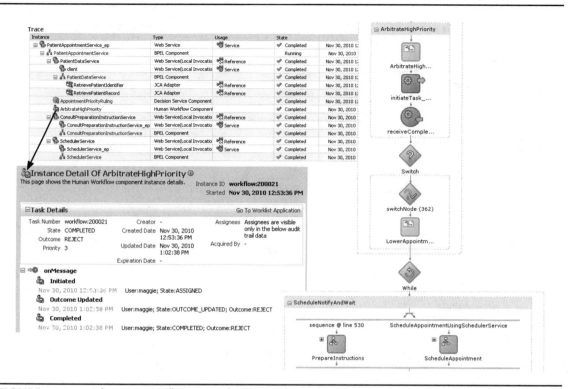

FIGURE 10-14.   *The message flow trace for PatientAppointmentService after the task has been completed*

The other flaw we will fix is the fact that given the workaholic that she is, even Maggie will have her time away from work—for sickness, vacation, or the odd conference. It is not a good idea to assign tasks to a single individual—unless we are prepared to accept an occasional cessation of task processing. Even better than assigning tasks to specific users by name is assigning tasks to a group or role. That way, the composite application is not coupled to the current staff members, and personnel changes are handled in the identity management system and thus not impacting the SOA composite application, forcing, for example, a change in code and redeployment.

Sending Task Notifications

Before we can use notifications in task definitions, we need to have a notification configured for the SOA Suite User Messaging Service as a whole. Appendix C describes this configuration.

Next, we need to go to the identity store to specify the e-mail addresses for the users who need to receive notifications. Using the default myrealm security realm, we can go to the Web Logic Server console (http://<host>:7001/console). Like before, navigate to Security Realms, select myreal, and go to the Users And Groups tab. Click the user Maggie and navigate to the Attributes tab. Locate the attribute "mail" and set it to the e-mail address you have configured to receive notifications (for Maggie or the user in your environment). Activate the changes in the console using the button in the upper-left corner.

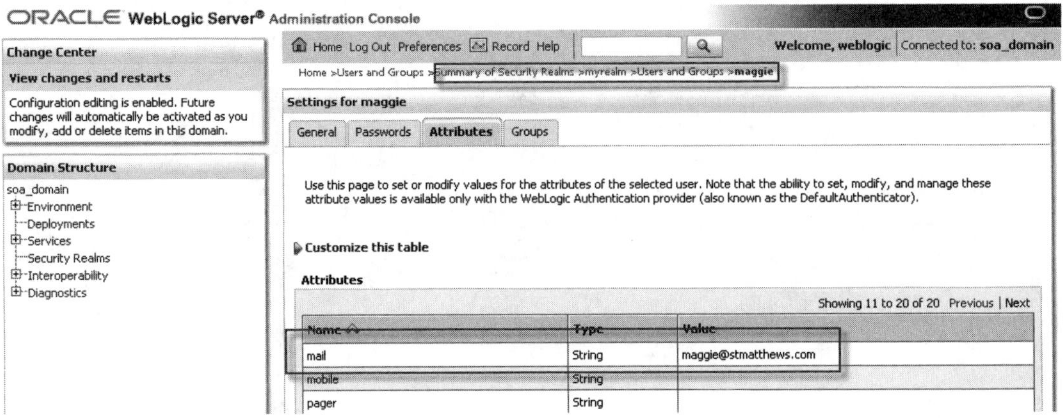

FIGURE 10-15. *Set mail attribute for user Maggie in the WLS Console*

When Maggie checks her Preferences page in the Worklist application, she'll find that a business e-mail address has been added on the Notification tab. This entry is derived from the identity store—and it cannot be maintained in the Worklist application.

We next need to configure the task definition, instructing it on the content of the e-mail it should send as "send notification" to the task assignee. Go to the Notifications tab in the task editor. You will see three notifications predefined: The default notification settings for tasks include notification upon assignment to the assignee and upon completion to the initiator (when set). You may wonder why, despite this default configuration, Maggie did not receive an e-mail to alert her of the task she had assigned to her earlier on. The answer is quite simple: As long as the identity store does not have an e-mail address set for a user, notifications cannot be sent.

Notifications can be configured for many different actions that take place on the task, including expiration, request for info, update, suspend, resume, and withdraw (see Figure 10-16). Various roles involved with the task can be specified as recipient of a notification: assignee,

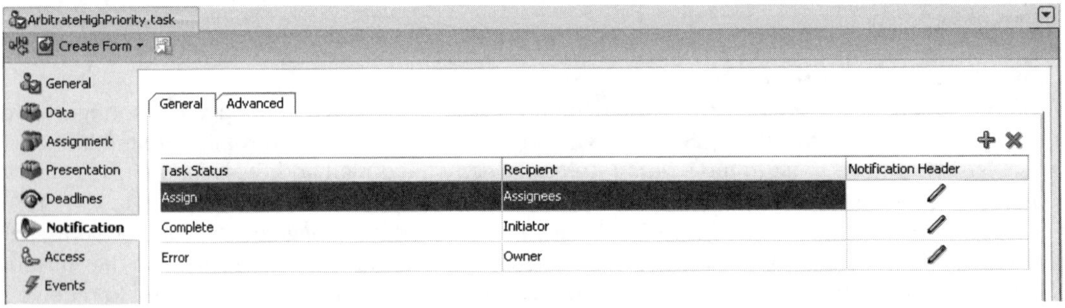

FIGURE 10-16. *Configuring a notification for task assignees*

initiator, approver, owner, and reviewer. The content of the notification can be defined, either as static text (typically not very useful) or through an XPath expression that combines static content with data from the task parameters.

Note that even though it may seem it is suggested that the notification will be sent in the form of an e-mail, that is not necessarily the case. The Task Service works with UMS to dispatch the notifications. UMS also supports channels other than e-mail: IM (chat), voice, and SMS. Addresses for messaging channels are fetched from the configured identity store. Users can specify through the preferences in the Worklist application what their desired channels of notification are. Whenever the Task Service emits a notification, these preferences determine through which channels the notifications are sent. Additionally, users can specify message filters—routing rules specifying that task notifications should be sent to a specific channel when the task attributes satisfy the conditions defined for the filter. We can specify custom headers for notifications in the task definition whose values are derived from the task parameters; these headers can subsequently be used in message filters to select the appropriate message channels.

Assigning Tasks to a Group

It is clear that assigning the task to Maggie and no one else is not a smart thing to do. When she is away for whatever reason, a task can be left unattended for several days or even weeks—which is clearly not desirable or acceptable. Notifications do not really solve this issue—even with a PDA or other mobile gadget, Maggie might not be able to respond to all tasks in a timely fashion.

In general, tasks are better assigned to a group or role for which the user membership is managed in the identity management system, entirely decoupled from the task definition. Tasks assigned to a group are a shared responsibility. All members of the group will find the task waiting for them in their to-do list. As soon as a user acquires the task, it disappears from the other users' list or workload. It is possible to assign tasks using XPath expressions that invoke advanced delegation rules that assign tasks to members of a group following patterns such as round-robin, most productive, and least busy. We can also create a custom Java class that implements (more advanced) task-assignment logic.

We keep things fairly simple in this example. We create a new group called AppointmentPriority Arbiter in the Security Realm section of the Web Logic Console. We add Maggie to this group. Next, we create a new user, Jenny, associate her with the new group too, and configure her e-mail address. Then we return to the task editor in JDeveloper and assign the task to the group. We remove the current assignment to user Maggie. See the online chapter complement for details.

Handling Tasks Through Actionable E-mails

When a task produces a simple outcome, one from a list of predefined possible outcomes (such as in simple Approve/Reject decision tasks), it is not necessary for the user to go into the Worklist application in order to perform the task. In such cases where the user only needs to select one outcome from a predefined list of values, the SOA Suite can send a special type of e-mail to the user that contains a number of hyperlinks—one for each possible outcome. When the user clicks one of these hyperlinks, a new e-mail message is created with the selected outcome for the task and is sent to the workflow engine, possibly even with attachments. It is processed as if that outcome were selected in the Worklist application. This type of e-mail is called "actionable."

Configuring the task for actionable e-mails is easy. Go to the Advanced tab on the Notification page in the task editor. Mark the check box Make Notifications Actionable, as shown in Figure 10-17.

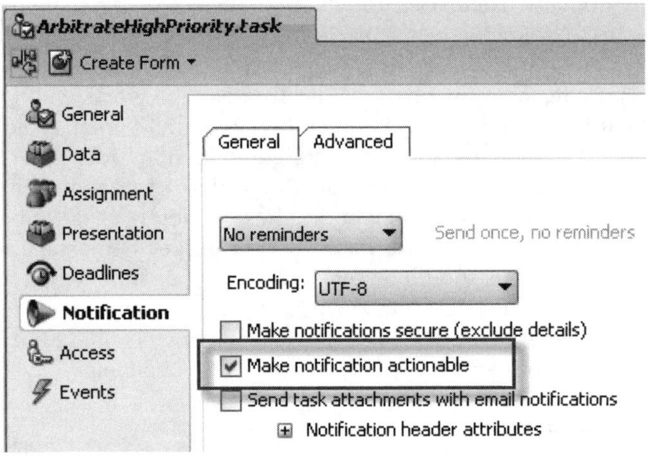

FIGURE 10-17.   *Configuring actionable e-mails for the task ArbitrateHighPriority*

It is as simple as that. However, the UMS needs to be configured, too. We need to specify which e-mail account should be listened to for incoming e-mails that are sent by users acting on actionable e-mails they received from the Human Workflow Service. In the FMW Control, select SOA Administration on the context menu for soa-infra and click the item Workflow Notification Properties in the ensuing menu. Set the actionable e-mail address on the page that opens. This should be an account on the incoming e-mail server that is configured through the FMW Control on the Email driver in the User Messaging Service.

Human Task with Group Assignment and Actionable Notifications

It is time to see the task in action again, with the refinements we have applied. Deploy the application to the SOA Suite and invoke the Web Service with an appointment request with High priority assigned in the request. The ArbitrateHighPriority task should be instantiated and assigned to the new group AppointmentPriorityArbiter. Both members of the group—Maggie and Jenny—should receive an e-mail, notifying them of the task that is assigned to them. They can execute the task by clicking one of the hyperlinks in the e-mail. When they do that, a reply e-mail is sent to the e-mail account that the UMS polls for such messages that convey task outcomes. The UMS triggers the Human Workflow Services and the task is updated with the final outcome (see Figure 10-18).

When first Maggie activates one of the possible outcomes in the actionable e-mail (and thus completes the task) and later on Jenny does the same, the e-mail sent from Jenny's account is ignored—the task has moved on and her e-mail cannot be meaningfully processed in conjunction with that task. Of course, when the task is of type Group Vote, her e-mail can still constitute a valid vote, as long as the task has not moved to the next stage. A user whose activation of the actionable e-mail comes in too late to be handled is not aware of that fact. Only when Jenny inspects the historic task view in the Worklist application would it occur to her that this task is not listed—Margaret is the one recorded as the person completing the task.

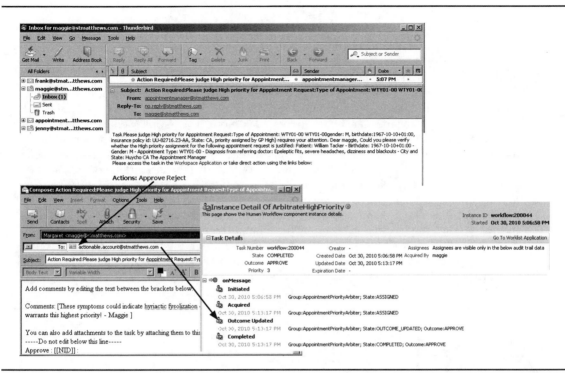

FIGURE 10-18. *The task ArbitrateHighPriority is assigned to the group AppointmentPriorityArbiter (Maggie and Jenny); Maggie utilizes the actionable notifications to execute the task*

Mediator and Human Task

Human Task service components are SCA components, just like Mediator, Business Rule, and BPEL components. Human Task components expose services that can be wired to other components within the composite and that also can be promoted to public services published by the composite to external consumers.

Much of the communication with a Human Task component requires a stateful, long-running consumer that can receive asynchronous callbacks. The initial creation of a task happens through a synchronous service call. Subsequent status changes in the lifespan of the task instance—such as reassignment, expiration, and completion—are reported back to the invoker using a callback interface. This nature of the interaction with the task service positions BPEL service components as the ideal partner for Human Task components—or other composites when the human task is reusable! The vast majority of human tasks in the SOA composite application will be initiated from BPEL components.

(Continued)

There are a few use cases where a task can also be instantiated from a Mediator component. In situations where neither the final task outcome nor the midway status changes are of relevance to the task initiator and the only requirement is to kick off the task, it might be logical to trigger the task from a Mediator.

One such fire-and-forget human task situation is when events that appear on the Event Delivery Network should be turned into a more human form of notification (telephone call, message posted on the message board in the break room, and so on). Mediators can consume such events from the EDN and invoke a Human Task service component to turn the event into a notification and possibly call for action targeted at a user or group of users.

The Mediator will not be able to wait for the outcome of the task or one of the callback calls. All it could do is use the synchronous reply from the Task Service and forward it to, for example, an event log. This reply contains task details such as the name of initial assignees, the expiration date, and the task instance identifier that can be used to look up the task through the Java API exposed by the Human Workflow Services.

Figure 10-19 shows how a Mediator component consumes the DoctorSickEvent from the Event DeliveryNetwork and then initiates a Human Task for the secretarial pool to let all relevant parties know about Dr. Steve Knuckles' illness.

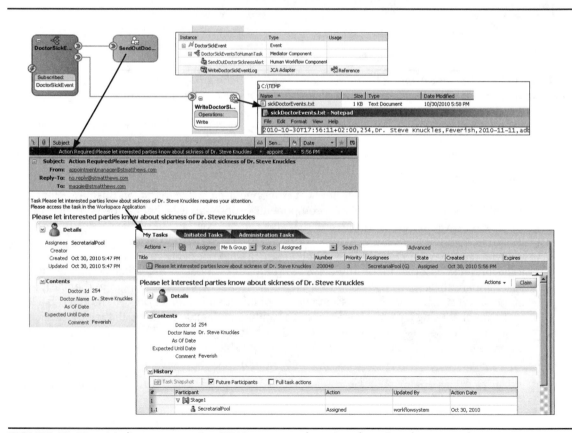

FIGURE 10-19. *Mediator consuming EDN events and turning them into human tasks*

The Scheduler Service—Beyond Mere Decisions

Our first encounter with the Human Task service component focused on one unique capacity of humans in the context of our composite applications: decision making beyond the purely rational, fact-based realm that the Business Rule component governs. When it comes to dealing with more subtle, fuzzy, or unstructured data or political considerations on which to base a decision, or when the impact of a decision is very large and requires a level of authority we are not (yet) prepared to hand to a machine, human staff members with special roles are brought in to make the final call. The outcome of this category of human tasks is fairly simple: In the first case, we discussed a simple yes or no (approve or reject). Decisions can range over a larger set of possible outcomes, but they essentially always result in one value being picked from a number of predefined values.

Other tasks have more interesting outcomes. Some tasks may require the user to not only inspect but also modify or complement the payload provided with the task. For example, in cases where we have an incomplete address or contact details for a patient, there could be a task assigned to the front desk to question the patient when she arrives at the hospital and complete these details. Such a task would result in updated patient details being returned to the task invoker.

Tasks with Complex Outcomes

We are now going to look at another task definition that produces a more complex result: the SchedulerService. First introduced in Chapter 6, the SchedulerService is invoked by the BPEL process PatientAppointmentService with data from the appointment request. This service is expected to produce a scheduled appointment with the appropriate doctor in a suitable room at a specific date and time. We wondered in Chapter 6 whether this service was in fact implemented by a fancy computer application or had a pool of human staff members lurking behind it. It turns out the latter is the case, although St. Matthews is looking for ways to have at least a subset of all appointments scheduled automatically or have an automated process come up with a number of suggestions that the human schedulers can then choose from or replace if necessary with their own schedule.

The human task we will define for scheduling appointments uses several task parameters, one of which is designed as editable in the task. This means that the user can create and manipulate values in the parameter, and the augmented parameter data is made available to the caller of the task service. This task will also work with a generated task form—a straightforward user interface that is embedded in the Worklist application.

Configure Parameters for ScheduleAppointment Task

To begin, open the composite application SchedulerService and then open the Composite Editor. Drag a new Human Task component to the composite and call the task **ScheduleAppointment**.

Double-click the new Task component to bring up the task editor. We need to define the parameters for the task on the Data tab. Task parameters are based on XML types or elements defined in the XSD documents available in the project (or MDS, see Chapter 18). The SchedulerService.xsd contains a SchedulingRequest element as well as a PlannedSchedule element. The former represents the input data that the human operator should be able to use to schedule an appointment for the patient. The latter contains the details for the appointment's schedule. This parameter needs to be modified, so enable the Editable Via Worklist application option. Create both task parameters,

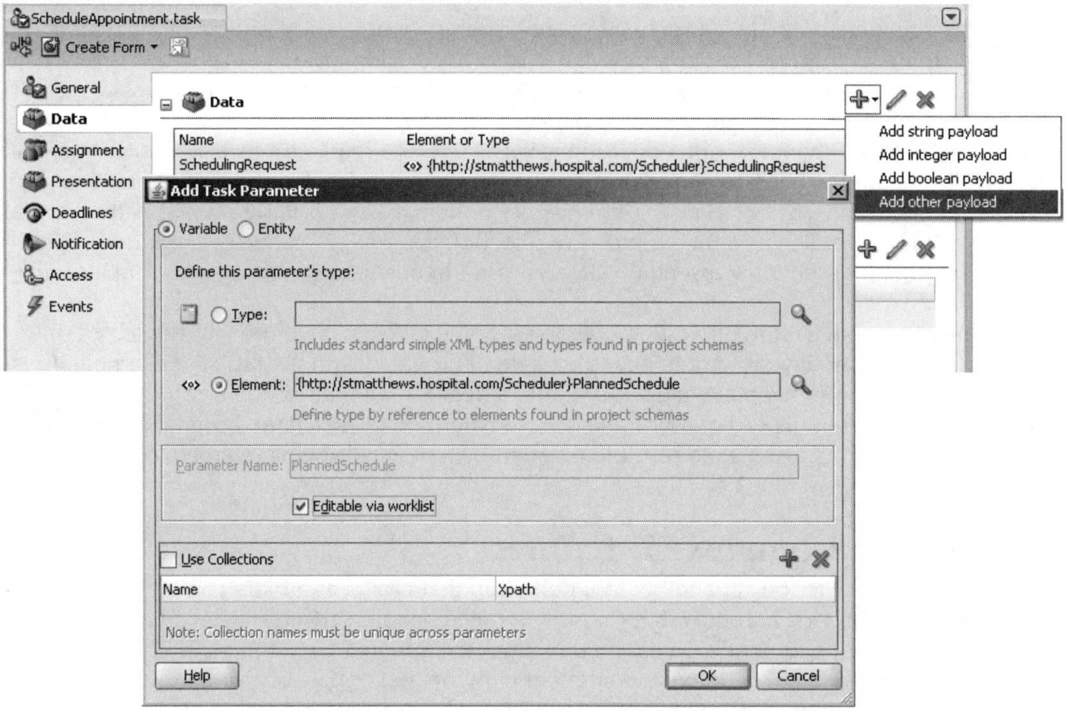

FIGURE 10-20. *Creating the PlannedSchedule parameter—editable in the Worklist application*

based on the elements in the XSD, as indicated, and set the parameter PlannedSchedule to be editable (see Figure 10-20).

Next, create an assignment of the task to a single user—Maggie, again, to keep things simple. You may want to specify a nondefault notification header to embellish the e-mail that Maggie is going to receive—however, once we have generated the task form, you will find the e-mail to be quite enriched as a result!

Add a Human Task to the BPEL Process

To start, return to the composite application and double-click the SchedulerService BPEL component. Drag a human task from the Component Palette to the BPEL process, drop it after the dummy activity Lot_of_Asynch_logic_to_determine_schedule, and select the ScheduleAppointment task component. Configure the mapping between the task parameters and the BPEL variables: Map the SchedulingRequest on the inputVariable to the first task parameter and the PlannedSchedule on the outputVariable to the second (updatable) task parameter (see Figure 10-21).

The OK branch of the taskSwitch should contain an Assign activity that copies the contents of the plannedSchedule task parameter to the BPEL outputVariable. We will ignore the other branches for now—they are not part of the "happy flow" we are focused on currently.

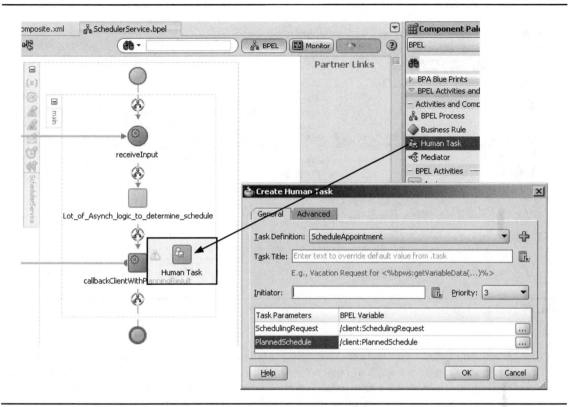

FIGURE 10-21.   *Adding the ScheduleAppointment task to the BPEL process*

Generate the ScheduleAppointment Task Form

Human tasks can have much richer user interfaces than we have seen so far in the Worklist application. We can create our own advanced custom applications—from scratch, using any user interface technology we fancy—for working on the tasks using the Human Workflow services API. At the near end of the task user interface spectrum, we find the generated task form. This is a generated ADF application that contains a so-called ADF Task Flow along with an ADF Faces page that is bound to the Human Workflow Service. It basically is a piece of user interface and flow logic in which one or more graphical components are combined in a single logically related user interface component. The ADF application that contains the task form is deployed to the same WebLogic domain as the SOA Suite. It is used at run time by the Worklist application with the appropriate parameter values to show the details for the selected task. The task assignee finds an overview of the values of the task parameters in a form layout. Fields associated with editable parameters are enabled and allow data manipulation. Changes made in the form to the payload data can be saved and will be persisted by the Human Workflow Services. We will have JDeveloper generate a standard ADF task form for the ScheduleAppointment task. This form can be used to inspect the details for the appointment request and enter the data for the appointment schedule.

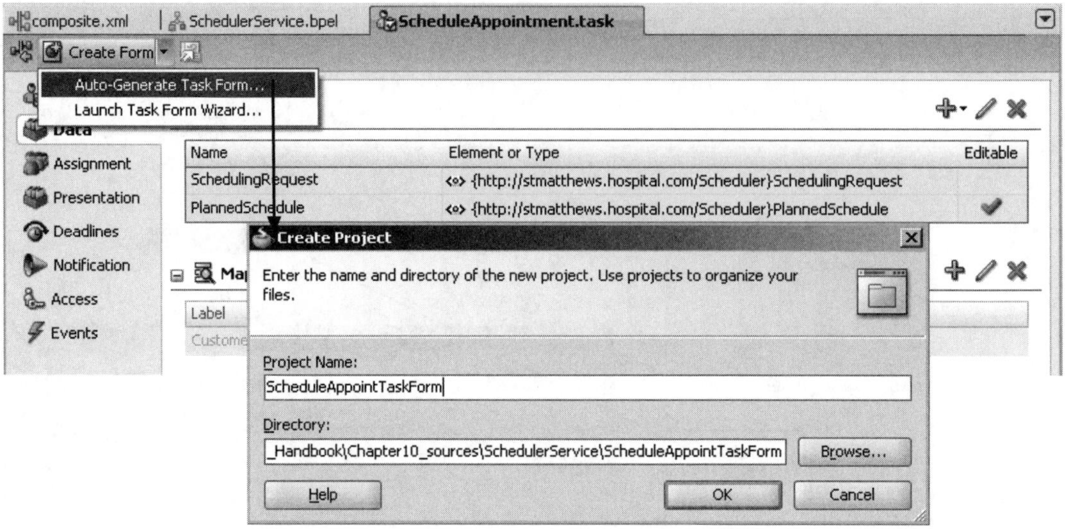

FIGURE 10-22. *Generating the task form for ScheduleAppointment*

ADF is the Oracle Application Development Framework used by Oracle for developing most of its own user interfaces, such as Fusion Applications, WebCenter, the BPM Worklist application, and the Enterprise Manager Fusion Middleware Control. Chapters 20 and 21 provide more details on ADF and explain how to customize the generated task form we will create next.

Generate the Task Form for the Task ScheduleAppointment

To generate the task form, go to the top of the task editor and select Auto-Generate Task Form from the Create Form drop-down menu. A pop-up window appears in which we need to enter the name of the project that will be created to hold the ADF artifacts that implement the generated task form. Click the OK button to kick off the generation of the form (see Figure 10-22).

At this point, your computer starts making whizzing or rattling noises with your hard disk activity indicator flashing excitedly. The new JDeveloper project is created, containing a number of XML files, derived in part from the ScheduleAppointment task definition. An interesting file to take a look at is taskDetails1.jspx. This is a JSF (JavaServer Faces) page that presents the task form. It contains fields corresponding to the contents of the task parameters, as well as controls required to manipulate the task. The page contains tables for comments and attachments that the user can add to.

Scheduling in Action

The PatientAppointmentService calls upon the SchedulingService to schedule the appointment. A good way of seeing the SchedulingService in action therefore is through a call to the Patient AppointmentService. That also gives us a good idea about whether the outcome of the task—the schedule itself—is properly set and returned to the invoker (first the SchedulerService BPEL process inside the composite and indirectly the PatientAppointmentService BPEL component).

First, we need to deploy the SOA composite application along with a web application that contains the generated task form. We deploy the SOA composite in the regular way—and we can

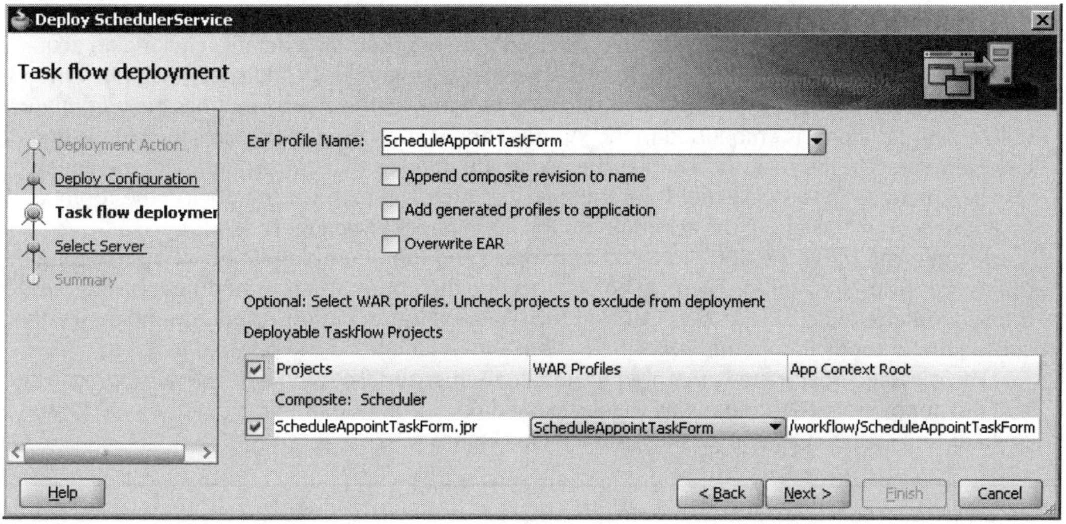

FIGURE 10-23. *Deploying the task form application as part of the SOA composite deployment to the SOA server*

indicate which web applications should be deployed alongside it, such as the ScheduleAppointment TaskForm project with the generated task form (see Figure 10-23).

The association between the Human Task service component and the ADF Task Form application can be inspected and manipulated in the FMW Control. Select the Scheduler composite in the tree navigator. When the dashboard for the composite appears, click the ScheduleAppointment task component. Navigate to the Administration tab, which lists the associations between the ScheduleAppointment Human Task component and task forms in the context of specific applications. Initially there is only the link to the SchedulerAppointmentTaskForm task form application in the context of the (BPM) Worklist application (see Figure 10-24). This registration is created upon deployment of the composite Scheduler.

Call the PatientAppointmentService with some appointment request. After some initial processing, a ScheduleAppointment task will be created and assigned to Maggie. She receives an

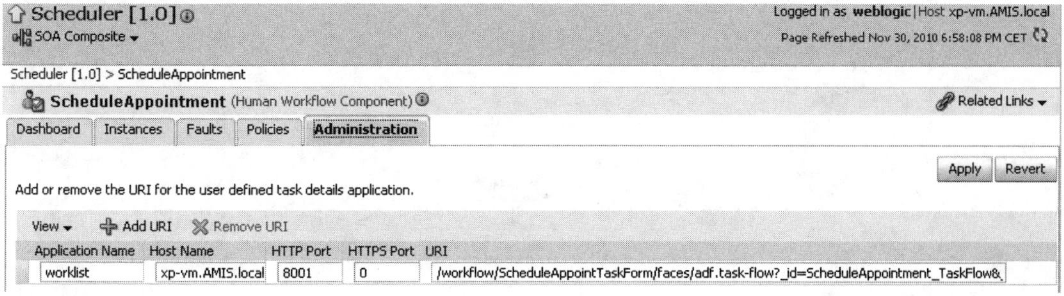

FIGURE 10-24. *The registered association between the human task and the ADF task form*

e-mail notification that is quite rich: It contains all the details that will also be presented in the task form inside the Worklist application in a HTML layout.

Because she needs to provide the actual appointment-scheduling details, clicking an actionable link in the e-mail will not suffice. Therefore, she needs to enter the Worklist application. When she selects the assigned task, the Worklist application will invoke the task form it has been configured to utilize. This task form is embedded in the Worklist application itself. It presents the details from the task parameters to the user and enables the user to fill in fields that correspond with the editable task parameters—in this case, fields for the date and time, the name of the doctor, the room, and additional comments about the schedule for the appointment (see Figure 10-25).

Maggie can fill in the fields, save her changes, and then complete the task by selecting the option OK from the Actions menu. The task result—the appointment schedule—is returned to the SchedulerService BPEL process and in turn handed to the PatientAppointmentService that subsequently sends it, together with the patient's instructions, to the original invoker.

The message flow trace is updated to reflect all this, and from the audit details, we can see that the appointment schedule was indeed passed back from the task form all the way to the original requesting SOA composite instance (see Figure 10-26).

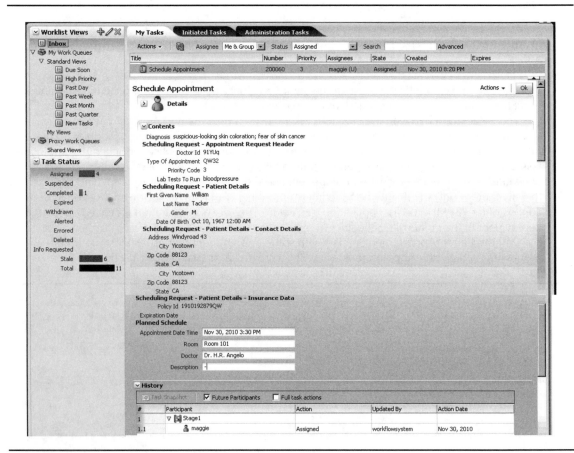

FIGURE 10-25. *The task form embedded in the Worklist application*

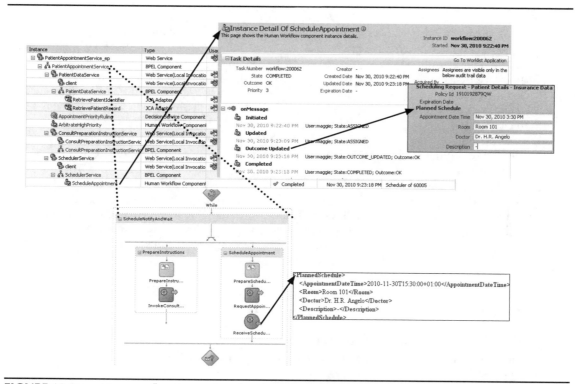

FIGURE 10-26. *Message flow trace showing the ScheduleAppointment task's results being passed back*

Just Press Next

It is a paradigm shift to approach applications from the angle of workflows and tasks rather than the data-oriented, global menu-powered, CRUD-style application angle that has been so common for the last decade or more. Traditionally, end users navigate their way through an extensive menu that takes them to pages where data is presented—usually a lot of data. And power users who work with the application, day in and day out, hardly need any UI features to perform their work. They operate on the records using shortcuts and years of routine. They select these records, for example, based on status flags that they query explicitly on in the page, or perhaps they select them working from a stack of paper forms.

This (traditional) way of working does not sit well with less experienced users. Nor does it appeal to a younger generation of computer users who were not raised with green-font terminals but rather grew up in the Internet era and are exposed to Web 2.0 user interfaces all over the World Wide Web. A more current approach to applications is one where user interfaces are task driven, presenting only data that is relevant for the task at hand and with guided, wizard-style navigation that takes the user through a workflow. The user only has to click the Next and sometimes the Previous button to visit the pages she needs for her tasks. Furthermore, the application knows what her tasks are and presents them automatically.

(Continued)

Instead of an application that consists of dozens of pages that are bound together in a central menu, we could have individual task UIs that are invoked by a workflow engine when the user embarks on a specific task. The workflow engine presents the user with a to-do list of tasks, the user selects a task, and the engine opens the corresponding user interface. When the user has completed the task, she can press the Next button and the workflow engine presents the page for processing the next task on the list—or shows the overview with tasks. Users can then decide for themselves what task to do next.

The human task in SOA composite applications, in conjunction with the Task and Workflow Services and the Worklist application, comes very close to achieving the scenario described here. E-mails can invite the user to come and execute a task. The Worklist application presents open tasks that should be attended to. When we define the process as a workflow with Human Task components in between the automated actions, we can have our users be guided by the engine, thus allowing them to focus on the highest priority task while presenting all relevant data in context. All the user has to do is click Next in order to be taken to the next task that requires typical human skills to be performed.

Acceptance of New Patient: Complex Task Routing

The human tasks we saw earlier were fairly simple and only involved a single actor—although selected out of potentially a much larger group. Tasks can be far more complex than that— involving multiple actors, each with their own responsibility. Some of these actors can work on the task at the same time, while others work in sequential order. Some actors or stages in the task may be conditional—only to be performed when certain conditions are met. It is possible to have steps within the task that require a consensus (unanimous) or majority in favor of one outcome or another. Task participants can be allowed to delegate their responsibility to another user, or they can escalate it to their manager. Tasks can also be escalated by the task service itself, when the deadline isn't met, for example.

We will take a look at some of these workflow aspects of human tasks when we implement the "acceptance of new patient" task.

Accepting a New Patient

The PatientAppointmentService calls upon the PatientDataService to retrieve the patient identifier and some key patient data. Sometimes it happens that an appointment request is being made for a new patient—one not yet known in Frank's database with patient records. The current implementation of this composite application ends with a fault when that is the case. Creating an appointment for an unknown patient is not supported. However, hospitals typically have to accept new patients from time to time, and St. Matthews is no exception. However, the hospital wants to carefully screen new patients before accepting them as such. So instead of simply aborting the BPEL process when a request is made for an appointment for a new patient, something else needs to happen.

When it turns out that the appointment request that is processed by the PatientAppointmentService is in fact one for a new patient, a workflow needs to be executed for screening the new patient, in various steps by a number of different actors.

First, every candidate patient is subject to a general admissibility check, which involves looking at criteria such as priority, address, the GP's diagnosis, and the "general impression" of the staff member. A patient is either outright rejected or moved to the second stage.

The nature of the second stage depends on whether the potential patient has valid insurance. When she does, the second stage consists of conferring with the insurance company and getting its approval. This is done by a group called "the insurance liaisers." The third stage for patients with insurance is the final go/no-go from the patient account managers at St. Matthews. A single account manager can make this final decision.

For patients without insurance, the second stage consists of a credit check, where credit assessors investigate the financial status and payment history of the applicant. Depending on their findings, they may decide to turn the patient away or nominate her for the third stage. The final stage is a group vote by the patient account managers.

Each of the stages has a maximum processing time assigned to it; the overall new patient acceptance flow should not take too long. Stage one must be completed within four business hours; stage two also has a deadline of four hours for patients with insurance and eight hours for patients without insurance. Stage three must be done in under two business hours for insured patients and in under four hours in case of a majority vote for uninsured patients.

Note that at each of the steps in this flow, the patient can be rejected and the task concluded immediately and the patient informed.

Parallel Activities

Although he is mighty proud of his database, Frank will have to admit that many patient records are incomplete. Contact details are incorrect or incomplete, essential information about birth dates or even gender may be lacking, and so on. The hospital management has urged the staff to be more diligent about gathering and entering complete and correct patient data. At the very least, new patient records should be immaculate.

It seems like a good idea to use this opportunity of the new patient acceptance workflow to have one of the secretaries work on the record for a candidate patient while various other actors work on their part of the task—dealing with the evaluation of the new patient. This ensures that at least for new patients, the record is complete and correct. It is accepted that in a minority of cases this work will have been in vain, because the patient for which the data has been assembled will not be accepted after all.

For Your Information: The Task's Carbon Copy

In the past, the financial controllers in the hospital were cc'd on e-mails regarding uninsured patients. They did not actually join in the decision process—although they could escalate it when they felt things went horribly wrong—but they liked to be kept in the loop. We will implement the same thing in the workflow we set up next by including them as a FYI participant. This type of assignment does not allow them to edit the task parameters or influence the task outcome. However, they can see what is going on and they can add comments or attachments to the task.

Developing the "Accept New Patient" Task Definition

Before we create the "accept new patient" task, it is useful to create the groups we are going to assign the subtasks to. We do this in the identity store from the WLS console. Create the following groups and assign at least two users to each group: FinancialControllers, SecretarialPool, PatientAccountManagers, CreditAssessers, InsuranceLiaisers, and PatientAdmissibilityCheckers.

Open the Composite Editor in the PatientAppointmentService application. Add a human task component to the application and enter **AcceptNewPatient** as the task name. Enter a meaningful namespace and then double-click the task definition to open the task editor.

Accept the default outcomes: Accept [new patient] and Reject [new patient]. Maggie is the owner of the task, so at least initially she can monitor the process and intervene when necessary.

On the Data tab, create an editable task parameter that is (again) based on the AppointmentServiceProcessRequest element in the PatientAppointmentService.xsd document. The parameter should be editable because patient details can be added or corrected by secretaries in this task.

Things start to get interesting on the Assignment tab. This is where we create the flow for this task, using various stages, both parallel and sequential. Click the default stage and change the name of the participant and the stage itself to **AdmissibilityChecker** and **AdmissibilityCheck**, respectively. Click the Advanced icon to open the editor for some advanced settings. These settings are for task stage deadlines, participant invitation, and skipping rules. The latter is used to specify under which conditions the stage can be skipped.

Click the green plus icon and select the option Parallel Stage. This creates a new stage in the task that is positioned next to the AdmissibilityChk stage, in a parallel flow. Edit this stage to set its name and participant label to **RefinePatient** and **SecretarialPool**, respectively. Select stage AdmissibilityChk, click the green plus icon, and add a sequential stage. Call this stage **CreditChk** with participant **CreditAssesser**. This stage has a sequential succeeding stage, Go/NoGo, performed by the PatientAccountManagers. Parallel to CreditChk is stage InsuranceChk, by InsuranceLiaiser, followed by the (sequential) stage Go/NoGo, by a single PatientAccountManager (see Figure 10-27).

Click the edit icon in the upper-right corner. In the pop-up dialog, specify that the task should be completed as soon as the outcome REJECT is set by a participant. This means that the task can be aborted at any stage.

Edit each of the participant types by selecting the appropriate group from the identity store. Allow the participants of the RefinePatient stage to invite other participants. Set the stage duration in the Advanced Settings section according to the functional description—four, four, and two business hours.

In the function description of this task, we defined deadlines in terms of business hours. Unfortunately, the Human Task component itself is currently not aware of business hours—it only works with plain clock hours. The next chapter discusses the BPM service engine that runs workflows defined through BPMN. This type of workflow is slightly more business oriented and is aware of opening hours and the work days of an organization.

Add the FYI Participant   Select the stage CreditCheck and then select the option Add Parallel Participant Block. A new participant is created parallel to CreditCheck. Set the participant type to FYI and set the label to FYIFinancialController. Note that it does not matter very much whether the FYI task is created as a sequential or as a parallel participant block because the task flow continues without waiting for an outcome of that particular participant.

Configure the Group Vote for the PatientAccountManagers   We want all PatientAccount Managers to be invited to vote on the candidate patient. Double-click the participant type. We need to change the participant type for the PatientAccountManagers from Single to Parallel. This turns the stage into a group vote. We can specify the minimum percentage required for an outcome to be selected. In this case, any outcome that reaches 51 percent of the vote (a majority) is selected as *the* outcome for this participant type (see Figure 10-28).

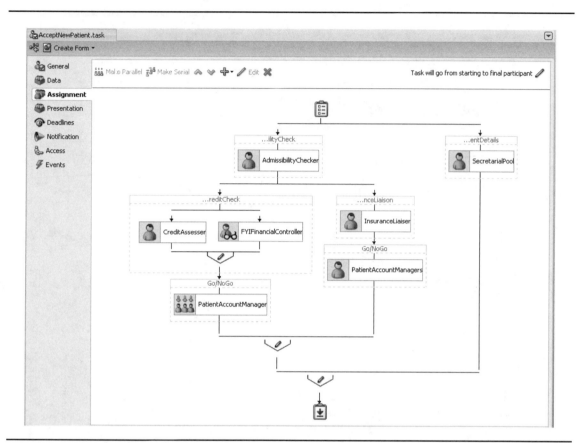

FIGURE 10-27. *Parallel and sequential stages in the task assignment flow*

Skip Irrelevant Branches   For a candidate patient without insurance, the parallel steps InsuranceChk and its subsequent Go/NoGo do not need to be executed. And for new patients who *do* have insurance, the CreditChk and subsequent Go/NoGo can be skipped. Go to each of these participant types that only need to be performed under certain conditions. Double-click to edit and expand the Advanced section. Mark the check box Specify Skip Rule. The field for entering the skip rule's XPath expressions appears. You use the XPath expression editor for creating the XPath expression that tests whether the policyId element has a value (see Figure 10-29).

Note that the use of the concat is a shortcut that prevents us from having to explicitly check the existence of the policyId element as well as its value.

Restrict Secretaries Through Limited Access Privileges   Not all participants in a task are created equal—not all of them have the same privileges. We can set authorization details on the Access tab—per role or, even more detailed, per participant type, and for content and actions.

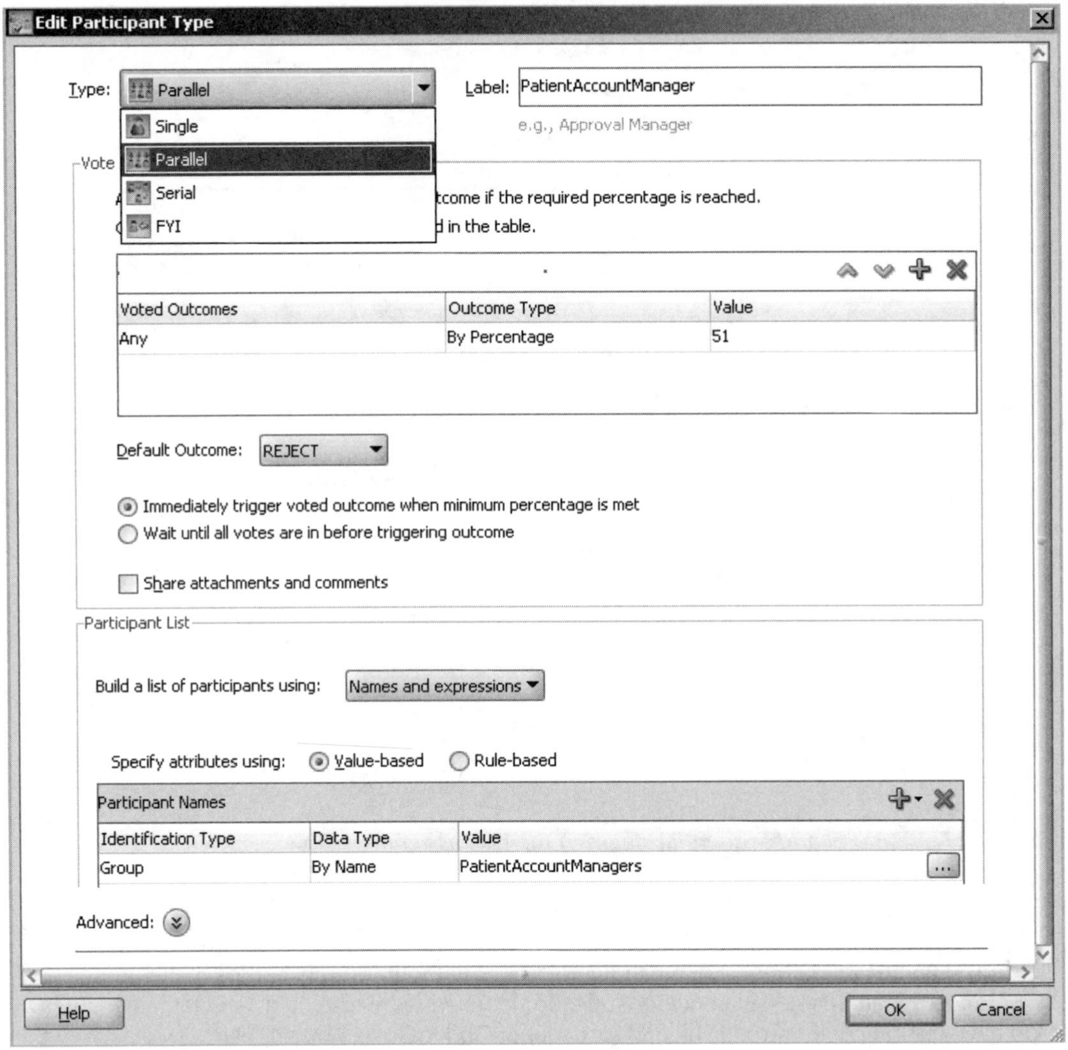

FIGURE 10-28. *Configuring the parallel participant type with a group vote*

In this case, we do not want secretaries to set the task outcome Reject—which means specifying a restriction on an action. Go to the Actions tab. Select the radio button Fine Grained (to switch from roles to participant types) and uncheck the check box in the column for SecretarialPool and the row for REJECT (see Figure 10-30).

Generate the Task Form   We need to provide our users with the information required to act upon the task. Therefore, we should generate the task form for the Accept New Patient task. In the same

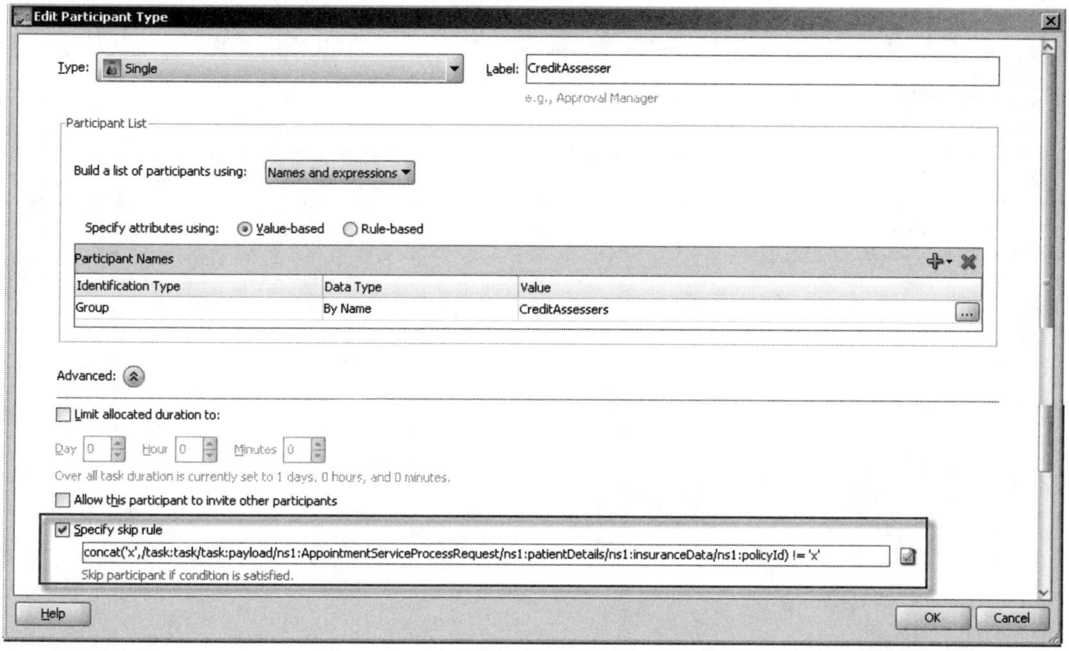

FIGURE 10-29.   *Specifying the skip rule for CreditChk to be only performed for uninsured patients*

way we saw in the previous section, select the option Create Form | Auto-Generate Task Form from the menu in the top bar of the task editor. Enter a project name of **AcceptNewPatientTaskForm**. The ADF web project is generated. We deploy it along with the composite application just like before.

Integrate the Task in the PatientDataService BPEL Component

Leave the task editor, return to the composite, and double-click the BPEL component to edit the PatientAppointmentService. Add a fault handler to the scope RegisterPatientData. This handler catches the fault client:PatientNotFoundFault. Add a human task to this fault handler. Select the AcceptNewPatient task and map the BPEL InputVariable's ApppointmentServiceProcessRequest part of the task parameter (see Figure 10-31).

In the Reject branch of the task switch, we should throw a fault—the situation we end up in cannot be resolved and is also not the desired end result.

In the Accept branch of the task switch, we should invoke the PatientDataService to create the new patient. Then we need to load the patient's data in the BPEL variable Patient. Subsequently, the PatientAppointmentService process can continue normally.

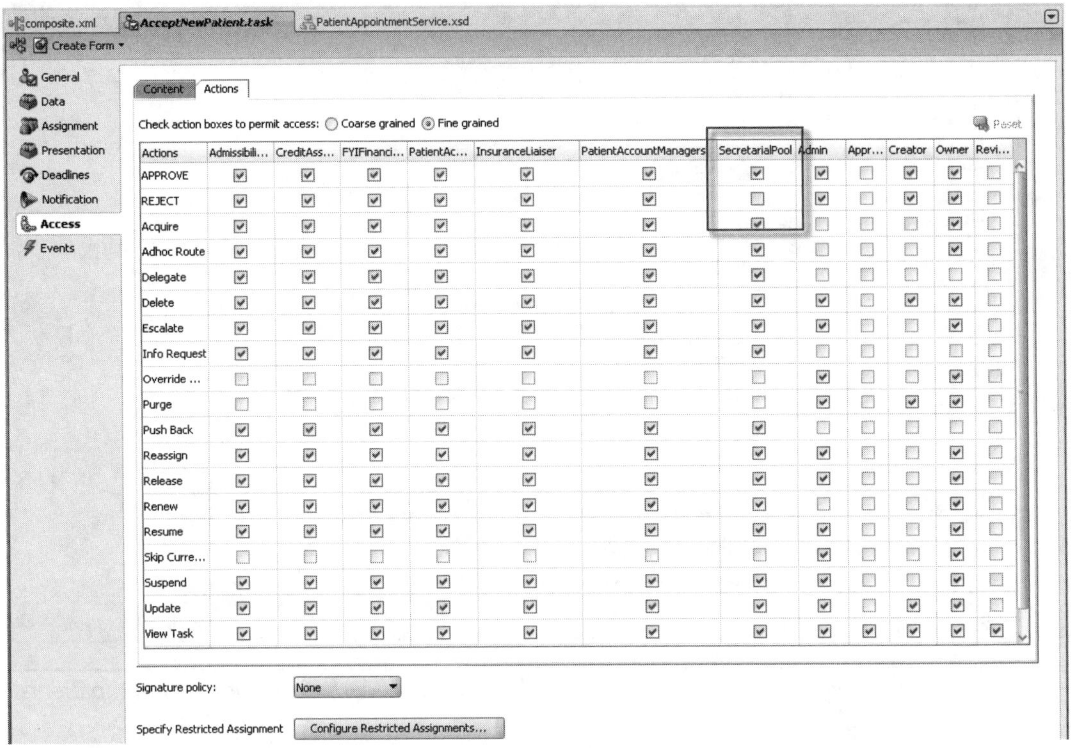

Tabs: composite.xml | **AcceptNewPatient.task** | PatientAppointmentService.xsd

Create Form ▾

General
Data
Assignment
Presentation
Deadlines
Notification
Access
Events

Content | Actions

Check action boxes to permit access: ○ Coarse grained ● Fine grained   Reset

Actions	Admissibili...	CreditAss...	FYIFinanci...	PatientAc...	InsuranceLiaiser	PatientAccountManagers	SecretarialPool	Admin	Appr...	Creator	Owner	Revi...
APPROVE	✓	✓	✓	✓	✓	✓	✓	✓	☐	✓	✓	☐
REJECT	✓	✓	✓	✓	✓	✓	☐	✓	☐	✓	✓	☐
Acquire	✓	✓	✓	✓	✓	✓	✓	☐	☐	☐	✓	☐
Adhoc Route	✓	✓	✓	✓	✓	✓	✓	☐	☐	☐	✓	☐
Delegate	✓	✓	✓	✓	✓	✓	✓	☐	☐	☐	☐	☐
Delete	✓	✓	✓	✓	✓	✓	✓	✓	☐	✓	✓	☐
Escalate	✓	✓	✓	✓	✓	✓	✓	✓	☐	☐	✓	☐
Info Request	✓	✓	✓	✓	✓	✓	✓	☐	☐	☐	☐	☐
Override ...	☐	☐	☐	☐	☐	☐	☐	✓	☐	✓	✓	☐
Purge	☐	☐	☐	☐	☐	☐	☐	✓	☐	✓	✓	☐
Push Back	✓	✓	✓	✓	✓	✓	✓	☐	☐	☐	☐	☐
Reassign	✓	✓	✓	✓	✓	✓	✓	✓	☐	☐	✓	☐
Release	✓	✓	✓	✓	✓	✓	✓	☐	☐	☐	✓	☐
Renew	✓	✓	✓	✓	✓	✓	✓	☐	☐	☐	✓	☐
Resume	✓	✓	✓	✓	✓	✓	✓	☐	☐	☐	✓	☐
Skip Curre...	☐	☐	☐	☐	☐	☐	☐	✓	☐	☐	✓	☐
Suspend	✓	✓	✓	✓	✓	✓	✓	✓	☐	☐	✓	☐
Update	✓	✓	✓	✓	✓	✓	✓	✓	☐	✓	✓	☐
View Task	✓	✓	✓	✓	✓	✓	✓	✓	✓	✓	✓	✓

Signature policy: None ▾

Specify Restricted Assignment   Configure Restricted Assignments...

FIGURE 10-30.   *Prevent the SecretarialPool from setting the task outcome to REJECT*

See Some Action: Requesting an Appointment for a New Patient

After deploying the PatientDataService composite with the AcceptNewPatient human task integrated into the BPEL component, it is time to see everything in action. Let's invoke the composite's "process" operation with an appointment request for a new, unknown patient. The BPEL process will enter the fault handler because of the (functional) "no patient found" fault thrown by the PatientDataService. At this point, the "accept new patient" task is instantiated and assigned (see Figure 10-32).

Advanced Features for Human Tasks

Human tasks in SOA Suite 11g do not end with what you have read in this chapter so far. Chapter 20, for example, describes how we can create custom (and customized) task forms—more tailored to the specific needs of the organization or specific users. Additionally, there is a series of advanced features and options that are beyond the scope of this book but should however be mentioned, no matter how briefly.

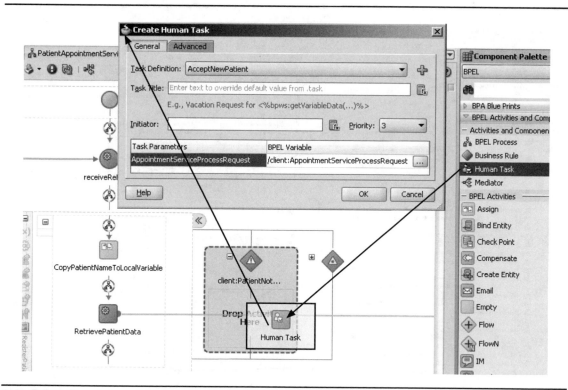

FIGURE 10-31.   *Integrating the accept new patient task in the BPEL process*

Business Rules for Task Allocation

When creating the participant list, we can select individual users or groups from the identity management system or use an XPath expression for creating straightforward logic to derive the task actors. There is a third, more advanced option: Build a list of the task participants using a Business Rule component. Upon selection of this rule-based option, a rule dictionary is created that contains predefined functions such as CreateResourceList and a series of fact types for various aspects of the task, including the parameters. This function creates a fact of a type understood by the task service and that contains the assignees for the task. A rule set is created in the dictionary that works on the facts that the task service passes to the Business Rule component. The rule set can use this function in its actions. The task definition refers to this rule set.

Java and WebService API for Human Workflow Services

The Human Workflow Services can be accessed through a Web Service API as well as a Java API—based on EJBs that can access the SOA Suite both locally for classes running in the JVM as well as remotely. The APIs allow applications to browse, query, and manipulate tasks—and can

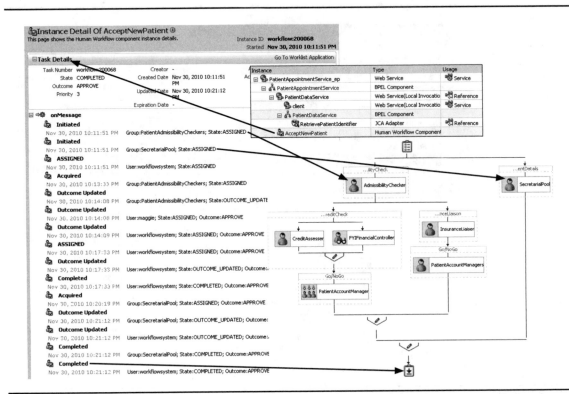

FIGURE 10-32. *An appointment request for a new patient has started the accept new patient task*

thus be used to develop custom applications that expose, modify, and/or complete tasks to assignees through tailor-made user interfaces. Appendix D provides some details on accessing this API.

Todo List Service Portlet in WebCenter

One prebuilt user interface that leverages the WebService API is the Worklist Service in WebCenter. This service consists of an ADF task flow that can be integrated in custom ADF applications as well as WebCenter spaces. The Worklist Service queries the Human Workflow Services API to find the 25 most recent tasks for the current user, presents them in a Todo List, and allows navigation into the Worklist application.

Database Views for Inspecting Task Details

Tasks are persisted in the database. We are not supposed to access those task tables directly, of course, nor is this supported. However, a number of database views has been published to give us insight in the tasks directly from SQL. Views such as WFUNATTENDEDTASKS_VIEW and WFPRODUCTIVITY_VIEW can be queried to report on task instances. There is no PL/SQL API for querying or manipulating tasks.

Using Excel as an Alternative Worklist Application

We can use Excel worksheets that connect to the Human Workflow Services as an alternative for the Worklist application. Such Excel worksheets can be sent to users as attachments to the notification e-mail. They can provide a great number of task details in a structured spreadsheet format. These worksheets can contain buttons that act like the actionable links in e-mails and send task updates to the task service. The Excel worksheets are powered by ADF DI (Desktop Integration) and can be created in a similar way to the ADF Faces browser-based task form.

Human Task Callbacks

The Workflow Service can be configured to call back (to the task initiating the BPEL process) or call out (to a Java class or the Event Delivery Network) upon certain events and status changes that take place for the task. The events that can trigger such a call are Assign, Update, Complete, Stage Complete, and Subtask Update. The callback sends a notification about what just happened with the task, including relevant details such as the user who updated the task, the new assignee, and the values of task parameters. Callbacks are configured for a task in the task editor on the Events tab. Three types of callbacks can be discerned:

- **Java callbacks**   A custom class that implements the interface IRoutingSlipCallback can be registered to be called upon task update.

- **Business events**   A task can be configured to produce events on the Event Delivery Network. These events are specified in a pre-seeded EDL file: HumanTaskEvent.edl. Mediators and BPEL components can subscribe to these task events.

- **BPEL callbacks**   When a human task is added to a BPEL process, the process is extended with a Receive activity based on the onTaskCompleted operation in the callback interface. However, the BPEL process can be made to accept other callbacks from the task service as well. On the bottom of the Events tab in the task editor is a check box marked "Allow task and routing customization in BPEL callbacks." When you check that box, open the Human Task activity editor in the BPEL process, and click OK, the BPEL process is extended again with a while loop and a Pick activity that has onMessage branches for the various callbacks the task can make. The BPEL process can do various things with the information received in a callback. Among those things is the option to invoke the task service to update the task instance—for example, with new parameter values or by ending the task.

Custom Task Allocation and Escalation Mechanisms

The Task Service works with a number of built-in algorithms for assigning tasks to users—such as least busy and round-robin. If you have a need for a specific, custom method for assigning a task to a user or a group (for example, based on task properties or parameter values), you can register a Java class that is invoked at run time to determine the assignee. In the same way the Task Service can work with a custom task-escalation method implemented in a registered Java class. The book's wiki contains an example of using a custom assignment function.

Summary

A business process typically consists of a combination of human activity and automated service calls that make computers perform some work. These actions are wired together in a process flow with additional logic, including decision points, loops, and parallel paths. The Human Task service component introduced in this chapter enables the implementation of the human activity in SOA composite applications. It seems almost as if the human actors come with a WSDL interface, just like truly automated services. Human tasks can be handled by the assignees through a generated or custom-created user interface and in some cases through actionable e-mails. The result of the human activity consists of the task outcome and possibly an updated task payload. Both are returned to the invoker of the Human Task component, which will frequently be a BPEL process component.

We saw in the last step—the process around the acceptance of a new patient—that a single task can be defined as a workflow with fairly complex routing that takes the task and its payload to various participants, who can be selected dynamically, work in parallel, and under specific conditions only. However, it is still a single task, a single packet of data, that is routed to human actors only. The routing logic is limited, and service calls are not part of the task route. The definition of the Accept New Patient flow was pushing the human task to the limits.

To implement business processes that consist of various tasks with different payloads and have both services and human agents to execute activities, we need to step outside the scope of a single human task component. Such a process can be implemented using a BPEL process that embeds multiple human tasks, service calls, and the flow logic to wire them all together. We will discuss such workflows in the next chapter.

In that chapter, we will also meet another service engine: the BPMN service engine that runs business processes developed using the Business Process Model Notation. Such BPMN processes also combine human operations and service invocations.

BPMN allows for a more intuitive, business-driven definition of processes and workflows than the combination of BPEL and Human Task. In addition, the run-time BPM Process Composer tool—somewhat similar to the SOA Composer we used for run-time editing of business rules and Domain Value Maps—allows business analysts and other run-time participants to maintain process definitions on the fly, after deployment, and in the production environment.

CHAPTER
11

Business Process
Management with BPEL
and BPMN

he previous chapter introduced the Human Task component. We have seen how human contributions can be integrated into SOA applications. Individual tasks that require decisions, data entry, and manipulation—based perhaps on interpretation of unstructured or graphical data, or verbal communication and deliberation, or even sensitivity, intuition, improvisation, or creativity—can be incorporated into otherwise automated applications. These tasks can be shared, escalated, and routed in various ways. They remain the same task, though, with the same task contents, and the routing patterns are fairly limited.

A business process or workflow typically consists of a combination of human activities and automated service calls that make IT systems perform some work. These actions are wired together in a flow with additional logic, including decision points, loops, and parallel paths. Human Task service components do not implement that typical workflow all by themselves. Instead, they implement the individual actions during the workflow—or at least trigger and represent the fact that they are (to be) executed.

To implement workflows or processes that consist of various tasks with different payloads and have both services and human agents execute activities, we need to step outside the scope of a single Human Task component. Such a workflow can be implemented using a BPEL process that embeds multiple human tasks, service calls, and the flow logic to wire them all together. We will study that approach in this chapter, and we will meet a new service engine—the BPMN service engine—that runs business processes developed using the Business Process Modeling Notation (BPMN). BPMN is often applied in the context of a broader Business Process Management (BPM) approach that focuses on cross-enterprise business processes for achieving business objectives. BPM is briefly discussed in this chapter, including the supporting tools that Oracle provides.

BPMN is an industry standard for modeling and visualizing business processes. Its original focus was not so much the execution of business processes but purely the ability to describe these processes in a clear, unequivocal notation. The initial users of BPMN, therefore, were business analysts who wanted to visualize and communicate the business processes as they took place. They then also started to refine and redesign these processes using BPMN. Many tools became available that supported the visual editing and publication of BPMN process models. Some advanced tools then also introduced process simulation, and at some point the first BPMN run-time engines appeared on the stage. These engines are very similar to BPEL engines in that they take the process blueprint and create concrete process instances based on the blueprint. Oracle provides one such BPM(N) engine, and SOA composite applications can incorporate BPMN components run by that engine—which turns out to be the same engine on the inside that runs the BPEL process components in the SOA Suite. We will see in this chapter how we can embed BPMN components in composite applications—and how such BPMN components can call out to services, possibly exposed by other composite applications.

The BPMN service engine comes with a special run-time editor called the Process Composer tool. It is somewhat similar to the SOA Composer that we used for run-time editing of business rules and Domain Value Maps, and it allows business analysts and other run-time participants to review and maintain process definitions through a browser-based environment. At development time, JDeveloper—with the special BPM 11*g* plug-in—is used to model processes.

NOTE
This chapter can only scratch the surface when it comes to the rich, complex BPMN process components and how to use them for designing and implementing applications. The online complement for this chapter provides a detailed example of the step-by-step implementation of the Treatment Approval business process discussed in this chapter—with many dozens of detailed screenshots and fine-grained instructions.

Business Process Management (BPM)

Business Process Management—briefly introduced in Chapter 2—is concerned with the management (design, improvement, execution, simulation, and so on) of *business* processes in an organization. It is a holistic approach to aligning all aspects of an organization with the ultimate business objectives and the needs of whoever the customers are. It promotes agility, flexibility, and innovation, and attempts to integrate business and (information) technology in order to achieve these goals. It is important to note that not everything within an organization can be modeled using processes: Ad-hoc questions by users, for example, can be modeled in processes but are usually not part of business process design. Also, out-of-the-ordinary events such as earthquakes are dealt with by an organization even though they are most likely not modeled by business processes.

BPM focuses on business processes—defined as a series of value-added automated or human activities that together achieve a business objective and that may involve participants across the entire organization and outside of it. The adoption of BPM in an organization mandates the use of a modeling technique such as BPMN for analyzing and improving business processes as well as possibly the utilization of a BPM run-time engine to automate the execution of these processes.

St. Matthews is anxious to have the entire organization act more as one, more streamlined—focusing on the patient and the overall business objectives. It embraces BPM as an approach that will also provide context and direction for the application of SOA. Mary, the enterprise architect engaged by St. Matthews, leads the way in the introduction of BPM. BPM and SOA are very complementary!

Mary decided to start the Business Process Management initiative with a process that is very visible to the patients: the appointment process that we have worked on in the previous chapter. She has analyzed the end-to-end appointment process and created a blueprint. She uses Oracle BPA Suite for this. The blueprint created with this tool can be imported as either a BPEL or BPMN process (or processes) into JDeveloper.

There are several reasons for selecting the first process to take on: the urgency of existing problems, the visibility throughout the organization, the largest chance of a quick success (the low-hanging fruit), and the toughest nut to crack that would provide the best possible proof for the validity of the approach.

The BPM cycle consists of the following stages:

- **Business process analysis**   In this phase, we identify business processes, capture and analyze existing processes, and/or design new ones. It is an activity that is usually executed by business analysts. Once the business processes have been modeled, they can be analyzed and simulated (for example, using what-if scenarios) to optimize them for reduced risk, duration and cost, and for increased flexibility.

■ **Business process execution**   The processes that are modeled are abstract and need to be translated into concrete processes that can be deployed and run.

■ **Business process monitoring**   The processes need to be monitored. When problems occur, we can rectify them by assigning tasks to other people, rerouting actions to other locations, and so on. After some time we evaluate the process. We can use historical data about the process to see what bottlenecks exist, what activity is the most time-consuming, and so on. This is input for the next step: optimizing the process.

■ **Business process optimization**   Optimizing the process starts the cycle again, beginning with business process analysis.

BPM from an Architectural Point of View

There are different types of processes. One category is formed by human-centric processes, where most of the work is done by humans and the most important challenge is to assign workload evenly and to monitor the progress of tasks. This is what is traditionally known as *workflow*. Another category is document-centric processes. These are very dynamic processes that evolve around documents, such as contracts or a press release for a website. Typically you will see this in document management and content management systems. There will be processes for scanning, editing, approving, and publishing the documents. The third category of processes is system-centric processes. This is what is traditionally called *orchestration*. One of the biggest improvements in system-centric processes in recent years has been the shift from batch processing to straight-through processing of one item.

In most IT environments, a system-centric process is implemented as a chain of batches. For example, suppose we have an appointment process in one of the departments of St. Matthews. There are four steps in the "happy path" of the process. Until recently, the administrators at St. Matthews used to run a batch every night to execute the steps in the process for all appointments (see Figure 11-1).

In process-oriented IT environments, a particular process will run in its entirety for every appointment (see Figure 11-2).

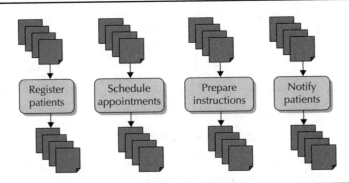

FIGURE 11-1.   *Batch processing of the appointment process*

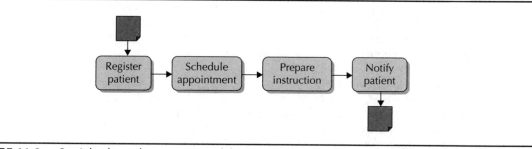

FIGURE 11-2. *Straight-through processing of the appointment process*

This has the following advantages:

- **A more even use of system resources**   No need for ever-growing batch windows anymore. Processes are running all the time, so the load on the systems doesn't peak at night.

- **Processes finish sooner**   Because we run a process immediately and complete every step, we can minimize the duration of individual process instances. There are fewer synchronization issues, too: Because the process runs immediately, we can postpone fetching data until we need it. This means that chances that data has changed between fetching it and using it are smaller.

So, does this approach have any disadvantages? Of course it does. If you have processes that are kicked off periodically, they can flood your system with instant straight-through processing. For example, a company that sells subscriptions will bill its customers every month. It is very inefficient from a database point of view to fetch one record at a time, for every individual subscription as it is processed. A batch process could use much more efficient bulk fetches of records. Another disadvantage is that related processes can interfere with each other because they might start at any time.

In cases where these disadvantages prove damaging, good-old batching may still be the way to go—or the process design needs to be improved further (for example, using the so-called Claim Check pattern). The architecture, therefore, cannot simply dictate that every process be run immediately, completely, and independently when there has been a trigger for an instance of that process; care needs to be applied to select the circumstances and (sections of) processes that qualify for real-time straight-through processing. BPM and associated tooling, along with SOA, at least offer the possibility.

The last category is called rule-centric processes. A rule-centric process is one that has many alternative paths, depending on existing business rules. An example in healthcare is case management. Case management focuses on delivering personalized services to patients to improve their care, and it consists of the following four steps:

1. Screening to find appropriate patients

2. Planning and delivery of care

3. Evaluating results for each patient and then adjusting the care plan

4. Evaluating overall program effectiveness and then adjusting the program

Every case has multiple possible outcomes, depending on the patient and the symptoms. This type of process depends very much on business rules and logic. Rules engines and decision services are appropriate for this type of process. Other examples of environments with many occurrences of rule-centric processes include health insurance companies and government agencies.

Apart from having different types of processes, we usually define different levels of processes in the process layer (see Chapter 1). Mary decides to use three levels: The first level contains value-added chains that may string several business processes together. (We saw an example in Chapter 1.) The second level contains the end-to-end processes. The third (and lowest) level is the one that is relevant for developers and end users: This is the process that will actually be implemented and run. It contains implementation details about the types of activities (automated, human step, and so on), and describes in detail the flow logic with loops and parallel flows that can be left out of the model at the second level.

Design Guidelines

As with SOA, certain principles apply when you design and execute processes:

- *Processes should be loosely coupled.* When defining the automated steps in business processes, we do not define the applications that execute those steps, but just the service interfaces that provide the required functionality. In short, we orchestrate autonomous services instead of IT systems. This also holds for human interaction: We define the task definition, not the actual implementation. The implementation of those services is outside the scope of BPM. This makes it easier to separate technical changes from changes in the process or the business logic. For example, the hospital might decide to replace the clinical information system. This does not affect the appointment process—as long as the new clinical information system implements the service interfaces on which the process relies. The other way around is the same: Suppose the hospital decides to change the appointment process. This does not necessarily mean that the IT systems that provide the services need to change.

- *Processes should not be too generic but also not too specific.* Designing business services is different from designing a process. In software you are looking for reuse, whereas in processes you are looking for efficiency and possibilities for improvement—goals that are at odds with generic, all-purpose designs. In our appointment process, we want to make a distinction between the first time we schedule an appointment and subsequent changes in the schedule. We want to minimize the latter and monitor occurrences separately.

- *Parallel execution flows should be used whenever possible.* One of the ways to speed up a process is to have activities not wait for unrelated events. For example, if we need permission from the insurance company before we treat a patient, we could do that parallel to the appointment process. A technical ramification of parallel flows is that they consume more execution threads and thereby present a larger load to the CPUs of the system.

Tools to Facilitate BPM Efforts

Oracle BPM Suite 11*g* and Oracle SOA Suite 11*g* offer several options for BPM. The components are discussed in detail in the next chapter. To design processes, you can use either Oracle BPA Suite or the lighter-weight Oracle BPM Studio—starting with BPM 11*g* available as a JDeveloper extension—if you don't need the full architecture features and the many dozens of diagram types that BPA Suite offers.

Oracle BPA Suite is a better option when there is a need for formal description and traceability. Mary has decided this is a good choice for St. Matthews: The hospital needs to describe the processes rigorously, top-down, to comply with rules and regulations. These descriptions can then be reused in the architecture to define services that are needed and to describe detailed activities that are used in the processes.

The BPA Suite offers several diagram types to model processes and other Enterprise Architecture (EA) artifacts. The first type is the value-added chain. This diagram specifies the functions in a company that directly influence the real added value of the company. The second type is Business Process Modeling Notation (BPMN). BPMN is based on flow charting for Business Process Modeling. BPMN became an OMG final adopted standard in February 2006. The specification defines the notation and semantics of a so-called business process diagram (BPD)—a standardized, cross-industry way of visualizing business processes in a structured manner. A BPD consists of flow objects, connecting objects, swimlanes, and artifacts. Business processes can be designed in BPMN using many different tools. These tools usually have some capability to publish the models as webpages on an organization's intranet, making the process visualizations available to all employees.

The 2.0 release of the BPMN standard has been in the works for several years and is scheduled to be completed in the second half of 2010. Associated with BPMN is the XPDL specification, which details how a process described in BPMN can be exchanged between BPMN tools.

After we designed the process, we want to actually execute it. This means that the business analyst is done and a developer comes in to enrich the process definition with data to make it executable. Unlike other modeling approaches, such as Visio or brown paper, the BPMN processes can also run on a server, and in such cases will never be out of sync with the living code (because they are living code). A BPMN process is created as a service component inside a SOA composite application and is deployed and executed as part of the application, in the same way BPEL processes as well as Human Task and Business Rule components are. Note, however, that the license for SOA Suite does not cover the BPMN Studio, Composer, and the run-time engine. You will need the BPM Suite license to be able to design, simulate, and run BPMN process components.

Alternatively, process models can be the basis for some other form of executable process definitions, such as BPEL processes. The Oracle tooling works together here to form a closed loop: Process models created in Oracle BPA can be generated into BPEL blueprints—abstract BPEL processes that provide the overall structure for the BPEL processes that need to be fleshed out by the developer. In the reverse direction, Oracle BPA can extract BPMN process models from BPEL processes.

Implementing Business Processes Through BPEL and Human Tasks

The missing link in the composite applications we discussed in the previous chapter was the human contribution that is indispensable in many processes—people can contribute unique skills such as fuzzy logic, improvisation, interpretation of unstructured information, and authority. The Human Task component was introduced, which on one hand is a service interface that makes it easy to wire a task into a composite application, like any other service component, and on the other hand is the task's user interface, the workflow engine, and the BPM Worklist Application that allow humans to easily interact with the task and perform the action required. BPEL processes can easily interact with Human Task components, in more or less the same way as with asynchronous automated services.

Human task definitions can be fairly complex, with serial or parallel subtasks that can even be nested, advanced rules for escalation, subtask skipping, and expiration. We have to be careful to find an appropriate balance when crafting human tasks. One or only a small number of tasks may initially sound attractive in terms of complexity and development effort compared to a larger number of tasks forged together into a workflow by an orchestrating BPEL process. However, the complexity of the individual task definitions, as well as their relative lack of flexibility, may well undo that perceived advantage.

Let's take a look at how a multitask business process with interspersed automated steps can be constructed using a BPEL process. Later on in this chapter, we will go through a similar exercise using the BPMN process approach—which is in many cases much easier and more intuitive. Note that the same human tasks used with BPEL process provide the implementation of human activities in BPMN processes.

"Accept New Patient" as a Multitask Process

The last human task discussed in the previous chapter was the "accept new patient" task (see Figure 11-3). This task really explored the boundaries of what we can do with a single human task definition in the SOA Suite today. This particular task contains several parallel subtasks; some internal routing; and the use of skip rules, deadlines, escalation rules, early task completion, and a number of different participant types, some in an FYI role and one in a group voting process. It was not easy to develop, and it is not trivial to track its progress in detail. On the other hand, a single task definition suffices to implement a complex workflow that determines whether a new patient is accepted by the hospital.

Considerations for Single Task vs. Breaking Up into Multiple Subtasks

The task definition for accepting new patients has two main parallel flows: one for the secretarial pool that has to enrich the patient details, and one that should lead to a decision about the acceptance of the new patient. This last flow starts with a initial check on some key aspects—a quick triage, if you will—performed by a user with the role AdmissibilityChecker. When a patient is accepted in this first stage, he enters the next, which is one of two flows, depending on whether he has health insurance. Both flows consist of two steps: It is either an interaction with the insurance company and the final decision by a single patient account manager, or a credit check followed by a group vote by (the majority of) the patient account managers. This entire workflow results in an enriched patient record and either an acceptance or rejection of the patient.

There can be several reasons to implement this task in a complex workflow rather than a single, complex, nested human task definition with multiple subtasks, like we did in Chapter 10. For example, the routing between the subtasks and participant types can be predefined in a static, linear, or parallel way, or it can be dynamic, governed by business rules that use the task payload and the outcomes of earlier participant types to choose the next participant type or decide on an early completion of the task. However, when the routing becomes very complex or depends on information that is not available as part of the task routing slip or payload, it can no longer be handled within a single task definition. Alternatively, when the various steps are quite

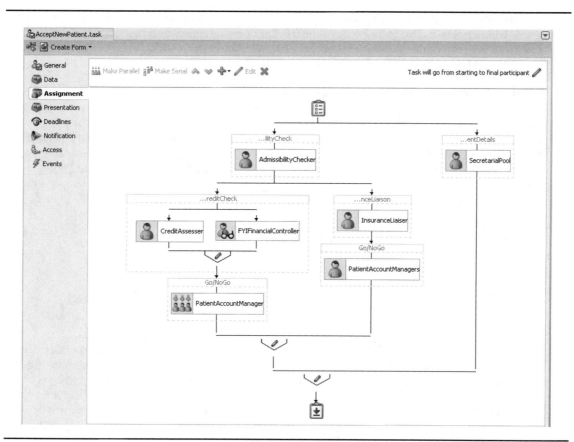

FIGURE 11-3.   *Accept New Patient—a complex human task*

distinct and each requires its own dedicated user interface, we should consider splitting the task up into several task definitions that have their own special task flow associated with them. Note, however, that a single ADF task flow associated with the human task may contain multiple view activities and special controller logic that can present a user interface dedicated to the current subtask.

When steps that are currently manual could at some point be automated through a service call or additional payload enrichment, routing or looping logic may be desired between the various manual steps in the task, which could provide a trigger for breaking up the task into multiple smaller tasks that are orchestrated together in a BPEL process that could easily include those additional elements as well. The BPEL process with multiple finer-grained tasks results in a more accessible, detailed audit trail than a more coarse-grained task will. And, frankly, developing smaller-scale, more-focused tasks and combining them in a BPEL process is easier on the developer than constructing a complex task with many subtasks and embedded routing logic. As with services, in general, complex, coarse-grained human tasks are probably less likely to be reusable than finer-grained tasks (although when they are, they can contribute a lot of value). That could be a consideration as well.

The downside of breaking up the task is that the number of artifacts to develop increases with every additional task. The complexity of the BPEL process increases and there is some run-time overhead because of the additional "context switches" between the BPEL engine and the Human Workflow Service—although these are usually negligible.

Implementing a Multistep Workflow Using BPEL

Instead of the single, coarse-grained human task definition AcceptNewPatient, we will create an asynchronous BPEL component with that same name in the PatientAppointmentService application. This BPEL will consist of more, simpler human tasks that together provide the same functionality. It will take the AppointmentServiceProcessRequest element as its input and return two response messages: one based on that same element—possibly enriched with additional patient details (the task payload altered by the assignee)—and the other based on a simple string-based type that either contains OK or REJECT (the task outcomes):

```
<element name="HumanTaskOutcome" type="ap:humanTaskOutcomeType"/>
<simpleType name="humanTaskOutcomeType">
  <restriction base="xsd:string">
    <enumeration value="OK"/>
    <enumeration value="REJECT"/>
  </restriction>
</simpleType>
```

The BPEL process starts with a Flow activity that contains two parallel sequences. One contains the human task EnrichPatientDetails, which is assigned to the role SecretarialPool. The other sequence starts with the human task Accessibility Check. Depending on its outcome (OK or REJECT), either the sequence is completed (with REJECT as the outcome) or a Pick activity is entered that checks whether the patient for whom the appointment request is made has an insurance policy. One case deals with insured patients and has two human tasks—the first InsuranceLiason, and the second the Go/NoGo decision by the patient account manager. The other case handles the uninsured patients and also has two human tasks—the first is the credit check, and the second is the group vote by the patient account managers. Both of these cases complete with either an OK or REJECT outcome. This outcome is returned in the response from the process, along with the potentially updated patient record.

The BPEL process that implements the Accept New Patient workflow is illustrated in Figure 11-4. All steps are clearly visible, and because they have been implemented as separate BPEL activities and individual human tasks, it is easy to rearrange them, to mix in additional flow logic and service calls or data manipulation, and to handle incoming events.

When we look at the composite diagram of the application, shown in Figure 11-5, it is clear how the flexibility we have gained in the workflow and the implementation of the user interface for each individual task come at a price: The application contains more artifacts that we need to implement and that increase in complexity as well. Striking a balance can sometimes be a challenge. What's more, the BPMN process component introduced in the next section makes the decision still somewhat harder by providing an alternative technique for the implementation of a workflow that combines business logic, human activities, and service logic.

Calling the AcceptNewPatient Service Component

The BPEL process PatientAppointmentService, which we left in Chapter 10 with a call to the Human Workflow Service for the task AcceptNewPatient from the fault handler that's handling the

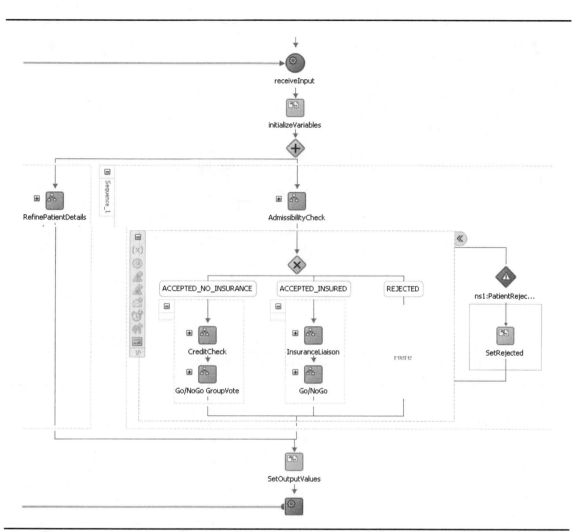

FIGURE 11-4.   *The BPEL process that implements the Accept New Patient workflow*

PatientNotFoundFault, requires only minor changes to invoke the AcceptNewPatient BPEL process instead. The human task is replaced with an Invoke to AcceptNewPatient—preceded by an Assign activity that prepares the input variable for AcceptNewPatient. Because this is an asynchronous service, we should also add a Receive to get hold of the outcome of the AcceptNewPatient workflow. This outcome consists of two parts: the enriched patient details (which can be copied to the inputVariable) and the decision (either OK or REJECTED). In case the result is REJECTED, the BPEL fault AppointmentFaultMessage is thrown, just like before when we handled the human task result.

Figure 11-6 shows how PatientAppointmentService now calls the BPEL process AcceptNewPatient instead of the human task of the same name that used to be invoked.

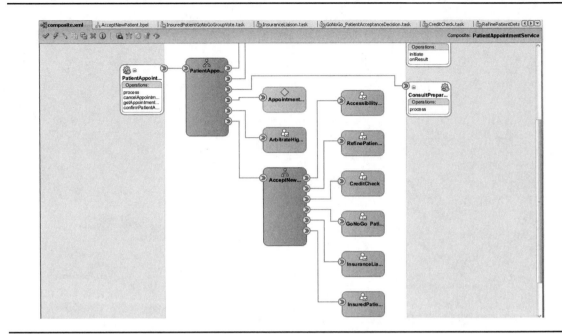

FIGURE 11-5. *The composite application overview for PatientAppointmentProcess*

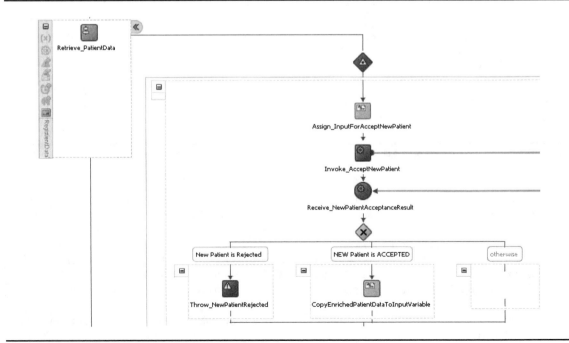

FIGURE 11-6. *The fault handler for PatientNotFound calling the AcceptNewPatient BPEL process that implements the workflow for thoroughly evaluating new patients*

Introducing BPMN Service Components

Business processes described through BPMN are workflows that combine human operations, business rules, and service invocations. The focus is often somewhat more on the business process and the human activities in comparison to BPEL, which plays a slightly more technical role and has its primary focus on service orchestration, with the task service and the human actors providing just another service. BPMN can be very system oriented as well—although at a slightly higher, more abstract level than BPEL.

BPMN can be used by both technical staff and business users, and is well suited to bringing these parties together. One of the main reasons for using BPMN in addition to or even instead of BPEL processes is exactly this fact—that business analysts and even end users can typically understand, help maintain, or even own definitions of business processes, as opposed to BPEL, which is mostly unreadable for business users.

Comparing BPMN and BPEL

BPMN is in several areas more intuitive and process oriented than BPEL—which is a rather technical language for service orchestration and composition. Creation of conditional flows and transitions, and even loops and iterations, for example, is quite straightforward in a BPMN process and requires no understanding of technical constructs or XML manipulation.

BPMN—quite unlike BPEL—makes use of "swimlanes" that represent organizational units or business roles or IT systems. Activities are assigned to a swimlane. This provides clear insight into the responsibilities for and contributions from each part of the organization to a business process. Additionally, the organization's hierarchy can be defined along with calendars that specify per organization unit or role the working hours, normal business days, and special holiday rules. However, this information is currently not carried over when a project is deployed and executed at run time. Unfortunately, it is not used in SOA Suite to allow, for example, deadlines defined in terms of business hours or days rather than normal calendar time.

Manipulation of data objects included in the business process (instance) is largely done through data associations that define how data is passed to and from script tasks, business rules, human tasks, external services, and external processes. These associations use data objects and expressions that are similar to but more (business) user friendly than the XSD elements and the XPath expressions used in BPEL processes. For extensive data conversions, BPMN processes can use XSL(T) transformations as well.

BPMN processes integrate with human tasks to provide the implementation of human activities in the same way BPEL processes do. Integration of business rules is straightforward to perform calculations on behalf of a business process or execute logic that returns the values that determine which conditional flows are to be executed. Calls to other services as well as to other business processes are easily included as well.

A BPMN process can also contain manual tasks. These represent activities that are part of the business process but are not managed by the BPMN service engine. They are included to provide a complete overview of the business process but are otherwise ignored. Note that these manual tasks are not the same as human tasks—although also executed by humans, those are still under the control of the SOA Suite's Workflow service engine. BPEL processes would have to use the Empty activity to approximate this concept of a manual task.

BPMN processes can broadcast signals and be initiated by the reception of signals, similar to BPEL processes. Signals correspond to events on the SOA Suite Event Delivery Network. This provides a second, more decoupled interaction mechanism between BPMN processes and other service components and composite applications—in addition to direct service calls. BPMN has an easy-to-leverage correlation mechanism that acts between BPMN process instances. However, at the time of this writing, there does not seem to be an all-around correlation mechanism that allows events or incoming request messages to be fed into specific instances of BPMN process instances. BPEL seems superior in this respect.

A BPMN process can expose a Web Service interface that can be invoked to initiate a new instance. Reception of a signal (which equals an EDN event) can also initiate a new instance, as can a timer event. The latter can cause an instance to be started at a specific date and time or on a specific interval. BPEL does not have a timer-based initiation mechanism.

BPM Studio—the JDeveloper extension for BPMN—has support for simulation of business processes. Through the simulations, analysts can examine what-if scenarios for a business process and achieve process optimization based on the results. BPEL does not offer anything like this.

BPMN processes can collect metrics during execution—similar to what BPEL sensors do—that can be collected and monitored using process analytics. These metrics can be tracked in the BPM Business Process Workspace application and Oracle BAM (see Chapter 19 for more on BAM).

Auxiliary Applications for BPMN Processes

The Business Process Workspace application (http://host:8001/bpm/workspace) has prebuilt dashboards per business process for monitoring process performance, task performance, and workload, and it also allows creation of custom dashboards. In a similar way to the BPM Worklist application discussed in the previous chapter, it also provides access to human tasks that need to be performed.

The BPM process composer (whose default location is http://host:8001/bpm/composer) provides a visual representation of the processes through a browser-based application that can make them accessible to a wide audience. Through this application, business analysts may document and refine the business processes. These refinements can either be deployed to the run-time SCA container or pushed back to JDeveloper, where the developer can evaluate and complete them before deployment.

Process Spaces—also shipped with Oracle BPM 11g—is a WebCenter Spaces application that brings together process participants and process owners. In Process Spaces, users can collaborate on and communicate about business processes and process instances, track progress, and inspect audit trails. The Process Work Space lists processes that the user can instantiate, shows tasks assigned to the user for running process instances, and provides charts with statistics. The Process Instance Space lists audit trails for running instances, provides a process calendar with deadlines and other important dates related to process instances, and shows the stakeholders for each of the running processes. The Process Modeling Space publishes a catalog with all deployed business processes. Additional custom spaces can be created based on a series of task flows that publishes details about business processes and instances. Note that you need to have WebCenter Suite licensed and installed in order to make use of Process Spaces.

Designing the "Treatment Approval" Workflow Using BPMN

The scope of this book allows us only a brief introduction to BPMN processes. We will create a composite application using a BPMN component that supports the business process through which a doctor gets approval for a special treatment she intends to apply to a patient.

Some treatments, though well established in medical practice and quite successful, are expensive—more expensive than perhaps less effective alternatives. Unfortunately, someone has to pay for those treatments and not all patients will be able to afford them or have insurance to cover the costs for them. Other treatments may be somewhat experimental or controversial.

Guided Business Processes

It is not uncommon for business processes to consist of a fairly large number of steps to be performed by a business user. These steps can frequently be clustered together in a milestone. Although all (mandatory) milestones must be completed in order to finish the entire process, users can be guided through the process in smaller, easier-to-understand stages that lead to intermediate milestones. The structure of a (guided business) process as well as the progress of the user in a specific process instance can be visualized very well using a breakdown structure with milestones that contain human tasks and possibly other service calls (including calls to other guided business processes).

A *guided business process* is an asynchronous BPEL process or a BPMN process that orchestrates a set of human tasks and provides a common user interface to complete and track these tasks. Such a guided business process is created by configuring a BPEL or BPMN process (for example, through the Activity Guide node or icon). Milestones are added to the process and human tasks are assigned to the milestones. Milestones have a name and display title, an associated image, the progress percentage, and an expiration date. When a milestone contains a required task, it is automatically required for the process as a whole, meaning that it must be finished before the process can be successfully completed. Alternatively, tasks and milestones can be optional as well.

When an instance of a BPMN or BPEL process configured as a guided business process is initiated, the service engine keeps track of the current, future, and completed milestones. These can be displayed in the client application used by the business users to access the process and perform the tasks. Guided business processes provide you with predefined ADF task flows that you can use to build an ADF application to display and run the guided business processes. Alternatively, information about instances of guided business processes and their milestones is available to client applications from Web Service and EJB-based APIs.

Such treatments should not be subscribed willy-nilly, and care should be taken to not expose the hospital or the doctor to bad publicity or legal actions by the patient, his relatives, or any other who may see a reason for doing so. St. Matthews has had some bad experiences in the past where treatments were given without proper consideration up front, with no documentation of this consideration nor a written consent form from the patient and no confirmation from the health insurance company. It is determined to prevent this from happening again.

Business analysts have conferred with doctors, the legal and financial departments, and representatives from health insurers. They have designed a business process that should not make life any harder on the doctors yet guarantees a proper decision-making process as well as an audit trail of the essential steps along the way. While they started with napkins and whiteboards, soon they resorted to BPM Studio to create the definition of the process using BPMN.

Outlining the Treatment Approval Business Process

The doctor who wants to start a specific treatment for a certain patient needs to get approval as well as create an audit entry. The Treatment Approval business process is initiated to take care of these two requirements. The input for the process consists of the identification of the doctor, some patient details (including gender, age, body weight, and medical insurance details), the proposed treatment, estimated total costs, as well as a motivation for administering treatment.

The first step in the process, after the request for treatment approval is created, is a business rule that checks whether the proposed treatment is one that requires formal approval. If approval is not required, the doctor may proceed as planned. If it is required, the request is evaluated by the financial department—in a human task. This department cross-checks the patient and treatment details with the patient's financial history and credit status as well as the insurance policy and then comes up with its verdict: It grants the approval, it rejects the approval, or it enlists the help of the health insurance company to make the decision. This last part is done via a service call to a Web Service available from the enterprise service bus.

When the approval for the treatment has been granted or denied, a service is called to make an entry in the audit trail, so as to create a traceable history of treatment requests and approval decisions. Subsequently, the doctor is notified of the decision (that is, whether the approval has been granted or denied).

Creating the BPMN Process Definition

A BPMN process is created in JDeveloper with the BPM (Studio) extension installed on top of the SOA (Composite Editor) extension. A BPMN process is just another service component in a composite application. The Treatment Approval process is created in a brand-new JDeveloper application of type BPM, called TreatmentApprovalProcess. Note that a BPM application is also an SOA application—with BPMN as an additional component.

The BPMN process component is called TreatmentApproval. It is based on the Manual Process pattern because it will be initiated by a doctor who, through a human task, requests approval to perform a certain treatment (see Figure 11-7).

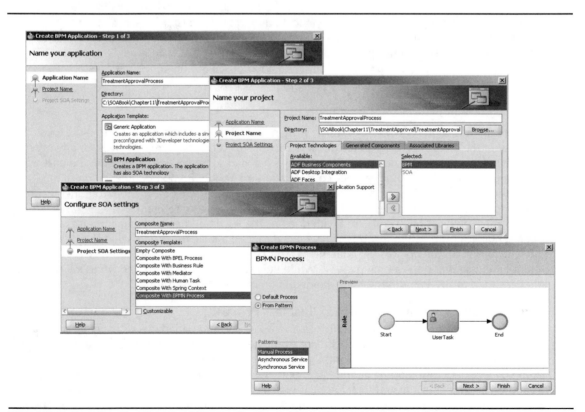

FIGURE 11-7. *Creating the new BPM application with the TreatmentApproval BPMN process component*

To begin, open the BPM Project Navigator if it is not open already. Select the node Organization. Open the Organization editor by right-clicking the node. Change the name of the default role (Role) to Doctor and then create these additional roles: FinancialDepartment, InsuranceCompanies, and HospitalPoliciesAndRegulations. Close the Organization editor.

Back in the BPMN editor, right-click the swimlane for Doctor. Select the option Add Role from the context menu. Select the role HospitalPoliciesAndRegulations from the list of roles. This will add a swimlane for this particular role. Add swimlanes for the other two new roles as well.

Create a Business Rule step in the HospitalPoliciesAndRegulations swimlane called Approval Requirement Check. Create a human task called Financial Cross Check in the swimlane for the Financial Department.

Add a Service Call activity called Request Insurance Company's Approval. Finally, create a service call with label "Create Audit Entry" in the Doctor's swimlane and another one called "Send Notification to Doctor." The BPMN component will now look as is shown in Figure 11-8—a series of currently unrelated activities.

Create the Flows and Gateways

To begin, create the default sequence flow through the activities in the order in which you have just created them. This is the happy path—the no-exception flow that results in a straightforward approval of the treatment.

Reroute the default sequence flow from the Initiate Request For Treatment Approval human task. It should get the Business Rule activity as its destination instead of the End node. Create a sequence flow from the Business Rule activity to the Financial Cross Check and from there to the service task that calls the insurance company. Link this activity to the Create Audit Entry activity and connect that to Send Notification To Doctor, which itself connects to the End node (see Figure 11-9).

However, processes are never that simple, and the facilities offered by BPMN for conditional flows, loopback constructs, and parallel paths are required to deal with the subtleties. Various types of gateways are used to create decision points: an *exclusive gateway* where the flow goes this way *or* that way (and start or merge parallel paths) as well as a *parallel gateway* and *parallel merge gateway* where the flow goes this way *and* that way or converges again into a single flow. Note that parallelization of flows is an important tool for process designers to achieve more efficient processes with a shorter duration.

Create an exclusive gateway in the swimlane HospitalPoliciesAndRegulations that's labeled "Is Approval Required?" The outcome from the business rule Approval Requirement Check is fed into this gateway. The flows from this gateway lead to the steps Add Audit Entry and Financial Cross Check. An exclusive gateway is a decision point: The process token is sent to one and only one of the outgoing flows. Each flow will be associated with a condition that determines whether the flow is the one selected; one flow can be the default flow—the unconditional one—that is executed when none of the conditions on the other flows are satisfied.

Also add an exclusive gateway after the task Financial Cross Check that's called "What is the outcome of the Financial cross check?" It will pick a flow to either the Insurance Company Consultation or the Create Audit Entry activity. The default flow from the Financial Cross Check should go to this gateway (see Figure 11-10).

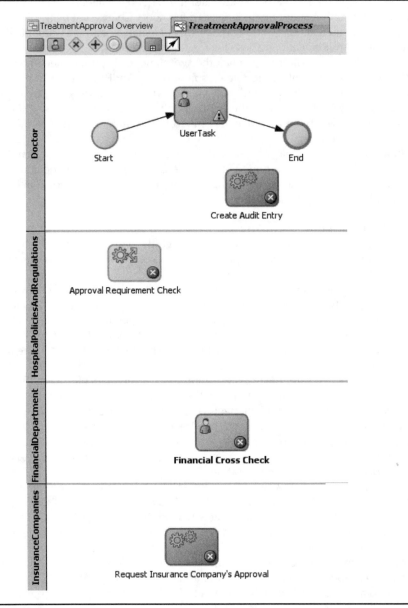

FIGURE 11-8. *Treatment Approval business process—all activities*

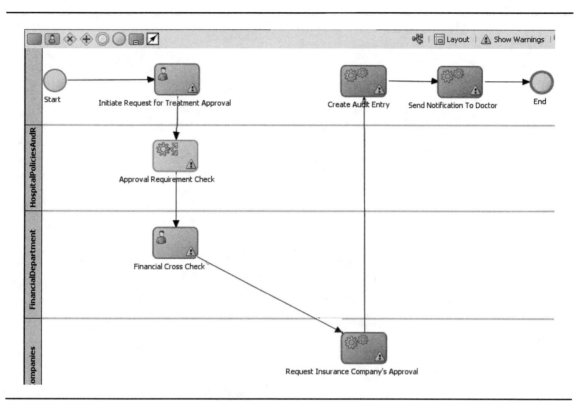

FIGURE 11-9. *The happy flow through the Treatment Approval process*

Simulate the Execution of the Business Process

One of the benefits of BPM Studio is its simulation capability. Even at this fairly early stage, where we have only created an outline of the process without going into any of the data structures involved or a discussion of the actual implementation of each of the steps in the process, we can start simulating the execution of the process—and improve the design if the simulation gives cause to do so.

Create the Process Simulation

To begin, open the node Simulations in the BPM Navigator. Select the node Simulation Models, open the context menu, and select New Process Simulation. Set the name of the new Process Simulation to **TreatmentApprovalSimulation**. Accept the default number of process instances to be created in the simulation at 100. Click the tab Flow Nodes. Each of the activities in the process can be selected and its costs and metrics can be set. Select the node for Financial Cross Check. Set the mean time to 6 hours and 30 minutes and the deviation to 2 hours. Set the duration for the other steps to small values in the order of magnitude of tens of seconds (see Figure 11-11).

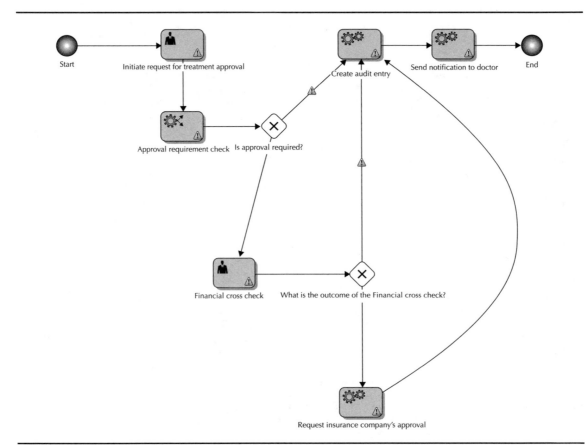

FIGURE 11-10. *Exclusive gateways to implement the decision points in the process flow*

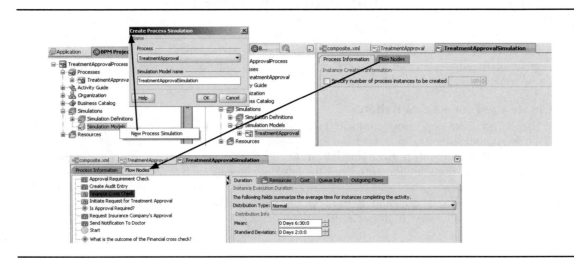

FIGURE 11-11. *Creating and configuring a process simulation*

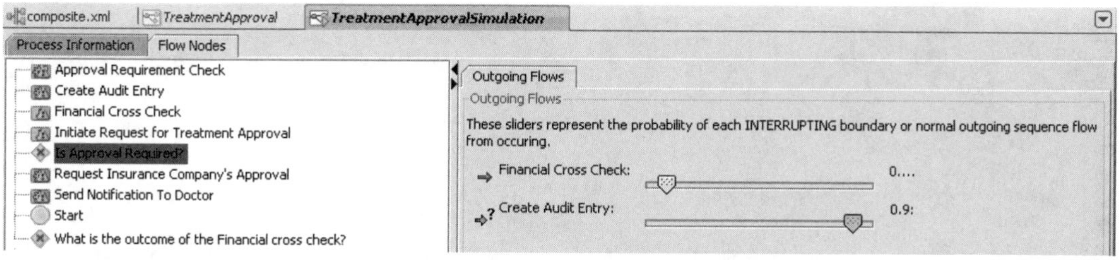

FIGURE 11-12. *Configuring the sequence flow ratios for the exclusive gateway "Is Approval Required?"*

Select the Flow node for the gateway "Is Approval Required?" We can indicate for each gateway what percentage of process instances will flow through which of the outgoing sequence flows. Set the percentage for the flow to Create Audit Entry to 0.9 to indicate that 90 percent of the treatment approval requests can be handled automatically. The Financial Cross Check probability is automatically set to 0.1, which means that 10 percent of all approval requests have to be evaluated by the financial department (see Figure 11-12).

Next, select the exclusive gateway "What is the outcome of the Financial cross check?" Seventy percent of the process instances flowing through this gateway are routed to Create Audit Entry (either because of rejection or immediate acceptance); 30 percent require consultation of the insurance company.

Create the Simulation Definition

In the BPM Navigator, select the node Simulation Definition and choose the option New Simulation from the context menu. Call the new definition **TreatmentApprovalSimulation**. Configure the simulation to represent a ten-hour period. Add a resource (capacity set to 1) for the role FinancialDepartment. Also add a resource for the role Doctor; set the capacity for this resource to some fairly high number.

Run the Simulation

Open the Simulations tab in the console (View | Simulations). Click the green triangle icon to start the simulation. The process editor shows the simulation in action: New instances are created, and the process token flashes across the screen according to the various flows and the relative weights that have been defined for the gateways (see Figure 11-13).

The Simulations tab can show a number of charts representing various metrics for the process. Important metrics include the average and maximum process time—for the entire process as well as for individual steps. We learn, for example, that the process activity that consumes most of the time spent on the process is Financial Cross Check. The average processing time is determined primarily by the mean processing time of this activity. If we could speed up this activity—or increase the number of resources available to perform the financial cross-check—that would help boost the overall performance of the entire process. Set the mean duration for Financial Cross Check to 2 hours and 30 minutes and run the simulation again. Both the average and the maximum wait time are substantially decreased.

Other ways to improve the process and achieve faster average processing speed include the introduction of some parallel flows, adding resources (assigning more staff members) to execute

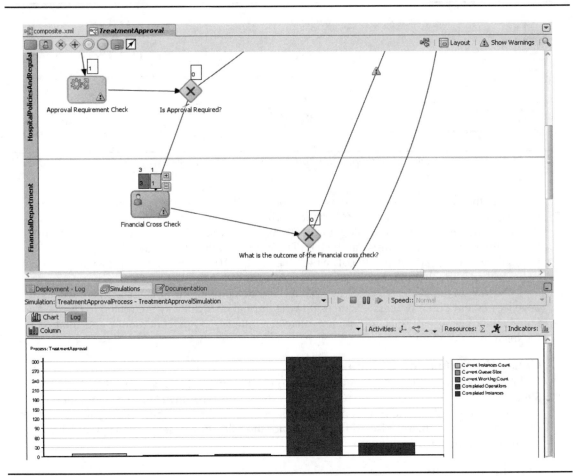

FIGURE 11-13. *Running the simulation for the BPM process Treatment Approval*

a certain step, and changing the percentages of the requests that require the more expensive manual Financial Cross Check activity (for example, by creating more sophisticated business rules to prevent too many requests from reaching a [slow] human operator).

Implement the Treatment Approval Process

At this point, the design of the business process that has evolved from the analysis of all requirements from various interested parties has been laid down in a formal BPMN-based design. The actors have been identified, the individual process steps have been specified, and the flow through the process has been charted. This involves both the happy flow as well as some variations on the happy theme. Gateways have been used to specify conditional transitions.

This design is a first step that allows us to communicate, discuss, simulate, and possibly further refine this process. However, nothing has been said about the actual implementation of the process. The implementation of each process activity is still to be created, and we have not yet even defined which data is associated with the process, each of the process steps, and the conditions that steer the execution.

The composite application at this point only contains the BPMN process component. Shortly, as we provide the implementation of the activities in the process, it will also have other components and references as well as wires to these from the BPMN component.

NOTE
Detailed descriptions and screenshots regarding the implementation of the various process activities are available in the online chapter complement.

Business Objects and Process Data Objects

A business process has data associated with it—data that represent the input and the output for human tasks or other activities such as automated services and business rules. Data objects are the equivalent in BPMN to variables in BPEL—the carriers of data in an actual process instance that are passed as input, modified by services, and returned as output. Data objects in BPMN can exist at the process (global instance) or activity (local) level, or even at the project level, spanning multiple related processes.

Data objects are based on business objects. The latter define the type and structure of the data, and the former *are* the data: XML versus XSD. Business objects correspond with elements defined in XSD documents. Business objects are created through BPM Studio—either from scratch or based on XSD elements. When the required complex business objects have been defined, the Process and Activity data objects can be defined.

We need a business object to describe the data carried by the TreatmentApproval process: the TreatmentApprovalRequest. It must contain attributes for all pieces of data required to evaluate the request. These include the name of the doctor, gender, age, body weight, ZIP code and insurance policy ID of the patient, the diagnosis, proposed treatment, and a motivation from the doctor.

To create this business object, right-click the Business Catalog node in the BPM Navigator, as illustrated in Figure 11-14. Select New | Business Object from the context menu. Enter **TreatmentApprovalRequest** as the name for the business object. Create and select a target module called **Data**. (We could now select an element defined in an XSD definition. Instead, we will specify the structure of the business object in BPM Studio.) Click OK.

Add the scalar attributes as described earlier.

Business Rule activities can only handle input and output based on nonscalar data objects defined through XSD. Even though the Evaluate Approval Request business rule needs only to return a string to indicate the outcome, we have to create a business object called BusinessRuleOutcome with a single attribute outcome of type String.

Process Data Objects—Variables to Hold the Process State
Process data objects are the variables that hold the state of the BPMN process. They are based either on scalar types—String, Decimal, and Time—or on business objects, such as the two we have just created.

We need a Process data object to hold the treatment approval request submitted by the doctor. In addition, we need Process data objects to hold the results from the Business Rule activity, the Financial Cross Check task, and the Insurance Company Result service call.

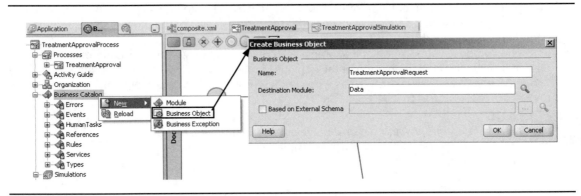

FIGURE 11-14. *Creating the business object TreatmentApprovalRequest*

To create the Process data objects, open the structure window for the BPM process. Select the node Process Data Objects and select the option New from the context menu. Create a Process data object called **treatmentApprovalRequest** based on the business object TreatmentApprovalRequest we just created (see Figure 11-15).

The Process data object approvalEvaluationOutcome is based on the business object BusinessRuleOutcome. Also create Process data objects called financialCrossCheckOutcome and insuranceCompanyDecision—both of type String.

Activity Instance Attributes   In addition to the data objects we create, the BPM engine provides a number of predefined activity instance attributes. These read-only attributes provide information, for example, about the number of times a loop or an activity has been executed. Values are retrieved using the XPath function getProcessInstanceAttribute(). Note that a BPMN

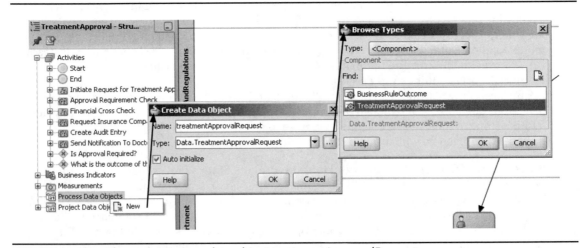

FIGURE 11-15. *Create the Process data object treatmentApprovalRequest*

can contain a subprocess—similar to a BPEL scope—that can be configured through the loop characteristics to run multiple times. Alternatively, loops can be implemented using gateways and loopback flows.

Implement the Human Task "Request Treatment Approval" to Initiate the Process

Our process contains two human tasks. However, other than identifying them and associating them with a specific role, we have not yet done anything to implement them. That is the reason for the alert indicators that these tasks—and the other not-yet-implemented activities—have in the editor.

Human activities in BPMN processes are implemented using the Human Task or Workflow Service component that was first introduced in the previous chapter. When we implement the human activities, what we really do is create a Human Task component and associate it with the human activity in the process.

Right-click the human task Initiate Request For Treatment Approval and select the option Properties. Click the green plus icon to create the human task that provides the implementation for this activity. In the Create Human Task pop-up, set the name of the task to **CreateTreatmentApprovalRequest**. Select Initiator as the pattern to specify that this task will create a new instance of this process. When you select this pattern, the Outcomes field is set to SUBMIT, because that is the only outcome required for a task of this type. Figure 11-16 shows these steps.

Next, we need to create the parameters for this task. All we need is single parameter, based on the treatmentApprovalRequest process data object. Click the green plus icon above the Parameters table. The Data Object window opens. Drag the treatmentApprovalRequest data object to the Parameters table. Mark the check box in the Editable column to make this parameter updateable by the task definition. Click OK to complete and close the Human Task dialog.

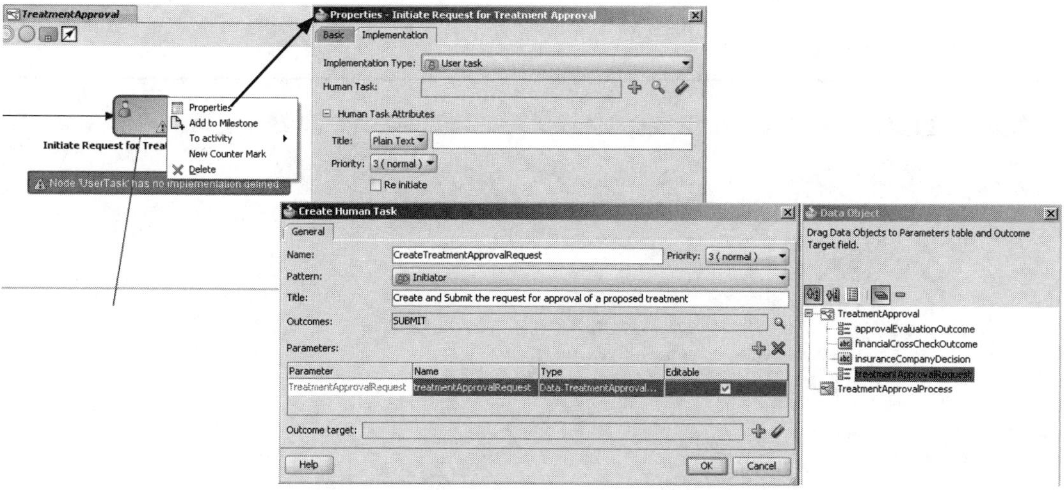

FIGURE 11-16. *Creating the Human Task to implement the process activity Request Treatment Approval*

When you open the Composite Editor, you can see that the BPMN service component is wired to the newly added Human Task component. We also need to create or generate the task form for this task, as was described in Chapter 10. Double-click the human task to open the task editor. Click the Create Form menu, select the option Auto-Generate Task Form, and specify the name of the project that is to be created for this task form. Click OK, and the project with the ADF page is now generated.

Implement the Human Task "Financial Cross Check"

Return to the process editor. Right-click the human activity Financial Cross Check and select the option properties from the context menu. The activity properties editor opens. Click the Implementation tab and then click the green plus icon to create a new human task definition as the implementation for this process activity.

The task creation window opens. Select the Simple pattern for this task and then specify a name (for example, **PerformFinancialCrossCheckForTreatmentApprovalRequest**). Click the looking glass icon behind the Outcomes field. The default outcomes APPROVE and REJECT are perfectly acceptable, but we need one additional (custom) outcome to indicate that the financial department can accept the proposed treatment but needs confirmation and consent from the health insurance company.

The Outcomes dialog appears. Click the green plus icon, enter the name for the custom outcome (for example, **OK_BUT_NEED_INSURANCE_APPROVAL**), and click OK. The Add Custom Outcome dialog closes. The new outcome is added and automatically selected as well. Click OK to return to the Create Task dialog.

Next, click the green plus icon above the parameters table. The Data Object window opens. Drag the treatmentApprovalRequest data object to the parameters table. Note that this time the parameter is not editable (see Figure 11-17).

Also, drag the financialCrossCheckOutcome process data object to the Outcome Target field. This ties the outcome from the human task to this process data object—which we will inspect later on in the conditions on the flows in the exclusive gateway.

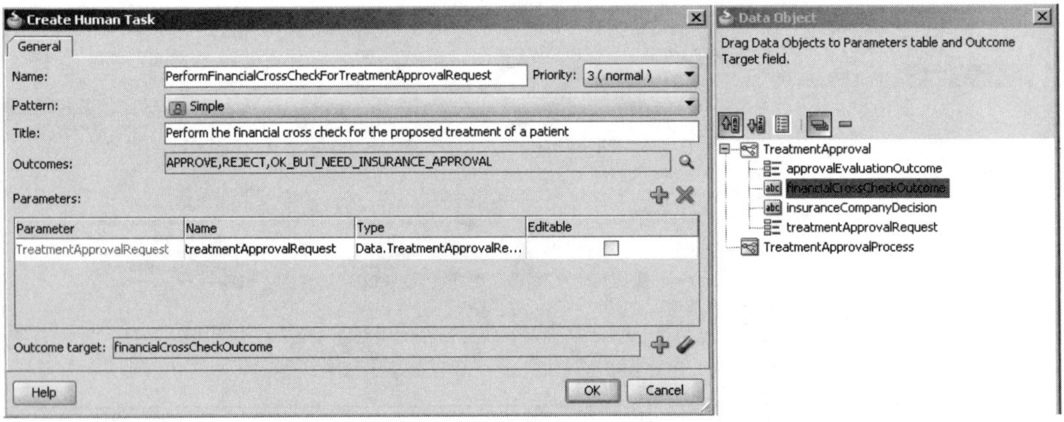

FIGURE 11-17. *Creating the human task PerformFinancialCrossCheckForTreatmentApprovalRequest*

A quick look at the Composite Editor tells us that a new Human Task service component has been added and wired to the BPMN process. This component requires implementation, in the same way we did for the first Human Task component, by auto-generating the task form.

Implement the Business Rule "Task Evaluate Treatment Approval Request"

The business rule activity in the BPMN process also needs to be mapped to an executable implementation that will perform the work. Open the process editor. Right-click the Business Rule task and select the option Properties. In the properties dialog, go to the Implementation tab. Click the green plus icon to create a new Business Rule component in the composite application that provides the implementation for this process activity. The Create Business Rule dialog opens. Type the name for the business rule (for example, **EvaluateTreatmentApprovalRequest**).

Next, click the green plus icon in order to add parameters for the business rule, as illustrated in Figure 11-18. The Data Object window is presented. Drag the treatmentApprovalRequest parameter to the parameters list. This is added as an input parameter. Switch the drop-down list labeled Direction to Output. Drag the data object approvalEvaluationOutcome to the Input and Output Data Objects table. This process data object will be set by the business rule. Click OK to close the dialog and complete the creation of the business rule.

Open the Composite Editor to see if indeed the component was added and wired to the BPMN process.

Next, we need to implement the Business Rule component in the same way we did in Chapter 8, where the business rules were first discussed. Double-click the component in the Composite Editor to bring up the business rule editor. See the online chapter complement for detailed instructions. Note that the business rule has two possible outcomes: NO_APPROVAL_NEEDED and APPROVAL_IS_REQUIRED.

Implement the Automated Service Tasks

Implementing a service task—such as the creation of the audit entry and the consultation with the insurance company—is done in two steps. The implementation is created as a component—Mediator or BPEL—in the BPMN composite application or added as reference binding to that application, such as a technology adapter binding or an (external) Web Service binding. The component or reference can be mapped to the service task in the BPMN process.

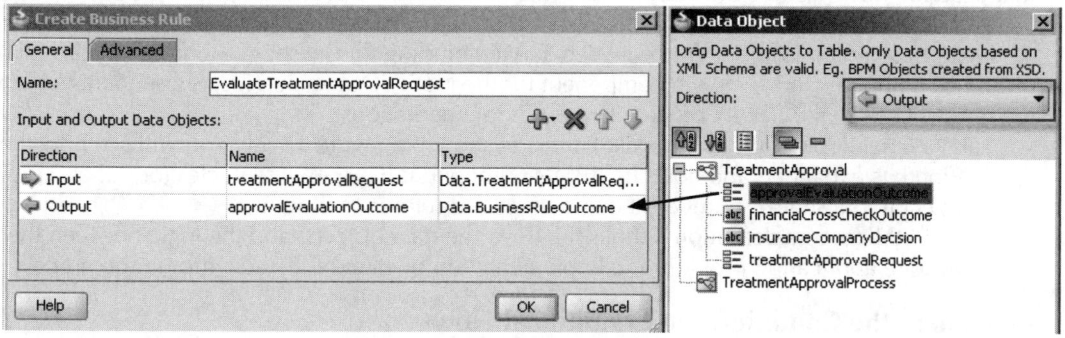

FIGURE 11-18. *Creating the business rule EvaluateTreatmentApprovalRequest*

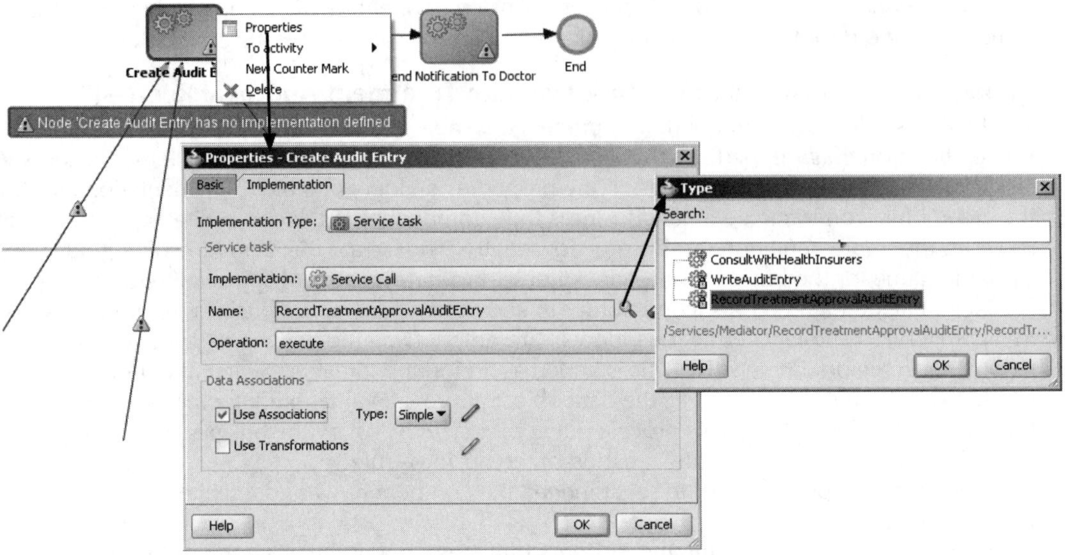

FIGURE 11-19. *Mapping the Service Task process activity Create Audit Entry to the service RecordTreatmentApprovalAuditEntry—provided by a Mediator component*

As an example, let's look at mapping of the Create Audit Entry activity. First, the implementation is prepared through a Mediator/file adapter combination. When the Service component is created, return to the BPMN process. The Mediator component is available now in the Business Catalog under the Services node. Right-click the Create Audit Entry activity and select the menu option Properties, as shown in Figure 11-19. In the properties dialog, select the Implementation tab. Select Service Call in the Implementation drop-down, click the search icon to select the service that provides the implementation for this service task, and then select the Mediator component RecordTreatmentApprovalAuditEntry from the list of services that appears.

After mapping the process activity to the service, we need to specify the data associations that describe how process data objects are mapped to the input and output of the service (see Figure 11-20).

Next, in a similar fashion, create a Web Service binding for the service to consult the insurance company and a service component for the Notify Doctor service. Subsequently, map the service tasks in the BPMN process to these implementations.

Take a quick look in the Composite Editor, as shown in Figure 11-21. You will see how the application has expanded and how the BPMN component has grown tentacles (or rather *wires*) that connect it to a serious number of component and reference bindings.

The BPMN process definition defines the flow, the data objects, and the logic between them; the composite application provides the implementation of each of the activities in the process.

Implement the Conditions on Conditional Flows

The two last remaining alert icons point out that we still have to indicate the conditions for two conditional flows: when will the process token be routed from the Business Rule activity to the

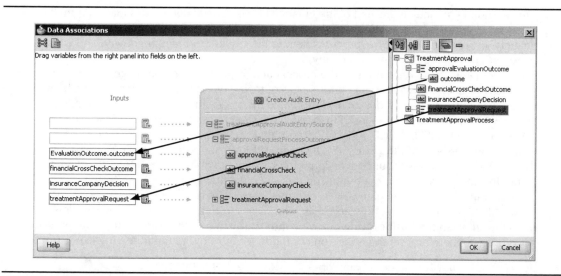

FIGURE 11-20. *Creating data associations for the mapping of the service task Create Audit Entry*

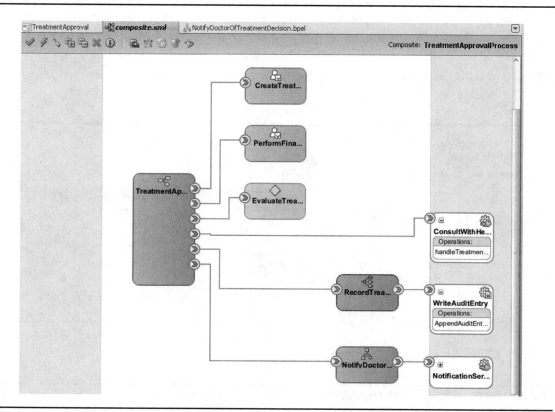

FIGURE 11-21. *The Composite Editor, showing the BPMN component and wires to the components and references providing the implementation of the process activities*

Create Audit Entry activity instead of the Financial Cross Check default destination from the gateway "Is approval required?" And when does the gateway "What is the outcome of the financial cross check?" send the process token to the Create Audit Entry activity, and when to the consultation with the insurance company?

Now that we have implemented the process activities, we have a fairly good idea about what each activity does and what it may return as its outcome (we could have been a little bit more conscious of that during the design and stipulated the to-be-supported outcomes in advance). We now know that the human task Financial Cross Check results in APPROVE, REJECT, or OK_BUT_NEED_INSURANCE_APPROVAL and that the business rule Approval Requirement Check produces NO_APPROVAL_NEEDED and APPROVAL_IS_REQUIRED. We have passed these outcome values without conversion into process data objects. Therefore, these are the values the gateways and the conditions on the sequence flows have to work with.

Select the flow from the gateway "Is approval required?" to Create Audit Entry, as shown in Figure 11-22. Right-click the flow and select Properties from the context menu. This flow needs to be followed when the business rule outcome indicates that a further formal approval procedure is not required. Therefore, set the transition condition for this flow to the following expression:

```
approvalEvaluationOutcome.outcome == "NO_APPROVAL_NEEDED"
```

Next, set the condition for the flow from the gateway "What is the outcome of the Financial cross check?" to Create Audit Entry. This flow is to be followed when either the Financial cross-check rejects the treatment approval request or when it accepts the request without further need for consultation with the health insurance company. Here is the condition expression that implements this logic:

```
financialCrossCheckOutcome == "APPROVE" or financialCrossCheckOutcome == "REJECT"
```

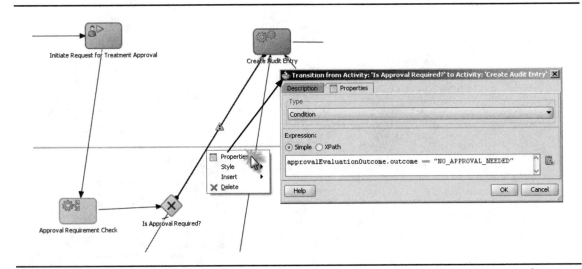

FIGURE 11-22. *Specifying the transition condition from "Is approval required?" to Create Audit Entry*

Role Implementation

For our fairly straightforward example, we will use a fairly simple approach—well, actually, an embarrassingly simple approach—to role implementation. Instead of defining groups on the WebLogic Server or an external LDAP and mapping the organization roles in our BPMN process to those enterprise roles, we will simply make user "weblogic" a member of all roles that need to execute human activities. To that end, select and open the Organization node in the BPM navigator. Select the first tab, Roles. Select the role Doctor, add weblogic as a member, and do the same thing for the role FinancialDepartment. It is left as an exercise to the reader to map roles to different groups and persons. The online chapter complement for Chapter 10 shows in detail how to add users and groups to an identity store.

Run the Business Process and Track Its Progress

In order to run the business process and execute the implementations of the process activities, we first have to deploy the composite application to a running SOA Suite environment—just like we have been deploying composite applications in previous chapters. So even though we deal with a BPM application, it is still an SOA composite application with a special service component (a BPMN process component) inside.

Publish the BPM Project to MDS

In addition to the deployment to the SOA Suite run-time container, BPM projects can be deployed to the MDS repository. BPM projects loaded in MDS are available for publication, review, and even editing through a shared browser application. Select the TreatmentApprovalProcess project node in the BPM project navigator. Right-click to open the context menu and then select the option Publish To BPM MDS. Select the MDS connection to use and the target folder to publish to.

The publication proceeds and gives no additional feedback. To verify that the publication was successful, either check in the BPM Composer application, which we will use later on, or open the BPM MDS Navigator in JDeveloper (BPM Studio, if you like) and check the contents of the Public folder.

Create a New Process Instance from BPM Workspace

To begin, open the BPM Workspace application, through which we can instantiate the TreatmentApprovalProcess. Note that this process does expose a Web Service interface and can therefore not be started from the FMW EM Console. However, once an instance is created, the message flow trace and audit details are available in that console, just as for other types of composite applications.

Go to http://host:8001/bpm/workspace and connect as weblogic. Initiate a new instance of the TreatmentApprovalProcess by clicking the link in the Applications box, as illustrated by Figure 11-23. A new process instance is created. The first step in the process is to create the treatment approval request. The task form appears in a pop-up window in which the treatment approval request is created. When the details have been entered and the task submitted, the BPMN process will run its course.

Because the cost category is 2, no formal approval is required and the process instance comes to completion without further human participation. For BPMN components, the message flow trace provides a visual flow diagram that provides insight in what routes were followed in the process and what its current status is (see Figure 11-24).

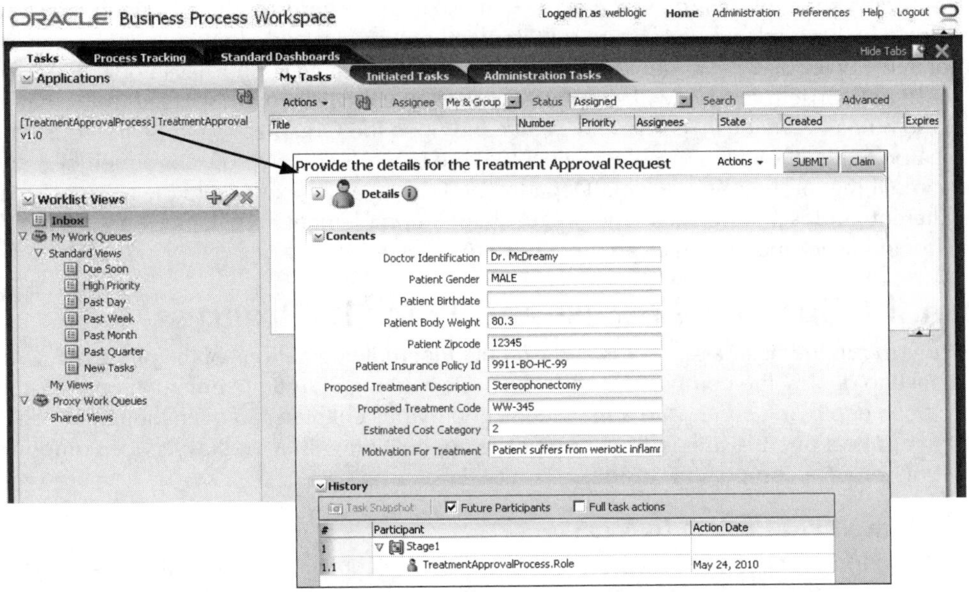

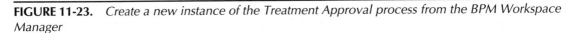

FIGURE 11-23. *Create a new instance of the Treatment Approval process from the BPM Workspace Manager*

Alternatively, the BPM Workspace application supports tracking the progress of process instances, with both tabular and graphical overviews. This is particularly useful because the FMW Enterprise Manager is typically not made available to end users and business analysts, whereas the BPM Workspace application is targeted at these user groups.

The Next Process Instance That Does Require Formal Approval
Create another new process instance in the BPM Workspace application. Provide treatment details that will lead to the full approval procedure. In other words, set the estimated cost category to 5.

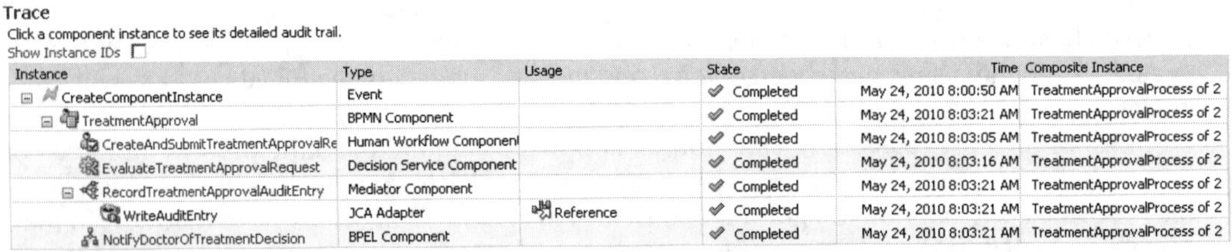

Trace
Click a component instance to see its detailed audit trail.
Show Instance IDs ☐

Instance	Type	Usage	State	Time	Composite Instance
⊟ CreateComponentInstance	Event		✓ Completed	May 24, 2010 8:00:50 AM	TreatmentApprovalProcess of 2
⊟ TreatmentApproval	BPMN Component		✓ Completed	May 24, 2010 8:03:21 AM	TreatmentApprovalProcess of 2
CreateAndSubmitTreatmentApprovalRe	Human Workflow Component		✓ Completed	May 24, 2010 8:03:05 AM	TreatmentApprovalProcess of 2
EvaluateTreatmentApprovalRequest	Decision Service Component		✓ Completed	May 24, 2010 8:03:16 AM	TreatmentApprovalProcess of 2
⊟ RecordTreatmentApprovalAuditEntry	Mediator Component		✓ Completed	May 24, 2010 8:03:21 AM	TreatmentApprovalProcess of 2
WriteAuditEntry	JCA Adapter	Reference	✓ Completed	May 24, 2010 8:03:21 AM	TreatmentApprovalProcess of 2
NotifyDoctorOfTreatmentDecision	BPEL Component		✓ Completed	May 24, 2010 8:03:21 AM	TreatmentApprovalProcess of 2

FIGURE 11-24. *Message flow trace for the Treatment Approval process*

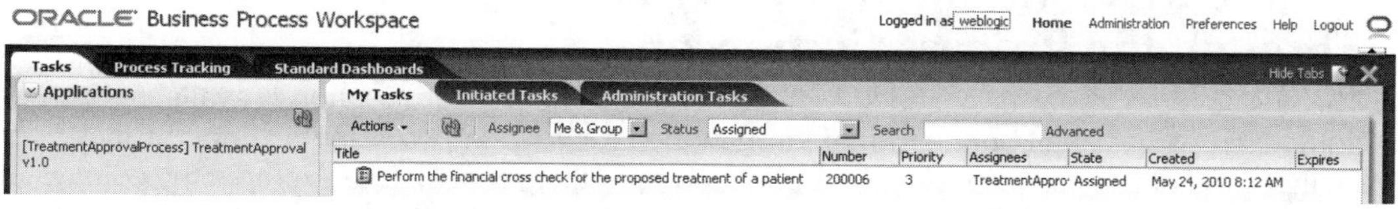

FIGURE 11-25. *Task list with the Financial Cross Check task*

When you click the SUBMIT button, the process will execute the business rule, and because this time it will indicate that the financial cross-check *is* required, a task will appear in the to-do list for the user weblogic (see Figure 11-25).

In the task list, select the pending task and select the outcome OK_BUT_NEED_INSURANCE_ APPROVAL. This allows the process to run its full course automatically—invoking the insurance company's service, writing the audit entry, and sending the notification to the doctor.

Revising the Business Process

The initial design of the Treatment Approval process has raised a number of questions and concerns, and some revisions are required. The functional changes that are to be applied are as follows:

- The business rule that performs the initial check whether a formal approval is required contains logic that refers to the estimated cost level of the treatment. Initially, any treatment in cost categories 1, 2, and 3 was automatically approved, while categories 4 and 5 required the formal approval of at least the financial department. This level is to be adapted: Category 3 is no longer automatically approved, but will also require the financial department to consent.

- It is concluded that although the financial department definitely has a say in whether a treatment can be performed, there is a need for a different type of evaluation as well. Medical treatment can be controversial for purely medical and ethical reasons, not necessarily directly connected with money issues. The business process should explicitly cater to this fact by introducing two new steps that can be performed in parallel with the financial validation. The first step is the peer review, where a fellow doctor needs to indicate whether the proposed treatment is the regular approach or whether it is something that is out of the ordinary that requires the stamp of approval from St. Matthews ethics committee, which is the (optional) second new step. This committee is composed of legal, medical, and public relational experts who together decide whether treatments deemed controversial in any way should be performed. Any decision by the committee needs to be carefully monitored and recorded.

Online Redefinition of the BPM Process Through the Process Composer

The business process as designed and implemented in the previous section is available to authorized parties in an online format through the Process Composer application. Business analysts and others can also use this application to further refine it—for example, by editing business rules or changing the flow in the application. These changes can be deployed to the run-time environment or they can be imported into BPM Studio in JDeveloper for consideration by the developers.

Open the BPM Composer, located at http://host:8001/bpm/composer. Projects that have been published to MDS can be opened, as well as BPM projects deployed to the SOA Suite. When changes are made, these are saved to MDS in both cases.

When the project has opened, the same process diagram is presented as we have been working on in BPM Studio (aka JDeveloper). Therefore, this browser-based facility presents the same visual overview of the business process (see Figure 11-26).

When we want to—and have the proper privileges—we can even start editing the process definition. Later on, we share the changed definition with other users and we can export it to further refine it in BPM Studio. We can also deploy the modified BPMN process definition to the running SOA Suite environment. Alternatively, Composer can export projects to an SAR archive that can then be deployed from the FMW Enterprise Manager console or through WLST (see Chapter 17 for details).

Edit the Business Rule

The proposed change to the business rule EvaluateTreatmentApprovalRequest can be made in various places. One is the SOA Composer, where the change will immediately take effect.

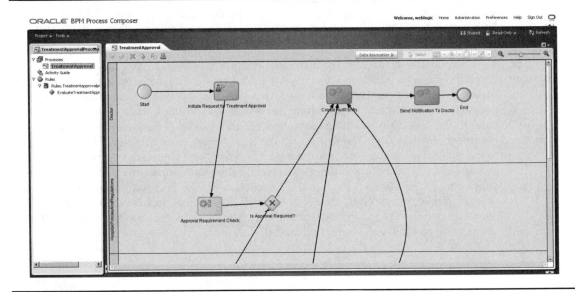

FIGURE 11-26. *BPM Process Composer with the TreatmentApproval process*

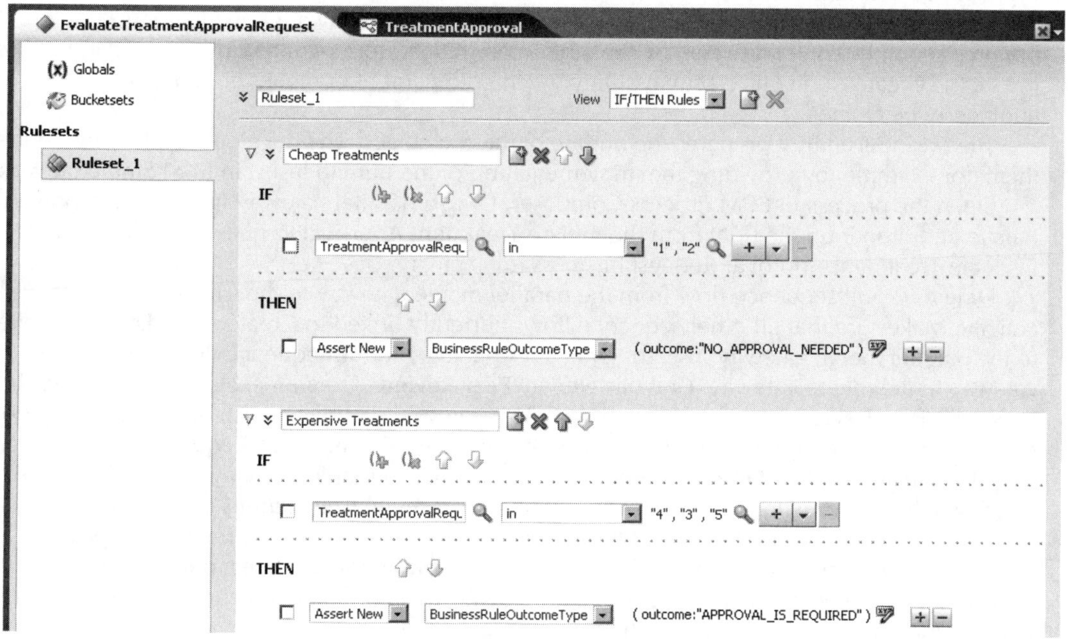

FIGURE 11-27.   *Update the business rule EvaluateTreatmentApprovalRequest*

Another is the BPM Process Composer, where the change is made, saved, published, and possibly deployed after review and approval. Chapter 8 discussed the online editing of business rules in the SOA Composer. The procedure is very similar in the BPM Process Composer—but without the immediate live run-time repercussions.

Open the TreatmentApprovalProcess in BPM Process Composer and switch to edit mode. Select the Business Rule component EvaluateTreatmentApprovalRequest and open Ruleset_1. Remove the string operand "3" from the first rule (CheapTreatments) and add that value as an operand to the second rule (ExpensiveTreatments), as shown in Figure 11-27.

Save the changes by clicking the Save icon. This will save a draft that is not yet visible to other users. Only when you stop editing and publish the modifications you have made will the changes be shared.

NOTE
Unlike in the SOA Composer, saving these changes does not immediately make them effective in any run-time environment.

Add a Parallel Flow with the Peer Review and Ethics Committee

Next up is a change in the process flow itself. After leaving the Initiate Treatment Approval Request, the process token should split into two parallel flows. One consists of the existing flow through business rule evaluation, financial cross-check, and insurance company consultation. The other one is a new flow, with as a first step the peer review by a fellow doctor and as an optional second step the decision by the ethics committee. Both parallel flows should merge just before the Create Audit Entry activity. Only when both parallel branches are complete should the audit entry be created.

The business analyst prepares the outline of these changes. The developer will further refine them (for example, by providing the implementation of the human tasks) in BPM Studio later on.

Open the process in BPM Process Composer. Drag a parallel gateway from the Component Palette and drop it on the flow from the Initiate Treatment Approval Request human activity to the Evaluate Treatment Approval Request business rule activity.

Drag a default sequence flow from the parallel merge gateway to the Create Audit Entry activity. Make sure that all other sequence flows currently linked to Create Audit Entry are linked to the parallel merge gateway instead. Drag a user activity to the sequence flow from the parallel gateway to the merge gateway. Call this activity **Peer Review**. Drag an exclusive gateway to the flow from Peer Review to the merge gateway. This gateway will distinguish between "yes or no ethics committee required." Call the gateway **Review Ethics Committee Required?** Next, add a User Task activity called **Ethics Committee** and link it to the merge gateway. Also link the "Review Ethics Committee Required?" gateway to this activity (see Figure 11-28).

This more or less completes what the business analyst can do in the Process Composer. It is now up to a developer working in BPM Studio to create additional process data objects and provide the implementations for the two new activities. The online chapter complement describes in detail the refinements applied by the developer.

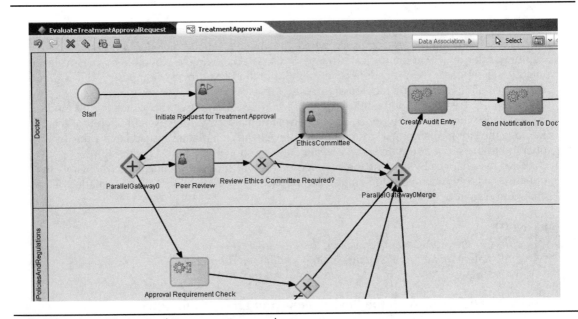

FIGURE 11-28. *The revised TreatmentApproval process*

Running the Revised Business Process

When the implementation of the process extensions has been done as outlined in the online chapter complement and redeployed as suggested, we can see the effects of these changes when we run a new instance of the business process from the BPM Workspace application. We can track the progress of each instance in either the BPM Workspace application or the FMW Enterprise Manager.

Create a treatment approval request for an expensive treatment (cost category 5). This will result in the most extensive variant of the business process to be executed. After clicking the Submit button, we will find two concurrent tasks for this process instance. The parallel gateway has been passed, and now both the Peer Review activity and the Financial Cross Check activity are waiting on their respective operators (see Figure 11-29).

Note that the only reason why these two tasks are shown in the same list is because user weblogic is wearing many hats—one for every role identified in the organization. Normally these different tasks require different persons to execute and will not be shown in the same task list for a single user.

Execute the Financial Cross Check task—suggest consultation of the insurance company. The message flow trace for this composite application instance in the FMW Enterprise Manager Console indicates what has been done and which step is currently pending—the Peer Review task.

The merge gateway has been reached by the flow from the insurance company. It is waiting for the flow currently halted at the peer review to catch up so the process token can be passed onward to the Create Audit Entry activity.

Let's complete the Peer Review task, indicating that this approval request should be reviewed by the ethics committee. The visual flow is shown in Figure 11-30.

A new task is instantiated, this one for the committee members to review and decide upon. Complete the task by granting the approval for the treatment. The process can now be completed automatically: Both tokens have arrived at the merge gateway, so the flow from this gateway can be executed.

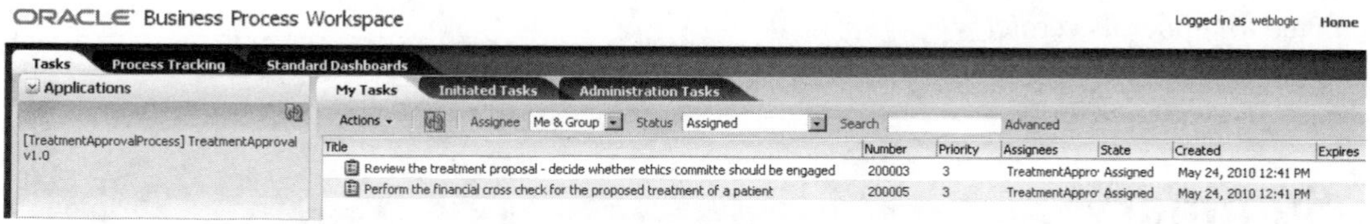

FIGURE 11-29. *Two parallel tasks for the same process instance*

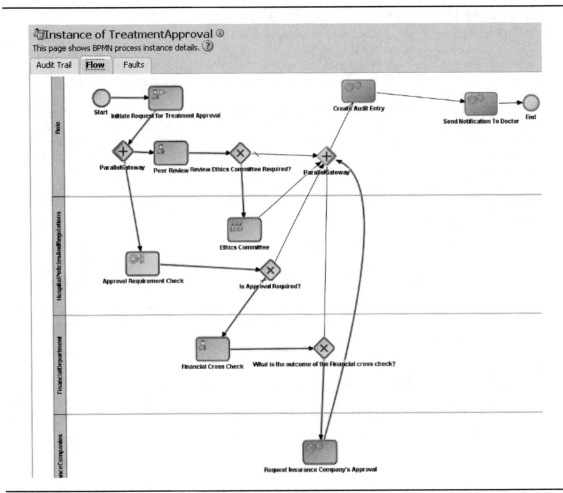

FIGURE 11-30. *Visual flow of the TreatmentApproval process instance, waiting for the ethics committee to render its verdict*

Summary

The objectives of an organization can only be achieved through the execution of business processes. This chapter introduced Business Process Management as a means to improve the performance of an organization through a constant focus on its business processes in an iterative cycle of design, execution, and improvement. BPM describes a structured approach to analyzing, designing and modeling, simulating, executing, and monitoring the business processes. BPMN offers a language for formally describing processes. In addition, BPMN run-time engines such as Oracle BPM are capable of executing the processes based on this formalized definition.

This chapter introduced the BPMN service component in SOA composite applications that is available through the BPM Studio extension to JDeveloper and the BPM extension to the SOA Suite WebLogic domain. Note that in order to use BPM with the SOA Suite, you need an additional license.

BPMN components contain business process definitions that are created from a purely business perspective, without focus on technical aspects and implementation details. A process is defined through flows—conditional, parallel, iterative—in combination with various types of activities allocated to different business roles. The process can be simulated—long before any implementation details have been specified.

In a next iteration—probably where the developer takes over from the analyst—the implementation for the process activities is created. The implementation is provided by other service components in the composite application—such as human tasks, business rules, and BPEL processes—or through external references bound to the composite application.

The SOA composite application with BPMN processes inside is deployed in the same way as the composite applications discussed in previous chapters. However, the run-time BPM environment offers various additional browser-based applications through which instances of BPM processes can be created and monitored (BPM Workspace) and the BPM process definition can be published, reviewed, and refined (BPM Composer).

Another way to implement business processes is through BPEL components. BPEL supports a similar set of flow, logic, and data-mapping facilities and can have more or less the same interaction with other service components and reference bindings. Workflows composed of several human tasks as well as automated steps with complex flow logic and data manipulation can be implemented well using BPEL. The run-time engine for BPMN and BPEL processes is exactly the same! However, the design experience for BPEL is far more technically oriented and less business (analyst) friendly than BPMN. If you approach applications from a business process perspective and your organization has acquired the BPM license, you will be able to make excellent use of BPMN components in your composite applications. Note that BPMN does not replace BPEL, which still has added value for designing and running complex, orchestrated services.

CHAPTER
12

Leveraging Java in
Composite Applications

n the previous chapters, we discussed the integration of human actors into SOA composite applications. When the standard service engines need help in areas such as interpreting unstructured data, making ultimate decisions, conferring and communicating with multiple human participants, or applying intuition and fuzzy logic, we can bring in the human touch using the Human Task component.

This chapter discusses the introduction of another element into the composites: Java. Oracle SOA Suite 11*g* offers many different ways in which Java and JEE can be engaged in SOA composite applications—from the Java Messaging Service (JMS) and EJB Adapter Services and the Spring Java Service component to intra component SDO entity binding, Java snippets in BPEL, and Java callouts in the Mediator.

There can be various reasons for introducing Java in composite applications. We may need our application to access third-party applications through existing, possibly remote, Java or JEE APIs for which no Web Service interface has been published. We will see an example of the finance department accepting requests through a JMS queue only.

We may also want to leverage capabilities of Java and JEE to perform calculations, specialized conversions, or device interactions that are perhaps much better implemented in Java than in one of the other service engines in the SOA Suite. We may be able to use packaged functionality from third-party libraries or just the flexibility of the programming language in general (possibly indirectly utilizing Groovy or Scala).

Java can also be used to extend the functionality of the SOA Suite by registering local Java classes and libraries on the SOA Suite server itself. For example, we can create new, specialized XPath functions by creating custom Java classes that we then register with the SOA Suite, or we may want to create our own OWSM (Oracle Web Services Manager) audit or security policy in Java or handle faults in Java code. Appendix D discusses the hooks provided in the SOA Suite to extend functionality of the run-time framework using custom (Java) code. That appendix also describes the Java API available in the SOA Suite to interact at run time with the SCA container to initiate, manage, or monitor instances of composite applications.

The online chapter complement provides more in-depth details and screenshots on the examples described in this chapter and adds some examples as well.

Java Integration in Various Ways

If you want to invoke business logic implemented in Java from an SOA composite application, the easiest way from the perspective of the SOA developer is quite obvious: Ask the Java programmers to deploy this logic as a Web Service using JAX-WS, the Java specification for publishing Web Services. Such Web Services can be invoked from composites like any other Web Service implemented in any technology stack.

At the same time, there can be various reasons why that approach is really too simplistic. The overhead of calling the Java code via SOAP and XML can be prohibitive. Perhaps the Java developers are not inclined or do not have the skills to publish their logic as a Web Service. They may already offer different public APIs via EJBs or JMS queues, for example, and think that is quite enough. We may not even know the developers and therefore simply have to work with whatever API is available in some legacy or third-party product. Then again, perhaps we need a tiny nugget of logic somewhere inside our BPEL process or just prior to the Mediator performing a transformation or filter operation. We do not want to call a full-blown Web Service at that point—we just would like to implement that snippet of logic in Java and inject it into the service

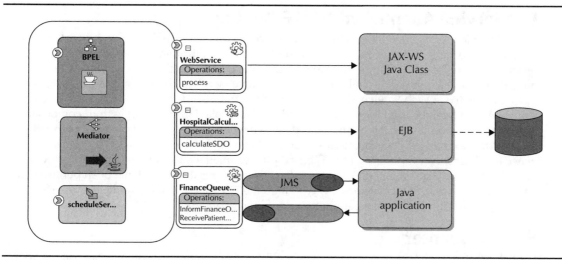

FIGURE 12-1. *Java inside and in sight—integration of Java into SOA composite applications*

component we are putting together. Or perhaps it is not just a snippet but a fair-sized chunk of functionality that needs to be executed inside the composite application, for which Java provides the superior implementation—over other service components such as BPEL, Business Rule, and Human Task. In that case, the Spring Context Component can be used to expose Java beans as component-level services inside the composite application.

This chapter discusses several ways to integrate Java and the logic implemented in Java into SOA composite applications (see Figure 12-1).

JMS Adapter Services

JMS is an API for messaging services provided by some messaging technologies. Messaging provides a decoupled, scalable, robust, and proven way to distribute messages to possibly unknown consumers. The Event-Driven Architecture (EDA) and the Event-Delivery Network (EDN) are based on the same concepts and largely the same infrastructure—yet they operate on a slightly higher level, more business event oriented and somewhat abstracted away from J(2)EE technology.

Many Java applications use messaging through JMS to achieve decoupled interaction—for example, using Message Driven Beans (MDBs, a special type of EJB) that listen to messages arriving on a JMS queue or topic. Applications can also publish events on a JMS topic that they thus make available to potential consumers—of which they do not specifically want to or need to be aware.

The SOA Suite has the JMS Adapter that integrates this JEE messaging world into composite applications. JMS adapter services can be inbound (they listen for messages to be published on a queue or topic and instantiate a new composite instance or update a running one) or outbound (they publish messages to a JMS destination). Through the JMS adapter, we get a decoupled integration with Java/JEE applications.

EJB Service Adapter and ADF Binding

The EJB Service Adapter facilitates interaction between composite applications and (potentially remote) Enterprise Java Beans. Functionality implemented in EJBs that run on either the same or a remote JVM can be invoked from the composite application in much the same way as stored procedures can be invoked through the database adapter service: To the composite, the EJBs are made to look like a Web Service, described by WSDL and XSD documents. Note that the EJB Service Adapter can be used for reference bindings (to invoke EJB-based logic from composite applications) as well as service bindings (to expose the composite application itself as an EJB).

The data exchange between composite and EJB can be done in two ways. The conventional way can be used over RMI, using POJOs based on Java Interface definitions. The second way is based on Service Data Object (SDO) parameters; this requires the EJB to have been published as an SDO data service. SDO provides a way to map the EJB interface and parameters to a Web Service (WSDL) and XML-based parameters (described in an XSD).

Socket Adapter

For tightly integrated, high-speed, low-level TCP/IP socket communication, we can use the Socket Adapter. This adapter supports both inbound and outbound communication patterns, both synchronous and asynchronous. Socket communication is fairly coupled—on several levels. However, in specific circumstances it can help bridge interoperability issues and provide a high-speed data-transfer connection. A Java application can be a partner at the other end of this connection, as well as any other piece of software that accepts TCP/IP.

Spring Context Component

The Spring Context component makes it possible to create service components that execute Java-based logic exposed through Spring Beans. Instead of deploying Java classes in a stand-alone application, exposed as JAX-WS Web Services or EJBs, we can include these classes in the SOA composite application and integrate them more directly, more privately (or encapsulated), and more natively as a Spring service component. Such service components are accessed like any other SCA component—through wires based on WSDL and XSD contracts.

Note that Spring service components can expose both services and references. In other words, they can be invoked by other components and other service components—for example, a Mediator or BPEL process and—can be injected into the Java beans to satisfy their dependencies.

Java Inside

At a finer level (inside service components), we can add specialized behavior programmed using Java.

Embedded Java in BPEL

We can embed Java snippets in special activities inside BPEL process components—at a more granular, tighter integrated, less formal, typically more specialized level than using partner links to other components or even external services. Embedded Java has access to all BPEL variables, both for reading and writing. It can bring the full power of Java, JEE, and other Java libraries installed on the SOA Suite server environment to custom BPEL activities, while fully integrating with the BPEL process instance. Using Embedded Java, however, does raise the issue of less decoupled code, less reuse potential, and harder maintenance as a result.

Embedded Java can be used for fairly small things—a calculation, for example—or for much more advanced effects, such as invoking EJBs or RESTful services.

BPEL Custom Sensor Action

BPEL processes can send signals out through so-called sensors. These signals inform the world of the progress in the process. Sensors can be targeted at a database table, a JMS queue or topic, or a custom Java class. Note that in this case the Java class is called and notified; it cannot respond to the process and it cannot manipulate its data or impact its flow. Chapter 16 introduces BPEL sensors as well composite sensors—the latter are defined at the composite level, and do not support custom Java actions.

Mediator Java Callouts

The Java callouts that we can specify on Mediator components can act on the data that comes into a routing rule before transformation takes place, as well as on the transformation result before it gets passed onward to the target service or event. The same applies to fault or reply traveling in the reverse direction. The Java callouts are typically used for special validation (beyond what XSD or Schematron can do), message enrichment (in a way that resembles the OSB XQuery manipulations introduced in the next chapter), advanced transformations, and fine-grained logging and auditing.

The online chapter complement contains an example of using the Mediator Java callout for debugging.

Registering Custom Classes with the SOA Suite

Other hooks for extending and customizing the behavior of the SOA Suite are available through the creation of custom XPath functions based on Java classes. These XPath functions are registered with the SOA Suite and are available in BPEL, Mediator, and other XPath expression editors. Likewise, we can create custom classes that, for example, assign human tasks to participants according to special rules, escalate tasks in specialized ways, provide special fact types in business rules, implement custom security assertions, preprocess files read by the file adapter, and handle run-time faults. These custom extensions are available across the SOA Suite, in any composite.

Another way of extending the SOA Suite is through the creation of a custom JCA adapter. The technology adapters shipped with the SOA Suite, such as the File Adapter, JMS Adapter, and Database Adapter, are all created according to the JCA (J2EE Connector Architecture) specification. We can implement our own adapter in Java, following this specification, and register this adapter with the SOA Suite. Subsequently, we can use this adapter—or any third-party custom JCA adapter—to create adapter services in SOA composites.

BPEL Entity Variables Bound to Service Data Objects

An intricate type of integration with the world of Java-powered components is the binding of BPEL variables to Service Data Objects (SDOs) offered by a Data Access Service (DAS), implemented by an ADF Business Components Application Module. BPEL variables that are bound like this are called *entity variables*. These variables are not just populated with data from the DAS at one moment in time. Instead, they contain a reference to the SDO that is maintained by the DAS acting against some back-end data store, which could be a database, a file repository, or something else altogether. Any change in SDO is immediately available in the BPEL process when it accesses the variable—no explicit refresh is required.

Additionally, updates of the BPEL entity variable are sent to the DAS to be applied to the SDO (and the underlying data store). Again, no explicit action is required on the part of the BPEL process. Although this all happens transparently, it is still nice to know that the SDOs can have a complex, nested structure of extensive data graphs and that the communication between the Data Access Service and its clients uses deltas to only communicate the changes in the graph instead of the entire structure.

The topic of BPEL entity variables bound to SDOs is discussed in Chapter 20, which also introduces ADF in more detail.

Invoking SOA Suite from Java

Most of these integrations between the SOA Suite and the world of Java are initiated from the end of the SOA Suite. The composite applications call out to engage Java-based logic. However, there are several ways to integrate in the other direction. Java applications can interact with SOA composite applications and with various facilities in the SOA Suite infrastructure.

Java applications can fairly easily call the Web Services published by the SOA composite application over SOAP/HTTP. However, both the EJB Adapter Service and the Direct Binding Service provide ways for Java applications to invoke the services in a faster, more native fashion and exchange messages over a remote (cross-JVM) method invocation (RMI). Another way to interact with composite applications is by exposing services using an ADF Binding. Such services can be invoked remotely over RMI through the SOA Suite run-time Java API. This interaction uses XML messages rather than plain Java objects.

The JMS Adapter provides another Java-based entrance to composite applications: This adapter listens to messages arriving on JMS queues or topics and initiates new instances or correlates into running instances.

The SOA Suite exposes APIs for querying, retrieving, and manipulating composite instances. Other APIs provide programmatic, Java-based access to the User Messaging Service (UMS) and the Human Workflow Services. The Business Rules engine also publishes a Java API through which business rules can be invoked from any Java application.

Appendix D provides more details about many of the APIs available to access the SOA Suite programmatically from your own applications. This chapter focuses on the interaction in the other direction: composite applications calling out to Java logic. The online chapter complement has detailed examples of invoking composite applications from Java, as well as the other way around.

Using the JMS Adapter to Loosely Couple with Java Applications

JMS (Java Message Service) is a Java standard (JSR-194) that describes an API for interacting with a messaging infrastructure. Many open-source projects and commercial vendors offer messaging technologies—such as Apache ActiveMQ, SonicMQ, WebSphere MQ (aka MQSeries) from IBM, Oracle AQ, and EMS from Tibco—that can be accessed via JMS, either directly or through adapters. JEE application servers also contain messaging frameworks that publish a JMS API—including JBoss Messaging, Glassfish Sun Java System Message Queue, and Oracle Enterprise Messaging Services (based on WebLogic JMS or Advanced Queuing).

Messaging according to JMS comprises two main models:

- Publish a message to a *queue* and have it consumed by only one consumer.
- Publish a message to a *topic,* where it can be consumed by potentially many consumers.

These fundamental models are embellished and refined in many ways, including topics that persist messages until all registered consumers have consumed them (even when they were unavailable at the time of publication), various retry patterns for delivering messages, high availability and performance features, transactional support, and so on.

Using the JMS Adapter to Integrate with the Finance Department's Java Application

The finance department at St. Matthews is very keen to know about new patients as early as possible. Even when the patients have never yet visited the hospital or are still in the process of making their first appointment, the accountants would like to know about them so they can start doing credit background analysis, confer with insurance companies, check against black lists, and so on. The finance department uses their own application—that they zealously guard against other departments. No one gets access to their system. They do not publish open APIs. Their application's only supported mode of communication is through a JMS queue that it monitors.

The finance department has requested to be notified of every new patient who is created through the PatientDataService, via a message that is to be sent to their JMS queue. Also, Margaret has been advised by the upper management echelon that it would be a good idea to heed this request. So there we go, as is depicted in Figure 12-2.

Preparing the Finance Department for JMS Communication

We have to do a number of things in terms of preparation. Set up the JMS queue financeNewPatients Queue (normally the finance department would do that, of course) according to the instructions in Appendix C and configure the JMS Adapter, also described in Appendix C (that is the part we always have to do ourselves—to hook into the queue we want to listen to). The JNDI name for the JMS adapter connection factory we will use is eis/Queue/patients, as stated in the appendix.

Next, we need a mock application that emulates the financial application. The mock application subscribes to the financeNewPatientsQueue and processes the messages it receives. In our simplified environment we will have the mock application write to the console about the new patients it receives from the PatientDataService. We can test the mock application by

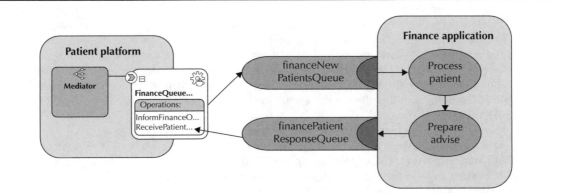

FIGURE 12-2. *Loose integration between the patient platform and the financial application based on JMS*

publishing dummy messages on the queue, either from the WebLogic Console or from a second Java program. The online chapter complement describes both procedures.

The steps for creating TheFinancialApplication—described in detail in the online chapter complement—are to create a generic application in JDeveloper and a project with this name and then add the library WebLogic 10.3 Remote Client to the project (we will need that to do programming against the JMS API).

Then, we create the class JMSQueueHandler. This will be the abstract superclass that does some of the JNDI and JMS plumbing, such as acquiring the JMS connection factory and finding the destination queue based on the JNDI properties, including host, user, password, and connection factory name (again, see online chapter complement for more details).

Next, we create the class NewPatientsQueueListener. This class extends from JMSQueueHandler, instructing it on the JMS queue name and registering itself as a listener to the destination. It implements the onMessage method described by the JMS MessageListener interface. This method is invoked by the JMS implementation for every message that arrives on the queue. The method expects a comma-separated string with data for the new patient. It writes the salient details out to the console—where, of course, the real application would start all kinds of interesting actions with this data.

A simple main method runs this mock financial application. See the online chapter complement for the source code and detailed description of the two classes that make up TheFinancialApplication.

Adding JMS Capabilities in SOA Composite Applications

Our next step can be approached in two ways. The first approach: We open the PatientDataService composite application, add a JMS adapter service, wire it to the BPEL component, and add an Invoke activity to the BPEL process. Fairly straightforward.

In the second approach, the PatientDataService composite application publishes an event on the Event Delivery Network when a new patient is created: a PatientDetailsChangeEvent. We can create a new composite that listens to that event and upon reception invokes a JMS adapter service.

Clearly the second approach should be picked, because it is much more decoupled than the first. The event already gets published on the EDN by the existing application, so we need not disturb the PatientDataService in order to grant the finance department's wish. What if we pick the first approach and then discover in a few months, time that the finance guys have changed their minds about receiving these messages—or they want to receive slightly different message formats?

By going with the second design based on the EDN event, we minimize the impact on our existing applications—now and in the future. It also gives us a nice demonstration of two very similar mechanisms: the Event Delivery Network and JMS, both for decoupled information distribution over a generic messaging infrastructure. One is fairly abstract and tightly integrated into the SOA Suite, and the other is somewhat lower level, more technical, and coupled with the Java/JEE platform.

Having made this clear design decision, we can move forward and create the implementation. The steps are fairly straightforward. To begin, create a new SOA application called **FinanceInformer**. Choose the Composite With Mediator template. Then indicate that this Mediator subscribes to the PatientDetailsChangeEvent that is specified in PatientEvents.edl, which we created in Chapter 9 (see Figure 12-3).

Time at last to meet the JMS adapter. Drag a JMS adapter service from the Component Palette to the References swimlane. Configure the adapter reference in the wizard. Enter **FinanceQueueInformer**

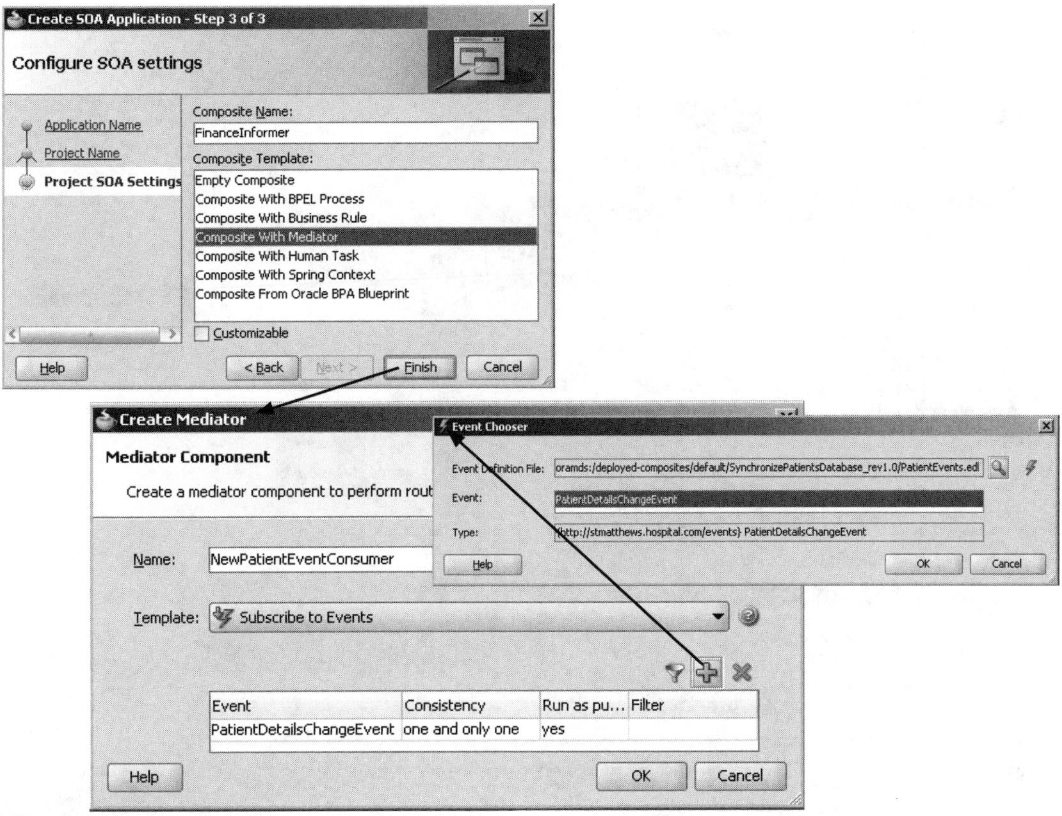

FIGURE 12-3.   *Creating the new composite FinanceInformer with the Mediator NewPatientEventConsumer*

in the first step as the name of the reference. On the JMS Provider page, select Oracle Enterprise Messaging Service and the WebLogic JMS implementation.

Select the same application server connection that you use to deploy SOA composite applications. Indicate that the adapter interface will be specified later from an operation and schema. For the operation, choose Produce (because this reference should publish messages to a JMS destination). Then specify an easy-to-understand name for the operation, something like **ProduceNewPatientMessage** (see Figure 12-4).

In Step 7, "Produce Operation Parameters," several important values must be set. The destination name (the JNDI name of the queue to publish to) is jms/financeNewPatientsQueue. Note that you can browse this queue directly from the application server.

We will allow the messages to live for 15 seconds—that will give us an opportunity to spot them in the administration console. The JNDI name for the JMS connection corresponds with the value specified in the outbound connection factory when we configured the JMS adapter (see

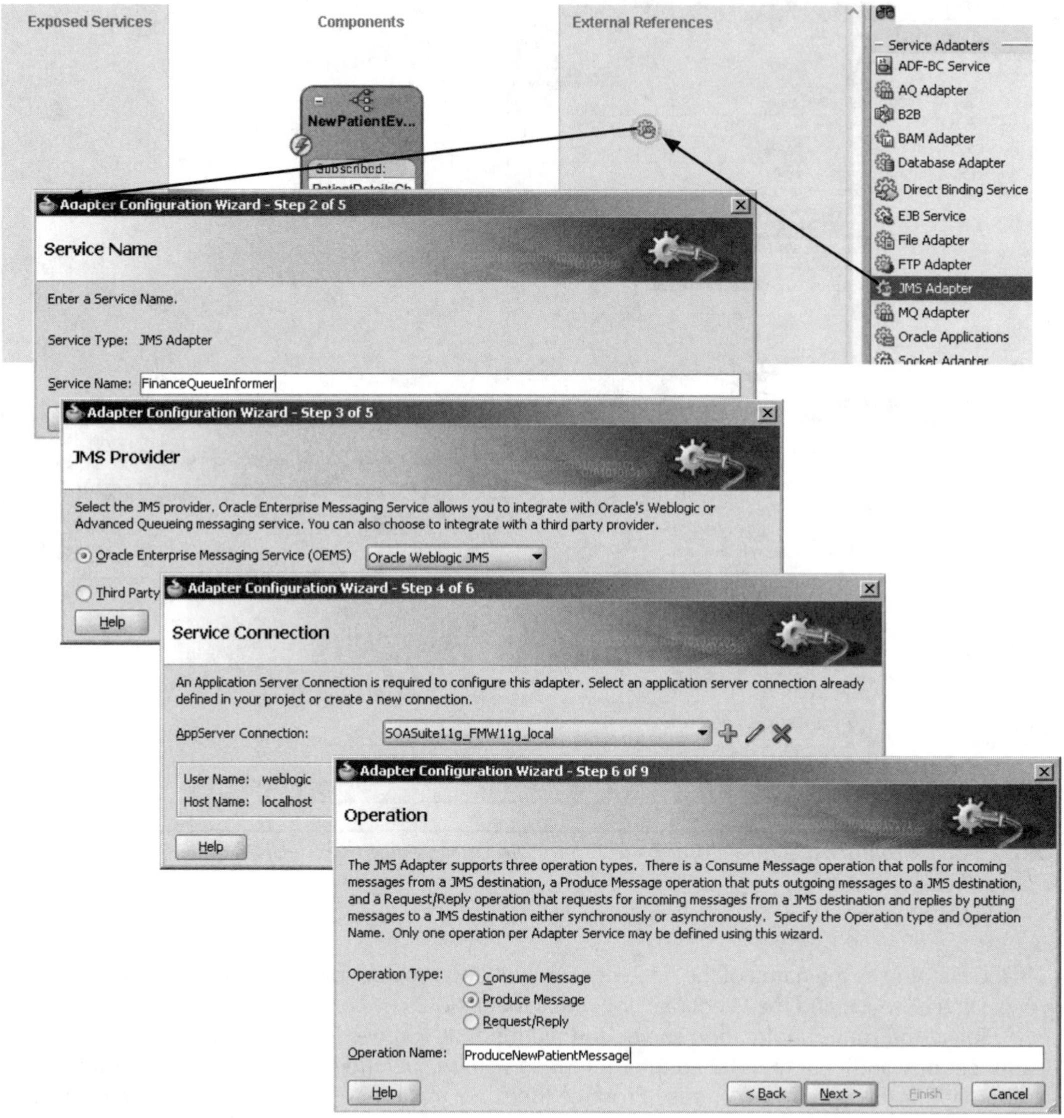

FIGURE 12-4. *Adding and configuring a JMS adapter service to publish messages to the* financeNewPatientsQueue

Appendix C). The name is eis/Queue/patients. Figure 12-5 illustrates these steps in the JMS Adapter wizard.

The Messages page is a familiar one—the same page is used in the database adapter and the file adapter. We can have the XSD created that goes with a comma-separated values format and enables the JMS adapter to take our XML message and create a CSV from it. Click Define

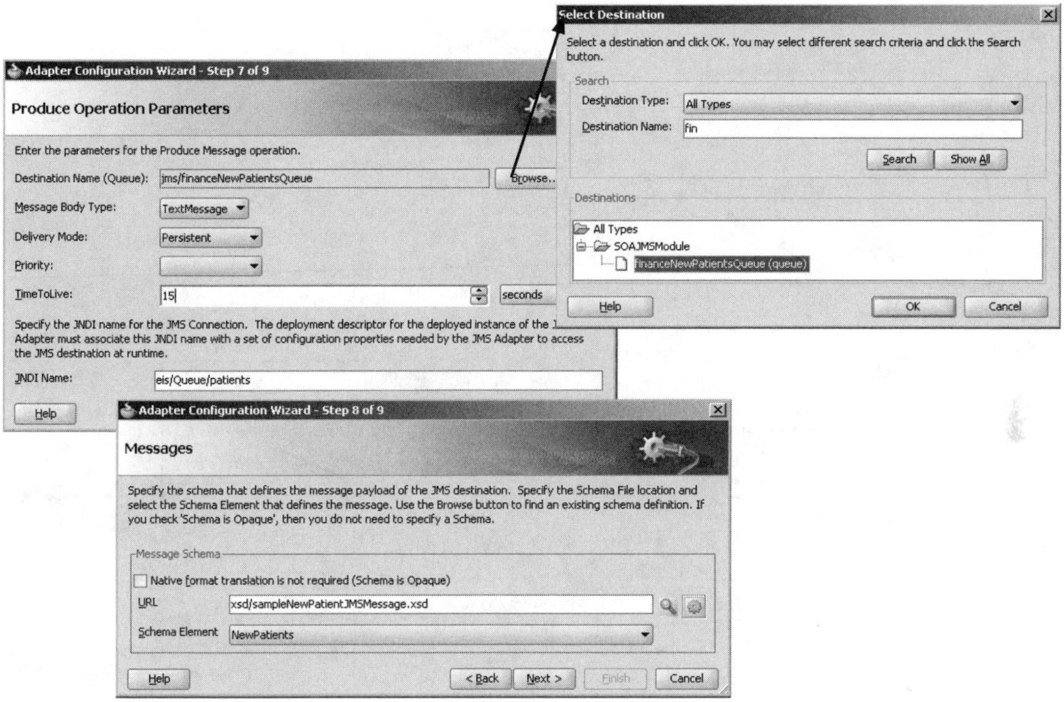

FIGURE 12-5. *Completing the configuration of the JMS Adapter Service*

Schema For Native Format and create a sample file with one or two lines of comma-separated patient details as an example of the format that the JMS messages will deliver to TheFinancialApplication. Let the native format builder do its job using that sample file.

When the JMS adapter service has been configured, wire the Mediator to the JMS adapter. Edit the Mediator. Create the mapping from the incoming event to the format required by the JMS adapter in the usual way.

This completes the composite application—which is really just a pipeline from the EDN event to the JMS message. We can deploy the application to the SOA Suite.

New Patients Communicated via JMS to the Finance Department

When the application has been deployed, we can invoke the RegisterNewPatient_ep service on the PatientDataService composite. Let's create a new patient by the name of James Ulohado of Qotica City in New Mexico, as shown in Figure 12-6. A database record is created, and the PatientDetailsChangedEvent is published to the Event Delivery Network.

This event is consumed by three different composites, one of which is the FinanceInformer through its NewPatientEventConsumer Mediator. The Mediator forwards the transformed message to the JMS Adapter Service.

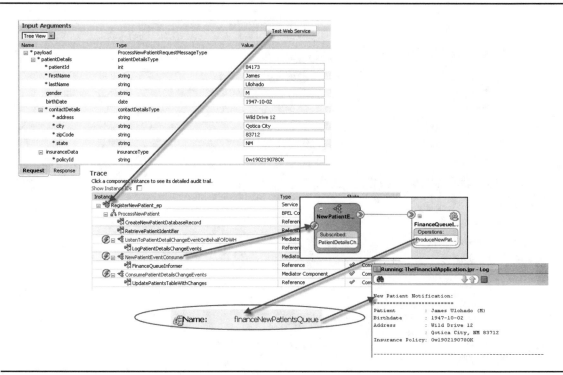

FIGURE 12-6. *TheFinancialApplication is notified via JMS of the creation of the new patient.*

The JMS adapter creates the JMS message with the CSV string and publishes it to the JMS queue. The message for new patient James Ulohado is consumed from the queue by TheFinancialApplication—which in this case writes the information to the console.

The essence here, of course, is the fact that through the JMS adapter we managed to inform the black-box Java application from the finance department using standard Java/JEE infrastructure without compromising the service-oriented nature of our application. In this case, the JMS adapter produced a message. It is important to realize that it can just as easily consume messages from a JMS queue or topic and instantiate (or correlate) a composite instance.

Return to Sender

As it happens, the financial guys are opening up a little. They think it is beneficial for all participants if they provide some instructions regarding the new patients in a very early stage. In fact, they have promised to respond to the new patient events that are published to their JMS queue with a message of their own on a second JMS queue within a five-second window. They indicate that their message can provide useful information with regard to the financial situation of a new patient.

To process their response in the same composite instance that sent the new patient event message, we will utilize a special mode of operation of the JMS adapter: the request/reply pattern. This mode is used to send out a request and consume the corresponding reply, thus turning the JMS adapter service into a two-way service.

This third mode (next to the regular consume and produce modes) is quite advanced—it supports a correlated message exchange with a third party, using one queue for sending out the request and another queue for consuming the response. The adapter itself is capable of correlating the reply with the response and presents itself to the composite as a two-way service (either synchronous or asynchronous). The correlation requires the header property JMSCorrelationId in the reply message to be set to the JMSMessageId header property value of the request message. The property JCA_JMSReplyTo is set in the request message with the name of the destination queue that the adapter listens on for the reply in case the client is not aware of the name of that queue.

The request/reply mode relieves us from implementing an explicit correlation ourselves where a BPEL process has a Receive activity connected to an inbound (consume mode) JMS Adapter service with an associated correlation set that was initiated by the earlier invoke of an outbound JMS Adapter service. The only requirements for leveraging this advanced mode with built-in correlation are the use of the correct queue for the reply message and the use of the JMSCorrelationId header property by the party at the other end of this JMS-based interaction. With explicit correlation—using separate outbound and inbound JMS adapter services, we would still have the requirement on the queues. The correlation could then be done on some custom element in the message payload.

Before we can receive any response messages, the queue for those messages must be created. This is done in the WebLogic Administration Console, as explained in Appendix C. The name of this second queue is jms/financePatientResponseQueue.

Modify TheFinancialApplication to Have It Send Response Messages   In the scenario we are implementing, we need the financial Java application to publish messages on the response queue, as was promised. In order for the JMS adapter to properly correlate those response messages with the original request messages and thus forward the messages to the correct composite instance, it is essential that the response messages contain a correlation ID property that is set to the message ID of the corresponding request message. Here's the essential snippet of Java code:

```
public void onMessage(Message msg) {
    String correlationId = msg.getJMSMessageID();
    ...
    jmsTextMessage.setJMSCorrelationID(correlationId);
    jmsTextMessage.setText(xmlPayload);
    jmsMessageProducer.send(jmsTextMessage);
```

The published message has its header property JMSCorrelationId set to the JMSMessageId value that was received in the incoming message.

The XML Payload is defined as follows:

```
String payload =    "<?xml version=\"1.0\" ?>" +
    "<NewPatientAdvise
  xmlns=\"http://com.stmatthews.hospital/finance/FinanceQueueTwoWayInformer\">" +
        "<PatientName>"+fields[0]+" "+fields[1]+"</PatientName>" +
        "<Advise>this patient poses no special financial risks</Advise>" +
    "</NewPatientAdvise>";
```

Create New JMS FileAdapterService with Request/Reply   Create a new XSD document with the definition for the NewPatientAdvise element that has child elements named PatientName and Advise.

Delete the existing JMS Adapter Service and create a new one under the name **FinanceQueue TwoWayInformer**. On the Operation page, select the operation type Request/Reply. Pick the Asynchronous option and specify operation names—for example, **InformFinanceOfNewPatient** for the request and **ReceivePatientAdvise** for the reply.

Specify the request operation parameters: These are the same as in the JMS adapter service we configured before, with jms/financeNewPatientsQueue as the destination and eis/Queue/patients as the JNDI name for the JMS connection.

The next page is for configuring reply operation parameters. The name of the destination is different this time: jms/financePatientResponseQueue. The JNDI name for the connection is the same.

The Messages page has us define the message types for the request (the same NewPatients element as before) as well as the reply. For the reply we can select the NewPatientAdvise element from the NewPatientAdviseJMSMessage.xsd document. Click Next and then Finish to complete the JMS adapter service (see Figure 12-7).

Reconfigure the Mediator   We can do several things with the advice we receive from the financial department as a response on our JMS message. We can turn it into an event on the EDN, or we can invoke an "update patient" operation on the PatientDataService. We can also just ignore it. The latter is what we will do for now.

When we wire the Mediator to the FinanceQueueTwoWayInformer JMS adapter service and open the editor for this Mediator, we will see a routing rule with the two sections. One is the same as before, for the forward direction to the JMS adapter service. And the other one is for handling the asynchronous response that the JMS adapter will return. Here is where we can forward to either an event or a specific target service.

To begin, create the mapping between the PatientDetailsChangedEvent and the request element configured for the JMS adapter service. Then close the Mediator editor and redeploy the composite. Make sure that TheFinancialApplication is running the latest version that publishes response messages on the response queue with their JMSCorrelationId set.

Now, call the RegisterNewPatient_ep service on the PatientDataService composite with data on some made-up patient. Check in the FMW Console whether the composite did indeed receive sound advice regarding the patient from the financial application (see Figure 12-8).

Embedding Java Logic in BPEL Processes

If you want to add Java-based logic to your BPEL process—not through invocations of partner links, but really embedded execution of Java code—you can make use of the Oracle-specific BPEL extension activity Exec. This activity contains a snippet of Java code that is executed by the JVM that executes the BPEL process—in the same JTA transaction context as the BPEL process and without any context switches.

Embedding Java like this is primarily useful for advanced validation and manipulation of BPEL variables and for auditing and debugging purposes. One usage is to fill the metadata attributes in the instance table in the dehydration store with functional data, such as the patient identifier, to be able to correlate composite instance IDs with meaningful instance data. This can be handy for error recovery.

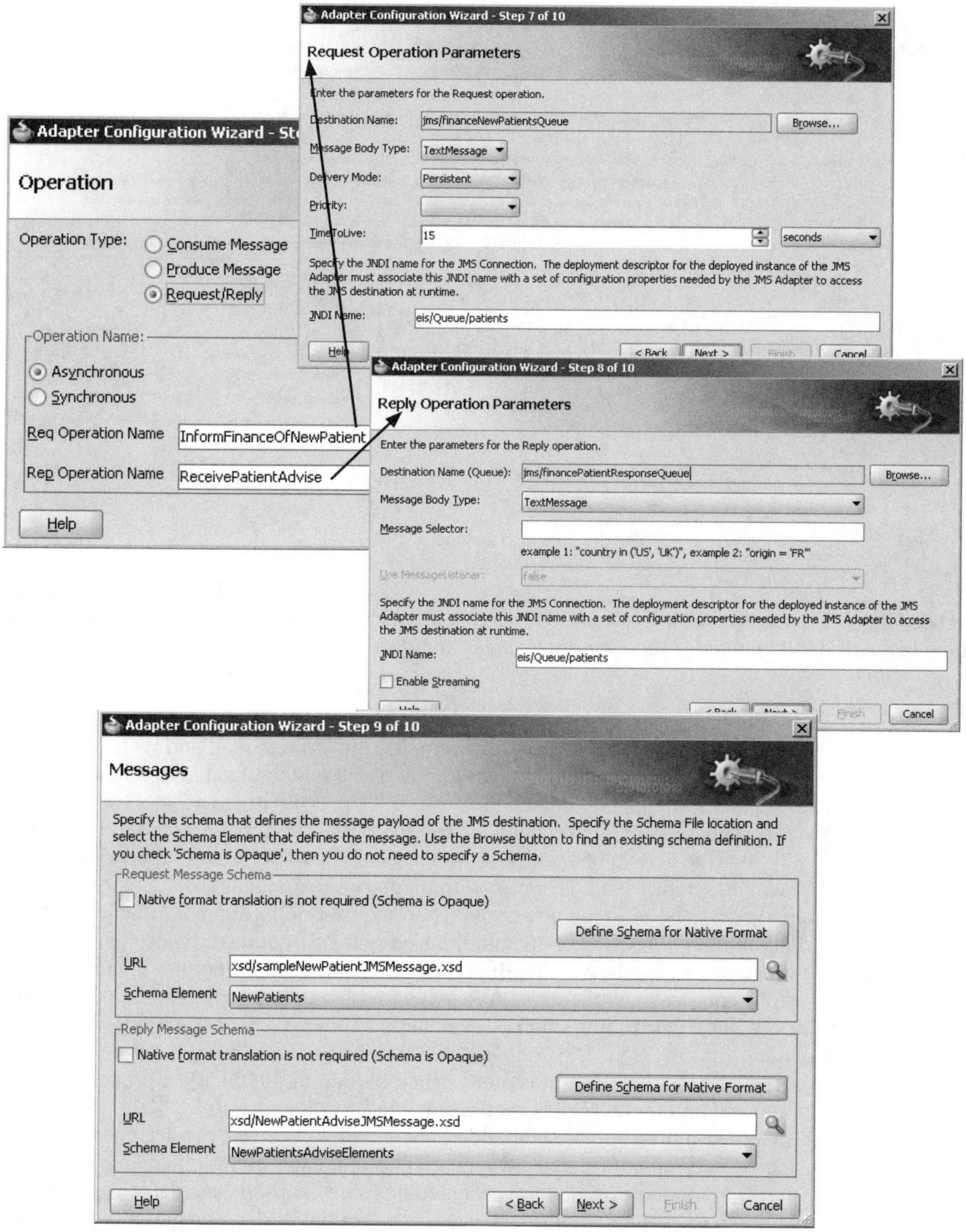

FIGURE 12-7.   *Configure the two-way request/reply JMS adapter service*

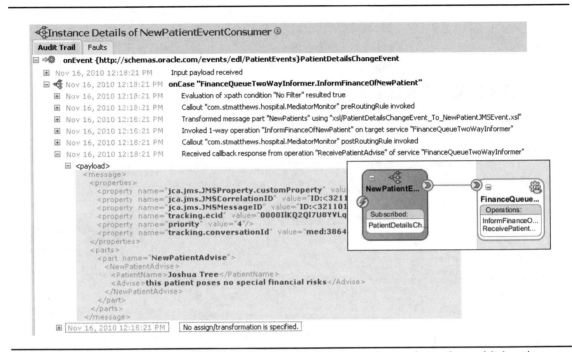

FIGURE 12-8. *The two-way request/reply JMS service in action: The Mediator that publishes the new patient event to the JMS adapter service now receives an advise in response.*

The Java snippet can use a number of special built-in methods that facilitate integration with the BPEL process instance. These methods, for example, allow direct read and write access to BPEL variables. Java exceptions thrown and not handled in the Embedded Java activity are converted to BPEL faults and can be dealt with in the BPEL process in the normal way.

The Embedded Java snippet can do JNDI lookup operations that make it possible to invoke EJBs from within the Exec activity. Note that although this is possible, it is certainly not the recommended way to interact with EJBs from within composite applications.

It sounds too good to be true: the power of Java in the best-performing, transaction-preserving way. Wow! Well, although it seems pretty good, it is very tightly coupled. Before you get too excited about the ability to use Java inside BPEL, remember why we do not use Java for all the functionality of our composite applications. We strive for decoupled, reusable components that bring us business agility. Embedding small or even large chunks of Java code inside BPEL processes threatens this ambition: The code is not reusable at all, and it is difficult to develop, test, and subject to version control, as it is pretty much hidden inside the BPEL process. However, for relatively localized and fairly small operations, it can be quite powerful.

However, before you dive into the Embedded Java in the bpelx:exec tag, I suggest you carefully consider whether that is the best way to go about it. Later in this chapter, you will meet the Spring Context component, which allows Java logic to be exposed as a regular service component in a much more service-oriented way, even though it is less integrated with the BPEL process—no direct access to BPEL variables, for example—and has somewhat more overhead when invoked from BPEL via a Partner Link.

Using Embedded Java in a BPEL Process

The Embedded Java can do very local, Java-specific manipulation or validation of a BPEL variable—or call out of the JVM to external components such as EJBs or RESTful services. The Exec activity is best used for fairly small-scale tasks because calling out to external services should probably be handled through references and possibly via the enterprise service bus (see the next chapter on Oracle Service Bus). However, to give you a taste of what you *can* do and show you how to do it, we will discuss how to call a RESTful service from the BPEL component ConsultPreparationInstructionService, which prepares the instructions to be sent to the patient along with the appointment schedule. The service we want to invoke will translate the instructions, which are originally in English, into Spanish to cater to the very mixed patient population.

In the near future, we intend to record every patient's preferred language and make sure all St. Matthews' communication with patients are in that language. For now we will offer the instructions in Spanish (or "Spanglish," depending on the quality of this translation service).

NOTE
The book's wiki has two other examples of leveraging this same RESTful service—one using the Mediator Java callout function and one using the Spring component. A third option would be engaging the OSB because it knows how to talk "RESTish."

Create Java Code That Does the Job

Our first step will be to create a stand-alone Java application—well, Java class—that has the logic we need to embed later on. We have no easy way to test the Embedded Java—only by deploying the composite and testing it can we test the Java logic in a very indirect way. It is a best practice to have as little Java code inside the Exec tag—only the direct interaction with the BPEL process and a call to a custom class that does the actual work. Note that this custom class needs to be explicitly imported in the BPEL process.

Download the JAR file json_simple-1.1.jar from http://code.google.com/p/json-simple/ and copy this file to the directory SCA-INF/lib.

Next, open the SOA application ConsultPreparationInstruction. Add the JAR file to the ConsultPreparationInstructionService project (on the Libraries and Classpath tab in the project properties dialog).

Finally, create the class StringTranslator. This class uses JSON-Simple to call out in a RESTful way (a simple HTTP Get request with JSON payload) to the Google translation service. The public method we can use to have some text translated is called translate. This static method will be used from the Embedded Java snippet in the BPEL process, as shown here:

```
public class StringTranslator {
   public static String translate(String sourceString
                            , String sourceLanguage, String targetLanguage)
   ...
```

NOTE
See the online chapter complement for the complete source code for this example.

Embed the Java Logic in the BPEL Process

We have the Java code working on its own; we can now leverage it from an Exec activity in the BPEL process and integrate it with the BPEL variables in that process.

Open the BPEL component ConsultPreparationInstructionService and add a bpelx:exec tag (in the source tab) as the first child of the process root element:

```
<bpelx:exec import="com.stmatthews.hospital.StringTranslator"/>
```

Create variables to hold the (English) instructions (the source text for the translation) and the translation result (the Spanish instructions):

```
<variable name="instructions" type="xsd:string"/>
<variable name="spanishInstructions" type="xsd:string"/>
```

Extend the Assign activity to copy the value of the instructions already set in the outputVariable to the new variable: instructions. Add an Embedded Java activity to the BPEL process and set its name to **RESTfulTranslation** (see Figure 12-9).

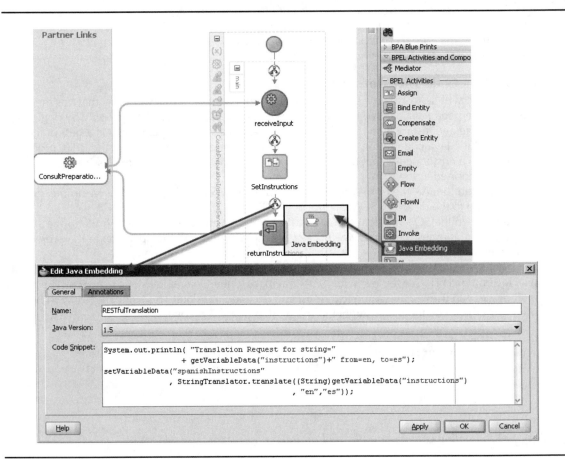

FIGURE 12-9.   *Adding an Embedded Java activity to the BPEL process*

Add the following code snippet to the Embedded Java activity:

```
<bpelx:exec name="RESTfulTranslation" version="1.5" language="java">
  <![CDATA[System.out.println( "Translation Request for string="
              + getVariableData("instructions")+" from=en, to=es");
setVariableData("spanishInstructions"
              , StringTranslator.translate
                ( (String) getVariableData("instructions")
                , "en","es"
                )
              );
]]>
</bpelx:exec>
```

Note that getVariableData and setVariableData are predefined methods that we can use in Embedded Java snippets to get and set BPEL variable values. Another built-in method we can use is addAuditTrailEntry(String). We can include calls to this method if we want information written to the audit trail of the BPEL process. Here's an example:

```
addAuditTrailEntry("RESTfulTranslation: Translation Request for string="
              + getVariableData("instructions")+" from=en, to=es");
```

Finally, add an Assign activity that takes the result of the translations and concatenates it with the original English instructions. This completes the BPEL process with Embedded Java logic. The real work is done, of course, in the StringTranslator class that is imported into the BPEL process and invoked from the Exec activity.

Run the Composite with Embedded Java Inside

With all the code in place, we can deploy the composite application. The json_simple-1.1.jar file is deployed along with the application, so you do not need to do separate server-side deployment of the JAR file—or any custom classes for that matter.

Deploy the composite and test the Web Service ConsultPreparationInstructionService. You will find the predefined (and somewhat simplistic) English instructions as well as the translated Spanish version of these instructions, obtained from the RESTful translation service that the BPEL process was able to invoke through an Embedded Java snippet that leveraged a custom class that used a third-party library to make the call (see Figure 12-10).

The Spring Context Service Component for Custom Java Service Components

The PS2 release of SOA Suite 11*g* introduced a new type of service component: the Spring Context component. This component allows us to publish Java interfaces implemented by Spring Beans—Java classes configured in a Spring Beans Configuration file—as services that can be used inside a composite application. This essentially means that we can implement part of the logic required in our SOA composite applications in Java and use it like any other service component. Unlike BPEL's Embedded Java, a Spring Context service component can be reused within the composite, invoked by various other components, and even exposed outside the composite, either as an EJB or as a Web Service. Additionally, the Java beans in the Spring Context component can call services exposed by other Service Components and Adapter Bindings.

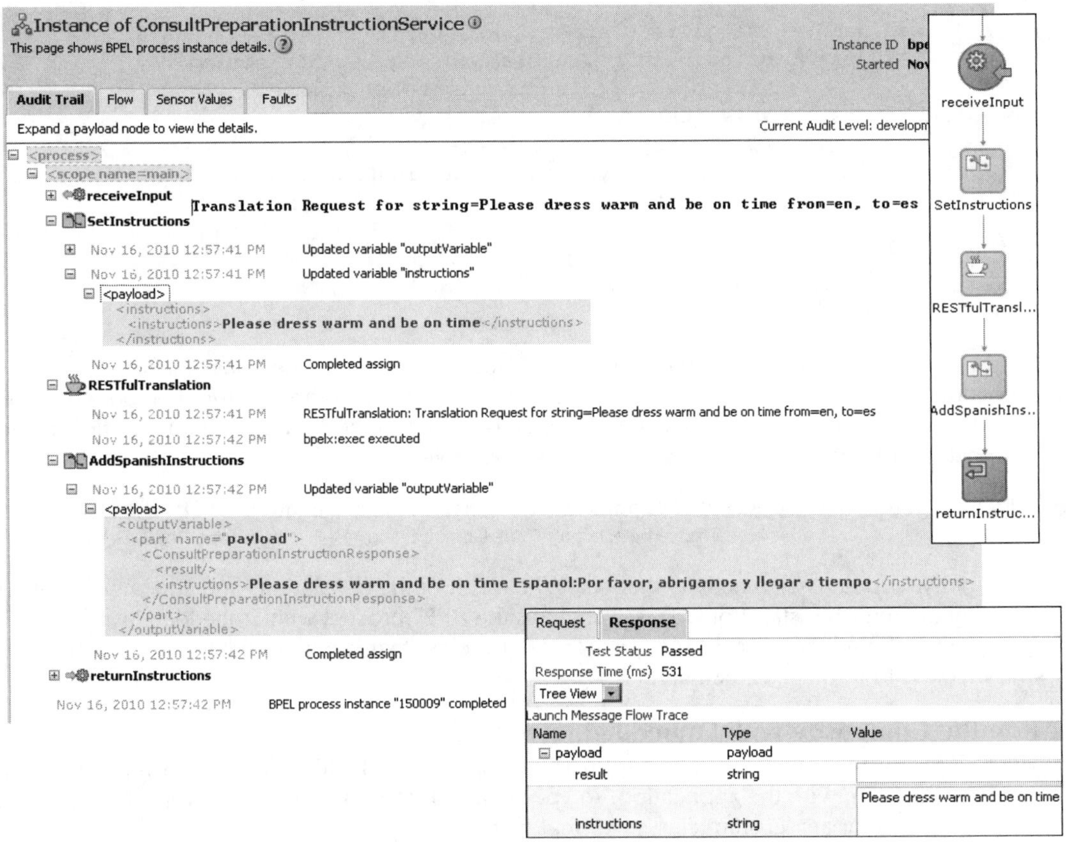

FIGURE 12-10. *The embedded Java activity invokes a RESTful translation service to retrieve the Spanish version of the instructions. Notice the message in the audit trail.*

This means, for example, that a Java bean can retrieve records from a database table using a Database Adapter service.

We can use the full breadth of the Java language and platform, including third-party libraries. The Java classes to be exposed as service components are developed as any Java application is, and they can be version controlled, unit tested, and debugged just like a regular Java application. All libraries and classes in the project are packaged and deployed along with the composite application, so you do not have to copy classes or JAR files to the SOA Suite classpath on the server. There are some definite advantages over Embedded Java in BPEL processes.

NOTE
You can add an extension for the Spring Framework to JDeveloper that makes working with Spring artifacts a bit easier. The book's wiki has an article describing the configuration and use of that extension.

Using the Spring Context Service Component

The Spring Context service component can make the hands of Java developers itch. Because it allows us to integrate almost any piece of Java logic into the composite applications, the temptation can be huge to forget about the other service components and technology adapters and implement all logic in Java. That would *not* be a good approach. It is highly recommended to use the service components and adapters for their respective tasks and leverage their built-in features, functionality, and facilities for configuration and administration.

Having issued that warning, it is clear that there are frequent circumstances where the standard service engines and adapters do not offer everything we want—or at least not in a very intuitive, productive way. Having Java—and the richness of the Java platform and community—at our fingertips through this Spring Context component is a real boon in such cases. When it comes to interaction with specialized interfaces for hardware equipment, or the generation of images or documents, the interpretation of information in binary formats, communication with non-JDBC databases, performing complex calculations, absorbing readings from physical sensors, and other use cases for which custom-built or standard third-party Java logic provides a solution, this component can be of tremendous value.

We will use the Spring Context component to enrich the SchedulerService. This service, which schedules an appointment based on an incoming appointment request, will generate a PDF document with the appointment details and write it to a central directory where the mail room can pick it up. A future version of the PatientAppointmentService could also process this PDF document and attach it to the e-mail notification that the patient receives when the appointment is scheduled.

NOTE
The complete source code for this example is available in the online chapter complement.

Implement the Java Code for Generating the PDF Document

We will take a very straightforward route here—we just implement a single class that does the PDF generation using the open source iText library. We will add a main method to be able to locally run, debug, and unit-test this class. When we have it working, we will move to the next step where the Spring Context is added.

Before we continue, you need to download the iText library that we will use for generating the PDF document. Go to http://itextpdf.com/ and download itext.jar. Add this JAR file to the SCA-INF\lib directory in the SchedulerService project.

Next, open the SchedulerService application in JDeveloper. Add the itext.jar file to the SchedulerService project (from the Libraries and Classpath tab in the project properties dialog).

Create the classes Patient and AppointmentSchedule—simple Java Beans with properties such as firstName, lastName, city, and state for the patient and appointmentDateTime, room, and doctor for the appointment schedule.

Create a new class called **PatientAppointmentPdfGenerator** (in the package com.stmatthews.hospital) and add the following method:

```
public byte[] createPDFforAppointmentSchedule(Patient patient
                                   , AppointmentSchedule schedule) {
  ByteArrayOutputStream buffer = new ByteArrayOutputStream();
  Document document = new Document();
  try {
    PdfWriter.getInstance(document, buffer);
    document.open();
    prepareDocument(patient, schedule, document);
  } catch (DocumentException e) {
  }
  document.close();
  byte[] bytes = buffer.toByteArray();
  return bytes;
}
```

This public method creates a new PDF document, calls upon a private method (prepare Document) to add the actual contents to that document, and then returns the document as a byte array. This is the method we will expose in the Spring Context to be invoked from the composite.

Now you can implement a very basic or more advanced version of the method prepareDocument. Here's a fairly simple implementation:

```
private void prepareDocument(Patient patient, AppointmentSchedule schedule,
                          Document document) throws DocumentException {
  Paragraph addressHeader = new Paragraph();
  addressHeader.add(new Chunk(patient.getFirstName()+" "+ patient
.getLastName()));
  addressHeader.add(Chunk.NEWLINE);
  addressHeader.add(new Chunk(patient.getAddress()));
  addressHeader.add(Chunk.NEWLINE);
  addressHeader.add(new Chunk(patient.getCity()+", "+patient.getState()+"
"+patient.getZipcode()));
  addressHeader.add(Chunk.NEWLINE);
  document.add(addressHeader);
}
```

The source code for this application on the wiki contains a more extended version of this method that creates a more verbose letter for our patients (see Figure 12-11).

Create the Spring Context Service Component

Now that we have the Java logic we want to expose as a service component, we will bring in the Spring Framework. First, open the context menu for the PatientAppointmentPdfGenerator and under Refactor choose the option Extract Interface. In the dialog that opens, provide the name of the interface (IPatientAppointmentPdfGenerator) and select the public method createPDFforAppointmentSchedule to be included in the interface.

In the Composite Editor, drag the Spring Context component from the Component Palette and drop it in the components area. Set the name of this new Spring Bean configuration to **scheduleService-beans.xml**. Double-click the newly added component to bring up the source editor.

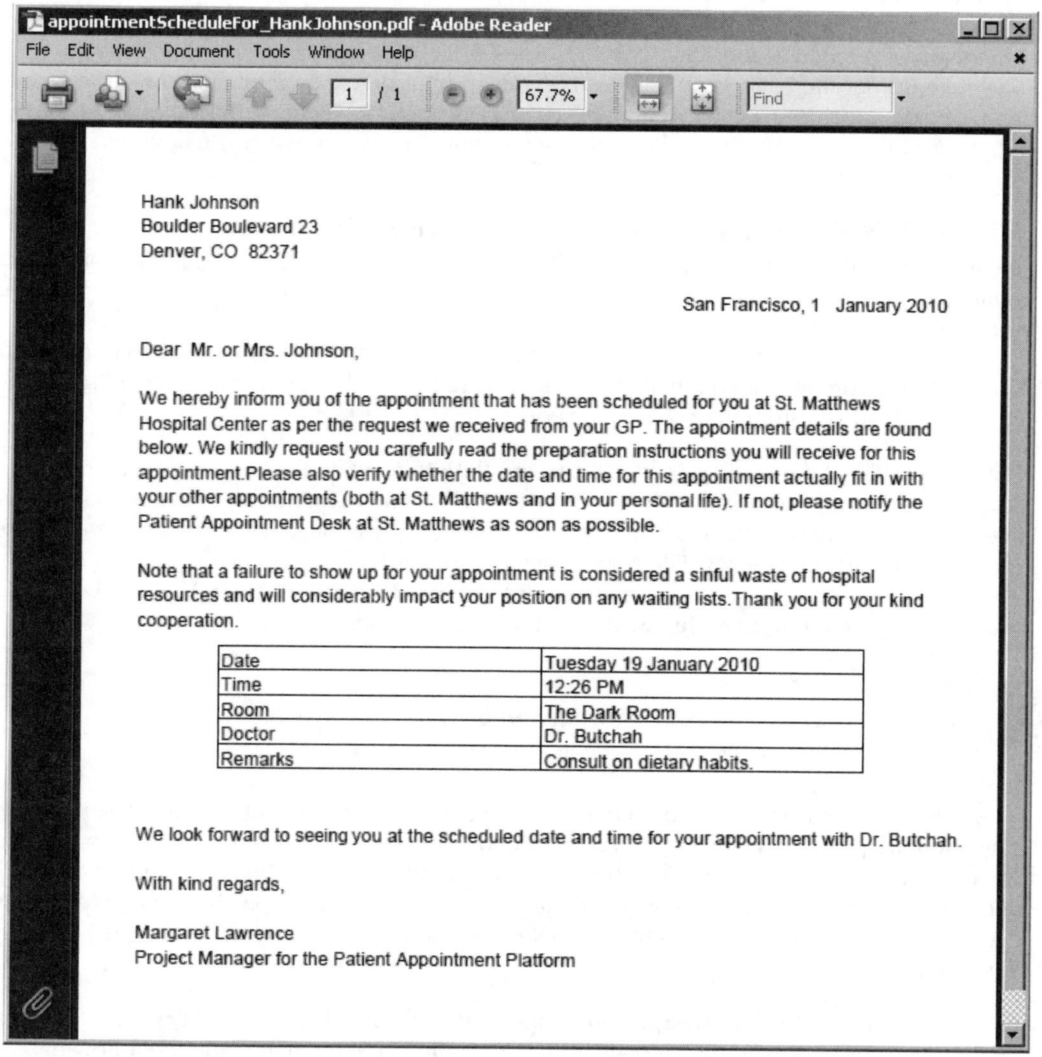

Hank Johnson
Boulder Boulevard 23
Denver, CO 82371

San Francisco, 1 January 2010

Dear Mr. or Mrs. Johnson,

We hereby inform you of the appointment that has been scheduled for you at St. Matthews Hospital Center as per the request we received from your GP. The appointment details are found below. We kindly request you carefully read the preparation instructions you will receive for this appointment.Please also verify whether the date and time for this appointment actually fit in with your other appointments (both at St. Matthews and in your personal life). If not, please notify the Patient Appointment Desk at St. Matthews as soon as possible.

Note that a failure to show up for your appointment is considered a sinful waste of hospital resources and will considerably impact your position on any waiting lists.Thank you for your kind cooperation.

Date	Tuesday 19 January 2010
Time	12:26 PM
Room	The Dark Room
Doctor	Dr. Butchah
Remarks	Consult on dietary habits.

We look forward to seeing you at the scheduled date and time for your appointment with Dr. Butchah.

With kind regards,

Margaret Lawrence
Project Manager for the Patient Appointment Platform

FIGURE 12-11. *The PDF document generated by the PatientAppointmentPdfGenerator*

Add the following bean definition to this file:

```
<bean  name="patientAppointmentPdfGenerator"
       class="com.stmatthews.hospital.PatientAppointmentPdfGenerator"  />
```

Configure an sca:service in the scheduleService-beans.xml file that declares this bean to be exposed as an SCA service:

```
<sca:service name="appointmentScheduleGenerationService"
     target="patientAppointmentPdfGenerator"
     type="com.stmatthews.hospital.IPatientAppointmentPdfGenerator"/>
```

The target attribute refers to the bean that implements the service, whereas the type attribute indicates the Java interface that describes the service. This interface is the starting point for the generation of the WSDL and XSD.

In the Composite Editor, you will see that the Spring Context component now has a service icon, based on the <sca:service> element we just inserted. However, at this point there are no WSDL or XSD documents created for this component. Only when we create a wire to the component will they be created.

Wire the PDF Generator to the SchedulingService BPEL Process

We will create a File Adapter service to write the PDF document to the central directory just mentioned. This service will receive a binary block of data and just write it out to the file without touching the contents.

A Mediator will be created next that first calls the appointmentScheduleGenerationService Spring service component and then forwards the response to this file adapter. We will then invoke this Mediator from the SchedulingService BPEL process.

Configure a File Adapter Service to Write the PDF to the File System   Add a File Adapter Service to the composite. Call the service **WritePDFDocumentToFile**. We'll define the adapter interface later (from schema and operation). On the next page, pick Write File as operation and specify **WritePDFDocumentToFile** as the operation name.

On the File Configuration page, enter the logical directory name **CENTRAL_PDF_DIRECTORY** and enter **AppointmentSchedule%SEQ%.pdf** for the filename.

NOTE
Later on we will set a file adapter header property to customize the filename using the name of the patient.

In Step 6, "Messages," we would normally either choose an element from an existing XSD or, even more frequently, use the Native Format Builder to create the XSD for some comma-separated values file format. Not this time: The content of the file to write is the binary definition of the PDF document. The file adapter can pass the contents without transformation. Therefore, we need to check the box marked Native Format Translation Is Not Required (Schema Is Opaque). Click Finish.

Create a Mediator to Call the Spring Component and the File Adapter Service   To prepare for the Mediator we are about to create, open SchedulerService.xsd and add the following element and type definitions that will define the input for the Mediator:

```
<xsd:element name="PatientAppointmentSchedule"
             type="PatientAppointmentScheduleType"/>
<xsd:complexType name="PatientAppointmentScheduleType">
 <xsd:sequence>
  <xsd:element name="patientDetails" type="ap:patientDetailsType"/>
  <xsd:element name="scheduleDetails" type="PlannedScheduleType"/>
 </xsd:sequence>
</xsd:complexType>
```

Spring Dependency Injection and SCA References

An important concept for Spring Beans is dependency injection. When a bean has dependencies on other objects that it needs to call to, these dependencies are not hard-coded in the bean's source code. Instead, the bean exposes a setter method through which an object reference can be set with an implementation of the interface required by the bean. In the Spring Bean configuration file, a bean that provides the implementation is wired to the dependency, exposed as a bean property. However, if no bean is available to satisfy the dependency, we can use an sca:reference element in the bean configuration file to expose that dependency at the level of the Spring Context Service Component. Another Service Component can then be wired to that reference.

For example: A Java Class ComplaintsHandler is to be configured as Spring Bean. The bean requires the injection of a file writer. It has information to write to a central patient complaints register, and it requires an object that implements the IMessageFileWriter interface that it can call upon to perform that action (and that should know where the destination file is and how to write to it). This class has a property with the associated setter method:

```
private IMessageFileWriter writer;
public void setWriter(IMessageFileWriter writer)
```

Note that we could express this in SCA terminology quite easily, replacing Java Class and Spring Bean with Service Component (such as Mediator) and dependency and property-to-set with reference.

The configuration for this bean would be as follows:

```
<bean name="complaintsHandler"
      class="com.stmatthews.hospital.ComplaintsHandler">
   <property name="writer" ref="theFileWriter" />
</bean>
```

and the Spring configuration file also needs to define theFileWriter that is referenced by the complaintsHandler bean in order to be valid. This *theFileWriter* can be just another Spring Bean *or* it can be an sca:reference element that exposes the dependency outside the Spring context component:

```
<sca:reference name="theFileWriter"
               type=" com.stmatthews.hospital.IMessageFileWriter"/>
```

We could now, for example, create a Mediator in the Composite application and wire it to the *theFileWriter* reference exposed by the Spring context component. The WSDL for the Mediator would be generated for us when we create the wire, based on IMessageFileWriter interface definition. This Mediator could, for example, route to a File Adapter service.

Add a Mediator to the composite and call it **WritePDFDocumentToFile**. Select the template for the one-way interface. Select the PatientAppointmentSchedule element from SchedulerService.xsd for the input and then click OK.

Wire the Mediator to the Spring Context service component PatientAppointmentPdfGenerator. At this point, JDeveloper generates the IPatientAppointmentPdfGenerator.wsdl document for the PatientAppointmentPdfGenerator. An alert to that effect is shown in Figure 12-12.

Open the Mediator to edit the mappings for the routing rule. First, create the mapping to the Spring Component. Using AutoMap will get you a long way in creating all the mappings—for both the patient details and the appointment schedule.

Next, select the target for the synchronous reply. Click the icon and select Service. Then select the WritePDFDocumentToFile operation in the File Adapter Service (see Figure 12-13).

Create the mapping from the reply from the Spring Component to the File Adapter Service. Include the initial request in the mapping by checking the box. Map the return element in the source—the byte array with the PDF inside—to the opaqueElement in the target and then close the mapping editor (see Figure 12-14).

Now you may wonder why you had to include the request in the mapping if we do not even use it! To the contrary, we *will* use it—to assign the name of the PDF file that is written by the file adapter, by setting one of the file adapter's header properties. We have to do this in a roundabout way, because we need to set the property using data from the initial request instead of the message we are now forwarding to the file adapter.

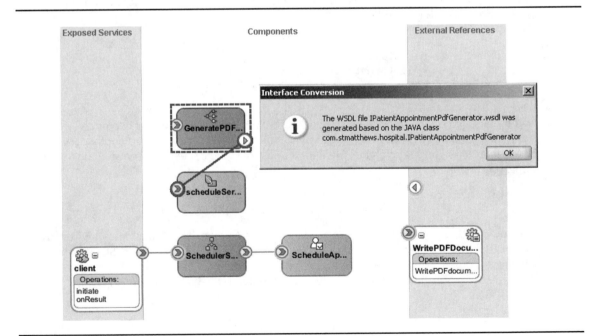

FIGURE 12-12. *Wiring the Mediator to the Spring Context component prompts JDeveloper to generate the WSDL for the PatientAppointmentPdfGenerator.*

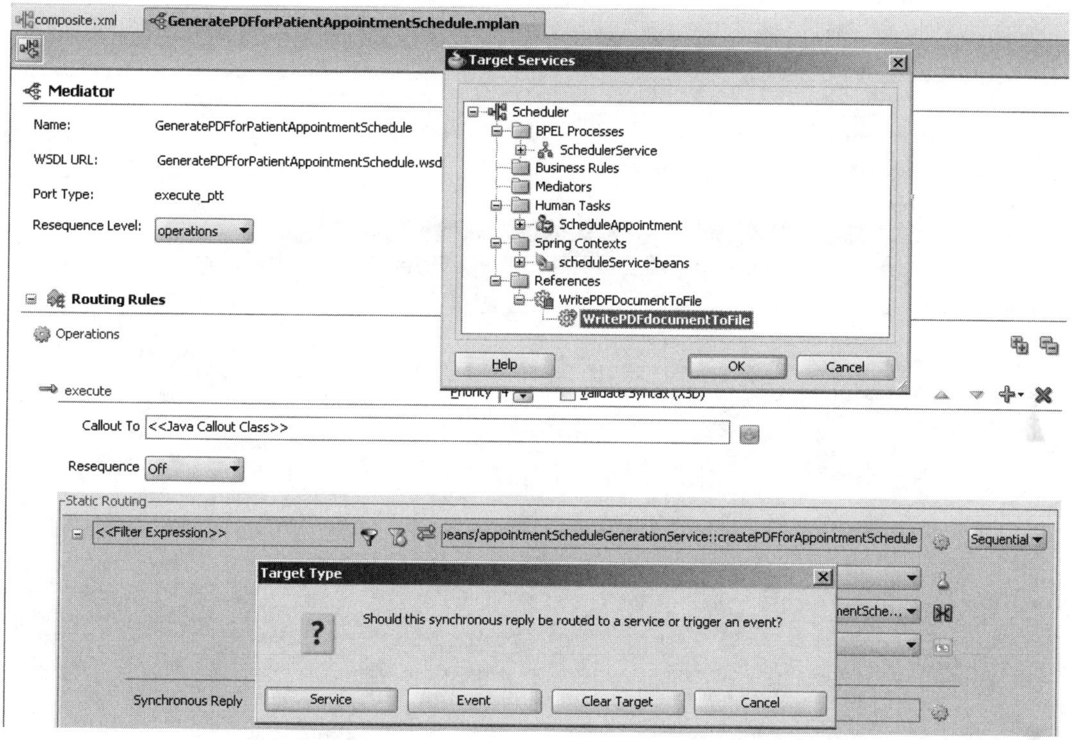

FIGURE 12-13. *Forwarding the reply from the Spring Component to the File Adapter Service*

Open the GeneratePDFforPatientAppointmentSchedule.mplan file. Open the Source tab and locate the <onReply> element. Insert the following XML snippet between the transform and forward elements:

```
<assign>
    <copy target="$out.property.jca.file.FileName"
        expression="concat('AppointmentScheduleForPatient'
        ,$initial.request/sch:PatientAppointmentSchedule/...
...sch:patientDetails/ap:firstGivenName
        ,$initial.request/sch:PatientAppointmentSchedule/...
...sch:patientDetails/ap:lastName
        ,'.pdf' )"
        xmlns:xpath20="http://www.oracle.com/XSL/Transform/java/...
...oracle.tip.pc.services.functions.Xpath20"
        xmlns:sch="http://stmatthews.hospital.com/Scheduler"
        xmlns:ap="http://stmatthews.hospital.com/patient/AppointmentProcess"
        />
</assign>
```

FIGURE 12-14. *Creating the mapping for the reply from the Spring Component to the File Adapter Service*

We assign a value to the header property called [$out.property.] jca.file.FileName. The value we assign is taken from the $initial.request and is the concatenation of a static string and the first and last name of the patient. Notice how we need to define the namespaces in order to extract the correct elements from the initial request message.

Invoke the Mediator from the BPEL Component   Open the Composite Editor. Create a wire from the Scheduler BPEL component to the Mediator GeneratePDFforPatientAppointmentSchedule.

Open the BPEL editor for the Scheduler component and add an Invoke activity immediately after the task switch. Wire the Invoke to the partner link that was created for the wire to the Mediator and then have a local input variable created.

Add an Assign activity to initialize the input variable. Use two copy steps to populate the two elements patientDetails and scheduleDetails in the input for the Mediator from the BPEL variables inputVariable and outputVariable. Then close the BPEL editor.

And Action: The SchedulingService Composite Generates PDF Documents

Open the Composite Editor. Click the File Adapter Service and open the property inspector. Set a proper value for the property CENTRAL_PDF_DIRECTORY (for example, c:\temp).

Next, deploy the composite application to the SOA Suite in the familiar way. Test the SchedulerService with proper patient details. It is an asynchronous service with a human task inside, meaning you will not get a response in the FMW control test window. Open the Worklist application, log in as Maggie, and check out the tasks assigned to her. Process the Schedule Appointment task that has been assigned as a result of the call to the SchedulerService. Fill in some meaningful scheduling details, save the data, and click the OK button to complete the task.

We can check the flow trace for the Scheduler instance to see whether it has completed—and successfully so. Also, we can verify on the file system whether the expected PDF is indeed written to the central PDF directory that we have configured—with the customized filename we specified through the header property (see Figure 12-15).

Leveraging the Outbound EJB Binding

An Enterprise Java Beans binding adapter reference allows an SOA composite application to invoke Enterprise Java Beans through RMI. The EJBs that are invoked in this way can be SDO enabled, or they can be defined through a (remote) Java interface.

The EJB binding reference is configured through the EJB Adapter Wizard. The wizard asks for the JNDI lookup name for the EJB, the Java Remote EJB interface, whether the EJB binding is WSDL (SDO) based or Java based, and in the former case the WSDL that describes the service provided by the EJB. The parameters sent into the EJB service and returned by it in that case are SDO types, which means they are described in an XSD that follows the SDO specifications. Because we have the parameter definitions generated for us, it is not a large burden to work with these SDO-enabled EJBs. However, it means that we have to morph the EJB into a shape that the EJB adapter can work with—and it requires us to manipulate the EJB, which may not be possible at all. Working with a Java (interface)–based EJB binding is usually the easier option.

NOTE
The online chapter complement has a detailed example of using the SDO-based EJB binding, as well as the step-by-step instructions and screenshots for creating the EJB binding based on a Java interface, as described next.

Create the EJBs and Configure the EJB Adapter Reference

We will go through two sets of steps: First, we create and deploy the EJB Session Bean. Second, we create a simple SOA composite application that calls upon the EJB to perform its mathematical wonders.

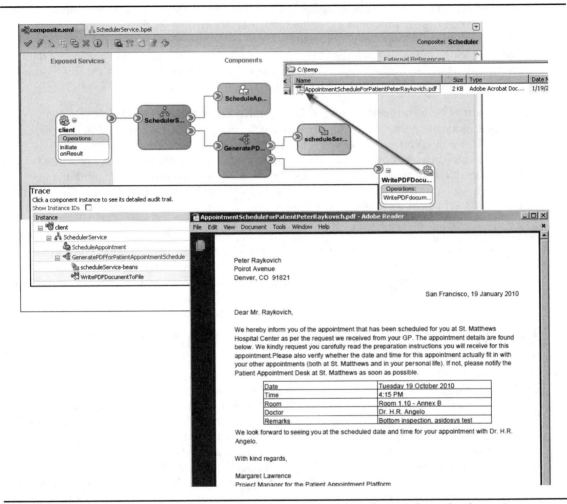

FIGURE 12-15.   *This instance of the Schedule composite produced a PDF letter for the patient.*

Create the EJB Session Bean

The steps for creating what is probably the world's simplest and least useful EJB Session Bean are as follows: To begin, open JDeveloper and create a new generic application. Create a generic project as well. Create a new EJB Session Bean from the New Gallery—Category Business Tier, Node EJB. The Create Session Bean Wizard appears. Enter **HospitalCalculatorEJB** for the name, set HospitalCalculatorBean as the mapped name, and accept all other defaults. Click Next. The Bean class is to be called HospitalCalculatorEJBBean, in the package hospital. Click Next and indicate that only a remote interface is to be created—called HospitalCalculatorBean. Click Finish. The class and interface are now generated, with some annotations.

Now, open the interface and add a single method signature:

```
public interface HospitalCalculatorBean {
    public Float calculate(int a, int b, String operation);
}
```

Go to class HospitalCalculatorEJBBean and add the implementation for the method calculate (for now, a very simple one):

```
public Float calculate(int a, int b, String operation) {
    return new Float(a+b);
}
```

Right-click the Session Bean in the project navigator. Select the option Create EJB JAR Deployment Profile. Enter a name and click OK three times in a row, accepting all defaults. Deploy the application according to this profile, using the Application Server connection that you also use for deploying SOA composite applications. Target the application at the soa_server1 server in the domain.

This next step is entirely optional: When deployment is done, you could try out the new remote EJB. When you select the option New Sample Java Client from the context menu on the EJB Session Bean class, you can let JDeveloper create a new project with a Java class that looks up the EJB in the remote server and invokes the method it publishes. Through a tiny bit of code editing, you can have this class write the result of the EJB invocation to the console.

With the EJB deployed and running, we can continue to create an SOA composite that will consume it.

Develop the SOA Composite with EJB Adapter Reference

We will create a simple SOA composite application from scratch—to have a clear view on what is needed to configure the EJB adapter reference that calls out to the Session Bean.

First of all, create a brand-new SOA application in JDeveloper—say ConsumeHospitalLogic, with a fresh project with that same name. Copy the Java interface HospitalCalculatorBean.java to the SCA-INF\src directory in the ConsumeHospitalLogic application (and remove the EJB annotation @Remote).

Open the Composite Editor. Drag the EJB Service Adapter from the Component Palette to the References lane (see Figure 12-16).

The Create EJB Service dialog appears. Enter the name for the reference (for example, **HospitalCalculatorBean**). Enter the JNDI name (binding name) for the EJB; you may know the name from the annotation in the EJB itself or from the sample Java client you generated earlier on for the EJB. Alternatively, you can browse through the JNDI tree for every server running in the SOA domain of our WebLogic instance and locate the binding name of Enterprise Java Beans. Browse to the Java interface that is the remote EJB interface (hospital.HospitalCalculatorBean) and select it. Select Java as the interface rather than WSDL, and then close the window.

An earlier version of JDeveloper scrambled the values you entered into the dialog a little. They did not end up quite correctly in the composite.xml file. To make sure that the right values

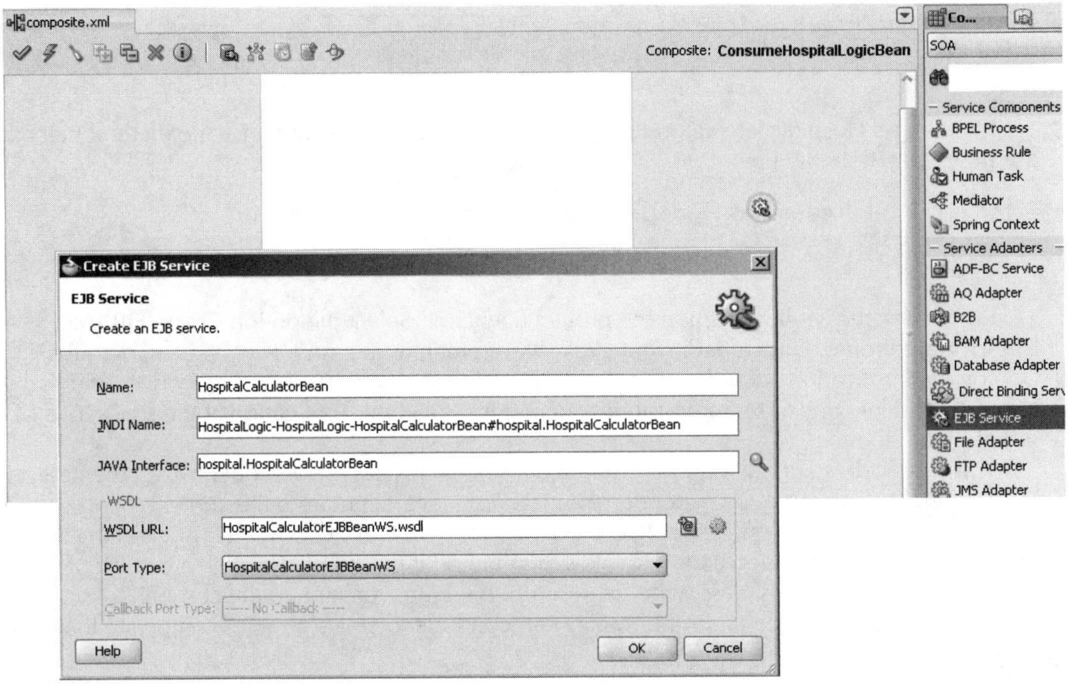

FIGURE 12-16. *Adding an EJB Service Adapter for HospitalCalculatorBean to the References lane of the composite*

are in the reference element, you should inspect this element on the Source tab of the composite.xml editor. Make sure that the value for the javaInterface is set.

```
<reference name="HospitalCalculatorBean">
   <interface.java
      interface="com.stmatthews.hospital.utilities.HospitalCalculatorBean"/>
   <binding.ejb
      uri="HospitalCalculatorBean#...
                     ...com.stmatthews.hospital.utilities.HospitalCalculatorBean"
      javaInterface="com.stmatthews.hospital.utilities.HospitalCalculatorBean"
      ejb-version="EJB3"/>
</reference>
```

The most important part is done. Let's create an XSD document that will underpin the service we are about to publish. It should define a request element called calculationRequest, with two operandi of type int and one string operator, and a response element called calculationResponse with a single float value.

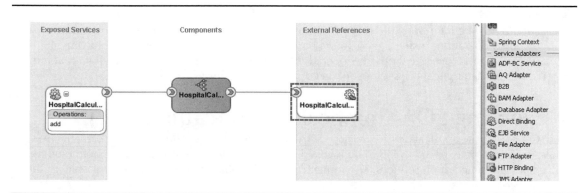

FIGURE 12-17.   *The SOA composite application that consumes the EJB HospitalCalculatorBean*

Now add a Mediator component called **HospitalCalculationService** that is exposed as a synchronous SOAP service at the composite level. Generate the WSDL for the Mediator's service based on the two elements defined in the XSD. Close the window and then wire the Mediator to the EJB reference. The composite application now looks as illustrated in Figure 12-17.

Open the Mediator editor. Create the mappings for the calculationRequest and calculation Response elements to the XSD elements generated for the EJB binding.

Deploy the composite application to the SOA Suite as always. We can now call the SOA composite application to help us with complex calculations as demonstrated in Figure 12-18; under the covers it will leverage the Enterprise Java Bean. To accomplish this, we did not have to adapt the EJB that is invoked, nor did we have to manually create XML mappings or derive WSDL files describing the Java interface.

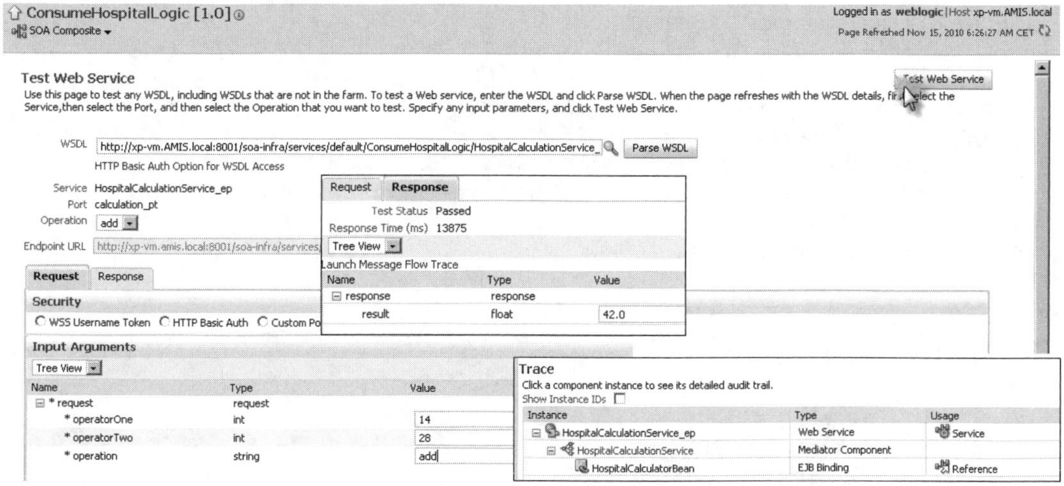

FIGURE 12-18.   *Testing the composite ConsumeHospitalLogicBean in FMW Control*

Next Steps

It would now be interesting to see if we can extend the logic of the HospitalCalculatorBean with additional operations (using the operation parameter to pick the operation), redeploy the EJB application, and leverage these new operations when testing the Web Service without touching the composite application; see the online complement for this next step.

Exposing SOA Composite Applications as EJB

SOA composite applications can expose SOAP Web Services—via binding.ws. Alternatively, services can be exposed as EJB to be invoked over RMI. SOA composites can use both binding. ejb and binding.adf on services. The former supports communication in native Java objects; the latter communicates with XML messages.

Inbound EJB Binding

To expose a composite application as an EJB, we need to define a Java interface that describes the contract for the EJB. You probably also need to create Java domain classes or Bean types describing the structure of the input and output of the methods on the EJB (which should correspond with the operations available in the composite application).

Next, create an EJB binding in the Services lane, based on this Java interface. Specify the JNDI name for this EJB; the EJB will be published on the WebLogic server when the application is deployed. You probably have to go to the source of the composite.xml to add the javaInterface attribute, which is often not set by the wizard.

Create a Mediator to connect the EJB binding to the rest of the composite application. When this wire is added, JDeveloper will create a WSDL for the inbound EJB binding, based on the Java interface and the domain objects. Next, create the mappings in the Mediator for the request and response message. When the composite application is successfully deployed, the EJB with the specified JNDI name will be listed in the JNDI tree in the WebLogic Administration Console and is ready to be invoked from a Java client.

```
public class RemoteSOAServiceClient {
public static void main(String [] args) {
  try {
    final Context context = getInitialContext();
    MyJavaInterface myJavaInterface =
(MyJavaInterface)context.lookup("JNDINameOfSOACompositeEJB");
    System.out.println("The result: "+myJavaInterface.getResult("hello world");
  } catch (Exception ex) {
  ex.printStackTrace();
  }
}
private static Context getInitialContext() throws NamingException {
    Hashtable env = new Hashtable();
    env.put( Context.INITIAL_CONTEXT_FACTORY
           , "weblogic.jndi.WLInitialContextFactory" );
    env.put(Context.PROVIDER_URL, "t3://localhost:8001");
    return new InitialContext( env );
  }
}
```

Inbound ADF Binding

There is another way to invoke an SOA composite as an EJB via RMI. This other way is through the binding.adf binding type. The main difference with the inbound EJB binding is that we communicate in terms of XML (over RMI) with the SOA Suite's generic Client API—and not directly to a service-specific EJB. We will expose the PatientDataService using this type of binding and then create a client to invoke this composite using binding.adf.

Expose the binding.adf Service

To begin, open the PatientDataService composite application. This application exposes services to retrieve data for a specific patient and to create a new patient. The former is to be exposed with binding.adf in order to make available to Java clients for invocation over RMI.

Open the composite.xml file. The service element named client describes the SOAP interface for retrieving patient data. Copy this element and configure the clone as binding.adf (based on the same WSDL):

```
<service name="PatientDataServiceEJBClient"
         ui:wsdlLocation="PatientDataService.wsdl">
    interface="http://stmatthews.hospital.com/patient/PatientDataService...
                            ...#wsdl.interface(PatientDataService)"/>
  <binding.adf serviceName="ejbPatientDataServiceClient" registryName=""/>
</service>
```

NOTE
The values for the attributes serviceName and registryName are not used in this example.

Deploy the composite with this new service of type binding.adf.

Create a Java Client for Calling the Composite Through Binding.adf

Create a new application and project. Add three libraries to the project: WebLogic 10.3 Remote-Client, SOA Runtime, and Oracle XML Parser v2. Create a class called **PatientDataService** that uses the Locator() class in the SOA Suite Java Client API.

```
private Locator locator = null;
...
private void prepareLocator() {
 Hashtable jndiProps = new Hashtable();
 jndiProps.put(Context.PROVIDER_URL, "t3://localhost:8001/soa-infra");
 jndiProps.put(Context.INITIAL_CONTEXT_FACTORY,
 "weblogic.jndi.WLInitialContextFactory");
 jndiProps.put(Context.SECURITY_PRINCIPAL, "weblogic");
 jndiProps.put(Context.SECURITY_CREDENTIALS, "weblogic1");
 jndiProps.put("dedicated.connection", "true");
 // connect to the soa server
try {
 locator = LocatorFactory.createLocator(jndiProps);
 } catch (Exception e) { }
 }
```

The salient part of the getPatientDetails method that interacts through the Locator with the SOA Suite and the PatientDataService is shown in part here (the complete source is shown in the online chapter complement):

```
...
prepareLocator();
Composite composite=null;
try {
composite = locator.lookupComposite("default/PatientDataService!1.0");
} catch (Exception e) {
}
Service service = composite.getService("PatientDataServiceEJBClient");
NormalizedMessage input = new NormalizedMessageImpl();
String uuid = "uuid:" + UUID.randomUUID();
input.addProperty(NormalizedMessage.PROPERTY_CONVERSATION_ID, uuid);

String inputPayload =
"<ns1:PatientDataServiceProcessRequest xmlns:ns1=\"http://stmatthews
.hospital.com/patient/PatientDataService\">\n"
 + "<firstName>"+firstName+"</firstName>\n"
 + "<lastName>"+lastName+"</lastName>\n" +
"</ns1:PatientDataServiceProcessRequest>";
input.getPayload().put("payload", inputPayload);
NormalizedMessage res = null;
try {
res = service.request("process", input);
} catch (Exception e) {
e.printStackTrace();
}
 Element payload =
      (Element) res.getPayload().get("payload");
}
```

Summary
The various service engines in the SOA Suite can run composites programmed in BPEL or BPMN, execute business rules and human tasks, and perform message routing and transformation through the Mediator. And still, that may not be enough. There may be a need to extend the functionality available in these engines using custom Java logic. This chapter explained how we add fine-grained Java functionality to Mediators (through Java callouts) and BPEL processes (using Embedded Java). We then made things much more interesting through the introduction of the Spring (Context) service component, which can expose Spring Beans as services that can be invoked within and even exposed from composite applications and that can call upon other service components that are injected to satisfy the dependencies of these beans.

In addition to adding functionality implemented in Java to composite applications, there are various ways for these applications to interact with external Java-based partners. One of the technology adapters in the SOA Suite is the JMS Adapter. This adapter caters to interaction with JMS queues and topics, both inbound and outbound. JMS is commonly used in Java and JEE applications for communications.

The EJB Binding Service Adapter makes it possible for composite applications to invoke externally exposed Enterprise Java Beans. Both SDO-enabled EJBs and regular EJBs can be called from SOA composite applications. The services exposed by the composite application itself can also be published as an EJB to allow Java clients to invoke the composite via RMI. The (inbound) EJB Binding and the ADF Binding are the two ways to expose an EJB interface—the first publishes a specific EJB and communicates in Java objects, whereas the second leverages the SOA Suite Java Client API using XML messages communicated via RMI.

The next chapter introduces the Oracle Service Bus—a product that adds support for even more communication protocols to our SOA infrastructure.

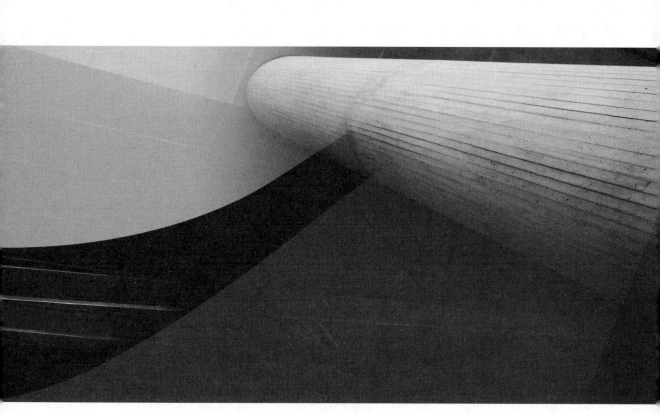

CHAPTER
13

Enterprise-Level
Decoupling with Oracle
Service Bus

hapter 2 introduced Service-Oriented Architecture and stressed the importance of decoupling in order to achieve BAD (Business Agility through Decoupling). In that chapter we also discussed the concept of an enterprise service bus (ESB) as a concept to manage all the connections (including message format and service location) between services and service consumers. The ESB facilitates interactions between potentially very disparate partners—without coupling them in a tight, inflexible manner.

An enterprise service bus in general adapts between the different realms that interacting partners may be living in—for example, in terms of security, physical location, business terminology and data structure, synchronicity, enterprise, and communication protocol. The ESB exposes services in ways that make them accessible to many and diverse potential consumers. As such, the ESB is a main factor in promoting reuse of services.

The Mediator component in the SOA Suite fulfills a role that comprises a number of the characteristics of an ESB: The Mediator facilitates interaction between partners that speak in potentially different data structures, protocols (WS vs. PL/SQL vs. RMI), and synchronicity. It does content-based message routing and makes a contribution to service virtualization—that is, hiding the exact service implementation and its physical location from the service consumer. Together with technology adapters, it also enables interaction across technology stacks—such as file system, database, and messaging infrastructures.

However, the Mediator plays its role primarily locally—between components in the same SOA composite applications and to a limited extent between composites in the same SCA domain. A true enterprise service bus is ideally introduced to mediate between different SCA domains within the enterprise and to connect the enterprise's composites to the outside world, and vice versa. Such a bus may also provide enterprise-level capabilities in areas such as security, handling peak loads through throttling, load balancing, and result caching.

In Oracle SOA Suite 11g—this enterprise service bus with true enterprise scope is provided through the Oracle Service Bus (OSB), which is shown in Figure 13-1.

NOTE
Many of the examples in this chapter are described in more detail and with many illustrations in the online chapter complement. When you want to follow through these examples, refer to this online complement.

Introducing the Oracle Service Bus

The Oracle Service Bus appears to all its consumers as a provider of a possibly very large number of services, exposed as HTTP-based Web Services, SOAP, and RESTful, as well as via JMS and e-mail interaction. What goes on inside the OSB and how it interacts with the "real" services that do the actual work is hidden from view—as it should be in a decoupled world. The services exposed by the OSB are called Proxies (or Proxy Services). They are invoked by clients as services for all intents and purposes, but they are really nothing but the store front. Inside the OSB there can be a lot of activity going on in the flow from consumer to the underlying services that do the actual work—called *business services*—and on the response's way out, as shown in Figure 13-2.

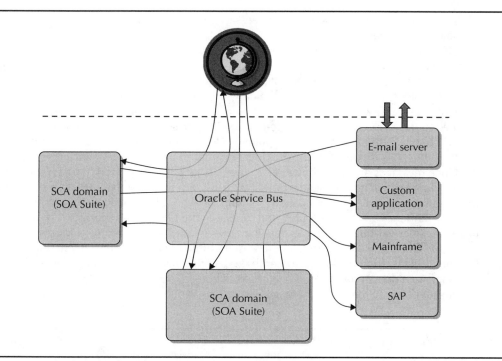

FIGURE 13-1. *The Oracle Service Bus is the two-way insulation layer between various SCA domains, other applications, and enterprise resources and external partners.*

Functions Performed by the Oracle Service Bus

Before the OSB can do anything, it first needs to properly receive a request message from a service consumer—either synchronously via a call or asynchronously through, for example, fire-and-forget or message polling. It is capable of receiving messages from a variety of transport protocols such as HTTP(S), e-mail, JMS, RMI (for EJB), FTP, and File System. OSB 11*g* also debuts "Java on the Bus"—native EJB 3.0 transport for inbound proxy and outbound business services and the ability to transmit native Java types and Service Data Objects (SDOs) through message flows

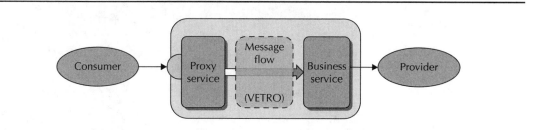

FIGURE 13-2. *OSB exposes proxy services that connect through a message flow (including routing and transformation logic) to business services.*

(no serialization to XML DOM objects necessary). The native Java objects can be passed along to JMS and Java callouts.

OSB can, of course, return response messages via those same protocols, and it can itself invoke services along those protocols. OSB has support ("native transport") to Tuxedo, Oracle Data Services Integrator, and SOA Suite, among others.

The contents of the messages are typically presented inside the OSB message flow as if they are XML messages, with header body and optionally MIME attachments. Non-SOAP messages are mapped to this paradigm—including e-mail bodies, messages in binary format, JMS messages, and REST-style requests with JSON or plain text. The processing in the message flow has easy access to header variables that provide metadata about the message.

Once messages are safely delivered to the bus, an ESB is expected to be able to perform several standard operations (see Figure 13-3). Most definitions of the term *enterprise service bus* include the so-called "VET(R)O pattern" that an ESB should implement. This acronym stands for Validate, Enrich, Transform, (Route), and Operate. The OSB has support for this integration pattern besides various other patterns, such as fan-in and fan-out, fire-and-forget, and so on. Note that the SOA Suite Mediator component is more limited when it comes to enrichment and has less functionality than OSB in the other three departments. This is partially due to the fact that OSB can store data in intermediate variables, whereas Mediator is mostly stateless when it comes to data—it does not have the concept of temporary variables.

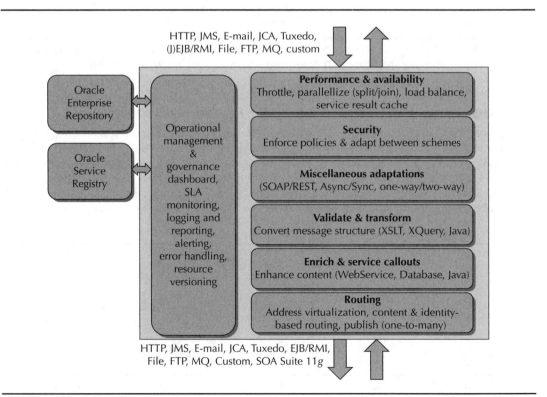

FIGURE 13-3. *Functions performed by an enterprise service bus such as the Oracle Service Bus*

Validation

Validation is supported, too, in OSB—again, like transformation, on various levels. The message can be validated as a whole against an XSD schema definition. However, it is also possible to define validations for smaller sections of the message, or even individual elements, also using XSD definitions.

Validation results can be stored in temporary variables, used for conditional flow logic or the updating of the message headers, for example. Alternatively, an error handler can be specified that may send alerts, report the error, or perform other actions. The use of temporary variables is a major boon in OSB over Mediator, not only for use with validation, but also for complex transformations and enrichments, to name but two circumstances.

Enrichment

One of the differentiators between the Mediator component and the OSB is the latter's capability to enrich a message both on the way in and on the way out. The OSB can invoke Web Services, query a database, or execute custom Java logic to get hold of data that is subsequently used to update the message. Existing message elements can be removed or have their contents replaced. New elements can be inserted into the message.

Complex and extensive enrichments are easier to implement and are typically better performing when executed in OSB.

Transformation

An important function of an ESB is the transformation of messages from the incoming structure to the structure required for invoking the business service(s). In Chapters 2, 4, and 7 we discussed the canonical data model (CDM) as the 'esperanto-like' enterprise-wide language for XML messages. The OSB will frequently transform incoming messages to and outgoing messages from the CDM-based structure.

OSB provides "any-to-any" mapping and uses XQuery as the primary transformation mechanism. Additionally, XSLT can be used, as well as custom Java transformation code. MFL (Message Format Language) is an Oracle proprietary XML-based language that is used to describe the format of a non-XML text document (similar to the Native Format created in JDeveloper to create a structured description for the presentation of plain-text documents read or written by, for example, the File Adapter). MFL can be used in XQuery transformation to map non-XML to XML, and vice versa.

It is easy to perform multiple transformations on a message or on selected parts of a message. OSB supports the use of variables in a message flow, making it possible and straightforward to do complex calculations and conditional processing. With OSB we can manipulate individual elements in messages. Note that these message manipulations can be performed both on inbound, intermediary messages and on outbound messages.

Other transformations to be performed on messages include those between communication protocols, message exchange patterns (synchronous to asynchronous), security protocols, and business dictionaries.

Operate

The Operate action in the VET(R)O pattern refers to the primary function of the ESB: the delivery of the message from the consumer through invocation of the target service or an interaction with the target application. OSB can have a message flow invoke a so-called "business service" using the many transports we discussed earlier for inbound messages. Additionally, or alternatively, it can use service callouts to Web Services or custom Java code.

Note that a single message flow can use multiple calls to external services to compose the response message. This means that we can use OSB to implement composite services from elementary or at least finer-grained services. This is another important distinction with the Mediator—which is not capable of implementing composite services (that is the role of the SOA composite as a whole). However, OSB is not suitable for service orchestration like BPEL is; its strength lies in short-timed interactions, not long-running processes. We can define error handlers at various levels to take actions that work around a problem, retry an operation, or send out alerts to have the administrator resolve the situation.

Routing

One aspect of routing is that a certain routing path can be chosen for the message, based on specific conditions such as contents of the message, the meta-information in the header or the identity of the requestor: content-based routing. OSB supports dynamic selection of the business service to invoke as well as the transport protocol used for the invocation. Note that the transformation to perform is dynamically selected depending on the target service that is to be invoked.

An advanced form of content-based routing can be achieved when, for example, the target database or database schema to access is dynamically determined, based on the content of the request message. This can be done by OSB in conjunction with the database adapter by setting the jca.db.DataSourceName header property. The book's wiki has a reference to a resource describing this special type of dynamic content-based routing.

Message Exchange Patterns

OSB supports various MEPs (message exchange patterns) or integration patterns—as well as the adaptation between some of them. This means that the proxy service exposed to consumers by the OSB may adhere to one style (say, asynchronous request and response) while the business service that is invoked itself has a synchronous request and response interface.

The messaging paradigms supported by the OSB include synchronous request/response, asynchronous publish to one consumer (fire-and-forget queue style), asynchronous publish to many consumers (fire-and-forget topic style), and asynchronous request/response.

Security

OSB has its own security framework that is based on WS-Policy. Security policies based on the WS-SecurityPolicy (WSSP) 1.2 specification (for transport only) or on the Oracle proprietary Web Services security policy schema can be attached to proxy services and business services. Through these policies, OSB can be instructed to enforce authentication (establish identity), authorization (establish and enforce access rights), encryption (for confidentiality), and signing (to verify integrity) on messages. (More on security in Chapter 15.)

In addition to the ability to enforce security policies itself, OSB can adapt between different security schemes when calling a business service. OSB can, for example, decrypt the messages received from the service consumer to perform validation, enrichment, transformation, and routing. It can then pass the unencrypted message to the business service—or encrypt in the way mandated by that service. OSB can forward the identity token from the service consumer, converting it if necessary from Basic HTTP Authentication to a SAML token, for example.

OSB can thus be used to add a security layer on top of business services that do not have any security constraints enforced: OSB exposes proxy services with the appropriate policies applied against them. OSB enforces the authentication, authorization, and so on, and only when the request satisfies the requirements will the (unsecured) business service be invoked. Oracle Web Service Manager implements a similar decoupled security approach—with more specialized focus obviously than Oracle Service Bus.

However, OWSM (Oracle WebServices Manager) is a component of SOA Suite 11*g* and is the preferred method for securing Web Services in either OSB or the SCA container. In the absence of OWSM, OSB is the preferred approach, using the patterns described earlier. Chapter 15 describes the use of OWSM.

Speeding Up and Slowing Down

The load on a particular service may be evenly spread out over time. No peaks—just a steady, constant flow of request messages. However, it is more likely that the load varies over time, with specific peaks at possibly even predictable moments. Note that the (web) service can become the object of denial of service (DoS) attacks, just like websites.

OSB supports throttling for business services. This means we can specify the maximum number of concurrent requests that can be sent to a business service. When there are more requests than that number, the remainder is moved to a queue and then sent to the business service when previous requests have completed. We can specify an expiration time for messages in the queue, waiting for processing by the business service.

Also, the total number of requests in a given timeframe may be regulated. You might specify that a particular service consumer can access a proxy service 100 times an hour and then specify that all requests exceeding that rate are returned with exception information.

Note that neither the SCA container nor the Mediator component has out-of-the-box defense mechanisms against peak loads of request messages. You can resort to queuing mechanisms such as JMS and AQ to decouple the destination composite from the incoming message flow, but that is a lot of additional work.

Speeding Up Using Split-Join   Almost the opposite of throttling is the use of Split-Join to speed up the processing of individual messages. Split-Join is used to process multiple small parts from the same message in parallel threads (split) before merging the results back together (join). Split-Join can be static (fixed number of branches) or dynamic (the payload of the message dynamically determines the number of branches).

St. Matthews could expose a service from the OSB that external healthcare organizations can invoke to request a number of appointments for multiple patients at once. Using a Split-Join in the message flow for this service, we can have each individual appointment request processed—in parallel with the others. Each request results in an appointment identifier; all appointment identifiers are joined back together in a single response message.

The Split-Join is somewhat similar to the Flow and FlowN activities in BPEL processes.

Service Pooling or Load Balancing   Multiple endpoint URIs (physical locations) can be configured for business services that are invoked from the message flows. This allows OSB to spread the load over multiple instances of the business service, using the selected load-balancing algorithm—such as round-robin, random, or random-weighted. Multiple endpoints are also useful to cater for downtime: When one endpoint is unavailable, OSB can be configured to revert automatically to one of the other endpoints.

Service endpoints that are removed from a pool (usually because they are not available due to network errors or a restart of the host machine) can be configured to automatically be reintroduced into the service pool after a specified time has elapsed. The helps to prevent the service pools from shrinking to zero service endpoints. It also eliminates the need to manually reintroduce these endpoints after they have "errored out" of the pool.

Service Result Cache   Some services are called fairly frequently from OSB—multiple times even with the same request message. Service calls can be expensive—in terms of performance overhead and perhaps literally in dollar cost. OSB 11*g* introduced the WebService Result Cache, functionality based on Oracle Coherence. This result cache makes it possible to cache results from service calls in order to reuse those results for subsequent service invocations. This feature is similar to the (PL/SQL) function result cache in Oracle 11*g* Database.

Simply put: When a result is available from a cache, the implementation behind the business service does not need to be invoked to provide the result. This means that the response from the business service is available much faster, near instantaneously, because it only needs to be retrieved from the cache, without burdening the underlying systems. Caching improves response time and decreases the load on system resources. The downside to caching results is that a request to the business service does not return a freshly calculated result but rather a preserved one that by now could be stale.

Operational Management

When in action, there can be a lot of activity in the OSB. It would not be uncommon to have many thousands of service requests per hour, involving dozens of consumers and service providers. Some of the interactions may fall under formal service level agreements, which gives us a special responsibility to guarantee their availability and responsiveness. But even for services that do not have such specific requirements, we probably want to ensure proper functioning.

The OSB has broad support for operational management. It offers a dashboard where (aggregate) metrics can be monitored about the activity in the service bus. This includes the number of invocations of a service, the average response time, recent trends with regard to service invocation and responsiveness, errors reported by error handlers, the status of business services (availability), and many other details.

SLA monitoring can be configured through alert rules regarding response time, number of messages, success and failure ratios, validation errors, and security violations. Note that SLAs apply both to proxy services (the service level the OSB must provide) and business services (the service level we expect from third parties). Alerts can be sent via e-mail, to an SMNP trap, through JMS, and to a custom reporting provider (custom Java code). Messages written by log actions are forwarded to the WebLogic AdminServer log; these can be inspected in the Server Health tab of the Oracle Service Bus Console.

Governance

The Oracle Service Bus can work closely with the Oracle Service Registry (a UDDI implementation) and a separate product from OSB. All OSB proxy services can be uploaded to the OSR and registered/published as services that can be consumed by others. Conversely, OSB can look up services in the registry to consume (business services). When the endpoint of a service in OSR changes and that service is a business service in OSB, then the change is propagated to OSB.

As stated before, the Oracle Service Bus is an important factor in achieving reuse of functionality—by exposing services in ways that make them easily consumable for a wide variety of consumers across the enterprise (typically a wider audience than the average SCA domain and composite application). In Chapter 2, we noted that services can only be reused when people know about their availability and can learn more about their characteristics, such as the functional interface, nonfunctional specifications, and operational metrics. It is important to expose such metadata on the services published from the OSB. One way to do this is through Oracle Enterprise Repository (OER), the tool offered by Oracle to support governance of SOA artifacts. OSB services can be harvested by OER, and through OER those services can be found, inspected, and then analyzed for dependencies and impact of changes. (More on OER in Chapter 18.)

OSB at St. Matthews

Margaret is introducing the Oracle Service Bus at St. Matthews as the bridge from the hospital to external parties (such as health insurance companies and third-party healthcare providers). Any service exposed by the hospital to external consumers will have to be published on the OSB, and likewise any external service that is invoked from within the systems at St. Matthews is to be invoked via the OSB. She is intent on providing this single, central gateway that can be monitored and managed, protected against security threats, and equipped with support for various transports, message exchange patterns, and protocol adaptations.

Through the OSB, for example, general practitioners can communicate via e-mail with the appointment-related services at St. Matthews. And through the OSB, composite applications can interact with insurance companies without each application having to keep track of the whereabouts and characteristics of the services of each individual insurance company. The OSB will help lower costs and speed up execution of applications through the Service Result Cache, which helps eliminate a substantial number of calls to external services that charge a fee per call.

Margaret is not just planning on using the OSB as a bridge between external and internal. She also wants to decouple various business domains from each other. Selected services from SOA Suite instances in various business domains will be published on the OSB, and that will be the only way for a domain to access services in another domain.

Oracle Service Bus Product History and Architecture

The OSB is the next generation of the well-established AquaLogic Service Bus (ALSB), acquired by Oracle when it bought BEA. After the acquisition, Oracle decided to make ALSB its strategic ESB product and proceeded to improve the ALSB with features such as the JCA technology adapters available with the SOA Suite (for example, the Database Adapter). The OSB 11*g* release became available in the spring of 2010—the first release to be (somewhat) integrated with SOA Suite 11*g*. Integration will continue to get tighter over subsequent releases. Oracle Service Bus 11*g* runs on the WebLogic Server and can share a WLS domain with the SOA Suite. However, it can just as easily be installed independently of SOA Suite 11*g*. Figure 13-4 shows the product architecture of OSB 11*g*.

The OSB exposes a browser-based user interface—the OSB Console—that is used for two purposes:

- Operational management, done at run time, by administrators
- Service development and configuration, done at design time, by developers, architects, and administrators

Most of the tasks developers need to perform can be managed through the browser in a multiuser, central repository-based development environment.

Additionally, developers can install Eclipse with the OSB Workshop plug-in to do file-based service development in relative isolation. In this chapter, we will only work through the browser-based console because it is slightly easier to get going with. However, several options are only

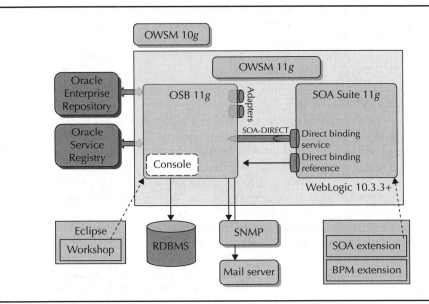

FIGURE 13-4. *The product architecture of the Oracle Service Bus 11g*

available through the IDE, so it is recommended that you get familiar with that environment too. The online chapter complement discusses Eclipse plus Workshop and shows screenshots of the IDE. A (near) future release of Oracle Service Bus will also use JDeveloper as its design-time environment.

Oracle Service Bus 11g runs in the same WebLogic Server (11g, and more specifically 10.3.3 or higher) as the SOA Suite (unlike OSB 10g, which does not run on WLS 11g). Along with the integration of OSB 11g on WebLogic Server 11g and the SOA Suite SCA container comes OWSM integration for OSB with centralized policies. Invocations from the OSB to SOA composite applications, and vice versa, are done using native bindings—the 11g SOA transport direct bindings—rather than as normal Web Services. In the future, the message flow can be traced from composites through OSB services and beyond.

Installation of Oracle Service Bus 11g

It is pretty easy to get going with the Oracle Service Bus. Details can be found in the installation guide and in the online chapter complement.

The main steps involve downloading the OSB 11g installation file, running it, and subsequently running the FMW Configuration Wizard to configure an existing or new WLS domain with the Oracle Service Bus. Ensure that the OSB server listens to a different port than the SOA server.

The installation file also contains the Oracle Enterprise Pack for Eclipse (OEPE), which in turn contains the OSB IDE plug-in.

Note that the SOA Suite 11g license includes OSB, so no separate licenses are required. Also, the decision between using a composite application with the Mediator component versus services on the OSB does not need to be financially driven.

Sending Invoices to Patients Who Had Appointments

The Finance & Accounting department at St. Matthews—which we briefly met in the previous chapter—offers an invoicing service to authorized consumers from various departments inside the hospital. The concept is pretty simple: A consumer sends in details about the patient, the address where the patient lives and the address the invoice should be sent to, and a list of the items for which the patient is to be charged. The F&A department's service will create the invoice, send it, and track its progress to ensure the bill is paid. This is a perfect example of functional decoupling, where the F&A department performs a reusable, encapsulated service for other parties in the hospital.

St. Matthews decides to extend the patient appointment process by adding billing to it. Once the appointment has taken place, the InvoiceService in the back-office system is called to start the billing process. The invoicing service is hosted on a different system in a different business domain, as explained later, and St. Matthews uses Oracle Service Bus to decouple the appointment process from the billing process.

Note that the term *domain* is used in several ways: one is the business domain—an area of related concepts, processes, data definitions, and terminology. Closely related to this conceptual business domain is the more concrete business domain that consists of one or several departments, individuals, systems, and applications responsible for executing the processes and managing the data. Then, of course, there is the WebLogic domain—a separate instance of the application server in potentially a distinct environment.

Decoupling Between Business Domains

An enterprise service bus provides a number of types of decoupling in areas such as security, transport protocols, message formats, peak loads, and message exchange patterns. Services offered to consumers across the enterprise typically require "more" decoupling than intradepartmental services. In this case, it is perfectly possible that some archaic legacy system is wrapped by OSB, its functionality exposed as an ordinary (standardized) Web Service. When the F&A department at some point migrates to a more modern application, it will probably be able to continue offering the same InvoiceService—with OSB then wrapping a completely different underlying application.

We will go through a number of steps in order to create this service. First, we implement a simple Invoice Web Service and then create (or register) a business service in OSB for this InvoiceService. Next, we create a proxy service—the service as we want the rest of the enterprise to see it.

The last step is to connect the business service and the proxy service with a so-called message flow. Figure 13-5 provides an overview of these services and their relation with the OSB.

Implementing the InvoiceService on Behalf of the F&A Department

There are many ways to implement an InvoiceService. We do not have the legacy system at our disposal that the fictional F&A department has. Any implementation will do for the purpose of demonstrating OSB in this chapter. The most simple route is probably to create a Web Service by using a simple Java class that serves as an invoicing implementation, annotating it with JAX-WS annotations, and deploying it to a JEE container. See the online chapter complement for the detailed steps.

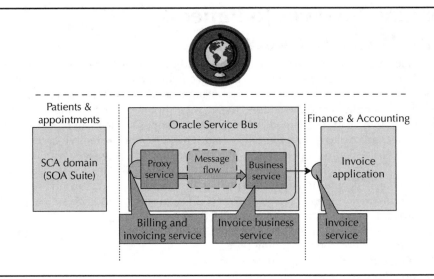

FIGURE 13-5. *The InvoiceService is exposed to other departments through the OSB*

Creating the Invoice Business Service

There are two ways to configure services in the Oracle Service Bus: through Workshop (a plug-in for Eclipse) or through the browser-based console. In this case, we will use the latter.

Access the Service Bus Console at http://localhost:7001/sbconsole and then log in as weblogic/weblogic1 (the default credentials).

All changes made through the console are made in so-called sessions that can be activated or discarded, like database transactions or WLS configuration changes in the WebLogic Server Administration Console. Therefore, before we can start doing anything, we have to start a new session. Click the Create button in the Change Center in the top-left corner of the console.

Create a new project by clicking Project Explorer in the bottom-left corner of the dashboard. Enter the new project name (**InvoiceProject**)and click Add Project. Next, create two folders in the InvoiceProject, called **Resources** and **BusinessServices**.

We need to register the WSDL for the InvoiceService that we want to use in the business service we are about to create. Enter the new Resources folder. Select the option Resources From URL in the Create Resource drop-down list. Enter the URL for the WSDL for the InvoiceService Web Service. Type **InvoiceService_WSDL** as the name for this resource. Indicate that resource type is WSDL and then click Next. In the next page, OSB shows us the resources it will actually import—the WSDL document and the associated XSD. Click the Import button to actually create the resources (see Figure 13-6).

Our next action is the creation of a business service based on this WSDL resource. Navigate to the folder BusinessServices and create a new business service by selecting Business Service from the Create Resource drop-down. Type **Invoice Business Service** as the name of the business service. Select the WSDL Web Service radio button and click the Browse button to open the Select A WSDL Browser. Select the InvoiceService_WSDL. A second window appears in which

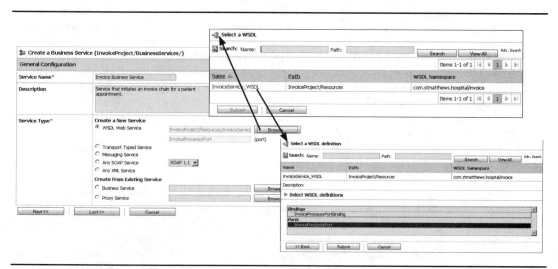

FIGURE 13-6. *Loading the InvoiceService WSDL as a resource into the OSB project*

we need to select the correct port (in this case, the InvoiceProcessorPort). Click the Submit button to confirm this choice (see Figure 13-7).

You can click the Last button to accept all further default values and complete the creation of the service. Alternatively, you can inspect the subsequent steps—HTTP Transport Configuration, SOAP Binding Configuration, and Message Content Handling. On the Summary page, click Save to actually submit the business service definition.

This is a good moment to activate the changes created in the current session. Click the Activate button in the Change Center in the upper-left corner (see Figure 13-8). The OSB Console will present a form into which change notes can be recorded for future reference.

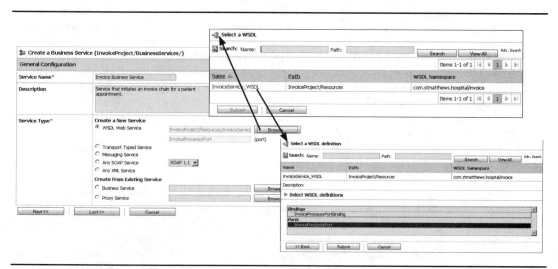

FIGURE 13-7. *Creating the Business Service Invoice business service*

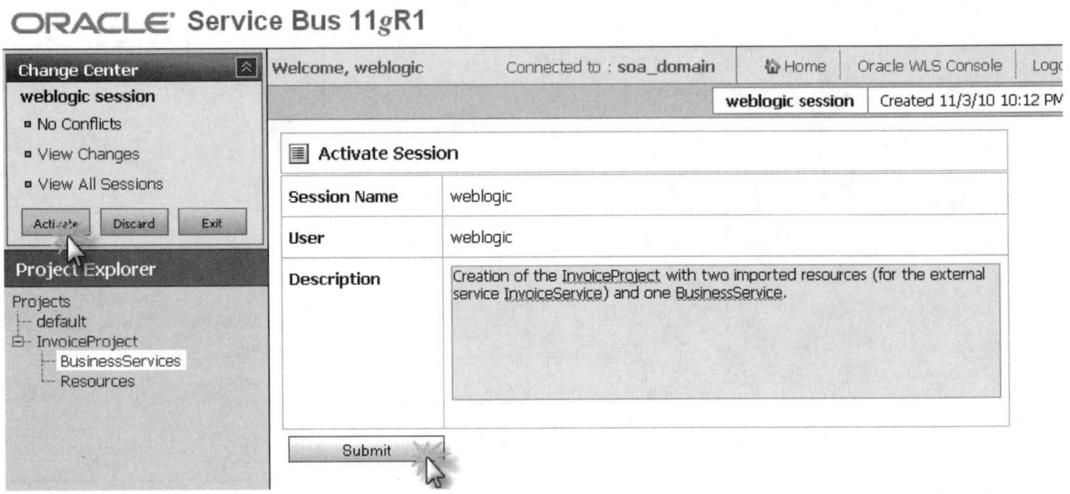

ORACLE' Service Bus 11*g*R1

Change Center ⌃	Welcome, weblogic	Connected to : **soa_domain**	🏠 Home	Oracle WLS Console	Log

weblogic session

- No Conflicts
- View Changes
- View All Sessions

[Activate] [Discard] [Exit]

Project Explorer

Projects
- default
- InvoiceProject
  - BusinessServices
  - Resources

	weblogic session	Created 11/3/10 10:12 PM

📋 **Activate Session**

Session Name	weblogic
User	weblogic
Description	Creation of the InvoiceProject with two imported resources (for the external service InvoiceService) and one BusinessService.

[Submit]

FIGURE 13-8. *Activating the changes in the current session through the Change Center*

Testing the Business Service

The business service we have just created can be tested from within the OSB Console. Open the Project Explorer and navigate to the BusinessServices folder under the InvoiceProject. The "actions" column has a bug-like icon; click that icon for the Invoice Business Service. This will bring up the embedded Test Console. Based on the XSD for the request message, a prepopulated XML document is shown that we can edit to add meaningful data. We can also manipulate the headers that will be sent in the message as well as add attachments.

Click the Execute button to have the service invoked. The Response Message is shown, along with the response metadata (see Figure 13-9). However sparse the response, the business service is working—the custom Java class InvoiceProcessor that implements the service is called and executed.

Creating the BillingAndInvoicingService Proxy Service

Now that the business service is working, it is time to move to the proxy service that will be exposed to consumers in other domains in the enterprise. Despite the fact that the proxy service is primarily a wrapper around the business service, it is still a service in its own right, with its own WSDL and XSD documents. Note that some proxy services call upon multiple business services or even no business services at all.

Select the InvoiceProject in the Project Explorer and create a new session in the Change Center. Next, create a folder called Proxy Services and then enter that folder.

Select Proxy Service in the drop-down for Create Resource. The Create A Proxy Service Wizard appears. Enter the name of the new service: **BillingAndInvoicingService**. Click the radio button Create From Existing Service business service in the Service Type section. Select the Business Service Invoice business service as the example to create the proxy service from. Then click Next. On the second page can we set transport configuration details, such as the protocol through which this proxy service can be accessed ("http" in this case; other options include jca, jms, local, sb, and ws). We can also specify the endpoint URI—the relative part of the URL at which the proxy service can be invoked. Accept the default for now (see Figure 13-10).

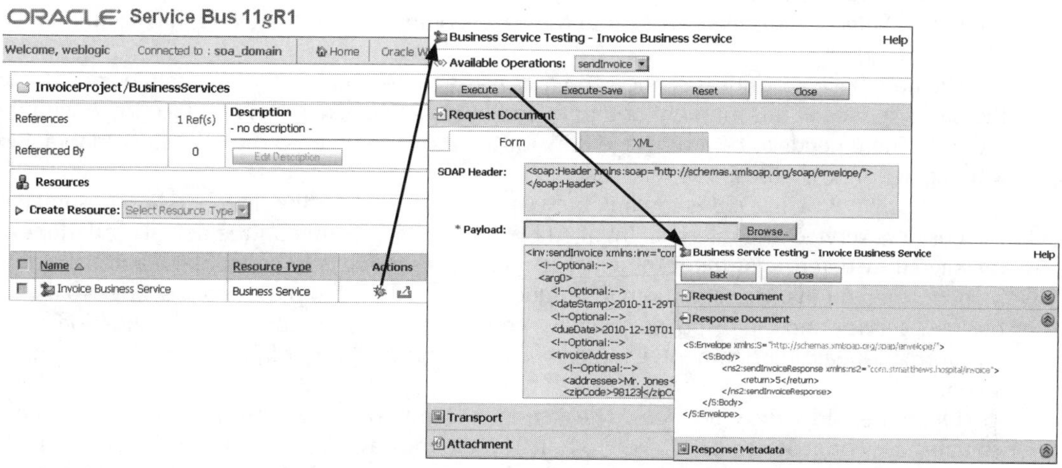

FIGURE 13-9. *Testing the business service*

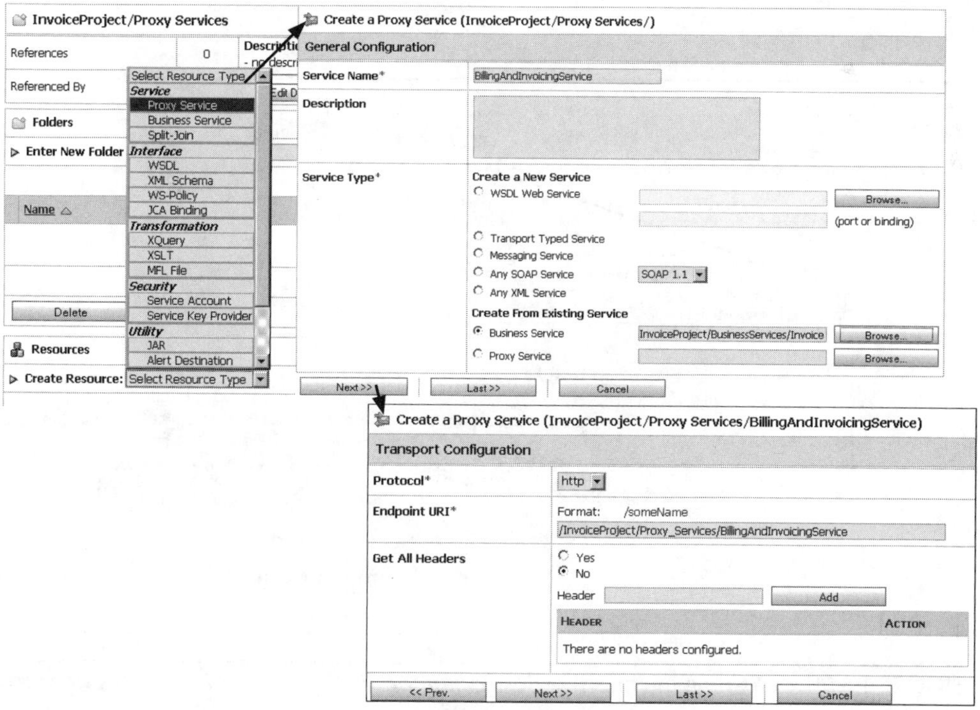

FIGURE 13-10. *Creating the proxy service*

Also accept the default settings on the next three pages—HTTP Transport Configuration, Operation Selection Configuration, and Message Content Handling. On the last (Summary) page click Save.

We now have a business service and a proxy service—but are the two connected? Is invoking the proxy service at this moment bound to end in tears because it has no place to go with the request? There needs to be a message flow for the proxy service—a message flow that includes a Routing action to the business service.

A message flow in OSB is the link between a proxy service (the interface for consumers) and the business service (the interface invoked by OSB to have [some of] the actual work done). The message flow determines the routing (which business service is to be invoked) and the actions to be performed on the message (both the request on its way in from the proxy service to the business service and the response on its way out). These actions can include validation, transformation, and enrichment; various types of reporting; Split-Join for parallel execution; and so on.

Open the folder ProxyServices. The Actions column for the BillingAndInvoicingService contains an icon that can be clicked to bring up the message flow editor (see Figure 13-11).

The message flow starts with the BillingAndInvoicingService start node. It also already contains a node of type Route connected to the business service. This is due to the fact that we created the proxy service based on the business service. If we had created the proxy service based on a WSDL instead of an existing business service, we would have had to create this routing node ourselves.

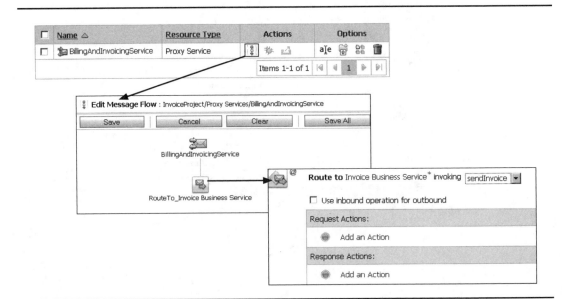

FIGURE 13-11.   *Opening the message flow editor for the BillingAndInvoicingService proxy service*

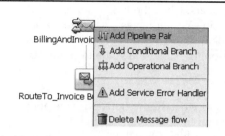

FIGURE 13-12.   *Adding a pipeline pair to the start node BillingAndInvoicingService*

Let's add a Report action to see at least some tangible benefit from having the OSB wrap the business service. Click the start node of the message flow and then select the option Add Pipeline Pair in the pop-up menu (see Figure 13-12).

A pipeline pair explicitly represents both the request and the response message path in a node. A pipeline consists of one or more stages. A *stage* is a container for a collection of related actions. A pipeline can contain multiple stages that may each fulfill a specific function. There are three types of pipelines: request pipeline, response pipeline, and error pipeline. You can add error handlers on the stage level or at the pipeline level. If no error handler is defined, the error will be handled by the default system error handler and results in a SOAP fault.

Click the Request Pipeline node and then select the option Add Stage in the pop-up menu. The stage is added to the message flow, inside the request pipeline. Click the stage and select Edit Stage from the pop-up menu. In the stage editor, click Add An Action and select the Report action from the Reporting menu (see Figure 13-13). This type of action will publish information from each instance of the proxy service; this information can be monitored on the dashboard. We will report the name of the patient for whom we want the invoice to be prepared.

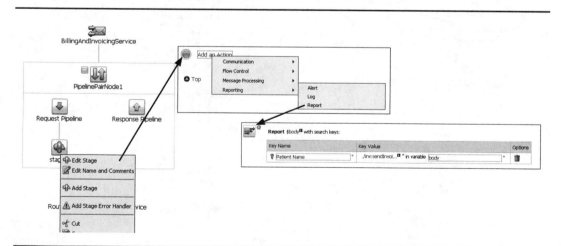

FIGURE 13-13.   *Editing the stage and adding a Report action*

The Report editor appears. Click the link "variable" and enter **$body** as the expression. Note that the dollar sign prefix in OSB indicates a variable. $body is the predefined variable that contains the body (payload) of the message. Enter **Patient Name** as the name of the key. Enter the following XPath expression to extract the value from the "body" variable:

```
./inv:sendInvoice/arg0/patientName
```

Click the Save All button to save the updated stage and message flow. Click the Activate button in the Change Center to commit the changes.

Open the ProxyServices folder. Click the "bug icon" in the Action column for the BillingAnd InvoicingService. The test console appears with the request message. Enter some details for a patient, especially the name of the patient, and then click the Execute button (see Figure 13-14).

The Response message appears, along with the Invocation trace. This trace provides some insight into what went on inside the proxy service.

One of the things that should have happened in the message flow between the entrance of the message in the proxy service and the routing action that invokes the business service is the Report action. The name of the patient must have been reported, and we should be able to find that message report in the dashboard.

Open the Operations tab in the navigator in the left section and then click the Message Reports link. A summary of message reports is displayed. The Patient Name key for the service call we just made is reported here, as shown in Figure 13-15.

You may feel that functionality would be nice to have for SOA composite applications, too. And, in fact, through the composite sensors (discussed in Chapter 16), we have a very similar mechanism.

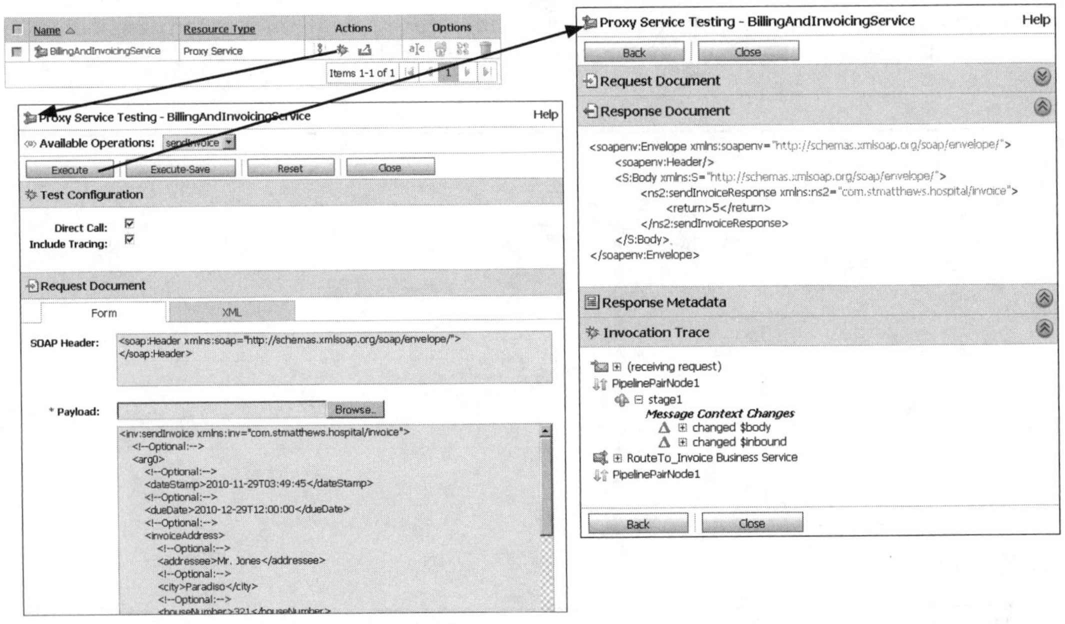

FIGURE 13-14. *Testing the BillingAndInvoice proxy service*

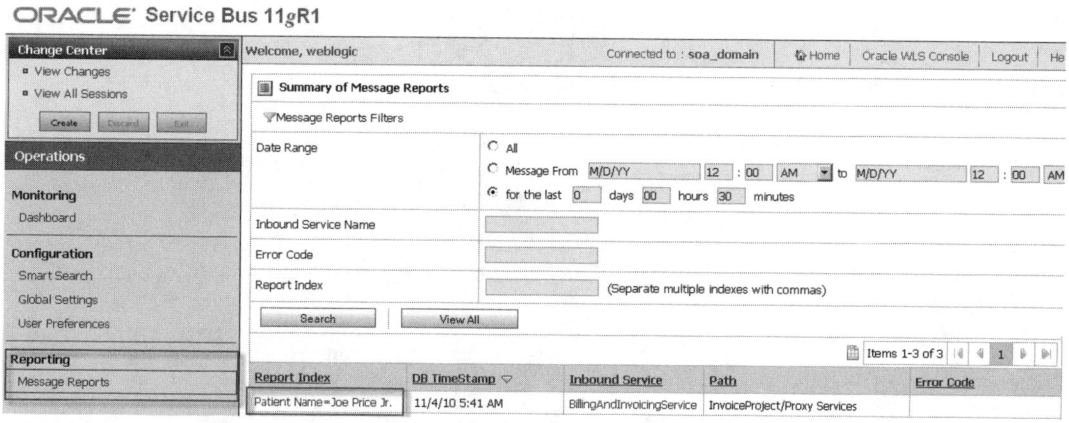

FIGURE 13-15. *Inspecting the result from the report action on the dashboard*

The PatientAppointmentService and External Parties

We created the PatientAppointmentService in Chapter 6—a service that can be invoked to request an appointment for a patient. We assumed at that point that the service would be invoked by general practitioners (GPs) referring their patients to the hospital and other healthcare providers.

However, we have not really given any thought to the fact that it may not be such a good idea to have external parties call into our services just like that. We would effectively open up our back-end systems to third parties, possibly leaving them vulnerable to misuse and attacks such as DoS (denial of service). The first figure in this chapter suggested that a real enterprise service bus be used as gateway between our service domain and the rest of the enterprise as well as the world at large to shield our primary systems.

So this interaction with the world outside of St. Matthews—family doctors calling into the PatientAppointmentService—should be mediated by our enterprise service bus implementation: the OSB (see Figure 13-16).

Apart from the increased security we gain, this also adds decoupling between the composite application and its consumers, the GPs. This insulation layer can help to shield the consumers from changes in the underlying service. The service can easily be exposed by the OSB in alternative ways—for example, through e-mail—that make it even more useful than the current composite-based service already is.

Adding a Virtualization Layer

The Oracle Service Bus is used to add a virtualization layer on top of the existing Patient Appointment Service composite application. This layer can render a number of services, including security enforcement, throttling of peak loads, message enrichment, endpoint

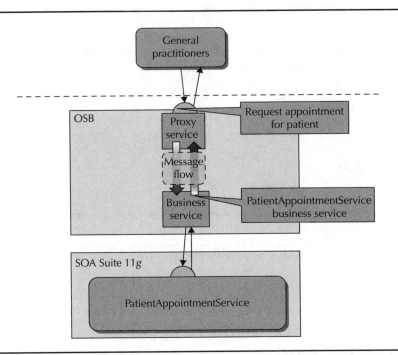

FIGURE 13-16. *OSB virtualizes PatientAppointmentService, decoupling it from external consumers.*

virtualization, validation, and logging. At this point, we are primarily interested in decoupling the general practitioners from the internal services domain—some of these other services are added later on.

Assuming that the SOA Suite is running, with the PatientAppointmentService application deployed and enabled, we will create the proxy service that exposes the RequestAppointmentFor Patient service to general practitioners. In the same vein as the previous section on the InvoiceService, we create a business service that is associated with the process operation on the PatientAppointmentService. We then prepare a WSDL and XSD for the proxy service as a variation on the definitions for the PatientAppointmentService, making life a little bit easier for the external consumers. We create a proxy service called RequestAppointmentForPatient, using the WSDL and XSD that were just prepared. Then we define the message flow for the proxy service, with a transformation step to construct the request message to be sent to the SOA composite application, a reporting step to help trace the incoming requests, and a routing step to invoke the business service configured for the PatientAppointmentService.

When these changes have been activated from the Service Bus Console's Change Center, we can test the proxy service. A call to the proxy service should result in a response, of course, a new instance of the composite application PatientAppointmentService in the SOA Suite, and a report message in the dashboard in the console.

Configuring the Business Service

Create a new project in the OSB Console and create a new session in the Change Center. Then click the Projects node in the Project Explorer and enter the name for the new project: **PatientAppointments**. Create the folders Resources, BusinessServices, and ProxyServices for this project.

Select the folder Resources and create a new resource as "Resources from URL"—just like we did in the previous section. Enter the URL for the WSDL for the PatientAppointmentService (which you can retrieve from the FMW Control). Specify the name for the resource, PatientAppointmentService_WSDL, and select WSDL as the resource type. Click Next. The Load Resources Wizard shows the selected WSDL document, along with two more WSDLs and three XSD documents; these are the (nested) dependencies for the WSDL of the PatientAppointmentService. We will accept the fact that we need all these resources. Click Import. When the Import operation is completed successfully, activate the current change session in the Change Center.

Finally, navigate to the folder Business Services. Create a new resource of type Business Service. Enter **PatientAppointmentService Business Service** as the name and provide a description. Select the radio button WSDL Web Service and select the WSDL resource we just created. Select the (only) port in the WSDL. Then click the Last button and click Save in the Summary page. Activate the changes in the Change Center.

Using SOA-DIRECT Transport to Access SOA Composite Application

Any Web Service can be accessed from a business service in OSB in the way described earlier. However, services exposed by SOA composite applications can be accessed in a much more direct way: The SOA-DIRECT transport provides native connectivity between Oracle Service Bus and Oracle SOA Suite service components. This native connectivity offers many advantages over using the normal, formal, SOAP-based Web Service transport. Among these are performance—the SOA-DIRECT transport is more direct, RMI-based, with less XML serialization and communication abstraction. This transport supports WS-Addressing, including optional auto-generation of ReplyTo properties for asynchronous callbacks. It also does identity and transaction propagation—and eventually propagation of the ECID conversation ID that will allow the FMW Enterprise Manager console to present a true end-to-end message flow trace. SOA-DIRECT can handle attachments and supports connection and application retries on errors.

In order for the PatientAppointmentService business service to be able to use the SOA-DIRECT transport, the SOA composite application PatientAppointmentService needs to expose a Direct Binding Service interface—in addition to or instead of the SOAP Web Service binding that it currently exposes. To do this, open the Composite Editor. Drag a direct binding from the list of service adapters and drop it in the Service lane. Specify **Direct_PatientAppointmentService** as the name and select the existing PatientAppointment Service.wsdl as the WSDL. Wire this service binding to the BPEL component (see Figure 13-17).

Back in OSB, we need to create a WSDL resource based on the WSDL of this new Direct Binding Service interface. To get hold of this WSDL, open the URL http://localhost:8001/soa-infra/ in a browser (replace "localhost" with the host that runs your SOA Suite environment). The page that appears lists all services and WSDLs exposed by the soa-infra application, including the one for Direct_PatientAppointmentService.

(Continued)

Next, create a new business service. Call the service **Direct PatientAppointmentService**. Select WSDL Web Service as the service type. Select the WSDL resource you created based on the corresponding Oracle SOA Direct Binding Service WSDL, and choose the appropriate port or binding. The protocol setting on the Transport Configuration page already defaults to soa-direct based on the selected binding in the WSDL and accesses the Direct Patient AppointmentService over the native WLS T3 protocol rather than SOAP/HTTP.

This business service can, of course, be called from the RequestAppointmentForPatient proxy service in exactly the same way as the not-so-direct PatientAppointment business service; it is totally transparent to proxy services how the business service they invoke does its stuff.

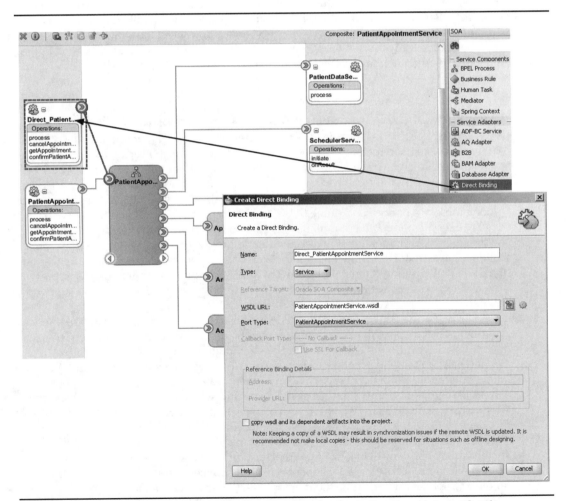

FIGURE 13-17. *Creating the Direct Binding interface for the PatientAppointmentService*

Defining the Proxy Service RequestAppointmentForPatient

The service that we will expose to general practitioners will be somewhat friendlier and more to the point than the current internal one. The WSDL specifies a proper operation name—RequestAppointment—instead of the meaningless *process* that accidentally slipped in as the default operation exposed by any BPEL process. Additionally, the schema definition for the request message has been redesigned—not complicating the message with multiple sets of contact details, for example.

This short paragraph is actually not trivial. It states the fact that St. Matthews will be decoupling the service consumer from the technical and application (BPEL) specific implementation details. This is a fine example of decoupling that directly leads to increased agility in the future.

Create a new session in the OSB Console. Navigate to the Resources folder in the Patient Appointments project and create a new resource of type Interface/WSDL. Enter the name for the resource—**RequestAppointmentForPatient_WSDL**—and select the file RequestAppointment ForPatient.wsdl. Finally, click the Save button.

The file is uploaded and the resource created, although with a validation error because of the missing XSD document on which the resource has a dependency. Create another new resource, of type XML Schema Definition, and upload RequestAppointmentForPatient.xsd as RequestAppointmentForPatient_XSD. Next, go to the RequestAppointmentForPatient_WSDL resource and edit its references: Select the XSD resource as its dependencies. With the validation error resolved, activate the session in the Change Center.

Next, we need to create the proxy service. Create a new session, go to the ProxyServices folder in the Patient Appointments project, and create a new proxy service. Specify the name—**RequestAppointmentForPatient**—and provide some description. Click the radio button WSDL Web Service and select the WSDL resource that was just uploaded. Select the PatientAppointmentServiceBinding—the only binding available in the WSDL document—and click the Last button. Then click Save in the Summary page and activate the session.

Defining the Message Flow for the Proxy Service

We have set up the business service—wired to the service exposed by the SOA composite application running in the SOA Suite—and the proxy service with its own public and friendly WSDL and XSD. The two are entirely unrelated at this point. Time, therefore, to add a message flow to the proxy service—a message flow that this time will have to do more than just route to the business service, although that is still an essential part of its job.

We will have to transform between the request message that is received by the proxy service and the message that must be sent to the business service. Transformations in OSB can be done using XSLT, XQuery, or a combination of the two. We will use a combination—primarily just to demonstrate how that is done. The XSLT part of the transformation is prepared outside of OSB, using the Mapping editor in either JDeveloper or Workshop (or in vi or Notepad if you are feeling brave). This file must now be loaded from the file system to the OSB, just like previous resources were loaded, such as WSDL and XSD. Create resource RequestAppointmentForPatient_to_ PatientAppointmentService_XSLT in the Resources folder of the Patient Appointments project, based on the file PatientAppointmentRequest_to_AppointmentServiceRequest.xsl.

Go to the ProxyServices folder. Click the message flow icon in the Actions column for the RequestAppointmentForPatient proxy service. Click the start node (RequestAppointmentForPatient) to add a Route node. Call this node **InvokePatientAppointmentService**. Click the node to edit it. Add

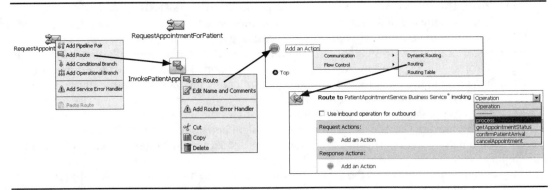

FIGURE 13-18. *Configuring the Route node in the message flow for the proxy service*

an action of type Routing/Route. Then, select the process operation on the PatientAppointmentService business service as the target for the Route node (see Figure 13-18).

Click the start node (RequestAppointmentForPatient) again to add a pipeline pair. Click the Request Pipeline node to add a stage. Call this new stage **Prepare Request Message for Business Service**. Click the stage to start editing in order to add actions, and then click Add Action and select the Message Processing/Assign action (see Figure 13-19).

We will first configure the main transformation in the message flow using this Assign action and a subsequent Replace operation. To configure the Assign, click the expression link. Click XSLT Resources in the XQuery/XSLT Expression Editor. Click the Browse button and select RequestAppointmentForPatient_to_PatientAppointmentService_XSLT. Type the XPath expression **$body/*[1]**. This refers to the first element in the body variable. Click the Save button to confirm these settings.

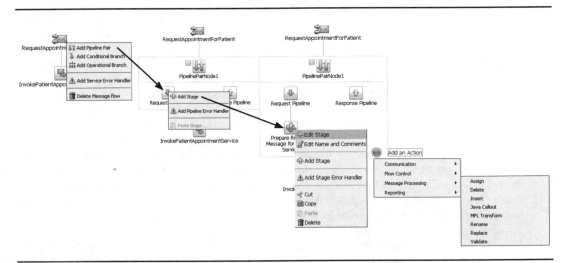

FIGURE 13-19. *Adding a pipeline pair, stage, and the first Assign action to the message flow for the proxy service*

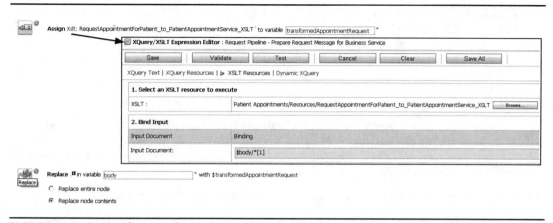

FIGURE 13-20. *Configuring the Assign and Replace actions that initialize a variable with the transformed request body and replace the body contents with that variable*

Next, click the Assign action to create a new action of type Message Processing/Replace. The name of the variable in which something is replaced is body. The entire contents of the body variable are replaced with the result of the XQuery expression $transformedAppointmentRequest: the current contents of variable transformedAppointmentRequest (see Figure 13-20).

There are two more things to do: The Gender element is set to either male or female in the incoming request, yet the business service expects M or F. A similar situation exists with the PriorityCode: The public service asks consumers to use strings such as lower, normal, and very high to specify the priority, even though the SOA composite expects an integer value in the range 0 to 4. We need to rectify these two.

Because we can create variables in the message flow, extending the transformation with additional steps to manipulate the message that is on its way to the business service is pretty simple—much easier than it would be in the Mediator. Even better, of course, would be to use a Domain Value Map (DVM), as is supported in Mediators. OSB 11*g* initially does not support DVM out of the box, although a later release will.

Updating the Message with the Proper Value for Gender   Using a temporary variable, it becomes quite easy to set the correct value for gender: Create an Assign action—as the first action in the message flow—and set the expression to the following:

```
fn:substring(fn:upper-case($body/app:PatientAppointmentRequest/...
                ...app:patientDetails/app:gender/text()),1,1)
```

The value should be assigned to a variable called Gender that is to be instantiated by this action. A simple Replace action is then used—after the body has been updated with the transformation result—to update the body with this derived value for Gender. Create a Replace action and set the expression to $Gender. The variable to be manipulated is body, and the XPath expression that selects the element that is to be updated is as follows:

```
./app1:AppointmentServiceProcessRequest/app1:patientDetails/app1:gender
```

Finally, select the radio button Replace Node Contents.

Enrichment of the Message with the Priority Code   The last thing we need to put right is the priority code. The XSLT transformation does not produce a Priority Code element in the body. So instead of replacing (the contents of) an existing node, we have to create a new one, using an Insert action. Create an Insert action as the last action in the stage and set the expression to the following:

```
<app1:priorityCode>{$PriorityCode}</app1:priorityCode>
```

This means that a new element called priorityCode in the namespace indicated with app1 is to be inserted into the document. Its value is set to the value of the XQuery variable PriorityCode.

This new element is to be inserted into the variable body as the first child of the element selected by the following XPath:

```
./app1:AppointmentServiceProcessRequest/app1:appointmentRequestHeader
```

Now you may—or really should—wonder where this variable PriorityCode comes from. Of course, that variable needs to be created in another Assign action to be added as the first action in the stage. This action assigns a value to the (new) variable PriorityCode, using the following expression:

```
fn:replace(fn:replace(fn:replace(fn:replace(
    fn:replace($body/app:PatientAppointmentRequest/app:Priority, 'lower', '1')
,'low','0'),'normal','2'),'very high','4'), 'high', '3')
```

This expression replaces the strings low, lower, normal, high, and very high with the numerical equivalents expected in the business service. It's not pretty and definitely an example of where a Domain Value Map would be preferable. The online chapter complement explains how this could be done with a DVM and some manual steps.

Click Save All to close the stage and the message flow. Click Activate in the Change Center to commit the session and all its changes.

Testing the Proxy Service

Go to the folder ProxyService and click the Test Console icon in the actions column for the RequestAppointmentForPatient proxy service. A prepopulated request message appears that you can refine. Click the Execute button to send the message to the proxy service (see Figure 13-21).

After a few seconds, you should receive the response message from the proxy service with the appointment identifier. Notice anything strange? Look closely: Is this the correct message you get? It is not! We have forgotten process the response from the business service in the message flow—so we are passing the response that arrived from the SOA Suite through to the consumer of the public service. That is not good! Therefore, we need to add another message-processing action in a stage in the response pipeline.

Go to the message flow for the proxy service. Click the Response Pipeline node and add a stage. Call the stage **Create Response Message based on BusinessService result**. Edit the stage. Create an Assign action that sets the variable AppointmentIdentifier with the following value:

```
$body/ap:AppointmentServiceProcessResponse/ap:appointmentIdentifier/text()
```

Before closing the XQuery/XSLT Expression editor with this expression, we first need to create a user-defined namespace by clicking the Add Namespace link. Type **ap** as the prefix and **http:// stmatthews.hospital.com/patient/AppointmentProcess** as the URI for this namespace.

```
Proxy Service Testing - RequestAppointmentForPatient                                    Help
   Back          Close
Request Document                                                                          ⊗
<soapenv:Envelope xmlns:soapenv="http://schemas.xmlsoap.org/soap/envelope/">
    <soap:Header xmlns:soap="http://schemas.xmlsoap.org/soap/envelope/">
    </soap:Header>
    <soapenv:Body>
        <app:PatientAppointmentRequest xmlns:app="com.stmatthews.hospital/public/appointments">
            <app:GPRegistrationNumber>pp
            <app:TypeOfAppointment>Q<
            <app:Priority>high</app:Priority
            <app:LabTestsToRun>Blood pre   Response Document                                                      ⊗
            <app:patientDetails>
                <app:firstGivenName>Willia    <env:Envelope xmlns:env="http://schemas.xmlsoap.org/soap/envelope/" xmlns:wsa="http://www.w3.org/2005/08/addressing">
                <app:lastName>Tacker</a          <env:Header>
                <!--Optional:-->                     <wsa:MessageID>urn:2057FBD06FF211DFBFDA770C14CC37E2</wsa:MessageID>
                <app:gender>male</app:g             <wsa:ReplyTo>
                <app:contactDetails>                     <wsa:Address>
                    <app:street>Main Str                     http://www.w3.org/2005/08/addressing/anonymous
                    <app:housenumber>2                   </wsa:Address>
                    <!--Optional:-->                 </wsa:ReplyTo>
                    <app:city>Hoevelake          </env:Header>
                    <!--Optional:-->             <env:Body>
                    <app:zipCode>3871T               <AppointmentServiceProcessResponse xmlns="http://stmatthews.hospital.com/patient/AppointmentProcess">
                    <!--Optional:-->                     <appointmentIdentifier>120005</appointmentIdentifier>
                    <app:state>TX</app              </AppointmentServiceProcessResponse>
                    <!--Optional:-->             </env:Body>
                    <app:emailAddress>string</app:emailAddress>
                    <app:phoneNumber>string</app:phoneNumber>
                </app:contactDetails>
                <!--Optional:-->
                <app:dateOfBirth>2013-11-23</app:dateOfBirth>
                <!--Optional:-->
                <app:insurancePolicy>string</app:insurancePolicy>
            </app:patientDetails>
            <app:InitialDiagnosisAndFindings>string</app:InitialDiagnosisAndFindings>
        </app:PatientAppointmentRequest>
    </soapenv:Body>
```

FIGURE 13-21. *The call to the public RequestAppointmentForPatient proxy service receives a response with the appointment identifier.*

Create an Assign action that sets the variable AppointmentIdentifierResponse from the following expression:

```
<PatientAppointmentResponse xmlns="com.stmatthews.hospital/public/appointments">
  <IdentifierForAppointment>{$AppointmentIdentifier}</IdentifierForAppointment>
</PatientAppointmentResponse>
```

Finally, add a Replace action that replaces the contents of the body variable with $AppointmentIdentifierResponse (see Figure 13-22).

The request pipeline accesses the business service that makes the call to the currently configured endpoint. It invokes the SOA composite application PatientAppointmentService, which will instantiate a new instance for this appointment request. Note that this instance will continue to be around after the response was sent and long after the OSB service instance has ceased to exist. We will access that same instance later on, using the appointment identifier, to learn about the status of an appointment.

Exporting the Project and Its Resources

The resources that comprise the Patient Appointments project—WSDLs, XSDs, business service, proxy service with message flow—can be exported to a single archive file (a JAR file). This file

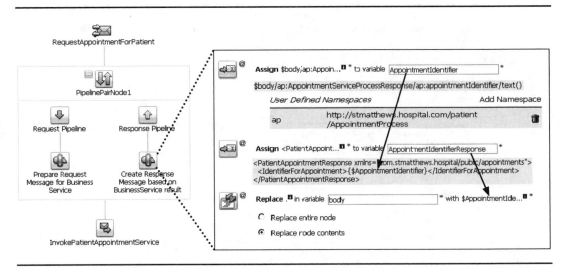

FIGURE 13-22. *Configuration of the response pipeline to produce the proper response message format and content*

can serve as the backup and is also the vehicle for transporting the project to other environments. You also can use it to export projects developed in Eclipse to the run time using the console.

To export the project, you need to go to System Administration in the navigation pane on the left of the OSB Console and click Export Resources. A list of the projects appears—that is, when the radio button Export Projects is selected. Mark the check boxes for the projects that you want to export and then click the Export button. A JAR file with the selected projects is downloaded to your local file system.

Requesting the Appointment Status via E-mail

We have exposed the PatientAppointmentService to third parties as a proxy service on the Oracle Service Bus, firmly decoupled from our internal service domain, with a slightly modified service interface, more aptly named operation, and somewhat improved schema design. The service is still a synchronous SOAP-based Web Service.

St. Matthews has received requests from general practitioners as well as patients who wanted to be able to retrieve the status of an appointment—not by invoking a SOAP Web Service, but simply by sending an e-mail and receiving the information as a reply mail message. This is what we will implement next.

Inbound and Outbound E-mail Transport in OSB

SOAP-based Web Services are fine for computers—but not so much for people when they need to use them directly. The Patient Appointment Service SOA composite application exposes a service from which the status of an appointment can be requested using the appointment identifier as the key. The functionality is valuable and is used by the Patient Portal application, published by

St. Matthews on its website. However, for direct consumption by general practitioners, it is less than ideal as they are not very much SOAP-enabled.

An alternative mode of communication supported by Oracle Service Bus is e-mail transport. OSB can receive e-mails into a proxy service as well as send e-mails from a business service. We will leverage this capability to implement the following scenario: A general practitioner sends an e-mail to a special e-mail address at St. Matthews. The subject of the e-mail ends with a colon followed by the appointment identifier. The GP will receive a reply message, typically after a few seconds, with the schedule details for the appointment. Figure 13-23 shows an e-mail from Frank that is sent to appointmentmanager@stmatthews.com to enquire after the status of appointment 130009; the reply produced by the Oracle Service Bus provides the appointment details.

The implementation of this functionality requires a number of steps: An e-mail server must be up and running. A so-called "service account" must be created in Oracle Service Bus that identifies the incoming e-mail server. A proxy service of type messaging with transport e-mail is configured to listen to this service account for e-mails and process them. The message flow for this service extracts the subject and the sender of the e-mail from the transport headers of the incoming e-mail. It then invokes a business service that is created for retrieving the appointment status from the PatientDataService SOA composite application.

The response pipeline for the proxy service composes the body for an e-mail message from the response from the business service—and indirectly the BPEL process in the SOA Suite—and makes a service call out to a generic e-mail proxy service and send e-mails to a given address with a given content. This proxy service calls the EmailBusinessService to do the actual work; this business service is a messaging service based on the e-mail protocol and is configured to use a preconfigured SMTP server that was set up in the System Administration section of OSB. Although such a configuration has a static endpoint URI—all e-mails are to be sent to the same e-mail address—we achieve dynamic destination e-mail address selection through manipulation of the transport headers in the generic e-mail proxy service (see Figure 13-24).

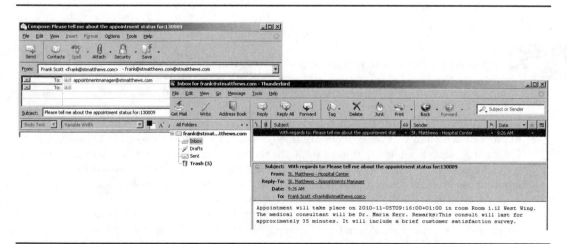

FIGURE 13-23. *A sample e-mail to appointmentmanager@stmatthews.com enquiring after the status of appointment 130009*

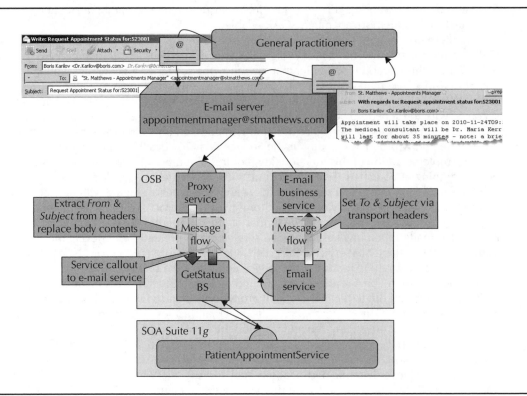

FIGURE 13-24. *Asynchronous request-response through e-mail in OSB*

NOTE
We assume that by now you are accustomed to working with change
sessions *that need to be created and activated in OSB Console, so
these are not explicitly mentioned in the steps described next.*

Preparation for E-mail-based Services

In order to send and receive e-mails, we need access to a mail server—as in Chapters 6 and 10.
On the mail server, we need to have multiple accounts—at least one to send the appointment
status requests from and one to act as the endpoint for service requests arriving by e-mail
(appointmentmanager@stmatthews.com). The wiki provides configuration details for setting up
a local e-mail server with these domains and accounts based on the JavaEmail project.

In order to use an e-mail account as a receiving endpoint for a proxy service, we need to
create a new resource in OSB of type Service Account. Go to the Resource folder for the Patient
Appointments project and create a new resource of type Service Account. Enter **StMatthewsEmail**

as the name and choose Static as the type. The username should correspond with the e-mail account (that is, appointmentmanager@stmatthews.com, with the corresponding password).

To be able to also send e-mails, we need to configure an SMTP server. Click System Administration in the navigator on the left side. Click SMTP Servers and then click Add to create a new SMTP server definition. Enter the name (**LocalJavaMailServer**), the server URL (**localhost**), and the SMTP port number (typically **25**). Depending on the server configuration, you may have to provide a username and password.

Creating the Generic E-mail Service

Sending an e-mail is a fairly generic operation and one that every organization should probably have an enterprise-level service for—a service that takes the e-mail content, subject, and destination as input and sends it on its merry way. Such a generic service is created next. This approach is based on several resources listed on the wiki.

To begin, create a new project called EmailSender and then create an XSD resource called EmailRequest_XSD that describes the input to the generic e-mail service. The source for this XSD should be like this:

```xml
<?xml version="1.0" encoding="UTF-8"?>
<schema xmlns="http://www.w3.org/2001/XMLSchema"
targetNamespace="http://www.example.org/EmailRequest"
xmlns:tns="http://www.example.org/EmailRequest"
elementFormDefault="qualified">
    <element name="Email" type="tns:EmailType"></element>
    <complexType name="EmailType">
        <sequence>
            <element name="to" type="string"></element>
            <element name="subject" type="string"></element>
            <element name="content" type="string"></element>
        </sequence>
    </complexType>
</schema>
```

Creating the E-mail Business Service   Create a business service called **EmailBusinessService**. The service type is Messaging, the request message type is Text, and the response type is None. The transport protocol is e-mail, and we need to provide an endpoint URI even though we will dynamically determine the "endpoint" or real destination e-mail address. Enter **mailto:dummy@ mail.com** as the value.

Select the SMTP server you created previously. Specify the From address—the e-mail account from which the e-mails will be sent: **appointmentmanager@stmatthews.com**. You may specify the From name, Reply To name, and address as the finishing touch. Accept the defaults for other fields and save the changes. If you now activate the change session, you can test the business service to verify whether an e-mail is sent.

This business service will always send the e-mail to the same destination—the endpoint URI we just configured. To send a mail message to a different address, we would have to create a new business service. Alternatively, a much more attractive option is to manipulate the transport headers that are propagated to the business service. We will now create a proxy service that will do precisely that.

Creating the Proxy Service EmailService   Create a new proxy service called **EmailService** and select Messaging as the service type. In step 2, select the XML radio button and the Email element in the EmailRequest_XSD resource for the request message type. Even though this service will not provide a meaningful response, we need to configure some response message type; otherwise, we will not be able to invoke this service in a service callout. Therefore, select XML and any type of element as the response message type. Click the Last button to accept all other default values and then click Save to create the proxy service.

We need to configure the message flow for the proxy service. Click the start node and select Add Route from the pop-up menu. Call the routing node **HaveBusinessServiceSendEmail** and edit the route. Select EmailBusinessService as the target for the routing node. Add a Request action of type Communication/Transport Headers. Select the outbound request as the one to add headers to. Set the Subject header to the expression **$body/ema:Email/ema:subject/text()**, and set the To header to **$body/ema:Email/ema:to/text()**. This last action will override the static endpoint URI and make the business service send the e-mail to the address thus copied. Then add a Message Processing/Replace action that replaces the XPath expression in the variable body with the expression **$body/ema:Email/ema:content/text()**. Finally, select the radio button Replace Node Contents.

This completes the creation of the proxy service. Activate the changes. Now you can test the proxy service—see whether you can send an e-mail to another recipient.

Implementing the RequestAppointmentStatusPerEmail Proxy Service

We will now create a service that is triggered by the reception of an e-mail, calls the Patient AppointmentService SOA composite, and then invokes the generic e-mail service we created in the previous section.

Creating the Retrieve Appointment Status Business Service

Go to the Business Services folder in the Patient Appointments project. Create a new business service called **Retrieve Appointment Status Business Service**. The service type is WSDL. Select the same PatientAppointmentsService_WSDL we used before and then select the port in this WSDL. Click the Last button and save the service definition.

Creating the Proxy Service RequestAppointmentStatusPerEmail

Create the proxy service RequestAppointmentStatusPerEmail in the Proxy Services folder of the project. Select Messaging Service as the service type and then select Text as the request message type and None for the response message type. On the Transport Configuration page, select e-mail as the protocol and set the endpoint URI to **mailfrom:localhost:110**. Click Next to go to the **EMAIL** Transport Configuration page. Select the StMatthewsEmail service account that was created in the preparation section. Note that this service account is specifically linked to the appointmentmanager@stmatthews.com account—the account that this proxy service will be listening to. Accept the default POP3 e-mail protocol setting as well as the other default settings on this page. Click the Last button and then the Save button to create the proxy service.

Open the message flow for the proxy service and click the start node RequestAppointmentStatus PerEmail. Add a Routing node, call it **Invoke_RetrieveAppointmentStatus**, and open the node for editing. Route to the getAppointmentStatus on the business service. Add an Assign action in the

Request Actions section and then assign the following expression to a new variable called **requestMessage**:

```
<app:AppointmentStatusRequest
xmlns:app="http://stmatthews.hospital.com/patient/AppointmentProcess">
   <app:appointmentIdentifier>{$appointmentIdentifier}</
app:appointmentIdentifier>
</app:AppointmentStatusRequest>
```

This variable, $appointmentIdentifier, will be initialized in the pipeline pair that we will add to the message flow.

Add another Replace action—replacing the node contents—that switches the XPath expression (that is a period character) in the variable "body" with the expression $requestMessage.

Next, add a pipeline pair to the start node. Create a stage in the request pipeline called **Prepare Request Message for Business Service** and then create three Assign activities for the variables from, subject, and appointmentIdentifier, with the following expressions:

```
$inbound/ctx:transport/ctx:request/tp:headers/email:From
$inbound/ctx:transport/ctx:request/tp:headers/email:Subject
fn:substring-after($subject, ':')
```

The first two expressions extract information from the incoming e-mail's transport headers. The last expression retrieves the appointment identifier from the e-mail subject based on the assumption that this identifier is formed by everything after a colon.

This completes the request pipeline. Let's turn our attention to the response pipeline. This pipeline is executed when we have first derived the three variables in the request pipeline and then invoked the Patient Appointment Service to retrieve the status of an appointment based on the identifier. The body variable is populated with the status information, and we are ready to invoke the EmailService that will send the e-mail to the original requestor (see Figure 13-25).

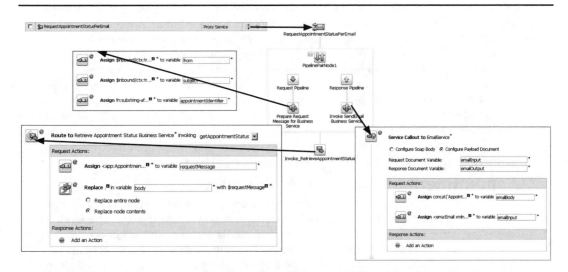

FIGURE 13-25.   *Configuring the message flow for the proxy service with the service callout to the EmailService*

Add a stage to the response pipeline. Edit the stage and add a Communication/Service Callout action that invokes the EmailService proxy service. Note that the service browser will only display a proxy service if it has a response type that is not set to None. Specify **emailInput** and **emailOutput** as the names for the Request and Response Document variables, respectively.

Create two Assign actions in the Request Actions section. The first one is used to set the value of a new variable called **emailBody**:

```
concat('Appointment will take place on '
,$body/app:AppointmentStatusResponse/app:plannedSchedule/...
                          ...sched:AppointmentDateTime
,' in room ',$body/app:AppointmentStatusResponse/app:plannedSchedule/sched:Room
,'. The medical consultant will be '
, $body/app:AppointmentStatusResponse/app:plannedSchedule/sched:Doctor
,'. Remarks:'
,$body/app:AppointmentStatusResponse/app:plannedSchedule/sched:Description)
```

The second one sets the value of the emailInput variable:

```
<ema:Email xmlns:ema="http://com.stmatthews.hospital/EmailRequest">
    <ema:to>{$from/text()}</ema:to>
    <ema:subject>With regards to: {$subject/text()}</ema:subject>
    <ema:content>{$emailBody}</ema:content>
</ema:Email>
```

Here, we also make use of the variables $from and $subject that were set in the request pipeline. This completes the proxy service.

Testing the E-mail Service Interface for the Proxy Service RequestAppointmentStatusPerEmail

We have implemented what we set out to do: Create a service interface that returns the status of an appointment in the form of an e-mail and that can be invoked itself through an e-mail. By sending an e-mail that has the appointment identifier included in the subject (everything behind the colon) to appointmentmanager@stmatthews.com, the service consumer will activate the proxy service that invokes the Retrieve Appointment Status business service—based on the SOA composite application Patient Appointment Service—and then performs a service callout to the EmailService to send an e-mail to the e-mail address from which the initial message was received.

Testing this service is simple: Send an e-mail with an actual appointment identifier to the configured e-mail address and wait for a response message that informs you about the appointment details. Refer back to Figure 13-23 to see the results.

Service Result Caching for the Retrieve Appointment Status Business Service

The status of an appointment consists primarily of the scheduling details: date and time, location, and doctor. When those details have been determined, they rarely change. The service that returns the status of an appointment is a candidate to have its results cached—especially when many calls are made for the same appointment. The steps to enable result caching are fairly straightforward: First, we have to make sure that service result caching is enabled for the OSB instance through a global setting. Then we need to enable result caching for the business service and specify the expression to derive the key from an incoming request message and specify the Time To Live for results in the cache. Let's go through these steps in detail and then see the cache in action.

Enabling Result Caching Through Global Settings

Before we can enable service result caching for any business service, this feature needs to be switched on for our OSB 11*g* instance. In the console, go to the Operations panel and select the Global Settings link. Make sure that the check box for Result Caching is checked.

Configuring Service Result Caching for the RetrieveAppointmentStatus Business Service

Any business service can be configured for result caching. This configuration has a few aspects: Enable result caching for the service, indicate the Time To Live for cached results, and specify the key that identifies the results.

The configuration of result caching for a business service requires us to indicate for how long the results can be considered fresh (and when they should be flushed). The Time To Live can be indefinite or zero (always cache or never cache), a fixed period, or a duration that is somehow calculated from the request or the response message in an XQuery expression.

Every result in the cache is identified by a key. The value of this key is derived from the incoming request message. All messages that produce the same value of this key will get the same value from the cache. When the key for an incoming message does not yet exist in the cache, the business service will execute normally, store the result in the cache, and return the result to the caller. Every subsequent caller with the same key in its request message will get the result from the cache, for as long as it is valid.

Locate business service RetrieveAppointmentStatus in the Business Services folder in the PatientAppointments project. Click the service to bring up its configuration. Click the edit icon for the Message Handling Configuration section to open the edit page for this section (see Figure 13-26). Check the Supported box for Result Caching. Also, specify the expiration time (set it at 30 minutes in this case).

Next, we need to specify the cache token expression. This is an XQuery expression that evaluates to the key that identifies each cache entry. The expression is evaluated against the request message. It should return a string that is unique for every set of input data that should result in a specific response message.

In our case, every status request for the same appointment identifier should result in the same response from the business service. Therefore, the cache token expression should evaluate to the value of appointmentIdentifier:

```
$body/app:AppointmentStatusRequest/app:appointmentIdentifier
```

Requesting the Appointment Status via REST

We have exposed the PatientAppointmentService to third parties as a proxy service on the Oracle Service Bus, firmly decoupled from our internal service domain, with a slightly modified service interface, and now as a standardized synchronous SOAP-based Web Service and with a more human friendly e-mail interface. However, there is call for more: both from internal development teams who are working on web applications that need to expose appointment-related functionality

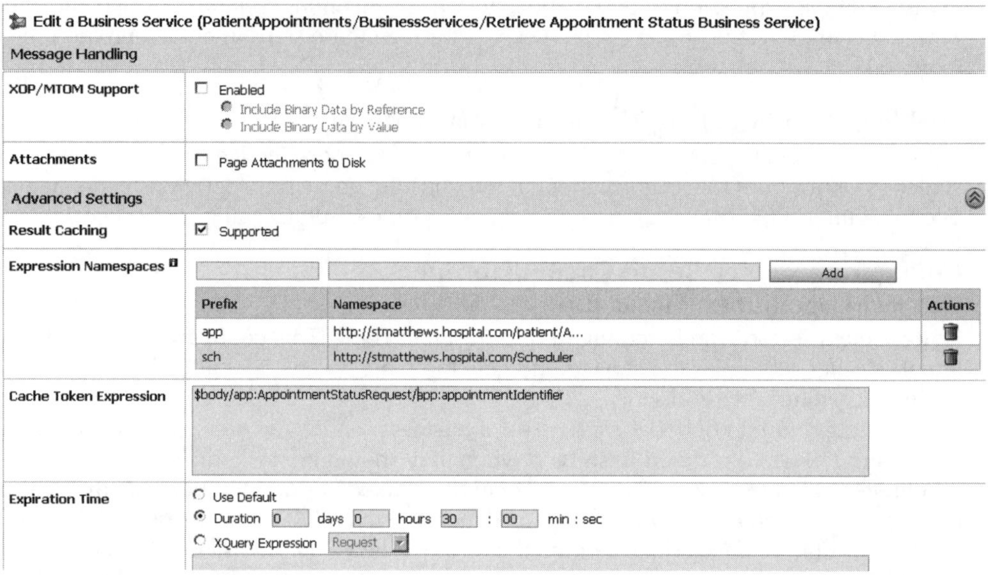

🗐 Edit a Business Service (PatientAppointments/BusinessServices/Retrieve Appointment Status Business Service)

Message Handling	

XOP/MTOM Support	☐ Enabled
	  ⦿ Include Binary Data by Reference
	  ⦿ Include Binary Data by Value

Attachments	☐ Page Attachments to Disk
Advanced Settings	⊗
Result Caching	☑ Supported

Expression Namespaces ⓘ

			Add

Prefix	Namespace	Actions
app	http://stmatthews.hospital.com/patient/A...	🗑
sch	http://stmatthews.hospital.com/Scheduler	🗑

Cache Token Expression	$body/app:AppointmentStatusRequest/app:appointmentIdentifier

Expiration Time	⦾ Use Default ⦿ Duration `0` days `0` hours `30` : `00` min : sec ⦾ XQuery Expression `Request ▾`

FIGURE 13-26. *Configuring service result caching for the RetrieveAppointmentStatus business service*

Alternative Service Interactions

The preceding approach opens up several avenues for direct interaction between end users—and even non-SOAP and XML-oriented applications—and services exposed by the OSB. When the same e-mail account is to be used for different types of requests—for example, cancellations of appointments in addition to status requests—it is good to know that we can use a Conditional Branch node instead of a regular Route node. We can create a message flow that enters one of several branches, depending on the evaluation of conditions that depend on the contents of request messages and the values of header variables. The conditional branch is similar to the Pick activity in BPEL.

Similar effects—but even more dynamic—can be achieved with the Dynamic Routing action, which allows us to specify the service and operation to invoke at run time through XQuery variables. The Routing Table action is another condition-based routing mechanism. Finally, there is the option of an If. Then action, which enables us to specify one or more actions that should only be executed when an expression evaluates to true.

The Service Callout action—and its counterpart, the Java callout—can play an important role, as we have seen, in engaging additional services. This can be used for special communication or reporting needs. However, these actions derive their value primarily from enrichment cases. For example, the incoming message needs to be extended with data that is to be looked up from a service before the business service can be invoked, or the response message from the business service needs to be complemented by data that needs to be retrieved from a service or database. Java callout actions can also provide special transformation capabilities—for example, to turn the JSON format returned by the business service into proper XML. The book's wiki has references to examples of implementing these enrichment scenarios.

as well as from external partners who want to embed "appointment portlets" into their own portal. These teams want a programmatic interface, but feel that full-blown SOAP is too complex for their needs (which may include calling a service in Ajax calls from JavaScript running in a browser). They have asked for a REST-style service to invoke with a simple HTTP GET request that will pass parameters in the URL.

RESTifying OSB Services

Oracle Service Bus will help us expose the Retrieve Appointment Status Business Service (which we created in the previous section and exposed through an e-mail-based proxy service) with a REST-style proxy service.

Inside the message flow, we have access to the (relative) URL used to access the service through the inbound transport headers. This helps us unravel the REST-style resource paths used in the URLs for accessing services.

The steps for exposing a RESTful service interface are relatively straightforward: Create a proxy service called **RESTAppointmentsService** and retrieve the relative URI from the incoming HTTP request in the message flow. We will make RESTful service calls with URLs constructed like this:

```
http://localhost:8011/REST/Appointments/appointmentIdentifier=531001
```

The last part (/appointmentIdentifier=531001) is where the request information is passed into the proxy service.

The relative URI is parsed to get hold of the parameters that may be used for invoking a business service. The online chapter complement describes the detailed steps and demonstrates them in many screenshots. Figure 13-27 shows an invocation of the RESTful service RESTAppointmentsService to retrieve the status of an appointment; this simple HTTP GET request engages OSB and SOA Suite.

Workshop: The Eclipse-based IDE for Oracle Service Bus

In this chapter we do all editing of OSB resources through the web-based console. This is a multiuser, centrally hosted, zero-install (at least on the client) development environment. The console is perfect to quickly get going with OSB.

However, there is an alternative to the console in the form of an IDE: the Oracle Service Bus plug-ins for Workshop WebLogic. This plug-in offers a richer development environment that allows for more interactive, right-click–enabled development activities. The Eclipse environment synchronizes with OSB and the resources worked on in the console through export and import operations. Integration with automated build operations and version control using, for example, Subversion can be done on the file-based resources in Workshop.

Some actions are only available in the Eclipse IDE and not in the console. Examples of these are the creation and manipulation of MFL resources—the Message Format Language used to describe the structure of non-XML resources—and the development of Split-Joins. Additionally, OSB services can be debugged from the Workshop IDE.

Workshop is installed as part of the OSB 11g installation. In the near future it will be complemented with an IDE for OSB that is integrated into JDeveloper. This will make it much easier to use the JCA technology adapters and features such as the Domain Value Map with OSB as well as with SOA composite applications.

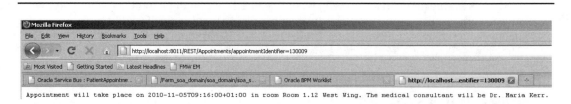

FIGURE 13-27. *Invoking the RESTful service RESTAppointmentsService to retrieve the status of an appointment*

Parallel Processing of Appointment Requests Using Split-Join

External parties can upload files with multiple patient appointment requests, instead of invoking the PatientAppointmentService for every individual request. We showed in Chapter 7 how a File Adapter Service together with a Mediator component took care of these files and every single request in it. The composite application developed in that chapter did not return the list of appointment identifiers to the sender of the file—one of its shortcomings.

Therefore, Margaret and her team have decided to expose a Web Service that allows a number of appointment request messages to be sent in one batch, rather than requiring individual calls for every appointment that is requested. Eventually it may be possible to send a file with the details for all requests as an attachment, either to an e-mail or to a Web Service call, or even as part of an HTTP POST request sent to a REST-style service. However, for now we'll focus on the Web Service call.

We will make use of OSB to expose that multi-appointment request service and enlist its Split-Join capability to still have all or at least a substantial number of appointment requests processed simultaneously. All appointment identifiers that are the result of processing the requests are combined into a single response message.

Parallel and Batch-wise Processing in OSB

Message flows occasionally have several actions that could be executed simultaneously given the logic to be performed: If these actions are, for example, lookups for or calculations on all elements in a collection, with no interdependencies between these operations, there is no logical reason for having these actions performed sequentially. In these situations we can use the Split-Join feature of OSB, which allows us to send message requests to multiple services concurrently and speed up the service's execution.

The Split-Join is a component that can only be called from a business service. It is based on a specific operation in a WSDL resource. Typically, a Split-Join contains a Parallel (static) or For Each (dynamic) node in which the concurrent actions are configured. The last action in these nodes typically is an update of a variable that collects the output for the response message through an Insert action. One thread is created for each path in a Split-Join, allowing for true parallel processing.

Note that a Split-Join must be created in the Workshop IDE and subsequently imported into the OSB console—the console does not support the creation of the Split-Join. The book's wiki has a detailed example of using the Split-Join for processing a batch of appointment requests.

Choosing Between OSB and SCA Composites (and Mediators)

Chapters 4 through 12 described SOA composite applications, built from components such as Mediator and BPEL. This chapter introduced the Oracle Service Bus. There is considerable overlap between the functionality of these two technologies; both can be used to implement similar services. This chapter has suggested a certain use case for OSB—primarily targeting it at mediating between business domains and between the enterprise and external parties. However, OSB can also be used for creating composite services (but not long-running, stateful orchestration!) as well as mediating between various technology stacks, message exchange patterns, and transport protocols. Besides, it has throttling capability, the cache for service results, and the Split-Join feature, which have no immediate equivalent in composite applications.

Sometimes the question will be, Do I use Oracle Service Bus or is it more appropriate to use an SOA composite application with BPEL and/or Mediator components? For a number of cases, the choice is easy to make. For example, if a long-running process is involved, where compensation and business rules are needed, you use BPEL. For large numbers of messages that require minimal response times, OSB seems more appropriate, provided these messages do not initiate business processes, need to invoke business rules, or involve human tasks. In many other circumstances, the choice is not as clear cut and it may well be that a mix of OSB and Composite application is optimal. The next section discusses some guidelines for making this choice.

Rules of Thumb for Choosing Between OSB and SCA Composite

Within the hospital, Mary—the enterprise architect—has heated debates with project developers, project managers, and system administrators about whether to use OSB or SOA Suite with BPEL and Mediator. For project managers and SCA developers, it is easier to use the Mediator (in composite applications) all the time, for all problems. For system administrators, services on the OSB may seem easier to manage because the console supports close monitoring, online redefinition of services, and a wide range of transports, all closely integrated with WLS. The OSB developers think it is easiest to develop everything in OSB.

Mary decides to create some general principles and guidelines for the use of the different tools, based on the goals of the hospital and the practical situation. She has so far come up with the following principles and guidelines:

Guideline 1	Enterprise services are exposed on and called from OSB.
Rationale	St. Matthews wants to standardize communication with external organizations. St. Matthews wants to minimize costs by reusing mechanisms and such. This approach also helps to hide the internal deployment architecture of St. Matthews from the service consumer, which gives the service consumers a single enterprise API for accessing services. It also frees up the St. Matthews operations folks, allowing them to move machines and scale-up service platforms without affecting any of the service consumers. Finally, it gives a central place to apply policies to all externally exposed and invoked services.

Consequences	Services that are called by other organizations need to be exposed on OSB using a proxy service (for example, the appointment service in this chapter that's exposed to general practitioners).
	A department that needs access to an external service has to expose it on the OSB, if it is not already there.

St. Matthews wants to avoid, for example, paying twice for a ZIP code service. In the past, every department that needed a ZIP code subscribed to a commercial service. Every department had logic to read in the data and merge it with the address data from patients, suppliers, and so on. Now St. Matthews only pays once for the service and maintains one OSB service to update the ZIP codes in systems that keep their own address book, and one ZIP code service that returns ZIP codes based on addresses and returns street names based on ZIP codes. Besides, in the future it may switch to another (cheaper, more reliable) provider of that service or implement a home-grown alternative. Such changes should be transparent to service consumers.

Guideline 2	Business services and elementary services that are used across domains are exposed on the OSB.
Rationale	**Flexibility:** It is easier to change a service provider if the consumers call the service from one place (the proxy service).
	Efficiency: It is cheaper to create a proxy once, instead of repeating the process in every Mediator component.
	Quality: We can communicate using the canonical data model on the bus. The consumer can optimize the model to its own specific process or business logic.
Consequences	A service consumer needs a service from another domain and needs to connect to a proxy service on the bus—not to the service directly.
	Services that are reusable in other domains need to be exposed using a proxy service.
	SCA composites that call other composites do so using OSB.

Services that are being used across business domains are exposed on OSB using a proxy service. If an SCA component wants to use this service, it calls the proxy service on the OSB. A typical example is the invoice service we built in this chapter. This service can be called from all the other domains, such as patient communication, patient care, human resources, and so on.

Guideline 3	Specific process logic stays within a composite.
Rationale	If you don't want other consumers to use the service, SCA can make sure these services are not visible.
Consequences	A service that is only relevant for the specific application should be called using a Mediator component.
	Process logic and business rules that are specific to the process and/or the business domain are built using SCA components.

An example is the appointment service. The service that provides the instructions to a patient for preparation for an appointment is very specific to the appointment-making process, and we do not want other consumers outside the business domain to call this service. Therefore, it is not exposed on the OSB.

Summary

The Oracle Service Bus adds functionality to the Oracle SOA stack that is not readily available through other means. This includes support for peak load throttling as well as support for transports such as e-mail, Tuxedo, and JEJB, the Service Result Cache, and several security protocol mappings. However, the importance of the OSB lies more in the fact that it fulfills the Enterprise Service Bus role that was first discussed in Chapter 2. The OSB provides the central decoupling point between the world outside the enterprise and the applications inside the enterprise, as well as between various business domains within the enterprise.

With its native integration from and into the SOA Suite's SCA container and the composite applications running on it, the OSB can mediate between external consumers—either outside the business domain or even outside the enterprise—and the SOA composite or legacy application exposing or implementing the service, and vice versa.

Note that OSB can be used on its own, without the SCA container running SOA composite applications—and the reverse is also true, as we have seen in the previous chapters. The two can complement each other, though, with OSB focusing on a larger scope with multiple parties and the SOA Suite primarily providing interapplication communication within the business domain.

There are no clear-cut, black-and-white rules about the respective roles of the OSB and SOA composite applications in general and the Mediator and BPEL components in specific. That is to some extent for each organization to discover and determine. It is important, though, that every developer realizes that in addition to the service engines already discussed for the SOA Suite, another service implementation option is available through OSB.

The integration of OSB and the SOA Suite SCA container has progressed a lot, but is not yet complete at the time of this writing. Some of the important pieces still missing are the integrated design time that allows developers to create OSB services in JDeveloper and the end-to-end message flow trace presented in a single, unified administration console used for managing OSB as well as SOA Suite components. The integration of JCA adapters and the use of Domain Value Maps in OSB, at the present, leave some room for improvement.

The online complement for this chapter has more details on the implementation of the services discussed. It also shows how to use the Workshop IDE plug-in for Eclipse. Additional topics in this online chapter include Split-Join, EJB and JEJB transport, the Service Result Cache, and the use of JCA adapters with OSB 11*g*.

CHAPTER
14

Service Components and Composite Applications According to SCA

ven though the SCA standard may not have been the first thing on our minds in the previous chapters, it has been the foundation for all applications we created in Chapters 5 through 12. Service Component Architecture is the specification that describes how service-oriented composite applications are assembled from smaller service components. SCA provides the guiding principle under the Oracle SOA Suite service fabric onto which the applications are deployed and executed. Thanks to SCA, the introduction of new service components (such as OSB and BPMN) is relatively straightforward, at least for administrators and developers, because these components are additional pieces of the composite puzzle that are similar in use, composition, and administration. Additionally, SCA makes life much easier for vendors such as Oracle that want to put together a service fabric that can run components on various service engines.

Even though SCA is a widely accepted industry standard, it does not provide portability of composite applications between SCA containers. An SCA application that has been developed for the Oracle SOA Suite will not run on Apache Tuscany or IBM WebSphere. Applications running on those platforms will have a similar structure, using the same SCA artifacts, but leveraging platform-specific service engines and bindings. The portability of developers and administrators across different vendors' SCA containers is much enhanced, though.

This chapter will look at some SCA artifacts to give you an overview of the files generated by JDeveloper during the development of composite applications. It introduces the SCA specification from a technical, bottom-up perspective that will help you understand the purpose of the files and their contents, how you can interpret them, and perhaps manually troubleshoot and edit them.

The second part of the chapter is more on the architecture and the design of composite applications. It will revisit some of the key SOA themes, such as reuse, decoupling, and encapsulation. It will also discuss the question of composite application granularity: How big or small should a composite application be?

Artifacts According to the SCA Specification

SCA is an industry standard that prescribes a structured approach for composing applications from service components. Service components are pieces of (potentially fairly coarse-grained) business logic that are used as building blocks when composite applications are assembled. The composite applications are the reusable functional units that provide meaningful business functionality. We will first look at the building blocks—the service components—and subsequently at the composites. Note, however, that in real life, frequently a top-down approach is adopted, starting from business-oriented functional requirements and drilling down into the actual implementation through various specialized components running in their dedicated engine.

The components, their assembly into composite applications, and their mutual dependencies and interaction within the composites are described in the SCA standard and defined by a series of XML files, created at design time and interpreted by the SCA container at run time. The composite.xml file is the file that describes the composite application as a whole. It is from this file that all other files are directly or indirectly referenced, and it is still this file that the SCA container will interpret first at deployment time.

Service Components

Each service component is described in a document with the .componentType extension. This file specifies the service(s) exposed by the component—through references to portTypes in WSDL documents or alternatively with references to Java interfaces.

However, a service component not only explains what it can do for the world; it also indicates what it needs the world to do in return. Every service component can specify one or more references. A reference is a dependency from within the component that needs to be satisfied. It is similar to the power plug that comes with electrical devices: The device promises to deliver a service, but only when you provide it with an electricity service. For Java developers, this mechanism of advertising a dependency and relying on it to be fulfilled in order to properly function is well known as "dependency injection," as performed by the Spring Bean Container or the JSF managed bean framework, for example.

References are, like services, usually described in terms of a portType defined in WSDLs or a Java interface: The service component describes the interface it needs for an injected service to implement in order to utilize it.

Additionally, a component can advertise the fact that it has properties that can be set by anyone who is including the component in a composite application or doing deployment, or even administering the composite at run time. Note that these various procedures are described in Chapter 17. A property has a name, type, and possibly a (default) value. Typically, the value of a property governs part of the behavior of the component.

Here's an example of a componentType definition, including a service, reference, and property:

```
<componentType xmlns="http://xmlns.oracle.com/sca/1.0"
               xmlns:xs="http://www.w3.org/2001/XMLSchema"
               xmlns:ui="http://xmlns.oracle.com/soa/designer/">

  <property name="preference.birthdateFormat" type="xs:string"
            xmlns:xs="http://www.w3.org/2001/XMLSchema">dd-mm-yyyy</property>
  <service name="PatientDataService" ui:wsdlLocation="PatientDataService.wsdl">

    <interface.wsdl
     interface="http://stmatthews.hospital.com/patient/PatientDataService...
                              ...#wsdl.interface(PatientDataService)"/>

  </service>
  <reference name="PatientRecordProvider.PatientRecordProvider">

    <interface.wsdl
        interface="http://stmatthews.hospital.com/patient/PatientDataService...
                             ...#wsdl.interface(PatientDataServices_ptt)"/>
  </reference>
</componentType>
```

Note that a service component initially is largely an interface definition that contains two types of interfaces: the services provided and the services required (the references that describe the dependencies or injection needs). So far we have not discussed how the service component intends to actually implement the services it promises to provide. The .componentType file does not describe this implementation or even an association with a specific service engine.

A second description of each service component is to be included in the composite.xml file whenever the service component is included in a service composite:

```
<component name="PatientDataService">
  <implementation.bpel src="PatientDataService.bpel"/>
  <property name="bpel.bpel.preference.birthdateFormat">mm/dd/yyyy</property>
</component>
```

This component element specifies a name that corresponds with the <name>.componentType document as well as an implementation. The implementation indicates the service engine that is used to run the service component—for example, BPEL, Workflow (for human tasks), Decision (for business rules), Mediator, Spring, or BPMN—and the source file that contains the actual implementation. Services, references, and properties that are defined in the componentType file are inherited by this component entry. Properties that have been defined in the componentType file can be overridden in the component entry in the composite.xml file.

Service Composites

Components cannot exist on their own—or at least not in the SCA run-time environment. They need to be part of a service composite (application) because that is the unit of deployment and execution. Usually a composite will contain more than just a single component, but it does not have to.

Composites are described through the composite.xml file as per the SCA standard, which is rendered in JDeveloper in the Visual Composite Editor. This composite.xml file includes entries for service components and the wires between these components.

Composite Services

A composite application usually exposes at least one service—a public interface for consumers of the composite. Note that a composite application could have as its only "interface" a component that consumes an event from the EDN. In that case, there is no explicit public service interface.

Multiple services containing multiple operations can be published by a single composite application. A public service exposed by a service composite application is a service published by one of the service components inside the composite that has been promoted to the composite level.

Adapter services are the special case in the Oracle SOA Suite—they provide entrance points into SOA composite applications, but frequently in a slightly indirect way that does not allow for direct invocation. Examples are the file system and database adapters that poll for new files or records and in response initiate a new composite instance with the new or modified data acting as the implicit request message. The JMS and AQ adapter do something similar with messages arriving on a queue or topic.

Composite References

Components declare their dependencies on external resources through references. Some of these references are satisfied by other components within the composite. These references can therefore remain private, hidden from public view—an example of encapsulation. Compare this with a desktop computer that has a motherboard inside with a dependency on electricity—a fact that is not advertised externally because it can be satisfied internally with a wire (quite literally in this case) to the internal power adapter that itself is published as a reference through the power cord that we connect to the power socket.

References that cannot be resolved using other components are exposed by the composite on behalf of those components that are still wanting. These references are promoted—just like services—to the composite level and need to be satisfied when the composite is deployed. At that time, it should be indicated in the composite.xml how those references are to be resolved. Component-level references have to be wired to their provider—which is either another internal component or a composite-level reference that gets bound to an implementation.

Whether or not another component or another composite fulfills the service is mostly determined by aspects such as reuse, encapsulation, and ownership. These design and architectural issues will be discussed in the second part of this chapter.

The next code fragment shows an abridged composite application definition that exposes a service (PatientDataService) and a reference (RetrievePatientRecord). The latter is provided through a database adapter reference and accessed via a JCA binding. A second reference is provided by an EJB (MedicalHistoryEJB) based on a Java interface, rather than a WSDL file. Figure 14-1 shows a visual representation. Note that some of the component-level references are defined in the componentType files rather than explicitly in composite.xml.

```xml
<composite name="PatientServices">
  <service name="PatientRecordService" >
    <interface.wsdl
      interface="...PatientDataService#wsdl.interface(PatientDataService)"/>
    <binding.ws port="..."/>
  </service>
  <component name="PatientDataService">
    <implementation.bpel src="PatientDataService.bpel"/>
      <property name="bpel.bpel.preference.birthdateFormat">mm/dd/yyyy</property>
  </component>
  <component name="PatientRecordProvider">
    <implementation.mediator src="PatientRecordProvider.mplan"/>
  </component>
  <reference name="RetrievePatientRecord">
    <interface.wsdl interface="...RetrieveRecord/#wsdl.interface(
                                       RetrievePatientRecord_ptt)"/>
    <binding.jca config="RetrievePatientRecord_db.jca"/>
  </reference>
  <reference name="MedicalHistoryService">
   <interface.java interface="com.stmatthews.hospital.MedicalHistory"/>
   <binding.ejb uri="MedicalHistoryEJB"
               javaInterface="com.stmatthews.hospital.MedicalHistoryProvider"
               ejb-version="EJB3"/>
  </reference>
  <wire> <!-- promote PatientDataService from component to composite -->
    <source.uri>PatientRecordService</source.uri>
    <target.uri>PatientDataService/PatientRecordService</target.uri>
  </wire>
```

```
<wire> <!-- satisfy reference RetrievePatientRecord in Mediator
      PatientRecordProvider with composite reference RetrievePatientRecord -->
   <source.uri>PatientRecordProvider/RetrievePatientRecord</source.uri>
   <target.uri>RetrievePatientRecord</target.uri>
</wire>

<wire> <!-- satisfy reference in Component PatientDataService with wire to
      Mediator PatientRecordProvider's service called PatientRecordProvider -->
   <source.uri>PatientDataService/PatientRecordProvider.PatientRecordProvider
   </source.uri>
   <target.uri>PatientRecordProvider/PatientRecordProvider</target.uri>
   </wire>
</composite>
```

The wires in the composite.xml file specify how references are satisfied by components or by composite references. The last wire, for example, defines how the dependency on a provider called PatientRecordProvider.PatientRecordProvider—which is specified in the componentType file we saw earlier for the PatientDataService—is satisfied by the service PatientRecordProvider, exposed by the PatientRecordProvider Mediator component (specified in the Mediator's componentType file, which is not shown here).

Wires also indicate the promotion from services exposed by components to the level of the composite. The first wire configures the composite-level service PatientRecordService to be based on the PatientDataService exposed by the (BPEL) component also called PatientDataService. It is only too convenient that we work through the visual editors most of the time, to handle the contents of the composite.xml file and its associates; for example, the structure view shown in Figure 14-2. Note that these files were designed in the SCA specification very much with development tools in mind, and not with the objective to have us manually edit every last byte of these configuration files.

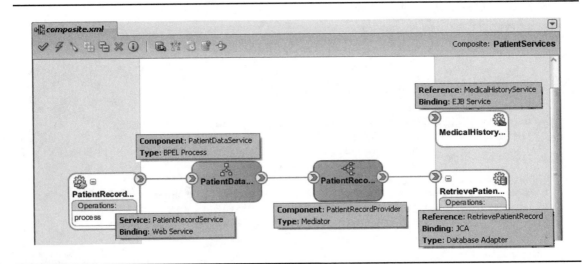

FIGURE 14-1. *Visual rendition of the composite.xml file*

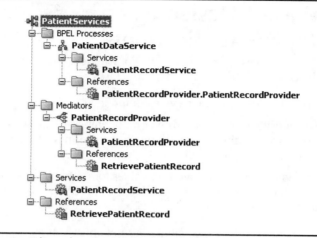

FIGURE 14-2. *Composite Editor showing the structure of the composite in a tree view*

Business Events

Business events were originally not part of the SCA specification. They are currently under discussion for subsequent inclusion. Advancing on that discussion, Oracle has defined its own approach for defining business events in which a component can act as a consumer or a producer (or both) of a business event. Note that the namespace used by Oracle for the SCA-based composite.xml file is http://xmlns.oracle.com/sca/1.0 and not the generic http://www.osoa.org/xmlns/sca/1.0; this is, in part, to cater to the business event notation currently used by the Oracle SOA Suite.

Business event consumption or production is not declared in the componentType files, only in the composite.xml document. That makes sense because business events can be seen as entry or exit points for the composite itself. The following snippet (taken from a composite.xml file) shows an example of a Mediator component that consumes the PatientDataRequestEvent and publishes the PatientDataResponseEvent:

```
<component name="ListenToPatientDataRequestEvent">
  <implementation.mediator src="ListenToPatientDataRequestEvent.mplan"/>
  <business-events>
    <subscribe xmlns:sub1= "http://schemas.oracle.com/events/edl/PatientDataEvents"
               name="sub1:PatientDataRequestEvent"
               consistency="oneAndOnlyOne"
               runAsRoles="$publisher"/>
    <publishes xmlns:pub1= "http://schemas.oracle.com/events/edl/PatientDataEvents"
               name="pub1:PatientDataResponseEvent"/>
  </business-events>
</component>
```

This component exposes neither a reference nor a service, so the only mode of communication for this component is through events. Note that, usually, components that consume an event do not also publish one, and vice versa.

The SCA Way of Designing and Developing Applications

The SCA specification promotes a service-oriented software engineering process—aimed at reuse and flexibility—that consists of a number of steps and tasks:

- Create (a collection of reusable) service components.

- Assemble composite applications from components—and nested composites that are acting as components—that are wired together. Determine which services and references to promote to the composite level.

- Just prior to deployment, set or override values for properties and provide the binding for the composite-level public references. (Note that most SCA containers support run-time management of these values.)

Oracle has implemented SCA in a way that does not entirely agree with this suggested way of working according to SCA, because it does not support the notion of nested composites.

The preceding approach is bottom-up. However, typically we will set out to provide a solution to a business challenge and we are likely to start at the other end, adopting a top-down way of designing the application. We would start with the (reusable) functionality required from the composite application, by defining its services and references (WSDL and canonical data structures) and then drilling down into the individual service components that each implement a piece of the functional puzzle addressed by the composite.

Reuse of Service Components and Composites

Service components are not developed as stand-alone units in JDeveloper. You always create service components in the context of a composite application. At the same time, service components are not available as reusable, stand-alone building blocks that can easily be assembled in various composite applications. A service component in the world of JDeveloper is not readily reused. The level of reuse is the composite. We can now discern the following approaches for reusing an individual service component:

- Expose the service(s) offered by the component at the composite level. A service component that is embedded inside a service composite cannot be reused outside of that composite (internally, it can typically be used by various consumers). However, reuse by external parties can be achieved by exposing the service(s) offered by the component at the composite level.

  Note that the context in which the component performs its duty—in terms of the values of properties and the providers used for satisfying the references—is beyond the control of external consumers of the component because they are determined within the composite that exposes the component. Optionally, the component can expose some of its properties or binding characteristics in the service interface, allowing consumers to influence such settings in service calls.

- Create a service composite that contains a single service component and exposes the service(s) exposed by the component. This new composite containing the reusable component can be invoked (or reused) from multiple composites; however, as just mentioned, this means we cannot set properties or bind references specific to the usage of the service component in a certain composite.

■ Create a service component, as just described, and copy (yikes!) the component resources into each composite application in which you want to reuse the component. Needless to say, this is not ideal, because maintenance becomes quite nightmarish when a change to the component needs to be distributed to all instances of that service component, in possibly many different composite applications. Reuse should not be about duplicating components. Therefore, this third option is really not an option after all (just so you know).

The second option is really the only one if you want to properly organize reuse. The first option, which has one composite application expose multiple independent services, will give us problems when these services turn out to have disparate security requirements and release schedules, versioning needs, SLAs, and so on. In general, an identified reusable piece of functional logic warrants its own composite application. You may need to intellectually "promote" the service component to become a full-fledged service and thus a stand-alone composite.

Nested Service Composites

The Service Component Architecture specification describes the notion of nested composites. This means that a service component in one composite application can have another composite as its implementation, at least according to the SCA specification. Oracle has chosen not to implement this particular aspect of SCA—and is even trying to have the specification altered and have this multilevel nesting removed. Two arguments Oracle has used for justifying this course of action are that the mechanism of nesting service composites is too complex for developers and application assemblers, and that nesting may produce infinite loops. It also argues that nesting is not necessary because service composites can be reused by simply invoking the service(s) they publish.

It is true, of course, that service composites can be reused through the services they publish. However, there is an essential distinction between nesting and invoking:

When a composite is nested—embedded in a higher-level composite as the implementation of a service component—its properties and references can be configured for that particular usage of the nested composite. Figure 14-3 demonstrates this principle: The composite application includes a component, C, that satisfies a reference from BPEL component A. Component C is implemented by service composite X, rather than a Mediator or BPEL component. This composite has two references that become references for component C upon embedding. The references for component C inside the higher-level composite can be satisfied either by other service components in that composite or by promoting these references to the composite level.

When the composite is merely invoked through the services it exposes, rather than embedded in the composites, its references and properties cannot be adapted to the context in which the composite is consumed (Figure 14-4). With true embedding, we can have the internal service component B provide the first reference of the nested composite. When composite X can only be reused by invoking its public services, we cannot wire the reference from X to component B.

You may argue that if you really insist on having component B as the provider for the first reference of composite X that you promote the service offered by X to the composite level and wire the reference from X to that service. This is true, but it has two disadvantages: We have to make public the service offered by B even though that was not the intention, and composite X will always be wired to use B as its reference satisfier, not just when X is called from the higher-level composite discussed here, but permanently.

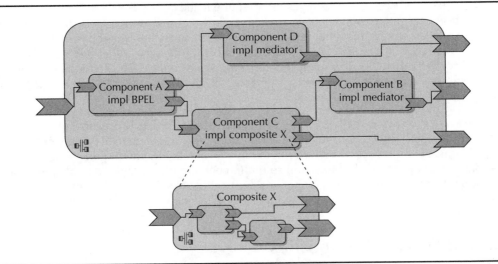

FIGURE 14-3. *Higher-level composite contains a service component that has another lower-level composite as its implementation*

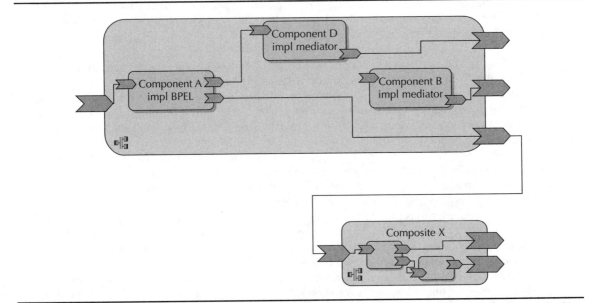

FIGURE 14-4. *The situation with the SOA Suite: Nested composites are not supported; composite X can only be leveraged by calling its public service(s).*

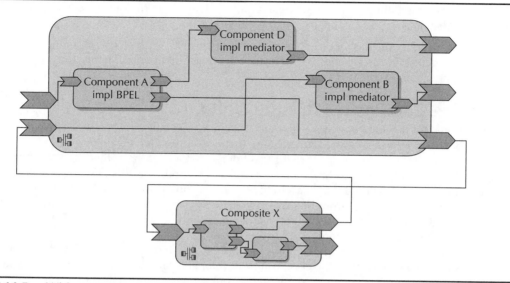

FIGURE 14-5. *Wiring a service composite that cannot be embedded to publicly expose a service component*

There is a third, easy-to-overlook distinction with the embedded case: With composite X embedded, a call to component B would be within the same instance of the higher-level composite. The situation depicted in Figure 14-5 shows how composite X can be wired to component B. However, a call from composite X to B results in a new instance of the higher-level composite; it would not be handled by the same instance in which component A initiated the call to X.

This gives an example of a composite with two, relatively independent publicly exposed services—from component A and component B. It would seem that because component B is reusable in its own right, it should be placed inside its own composite B. This composite is then invoked by other composites. That way, component B remains hidden (encapsulated).

Granularity of Service Composites

When designing and developing service composites (aka SOA composite applications), we have to decide on the granularity of those composites. How much functionality should be assembled into a single composite application? When should we break up a composite or merge multiple composites together?

These questions are very similar to the ones we discussed in Chapter 2 with regard to service granularity. And just like in that discussion, there are no one-size-fits-all answers. "It depends" is really all you can say, in general.

Well, there is a little bit more that we should realize about service composites—considerations that help decide on how to organize the service composites. Two things are of primary importance:

■ **Reusability** If a service component is to be (offered as) reusable, it should be in a separate composite—which you might want to use from a non-SCA context. When it is not, it should be put inside the composite to which it belongs. This is also the most important thing (from a functional point of view) when migrating from 10*g* to 11*g* (that is, deciding on the composition of the composites).

■ **Flexibility (or the required frequency of changes)** When a piece of functionality will see lots of changes and we don't want to impact other components, that, too, warrants a new composite.

Service Composites Are the Unit Of...

Composites are the level that make sense to consumers and business analysts—they don't even care about a more fine-grained level because that is encapsulated away from them.

As we have seen, composites are the level of reuse. Only at the composite level can services be exposed as reusable units, based on encapsulated components, because the composite is also the level of encapsulation. In addition to the services exposed at the composite level—which provide the reusability—a composite will also publicly expose those references from its internal components that cannot be satisfied internally. This could be seen as somewhat breaking the strict encapsulation requirements.

The service composite (application) is the level at which developers work in JDeveloper. There is nothing smaller than the composite—developers can work on service components like BPEL processes and Business Rule components, but always in the context of a composite.

The composite is also the level of deployment—composites are deployed in their entirety. You cannot redeploy part of a composite. Multiple composites can be deployed together, but they are not grouped together in the eyes of the SCA container. The only type of grouping available in the SOA Suite is the partition, a logical clustering of composites, with no functional consequences. Composites can be migrated between environments and shipped to remote teams or external parties—not individual service components.

Governance and Lifecycle Management

In addition to the unit of deployment, the composite is (unavoidably) also the unit of versioning. We can create and discern the version of composites—not versions of something smaller (such as individual components) or something larger (such as a collection of composites). Versioning is a means to enable the modification/evolution of composites that are reused by more than one consumer. Consumers can gradually move to the new version and are not forced to use the new version as soon as it is introduced. Multiple versions of the same composite will be available at run time.

It seems likely that from a governance perspective, we will look at individual artifacts that stretch beyond the boundaries of composites (such as event definitions, XSDs, and WSDLs) on the one hand, and service composites on the other. Talking about lifecycle management, ownership, availability, performance and the Service Level Agreement only seems to be meaningful with respect to a composite, not to individual service components, given the way these are represented in the tooling, both at run time and at design time. When it is important that governance be done, for example, on individual human tasks or business rules, these should live inside their own composite rather than being embedded in complex composites as internal components.

Security policies—discussed in detail in Chapter 15—are applied mainly at the composite level (some simple policies can be attached to individual components) and not across components.

Testing

Testing, as we shall see in Chapter 18, is supported by an out-of-the-box unit testing framework in Oracle SOA Suite, next to a plethora of external, standard black-box Web Service test tools such as soapUI. All external tests work at the composite level, interacting with the publicly exposed service. The shipped unit-testing framework supports unit testing of service components, even those that are not publicly exposed.

We can add test suites with test cases to a composite application. The test cases consist of assertions—conditions on the contents of messages—and are associated with wires inside composite applications. Testing applies to interactions at the component level, including components that are not exposed at the composite level. The scope of test cases is at the level of such an interaction.

Test suites that bundle test cases are associated with service composites. Test suites are the unit of running tests; therefore, the service composite is indirectly the unit of testing, too. The structure of the composites, however, is not relevant when it comes to determining exactly what you can have unit tested.

Tracing Composite Instances and Messages

Composite sensors—defined at the entrance points of composites (services) as well as the exit points (references), and discussed in Chapter 16—can be used to monitor the values of important variables. The results from these sensors can be used to locate composite instances. Monitoring and the management of instances, including purging of instances, are done at the composite level.

However, message flow traces go across composites: When we inspect the route of a message from the moment it enters the SCA domain until the time that the response is returned, the flow trace is reported across composite applications. It is not at all intuitive to find out from the message flow trace which composites participated in it. Usually it is not entirely relevant, either, until the time of an error that you want to be able to pin down a specific composite (or version of a composite).

Even more importantly, communication within a service composite is usually equally expensive as communication between composites running in the same SCA container. The container will leverage native bindings for such intra container interactions between different composites with the same minimal overhead that is achieved for communication between components in the same composite. The exception to this situation is when local optimization between composites is disabled for security reasons—to have policies enforced in the interaction between composites (see Chapter 15). Note that most security policies are applied on entrance to and exit from composites and *not* on the interaction between components within a composite.

Exception Handling

Error or exception handling in SOA composite applications can be configured at different levels, each with a different purpose. BPEL components can have exception handling inside, as we have seen in Chapter 6, to be used for handling business faults.

The fault policy infrastructure in SOA Suite can be instructed to activate certain fault policies when faults occur in a specific component or when faults occur anywhere in the composite. This is useful for technical (or unexpected) fault handling.

Faults can be handled per component or per composite. We cannot define fault policy bindings for multiple composites at the same time. Recovery from faulted instances is at the composite level. Note that transactions may very well involve (instances of) multiple composites and/or components if that is how the message flows.

Splitting or Merging Service Composites

Does it matter very much how we design the service composites? Are early decisions irreversible? Is it very hard to break up or combine composite applications later on? Fortunately, although the answer is, of course, "yes" to the first question, it is a resounding "no" to the other two. We have to be aware of what we can and cannot do with composites—and we have to get going in some direction. However, it is fairly easy to change directions and design the composites differently later on.

We will briefly discuss the steps we have to go through when we want to break up a composite application or combine several into one.

Splitting Up a Service Composite

We may have started out with a single composite application that contains all the service components, interacts with many references (adapters and external Web Services), and exposes a substantial number of services.

Then, at some moment, we may come to the conclusion that certain parts of the composite should branch out—for example, because they need to be modified quickly to meet a new business requirement, are subject to a different security scheme than the rest of the composite, or should be shipped offsite to be deployed somewhere else. Whatever the reason, the procedure for creating two composites from one is straightforward. First, we have to copy the existing composite application in its entirety, so we get a "Part One" and "Part Two" that are exactly the same at this point. Open Part One (one of the two clones of the composite) and then follow these steps:

1. Drag services to the composite level that are currently provided to components that will be in Part Two (if they are not already publicly exposed), as is shown in Figure 14-6.

2. Drag the references currently satisfied by Part Two components to the composite-level references swimlane.

3. Replace wires to Part Two components with wires to the new composite-level references—primarily in Mediator and BPEL components.

4. Remove the Part Two components from the composite.

5. You may need to change the name of the composite (at least either of the two must be renamed, but for clarity's sake it is probably best if both are given new names).

6. Remove all resources that were only referenced by the Part Two components that have now been removed from the composite.

Now open Part Two. Perform the reverse of the operations just executed for Part One on the components in Part Two, as shown in Figure 14-7.

For example, drag services to the composite level that are currently provided to Part One components (if they are not already publicly exposed), and expose as public any reference that is provided by a Part One component. The final result of breaking up the composite into two smaller composite applications is shown in Figure 14-8.

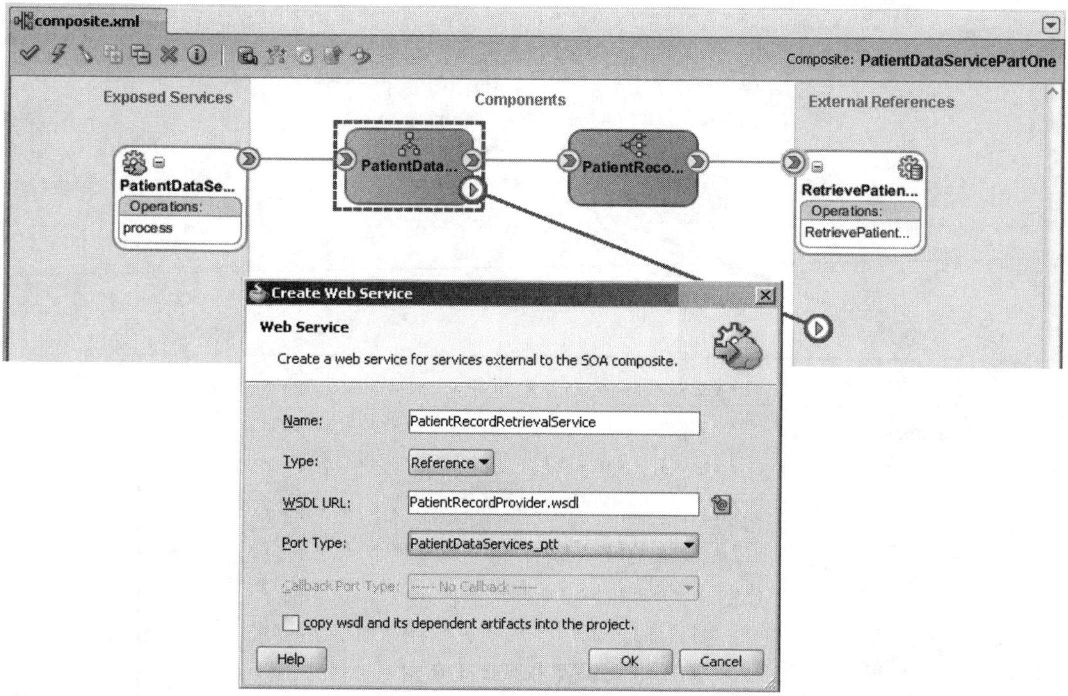

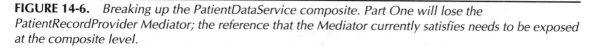

FIGURE 14-6.   *Breaking up the PatientDataService composite. Part One will lose the PatientRecordProvider Mediator; the reference that the Mediator currently satisfies needs to be exposed at the composite level.*

Note that in this case, we would deploy Part Two first and subsequently bind the reference PatientRecordRetrievalService in Part One to the end point of Part Two, or use deployment plans (see Chapter 17) and/or local references to WSDLs to remove dependencies at design time. Also note that sometimes instead of copying an entire application and subsequently removing and renaming components and other artifacts, it may be better to create a new application from scratch and only copy individual artifacts such as XSD and XSLT documents.

Merging Service Composites Together

The reverse procedure from breaking composites into multiple smaller parts is quite straightforward as well. Constructing a composite application by merging together components from multiple composites can be useful when composites have been created on a too-fine-grained level. We may conclude that reuse will only occur for one out of a related collection of composites or that versioning and deployment will always concern a combination of composites.

The steps for the merge procedure are roughly as follows:

1.   Pick one of the composites (usually the one with the largest number of components) as the merge target.

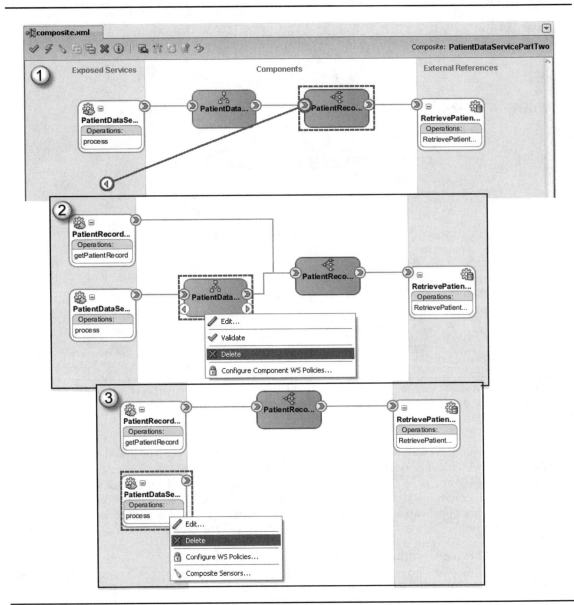

FIGURE 14-7. *Editing PatientDataService Part Two*

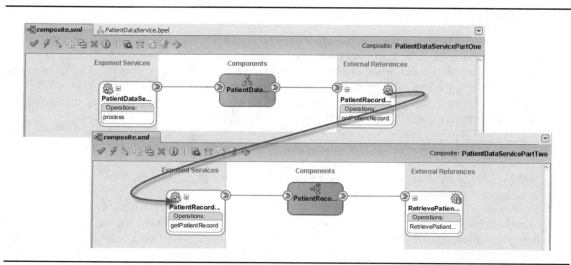

FIGURE 14-8.   *The end result of breaking up the PatientDataService composite: Two stand-alone composites that can be independently managed, developed, and deployed*

2.   Iterate through the other composites. Identify the components that must be merged into the target. All resources associated with a component must be copied to the target application via the file system (JDeveloper does not support such operations). A service component will have, at the very least, a componentType file and an implementation file (.bpel, .mplan, .bpmn, .decs, or java). It will have associations with a WSDL and XSD, and it may use XSLT files. These resources are ideally stored in the MDS and do not need to be copied between JDeveloper applications. (More on MDS in Part III of this book.)

3.   The component entry in the source composite.xml file needs to be copied to the target composite.xml.

4.   References based on technology adapters can also be copied: The reference entry should be transferred to the target composite.xml file, and the .jca file that contains the configuration for the technology adapter must be copied to the target application. The associated XSD and WSDL may be referenced in the MDS, or should be copied along with the .jca file.

5.   The dependencies from the components thus copied to the destination composite need to be satisfied: Wires need to be created from these components to the providers of the required services in their new "composite environment." Some of these dependencies may result in references at the composite level. Note that it may also be the case that the original components in the composite have promoted references that can now be satisfied within the composite itself by the components merged into the composite.

6.   When the components that have been added to the combined composite provide services that we want to have publicly exposed, we should also create wires from these components to the composite level.

Summary

Although we have been creating composite applications since Chapter 5, this chapter is the first to take a closer look at the nature of these applications. The Service Component Architecture (SCA) specification describes the construction of composite applications from service components and the wires that connect them. It also specifies the mechanism through which composite applications expose services to external consumers as well as references that during deployment of a composite must be satisfied through injection of external providers.

The SCA standard is extended with a specification regarding business events, as an alternative public interface for composites. Instead of accepting an incoming service request through its publicly exposed interface, a composite can trigger itself by the consumption of a business event. And likewise, instead of invoking a reference, a composite can produce its outcome in the form of an event it publishes.

Business functionality as designed by analysts is projected on composite applications. Composites are reusable units, with a well-defined public interface, that encapsulate their internal implementation. Thus, they help achieve the SOA objectives of reuse, decoupling, and agility. As developers and administrators, we need to learn how to design and implement composites; how to test and deploy them; how to secure them; how to monitor, trace, and troubleshoot them; how to do governance on them; and also how to break them up or merge them. Chapters 15–18 discuss these activities.

PART
III

Administration, Security, and Governance

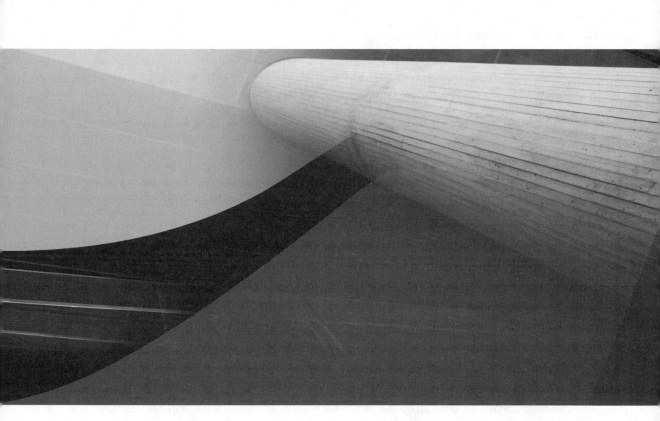

CHAPTER
15

For Your Eyes Only

T security has become more and more important over the last decades. Although at first security was frequently treated as a necessary evil, nowadays it has matured into a separate area of expertise. Recent drivers for applying security are changing government regulations, avoiding fraud, ensuring privacy, adhering to (stricter) auditing and compliancy rules, and providing more integration of both internal and external IT components using, for example, SOA and cloud computing.

For St. Matthews—and hospitals in general—security is a priority and an area of concern. Hospitals gather, store, and share sensitive personal information about patients. Medical records are strictly confidential and protected by government regulations. St. Matthews needs to be sure that information cannot be accessed by persons or organizations that are not authorized. Suppliers of medical equipment are allowed access to supplier services, not to services providing patient information and their medical history. Even more important, the hospital needs to rely on the quality of information and needs assurance that information is not unrightfully altered. Think about information on upcoming medical procedures (do we need to operate on the left or right leg?) and prescribed medication in combination with a patient's condition (is the patient allergic to a particular antibiotic?). When the integrity of information is violated, St. Matthews needs to know immediately. Although security measures can greatly reduce these risks, they can never be avoided altogether. In case something goes wrong, St. Matthews needs audit trails to be able to know what went wrong when, where, and why.

A complicating factor is an organization's increasing need to interact and share information with several stakeholders. In the case of St. Matthews, these include suppliers of medical equipment and drugs, other hospitals, emergency services, insurance companies, patients and their families, employees (medical staff, managers, IT department, and so on), physiotherapists, general practitioners (GPs), government agencies, and so on. This is a common "area of conflict": the increasing need and drive to share more information versus the need and drive for strict(er) security demands and measures. Patients, their relatives, insurance companies, and so on expect more information in a more timely manner while at the same time they expect their information to be treated strictly confidentially. Good risk assessment is the key to balancing these (sometimes) conflicting requirements.

This chapter consists of the following sections:

- We begin with a brief discussion of IT security in general. Then we'll discuss if and why security is different for service orientation as compared to "traditional" system development.

- Then we will move on to security within Oracle Fusion Middleware 11*g*. Oracle Fusion Middleware uses a policy-based model to manage Web Services. The chapter will zoom in on Oracle Web Services Manager, which is used to secure SOA composites.

- Next is a step-by-step demonstration in which you will secure an SOA composite using various policies, including a custom-defined policy.

- We will end with a short summary.

The Case for Security

Both St. Matthews and healthcare insurance companies want to automate the claim-handling process to increase effectiveness, decrease administrative efforts, reduce errors, and thereby lower costs. In this process, insurance companies handle customer claims and decide upon reimbursement. The insurance companies need information about provided healthcare and treatments from healthcare providers such as St. Matthews to be able to decide whether clients are reimbursed.

This process used to be a sequence of human (labor-intensive) activities involving phone calls to the hospital, verifying paper hospital records received by mail, and so on. Automating this process will save money, reduce the number of errors, and speed up the process—both for hospitals as well as healthcare insurance companies.

Following the service-orientation paradigm, St. Matthews decides to provide a service to the insurance companies it has an agreement with. These insurance companies can retrieve patient information—including treatment history—in an automated fashion by invoking this service.

But wait a second: Does a patient want his or her medical records to be available to just any invoker of this service? For example, banks providing mortgages and loans, life insurance companies, or (future) employers? Of course not. This information is highly confidential and personal! St. Matthews needs to apply security so this service can only be used by the healthcare insurance companies it trusts. St. Matthews also needs to make sure the client invoking this service is who it claims to be. The hospital finally needs to make sure that the inbound and outbound information of this service cannot be seen or tampered with by third parties that possibly want to take this information and misuse it.

The remainder of this chapter investigates how to apply security to SOA composites in order to achieve the stated objectives for the externally available insurance service.

IT Security

This section introduces IT security and investigates if and how security is different for service-oriented environments. It continues by providing some "best practices" for applying IT security. The section concludes by diving into some important aspects for IT security in a SOA environment, such as transport versus message security and the agent and gateway pattern.

Security and SOA

When compared to traditional software development, the important question is not whether security in a service-oriented environment is important, but if it is any different and should therefore be designed and implemented differently. The answer to both questions is yes.

To understand why security should be handled differently, we first need to understand the characteristics of SOA that are key to IT security, compared to those of traditional software development:

- There is more machine/machine interaction (versus human/machine interaction) in a service-oriented landscape. This means there is a greater need for automating security mechanisms for the purposes of authentication, authorization, encryption, and so on. In addition to this, security traditionally revolved around human actors who were assigned identities in the computer systems they interacted with. These identities are associated with roles and privileges. In a service-oriented environment, it is also services that interact with various systems, just like the human actors do. These services are also assigned identities—with associated roles and privileges.

- An SOA-environment generally contains more intermediary stations such as ESBs and other middleware components. As messages are flowing around the system, passing various stations, there are more opportunities for users and administrators to view possibly confidential message contents such as credit card information or medical details. In this case, transport security alone is not enough; message security is required. As will be explained later on, transport security only secures information that is in transmission, whereas message security secures the information itself, regardless of whether it's in transport or stored in some intermediary component.

- Service are to be invoked in a loosely coupled manner, without tight links between consumer and service. This loose coupling, however, should not make it possible for just any application to invoke services that should enforce a minimum security clearance level for its clients. For example, not every client can be allowed to invoke a medical-records service or insurance service.

- SOA results in more straight-through processing (STP), meaning processes are more frequently executed in an entirely automated fashion without human interference. Appropriate security enforcement is important because consequences of possible security breaches could be detected in a later stage than is the case when human activity is involved. Also, the consequences of security breaches in an STP environment can be graver due to the possible large amount of messages that are rapidly processed.

- Service orientation aims for reuse. Reuse of a service requires trust from the clients that are using or will be using the service. Trust is based on Quality of Service (QoS) aspects of a service, including the security level guaranteed and enforced by a service. That security level is generally determined by the service owner. In case of external services, security will be largely determined and enforced outside your own span of control. Possible consumers want to know what happens with their data if a service is not secured. Can they trust a service's result? If you want your services to be used, you need to make sure that it has appropriate Quality of Service, including appropriate security. Conversely, if you want to use external services, you need to make sure the right amount of security is applied by the service provider.

Various aspects, such as the (type of) service consumer, the location from which a service is invoked, and the information flowing to and from a service, impact the type of security and security measures that are needed. For example, a service provider might enforce message encryption when services are invoked by employees working from their home location as opposed to employees working from a company building with a secured network.

These characteristics and differences clearly impact the way IT security should be designed and implemented within an SOA environment. It furthermore warrants the need for an integrated and holistic approach to security beyond the boundaries of your own organization.

So What Exactly Is IT Security in a World of Services?

Although we touched upon the implications of service orientation on IT security, we have not yet discussed what we actually mean by "IT security." Does it include Identity and Access Management (IAM)? Is it also about securing buildings and using metal detectors? There can be a lot of confusion about what encompasses IT security and Identity and Access Management. When discussing these topics, we first need to agree upon the scope before delving into it.

Identity Management

Identity management is the administration of identities and relevant information (name, job title, password). It provides services for the retrieval and administration of identity information. Identities can represent both human actors, such as employees, patients, suppliers, and applications, as well as virtual entities, such as (internal and external) services and applications. Different rules, responsibilities, and administration may apply to each of these categories.

Identity management includes identity propagation: the mechanism to "pass" identity information within a chain of IT components invoking each other. For example, a client might invoke an order service that in turn invokes a payment service. Usually you want a service provider to authenticate the original consumer: the person (or service) that started the chain of service calls, and not some intermediary component such as an ESB. The *initial* service consumer is allowed (or denied) access to your services and information, not intermediary infrastructure components (middleware) that can never act on their own accord. In this example, the payment service needs to authenticate and authorize the client, not the order service or ESB. This implies that intermediary components between service consumer and provider need to be able to transport identity information such as certificates and possibly transform these from one format or protocol into another (for example, from SSO token into a username/password combination, or from HTTP Basic Authentication to a WS-Security username token). Figure 15-1 shows another example of identity propagation.

Note that besides authentication and authorization by the payment service, the client also needs to be authenticated and authorized by the Portal application.

Every identity in the identity store usually maps to a specific person or IT component. These identities can be members of a larger organization structure such as a department of the company. This results in a hierarchy of identities. In case of external organizations that are allowed access to your services, you should consider the tradeoff between using specific identities (employee "Doe" of organization "Acme") versus more general identities (organization "Acme" as a whole). Specific

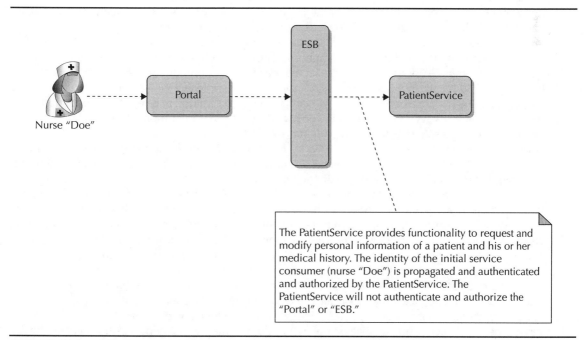

The PatientService provides functionality to request and modify personal information of a patient and his or her medical history. The identity of the initial service consumer (nurse "Doe") is propagated and authenticated and authorized by the PatientService. The PatientService will not authenticate and authorize the "Portal" or "ESB."

FIGURE 15-1.   *Identity propagation*

identities result in better traceability and can provide for more fine-grained access control, whereas more "coarse-grained" identities result in less administrative burden. You might want to avoid generic identities such as "consultant" and "trainee" altogether due to lack of traceability.

Provisioning is the process of synchronizing identity-related information between various identity management systems (in an automated fashion). One of these systems is usually the "source" identity store that provisions (sends) changes to other identity management solutions. For example, when St. Matthews hires a new employee, her identity information (such as e-mail address and password) might be stored in Oracle Internet Directory. Using Oracle Identity Manager, this information is provisioned to Microsoft Active Directory, which is used as the identity store for Windows workstations and Outlook.

When identity propagation and administration span more than one organization (crossing an organization's boundary), we speak of "identity federation."

A best practice is to use as little centralized identity stores as possible. This avoids duplicate or inconsistent identities and decreases user management efforts. Be careful in allowing externally hosted services and other organizations direct access to your identity management solution. Consider provisioning to an external organization's IAM solution as an alternative in such cases to minimize security risks.

Authentication

Authentication (or identification) is the process of verifying that an identity is who he, she, or it claims to be. Authentication mechanisms are usually based on something an identity *knows* (username/password combination), something an identity *possesses* (key, telephone, private key), a unique *property* of an identity (fingerprint or iris pattern), or a combination of all these.

Best practice is to define a limited set of authentication levels based on the mechanisms described here. For example, "basic" authentication requires knowledge (username/password), "medium" authentication requires knowledge and possession (username/password and token), and "high" authentication requires verification through a biometric property (iris scan).

Authentication also includes Single Sign-On (SSO), a mechanism in which an identity only needs to authenticate once while getting access to several IT components. SSO improves user friendliness and results in a better user experience. For example, a user logs on to a Windows workstation and because of SSO does not need to log in to Outlook and intranet applications. SSO is all about trust: A service needs to verify and trust the SSO component to which it delegates authentication. It also needs to trust the identity-related information received by the SSO component. SSO infrastructure can be used for identity propagation using, for example, Security Assertion Markup Language (SAML) tokens. Identity propagation can be seen as a way to achieve SSO. Single Sign-Off is the opposite of Single Sign-On.

A best practice for SSO is to grant access to IT components based on authentication level; if you successfully authenticated using "medium" authentication, SSO may only grant you access to IT components requiring the same or a lower authentication level, not to IT components requiring "high" authentication. Consider if you want to apply SSO for your most classified services. SSO can provide (unauthorized) access to a multitude of IT components due to a security breach in only one of the IT assets. This is called the "keys to the castle" principle.

SSO is often associated with one-time authentication for users accessing various web applications. How about SSO for application-to-application integration? Automated authentication (possibly using SSO) is a prerequisite for service automation in which a user interaction or an event results in a chain of services being invoked in an automated fashion. We do not want to reauthenticate the initial user every time a new service is invoked. With standards such as SAML, WS-Federation, WS-Security, and WS-Trust identity propagation, federation and SSO become possible in a service-oriented environment.

Authorization

Authorization involves the administration, establishment, and enforcement of access rights for *authenticated* identities within a given context. Authorization should be based on the function someone or some organization needs to do and know; no more, no less. A best practice is to avoid "super users"; that is, staff (usually management and IT administrators) who over time have gathered more privileges than they are entitled to.

A very common authorization model is Role-Based Access Control (RBAC). In this model, identities belong to one or more groups. Access rights to IT components are granted to groups instead of being directly coupled to identities (no "lock-in" on specific employees). This greatly reduces the cost and effort to administer authorizations and keep them up to date. Groups are often based on attributes that do not frequently change over time, such as organizational units (finance, IT, marketing) and functions (senior controller, database administrator, nurse), even when the identities belonging to those roles *do* change. RBAC can furthermore simplify "separation of concerns" so that different roles (and thus different persons) need to be involved in decision making within a single process. We used RBAC in Chapter 10 when discussing the assignment of human tasks. This prevents a single user from executing a process entirely on his own. For example, the same employee cannot be allowed to order a laptop, approve the order, and approve payment of the laptop supplier's invoice.

A frequently used term is "anonymous" to indicate an unauthenticated identity as well as a special authorization role that usually indicates that everyone has the right to access certain information or services, including unauthenticated identities.

"Hard" IT Security

This type of security includes confidentiality and integrity of data and more technical security, including the protection of networks and infrastructure using firewalls, (reverse) proxies, intrusion detection systems (IDS), intrusion prevention systems (IPS), virus scanners, and so on.

Confidentiality (or exclusivity) of information is about restricting access to data and messages to those identities that are allowed to view (and possibly modify) this data. Integrity (or reliability) of information is about ensuring data and messages to be complete, valid, and unaltered by (possibly malicious) unauthorized identities. Encryption using Public Key Infrastructure (PKI) is a common implementation to ensure confidentiality and detection of integrity violations. See the "WS-Security (WSS)" section for more information on the use of encryption for message confidentiality and integrity.

Together with confidentiality and integrity, availability forms the so-called "CIA triad." Availability of information, availability threats (denial-of-service attacks, single points of failure), and measures to ensure availability (clustering, failover) are out of scope for this book.

"Hard" IT security is often divided into various layers such as network security, platform and operating system security, application security, integrity and confidentiality, content security, and mobile security. For each layer, specific measures can be applied to increase overall security. Examples of such measures include dividing networks in segments and specifying fixed network routes (network security), having a central list of allowed and non allowed file extensions for inbound and outbound traffic (content security), and the use of hardening (platform and application security). *Hardening* refers to the process of securing a system (operating system, application, and so on) by means of ridding it of all unnecessary features (for example, removing unnecessary OS services).

"Soft" security, such as security education and awareness (employees Twittering sensitive information), as well as "physical" security, including fire alarms, metal detectors, and bodyguards, are out of scope for this chapter and this book.

Logging, Monitoring, and Auditing

Logging, monitoring, and auditing encompass the following activities within the scope of authentication, authorization, and security:

■ Storing and accessing relevant events and related information such as the time and location of (failed) authentication attempts.

■ Notifying stakeholders (such as administrators) in case of certain (usually suspicious) behavior. For example, warning an administrator by sending a text message in case an identity accesses a secured service from different geographical locations within a few minutes.

Functionality and processes in an SOA are spread over different loosely coupled components. Some logging and monitoring needs to be executed on a higher level—composite service or process level—than on the level of an elementary service. This gives rise to the need for a central logging and monitoring component that is able to combine and correlate decentralized logs and enable monitoring on the process level. The "Wire Tap" pattern can be used to publish logs, notifications and monitoring events, and other types of messages from services and middleware components to a centralized monitoring component. Notifications can be implemented and managed separate from the logging itself. Notifications can be published by the central monitoring component. Note that this requires the synchronization of the system clocks of all managed components to enable correct correlation.

You need to determine for every service if it is allowed to continue operation in case the central monitoring component fails. Is it allowed, for example, from a security point of view to switch to local logging and monitoring in case the central monitoring component is down?

Note that monitoring for Oracle SOA Suite in general will be covered in the following chapter. This chapter introduces some security-specific logging capabilities of Oracle SOA Suite.

Overview of IT Security

The previous sections discussed different aspects of IT security. Identity management, authentication, and authorization together are named Identity and Access Management (IAM). IAM is important for both *functional usage* of services (clients need access to services and data) as well as *administration* of services (administrators need access to service repositories, rule configurations, ESB and BPM consoles, and the platforms on which the services run).

The definition of IT security as provided here is not an "absolute truth." Other definitions of IT security can also be perfectly valid. The key thing is to mutually agree on a definition for IT security before discussing it further with stakeholders.

Best Practices for Applying IT Security

This section discusses the best practices for applying IT security in general.

Externalize Security

For a number of reasons it is a good design principle to externalize (or decouple) security from service and process implementation. There may be different security requirements for the same service based on the type of service consumer and related aspects, such as the location and network used to invoke the service. Implementing security as an integral part of a service can result in inflexible and under- or over secured services.

Besides, IT security is designed and implemented by different persons with different skills and expertise than those responsible for implementing processes and services. The lifecycle, release management, and administration of IT security also differs from those of processes and services. These are additional reasons for separating IT security from the design and implementation activities.

Security-related information such as the use of SSL/TLS and WS-Security is normally not advertised in a Web Service's WSDL document. This further promotes the separation of concerns. Standards such as WS-Policy can be used to define a Web Service's constraints and requirements separately.

An SOA environment frequently consists of heterogeneous infrastructure components, each possibly having its own IAM and security design and implementation (for instance, security that is embedded in an ESB product or application server). These different products will most likely support different versions and implementations of security standards and protocols. The application server might support WS-Security 1.0, whereas the ESB product supports WS-Security 1.1. This is worsened if the external infrastructure supports yet another subset of standards and protocols. This can cause poor interoperability and result in more security customizations and a higher risk of security breaches.

Best practice regarding these issues is to use a separate and specialized component aimed at IT security. This means "doing things in the right place" and promotes reuse of security artifacts and separation of concerns through decoupling. Just like business rules are used to externalize business decisions from processes, you can use a specialized component to externalize security from services and processes. The agent and gateway pattern, which is introduced later on in this chapter, is very well suited to externalize security from services.

Apply Defense-in-Depth

Does Great Britain rely on 007 alone to defend the country? You can ask the same question for IT security. Are your processes, services, and information secure when you only use a firewall? No! It is like Shrek said in the movie: "Onions have layers. Ogres have layers." IT security should also be layered, involving measures on multiple levels (awareness, logical access control, network security, and so on). Trying to implement security on one (and only one) level, such as an ESB, is not enough. Using a layered approach on various levels to secure an organization against a wide variety of security threats is called "defense-in-depth."

Classify Your Services

In traditional system development, IT components and information are often categorized into subsets for which the same security regime applies. Such a categorization can be based on the CIA triad (confidentially, integrity, and availability) with classification levels ranging from "public" to "highly confidential," for example. For each classification level, a set of minimum security measures is defined; for example, a system that is classified as "confidential" should enforce authentication and role-based authorization and apply message encryption. Using a security classification results in just the right amount of security to be applied while saving money by striving for the lowest possible (and allowed) classification levels without endangering security.

Just as in traditional system development, you can use a security classification system in service-oriented environments, as shown in Figure 15-2. Here, services and their operations are categorized to determine the required security measures. For example, St. Matthews classifies its "patient service" that allows retrieval and modification of personal information as "highly confidential" and "highly available." This, among others, implies that the service may only be invoked from within St. Matthews and its private and secured network.

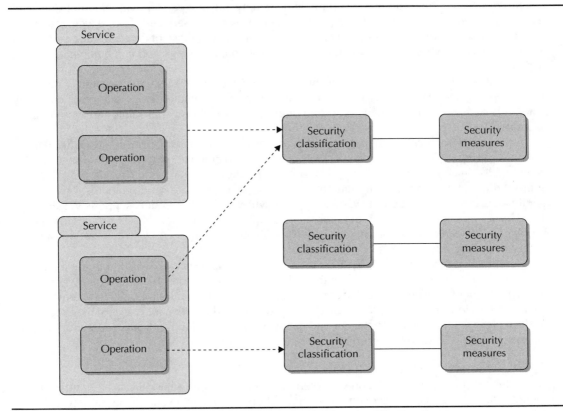

FIGURE 15-2.   *Categorizing services according to a security classification*

Best practice is to define a limited set of security classifications and corresponding measures. For each new service and its operations, determine the classification levels; this is usually the responsibility of the service owner. A classification per service as a whole is preferable over a classification level for every operation, although sometimes this granularity may be required (for example, when the remove operation of a DocumentService is accessible to fewer people than the read operation of the same service). The classification information should be part of your service repository and incorporated into governance processes. This results in transparent security regulations, provides better insight in the current and future security of your environment, results in better reuse of existing security policies, and prevents reinventing the wheel.

Standardize
This may appear trivial but I'll keep on stressing the importance of using standards to achieve interoperability. This also includes the usage of security standards such as LDAP, SSL/TLS, SAML, X.509, and WS-Security (WSS). The use of standards results in secured services being more reusable by consumers that may have heterogeneous infrastructures. Next to that, standardization also results in more manageable IT systems, which is important when operating at scale. Note that SSL/TLS and WS-Security will be covered in more detail later on in this chapter.

The mission of the open-industry organization Web Services Interoperability (WS-I) is to promote interoperability of Web Services that are implemented using various technologies and platforms. One of WS-I's publicly available resources is the so-called "Profiles," implementation guidelines that state how related Web Service specifications should be used for best interoperability. WS-I has finalized the Basic Profile, Attachment Profile and Simple SOAP Binding Profile, and a Basic Security Profile is currently underway. Such a profile can—among other things—be used to test security compliance of Web Services. See www.ws-i.org for more information.

Transport Versus Message Security

There are roughly two main security mechanisms for exchanging messages: transport security and message security.

Transport security secures a message only during transport between service consumer and service provider by using a secured transport layer—for example, using HTTP over SSL/TLS (HTTPS). That means messages are not protected in intermediary components such as an ESB and are equally unprotected directly after being received by the service endpoint. This implies that even though the message was secure during transport, *after* its delivery to an SOA composite, the message contents are directly visible to the components within the composite and are also readable to administrators who can view the message flow within composites in a console such as Enterprise Manager. This might not be acceptable for very sensitive information such as credit card data or patients' medical records.

Message security secures the message itself, often through encryption of the payload using, for example, Public Key Infrastructure (PKI) and WS-Security (WSS). Because message security can provide security in the scope you want and need—and also in intermediaries and after the message has been received—it is generally preferable over transport security in implementing stricter security requirements. The difference is shown in Figure 15-3. The top part of the figure displays message security, and the lower part displays transport security.

Both transport and message security can be used for authentication purposes and to guarantee message integrity and confidentiality. The following sections dive into the most common implementations in Oracle SOA Suite for transport security using SSL/TLS and message security using WS-Security, as well as how authentication, integrity, and confidentiality can be achieved.

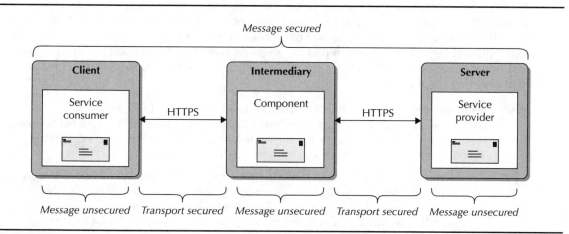

FIGURE 15-3.   *Transport security (bottom) versus message security (top)*

Secure Sockets Layer (SSL) or Transport Layer Security (TLS)

A frequent interaction pattern in a service-oriented landscape is invocation of Web Services using SOAP (or REST) over HTTP. The HTTP transport layer can be secured using TLS (Transport Layer Security). TLS is an encryption protocol and IETF standard for securing network communications such as over the Internet. Secure Sockets Layer (SSL) is the predecessor of TLS. TLS can be used in combination with other protocols such as HTTP, FTP, SMTP, and LDAP. TLS is a possible implementation to realize a virtual private network (VPN). Current versions are TLS 1.2 and SSL 3.

This section won't go into the nitty-gritty details of the protocol but rather outlines its mechanism. TLS can be applied one way (or unilaterally), meaning that the server authenticates to the client using a signature. Server authentication is required, for example, for online banking. A client wants to know that he is really using the bank's online banking application and not some look-a-like website used by a hacker to retrieve his banking data (known as "website spoofing").

Authentication in SSL/TLS is achieved by means of a signature that's generated by the server using its private key. The private key used for authentication should only be known to the server. The client validates the signature using the corresponding public key by means of a trusted digital certificate that is issued by a certificate authority (CA). If validation succeeds, the client knows that the server is who it claims to be (server authentication). This ends the "handshake" between server and client. Two-way TLS (mutual authentication) is also possible. This means that the client also sends a signature using its private key to the server so the server can verify the client's identity.

The public and private key pair and a mutually agreed random number are then used to encrypt, hash, and decrypt the information that is sent from client to server, and vice versa, thus ensuring integrity and confidentiality.

SSL/TLS support—enabling HTTPS communication—is realized through Oracle WebLogic Server on which Oracle SOA Suite, Oracle Service Bus (OSB), and Oracle Web Services Manager (OWSM) run. The step-by-step tutorial later on in this chapter demonstrates how to enable secure message transport by invoking a service over HTTPS.

WS-Security (WSS)

WS-Security is the most important Web Service standard to achieve message security. The WS-Security standard is supported by the policy-based security framework of Oracle Service Bus and Oracle Web Services Manager that can be used to secure SCA composites. WSS is an OASIS standard that uses SOAP messaging to secure messages independent of the transport layer that is used. WSS provides end-to-end security, from service consumer to service provider, through all intermediate components as compared to the point-to-point security provided by SSL/TLS. OASIS released WSS version 1.0 in 2004 and version 1.1 in 2006. WS-Security supports authentication, confidentiality, and integrity:

- **Authentication** WSS adds authentication data—which identifies the service consumer—to a SOAP message using one of the different token types: UserNameToken Profile (username with clear text or digest password combination), X.509 Certificate Token Profile, SAML Token Profile, or Kerberos Token Profile.

- **Confidentiality** The identity that sends a message uses the public key of the identity that *should* receive the message (for example, the service provider) to encrypt the message contents using an encryption algorithm such as RSA. Only the owner of the corresponding private key (again, the service provider) is able to decrypt the message contents.

■ **Integrity** The identity that sends a message uses its private key to generate a signature. The signature contains a "digest" of the message contents; this is called "hashing." You cannot re-create a message from its digest. Any change in the message can be detected because the digest in the signature no longer corresponds to the altered contents of the message. The identity that receives the message uses the sender's public key to decrypt the signature. If the signature is decrypted successfully, it knows the sender is authentic because only the holder of the private key could have created a signature that can be decrypted using the public key. The receiver can then use the digest to verify the message contents have not been altered during transport. The XML Digital Signature (XML-DSig) standard is often used as XML syntax for digital signatures.

Figure 15-4 shows what it looks like when all these WS-Security aspects are applied to a SOAP message (header and body).

Consider the following unsecured SOAP message. This is a sample request message for the Acme Web Service that exposes the operation "echoMe":

```
<soapenv:Envelope
    xmlns:soapenv="http://schemas.xmlsoap.org/soap/envelope/"
    xmlns:acme="http://acmewebservice/">
    <soapenv:Header/>
```

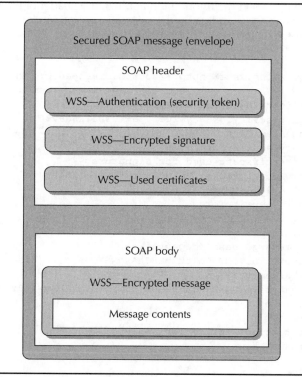

FIGURE 15-4. *Secured SOAP message with WS-Security*

```
        <soapenv:Body>
            <acme:echoMe>Hello World!</acme:echoMe>
        </soapenv:Body>
    </soapenv:Envelope>
```

We now use the WS-Security standard to apply security to the Web Service request message enforcing authentication, integrity, and encryption. When trying to invoke the Web Service without adding the corresponding WS-Security information, we might get the following fault message:

```
<env:Envelope xmlns:env="http://schemas.xmlsoap.org/soap/envelope/">
    <env:Header/>
    <env:Body>
        <!-- Fault message -->
        <env:Fault xmlns:wsse="http://docs.oasis-open.org/wss/2004/01/...
                                 ...oasis-200401-wss-wssecurity-secext-1.0.xsd">
            <faultcode>wsse:InvalidSecurity</faultcode>
            <faultstring>Missing <wsse:Security> in SOAP Header</faultstring>
            <faultactor/>
        </env:Fault>
    </env:Body>
</env:Envelope>
```

With the required WS-Security information applied, the header of the resulting secured message may look like this (depending on the selected encryption algorithms, key identifier type, and so on):

```
<soapenv:Header>
    <wsse:Security xmlns:wsse="http://docs.oasis-open.org/wss/2004/01/...
                                 ...oasis-200401-wss-wssecurity-secext-1.0.xsd">
<!-- X.509 certificate used for encryption -->
        <wsse:BinarySecurityToken ValueType="wsse:X509v3">
        MIICUTCCAbqgA...awxekHKkTWS2az
        </wsse:BinarySecurityToken>
        <!-- X.509 certificate used for signature -->
        <wsse:BinarySecurityToken ValueType="wsse: X509v3">
        MIICRzCCAbCgA...9ssBsDFmgT2AS0=
        </wsse:BinarySecurityToken>
        <Signature>
            <SignedInfo>
                <!-- message hash (digest) -->
                <DigestValue>odVp0oTtu7BRBJhAxgxSMQssRdI=</DigestValue>
                <!-- signature -->
                <SignatureValue>H7MoXu2JdPx2...HOVdTqrylXDAg=</SignatureValue>
            </SignedInfo>
        </Signature>
        <!-- clear text authentication -->
        <wsse:UsernameToken>
```

```
          <wsse:Username>acme</wsse:Username>
          <wsse:Password>mypassword</wsse:Password>
      </wsse:UsernameToken>
    <!-- timestamp -->
    <Timestamp>
        <Created>2010-04-16T21:10:09Z</Created>
        <Expires>2010-04-17T05:10:09Z</Expires>
    </Timestamp>
  </wsse:Security>
</Header>
```

The following snippet shows a SOAP message body containing the encrypted request data:

```
<soapenv:Body>
    <!-- header indicating the message body contains encrypted data -->
    <xenc:EncryptedData
        Id="_Dff7ySASsISfb2H31osV8A22"
        Type="http://www.w3.org/2001/04/xmlenc#Content">
    <!-- encryption algorithm -->
    <xenc:EncryptionMethod Algorithm="http://www.w3.org/2001/04/...
                                            ...xmlenc#aes128-cbc"/>
    <!-- encrypted message data -->
    <xenc:CipherData>
        <xenc:CipherValue>LljX08Z3ujA3lsA1+p0E...TaG3WiWm7qA==</xenc:CipherValue>
    </xenc:CipherData>
  </xenc:EncryptedData>
```

Note that applying security such as WS-Security introduces additional challenges. Messages are encrypted and additional information is scarce (because elaborate error messages containing implementation details may pose an additional security risk). The very reason to shield unauthorized people also results in the administrator's job becoming more difficult.

We'll continue with a frequently used pattern for securing services: agents and gateways.

Agents and Gateways Pattern

As discussed earlier, it is a good principle to externalize security from service providers and consumers. One way to achieve this is through agents and gateways. In this pattern, agents contain a service-specific security configuration (also called "policies"), while gateways contain more generic security configurations that should be enforced for more (or all) services. Both agents and gateways can consist of one or more policies that are applied sequentially. Some middleware component is usually responsible for intercepting inbound and outbound messages and enforcing these policies. When all policies are successfully enforced, the message may proceed.

An example is shown in Figure 15-5. Services A and B are secured using a gateway. The gateway might enforce authentication using the WS-Security UsernameToken profile. Services C, D, and E are secured using agents. In this case each service has its own security requirements that are fulfilled by its corresponding agent. For example, service C might require transport security

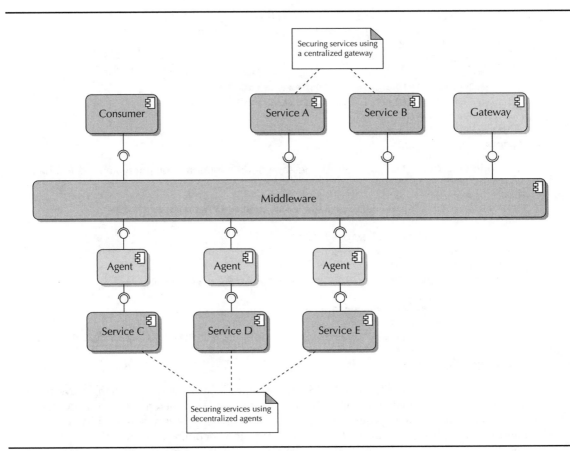

FIGURE 15-5. *Agents and gateways*

requiring two-way SSL/TLS; service D might require authentication, authorization and message integrity, and confidentiality; whereas service E might require that it only be invoked with requests originating from a specific IP address.

A best practice is to use a mix of gateways and agents. Use gateways to apply common security policies and agents for more service-specific security policies. A gateway can introduce a possible "single point of failure" or performance bottleneck, because messages for all secured services have to flow through the gateway. Investigate the impact of gateways and agents on the high availability of secured services.

Security in Oracle Fusion Middleware 11*g*

This section provides an overview of the security capabilities in Oracle Fusion Middleware 11*g*. Next, we will dive into Oracle Web Services Manager, which can be used to secure SOA composite applications.

Security Overview

Developers and security architects can leverage the following security services and products in Oracle Fusion Middleware:

- **Identity- and access-management products**   Oracle Fusion Middleware provides a comprehensive stack of products for identity administration (including provisioning and federation), authentication (including SSO), and authorization. These products include Oracle Internet Directory (OID), Oracle Virtual Directory (OVD), Oracle Access Manager (OAS), and Oracle Identity Manager (OIM). The IAM capabilities that these products provide can often be leveraged by applications and services running on Oracle WebLogic Server through the integration of these products with the application server. Oracle WebLogic Server, for example, virtualizes the underlying identity store, username and password authentication, and role-based authorization through its "Authenticator" mechanism. The underlying provider can be WebLogic's file-based default store, but also OID or third-party identity management offerings. This is transparent to applications and services that delegate identity management, authentication, and authorization to WebLogic Server.

- **Java security**   Oracle WebLogic Server is a Java EE–compliant application server and, as such, implements Java and Java EE security standards such as Java Authentication and Authorization Service (JAAS) and Java Authorization Contract for Containers (JACC). Applications and services running on Oracle WebLogic Server can use these implementations to provide security through standards.

- **Oracle Platform Security Services (OPSS)**   OPSS is WebLogic's abstraction layer on top of security functionality and tooling. OPSS provides a set of APIs that can be used by Java and Java EE applications to realize security. These APIs cover authentication, authorization, SSO, auditing, policy management, user and role management, and so on. OPSS supports the SAML, XACML, JACC, and JAAS standards. OPSS is used by Oracle's own components running on WebLogic Server, including Oracle SOA Suite, Oracle Web Center, OWSM, Oracle Entitlements Server, and ADF Security as well as Oracle WebLogic Server itself.

- **Transport security**   Oracle Fusion Middleware components run on Oracle WebLogic Server, which supports SSL/TLS using PKI and keystores to achieve transport security.

- **Oracle Fusion Middleware Audit Framework**   A central auditing facility that can be used by Oracle components running on Oracle WebLogic Server.

- **Policy frameworks for Web Services**   Policies describe the (security) requirements and capabilities for services. Policies are used by service clients to *apply* security to outbound messages (for example, WS-Security headers) or service providers to *enforce* inbound security. Policies are often applied using agents and gateways. The following section will dive into Oracle Fusion Middleware's policy frameworks, which can be leveraged to secure Web Services.

The wiki for this book provides links to relevant documents that provide more in-depth information on the security offerings of Oracle Fusion Middleware.

Web Services and Policy Frameworks in Oracle Fusion Middleware

With respect to (security) policies, Oracle categorizes Web Services as follows:

- **"Plain" Java Web Services**   Java and Java EE components that are exposed as Web Services using the JAX-RPC or JAX-WS standard and run on Oracle WebLogic Server. Oracle calls these "WebLogic (Java EE) Web Services."

- **Fusion Middleware–related Web Services**   These include SOA Suite, ADF, and WebCenter services. SOA composites can be exposed as Web Services. These composites can also reference other Web Services. ADF components such as ADF Business Components (ADF BC) can be exposed as Web Services. ADF uses Web Service Data Controls and Web Service Proxies to reference other Web Services. WebCenter provides Web Services and REST APIs to expose portlets and Web 2.0 technologies such as wikis, RSS, and blogs. Web Center can consume other Web Services. Oracle terms these "Oracle Infrastructure Web Services."

Security in Oracle SOA Suite is largely externalized in separate security products or frameworks and is therefore loosely (de)coupled with the actual implementation of services themselves. The security frameworks are mostly policy based. These policies are based on standards such as WS-Security. Policies can be applied and configured using management consoles or IDEs and reused by processes and services. Policy violations such as unsuccessful authentication attempts can be monitored using management consoles.

There are three policy frameworks in Oracle Fusion Middleware 11*g* to secure Web Services:

- **OWSM policies**   OWSM's policy framework is leveraged to secure Oracle Infrastructure Web Services. Only OWSM *security* policies (and not other types of policies, such as management policies) can be applied to JAX-WS Web Services.

- **WebLogic Server policies**   WebLogic Server policies can be used to secure both JAX-RPC and JAX-WS Web Services.

- **Oracle Service Bus policies**   Oracle Service Bus uses its own policy framework to secure business and proxy services. As stated in OSB's Statement of Direction: "The ability to attach, detach, author and monitor policies in a central fashion will be extended to the Oracle Service Bus (as it is has been extended to all other components in the SOA Suite 11*g*)." See the next section "OWSM and OSB" for more details.

You cannot secure the same Web Service using a combination of OWSM and WebLogic Web Service policies. Oracle recommends using OWSM policies over WebLogic Server policies where possible.

OWSM and OSB

Oracle SOA Suite Patch Set 2 (11.1.1.3) introduced an OWSM agent for Oracle Service Bus. This means you can secure OSB business and proxy services of types "WSDL" and "Any SOAP" using OWSM. The support is not yet complete, but will probably be enhanced in future releases of Oracle SOA Suite. Because OWSM will gradually replace OSB's own policy framework based on WebLogic Server policies, it is recommended to use OWSM for securing new OSB projects. Note that there are limits to the degree in which you can mix OWSM and WLS policies for OSB projects.

You will need to perform some additional configuration steps, such as enabling the OSB domain for OWSM. These steps are explained in detail in the Oracle Service Bus guides on Oracle Technology Network (OTN).

Oracle Web Services Manager (OWSM)

OWSM is used to secure JAX-WS Web Services, Oracle Infrastructure Web Services such as SOA composites, and from Oracle SOA Suite Patch Set 2 (11.1.1.3) onwards OSB business and proxy services. This section provides an overview of OWSM's architecture and briefly discusses all relevant concepts of OWSM, such as policies, assertions, policy store, and policy administration.

OWSM 11*g* is tightly integrated with Oracle WebLogic Server. It can only secure Oracle WebLogic services and does not provide agents for third-party application servers as OWSM 10*g* did. Note that with the acquisition of AmberPoint, Oracle has acquired tooling that provides security enforcement for multiple application servers, such as IBM WebSphere, Apache Tomcat, and Microsoft IIS.

Architecture of OWSM

OWSM's policy framework is based on the WS-Policy standard. A *policy* is a concrete, bounded, and specific piece of security functionality—for example, an authentication policy that verifies a given username/password using an LDAP server or a management policy that logs request and response messages. One or more policies can be applied to a service to provide both inbound and outbound security, thereby fulfilling its security requirements. A policy is reusable, meaning that the same policy can be applied to more than one service. Policies often need to be *configured* for the specific service they are applied to—for example, when providing a username/password combination for an authentication policy.

Figure 15-6 depicts the various components of the OWSM framework.

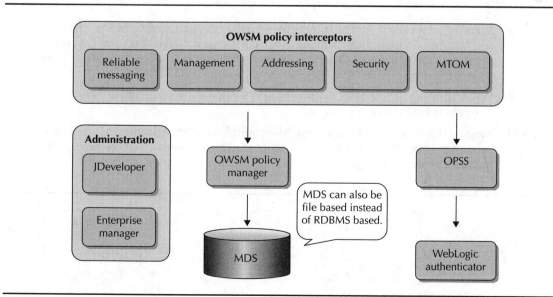

FIGURE 15-6. *Overview of OWSM*

The actual enforcement of policies that are applied to services is achieved using *policy interceptors*. These make sure that inbound and outbound messages are intercepted and the policies are also executed.

For some policies, the actual security implementation is delegated to Oracle WebLogic Server using the Oracle Platform Security Services (OPSS) APIs—for example, authentication and authorization policies that leverage WebLogic's LDAP-based authentication and authorization provider.

Policy definitions are stored in the Metadata Store (MDS). The MDS can either be file based or RDBMS based. For the production environment, it is recommended to have a database store. Access to the policy definitions in the MDS is achieved through OWSM Policy Manager. This means that policies are centrally managed (MDS, Policy Manager, and Enterprise Manager) and enforced at run time per service.

You can use Enterprise Manager to define, apply, configure, manage, and monitor policies. JDeveloper can only be used to *apply* policies to services.

Policies and Policy Assertions

Policy assertions are the smallest building blocks when it comes to security (see Figure 15-7). Assertions provide a basic security capability such as a logging capability, encryption capability, or authentication capability. Policies are created by combining one or more assertions in a sequence (a "pipeline") to provide a larger reusable piece of security functionality—for example, a policy that contains an assertion to log an inbound encrypted message, followed by an assertion to decrypt that message, and finally another logging assertion to log the decrypted message. Another example is a policy containing an authentication and subsequent authorization assertion.

OWSM provides a set of out-of-the-box policies and assertion templates on which concrete assertions are based. Next to that, OWSM provides a mechanism to create your own policies and assertions.

OWSM differentiates assertions and policies into the following categories:

- **Security**   Policies for identity propagation, authentication, authorization, confidentiality, and integrity. These policies, among others, implement the WS-Security 1.0 and 1.1 standards. This is the only OWSM policy type that can be applied to JAX-WS Web Services.

- **WS-Addressing**   Policies that support the WS-Addressing standard for including transport information in messages.

- **Message Transmission Optimization Mechanism (MTOM) Attachments**   Policies that support the transmission of binary content (attachments) between services. MTOM is applied to reduce message size.

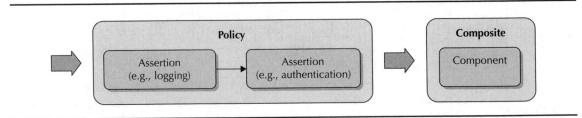

FIGURE 15-7.   *Policies are composed of assertions.*

- **Reliable Messaging** Policies that support the WS-Reliable Messaging standard. This standard is used for guaranteed (one-time) delivery of messages and to guarantee the order in which messages are delivered.

- **Management** Policies that provide logging capabilities for messages (request, response, and fault messages).

Applying Policies

Policies can be applied to service consumers as well as service providers. Suppose message confidentially is required between a service and its clients and message security is used to realize this. In this case, the service consumer—for example, a reference binding in a composite—can apply a policy to encrypt an outbound message, whereas the service provider uses a policy to decrypt the inbound message.

Looking specifically at SOA composites, policies can be applied to the following:

- **Service bindings** Securing exposed services for inbound messages.
- **Reference bindings** Applying security to outbound messages.
- **Components** A subset of management (logging) and security (authorization) policies can be applied to components within a composite.

Policies can be associated with services using Enterprise Manager or JDeveloper. Policy definition, configuration, and management can only be done through Enterprise Manager.

Policy Enforcement

Policies are enforced using so-called "interceptors." Policies are executed in a specific order based on their type, as shown in Figure 15-8.

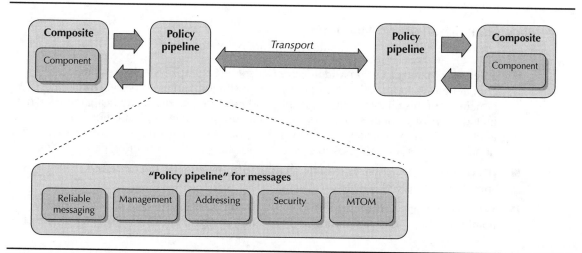

FIGURE 15-8. *Policies are executed in a specific order.*

Policies are "two-way" by default, meaning that they are enforced on inbound and outbound communication channels, but in reverse order. For example, if you attach a policy that enforces encryption through WS-Security to an exposed synchronous two-way service (request/reply), you will enforce encryption on the incoming payload (request) as well as the outbound payload (response). This is only the case for applicable policies; for example, applying authorization to a request message will not result in outbound authorization for the response message that is sent back to the client.

Local Optimization

Oracle SOA Suite uses various protocols and bindings based on its run-time environment and configuration. In case composites run in the same Oracle WebLogic Server or Oracle WebLogic Server cluster, local optimization is applied for invocations from one composite to the other, where possible. This means native Java calls are used instead of the SOAP protocol. In this case, some OWSM policies will not be enforced. If you want to make sure policies are enforced, you can use one or both of the following options:

- Disable local optimization between composites. This will result in OWSM policies being enforced but also introduces a slight performance penalty. You can turn off local optimization by adding a property to a reference in the composite.xml file of the client composite. The composite will invoke another composite using SOAP/XML via HTTP rather than the optimized native binary binding.

```
<reference name="MyExternalService" ui:wsdlLocation="MyReference.wsdl">
  <property name = "oracle.webservices.local.optimization">false</property>
</reference>
```

- Set the "local optimization control" property of a policy in Enterprise Manager. You can indicate per policy if local optimization is used. See the "Configuring Local Optimization" section in *Oracle Fusion Middleware Security and Administrator's Guide for Web Services 11g* for more information and the default settings for local optimization per policy.

Policy Administration and Monitoring

Oracle provides the following tools for the administration of policies:

- **Enterprise Manager Fusion Middleware Console**   Enterprise Manager is the most comprehensive tool available for policy administration and monitoring. During the remainder of this chapter, you will explore some of its security-related capabilities. These include applying policies to composites, configuring policies and assertions that are applied to composites, viewing the available policies and assertions, run-time monitoring of policies, assertions and possible security violations, and configuring new policies.

- **JDeveloper**   JDeveloper can (only) be used to apply policies to composites. This chapter shows an example of how to do this.

- **WLST (WebLogic Scripting Tool)**   WLST provides OWSM-specific scripts for policy administration, such as importing and exporting policies. WLST is outside the scope of this chapter.

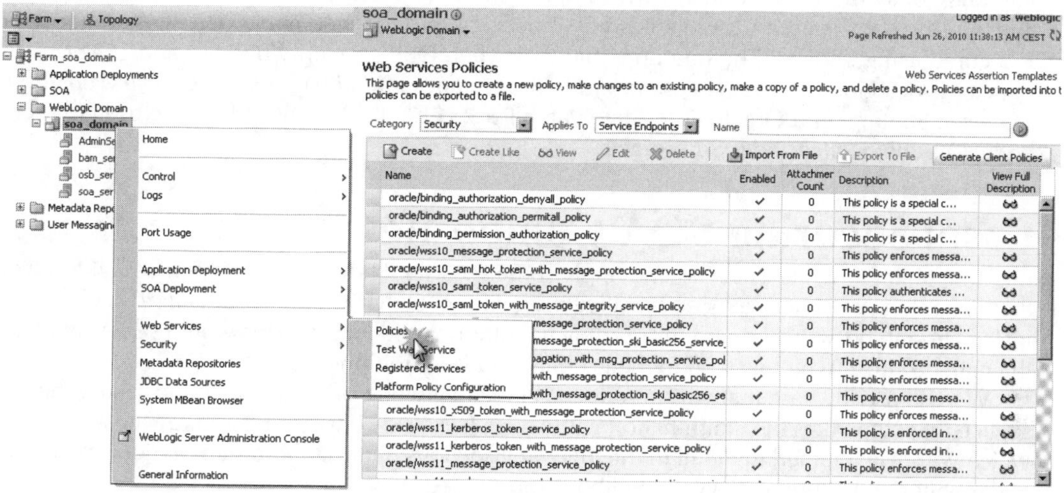

FIGURE 15-9. *Using Enterprise Manager to view the available policies*

Let's inspect the policies and assertions that are available "out of the box." Log in to Enterprise Manager. In the overview panel, open the WebLogic Domain node, right-click the SOA Suite domain, and select Web Services | Policies (see Figure 15-9).

This will open the Web Services Policies overview. Here, you can filter on category (MTOM, security, and so on), view policy descriptions, and more. Click the Web Services Assertion Templates link to view the available assertion templates. The out-of-the-box policy and assertion template names have a specific format. It is a best practice to follow these naming conventions when we create our own policies and assertions later on.

Custom Policy Assertions
You can create custom policy assertions if you need security features above and beyond those provided by the default set of out-of-the-box policy assertions. A custom policy assertion needs to be implemented in Java. An overview of the steps involved and use of a custom policy assertion is out of scope for this chapter. See *Oracle Fusion Middleware Security and Administrator's Guide for Web Services* and *Java API Reference for Oracle Web Services Manager* for more information.

Gateway
The attentive reader might have noticed that the previous sections were all about support for the agent pattern and did not include gateways. Currently, OWSM 11*g* does not offer a gateway. A gateway is, however, part of OWSM's roadmap for the future. Deployment and use of the OWSM 10*g* Release 3 gateway is an option if you need gateway functionality.

Interoperability
As mentioned before, Oracle Service Bus and Oracle SOA Suite have different default security frameworks: OSB's own security framework and OWSM 11*g*. Both are based on policies. Security

interoperability is a main concern when implementing services that span (and include) both OSB and SOA composites. An example is an OSB business service that invokes an SOA composite that is secured using OWSM. The interoperability between OSB's security policies and OWSM's policies is described in *Oracle Fusion Middleware Interoperability Guide for Oracle Web Services Manager*. Starting with Oracle SOA Suite Patch Set 2 (11.1.1.3.0), OWSM can be used to secure both SOA composites and OSB projects.

Case: Securing SOA Composites

It is time to get down to business and apply some security. St. Matthews recognizes all too well that several of its services expose sensitive information. St. Matthews cannot afford such information to be accessed and misused by unauthorized identities. This would seriously harm the patients' trust, which is vital to the hospital and its ambitions.

We will use the case that was introduced at the beginning of this chapter and secure the service that automates the claim-handling process. The case consists of the following main steps, which will be explained in detail in the following sections. During these steps various management and monitoring features of OWSM will be demonstrated.

- Inspect, deploy, and test the SOA composite that the hospital exposes for insurance companies to retrieve patient information.

- Add identities that represent the insurance companies to WebLogic's default identity store.

We will continue by using Enterprise Manager to do the following:

- Enforce authentication from service clients (insurance companies) using WS-Security.

- Enforce authorization. Not every insurance company may use this service—only insurance companies that have a specific contract with St. Matthews. To achieve this, we will create a new authorization policy based on an existing policy.

- Enforce transport security using SSL/TLS to guarantee message integrity and confidentiality during transport.

- Log access to a BPEL component that is part of the composite.

We will finish by using JDeveloper to add a policy reference to the composite.

This section uses soapUI as a client to test invocation of secured SOA composites. The soapUI tool provides functionality to add security information to Web Service invocations. Alternatively, you can use any other Web Service test tool that supports WS-Security and SSL/TLS. We will use versioning of composites so that the same SOA composite can be used simultaneously, with every version having different security measures applied.

The detailed step-by-step instructions as well as the screenshots for all intermediate stages can be found in the online chapter complement.

Inspecting the SOA Composite

The initial SOA composite used to demonstrate the security features of OWSM is a simplified composite named InsuranceComposite. The composite exposes a Web Service for insurance companies to retrieve patient details and their treatments. Insurance companies use this information in their claim-handling process. Note that at a later stage, this service will be exposed via the enterprise service bus—implemented using Oracle Service Bus 11*g*.

The input of the composite consists of a patient's Social Security number and a start and end date. The output consists of relevant patient details and the hospital records containing treatments for that particular patient between the start and end date. As you can imagine, this information is highly confidential and should be well protected. The input and output are described in the insuranceMessages.xsd document that is shown in Figure 15-10.

The SOA composite contains a single synchronous BPEL component that receives the request message and creates a response message that always contains two hospital records for the patient "John Doe."

Deploy this composite to your Oracle SOA Suite installation as version "1.0." Use Enterprise Manager to inspect the deployed SOA composite and to discover the WSDL location of the exposed Web Service. Test the composite using soapUI, as described in the online chapter complement. In the next sections, we will be using soapUI to also add security-related headers to the Web Service calls.

When everything works, we will continue by applying security to this composite.

Identity Administration

As you can imagine, not everyone is allowed to invoke the SOA composite. The first step toward sufficient security is to add authentication—making sure only insurance companies that St. Matthews knows and trusts can access this service and get hold of the sensitive information it returns.

To achieve this, authentication details need to be transmitted between service consumer and service provider using either the transport or message level. SSL/TLS is the most common approach for the transport level. At the message level, WS-Security profiles are a common implementation.

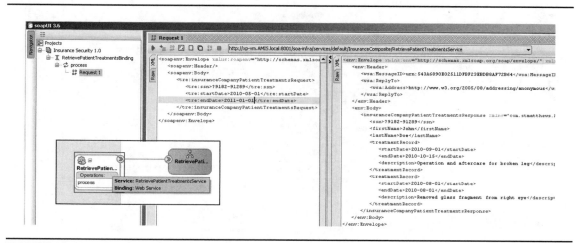

FIGURE 15-10. *Invoking the InsuranceComposite from soapUI*

For our composite we will be using the WS-Security UserNameToken Profile in which a name/password combination is added to the request message. You might think this is pretty insecure because the message itself can be intercepted and the sensitive authentication information (including the password) can be captured. And right you are. We will address this issue in the remainder of this case.

By default, Oracle WebLogic Server uses a file-based store. Note that you can use Oracle Internet Directory (OID) or any other third-party LDAP-compliant solution, such as Microsoft Active Directory (AD), instead. It is recommended to use the file-based solution only for development and test purposes and use a dedicated IAM solution, such as OID, for production environments.

We add the identities of insurance companies using the Oracle WebLogic Administration Console. Log in to the console and browse to the "users and groups" section in the "security realm," as explained in Chapter 10. The console should at least list the "weblogic" user.

Add the following identities and their respective usernames and passwords to the default authenticator of Oracle WebLogic Server, as shown in Figure 15-11:

- **Platinum Insurance**   Username: platinumInsurance. Password: platinumInsurance1.

- **Acme Insurance**   Username: acmeInsurance. Password acmeInsurance1.

- **Insurance for All**   Username: insuranceForAll. Password: insuranceForAll1.

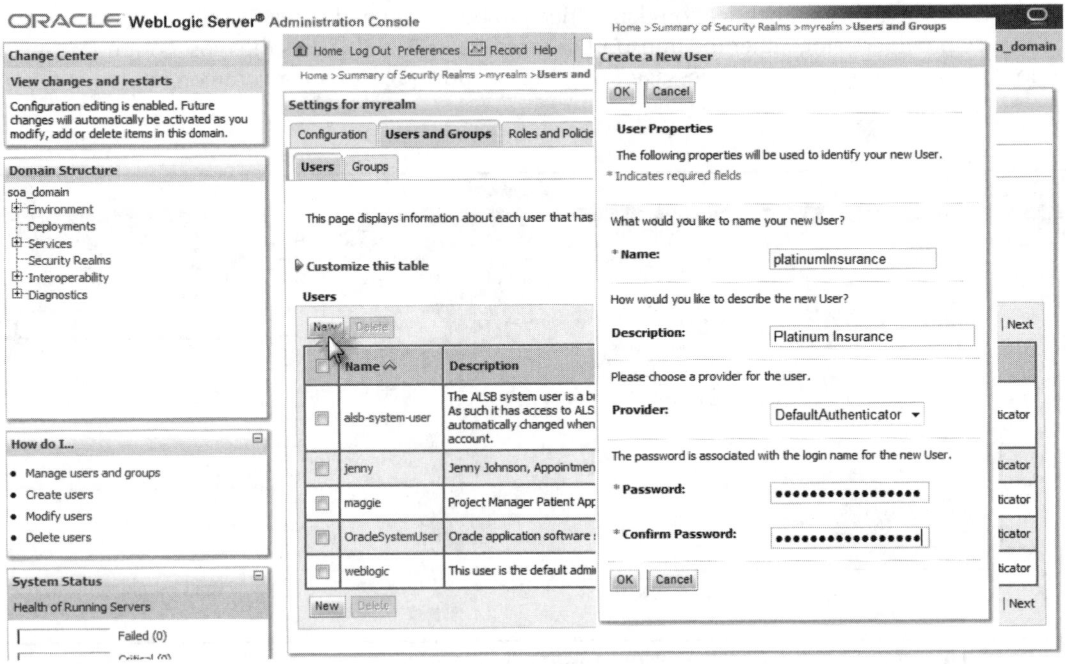

FIGURE 15-11.   *Adding Platinum Insurance as an identity*

IdentityService

Oracle SOA Suite ships with several APIs and Web Services that provide access to its functionality and can be used for building custom clients. Examples of these Web Services are the TaskService, the TaskQueryService, and the IdentityService. See Appendix D for more information.

The IdentityService can be used to search for users and groups, retrieve permissions for users, authenticate users, retrieve the manager of a user, retrieve a property of a specific user or group (such as an e-mail address or telephone number), and so on. The default endpoint for the IdentityService is http://server:port/integration/services/IdentityService/ identity.

Next to the Web Service interface, you can access the IdentityService using the out-of-the-box XPath functions. These functions can be integrated in transformations and assignments within composites.

Authentication Using WS-Security

So where do we check the authentication details that are sent as part of the request message? In other words, where and how is authentication enforced and how is this information delegated to our identity and access management solution?

We will use an OWSM policy to enforce authentication of service clients using WS-Security. When we add this policy to the composite, OWSM will intercept the inbound request message and enforce authentication. This is achieved by extracting the username and password from the request message and delegating authentication to Oracle WebLogic Server's default authenticator, which in turn will validate the username and password.

Deploy InsuranceComposite as Version 1.1

Deploy the original SOA composite again, but this time as version 1.1. The composite is unchanged—and will remain unchanged. The difference with version 1.0 is that the 1.1 version will have a security policy applied to it. Note the separation of concerns: Security stays outside the composite.

Apply the Authentication Policy

We will use Enterprise Manager to apply the authentication policy to the SOA composite. Log in to Enterprise Manager, expand the SOA node, and browse to version 1.1 of InsuranceComposite. Right-click the composite and select Policies.

Click Attach To/Detach From in the Policies view and select the RetrievePatientTreatmentsService service, as shown in Figure 15-12. This opens the Attach/Detach Policies dialog. In this dialog, filter on policies that are in the Security category and select the policy named oracle/wss_username_token_ service_policy.

This policy will accept a WS-Security UserNameToken as the authentication mechanism—both plain text as well as digest. Click OK to apply the policy to the SOA composite. The policy is enabled by default. You can enable and disable policies per SOA composite using Enterprise Manager, as illustrated in Figure 15-13.

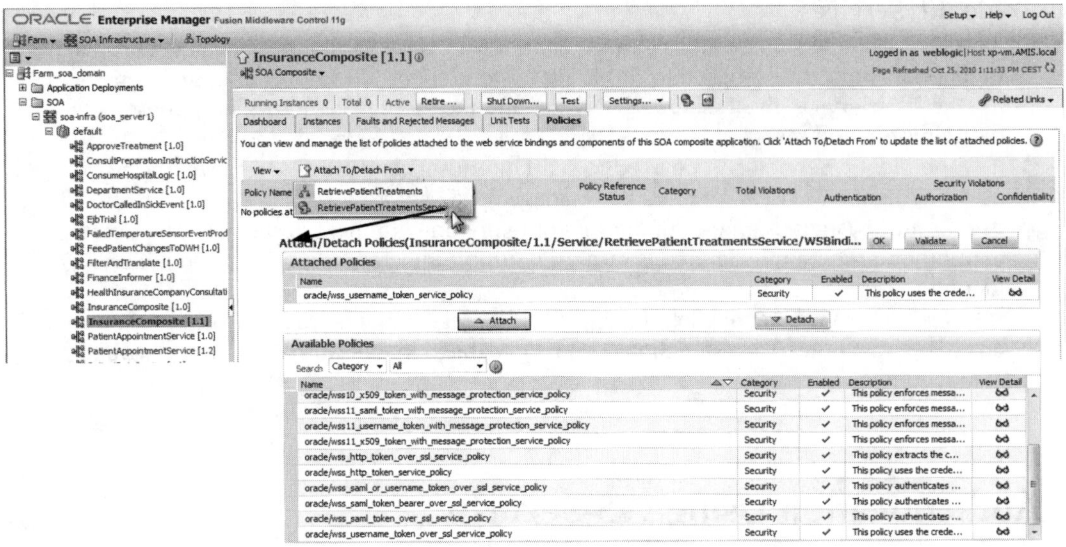

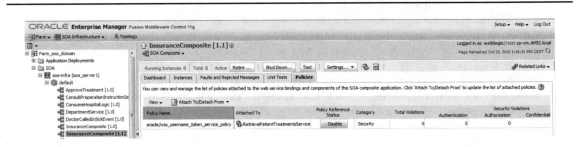

FIGURE 15-12. *Attaching oracle/wss_username_token_service_policy to the InsuranceComposite*

Put the Authentication Policy to the Test

Create a new soapUI project named "InsuranceComposite 1.1" to test the new version of our insurance service. Enter a Social Security number and start and end date in the default request message, and then invoke the service. The response message will not contain John Doe's medical treatments, but instead a fault message with the following description (see Figure 15-14):

```
InvalidSecurity : error in processing the WS-Security security header
```

Return to Enterprise Manager and refresh the Policies view. You will see that there is one security violation. Note that the violation is not listed in the Authentication column; only the number of incorrect authentication attempts will be listed there, as shown in Figure 15-15. In this case, the security headers (and authentication details) were missing altogether.

FIGURE 15-13. *The policy overview after a policy has been added to the SOA composite*

FIGURE 15-14. *Fault message after invoking a secured SOA composite*

Return to soapUI to add the required WS-Security authentication headers. Select the Request 1 message in the Navigator view. In the Request Properties view, add the following properties: **acmeInsurance** as the username and **acmeInsurance1** as the password. Right-click in the Request 1 message and select Add WSS Username Token. A new dialog opens. Select PasswordText as the password type and click OK.

This will add a WS-Security UserNameToken to the request message. Note that this OWSM policy does not require WS-Security Timestamp information to be included in the message.

The request message now looks like the following:

```
<soapenv:Envelope xmlns:tre="com.stmatthews.hospital/treatments"
                   xmlns:soapenv="http://schemas.xmlsoap.org/soap/envelope/">
   <soapenv:Header>
      <wsse:Security soapenv:mustUnderstand="1"
                     xmlns:wsse="http://docs.oasis-open.org/wss/2004/01/...
                            ...oasis-200401-wss-wssecurity-secext-1.0.xsd">
         <wsse:UsernameToken wsu:Id="UsernameToken-1"
                             xmlns:wsu="http://docs.oasis-open.org/wss/...
                ...2004/01/oasis-200401-wss-wssecurity-utility-1.0.xsd">
            <wsse:Username>platinumInsurance</wsse:Username>
            <wsse:Password Type="http://docs.oasis-open.org/wss/2004/01/...
               ...oasis-200401-wss-username-token-profile-1.0#PasswordText">
            platinumInsurance</wsse:Password>
            <wsse:Nonce EncodingType="http://docs.oasis-open.org/wss/2004/...
               ...01/oasis-200401-wss-soap-message-security-1.0#Base64Binary">
            5oXaNox3LMvKnDBB/oGeXg==</wsse:Nonce>
            <wsu:Created>2010-01-02T21:18:53.957Z</wsu:Created>
```

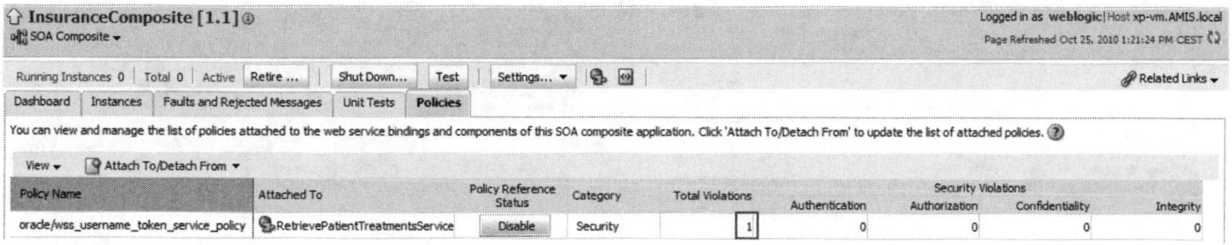

FIGURE 15-15. *Security violation after the secured SOA composite has been invoked*

```
        </wsse:UsernameToken>
      </wsse:Security>
  </soapenv:Header>
  <soapenv:Body>
...
```

Invoke the service again. This time, a valid response is returned.

Edit the request message in soapUI and enter an invalid password for the acmeInsurance identity. The response after the service has been invoked now returns the following fault message:

```
... <env:Fault xmlns:ns0="http://docs.oasis-open.org/wss/2004/01/...
                      ...oasis-200401-wss-wssecurity-secext-1.0.xsd">
    <faultcode>ns0:FailedAuthentication</faultcode>
    <faultstring>FailedAuthentication : The security token cannot be
                        authenticated or authorized.</faultstring>
    <faultactor/>
  </env:Fault>
```

Return to Enterprise Manager and refresh the Policies view for the InsuranceComposite service. The overview will list a new authentication violation.

You can more closely inspect a security violation in the "Faults and Rejected Messages" region of Enterprise Manager. To do so, expand the soa-infra node in the navigator and select a composite. Click the Faults And Rejected Messages tab in the composite overview. In the new view, you can search and filter on faulted and rejected messages, including messages that have caused policy violations. Filter on the fault type and select OWSM Policy Faults Only. The table will now list all OWSM security violations with their corresponding fault time, fault location (such as the component), and a link to the corresponding log file. Click the error message to open a summary dialog in which you can view the payload of the rejected message. As you can see in Figure 15-16, no authentication details are included in the request message.

We have now added authentication enforcement to the composite. As you might have guessed, every identity that is in the identity store is a valid user—as long as the correct username and password are provided.

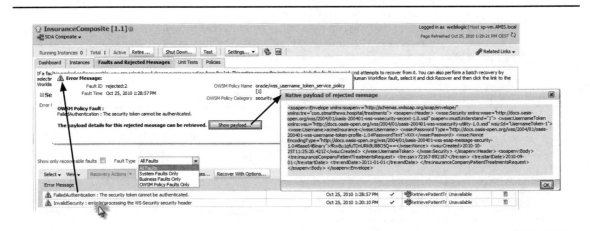

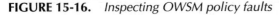

FIGURE 15-16. *Inspecting OWSM policy faults*

Authorization Using WS-Security

Not every identity in our identity store should be allowed to access the insurance composite—not even after successful authentication (for example, administrators who are using the "weblogic" identity or insurance companies that do business with St. Matthews but do not have a specific contract for automated retrieval of patient records). That is where authorization comes into play. We need to make sure that the authenticated identity actually has rights to access the service. We will apply a second policy to the service for this purpose.

Create a Role in the Identity Store and Assign the Role to Users

To begin, create the role TrustedInsuranceCompanies in the identity store. All members of this role will be allowed (authorized) to invoke the InsuranceComposite service. Next, add the selected insurance companies—Insurance for All and Platinum Insurance—to this role. Do not add Acme Insurance because the hospital does not have a contract with Acme Insurance for this specific service.

Apply an Authorization Policy to the InsuranceComposite

Now we add a policy to the SOA composite to make sure that only identities belonging to the TrustedInsuranceCompanies group may access the service. Deploy the SOA composite as version 1.2 and first apply the authentication policy from the previous step to ensure authentication is enforced. After all, an identity needs to be authenticated before it can be authorized.

OWSM provides some out-of-the-box authorization policies—for example, oracle/binding_authorization_denyall_policy, which denies all roles access, and oracle/binding_authorization_permitall_policy, which permits all roles access to a service. We will need to create our own policy based on such an out-of-the-box policy so that only members of the group TrustedInsurance Companies can access the composite.

Log in to Enterprise Manager. In the overview panel, open the WebLogic Domain node, right-click the SOA Suite domain, and select Web Services | Policies. Inspect the policies oracle/binding_authorization_denyall_policy and oracle/binding_authorization_permitall_policy by selecting them and clicking View. Next, we create a new policy that is based on these authorization policies. Select either one of the two authorization policies and click Create Like, as shown in Figure 15-17.

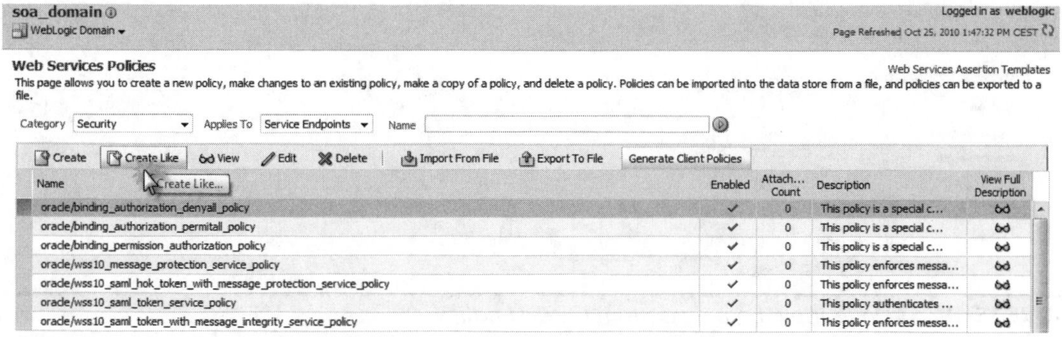

FIGURE 15-17. *Creating a new OWSM policy based on an existing policy*

In the Create Policy view, enter **soasuite11gbook/binding_authorization_permit_trusted_ insurance_companies_policy** as the policy name, as shown in Figure 15-18. In the Roles region, click the radio button Selected Roles as the Authorization Setting. Add TrustedInsuranceCompanies as an authorized role.

Use Enterprise Manager to add this newly created policy to version 1.2 of the InsuranceComposite service (see Figure 15-19).

Trying Out the Authorization Policy

It is time to test the authorization capabilities of the service. Create a new test project in soapUI for version 1.2 of the InsuranceComposite. Add a valid WS-Security UserNameToken to the request message, as explained before. Use acmeInsurance as the username—an identity that is not a member of the TrustedInsuranceCompanies group and that should therefore not be able to access the service. Invoke the service.

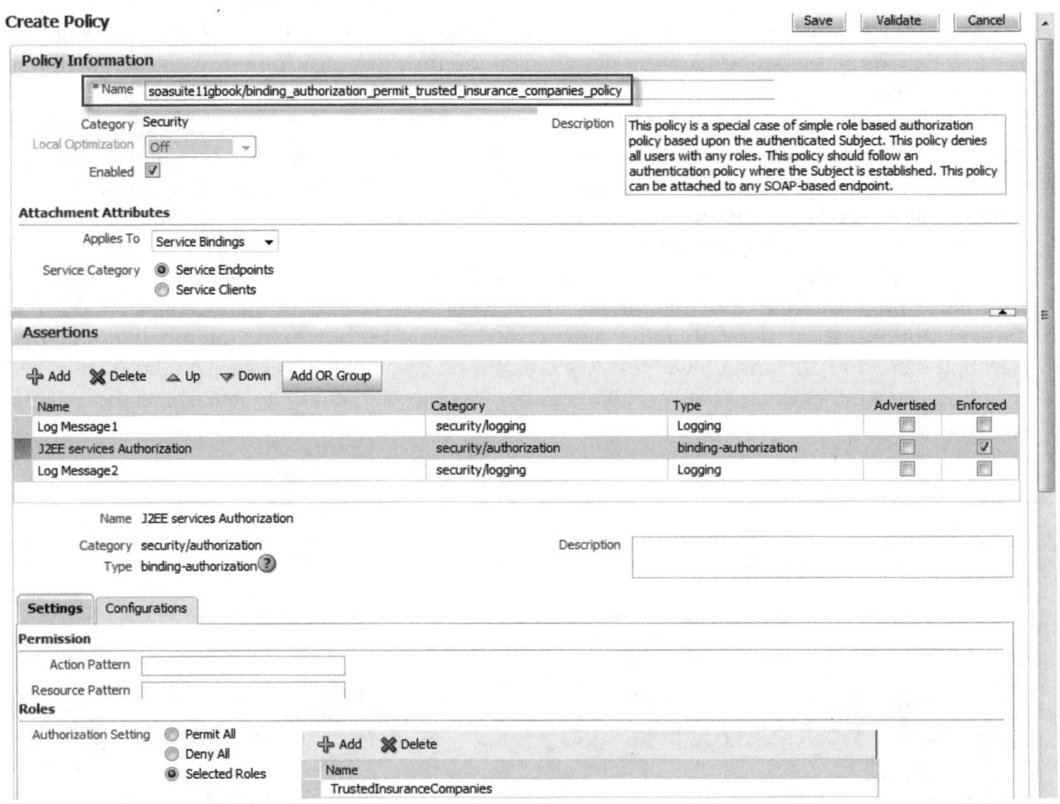

FIGURE 15-18. *Configuring the new custom OWSM policy*

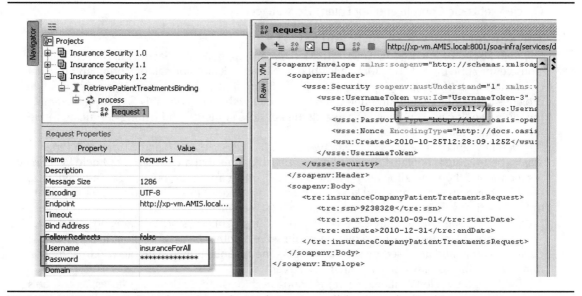

FIGURE 15-19. *The InsuranceComposite service after the policies have been attached to it*

The response message will include the following authorization fault:

```
... <env:Fault xmlns:ns0="http://docs.oasis-open.org/wss/2004/01/...
                       ...oasis-200401-wss-wssecurity-secext-1.0.xsd">
    <faultcode>ns0:FailedAuthorization</faultcode>
    <faultstring>FailedAuthorization :
                          failure in authorization</faultstring>
    <faultactor/>
  </env:Fault>
```

Return to Enterprise Manager and browse to the Policies view for the InsuranceComposite service. The overview will list an authorization violation.

In soapUI, replace the credentials in the request message with those for the Insurance for All insurance company and then invoke the service again (see Figure 15-20).

This time you should see a valid response message containing John Doe's medical history.

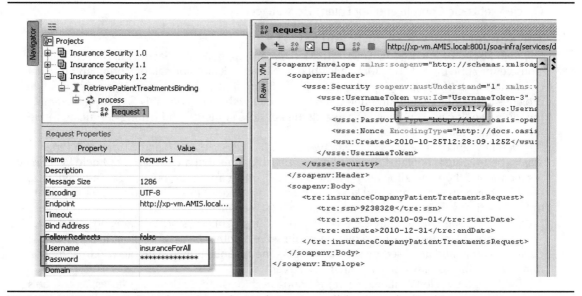

FIGURE 15-20. *Setting credentials on the Web Service call for an authorized insurance company*

Authorization at the Record Level

Note that authorization on the data level is out of scope for this chapter. We will not check that an insurance company can only request patient information from its own clients. You could, for example, expand the composite to check for this or apply Oracle Virtual Private Database (VPD) and identity propagation from the composite to the database to enforce authorization on the data (database row) level.

Ensuring Integrity and Confidentiality Using Transport Security

Although we have enforced authentication and authorization for this service, it is far from secure. Third parties that intercept request and response messages to this service are able to see the message contents containing an overview of patient's medical treatments and the username and password used by insurance companies to invoke the service. Furthermore, St. Matthews is at this point still unable to guarantee messages have not been altered during transport or even tell whether that has happened. In other words, we need to add message integrity and confidentiality capabilities to the service.

For this we can either use WS-Security or SSL/TLS. As explained in the section "Transport Versus Message Security," both WS-Security and SSL/TLS apply data encryption so that intercepted messages remain confidential (unreadable) and add a checksum (or hash) so that data integrity can be verified.

Both WS-Security and SSL/TLS (can) use Public Key Infrastructure (PKI) as the underlying encryption mechanism to enable integrity and confidentiality. OWSM provides policies to ensure data integrity and confidentiality. These policies are either based on WS-Security for message security or ensure that SSL/TLS is used in the transport layer. The keys used for WS-Security policies can be managed using Enterprise Manager. Because transport layer security is managed by the underlying Oracle WebLogic Server, the key management for SSL/TLS is provided by Oracle WebLogic Console and *not* Enterprise Manager.

The Keystores for WS-Security and SSL/TLS

Different keystores are used by Enterprise Manager for applying WS-Security and WebLogic Console for applying SSL/TLS. Oracle WebLogic Server's default format for storing and managing certificates and keys is Java Keystore (JKS). The JKS format is defined by Sun Microsystems. Sun provides the key tool command-line utility to interact with a keystore; this is used, for example, for adding certificates, creating keys, listing the keystore contents, and issuing certificate requests for certificate authorities (CAs).

Oracle WebLogic Server ships with two demo JKS keystores: an identity store and a trust store. The trust store contains the certificates of third parties that are trusted by Oracle WebLogic Server and are therefore allowed to create SSL/TLS connections with our server. The identity store contains our own certificates and keys (including private keys) that are used to identify ourselves to third parties with whom we want to create SSL/TLS connections. Both keystores should be well protected, although the identity store is the most critical. This keystore contains our private key(s). Trust keystores are usually spread over multiple servers within an organization or stored in a central location and accessed by several servers. The organization as a whole will trust the same third parties; this usually does not differ per server.

By default, Oracle WebLogic Server is configured to use these demo keystores, as can be seen and modified in the WebLogic Console. The Keystores property is initially set to "Demo Identity

and Demo Trust." These keystores are located at [Oracle Home]/wlserver_10.3/server/lib/
DemoIdentity.jks and [Oracle Home]/wlserver_10.3/server/lib/DemoTrust.jks. The keystores'
passwords are DemoIdentityKeyStorePassPhrase and DemoTrustKeyStorePassPhrase, respectively.
You can use the command-line utility keytool to list the contents of these keystores—see the
online chapter complement for instructions.

The demo keystores and the demo certificates can be used for development and testing
purposes. However, for production environments it is recommended to use "real" keystores
containing actual certificates that are signed by trusted certificate authorities. For now, we will
use the default demo keystores and certificates.

Configure SSL/TLS in WebLogic Console

We are going to enable integrity and confidentiality based on transport security; therefore, we'll
make use of SSL/TLS. We will be using one-way SSL/TLS. We need to configure SSL/TLS for
Oracle WebLogic Server and apply an authentication policy to the InsuranceComposite that uses
SSL/TLS.

In the WebLogic Console, select the SSL tab and inspect the SSL settings. You can, among
other things, configure whether you want to use one-way or two-way SSL. In two-way SSL, the
client also needs to send a certificate that needs to be accepted by the server. Two-way SSL can
be used for mutual authentication. In our case, however, client authentication is achieved
through WS-Security. Therefore, we do not require two-way SSL. For now, we will accept the
default values—and thus one-way SSL.

Select the General tab and make sure that the check box SSL Listen Port Enabled is checked
so that incoming SSL/TLS connections are supported.

Add Transport Security to the InsuranceComposite

We will now add transport security to our SOA composite. Deploy the SOA composite as version
1.3. Instead of adding the authentication policy oracle/wss_username_token_service_policy that
we used in the previous versions, we will now use the oracle/wss_username_token_over_ssl_
service_policy. This policy ensures that the message is sent over SSL/TLS rather than using a
nonsecured protocol. We also apply our own authorization policy to it.

Secured Transport in Action

Create a new test project in soapUI for InsuranceComposite version 1.3. Add a valid WS-Security
UserNameToken to the request message. Use either the identity Insurance for All or Platinum
Insurance.

Bulk Attachment of Policies

Using Enterprise Manager, you can attach one or more policies to more than one service in
a single operation. This is known as "bulk attachment."

The steps for bulk policy attachment are as follows: Expand the SOA Domain node in
Enterprise Manager, right-click the SOA server node, and select Web Services. In the Web
Services overview, select the SOA tab and click the Attach Policies link. This opens a
wizard in which you can select all services, references, and/or components to which you
want to apply policies, the policies you want to apply to them, and a summary page to
confirm this bulk attachment.

The policy oracle/wss_username_token_over_ssl_service_policy also requires request messages to include a WS-Timestamp header containing the creation and expiration time of the message. The WS-Timestamp header can be placed either before or after the WS-Security UserNameToken header. The order of these elements is not specified by the WS-Security standard. Right-click the request message and select Add WS-Timestamp. Enter **3600** as the Time-To-Live value.

NOTE
When using headers containing timestamps, you may need to regenerate these headers in soapUI because they can become outdated after a while and will be rejected by OWSM.

Invoke the service. The following fault message is returned:

```
... <env:Fault xmlns:ns0="http://docs.oasis-open.org/wss/2004/01/...
                        ...oasis-200401-wss-wssecurity-secext-1.0.xsd">
    <faultcode>ns0:FailedCheck</faultcode>
    <faultstring>FailedCheck : failure in security check</faultstring>
    <faultactor/>
</env:Fault>
```

This error is returned because InsuranceComposite 1.3 can only be accessed over HTTPS due to the policy we have applied to it. Our attempt to call it on unsecured HTTP was rejected. We will try again, this time using HTTPS.

Create a new test project in soapUI, for the same version 1.3 of the composite. Add the WS-Security UserNameToken and WS-Security Timestamp headers.

Add a new endpoint for the request; this time, use the endpoint derived from the WSDL, but replace "http" with "https" and replace the port number (default is 8001) with the SSL port number, as configured in the Oracle WebLogic Server Console (the default SSL port is 8002). This is shown in Figure 15-21.

Now invoke the service, calling the new endpoint. This time, the correct response message will be returned by the SOA composite. Click the "SSL Info (1 certs)" tab in the response window to see the certificate returned by Oracle WebLogic Server (see Figure 15-22).

Monitoring Access to the BPEL Component

OWSM policies do not all apply at the composite level. Some policies can be applied to individual components within composites. We will add logging capabilities to the BPEL component in the

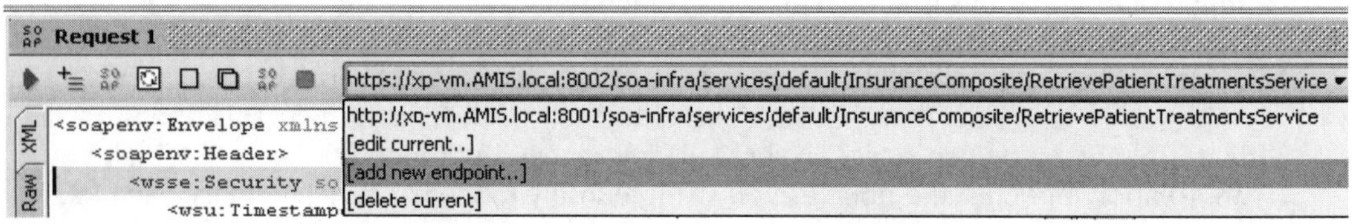

FIGURE 15-21. *Configuring a new, HTTPS-enabled endpoint in soapUI*

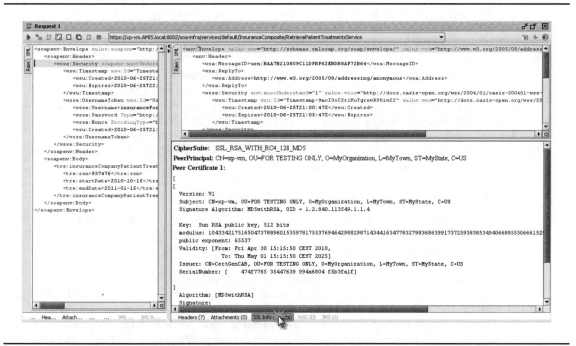

FIGURE 15-22. *Inspecting the certificate used to set up the SSL/TLS connection*

InsuranceComposite, using a OWSM policy. The logging assertion that is used will log messages to the following file: [Oracle Home]/user_projects/domains/[SOA domain]/servers/[SOA server]/logs/owsm/msglogging/diagnostic.log.

Deploy the InsuranceComposite as version 1.4 and add the previously introduced OWSM policies (authentication over SSL/TLS and authorization) to it in the Enterprise Manager console. Now continue by adding the policy oracle/log_policy to the BPEL component. As you can see in Figure 15-23, we add this policy to a component, although it can also be applied to a service or reference.

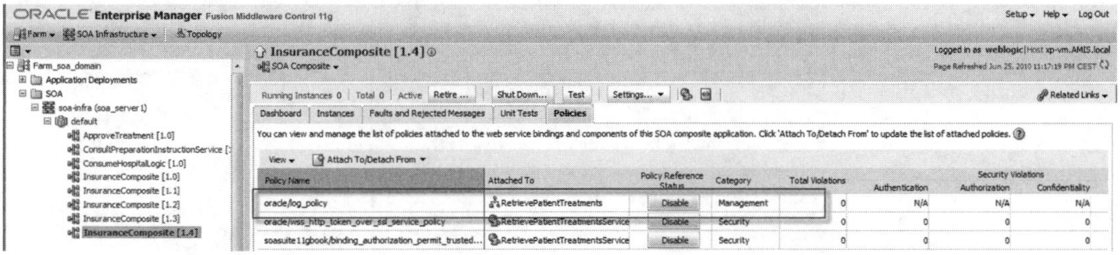

FIGURE 15-23. *InsuranceComposite version 1.4 with the logging policy applied*

Create a new test project in soapUI for InsuranceComposite version 1.4. Remember to provide valid credentials. After successful invocation of the service, the diagnostic.log file should contain an entry that holds the payload and metadata of the message that is sent to and from the BPEL component.

Several out-of-the-box policies also include the logging assertion. However, most of these assertions are disabled by default—not advertised or enforced. Enforcing these assertions will cause the messages to be logged to the diagnostic.log file after successful authentication. Advertisement is about exposing the policies in the Web Service's WSDL using WS-Policy.

If, for example, you want to log incoming messages before and after processing of WS-Security headers, you can enforce (and advertise) these logging assertions. See the online chapter complement for instructions and screenshots.

Applying Security Using JDeveloper

As shown in the previous examples, Enterprise Manager can be used to apply, configure, monitor, and manage OWSM policies for SOA composites. This section demonstrates how to add OWSM policies at design time in JDeveloper. When deployed, these policies will be visible in Enterprise Manager.

You cannot use JDeveloper to configure, monitor, or manage policies and assertions or create your own custom policies. This makes sense because security configuration is often an administration task rather than a development task.

To illustrate JDeveloper's policy capabilities, we will return to one of the first scenarios in which we enforced authentication. Open the InsuranceComposite project in JDeveloper and open the SOA composite by double-clicking the composite.xml file. This displays a graphical overview of the composite. Right-click the exposed RetrievePatientTreatmentsService service binding and select Configure WS Policies...., as illustrated by Figure 15-24.

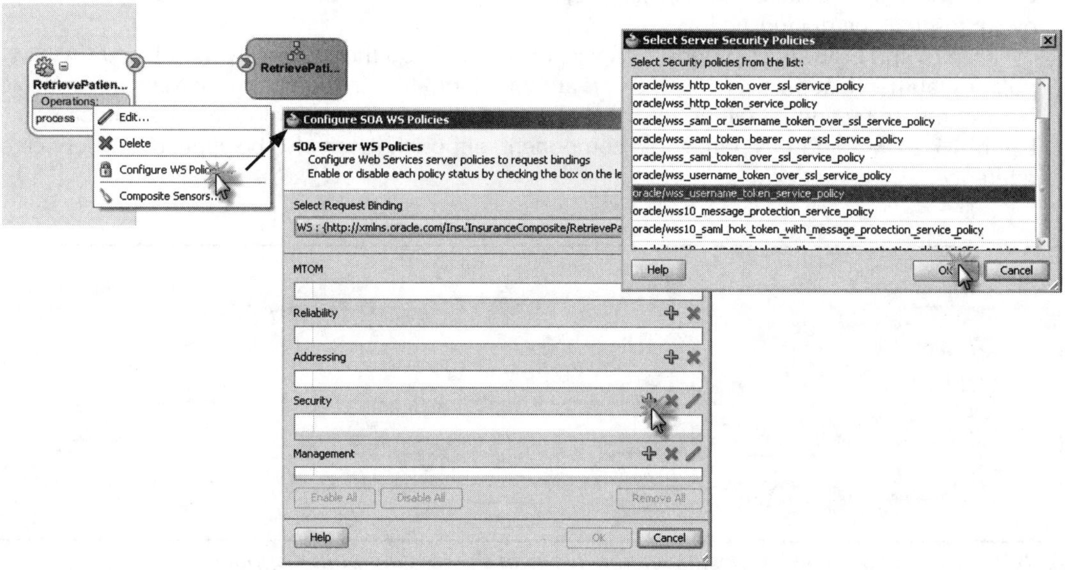

FIGURE 15-24. *Adding policies to a SOA composite using JDeveloper*

JDeveloper will now load the available policies from its internal policy repository that is located in the [Middleware Home]/jdeveloper/jdev/bin/owsm directory. The repository contains assertion templates and policies. This means that JDeveloper will not display the custom policies you have defined in Enterprise Manager. You will need to copy these to the local repository in order to apply them using JDeveloper.

Just as in Enterprise Manager, JDeveloper categorizes policies into different categories: MTOM, Reliability, Addressing, Security, and Management. Click the green plus sign icon next to security. This will open a dialog that displays the available security policies. Select the policy oracle/wss_username_token_service_policy and click OK. This is the same policy that we previously added using Enterprise Manager.

Back in the Configure SOA WS Policies dialog, you will notice that the policy is added to the RetrievePatientTreatmentsService service binding. You can select (or deselect) the check box next to policies to enable (or disable) them. This setting is included when the SOA composite is deployed to the run time and can be changed using Enterprise Manager.

In the SOA Composite Editor, notice the yellow lock symbol in the top-right corner of the exposed service. When you switch to the Source view of the composite.xml file, you will see that a policy reference is added to the service binding and its status is set to enabled:

```
<service name="RetrievePatientTreatmentsService">
  <interface.wsdl ... />
  <binding.ws port="...">
    <wsp:PolicyReference URI="oracle/wss_username_token_service_policy"
                         orawsp:category="security" orawsp:status="enabled"/>
  </binding.ws>
</service>
```

When we deploy the composite as version 1.5, we would find in Enterprise Manager that this authentication policy is already in place—and does not need to be added after deployment. However, any further configuration, monitoring, and managing need to be done through Enterprise Manager.

Summary

IT security has become increasingly important over the last decades. This is even more true for businesses and organizations dealing with sensitive information, including hospitals. This chapter introduced general security concepts such as identity and access management, encryption, transport versus message security, and agents and gateways. It discussed the implications of the service-orientation paradigm for security.

Oracle SOA Suite and WebLogic Server on which it runs provide numerous security capabilities. One of these is Oracle Web Services Manager (OWSM), which can be used to secure Web Services. This chapter described the main features and workings of OWSM and provided a step-by-step case on how to use OWSM to secure your SOA composites and protect valuable and sensitive data.

Security needs a holistic approach. Securing SOA composites alone is not enough. You also need to consider securing Oracle WebLogic Server itself (for example, access to the various consoles and the file system on which it runs). Also remember to secure access to the human tasks that are created and managed by Oracle SOA Suite.

Finally, Oracle's acquisition of AmberPoint will probably impact the future security offerings and functionality of Oracle SOA Suite and the OWSM roadmap.

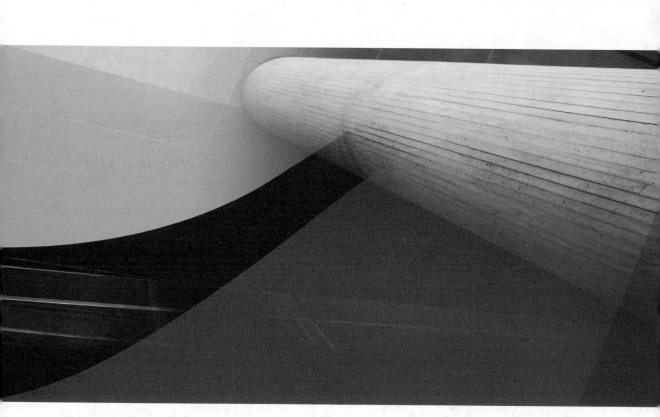

CHAPTER
16

What Is Going On:
Monitoring SOA
Composite Applications

t is sometimes easy to forget that for a developer, his or her work is only the tip of the iceberg. When the applications are developed, it may feel as if everyone can lean back and relax because the most important part of the job is done. Okay, a little testing and, of course, deployment to a production environment (see Chapter 17), but that's it. Job done.

Of course, we all know that it is only after deployment that applications can start to add value to the organization. Production usage is the only reason for being when it comes to applications—and ultimately developers. At that time, we know longer only care about composites but also about instances. Every instance of a composite may represent a business transaction—an interaction with a business partner, a patient or doctor, or insurance company. A transaction can be associated with strong emotions, large amounts of money, or people's health.

Monitoring instances of the composite applications, ensuring their timely and correct completion, intervening when instances have faulted, and archiving and purging instances are all extremely important operations required for successful execution of business processes.

This chapter takes a look behind the scenes of running SOA Suite containers. We will look at facilities in SOA Suite to monitor ongoing operations and to recover from errors in running instances. It introduces several ways to provide an administrator with all relevant details about running and completed instances. Most of what we do in this chapter will take place in the Fusion Middleware Control Console—the run-time tool we have used ever since we deployed our very first HelloWorld composite back in Chapter 3.

Monitoring Instances of Composite Applications

Composite instance monitoring happens at various levels. We are usually interested in performance and throughput at an aggregate level where all instances are taken together, grouped by time slice, for example. Individual instances and their state and content are not relevant at this level. Overall metrics and how they compare to predefined objectives as perhaps laid down in Service Level Agreements are what we are chiefly after.

Occasionally, we need to find and inspect a specific instance of a composite application—usually because one of the parties involved somehow with the instance has questions about the result or wants to know the current status. When instances have failed—that is, ended with an exception—administrators typically need to know and possibly act on it.

Dashboard and Aggregate Metrics

By now you must have seen the Fusion Middleware Control Console dozens if not hundreds of times. It provides a wealth of information on what's going on in the SOA Suite, both at an aggregate level as well as per service engine, per composite, and per composite instance. Through the console, we can access real-time performance charts, get hold of live statistics, inspect fine-grained log files, and analyze the message flow trace for composite instances. The console currently does not offer SLA monitoring—although that may be available in the near future in the console itself, in the add-on SOA Management Pack, or through products from the newly acquired AmberPoint portfolio. The console will not alert us when performance is degrading, for example, or when an unusual high percentage of composite instances is failing. Note that the Oracle Service Bus does have support for such SLA alerts.

Dashboards at the Container, Composite, and Component Levels

The console presents a dashboard in the context of the node selected in the tree navigator on the left. When the soa-infra node is selected, the dashboard covers the entire container with all instances for all components. It will show the status for all deployed composites in all partitions—for recent and running instances. It also lists recent faults in composite execution and rejected messages (messages from adapter services that failed to reach a composite). By selecting a specific partition node, we will get the same information for all composites in that particular partition.

When we select a node for a specific composite (or version of a composite), as in Figure 16-1, its dashboard is shown with instances and faults for the selected composite and the metrics for its components, services, and references: the number of instances, faults, and the average processing time. It is possible to drill down to individual components, services, and references in the composite by clicking them in the composite dashboard.

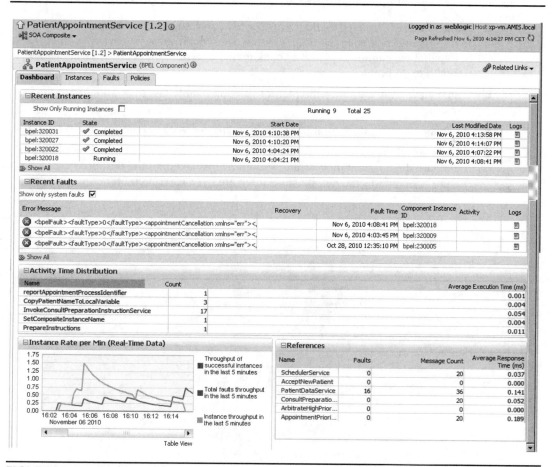

FIGURE 16-1. *Dashboard for a BPEL component inside the PatientAppointmentService composite*

A detailed dashboard is shown with information about the activity—past and present—of the selected component, service, or reference. The dashboard lists instances, faults, and throughput (number of instances per minute). Depending on the type, different data is shown. For example, the Human Task Component dashboard provides insight into the variation in the business outcomes of the task and into the average time taken by the human actors for executing the task. For BPEL components, the dashboard shows an overview of the activity time distribution, a listing of the average time spent on each activity in the BPEL process.

Performance Monitoring

The FMW Control Console provides a real-time graphical performance dashboard with a customizable selection of charts or listings that indicate the recent past and present of composite processing in the SOA Suite. This dashboard is accessed from the context menu on the soa-infra node: Right-click this node to bring up the context menu, open the Monitoring submenu, and select Performance Summary (see Figure 16-2).

The presentation of the performance information can be configured in several ways:

- **Time window**   Using the slider, the Zoom In and Zoom Out icons, or the time entry pop-up, we can specify the time window over which we want to review the metrics. (Note that we cannot look farther back than the startup time of the SOA Suite and never more than 24 hours.)

- **Table view**   We can have the metrics listed in a table layout in addition to the graphical presentation.

- **Overlay**   Metrics from multiple SOA Suite instances can be combined in the dashboard.

- **Metric selection**   The Metric Palette, shown in Figure 16-3, can be brought up to configure the different metrics that should be displayed on the dashboard. Brace yourself before opening this palette, because there are over 150 different metrics you can select

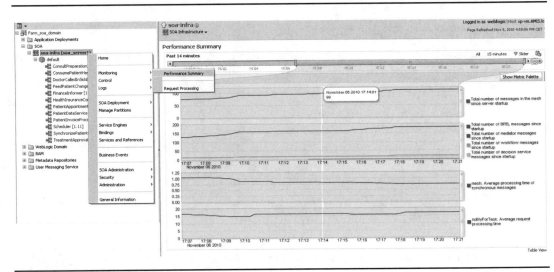

FIGURE 16-2.   *Real-time Performance Summary*

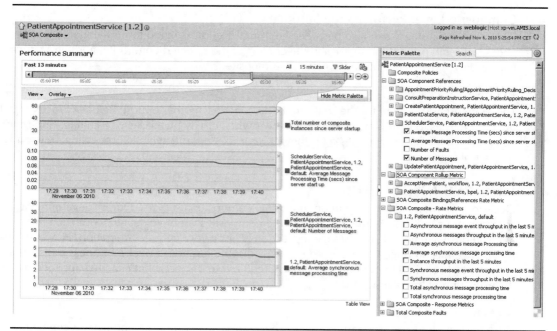

FIGURE 16-3. *The Metric Palette for Performance Summary to select the metrics to visualize*

to have displayed on the dashboard; these metrics range from the number of messages arriving at the SOA Suite and specific composites and engines, to the average processing time of individual services and references.

- **Dashboard composition**   You can reorder these charts by simply dragging and dropping them into the desired position.

Performance Summary is a great tool for quickly getting insight into the current state of affairs. Multiple browser windows can be opened with focus on various aspects of the operations. However, the tool lacks a number of functions that one may desire from it:

- It does not save the configuration of the dashboard; when you close the page, you will have to reselect the metrics to display.

- It does not allow us to set goals or thresholds for the metrics that would show up in the charts.

- It does not do any form of SLA monitoring, raising alerts when performance falls short of the specified minimum levels.

- It does not cater for exporting metrics in any form.

The Business Activity Monitor product that we will discuss in Chapter 19 can be used to address some of these requirements.

Composite-Level Performance Summary

Performance Summary can also be accessed from the context menu for individual composite nodes. This will present the metrics in the context of the selected composite, and the Metrics Palette only shows relevant options for the composite.

Request Processing

The Monitoring submenu for the soa-infra node contains another option: Request Processing. This option brings us to a fairly high-level overview of the activity by the Service Engines and Binding components: the number of messages they have processed, the average processing time, and the number of faults.

Instance Inspection

Occasionally we need to zoom in on individual composite instances. During development, this is common practice to verify the behavior of the composites we have developed. When the applications have gone live, instance inspection is not a very frequent operation. However, when an instance has produced unexpected results, a dispute has arisen over a business transaction, or an instance has failed to complete, it may be required to inspect what exactly happened during the execution of the composite.

Message Flow Trace

We have seen in previous chapters that each instance of a composite application can be tracked through the message flow trace. This trace visualizes the path a message has followed from the moment it entered the SOA Suite, until such time all activity in the composite instance has completed. All components that were visited appear in the flow trace, as well as other composites that were invoked and all other bindings such as external Web Services and adapter references. The flow trace shows the status of each component invocation and also the start time and end time. For faulted instances, the flow trace presents details about the exception that occurred.

We can drill down from the flow trace to the detailed audit trail for the service components. This, in turn, presents fine-grained trace information about the execution of the component. Each BPEL activity, Human Task update, or Mediator action can be tracked in this way.

Audit-Level Settings

The validity of those last statements depends on the audit-level setting. The audit level for the entire instance of the SOA Suite as well as for individual composites can be one of three settings: Development, Production, or Off. Composites can also inherit the value set at the soa-infra level. The Development setting results in the most detailed audit information—down to details about each Assign activity in BPEL processes. With the audit level set to Off, we will not get *any* information about composite instances: They will still run, but no trace of them is found in the FMW Control Console. The audit level Production is the most common setting in—this may not come as a surprise—production environments.

You can set the audit level for composites by clicking the Settings button for a composite and selecting the desired audit level, as shown in Figure 16-4.

Log Files

In addition to the fairly structured message flow trace that helps us analyze individual composite instances—provided the audit-level setting is appropriate, of course—the SOA Suite writes out information about its activities to several log files. These files are located on the server on which

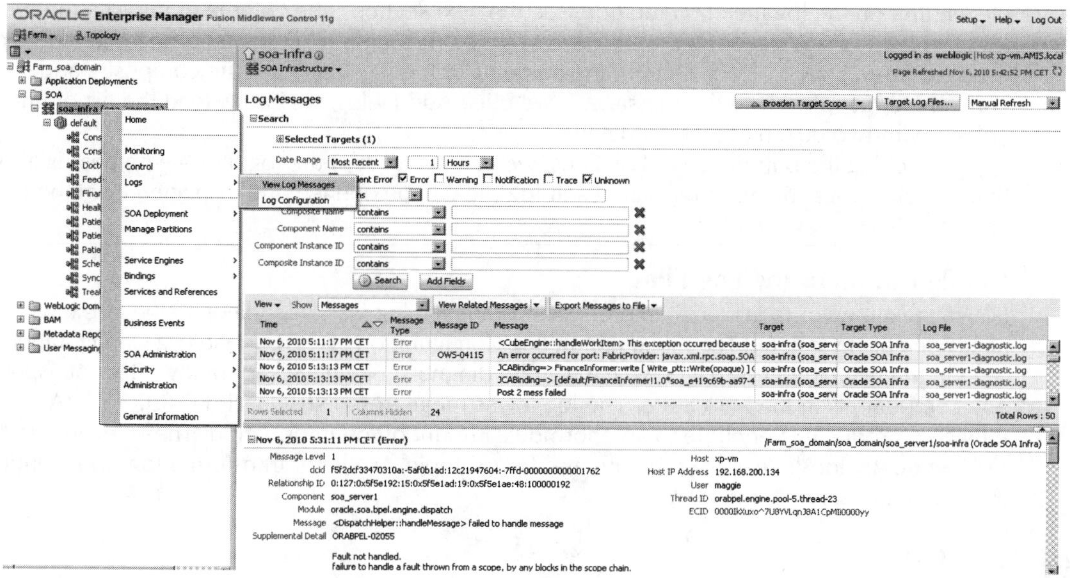

FIGURE 16-4. *Setting the audit level for the PatientAppointmentService composite*

the SOA Suite runs, and can also be inspected from the FMW Control Console. You can find the log files in the console from the context menu on the soa-infra node, picking the option View Log Messages from the Logs submenu, as shown in Figure 16-5.

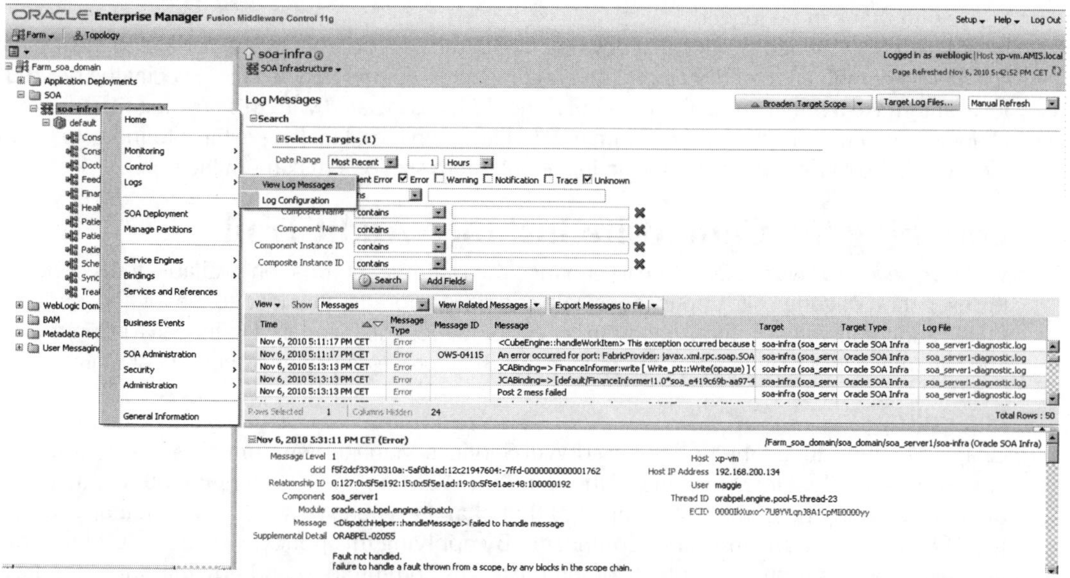

FIGURE 16-5. *Inspecting the SOA Suite–wide log messages*

The Log Messages page provides access to all messages written to one of several log files. Depending on the log file configuration (see the next section), the volume of information in the logs can be huge. We can filter our view on the log messages by date and time range, the type of message (from Error to Trace Detail), the contents of the message, and the composite and component that produced the message. If we click Add Fields, we can extend the list of filter criteria with two dozen additional details.

By clicking the button Target Log Files, we can get a list of the log files—with details about their physical location and their size. Each log file can be opened and inspected from the console and can also be downloaded.

Configuration of the Log Files

SOA Suite allows us to instruct it to produce customized log files, in addition to the files it will already create by default. The menu option Log Configuration takes us to the Log Configuration page.

On the first tab of this page, we can set the diagnostic log levels for many different aspects of and components in the SOA Suite. The log levels range from INCIDENT_ERROR to TRACE:32 (FINEST), producing very little to an enormous amount of log information. These levels can be set independently for dozens of components—for example, Mediator transformation, BPEL entity, and Metadata Services (MDS).

NOTE
Make changes to these settings with some care, because you can easily and inadvertently instruct SOA Suite to produce tens of megabytes' worth of logging data per hour, which may not necessarily be very helpful and is even less likely to endear you to your system-administrating colleagues.

The second tab of this page has us configure the log files that are being written. We can add our own specialized log file, with our special selection from the many events taking place in the SOA Suite that can be logged.

Click the Create icon to create a new log file. In the pop-up, specify the name and the log path—a server-side combination of directory path and filename—for the new log file. Specify the desired log level and make a selection of all loggers that should be associated with this new log file—for example, all loggers that have to do with the Human Workflow services. Finally, we have to indicate how these files should be rotated, either by specifying a maximum size or a maximum lifetime.

Enriching the Composite Instance Audit Trail

We have several ways in SOA Suite to enhance the run-time information available to us concerning the execution of composite applications. We can have information added to the log file, enrich the (BEPL) audit trail, make composite instances easier to recognize and find in the FWM Control Console, and even have information about the progress of BPEL processes reported via JMS or Database.

Log Policy

Chapter 15 introduced the policy-based WebServices Management framework, primarily in the context of security. However, one of the standard WSM policies is a logging policy, as was demonstrated in one of the last sections of that chapter when we added the oracle/log_policy to the BPEL process in the InsuranceComposite. By applying this policy, we can extend the logging with exact entries with the contents of the messages coming in to and flowing out of the targeted composites and components.

For example, to log the request and response message to and from the PatientDataService—in the console, because we only have a temporary need for this additional logging—select the node PatientDataService in the FMW EM Console. Select the Policies tab, where policies can be applied to and detached from composites and their components, and then open the drop-down on Attach To/Detach From and select the BPEL component PatientDataService. The Attach/Detach Policies pop-up opens. Select the oracle/log policy and click Attach. Click OK to close the pop-up. The log policy is now in place, as shown in Figure 16-6.

Let's see the log policy in action: To begin, invoke the PatientApppointmentService that in turn calls the PatientDataService. Then go to the Instances tab for the PatientDataService. Click the icon in the Logs column for the instance that was just created and then click the button Target Log Files. Select the diagnostic.log file and click View Log File. The most recent two entries of type Notification are created by the WSM logging policy that we have applied before; this, too, is

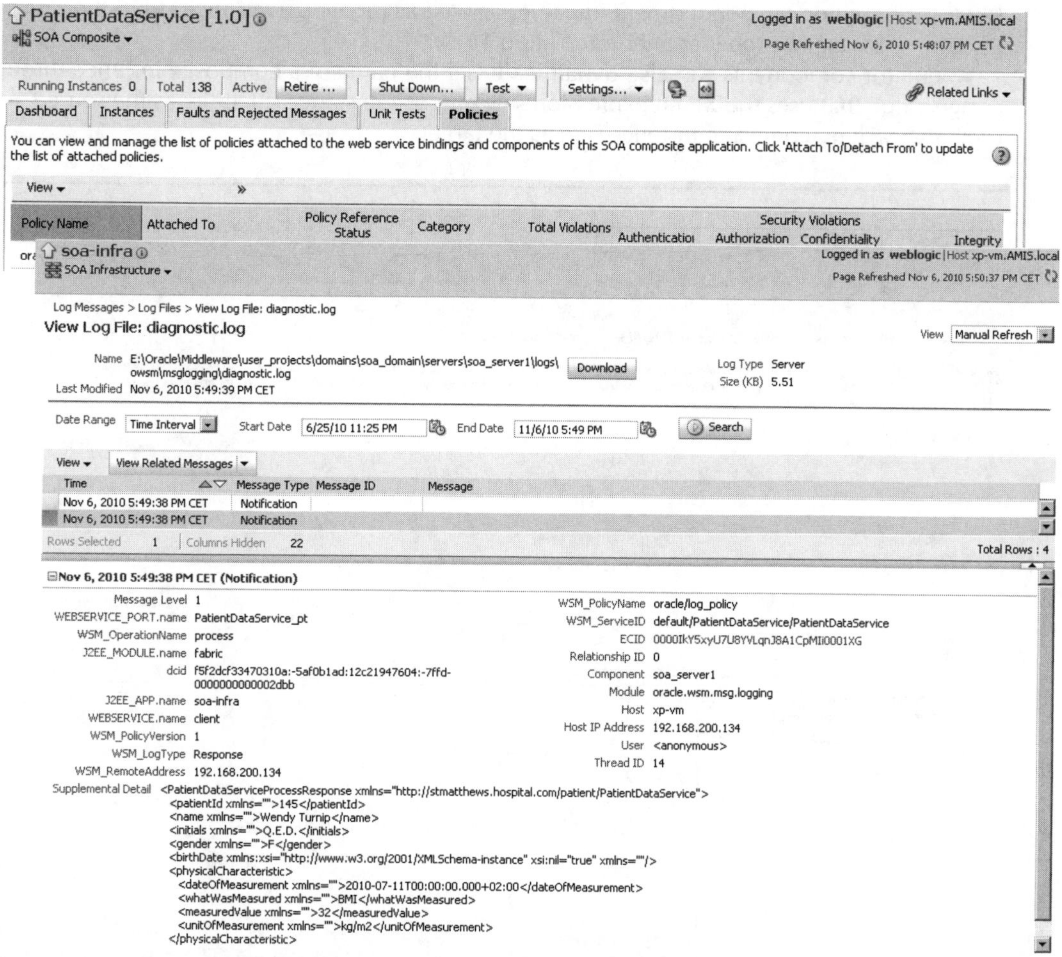

FIGURE 16-6. *Applying the log policy to the PatientDataService component and seeing the resulting log entries*

shown in Figure 16-6. Alternatively, you can inspect the log file on the file system to verify whether the WSM policy creates the log entries as intended.

Setting the Name of a Composite Instance

Composite instances all look the same in the console. The only way really to distinguish one from the other is based on their start time—which is not terribly much to go on. Fortunately, there are several ways to make it easier to discern between instances. One is by dynamically assigning a meaningful name to an instance of a composite. For example, we can add an Embedded Java activity to the BPEL process PatientAppointmentService—as described in Chapter 12—that sets the name of the composite instance to the appointment identifier, as shown here:

```
setCompositeInstanceTitle("Appointment Id:"
             +getVariableData("processIdentifier"));
```

When we deploy the composite with this activity added to it, we will be able to search for instances based on the appointment identifier as well as recognize instances from their names because these expose the identifier (see Figure 16-7).

Mediator components can also dynamically set the name of a composite instance through an Assign value that uses the XPath expression setCompositeInstanceTitle(title) as the source and the property tracking.compositeInstanceTitle as the target.

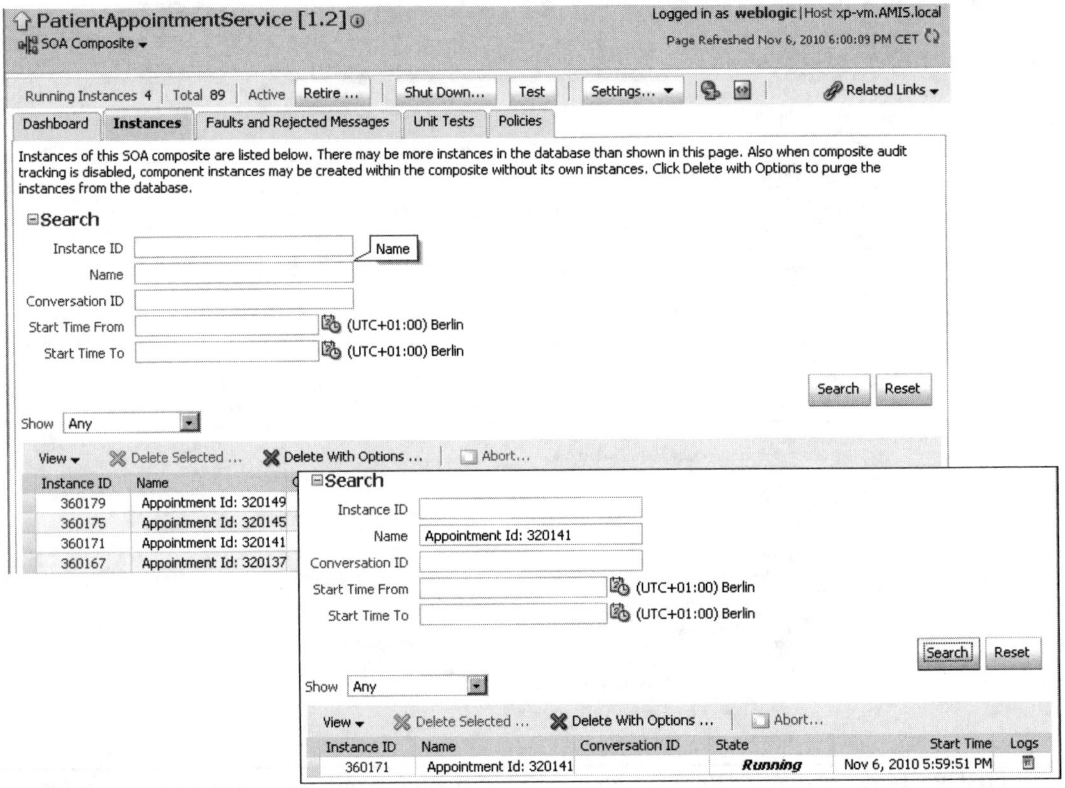

FIGURE 16-7. *Instances for which the name has been set are easier to identify and find.*

Composite Sensors

Composite sensors make our life easier by allowing us to expose information from within composite instances. These sensors are typically used to expose data such as the name of the patient, the appointment identifier, or other information that represents the composite in a meaningful way. This information can subsequently be used to find instances we may have a special interest in or to learn something about an instance already under scrutiny. Composite sensors report values for services or references in a composite—the internal processing in the composite is not exposed. Composite sensors are defined in JDeveloper, in the Composite Editor.

Adding Composite Sensors to Composite PatientAppointmentService Let's add a few sensors to the PatientAppointmentService composite to make it easier to find instances of this composite and also to better appreciate the composites we see listed in the console. Click the screwdriver icon in the Composite Editor. Select the service or reference on which a sensor is to be defined. In this case, select the PatientAppointmentService_ep service and click the green plus icon (see Figure 16-8).

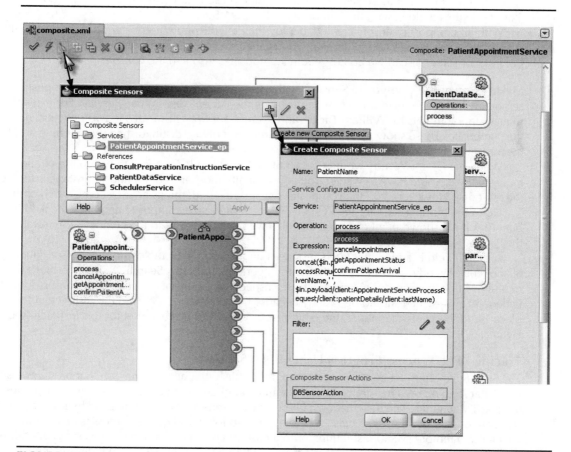

FIGURE 16-8. *Creating the composite sensor PatientName for composite PatientAppointmentService*

Enter a name for the sensor in the Create Composite Sensor pop-up—for example, **PatientName**, because our first sensor will expose the name of the patient for whom an instance of the PatientAppointmentService is created. Select the initially invoked process operation on the service. Specify the expression for the value that this sensor should expose. In this case, we expose the result of concatenating the first and last name of the patient.

A filter can be used to specify that the sensor should only report a value under a special condition. The sensor's actions need not (and cannot) currently be set, because only the DBSensor action is supported for composite sensors. Click OK to complete the creation of the first sensor.

Continue to also create composite sensors on the patient identifier (set by the reference PatientDataService) and the appointment identifier (set in the same process operation that we just created the PatientName sensor for). Finally, also create a composite sensor on the getAppointmentStatus operation in the composite's publicly exposed service.

The composite sensors are depicted in the Composite Editor by little icons on each service or reference that has sensors defined on it.

A new file called sensor.xml is created in the root of the project. This file contains the detailed definitions of all composite sensors. Additionally, the file sensorAction.xml defines the action taken for each of these sensors—which at the present can only be DBSensorAction. These files are deployed along with the composite to the SOA Suite.

With all composite sensors created, deploy the PatientAppointmentService composite to the SOA Suite. Note that we cannot find any metadata about the composite sensors in the FMW Control Console, nor can we add or modify composite sensors in the console.

Making Use of the Composite Sensors in the Console To see the effect of the composite sensors, we have to create some new instances of the PatientAppointmentService. For example, request appointments for William Tacker and Wendy Turnip. This results in two new instances of the composite. These show up in the console and can only be distinguished by start time and the meaningless composite instance identifier.

When the GP for Wendy would contact St. Matthews to learn about the appointment he has requested, we would have to wade through potentially thousands of composite instances to find the right one. However, with the composite sensors attached, things have become much easier.

Go to the Instances tab for the PatientAppointmentService composite and click the Add Fields button. A list is shown of all extra search fields we can use thanks to the composite sensors. Select the Patient Name field.

A search field is added that filters instances on their value for the composite sensor Patient Name. Enter **Wendy**, select Like as the search operator, and click Search. A single instance is returned. Click the Composite Sensor icon to inspect the values of the composite sensors for Patient Name—which should be Wendy because that is how we retrieved the instance in the first place—and the Patient Identifier, the other sensor value that has been set for this instance (see Figure 16-9).

Tracing BPEL Process Progress Using BPEL Sensors

The SOA Suite offers yet another mechanism for publishing trace information that provides insight into what is going on. Fine-grained sensors can be applied to BPEL processes to track activities, variables, and faults. The information gathered by the sensors can be processed by sensor actions that can forward the sensor signals to the database, to local JMS queues or topics or via a JMS adapter to a remote JMS infrastructure, or to a custom Java class. Important sensor signals can be turned to EDN events via a JMS or custom Java action. In Chapter 19, we will discuss the BAM

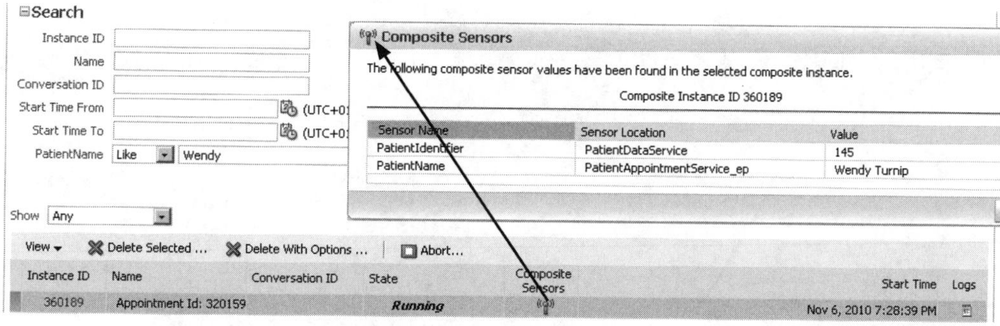

FIGURE 16-9. *Retrieving the PatientAppointmentService composite instance for patient Wendy and inspecting the composite sensor values*

sensor action, which reports BPEL sensor signals to the Business Activity Monitor server, for example, for use in real-time operational management dashboards. We will then also learn about the BPEL Monitor framework that provides declarative integration with BAM for reporting counters, business indicators, and intervals that result in detailed insight into the metrics of the BPEL process through real-time BAM dashboard reports.

Adding Sensors to the BPEL Process BPEL sensors are added and maintained in the BPEL process editor. This editor first needs to be switched to monitor mode using the Monitor button in the upper-right corner, as shown in Figure 16-10. In monitor mode, we can add sensors to a BPEL scope or activity simply by right-clicking and selecting Create Sensor from the context menu.

Let's create a sensor to monitor the RegisterPatientData scope and include the PatientIdentifier in the sensor signal. Right-click the RegisterPatientData scope, open the Create submenu, and select the Sensor menu item. The Edit Activity Sensor pop-up opens. Enter the name for the sensor: **RegisterPatientDataScopeSensor**. Accept All as the value for the evaluation time, which means that for normal execution we will have two sensor signals: one upon activation and one upon completion of the scope. Specify the XPath expression to retrieve the value of the patientId:

```
$Patient/payload/ns1:PatientDataServiceProcessResponse/patientId
```

This means that the result of this XPath expression is added as payload to the sensor signal. Note that we can add XPath expressions to this sensor.

Let's also create a variable sensor to monitor the value of the appointment identifier. Open the structure window if it is not already open (from the View menu, select the Structure option or use the default shortcut key combination CTRL-SHIFT-S). Select the Variable node and click the green plus icon to create a variable sensor. Call this sensor **AppointmentIdentifierVariableSensor** and set target to **$processIdentifier**.

Associating Sensor Actions with BPEL Sensors At this point, we have done nothing yet to send the sensor signal to even a single destination. It is time to associate at least one sensor action—of potentially several—with the sensors we have created.

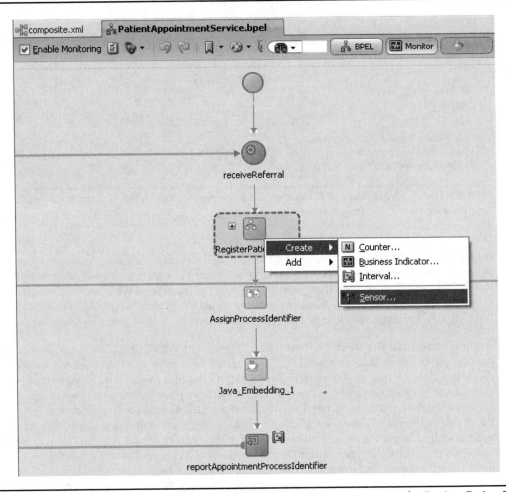

FIGURE 16-10. *Switching to monitor mode and adding an activity sensor to the RegisterPatientData scope in the PatientAppointmentService BPEL process*

Click the plus icon on top of the Sensor Actions box. The Sensor Action Chooser opens—with no sensor actions to choose from. Click the green plus icon to bring up the Create Sensor Action. Enter **GenericDBSensorAction** as the name and accept the default value Database as the publish type.

Select the AppointmentIdentifierVariableSensor and click the edit icon. Add the GenericDB SensorAction as the sensor action for this sensor.

We can now redeploy the PatientAppointmentService with the embedded sensors to expose additional information about the progress of the BPEL process. Deployment is done in the same way as before, when we did have the sensors. However, this time the two files created by JDeveloper for the sensors and sensor actions—PatientAppoinmentService_sensor.xml and PatientAppoinmentService_sensorAction.xml—are deployed along with the application.

NOTE
See the wiki for an example of a custom sensor action—a Java class that writes selected information to a log file in a format that can perhaps be used for additional reporting.

Inspecting the Output from BPEL Sensors   With the application deployed and sensors inside, we can now create a new instance of the PatientAppointmentService to see what the sensors will do for us.

It depends on the sensor actions that have been associated with the BPEL sensors where the output from the sensors will be available—JMS queue or topic, database tables, BAM server, or just about anywhere, including potentially Twitter when the Custom action has been used.

Output from Database sensor actions is visible in the FMW Control Console: Open the message flow trace for the composite instance and then open the BPEL component instance. Select the Sensor Values tab. This tab lists the sensors and the associated sensor signals and their (variable) values. This tells us, for example, that the RegisterPatientDataScope took 145 ms to complete (see Figure 16-11).

When the sensors are associated with the Database sensor action, we can retrieve the same output we find in the console through a number of database views: BPEL_PROCESS_INSTANCES, BPEL_ACTIVITY_SENSOR_VALUES, BPEL_FAULT_SENSOR_VALUES, and BPEL_VARIABLE_ SENSOR_VALUES. Here's an example:

```
select  s.activity_name
    ,       s.activity_type
    ,       v.creation_date
    ,       s.eval_point
    ,       s.eval_time
    ,       v.variable_name
    ,       case v.value_type
            when 2 then to_char(v.number_value)
            when 12 then to_char(v.varchar2_value)
```

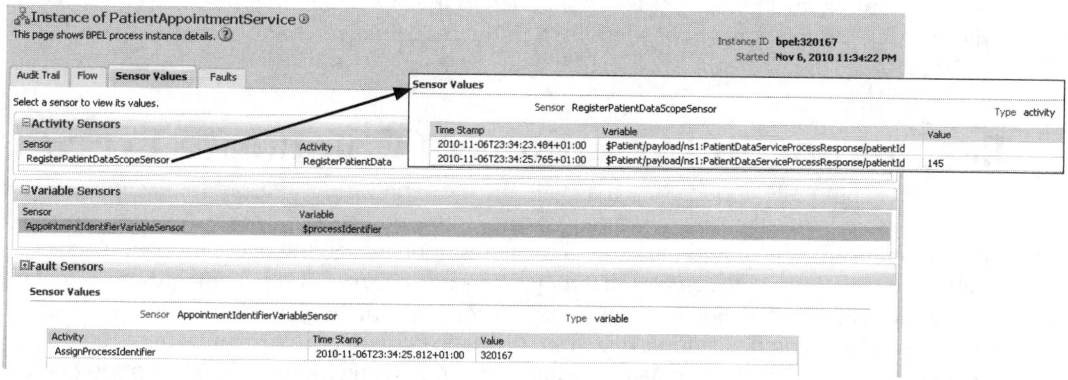

FIGURE 16-11.   *BPEL sensor signals for the PatientAppointmentService in the FMW Control Console*

ACTIVITY_NAME	ACTIVITY_TYPE	CREATION_DATE	EVAL_POINT	EVAL_TIME	VARIABLE_NAME	VARIABLE_VALUE
RegisterPatientData	scope	06-NOV-10 08.18.48.015 PM	completion	1485	Patient	
RegisterPatientData	scope	06-NOV-10 08.18.49.500 PM	completion	1485	Patient	145

FIGURE 16-12. *Result of querying the sensor signal values from the database*

```
        else to_char(substr(v.clob_value,1,100))
        end variable_value
from    bpel_activity_sensor_values s
        left outer join
        bpel_variable_sensor_values v
        on (s.instance_key = v.instance_key)
where   s.instance_key = 90015
```

The result of this query in this case is shown in Figure 16-12.

Monitoring by sensors can easily be switched on or off, without removing any of the sensors. The Settings drop-down in the Composite Dashboard tab in the FMW Control Console includes this option to toggle sensor monitoring.

Additional Custom Logging

Chapter 12 demonstrated various ways of extending the default processing of the SOA Suite using Java. We discussed the Mediator Java callouts and the Embedded Java activity in BPEL processes as well as the Spring Java component. It should be obvious to you that we can use Java to provide additional trace reports from our components.

Adding messages to the BPEL audit trail is pretty simple: Just add an Embedded Java activity to a BPEL process and include a call to addAuditTrailEntry(String), as shown here:

```
addAuditTrailEntry("An additional piece of audit information on patient "
                + getVariableData("patientIdentifier"));
```

Note that in the current release of SOA Suite, logging written by Java code in the Mediator callouts or Spring Java components is not added to the SOA Suite log files. We can, of course, write messages to the console or send them through alternative channels such as JMS, e-mail, and the database.

Responding to Exceptions in Composite Execution

Execution of composite applications may fail. There can be various reasons for exceptions to occur. Bugs in the software, either the infrastructure or the custom developed code, are one option. Much more common are system and infrastructure failures or unavailability of components such as database, queue, or remote services that may lead to errors and full disks or tablespaces that may prevent successful completion of composite instances. At a higher level, business exceptions may occur that cause a composite to deviate from the happy flow. These can range from request messages that do not contain correct information or are sent at the wrong moment, to attempts to book or buy something that is (currently) not available.

Some exceptions are recoverable; that is, they are caused by a temporary issue that can be resolved after which the composite could continue to run and complete successfully. This is the case, for example, when the instance faulted because a remote service is unavailable. Once the service is up again, the error condition has ceased to exist and the instance can continue processing. Another example of a recoverable exception is a request message that does not pass validation and that with a simple manual correction can be made to comply and be put forward for continued processing.

Other exceptions are irrecoverable—at least within a decent amount of time. An appointment was requested for a type of appointment that St. Matthews does not offer, or details were requested for a nonexistent patient. When the exception is caused by a bug in the composite application, the exception is only recoverable after the bug has been fixed and a patch has been applied. When a service is protected by an OWSM security policy and the request did not fulfill the policy's requirements—due to, for example, an unknown identity, insufficient access privileges, or an incorrectly encrypted message—it will fail in an irrecoverable way.

We need to decide how to deal with exceptions. We can probably not afford to simply ignore them. Instead, we can choose for some exceptions to result in faults that are returned to service consumers—preferably meaningful faults, defined in the WSDL, that do not give away information about the internals of the service implementation, such as a proper fault message that advises the consumer about the fact that an appointment type is not known rather than an "ORA-1403: no data found" error. Other exceptions can be dealt with in an automated fashion—for example, through the catch (exception) and compensation handlers in BPEL processes that were described in Chapter 6.

We will next discuss the fault policies in the SOA Suite that help administrators deal with errors that have bubbled up from within composite instances—by properly reporting on them, by automatically retrying them, by executing a custom action for them, or by providing the option for manual recovery from the console with possibly payload correction and the option to restart.

All exceptions that cannot be dealt with in an automated fashion should be and are reported in the console for administrators to act upon or at least learn about. Note that faults that are not dealt with by explicitly configured policies are handled by the default policies embedded in the SOA Suite. These default policies have a coarse-grained filter for discerning recoverable exceptions—for which the faulted instance can be retried in the console—and irrecoverable faults that are reported in the console and also lead to some form of fault being returned to the service consumer. Human intervention is the default action for errors that do not have a fault policy defined.

Policy-based Fault-Handling Framework

SOA Suite 11g provides a policy-based system for fault handling. *Policy based* means that we create a potentially wide range of policies to configure a response to a specific type of exception. These policies are created apart from the applications and components they apply to—just like the security policies discussed in Chapter 15. This means decoupling: The policies can easily be reused across composites and components, and they can be centrally maintained. Policies are defined in a file that by default is called fault-policies.xml. It is important to realize that this fault-handling framework covers all types of components—from Human Task and Spring Context to Business Rule and BPEL—and deals with entire composite applications.

Policies for fault handling consist of two main elements:

■   The condition under which the policy is activated—we specify what type of fault(s) the policy is relevant for, and we may add a finer-grained test on the payload of the fault; through such a payload-based condition, we can very precisely associate the policy, for example, with specific database error codes, Java exceptions, or WSDL fault metadata, or create conditions that distinguish between Mediator faults, business and SOAP faults (including BPEL faults), and adapter faults.

■   The action(s) that should be performed when the condition is satisfied; note that actions can be chained—for example, first retry several times and upon repeated failure, go on to manual intervention.

The fault-handling framework provides a number of actions that can be used in fault policies: retry, human intervention, abort, rethrow fault, and custom Java action.

Human intervention will make the composite instance available in the FMW Control Console in a recoverable state. The administrator can manipulate the payload and then decide to retry, replay a single BPEL scope, continue (ignore error), or abort the instance.

Fault policies by themselves do nothing. They need to be explicitly associated with composites, components, or references. This is done in a file fault-bindings.xml (this is the default name that can overridden). Fault bindings link the composite, specific components in the composite, or specific references in the components on the one hand to one of the fault policies on the other. Any policy for a specific fault at the component level overrides (that is, replaces and not complements) a policy defined at the composite level, and a policy defined for a reference of a component will take precedence over a component-level policy.

We will now first look at the default behavior of the SOA Suite when a composite instance faces the problem of an unavailable external service. Then we create a fault-policies.xml with some policies that we may want to use for our composites later on for this situation. These policies include retry and human intervention for availability issues with calling remote services.

Once the policies and their actions are available, we will create a fault-bindings.xml to configure how the policies should be applied to composite PatientAppointmentService.

Finally, we will create a custom Java action that sends an alert to an administrator for a fault that requires human intervention.

Default Behavior in Case of Unavailable Remote Services

An easy way to find out what the default behavior is for the "remote service not available" case is by turning off the PatientDataService composite from within JDeveloper—or shutting down that composite in the FWM console—and then invoking the composite PatientAppointmentService, as shown in Figure 16-13. This composite relies on the PatientDataService, and when it is not available, something will go wrong.

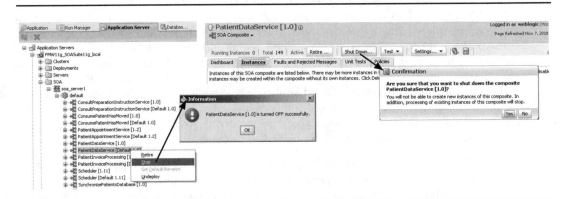

FIGURE 16-13.   *Turning off the PatientDataService from JDeveloper or shutting it down from the console*

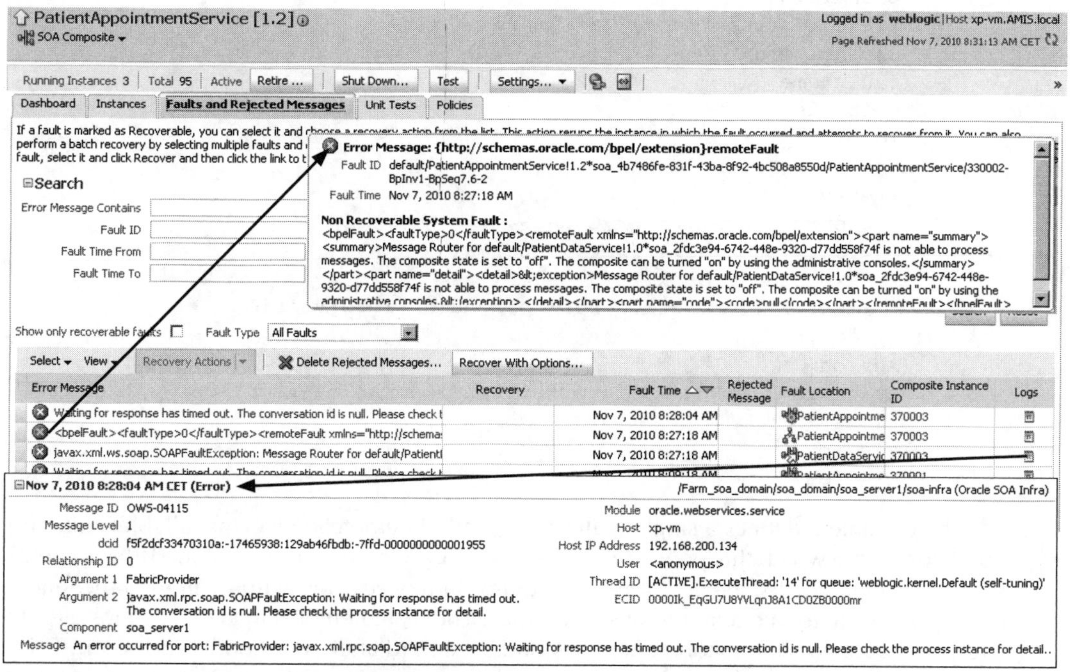

FIGURE 16-14. *FMW Control Console with the faulted instance of composite Patient AppointmentService*

After we have shut down/turned off the PatientDataService composite, the request to the PatientAppointmentService times out. Checking the FMW Console, we will find the faulted instance, along with an indication of a nonrecoverable system fault, as shown in Figure 16-14. That is somewhat unfortunate, because we could easily have retried the instance after turning on the PatientDataService composite again. However, because the instance is marked unfit for recovery, all is lost. We clearly need a policy that prevents PatientAppointmentService instances from completely falling apart when one of its references is unavailable for just a little while.

Fault Policies for Retry and Human Intervention

Open the PatientAppointmentService application in JDeveloper. Create a new XML document called fault-policies.xml with the following content:

```
<?xml version="1.0" encoding="UTF-8"?>
<faultPolicies xmlns="http://schemas.oracle.com/bpel/faultpolicy"
               xmlns:xsi="http://www.w3.org/2001/XMLSchema-instance">
  <faultPolicy version="1.0" id="RemoteServiceUnavailableFault">
    <Conditions>
      <faultName xmlns:bpelx="http://schemas.oracle.com/bpel/extension"
                 name="bpelx:remoteFault">
```

```
            <condition>
              <action ref="retry-medium"/>
            </condition>
          </faultName>
        </Conditions>
        <Actions>
          <Action id="retry-medium">
            <retry>
              <retryCount>7</retryCount>
              <retryInterval>4</retryInterval>
              <exponentialBackoff/>
              <retryFailureAction ref="ora-human-intervention"/>
            </retry>
          </Action>
          <Action id="ora-human-intervention"><humanIntervention/></Action>
        </Actions>
      </faultPolicy>
</faultPolicies>
```

The document defines a single fault policy, called RemoteServiceUnavailableFault. The condition under which this policy will take an action is the occurrence of the BPEL remoteFault. When that fault occurs, the action retry-medium is invoked. This action will retry the failed step in the composite for a maximum of seven times. The first attempt is made 4 seconds after the exception occurred, the second after 8 seconds, the third after 16 seconds, and so on. This exponential increase of the wait time is caused by the exponentialBackOff element in the retry action.

If after seven attempts the remote service is still not invoked successfully, the administrator-action is invoked. This action is of type humanIntervention, which means that the failed instance is presented in the console as recoverable.

Binding the Fault Policy to the PatientAppointmentService

With the definition of the policy in place, we can configure the binding of this policy to the PatientAppointmentService. Create a new XML file, called fault-bindings.xml. In this case, the contents of this file should be the following:

```
<?xml version="1.0" encoding="UTF-8"?>
<faultPolicyBindings version="2.0.1"
                     xmlns="http://schemas.oracle.com/bpel/faultpolicy"
                     xmlns:xsi="http://www.w3.org/2001/XMLSchema-instance">
    <composite faultPolicy="ConnectionFaults"/>
</faultPolicyBindings>
```

This configures the fault policy ConnectionFaults, defined in the fault-policies.xml file, to be bound to the composite [PatientAppointmentService]. We can create more fine-grained bindings by using the <component> element with <name> child elements that contain the name of the components to which the fault policy should be applied. Fault policies can be bound to component references using the <reference> element.

With both fault-related files in place, we can deploy the PatientAppointmentService and see what these policies do.

Note that we can decide to use different policies for the unavailability of the reference for PatientDataService and the reference for the SchedulerService, because fault-policy bindings can be as fine grained as the reference level.

Fault Policies in Action for the PatientAppointmentService

Invoke the PatientAppointmentService—with the PatientDataService turned off. When we check the progress of the new composite instance in the console, we will find that the instance has faulted. On inspecting the message flow trace, we find that the retry action has kicked in. Even though the instance has the status faulted, it is still alive thanks to our fault policy. Figure 16-15 shows the flow trace after six retry attempts have been made and failed to invoke the PatientDataService. Note how the time between the attempts increases exponentially, up to 128 seconds between the fifth and sixth attempt.

When we turn on the PatientDataService before the seventh and last attempt is made, we may be able to yet have the instance continue successfully.

However, when the final retry has failed, too, because we did not react in time, the human intervention action is invoked. This means that the instance is hospitalized: Without treatment by the administrator, it will go nowhere from here.

When we check the Faults and Rejected Messages tab for the PatientAppointmentService composite, we will find the faulted instance—with an indication that it is recoverable. That means we have a number of actions that the SOA Suite allows the administrator to perform. These actions are Retry, Abort, Continue, Rethrow, and Replay (see Figure 16-16). In this case, the administrator needs to turn on the PatientDataService component and then retry the instance from the console.

In this case, we just retry the instance without changing its payload. Sometimes, however, we may need to correct the input payload or set a BPEL variable with the value that should have been provided by a remote service call that fails. When you click the link Recoverable on the

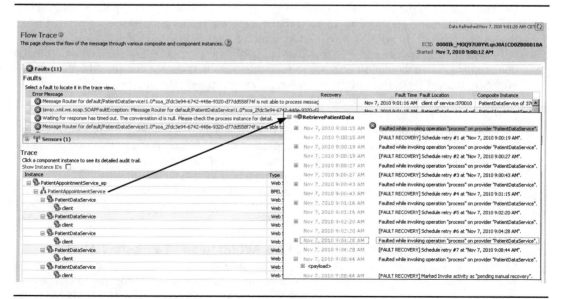

FIGURE 16-15. *Message flow trace for faulted PatientAppointmentService with retry at work*

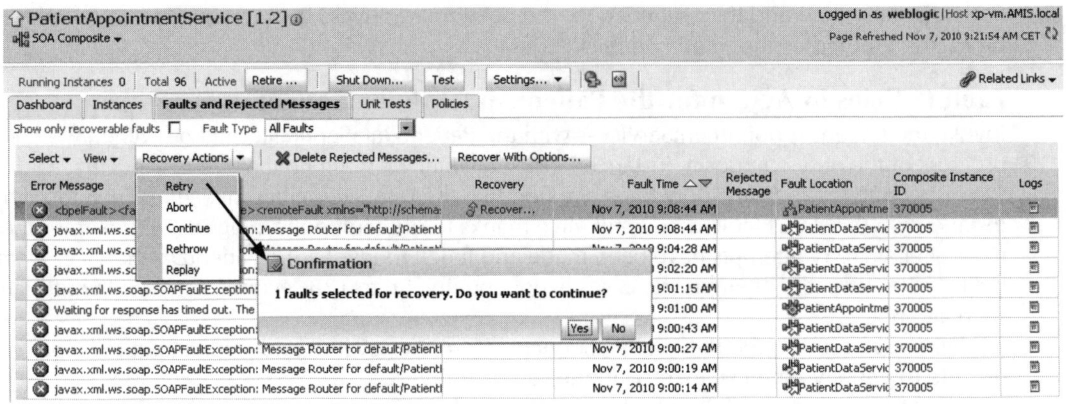

FIGURE 16-16. *Human intervention on the faulted PatientAppointmentService instance*

Faults and Rejected Messages tab, a pop-up appears where the instance can be recovered. In that pop-up, we can review and manipulate the value of all BPEL variables.

Important Facts on Fault Policies

Fault policies can be bound to Mediator components. However, they will only catch and handle faults for parallel routing rules in Mediator components. This has to do with the transaction context: For sequential routing rules that execute in the same thread and transaction context as the caller, the transaction in which the exception occurs can contain many earlier actions performed by actors earlier in the call chain than the Mediator component. The exception is returned to the caller to handle and decide what to do with the transaction. For parallel routing rules, a new thread and transaction context is created for which a fault policy can safely handle faults.

Another thing you should realize is that fault policies will not be triggered when a Mediator component raises a validation error for request messages that do not comply with the XSD. Such errors are thrown before any of the routing rules are executed. The alternative for message validation in the Mediator—based on Schematron—can be handled by fault policies because this type of validation occurs later in the Mediator lifecycle, for every routing rule.

Note that fault policies take precedence over BPEL catch activities. This is a good thing because policies can be applied without impacting the BPEL components they are applied to. However, if the BPEL catch should be executed (too), the fault policy needs to rethrow the fault to have it bubble up to the BPEL component's own embedded fault handling.

When you want to use different names and locations for the fault policies and fault bindings files, you can use the properties oracle.composite.faultPolicyFile and oracle.composite.faultBindingFile in the composite.xml to configure those custom files.

Creating and Integrating a Custom Java Action to Send an E-mail Alert

Of course it is great that the instances that are eligible for manual recovery are presented in the console. However, only when the administrator actively goes into the console to check for such instances will action be taken. It would be so much nicer if the administrator is alerted through e-mail, for example, every time an instance requires human attention.

Through the custom Java action, it is quite straightforward to make this happen. When the automatic retry has failed to successfully recover the instance, the custom Java action to send an e-mail is executed and, when done, is chained through to the human intervention action.

Therefore, we need to create the Java class that implements the interface IFaultRecoveryJavaClass, configure a custom Java action for it in the fault-policies.xml file, configure a properties set with e-mail settings, and deploy the class (the easiest way is to include the class in a composite application). The online chapter complement provides detailed instructions for creating class FaultEmailAlerter and configuring it in a custom fault handler. The class implements interface IFaultRecoveryJavaClass, which defines two methods: handleRetrySuccess and handleFault. Our Java class has access to the IFaultRecoveryContext, which makes information available about the composite, the fault, and the policy. Depending on the origin of the fault, this context may be an instance of MediatorRecovery Context (which exposes the mediator message) or the IBPELFaultRecoveryContext (which allows us to write messages to the BPEL audit trail, inspect the current activity, and read and update the values of BPEL variables). The next code snippet shows how the handleFault method could be implemented:

```java
public String handleFault(IFaultRecoveryContext iFaultRecoveryContext) {
    StringBuffer msg = new StringBuffer("Dear Administrator,\n\n");
    msg.append("Fault policy id: " + iFaultRecoveryContext.getPolicyId()+"\n");
    if (iFaultRecoveryContext instanceof IBPELFaultRecoveryContext) {
        IBPELFaultRecoveryContext ctx =
                        (IBPELFaultRecoveryContext)iFaultRecoveryContext;
        msg.append("Fault: " + ctx.getFault()+"\n");
        msg.append("Activity: " + ctx.getActivityName()+"\n");
        lastName =  ((XMLText)ctx.getVariableData("inputVariable", "payload"
                            , "/client:AppointmentServiceProcessRequest"
                            + "/client:patientDetails/client:lastName/text()")
                ).getData();
        msg.append("Patient: "+lastName+"\n");
        ...
```

Injecting the "send email alert action" in fault-policies.xml

The fault-policies.xml file needs to be modified to make sure the e-mail alerts are sent whenever an instance has failed with a remoteFault and the retry action was not successful.

First, we change the retryFailureAction in the retry-medium action to chain to a new action called alert-and-human-action:

```xml
<retryFailureAction ref="alert-and-human-action"/>
```

Then we create this new action:

```xml
<Action id="alert-and-human-action">
    <javaAction className="com.stmatthews.hospital.FaultEmailAlerter"
            defaultAction="ora-human-intervention"
            propertySet="emailSettings">
        <returnValue value="OK" ref="ora-human-intervention"/>
    </javaAction>
</Action>
```

When the e-mail alert has been sent by the custom Java action, the next action should always be ora-human-intervention.

The attribute propertySet with the value emailSettings is a reference to a list of properties defined in the fault-policies.xml file that are passed to the custom Java action. In this case, these properties provide e-mail configuration settings:

```
<Properties>
  <propertySet name="emailSettings">
    <property name="emailServer">stmatthews.com</property>
    <property name="emailPort">25</property>
    <property name="emailToAddress">frank@stmatthews.com</property>
    <property name="emailFromAddress">appointmentmanager@stmatthews.com
    </property>
  </propertySet>
</Properties>
```

E-mail Alerts Sent for Failing PatientAppointmentService Instances

Invoke the PatientAppointmentService—with the PatientDataService still turned off. The fault policy will be activated and perform the automatic retry. When the retry has run out of steam, the custom Java action should be invoked—resulting in an e-mail being sent to the administrator (see Figure 16-17). The audit trail of the BPEL process is also updated by the Java action. Subsequently, the human intervention is activated and the failed instance ends up as recoverable in the console.

Java actions can, of course, be used for many more things than sending e-mails; they can perform a lot of actions that resolve the issues that caused them to be invoked in the first place—such as updating BPEL instance variables and changing properties and endpoints in the SOA Suite. Writing logging information to a database and custom log file is another frequent task for these actions.

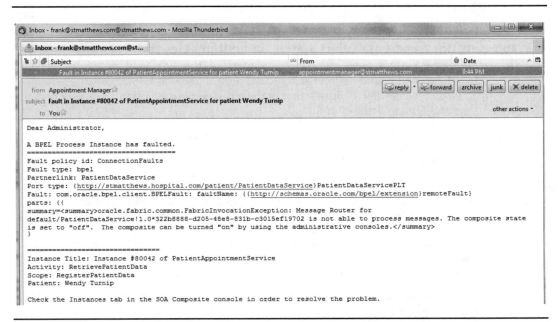

FIGURE 16-17. *E-mail advising the administrator of an instance that requires attention*

Rejected Messages

There is another category of exceptions that we have not yet discussed. These exceptions do not occur in composite applications. Instead, they happen before the service infrastructure is even reached. Such exceptions take place, for example, in the file adapter when it reads a file for which it expects a certain format and the translation based on the native format to a proper XML message fails because the file is corrupt. Before the file adapter can hand the message to a newly created composite instance, it has already rejected it.

Because the fault policies apply to service composites, components, and references, these rejected messages do not fall under their dominion. Rejected messages are handled differently: They and their payload are stored in the database, and we can specify the procedure for dealing with them through so-called "rejection handlers."

Rejection handlers are a special type of faultPolicy in the faultPolicies.xml file. They are bound to a service or reference (to handle failures with outbound messages after they have left the service fabric).

Implementing a Message Rejection Handler for the DoctorAppointmentRequestsProcessor

We created the DoctorAppointmentRequestsProcessor in Chapter 7. It uses an inbound file adapter service to read requests for patient appointments from a file. These requests are forwarded to a Mediator and from there are processed to either external healthcare providers (dentists and chiropractor) or to the PatientAppointmentService. Sometimes the files with appointment requests received by St. Matthews from the general practitioners are not correct. These files should have the agreed-upon comma-separated values format with the specified number of values per record—but occasionally, they do not. When these corrupt files are processed, the file adapter will throw an exception, even before an instance of the DoctorAppointmentRequestsProcessor is created. A normal fault policy will not catch and handle the exception, because it acts on a composite and not on a rejected message.

The fault policy for rejected messages is defined in the faulty-policies.xml file as follows:

```
<faultPolicy version="2.0.1" id="RejectedMessages">
  <Conditions>
    <faultName xmlns:rjm="http://schemas.oracle.com/sca/rejectedmessages"
               name="rjm:ReadFileDoctorsAppointmentRequests">
    <!-- name refers to the composite service -->
      <condition>
        <action ref="logInFile"/>
      </condition>
    </faultName>
  </Conditions>
  <Actions>
    <Action id="logInFile">
      <fileAction>
        <location>c:\temp\stmatthews\logs</location>
        <fileName>AppointmentRequest_%ID%_%TIMESTAMP%.xml</fileName>
      </fileAction>
    </Action>
  </Actions>
</faultPolicy>
```

The namespace http://schemas.oracle.com/sca/rejectedmessages is used to identify the "rejected message exception" category. The (local part of the) name of the fault must match the name of a service or reference in the composite. Various actions are available for use in rejection handlers: Web Service Handler, Custom Java Handler, Queue Handler, and File Handler.

In this case, every corrupt message will result in two files in the specified directory: one a literal copy of the rejected message, the other a file that describes the exception.

The fault policy must be bound to the service or reference in the composite through the fault-bindings.xml:

```
<faultPolicyBindings version="2.0.1"
                   xmlns="http://schemas.oracle.com/bpel/faultpolicy"
                   xmlns:xsi="http://www.w3.org/2001/XMLSchema-instance">
      <service faultPolicy="RejectedMessages">
              <name>ReadFileDoctorsAppointmentRequests</name>
      </service>
</faultPolicyBindings>
```

If a composite does not have custom-rejected messages handlers for its services and references, the default message rejection handler is activated upon inbound or outbound exceptions. This handler writes the failed message to a file in the directory [FMW_HOME]\user_ projects\domains*soa_domain*\rejmsgs*soa_server1*\DoctorsAppointmentRequestsProcessor— where soa_domain and soa_server1 are the names, respectively, of the WLS Domain and Managed Server running the SOA Suite.

Rejected messages are also written to the database and can be inspected using queries against the tables REJECTED_MESSAGE and REJECTED_MSG_NATIVE_PAYLOAD. Rejected messages are also available in the FMW Control Console, on the tab Faults And Rejected Messages for the SOA composite that the rejected message should have reached.

Retrying Inbound and Outbound Adapter Actions

In addition to the rejection handlers just discussed, most technology adapters can be configured to retry failed operations. The retry configuration is done through properties on the binding.jca element in the composite.xml file or through the FMW Control Console (see Chapter 17). The next example instructs the inbound database adapter service to retry on failure for a maximum of five times:

```
<service name="RetrieveDatabaseDoctorsAppointmentRequests">
   <interface.wsdl
     interface="DocApp/GetDBDocAppReq#wsdl.interface(RetrieveDBDocAppReq_ptt)">
   <binding.jca config="GetDBDocAppReq_db.jca">
     <property name="jca.retry.count">5</property>
     <property name="jca.retry.interval">1</property>
     <property name="jca.retry.backoff">2</property>
   </binding.jca>
</service>
```

Managing Composite Instances

In the previous sections we have seen several ways to learn about the instances of composite applications that are currently executing or that have concluded—either successfully or in a failed state. We have learned how we can implement automated and manual strategies for dealing with the faulted instances. Now it is time to discuss the next stage in the lifecycle of composite instances: their demise.

Composite instances can have a lot of data associated with them—depending on the audit-level settings. Instance payload in various stages of the composite instance lifecycle can be captured along with various types of metadata. This wealth of information can be tremendously useful for problem resolution and for (aggregate) reporting purposes. However, when the number of instances increases, the data volume can expand rapidly. Some form of pruning is in order; otherwise, you run a serious risk of performance degradation and disk space shortage.

Deleting Composite Instances

The Instances tab for a specific composite application provides an overview of all instances that are running, have faulted, have completed, or have become stale (because they were run for a previous deployment of the composite application). We select instances and delete them. Alternatively, we can click the Delete With Options button, which brings up a window that allows us to specify criteria used to select the instances to delete, such as the time window in which the instances were created (see Figure 16-18). Before the instances are actually purged, we get a last notification of the number of instances the SOA Suite is about to delete and a last opportunity to back out of the delete operation.

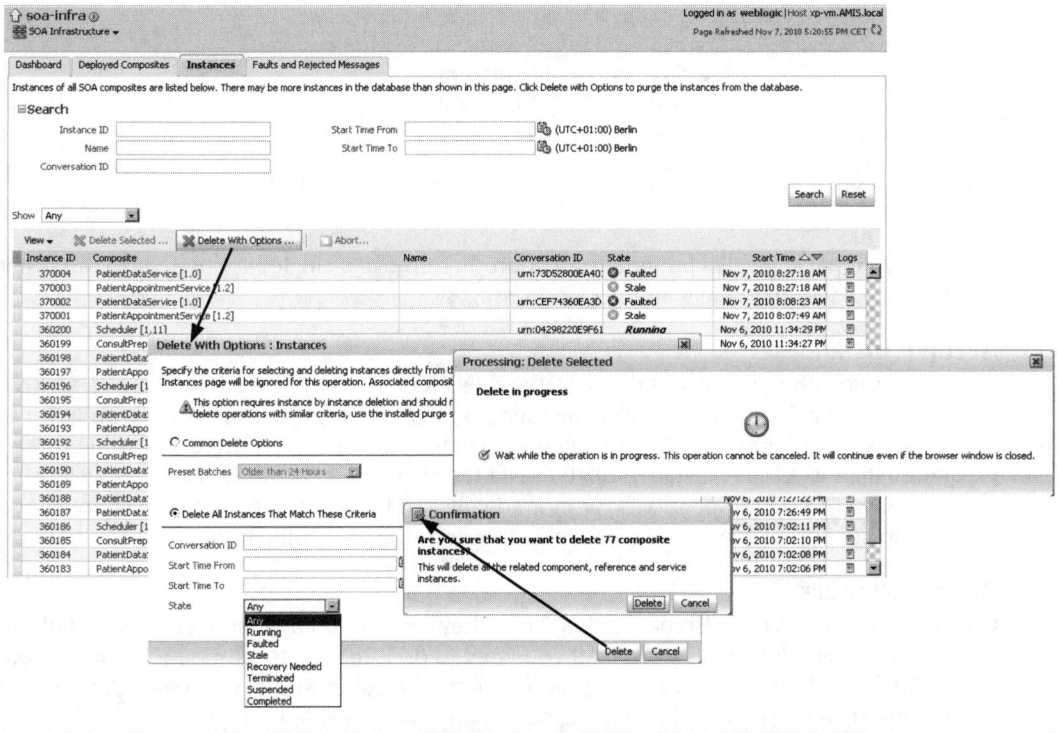

FIGURE 16-18.   *Deleting composite instances through the FMW Control Console can be done in the Instances tab for a specific composite or for all composites in a specific partition.*

The SOA Suite will happily allow us to delete some but not necessarily all instances that are part of a message flow trace. For example, we can delete an instance of PatientAppointmentService while not deleting the instances of PatientDataService and SchedulerService that were invoked by the deleted instance. When we try to reconstruct the message flow trace that led to the instantiation of the PatientDataService instance, we will not be able to. This is not necessarily a problem because it is all in the past anyway, but it's something you should be aware of.

Bulk Instance Purgatory

Although the console has the means to select a substantial number of composite instances for deletion, Oracle recommends using the PL/SQL API to purge large numbers of instances (over a thousand). This package can also be used for automatic, scheduled removal of instances—for example, daily or weekly purging of all successfully completed instances that are at least two days old.

The PL/SQL package FABRIC can be used by an administrator to get rid of instances of composite applications, as shown here:

```
declare
  l_number_removed integer;
  l_instance_filter instance_filter := instance_filter ();
begin
  l_instance_filter.composite_name := 'PatientDataService';
  l_instance_filter.composite_revision := '1.0';
  l_instance_filter.max_created_date := sysdate - 1;
  l_number_removed:= fabric.delete_composite_instances
                   ( filter => l_instance_filter
                   , max_instances => 1000
                   , purge_partitioned_data => true
                   );
  dbms_output.put_line('Purged '||l_number_removed||' instances.');
end;
```

This same package also provides procedures to remove a single instance, purge all instances for all composites, and delete all rejected messages.

Archive Instances

The SOA Suite either retains instances or it purges them. It does not have facilities to archive instances—taking them offline or moving them to a set of history tables. Deleting an instance means giving up all information associated with that instance. However, it is possible to programmatically retrieve instance-related data through several database views as well as by using the Java API (see Appendix D for more details) and create some form of custom archive. There is no supported way for re-creating instances in the SOA Suite from such a custom archive.

Abort Instances

Composite instances can also be deleted when they are still running. However, all details about such instances are deleted as well. If all you want to do is terminate a running instance, you can also abort the instance in the Instances tab for either the composite or the soa-infra node. An aborted instance is not purged and all its details are still available for review.

Summary

For successful operation of the SOA Suite, it is important for administrators to know what is going on inside. Especially when instances of SOA composite applications fail for unknown or unexpected reasons, it is essential to trace the history of failed instances in order to uncover when, where, and why the instance failed. Another reason for administrators to closely scrutinize the current proceedings inside the SOA Suite is performance: Response times need to stay under the levels agreed upon in the SLA, and should in general be as short as possible. This chapter showed various ways of learning about the activity in the SOA Suite—through the instance audit details in the console, the Performance Summary, and preconfigured and custom log files. Additional information can be exposed in the FMW Console through sensors—both at the composite level as well as inside BPEL processes.

When the administrators learn of failed instances through one of the monitoring channels just listed, usually some form of action should be taken. Depending on the type of fault that has occurred, this could be an automated action or require a manual intervention. The SOA Suite contains a fault policy framework that allows us to specify the required action for specific types of faults and exceptions in specific components or service/reference bindings. Among these actions are retry, log, human intervention, abort, rethrow fault, and custom Java action. Through this latter option, we can extend the SOA Suite to do anything we want it to upon a specific fault occurrence.

Even for the instances that do not end in tears—the vast majority, one would expect—some administration is required. To prevent the SOA Suite from clogging up, we must implement some form of purging strategy. Even with the most restricted audit policy, at least some trace remains of every instance that happened. In general, instances should be removed when they serve no immediate purpose any longer. This can be done both through the console as well as through a PL/SQL API.

Of course, there is much more to the administration of the SOA Suite than security (discussed in the previous chapter) and monitoring, fault handling, and the pruning of instances. In the next two chapters, we will discuss deployment, lifecycle management, automated testing, and governance of composite applications.

CHAPTER
17

Lifecycle Management:
Testing and Dealing with
Environmental Change

he world is not as simple as we made it look in the previous chapters. This is certainly true for the world at large, but it is also the case for the run-time environments into which our SOA applications are deployed. So far we have only dealt with a straightforward development environment to deploy the application into. However, in reality, the application will have to run in different environments—such as integration test, acceptance test, and production. These environments will not be identical—external services are exposed at different endpoints, different directories are used for the file adapter, and adapter properties such as polling intervals and JDBC settings may have different values for the various environments. In this chapter, we will see how we can work effectively with such variations between environments, using environment-specific configuration plans that are attached at deployment time.

In the previous chapters we have deployed SOA composites several dozens of times, at least, to see the work we had done on the application in action. But we have not really looked in any detail at how deployment is done. That is an oversight that will be corrected in this chapter, as we look at the various methods for packaging and deploying applications—from JDeveloper, the command line, and the FMW Enterprise Manager Control.

At some point in the deployment procedure we should establish the correctness of the composite application by executing unit tests against it. We will leverage the embedded unit testing framework in the SOA Suite, which allows us to create test cases in JDeveloper and carry out the automated unit tests on the deployed application.

After composite applications are deployed and have been happily processing requests, we are not likely to reach a status quo. In this world in which we embrace change "for a living," we will be faced with changes—in the environment (for example, the location of services), in the functional requirements, or in nonfunctional aspects such as security, performance, and audit levels. We will discuss several ways in which we can respond and accomplish the desired changes: through run-time property adjustment and management of metadata, redeployment of a modified application, and the creation of a new version. Managing the evolution of services, events, and composite applications as well as dealing with multiple versions of a composite service are special challenges that we introduce in the last part of this chapter. The next chapter, on SOA governance, further elaborates on this topic.

Building and Deploying SOA Composite Applications

Deployment is the process that delivers an SOA composite application to a run-time environment. This can be straight from the development environment in which it is created (JDeveloper), from a source code control system where all constituent parts of the application are gathered, or even from another run-time environment. Before the application is in a format that the SOA Suite run time can handle, the application needs to be compiled, built, and packaged into a properly constructed archive. Note that faultless deployment may not be enough for successful execution of the composite application because the application may depend on data sources, JMS objects, and external references that need to be configured and made available to the composite application.

There are several methods for building, packaging, and deploying SOA composite applications that are suitable for different roles and environments. Developers tend to use JDeveloper for developing as well as building and deploying the application to non-production environments, because it is the fastest way to go through development iterations. Automatic build procedures are typically in place for testing environments and sometimes for production environments as well (especially when these become too complex to handle manually); these procedures use the command-line facilities—either using Ant or through the WebLogic Scripting Tool (WLST) and Python scripts (all supported by WebLogic Server)—to automatically build the applications, package and deploy them, and subsequently test them. Production environments will usually not have such frequent rollouts through automated deployment procedures. The prepackaged archive that was deployed to the acceptance test environment is taken and deployed by the administrators to the production environment—typically through the Enterprise Manager Console. Note that the administrator can export the application from acceptance test and import it to the production environment.

We will discuss and perform each of these three deployment methods in the coming sections.

Pre- or Post-Deployment Operations

Deployment of composite applications themselves is, of course, an important step in enabling the publication and subscription of events and successful invocation of the services exposed by the SOA composites. Note that many applications have several dependencies on other objects and configurations that we need to take care of—either before or after deployment of the composite applications themselves—but at least before we attempt to invoke the composite's services. Some examples of these dependencies are listed here, but note that this list is not exhaustive. Note that these steps that complement the deployment of the SOA composite applications are required, regardless of whether deployment is done from JDeveloper, through a command-line script, or from the FMW Enterprise Manager Console.

SOA composite applications may contain technology adapter services that depend on other JEE resources or resource adapters. For example, database adapter services reference a database resource adapter connection pool through a JNDI name that needs to have been set up—for example, through the WebLogic Server Administration Console or the WLST command-line interface. This connection pool is associated with a data source that connects to a database schema that needs to expose the expected database objects such as tables and views, AQ queues, or PL/SQL program units.

Likewise, JMS adapter services depend on a connection pool set up for the JMS adapter that links to a JMS connection factory and on a JMS queue or JMS topic to consume from or publish to.

XPath expressions, in, among others, business rules, human tasks, and BPEL notification activities, may refer to roles and individual users that need to have been set up in the identity service configured for use in the SOA Suite.

Human tasks in the composite application may depend on ADF task flows (discussed in Chapter 20) to provide the user interface for the task. Those task flows need to be deployed, either before or after the composite application is deployed.

Compiling, Building, and Deploying from JDeveloper

Deployment is done in JDeveloper based on *deployment profiles*. These profiles specify what type of archive is to be created in which location—for example, simple JAR, ADF library, Service Archive (SAR), Web Application Archive (WAR), or Enterprise Application Archive (EAR). When a new SOA composite application is created, JDeveloper auto-generates such a deployment profile for it. That default profile is the one we have used throughout this book to deploy our composite applications.

We can create a new deployment profile for an SOA-SAR file from the New Gallery—which is really only useful when the project does not already contain one (that is, the auto-generated one). There are no special settings to be made on this profile.

There are two other types of deployment profiles that cannot be created in the New Gallery, but only from the application properties editor. These are called SOA Bundle and MAR File (Metadata Archive).

The SOA Bundle is a collection of SOA composite application archives that can be distributed and deployed as one bundle. When you create an SOA Bundle–style deployment profile, you have to select the projects from which the SAR and MAR deployment profiles provide the archives to include in the bundle. Note that, annoyingly enough, you cannot combine composite applications that call each other in a single bundle. You first have to deploy the application that is being called. Of course, this helps you to continue your strive for decoupling and reuse.

The Metadata Archive is used to deploy shared metadata, such as XSD documents and EDL files. Instead of these artifacts being deployed as part of every application that uses them, they can be stored in and exposed from a central location—the MDS repository. The next chapter discusses the use of MDS and shared metadata to avoid duplication of shared artifacts.

Deployment for the various types of profiles—including SAR, WAR, and EAR—can be to the file system or to a running application server over a predefined application server connection (or both). This is what we have done over and over again in the preceding chapters. What you may not have realized is that every deployment directly to a running SOA Suite instance was preceded by the creation of a service archive in the deploy directory of the composite application. That JAR file can also be used on its own—outside of JDeveloper—for deployment from an Ant or WLST script or from the FMW Enterprise Manager Console.

The service archives are typically quite small: They consist of an initially fairly small number of XML files that are not very large to begin with and compress quite well. Entire composite applications result in archives of tens to a maximum hundreds of kilobytes, nothing like the multimegabyte enterprise archives produced for most JEE web applications. Note that when a composite application uses Java and relies on external libraries that are deployed with the composite application, the size of the archive can increase rapidly.

We have to make several decisions before the deployment can proceed—either in JDeveloper or in our automated build scripts—in order to specify exactly how the composite application is to be processed in the SOA Suite. For example, what is the intended revision ID of the composite? And if the target environment already has a composite with the same name and revision, should it be overwritten, or should that not occur? Is the composite revision we are about to deploy considered the default revision? In other words, all consumers that do not explicitly indicate which revision of a service exposed by this composite are to be routed to this specific revision (or to the current default revision if there is one). Also, should a configuration plan be applied during deployment? The configuration plan will help morph the composite for a specific target environment—more on this in the next major section of this chapter.

The last questions to be answered during deployment from JDeveloper to a running application server are, to which target server(s) should the application be deployed? And into which partition should the application go on each target server?

Figure 17-1 shows the deployment wizard in JDeveloper and how it presents the questions discussed earlier.

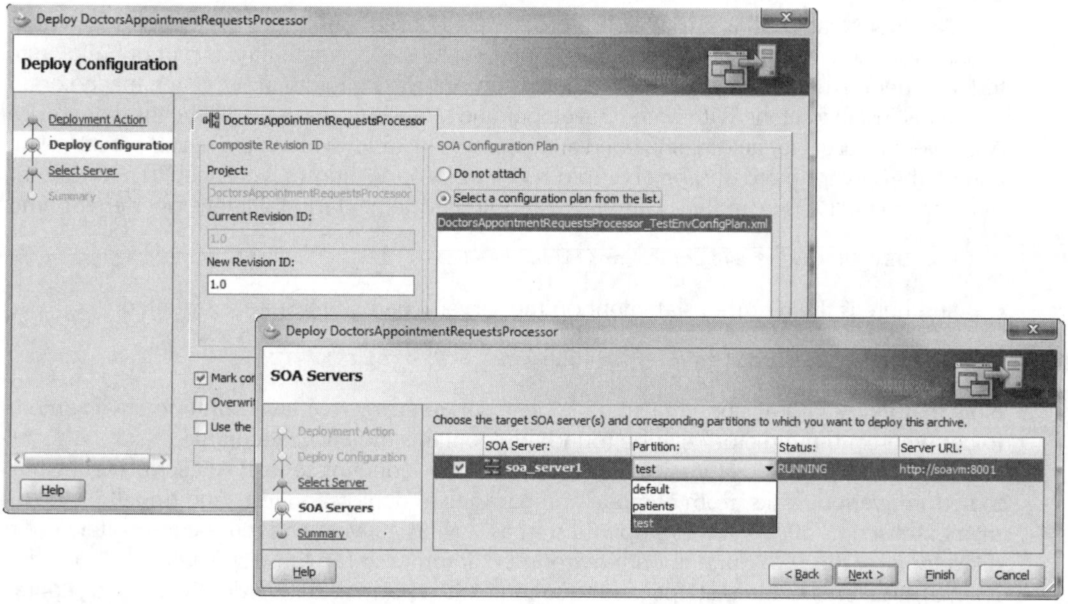

FIGURE 17-1. *Deployment from JDeveloper—setting deployment options and choosing the target server and partition*

When the deployment is concluded by clicking the Finish button, the composite application(s) is validated, compiled, and built; packaged into archive files; and deployed to the application server. The console window in JDeveloper contains the logging for these actions.

Building and Deploying from the Command Line

Packaging applications from JDeveloper is fine for developers going through many trial-and-error cycles, but usually not as appropriate for administrators and certainly not when automated build scripts are used to set up the environment. For example, test environments are typically created using build scripts that are executed periodically, on request, or even with every check into a source code control system.

Such build procedures start with a checkout of the tip of the trunk or some designated branch in a source code control system (such as Subversion or CVS). This checkout creates a temporary folder structure on the file system with all constituent parts that make up the application. Then command-line scripts are run to compile the applications and package them into deployable units (archives). Subsequently these archives are sent to one or more running WebLogic servers with SOA Suite configured on them.

SOA Suite 11*g* supports two main categories of scripts that can be used to build and deploy SOA composite applications: the Ant build-scripts, based on the popular Java-based Apache Ant build tool, and the Python-based WLST scripts that are executed via the WLST command-line scripting interface to WebLogic Server.

Using Ant

Ant (Another Neat Tool) is a rock-solid, proven Java-based tool under the Apache Software Foundation, used for programmatically executing batch tasks, frequently as part of build, automated test, and deployment procedures. More details on Ant can be found at http://ant.apache.org.

Ant is installed along with both JDeveloper and WebLogic Server. This means that you will have Ant at your disposal for automating build and deployment tasks, both on the development environment and on the server. In order to be able to run Ant tasks on Windows, you need to add the Ant bin directory to the PATH variable. Here is the required statement for the JDeveloper environment:

```
PATH=<JDEV_HOME>\jdeveloper\ant\bin;%PATH%
```

And here is the required statement on the server where SOA Suite is installed:

```
PATH=<FMW_HOME>\modules\org.apache.ant_1.7.0\bin;%PATH%
```

Note that JAVA_HOME should also have been set, referring to a Java Runtime Environment—a folder where a bin directory can be found that contains the Java executable.

The <FMW_HOME>\Oracle_SOA1\bin directory contains several Ant scripts that can be used to perform various tasks, from compile and package to deploy and test. Additionally, the ant-sca-mgmt.xml scripts allows Ant to stop and start as well as activate and retire composites. We need JDeveloper or the SOA Suite in our environment in order to run these special Ant targets due to the internal structures of build scripts and required JARs. This makes it harder to create a separate, standalone build server. Note that when you deploy SOA composite applications directly from JDeveloper, the compilation is done behind the scenes through the same ant-sca-compile.xml task that we can invoke ourselves.

A simple first test to see how to work with the Ant scripts would be to open a command-line window and submit the following command in the directory <FMW_HOME>\Oracle_SOA1\bin, which contains the Ant scripts for the SOA Suite:

```
ant -f ant-sca-mgmt.xml listDeployedComposites
    -Dhost=localhost -Dport=8001 -Duser=weblogic
```

You will be prompted for the password of user weblogic. Then the script will produce a list of the currently deployed composites on the SOA Suite. The ant-sca-mgt.xml script can be used with various targets (in addition to listDeployedComposites).

These targets include listPartitions, to get a list of the partitions in the SOA Suite target server; listCompositesInPartition, to list the composites in a specific partition; startComposite/retireComposite/stopComposite/activateComposite, to start, retire, activate, and stop, respectively, a specific composite; and startCompositesInPartition/stopCompositesInPartition, to bulk start or stop all composites in a specific partition. Management of partitions is further supported with the targets createPartition and deletePartition.

The SOA composite application can be packaged with an Ant script. Packaging means creating a service archive (SAR), which is just a JAR file whose name starts with sca_, in the "deploy" directory of the project root. This JAR file can then be deployed using the ant-sca-deploy.xml script, as shown here, or from within JDeveloper or using the FMW Enterprise Manager Console:

```
ant -f ant-sca-package.xml -DcompositeDir=C:\Patients\PatientDataService
    -DcompositeName=PatientDataService -Drevision=1.0
    -Dscac.application.home=C: \PatientDataService
```

Ant-based deployment of a service archive to a running SOA Suite instance is done with the ant-sca-deploy.xml script—whether the archive is created from JDeveloper or from the command line or as an export from another SOA Suite instance is irrelevant. The following statement is used for deployment and transfer of the archive to the running SOA Suite:

```
ant -f ant-sca-deploy.xml -DserverURL=http://localhost:8001
    -DsarLocation=C:\PatientDataService\deploy\sca_PatientDataService_rev1.0.jar
-Doverwrite=true
-Duser=weblogic
-DforceDefault=true
-Dpartition=Patients
```

When the script is executed, you will be prompted for the password. Alternatively, to truly run in batch mode, you can pass in the password as one of the parameters.

It is, of course, possible to create command scripts (.bat or .sh) that chain multiple calls to Ant scripts. Alternatively (and preferably), new Ant scripts or, for example, Maven scripts are created to compile, package, and deploy (and test) SOA composite applications as part of automated build procedures.

WLST

The WebLogic Scripting Tool is a command-line scripting environment that allows interactive and scripted (file-based, batch-wise) execution of administrative actions for the core WebLogic Server as well as other Fusion Middleware components such as WebCenter, MDS, the Identity Infrastructure, and SOA Suite. It is based on the Java scripting interpreter Jython (a.k.a. Python for the Java platform), which supports local variables, conditional variables, and flow control statements. WLST provides an additional set of scripting functions (commands) that are specific to WebLogic Server.

We can create WLST scripts that perform various activities, including configuring WLS domains and servers, creating JDBC and JMS resources, configuring the User Message Service, and managing SOA composite applications. These scripts cater to different environments and adapt themselves to the specific environment for which they are used because they can inspect the destination environment and set local variables, perform logical evaluations, and conditionally execute specific code branches.

The WLST command-line interface is accessed from the command line under Windows or Unix/Linux in the <FMW_HOME>\Oracle_SOA1\common\bin directory using the wlst.cmd (or wlst.sh) command script. Note that you will find multiple occurrences of wlst.cmd in various folders of the WebLogic Server installation. However, the one under the Oracle_SOA1 node is the only one to support the specific WLST command for SOA composite applications.

The WLST commands for management of SOA composite applications are analogous to the set of Ant scripts we discussed before. For example, here's how to list all currently deployed composites—for all partitions:

```
sca_listDeployedComposites('localhost', '8001', 'weblogic', 'weblogic1')
```

And here's how to "undeploy" a composite application:

```
sca_undeployComposite('http://localhost:8001','Project1', '1.0')
```

NOTE
When this statement is executed, you will be prompted for the username and password.

The WLST can run scripts using the execfile('someFile.py') command. A simple .sh or .bat script can be created that starts WLST and runs a potentially complex script that prepares a managed server by creating and configuring JEE resources such as data sources and a database adapter connection pool, a JMS queue, and a connection factory, and then compiles, packages (or exports), and deploys one or more composite applications and executes test cases for those applications. WLST also provides commands for starting and stopping, activating and retiring, and undeploying individual composites.

Deploying Through the Enterprise Manager Console

SOA composite applications can be deployed using the FMW Enterprise Manager Console. This method is typically used for deploying applications to production systems. Note that the application needs to have been packaged into a service archive—the Enterprise Manager can only deploy already-built and packaged applications. This archive, as we have seen, can be created from JDeveloper and through Ant or WLST scripts run from the command line or as part of automated build processes, or through an export from the SOA Suite.

To deploy an SOA composite application from a service archive through the EM Console, select the soa-infra node or any composite node and then open the Select SOA Deployment submenu from the context menu. Select the option Deploy (or Deploy Another Composite from a Composite Node). The three-step deployment wizard appears.

In the first step of the deployment wizard, select the archive to deploy through the browse file dialog in the web browser and then click the Next button. In the second step, after the selected archive has been uploaded and validated, select the target partition to deploy the composite application(s) to. The third step provides an overview of what will happen: that is, which revision of which composite is to be deployed to which partition. This step offers the option to set the deployed revision as the default revision or to keep the current default. Note that we cannot deploy a composite revision into a partition that already contains that same revision of that same composite. We accept the information in this third step by clicking the Deploy button, which will initiate the deployment of the application on the target partition.

Exporting Composite Application from Running SOA Suite

A service archive can also be retrieved from the Enterprise Manager console itself: A single composite application can be exported, for example, from an acceptance test environment to an archive on the file system. This archive is a normal service archive that can subsequently be deployed from the console, for example, into a production environment. Note that there is no special import operation—we use the normal deploy action to do the import.

To export a composite application from the console, select the composite in the navigator. Then open the SOA Composite drop-down menu just below the title of the composite and select the menu option Export. The Export dialog appears, which allows us to specify what exactly should be exported: the application as it was originally deployed or the application along with changes in properties and metadata that have been applied through the console post deployment (see the next section for details on such changes). Export processes a single composite application—you cannot create a composite bundle with multiple applications through exporting. The result of an export operation is a JAR file that is initially created on the server side and can next be downloaded from the browser to the client. This JAR cannot be told apart from a JAR file that is the result of a command-line-driven compile-and-package operation or a deployment from within JDeveloper.

Environmentally Friendly Customization Using Configuration Plans

SOA composite applications will be used in environments that will be similar but probably not equal. Development and various testing and production environments will use different servers with possibly different ports, directory structures, polling times, and different values for other properties that govern the behavior of service components or adapter services as well as different security policies. Also, some environments will be configured for high availability and will be clustered or have different transactions settings and so on. This might influence the configuration settings for nonconcurrent adapters.

The service archive that gets deployed consists of the composite application as it has been developed. However, during deployment a configuration plan can be applied to the composite application. This plan is used to add policies and replace designated properties and references to service endpoints and the physical location of WSDL and XSD documents in the composite application with environment-specific values as they apply to the deployment target environment. This means that a single composite application can be customized for each target environment through the creation and application of configuration plans that have been especially prepared for those environments. A composite can reference only one configuration plan during deployment.

Note that as an alternative to the use of configuration plans, the references to endpoints of services in composite applications can also be environment independent through the use of a run-time service virtualization layer—for example, a UDDI v2 directory service (such as Oracle Service Registry) or an enterprise service bus. The composite application can use the same *virtual* endpoint in every environment, leaving it up to the service virtualization layer to route the calls to the appropriate endpoint in the current environment. However, we might still need different endpoints from the ESB or registry for different target environments, so we never truly solve the endpoint problem using this approach—while we introduce additional overhead and potentially a single point of failure. Note that rewrite rules on web servers, load balancers, proxies, or other elements participating in routing messages over the network could help discern between and routing within different environments.

A last remark before we embark on the discussion of configuration plans is that—as we shall see later in this chapter—all properties that we can automatically customize during deployment using configuration plans, can also manually be configured through the Enterprise Manager Console after deployment.

Creating Configuration Plans

A configuration plan is, by and large, an elaborate set of search-and-replace expressions expressed in XML that prescribe which settings from the base application should be replaced with environment-specific values. When the configuration plan is applied, the composite.xml file (and the import statements in the listed WSDL and XSD files) are scanned for the search expressions that, when encountered, are replaced with the value defined in the configuration plan. Replacement is done for the following values:

- References to (the location of) WSDL files can be replaced in the composite.xml.

- References to (the location of) XSD files can be replaced in the composite.xml and also in WSDL and XSD files.

- Values for port and location attributes in binding elements (specifying the endpoints of references) can be replaced.

■   Values for properties at any level in the composite.xml can be replaced. Note that only values for properties that are explicitly defined in the composite.xml can be customized through the configuration plan; for example, the (implicit) default values of technology adapter bindings are not adapted through the configuration plan unless they have been explicitly included in the composite.xml file.

Additionally, the configuration plan can add policy references for service/reference bindings and components. Note that it will not remove or make changes to existing policy attachments.

A configuration plan is created in JDeveloper using the option Generate Config Plan in the context menu on the composite.xml file. The sca_generatePlan() command is available through WLST for the creation of a configuration plan. We need to provide the name of the configuration plan; typically, the name will refer to the environment the plan is intended for—using abbreviations such as dev, tst, acc, and prd. The configuration plan itself is a simple XML file that is, by default, created in the root of the project.

Right after the creation of the plan by JDeveloper, it will not yet cause any replacements to be made when applied during deployment. At this point, the plan only provides the skeleton in which we can specify the replacements that should be made. JDeveloper creates entries for replaceable properties and attributes at the composite and component level as well as for services and reference bindings. Here are two examples:

```
<property name="some.custom.property">
     <replace>valueOfPropertyInApplication</replace>
</property>
```

and

```
<reference name="HW_Service">
     <binding type="ws">
        <attribute name="port">
          <replace>com.me/HW#wsdl.endpoint(HW_ep/HW_pt)</replace>
        </attribute>
        <attribute name="location">
           <replace>http://devhost:8001/soa-infra/services/HW_ep?WSDL</replace>
        </attribute>
     </binding>
```

Additionally, it contains suggestions for search-and-replace rules for the import section of the composite.xml file—where WSDL documents are imported. The plan contains an example of a policy that could be attached to service or reference bindings and components. Finally, the wsdlAndSchema element in the generated plan can be used to specify rules to search and replace references to (the location of) imported WSDL and XSD documents; these rules can be applied to all WSDL and XSD documents that are part of the composite application—not just the composite.xml file.

Example of a Configuration Plan

Let's create a configuration plan for the DoctorsAppointmentRequestsProcessor composite application that we first worked on in Chapter 7. This application polls the file system and a database table for new appointment requests from general practitioners in the region on behalf of their patients. Some of these requests are, in fact, for dental appointments or chiropractical treatments—these are registered by the application and subsequently routed to external services for the dentist's service center and the chiropractors' association. Most requests are to be handled by St. Matthews, and those are routed to the PatientAppointmentService. All requests are routed to a logging service that uses the file adapter to write details about the request to a log file.

This application has quite a few settings that require environment-specific values—for example, the directories the file adapter services read from or write to, the properties that govern the polling times, and the physical endpoints for the test and production services exposed by the central organizations for dentists and chiropractors. We will first generate a configuration plan and then start to make the environment-specific replacements.

Inspecting the DoctorsAppointmentRequestsProcessor Application   Open the DoctorsAppointmentRequestsProcessor application. Double-click the composite.xml file to open the editor and then select the Source tab. Note the properties, such as DOCTOR_ APPOINTMENTREQUESTS_DIRECTORY and LOG_DOCTOR_APPOINTMENTREQUESTS_ OUTPUT_DIRECTORY. Also note that several properties are *not* in the composite.xml, such as the PollingFrequency for the ReadFileDoctorsAppointmentRequests Service binding. And remember that the configuration plan cannot replace properties that are not in the composite.xml file.

The Reference elements contain binding.ws elements that specify the endpoint location for the external services such as DentistServiceCenter and ChiropractorsAppointmentProcessorService.

Generating the Configuration Plan for the Test Environment   Select the composite.xml file in the navigator tree. Open the context menu and select the option Generate Config Plan. Type **DoctorAppointmentRequestsProcessor_TestEnvConfigPlan.xml** as the name for the file to be generated. Next, click the OK button. JDeveloper will now generate the configuration plan, with entries for properties that can be replaced.

Now suppose that the edition of the DentistsServiceCenter service to be used in the test environment has been deployed to a *test* partition on the SOA Suite, which means that the endpoint for that particular reference binding needs to be replaced in the configuration plan, as shown here:

```
<reference name="DentistServiceCenter">
  <binding type="ws">
    <attribute name="location">
      <replace>http://xp-vm:8001/soa-infra/services/test/...
        ...DentistsServiceCenter/HandleDentistAppointmentRequest?WSDL</replace>
    </attribute>
  </binding>
</reference>
```

Note that this entry was generated into the configuration plan; the only thing we need to do is to provide the new value for the location attribute.

The import statement for the WSDL for this DentistServiceCenter service also needs to be replaced:

```
<import>
  <searchReplace>
    <search>http://xp-vm:8001/soa-infra/services/default/...
      ...DentistsServiceCenter/HandleDentistAppointmentRequests.wsdl</search>
    <replace>http://xp-vm:8001/soa-infra/services/test/...
      ...DentistsServiceCenter/HandleDentistAppointmentRequests.wsdl</replace>
  </searchReplace>
</import>
```

Another change between the development and test environment is the directory that is used to write the log file with entries for every doctor's patient appointment request. This directory is set through the property LOG_DOCTOR_APPOINTMENTREQUESTS_OUTPUT_DIRECTORY, also defined in the file composite.xml. In the development environment it is set to c:\temp\ stmatthews\logs, and that is the value generated by default into the configuration plan. However, the test environment uses the directory c:\test\logs. We need to edit the configuration plan, as follows:

```
<reference name="LogDoctorsAppointmentRequests">
    <property name="LOG_DOCTOR_APPOINTMENTREQUESTS_OUTPUT_DIRECTORY">
        <replace>c:\test\logs</replace>
    </property>
    <binding type="jca"/>
</reference>
```

We have decided that for the test environment we would like every message that is sent into the HandleDoctorsAppointmentRequest Mediator component to be logged. To achieve this, we add the following entry to the configuration plan for the test environment:

```
<component name="HandleDoctorsAppointmentRequest">
    <wsp:PolicyReference orawsp:category="management"
                         orawsp:status="enabled" URI="oracle/log_policy"/>
</component>
```

Replacing Properties for Technology Adapter Bindings   Oftentimes, the properties for technology adapter bindings are specified in the special .jca files that are created by the adapter wizard. These files are not touched by the configuration plan. If we want those properties to be set to environment-specific values, we first need to "promote" those properties to the composite.xml file. We would like to set the polling time for the file adapter service ReadFileDoctorsAppointment Requests to a value of 20 seconds for the test environment. Here are the steps for doing this (see Figure 17-2):

1. Bring up the Composite Editor and click the ReadFileDoctorsAppointmentRequests service.

2. Open the property editor for this service, locate the Binding Properties section, and click the green plus icon to create a new property.

3. Select the PollingFrequency from the drop-down list of properties, set the value to 10 seconds (the value used in the development environment), and click the OK button.

This will create a property element for the PollingFrequency property in the composite.xml file inside the binding.jca element:

```
<binding.jca config="ReadFileDoctorsAppointmentRequests_file.jca">
    <property name="PollingFrequency" type="xs:positiveInteger" many="false"
              override="may">10</property>
</binding.jca>
```

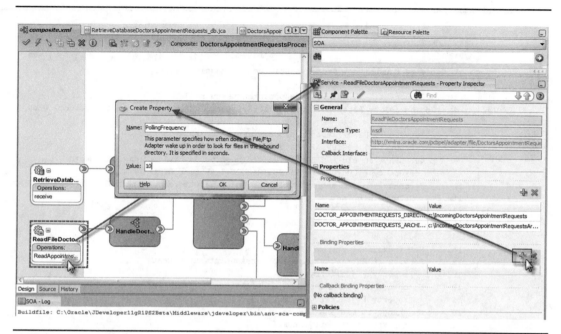

FIGURE 17-2. *Promoting a technology adapter service-binding property to the composite level*

When we next generate the configuration plan, it will include an extra element that allows us to replace the value of the PollingFrequency for the service ReadFileDoctorsAppointmentRequests from its current value of 10 (seconds):

```
<!--Add search and replace rules for the binding properties-->
<binding type="jca">
   <property name="PollingFrequency">
      <replace>10</replace>
   </property>
</binding>
```

Set the value inside the <replace> element to 20.

Validation of the Configuration Plan

To verify the syntactical correctness of a configuration plan and to see the modifications it will cause, the plan can be validated. Plan validation results in a log file that provides an overview of all additions and replacements that would be made to the composite.xml (and possibly other files) by the configuration plan as it currently stands. When the syntax of the plan is not correct, the validation step will fail with messages indicating the problems in the search and replace rules. The validate option can be accessed either from the context menu on an individual configuration plan or on the composite.xml.

```
 1  Modified Composite [ DoctorsAppointmentRequestsProcessor ]
 2    Component
 3      Component  [ HandleDoctorsAppointmentRequest ]
 4    Adding policy Reference <wsp:PolicyReference orawsp:category="management" oraw
 5    Service
 6      Service  [ ReadFileDoctorsAppointmentRequests ]
 7        Property [ DOCTOR_APPOINTMENTREQUESTS_DIRECTORY ]
 8      No change in old and new value c:\IncomingDoctorsAppointmentRequests
 9        Property [ DOCTOR_APPOINTMENTREQUESTS_ARCHIVE_DIRECTORY ]
10      No change in old and new value c:\IncomingDoctorsAppointmentRequestsArchive
11        Service Bindings
12        Binding [ jca ]
13        Property [ PollingFrequency ]
14      Old [ 10 ]
15      New [ 20 ]
16      Service  [ RetrieveDatabaseDoctorsAppointmentRequests ]
17        Property [ jca.retry.count ]
18      No change in old and new value 2147483647
19        Property [ jca.retry.interval ]
20      No change in old and new value 1
21        Property [ jca.retry.backoff ]
22      No change in old and new value 2
23        Property [ jca.retry.maxInterval ]
24      No change in old and new value 120
25        Service Bindings
26        Binding [ jca ]
27    Reference
28      Reference  [ LogDoctorsAppointmentRequests ]
29        Property [ LOG_DOCTOR_APPOINTMENTREQUESTS_OUTPUT_DIRECTORY ]
30      Old [ c:\temp\stmatthews\logs ]
31      New [ c:\test\logs ]
32        Reference Bindings
33        Binding [ jca ]
34      Reference  [ PatientAppointmentService ]
35        Reference Bindings
36        Binding [ ws ]
37    Attribute name=port
38      No change in old and new value http://stmatthews.hospital.com/patient/Appoir
39    Attribute name=location
```

FIGURE 17-3. *Validation report for the configuration plan*

The validation reports—shown in Figure 17-3—clearly logs the (test) environment-specific changes that the configuration plan will bring about when applied during deployment:

```
Modified Composite [ DoctorsAppointmentRequestsProcessor ]
    Import Locations
      Old [ http://xp-vm:8001/soa-infra/services/default/...
              ...DentistsServiceCenter/HandleDentistAppointmentRequests.wsdl]
      New [ http://xp-vm:8001/soa-infra/services/test/
              ...DentistsServiceCenter/HandleDentistAppointmentRequests.wsdl]
```

```
     Component  [ HandleDoctorsAppointmentRequest ]
       Adding policy Reference <wsp:PolicyReference
                 orawsp:category="management" orawsp:status="enabled" ...
   Service  [ ReadFileDoctorsAppointmentRequests ]
     Service Bindings
       Binding  [ jca ]
         Property [ PollingFrequency ]
           Old [ 10 ]
           New [ 20 ]
   Reference  [ LogDoctorsAppointmentRequests ]
     Property [ LOG_DOCTOR_APPOINTMENTREQUESTS_OUTPUT_DIRECTORY ]
       Old [ c:\temp\stmatthews\logs ]
       New [ c:\test\logs ]
   Reference  [ DentistServiceCenter ]
     Reference Bindings
       Binding  [ ws ]
         Attribute name=location
           Old [ http://xp-vm:8001/soa-infra/services/default/...
               ...DentistsServiceCenter/HandleDentistAppointmentRequest?WSDL]
           New [ http://xp-vm:8001/soa-infra/services/test/...
               ...DentistsServiceCenter/HandleDentistAppointmentRequest?WSDL]
```

Applying a Configuration Plan During Deployment

Configuration plans can be attached to composite applications during deployment. The applicable plan can be selected as part of the deployment dialog in JDeveloper and in the FMW Enterprise Manager Console as well as in the Ant and WLST deploy commands. When a configuration plan is attached during deployment, then prior to moving the composite to the SOA Suite, the composite. xml file is extracted from the service archive, the replace actions are performed, and the result is put back in the archive. The same happens to all artifacts processed by the configuration plan files in the service archive, such as WSDL and XSD.

Attaching a Configuration Plan upon Deployment from JDeveloper

Now that we have created the configuration plan for the test environment, we can use it whenever the composite application is deployed to that environment. We will probably end up having configuration plans for every environment that we deploy the application to. Whenever we deploy the application, we should pick the configuration plan appropriate for the target environment.

Let's deploy the composite application to the test environment and apply the configuration plan at that time. When the deployment dialog appears, choose Deploy To Application Server and click Next. Select the radio button Select A Configuration Plan From The List. Next, select the DoctorAppointmentRequestsProcessor_TestEnvConfigPlan.xml plan in the list box and click Next (see Figure 17-4).

Select the Application Server connection for the SOA Suite 11*g* instance you want to deploy into and then click Next. On the SOA Servers page, check the box for soa_server1. Select the "test" partition from the drop-down list to direct this composite application deployment to that particular partition that we use as the test environment, as shown in Figure 17-5. (Note that this partition is created in the FMW Enterprise Manager Console on the Manage Partitions page that is opened from the context menu on the soa-infra node.)

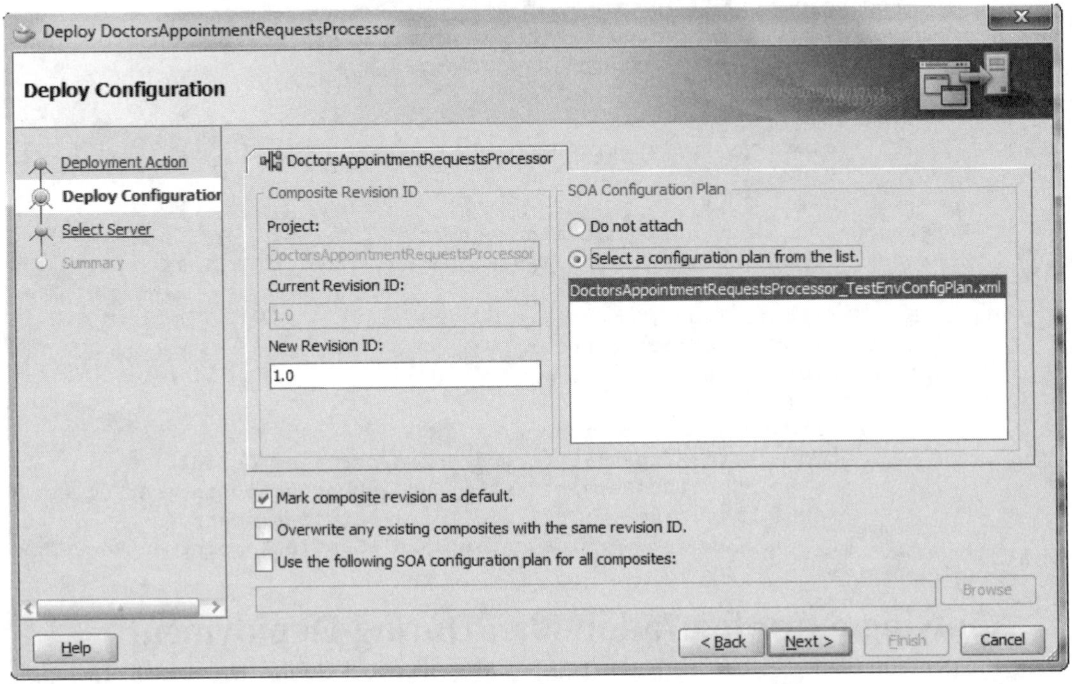

FIGURE 17-4.   *Attaching the configuration plan during deployment*

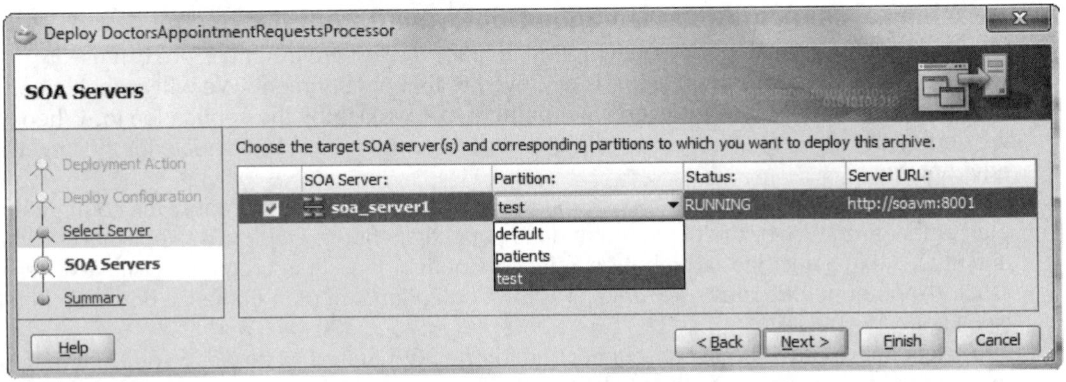

FIGURE 17-5.   *Selecting the "test" partition as the deployment target*

Click Finish to start deployment of the application. During this deployment, the configuration plan is applied before the resulting SAR is deployed to the running server.

Verifying Deployment in the FMW Enterprise Manager Console

When the deployment is complete, we can open the Enterprise Manager console to check on the effects of the configuration plan. Select the node for the composite DoctorsAppointmentRequests Processor in partition "test."

Click the Policies tab—this tab contains the logging policy that is added in the configuration plan to the component HandleDoctorsAppointmentRequest.

From the composite menu, open the submenu Service/Reference Properties and then select the item ReadFileDoctorsAppointmentRequests on this submenu. The Properties tab for this incoming file adapter service binding contains the property PollingFrequency with the value 20, as was set in the configuration plan. Note that this—and all other file adapter properties—can be edited in this page. See Figure 17-6 for an illustration.

From the composite menu, open the submenu Service/Reference Properties and then select the item LogDoctorsAppointmentRequests on this submenu. The Properties tab for this item displays the LOG_DOCTOR_APPOINTMENTREQUESTS_OUTPUT_DIRECTORY property, which contains the (modified) value c:\test\logs for the output directory, as was specified in the configuration plan. Note, again, that most properties on this file adapter reference binding can be manipulated at both design time and run time.

The fourth change brought about by the configuration plan was the location attribute for the Web Service binding in the DentistServiceCenter reference—to use the service in the test partition. This change is slightly harder to find: Open the System MBean Browser using the Administration submenu

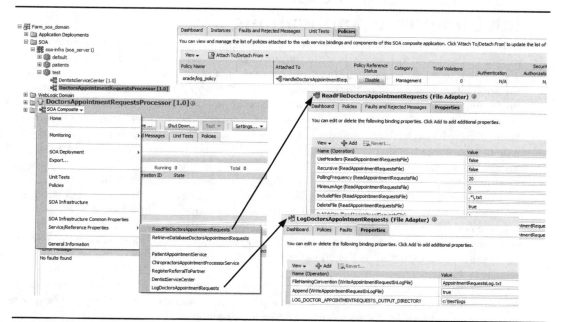

FIGURE 17-6. *Inspecting the effects of the configuration plan in the FMW Console*

on the context menu on the soa-infra node. In the browser, locate Application Defined MBeans and select oracle.soa.config/Server: soa_server1/SCAComposite/DoctorAppointmentRequestsProcessor/SCAComposite.SCAReference/DentistServiceCenter. The Attributes tab displays the wsdl-file attribute that refers to the WSDL document in the test partition. The location attribute that we replaced in the configuration plan on the ws.binding element can be inspected when we select the grandchild node SCAComposite.SCAReference/WSBinding.

Attaching Configuration Plans on the Command Line

The ant-sca-deploy.xml script can be invoked with the following optional parameter to apply a plan:

```
-Dconfigplan=<location and name of configuration plan file>
```

The WLST command sca_deployComposite can be invoked with a last optional parameter to specify the configuration plan:

```
sca_deployComposite(...,
configplan="c:/temp/DoctorAppointmentRequestsProcessor_TestEnvConfigPlan.xml")
```

Exporting Composite Applications from the Console

Note that the resulting service archive that is created when you export a composite application through the EM Console contains the composite application, including the environment-specific values that were applied from the attached configuration plan at the time of deployment. However, when the exported archive is redeployed, you can still attach another configuration plan.

Automated Unit Testing for Composite Applications

Most software developers will—albeit perhaps a little grudgingly—agree that it is probably a good idea to test applications before they are thrown at production environments and real end users. This applies to the first time an application sees the light of day as well as to later incarnations of the application (regression testing). Our desire for agility and the ability to flexibly embrace and implement changes leads to a constant production of new incarnations that all need testing. This is impacted because we deliver smaller pieces of functionality (services) instead of monolithic applications. So we have more frequent (but often) smaller changes, leading to a more dynamic type of release management. This alone is a powerful trigger for the introduction of automated testing of applications.

Various types of testing should be considered (for example, targeted at functionality or performance) as well as different levels, such as unit and (composite) application or service and integration (across multiple services and entire business processes). In addition to the scope of the test, we need to consider various types of components or aspects that require testing—for example, user interfaces and (programmatic) service interfaces—and how exactly do we test a composite that is triggered by the consumption of an event on the EDN or the arrival of a file on the file system?

Most modern testing methodologies heavily rely on interfaces and contracts to provide the foundation for both the tests and the implementation of the software; this is sometimes referred to as "contract and test-driven development." Service-oriented applications are, by their very nature, based on interface definitions and functional contracts. Adoption of automated testing based on design contracts is, therefore, fairly easily achieved for SOA composite applications.

Automated Testing

Automated testing of SOA composite applications can be done from the outside of the applications by simply invoking the public services and operations exposed by the applications and checking the responses received. In a simplistic approach, we consider the application a black box where we need no more than the public WSDLs and associated XSDs to create test cases (and probably the functional design to be a little smart about it).

A slightly more advanced approach is called "white box testing," where we make use of our knowledge of the internals of the composite application to devise the test cases we should throw at the application in order to cover as many different paths and special conditions.

Both black box and white box testing require tools that can invoke Web Services in an automated fashion, but do not require any knowledge about the implementation of the application or the SOA Suite. A well-known tool that is frequently used for functional testing of Web Services is soapUI. When the test is specifically focused on performance and the behavior of the application under a substantial load, Apache JMeter is a frequent test tool.

However, the automated test scenarios described here are fairly coarse grained: They test the application in its entirety (and are beyond the scope of this book). Before we embark on these application-wide tests, or at least as a complement to them, it is probably a good idea to do unit testing. In a unit test, we try to establish the correct behavior of a unit or part of an application or service. We do so by testing the unit in isolation—without any dependencies on external components.

Unit Testing in SOA Suite 11g

It would seem like a contradiction in terms to test parts of an SOA composite application because—with the exception of the simplest BPEL process components or the Mediator, which only does an echo of the request message—all components or other sub entities in composite applications seem to have dependencies. Messages are passed to other components, external services are engaged to provide information, and interaction is sought with technology adapters. Stand-alone units are hard to find.

Fortunately, the SOA Suite comes with a unit-testing framework that allows us to define units inside composite applications by arbitrarily selecting services, components, and references. All calls from within this *unit* to external references—other components, technology adapter references, or to external services—can be handled by the unit-testing framework and responded to with predefined mock response messages. When the unit test is done, no real calls are made to any element outside of the unit, so we can test the unit in isolation.

We define a test suite for such a custom defined unit and create test cases in it. Each test case is the combination of the following:

- The request message sent into the unit to one of the services it exposes (called *initiation*). Note that we can also emulate events that enter the composite during the test.

- The mock response messages to be fed into the unit during the test for each of the wires coming out of the unit (known as *emulation* in the unit-testing framework).

- The expected result that the unit should produce for the test case given the request message (indicated with an *assertion*). This is usually a response but can be any other message travelling out of the unit as well.

The assertion does not take into account any possible side effects the test case may have—for example, in a situation where not all outgoing wires have been plugged through an emulation and the execution of the unit test should result in a change in a file or a database table. The unit-testing framework does not have special setup and tear-down facilities to prepare for and clean up after the test.

Test suites for automated unit tests are created in JDeveloper as part of the composite application that they test. They are deployed along with the application. A test suite can be executed from the FMW console, as well as from an Ant script or a WLST command. These last two options make it possible to execute unit test suites automatically, as part of Maven and Ant-based build procedures, for example.

We will next create a unit test suite with test cases for the DoctorsAppointmentRequestsProcessor application. One of the things we want to test is whether the AppointmentRequestRouter component will send requests that are intended for external care providers to the HandleAppointmentRequestFor ExternalPartner that takes care of these appointment requests. The condition for this decision is a weak spot in the design—based on the first character of the appointment type being a "W" (chiropractors) or the appointment type containing the string values Q1, Q2, or Q4 (dentists).

Creating the Test Suite for the DoctorsAppointmentRequestsProcessor Application

A new test suite is created from the context menu on the node testsuites in the project navigator; the relevant menu item reads Create Test Suite. The test suite has a name that typically conveys the purpose of this particular collection of test cases. All cases could focus on a specific component in the composite—the name of this component is then a logical element in the suite name. In our case the test suite is called ExternalPartnersTest_AppointmentRequestRouter.

After the test suite is created, JDeveloper immediately prompts us to create the first test case. We can add many test cases later on, from the context menu on the node for the test suite.

Creating Test Cases for the AppointmentRequestRouter Mediator

Let's create a first test case from the context menu on the node for the test suite. Select the option Create Test. Call this first test case **ChiropractorAppointmentRequest_test**. In this test, we send in an appointment request for an appointment type that starts with W. Our functional design prescribes that this type of appointment should be routed to the external Chiropractor Service Center. For the purpose of our test case, this means that the AppointmentRequestRouter should send this request to the HandleAppointmentRequestForExternalPartner Mediator (and from there onward to the Web Service reference binding ChiropractorsAppointmentProcessorService—but that is outside the scope of this unit test). Note that when we click the OK button to complete the creation of the test case, the Composite Editor visualizes in a subtle way (yellow background in the swimlanes and an additional icon in the toolbar) that we are not looking now at the definition of the composite application, but at the editor for a new test case of that application instead.

Initial Chiropractor Appointment Request Message   To initiate this test case, we create the initial message on the service that acts as the test case's entry point, as shown in Figure 17-7. Right-click the ReadFileDoctorsAppointmentRequests service. The menu has a single option that you should activate: Create Initiate Messages. The Initiate Messages dialog appears in which we can specify the message(s) to send into the composite during this unit test. Click the Generate Sample button. This will create an XML document that contains three request messages. Remove two and make sure to set the appointment type element in the remaining one to any string value

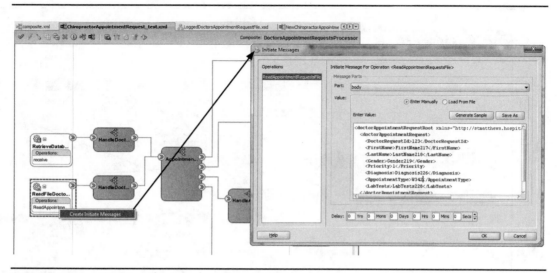

FIGURE 17-7. *Creating the initial message for the test case*

that starts with W. Click the OK button. The dialog closes and a small icon marks the service in the editor to indicate that a message from this binding initiates the test case.

Assert Message to HandleAppointmentRequestForExternalPartner   The expected behavior of the unit that we are testing in this test case is that it routes the message through to the HandleAppointmentRequestForExternalPartner Mediator because it is a request for an external appointment. This expectation is laid down using an assertion on the wire from the AppointmentRequestRouter to the HandleAppointmentRequestForExternalPartner Mediator. Right-click the wire. The context menu has a single option: Create Wire Actions. Activate that option, and the Wire Actions dialog appears.

Click the green plus icon to create a new assertion. We want to assert that the initial appointment request that was sent into the composite is forwarded through this wire. An easy way of doing so is to test for a message that contains the same appointment type as the initial message. Select the appointment type element as the Assert Target and set the Assert Value to the value for Appointment Type that we used in the initial message (see Figure 17-8).

You should realize—and I consider it a shortcoming in the unit-testing framework—that the only thing we will be able to test here is that *if* the message is routed via this wire, then the appointment type is the same as in the initial message. However, if it is not routed via this wire, the absence of the message does not trigger a failure.

In this case, we do not expect the unit to call out through other wires to retrieve responses, so we do not need to emulate those services on the outgoing wires. Note that for the unit test we would prefer no external calls at all, but we cannot prevent calls to the one-way reference bindings LogDoctorsAppointmentRequests and RegisterReferralToPartner.

If we want to ascertain that the chiropractor-oriented appointment request in this case is not accidentally forwarded to PatientAppointmentService and incorrectly treated as an internal appointment request, we can create an assertion on the wire to that external service and have that assertion fail on any message content—there should never be a message, so every message should trigger a test failure.

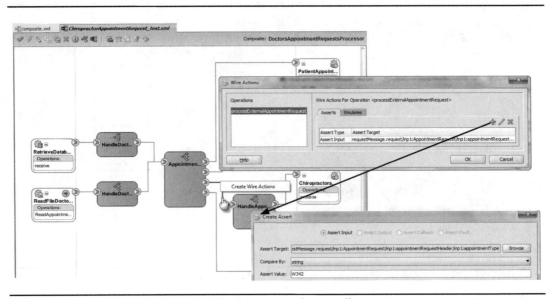

FIGURE 17-8. *Creating an assertion for the wire to the HandleAppointmentRequestFor ExternalPartner*

Other Test Cases in the Appointment Request Router Test Suite

In addition to the test case for the chiropractor appointment, we can create a similar test case for an appointment with a dentist—the appointment type contains Q1, Q2, or Q4. The same assertions as with the chiropractor will do. An internal appointment—that is, an appointment type that does not start with W and does not contain Q1, Q2, or Q4—is slightly more interesting: It should be routed by the AppointmentRequestRouter to the external Web Service binding PatientAppointmentService (and *not* to the HandleAppointmentRequestForExternalPartner Mediator). We can create corresponding assertions on the two wires.

Because we do not want the PatientAppointmentService to be really called for this unit test, we can emulate this service and its response. Right-click the wire to the service and select Edit Wire Actions from the menu. The Wire Actions dialog appears, with two tabs: Assertions and Emulations. Activate the latter tab. Create a new emulation—for the output from PatientAppointmentService's process operation. Click the Generate Sample button to have a sample response message generated (see Figure 17-9).

Testing the First Development: The Test Case for the New Functionality

A good practice before starting the development of new functional requirements is the up-front creation of the test cases for the new functionality. Suppose our new requirement is that in addition to Q1, Q2, and Q4, an appointment type value of Q7 is also used to indicate an appointment with a dentist. Before we adapt our composite application for this latest requirement, we can create the test case for it. This test case can be a clone of the ChiropractorAppointmentRequest_test. There is no simple clone operation; however, we can create a new test case and copy the contents from the Source tab in the original to the clone, which will do the trick nicely. Edit both the initial message and the assertion on the wire to HandleAppointmentRequestForExternalPartner—to cater for

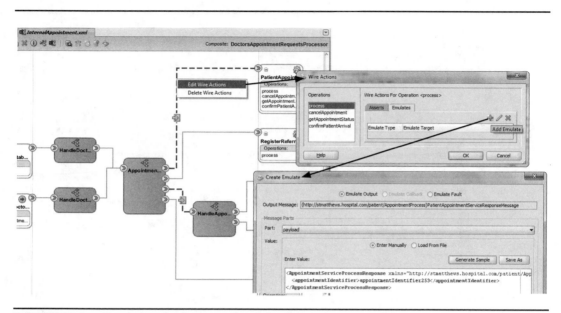

FIGURE 17-9. *Emulating the response from the PatientAppointmentService (to prevent this service from being called during the unit test)*

appointment type Q7. Make sure an "anti-message" assertion is in place on the wire to the PatientAppointmentService: No message should go that way, but during the test we can expect one anyway because we have not yet modified the AppointmentRequestRouter to cater for Q7.

Deploying and Running the Test Suite
Unit test suites are part of the composite application. When the application is packaged and deployed, the test suites are taken along for the ride. So by redeploying the composite application, we automatically deploy the unit test suite.

Test suites can be run from the Unit Tests tab on the composite application's dashboard. We can select the test suite to run and pick the test cases that should be executed (see Figure 17-10).

The result of running the unit test is as to be expected: One failure (for the not-yet-implemented Q7 appointment type) and three successes. We can inspect the reason for the failure by looking at the violated assertions. In this case, the message across the wire to the PatientAppointmentService violated the assertion (which basically says that any message on that wire is an unexpected result for this test case).

Unit tests produce new instances of the composite application. These are marked as test instances and have visual indicators in the FWM Console. Calls to external services or internal components outside the test unit that have been emulated are not really made—the message trace makes that clear. In the figure, for example, we see that the components we know live inside the PatientAppointmentService and that the calls normally made from the PatientAppointmentService are missing. This is because the emulation wire action handled the call and the PatientAppointment Service composite was never actually accessed in the unit test.

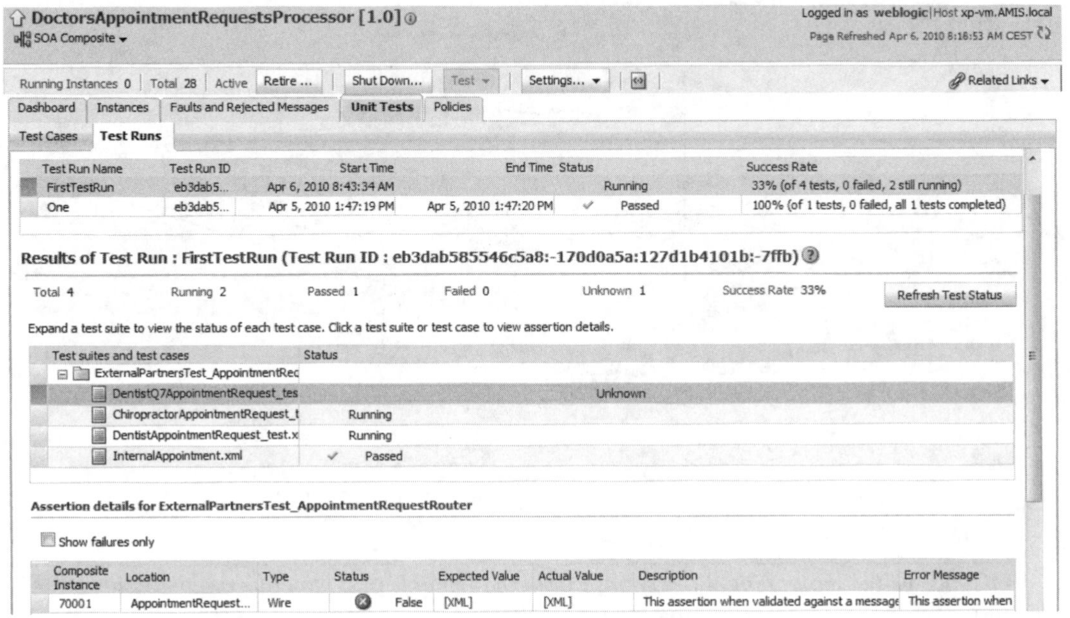

FIGURE 17-10. *Running the test suites from the FWM Console*

Limitations in the Unit-Testing Framework

The unit-testing framework is undoubtedly useful, but it does have several limitations that you should be well aware of. We cannot test for the fact that a message is sent; when a message is not sent, there will never be a failure reported. An assertion will succeed in the absence of a message, even though the message should have been sent. In our example, we cannot test for the fact that a request for an appointment type W61 is sent onward to the HandleAppointmentRequestFor ExternalPartner Mediator. We can check for a message sent to the (alternative) PatientAppointment Service reference binding and declare any message sent that way a failure. But the test cannot conclusively prove that the correct message was sent (only that if it was sent, then it was correct).

We cannot emulate (the response from) one-way services and thereby prevent a real call from being made. This means that our unit test will, for example, call out to the outbound file adapter service that logs the test request just like any other (real) appointment request. Side effects from one-way services invoked from the unit under test scrutiny cannot be prevented, nor can those side effects be tested for by the framework.

We also cannot emulate the publication of a business event. A composite that is triggered through the consumption of an EDN event cannot itself be tested using this unit-testing framework.

Including Testing in Automatic Deployment

The previous section showed how we can manually start execution of a test suite from the FMW Console. However, unit testing is ideally incorporated in automated build scripts that may run periodically or even following every check-in for an integrated testing environment—coordinated by tools such as Continuum, Hudson, and Cruise Control. Fortunately, we can execute test suites for composite applications in the SOA Suite from the command line, using an Ant script or a WLST command.

Running the test suite from Ant is done through the ant-sca-test.xml script:

```
ant -f ant-sca-test.xml -Dscatest.input=DoctorsAppointmentRequestsProcessor
-Dscatestsuite.input=testSuite1,testSuite5
-Dscatest.partition=test -Dscatest.format=junit
-Dscatest.result=c:\temp\test\reports
-Djndi.properties=c:\temp\test\soasuite11g_jndi.properties
```

The file soasuite11g_jndi.properties contains JNDI properties that are needed to connect to the SOA Suite instance in which a composite application needs testing; this includes the server name, port number, and user account. We get prompted to provide the password.

The format property instructs the SOA Suite to produce a JUnit-style HTML-based test report; it is created in the directory c:\temp\test\reports, specified through the result property.

Most command-line operations can be performed using Ant as well as using the WLST interface. Testing of SOA composite applications is no exception. The WLST command for running a test suite is sca_test. It takes parameters for the composite name, partition and revision, the name of the test suite, and the jndi-properties filename. Note that the WLST command invokes the Ant script to run the test suite:

```
sca_test('DoctorsAppointmentRequestsProcessor', '1.0'
        , 'testSuite1,testSuite5'
        , 'c:\temp\test\soasuite11g_jndi.properties', partition='test'
        )
```

Embracing Change

One of the main objectives of SOA in general is to achieve business agility. Agility can be defined in various ways, but a central element of all definitions will be an ability to adapt to changes in a flexible, quick, and controlled manner. A constant willingness and preparedness to embrace change is what we try to instill in people as well as install in the applications we develop.

This section discusses various ways of dealing with changes—both by leveraging the intrinsic facilities of SOA Suite for absorbing changes in the environment and embedding a degree of dynamic customizability in the SOA composite applications as well as through changing and redeploying (new versions of) composite applications.

Dynamically Adjusting Application Behavior

A portion of the changing requirements we face for our composite applications can be resolved by an administrator, at run time, without the need for changing and redeploying the application. For example, endpoints of external services that are invoked from composite applications can be adjusted. The configuration of technology adapter services is another aspect that can be altered at run time. When it comes to the more functional aspects of the application, there are several options to make those subject to on-the-fly manipulation too. When applications make use of SCA properties and facilities such as Domain Value Maps and business rules that can be edited at run time, parts of their behavior become manageable.

Run-time Management of Adapter Configuration and Endpoint Settings

SOA Suite has built-in support for run-time adjustment of various types of properties. The administration pages for composites and their service and reference bindings offer access to the same properties that we can replace using configuration plans during deployment. When we inspected the effect of the configuration plan a few paragraphs back, we visited those pages that we can now also use to apply run-time modifications to those same properties.

Changing the Endpoints of Services   A possible change that we may need to make to a deployed composite application is a readjustment of the endpoint of one of the services referenced by the composite. The service referenced by the composite may simply be moved to a different server, and we need to use a different address to access it. Or it may be the case that the owner of the service offers a new, improved version of his service that we want to make use of (and because the port and message definitions have not changed, we will be able to). Or a virtualization layer—wrapper service, enterprise service bus, service registry—is to be inserted between the composite and the referenced service and therefore the reference binding needs to switch to a different address.

Whatever the occasion, when the endpoint of a referenced service needs to be changed, the steps are as follows: Select the composite application for which the reference binding needs adjustment. From the SOA Composite drop-down menu, open the submenu Service/Reference Properties and select the reference that needs changing. The Reference Binding dashboard opens. Click the Properties tab. The new endpoint address for the referenced service can be entered into the Endpoint Address field, as shown in Figure 17-11. Click the Apply button to save this change. From then on, whenever the composite invokes the reference, the call is routed to this new address.

Note that the use of an enterprise service bus (for example, using Oracle Service Bus) or a directory service such as the Oracle Service Registry to virtualize Web Service addresses at run time in the first place would prevent most if not all of these changes to the composite's reference binding properties. Changes in the location of the services accessed through the OSB or service registry would be handled inside that service, transparent to the composite application.

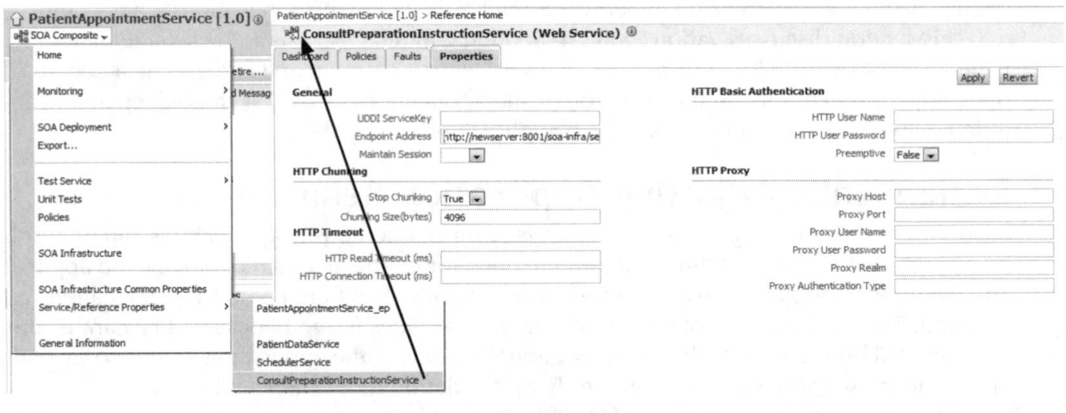

FIGURE 17-11.   *Changing the endpoint address of a reference binding of an external service*

Modifying Properties for the Composite, Components, and Technology Adapter Services   Both the custom properties that we may define on the composite or one of the components (as we will see in the next section), as well as the standard properties for the technology adapters, can be manipulated in the FMW Console. Earlier we checked on the effect of the configuration plan on the properties logging directory for the outbound file adapter service and the polling time for the inbound file adapter service. The console pages that we used for this inspection can also be used for manipulation of the values of these properties.

All aspects of the composite application and its adapter bindings that are controlled through properties that can be set at design time are also up for adjustment at run time.

Reapplying Configuration Plans   Configuration plans can almost be seen as run-time themes— snapshots of a coherent set of property and endpoint values that make sense in a certain context. It would be quite nice if we could apply configuration plans to deployed composites—without redeploying—as an efficient way to apply a meaningful set of logically related changes that, for example, switches a composite from development settings to acceptance test settings, or to reapply the same set of configuration settings to the new version of the composite in the same environment. In that light, it would also be useful to be able to export the current set of property values as they have been set through the console as a configuration plan (or "theme") that can be reused. At the present, however, that functionality is not available in SOA Suite.

Designing Customization into Composite Applications

We have seen how the configuration and behavior of composite applications can be manipulated, prior to deployment, by attaching the right configuration plan and at any point after the application has been deployed from the FMW Enterprise Manager. In addition to the standard properties in bindings and the technology adapter we tweaked in the previous section, we can also expose custom properties from our composite application that influence the application behavior and that can be altered at run time to implement changes in the behavior. Note, however, that next to these properties there are other ways to influence applications after they have been deployed.

Let's investigate an example. We have currently implemented an implicit business rule in the PatientAppointmentService: to change the status of an appointment to "No Show" when the patient has not arrived for the appointment within four hours of the scheduled appointment time. This "deadline" period of four hours is rather arbitrarily chosen—and it is a candidate for post-deployment readjustment. Several customization strategies are available to turn this value into one that can be manipulated at run time. The value of this setting can be

- Set using a Business Rule component (that itself can be manipulated in the SOA Composer at run time);

- Read from a database table, PL/SQL package, or properties file;

- Retrieved from a Web Service, singleton BPEL process, EJB, or (static) Java object (which may act as a properties cache);

- Read from properties defined in the composite.xml file and manipulated through the MBean browser in the SOA FMW Console.

For simple properties that are used in BPEL processes, using custom SCA properties at the component (or composite) level is the leanest approach. These properties are defined in the component element in the composite.xml and in the componentType file—for example, for

Mediators and BPEL components. These properties can be accessed inside these components using special XPath operations (for example, in the BPEL Assign activity). The value of these properties can be inspected and modified through the System MBean browser.

We will now edit the PatientAppointmentService BPEL component to make the no-show deadline a customizable property. Subsequently, we will see how to find and manipulate this property after deployment.

Configuring the noShowDeadline Property in composite.xml Defining SCA properties is done in the composite.xml file, at the composite level or at the component/service/reference level—either directly in the source file or through the Property Inspector. Properties can also be defined in the componentType file that describes the abstract definition of a component.

A property definition consists of the name and type of the property—and may also indicate whether the value can be overridden, whether multiple values are allowed, and what the source of the property value is when the component-level property inherits its value from a composite-level property. Note that the name for properties for BPEL components has to start with "preference."

In this case, the property is called preference.noShowDeadline, is of type duration, and has the initial value of P0Y0M0DT4H0M0S (which means four hours):

```
<component name="PatientAppointmentService">
  <implementation.bpel src="PatientAppointmentService.bpel"/>
  <property name="preference.noShowDeadline" type="xs:duration">P0Y0M0DT4H0M0
S</property>
</component>
```

As an aside, custom properties like the noShowDeadline property are among the elements that can be customized by configuration plans. When we generate a new configuration plan for the composite.xml in which we added the property definition, the following entry is created to support environment-specific customization of the property value:

```
<component name="PatientAppointmentService">
    <property name="preference.noShowDeadline">
       <replace>P0Y0M0DT4H0M0S</replace>
    </property>
</component>
```

Accessing the noShowDeadline Property in the BPEL Process PatientAppointment Service The BPEL process needs to be altered to have it make use of the noShowDeadline property. Values of BPEL component properties are retrieved in Assign operations using the getPreference() XPath function that is part of the BPEL XPath Extension Functions. We have to pass the name of the property to the getPreference() function—without the prefix "preference." The following copy operation populates the BPEL variable NoShowDuration with the duration set in the property that was defined on the BPEL component:

```
<copy>
  <from expression="ora:getPreference('noShowDeadline')"/>
  <to variable="NoShowDuration"/>
</copy>
```

Inspecting and Adjusting the noShowDeadline Property Through the Console   We can deploy and run the PatientAppointmentService composite application with these changes applied, and initially everything would be the same as before. However, we now have the option of changing the behavior of the BPEL component: The noShowDeadline is exposed by the application and can be adjusted through the FMW Console.

Open the console and then open the context menu on the soa-infra node. Open the submenu Administration and the item System MBean Browser on this menu. Locate the node Application Defined MBeans in the tree and find its child node oracle.soa.config. Expand this node and its child Server: soa_server1. Expand the SCAComposite child node. You will now see a list of all deployed SOA composite applications. Open the node for the composite application PatientAppointmentService. It has three children: one for components, one for services, and one for references. Expand the node for the component and, finally, select the node for the BPEL component PatientAppointmentService. All attributes of the selected MBean are shown on the right side of the page, as is illustrated in Figure 17-12. Click the attribute called Properties and locate the property called preference.noShowDeadline. You will see the value that was specified in the composite.xml file—or in the configuration plan that was used to deploy the application. You may now decide to change the property value and click the Apply button. From now on, whenever the PatientAppointmentService component refers to this property through the getPreference() method, it will retrieve the value that has just been set.

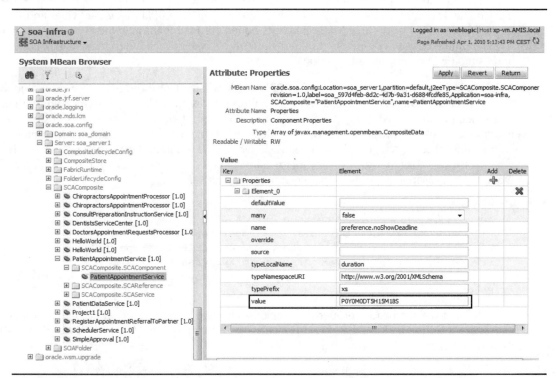

FIGURE 17-12.   *Inspecting and manipulating the noShowDeadline property for the PatientAppointmentService component*

NOTE
This applies immediately and to all instances—new ones and instances that are already running and have not yet retrieved the value of the noShowDeadline preference.

Design Time at Run Time Through Rules and DVM in SOA Composer

SOA Suite ships with the SOA Composer, a web-based tool that is used at run time to edit the definitions of business rules and Domain Value Maps. This opens up another way of modifying the behavior of deployed composite applications: When these applications use a Business Rule component or a Domain Value Map to govern part of their behavior, then that part of their conduct can be influenced through SOA Composer. Chapter 7 briefly introduced the Domain Value Map in combination with the Mediator component. Chapter 8 discussed the Business Rule component as well as the SOA Composer; it contains an example of how a custom System Parameters rule set can be created that also offers a way to make centrally defined properties available to applications that can easily be managed at run time.

Let's take a brief look now at a special kind of Domain Value Map that we could introduce as a fairly generic way of influencing run-time characteristics of composite applications.

This Domain Value Map could be called something like Properties, and it contains two columns: PropertyName and PropertyValue. It contains properties that are used in composite applications, and whose values need to be customizable at run time.

The values in the domain value map are accessed through XPath expressions that can be used in Mediator Transformations and Assign Value steps as well as in BPEL Assign activities and transformations. Domain Value Maps are easily edited at run time through the SOA Composer tool.

The online chapter complement demonstrates the steps for creating this Domain Value Map and using it in a composite application.

Referencing the Domain Value Map in BPEL and Mediator Components   Domain Value Maps are accessed in composite applications through the XPath extension function dvm:lookupValue. This function can be used in XPath expressions in BPEL and Mediator. An example of using this function to set header properties or message elements on the outgoing message in a Mediator component using the Assign Values dialog is shown next. It is part of the Mediator's .mplan file where it is used to set the value of a property called temp.chiro using an entry in the Properties Domain Value Map that has its PropertyName set to CHIRO:

```
<assign>
  <copy target="$out.property.temp.chiro"
        expression="dvm:lookupValue('Properties.dvm',
                        'PropertyName','CHIRO','PropertyValue','Q1')"
        xmlns:dvm="http://www.oracle.com/XSL/Transform/java/...
                                ...oracle.tip.dvm.LookupValue"/>
</assign>
```

Note that when a header property has been set by one Mediator, the value of that property is accessible to subsequent Mediator components—both in the Assign Values dialog and in XSLT transformations:

```
<xsl:value-of select='mhdr:getProperty("in.property.temp.chiro")'/>
```

BPEL Assign activities can use this same lookupValue function to retrieve values from the Domain Value Map. In a similar way, a property value can be extracted in the filter condition for a routing rule or in the transformation performed in the routing rule or in the BPEL transform activity:

```
<xsl:value-of select="dvm:lookupValue( 'Properties.dvm',
                  'PropertyName','CHIRO','PropertyValue','Q1') "/>
```

Run-time Administration of Domain Value Map   Domain Value Maps—like business rules— can be edited at run time from the SOA Composer. This browser-based editor can be accessed at http://localhost:8001/soa/composer/ (replace localhost with the host on which you run your instance of SOA Suite). Open the properties for the Domain Value Map. This is deployed in the DoctorAppointmentRequestsProcessor composite. Click the Edit button to go into edit mode. Click the row for the property that you want to change and click the edit icon. Change the property value and click the Commit button. At this point, the changed property value is loaded in memory and any subsequent access to this property through the dvm:lookupValue function will return this modified value.

Process Composer for Dynamic Business Process Management   As we have seen in Chapter 11, the BPM Composer—shipped as part of BPM 11*g* and completely integrated with SOA Suite 11*g*—is another application that is used for "design time at run time." The BPM Composer is used to modify the design of business processes, or even create new ones. Through this application, service invocations can be introduced, variable assignments manipulated, human tasks added or modified, and the flow logic of business processes rearranged. This capability to dynamically reorganize and manipulate business processes is an intrinsic quality of the BPM Suite 11*g* and not something we have to build into the application.

Changing Composite Applications

The previous section showed how a certain category of functional changes in a composite application can be handled at run time, through the console, without changes in the implementation of the application and thus with no need for redeployment. However, that will be the exception, not the rule. Usually, functional changes will require changes in the implementation of the application. These changes can be of various types:

- **Bug fixes, refactoring, or performance enhancements**   The functionality does not deviate from what was intended, the interface does not change, and the metadata describing the services does not require an update.

- **Functionality changes**   The functionality is changed even though the interface and contract do not change; the service behaves differently, but those changes fit within the predefined boundaries of the schema definition, the existing message type, and the port type definition in the WSDL.

- **Interface changes**   The schema definitions for the message types and/or the operations in the port type change; some of these changes are merely extensions that are fully backward compatible (only optional elements added to request message types; new operations but no changes to existing operations), and others break the existing contract and force consumers to adapt.

The SOA Suite provides various ways of dealing with changes to composite applications: A deployed application can be replaced through redeployment with a changed implementation, a new version of a deployed application can be deployed in parallel with the existing application, and an application can be renamed and deployed as an entirely new application.

Adopting a Change Procedure for SOA Composite Applications

Before we start making decisions, we should discuss two important characteristics of the SOA Suite.

Versions of Composite Applications and the Default Version We need to look at the endpoint address resolution in the SOA Suite. The services exposed by the composite applications are available at an endpoint that looks like this URL:

```
http://xp-vm:8001/soa-infra/services/default/...
             ...PatientAppointmentService!2.0/PatientAppointmentService_ep
```

There is some logic built into this URL: It first identifies the partition and the composite, then it names a specific version of the composite. Consumers of the service can use this full-blown URL that determines exactly which version of the (services exposed by the) composite they will access. Alternatively, they can use a URL that does not contain the version information, like this:

```
http://xp-vm:8001/soa-infra/services/default/...
             ...PatientAppointmentService/PatientAppointmentService_ep
```

In this case, they leave it to the SOA Suite to decide which version of the composite will be accessed to handle the request. This is where the concept of the default version makes its appearance: When we deploy a version of composite application, we can indicate whether that version will be the default version; we can also designate the default version of a composite through the FMW Console using the Set A Default button on the composite revision's dashboard. This default version is the version that will handle all requests to the composite that do not explicitly name a version in the URL. It is also the version that will be activated by inbound adapters (for example, Database, JMS, or File). Note that EDN events will be consumed by all versions of the composite.

NOTE
If changes from one version of a composite to the next are not backward compatible, consumers that access the composite's services using a version-free endpoint designation—effectively using the default revision of the service—can be severely impacted if we adopt the new incompatible version as the default revision.

Effects of Redeployment of a Composite When a composite application is changed and redeployed, all URLs—whether version specific or relying on the default revision—stay the same and continue to work. No consumer may even know that the redeployment has taken place, except for two important facts: During redeployment, there will be a period of unavailability that may result in timeout exceptions for service consumers. Even more dramatically, the status of running instances of the composite that is redeployed is changed to "stale." Stale instances have ceased running—they are effectively aborted. And, of course, it is obvious that when the WSDL changes during the redeployment, the consumer may no longer be compatible with the deployed composite and the consumer will very much become aware of the redeployment.

Before starting redeployment of a composite, you can first retire it. This will prevent new instances from being started. Running instances will continue normally. Short-running instances can be allowed to complete. Then redeployment is performed and the composite can be activated again. Note that the composite is unavailable to consumers as soon as it is retired.

Long-running instances of a composite application do not survive redeployment of that composite, and redeployment is probably not a useful strategy for composite applications that can be long running.

Versioning of Web Services

Versioning of services is a little more complex than versioning in a traditional architecture. The number of artifacts that each potentially have their own individual life cycle is much larger than in traditional monolithic applications. And even though through decoupling we try to minimize direct dependencies between these artifacts, they still rely on each other and on their interface definitions (WSDL and XSD). The impact of changing the interface of a single service artifact can be quite huge.

Another aspect of versioning in our service-oriented world is the fact that unlike with the monolithic applications, we can have multiple versions of the same artifacts active at the same time. Provided, of course, that we carefully manage the access of the consumers to the specific version they can work with.

Because a service consists of three parts, all three parts can change independently. Suppose we have a service that can be invoked to update the medical records for a patient. The interface definition for the operation addLabResult has two parameters: patient identifier and the laboratory test result. The implementation will return the result code and the current number of results. The contract of this service states that you need to authenticate with an X509 certificate and that HTTPS is used to encrypt the message during transport.

Now the business decides that the patient's medical information is confidential and that they want the message itself to be encrypted using WS-Security instead of just securing the transport layer. Do we consider this a new service, or a new version of the existing service?

What if we fix a bug in the (encapsulated) implementation of the service? Do we consider this a new version of the service, even if the contract and the interface are unchanged, or just a new version of the component that implements it? Or does this constitute a new service altogether? And what if the interface is changed, but the change is fully backward compatible, such as a new operation or support for a new optional input parameter? Should we then declare a new version of the service or an entirely new service?

Many books and blogs have been written about this topic. In our experience it is a best practice to keep it simple. In general, when the interface, the component, or the contract changes, it is a good idea to consider this to be a new service altogether. In our repository we can deprecate the old service and then retire it as soon as the new service is live, or as soon as all the consumers have switched to the new service. This is clear for the service consumers and keeps the complexity of backward compatibility to a minimum.

Redeploy, Revise, or Re-create?

For all intents and purposes, a new version of a composite application is not really any different from a new composite application. The only difference is in the default revision mechanism that allows administrators to automatically transfer consumers to a version without them realizing it. This automatic transfer can only be done for changes that fully respect the service contract and are fully backward compatible.

Changes to a composite application that change the contract and are not backward compatible should probably not be regarded as producing the next version of the application but rather as the birth of a new composite application—conceptually at least. Automatic rerouting using the default revision mechanism cannot be allowed for such drastic, incompatible changes.

One intermediate strategy to consider could be something like this:

- Backward-compatible changes are labeled with the second digit in the revision indication (1.2 leads to 1.3); the new version is immediately designated as the default revision; consumers relying on the automatic routing to the default revision always use the latest compatible revision. Running instances of previous revision can continue to run. Consumers with a specific preference can continue to use prior revisions.

- Substantial changes that are *not* backward compatible are labeled using the first digit in the revision label (1.2 leads to 2.0); this new revision is *not* immediately designated as the default revision. A grace period is defined during which consumers can choose to either adopt the new version or change their application to specifically consume the previous (1.2) revision of the service. The grace period is the phase during which the new situation is not yet forced upon everyone, even though from the provider's perspective that is what we probably would prefer to be doing. The grace period gives consumers a chance to make a decision about the new version and act on it. After the grace period, the latest version (2.0) is designated the default revision.

- Another procedure should be set up to determine when older revisions of services will be terminated; this is part of SOA governance that is further discussed in the next chapter.

The major new revision—the second step in the preceding strategy—will always require work to be done by the consumers of the service. The fact that it is a new revision of an existing composite instead of an entirely new service is perhaps somewhat useful in a semantic or symbolic way, but it does not really help our tools at all.

Note that changing a shared artifact like a publicly exposed service is a tricky business with a serious responsibility on the part of the party initiating and making the change. It requires a lot of communication, planning, coordination, (impact) analysis, and more. The next chapter, on SOA governance, will discuss this in somewhat more detail.

Summary

This has been a very hands-on chapter. The initial discussion was on how to package composite applications to prepare them for deployment and subsequently on how to deploy the application. Build and deployment can be done from JDeveloper or the command line using Ant or WLST. Deployment of a service archive can also be done from the FWM Console.

To cater to differences between environments into which composite applications are deployed, we can create configuration plans—one per target environment. A configuration plan contains the environment-specific values for properties and endpoint addresses. During deployment, a specific configuration plan can be selected to be applied.

The properties that can be set by the configuration plan during deployment can also be manipulated through the FWM Console. Note that through custom properties, such as BPEL preferences, business rules, and Domain Value Maps, we can integrate a form of customizability into the composite applications: the behavior of components can be implemented to depend on these elements. These elements can all be configured at run time through the FMW Console. The same applies to technology adapter bindings and the endpoints of external Web Services.

Between development and deployment (to a production environment at least), we should test applications. The SOA Suite comes with a built-in framework for unit testing. Unit tests are created in JDeveloper. Test suites contain test cases that consist of input messages or events, emulated (mock) response messages, and assertions about the expected results from the unit that is tested. Test suites are deployed along with the composite application and can be executed in the FMW Console—or from the command line using Ant or WLST.

Somewhat advancing on the discussion of governance in the next chapter, we concluded this chapter with a discussion on changing (the implementation of) composite applications and guidelines for versioning services. The SOA Suite supports the notion of versions of composite applications. Multiple versions can be active at the same time. One version can be designated the default version—that is the version that will handle all requests that do not target a specific service. When this default version mechanism is used, a policy could be adopted to only version a service when the changes are backward compatible and create an entirely new composite for substantial, incompatible changes.

CHAPTER
18

Tactical Management
and Governance

e discussed the overall objectives with SOA in the first part of this book. "Business Agility through Decoupling" was in the book's opening sentence (SOA is BAD!):

- Decoupling through encapsulated, reusable, stand-alone services and events with well-defined interfaces and contracts that are orchestrated together into processes

- Reuse of proven assets resulting in shorter time to market, lower development costs, higher quality, and the IT department's ability to eagerly follow business desires and even lead the way in spotting opportunities for improvement

After stating those objectives, we have spent many pages discussing the technical concepts of services, Service-Oriented Architecture, SOA composite applications, and the service components at our disposal in the Oracle SOA Suite for implementing these applications and fulfilling the service contracts. However, the tools and technology by themselves are not enough to deliver the goods required by an organization.

Reuse, for example, requires a paradigm shift—it requires developers to shake off their not-invented-here intuition and look for already existing functionality (services) outside their own scope and span of control.

And first of all, this requires very easy access to the reusable assets: They need to be easy to find, easy to understand and trust, and easy to adopt. Organizations that really want to achieve reuse need to work on a culture—and before that probably an obligatory but also stimulating process—that makes it hard and/or expensive not to reuse or to create nonreusable services if they could be reusable, and rewarding those who do reuse or develop reusable services. In order to build an inventory of reusable assets, the design and development of new artifacts need to be done in the spirit of reuse and flexibility—and not with only the immediate utilization of the artifact in mind. Developers are not only developing and delivering services for their project but possibly for all projects within their organization (or even outside the organization). This usually requires them to make a service more generic than would be the case if it concerns only a local project's artifact.

Additionally, when assets are being reused, new challenges stare us in the face, such as dependency management, ownership, versioning, and lifecycle management of the reused assets. Because of the reuse, the number of involved parties and dependent assets has increased. Evolving the reusables or discontinuing them is no longer a matter of a single owner or team—much more is at stake. One cannot just modify a service because one of its users asks for a change. What if other consumers will "break" due to a modification?

The process of *governance* (of software artifacts) deals with the challenges just described. This chapter will introduce governance and discuss some of the objectives, concepts, and high-level approaches.

The MDS (Metadata Services) repository offers a small, down-to-earth aspect of managing shared SOA artifacts that is used from JDeveloper (design time) and the run-time SOA Suite environment. Use of the MDS repository helps to prevent duplication of artifacts and the synchronization challenges that are the unavoidable result of such duplication. This chapter demonstrates the use of MDS for straightforward assets such as XSD, WSDL, and EDL (event) definitions.

MDS is a great facility for some operational governance aspects. However, as soon as organizations take a step back to take a more tactical look at things, they will quickly realize that some form of service inventory should be created, too, to record and share information about services and other SOA assets. Such inventories can be simple and straightforward, created using a wiki or just a spreadsheet, used for design-time activity. A more formal inventory can be implemented using service directories—such as those based on the UDDI standard, including Oracle Service Registry. These directories support both design-time gathering and communication of metadata, as well as run-time (automated) sharing of artifacts.

This chapter also very briefly discusses the Oracle Enterprise Repository, a tool that integrates with JDeveloper, Oracle Service Bus, Service Registry, and the SOA Suite to support the next (enterprise) level of governance in a largely automated fashion.

We can only briefly touch upon governance in this book—unfortunately it is by and large outside its scope. The field is too vast, the topics and discussions too specialized for us to be able to really do them justice and have a truly thorough discussion. This chapter has a modest ambition and is meant to provide a first introduction, high-level overview, and a down-to-earth small example using MDS.

Introducing Governance

Traditionally, stand-alone applications were developed by dedicated teams that remained attached to the application during subsequent stages in its lifecycle. The assets that formed the application were completely owned, controlled, and exclusively used and modified by this relatively small team.

Packaged applications have by now been introduced in most organizations. The evolution of those applications is largely out of the hands of an organization—it can only decided to upgrade to a next release or (temporarily) refrain from doing so. Yet many organizations will have custom extensions and integrations developed around these off-the-shelf applications that are managed in a similar way to the stand-alone custom applications. However, the manufacturer of the packaged application is in a somewhat different situation—one that is close to where, as a result of a service-oriented approach, most development teams will be.

Services are usually initially designed and built for one or more specific consumers at the time being, but they are created with additional future reuse in mind. Reuse and flexibility are things we want to achieve. However, reuse can also lead to new challenges. When a service is deployed, it might be—and hopefully will be—used by others than just the consumer it was originally built for. In a Service-Oriented Architecture, most assets therefore end up very much not (exclusively) owned by any team or even department: They are (in theory, at least) co-owned by the enterprise, targeted at widespread reuse, and not naturally controlled by an individual or group. Note, however, that every service needs to have a designated *owner* who is responsible for the services delivered. Because the service delivers business value, it is a business unit that owns it. And this unit needs to work together with other interested parties in the enterprise when it intends to evolve the service artifacts.

Management of the lifecycle of these assets is important, especially given the extent of reuse we are trying to achieve. To realize reuse, the availability of assets needs to be made public, and the assets need to be found, understood, and trusted. Once reuse has happened, the process of evolving those assets becomes more involved: Multiple parties have a stake in the assets and may have specific requirements with regard to their evolution. The designated owner of an asset—or the body governing the lifecycle of the asset—needs to be aware of all the usages of the asset. Other aspects of governance include: How do we ascertain that assets have the required quality and deliver on their (functional) promise? How do we define and record the required service and security levels and subsequently (at an operational level) monitor the actual performance of assets?

Implementing Governance

Before the management of the assets themselves is in full swing, governance is also required to enforce the architectural principles laid down for the organization. What processes must be implemented to ensure that all teams stick to the rules and are stimulated to do so (not only the service police!)? And how do we ensure that teams do not create the same or overlapping assets? How do we decide which reusable assets should be created? What should the interface be for a new reusable service, and how much functionality should it comprise? Or at a higher level, what should the process look like that determines which assets will be created and how they should look? How do we organize the process to create and control the canonical data model?

We also need strategic governance to link corporate goals to SOA and to have a process in place to check and possibly modify the governance processes for SOA. (And, of course, governance processes themselves are also subject to improvement and change. How do we govern this evolution?)

Governance must be implemented at every stage of the SOA lifecycle to track ongoing changes to the architecture, design, and implementation—and to define, implement, and execute the processes around the creation of new assets and changes to existing ones. An architecture board or (SOA) competence center can be considered with representatives from different departments to align SOA initiatives—and to help overcome each department's not-invented-here tendencies, which stand in the way of true reuse and flexibility. Governance should be aimed at stimulating and enforcing desired behavior. And the one most important behavior we try to achieve is collaboration—opening up applications can only be successful when we open up inward-looking departments and have them collaborate with other units in the organization.

Governance should be aimed at getting all involved parties to do the right things and to do these things right. Not only by laying down rules that are enforced, but mostly by inspiring the people involved, leading the way by setting the right example, and taking care of clear, timely, and open communication. Acting in a truly service-oriented, decoupled, reuse-focused way will take time. Knowledge and skills are required, as well as internalization of the objectives and approach. Ownership must be taken—like Frank did, back in Chapter 4—and cannot just be assigned. Coaching of teams that start out in the spirit of SOA by members of the architecture board or representatives from more experienced teams is valuable in order to inspire confidence, to help prevent making common mistakes and reinventing the wheel, and to guide the way through the acronym jungle, the technology challenges, and the adopted practices and mantras of the organization.

All of this requires organizational courage—and real leadership. Governance is not a problem you can simply throw money at, nor can you hire consultants to do it for you. It is organizational change. Therefore, an important aspect of SOA governance, especially in the early stages of adoption of SOA in an organization, is spreading the word (evangelizing), demonstrating the success, celebrating the measurable results, and thus building the case for SOA. Think big, act small, start successful.

Asset Registration and Publication

Reuse can only happen when assets are first of all identified as reusable and then created and subsequently made available to potential consumers. The latter requires assets to be discoverable, along with metadata that clearly states the status, QoS provided, and meaning of assets and also helps establish the credibility through insight in the current usage of assets, QoS, and the satisfaction of the current consumers. The exact location, security measures, conditions for reuse, and future plans for the asset should be clear as well.

Registration is essential as part of SOA governance—to record a description and status of a service and some of its assets (XSD, WSDL, and so on) as well as to gather and record metadata and metrics. Subsequently, the metadata about the assets must be made available throughout the enterprise. A central repository, here called the "asset manager," provides a single source of truth for what was intended—the to-be architecture design—and what has been and is being implemented (the as-is architecture).

Note that there is typically a grow path here: Start with a run-time registry, which can be very lightweight with only service descriptions and an indication of the status and owner of service. Later on the organization could move to a more elaborate registry. The next stage along the path could be the move to a thin repository (initially only XSD and WSDL artifacts) and finally to a complete repository. The registry is by far the most important when starting with SOA. A full-blown design-time repository loaded with metadata is quite possibly overkill in the early days of SOA adoption in an organization.

At the advanced stage, assets must be managed across every stage of the lifecycle, from conception to implementation, and from deployment to retirement. Ideally, an asset manager includes functionality for automated harvesting of assets and metadata on assets, as well as customizable asset-approval workflows, notifications, and event infrastructure.

The assets themselves as well as this metadata must be easily searchable. The asset manager or SOA artifact registry is the primary means for architects, designers, and developers to learn about the assets available for reuse.

The administration of assets and their metadata can be done in various ways with different levels of sophistication. Most organizations will start out with spreadsheets and text documents, based on predefined templates, collected in a central directory. As the number of assets and the volume of metadata increases, simple content management systems, custom-developed administration tools, or standard governance tools, such as the Oracle Enterprise Repository and Service Registry and BPA Suite, may be adopted.

Life Cycle Stages for SOA Assets

One of the concerns of SOA governance is the evolution of services and other SOA assets or artifacts (these terms are used interchangeably). An organization that starts with SOA must have clear rules about what happens when a service needs to be changed. This applies to change management, configuration management, release management, and for the planning of projects. It also needs to label each asset in such a way that everyone involved understands the status of an asset. At St. Matthews, Mary has defined the following states of a service (or other SOA artifact):

- **Identified**   The service is identified, either by a project as something they need or in the to-be architecture.

- **Development**   A service is being created but not yet in production.

- **Released**   The service is released and ready to be used or already used by service consumers.

- **Deprecated**   The service is still working, but (new) service consumers are not supposed to use it anymore because the organization plans to discontinue the service. Information that could be stored with this status is a pointer to the alternative and/or a planned retirement date for the service. Services should be deprecated before a replacement has been made available. Some organizations introduce an additional service state called "Sunset." This state is a specialization of Deprecated in that it not only declares the intent to discontinue the service, but also provides an official date for retirement.

- **Retired**   The service is not available anymore.

The states apply to the service as whole. It is not meaningful to have separate states for the service implementation, contract, and interface.

To use services, the organization needs to be aware of the state of the services. Knowing who owns a service and what interface and contract are associated with it is also very important in deciding whether the service can be reused in a certain situation. These and other governance issues can be addressed using tools. But more importantly, the organization has to define and communicate this information to stakeholders in order for services to be (re)used safely. Required information includes the state, owners, and terms and rules for reusing and changing the services (for example, payment, security, and so on). This information is typically published through the SOA Asset Manager.

Versioning

When we talk about the various states of a service through its lifecycle, a discussion on versioning cannot be far away. We briefly touched upon versioning in the last chapter, concluding that, in general, having multiple versions of the same service does not seem to be a good idea: As soon as the interface or the contract of service changes, it is best to create a new service altogether rather than try and establish a series of versions. However, with smaller changes that are backward compatible, for example, versioning may be useful. The SOA Suite has some support for the notion of versioning services—allowing the use of a revision ID in the identification of composite applications and in the URL used to access them. Clearly, when versioning is applied to specific artifacts, it should very much be part of the governance process.

MDS Repository for Managing and Reusing Shared Artifacts

Many development and deployment strategies that involve reuse sooner or later end up having to rely on copying artifacts. When an XSD definition or XSLT stylesheet is reused, it seems always necessary at some point to create physical duplicates of these artifacts. And in general, duplication of assets in the long run becomes a problem that frustrates the very reuse we try to achieve. Although some level of duplication is acceptable—between environments such as System Test, Acceptance Test, and Production, and across multisite production environments—in general it should be prevented. The effort required to keep duplicate artifacts synchronized is huge and typically will fail at some point. On the other hand, if we do not replicate the thing that stores all artifacts, it becomes a single point of failure, also during development.

SOA Suite provides a central store for shared artifacts that can be accessed at design time from JDeveloper and at run time from deployed SOA composite applications. This central store, the MDS repository, along with the Metadata Services on top of it, helps to organize reuse of cross-application artifacts such as canonical data model definitions and business event definitions. Note that the MDS repository is an intrinsic part of the SOA Suite run-time environment, not something that you need to install separately and additionally. However, also note that during development, the JDeveloper IDE can also make use of a local, file system–based MDS repository (see the section "JDeveloper and the Split-Brain MDS" for the background on this).

Using MDS with SOA Suite 11g

Resources in the MDS can be directly accessed at design time as well as at run time using a URL that starts with "oramds:". This URL is valid at design time as well as at run time, resolved against the local or the central MDS service. When a composite application is developed in JDeveloper, it can refer to artifacts in the MDS, and when that application is deployed, those same references into the central MDS are valid.

The MDS repository is organized in partitions, container structures similar to file system directories. Resource names must be unique within a partition. MDS contains three types of resources: (pre)seeded, application specific, and shared.

The pre-seeded resources are the run-time artifacts shipped with the SOA Suite and required out of the box. This includes RuntimeFault.wsdl, HumanTaskEvent.edl, and ws-addressing.xsd. These resources are stored in the partition path /soa/shared.

The second category contains SOA composite applications and their artifacts (business rules, DVMs, and so on) that end up in the MDS repository when they are deployed to the SOA Suite container. Each composite, and in fact each revision, has its own store (or MDS partition) for artifacts such as XSD, WSDL, XSLT, EDL, adapter configurations, and the composite.xml file. These application-specific artifacts are in a path that starts with /apps/.

The last category of shared resources is created by users and deployed in a special type of archive (MAR, or Metadata Archive). It consists of artifacts that are shared by multiple applications. Examples are XSD with common (canonical) definitions, Domain Value Map definitions, and EDL files with business event definitions.

Using MDS to store shared artifacts and references to MDS to reuse those artifacts is an important method for reducing duplication (such as local copies) of artifacts. We will next define a shared artifact—an EDL file with a business event definition. This artifact is deployed to MDS. Subsequently, this artifact is used in a composite application—first at design time and subsequently at run time. We will also briefly look at how the MDS and its resources can be managed.

JDeveloper and the Split-Brain MDS

Duplication is evil, and the MDS is here to coordinate and facilitate reuse of shared artifacts. That, in short, is the summary of the previous section. So it may come somewhat as a surprise that in fact the MDS itself is duplicated—for a very pragmatic reason.

The central MDS repository is available only when SOA Suite 11*g* is up and running. This repository is part of the WebLogic domain that runs the SOA Suite and is integrated inside the soa_server1 managed server and the MDS schema of the database. References to MDS resources can only meaningfully be used during development when the central MDS is available. However, it would be inconvenient if development on SOA composite applications can only be done when the server is up and running.

The team behind the SOA Suite came up with a solution where a local MDS repository is created in the JDeveloper directory during installation of the SOA Suite plug-in for JDeveloper. This local repository contains the pre-seeded artifacts such as RuntimeFault.wsdl and ws-addressing.xsd. You will find this repository at the following location: JDEVELOPER_HOME\jdeveloper\integration\seed.

JDeveloper knows how to find this local MDS store and uses it during development of the composite application to retrieve common definitions—for example, when a Notification activity or Human Task is added to a BPEL process.

The resources in the seed partition of this local MDS store are also available in the central MDS repository in the SOA Suite server. This repository is created during installation by the repository creation utility in the FMW database.

We can also use this local MDS repository to store our own shared artifacts. Although ideally these artifacts are always and only stored in the central MDS, it can be convenient to employ the local MDS to reduce the complexity and dependencies of the development environment—and allow development of shared artifacts in relative isolation. We can add resources to the local file-based MDS repository by copying them to (a child folder under) the directory JDEVELOPER_HOME\jdeveloper\integration\seed\apps.

Composite applications that refer to custom shared artifacts from the local MDS use the same type of references that are used for resources in the central MDS. This means that during deployment, nothing needs to be changed to those references. However, we do need to ensure that the shared artifacts in the local MDS are also available in the central MDS; otherwise, the deployment will not be successful. Deployment of shared artifacts to the central MDS is done using a MAR (Metadata Archive) deployment profile; this is discussed later in this chapter.

IDE Connection to MDS Repository

In order to be able to access MDS resources from applications developed in JDeveloper, we need to create a special type of connection on the Resource Palette: an SOA-MDS connection. This type of connection comes in two flavors: one to connect to the local file-based MDS repository, and one to connect to the central MDS repository stored in a database.

An SOA-MDS connection is created using the New Connection dialog on the Resource Palette. Select File Based MDS under Connection Type and specify the root folder **JDEVELOPER_HOME\ jdeveloper\integration\seed**. Test the connection and, when successful (which only means that the directory exists), close the dialog. We can now browse the contents of the local MDS repository on the Resource Palette. Then, whenever during development of composite applications we browse for a resource—such as an EDL file, a WSDL document, or an XSD definition—we can also select from the contents of the MDS repository.

The SOA-MDS connection to the central (shared) MDS repository is created in a similar fashion. However, this connection is of type DB Based MDS. We need to provide the connection details to the MDS database schema that was created by the repository creation utility during the installation process of SOA Suite 11g. For this connection we also need to select the appropriate MDS partition, which in our case is soa-infra. When we have verified the success of this connection, we can use it in the same way as the local SOA MDS connection: to browse (and search) the repository for resources and to create references from our composite applications to those resources (see Figure 18-1). Note that the MDS does not only contain resources designated to be shared: It contains and exposes all artifacts that have been deployed as part of composite applications as well.

Sharing the ContagiousDiseaseBusinessEvent Definition

It is good practice to identify shared artifacts and adopt governance procedures for their design, development, lifecycle management, and administration. Shared artifacts are reused, and this should be facilitated without the need for duplication through local copies. MDS is the appropriate way for exposing and accessing shared artifacts. Governance tools such as the Enterprise Repository will contain the metadata assets describing these shared artifacts, including details about their history, current usage, status, rating, and location.

Let's take a look at how some shared artifacts can be created, deployed, and exposed and can subsequently be reused. In order to be able to respond promptly to suspicions of contagious diseases, the analysts at St. Matthews have defined a new type of business event: the SuspectedContagiousDiseaseEvent. This event is a shared artifact, just like the XSD definition that specifies its payload. The underlying .xsd and .edl sources are to be deployed to the MDS repository and subsequently reused without local duplications.

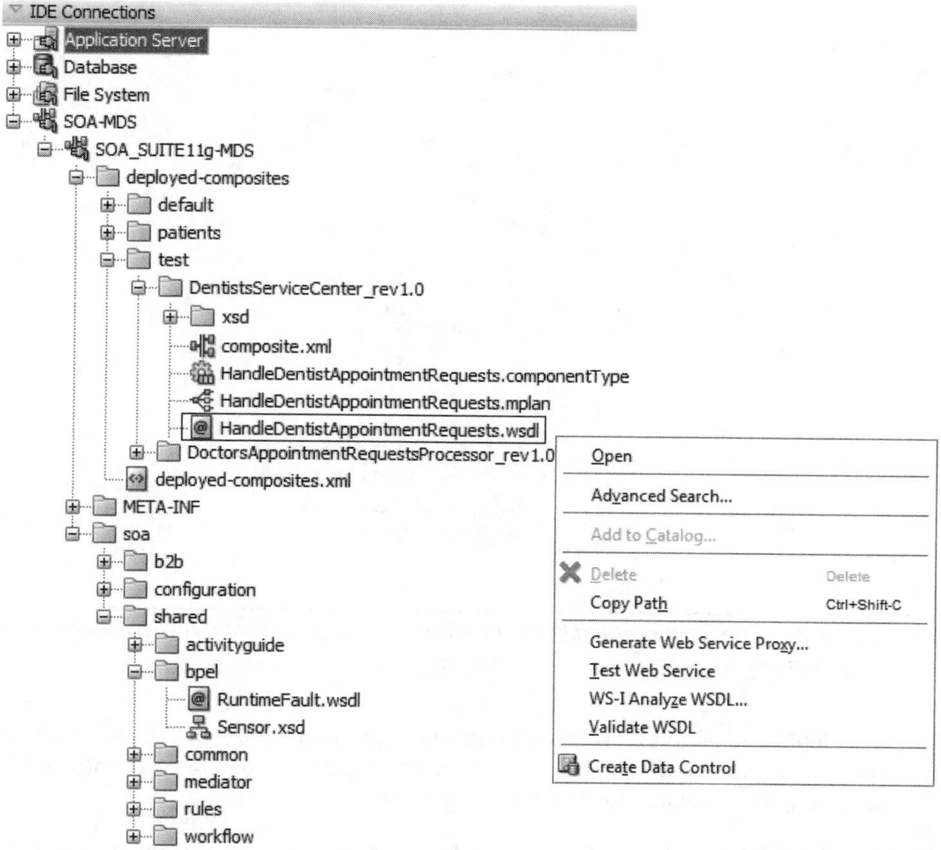

FIGURE 18-1.   *Browsing the central MDS repository through the SOA-MDS connection*

Note that the online chapter complement for this chapter contains detailed descriptions of the steps outlined next as well as source code and screenshots for each step.

Creating and Deploying Shared Artifacts   The SOA composite application SharedArtifacts is created to be the container for the artifacts we are about to create and deploy to the MDS. The PatientEvents.xsd schema definition is created with the definition of the element Suspected ContagiousDiseaseEvent that describes the payload of the SuspectedContagiousDiseaseEvent that is created next in the new PatientRelatedEvents.edl file.

In order to deploy these artifacts to an application-spanning section of the MDS repository, we will create a simple JAR deployment profile that contains the artifacts. Next, we have to create a deployment profile of the type SOA Bundle at the level of the composite application. Specify a dependency for this profile on the simple JAR deployment profile. We can then deploy the application according to this new SOA Bundle deployment profile.

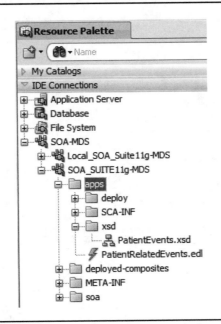

FIGURE 18-2. *The shared artifacts for the ContagiousDiseaseEvent are available from the MDS after deployment.*

After deployment, go to the Resource Palette, refresh the SOA-MDS connection, and expand the apps node. The shared .edl and .xsd artifacts that were just deployed are now visible under this node and thus available for reuse (see Figure 18-2).

Reusing Shared Artifacts in a Composite Application   The PatientAppointmentService should publish the ContagiousDisease event whenever it suspects—based on the requested appointment type and the diagnosis from the general practitioner—that the patient is carrying a transferable and potentially dangerous disease. For now we will not go into the logic of making that evaluation—we will just look at the publication of an event type defined by a shared MDS artifact.

Add an Invoke activity to the BPEL process PatientAppointmentService. Open the editor for this activity and select Event as the interaction type—instead of Partner Link.

Click the looking glass icon to browse for the Event Definition Language file, as illustrated in Figure 18-3. Select the Resource Palette in the top drop-down list. Open the IDE Connections node and expand the SOA-MDS node. Two connections are available: the local MDS store and the central MDS repository to which we have deployed the SharedArtifacts project with the .edl file we are now looking for. Open the SOA-MDS connection to the shared, central MDS repository. Under the apps node, we see the PatientRelatedEvents.edl. Select this file and click OK. Select the SuspectedContagiousDiseaseEvent and click OK. Have a local input variable created that will be populated to provide the payload for the event (based on the element definition in the PatientEvents.xsd document referenced from the EDL file and stored in the MDS repository). This completes the Invoke activity. Next, create an Assign activity to populate the local input variable auto-created for the Invoke activity.

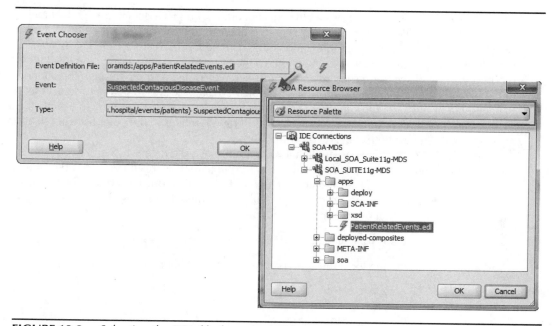

FIGURE 18-3. *Selecting the EDL file from the MDS repository for reuse in a composite application*

Here's the import element added to composite.xml file for the EDL file used from the MDS:

```
<import namespace="com.stmatthews.hospital/events/patients"
        location="oramds:/apps/PatientRelatedEvents.edl" importType="edl"/>
```

The PatientAppointmentService.wsdl document has a new schema import that references oramds:/apps/xsd/PatientEvents.xsd.

The prefix oramds is an indication for the MDS repository. At run time it is resolved using the registered MDS repositories for the soa-infra application. At design time—during the compilation and build from JDeveloper—the resolution depends on the adf-config.xml file. This file contains <metadata-store-usage> elements that specify connections to the central MDS repository and local file-based repositories.

Using the Local MDS Repository for Custom Shared Artifacts

We have discussed previously how the seeded reusable artifacts are available from not only the central MDS repository but from the local file-based MDS store as well—primarily for practical purposes and a less complex development environment. Custom shared artifacts such as the EDL and XSD files for the ContagiousDiseaseEvent can also be added to this local MDS repository. This allows reuse of these resources across composite applications without the need to have access to a full-blown running SOA Suite environment. The main drawback of using the local MDS store is, of course, the artifact duplication that may lead to inconsistencies between the various copies of the artifacts as well as among all local MDS repositories.

In the example of the PatientRelatedEvents.edl artifact and its associated XSD document, we can simply put the files representing the shared artifacts into the local file-based MDS repository: <JDeveloperHome>\jdeveloper\integration\seed. Create a subdirectory called **apps** and copy the two files to this directory. When we now refresh the SOA-MDS connection to the local file-based repository, we will see these shared artifacts just like we could see them through the connection to the central database–backed repository. The Browse dialog we used before to select the PatientRelatedEvents.edl file can select artifacts from the local MDS repository in exactly the same way as from the central MDS repository. The resulting references in the composite application are also exactly the same: Both start with oramds:/apps.

The only difference between applications that reference the local MDS and applications that reference the central MDS repository is in the adf-config.xml file; this difference is relevant at design time only, during editing and compilation of the application. The adf-config.xml has a namespace element that associates the /apps path with a metadata repository connection and a metadata-store-usage that defines that connection:

```
<namespace metadata-store-usage="mstore-usage_3" path="/apps"/>
```

When it references the local file-based repository, this element is defined like this:

```
<metadata-store-usage id="mstore-usage_3">
    <metadata-store
              class-name="oracle.mds.persistence.stores.file.FileMetadataStore">
      <property
        value="C:\Oracle\JDeveloper11gR1PS2Beta\Middleware\jdeveloper\integration"
              name="metadata-path"/>
      <property value="seed" name="partition-name"/>
    </metadata-store>
  </metadata-store-usage>
```

Then, when /apps is associated with the central, database-backed repository, the element is configured like this:

```
<metadata-store-usage id="mstore-usage_3">
    <metadata-store class-name="oracle.mds.persistence.stores.db.DBMetadataStore">
      <property value="FMW_MDS" name="jdbc-userid"/>
      <property value="fmw" name="jdbc-password"/>
      <property value="jdbc:oracle:thin:@xp-vm:1521:orcl"
              name="jdbc-url"/>
      <property value="soa-infra" name="partition-name"/>
    </metadata-store>
  </metadata-store-usage>
```

Note that these configurations are maintained by JDeveloper—you do not have to create them manually. Also note that you cannot reference resources in both the local and central MDS repository at the same time: The /apps path is resolved to either one.

Administration of MDS Repositories

MDS repositories are a special component in the run-time infrastructure that require appropriate administrative attention. This attention from the administrator includes well-known aspects such as backup and recovery. More specific are tasks associated with the versioning capabilities of the

MDS repository: Every import or deployment of an artifact to the MDS repository (when it is backed by a database) produces a new version of the artifact. An impressive version history with a substantial number of documents can be created over time. The purge operation allows the administrator to remove redundant revisions of the artifacts in the MDS repository.

The administrator can create a version label in the MDS repository, a named collection that consists of the latest version of each document in the partition at the time the label is created. When new revisions of the composite applications are deployed and new versions are added for the document in the repository, the label is still available as a logically coherent collection of document versions that can be manipulated as a group.

Administration of the MDS repository is partly done through the FMW Control Console, via the command line with Ant and WLST, and possibly directly against the underlying database schema.

Migrating Artifacts in the MDS Across Environments

The contents of an MDS partition can be exported from the FMW Enterprise Manager console and by using the WebLogic Scripting Tool (WLST). An import can be done from Ant, the WLST command-line interface, and the FMW Control Console. The export and import operations can be performed for backup and recovery reasons and to migrate between environments, such as from development to testing and onward, all the way to production.

Note that the current export and import functions are not at all very refined or fine grained; you may be better off hanging on to the JAR file that was originally used to load shared artifacts to MDS and use that when these artifacts are required in another MDS or MDS partition. Perhaps—though probably quite unsupported—it may be useful to do management, export, and import at the level of the database tables that contain the MDS resources. The wiki has an article that goes into this particular option.

Exporting MDS Resources from the Console   The export and import operations in the console are accessed as follows: Select the soa-infra node in the FMW Control Console. Open the context menu and select the option MDS Configurations from under Administration. The MDS Configuration page is displayed with support for three operations—export, import, and purge partition—and two links that provide access to MBeans for more fine-grained operations.

The export operation (a very indiscriminate procedure that will export the entire MDS partition, which adds up to more than 9MB's worth of pre-seeded artifacts) has us specify the target directory (on the server) for the export and subsequently exports all documents in the MDS partition soa-infra.

Alternatively, we can go to the Runtime MBean Browser and click the Operations tab, select the operation exportMetaData, and export selected documents to a location on the server. This operation allows us to specify a particular label to process, to export a specifically labeled version of artifacts in the repository.

Exporting Through WLST and Ant   The export of artifacts in the MDS repository is supported on the command line through Ant scripts as well as WLST commands. The file ant-sca-deploy. xml is the Ant script that contains the task that exports MDS data. Here's the basic statement to run this Ant-based export:

```
ant -f ant-sca-deploy.xml exportSharedData
```

The script takes additional parameters to connect to the SOA Suite instance, select the artifacts to export, and specify the name and location of the JAR file created by the export task.

The WebLogic Script Tool supports a command called exportMetadata. It takes parameters to specify the application (always soa-infra), the managed server running the SOA Suite, the target location for the export, and a document selector. Other parameters can specify a version label to filter documents by. Here's an example:

```
exportMetadata
( application='soa-infra'
, server='soa_server1'
, toLocation='c:\temp\MDS_XSD_export'
, docs='/**'
)
```

Importing Metadata from an Export   Importing resources into the MDS repository can be done in the console, on the MDS Configuration page. Click the Import button, specify the location on the server (either a directory or an archive file) that contains the resources to import, and click OK.

On the command line, we can use the importMetadata command through WLST to perform an import. This command takes the name of the application (which is soa-infra for SOA composite applications), the name of the managed server, the source location, and the docs (a list of comma-separated, fully qualified document names or document name patterns, or both).

Service Inventory for Gathering and Publishing

As stated previously, governance is a collection of processes and agreements that have to live in the minds, and preferably the hearts, of many different stakeholders involved in the architecture, planning, design, implementation, testing, and administration of service-oriented artifacts such as Web Services, canonical data models, and events. These processes together have to enable the organization to achieve the objectives with SOA, such as agility through decoupling and reuse.

Implementing governance is, to a large extent, a matter of communication, building awareness and involvement, making information available about procedures and reusable artifacts, collaborating on the creation of services and the design of the canonical model, and so on. Many of these governance processes require registration and publication of metadata about these processes themselves as well as about artifacts and dependencies between the assets. Various approaches and tools can be adopted for the management of this metadata—some simple DIY tools, others more formal, such as UDDI directories (for example, the Service Registry), or even a full-blown enterprise-level system like the Oracle Enterprise Repository (OER).

DIY Service Registry

Especially in the early stages of SOA adoption, organizations do not need complex, advanced, enterprise-level artifact registration infrastructures. They need simple, accessible, lightweight mechanisms for recording the key data about services and other SOA assets—and for making these details readily available to any interested party. Core aspects to be recorded about services include their name, a description, the status and owner, and the dependencies. And in the beginning, when the number of services is still relatively small, this can be just unstructured text that is maintained in a corporate wiki or even a spreadsheet on a central file share.

Teams that create new assets should describe them in the service registry—in the format and with the details that the organization has agreed on. And before they do so, they should browse through the registry to see whether perhaps what they want to create has been created already—or at least something that is similar to it. Note that services that have been identified should be recorded in the registry, even if they have not yet been implemented.

A common experience is that organizations that may have had a lukewarm start with some of the abstract concepts and intangible objectives of SOA quickly start to pick up some enthusiasm when a tangible, commonly owned service inventory is introduced and the first real assets have been recorded. An important aspect of the inventory is to provide recognition, celebrate successes, and foster a sense of achievement.

Oracle Service Registry

As the SOA matures, and the size and complexity of the collection of SOA assets increases, an organization may outgrow the informal inventory and move to a more formal and structured service inventory. Various vendors, including Oracle, have products on offer, many of which implement a UDDI-based registry.

Oracle Service Registry is a fully V3-compliant implementation of the UDDI (Universal Description, Discovery, and Integration) specification. A UDDI registry in general provides a base foundation for locating services, invoking services, and managing metadata about services (security, transport, or quality of service). A UDDI registry can store and provide these metadata using arbitrary categorizations—called "taxonomies"—that are used to describe the assets and to support richer search facilities.

Services and their artifacts are recorded in the Oracle Service Registry (OSR) through the Registry Managed console. Here are the essential asset types in OSR:

- **Business entity**   Organizational units such as groups, roles, projects, departments, or individuals who are responsible for other assets.

- **Business service**   Functionality or resource provided by the business entity; a business service can be a (SOAP/HTTP) Web Service, but just as well a service available through different transports and protocols (for example, EJB, CORBA, or REST style).

- **Binding template**   Represents the technical details of how to invoke the service, including the endpoint URI and a specification of the protocol.

- **tModel**   Referenced from binding templates to describe the interface (often a WSDL) of the business service; also used to link additional categorization information to the business service.

The OSR publishes the information recorded about these four core asset types. Using the Business Service Control, developers, architects, and business users can browse the various perspectives of the registry, including business-relevant classifications such as service and interface lifecycle, compliance, and operational/readiness status. They can browse information through business-relevant abstractions of SOA information such as schemas, interface local names, and namespaces. Just as in the basic inventory discussed in the previous section, the core attribute of the assets include their name, status, description, keywords, release date, version, and availability, as well as an indication of their dependencies and current usages. OSR allows subscriptions on assets that result in notifications sent to interested parties for meaningful changes to these assets.

Note that the OSR can be for design-time use by developers and architects as well as for run-time dynamic discovery by consumers of services. In the latter case, the consumer does not refer directly to the endpoint of the service itself, but uses the registry like the telephone operator of old to connect through to wherever the service currently may be hiding out.

NOTE
The OSR does not contain the artifacts themselves. It only has references to them and metadata about them. The OSR helps you to learn about the existence and characteristics of assets and shows you the way to them.

Integration with the SOA Suite

The Oracle Service Registry is a reference point for services that have been deployed into the run-time environment. It is primarily used for programmatic, dynamic discovery, and binding by elements of the SOA infrastructure. The Oracle Service Registry typically contains a subset of the metadata from the Oracle Enterprise Repository for runtime discovery. A major use case for Oracle Service Registry is to provide a UDDI interface by which selected OER content may be accessed or published. More on OER in the next section.

The Service Registry integrates with various components of SOA Suite, both design time and run time. For example, connections can be created in JDeveloper to OSR servers, to look up business services that are to be invoked from, for example, SOA Composite applications.

References to services exposed by the OSR can be set to "dynamically resolved [endpoint]." This means that the actual endpoint of the service is looked up at run time in the Service Registry. For this to work, you need to configure the UDDI Inquiry URL in the FMW Enterprise Manager Console. The SOA Suite run-time engine will consult the OSR to get hold of the real endpoint of the service that needs to be invoked. This means, for example, that if you move the business service WSDL from one host to another, you only need ensure that you change the location in the Registry Control, and no change is required in the WSDL location in Oracle JDeveloper or in the configuration of the WebService binding in the Oracle Enterprise Manager Fusion Middleware Control Console.

The services exposed by SOA Composite applications can be registered with and subsequently published by the OSR. This applies to SOAP/HTTP service bindings but other transports as well.

You can use Oracle Service Bus to import services from Oracle Service Registry and then publish Oracle Service Bus proxy services back to Oracle Service Registry. Oracle Service Bus imports business services from Oracle Service Registry. Proxy services are configured to communicate with the business services in the proxy service message flow. The proxy services can then be published back to Oracle Service Registry and made available for use by other domains.

Oracle Enterprise Repository

The OER provides organizations with a central repository of metadata about software assets, facilities for importing and harvesting such metadata from design-time and run-time SOA environments, functionality for providing access to the metadata, and BPM processes for coordinating the lifecycle of the metadata (and the underlying assets). The OER has a number of special integration points with the SOA Suite and JDeveloper that make it an attractive option for supporting SOA governance in organizations that primarily use Oracle's SOA technology.

Note that OER is an enterprise-level infrastructure for governance. It is relevant only in larger organizations with fairly mature SOA environments where processes have evolved sufficiently and departments have embraced service orientation. Implementing OER is not the first step organizations should take when starting to adopt SOA.

You will find more details on the OER and some of its features and functions in the online chapter complement.

It's about Assets

Fundamentally the Enterprise Repository (OER) is a very generic data store that contains things that have relations to other things. They don't come more universally applicable than this. The things stored in the OER are assets—such as WSDL, XSD, and XSLT artifacts—but also noncode elements such as design documents, test scenarios, payment/cost models, and application screen designs. The OER ships with a number of predefined assets and asset types, as well as definitions of meaningful relationship types between these asset types.

Assets are registered in the OER by their creators, owners, architects, or sponsors. Upon registration and throughout their lifecycle, metadata providing additional information about the assets is recorded. Users may browse the repository in order to learn more about the assets they intend to use in some way, or to first discover assets that they might want to reuse. Browsing can be done through the OER web console and also directly from JDeveloper via a connection on the Resource Palette.

Ideally, users also record feedback—reviews, cost-saving information—about the assets they reuse, so as to inform other potential users about the value and trustworthiness of the assets.

The OER can be configured in such a way that new assets or changes to assets are not simply recorded, but have to go through an evaluation and approval workflow. In such a workflow, subsequent roles have to evaluate the asset or the proposed changes, leading to acceptance or rejection.

Each asset has indicators that mark its status along various dimensions: unregistered or registered; under review, approved, rejected; active, inactive, retired, deleted, and more. Both the workflow steps and associated roles, as well the status values that can be assigned, are fully configurable.

The Enterprise Repository can also be set up to perform automated quality reviews on the assets that are submitted to it. These reviews can verify, for example, whether all required (metadata) details have been provided for an asset and whether all dependent assets have been submitted as well.

Search and Publish   An important function of the OER is to facilitate the discoverability of the assets it contains. To that end, it has extensive search capabilities that allow users to search for assets based on many asset properties, including custom properties. Search forms are available with fields per property as well as advanced search filters on extended metadata fields using XPath expressions.

Workflow (BPM)   Not just any asset submitted to the OER should be accepted and published just like that. There may be rules and procedures to apply in order to establish the status of new or even changed assets. Some form of workflow can be designed to implement these parts of governance processes, specifying which roles need to act in order to get a new asset or changes to an existing asset approved for an asset of a specific type and submitted by a user with a certain role from a certain part of the organization.

Events and Notification   Ideally you quickly learn about changes to assets that you have an interest in—such as the approval of a new version or the deprecation of another version. The OER fires events when assets reach the lifecycle stage. Users subscribed to an asset are automatically notified by e-mail if a new version has been created or registered. Manual notification can also be used to communicate any metadata changes to the asset.

Reporting and Quality Assurance   Various reports on the assets and their usage can be generated from the Oracle Enterprise Repository. Oracle Enterprise Repository offers more than 20 preconfigured reports—on projects and on assets—that provide insight into asset status and usages, reported value and cost savings, project compliance, (quality) policy status, and asset ratings and rejections.

Dependencies and Impact Analysis   The visual navigator tool in the OER web console provides very good insight into how assets hang together. It visualizes which assets have dependencies on one another and what the nature of those dependencies is. The tool supports traversal of dependency chains, in both directions, to do impact analysis (what may be impacted upon a change in some asset) and lineage analysis (what an asset depends on, and what it derives its meaning from).

How to Use the Enterprise Repository in Combination with SOA Suite

As stated before, the Oracle Enterprise Repository has a special, tight relationship with WebLogic Server, the Oracle Service Bus, and the SOA Suite when it comes to harvesting assets. Furthermore, the OER integrates with JDeveloper—bidirectionally, in fact, both for harvesting artifacts from SOA projects in JDeveloper to the Enterprise Repository, and vice versa, by searching, browsing, reusing, and inspecting assets in the repository from within JDeveloper.

   The online chapter complement describes and shows the detailed steps for harvesting assets from SOA composite applications into the OER as well as for browsing the repository from the context of JDeveloper. Harvesting can be done—as shown in this complement—from JDeveloper, directly against the file system and against managed WLS servers running SOA Suite and Oracle Service Bus.

Integration Between the Enterprise Repository and JDeveloper

The Oracle Enterprise Repository is one of the servers that can be exposed in JDeveloper on the Resource Palette. Just like with connections to databases, application servers, and UDDI directories, we can also create a connection to the Enterprise Repository by providing the URL (such as http://localhost:7111/oer) and the username and password (such as admin/admin). When this connection is created, the contents of the repository can be browsed through and assets can be inspected in JDeveloper, as shown in Figure 18-4. Note that assets cannot be edited, copied to the project, or directly referenced.

   An SOA composite application can be associated with a project in an Oracle Enterprise Repository instance, from the Repository tab in the Application Properties editor in JDeveloper. Projects in the application can be harvested (or published) to the repository. The artifacts in the project are registered in the OER as assets with mutual relationships.

Harvesting from Run-time SOA Suite and Oracle Service Bus

As discussed previously, the Oracle Enterprise Repository ships with a tool called the Harvester. The Harvester can read artifacts from various sources, including the file system, a running

FIGURE 18-4. *Browsing the Enterprise Repository in JDeveloper through the connection on the Resource Palette*

WebLogic Server, a running SOA Suite, and an Oracle Service Bus environment. The Harvester connects to the indicated environment, retrieves the artifacts, and offers these artifacts as assets to the configured OER instance (see Figure 18-5).

Feeding Run-time Metrics to the OER

Part of the metadata gathered in the Enterprise Repository consists of run-time metrics about performance (load and response times) and availability. Such metrics are collected by Oracle's Enterprise Manager Management Pack Plus for SOA, part of the Enterprise Manager Grid Control, which also provides dynamic discovery and service-level monitoring of all artifacts deployed within a Java application server.

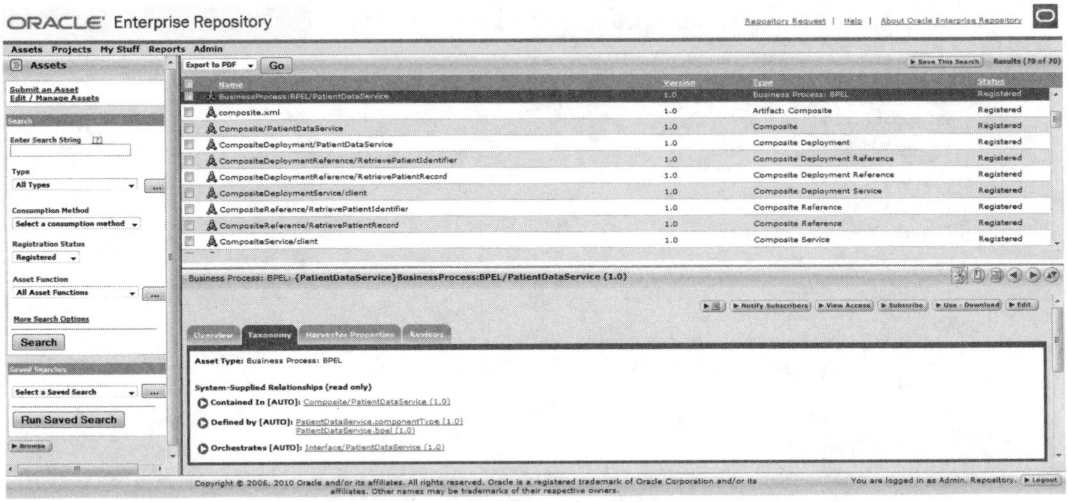

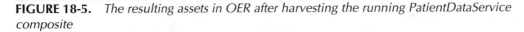

FIGURE 18-5. *The resulting assets in OER after harvesting the running PatientDataService composite*

The Enterprise Manager Grid Control and several (until recently) third-party tools, such as AmberPoint, collect statistics that include latency, invocation counts, and exceptions for each of the service components. These are aggregated and stored over various aggregation periods to provide a rich dashboard of metrics presented across a user-selected set of time periods. The EM Integration utility closes the loop between EM and Oracle Enterprise Repository by migrating metrics from EM into Oracle Enterprise Repository. The EM Integration utility pulls the statistics into the Oracle Enterprise Repository from EM feeds, in some cases via the Service Registry. They help complete the picture about the service assets exposed in the repository.

Note that the OER can publish Web Service assets directly to the Oracle Service Registry or other UDDI directories through the Exchange Utility.

Summary

SOA governance is a term that covers a wide range of activities, agreements, and processes aimed at making SOA a success in an organization by ensuring that the key SOA objectives are realized: agility through decoupling and reuse. At a higher level of abstraction and detachment than design and implementation of concrete SOA components, SOA governance tries to instill a fairly new way of thinking among the many stakeholders involved with the SOA initiatives. It also puts supporting procedures in place, identifies proven best practices, and possibly provides tools to support communication, coordinated execution of agreed-upon workflows, and automated quality assurance. SOA governance first and foremost strives to provide everyone involved with inspiration, timely information, and required facilities to think and act "service oriented." SOA governance is part of and/or related to other types of governance such as corporate governance, Enterprise Architecture governance, and general IT governance.

One of the very tangible aspects of SOA governance is the publication of metadata about potentially reusable SOA assets—such as services, schema definitions, and business events. This metadata should make it possible to discover assets; understand their meaning, history, and planned future; assess their applicability and trustworthiness; and get hold of the physical location or the contents of the assets themselves. From the perspective of the owners of assets, the governance infrastructure supports the asset lifecycle management and provides insight in the dependencies and extent of reuse of the assets. As such, it should enable the organization to measure and demonstrate the results and the success of the implementation of SOA concepts.

Metadata Services (or MDS) are a built-in facility in the SOA Suite that offers capabilities to share artifacts across composite applications and across design-time and run-time environments. MDS is an important weapon against unwanted duplication of documents such as XSD, WSDL, EDL, and XSLT. This chapter demonstrated how artifacts can be deployed to the MDS repository and reused from it.

Early on in their adoption of SOA, organizations should implement a service inventory. Its purpose is to record and communicate information about all services and other relevant SOA-related artifacts (including canonical data models and policies) that are available to all stakeholders. This SOA governance infrastructure can be as simple and informal as a wiki or a bunch of spreadsheets to communicate the services and other reusable artifacts, or as advanced as tools such as the Oracle Service Registry or even the Oracle Enterprise Repository.

Both OSR and OER provide a number of integration points with SOA Suite, JDeveloper, and each other, and have enterprise-level support for a wide range of governance procedures. The OER can also be customized in many aspects, including the definition of custom asset types and their attributes as well as tailor-made governance workflows.

PART
IV

Beyond the Basics

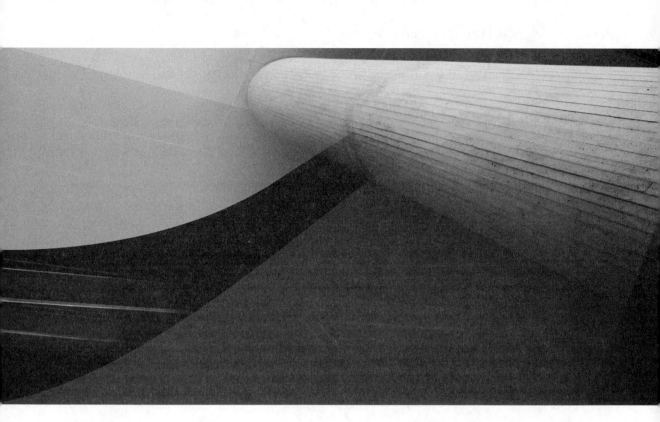

CHAPTER
19

From Live Data to Real-time Insight and Action Using Complex Event Processing and Business Activity Monitoring

hat good is data if you cannot extract information from it? And only when you can turn the information into meaningful conclusions and relevant actions will it be truly useful and understood. Our objective with IT in general is to better run our business—more cost effective, with higher quality, and faster throughput. SOA aims to help with that and explicitly add the ability to quickly adapt to changing requirements, which we have dubbed business agility. Data about the business processes and the components that constitute and execute these processes is needed, not only to measure whether we meet our objectives, but also to improve, adjust, and even intervene.

This chapter is about understanding the ongoing events in our organizations in general, and more specifically our IT systems and the SOA applications in particular. And doing something with that understanding—be it redesigning a process at a tactical level, changing systems parameters or business logic on a more day-to-day pace, making snap decisions, or taking immediate action under exceptional circumstances.

We will be using two very specific components in the SOA Suite that help us to deal with events. One is the Complex Event Processor (CEP), which can sift through large volumes of continuously streaming data, producing aggregates, trends, exceptions, and patterns. The other is the Business Activity Monitoring (BAM), a component for creating real-time dashboards. BAM can turn information received from CEP, SOA composite applications, or external sources into meaningful visual displays that human operators can base operational decisions and actions on.

As with most chapters in this book, you will find detailed hands-on instructions and many dozens of screenshots in the online chapter complement.

Sorting Out the Real-time Data Avalanche

The term *ongoing events* can refer to many different things—from fairly high-level business events such as signing a long-term agreement with some vendor or the arrival of a large order from a wholesaler, to tiny crumbs of information such as the current temperature in a fridge, a click on a navigation link in the patient self-service web application, the heartbeat of some device, or the fact that some security badge was scanned to gain entry into a storage room. The higher-level events typically have a much lower frequency—counted in occurrences per hour or day—than the lowest-level data grains, arriving in up to thousands per second. The information contents of these two ends of the events spectrum tend to range from rich for the high-level, low-frequency events, to quite sparse for highly frequent packets.

An important aspect of the processing of these events is that much of it must be done in real time. Ongoing business leads to continuous streams of events that may require instantaneous actions. We cannot afford to just dump all the data into data warehouses that we will analyze later on, even though for some of the data that is, of course, exactly what we will do. The urgency of some of the reactions the events may prompt us to come up with is one reason. The sheer volume of the data is another: Thousands of low-level events occurring every second represent tons of data that a data warehouse cannot comfortably handle—and should not handle, as the vast majority of those events represent entirely useless information, especially when considered by themselves.

Therefore, we need a way to process the zillions of events that the business operation keeps on producing. A processor that turns these events into information—usually by producing a higher-level type of event that has some special business meaning, carries a larger information payload and is produced at much lower frequencies. This is illustrated in Figure 19-1.

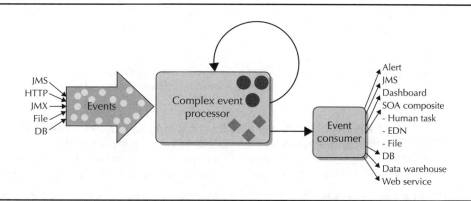

FIGURE 19-1.   *Event processing—increasing information content and decreasing frequency*

Typically the events produced by the processor are propagated in a more generic, canonical way, both in terms of protocol and channel as well as information structure.

After the first stage of event processing, downstream consumers absorb the higher-level events. These consumers can do several things, including sending out alerts or notifications, updating a real-time report or dashboard, taking actions such as invoking a Web Service or starting a human task, or loading data into a data warehouse. These downstream consumers can also further process the events—into even higher-level, more meaningful events. These events are then propagated through a next iteration of event processing.

Complex Event Processing

Finding the needles in the haystacks of large volumes of continuously arriving, largely individually meaningless events is the purpose of Complex Event Processing (CEP), also known as Intelligent Event Processing (IEP). CEP is a field that came to existence in the early 1990s, first in academic circles, such as Stanford University and the California Institute of Technology, and later in the IT industry. Over a dozen vendors are active in this space, including Progress Software, Aleri, IBM, Tibco, Oracle (also through BEA and Sun), JBoss, and EsperTech. These vendors offer various software products that provide "operational intelligence" through real-time computing that involves pattern matching with their respective intelligent or complex processors of event streams.

Event processors consume events from heterogeneous sources—such as JMS queues, JMX MBeans, incoming HTTP requests and native API calls, Message Driven Beans, and databases. The outcome of processing consists primarily of another generation of events that are sent through usually more homogenous channels in canonical data formats. Note that the event processors are decoupled from both the producers of the events they process and the consumers of the events they produce.

The processors perform the following operations on incoming events resulting in the events they publish:

- ■ **Filter**   Finding the needles in the haystack, those rare events that indicate exceptions
- ■ **Enrich**   Adding context and thereby (business) meaning to events

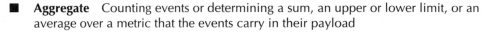

■ **Aggregate**   Counting events or determining a sum, an upper or lower limit, or an average over a metric that the events carry in their payload

NOTE
An aggregate is frequently calculated over a window that consists of all events in the specific timeframe or a specified number of the latest events.

■ **Pattern detection**   Spotting a trend by comparing correlated events over a period of time, finding a special sequence of values or value changes that is known to herald a certain incident, and discovering the absence of an event that should have occurred are all examples of the detection of meaningful patterns among a string of correlated events.

■ **Promote or propagate**   The result of the preceding operations can be to propagate the event, either as is or in an enriched or promoted state, or to publish entirely new events that carry an aggregated value, some indicator, or an alert.

To be clear: The word *complex* in Complex Event Processing does not refer to the events—they are usually extremely simple—but rather to the processing that takes place. Especially the detection of patterns can be very advanced, considering the complexity of the patterns and the addition of the challenges of continuously processing very large volumes of events in real time.

The Event Processing Language
Complex event processors need to be programmed. They are like query engines that need to query events—not static sets of records, but incessantly changing collections of data granules. Event queries are not executed just once. They are instead attached to an event stream and continuously executed. Every new arriving event may cause the event query to produce a new result. Results are constantly being published in the form of events.

Over time, special languages have evolved for programming the event processors, under the generic label of Event Processing Language (EPL). However, no single standard unified EPL has emerged in the industry. Several quite dissimilar EPLs are used for various CEP products. Some EPLs are derived from or inspired by Business Rule Languages—such as Tibco BEPL and JBoss DRL. Other EPLs are inspired by, derived from, or even integrated with SQL—such as CCL, StreamSQL, EQL, and CQL. It turns out to be quite handy to be able to combine event streams and relational data sources in a single query (for example, to join historical and reference data with the live event feed). The SQL-based EPLs typically facilitate this union to some extent.

As of late, it seems like out of this union of SQL and EPL, a standard EPL is evolving: CQL, the Continuous Query Language, which has its root at Stanford University. At least Oracle is putting its weight behind this event query language, using it for its CEP product. As it happens, the Intelligent Event Processor that Sun provided in Glassfish OpenESB also makes use of CQL. It seems likely that Oracle will also implement (parts of) CQL in the query engine in its RDBMS at some point in the not-too-distant future.

CQL queries select from an event channel, often with some range or time window applied, using a where clause to filter on the events that are returned by the query. The select clause refers to event properties and uses functions and operators to derive results.

Here is a simple example of a CQL query that produces an output event whenever the number of input events with a payload value larger than 15 changes, looking at a five-second window:

```
select count(payloadValue) as countEvents
from    someEventStream [range 5]
where   payloadValue > 15
```

We will be using CQL later on in this chapter when we use the Oracle Complex Event Processor to monitor the temperature sensors around St. Matthews.

Downstream Event Consumers

The Complex Event Processor brings us only part of the way from data to insight and action. It only speaks in events on channels such as JMS—not directly with people or even Web Services—and it has no user interface of its own. The events published by the CEP—no matter how advanced and enriched they may have become—need to be consumed and turned into something else: a report or dashboard, an alert or an action.

Complex Event Processors typically publish their findings in the form of fairly generic messages on a JMS queue or HTTP channel, or requests to a Web Service interface or to some other standard facility. Many different products can therefore be used downstream of the CEP to absorb the events and do something with them: load in a data warehouse, use to refresh a real-time dashboard, update a database record, notify a Web Service, send an e-mail or text message, create a human task, or publish on a website or RSS feed.

Business Activity Monitoring

A special category of event consumer is the Business Activity Monitoring (BAM). Wikipedia gives the following definition for BAM:

> "The goals of business activity monitoring are to provide real time information about the status and results of various operations, processes, and transactions. The main benefits of BAM are to enable an enterprise to make better informed business decisions, quickly address problem areas, and re-position organizations to take full advantage of emerging opportunities."

Note the use of *real time* in this definition—which is a key reason for the link between BAM and CEP.

BAM products usually publish a real-time dashboard that provides visual (graphical) insight into the key performance indicators of a business and its processes. This dashboard is continually refreshed as new data arrives and gets pushed to the dashboard. Besides looking pretty, the Business Activity Monitoring also applies rules to detect (pending) exceptions, threshold surpassing, deviations, trends, and other situations that require attention. Attention can be drawn through visual means on the dashboard and by sending alerts to human operators and/or automatic agents.

BAM may seem very similar to Business Intelligence (BI) as you know it, and of course there is a lot of similarity if not overlap. The key differentiator is the real-time aspect of BAM, along with the active alerting responsibility it has. The scope in time of BAM dashboards is usually fairly short—up to hours or days—and would hardly ever cross the quarter or year boundary, whereas traditional BI tends to take a look at data from a more historic, longer-term perspective in a more passive way.

Event Processing and Monitoring in the SOA Suite

Processing event streams is handled in the SOA Suite through the CEP 11*g* product—the successor to BEA's WebLogic Event Server. CEP runs CQL and still supports its own EPL (primarily for reasons of backward compatibility).

Note that the Complex Event Processor is not directly integrated into the SCA container—it is not a service engine like BPEL and Mediator. It even runs outside the WebLogic Server—it has its own stand-alone lightweight Java Application Server. See Figure 19-2 for an overview of the architecture of CEP and its relation with SOA Suite and other components. CEP consumes events from sources such as JMS, incoming HTTP requests, and other sources, including files, MBeans (JMX), and sockets through custom adapters. These events are then transported through channels to processors that execute CQL and/or custom Java. The results from the processors are carried across outgoing channels to destinations such as other processors, JMS queues, and registered HTTP consumers.

The higher-level events produced by CEP are typically published on JMS queues or topics. Selected events can be consumed into the SOA Suite via JMS Adapter Services, which could create business events on Event Delivery Network (as discussed in Chapter 9) or directly forward the events via a Mediator to other service components. Either directly or via the EDN, these

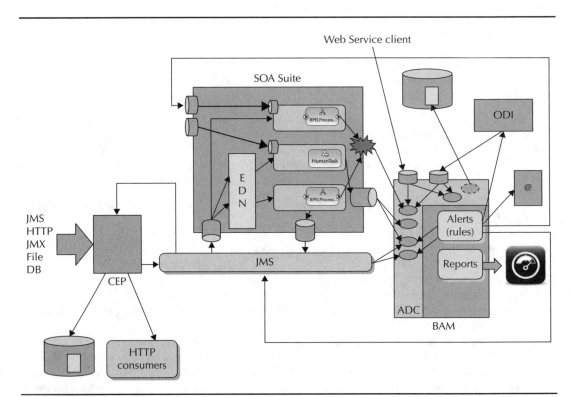

FIGURE 19-2. *Complex Event Processing working with SOA composites and Business Activity Monitoring*

events that originated with the CEP will trigger a BPEL process and notifications, a human task, or some adapter services, including possibly the BAM adapter that sends information to the Oracle Business Activity Monitoring. Note that composite applications can also produce messages on JMS queues that are consumed by CEP.

Part of the SOA Suite is Oracle BAM—a product that typically runs in the same WebLogic domain as the SOA Suite, but using its own server. It is not part of the SCA container. However, through the BAM adapter and the BPEL sensor framework, events can be channeled from composite applications to the Business Activity Monitoring in a fairly direct way.

BAM maintains an in-memory data cache with potentially a large number of active data objects. These objects can be refreshed via messages arriving from the SOA Suite BAM adapter, over JMS, in Web Service requests, from Oracle Data Integrator (ODI), or via the BAM ICommand interface. Web-based real-time dashboards can be created on top of this data cache—with lists, charts, dials, and gauges and cross-tab displays that are automatically refreshed in the browser when the server-side data cache is refreshed by newly arriving events.

BAM is more than a visual dashboard: It can also execute rules against the data objects— testing values or aggregations against thresholds or other conditions. The rules allow BAM to do event processing somewhat similar to CEP, though in a simpler way and with much smaller volumes of events. When the rules are triggered, various types of actions can be executed by the BAM engine. Among these actions are onscreen indicators, e-mail alerts, and calls to Web Services (which in turn could publish events on JMS or invoke SOA composite applications that create human tasks, update a database, generate a file, or execute business processes with BPM or BPEL).

In the next chapter we will see how ADF provides us with a BAM data control that acts against the Active Data Cache and allows us to create custom user interfaces with ADF that are refreshed live, thanks to server push from the BAM engine.

Analyzing Continuous Data Streams Through Complex Event Processing

The first line of defense in situations with lots of real-time information is likely to be some form of Complex Event Processing. This will act to filter, aggregate, and enrich the fine-grained, largely meaningless events that come streaming in to the level of businesswise, meaningful packets of information that are fed to downstream consumers—such as the EDN of the SOA Suite or the Business Activity Monitoring.

St. Matthews has a number of areas where voluminous event streams provide the hospital potentially with a lot of useful information. However, the challenge is to sift the information from the real-time data overload and turn it into insight and action. We will discuss a number of business situations at St. Matthews where Complex Event Processing would be useful to do exactly that.

Data-rich Business Areas, Ready for the Harvest

Areas in the hospital where events are more or less constantly generated range from signals from physical devices and biometric sensors to security and detection appliances, as well as from clicks and fine-grained traces from within websites and computer systems to business process metrics. These pose a wide variety to us: various business areas, very different types of events, with a wide range of frequency. Note that CEP excels at sifting through large volumes of real-time events and also at detecting complex patterns within events collection, be they small or very large. The conclusions CEP arrives at need to be communicated to relevant recipients. This will often happen through reporting tools and a real-time dashboard (for example, Oracle BAM). And that is what we will discuss later in the chapter.

Emergency Room

Events in the emergency room should be closely monitored and acted upon: the entrance of new patients, the first triage and priority assignment, the actual consult for the real diagnosis and subsequently treatment, which could even mean an operation, and finally checking in to the hospital or the dismissal to go home again. Patients go through various stages. By monitoring each new stage for each patient as events, the hospital can assess the overall waiting time against preset performance indicators as well as predict whether more staff is needed to handle the influx of patients. Patients that for some reason do not get to the next stage—for example, they may have lost their consciousness—can be identified.

Biometrics

Thousands of devices at St. Matthews are making biometric measurements, more or less constantly—checking on heart rhythm and pulse, on temperature and blood composition, on breathing, and on many other bodily functions. These measurements need to be monitored constantly, in real time, though typically we only care about exceptions and deviations. The heart rhythm is distorted for longer than a few seconds. The temperature drops beyond the safe range, or the sugar content in the blood reaches a level that warrants closer scrutiny. CEP can collect thousands of readings per second, aggregating them where necessary and forwarding only the situations that require attention. In addition, CEP can monitor the devices themselves: If a device is not delivering the events it should produce, CEP can detect the malfunction and report an alert.

Security

The hospital has several security zones. Public facilities are areas where patients are allowed—and relatives during visiting hours only. There are areas accessible to staff, with various degrees of security clearance. Some areas—where dangerous drugs are stored or where the data center is located—are off limits to everyone except a select number of employees. Surveillance cameras are used to monitor movements in the most sensitive areas. Additionally, staff as well as patients have badges with RFID tags that are scanned in hundreds of places in the hospital buildings. These badges are also used to gain entrance to secure zones. Tens of thousands of scan events are generated every hour, potentially providing insight into failed entry attempts, popular routes, the number of people (and even their identities) in every area at any one moment, and the fact that a person went into a zone but did not emerge within a certain period of time. This information is very useful in the event of fires or other emergency situations where parts of the hospital need to be evacuated. On a less dramatic level, the information can be used to guide patients to their destinations in the hospital (for example, with a wireless handheld device that is fed with directions based on the information produced by CEP about the position and movement of the patient).

Customer Service Levels

Customer service is a top priority at St. Matthews. Patients complained a lot in the past about not getting through on the phone or being left on hold for ages by rude operators. CEP can analyze the events that each phone call generates—the connection with the St. Matthews telephone system, the start of the actual conversation, and the end of the conversation as well as all through connections and their respective waiting times, and also the calls that ended with the caller hanging up while waiting. It will know the date and time of the day for each call, the different departments and operators that handled the call, and the identity of the patient who made the call. CEP will help identify increasing wait times as they start to occur—allowing for immediate and targeted reactions. It provides insight into the bottleneck departments across the hospital when it comes to dealing with phone calls. It tells us when and where in their interaction people hang up on St. Matthews. CEP and consumers of its findings, such as BAM, can prove tremendously valuable in increasing customer service levels and customer satisfaction.

Performance of Computer Applications

Events are produced in the zillions by our computer systems. Some represent a very technical level of detail—for example, hardware statistics or database trace information. Some are more functionally meaningful, including the search, click, and navigation behavior of users on the website. Yet others are a direct representation of the progress of business processes—for example, signals from SOA composite sensors, human task callbacks, and other trace signals. CEP can help analyze those signals—in real time, acting before real problems start to emerge and unfold.

The Product Architecture of Complex Event Processor

Oracle CEP consists of a number of components: the Server and Visualizer for the run time, and the Oracle CEP IDE inside Eclipse for the design time. This section gives a very brief introduction to the product architecture, illustrated in Figure 19-3. More details on installation and getting started are in Appendix C and on the wiki.

Run-time CEP Components

The Oracle Complex Event Processor is part of the SOA Suite license. However, it is not part of the SOA Suite SCA container—it does not even run in the same WebLogic Server as the SOA Suite does. It runs on its own streamlined, lightweight server—which is POJO based, founded on Spring DM and an OSGi-based framework to manage services. This server comes with Jetty, an HTTP container for running servlets, and support for JMS and JDBC. It has caching and clustering

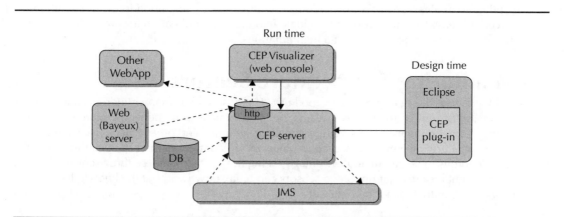

FIGURE 19-3. *Architecture of CEP*

facilities—possibly backed by an Oracle Coherence grid. To provide real-time processing of substantial event loads, it works with special JVMs: JRockit or WebLogic Real Time. CEP can handle thousands of concurrent queries and process hundreds of thousands of events per second. The average message latency can be under 1 ms.

Messages are typically read from JMS—for example, a queue in the SOA Suite WebLogic server. However, tables can be used as an event source as well, and through custom adapters, we can consume messages from virtually any source, including files, sockets, and JMX.

The CEP server provides an HTTP Pub/Sub event channel based on the Bayeux protocol; this allows the CEP application to consume messages pushed from a Bayeux-compliant server as well as allows clients to subscribe to messages published by the CEP server. Clients can also publish to an HTTP channel without having to be explicitly connected to the HTTP Pub/Sub server.

Event messages are typically processed by CQL processors—nodes in the event processing network (EPN) that receive messages from stream sources and act on them to produce new event messages. The outcome of a CQL query is typically a stream of events. For backward compatibility, CEP also still supports its own EPL.

Oracle CEP provides additional facilities, such as the ability to record events flowing through an event processing network and store them. They can later be played back from the event repository.

The Oracle CEP Visualizer is a Web 2.0 application that is the administration console. CEP applications can be deployed, paused and resumed, and uninstalled from the Visualizer. Current operations can be monitored, including all console output. It also has support for visual and run-time CQL Query editing. Events published on an HTTP Pub/Sub channel can be monitored in the Visualizer, asynchronously pushed by the server to the browser.

CEP at Design Time

The design time for the Complex Event Processor is not—at present—JDeveloper, as you might expect, given that JDeveloper is the strategic integrated development environment of Oracle. CEP may move into JDeveloper at some time, but for the moment the design time is Eclipse with the Oracle CEP plug-in. The installation process consists of downloading and installing Eclipse and then adding the Oracle CEP plug-in through the standard Eclipse plug-in mechanism.

The CEP Eclipse environment has pretty good capabilities for productive development of CEP applications—such as visual editing of the event processing network (EPN), validations on all CEP configuration files (XML based), including the CQL queries, and good integration with the CEP server. It is easy to add your own Java logic into the CEP application for producing or consuming event messages, or performing data manipulations.

Monitoring Temperature Sensors

St. Matthews is going to put CEP to good use. The hospital has many hundreds of temperature sensors, in dozens of areas (floors, wards, buildings), measuring the temperature in maternity wards, normal patients' rooms, refrigerating storage units, and other places. These sensors report the temperature once every few seconds. Sensors are configured in clusters of three, and the temperature is to be calculated per unit by taking the average of these three sensors. This cluster arrangement ensures that up to two sensors can break down without the knowledge of the temperature at that location being lost.

All these sensors produce up to 100,000 signals per hour. And CEP comes to the rescue—because most of these can be discarded right away. In other words, if we learn about the temperature in a room or fridge once every minute, that would be quite enough.

Here is some of the information we hope to learn from all the temperature signals—and the actions we may need to trigger as a result:

- Find failing heaters and open windows (detected from sudden temperature drops, steady declines, deviation of more than 4 degrees Fahrenheit from 66 degrees Fahrenheit).

- Discover potential fires.

- Find failing refrigerating equipment (steady increase in temperature above the preset temperature).

- Report on average temperature in special areas such as maternity wards and intensive care units.

- Find faulty sensors (no signal for longer than 30 seconds).

Let's see how we can set up CEP to get some of these answers.

Getting Started with CEP

Install the CEP Server and Eclipse with CEP development environment, as per the instructions on the wiki and in the online chapter complement. Also follow the instructions for setting up some JMS queues—called temperatureReadingsQueue, temperatureFindingsQueue, and failedTemperatureSensorsQueue—for the examples in this chapter.

Preparing Temperature Sensors Simulator

In your development environment, you may not have hundreds of temperature sensors that send temperature readings to JMS queues every other second—and neither have I. In preparation for the next steps, where we want CEP to find the average temperature per room or clinic and detect faulty sensors and spot fires, we need to set up a simulation of those sensors. One way of doing this would be to create a simple Java application that puts messages onto a JMS queue. However, we can also use CEP itself to do this. A simple CEP application will be able to do the following:

- Use a custom adapter to create temperatureReadingEvents—simple POJOs that carry the temperature value and the sensor's identification.

- Channel these events to a JMS queue that makes these events available to various consumers, including a second CEP application (one that could also be used to process the real temperature sensor readings).

Such an application that simulates or provides a mock implementation of the real event producers is frequently useful to develop and test a CEP application, because we may not have access to real events during development and we definitely have a need to explicitly hide needles in haystacks in order to thoroughly test our CEP application's capability to find those needles.

The first step in this process is to create a new Oracle CEP project in Eclipse, based on the HelloWorld template; this template adds some initial objects to the application that serve as a good example of what we need to develop ourselves, including a simple EPN, and an example of a custom adapter (class HelloWorldAdapter).

Rename the META-INF/spring/helloworld-context.xml file to **temperatureSensorSimulator-context.xml**. This file contains the EPN, the heart of the application (or rather the brains).

Create a new class called **TemperatureSensorSimulator**. It implements the CEP interface StreamSource with a single method (setEventSender) that allows the CEP framework to inject the StreamSender object through which our adapter can start emitting events. The class also implements the interface RunnableBean (with the methods run and suspend)—it will run in a thread and suspend itself to be reactivated some time later and fire another burst of events when the run() method is invoked. The class initializes a list of TemperatureSensor objects that each emulates a temperature sensor, with its identifier, a cluster reference, a base temperature, and a range of variation over which the sensor's reported value will randomly swerve.

In every burst of activity, all sensors are iterated, and for each one an event (pojo TemperatureReadingEvent) is filed with the injected EventSender. Every 50 bursts, one sensor is randomly selected and "disabled," not to emit temperature readings anymore. This is the needle we will later need to have our CEP application detect. See the chapter complement for the Java source code involved.

Open the temperatureSensorSimulator-context.xml file (in the folder META-INF/spring) in the EPN editor. It will visually show the event processing network—currently the HelloWorld network that we will delete later on, but now serves as a good example.

We can create new components in the EPN from the context menu. Right-click anywhere on the pane and select Adapter from the list of supported components. Call the adapter **temperatureSensorsSimulator**. Add a channel called **temperatureReadingsChannel** and another adapter, called **temperatureReadingsQueueJmsOutbound**. Wire the channel to this outbound adapter and likewise the temperatureSensorsSimulator adapter to the inbound side of the channel. The result is shown in Figure 19-4.

Open this file in edit source mode—for example, by double-clicking any of the components in the EPN. Add an event type, TemperatureReadingEvent, to the element event type repository, based on a class with the same name. Set the event-type attribute of the channel you created to this event type. Set the provider attribute for the outbound JMS adapter to jms-outbound. You may now remove all elements that refer to Hello World in any way. Configure the JMS provider in the file META-INF/wlevs/config.xml.

Open the Servers view—using menu path Window | Show View | Others | Server/Servers. The view that opens contains the CEP server we configured in the previous section. From the context menu on this server, select the option Add And Remove. In the window that pops up, select the TemperatureSensorsSimulator application to add to the server and then click Finish. The server is started, if it is not already running, and the application is deployed and starts running right away.

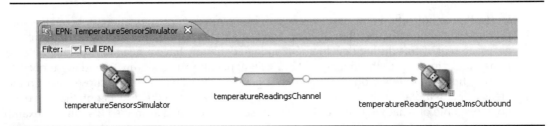

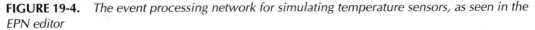

FIGURE 19-4. *The event processing network for simulating temperature sensors, as seen in the EPN editor*

We can check for messages being published to the JMS queue in the WebLogic Administration console.

NOTE
Because we are using a JMS queue in WebLogic soa_server1, we have to ensure that this server is up and running before trying to execute the CEP application.

Creating the CEP Application TemperatureReadingsProcessor

After our first introduction to CEP applications and an EPN, we are ready to create an application with some real CEP logic in it. The TemperatureReadingsProcessor will take the incoming temperature sensor readings from the JMS queue jms/temperatureReadingsQueue and analyze them in two ways:

■   The complex event processor is enlisted to consolidate the very large number of temperature readings, in two ways: The application publishes the average temperature per cluster of three sensors, every 30 seconds, using the readings from the last 60 seconds. The derived aggregate temperature findings are published on a second JMS queue, called TemperatureFindingsQueue. This queue feeds into the Business Activity Monitoring, with more meaningful information at a sensible pace.

■   The CEP will also be tasked with finding faulty temperature sensors. A sensor is considered faulty if it has not produced a signal for longer than 30 seconds. Failed detectors are reported on another JMS queue, this one called failedTemperatureSensorsQueue.

The logic of this application is defined through two processor elements that each run a CQL query that continuously scans incoming events and produces finding events. Here are the steps for creating this application:

1.   Create a new CEP project in Eclipse called TemperatureReadingsProcessor.

2.   Configure the JMS adapters in the META-INF/wlevs/config.xml file, in the same way we saw before, using the queue names mentioned previously and using the event types TemperatureReading, TemperatureFinding, and FailedSensorDetection. These event types are defined in the event repository in temperatureReadingsProcessor-context.xml, referring to POJOs with simple properties.

3.   Open the context file in the EPN editor. Add an adapter, called consumeTemperature Readings, that consumes events from the inbound JMS queue with temperature readings. Add two processors, called temperatureAggregator and failedSensorDetector. Add two other adapters—temperatureAggregatePublisher and failedSensorDectectionPublisher— both outbound JMS Queue publishers. Create the temperatureReadingsChannel (with event type set to TemperatureReading) that is the conduit between the incoming adapter and the two processors. Also create the channels temperatureAggregatesChannel (connecting temperatureAggregator to temperatureAggregatePublisher carrying event type TemperatureFinding) and failedSensorDetectionsChannel (which links failedSensorDetector to failedSensorDetectionPublisher with the event message of type FailedSensorDetection). The final situation is shown in Figure 19-5.

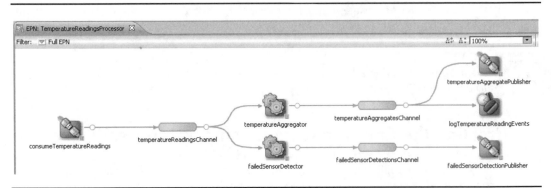

FIGURE 19-5. *The event processing network for TemperatureReadingsProcessor*

Configuring the Temperature Aggregator Processor with a CQL Query

Double-click the processor temperatureAggregator to edit the CQL query it needs to execute. Edit the XML file that opens and specify the query as follows:

```
<query id="aggregateTemperatureReadings">
      <![CDATA[
       select avg(temperatureReadingsChannel.temperature)  as temperature
       ,       temperatureReadingsChannel.clusterId as clusterId
       from    temperatureReadingsChannel [range 60 slide 30]
       group by temperatureReadingsChannel.clusterId
       ]]>
  </query>
```

This relatively simple CQL statement processes events (of type TemperatureReading) that appear on the temperatureReadingsChannel. Range 60 instructs the CQL engine to take the events in this channel for the last 60 seconds, and slide 30 is an instruction to produce a result every 30 seconds. The average temperature is calculated over all temperature reading events in the 60-second window and all sensors grouped per cluster. The events that are produced by this query have two properties set: temperature and clustered.

Keep in mind that this query may look a lot like the regular SQL used in queries against relational data sources. However, there are some really important distinctions. The CQL query operates on a stream of events, a dynamic data source that can change all the time. Also, the work of the query is never done—as events continue to arrive on the stream, the query continuously executes and potentially publishes events.

Detecting Non-Events to Identify Faulty Sensors with a CQL Query

The other processor we have to program with a CQL query is the failedSensorDetector. It has a tougher job to perform than the first processor we created. Spotting a faulty detector is done by finding a lack of events—one of many event patterns that CQL can unravel.

The MATCH_RECOGNIZE section of the next query is where the pattern must be matched. This section is partitioned by sensorId because we want to find events—or spot missing events—per sensor. The values returned by this section are sensorId and clustered, the two measures that are defined. The pattern clause indicates what combination of occurrences we are looking for—using a simple regular expression—like syntax. Here we have indicated that we are looking for an occurrence of A followed by one more occurrences of B. A is an anchor event for this pattern: Every temperature reading fits the bill for A. B occurs when there is an event that has a different sensorId value than the A event. However, because we have partitioned the events by sensorId, this really should not happen...wouldn't you say so?

If a sensor fails, the last A event is not followed by an event with the same sensorId; instead, it will be followed by a heartbeat event—a null event. The combination of "include timer events" and "duration multiples of 30" is responsible for producing the null event when the duration expires—that is, after 30 seconds. The null event does not have the same sensorId as the A event it follows, which means that the (A B*) pattern is detected. An output event is produced with the measures set as specified:

```
<query id="failedSensorDetection">
   <![CDATA[
        select  sensorReadings.sensorId  as sensorId
        ,       sensorReadings.clusterId as clusterId
        from    temperatureReadingsChannel
        MATCH_RECOGNIZE(
               partition by sensorId
          MEASURES A.sensorId as sensorId
          ,        A.clusterId as clusterId
          all matches
          include timer events
        PATTERN(A B*)
        duration multiples of 30
        DEFINE A as A.temperature > -100, B as B.sensorId != A.sensorId)
          as sensorReadings
   ]]>
</query>
```

The temperature readings taken from the inbound queue are forwarded through the channel to the CQL-based processor. This processor detects the absence for 30 seconds of a signal from a sensor that previously sent in messages—or at least one. This absence detection is reported through a FailedSensorDetection event that is sent through the channel to the outbound JMS adapter failedSensorDetectionPublisher to be put on the outgoing JMS queue. In the next section, we will see how this event is consumed into the SOA Suite's Event Delivery Network to produce a human task.

Test Run: Pinpointing a Malfunctioning Sensor

We have created two CEP applications—one to simulate a bunch of hyperactive temperature sensors and produce a load of events on a JMS queue, and the second one to process and analyze those temperature readings. This yields consolidated average temperature values once every 30 seconds and the detection of faulty sensors. Both results are published to JMS queues.

We can deploy these applications to the CEP server and have them run. There would be no spectacular displays—in fact, no visual output at all, except the arrival of messages on the JMS queues that we can monitor in the WebLogic Administration console.

A third and very small CEP application can also be used to tap into the JMS queue for failed detector events—at jms/failedTemperatureSensorsQueue. This application feeds events through a channel into an EventBean component based on the custom class FailedSensorTrapper that implements the EventSink interface. This class writes a message to the console for every failed sensor event it receives. This gives us an easy way, with almost no programming, to monitor the CEP applications.

All three CEP applications can now be added to the CEP server. This will deploy and start them. And this time we will be using the browser-based CEP Visualizer tool, an Administration console with run-time application-editing capabilities (for example, to edit CQL queries). The CEP Visualizer can be accessed at http://localhost:9002/wlevs. You can connect with wlevs/wlevs. We can find the console output in the Visualizer tool under Non Clustered Server/Services.

When the simulator decides to take a sensor offline, it writes a message to the console. Approximately 30 seconds later, the CEP processor failedSensorDetector has detected the lack of events from this sensor and produced a FailedSensorDetection event on the failedTemperatureSensors Queue queue. The TrackFailedSensors application consumes messages from that particular queue and logs them. The console output in the CEP Visualizer shows how various sensors start to fail from the simulator and after some time are being detected (see Figure 19-6). The figure highlights the case of sensor NU.0191 that fails and is detected as having passed away.

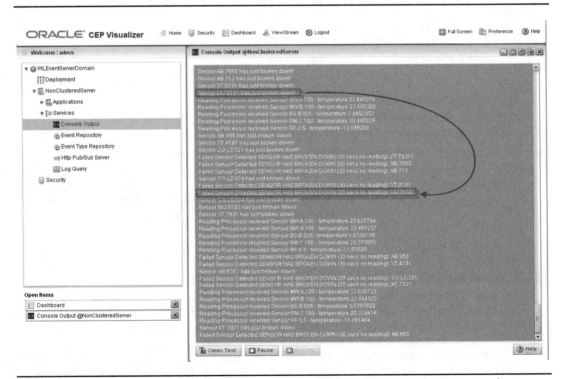

FIGURE 19-6. *Monitoring the console output of the CEP applications in the CEP Visualizer Administration console*

Promotion from a Simple, Anonymous Signal to a Business Event

CEP processes up to thousands of signals and low-level events per second. CEP applications filter, aggregate, and analyze those events to produce a far smaller number of facts that are truly meaningful at the level of human operators or the business processes. In the situation we have discussed in the previous section, where hundreds of temperature sensors post their readings with a JMS queue, the Complex Event Processor distills two new streams of events:

- Average, consolidated TemperatureFindings per sensing unit and per half-minute
- FailedDetectorEvents that are sent whenever a sensor is found to be absent for 30 seconds in a row

These two types of events are to be treated differently: The average temperature findings can be presented in a dashboard that consolidates lots of monitoring details relevant to operators in the control room for the hospital facilities. They can be used in that dashboard to create alerts when the temperature starts to deviate too far from the preset value or when it rises so high a fire is suspected. The events that indicate a failed sensor should be turned into a human task for a technician to inspect and potentially replace the detector.

Reporting, possibly alerting, and triggering specific follow-up actions are typical ways to handle the outcomes of a complex Event Processing application. However, these are not normally the responsibility of the CEP product itself. Through the queues, CEP produces the findings in a generic, decoupled way, independent of the consumers (and even in the absence of any consumers).

We will discuss two consumers of CEP outcomes in the remainder of this chapter. First, we take a look at SOA composite applications and how they consume CEP findings. Next up is the Business Activity Monitoring, which can also consume the CEP output.

Integrating CEP with SOA Composites

The integration from CEP to the SOA Suite is not a direct, native one on either end. CEP publishes events, usually to a JMS queue. And the SOA Suite—or rather composite applications running inside the SOA Suite—can consume messages from JMS queues through the JMS adapter, first introduced in Chapter 12.

The business scenario we will implement here is that whenever a failed sensor event is consumed from the JMS queue failedTemperatureSensorsQueue, an event of type FailedTemperatureSensorEvent is published on the Event Delivery Network inside the SOA Suite. The EDN was introduced in Chapter 9.

We will create a composite application that creates a human task assigned to the engineering pool to do something about this sensor. Because the JMS message only contains the identifiers of the sensor and sensing cluster, which is not enough information for the technician to go on, we will use a database adapter to retrieve location-specific details from a database table that contains information about the sensing clusters and their whereabouts in the hospital.

Alternatively, we could have a BPEL process just send an e-mail notification to the general e-mail account for the engineering department, bypassing the more formal human workflow mechanism.

Promotion from CEP to the Event Delivery Network

CEP and EDN both handle events. However, these events are usually not quite the same: CEP handles large numbers of small, largely meaningless events, and the Event Delivery Network works with much smaller numbers of events that each have a business meaning and represent a noteworthy occasion in the business processes. However, the Complex Event Processor may very well produce the kind of events that EDN deals in.

In the case at hand, the EDN can get hold of such meaningful events produced by CEP from the failedTemperatureSensorsQueue. We need to go through a few straightforward steps to define a new type of business event and broadcast this event on the EDN based on messages on the queue fed by CEP.

1. Create a new composite application in JDeveloper. Call it **FailedTemperatureSensor EventProducer**.

2. Create a new XSD document, called **TemperatureSensors.xsd**, with the definition of the payload element for the event (see Figure 19-7).

   Note that the FailedSensor element is not specific for temperature sensors, because failed sensors can be found in various measuring categories.

3. Define a business event called **FailedSensorEvent** by clicking the Event Creation icon in the Composite Editor. See Figure 19-8 and the next step for this.

4. Call the EDL file **TemperatureSensorEventDefinitions** and set the namespace to http://com.stmatthews.hospital/facilities. Select the FailedSensor element that was defined in the XSD document.

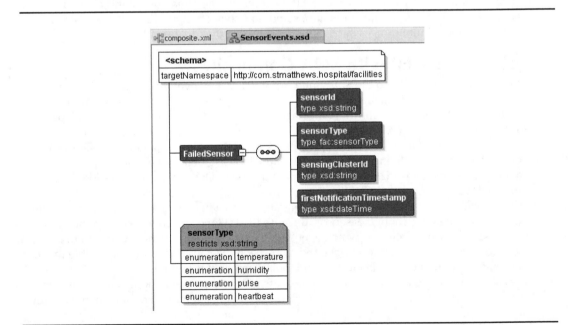

FIGURE 19-7. *Documenting SensorEvents.xsd with the FailedSensor element—the event's payload*

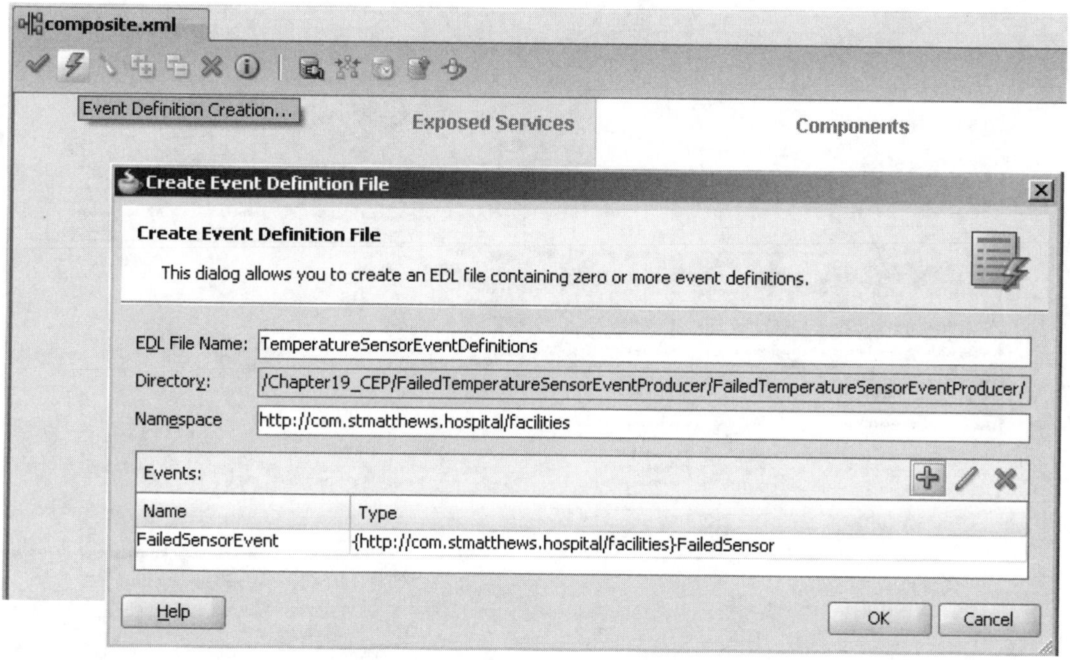

FIGURE 19-8.   *Defining the EDN event type FailedSensorEvent*

5. Create a JMS adapter service (FailedTemperatureSensorEventConsumer), inbound, in the Service lane of the composite. Configure this adapter service to consume messages from the queue jms/failedTemperatureSensorsQueue. Note that for simplicity's sake, we use the existing JMS adapter's connection pool (eis/Queue/patients).

6. Add a Mediator component to the composite, called **PublishFailedSensorEvent**. Wire the JMS adapter service to this Mediator. Create a static routing rule in the Mediator that has the FailedSensorEvent as its target. Create the mapping from the JMS map message to the event payload. Note that this may not be as trivial as it sounds, because the JMS messages arriving on this queue are MapMessages—a type of message that carries key/value pairs. The following snippet of the XSL mapping code illustrates how to process these messages:

```
<xsl:template match="/">
  <fac:FailedSensor>
    <fac:sensorId>
      <xsl:value-of select="/implmap:MapMessage/entry[
                                         @name='sensorId']"/>
    </fac:sensorId>
...
```

Note how we extract the sensorId from the map entry elements.

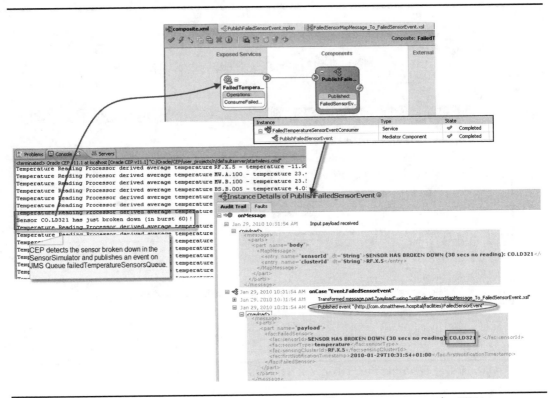

FIGURE 19-9. *Promoting the CEP failed sensor events to business events on the EDN*

We can now deploy and test the composite—to see whether events are published on the Event Delivery Network after being produced by the CEP application. See Figure 19-9 for confirmation.

From EDN to Human Task

The next step in deriving insight and actions from the data avalanche is a simple one, with everything we have discussed so far. When a FailedSensorEvent appears on the Event Delivery Network, it should be turned into the human task SensorInspection and assigned to a technician. Therefore, we will create a new composite application with a Mediator that subscribes to this event. Unfortunately, the event does not have enough information for the task to be created right away: We need to add the exact location of the sensor that has broken down.

Frank's database-of-all-trades contains two database tables that together provide this information: TEMPERATURE_SENSOR_CLUSTERS and HOSPITAL_AREAS. The latter has a self-referencing foreign key that represents the hierarchical relationship in areas—zooming in from the main building via the west section of the second floor to a specific room somewhere in that section. A hierarchical query can be used to retrieve a "zooming" identification of the exact position of a temperature sensor cluster given that cluster's identifier.

The steps for creating a composite application that creates the human task from the EDN event are as follows:

1. Create a new SOA composite application called **SensorInspectionCoordinator**. Drag the database adapter service to the external references lane. Configure the adapter service as RetrieveLocationOfSensorCluster using the database connection to Frank's database. The operation type is Execute Pure SQL. We use this operation type because we use a hierarchical query to retrieve the location path for the cluster, and this type of query cannot be handled in the regular query editor.

2. On the next page, enter the following slightly advanced SQL statement (and see the corresponding XSD created for it):

```
select tsr.id cluster_id
,      haa.full_location
from   temperature_sensor_clusters tsr
       join
       ( select sys_connect_by_path(location,'/') full_location
         ,       id location_id
         from    hospital_areas
         connect
         by      parent_area = prior id
         start
         with    parent_area is null
       ) haa
       on (tsr.location_id = haa.location_id)
where tsr.id = #clusterId
```

This SQL creates a hierarchy of areas in the hospital—starting with the buildings and drilling down into individual rooms and storage units—and then joins it with the sensor cluster we are looking for. The sys_connect_by_path operator helps us construct the route from the top-level location all the way down to the actual location of the cluster.

The query has a single input parameter—clusterId—that we will need to set when invoking this database adapter service.

3. Create the human task SensorInspection. See Chapter 10 for more details on human tasks and how to create them.

Eventually we need to set up the group TechnicalEngineeringStaff in WebLogic and assign this task to that group. However, to keep things simple and moving forward, let's just assign it to Margaret for testing purposes. After all, we are only trying to demonstrate how low-level event (and non-event) detection is turned into a technician dragging his feet down a hallway in search of a faulty sensor. We will keep things really simple for this task: A BPEL process will initiate the task and assign a title that contains the required context information. No task form is required, nor are any routing flows or escalation rules.

4. Create a BPEL process component, called **FailedSensorInspectionPlanner**, that subscribes to the failed sensor event. Select this event through the MDS connection, and browse for the EDL file in the deployed composite FailedTemperatureSensorEventProducer.

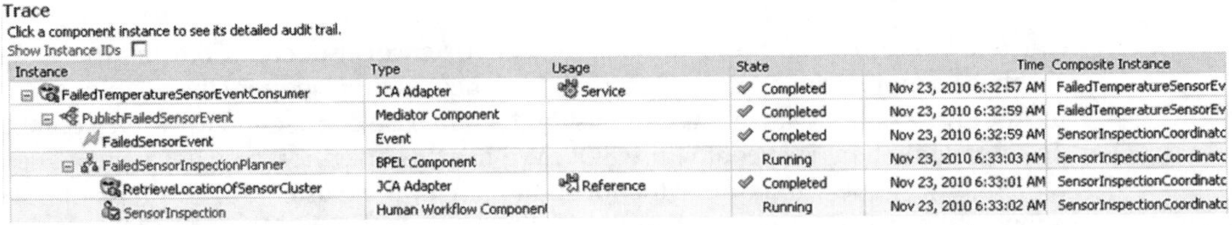

Trace
Click a component instance to see its detailed audit trail.
Show Instance IDs ☐

Instance	Type	Usage	State	Time	Composite Instance
⊟ 📇 FailedTemperatureSensorEventConsumer	JCA Adapter	🔧 Service	✓ Completed	Nov 23, 2010 6:32:57 AM	FailedTemperatureSensorEv
⊟ 🔷 PublishFailedSensorEvent	Mediator Component		✓ Completed	Nov 23, 2010 6:32:59 AM	FailedTemperatureSensorEv
〰 FailedSensorEvent	Event		✓ Completed	Nov 23, 2010 6:32:59 AM	SensorInspectionCoordinatc
⊟ 🔀 FailedSensorInspectionPlanner	BPEL Component		Running	Nov 23, 2010 6:33:03 AM	SensorInspectionCoordinatc
📇 RetrieveLocationOfSensorCluster	JCA Adapter	🔧 Reference	✓ Completed	Nov 23, 2010 6:33:01 AM	SensorInspectionCoordinatc
📇 SensorInspection	Human Workflow Component		Running	Nov 23, 2010 6:33:02 AM	SensorInspectionCoordinatc

FIGURE 19-10. *From CEP to human task—failed sensor events from CEP flow through JMS and EDN to BPEL and finally to a human task, assigned to "the fixer."*

5. Create a BPEL variable called **FailedSensorEvent** based on the same element as the event's payload. Set this variable as the input variable in the Receive activity.

6. Wire the BPEL component to the Database Adapter Service RetrieveLocationOfSensor Cluster. Have local variables generated. Add an Assign step to set the input—called clusterId, taken from variable FailedSensorEvent—for the database service.

7. Add a Human Task activity to the BPEL process, associated with the SensorInspection task we created earlier. Set the title to this fairly long expression—the easiest way to convey task details to an assignee.

Now is the time to deploy this composite application to the SOA Suite and see how it all comes together—from the CEP simulator that randomly breaks down the temperature sensors, to the technical staff (just Margaret for now) that starts receiving notification e-mails, prompting them to do something about the fictitious malfunctioning sensor. Figure 19-10 shows the message flow trace that is the result of an instance of the FailedSensorEvent.

The human task that is instantiated as the last step in this flow trace results in the e-mail notification to Margaret shown in Figure 19-11.

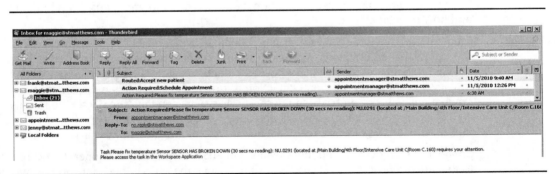

FIGURE 19-11. *The e-mail received by Margaret, prompting her to do something about a failed detector*

Oracle BAM: Real-time Business Activity Monitoring

Real-time insight into what is happening in your organization, through the actual values of relevant KPIs, presented in a visually attractive dashboard, with special alerts being raised and appropriate action being taken upon violations of predefined rules, such as crossing thresholds—that, in short, is the promise of BAM.

BAM maintains an active set of data that is constantly being refreshed, added to, and updated. Reports and charts can be defined against the data objects—and are updated in the browser that displays them whenever the underlying data objects are refreshed by incoming events.

Rules can be specified to identify exceptional situations that may require instant action. These rules are evaluated when the data objects they are defined against are refreshed. When a rule is violated, a visual alert can be displayed in the dashboard and the configured actions can be executed—including sending an e-mail and calling a Web Service. The rules can be quite advanced, thus allowing BAM to do a fair bit of filtering, aggregation, and pattern matching against its data objects and the events that update them.

BAM collects data in its Active Data Cache, an in-memory collection of data objects that are created and updated from the incoming events. Reports can be defined against these objects—dashboards containing one or multiple lists, charts, and other visualizations of the active data. The dashboard report is published in a web browser. BAM uses server push—an advanced technique where the server actively updates a web client—to ensure that it always displays the actual situation.

BAM is accessed through a browser-based web application, both for development activities such as creating the data objects and designing the reports, as well as for accessing the live dashboards. The BAM server can also take initiative in the form of two types of outbound actions: sending e-mails and calling Web Services, which in turn, of course, can start SOA composite applications, create human tasks, write files, update databases, and produce JMS messages.

Business Scenarios for BAM

Business Activity Monitoring is the business front-end of the SOA Suite. It is where we come full circle: Having started with (high-level) Business Process Analysis, including the definition of processes, interactions, business objectives, and key performance indicators, the BAM Dashboard is the live visualization of the execution of those business processes and their effect on the KPIs. Any organization with an interest in how its processes are performing should consider creating BAM reports—usually as a complement to their Business Intelligence initiatives based on more historically oriented, longer-term data warehouses. Once again, BAM is very much for real-time insight.

BAM complements CEP with the visual presentation of findings and the ability to take actions. At the same time, there is some overlap with CEP, because both products analyze events in real time, aggregating and detecting patterns. CEP is geared toward more intense event streams with generally simple, virtually meaningless, almost payload-less signals and events. Through CQL, it has far more advanced capabilities for analyzing complex patterns and executing advanced event queries. CEP is not meant as the final destination for events: It emits events that report its findings to downstream consumers to take advantage of. BAM is one of the usual suspects as a consumer.

In situations where substantial numbers of events need to be processed or complex patterns are to be analyzed, CEP is a perfect gateway. It can feed into BAM as well as into other consumers, such as the Event Delivery Network. When the events are not as frequent and maybe more meaningful in a business sense, they may be absorbed directly by BAM—for example, SOA composite applications sending EDN events or other signals to the BAM engine.

BAM for Business

Typical users of BAM are business representatives responsible for the execution of specific business processes and their managers. Whether monitoring the status of physical equipment, tracking the vital life signs for the newborn babies in the maternity ward, managing the waiting times and number of calls processed by the hospital's helpdesk, analyzing the load on and efficiency of the emergency room, or studying the efficiency of the invoicing process and the effect of the "get better, pay faster" campaign, BAM can be used to collect the data, events, and statistics needed for deriving the values of performance indicators and visualizing the progress of the operations, as well as to put together the dashboard that updates in real time.

BAM even allows business users to create or enhance reports and dashboards themselves—just like they could do in Excel. When the developer has set up the data objects in BAM—and made sure that those are loaded with the live data feeds—it is an easy, declarative, browser-based task to create the charts, lists, and KPI visualizations.

BAM for System Administration

In addition to its importance for analyzing and visualizing the events on the business and process level, BAM dashboards can be very useful for lower-level, more-detailed technical tasks, such as operational control of computer applications and service infrastructures, including the SOA Suite and the applications it is running.

Events at this level include the number and time of invocations of composites and components, the time it takes to complete each instance, the number and types of faults that occur, the values of variables, changes in environment settings, and so on. The data available from these events can be retrieved from various systems across the enterprise. The data is aggregated in dashboard reports that help to provide insight into bottlenecks in the system—both historic and actual—in terms of performance and functionality (looking at the number of faults originating from specific components). The BAM server can take even some forms of corrective action, or at the very least can alert administrators when the performance of a specific component seems to be degrading very rapidly. Monitoring of Service Level Agreements could also be supported if not implemented using BAM.

The BAM Product Architecture

Oracle Business Activity Monitoring is a product that consists of several components, including a web application, application server components, and a database. The BAM server runs in its own WebLogic server (default name, bam_server1). This server is managed from the WebLogic Administration console— for configuring users, groups, application roles, adapter settings—and the Oracle Enterprise Manager Fusion Middleware Control for most operational tasks, such as performance and load monitoring. The FMW Repository hosts a database schema for BAM that contains all metadata (such as data object definitions and report definitions) and all active data for the data objects.

BAM is logically built from a number of components:

- **The Active Data Cache (ADC)**   An in-memory store of the data in the data objects. Incoming updates, events, and messages are pushed to the ADC and made available to the Report Cache and the Event Engine; the ADC is driven by metadata that describes the structure of the data objects.

- **Enterprise Message Sources**   Defines and connects to JMS queues and topics, consuming messages and forwarding them to data objects in the ADC.

- **The Event Engine**   Validates alert rules in response to events (updates of data objects) and takes action when appropriate.

- **The Report Cache**   Runs the reports, making them available for the Active Viewer web application and for dispatching via e-mail messages.

BAM publishes a service API, both as a SOAP Web Service as well through RMI to EJBs. It also supports external data objects that are based on tables or views in a database schema accessed through a JNDI data source. BAM is integrated with Oracle Data Integrator in two ways—both as a source and as a target. ODI ships with knowledge modules that implement specific data-integration patterns. It has several knowledge modules for integrating with BAM—using BAM both as a source for data that it transfers to another target store, and also as a target, where ODI loads data from one or more sources to the BAM server's data objects in the ADC.

The Oracle ADF framework ships with a BAM data control that makes it quite an easy task to develop custom, rich user interfaces against the data objects in the BAM Active Data Cache. These user interfaces have the same server push facility as the BAM dashboards themselves, meaning that changes in the ADC are pushed to a custom-developed ADF user interface. ADF has many different types of user interface components, charts, and other rich data visualizations as well as trees and tables. We will discuss ADF in the next chapter and also see how we can make use of this BAM data control to embed a BAM dashboard in a custom application.

The event engine can execute actions that include sending e-mails and invoking external Web Services. BAM uses the User Messaging Service (UMS), which is also used by the BPEL and Human Task service engines to send notifications. The UMS needs to be configured for the BAM server in the FMW Control. The outgoing e-mail server and send-from e-mail account need to be configured.

An incoming e-mail account and server can be specified too, because BAM supports a specific type of action that sends an e-mail with a link that the addressee should click to acknowledge the receipt of the message; upon that click, a reply e-mail is sent to the BAM engine's incoming e-mail account and the action is completed. If the incoming e-mail is not received within the specified period of time, the action is escalated and the next person on the list is notified via e-mail.

Developers and administrators will access BAM through the BAM Architect (for managing data objects and Enterprise Message Source), the Active Studio (for development of reports), and end users go through the Active Viewer (for running reports and watching dashboards).

User Administration

Users of Business Activity Monitoring are all defined in the Identity Store that is configured with WebLogic Server. Initially this will be the default, file-based repository.

Management of the user accounts takes place primarily in WebLogic and to a smaller extent in BAM Administrator. In WebLogic, a number of BAM-specific groups has been defined during installation: BamAdministrators, BamReportArchitects, BamReportCreators, and BamReportViewers. These groups have been granted the corresponding BAM application roles. When a user is added to one of these groups, that user inherits the application role that defines the level of access in the BAM web application.

Privileges on specific reports, data objects, and even rows within data objects can be assigned in BAM Architect and BAM Active Studio.

Note that users are added to the BAM Administrator the first time they connect to the product—or when the administrator actively registers the users defined in the WebLogic Identity Store into BAM.

Feeding the Output from the Complex Event Processor into the Business Activity Monitoring

In the first part of this chapter, we have developed a Complex Event Processor application that processes thousands of temperature readings per second produced by hundreds of temperature sensors all over the hospital. The CEP application consolidates the temperature readings from the sensors into temperature findings averaged per sensor cluster and per half-minute. It emits these events on a JMS queue—TemperatureFindingsQueue—from where it can be consumed by consumers such as BAM.

Our business objective in this section is to create a dashboard that displays the actual temperature for every area in the hospital and, even more importantly, to send out alerts when the temperature in any area starts to deviate from the predefined value. Thus, someone can act to shut the window that is left open near the incubators, close the refrigerator lid before the vaccines go bad, or extinguish a potential fire before there really is one.

Reporting on Temperature Sensor Readings

We will have to go through the following steps to create such a dashboard. All of them are done in BAM Architect, except for the last one:

- Create an external data source—a lookup database schema.
- Create a ReferenceTemperatureSensorCluster data object that is based on a database view.
- Define a TemperatureSensorCluster data object that represents a live temperature sensor cluster.
- Configure an Enterprise Message Source—a bridge between the JMS queue TemperatureFindingsQueue and the TemperatureSensorCluster data object.
- Create a report based on the data object in BAM Active Studio.

Configuring the Active Data Cache in BAM Architect

The BAM development environment is entirely web based. Before we can access Oracle BAM, we need to start up the BAM server, which is one of the managed servers in the WebLogic domain—next to soa_server1 for the SCA container. You can start this server in almost the same way, replacing the string "soa_server1" with "bam_server1." Administration is done in the WebLogic Administration console and the Enterprise Manager Fusion Middleware Control.

Access BAM in Internet Explorer 7 or 8 at http://localhost:9001/OracleBAM. Mozilla Firefox, Google Chrome, and other browsers are not currently supported, unless you install the IE Tab plug-in for Firefox 3.0. Connect with the same weblogic user that you also use for the soa_server1.

Go to the BAM Architect. Select External Data Sources from the drop-down list in the upper-left corner and click the create link in the right pane. Create an External Data Source called **FranksDatabase** using the database connect details for the database schema that contains the tables for St. Matthews. The External Data Source is used to retrieve static lookup information that we can use to enrich a (dynamic) data object. Click the Create button to commit the changes.

Next, select Data Objects from the drop-down list. Select the folder Data Objects, click Create Subfolder, and create a folder called **HospitalFacilities**.

Now, click this new folder in the folder navigator tree on the left side and then click Create Data Object. Enter **ReferenceTemperatureSensorCluster** as the name for the new data object. Mark the check box External Data Object to indicate that this data object is based on a database table or view. Select the External Data Source FranksDatabase and subsequently VW_TEMPERATURE_SENSOR_CLUSTERS for the External Table Name setting. This view provides the static lookup information for the clusters: the location and the target temperature it is supposed to find. Click the Create Data Object button to go ahead and really create the object. Click the contents link to review the data in the external data object—retrieved from the underlying database view. Figure 19-12 shows this data object.

Next, click the link Create Data Object and enter **TemperatureSensorCluster** as the name. This object represents a live temperature sensor cluster and includes the current temperature value as well as the lookup values location and target temperature retrieved from the Reference TemperatureSensorCluster object. Figure 19-13 demonstrates how this object is created.

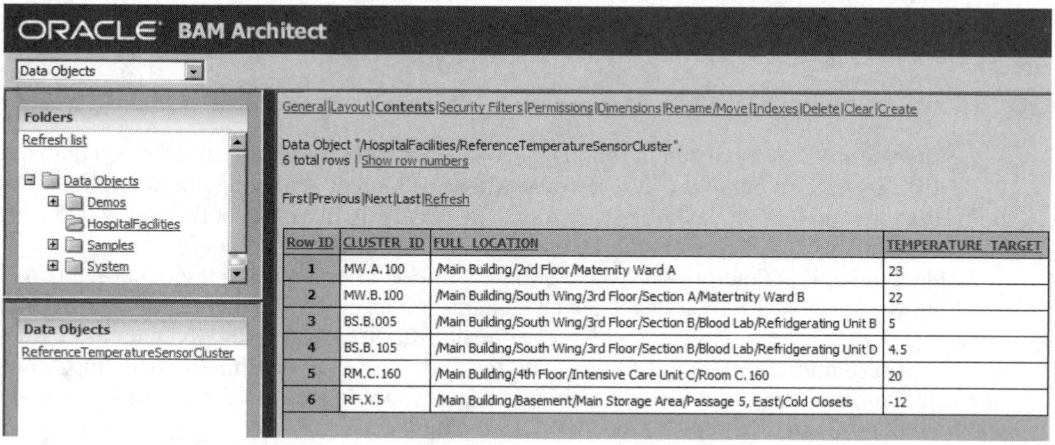

FIGURE 19-12. *Inspecting the contents of the external data object—the data retrieved from the database view*

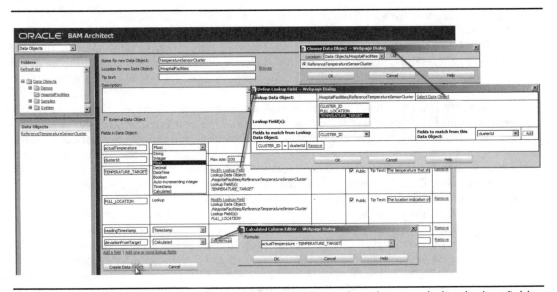

FIGURE 19-13. *Configuring the TemperatureSensorCluster data object, including lookup fields*

Create the fields actualTemperature of type Float and clusterId of type String. Then create two lookup fields—TEMPERATURE_TARGET and FULL_LOCATION—that are both retrieved from the external data object ReferenceTemperatureSensorCluster.

BAM data objects can have auto-generated fields—the last modified timestamp or a version field that is incremented with every update. Calculated fields can be added to provide values derived through some formula to make life easier for report developers. Expressions for calculated fields can refer to other fields in the data object and make use of operators and system functions such as now() for the current timestamp. Quite powerful and frequently used in formulas is the if-then-else syntax. For example, here's a formula for the target room temperature (in degrees Celsius) depending on whether it is currently night or daytime:

```
if ((Hour(now())>21) ||(Hour(now())< 6))  then (16) else (22)
```

Note that the views created in reports can also have their own specialized calculated fields.

Next, we need to configure an Enterprise Message Source—the bridge between the messaging infrastructure and a BAM data object, or more specifically in our case, between the JMS queue TemperatureFindingsQueue and the TemperatureSensorCluster data object.

Select the option Enterprise Message Source in the drop-down list in the upper-left corner. The page shown in Figure 19-14 appears. Specify a name (for example, **TemperatureFindingsQueue**). Set the URL details for the JNDI provider: **t3://localhost:8001**. Provide the JNDI names of the queue (**jms/TemperatureFindingsQueue**) and the connection factory (**jms/patientsJmsCF**). Enter the username and password for user weblogic. Select MapMessage for the message type—that is the type of message produced by the CEP TemperatureReadingsProcessor.

Select the data object that this message source will feed into—obviously this should be the TemperatureSensorCluster object we have just created. Now we need to make an important decision: What operation should be performed on the data object? Should a newly arriving

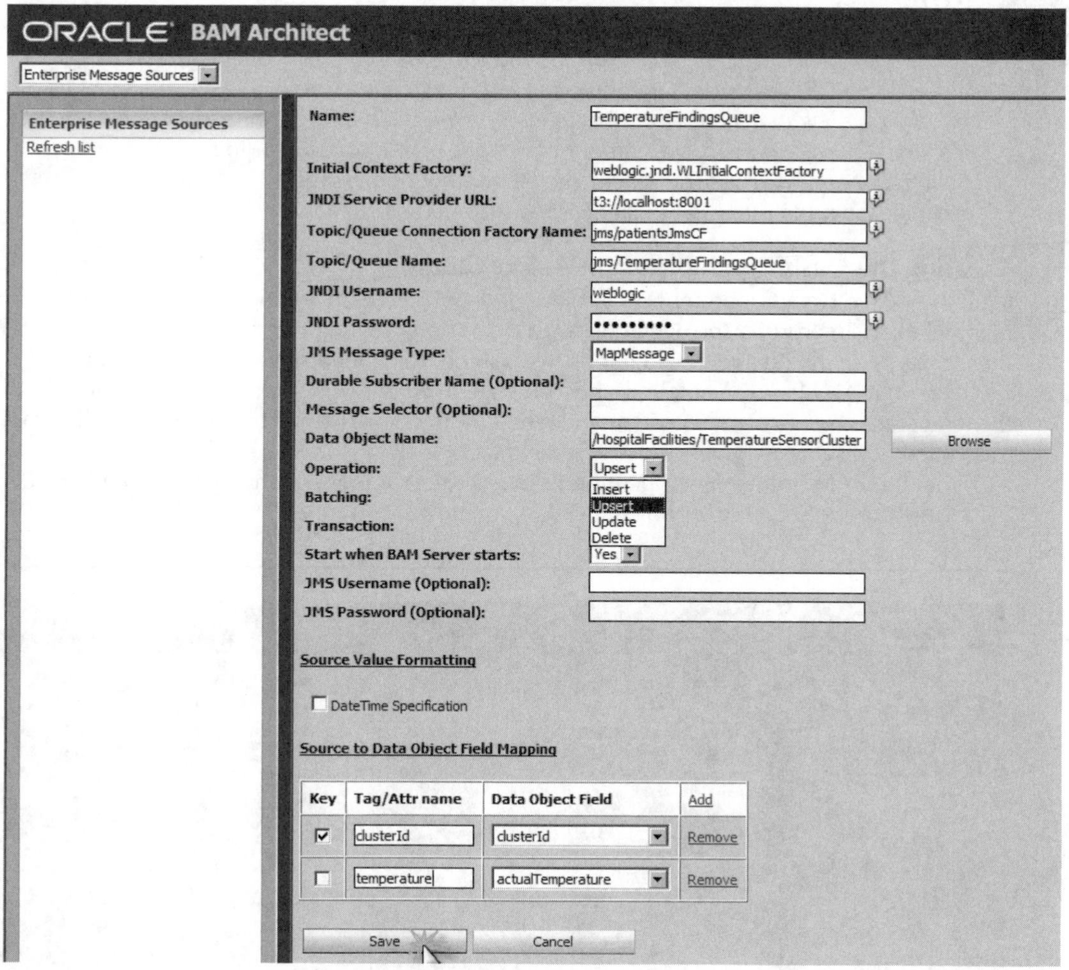

FIGURE 19-14. *Defining the Enterprise Message Source—mapping the JMS queue to the data object*

message on the queue always create a new data object instance? Or should a new message first attempt to update an existing data object before—when necessary—creating a new one? In this case, we want the TemperatureSensorCluster data objects to represent the actual situation of a cluster of sensors—and we do not care about historical reading. Therefore, we pick the Upsert operation type, which instructs BAM to update a data object when it can find one (based on a key that we will specify shortly) and insert one if no object is available to update.

The MapMessages contain two attributes that we care about, with tags clusterId and temperature. We should map these two attributes to the fields clusterId and actualTemperature in the TemperatureSensorCluster data object. Check the box Key for the clusterId field. Click Save to commit the changes.

NOTE
An Enterprise Message Source (EMS) must explicitly be started in order to commence the process of consuming messages from the JMS queue and feeding them into the data objects in the Active Data Cache. When you click the Enterprise Message Source name in the list on the left side, the right pane has a number of options on the top, including Start, Stop, and Metrics. The latter lists the number of messages received from the queue since the EMS was started.

Creating the Dashboard Report in Active Studio

With the Active Data Cache set up—and the data objects ready to go, one external and one mapped to an Enterprise Message Source—we can start creating the reports and alerts on top of these objects. In the next few paragraphs, we will put together a report on the temperature situation at St. Matthews. A single dashboard-style overview will make visible in real time what the temperature sensors are reporting and where hotspots may appear. The report will combine four different displays, all on top of the same data object.

From the BAM home page, open the Active Studio component and click Create New Report. Select the four-tile report layout by clicking it, as shown in Figure 19-15.

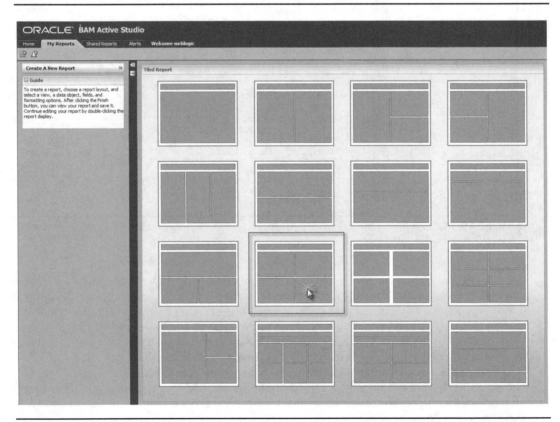

FIGURE 19-15. *Creating a new report with the four-tile layout style in BAM Active Studio*

Live List of Temperature Cluster Values   The first tile in the new report will display a list of all temperature sensor clusters, with their actual temperature value as well as an indication of their location in the hospital and the target temperature they were set to. The Updating Ordered List view type displays a list of data object instances and processes, and displays the updates to these objects that are pushed in real time. Click the icon for this view type.

On the first tab that appears, choose the TemperatureSensorCluster data object. On the second tab, select all fields except readingTimestamp. Click Next and then Finish (see Figure 19-16). This basically completes the first part of the dashboard.

The Arrow: A Quick-Glance Temperature Indicator   Click the Arrow view type in the second report tile. We will use the Arrow to indicate in a loud and clear way whether all temperature clusters report a value in the safe range (a big green upward-pointing arrow) or if one or more clusters measure a value that's outside that range (a red arrow pointing downward).

Select the TemperatureSensorCluster data object. On the Data Fields tab, select the Maximum of the readingTimestamp for the top value. Accept the default for the KPI value itself; we will create a calculated field to determine this KPI that dictates the arrow style.

Click Next and then click Create A Calculated Field. Enter the following expression, as shown in Figure 19-17:

```
if ((deviationFromTarget > 2) || (-2 > deviationFromTarget))
then (-1000) else (1)
```

This expression returns 1 for all clusters that are within the designated temperature range and –1000 for any cluster outside that range. Click Enter. A new calculated field is created. Rename the field **SeriousDeviation**.

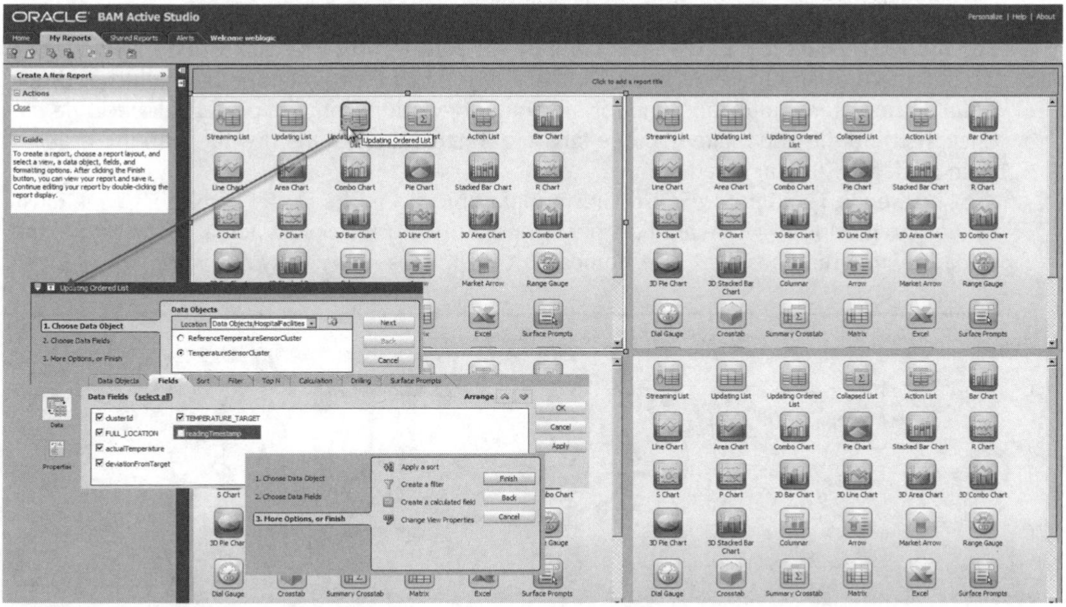

FIGURE 19-16.   *Creating the Updating Ordered List view for temperature clusters in the first report tile*

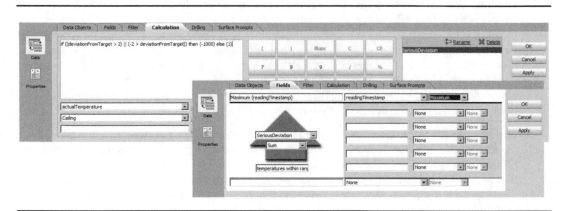

FIGURE 19-17. *Creating the calculated field SeriousDeviation to use (summarized) as the KPI value*

Return to the Fields tab. Set the KPI value—in the center of the arrow—to SeriousDeviation. Select Sum as the aggregation method and set the bottom title to "temperatures within range."

Click Properties and edit the View Title in the General tab. Then click the tab Value Format (see Figure 19-18). We can specify the display format for readingTimestamp—select the Time category and H:mm:ss for the format.

And we can set the format for SeriousDeviation: Select the Number category and mark the check box Round To The Nearest [Thousands]. We can also effectively hide the value from the arrow—set the font size to 1 for the Delta Value on the Font tab.

Finally, click OK to save the view definition.

The 3-D Bar Chart for a Live Overview of All Temperature Sensor Clusters
Let's add a 3-D bar chart to the third tile. This chart will have two bars for every temperature cluster: one for the actual temperature value, and one for the actual deviation from the preset value for the cluster. Click the third tile and make it a little larger, at the expense of the first tile with the ordered list. Then click the 3-D Bar Chart icon.

Choose the TemperatureSensorCluster data object. On the Data Fields tab, check clusterId as the field to group by—we want bars per temperature cluster. Select actualTemperature and deviationFromTarget as the Chart Values. Click OK to save the view definition.

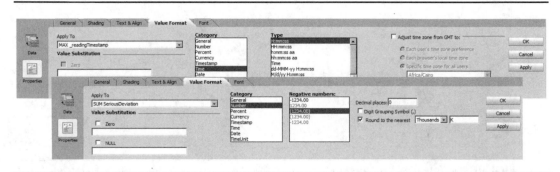

FIGURE 19-18. *Setting the value format for readingTimestamp and SeriousDeviation*

A Range Gauge to Visualize the Number of Temperature Deviations For the fourth tile, select the Range Gauge as the view type. Then select the familiar TemperatureSensorCluster data object. Click Next (to go to the Fields tab) and Next again to accept the default field settings. Then click Create A Calculated Field and create a new calculated field based on this expression:

```
if (deviationFromTarget>2 ||-2 > deviationFromTarget) then (1) else (null)
```

Now return to the Fields tab and select Deviant as the KPI value with Count as the aggregation method. Note that Count does not count "nulls," so we are only counting the clusters for which the deviation is larger than 2 degrees.

Click Properties. On the General tab, specify a relevant title. Set the value display ranges that determine which value range the gauge will cover and which values are the boundaries between the green, yellow, and red zones. The values for Low, Low/Medium Boundary, and Medium/High Boundary are 0, 1, and 3, respectively, with 15 being the upper limit for the Range Gauge.

Click OK to complete the definition of the view.

Running the Dashboard

After the report has been saved, it is ready to be used. The Active Viewer is the read-only section of Oracle BAM, where reports can be opened. Open the HospitalTemperatureDashboard report in the Active Viewer (see Figure 19-19).

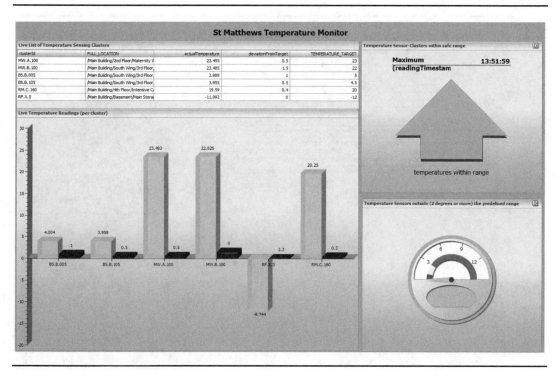

FIGURE 19-19. *Running the Temperature Monitor report—with all systems clear*

The report is based upon two data objects in the Active Data Cache that need to be fed from the JMS queue that itself has its messages published by the CEP application. Therefore, you have to make sure the following have been started to ensure the report will give you anything to monitor:

- The WebLogic Admin server, SOA server, and BAM server
- The CEP server and the CEP applications TemperatureSensorSimulator and TemperatureReadingsProcessor
- The Enterprise Message Source TemperatureFindingsQueue

NOTE
The TemperatureSensorSimulator application that runs in the CEP server to simulate the output from temperature sensors has been tampered with to have it randomly apply incidents to the temperature clusters—the window or door to a room that should stay warm may have been left open (resulting in a gradual drop in temperature), the lid of a refrigerator was not closed properly (resulting in an increasing temperature), or a fire may have started. Our dashboard will help us spot these situations, as is shown in Figure 19-20.

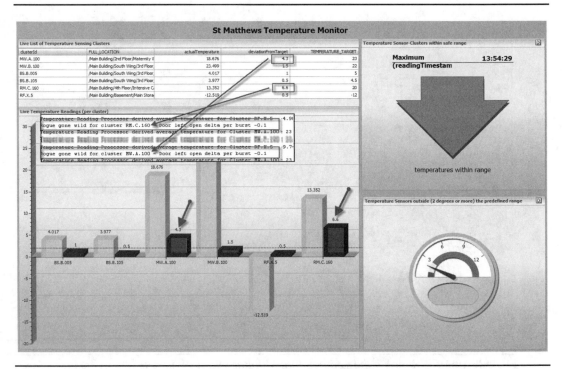

FIGURE 19-20. *Temperature Monitor dashboard with visual indications of exceptions*

Exporting and Migrating the Report

Oracle BAM comes with a component called ICommand. It is a command-line interface on the BAM server that supports a number of administrative operations, including the export and import of data objects, reports, and alert definitions to and from XML files. The XML-based definitions can be moved to different environments and imported into remote BAM server instances.

ICommand is started from the command line in the directory <Oracle Middleware Home>\ Oracle_SOA1\bam\bin. To export the metadata definition of data object TemperatureSensorCluster to a file that can be imported into other BAM environments and include the current data contents as well, we can execute the following command on the command line:

```
icommand -cmd export -file c:\temp\BamExport_DO_TemperatureSensorCluster.xml
 -name /HospitalFacilities/TemperatureSensorCluster
```

The essential connection details for locating and accessing the BAM server are read from the file <Oracle Middleware Home>\Oracle_SOA1\bam\config\BAMICommandConfig.xml by ICommand. If your environment does not use the default username, password, host, or port number for the BAM server, you will have to update this file.

Instead of typing all the commands on the command line, we can create a file that contains a number of ICommand statements and have that "script" executed using the following:

```
icommand -cmdfile c:\temp\icommand_exportDashboard.xml
```

The BAM ICommand Web Service offers a subset of the operations available through the command-line interface. These include exporting reports and importing rows into data objects. The Web Service interface is available at http://host_name:7001/OracleBAMWS/WebServices/ ICommand?WSDL.

Producing an Alert upon Fierce Temperature Deviations

When we have a strong indication of a potential fire, we want BAM to do more than just display the dashboard—even though that provides a strong visual clue as to what might be going on. We want BAM to raise an alert, through the web interface, by sending an e-mail and by calling a Web Service that in turn will start paging the hospital's fire brigade.

BAM has support for alerts that can take various actions when raised. The condition under which the alert is activated is specified through rules. Alerts and their rules can be defined through the Architect as well as the Active Studio.

Defining an Alert Rule

Go now into Architect. Select Alerts from the drop-down list in the upper-left corner and click Create A New Alert. Figure 19-21 illustrates the next steps. Specify the name of the alert, **FireWarning**, and then click Create A Rule. A window appears with the list of various types of rules—some referring to a time schedule that's used to plan certain actions to be taken periodically. Other rules refer to changes and conditions that may be met as a result of those changes. Select "When a data field in a data object meets specified conditions." Click the link "this data field has a condition of x" in the Rule Expression window to open the editor in which to specify the data condition that this rule will be evaluating. The Alert Rule Editor that pops up allows us to configure the expressions that together make up the filter for this rule. In this case, we want the alert be activated when any temperature sensor cluster reports a temperature of over

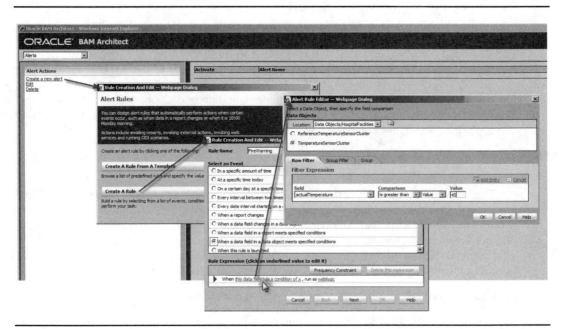

FIGURE 19-21. *Creating a new alert for fire warnings and configuring the associated rule expression*

45 degrees (Celsius, that is, over 110 degrees Fahrenheit!). We select the TemperatureSensorCluster data object, the field actualTemperature, and the comparison operator Is Greater Than. The threshold value we compare against is 45. Click OK to close the editor.

Click Next to go to the Rule Alert Action window. We can specify now what should happen when this alert is triggered. We can select actions by checking the boxes for sending a message or a report via e-mail, for launching another rule, for deleting data object instances, and for calling a Web Service.

We will stick to sending an e-mail message for this alert. Note that the wiki has an example of invoking a Web Service from a BAM alert.

After selecting the action Send A Message Via Email, we are invited to define the message—using field values from the data object. We also have to specify to which user or group we want to send the message. Note that we select users from the WebLogic Identity Store—and rely on the e-mail address configured in the Identity Store as the destination for the e-mail.

After you have finished, click OK to save and immediately activate the alert. Alerts can also be deactivated, in which case they do nothing at all. Figure 19-22 illustrates how to complete defining the FireWarning alert rule.

Alerts in Action

Suppose one of the temperature clusters reports a very high temperature value—in this case in a maternity ward. As soon as the data object for this cluster is updated with the actual temperature value, the alert rule is verified and the alert is raised. That means that the e-mail is sent to the indicated users or groups and the alert is also added to the Alert History, retained within the BAM server, as is shown in Figure 19-23.

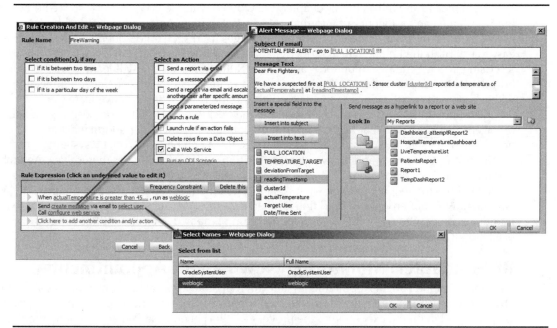

FIGURE 19-22.   *Completing the definition of the FireWarning alert rule*

Integrating SOA Composites into Business Activity Monitoring

SOA composite applications coordinate the execution of business processes or at the very least execute crucial steps in the business processes. A lot of essential information flows through these applications—information that could provide valuable insight for people monitoring the business activities. It seems obvious that the composite applications have a lot to offer to BAM—details on the progress of process instances that help to keep dashboards up to date, and information that BAM can analyze and use to trigger an alert and undertake an action.

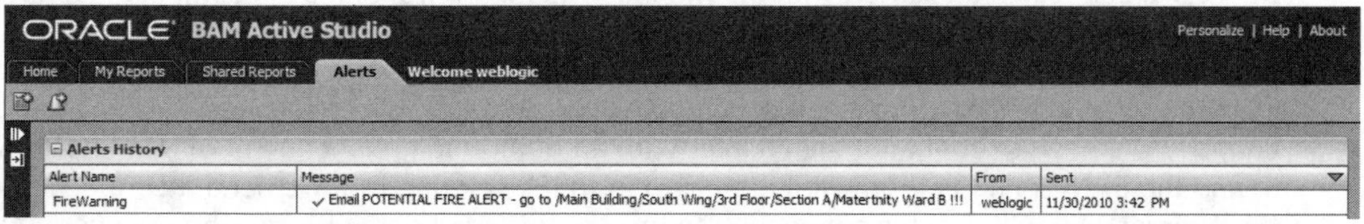

FIGURE 19-23.   *Alert History overview in Active Studio, listing the FireWarning alert that was raised for Maternity Ward B*

In Chapter 12 as well as in this chapter, we worked with the JMS adapter—so we know that the SOA Suite can easily put out information on a JMS queue. And we have seen how BAM can use an external message source to consume messages from such a JMS queue. So it should be easy to establish the link between SOA composites and BAM.

Using JMS is certainly an option—although not the best one. We will learn in this section how the BAM adapter in the SOA Suite provides a more-direct, better-integrated connection from within composite applications to the data objects in the BAM server's Active Data Cache.

In addition to information that is relevant at the business level, SOA composites generate a lot of lower-level trace data that harbors information about the structure, performance, and potentially fault-sensitive areas of the applications. BAM can be used, too, by system administrators to monitor and analyze the applications and their activities themselves. As such, BAM, and the integration from BPEL process components in particular, is a valuable complement to the facilities for keeping track of what is or was going on, as we discussed in Chapter 16. We will see how BPEL sensors can send fine-grained data to BAM. Subsequently, the Monitor Express introduces an easy-to-use infrastructure for monitoring many details about BPEL process execution through BAM.

BAM Adapter: Monitoring New Patient Appointments

As manager of the Patient Appointment Platform, Margaret wants to know as much as she can about how new appointments are created, confirmed, and either cancelled or kept. She wants to keep a close tab on the execution of the process as it has been designed and implemented using SOA concepts and technology. She wants to see if the overall performance of the process meets the business objectives and helps bolster customer satisfaction—and to find out if the process may have some weak spot, an Achilles heel that proves to be a bottleneck when the entire patient appointment flow is handled by the SOA platform.

What better way for her to monitor the execution of the process than through the Business Activity Monitoring, which can provide real-time insight into data gathered directly from the application instances running inside the SOA Suite? In this section, we will create a BAM report that visualizes the Patient Appointment process. Every incoming appointment request is fed into the BAM server, leading to a row in the PatientAppointment data object. When the appointment request goes through meaningful stages—scheduled, confirmed, cancelled, completed (and in the future, perhaps invoiced and paid as well)—the data object will be updated.

We will add some event-processing activity in the BAM server—to have it trigger an alert when some business performance indicator is not met for a particular appointment. In this particular case, it will detect a non-event—the absence of an expected update to a data object.

Preparing for the Integration Between SOA Suite and BAM

Before we can really get started with the integration to BAM from an SOA composite application, there are a few steps we need to go through.

First of all, the BAM adapter is another one of the JCA connectors, like the JMS, AQ, and Database adapters, that is managed outside the SOA Suite from the WebLogic Administration console. We need to configure the adapter with an outbound connection pool that knows where to find the BAM server and how to connect to it. In JDeveloper, too, we need a connection to the BAM server. We will use this connection to browse for target data objects when we configure the BAM Adapter Services. Instructions for configuring the BAM adapter and the BAM server connection in JDeveloper are provided in the online chapter complement.

Open the SOA composite application PatientAppointmentService to which we are going to add integration with BAM. Next, click the BAM Server connection in the Resource Palette and from its context menu select the option Add To Application.

Preparing the BAM Side of Things

In order to specify through a BAM adapter service which data objects should be updated, we need first to make sure that these objects actually exist by defining them through the BAM Architect.

Enter BAM Architect and create a new folder called **PatientAppointmentsPlatform** that will be the container for data objects that are related to appointments. Note that we will take a simplistic approach here, where we, for example, do not link to other information than the data delivered from the SOA composite application.

Create a new data object called **PatientAppointment** and specify the following fields (see Figure 19-24): AppointmentIdentifier, Name, Gender, Birthdate, City, State, TypeOfAppointment, AppointmentRequestDate, AppointmentStatus, StatusTimestamp, AppointmentDateTime, and Priority.

Add a calculated field called **Age** that will calculate the patient's age from his or her birthdate. Specify the formula for this field as follows:

```
Year(now()) - Year(Birthdate) + ( Month(now()) - Month(Birthdate))/12
```

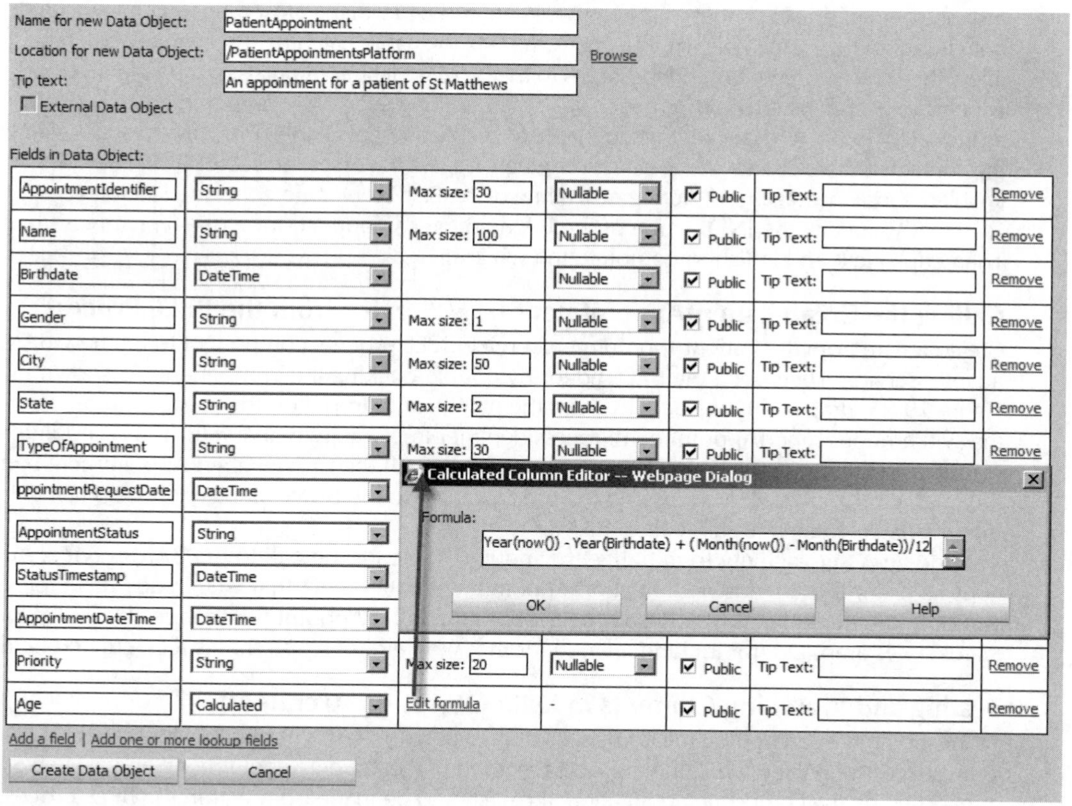

FIGURE 19-24. *The PatientAppointment data object in BAM Architect*

With these preparations done, we can start on the BAM adapter service that will create and update the data in the PatientAppointment data object.

Creating the CreatePatientAppointment BAM Adapter Service

The new PatientAppointments will be sent to the BAM Active Data Cache from within the BPEL component PatientAppointmentService using a BAM adapter service. As soon as the appointment identifier is reported back to the consumer of the service, the BAM adapter service is invoked to instantiate the new PatientAppointment instance in the ADC. We need to create the BAM adapter service, wire it to the BPEL component, and add the Invoke activity in the BPEL process.

BAM adapter services can be created in the Composite Editor or in the BPEL process editor, just like other adapter services. The BAM adapter is always used in an outbound fashion: The composite calls out to BAM, never the other way round—although a BAM alert can invoke a Web Service that can be a public service exposed by an SOA composite application.

Open the Composite Editor for the PatientAppointmentService application and add a BAM adapter service to the composite in the External References lane. Call the service **CreatePatientAppointment**. Select the BAM server connection that we created earlier in the IDE and added to the application. Click the Browse button to access the BAM server through the connection to locate the data object that this service will be targeting. Select the PatientAppoinment object.

Choose the operation Insert—we will be using this service exclusively to create PatientAppointment instances. Note, however, that a BAM service can also perform the Upsert operation—which does both Insert and Update. Make sure to check the box to enable batching. By enabling batching, we allow the SOA container to send messages to the BAM container in bursts of multiple messages— which can be much better performance-wise than sending every little burp immediately over. At least as important is that it means that when the BAM server is not available, the messages are retained by the container to be fed into the BAM server when it again becomes available. When batching is not enabled, those messages sent during downtime of the BAM server are gone and lost forever.

Finally, specify the JNDI name of the BAM adapter's connection pool—typically eis/bam/rmi. Then click Next and Finish to complete the wizard.

Calling the CreatePatientAppointment BAM Service from the BPEL Process

Create a wire from the PatientAppointmentService BPEL process component to the new BAM adapter service. Then open the BPEL editor by double-clicking the component. As shown in Figure 19-25, drag an Invoke activity from the palette and drop it on the process, immediately after the synchronous reportAppointmentProcessIdentifier Reply activity that returns the appointment identifier to the consumer. Associate this invoke step with the CreatePatientAppointment partner link that was created when we wired the BPEL process to the BAM adapter service. Have a local input variable created for the call to BAM.

Add an Assign activity to initialize the input variable for the call to the BAM service. Add copy steps for those fields of the PatientAppointment data object that we already have relevant values for. Include the currentDataTime for both the InitialAppointmentRequestDate and the StatusTimestamp. Do not include a value for the Age field, because that is a calculated field.

Testing and Watching Contents in Data Object (in Architect)

At this point, we can deploy the composite application and test whether the integration of BAM has been successful. When we call the process method of the PatientAppointmentService Web Service as exposed by the composite application, a call should be made from within the BPEL process to the BAM adapter service that should lead to the creation of a row in the data object. That fact can be inspected in the BAM Architect by looking at the contents of the PatientAppointment data object, as Figure 19-26 illustrates.

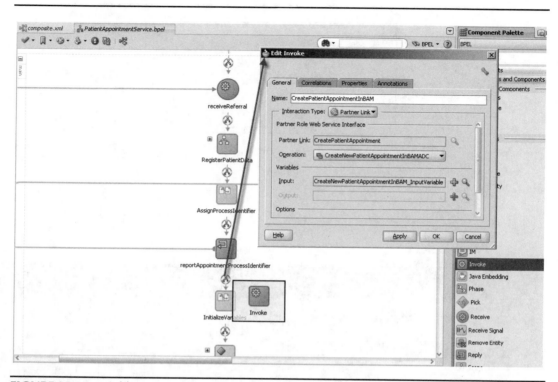

FIGURE 19-25.   *Adding an Invoke of the BAM CreatePatientAppointment service to the BPEL process*

Sending Appointment Status Updates to BAM

Margaret feels that while we have made a good start, she would like the composite application to provide a little bit more information about the Patient Appointment process to the BAM server. She is primarily interested in the time it takes to get an appointment from one status to the next—so she can try to identify bottlenecks in the process and, of course, alert staff to appointment requests that are not serviced within the agreed response time. Therefore, she asks us as SOA developers to extend the BPEL process with calls to the BAM server whenever the status of an appointment changes. These calls should lead to updates of the PatientAppointment objects that were created earlier in the same process instance.

Adding the BAM Adapter Service for Updating the PatientAppointment Data Object

In the Composite Editor, we drag a BAM adapter from the Component Palette to the references area. The BAM Adapter Service Wizard appears (see Figure 19-27) to have us configure this service that will update existing rows in the PatientAppointment data object. Call the new service **UpdatePatientAppointment**. Select Update as the operation this time. Select the field AppointmentIdentifier as the identifier for the PatientAppointment in the BAM server that should be updated.

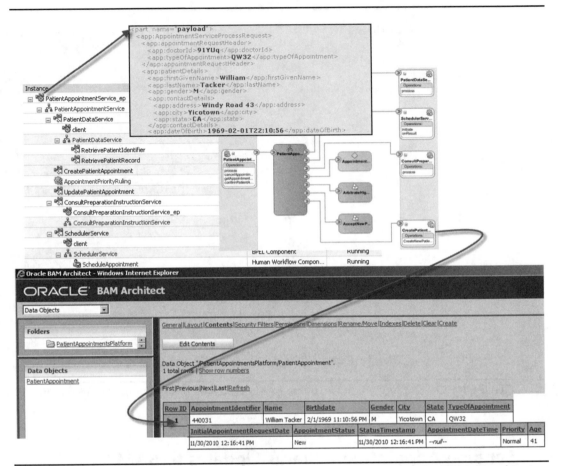

FIGURE 19-26. *The call to the PatientAppointmentService is reported to the BAM data object.*

The UpdatePatientAppointment partner link will be invoked on several occasions during the BPEL process (see Figure 19-28):

- **Right after the scheduling service completes** The status goes from New to Scheduled.

- **When a cancellation of the appointment is received** The status becomes Cancelled.

- **When the patient shows up** The status is set to Completed.

- **Upon a patient no-show** The status is updated to NoShow.

These invokes only need to set a few elements in the input variable: the appointment identifier, the new status, and the current date time to set the StatusTimestamp in the data object. When the appointment has been scheduled, the scheduled time is passed to the AppointmentDateTime field. When the priority has been established, that fact should be forwarded to BAM as well—without status change.

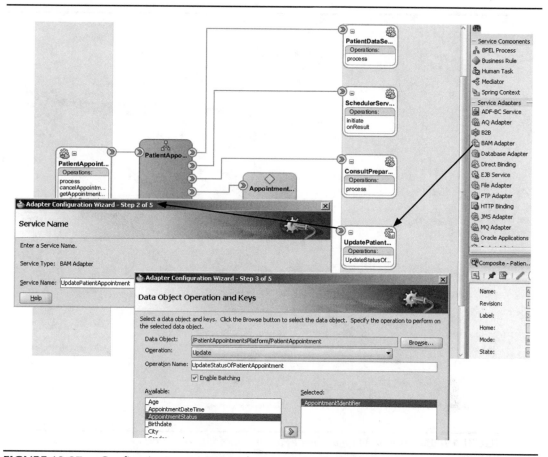

FIGURE 19-27. *Configuring a new BAM adapter service for updating the PatientAppointment data object*

It is time now to create that dashboard that Margaret has in mind. The SOA composite application is delivering through the two BAM adapter services all the information we need to provide real-time insight into the patient appointment process. Let's go to the BAM Active Studio.

Creating the St. Matthews Appointment Dashboard

Open Active Studio and create new report (choose a style with two columns and two tiles in the right column). Create a view type of container in the left column and select the four-tile layout for this container. Type **St. Matthews Appointment Process Monitor** as the report title.

We can include many different view types in the report. We will discuss a few simple ones to get started. We can always extend and refine based on the feedback we will get from Margaret on our first attempt.

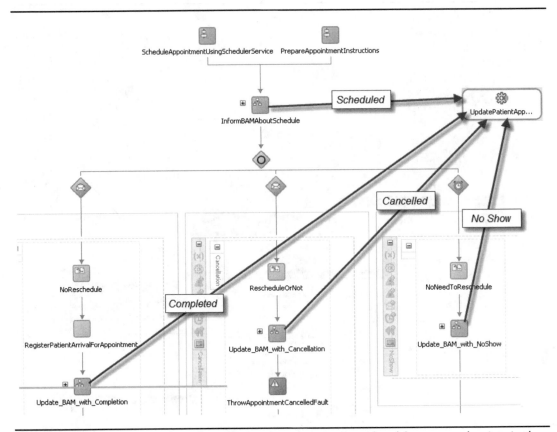

FIGURE 19-28. *The BAM data object PatientAppointment is updated from several points in the BPEL process.*

Live List of Appointment Inserts and Updates

Let's start with a simple one: a live list of the most recent new appointments and status updates to existing ones, ordered by the time of the most recent update, with the latest updates first. Double-click the tile in the lower-right corner, select the Updating Ordered List view type, and select the PatientAppointment data object. Check the boxes for the fields AppointmentIdentifier, AppointmentStatus, StatusTimestamp, Priority, and Age. Specify a sort order by StatusTimestamp, descending. Note that you toggle ascending and descending by clicking the AZ or ZA icon in the Sorted Fields list in the Sort tab. Go to the TopN tab to specify that we only want the last 25 appointment changes to be displayed.

Go to the Properties section and set a title for the view Live Appointment Updates. Go to the Value Format tab and select the StatusTimestamp field in the drop-down list. Select the Time category and set the Type to the time format you prefer. Close the view editor.

Appointment Summary per Status

The upper-right tile is reserved for a summary of the appointments, per status. Choose the 3-D bar chart for this tile. Pick the PatientAppointment data object, specify Group By AppointmentStatus, and then select the AppointmentIdentifier field in the Chart Values box and select the Count summary function.

This is all it takes to create the bare-bones bar chart. We now can add a filter to base the summary only on a subset of all the appointments (for example, only those that were received in the last month or quarter).

We can also refine the layout of the chart. Let's set the title to Appointment Overview (per status). Set the vertical axis label to # appointments, and make any other refinements you deem appropriate.

Appointments Summary

The first tile is reserved for a small summary, a quick-glance listing of pretty straightforward numbers. The list has an entry for each distinct appointment status value. And each entry contains the number of appointments that currently have that status, the most recent addition to that group, and the ages of the youngest and oldest patients in the group.

The view type used for this tile is the Collapsed List. After clicking the icon for this view type and selecting the PatientAppointment data object, you come to the Data Fields page. Select AppointmentStatus, StatusTimestamp, AppointmentIdentifier, and Age. We will group by the status field, so that field does not need a summary function. The others, however, do. Select the StatusTimestamp field and check the box for Maximum. Pick Count for AppointmentIdentifier and both Minimum and Maximum for Age. Set a proper title on the General tab in the properties section—something like **Summary of Appointments per status**. We need to specify better column headings for all fields and a nicer-looking display format for MAX StatusTimestamp. Go to the Text & Align tab for the headings and to Value Format to set the pretty time format.

Priority Distribution Pie Chart

We focus next on the second tile in the left column. Here we want a quick overview of the priority distribution of the appointment requests. The assumption that drives the appointment process is that the number of high-priority appointment requests is about 10 percent. In Chapter 8, we enlisted the Business Rule service engine to help establish priorities, based on a number of input parameters. It is quite important to Margaret to see whether that has helped to drive down the percentage of appointments that are assigned high priority—as those appointments get preferential scheduling, blocking the way for lower-priority requests. A simple pie chart will be used to show the distribution of the appointments over the three priority values: low, normal, and high.

Click the Pie Chart icon. Select the data object as before. Select Priority to group by and also Priority as the chart value—associated with the Count summary function. Figure 19-29 demonstrates this, and the next steps.

Set the title for this view—for example, **Priority Distribution**—and go to the Data Labels tab to mark the check box Series Name. This will make sure that the value of the priority is displayed in the pie chart.

Keeping an Eye on the Unscheduled Appointments

Appointment requests that have not yet been scheduled are not a good thing. There are bound to be some, but their number should be kept small and manageable. Of course, the more important KPI here is the actual time between the reception of the request and the moment of scheduling.

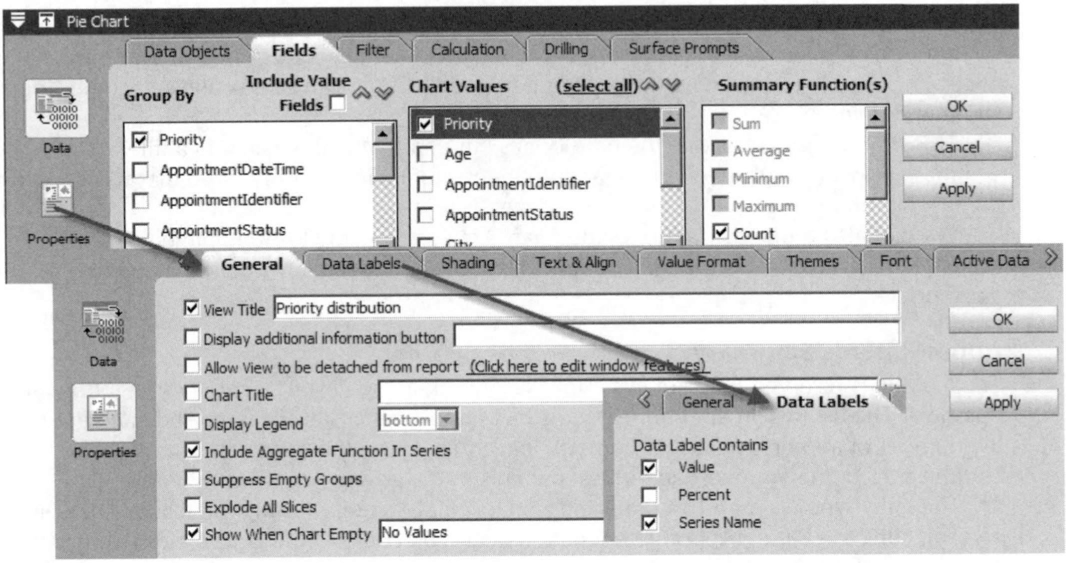

FIGURE 19-29. *Creating the Appointment Priority distribution pie chart*

First, though, we look at a simpler metric: the number of open, unscheduled requests. We will create a range gauge in the third tile on the left that shows the current number of new (new means unscheduled) appointments—against the predefined range values.

Click the Range Gauge icon to set the view type for this tile (see Figure 19-30). Select the PatientAppointment data object and then select the AppointmentIdentifier field and the Count aggregation operator as the KPI drivers. Select them again to provide the bottom label. Type **Number**

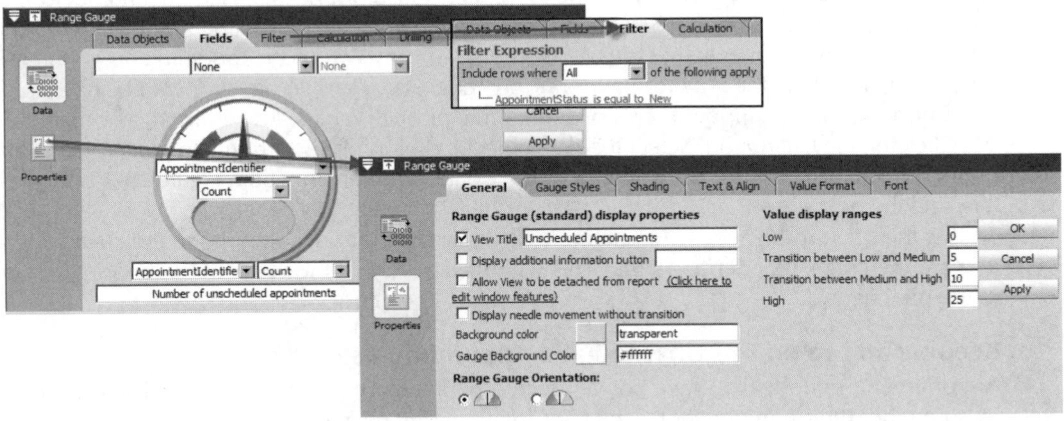

FIGURE 19-30. *Configuring the Range Gauge for unscheduled appointments*

of unscheduled appointments for the bottom title. Define a filter that only accepts rows for which the AppointmentStatus is equal to New—as those are the appointments that we want to count.

In the General tab in the properties section, type a nicer title for the view—for example, **Unscheduled Appointments**. More importantly, schedule the ranges and threshold values for the gauge—normally depending on the KPIs agreed upon with the business. Here we use 5 as the boundary between the green and the yellow zone, and 10 for the transition to the red zone of imminent danger.

Time and Again: New Appointment Requests

The final tile will display a bar chart with the number of new appointment requests per quarter time slot. This view will offer quick insight in the evolution over time: Is the pressure mounting, is the rate of new requests constant, or are the numbers going down?

Select the Bar Chart icon, select the PatientAppointment data object, and then select InitialAppointmentRequestDate in the Group By box. With that field selected, the Time Groups area appears. Mark the check box Continuous Time Series. Select Minute for Time Unit and set the quantity to 15 (minutes). Make sure the radio button Use Time Series is selected. Select the AppointmentIdentifier as the chart value. With that field selected, select the Count summary function.

Go to the properties, and after typing a better title on the General tab, go to the Value Format tab (see Figure 19-31). Select the field InitialAppointmentRequestDate. Select TimeUnit in the Category list box, and select Hour, Minute in the Type box. Thus, we specify the display format that is used for the time displayed under the bars as HH:MM (for example, 12:15 or 3:45).

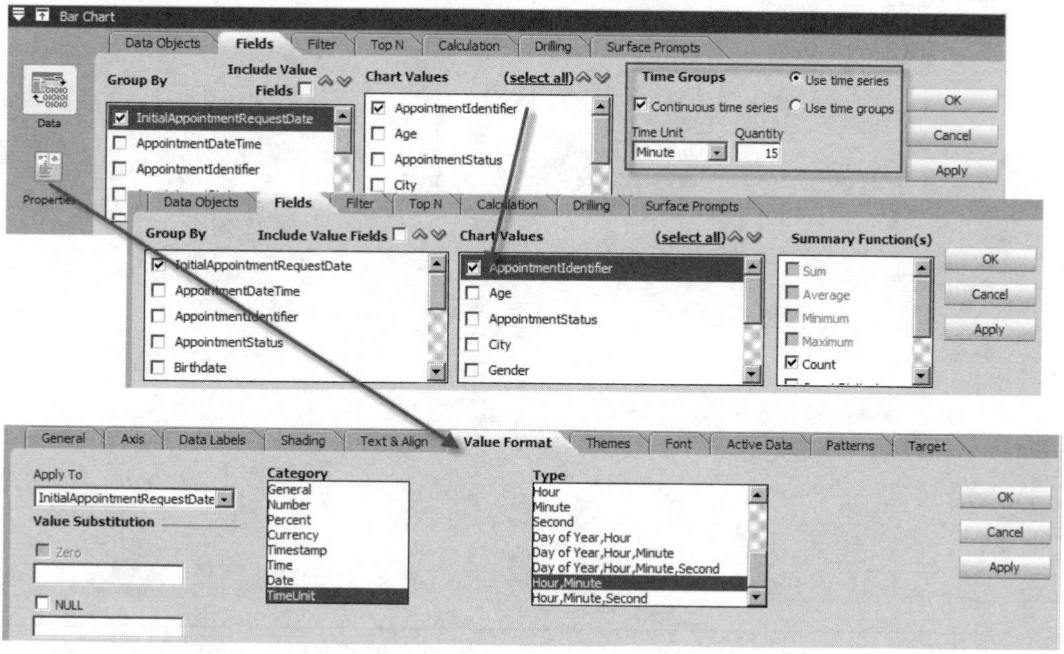

FIGURE 19-31. *Bar chart with appointments count per 15-minute time unit*

Saving and Testing the Appointments Dashboard

Save the report as StMatthewsAppointmentDashboard. Open the Active Viewer and select the newly created report. Depending on the appointment request that your PatientAppointmentService is and has been processing, the report will show different metrics (see Figure 19-32).

You may want to use ICommand to save the definition of the report and load into a version control environment. From personal experience, I can inform you of the fact that report definitions are easily inadvertently changed and even lost—so some safeguarding is worth considering.

BAM Detecting the Scheduling Non-Event

Non-events—or the absence of an expected event—can be quite telling, as we have seen earlier in this chapter (death of sensor) as well as in Chapter 9 on the Event Delivery Network. The Business Activity Monitoring can also be used to identify non-events, as we will see shortly. In this case, Margaret has stated that she wants to be notified whenever an appointment request goes without scheduling for longer than three days. It is against the performance criteria that have been agreed upon with the business to keep patients waiting for longer than 96 hours—and Margaret secretly considers 72 hours an attainable and more desirable target. By getting notified after three days, she also has a window of 24 hours to prevent such appointments from actually going over the real business threshold.

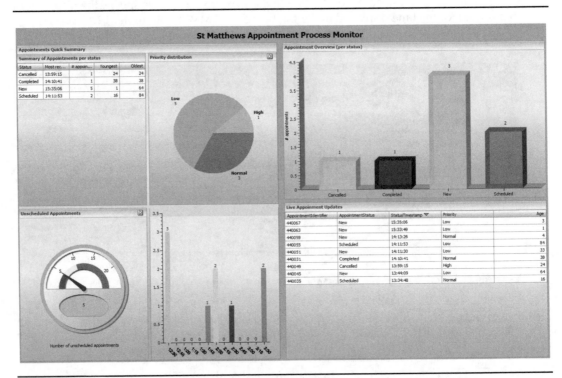

FIGURE 19-32. *The St. Matthews Appointment Process Monitor report in BAM*

You probably have long seen the non-event coming: How do we know an appointment request has not been serviced for 72 hours? Because the scheduling event that would promote the appointment from the "new" to the "scheduled" status never happened. If we spot that non-event, we have trapped the appointment request that we should tell Margaret about.

The steps to set up a BAM alert rule for such a non-event are straightforward. The most important part is the creation of a calculated field that sets the time at which the expected event should have happened. The rule then compares this date with the current date for all appointments that still have the status "new." Any new appointment for which the "expected event date" is in the past has undergone the non-event (that is, has not been scheduled while the deadline has come and gone).

Adding the SchedulingDeadline Field

Go into the BAM Architect. Select the PatientAppointment data object and click Layout. Click the Edit Layout button and then click the link Add A Field. Enter **SchedulingDeadline** as the name for the field. Select the Calculated type from the drop-down list.

Click Edit Formula and specify the expression for calculating this field as follows:

```
DateAdd( InitialAppointmentRequestDate, 0,0,0,72,0,0,0)
```

This will calculate the value of SchedulingDeadline by adding 72 hours to the value of InitialAppointmentRequestDate. This value can be used subsequently in the alert rule.

Creating the Alert Rule

While still in the BAM Architect, select Alerts in the drop-down list in the upper-left corner. Click the link Create A New Alert and then click Create A Rule. The next steps are illustrated in Figure 19-33. Select the radio button "When a data field in a data object meets specified conditions." Select the PatientAppointment data object and then add a new entry in the Filter Expression pane for the

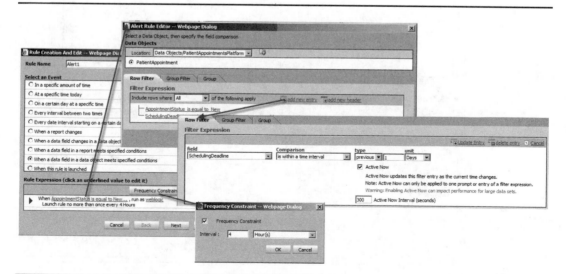

FIGURE 19-33. *Creating the non-event alert for not scheduling the appointment (on time)*

row filter. This entry specifies that the value of AppointmentStatus must be equal to New in order for this alert to trigger. The second entry makes this more specific, by filtering on rows where the value of SchedulingDeadline is in the past. Create this entry, select the SchedulingDeadline field, and select "is within a time interval" as the comparison operator. Then select "previous" as we look for dates in the past. The unit can be set to Days—the issue should be resolved before the deadline is more than one day in the past. Check the box for Active Now because we want to make "one day in the past" relative from the current day.

Click the Frequency Constraint button to have this alert activated only once every four hours for a particular appointment. Then click Next to go and configure the actions to be taken when this alert is triggered, as shown in Figure 19-34.

Select the action Send A Message Via Email. Specify the text for the mail message as well as the recipient (Margaret, of course). The message can contain dynamic values taken from the PatientAppointment data object for which the alert triggers.

Click the OK button to create the alert rule and make it immediately active. From this moment on, Margaret will know when an appointment goes unscheduled for more than 72 hours.

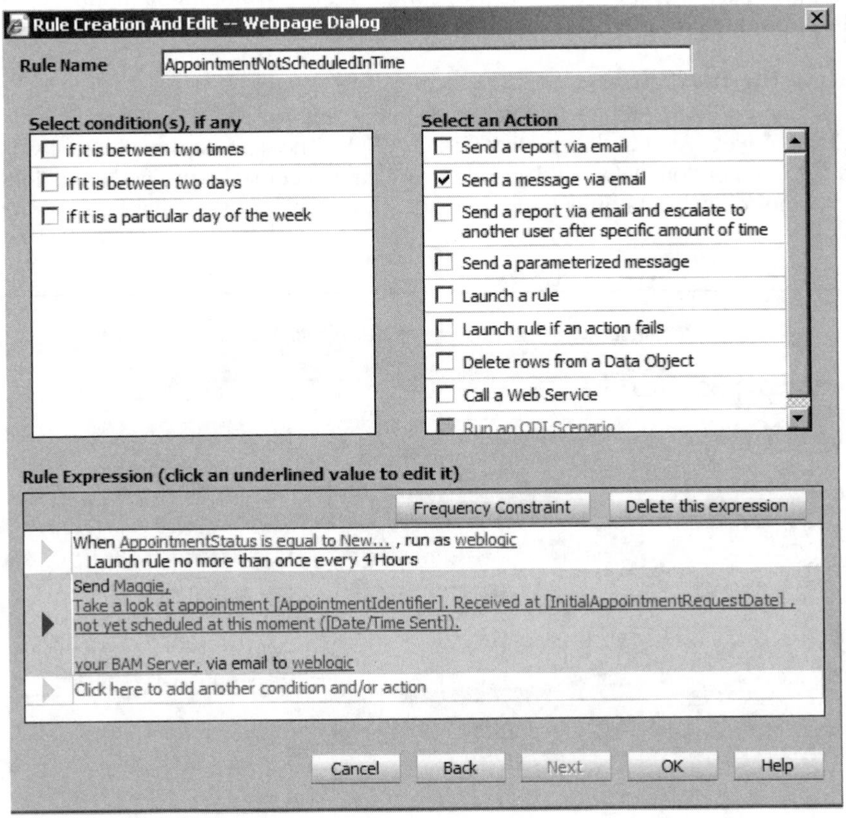

FIGURE 19-34. *Specifying the action for the non-event alert for not scheduling the appointment*

To test this alert, you could go into the BAM Architect, look at the content of the PatientAppointment data object, and update a row to have the status New and an initial appointment request date set to a date between 72 hours and 96 hours in the past. Then in the Active Studio look at the list of alerts to see whether our change in the data object did indeed activate the alert.

Fine-grained BPEL Tracking Using BAM Sensor Actions

Chapter 16 described the various ways in which we can learn what's going on (or has been going on) inside the SOA Suite. It showed how we can track running instances of composites as well as completed instances, following the message flow from component to component and depending on the audit-level settings even within components. We can learn about the payload of the messages—and how it changes—while flowing through the composites and through the components.

The FMW Control lets us query instances on their state, start time, or end time, and on the values of composite sensors. The console also provides access to the logging files where more raw trace details can be found. Additionally, the SOA Suite exposes a Java API through which we can query and retrieve information about composite instances.

We can extend the logging from within composites using Mediator Java callouts, human task Java callbacks, BPEL Embedded Java, and logging statements in Business Rule and Spring components. BPEL processes offer one further option to have their progress monitored, namely, through sensors. Using these BPEL sensors, we can collect information about the evolution of variable values or the time spent in scopes or activities. The sensors can publish information to a JMS queue, have it stored in a database, or update a BAM data object, as we will now see.

Introducing the BAM Sensor Action

The sensors for BPEL processes were first introduced in Chapter 16. We have seen how sensors can be attached to a BPEL process to report on activities and variables as well as faults. The sensors can emit different metadata about the process instance in which they are triggered, and they specifically report about the activity or variable they have been associated with. The information is reported to various output channels. And we will see now how a BAM data object can be one of those channels.

In Chapter 16, we created sensors and sensor actions that were attached to those sensors. We ignored at that time the special sensor action called BAM Sensor Action. Now that we have been introduced to BAM, we are ready to take on this special sensor action. In short, BAM Sensor Action provides us with a lightweight manner to have a BPEL process insert or update a BAM data object (lightweight in the sense that we do not need to configure a BAM adapter service to achieve this flow of data to BAM). Additionally, we do not make changes to the composite definition or even the BPEL process definition, because the definition of the sensors and the sensor actions, as well as the special configuration data and the mapping from the sensor variable and metadata to the BAM data object, are all stored outside the process in separate files. Also note that we have access to various metadata in the BAM sensor action that we do not have access to in normal BPEL activities—such as the time it took to complete an activity.

BAM sensor actions are typically used to gather information about the BPEL process itself and are more for monitoring the technical aspects of the BPEL process than the business aspects of it—although there is no clear distinction between the two, of course. Tracking the time it takes to get a response from an external service or the duration of a human task is a typical example of a metric sent to BAM from a sensor.

Note that the BAM adapter needs to be configured before the BAM sensor action can be used (just like it needs to be in order to use a BAM adapter service).

Monitoring the Service Level of the Patient Data Service

The PatientAppointmentService is but one of many applications that heavily depends on the PatientDataService. Various consumers throughout the hospital make use of this service—and more seem to be on the way. St. Matthews has not been very rigorous about defining, let alone monitoring and enforcing, Service Level Agreements. However, as we discussed in the previous chapter when we spoke about governance, we cannot simply leave the service levels to assumptions, good intentions, and intuitive impressions of actual performance. We need to monitor what exactly is going on—and then start making (requests for) improvements if those are required.

In this case, instead of asking the owner of the external service we invoke from our application, we will use the sensor mechanism linked to BAM to collect statistics about service performance ourselves.

We need to create the data object in the BAM server that we can send the statistics to in the BAM sensor action. Based on this object, we probably would like to create a report that visualizes the details for the activities that we monitor in this way.

In the BPEL process component, we first add a sensor to the RetrievePatientData Invoke activity. Then we create a sensor action that we associate with this sensor. The sensor action is actually a BAM sensor action that performs an Upsert on a BAM data object. We select the target data object and then create an XSL file to map the metadata available in the Activity Sensor to the data object.

Creating the BAM Data Object BPELActivityMonitor

Go into the BAM Architect. Create a new Data Object called **BPELActivityMonitor**. Specify the fields for this object, including the name of the composite application and the activity, the application instance identifier, the duration for executing the activity, and the time at which the activity was completed.

Creating and Attaching a BPEL Activity Sensor to the Invoke Activity

Open the BPEL Process editor for PatientAppointmentService. To activate the Monitor view mode, click on the Monitor button in the top-right corner (see Figure 19-35). Right-click the activity RetrievePatientData. From the context menu, select the option Create Sensor. Enter a name for the sensor—for example, **RetrieveData_Invoke_PatientDataService**. Select the Completion value from the Evaluation Time drop-down. We need to associate the sensor with a variable—even though in this particular case we do not need any values from the variable. Select the payload from the patient variable. Click OK to create the sensor, attached to the Invoke activity. This is half the work in the BPEL process—creating the BAM sensor action is the other half.

Creating the BAM Sensor Action for the Activity Sensor

The BAM Sensor activity describes what to do when the sensor that the activity is associated with is triggered. We need to indicate that when the sensor is fired, a sensor action is executed that updates a BAM data object.

With the BPEL editor still open, in the Monitor view mode, open the Structure window from the View menu—if it is not already open (see Figure 19-36). Select the node Sensor Actions and

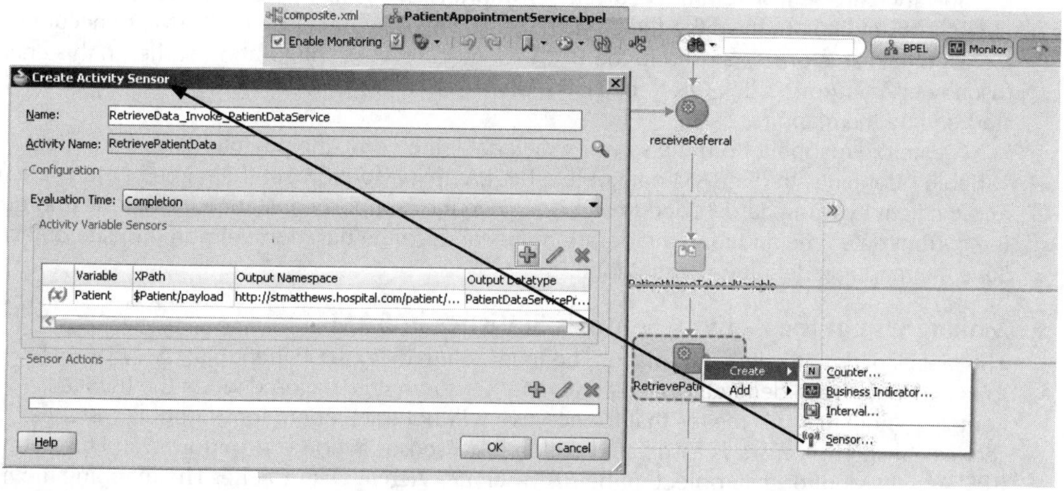

FIGURE 19-35. *Creating the BPEL sensor for the Invoke activity PatientDataService*

from the context menu pick the Create BAM Sensor Action option. The dialog for creating the BAM sensor action appears. Enter the name **FeedActivityMonitor**. Select the sensor for which this will be an action. Select the BPELActivityMonitor data object and select Upsert for the operation and _ApplicationInstanceId as the key field (used for finding the existing row to update).

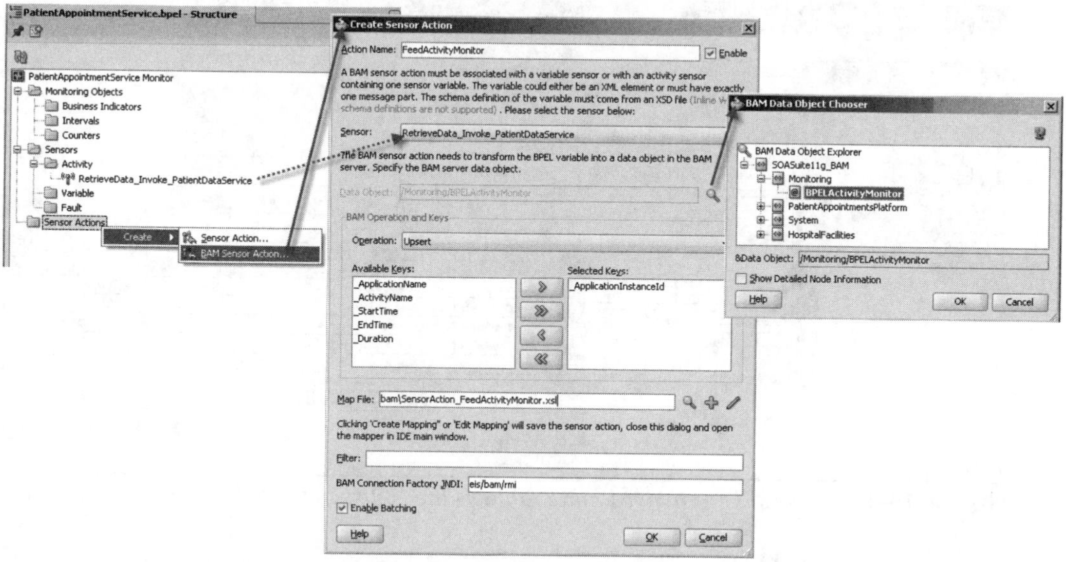

FIGURE 19-36. *Creating the BAM sensor action from the Structure window*

Specify **bam\SensorAction_FeedActivityMonitor.xsl** for the name of the mapping file and click the green icon to have the file created for us. Enter the name for the BAM connection factory—the same one you used in the BAM adapter service configuration earlier in this chapter (usually eis/bam/rmi). Click OK to close the dialog or click the edit icon behind the XSL field to start editing the mapping.

Create the mapping from the sensor's metadata, including the payload with the patient variable's contents, to the BAM data object BPELActivityMonitor. Set the name of the application and the activity using hard-coded text nodes. Map the composite instance ID. Set the end time to the current date time and map the durationInSeconds to the duration field on the data object. Save the mapping definition when done.

Making Use of the Activity Sensor's Statistics in BAM

The pieces of the puzzle are in place: The Invoke activity to the Patient Data Service that we want to analyze has been decorated with an activity sensor that is triggered when the Invoke is complete (note that this means that for now we will not track open, long-running instances of service calls). This sensor is associated with a BAM sensor action that performs an Upsert on the BPELActivityMonitor data object in the BAM server's Active Data Cache. The mapping file makes sure that the application name, activity name, instance ID, and total duration are set, as well as the time of sensor action execution.

We can deploy the composite application with the sensor and sensor action definition files inside. When we next invoke the PatientAppointmentService application, the activity sensor starts doing its job by sending the trace information to the BAM server, the results of which are displayed in Figure 19-37.

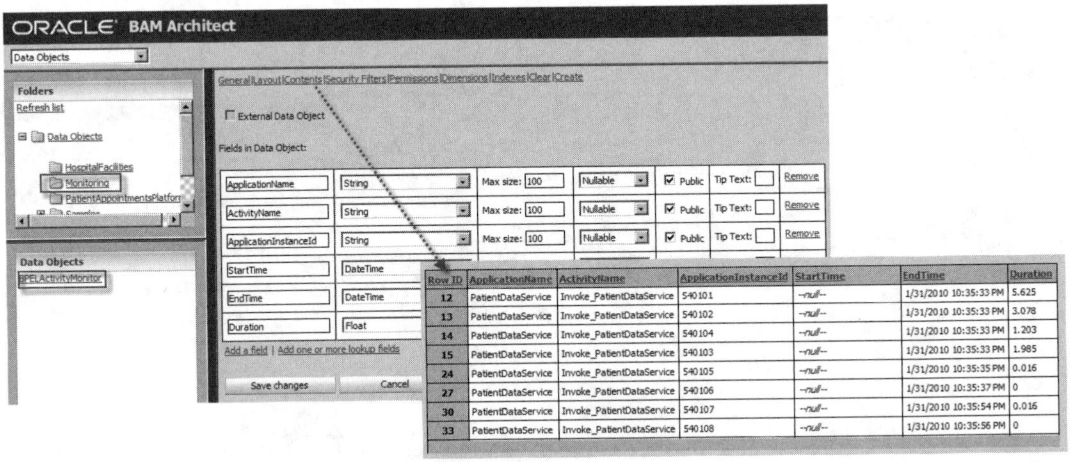

FIGURE 19-37. *The BPELActivityMonitor collects the statistics from the BAM sensor action.*

This information obviously begs for a nice BAM report with live counters and gauges and other visualizations of the calls to the PatientDataService and their key characteristics, such as average processing time, total number (per time slice), and the trend in the number (and the performance). We could easily create such a report—the fact that the data object is fed from BPEL sensors is not relevant at all for the report developer, and we can do the same things as with the Temperature dashboard and the Appointment report. However, the next section introduces the Monitor Express—a feature that perhaps will save us the work.

Tracking BPEL Process Execution Using Business Activity Monitoring and the Monitor Express

Oracle has made life easier even than it already had become with the BAM sensor action. It can still be a lot of work to add all required sensors and sensor actions to a BPEL process and to feed statistics to BAM—and that is where the activity monitors come in. Through a small number of simple, declarative steps we can add straightforward monitoring to the processes. These monitors can count the number of executions for any activity or scope in the BPEL process, they can time the intervals between two events in the process, and they can report the values of BPEL variables at specific points in the BPEL process execution.

When activity monitors are added to a BPEL process, the composite application will deploy the associated data objects to the BAM server—several data objects are generic and apply to all BPEL processes that are monitored, and one is specific to the process for capturing the values of BPEL variables. The monitors feed their data directly into these Monitor Express data objects, as illustrated by Figure 19-38. The BAM samples collection contains a set of predefined Monitor Express reports that visualize the contents of these data objects in a dashboard that helps to track the progress of BPEL processes and helps analyze bottlenecks or sources of unexpected faults.

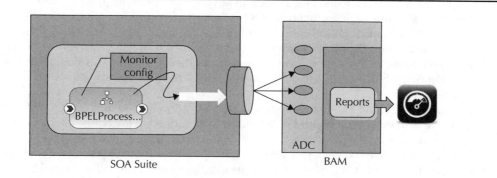

FIGURE 19-38. *Architecture of Monitor Express—BPEL process trace data loaded into the BAM ADC and exposed through a dashboard report*

Applying Monitors to the PatientAppointmentService BPEL Process

We will add three types of activity monitors to the PatientAppointmentService process:

- **Business Indicator** A monitor of type Business Indicator keeps track of the values of one or more metrics, specified through XPath expressions against BPEL variables. Each Business Indicator is evaluated—and reported to BAM—at specific moments, specified through "snapshots." Each snapshot indicates an evaluation event on an activity. That means that we can specify for a Business Indicator to have its values reported for each of the events or stages on an activity. The data object that records the data captured by all metrics in all Business Indicators in a BPEL process is called BI_<Domain_Name>_<Composite_Name>_<BPELPROCESS_Name>.

- **Counter** Counter is attached to an activity, reporting the completion of the specified stages in every execution of the activity to the BAM data object COUNTER, by creating a new row with a timestamp in the SNAPSHOT_TIME field.

- **Interval** Interval is attached to two activities; it will determine the interval between the specified evaluation moments on these activities and report it to the BAM engine, to the INTERVAL data object. The new row in this object may be referenced by two rows in the Business Indicator data object, with the value for the indicator at the start of the interval and at the end of it.

These will send their trace data to the predefined and the custom data objects in the BAM server, to be used in either the shipped or any custom reports.

Preparing the BAM Server

An SOA composite application that is decorated with monitors also contains the required BAM data object definitions. When the application is deployed, these data objects are automatically deployed to the BAM server.

You may want to create these objects in advance (for example, because you want to create reports or alert rules against them). The BAM Samples directory contains a sample Monitor Express application. This application also contains the data objects as well as a preconfigured BAM report against the Monitor Express objects—providing a generic overview of metrics for BPEL processes, their instances, and the timings for their activities. This sample dashboard can be used out of the box, tweaked to better fit your needs, or serve as inspiration for a report you create yourself.

You can load the Monitor Express sample application, including the data object definitions, using the ICommand command-line interface, as described in the online chapter complement.

When we start adding activity monitors to the BPEL process, two files are added to the application: monitor.config and <BPELComponentName>.monitor. The latter contains the configuration details of all monitor elements that have been attached to the BPEL process. The former indicates the JNDI name of the BAM adapter (default is eis/bam/rmi) and the name of the folder on the BAM server for the Monitor's data objects. You should verify whether the default settings in this file are correct for your environment.

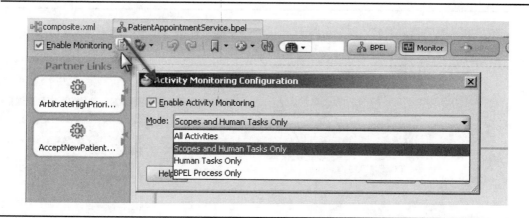

FIGURE 19-39. *Initial setup to enable activity monitoring on a BPEL process*

ActivityMonitoring in a BPEL Process

To enable ActivityMonitoring on a BPEL process, we first need to switch to Monitor mode, just like we have to do for creating sensors and sensor actions. The check box Enable Monitoring should be checked (see Figure 19-39). Then you click the icon next to Enable Monitoring to bring up a dialog that allows us to check Enable Activity Monitoring. We then also get to set the level at which the monitoring will take place.

Adding ActivityMonitoring in the PatientAppointmentService

Let's add ActivityMonitoring to the PatientAppointmentService—to provide us a little more run-time insight into what is going on. We will make use of the three types of monitors available to us. First, we use a Counter to simply count the number of calls we make to the PatientDataService (see Figure 19-40). We can add a call to an activity in a BPEL process by selecting the option Create | Counter from the context menu on the activity (when the BPEL editor is in Monitor mode!). Then we add an Interval monitor that will record the time from the moment the process receives the incoming request to the time it returns the appointment identifier to the caller. The most important activity during that interval is the call to the PatientDataService.

The Interval is created from the context menu on the Receive activity (see Figure 19-41). The dialog that appears allows us to select the end activity that forms the conclusion of the interval. We can specify exactly at which evaluation moment for the begin and end activity the interval should start and end. And we can add Business Indicators to have them evaluated at the start and end of the interval.

Business Indicators can be created in the structure window or from the drop-down menu at the top of the BPEL editor. We will create a Business Indicator for the priority assigned to the appointment. We know that an appointment request comes with a priority indication from the referring doctor. The EstablishAppointmentPriority invokes the Business Rule service component to establish the real priority based on St. Matthews business logic. We would like the activity monitors to report the priority both as initially received and formally established by the Business Rule component.

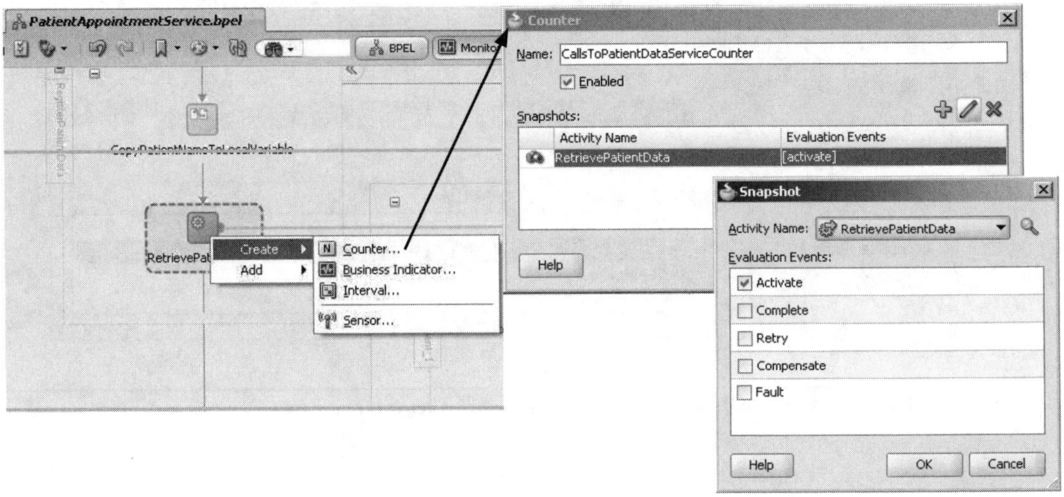

FIGURE 19-40. *Adding a Counter activity monitor to the PatientAppointmentService BPEL process*

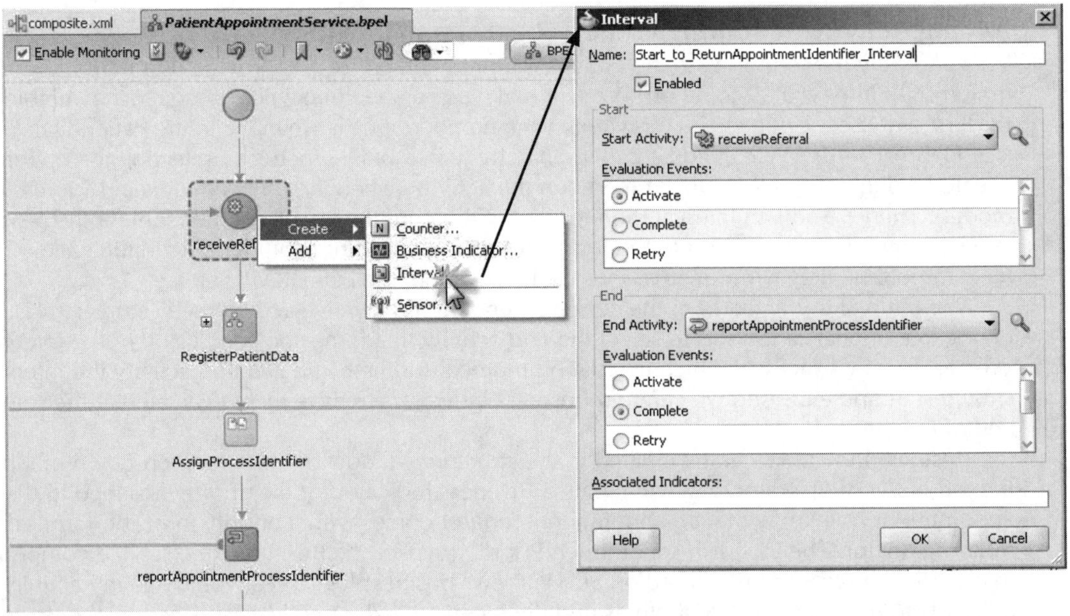

FIGURE 19-41. *Adding an Interval monitor to the PatientAppointmentService BPEL process*

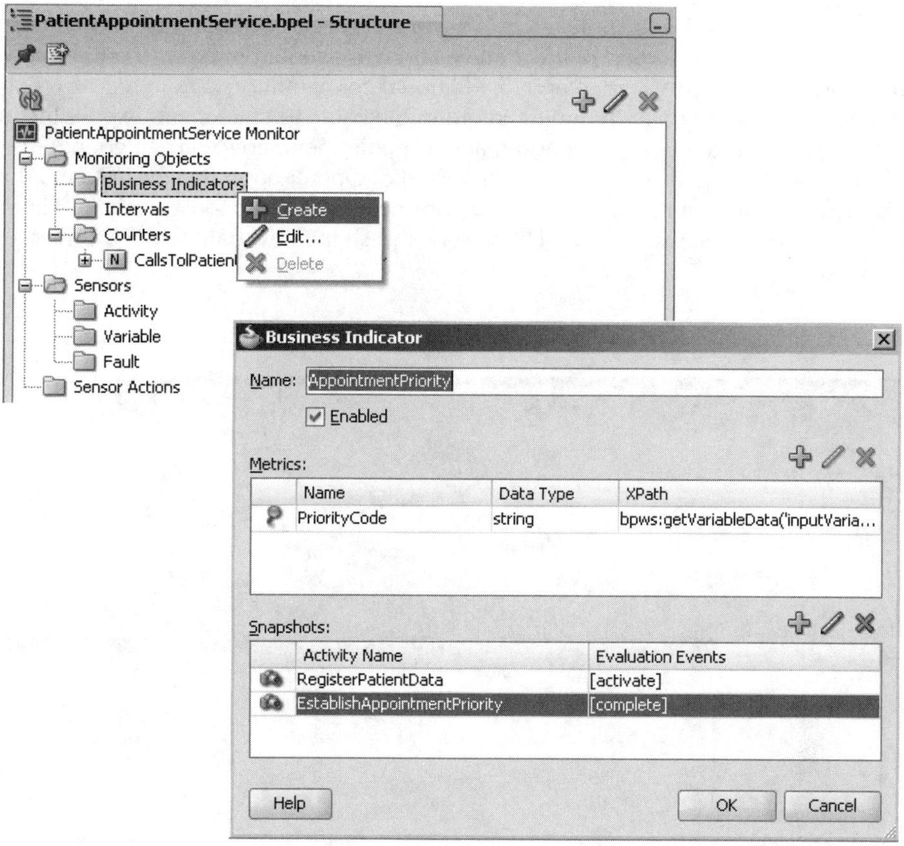

FIGURE 19-42. *Defining the Business Indicator AppointmentPriority in the PatientAppointment Service BPEL process*

Create a new Business Indicator and set the name to **AppointmentPriority** (see Figure 19-42). Create a new metric, called **PriorityCode**, that's based on an XPath expression that queries the priorityCode element in the appointmentRequestHeader element in the inputVariable. We want this metric to be reported at two times: immediately after the start of the process and when the call to the Business Rule component is completed. Therefore, we need to define two snapshots for this indicator. The first is activation of the RegisterPatientData scope—the first scope after the Receive activity (Note: It is recommended not to evaluate variables in a snapshot associated with initial Receive activity because the variables may not have been initialized at that moment and therefore XPath query might fail). The second is the completion of the scope EstablishAppointmentPriority.

With these activity monitors in place, we can go ahead and deploy the SOA composite.

Seeing Monitor Express in Action

Deploy the SOA composite application like you always do. The monitor instructions associated with the BPEL process are part of the archive and will be interpreted by the BPEL service engine that interacts with the BAM adapter. No additional configuration is required—except that the BAM server should be up and running in order to be able to collect and expose the monitor data.

Run several instances of composite PatientAppointmentService. Then go into the BAM web application and navigate to the BAM Active Studio. Open Report Samples/Monitor Express. See the summary of the test runs that you just performed, which will look similar to Figure 19-43. You could run another instance and watch the server push the new data to the browser, updating the dashboard.

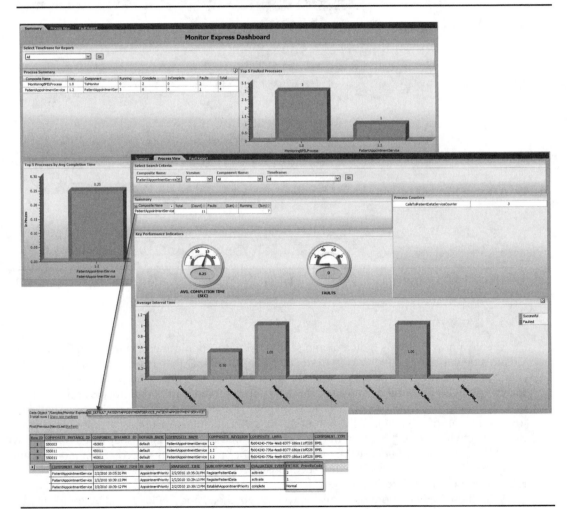

FIGURE 19-43. *The sample BPEL Monitor Express dashboard report after several instances of PatientAppointmentService have been started*

To see the results of the Business Indicator—which are process specific and therefore not part of the generic Monitor Express reports—go into the BAM Architect and check out the data object that was specifically created for this BPEL process. It is called BI_DEFAULT_PATIENTAPPOINTMENTSERVICE_ PATIENTAPPOINTMENTSERVICE. This data object contains two rows for each instance of the PatientAppointmentService BPEL process. The first one shows the value of the Business Indicator (the appointment's priority) at the time of instantiation, and the second one contains the value for that same indicator after the Business Rule component has performed its magic.

Custom BPEL Activity Monitor Reports

The Monitor Express consists of three parts:

- The configuration of the BPEL process that is interpreted by the BPEL engine and translated into appropriate calls via the BAM adapter to update the BAM Active Data Cache

- The definition of the data objects that get updated from the BPEL process

- The sample Monitor Express dashboard report

The first two components are the real boon—without hardly any effort at all, we get several useful BAM data objects that collect tons of information about running BPEL processes. The pre-built report that ships with Monitor Express is just one very generic example of how this information can be exposed in a dashboard.

It is very well possible for us to create our own reports using the Monitor Express data objects. This allows us to prepare reports that are not generic for all possible BPEL process definitions, but specifically geared toward a specific process to provide business users with meaningful insight into that process. Such reports can, of course, include alerts that take action under certain circumstances (for example, when a human task is taking too long to execute, an external service is not available, or the result of a service call has some unexpected, extreme value). BAM and the Monitor Express for BPEL can complement the exception policy framework in the SOA Suite as well as the escalation and notification mechanisms in the Workflow Services.

Summary

This chapter introduced a wide range of subjects, most of them revolving around the central notion of events. An event describes a change somewhere in the world, at a certain moment in time, of a certain type, and usually with some data associated with it. Events can be extremely fine grained, arriving at high volumes and frequencies, or come at a much slower pace with possibly a substantial payload.

This chapter discussed the Complex Event Processor that deals with the challenge of interpreting continuous event streams, detecting patterns and exceptions, and calculating aggregates. It does so using Event Processing Networks that tap into JMS queues or other event channels. These EPNs then apply CQL-based adapters that perform continuous queries on the streams of arriving events. CEP publishes its result in the form of a higher, more advanced level of events, over an outbound JMS channel, for example.

The Oracle BAM (Business Activity Monitoring) server is one of the potential consumers of these promoted business events. It can absorb them into the Active Data Cache, combine them with other data sources, and present real-time dashboards that visualize the current state of affairs as described by the events. BAM dashboards and alerts can be used to monitor for (looming) threshold transgressions, exceptions, and missing events, both visually and through concrete actions such as sending an e-mail notification and invoking a Web Service.

SOA composite applications can integrate tightly with the BAM server, in several ways. One is the use of the BAM adapter, which can be used in composites to report business events and the actual state of data objects. BPEL process components can also make use of the BAM sensor action in BPEL sensors to report events in the execution of BPEL process instances. Another convenient integration between BPEL and BAM is provided by the monitors—Counter, Interval, and Business Indicator—which allow declarative definition of non-intrusive spies to report on the statistics of BPEL process execution. Metrics on the number of executions, the average time required for an activity or service call to complete, and the evolution of values during process instances are published to the BAM data objects and reported in pre-built or custom-developed dashboards.

CHAPTER
20

ADF as UI Glue
(and More) in FMW

ver the past dozen years or so, Oracle has been working on components and infrastructure for enterprise Java applications: Business Components for Java (BC4J) for tight integration with relational databases from Java applications; JavaServer Faces components that help create rich, visually attractive, Ajax-enabled user interfaces; ADF faces; and the Model and Data Binding layer that insulates the Java web application from the underlying business services through data controls on top of various enterprise sources such as a database, content repository, BI database, Web Service, or BAM Active Data Cache. All these capabilities together make up the Oracle Application Development Framework (to be called ADF from now on).

ADF is the strategic framework for developing enterprise Java/JEE applications. In Oracle's view, that applies to the development of custom applications by its customers and also to all Java web applications that it creates itself, to be sold as products to customers. Fusion Applications is the pinnacle in application development at Oracle—and it is built in ADF, along with all the other parts in Fusion Middleware. Modules in other Oracle Applications' offerings—in eBusiness Suite, for example—are also developed using ADF. The Fusion Middleware Enterprise Manager console that we have used throughout this book was also developed with ADF, and the same applies to other run-time user interfaces such as Oracle Business Intelligence, WebCenter Spaces, Universal Content Manager, and, of course, the SOA and BPM Composer, the BPM Worklist application, and the BPM Workspace application that we have used in Chapters 10 and 11.

ADF has a number of special areas of interaction with the SOA Suite—situations in which we can leverage ADF to achieve some additional functionality or productivity. These include the ability to raise events onto the Event Delivery Network from ADF Business Components (ADF BC), the implementation of customized user interfaces for human tasks that can be embedded in the standard BPM Worklist application as well as custom web applications, and the BAM data control, which allows the development of custom dashboards and the integration of BPEL entity variables with ADF BC through an SDO binding.

This chapter will introduce these special integration areas between ADF and the SOA Suite. It will also demonstrate how ADF applications can invoke Web Services exposed by composite applications that run in the SOA Suite. Note that given the range of topics and the sometimes substantial number of steps required to demonstrate an integration point in a running application, this chapter can only scratch the surface. Please take a look at the online chapter complement for detailed descriptions, step-by-step hands-on instructions, and fine-grained screenshots.

Of course, ADF applications, like other Java applications, can leverage the Java and WebService APIs of the SOA Suite—to have business rules applied, human tasks created or manipulated, and composite instances searched and analyzed. Through JMS and other means, ADF applications (again, like any Java application) can leverage complex event processing—both as a consumer and provider of events—and feed information into Business Activity Monitor. These APIs and interactions, however, are not within the scope for this chapter. Appendix D goes a little into the Java and Database APIs, Chapter 12 gave some clues, and the wiki contains a number of examples of interaction from Java (and ADF) applications to the SOA Suite and its service engines.

Very-High-Level Architecture of ADF

ADF applications typically consist of two parts: the Model and the ViewController, implemented in separate JDeveloper projects in a single application. The Model project usually contains the business objects that implement the business logic and provide the business service. These objects frequently have interaction with enterprise resources such as databases, file systems, Web Services, or queuing infrastructures. The ViewController is the part of the application that provides the interface for interaction with external parties, typically end users and sometimes other applications. The ViewController renders the user interface, injecting data that it gets handed by the Model project through the data bindings. A page in the ViewController consists of components that can render or paint themselves. They are, for example, a calendar, a drop-down list, a form input field, or a button. They can make themselves look pretty on the screen and they can typically engage in some form of interaction—click, type, or select. The data content of these components is pulled by the ViewController from the Model, via the data bindings and data controls. Figure 20-1 visualizes the architecture of ADF.

ADF implements its own type of decoupling: It decouples the application—web application, desktop application, or Web Service—from the business service(s) it uses. The business services offer data and operations—usually against enterprise resources such as a database, content repository, files, BAM server, or Web Service (RESTful or SOAP based). These business services can be implemented in various technologies—for example, ADF Business Components (ADF BC), JPA using EclipseLink, and POJOs (Plain-Old Java Objects). However, regardless of the implementation technology, all services can be described in a generic way: They offer data collections that can be iterated over, from which records can be retrieved and removed and into which records can be added or updated. A record is a collection of key-value pairs. Business services can also expose operations that can be invoked to achieve a certain effect and/or retrieve information.

ADF Model is the insulation layer between applications that want to consume the business services and those business services themselves. ADF Model wraps all business services in data controls, abstracting them to the generic interface (just introduced) of data collections, with

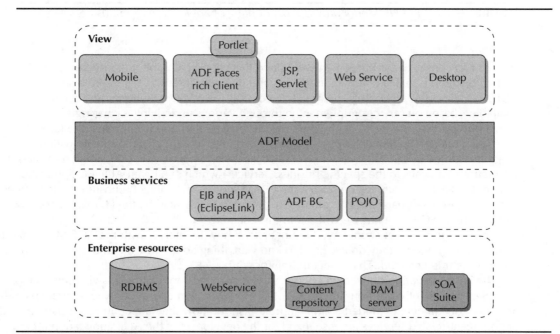

FIGURE 20-1. *Overview of the architecture of ADF*

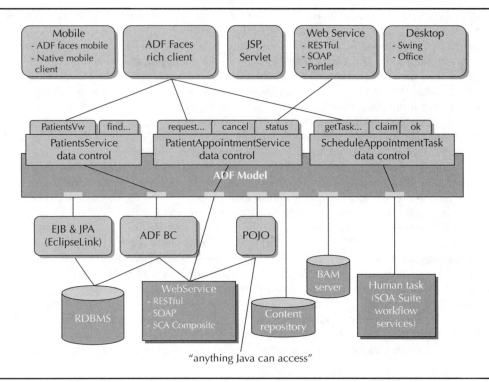

FIGURE 20-2. *The ADF Model provides decoupling of application from business services.*

records that consist of attributes with values and that support a number of standard actions and custom operations that take input parameters and may return results. Figure 20-2 shows how the ADF Model exposes technology-neutral data controls that make collections and operations available—based on services implemented through various underlying technologies.

Applications only have to deal with these basic elements—they do not need to know anything about the implementation of a business control, and they communicate with the data controls exposed by the ADF Model layer in those generic terms. The ADF Model translates these interactions into calls to the specific business service—which can be an ADF BC application, a JPA Entity Manager, a remote Web Service, a BAM server, or a content repository. The business service exposed as a data control can also be a human task hosted by the Human Workflow Services in the SOA Suite, as we will see in this chapter.

Application developers only need to understand how to interact with the ADF Model and the data controls it offers—they do not need to know anything about how the underlying business services are implemented. That's decoupling for you!

The implementation of the data control can be changed—for example, switching from one Web Service to another or from JPA to ADF BC. However, that operation is not entirely painless and is not one frequently undertaken. Figure 20-3 shows how the data controls for patient- and appointment-related services are visualized for the developers of the ADF application for requesting an appointment.

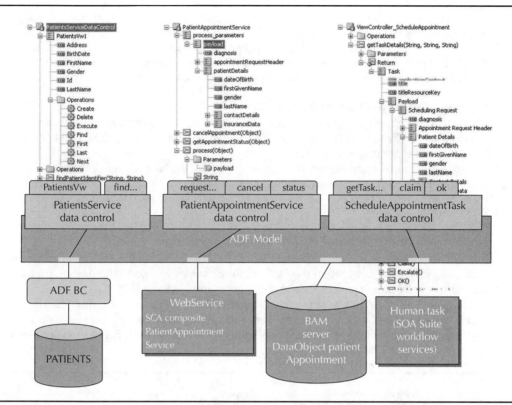

FIGURE 20-3. *Data controls abstracting business services away from applications*

Custom User Interface to Request an Appointment

The first task we will undertake is the development of a custom web application that can be used by general practitioners, by the staff at St. Matthews, and in the near future perhaps by registered patients themselves to request an appointment. This user interface will invoke the PatientAppointmentService published by an SOA composite application running in the SOA Suite. The application gathers patient and appointment details, sends them to the Web Service, and presents the user with the appointment identifier that is received in return.

As a second step, we will extend the application with the ability to check on the status of the appointment and to cancel it with or without a request to reschedule. These extensions all consume operations on the PatientAppointmentService.

Developing the Web Application Using ADF

This application makes use of the WebService data control provided in ADF. This data control interacts with a Web Service based on the WSDL. It completely insulates the application from the SOAP, XML, and other Web Service–specific details. When you create the application against the data control, the work is no different than when the underlying business service would have been a database or content repository.

The essence of the page on which the appointment can be requested lies in the form with input fields that the user completes and submits (to the Web Service). This form is automatically created when the WebService data control is dragged to the page editor. The developer can refine the UI using the rich components, selection lists, built-in validations and derivations, and styling mechanisms to produce an even more attractive and functional page.

Getting Started with an ADF Application

The ADF application for requesting appointments for patients is created in JDeveloper—the development environment not only for SOA applications but also for ADF applications. We need to go through some preparatory steps.

To begin, create a new Fusion Web application from the New Gallery called PatientAppointment FrontEnd. Enter **com.stmatthews.hospital.appointments** for the application package prefix and then click the Finish button. The new application will be created, including two projects: Model and ViewController.

Implementing the Request Appointment Application

To complete these steps, you will need the URL for the WSDL of the PatientAppointmentService. You can get hold of this URL in the FWM Control, when you go to the dashboard for the PatientAppointmentService composite application and click the WSDL icon.

Begin by selecting the Model project. Open the New Gallery, open the Business Tier category node, and select WebServices. Select the item WebService Data Control and click OK. The wizard for creating a data control for a Web Service opens (see Figure 20-4). Enter **PatientAppointmentService** as

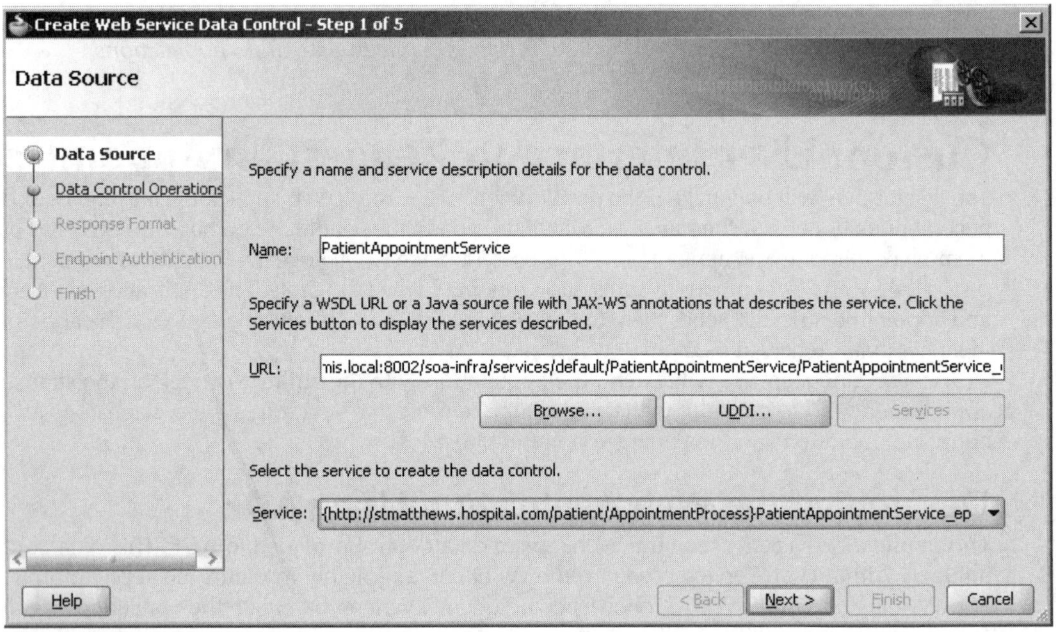

FIGURE 20-4. *Creating the WebService data control for the PatientAppointmentService*

the name and then type or copy and paste the URL of the WSDL to the corresponding field. The PatientAppointmentService is automatically selected because it is the only service exposed in the contract.

Click Next. JDeveloper extracts the names of the operations that are exposed by the Web Service. Select the operations *process, getAppointmentStatus* and *cancelAppointment*. We will only need the operation process for now, but intend to extend the application later on with functionality to check on the status of an appointment or cancel it. You can click Finish because the default settings on the other pages of the wizard are acceptable.

The data control PatientAppointmentService has now been added to the Data Control palette. If the palette is not already visible on the left side in the IDE, you can bring it up from the View menu. The new data control has three methods on offer for binding in webpages as well as three sets of parameters for which input forms can be created—as we shall see shortly. You should realize that for the WebService data control the PatientAppointmentService is just another Web Service—it has not done anything special because it happens to be a service that is exposed from the SOA Suite. The behavior we are getting is the same for any other WSDL-based SOAP Web Service.

Select the ViewController project. Go again to the New Gallery, this time to create the webpage that we will develop for requesting appointments for patients at St. Matthews. Open the Web category and select the JSF node. On the right side, click item JSF Page and click OK. A simple dialog appears for creating a new JSF (JavaServer Faces) page. The only thing you need to type or choose is the name of the file: PatientAppointmentForm.jspx. Click OK to have the page created.

We will focus only on functionality with no regard whatsoever for look and feel. The result will work but will be disappointing, visually speaking. So be prepared!

NOTE
Making the page better looking when it is already doing the job it is supposed to do is much easier than creating a pretty page and trying to wire it up to a Web Service.

On the Data Control palette, expand the node PatientAppointmentService. Expand the node process_parameters. Drag the child node "payload" to the page and drop it in the center facet as an ADF form. The Edit Form Fields dialog appears with entries for all first-level elements in the request message that we need to send to the Web Service. You can define display labels—those are shown as the prompts for the fields. Do not include a Submit button. Click OK when you have nothing more to inspect or to add. The fields are created in the webpage (the .jspx file). At the same time a new file is created called PatientAppointmentFormPageDef.xml. This file defines the data bindings—the usage by the page of the parameters as well as the collections and methods exposed by the PatientAppointmentService data control. All form fields refer in their value attribute to a data-binding element in this page definition and thereby indirectly to an element in the XML request message to be sent to the Web Service.

This first drag-and-drop operation gets us part of the total form we need. We need to separately drag and drop the nested child elements to the page. Through five drag-and-drop operations, we assemble a form that allows entry of all data required for submitting an appointment request to the Web Service. Now we need a button to actually make the request. Select the operation node "process(Object)" in the Data Control palette and drop it on the page as a command button. This results in a button that is wired to submit the request to the Web Service, carrying all the data entered in the form fields as the payload.

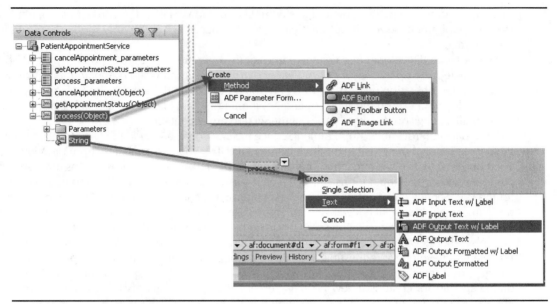

FIGURE 20-5. *Dragging the operation and result to the page and dropping them as a button and output text, respectively*

The PatientAppointmentWebService returns a response message—a simple one, but still one with a meaningful value: the appointment identifier (which we need to enquire after the status of the appointment request and when we want to cancel it). The last thing we will add to the page is an element that displays this return value. Drag the String return value under the process operation node to the page, dropping it behind the button as an output text element with a label. These steps are visualized in Figure 20-5.

Deploying the PatientAppointmentFrontEnd

We will deploy the ADF application to the soa_server1 server, which also runs the SOA Suite. At the top of the Application Navigator window is a drop-down list with the name of the currently opened application—showing PatientAppointmentFrontEnd. Behind that drop-down is a drop-down menu. Select the option Deploy in this menu. The Deployment Wizard appears. Select the same application server connection that we use for deploying SOA composite applications. Then we get the opportunity to indicate the location and other environment characteristics of the PatientAppointmentService that our application accesses through the WebService data control. For our simple development environment, we do not need to make any changes. Click the Deploy button.

When the deployment has finished, we are ready to run the form in a browser window and start submitting appointment requests in our own custom-developed ADF web application. The application is available at the following URL (if you used the same names for the application and the page as used previously):

```
http://localhost:8001/PatientAppointmentFrontEnd-ViewController-context-root/
faces/PatientAppointmentForm.jspx
```

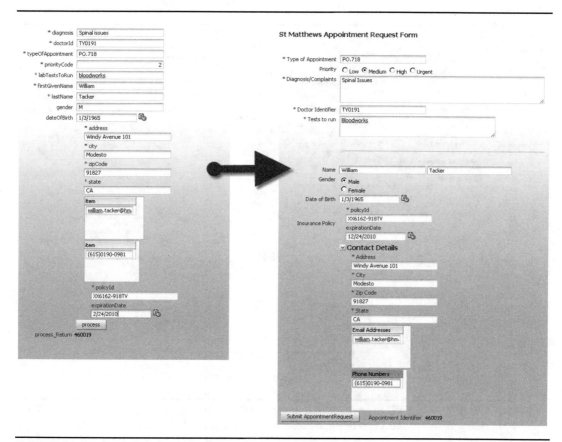

FIGURE 20-6. *Running the PatientAppointmentFrontEnd application and submitting an appointment request*

Let's enter the details for an appointment request on behalf of William Tacker. The user interface is quite straightforward, offering the user very little in the way of easy data entry and selections, automatic derivations, and visual adornments. Figure 20-6 shows, on the left, the original no-thrill form; the right side shows the result of five minutes' worth of decorating the form.

After the user clicks the button and waits for a little while, the synchronous response from the service comes in and the appointment identifier is displayed on the page. A new instance of the PatientAppointmentService was created and is still running after the ADF application has received the appointment identifier. These behind-the-scenes actions are illustrated by Figure 20-7.

Extending the Custom ADF Application: Checking on the Status of the Appointment

Way back in Chapter 6, we implemented the PatientAppointmentService in a BPEL process. This process can be fairly long running, and it is able to accept multiple requests during its lifetime. Using the correlation mechanism, matching the process instance on the appointment identifier, we can invoke operations to check on the status of the appointment and cancel the appointment.

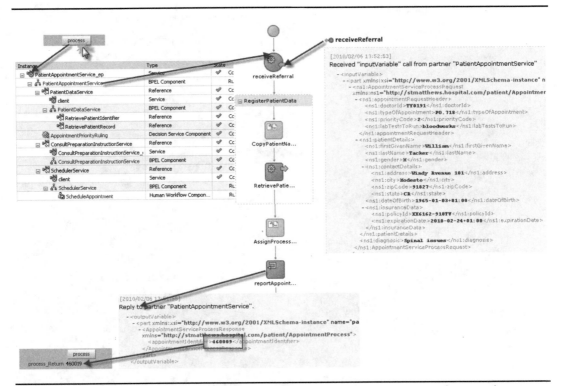

FIGURE 20-7. *The instance of the PatientAppointmentService composite application that was started as a result of the Web Service call from the custom ADF web application*

We will create an entirely new page, as equally unattractive and functional as the previous one, that allows the user to check on the status of an appointment. All the user needs to do is enter the appointment identifier and click the button.

Create a new JSF page called PatientAppointmentStatusCheck.jspx. Open the getAppointmentStatus_parameters node in the Data Control palette and drag the payload to the page and drop it as an ADF form. Next, drag the getAppointmentStatus operation node to the page and drop it as a command button. Finally, drag the plannedSchedule node under the Return node under the getAppointmentStatus operation node to the page and drop it as a form (see Figure 20-8).

The application can be redeployed in the same way as before. When done, we can use the new page to find out what the status is of an appointment we requested. Type the appointment identifier and click the button. The planned schedule—if it is available—is returned from the Web Service and displayed in the page.

ADF and Invoking Web Services
We have seen two examples of creating a custom ADF webpage bound to a Web Service—which could be a service exposed by an SOA composite application. In general, it is quite

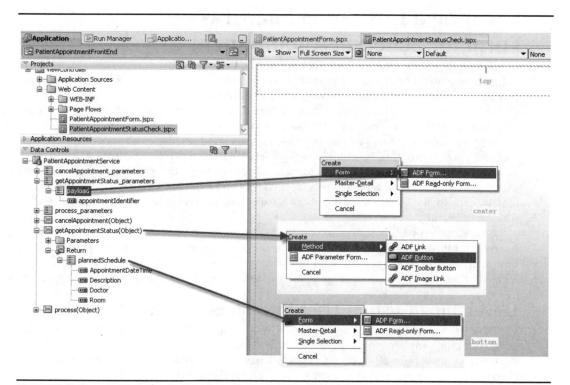

FIGURE 20-8. *Putting the PatientAppointmentStatusCheck form together using three drag-and-drop operations*

simple to make use of any Web Service and also any SOA composite application. ADF helps us to create the form elements required to collect the data for invoking the Web Service and displaying the response from the service. It also takes care of all the technical details for actually making the call.

The ADF page developer hardly has to be aware of the fact that her page is based on a Web Service and indirectly on an SOA composite. The data controls hide the Web Service intricacies from the ViewController project and the page developer.

Our conclusion can be that creating user interfaces that provide access to SOA composite applications is easily done using ADF. Even though this does not involve any special relationship between ADF and the SOA Suite, it is still an extremely convenient way of creating rich, attractive (although that still needs to be proven, of course) front-ends for composite applications. Note that ADF applications can also easily call Web Services from (plain-old) Java classes and present a more specific business interface to the ViewController project, possibly based on several Web Services whose results are combined. Creating a WebService proxy is again an automated operation in JDeveloper (leveraging JAX-WS), and publishing a POJO as a data control is a two-click action. Finally, SOA Composite applications can easily expose services with EJB binding instead of or in addition to a SOAP WebService binding, as we have seen in Chapter 12. ADF applications can easily make use of POJOs to invoke such bindings.

Creating a Custom Human Task Form for ScheduleAppointment

Chapter 10 introduced the Human Task service component. This component makes it possible to integrate manual operations and other tasks performed by people as an integral part of composite applications—which is only too logical because oftentimes a process has a step where communication, intuition, improvisation, chain of command, or fuzzy logic comes into play and an automated service simply is not good enough.

We have seen how a task can be as simple as acknowledging the receipt of certain information by choosing either "accept" or "reject." Sometimes a task can be much more complex, involving quite a bit of associated data to review or even to manipulate. And with such complex tasks, we benefit from a user interface that presents data to provide a context and more background for the task at hand. The user interface for the human tasks is perhaps ideally integrated with the enterprise portal or with other web applications.

It turns out to be fairly straightforward to build a custom ADF application to provide the user interface for the human tasks managed by the SOA Suite's workflow services. This section shows how to create such applications—and how to register them with the SOA Suite to have them merged into e-mails, linked from notifications, and embedded in the BPM Worklist application.

Developing Custom User Interfaces for Human Tasks

We have seen in Chapter 10 how we can generate a (default) task form for a human task. This generated task form lives in its own project. The form is created using ADF Faces Rich Client components. It supports all elements in the task payload, including update of the payload when that is allowed. The project with the generated task form is deployed as a stand-alone web application that is linked in FMW Control with the human task it supports.

Generation gives us a form with elements that are wired to the human task and its payload. However, what we get is also just a normal ADF Faces page that we can manipulate any way we like. We can add layout elements, apply styles, and include illustrations. The layout of the page can be reorganized, positioning the generated elements in a different way, using elements such as the panel splitter, tabs, and pop-ups. We can also add new elements—potentially bound to other data controls to provide richer context for the task.

There is another, semi-automated way of creating a task form. The context menu for Human Task activities in the BPEL process editor has an option called Launch Task Form Wizard. This action will also generate a task form, but will first guide the developer through a multistep wizard that allows configuration of many aspects of the generated task form.

Instead of generating a task form and then manually refining it, we can also work from the bottom up: Create a new ADF Faces page, using page templates and other foundational elements, and then bind it to a Human Task component deployed to the SOA Suite that is made available as a data control. We can use this data control to add components to the page that are wired to elements of the task payload. When we have completed the custom task form, we can deploy it to the WebLogic Server running the SOA Suite. In the FMW Control, we configure the Human Task component to associate it with the custom task form. This is for the benefit of the Worklist application, which needs to embed the custom task form when a user is acting on an instance of a task for this particular task component.

Developing a Custom Task Flow to Work on a Human Task

We will create a new, stand-alone Fusion web application called AppointmentScheduler that contains an ADF task flow that is bound to a Human Task definition; this is illustrated in Figure 20-9. The task flow will contain a single page that is initially populated using the data control and subsequently refined.

Select the ViewController project. Open the New Gallery, go to the Web Tier category, and select the node JSF. In the right pane, select ADF Task Flow Based On Human Task. The SOA Resource Browser appears to allow selection of a Human Task definition. Toggle the browser to the Resource Palette to use the MDS connection. Find the Scheduler composite application and expand it. Select the ScheduleAppointment.task definition and then click the OK button.

Next, the Create Task Flow dialog appears. We can safely accept all default settings here. Note that the name of the task flow definition file and the task flow ID will be required later on to register this task flow as the task form for the ScheduleAppointment task in the Fusion Middleware Control. Click OK to complete the creation of the task flow. The task flow editor appears—a pane with a single page and a task flow Return activity. The task flow has a substantial number of input parameters that will be populated by the Worklist application when it embeds and invokes the task form for a specific instance of the ScheduleAppointment task. If you want to use the task form in another context, you will have to provide the values for most of these input parameters.

Expand the data control ViewController_ScheduleAppointment node that was created when we created the task flow based on the human task. Nested under this node, you will find a node called Task. Drag this node to the page and drop it as Complete Task With Payload. Accept all default

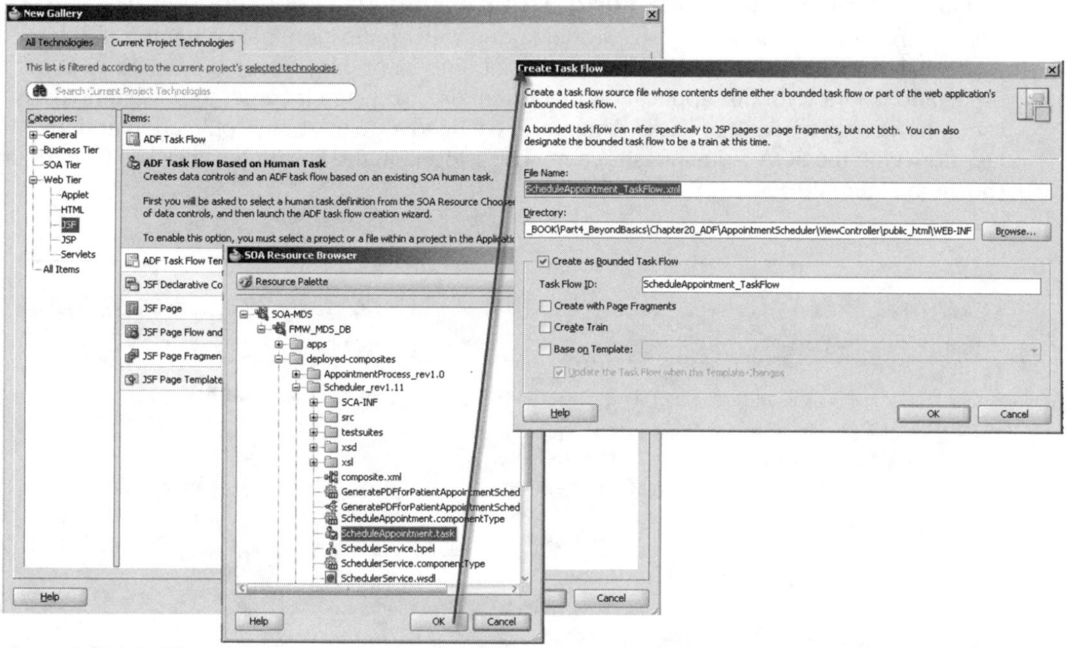

FIGURE 20-9. *Creating the task flow based on the human task ScheduleAppointment*

values in the two windows that appear when you click the OK button. The page will be refreshed with a large number of components in it, based on the task header, the actions, and the payload. Those elements in the payload that are updateable are bound to enabled input components.

We can now start to make changes to the page. We can add images and collapsible layout containers, and retrieve data from other data controls, such as a list of all rooms in the hospital and a collection of all the doctors working at St. Matthews.

In this case, we make a few small changes: The address data is wrapped in an initially collapsed panel box, the updateable description is converted to a rich text editor, the appointment date and time can be set using a date/time component, and the room can be selected from a drop-down list.

Of course, we can do much more to the page to make it richer and more attractive—but the focus of this chapter is on the integration between ADF and SOA Suite, not on the ADF specifics, so we'll leave it at that.

Deploying the AppointmentScheduler Application

After making these changes, we can deploy the AppointmentScheduler. Select Deploy from the drop-down on the right of the application name in the Application Navigator. Pick the (default) profile AppointmentScheduler_application1, as shown in Figure 20-10.

Select the same application server connection we use for deploying the SOA composite application to the SOA Suite. Select soa_server1 as the target server. Click Next and then click Finish. Deployment commences.

A pop-up window may appear regarding MDS. Select mds-soa as the repository and enter **tasks** as the name of the partition. Click the Deploy button.

Registering the Custom Task Form with the Human Task Component

When deployment is done, we have a standalone web application that contains a task form that supports processing instances of a Human Task component. However, no one knows about it—especially not the Worklist application that is the director when it comes to presenting users with a user interface for working on tasks. Therefore, we need to register our application and the human task flow with the SOA Suite infrastructure. This is done in the Fusion Middleware Control, as shown in Figure 20-11.

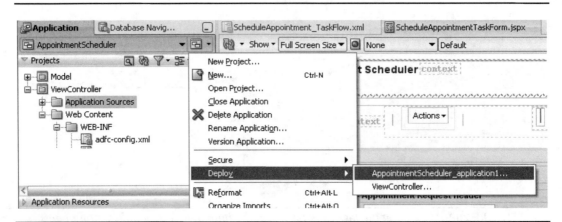

FIGURE 20-10. *Starting deployment for the AppointmentScheduler application*

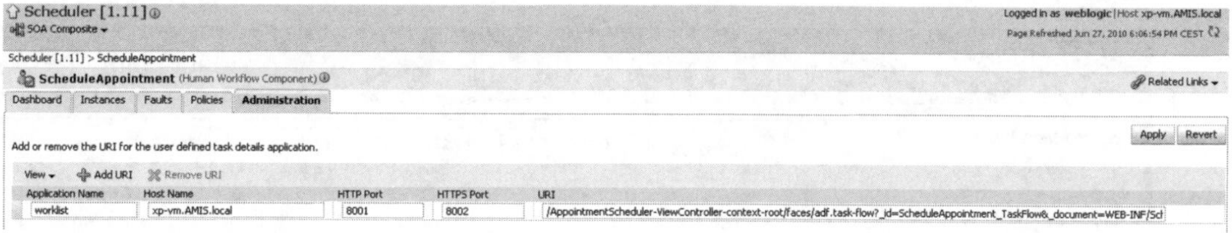

FIGURE 20-11. *Registering the custom task flow as the task form for the human task* *ScheduleAppointment*

Open the FMW Enterprise Manager Control. Open the SOA and the soa-infra node. Select the Scheduler Composite application, which contains the Human Task component ScheduleAppointment. Click the Human Task component.

The configuration page for the Human Task component appears. Here we can associate the custom task flow with the Worklist application in the context of the ScheduleAppointment task component. The application name should be set to **worklist**. Set the hostname (localhost, 127.0.0.1, or whatever is the name of the host that runs the Worklist application) and the port number (default value is 8001).

The URI is composed of the name of the application, the ID of the task flow, and the name of the task flow definition file:

```
/AppointmentScheduler-ViewController-context-root/faces/adf.task-
flow?_id=ScheduleAppointment_TaskFlow&_document=WEB-
INF/ScheduleAppointment_TaskFlow.xml
```

Here, AppointmentScheduler-ViewController-context-root is the (JEE) name of the application that contains the task flow, ScheduleAppointment_TaskFlow is the ID of the task flow that is based on the ScheduleAppointment task, and WEB-INF/ScheduleAppointment_TaskFlow.xml indicates the location and name of the task flow definition file.

The Worklist application contains an iframe that loads the task flow from the Appointment Scheduler application, using a URL and passing enough context information that allows the embedded task flow to interact with the human workflow service APIs regarding the correct task instance and user context.

Working on a ScheduleAppointment Task in the Custom Form in the Worklist Application

The custom task form that we have just created and registered is now ready for use by the BPM Worklist application for occurrences of the human task ScheduleAppointment.

Open the Worklist application, log in as Maggie, and select an open ScheduleAppointment task. The custom task form is opened with the details for the selected task. Maggie can benefit from the huge (!) enhancements we have implemented compared with the original, auto-generated task form (see Figure 20-12).

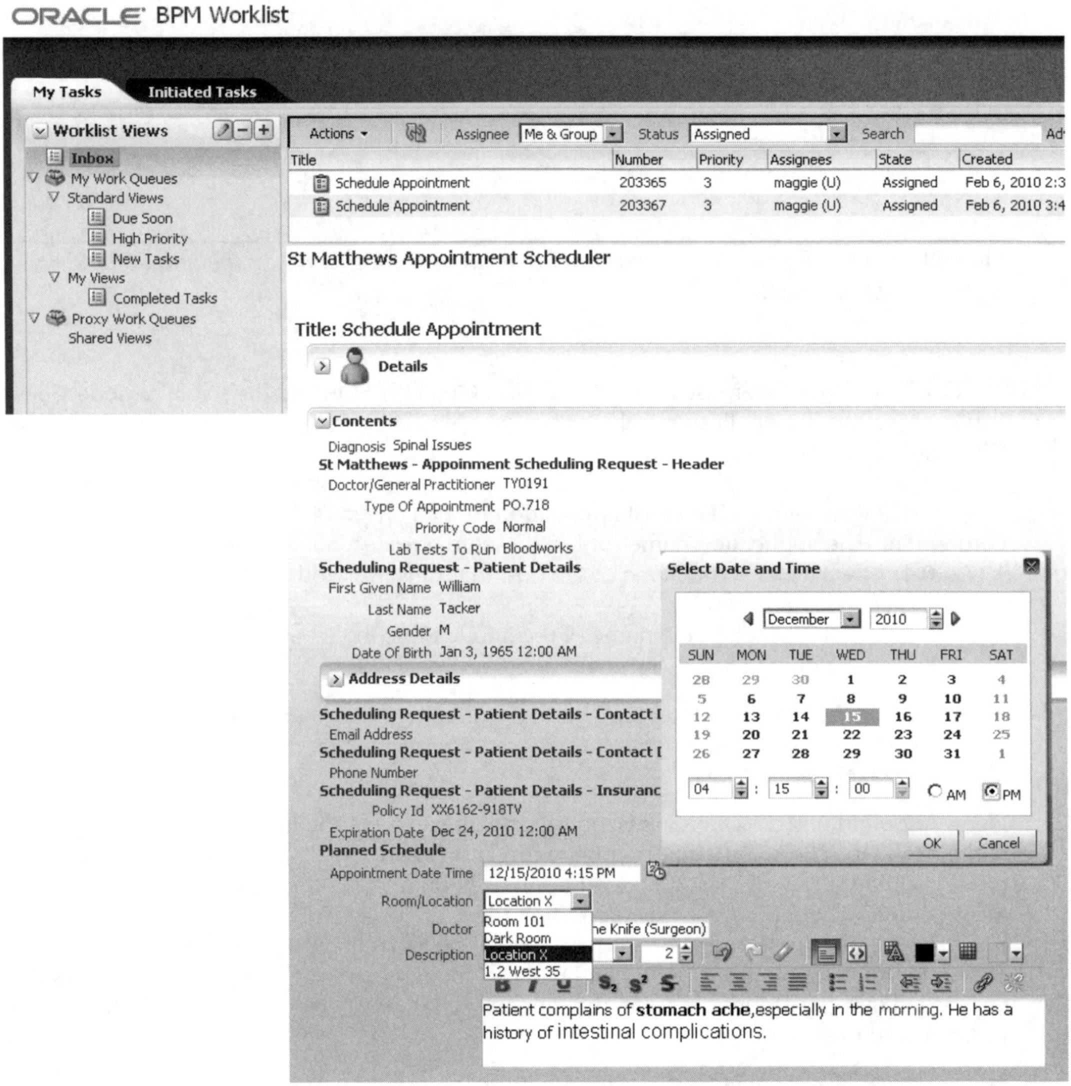

FIGURE 20-12. *The customized task form for an instance of the ScheduleAppointment task*

Note that we can continue to refine the AppointmentScheduler application. When we reach a new stage, we can redeploy the application and the Worklist application will automatically pick up the latest version of the task flow ScheduleAppointment_TaskFlow. Even though the Worklist application relies on our custom application, the two are well decoupled, allowing changes in one without impacting the other.

Creating Real-time Dashboards Based on BAM in Custom ADF Applications

In the previous chapter, we discussed Oracle BAM for business activity monitoring. In that chapter, we made use of the BAM Active Studio to create reports and real-time dashboards on top of the Active Data Cache. We can also use ADF Faces to create a custom dashboard or embed visualizations of BAM data in a custom web application. ADF comes with the BAM data control that connects to the Active Data Cache, consumes specific data objects, and exposes them for use in data bindings. This means we can just as easily create a rich table or 3-D bar chart in ADF Faces based on a relational database table exposed through ADF Business Components, based on a Web Service or based on a BAM data object.

A special feature of the BAM data control is the Active Data Service or server push. This means that changes in the Active Data Cache—for example, pushed through the BAM adapter from SOA composite applications—are pushed to the View component of the ADF application and from there even further to the browser. Just like the BAM Active Studio renders reports that are updated in real time to represent the actual state of the data, an ADF application based on the same BAM data objects will also have this live update functionality.

Implementing the Appointment Dashboard as a Custom ADF Application

In the previous chapter, we created the St. Matthews Appointment Dashboard using BAM Active Studio, based on the PatientAppointment data object in the Active Data Cache. We will discuss next how we can use the BAM data control in ADF and the ADF Faces Rich Client components to create a dashboard in an ADF web application. Apart from the slightly different set of components that ADF offers for creating the user interface, this can be interesting because it allows us to integrate the real-time visualization of data from BAM into applications that also work against Web Services and the database to execute actions. Whereas a BAM report is a read-only dashboard (a live indication of what is going on), an ADF application can offer not just the BAM-based real-time insight but also the functionality to act on that information. Additionally, ADF applications run in more browsers—such as Firefox and Chrome—than just IE 7.0 and 8.0, the current limitation for BAM Active Viewer.

Creating a comprehensive dashboard in ADF is a challenge that is somewhat beyond the scope of this chapter, so we will limit ourselves to a very simple example that makes clear what the basic steps are. We will create an ADF web application, create a new JSF page, and add a little basic layout to it. Then we will create a BAM data control for a data object that we select from the connection to the BAM server. The creation of such a BAM data control is very similar to the first part of the creation of a report in Active Studio, including the creation of calculated fields, filters, and groupings. Next we can create a representation of the data from the data control using rich components such as the table or one of the many ADF Data Visualization Components, a large collection of charts, gauges, and other graphics.

Because we are working on a regular JSF page in a standard ADF application, we can add many other things to the page besides the component bound to the BAM data control. And we can wire the BAM-based component to other components. For example, a BAM-based component could show a bar chart of appointment requests, and when we click one of the bars, a form that is bound to a Web Service is exposed by an SOA composite that can be updated based on that click.

Preparation for the BAM-Powered ADF Application

To keep things as simple as can be, we will work in a new ADF application called PatientAppointment Dashboard. In the previous chapter, we created a new IDE connection to the BAM server. Find this connection in the Resource Palette and add it to the PatientAppointmentDashboard application, using the context menu on the connection.

Creating the BAM Data Control for the PatientAppointment Data Object

Open the view on the Application Properties and select the connection to the BAM server. Expand the node for this connection. The data objects in the BAM server are listed in their folder structure. Select the PatientAppointment object and select Create Data Control from the context menu.

The Edit BAM Data Control Wizard appears—with steps that are very similar to those you go through when you create a new view in a report in Active Studio. We will use only a fraction of the functionality available to us, completely by-passing parameters, filters, and calculated fields and advanced groupings such as time series.

On the first page, specify **PatientAppointmentStatusGrouping** as the name for the data control. Accept the default setting of Group Query for the query type and leave the check box Collapsed unchecked.

Go to the Groups page and select the AppointmentStatus field as the one to group by: We want one bar for every distinct status value. On the Aggregates page, specify count for the appointment identifier (or the status or any other field that will always have a value). Click the Finish button to complete the creation of the data control.

We will now make use of this data control to wire a graph to the underlying active data source. Note once more that we can bind almost any ADF Faces component to the data control, including components that do not support server push—the BAM data control is just as easy to use as the WebService data control we saw earlier in this chapter and the ADF Business Components data control that we will see next. All data controls expose data attributes, collections, and operations to the ViewController project and allow components that work with single or multiple values or that know how to invoke operations to be bound to those exposed elements.

Creating the Leanest Dashboard Page Imaginable

To see the BAM data control in action, we will create a JavaServer Faces page that has almost no content—except for a bar chart based on the data exposed by the data control. Drag a Panel Header component to the top facet and set its text to **St. Matthews Appointment Dashboard**. Drag a Panel Box component to the center facet and set its title to **Appointment Overview per Status**.

We will create a three-dimensional bar chart that indicates the number of appointments and appointment requests per status—such as new, scheduled, cancelled, and completed. Note that we did the same chart using the BAM Active Studio, in the context of the BAM report (see Figure 19-32).

Select the BAM data control PatientAppointmentStatusGrouping in the Data Control palette and expand the node. Also expand its Query child node. This node has a child node called _ AppointmentStatus. Drag this node to the Panel Box and drop it as a graph. In the Graph selector that appears next, select the Bar Chart type. Note that we have many dozens of chart types to choose from that each come in various configurations and themes. These charts all have support for active data—meaning that they accept server push to update them in real time.

Next we have to edit the bar chart, to indicate which attribute from the BAM data control indicates the value visualized by the height of the bars and which attribute describes the group or bar value. Drag the COUNT_AppointmentIdentifier attribute to the Bars field, and drag the value tag to the X Axis field. Change the label for the first attribute to Number of Appointments. Accept the default of "Use Attribute Value" for the value tag attribute.

We need to do a little extra tuning on the bar chart—to set the 3-D effect and define the titles for the axes: **Appointment Status** for the X-axis and **Number of Appointments** for the Y1-axis.

Deployment and Server Configuration

Deployment of the PatientAppointmentDashboard application to the soa_server1 is done following the same procedure we used earlier in this chapter. The dashboard in all its simplicity can be accessed in a browser (and not just Internet Explorer) at

```
http://localhost:8001/PatientAppointmentDashboard-ViewController-context-root/
faces/Dashboard.jspx
```

The BAM-based live updated bar chart with appointments per status embedded in a custom ADF application is shown in Figure 20-13.

Multiple Consumer Components of the Same BAM Data Control

When you are ready to take on more complex pages, which contain multiple components based on the same BAM data control, these components must be in separate task flows that you combine in the same page. These task flows must have their data control scope property set to isolated (a BAM data control cannot be shared by components).

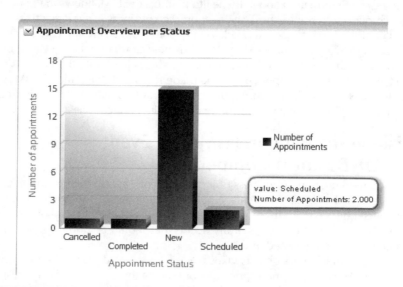

FIGURE 20-13.   *The ADF dashboard page with a BAM-powered bar chart*

ADF Business Components Feeding Events into the EDN

St. Matthews likes to think of its patients in terms of modern customer intimacy. Patients are health consumers and as such are just a special type of customer. Modern marketing techniques should be employed to build relations with these customers, and every contact should be recorded in the CRM system. Advanced campaigns will be developed to attract customers to products that are perhaps less urgent medically speaking but more profitable for the hospital.

The foundation of this customer intimacy thinking is, of course, a robust patient or customer administration. And, of course, being all Oracle minded and looking for optimal integration with the SOA platform, St. Matthews will develop the application for customer administration using ADF. Initially there will be an application for internal usage—and later on a more self-service style of patient administration is envisioned. In this section, we will create a simple Patient Management application in the most straightforward manner using ADF: ADF Business Components on top of database tables as the Model, and pages created using drag-and-drop from the Data Control palette in the ViewController. Getting this very basic-looking application up and running takes but a few minutes.

Even though the application is still simple, users will be able to look up patients as well as update patient details. Address changes, for example, can be applied, as well as modification of insurance details or e-mail address.

The fact that a patient has moved to a new address could be of importance—not only should all records for the patient be updated with the latest information, but depending on where the patient is going to live, he may qualify for a higher (or lower) priority assignment for scheduled appointments, he should be sent information about the health partners of St. Matthews in the neighborhood, or he triggers processes in some other way. In short: The business event PatientHasMoved should be published on the Event Delivery Network for any potentially interested consumer.

Data changes that are processed by ADF Business Components can easily be turned into EDN events—because the business components have a direct hook into the EDN. We will demonstrate how the Patient business component can be made to publish the PatientHasMoved event to the Event Delivery Network, thus ensuring that any relevant update of the patient record is brought to the attention of registered event-consuming composite applications.

Publishing the PatientHasMoved Event from ADF Business Components

Creation and modification of business objects—patients, appointments, invoices, employees—are frequently regarded as business events. Not every little change needs to be broadcasted on the EDN, of course, but changes in important attributes—such as status or address—and the creation of essential business entities are generally events that should be published, as other parties in the organizations may be interested in them.

Manipulation of business objects takes place in automated processes and services and through user interfaces. Any component responsible for making these changes is also responsible for publishing the associated business event. In an environment based on Oracle Fusion Middleware, many of these components will be implemented using ADF. The manipulation of business objects in these ADF-based components usually takes place in ADF BC.

Looking at these two findings—that data manipulation frequently should trigger the publication of a business event and that data manipulation frequently takes place through ADF Business

Components—it would be only too convenient if ADF BC could publish events to the Event Delivery Network—and it can.

We will work here with ADF Business Components on top of a simple database table for records for patients. The ADF BC objects need to implement a business service that will support an ADF Faces web application that provides patient record query and manipulation functionality. Later in this chapter, we will use the same business service exposed as a Web Service to provide tight data integration capabilities with a BPEL process. At the core of the ADF BC business service is the entity object that is mapped directly to the table. Every instance of the entity object corresponds with a patient record in the table.

On top of this entity object is a view object—the representation of the business object that applications will see and interact with. View objects wrap entity objects to present a data view that is not necessarily closely aligned with the table structure in the underlying database—as are the entity objects—but that is prepared for (re)use in applications. The view object decouples consumers such as web applications from the database structure. View objects expose operations such as query, navigate through recordset, create, delete, and update a row.

What I call the business service—comparable with the portType in a WSDL—is implemented in ADF BC by the application module. The application module exposes the service interface that clients interact with. This interface typically consists of a number of view objects and their intrinsic operations and possibly some additional custom operations.

Requests for data manipulation, either from the user interface in the ADF Faces application or from one of the consumers of the Web Service, are handled through the view objects and then access the underlying entity objects. The entity objects post the DML statements to the database. When all statements have been posted successfully and all validations have been successful, the transaction can be committed. As part of this transaction, the entity objects may publish events to the SOA Suite Event Delivery Network, when so configured. Figure 20-14 demonstrates this application architecture.

The configuration of business events can be fine-tuned in several dimensions: for which DML event should an event be published, what should be the payload of the event, and what are the exact conditions? This is based, for example, on the old and new values of the entity under which the event is to be published.

The main steps we go through to make this happen are as follows: In a new Fusion web application, create an entity object called Patient that's mapped to the database table PATIENTS, and then create an updateable view object called PatientsVw on top of this entity object. Create an application module called PatientsService that exposes PatientsVw. Create an ADF Faces page with a form based on PatientsVw. So far, this is standard ADF development (see the online chapter complement for the details).

The one step that is different here is the configuration of the Patient entity object to publish the business events with the appropriate payload at the desired moments. We can then deploy the application and run it. Any change in the address details of a patient made through the web application will result in a business event appearing on the Event Delivery Network in the SOA Suite, potentially triggering composite applications.

Preparation

Before we start developing the ADF BC objects and the web application, we need to start JDeveloper and create a new ADF Fusion web application called PatientManagement (from the New Gallery). When the application is created, add FranksPatientDatabase data connection to the application.

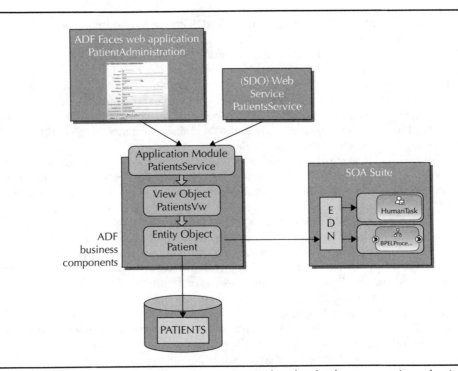

FIGURE 20-14. *ADF Business Components mapped to the database, exposing a business service and publishing events to the EDN*

Creating the ADF Business Components

Our simple and straightforward ADF application will use ADF Business Components to communicate with Frank's database. We need to create an entity object that is mapped to the Patients table, a view object to expose the patient data to consumers, and an application module to act as the overall business service.

Application Deployment to Another WLS Instance

When the application using the ADF Business Components that publish EDN events is deployed to the same WebLogic server that runs the SOA Suite, the events will be received into the EDN infrastructure without further ado. However, when the application is deployed to a different WLS instance, we need to do some additional configuration steps: ADF BC relies on two data sources being available for publishing to the Event Delivery Network. These are called EDNDataSource and EDNLocalTxDataSource—and you will find them in the WebLogic Server Administration Console. We need to make sure that the EDNDataSource is available in the WLS container into which ADF application is deployed—targeting the same database as the original data source.

In the New Gallery, find the Business Tier category and select the child node ADF Business Components. Select the item Business Components from Tables. Then select the database connection to Frank's database. Query the tables that are available from that database connection and select the PATIENTS table to create an entity object for. Specify **Patient** as the name of the entity. On the next page, configure a single updateable view object, PatientsVw, based on the Patient entity object. Skip the page for the read-only view objects. Mark the check box for Application Module on page four and enter **PatientsService** as the name of the application module. Click the Finish button to have the business components created.

When you open the Data Control palette, you will see a data control called PatientsService with a collection called PatientsVw1, based on the view object. The collection contains the attributes created in the view object. It also exposes operations such as first, next, previous, and last, as well as create, delete, find by key, and query. The collection, all attributes, and all operations are available for binding in webpages: ADF Faces components can be added to a page and wired to one of the elements on the Data Control palette.

NOTE
You can now run the PatientsService application module (choose Run from the context menu) to start the ADF BC browser that makes clear whether the business components have been configured correctly.

Creating the PatientAdministration Page

The patient records can be reviewed and manipulated in a simple webpage. This page shows a form with all the fields in the records, along with navigation buttons and a button to save the changes. Create a new page called PatientAdministration.jspx. From the Data Control palette, drag the PatientsVw1 collection to the page and drop it as an ADF form, as shown in Figure 20-15. Check the boxes to include the navigation buttons and the Submit button. Next, drag the Commit operation from the Data Control palette and drop it as a command button.

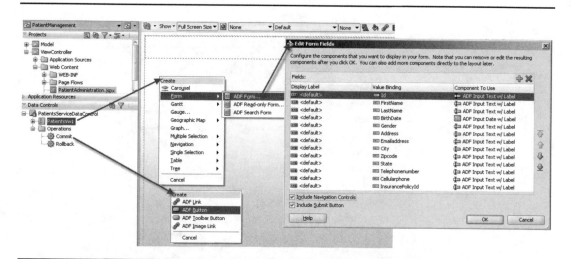

FIGURE 20-15. *Composing the PatientAdministration page through dragging and dropping appropriately from the Data Control palette*

You may further embellish the page—but for our purpose we are done. We have all we need to retrieve patient data from the database, present it in the form, modify it, and save it back to the database.

Deploy and Run

Deploy the application using the Deploy option in the drop-down menu found at the top of the application navigator window—just as we did before. Again, use the same application server connection that you have used to deploy SOA composite applications. It is the easiest way to get the ADF application running and interacting with the SOA Suite's EDN a little bit later on. You may limit the deployment to only the soa_server1 instance. See the online chapter complement for instructions on how to set up the data source in the WebLogic server for the ADF BC application module as well as the associated configuration of the application module itself.

The application can be accessed using the following URL:

```
http://localhost:8001/PatientManagement-ViewController-context-root/faces/
PatientAdministration.jspx
```

The rather basic form appears, as shown in Figure 20-16, and we can inspect and modify patient records. Keep in mind that the form is "basic" only in terms of visual attractiveness; it does have all the fields, it supports navigation through the patients collection, and it allows data manipulation against the underlying database. Therefore, functionally speaking, it is *not* that basic.

We will now extend the business components to have events published to the Event Delivery Network when the address in a patient record is changed.

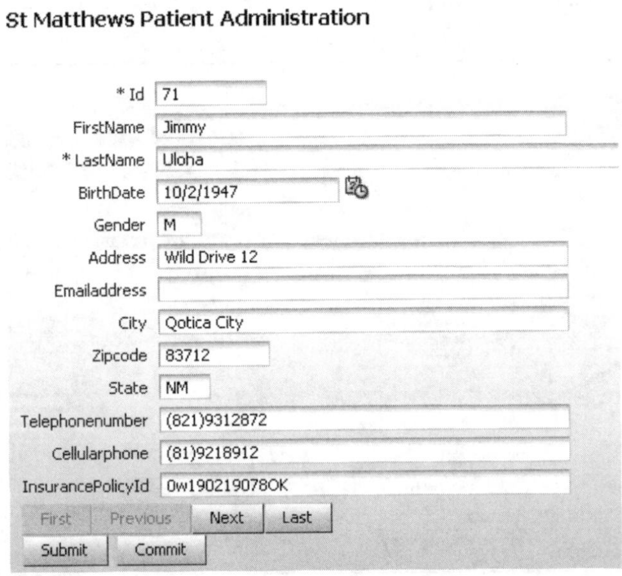

St Matthews Patient Administration

* Id	71
FirstName	Jimmy
* LastName	Uloha
BirthDate	10/2/1947
Gender	M
Address	Wild Drive 12
Emailaddress	
City	Qotica City
Zipcode	83712
State	NM
Telephonenumber	(821)9312872
Cellularphone	(81)9218912
InsurancePolicyId	0w1902190780K

First   Previous   Next   Last

Submit   Commit

FIGURE 20-16. *The PatientAdministration form in action*

Configuring Business Components to Publish Events to EDN

Open the Model project and select the Patient entity. Click the Business Events tab and then click the green plus icon to create a new business event. Call the event **PatientHasMoved**. Define the payload for the event by selecting the attributes Id, Address, City, Zipcode, State, and Telephonenumber. The Id attribute should always be included; otherwise, we cannot identify the patient to whom the event refers. The other attributes need only be included when they have changed. Of course, you could elect to also include FirstName and LastName or other attributes that make sense to make available in the event's payload.

Next we need to indicate when the event is published: which operation on the Patient entity object should be cause for sending a PatientHasMoved event to the Event Delivery Network. Well, clearly that should be an update event, because we are after changes in address.

JDeveloper creates an event definition for the PatientHasMoved event in a new .edl file that is written in a subdirectory called "events," under the directory that holds the definition file for the entity object. In the same directory, an XSD file is created that describes the payload of the business event.

We are now ready to redeploy the application. Not much has changed, really. However, every time we make a change in the address attributes of an existing patient record and commit that change (note: the PatientHasMoved event is only published when the change is committed to the database), the application publishes the event to the Event Delivery Network. And that can be quite meaningful because now the SOA composite applications can have themselves notified when a patient moves—at the same time as that piece of information formally enters the hospital (or the hospital's database).

Deploy the application in the same way as before. The EDL and XSD files are included, and this will make the new event definition known to the SOA Suite and the EDN infrastructure. After deployment, you can check the Business Events page (accessed from the context menu on the soa-infra node) for the PatientHasMoved event. You will find that it has no subscriptions...yet.

Creating a SOA Composite Application to Consume PatientHasMoved Events

We may very well claim that our PatientManagement ADF application is now capable of publishing the PatientHasMoved event—but that should be demonstrated for real. An easy way to provide the proof that the event appears on the Event Delivery Network when we change the address of one of the patients is by explicitly subscribing to that event and doing something with it. To do just that, follow these steps:

1. Create a new SOA application called **ConsumePatientHasMoved** that contains a Mediator that subscribes to the PatientHasMoved event.

2. Drag a File Adapter Service to the External References lane: We will write all PatientHas Moved events to a log file. This will give us a concrete demonstration of the event-publication capabilities of the ADF BC Patient entity object, as the next figure illustrates. Configure the File Adapter Service to write a log entry for each event to a comma-separated log file (for example, c:\temp\patientHasMovedEventsLog.txt).

3. Wire the Mediator to the File Adapter Service. Create the mapping from the PatientHas Moved event's payload to the File Adapter Service input. Note the nesting of the elements in the event payload (for example, Address\newValue\value).

When the deployment for this application is complete, you could verify whether the Business Events page in the Enterprise Manager FWM Control displays the event subscription from the Mediator in this application on the PatientHasMoved event. You can also go straight to the PatientAdministration form, make a change in the address details of a patient record, and commit the change. When you do so, a few things should happen: A new instance of the ConsumePatientHas Moved composite application should be created and executed, and a file called patientHasMoved EventsLog.txt should appear with an entry that corresponds with the changes you made in your browser in the ADF PatientManagement application. If you find that this indeed has happened, you have successfully integrated your ADF application with the Event Delivery Network.

Improving the Efficiency and Elegance of the PatientDataService Using SDO-Bound BPEL Variables—Tighter Data Integration for BPEL Processes

The same application module used in the previous section can also publish a generic SOAP Web Service interface to expose operations on patient records to potentially many different clients. And it can publish a specialized type of service interface, one that turns the application module into a Data Access Service (DAS) that publishes Service Data Objects (SDOs).

Service Data Objects is another industry standard, created by the Open Service-Oriented Architecture Consortium. It aims at creating a standard for interacting with business data in a technology- and protocol-independent manner. SDO is based on the concept of disconnected data graphs—XML representations of a data object and its children or dependencies. These data graphs are used to transfer the business data in a technology-agnostic manner, similar to messages to and from Web Services. SDO describes a wrapper around existing data sources that may be based on EJB/JPA, a non-(SDO)-standardized Web Service, JDBC and SQL, RESTful services, an in-memory data grid, Google BigTable, or any other data service or source.

Remote consumers can retrieve data as well as manipulate it according to the SDO standard, interacting with a Data Access Service (DAS) that provides the graphs of data objects. The DAS is somewhat similar in its role to the Entity Manager in JPA.

Through SDO, it becomes relatively easy to retrieve data: The operations to get hold of the data are standardized, as is the format in which the data is provided along with associated metadata that allows consumers to introspect the data graph to learn about the structure.

SDO is of particular interest to us at this stage because the SOA Suite and ADF can forge a special bond based on SDO: ADF Business Components can easily implement a Data Access Service and make view objects available as SDO data graphs. Any SDO-enabled tool can leverage these services, interacting with the ADF BC business service—and indirectly the underlying database—through a standardized, remote interface.

Additionally, the SOA Suite 11g BPEL component has functionality around SDO: a BPEL process can have one or more variables that are directly bound to an SDO. These so-called "entity variables" are indirectly bound to a row in the view object, and usually thereby also to an instance of an entity object and a record in some database table.

Manipulation of the entity variable—using the same Assign operations we use for other BPEL variables—has us directly interacting with the SDO and thereby the back-end data source.

This gives us a very simple, straightforward way to work with data in a database that's much more direct than through the use of a database adapter.

A huge extra benefit of working with entity variables bound to SDOs is that the data graph itself is not held within the BPEL process instance. When the instance is dehydrated, for example, only a reference (based on the primary key) to the SDO is saved, not the data itself. When the instance resumes and needs to access the data of the entity variable, the current state of the data is retrieved from the DAS. Note that all of this happens automatically—we just work with an entity variable like any regular BPEL variable.

In general when BPEL processes have frequent interaction with database adapter services for manipulating data, especially when the same record is accessed multiple times, it is worthwhile to consider using SDO and entity variables to make the process more efficient—both for the developer as well as for the run-time infrastructure. The volume of state data that your process may gather from back-end databases and hang on to can be another driver for SDO-bound entity variables, because these reduce the state to just a reference to a data graph instead of the data itself.

BPEL Entity Variables Bound to Service Data Objects

In Chapter 12, we discussed various types of integration between the SOA Suite and Java. Probably the most advanced integration with the world of Java-powered components was not discussed: the binding of BPEL variables to Service Data Objects offered by a Data Access Service—in this case implemented by an ADF Business Components application module. These entity variables are not just populated with data from the DAS at one moment in time. Instead, they contain a reference to the SDO that is maintained by the DAS acting against some back-end data store, which could be a database, a file repository, or something else altogether. Any change in SDO is immediately available in the BPEL process when it accesses the variable—no explicit refresh is required. Additionally, updates of the BPEL entity variable are sent to the DAS to be applied to the SDO (and the underlying data store). Again, no explicit action is required on the part of the BPEL process. Although this all happens transparently, it is still nice to know that the SDOs can have a complex, nested structure of extensive data graphs—and that the communication between the Data Access Service and its clients uses deltas to communicate only the changes in the graph instead of the entire structure.

Our very first SOA composite application in this book—well, not counting the HelloWorld process in Chapter 3—was the PatientDataService of Chapter 5. This composite application used the database adapter to retrieve and update patient information and create new patient records. We will now create a new implementation of this composite application: a PatientDataService that does not rely on the database adapter and indirectly on knowledge about database objects, but instead calls an SDO-enabled service—backed by ADF Business Components—to perform operations on data. The composite application does not know that ADF BC is used for the implementation of the DAS, and it is also unaware that further down the DAS has a relational database underneath it. For all it knows or cares, there could be an in-memory grid or an SaaS-based data cloud such as BigTable—which can be located anywhere.

The Implementation of DAS- and SDO-based Entity Variables in BPEL

We will slightly extend the ADF BC application PatientManagement that we created in the previous section to demonstrate the integration with the Event Delivery Network. We will use the same objects as before, and this time also expose them as a Web Service with support for SDO. This application is deployed to WebLogic as a stand-alone application that offers Web Services.

The SOA composite application PatientDataService is revisited. We will add an ADF BC reference to the composite, configured to interact with the PatientManagementSDO service. This ADF BC reference is wired to the BPEL process Patient Data Service, to provide the source for an entity variable bound to an SDO exposed by the PatientManagementSDO service.

At first we will use an entity variable for creating a new patient record in the database without using a Database Adapter Service. The entity variable is bound to the SDO that the ADF BC reference makes available. We set the patient attributes on the entity variable from the request message. Then we can use the Create Entity activity to persist the SDO to the Data Access Service.

Updating patient records is even more interesting, because we will then encounter another benefit of SDO-backed variables: If the underlying Data Access Service were to modify or enrich the record during creation or update—which could happen in the view object, the entity object, and also through database triggers—then the changes in the SDO are immediately available in the BPEL process. When we are using the database adapter, these changes applied by database triggers and other business logic are not pushed back to the BPEL process, but now they are.

Making ADF BC Expose an SDO-Enabled Web Service

In the previous section, we developed the PatientManagement application. This application consisted of two projects: Model (with ADF BC) and ViewController (with the ADF Faces web application that used the ADF BC objects). We will focus now on the Model project. An easy way to get going is to create a new Fusion web application called PatientManagementSDO with empty

Service-Enabled Entities

One of the potential consumers of an SDO service published by an application module is an entity object in a remote ADF BC application. An entity object (usually mapped to a table or view in an underlying database) can also be based on a Service Data Object. These service-enabled entities are useful to make data services available to the (local) web application through the familiar data controls that are used to bind data and operations in ADF Faces components—even when those data services originate with some remote SDO provider. This provider cannot directly be used to create data controls from, so the service-enabled entities act as the intermediary—potentially also transforming the service interface from whatever is on offer remotely to what best suits the needs of the local application.

To create an entity object that is based on an SDO and not on a database table or view, we can create a new entity object (from the New Gallery) and select Service Interface instead of Database Schema Object in the first step of the wizard. We then need to provide the URL for the WSDL of the remote SDO provider. JDeveloper will retrieve and parse the WSDL and then present a list of the service-enabled view instances on offer from the remote provider.

We pick the view instance we want to base the entity object on and then select the attributes from the remote view that should be in the entity object. If necessary, we can make changes to the attribute definitions.

View objects can be based on these service-backed entity objects, just like more regular database object–backed entity objects. View links can be created between VOs defined against EOs on database objects, and VOs on top of service-backed EOs. Some restrictions apply to the creation of entity-backed VOs that use multiple EOs based on a service interface.

Model and ViewController projects. Then remove both projects from this application and open (a copy of) the Model project from the PatientManagement application. Alternatively, you can create the PatientManagementSDO application from scratch with a single project called Model.

Select the application module PatientsService. Go to the tab Service Interface and click the green plus icon. The Create Service editor appears. On the first page, enter **PatientsService** as the Web Service name. Accept the default value for the target namespace. Skip the second step, because for now we will not expose any custom methods (we will do so later on).

On page three, select the view object usage PatientsVw1 as the one that is to be exposed. Check the Enable check box for all basic operations. Click Next, inspect the summary, and click Finish.

JDeveloper will now create a number of files, including a WSDL for the PatientsService with a supporting XSD document as well as the JAX-WS annotated Java interface and implementation class.

Preparing for Deployment of the ADF BC Application

Before we can deploy the application, we need to configure some values. See the online chapter complement for the specifics, apply all changes, and deploy the PatientManagementSDO application.

When the deployment is complete and successful, we can test the Web Service that this application exposes. Note that even though this service supports SDO, it can also be used by clients that are not aware of SDO. The service has a normal WSDL and XSD.

The Web Service is published at http://localhost:8001/PatientsServiceSDO/PatientsService. This URL takes you to a test page where you can try out all operations in the service interface. This page also contains the URL for the WSDL that we need when configuring the ADF BC reference.

Infusing the PatientDataService Application with SDO Interaction

We will enhance the PatientDataService composite application with SDO interaction. This application exposes two Web Services—one to create new patient records and one to retrieve patient details. Each of them is implemented using a BPEL Process component that interacts with a Database Adapter Service. The Database Adapter Services connect to Frank's Patients database—one to insert directly into a table and the other one to invoke a PL/SQL package.

We will introduce an ADF BC reference connecting to the DAS published by the ADF BC application module as a more straightforward and potentially leaner-yet-richer way of interacting with the back-end data store.

Creating the ADF BC Binding

Open the PatientDataService composite application. Drag the ADF BC Service Adapter from the Resource Palette to the References lane. The ADF-BC Service editor appears, as shown in Figure 20-17.

Enter **PatientsServiceSDO** as the name of the reference. Copy the URL for the WSDL for the PatientsServiceSDO—http://localhost:8001/PatientsServiceSDO/PatientsService?WSDL—to the WSDL URL field. When you tab out of this field, JDeveloper will fetch the WSDL document and parse it to extract the PortTypes.

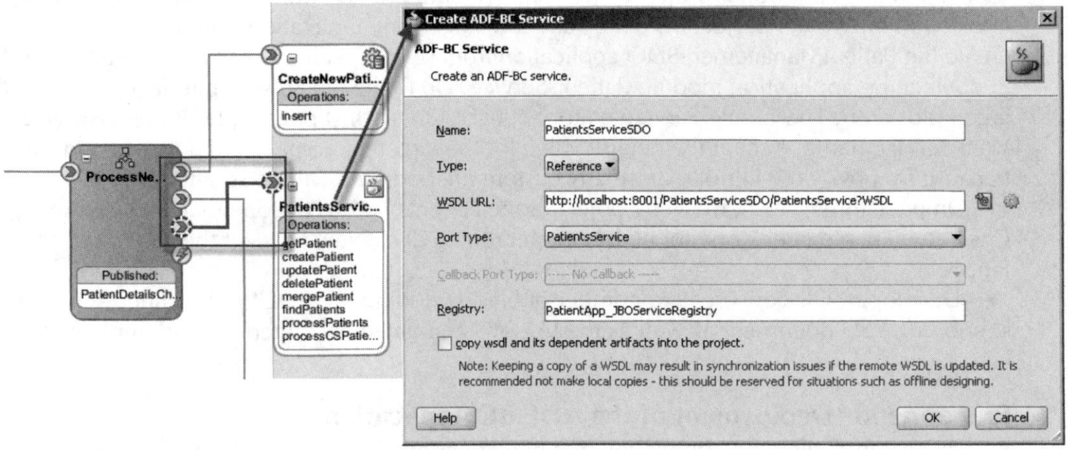

FIGURE 20-17. *Adding the ADF BC reference to the composite*

An important and nontrivial field in this dialog is the Registry field. This field specifies the key used by the SOA infrastructure to look up the ADF BC application that exposes the SDO service in order to invoke it using RMI rather than SOAP over HTTP. The value you need to set is PatientApp_JBOServiceRegistry. This value is composed from the name of the enterprise application, as specified in the deployment profile, with the standard suffix _JBOServiceRegistry.

Click the OK button to complete the reference definition.

Connecting the ProcessNewPatient BPEL Component to the PatientsServiceSDO Binding

Wire the BPEL Process component ProcessNewPatient to the PatientsServiceSDO reference. Then double-click the BPEL component to open the editor.

Open the structure window and expand the Variables node. Select the child Variables node under the Process node and then click the green plus icon to create a new variable.

In the Create Variable dialog that appears, mark the check box Entity Variable. Select the PatientsServiceSDO as the partner link that provides the SDO backing for the entity variable. Select the radio button Element in the Type radio group. In the Type browser, select the patientsVwSDO, which can be found in the inline schema in the PatientsService.wsdl that is imported from the PatientsServiceSDO.wsdl that describes the partner link. Figure 20-18 illustrates the variable definition.

Create a second new variable (*not* an entity variable) called Patient_temp that is based on the same element used for Patient_Entity. This new variable will be used to gather the data that is then moved into the entity variable.

Open the scope InsertNewPatientRecord. Add a Transform(ation) step in which the inputVariable is transformed to the Patient_temp variable.

Add a Create Entity activity immediately after the Transform activity. Set the name of the activity as **CreateEntity_Patient**. Select the Patient_Entity as the target entity to initialize. Set the From field to the following expression:

```
bpws:getVariableData('Patient_temp','/ns7:patientsVwSDO')
```

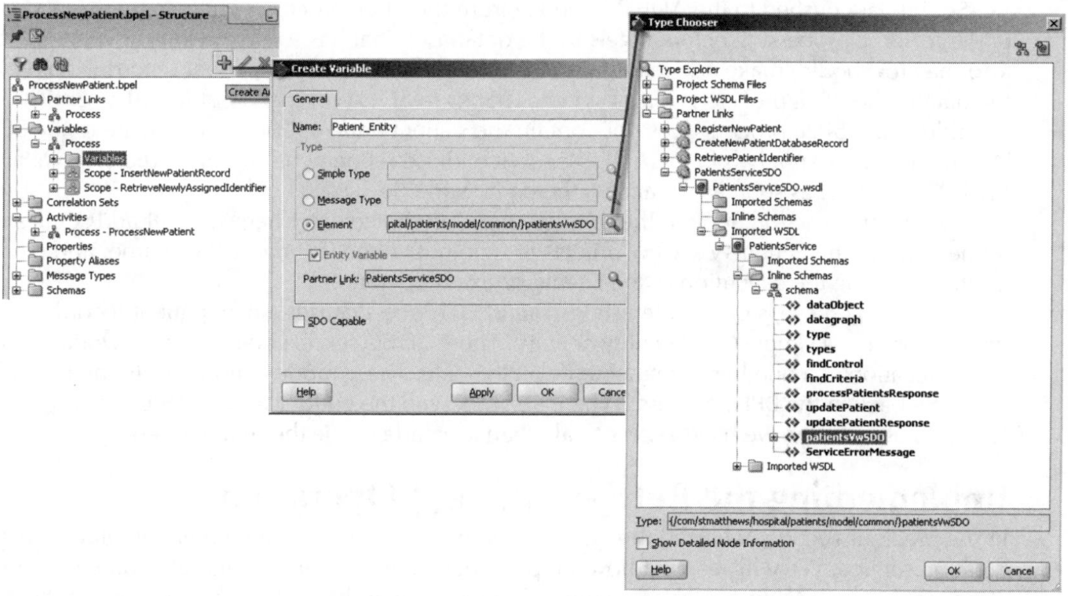

FIGURE 20-18. *Creating the Patient_Entity entity variable*

This extracts the value from the Patient_temp variable and pastes it into the Patient_Entity variable.

Remove the existing Transform and Invoke activities used in conjunction with the Database Adapter Service. Also remove the local scope variables associated with the Invoke activity. At this point, we can deploy the application to the SOA Suite—in the same way as before (the fact that we now have an SDO interaction inside does not alter the deployment process).

Running the SDO-Enabled PatientDataService Application

When we test the PatientDataService application—more specifically, its ProcessNewPatient service—what we expect to get is a new record in the PATIENTS table that is created by the ADF BC application that gets invoked from the BPEL process when the Create Entity activity causes the SDO dependency to be established. This shows that we can make an SOA composite application interact with the database without using the database adapter, but instead using an SDO powered by ADF Business Components.

An Entity Variable Has a Live Connection with the SDO

The ADF BC service can do more or less the same thing as the database adapter did—mapping one-on-one to a database table or view. However, it is easy to add functionality in the ADF BC objects: to calculate and derive values; to refine, enrich, and correct; to validate and to propagate to other targets besides the database; and to do specialized logging. Additionally, the entity objects can be configured to "refresh after insert and update" in order to capture any changes to the data that may be made by database triggers.

So the data pushed to the ADF BC service from the BPEL process's entity variable can undergo some processing before it gets to the database. That has some obvious advantages, but also may (or should) make you fear that even before the insert of the patient record is completed, the data in the BPEL process is out of synch. Thanks to SDO, you need not fear. The entity variable in the BPEL process does not contain the patient data, but only a reference to the SDO. When the data is enriched in the ADF BC service, those refinements are immediately available in the BPEL process, as soon as we access the entity variable.

To see this in action, look in the online chapter complement where we will add some small refinements to the PatientsVw view objects to manipulate the first name, last name, and city attributes during the execution of the Create or Insert operation.

What we achieve is pretty interesting: The BPEL process causes a new patient record to be created through a simple Create Entity activity. The ADF BC service does the hard work—including the application of a number of refinements on the data. These modifications are immediately available back in the BPEL process: When we work with the entity variable Patient_Entity after the Create Entity activity, we have access to all changes made inside the ADF BC service.

Implementing the Retrieve Patient Operation

In the previous section, we used the SDO-bound entity variable to implement an elegant patient-creation service. We will see next how simple it becomes to perform data retrieval based on the same mechanism. Additionally, we will see how we can add a custom Java method to the ADF BC application module and to the service interface and subsequently invoke that method from the BPEL process.

Adding a findPatientIdentifier Operation to the ADF BC Web Service

Open the editor for the application module PatientsService and select the Java tab. Click the edit icon in the upper-right corner and then check the box Generate Application Module Class.

Open the PatientsServiceImpl class that is generated. Add a custom method called **findPatientIdentifier** with the following code that retrieves the primary key value for firstName and lastName:

```
public Long findPatientIdentifier(String firstName, String lastName) {
   getPatientsVw1().setWhereClause("first_name ='"+firstName
                                 +"' and last_name ='"+lastName+"'" );
   getPatientsVw1().executeQuery();
   if (getPatientsVw1().getEstimatedRowCount()>0) {
     return ((oracle.jbo.domain.Number)getPatientsVw1().first()
                                   .getAttribute("Id")).longValue();
   }
   else return null;
}
```

Go to the Service Interface tab for the application module and click the edit icon in the Service Interface Custom Methods header. Move the findPatientIdentifier method to the selected box and then click the OK button.

We can now redeploy the ADF BC application. The Web Service published by this application has been extended with a new operation, called findPatientIdentifier. We will use this operation in the BPEL process to retrieve the patient identifier that will be used for binding the entity variable.

Implementing the RetrievePatient BPEL Process

The BPEL Process component PatientDataService (in the SOA composite application with the same name) is called to retrieve details on a patient. The request contains either the patient identifier or the first and last name of the patient. In the latter case, the patient identifier is first retrieved—currently using a Database Adapter Reference that calls a PL/SQL function. Another Database Adapter Reference is then used to retrieve the patient details based on the identifier.

We will make two changes to this process:

■   Use the findPatientIdentifier operation added in the ADF BC service to get hold of the patient identifier.

■   Use an entity variable and the Bind Entity activity to initialize the entity variable with a reference to the Patient SDO.

The two Database Adapter References can subsequently be removed—along with their associated variables, Assign steps, and Invoke activities. Here are the implementation steps:

1.   Open the Composite Editor for the PatientDataService application. Wire the PatientData Service BPEL component to the PatientsServiceSDO reference.

2.   Edit the PatientDataService BPEL component as shown in Figure 20-19. Add an Invoke activity called **Invoke_FindPatientIdentifier** to the flow for the case that the request does not contain the patient identifier. Configure it for the PartnerLink PatientsServiceSDO and the operation findPatientIdentifier, which is based on the new custom method that we have just added to the Service Interface.

3.   Remove the existing Invoke activity (which calls the Database Adapter Reference RetrievePatientIdentifier). Edit the Assign activities before and after the Invoke step to set the input for findPatientIdentifier and copy the output to the BPEL variable patientIdentifier.

4.   Add a new variable to the BPEL process called Patient_Entity. This variable is an entity variable (so check the box) based on the PartnerLink PatientsServiceSDO. This variable is based on the element patientsVwSDO.

5.   Add a Bind Entity activity right below the Flow activity. Set the name to **Bind_PatientEntity**. Choose the Patient_Entity variable as the variable to bind. The value for the key of this variable is derived from the patientIdentifier variable, which is set in the Flow activity (see Figure 20-20).

6.   Add a Transform activity called **PopulateOutputVariableFromPatientEntity**. The source variable is Patient_Entity, and the target is the BPEL variable outputVariable. Specify the name of the XSL Mapper file as **PopulateOutputFromPatient_Entity**. Edit the mapper file, mapping from source to target.

7.   We should remove several activities that are left over from the old database adapter–based approach: Remove the Assign_PatientIdToInput, Invoke_RetrievePatientRecord, and Assign_PatientRecordToOutputVariable activities.

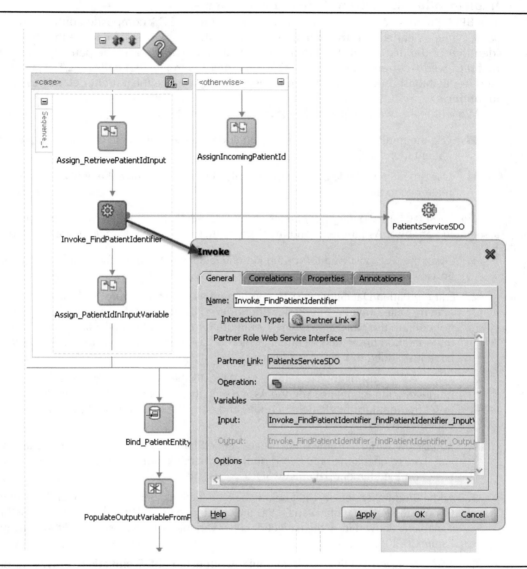

FIGURE 20-19. *Configuring the Invoke_FindPatientIdentifier activity*

Deploying and Running the Composite PatientDataService

Deploy the PatientDataService. Test the Web Service exposed by the PatientDataService application and choose the operation "process" on the client interface. Enter the first name and last name for one of the patients in the PATIENTS table and click the button Test Web Service. The response provides some details for the patient—not queried through the database adapter but elegantly provided by the SDO service.

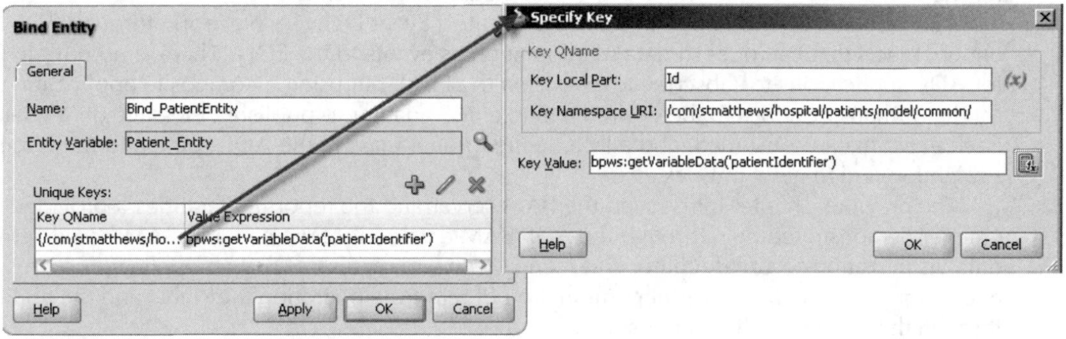

FIGURE 20-20. *Adding a Bind Entity activity, tying the Patient_Entity entity variable using the patient identifier*

The composite application has swapped two database adapter references for a "regular" Web Service call and a Bind Entity activity, and still has immediate access to data originating from the database. In fact, we have a live wire to the SDO data service: The entity variable is bound to the SDO. This gives us access to the patient data in the BPEL process.

Live Wire from BPEL Entity Variable to SDO

But wait, there's more: This "live wire" also means that when we change contents of the entity variable Patient_Entity with simple Assign statements, these changes are pushed to the SDO Data Access Service, implemented by the ADF BC service, and thus all the way to the database! An assign in BPEL on the Patient_Entity has now become more or less equivalent with an update on the PATIENTS table.

Summary

The Application Development Framework (ADF) is primarily intended to provide a user interface for people to use to perform tasks in business processes. Pages in ADF web applications are typically created using ADF Faces—a rich client component library that renders a modern, Web 2.0, fully Ajax-enabled interface. These components frequently work in conjunction with ADF Model data controls that supply the components with collections of data records and operations on these records and their attributes. The data controls in ADF Model encapsulate underlying business services, which can range from Web Services, Plain-Old Java Objects (POJOs), and ADF BC, to content management systems, BAM servers, and BI servers.

ADF applications can thus leverage SOA composite applications by wrapping the functionality provided by the services exposed by the composite applications in data controls and binding these to the webpages. In this way, the ADF application can, for example, trigger a business process from a webpage or retrieve required data from composite services.

The composite applications themselves make use of ADF to provide the user interface for human tasks. Many BPEL processes and BPMN processes require contributions from end users; these are implemented in the composite applications through human tasks that are exposed through the BPM Worklist application. This application uses ADF task flows specifically created for the task at hand to present the users with a customized task UI.

ADF applications can hook into the SOA Suite's Event Delivery Network, through ADF BC entity objects that can publish data manipulation as events to the EDN. There is no built-in facility for ADF applications to subscribe to events on the EDN, but using a composite application with a Mediator that subscribes to the desired event, a JMS adapter to publish a message on a queue for each event that is consumed, and a JMS queue listener class in the ADF application, it is fairly straightforward to get it to work.

The previous chapter introduced the BAM server and the reporting facilities it provides. This chapter demonstrated how through the ADF BAM data control we can add BAM-based active data visualizations—tables, charts, trees, and so on—to regular ADF web applications. This allows for a potentially powerful combination of real-time operational insights and the ability act through the other (non-BAM) parts of application.

The final integration between the SOA Suite and ADF discussed in this chapter is the Service Data Object (SDO) binding that we can create between an ADF BC application module that is published with an SDO-enabled service interface and variables in a BPEL process. The SDO-based entity variables in BPEL processes allow direct, lean, and real-time integration from the variable to the ViewObject row. This SDO-based link provides an alternative for the use of the database adapter, which can especially be helpful for chatty BPEL processes that almost require a stateful conversation with a database.

CHAPTER
21

The Bigger Picture: SOA for User Interfaces, SaaS, and the Cloud

he most visible part of most applications is the user interface—that tip of the iceberg that takes care of the interaction with us human users. This is despite the fact that the bulk of the functionality of most applications is in the services that perform the actual work, leveraging enterprise resources such as databases and various calculation engines. Chapter 10 (on human tasks) and Chapter 11 (on BPM) as well as the previous chapter (on using ADF to create advanced user interfaces) discussed the human-oriented interface that facilitates the interaction between users and (service-oriented) applications. We will take that discussion a little further in this chapter, when we look at the application of the concepts and principles of SOA—decoupling and focusing on reuse with agility as the main objective—to user interfaces.

We will briefly discuss mash-ups and portals, Portlets, and task flows. Our primary technology focus in this discussion is Oracle Fusion Middleware and ADF and WebCenter in particular, although most considerations apply more generally.

A growing number of applications will be consumed in or deployed and exposed in a SaaS (Software as a Service) manner, depending on your perspective. A SaaS application is offered remotely with regard to the users, as a more or less standard application for potentially large numbers of users who may belong to multiple distinct organizations. Usage of SaaS applications can be free, although customers are normally charged based on their usage metrics. SaaS applications will typically expose both a user interface as well as a programmatic interface through Web Services.

SaaS applications (running in the cloud) will somehow need to integrate with other SaaS applications and with non-SaaS applications running inside the organizations using them. We will look at typical requirements for SaaS applications and briefly look at what we can do to make them fit into the local SOA landscape of and work together with locally controlled applications.

Given the scope of these topics, we will only be able to scratch the surface. However, this chapter should provide you with insights in how the objectives, concepts, and ways of working for SOA and the SOA Suite, as discussed in the previous chapters of this book, by and large, can and perhaps should be applied to development of user interfaces to support human activities. The impact of SaaS-style deployment of applications—both on the user interface of SaaS applications as well as on the service-based interface—will be outlined, and we will discuss some generic considerations and guidelines. The online chapter complement provides more detail, suggestions, and references.

Integration at the User Interface Level

In all the discussions and examples in the book so far we have worked on the assumption that our SOA composite applications as well as the Oracle Service Bus perform all the integration that may be required for our user interfaces. The user interface is then created on top of the services provided by the SOA infrastructure.

This user interface could be a monolith, a conglomerate of pages and components that each use one or more of these services. The fact that services represent a heterogeneous environment with databases, content management stores, external Web Services, and other enterprise stores and facilities is hidden from the view of the application and its developers. This approach is indicated as option I in Figure 21-1.

However, there are other approaches for creating a user interface on top of the services in a SOA environment that should be considered, especially because they promote the same principles that form the foundation of SOA to the development of user interfaces.

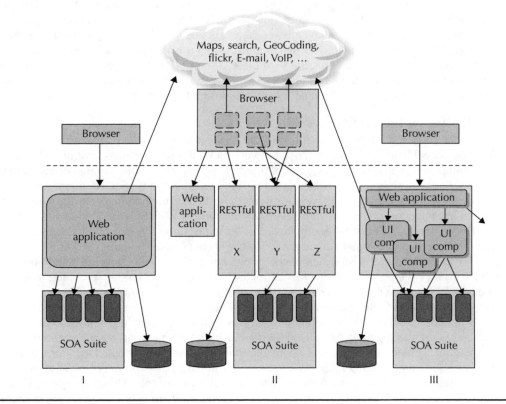

FIGURE 21-1.   *Three architecture styles for user interface applications*

Alternative Methods for User Interface Integration

In the approach we have assumed thus far, we use SOA composites and the Oracle Service Bus to bridge the gaps between technology platforms for us, to gather data from various sources and make them available in an uniform way to composite services.

An alternative approach is one in which the user interface itself is where the integration takes place—option II in Figure 21-1. For example, JavaScript widgets can be combined together in rich webpages. These widgets present data and operations to the end users and typically communicate with RESTful services to retrieve data and propagate manipulation of data. The widgets can be developed in separate files that can be assembled into what is sometimes called a *mash-up:* a simple HTML document that loads one or more stylesheets (CSS) as well as the widgets from their respective JavaScript files. Note that some of the widgets loaded may be located at remote locations. Google Maps is an example of such a remote widget that can be assembled into a mash-up. In this approach, some of the services exposed by our SOA infrastructure should be published in a RESTful way, with simple (non-SOAP) HTTP bindings, and usually with JSON as the format for data exchange. We have seen in Chapter 13 how the Oracle Service Bus can help us expose these RESTful services.

A third approach—option III in Figure 21-1—also does integration at the user interface level, but does so on the server side. In this approach, user interfaces are composed from multiple UI components that each represent an area in a page with a special focus or supporting a specific task. These UI components are typically reusable, encapsulated, and with well-defined interfaces, developed independently according to loosely coupled release schedules, very similar to how we have defined services in this book. Some of these UI components are just the front-end for a single composite service; others combine several composite services into a report or complex page. The components are assembled together at design time and/or run time.

Portlets for UI Integration

Portlet is a category of UI components that can be seen as a "service with a UI." Portlets are designed, developed, and even deployed in very much the same way as "normal" Web Services. They can be invoked remotely by a portal or other type of framework capable of consuming Portlets. Such calls are usually done via HTTP and based on the Portlet's contract specification expressed using WSRP (Web Services for Remote Portlets). The WSRP specification defines a Web Service interface for interacting with presentation-oriented Web Services.

The contract for a Portlet—and in fact most reusable, stand-alone user interface components—describes the parameters that can be passed to the Portlet (when initiating the Portlet) as well as which types of events are published by the Portlet and which it will consume. In addition, the contract may indicate which style class attributes have been used for the key elements in the UI. The page consuming the Portlet can use these style class names in a custom CSS stylesheet to apply its own styles to the content returned by the Portlet.

Note that Portlets can be developed in various technologies, including Java, .NET, PHP, and PL/SQL. As long as they support the WSRP standard, such Portlets can be consumed into web applications with portal facilities, across technologies, as well as distributed locations. The portal that integrates various remote Portlets into a single webpage has a role very similar to the Enterprise Service Bus that integrates various (non-UI) Web Services into a (non-UI) composite service. Like Web Services, Portlets are exposed from their own, potentially remote, run-time environments. They can be published under a certain SLA, available only to authorized consumers.

Portlets will use their own, local resources to provide data and services. Portlets may use databases, content management servers, and Web Services to implement the functionality they provide. Consumers of the Portlet typically do not need to be aware of resources consumed by a remote Portlet.

SOA Suite 11*g* does not publish or consume Portlets itself. However, the WebCenter Framework—another component in Oracle Fusion Middleware—contains facilities both for publishing and consuming Portlets. Webpages in ADF applications can consume one or more Portlets. In fact, using these WebCenter Portlet producers that make Portlets available for embedding in an ADF Faces page, we can create pages and entire applications that are nothing more than the assembly and wiring of external Portlets. Such a page is very similar to a composite service, integrating and wiring UI components together rather than programmatic services components.

Portlets require similar run-time administration and design-time governance as "simple" (non-UI) services. For example, identifying the existing Portlets available for reuse by new user interfaces is similar to finding out about services available for reuse. Deciding on the Portlets that are to be developed in order to support the expected reuse scenarios as well as managing the life cycle of those Portlets is required for Portlets just as much as for non-UI services.

ADF Task Flows: The Advanced Alternative to Portlets

ADF has its own concept of a stand-alone, encapsulated, reusable, service-like UI component: the (bound) task flow. A task flow can be developed, tested, and distributed as a stand-alone component. A task flow can be embedded in another task flow as well as directly in a webpage. A task flow usually provides its consumer with a UI that may consist of a single page fragment or multiple (multistep) fragments. A task flow can contain Java classes, make use of ADF BC against database objects, or invoke Web Services. Usually, a task flow is implemented as a self-contained unit that takes care of its own resources.

The contract of a task flow consists of input parameters that the consumer can specify to configure the behavior of the task flow. Additionally, task flows can produce events to report special conditions to the consuming page, and it may subscribe on events that the consuming page—or other task flows consumed by that same page—produce. The communication between consumer and task flow after the initial instantiation of a task flow is through events—somewhat similar to the communication with a running BPEL process instance from other components or from outside the composite application.

Page fragments in a task flow can make use of specific (CSS) style class names that the consumer can provide the style definition for. For example, a task flow may set a specific style class called dateField on every inputDate component that it contains. This allows the consumer to apply a special styling to all date fields in the whole application, both the part developed from scratch as well as the parts assembled from embedded task flows.

Task flows can be developed as stand-alone ADF applications. They can be deployed as a ADF Library, a special type of JAR file. This JAR file can be imported into one or potentially many ADF applications that want to reuse the task flow. After the ADF Library is imported into an ADF application, each task flow in that library can be embedded into every page in that application (or even several times into the same page).

WebCenter Services A very good example of reusable task flows that play a role very similar to reusable (web) services in an SOA environment is provided by WebCenter Services. This WebCenter component adds over a dozen reusable functional extensions to ADF applications, in areas such as Web 2.0, social networking, and collaboration. The WebCenter Services are implemented as task flows that can be embedded into the pages of the application—for example, to add document-browse and document-management functionality, tagging and linking support, discussion forums, and wiki integration.

One of the WebCenter Services is the Worklist service. This is a task flow that uses a connection to the SOA Suite's Human Workflow Services to retrieve all currently outstanding tasks for the user. These tasks are listed as a series of links that take the user right into the Worklist application from which the task can be handled.

Here we see a good example of the UI service (the Worklist service task flow) that itself uses a service (the Human Workflow service) of which the consuming page does not need to have knowledge. Well, that is, the connection to the Human Workflow service needs to be configured when the first occurrence of this task flow is added to the application.

Publishing ADF Portlets The manual creation of a Portlet requires knowledge of the JSR-168 or JSR-286 specification. These are produced by the JCP (Java Community Process) to lay down the requirements for standards-compliant Portlets. In addition, if the Portlet that is to be created should be accessible from distant locations, it should be published with a WSRP definition alongside of it.

To deploy the Portlet and make it available to external consumers, a WSRP-enabled Portlet container infrastructure is required.

When you want to create Portlets developed using ADF, you have two options. The open-source way has you use an open-source Portlet container and manual development of the Portlets. Note that Portlet development using vanilla ADF can be challenging, because a number of limitations apply to applications that need to be Portlet-enabled.

WebCenter Framework adds the JSF Portlet Bridge to ADF applications, which makes publishing Portlets based on ADF applications a purely declarative exercise. With this bridge, the limitations on the development of the applications largely go away. An ADF-based Portlet is created by publishing a task flow as a Portlet. A Portlet can be exposed by a WebLogic Server that has both the ADF and WebCenter Framework libraries installed. An ADF-based Portlet can be consumed by any WSRP-enabled portal framework.

Figure 21-2 shows an ADF application that reuses Taskflows from local ADF Libraries at design time and invokes remote Portlets at run time as well. These Portlets have also been implemented through ADF Taskflows. They have been independently deployed and have been configured for their own access—apart from the consuming application—to enterprise resources, such as Database and SOA Suite.

Comparing Portlets and Task Flows   At least when applications are developed using ADF there seems to be two options for "SOA style" development of user interfaces. We can make use of the native ADF mechanism of the task flow as the encapsulated, reusable user interface component. Alternatively, we can go with the standards-based mechanism of the Portlets.

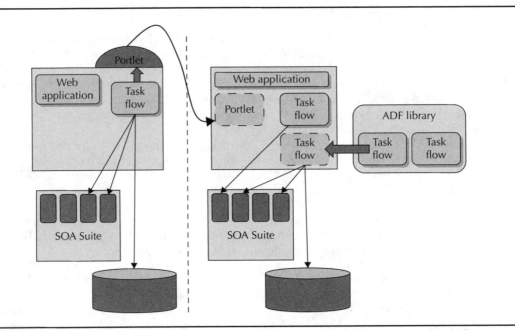

FIGURE 21-2.   *Web application assembly using both a remote Portlet and a local task flow*

Both options are similar in that they are stand-alone, reusable units with clear interfaces and an encapsulated implementation that can be developed, tested, and distributed in isolation. There are very clear distinctions that we should look at when choosing either approach. Note, though, that we can combine task flows and Portlets to create a "composite user interface application."

Portlets can be used across technology stacks. That means, for example, when Portlets are implemented in the .NET stack, they can be consumed in an ADF application and, conversely, an ADF task flow–based Portlet can be consumed by any WSRP-enabled portal framework. If you are creating integrated user interfaces in more than one user interface technology, Portlets are your only option because task flows are a proprietary, ADF-only feature.

NOTE
Using IFrames, you could find a way to embed an ADF page in a non-ADF HTML application, but without any of the event interaction and UI integration that real Portlets would give you.

In order to publish Portlets developed in ADF, you need a license to use WebCenter Framework with the JSF Portlet Bridge. For consuming Portlets into an ADF application, you also need WebCenter Framework.

Integration of Portlets happens at run time. That means it carries a little extra overhead compared to integration of native ADF task flows (although less than half a second per full page request). The fact that integration is done at run time makes it very easy to deploy new versions of Portlets without impact on the consumers (provided, of course, that the contract does not change). ADF task flows are integrated at design time—from the distributed ADF Libraries—and are deployed as part of the application that consumes them. Task flows do not run independently in their own server environment; they are merged with the consuming application. Portlets can be consumed from remote servers—task flows clearly are local. Note that by creating separate WLS shared libraries for the task flows, and subsequently creating library references in the weblogic-application.xml file to these libraries, it becomes possible to separately deploy the task flows and the applications that consume them.

The interaction patterns supported by task flows are more refined than those available with Portlets. This distinction depends on the version of the Portlet specification applied. Task flows can both publish and consume fine-grained contextual events with a complex, strongly typed payload. They also support navigation listeners, parent task flow actions, and other interaction facilities.

Task flows are better integrated into the IDE—it is easier to embed and configure a task flow into an ADF application than to integrate a Portlet. In addition, task flows can share the transaction used by the "rest of application" as well as ADF data controls—although from a perspective of decoupling, which is not something to be done lightly.

Task flows inherit the ADF skin in use by the consuming application—so they adapt their look and feel. Also, task flows have a very special characteristic: They can be extended and customized by the consumer. ADF customization is a generic mechanism through which application artifacts such as JSF pages can be customized for different situations. This same mechanism can be used to customize a task flow that is reused from an ADF Library. Customizing task flows breaks encapsulation, and should therefore be applied with great care and restraint. However, at times, it may make the difference between reuse or rebuild.

Presentation Services

Increasingly, customers of an application will request to not only have access to the application via a user interface, but via a programmatic interface as well. Oracle, for example, has addressed this requirement by creating a Web Service for every task flow in Fusion Applications. Task flows implement a workflow with associated operations that presents certain records and supports specific manipulations. Every task flow has a Web Service counterpart that supports those same operations as well as data retrieval and manipulation. Note that these services could be the foundation for the task flows themselves.

In general, services consumed by applications to support user interfaces are somewhat special. A user interface has a user waiting for its response. The interaction with the end user is usually bound by specific response times—typically sub seconds—and performance requirements. The service response times in business process execution are usually not as critical as those for services directly supporting end-user applications.

This means we might put additional work in reducing the overhead for user interfaces to get responses out of our services. Several aspects should be considered. First of all, you get the best performance for an action if you do not have to perform that action at all. The overhead of invoking a service from the application via the service bus will be incurred for every call, so we should try to limit the number of calls per browser request. The easiest way of doing this is to provide composite services that expose exactly the information required for a certain page. Instead of letting the application invoke multiple services to get all the pieces required, we can work with "presentation services" that make the exact data in the correct format available to the application. This can be compared with database views or ADF BC view objects that are created for similar purposes. Figure 21-3 shows various types of presentation services that provide tailor-made support for user interfaces.

Another way of reducing the response times suffered by the web application invoking the services is by shaving time off the service calls. This could, for example, be achieved by not making the service calls through SOAP/HTTP/XML all the time, but using other bindings such as the EJB binding, JMS adapter and queue interaction, or socket or direct binding. Additionally, perhaps the services should not be run as SOA composite applications. Perhaps the services should be implemented using Servlets, PL/SQL packages, RSS feeds, and so on.

Depending on the application architecture that is adopted in the organization, the presentation services may need to directly support special clients such as JavaScript programs that require access to RESTful services that accept simple HTTP requests and want JSON objects in response.

Run-time Assembly of the User Interface

Most user interfaces are designed at design time, by developers and according to functional specifications. However, many portal frameworks allow online maintenance by application administrators or end users. At run time, through the browser interface, the arrangement of the Portlets can be changed. New Portlets can be added and existing ones removed or reconfigured.

Oracle WebCenter Framework offers the Composer component. Composer allows an ADF application to be editable at run time (sometimes called "designtime@runtime" by Oracle). This means, for example, that authorized users can rearrange containers on the page and add new Portlets, as well as add new task flows to the page. When pages are editable, they can be switched to edit mode, where changes can be designed and applied. The definition of the page is partly created at design time and deployed to the run-time container, and partly created at run time and stored in and interpreted from MDS.

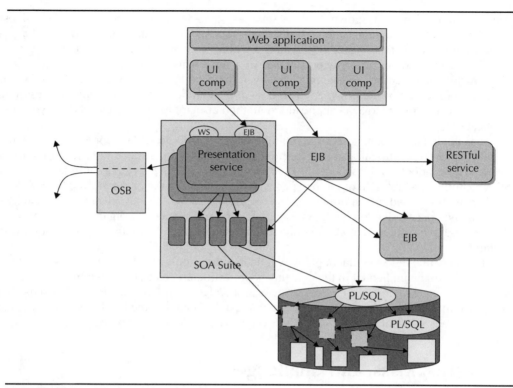

FIGURE 21-3. *Presentation services*

One similar example of run-time assembly occurs for human tasks when the Worklist application embeds—using an iFrame and a remote task flow call—a specialized task flow as the user interface for the service. That, too, is a mechanism we can make use of for our own applications.

Software as a Service and SOA Across the Cloud

The cloud is that somewhat intangible, omnipresent realm of services at the infrastructure, platform, and software level that exists "somewhere out there." IT facilities (such as server capacity and storage), application server environments, and ready-to-use business applications can be utilized from the cloud, like water and electricity. Cloud-based services are provided from a centrally managed 24/7 environment, are highly scalable, benefit from the economies of scale, are paid for per real usage (typically without large investments up front), and thus offer a lot of benefits to organizations with IT requirements. Additional benefits are typically the quick implementation, rapid availability of new functionality, and a user community to share experiences with.

Not only customers of cloud-based services such as IaaS (Infrastructure as a Service), PaaS (Platform as a Service), and SaaS (Software as a Service) benefit from said characteristics. Providers of such services also experience cost savings, easier entry levels for new customers (with less sales effort), and a global market with a potentially much larger customer base.

Amazon, for example, has grown its cloud services—IaaS and PaaS—into substantial business units based on the experience and cost efficiency it gained with establishing and managing its own IT infrastructure that runs 24/7, servicing a global audience of tens of millions of users.

This chapter focuses primarily on software as a service and does not further discuss infrastructure and platform as a service. However, IaaS and PaaS provide fine opportunities for organizations to deploy their own applications "in the cloud." Some of the topics discussed in this chapter with regard to SaaS application will then also apply to those cloud-deployed custom applications.

SaaS applications relate to SOA in multiple ways. In order to replace some homegrown, locally deployed functionality in an enterprise with one or more SaaS modules, the organization needs to have adopted a loosely coupled application architecture—such as SOA advocates and SOA technology enables. In order to expose functionality from the cloud in "the SaaS way," an implementation based on the principles and technology of SOA seems advantageous. And very importantly: Successful adoption of SaaS applications and services by organizations that themselves have embraced SOA can only be achieved by providing multiple service-oriented facilities.

It is likely that the SaaS functionality will have to be exposed with a user interface that can be integrated into the unified UI in the consumer's infrastructure, as discussed in the previous section, for example, through Portlets or JavaScript widgets. And the functionality also has to be published through a programmatic interface that can be bound to the local SOA infrastructure, with RSS feeds, RESTful services, and SOAP WebServices along with an event handling mechanism.

Concerns, Risks, and Challenges

Even though few would deny the potential benefits of cloud-based solutions, many have voiced concerns over certain aspects of the "as a service" approach. Although some concerns seem to be somewhat emotionally driven, others have merit and need to be addressed. We will see how this leads to a number of special requirements for SaaS applications, some of which are of immediate relevance from the perspective of SOA and the use of SOA Suite.

Out of Control

Part of cloud-based services is obviously relinquishing some control over components in the organization's IT infrastructure to the service provider. That means, for example, that the performance and plain availability of the SaaS application is no longer controlled by the local, in-house IT department but by the provider. Usually, a Service Level Agreement (SLA) will formally define the quality of service provided by the provider as well as financial penalties in case those levels are not met. Furthermore, cloud service providers benefit from economies of scale that allow for around-the-clock professional staff and enterprise-level facilities to monitor systems and handle or even prevent failures, which may be out of reach for many organizations that may consume the cloud services. Cloud-based infrastructures typically have satisfactory response times compared to in-house infrastructures, so handing over control to a better-equipped, more-professional IT organization may not be such a bad deal after all. There will be, however, some overhead incurred from cross-cloud communication that should be taken into account.

However, you are not just handing over daily control over your application in the case of a SaaS application—you leave your data in the hands of the cloud provider as well. The good news is typically the very low cost of storage space in a cloud-based scenario, compared to investing in an on-site SAN. The potential risk you may need to address is the fact that you may not at all times have access to what is essentially a core asset of your organization: your data. As long as you can get access to that data, at any moment in time and in more ways than only through a user-oriented interface, that should not have to be a problem. Of course, there is the small matter of availability, especially in the light of catastrophes befalling the cloud service provider. What are the risks of a long-term failure (the aftermath of a power outage, earthquake, or plane crash) or even permanent failure (for example, when the provider goes bankrupt)?

Additionally, what will be the physical, geographical location of your data and what could be possible consequences of that locality? Your data may be subject to legislation that you did not necessarily want to be governed by—for example, with regard to your customers' confidentiality.

Security is an aspect closely related with the previous consideration. What is the level of security guaranteed by the provider, and how can you be sure of it? And it is not just the location of the data when in storage; it is the security of that data in transit. When you're leveraging a cloud-based service for what could also be an on-site, behind-the-firewall intranet back-office application, data is moving across the Internet to a remote location beyond the firewall where it did not have to go. This poses an extra security risk that needs to be justified and addressed.

A certain lock-in with the SaaS provider will be inevitable. However, it may be wise to keep open as much as possible the options of moving from one provider to another. What, for example, would be the consequences for your business if the functionality provided by the SaaS application would overnight no longer be available to you, even if you had a dump of all data in the system? That's where open standards come into play—make these an important selection criteria when choosing a provider of cloud services.

Cloud Service Is an Off-the-Shelf, Standard Offering

Most organizations feel that they are special. No one is exactly like them. That led in the past frequently to custom development of entire applications. The trend in recent years has somewhat shifted to the use of commercially available "off-the-shelf" applications, which are frequently implemented with a customized configuration and/or complemented with custom-developed extensions to address the organization's specific characteristics.

A concern regarding SaaS applications is that they are not only obviously standard—many organizations (potentially thousands) use the same cloud-based instance of a single application— but probably not easy to configure for the specific needs of the organization, nor are they easy to extend with custom application components.

Integration with Other Systems and Infrastructure

It is unlikely that the only application used by an organization is a single SaaS application. It seems much more realistic, and increasingly so, for organizations to use a mix of onsite standard and custom(ized) applications and cloud-based SaaS applications. And those SaaS applications may be offered by different providers, each running its own cloud.

This obviously raises the topic of integration. What if more than one application works with the same data? Where is that data held? How are changes managed? And how are business events originating in the cloud-based application made available to the local, onsite event handlers such as the SOA Suite's Event Delivery Network as well as other SaaS applications used by the organization? Another aspect is the user interface. Many organizations want their users to work in a portal-like environment where all applications are visually integrated into a single user interface. The applications share a number of facilities, including Single Sign-On against the local identity infrastructure, and are capable of passing context information back and forth among each other for mutual alignment.

Additionally, when an application sends out an e-mail to a customer, that e-mail probably must come from the organization's e-mail server, not some SaaS provider's domain. And a batch print job should end up on a printer on the site of the SaaS consumer, not the provider. In short, cloud-based applications should be able to make use of services on offer within the consumer's infrastructure.

Consuming Cloud-based Software Services

Services provided by cloud-based SaaS applications can come in various forms. Some of the most common ways of consuming these services are listed here:

- The SaaS offering can be run as a stand-alone application in an isolated browser window. Examples of full-blown SaaS applications capable of running in stand-alone mode are SalesForce.com, AMIS APS, Connexys Recruitment solutions, Google Health, and Oracle CRMOnDemand.

- A SaaS application (or part of it) can also be visually embedded into another SaaS app or a local custom app, typically using an iFrame inside the embedding web page; when only a part of a SaaS application's page is embedded, this is frequently done using a technique called Web Clipping, which is, for example, supported by the standard WebClipping Portlet in Oracle WebCenter.

- Instead of leveraging the SaaS application's user interface, the consuming application can instead utilize RSS feeds and RESTful services, or make use of JavaScript libraries, images, or gadgets published by the SaaS application. Examples of these services that are consumed on the client slide, from within the browser, are Google Maps, the SlideShare presentation widget, social networking gadgets based on the OpenSocial API, and the reCaptcha gadget.

- A more formal, standardized, and potentially rich form of user interface integration involves the consumption of a Portlet. An example is the Oracle CRMOnDemand top-sales Portlet or the Task List Portlet exposed by the SOA Suite.

- Applications can consume Web Services (RESTful or SOAP based) exposed by the SaaS application, either directly or preferably via an enterprise service bus, and then use that service to create application logic or a custom user interface. Note that some SaaS applications do not have a user interface at all and are only available as a Web Service. Examples include Geo Coding, translation such as Babel Fish, currency exchange rates, weather forecasts, stock prices, and sending SMS messages.

- Specific forms of consumption of cloud services may leverage cloud-based infrastructure, such as storage, encryption, VoIP, and e-mail; examples include Amazon EC2 for storage, Google's Gmail, and Oracle BeeHive.

The wiki and online chapter complement provide some examples of these various SaaS consumption patterns.

Requirements for SaaS Applications

The concerns and risks discussed in the previous section come into play in several situations. When your organization is considering the use of an SaaS application or some cloud-based service, the concerns listed before might be used to compare various SaaS offerings and to compare them with on-premise solutions, either commercial off-the-shelf or custom-developed solutions. When your organization is involved in offering applications or other IT services, and you are already doing so from the cloud or considering going there, these considerations may be useful to decide on the functionality and architecture required for such SaaS-style offerings. This section will briefly introduce a number of facilities that your applications ideally should offer, in order to address concerns from your (potential) customers. Figure 21-4 illustrates some of the facilities that are required in order to achieve "cross-the-cloud" integration between (web) applications and SOA infrastructures.

NOTE
It would seem that many if not all applications would benefit from having the suggested characteristics, even when SaaS deployment is not relevant. Or, perhaps, the onsite IT infrastructure is a cloud of sorts and therefore even on-premise applications should be considered SaaS applications in most cases.

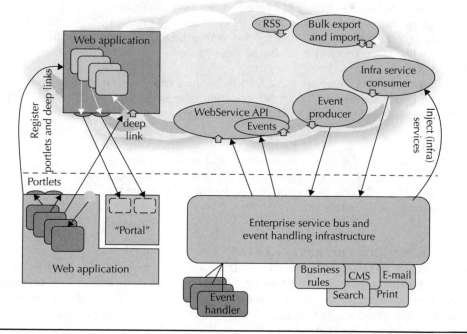

FIGURE 21-4.   *SOA across the cloud—facilities for integration between local and cloud-based SaaS application*

Web Service API

In addition to the user interface, every task, report, and operation supported by the SaaS application should be accessible through a WebService API. This allows customers of the application to create their own user interfaces that can be integrated into their enterprise portals and workflow systems and that can be developed for alternative channels and devices. It also makes it possible to integrate the SaaS application into the enterprise service bus of the consuming organization, making programmatic access possible. Oracle Fusion Applications as well as SalesForce.com are examples of SaaS applications with Web Services for all functionality available through the user interface.

In addition to regular (SOAP) Web Services, this service API could also publish RSS feeds for specific types of events as well as RESTful services that are easier to integrate through client-site widgets and gadgets.

Bulk Data Import and Export

To reduce the dependency on the SaaS provider and mitigate some of the perceived risks, it should be possible for SaaS consumers to get an export of all their data. In order to start using the SaaS application, or when dealing with substantial changes in the organization (such as mergers, acquisitions, or even legislation), bulk imports or updates into the cloud-based data store are highly desirable.

Dependency Injection of Services

Oftentimes, SaaS applications have a need to perform fairly generic actions, such as authenticating users, handling e-mail, printing (in batch), sending out alerts to human operators, executing enterprise-wide searches, maintaining calendars, managing documents in a content management system, logging business events of interest, performing organization-specific validations and calculations, and keeping track of the presence of users of the application. Most enterprises have their own specialized infrastructures for performing these tasks. SaaS applications typically should use these specialized, locally available services (or perhaps acquired from some other cloud), instead of their own cloud-based facilities.

This means that consumers of SaaS applications should be able to inject their implementation of the required services into the SaaS application. The SaaS application then should call out to the injected services to send the e-mail, authenticate the user, or print the report.

> **NOTE**
> *This requires of the SaaS customer that local services are exposed to the SaaS application, using the interface prescribed by the SaaS application. The Oracle Service Bus is an obvious medium for exposing such services.*

Event Subscription for Remote Listeners

In Chapters 9 and 19 we discussed Event-Driven Architecture, the SOA Suite Event Delivery Network, and complex event processing. Identifying business events and ensuring that these get published to a central event handler that manages subscriptions from all interested parties is crucial in successfully adopting EDA. This will only work when all potential event producers take their responsibility and publish their events.

SaaS applications are potentially the source of events and should therefore publish these events to the central event handler *in the infrastructure of the SaaS consumer.* Of course, the SaaS application has no way of knowing beforehand how to contact the event handler for each of its consumers. SaaS consumers, therefore, need to be able to register event handlers with the SaaS application. These handlers are implemented as Web Services that are invoked by the SaaS application when an event of the type they have registered for occurs.

The WebService API we discussed before should also provide interfaces for the publication of events onto the cloud. The SaaS application could be interested in business events that originate outside its own scope. In that case, the SaaS consumer should be able to publish such events through Web Service calls.

Visual User Interface Integration

Ideally, end users need to make use of as few different user interfaces as possible. It is best if all user interfaces required for an individual user to perform his or her tasks are integrated into a single UI, such as a portal or dashboard. Even the user interfaces required to access remote SaaS applications should be integrated into this single UI. Note that this does not mean that all users would use the same, single UI—only that a user should not have to access many different ones. Of course, the various components, gadgets, and widgets brought together in this single interface should interact: When a selection is made in one, this should be passed as an event to another one to have it synchronized.

The most obvious way to integrate remote user interfaces into a local interface is through the use of Portlets. SaaS applications should therefore typically publish their user interfaces in the form of Portlets that can be consumed into enterprise portals by SaaS customers. As an additional option, the SaaS applications could publish various gadgets that can be consumed on the client side and/or RESTful-style services that rich-client components can consume to produce the SaaS-based user interface components.

Note that when ADF is used, integration of remote user interface components can be achieved through task flow calls with the remote-app-url attribute set, in the same way the BPM Worklist application does with task flows especially created and registered for a specific human task. The UI rendered by the called remote task flow is embedded in an Iframe in the consuming page.

Registering Portlets with the SaaS Application   Although it seems most logical for Portlets exposed by the SaaS application to be consumed in a local portal-like application, there may be a requirement for the reverse situation as well: If the SaaS application, for example, does CRM, with the focus on customers, orders, and marketing activities, and it wants to provide users, if so desired, with additional product details about the products purchased by a customer, it could allow registration of a Product Details Portlet. Such a Portlet would have to be exposed by the SaaS customer and it would have to accept the input parameters as specified by the SaaS provider. After this registration, whenever a user of the SaaS application desires more information about the product ordered by a customer, the SaaS application will consume the Product Details Portlet that was registered to provide these details.

Deep Link Navigation   Business users typically will use enterprise applications to perform tasks that are part of business processes. Some of these tasks are performed in local applications, and some in SaaS applications. When the user accesses a task he is about to process, frequently from some form of to-do list, he prefers to be taken directly to the page that implements the user interface for that task, with the page initialized for the appropriate task detail context. This requires applications to support the notion of *deep link navigation*—URL requests that directly access pages in the application that are initialized in the appropriate context as indicated by request parameters.

SaaS applications should allow such deep link navigations from the applications used by their customers. Conversely, they may allow their customers to register deep link navigation paths that enable the SaaS application to access pages that, for example, provide additional details regarding the data currently in focus in the SaaS application.

Joining Clouds (the Internet Service Bus)

Organizations may very well make use of multiple SaaS applications. And each of these applications comes with similar challenges, such as dependency injection and event handling, as discussed before. One SaaS application used by an organization may provide the service that is to be injected into another SaaS application used by that same organization. And events produced by one SaaS application on behalf of a customer may have to be published into another cloud application used by that customer.

The enterprise service bus, as shown in Figure 21-4, is part of the SaaS customer's infrastructure. However, organizations that only use SaaS applications (or want to) are probably not interested in having to implement a local enterprise service bus in order to link together all SaaS applications they consume. Ideally, such a service bus would also be available in the cloud. And it would be useful to have an industry standard for SaaS applications to have them all implement a similar interface for injecting dependencies, registering event listeners, accepting deep link navigation, and so on.

Customization

One of the concerns discussed before is the potential one-size-fits-all nature of SaaS applications. To address that concern, typically a SaaS application, even though a single instance, is accessed by all users, should allow for customizations for various organizations, user groups, and/or customers. Organizations that use the SaaS application should be allowed to give their own look and feel to the application—both the user interface as well as the service interface. Note that these configurations should be possible to make via a self-service interface by the customers themselves.

Here are some typical customization hooks that an SaaS provider—and perhaps any application development team—may consider adding:

- Allow the upload of a customer-specific logo; also allow the definition of customized styles and the upload of a CSS stylesheet that defines a customer-specific look and feel.

- Enable customers to define their own business terminology to be used for prompts, titles, messages, button labels, and other boilerplate text elements.

- Have customers edit the context-sensitive help to align with their organization's procedures.

- Allow items that are not relevant to a particular customer or user group to be hidden by the customer.

- Enable customers to add new items to satisfy their specific requirements—for example, to record address elements or product properties that very specific to their geography or business processes.

- Enable customers to determine the composition of the dashboards in the application: which elements are shown, which are hidden, what is the order of the components is.

- Use application settings or preferences to govern many aspects of the application's behavior, such as default values, date and number display formats, and currencies and units used. These preferences can be set per customer.

- Enable domains with allowed values used for drop-down lists and radio groups to be customized by organizations.

- Have organizations configure their own business rules.

- Allow SaaS consumers to configure RSS feeds for their own needs—for example, by specifying filters.

- Enable customers to modify the XSD used for the WebService API and the payload for the events published by the SaaS application.

Note that customization can be done at various levels: Customization can be applied per SaaS customer—at the organization level—and could additionally be supported for specific departments or roles within those customer organizations. Finally, customization can be facilitated for individual users; typically it is then called "personalization."

Customization and Personalization in ADF

ADF has special built-in support for both customization and personalization. Many ADF Faces components can be configured in some way—for example, the collapsed state of collapsible panel boxes, the position of a panel splitter, the default selected tab, the state of accordion items, or the width and visibility of columns in a table. ADF supports the "cross-session state persistence" mode in which these configuration settings of the ADF Faces components are remembered for the end users.

Additionally, on top of a regular ADF application, developers can create customizations: modifications with regard to the base application that are associated with a specific context. This allows us to easily create versions of a page for specific industries, countries, and user roles, for example. At run time, the relevant customization context is determined and the specific customizations are applied on top of the base page before the result is rendered to the browser. Among the features that can be easily be customized in this way are the sequence and visibility of fields and other components on the page, the validation rules to be applied to input items, the style class, and other display characteristics of components.

We can safely conclude that ADF can easily satisfy the customization requirements for SaaS applications.

Summary

Integration is one of the important objectives sought after through SOA and the SOA Suite. It has been a recurring theme in most of the chapters in this book. This chapter discussed integration, too, although in two new ways. First, we looked at integration at the user interface level.

Instead of programmatic integration at the level of SOA composite applications and the enterprise service bus, we discussed user interface integration. Both client-side integration—for example, with rich user interface widgets leveraging REST-style services—and Portlet-based integration results in a seamlessly integrated user interface based on a services infrastructure that may not be integrated at all. Presentation services can be used to support these integrated user interfaces. Given the special response time requirements from presentation services, we may need to consider services specifically tailored to support application pages. And these services—for this same reason—may well need to be exposed via protocols with less overhead than SOAP.

Integration across the cloud was the second major topic in this chapter. With organizations increasingly making use of cloud-based services, integration between the applications used by an organization suddenly may involve SaaS applications that run on the cloud. For the integration of user interfaces, for programmatic integration, and for the implementation of business processes, this means that remote and local components need to work together. A number of facilities required for seamless integration across the cloud were discussed, including a WebService API, event listeners (and their registration), deep link navigation, Portlets, and the injection of infra services.

APPENDIX

Migration from SOA Suite 10g to 11g

any organizations have adopted Oracle SOA Suite 10*g* in the recent past, using BPEL Process Manager, the Enterprise Service Bus, Human Workflow services, and/or Web Services Manager. Such organizations typically have made considerable investments in their environment, the SOA applications, and the skills required to develop the applications and administrate the infrastructure.

With SOA Suite 11*g*, these organizations may feel like they are up against the "dialectics of progress." They were the first to adopt Oracle's SOA offerings and as a result they now have to make additional investments to upgrade to this latest release, even though it may seem the upgrade does not have immediate benefits. However, much of the investment is not lost, but can simply be applied to SOA Suite 11*g*. And these early adopters are best equipped to appreciate many of the improvements available in Oracle SOA Suite 11*g* over the previous releases of the SOA Suite. Finally, Oracle has provided various tools that support the migration. As a result, it may not be as earth-shattering, risky, or costly as it appears from a distance. On the other hand, migration is not something that can be done overnight in a few hours.

This appendix helps you by providing some best practices and tips and tricks to perform the migration from 10*g* to 11*g*. Note that the book's wiki contains a supplement to this appendix with additional (technical) details on the migration to Oracle SOA Suite 11*g*.

Overview of the Migration

The migration to SOA Suite 11*g* involves several aspects:

- The skills, processes, standards, guidelines and best practices need to be revised and refined. Many of the adopted ways of working, the existing knowledge, and the (automated) procedures and scripts currently used around SOA Suite 10*g* no longer apply—in exactly the same way at least—to the 11*g* release. The introduction of composite applications as a means to bundle multiple components together, for example, will impact both design and development of applications. The integrated console and end-to-end message flow trace will strongly influence daily operations and administration of the run-time environment.

- The tooling and infrastructure are upgraded. The 11*g* run-time infrastructure is composed of Oracle WebLogic Server instead of OC4J. JDeveloper needs to be upgraded from 10*g* to 11*g*. This aspect also includes the security framework and identity and access management tools.

  Also, the components that are used from Oracle SOA Suite but not implemented as ESB or BPEL processes, need to be migrated to the new infrastructure. The most important of these components are EJBs and Web Services that run on OC4J and are invoked from ESB and BPEL 10*g* processes. These projects need to be migrated to JDeveloper 11*g* and WebLogic Server and will then be used from SCA Composites.

- The BPEL and ESB applications developed on 10.1.3 and currently running on OC4J need to be migrated to SOA composites according to the SCA standard. This can be a one-to-one migration, meaning a BPEL 10*g* service is migrated to a single 11*g* SOA composite containing that same BPEL component or an ESB project is migrated to an 11*g* Composite application with a single Mediator component derived from the ESB service. However, it could also involve the migration of several BPEL and ESB 10*g* projects into a single SOA composite in 11*g*.

- Any long-running (and still open) BPEL process instances need to be migrated.

■   Human task display forms generated in 10g using JSPs and the .tform specification file in 11g need to be replaced with rich webpages created using ADF Faces 11g Rich Client.

■   Client applications that hook into the services running on Oracle SOA Suite and the client applications using Oracle SOA Suite's API's such as the TaskQueryService need to be revised, as these services are accessed differently in 11g.

■   Ant build scripts used for ESB 10g and BPEL 10g projects need to be "updated."

■   New features in SOA Suite 11g are adopted for development, deployment, and administration.

Some of these different aspects will be addressed in the following sections. Before we dive into the nitty-gritty details, we quickly recap some of the most striking changes when moving from SOA Suite 10g to 11g that need to provide the business case for embarking on the migration in the first place:

■   The SCA-based architecture and the notion of composite applications that may contain several (private) service components exposing one or more services

■   New service components: BPMN and Spring Java

■   Support for Service Data Objects (SDOs) through ADF Business Components and BPEL entity variables

■   The User Messaging Service (UMS) for sending and receiving notifications via e-mail, instant messaging, and Voice over IP (VoIP)

■   The Event Delivery Network for highly decoupled publish/subscribe-style component interaction

■   (Somewhat) integrated Oracle Service Bus 11g, which can be used to implement an enterprise service bus to connect SOA composite applications to other business domains and external business partners

■   Business rules as stand-alone service components with an enhanced editor in JDeveloper.

■   The run-time SOA Composer, which allows run-time editing of Domain Value Maps and business rules.

■   MDS (Metadata Services) repositories, which allow sharing of common artifacts such as XSD documents and event definition files (EDLs).

■   Integrated security through the WSM policies managed from the EM Console and integrated with WebLogic Server's platform security.

■   Composite-level, cross-component, policy-based, fault-handling framework.

■   End-to-end tracing of messages, across all composites and components.

■   Fusion Middleware Enterprise Manager Control as the integrated management console for all components and composites as well as for administration.

■   SOA Suite 10g uses OC4J as its underlying infrastructure, and WebLogic Server 11g is the foundation for SOA Suite 11g. Therefore, any changes and advantages introduced by WLS over OC4J will automatically apply when migrating to SOA Suite 11g.

■   Improved human workflow, including ADF Faces 11g Rich Client as the development framework for the user interface for human tasks.

In the next sections, we will first discuss the migration of the run-time environment—the application server and the SOA Suite run-time engine—and the additional software components running on OC4J, such as EJBs and WebServices.

We also discuss the adoption of SCA and the concept of composite applications, and how this will impact our BPEL processes and ESB services when we migrate them. Subsequently we describe in detail the migration of these BPEL and ESB components into composite applications. The online complement to this appendix discusses additional advanced topics, including migration of OWSM and adapter configurations.

Run-time Environment

The migration of the run-time environment is, in reality, a fresh install of Oracle SOA Suite 11*g* instead of an update of an existing 10*g* instance. Oracle SOA Suite 10*g* runs on Oracle Application Server, based on the OC4J container, whereas the 11*g* release runs on WebLogic Server. The 11*g* environment cannot be created by somehow migrating the existing infrastructure. Follow the install instructions as discussed in Chapter 3 and documented on Oracle Technology Network (OTN) in the installation guide for a fresh install.

Oracle SOA Suite uses a database as a dehydration store, among other things, to store process instance data. You may need to upgrade the database when moving from 10*g* to 11*g*, because Oracle SOA Suite 11*g* requires a later version of the RDBMS than is needed for SOA Suite 10.1.3. Also, different database schemas are used in 11*g* compared to the previous SOA Suite version; for example, MDS is new in Oracle SOA Suite 11*g*. The new database schemas are installed as part of the fresh 11*g* installation by the Repository Creation Utility. Afterwards—when you have phased out 10*g*—you can remove the 10*g* schemas.

Software Running on OC4J

Oracle SOA Suite components use other components—outside SOA Suite—to "get the job done." When these artifacts run on OC4J, they also need to be migrated to WebLogic Server and JDeveloper 11*g*. The most prominent examples will be EJB Sessions Beans and Web Services that run on OC4J and are used from BPEL 10*g* processes. An example could be an EJB project providing financial services that are exposed as a Web Service using JAX-WS. The next section discusses some migration issues for such projects.

Web Services

In general we have the following options when designing Web Services:

- **Top-down or contract first**   In this scenario, you first design the WSDL (contract). You can then use tooling to create skeleton code. This skeleton code can be elaborated so the service is fulfilled. The WSDLs and XSDs are fixed. When you change these contracts, you need to modify the code and possibly regenerate the "skeletons."

- **Bottom-up**   In this scenario, you start from working code. You use tooling to generate the Web Service artifacts such as WSDLs and XSDs. These contracts are partially not under your control because they are automatically generated. When the code changes, you need to regenerate the WSDLs and XSDs, possibly changing the service interface.

■   **Meet-in-the-middle**   In this scenario, you create both WSDLs and XSDs and the code. You then use tooling to create the "glue in between," such as JAXB mappings and JAX-WS annotations. This is the most flexible approach but also the most time intensive (in the beginning at least).

So why is this important for migration to 11*g*? Well, if you use a bottom-up approach for Web Services, the tooling (JDeveloper and OC4J in this case) has an effect on the generated WSDLs and XSDs. So when you're using other tooling such as JDeveloper 11*g* and WebLogic Server, there is a slim chance these artifacts will be generated a little bit differently, thus making service interfaces change and break interoperability. And that's exactly what happens.

Migrating EJBs That Expose Web Services to SOA Suite 11*g*

One such case where the preceding happens and manual intervention is needed involves EJB 3 Session Beans that are exposed as Web Services using JAX-WS annotations. In case these Web Services are used by ESB or BPEL 10*g* components, we will need to verify interoperability after migrating to SOA Suite 11*g*. When you use the EJB 3 Session Bean Wizard in JDeveloper 10*g* and select the option to create a Web Service interface, a separate Java interface containing JAX-WS Web Service annotations will be generated. This option is not available in JDeveloper 11*g*. The alternative is to right-click an EJB Session Bean and select the Generate Web Service option, which will give the same result.

Most migration activities are "automagically" performed when the 10*g* workspace is opened in JDeveloper 11. This includes the updating of the workspace and project files and the conversion of existing deployment plans, among other things.

When you deploy the project to a WebLogic Server, such as the integrated WebLogic Server, the project seems to deploy and run just fine. However, if you expand the deployment in the WebLogic Server Administration Console, no Web Services will be listed, only EJBs.

We will need some simple manual steps to correct this, as discussed later. After we have applied the corrective changes and redeployed the project, the Administration Console of WebLogic Server will show both the EJB and Web Service. In the project properties dialog, replace the JDeveloper 10*g* JAX-RPC project libraries with the (newer) JAX-WS Web Services libraries. Remove the Java interface containing the JAX-WS Web Service annotations. These annotations, which were generated in JDeveloper 10*g*, need to be (partially) moved to the EJB 3 Session Bean implementation class. This means adding an "@WebService" annotation to the EJB 3 Session Bean consisting at least of the following arguments: name, serviceName, and portName. You can possibly check the existing WSDL of the Web Service generated with JDeveloper 10*g* that runs on OC4J to obtain information such as name, namespace, and port name. Use these values in the @WebService annotations of the project in JDeveloper 11*g*. This lessens the chance that the Web Service project's clients "break" due to different endpoint locations, namespaces, port names, endpoints, and so on.

You can also use additional JAX-WS annotations to influence the endpoint, operations, and interface of the Web Service. These can be standard JAX-WS annotations or WebLogic Server–specific JAX-WS annotations. In the latter case, be aware of interoperability issues because these annotations are not portable to other JEE run-time infrastructure environments. The JAX-WS stack in some versions of WebLogic Server—and more specifically the JAXB implementation—does not support Collection-like types such as java.util.Map and java.util.Collection as return or input types of Web Service operations. When these types are used, deployment fails with the messages "java.util.Map is an interface, and JAXB can't handle interfaces" and "java.util.Map does not have a no-arg default constructor." A workaround would seem to replace these types with concrete implementations that have a no-argument constructor (for example, java.util.HashMap). Although deployment then succeeds, the information contained in the map is lost at run time when requests and responses are (un)marshalled. Another workaround is to replace these types with an array or two-dimensional array.

This is a typical case of migrating Oracle Fusion Middleware components to 11*g,* where almost everything is done automatically, whereas the final steps need some manual coding or configuration to make everything work or to make it work as you want to.

Moving from Different Standards and Technologies to SCA

Oracle SOA Suite 11*g* is based on the Service Component Architecture (SCA) standard. SCA defines composites that expose services. Those composite services are assembled out of components. Not every component in itself needs to be "published" as a service, meaning you do not need to expose low-level Mediator services and adapter functionality as a separate external service. It can be a local component to a composite and therefore invisible to other service composites. This promotes much better integration and encapsulation of low-level functionality. You only need to expose those artifacts that are reusable. This is referred to as *encapsulation.*

Historical Proliferation of ESB and BPEL Components

Oracle acquired the BPEL PM product in 2004 through its acquisition of Collaxa. At that time there was no Oracle ESB, meaning that all adapters such as the database, file, and FTP adapters were directly integrated in (and part of) BPEL processes. A few years later the Oracle ESB product was introduced, and it was advocated to place all adapters in the ESB instead of BPEL PM. This results in better separation of concerns (infrastructural adapters versus process logic). A bit of a downside, however, is that placing adapter functionality in the ESB layer can result in lots and lots of ESB projects in a real-life SOA environment. There may be tens or even hundreds of BPEL processes. Most of these processes will be using ESB projects that act as wrappers to technology adapters and contain logic for routing and/or transformation. This can result in "over-servicing" because lots of these ESB projects are not reusable, but rather "local" to a BPEL process.

When using SCA for service assembly, you can migrate these "local" ESB projects to "private" components inside a composite, thereby reducing the number of services (and artifacts) and hiding software within composites that are on their own account no services at all.

Reusability Is the Key!

So, in what cases do we do a "plain" one-on-one migration of a single ESB 10*g* or BPEL 10*g* project to a single SCA composite, and when do we elect to redesign the composite applications? That really depends on one thing: reusability! Chapter 14 discussed SCA and the design of composite applications. Also remember from the previous section that SCA can be used to encapsulate "fake" services that are not meant to be reusable. The rule of thumb when migrating a 10*g* artifact is as follows (note that *artifact* denotes an ESB 10*g* project, a BPEL 10*g* component, and so on):

- Is the artifact by itself reusable? If so, migrate it on a one-on-one basis to a stand-alone SCA composite. This could mean that a reusable ESB 10*g* component is migrated to a SCA composite containing a single Mediator. This Mediator component has (almost) the same implementation as the ESB 10*g* project, meaning the same transformations, (content-based) routings, and so on. A reusable BPEL process also results in a stand-alone composite application that contains a single BPEL process component with its services exposed at the composite level.

■ Is the artifact not intended to be generally reusable and only used by a single other 10g artifact such as a BPEL process? If that is the case, the artifact should be migrated into the same SCA composite that contains this single consumer of the artifact.

Using this simple guideline, you will probably migrate your heterogeneous 10g artifacts—ESB and BPEL—to fewer SCA composites that more closely resemble "real" services and that contain more than one BPEL or Mediator component.

We will dive into some specific migration considerations concerning SOA components in subsequent sections.

Using Partitions to Organize the Composites

As of SOA Suite 11g Patch Set 2, we can also use the partitioning mechanism provided by SOA Suite 11g to organize composites similarly to how we used to do in SOA Suite 10g, with ESB systems, ESB service groups, and BPEL domains. Note that organizing the composites into partitions is a manual operation following the migration of the 10g artifacts, not something taken care of by the automated migration process. Also note that in 11g, partitions do not have the exact same role as BPEL domains and ESB systems in 10g. In 11g they provide naming containers and support some bulk management operations such as shutting down all composites in the partition. There is no partition-level authorization or logging. Partitions do not have specific configuration settings, as is the case for BPEL domains and to some extent for ESB systems in 10g.

Migrating ESB and BPEL 10g Projects

The migration of your SOA Suite 10g projects to 11g can be done in an automated fashion using either JDeveloper 11g or Ant scripts. They both do the migration to 11g but only JDeveloper can also upgrade your Workspace and Projects files. Ant, on the other hand, has the advantage that it can combine one or more BPEL projects into one SOA composite application. If you don't need to automate this migration in a build tool and if you don't need to combine BPEL projects, then you should use JDeveloper 11g for your migration. Manual migration might be a viable alternative when you want to make sure you have a clean environment and want to know exactly what is going on. The downside of the manual approach is that it will probably take much more time.

Before you can start the automated migration, you need to do the following:

■ Upgrade your ESB and BPEL projects to (JDeveloper and) SOA Suite 10.1.3. Note that there is no supported migration path from SOA Suite 10.1.2 to 11g in JDeveloper; you will have to perform an upgrade from 10.1.2 to 10.1.3 first.

■ Expose the service of the ESB routers that are used by other BPEL or ESB projects as "formal" Web Services. Even though SOA Suite 10g can internally invoke these ESB services, the 11g migration wizard needs to read the formal WSDLs for creating the composite references.

■ Remove the mcf attributes of the jca:address element in all the adapter WSDLs. These attributes are only used by JDeveloper 10g.

When you are performing these migration steps, SOA Suite 10g and the external Web Services must be running.

```
[7:54:57 PM] Migration started.
Migration log file for EmployeeSalaryApproval: C:\oracle\MiddlewareJdev11gR1PS1\jdeveloper\upgrade\logs\EmployeeSalaryApproval22010-03-01-19-55-01PM.log
Warnings: 1
Migration successfully completed for the following file(s):
    C:\projects\11gR1\Employee\EmployeeSalaryApproval2\EmployeeSalaryApproval.jpr
[7:55:14 PM] Migration finished.
```

FIGURE A-1. *Migration results in JDeveloper 11g*

Upgrading SOA Suite 10*g* Projects Using JDeveloper 11*g*

Open the ESB or BPEL 10*g* workspace—or a single project—in JDeveloper 11*g*. This will automatically start the migration process. After JDeveloper asks you if you want to migrate these projects and you have replied in an affirmative way, JDeveloper will make a backup of your 10*g* workspace and projects before continuing the migration.

An output window will display the results of the migration, as shown in Figure A-1.

Check the migration overview for warnings and errors, and then click the link to open the log file for detailed information, as shown in Figure A-2.

This log tells us that the BPEL project has a partnerLink warning. This means that in the composite there is a reference with no binding. You will need to resolve such errors before you can actually deploy your newly created SCA composites.

Upgrading SOA Suite 10*g* Projects Using Ant

The Ant migration script will also make a backup of your 10*g* project before the migration start. The Ant upgrade script will not copy the workspace or project files. It will only copy all the BPEL or ESB projects files to a new folder.

Before you can start the Ant migration, you need to check whether your own JDeveloper 11*g* R1 with the SOA Suite extension is installed correctly. Check whether your jdeveloper\bin folder contains the following files:

■ **soaversion.cmd**   This file is used for setting the environment variables.

■ **ant-sca-upgrade.xml**   This file does the migration.

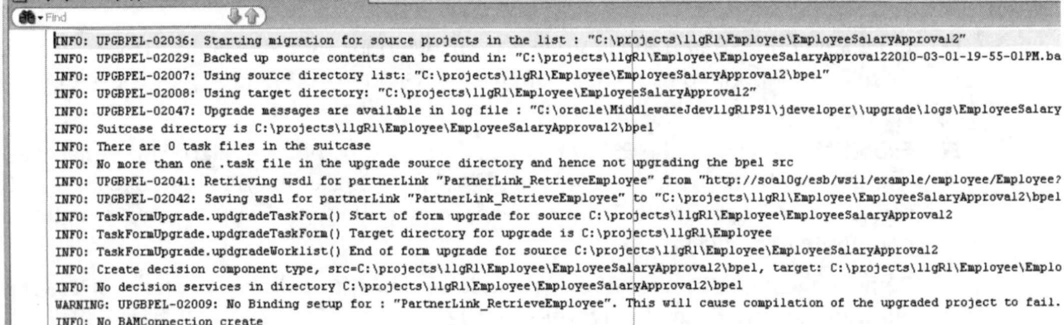

```
EmployeeSalaryApproval22010-03-01-19-55-01PM.log
Find
INFO: UPGBPEL-02036: Starting migration for source projects in the list : "C:\projects\11gR1\Employee\EmployeeSalaryApproval2"
INFO: UPGBPEL-02029: Backed up source contents can be found in: "C:\projects\11gR1\Employee\EmployeeSalaryApproval22010-03-01-19-55-01PM.ba
INFO: UPGBPEL-02007: Using source directory list: "C:\projects\11gR1\Employee\EmployeeSalaryApproval2\bpel"
INFO: UPGBPEL-02008: Using target directory: "C:\projects\11gR1\Employee\EmployeeSalaryApproval2"
INFO: UPGBPEL-02047: Upgrade messages are available in log file : "C:\oracle\MiddlewareJdev11gR1PS1\jdeveloper\\upgrade\logs\EmployeeSalary
INFO: Suitcase directory is C:\projects\11gR1\Employee\EmployeeSalaryApproval2\bpel
INFO: There are 0 task files in the suitcase
INFO: No more than one .task file in the upgrade source directory and hence not upgrading the bpel src
INFO: UPGBPEL-02041: Retrieving wsdl for partnerLink "PartnerLink_RetrieveEmployee" from "http://soa10g/esb/wsil/example/employee/Employee?
INFO: UPGBPEL-02042: Saving wsdl for partnerLink "PartnerLink_RetrieveEmployee" to "C:\projects\11gR1\Employee\EmployeeSalaryApproval2\bpel
INFO: TaskFormUpgrade.updgradeTaskForm() Start of form upgrade for source C:\projects\11gR1\Employee\EmployeeSalaryApproval2
INFO: TaskFormUpgrade.updgradeTaskForm() Target directory for upgrade is C:\projects\11gR1\Employee\EmployeeSalaryApproval2
INFO: TaskFormUpgrade.updgradeWorklist() End of form upgrade for source C:\projects\11gR1\Employee\EmployeeSalaryApproval2
INFO: Create decision component type, src=C:\projects\11gR1\Employee\EmployeeSalaryApproval2\bpel, target: C:\projects\11gR1\Employee\Emplo
INFO: No decision services in directory C:\projects\11gR1\Employee\EmployeeSalaryApproval2\bpel
WARNING: UPGBPEL-02009: No Binding setup for : "PartnerLink_RetrieveEmployee". This will cause compilation of the upgraded project to fail.
INFO: No BAMConnection create
```

FIGURE A-2. *The detailed migration log*

If you do not encounter these files, you need to (re)install JDeveloper 11g's SOA Suite extension.

Next, check whether the soa-infra-wls.ear is located in the jdeveloper/soa/applications folder. If it is not, copy this EAR from the SOA Suite 11g server installation (Oracle_SOA1/soa/applications) to your local jdeveloper\soa\applications folder.

To start the Ant migration, you need to open a cmd console in Windows or a terminal session in Unix. You need to execute the following command in Windows:

```
set ORACLE_HOME=C:\oracle\MiddlewareJdev11gR1PS1\jdeveloper
cd %ORACLE_HOME%
bin\soaversion.cmd
```

To test Ant and the build script, you can execute the following statement:

```
ant -f %ORACLE_HOME%\bin\ant-sca-upgrade.xml
```

Figure A-3 shows the output that is generated by the Ant script.

Now that you have tested that the Ant script is working, we will continue by migrating a real-life 10g project. We will start with an ESB 10g project and continue with two BPEL 10g projects that will be migrated to one SCA composite application. We finish by making new workspace and project files.

Migrating an ESB 10g Project to an 11g Composite Application

Locate the ESB project in the projects/10.1.3/Employee/EmployeeService folder. The ESB project will be migrated to projects/11gR1. This is a simple ESB project that contains a database adapter that retrieves an employee record from the employee table of the HR demo schema. The ESB project contains a router that exposes the adapter to the outside world. Because this is a (highly) reusable service, we choose to migrate it to a separate SCA composite instead of merging it into another composite.

There is no need to create the same project folder structure under the 11gR1 folder; Ant will do this for us. The Ant migration script will use the appName parameter for the folder name (appName is the workspace folder) under the target folder. Inside this appName folder, Ant will create a project folder with the same name as in 10g, as shown in Figure A-4.

```
C:\oracle\MiddlewareJdev11gR1PS1\jdeveloper>set ORACLE_HOME=C:\oracle\MiddlewareJdev11gR1PS1\jdeveloper

C:\oracle\MiddlewareJdev11gR1PS1\jdeveloper>cd %ORACLE_HOME%

C:\oracle\MiddlewareJdev11gR1PS1\jdeveloper>bin\soaversion.cmd
*****************************************************************
Oracle SOA Server version 11.1.1.2.0
        Build: 0
        Build time: Tue Nov 03 13:48:58 PST 2009
        Build type: release
        Source tag: PCBPEL_11.1.1.2.0_GENERIC_091103.1205.1216

Oracle BAM Source Tag:ORABAM_11.1.1.2.0_GENERIC_091101.2156
C:\oracle\MiddlewareJdev11gR1PS1\jdeveloper>ant -f %ORACLE_HOME%\bin\ant-sca-upgrade.xml
Buildfile: C:\oracle\MiddlewareJdev11gR1PS1\jdeveloper\bin\..\bin\ant-sca-upgrade.xml

BUILD FAILED
C:\oracle\MiddlewareJdev11gR1PS1\jdeveloper\bin\ant-sca-upgrade.xml:18: Please specify the fully qualified source directory name
named source, before proceeding.

BPEL Upgrade Usage: ant -f $ORACLE_HOME/bin/ant-sca-upgrade.xml -Dsource srcDir -Dtarget tgtDir -DappName application
ESB Upgrade Usage: ant -f $ORACLE_HOME/bin/ant-sca-upgrade.xml -Dsource srcDir -Dtarget tgtDir -DappName application mediator
XRef/DVM Upgrade Usage: ant -f $ORACLE_HOME/bin/ant-sca-upgrade.xml -Dsource srcDir -Dtarget tgtDir upgrade-xrefdvm

Check the documentation for more information.

Total time: 0 seconds
C:\oracle\MiddlewareJdev11gR1PS1\jdeveloper>
```

FIGURE A-3. *Output from running the Ant migration script*

FIGURE A-4. *Project structure after migration using Ant*

Note that the Ant target has to be a Mediator when you want to upgrade your ESB 10*g* project to a SOA composite 11*g* application. The next code snippet demonstrates how Ant is used to upgrade an 10*g* ESB service to an 11*g* Composite application with Mediator component.

```
ant -f %ORACLE_HOME%\bin\ant-sca-upgrade.xml mediator
-Dsource C:\projects\10.1.3\Employee\EmployeeService
-Dtarget C:\projects\11gR1
-DappName Employee
```

The CMD console displays the output of the migration (see Figure A-5). This output is also located in the JDeveloper upgrade folder jdeveloper/upgrade/logs. Always check this log file for possible warnings and/or errors.

In this case, there are no errors when performing the ESB migration.

Migrating and Merging One or More BPEL Projects to One Composite

The BPEL Ant migration is a little bit different from the ESB migration. First, the BPEL upgrade will back up your source project and delete some files from your source project (see Figure A-6).

```
INFO: UPGMED-02003: Upgrading ESB 10.1.3 to AS 11 Mediator started
INFO: UPGMED-02004: Upgrading project EmployeeService under C:\projects\10.1.3\Employee
INFO: UPGMED-02077: Upgrade messages are available in log file : "C:\oracle\MiddlewareJdev11gR1P
INFO: UPGMED-02078: Upgrade messages log level : "INFO"
INFO: UPGMED-02032: Back up of source directory is not required. C:\projects\11gR1\Employee\Empl
INFO: UPGMED-02030: Setting end point properties for example.employee.Employee[GUID:6C68F2E018C7
INFO: UPGMED-02031: End point properties not found for example.employee.Employee[GUID:6C68F2E018
INFO: UPGMED-02030: Setting end point properties for example.employee.EmployeeAdapter[GUID:C083F
INFO: UPGMED-02031: End point properties not found for example.employee.EmployeeAdapter[GUID:C08
INFO: UPGMED-02009: Upgrading Adapter Service example.employee.EmployeeAdapter[GUID:C083F97018C6
INFO: UPGMED-02042: Parsing wsdl from location "file:C:/projects/11gR1/Employee/EmployeeService/
INFO: UPGMED-02044: Fetching Porttype "{http://xmlns.oracle.com/pcbpel/adapter/db/EmployeeAdapte
INFO: UPGMED-02043: Parsed WSDL for service "example.employee.EmployeeAdapter[GUID:C083F97018C61
INFO: UPGMED-02011: Upgrading Routing Service example.employee.Employee[GUID:6C68F2E018C711DFBFD
INFO: UPGMED-02042: Parsing wsdl from location "file:C:/projects/11gR1/Employee/EmployeeService/
INFO: UPGMED-02044: Fetching Porttype "{http://oracle.com/esb/namespaces/example_employee}execut
INFO: UPGMED-02043: Parsed WSDL for service "example.employee.Employee[GUID:6C68F2E018C711DFBFDC
INFO: UPGMED-02015: Upgrading Xsl EmployeeAdapterSelect_employeeIdInputParameters_To_EmployeeAda
INFO: UPGMED-02015: Upgrading Xsl EmployeesCollection_To_Employees.xsl
INFO: UPGMED-02012: Upgrading ESB 10.1.3 to AS 11 Mediator successfully completed
```

FIGURE A-5. *The output log of the Ant migration*

FIGURE A-6. *The Ant BPEL upgrade will make a backup and delete the BPEL folder in the 10g project.*

The BPEL Ant upgrade script can merge two or more BPEL projects into a single composite application. In this test case, EmployeeInfo and EmployeeSalaryApproval will be migrated to one composite application, as shown in Figure A-7. Both BPEL projects have a reference to the ESB project we just migrated into a 11g composite application with Mediator component.

If you want to upgrade your BPEL project to 11g, you need to use BPEL as the Ant target. For migrating and merging two or more BPEL projects to one composite application, you need to use a colon (:) in Unix or a semicolon (;) in Windows between the different BPEL projects and enclose the source input variable with double quotes, as shown here:

```
ant -f %ORACLE_HOME%\bin\ant-sca-upgrade.xml bpel
-Dsource "C:\projects\10.1.3\Employee\EmployeeSalaryApproval;c:\projects\10.1.3\...
...Employee\EmployeeInfo"
-Dtarget C:\projects\11gR1
-DappName Employee
```

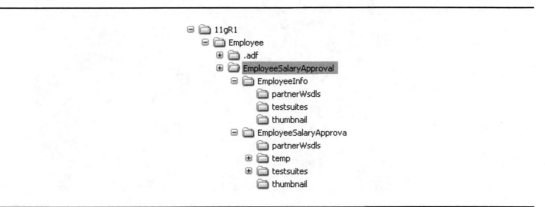

FIGURE A-7. *The result of the migration; the two BPEL projects are under the project folder.*

The BPEL 10*g* project listed first in the "source" parameter will be used as the project name under the Employee application, and both projects will be added under this folder.

Note that SOA Suite 11*g* cannot handle such subfolders very well. For example, if you want to change your composite by adding a new wire between a BPEL component located in a subfolder and a Web Service reference, JDeveloper will look for the WSDL in the wrong path. To solve this, copy the subfolder contents to the main project folder and change the composite.xml accordingly. Copy the BPEL componentType files of the subfolder and project folder, and finally remove the subfolders.

Another issue in this scenario is that the client partnerLink service of the first BPEL project will only be migrated to a composite service; the other client partnerLink service will be ignored. If the second BPEL process should have its client partnerLink exposed as a SOAP Web Service at the composite level, too, you need to manually correct the migration outcome.

The next step in the Ant migration is to add a workspace file and the project files.

Making an Application Workspace and Creating Project Files in JDeveloper 11*g*

The Ant migration script does not create the necessary JWS and JPR files, unlike the migration performed by JDeveloper. These files can also be created in JDeveloper 11*g* by simply creating a new SOA application, as shown in Figure A-8.

On the next page, enter the project name as **EmployeeService** and click Next. On the third page of the wizard, make sure you choose the Empty Composite Template.

JDeveloper 11*g* detects the composite.xml, and the pop-up shown in Figure A-9 appears. Choose to reuse this composite.xml.

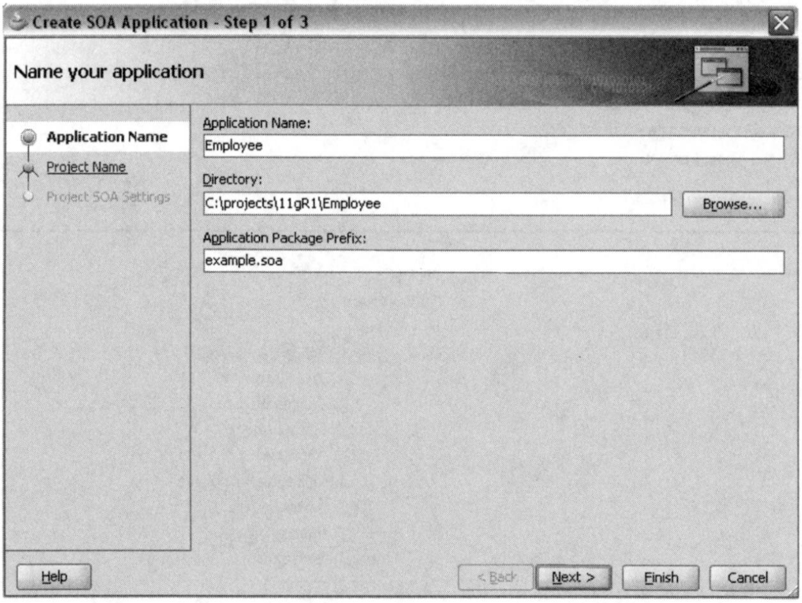

FIGURE A-8. *New SOA application dialog box*

FIGURE A-9.   *The composite.xml file that was the result of the migration is detected; elect to reuse this file.*

The resulting workspace and composite are shown in Figure A-10.

You can do the same for the BPEL composite. If this composite needs to be in the same application, you only need to create a new SOA project this time, in the same JDeveloper application. As can be seen Figure A-11, the two BPEL projects are merged into one composite application.

Comparing 10*g* and 11*g* Project Files

The following mapping exists between the composite and 10*g* files. Especially for the migration, it is extremely useful to know which project artifacts end up where:

- *.bpel files → composite.xml (BPEL main project file)
  - EmployeeSalaryApproval.bpel → EmployeeSalaryApproval.bpel
  - EmployeeSalaryApproval.bpel → composite.xml

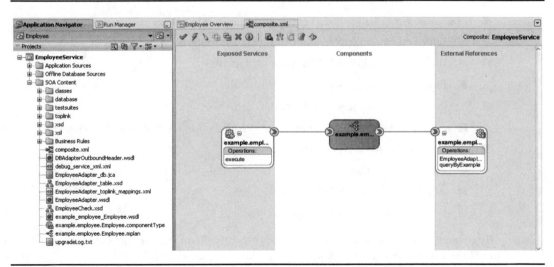

FIGURE A-10.   *The composite.xml created by the migration in the newly created JDeveloper application and project*

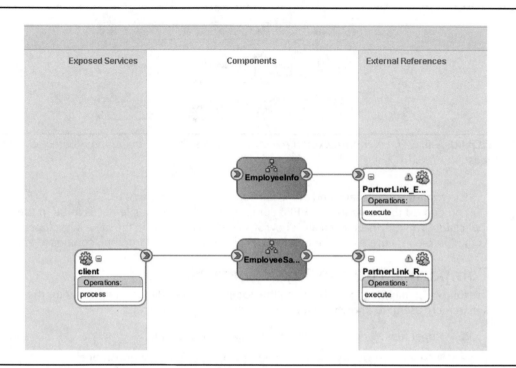

FIGURE A-11. *The composite.xml file resulting from the migration of two BPEL project into a single composite application*

- bpel.xml → xxx.componentType (partnerLinks references)
  - bpel.xml → EmployeeSalaryApproval.componentType
- esb file → composite.xml (ESB main project file)
  - EmployeeService.esb → Composite.xml
- *.esbsvc → *.mplan (ESB Router to Mediator files)
  - example_employee_Employee.esbsvc → example.employee.Employee.mplan
- Adapter WSDL files → Adapter XX.jca
  - EmployeeAdapter.wsdl → EmployeeAdapter_db.jca
  - AQ_Queue.wsdl → AQ_Queue_aq.jca
  - JMS_Queue.wsdl → JMS_Queue_jms.jca

By default, XSLTs and XSDs are migrated, respectively, to the xsl and xsd folders that are part of the SOA composite 11*g* root folder.

Summary

Organizations that have adopted SOA Suite 10g will probably think about migration to the SOA Suite 11g release. Many rewards can be reaped from such a migration. Undoubtedly, SOA Suite 11g will offer potential benefits due to the many enhancements over the 10g release. However, it depends on the specific situation of an organization whether and which of these potential rewards are relevant and outweigh the effort required by and risks posed by the migration.

Migration from SOA Suite 10g to the 11g release is not to be undertaken lightly. Even though the migration process is relatively straightforward, it certainly is not trivial. It requires some (substantial) effort, in several areas. Migration will impact the run-time infrastructure, the currently deployed applications, the procedures and automated scripts for building, deploying, administering, and testing, and possibly the consumers of the services. During the migration, care must be taken to prevent (prolonged) periods of downtime. The developers and administrators of SOA applications will experience considerable changes, too. Although this forces a relatively short learning curve on them, they will soon benefit from richer functionality and higher productivity.

The most notable differences are the new underlying infrastructure (WebLogic Server versus OC4J) and a new paradigm of designing services (SCA composites with integrated components versus separate ESB and BPEL components).

The online complement for this appendix discusses several detailed scenarios for specific components and artifacts that may not be relevant in all situations. Among the topics discussed in this online extension are the following:

- Domain Value Maps

- Custom XPath and XSLT functions

- Advanced BPEL characteristics, fault policies, unit test suites

- Oracle Web Services Manager (OWSM)

- Technology adapters (WebService, JMS, AQ, and Database)

Index

F

P

Q

GET YOUR FREE SUBSCRIPTION
TO *ORACLE MAGAZINE*

Oracle Magazine is essential gear for today's information technology professionals. Stay informed and increase your productivity with every issue of *Oracle Magazine*. Inside each free bimonthly issue you'll get:

- Up-to-date information on Oracle Database, Oracle Application Server, Web development, enterprise grid computing, database technology, and business trends
- Third-party news and announcements
- Technical articles on Oracle and partner products, technologies, and operating environments
- Development and administration tips
- Real-world customer stories

If there are other Oracle users at your location who would like to receive their own subscription to *Oracle Magazine*, please photocopy this form and pass it along.

Three easy ways to subscribe:

① Web
Visit our Web site at **oracle.com/oraclemagazine**
You'll find a subscription form there, plus much more

② Fax
Complete the questionnaire on the back of this card
and fax the questionnaire side only to **+1.847.763.9638**

③ Mail
Complete the questionnaire on the back of this card
and mail it to **P.O. Box 1263, Skokie, IL 60076-8263**

ORACLE®

Want your own FREE subscription?

To receive a free subscription to *Oracle Magazine*, you must fill out the entire card, sign it, and date it (incomplete cards cannot be processed or acknowledged). You can also fax your application to +1.847.763.9638. **Or subscribe at our Web site at oracle.com/oraclemagazine**

O **Yes, please send me a FREE subscription** *Oracle Magazine*.   O No.

O From time to time, Oracle Publishing allows our partners exclusive access to our e-mail addresses for special promotions and announcements. To be included in this program, please check this circle. If you do not wish to be included, you will only receive notices about your subscription via e-mail.

O Oracle Publishing allows sharing of our postal mailing list with selected third parties. If you prefer your mailing address not to be included in this program, please check this circle.

If at any time you would like to be removed from either mailing list, please contact Customer Service at +1.847.763.9635 or send an e-mail to oracle@halldata.com. If you opt in to the sharing of information, Oracle may also provide you with e-mail related to Oracle products, services, and events. If you want to completely unsubscribe from any e-mail communication from Oracle, please send an e-mail to: unsubscribe@oracle-mail.com with the following in the subject line: REMOVE [your e-mail address]. For complete information on Oracle Publishing's privacy practices, please visit oracle.com/html/privacy/html

X	
signature (required)	date
name	title
company	e-mail address
street/p.o. box	
city/state/zip or postal code	telephone
country	fax

Would you like to receive your free subscription in digital format instead of print if it becomes available? O Yes O No

YOU MUST ANSWER ALL 10 QUESTIONS BELOW.

① WHAT IS THE PRIMARY BUSINESS ACTIVITY OF YOUR FIRM AT THIS LOCATION? (check one only)

- ☐ 01 Aerospace and Defense Manufacturing
- ☐ 02 Application Service Provider
- ☐ 03 Automotive Manufacturing
- ☐ 04 Chemicals
- ☐ 05 Media and Entertainment
- ☐ 06 Construction/Engineering
- ☐ 07 Consumer Sector/Consumer Packaged Goods
- ☐ 08 Education
- ☐ 09 Financial Services/Insurance
- ☐ 10 Health Care
- ☐ 11 High Technology Manufacturing, OEM
- ☐ 12 Industrial Manufacturing
- ☐ 13 Independent Software Vendor
- ☐ 14 Life Sciences (biotech, pharmaceuticals)
- ☐ 15 Natural Resources
- ☐ 16 Oil and Gas
- ☐ 17 Professional Services
- ☐ 18 Public Sector (government)
- ☐ 19 Research
- ☐ 20 Retail/Wholesale/Distribution
- ☐ 21 Systems Integrator, VAR/VAD
- ☐ 22 Telecommunications
- ☐ 23 Travel and Transportation
- ☐ 24 Utilities (electric, gas, sanitation, water)
- ☐ 98 Other Business and Services _____

② WHICH OF THE FOLLOWING BEST DESCRIBES YOUR PRIMARY JOB FUNCTION? (check one only)

CORPORATE MANAGEMENT/STAFF
- ☐ 01 Executive Management (President, Chair, CEO, CFO, Owner, Partner, Principal)
- ☐ 02 Finance/Administrative Management (VP/Director/ Manager/Controller, Purchasing, Administration)
- ☐ 03 Sales/Marketing Management (VP/Director/Manager)
- ☐ 04 Computer Systems/Operations Management (CIO/VP/Director/Manager MIS/IS/IT, Ops)

IS/IT STAFF
- ☐ 05 Application Development/Programming Management
- ☐ 06 Application Development/Programming Staff
- ☐ 07 Consulting
- ☐ 08 DBA/Systems Administrator
- ☐ 09 Education/Training
- ☐ 10 Technical Support Director/Manager
- ☐ 11 Other Technical Management/Staff
- ☐ 98 Other

③ WHAT IS YOUR CURRENT PRIMARY OPERATING PLATFORM (check all that apply)

- ☐ 01 Digital Equipment Corp UNIX/VAX/VMS
- ☐ 02 HP UNIX
- ☐ 03 IBM AIX
- ☐ 04 IBM UNIX
- ☐ 05 Linux (Red Hat)
- ☐ 06 Linux (SUSE)
- ☐ 07 Linux (Oracle Enterprise)
- ☐ 08 Linux (other)
- ☐ 09 Macintosh
- ☐ 10 MVS
- ☐ 11 Netware
- ☐ 12 Network Computing
- ☐ 13 SCO UNIX
- ☐ 14 Sun Solaris/SunOS
- ☐ 15 Windows
- ☐ 16 Other UNIX
- ☐ 98 Other
- ☐ 99 None of the Above

④ DO YOU EVALUATE, SPECIFY, RECOMMEND, OR AUTHORIZE THE PURCHASE OF ANY OF THE FOLLOWING? (check all that apply)

- ☐ 01 Hardware
- ☐ 02 Business Applications (ERP, CRM, etc.)
- ☐ 03 Application Development Tools
- ☐ 04 Database Products
- ☐ 05 Internet or Intranet Products
- ☐ 06 Other Software
- ☐ 07 Middleware Products
- ☐ 99 None of the Above

⑤ IN YOUR JOB, DO YOU USE OR PLAN TO PURCHASE ANY OF THE FOLLOWING PRODUCTS? (check all that apply)

SOFTWARE
- ☐ 01 CAD/CAE/CAM
- ☐ 02 Collaboration Software
- ☐ 03 Communications
- ☐ 04 Database Management
- ☐ 05 File Management
- ☐ 06 Finance
- ☐ 07 Java
- ☐ 08 Multimedia Authoring
- ☐ 09 Networking
- ☐ 10 Programming
- ☐ 11 Project Management
- ☐ 12 Scientific and Engineering
- ☐ 13 Systems Management
- ☐ 14 Workflow

HARDWARE
- ☐ 15 Macintosh
- ☐ 16 Mainframe
- ☐ 17 Massively Parallel Processing
- ☐ 18 Minicomputer
- ☐ 19 Intel x86(32)
- ☐ 20 Intel x86(64)
- ☐ 21 Network Computer
- ☐ 22 Symmetric Multiprocessing
- ☐ 23 Workstation Services

SERVICES
- ☐ 24 Consulting
- ☐ 25 Education/Training
- ☐ 26 Maintenance
- ☐ 27 Online Database
- ☐ 28 Support
- ☐ 29 Technology-Based Training
- ☐ 30 Other
- ☐ 99 None of the Above

⑥ WHAT IS YOUR COMPANY'S SIZE? (check one only)

- ☐ 01 More than 25,000 Employees
- ☐ 02 10,001 to 25,000 Employees
- ☐ 03 5,001 to 10,000 Employees
- ☐ 04 1,001 to 5,000 Employees
- ☐ 05 101 to 1,000 Employees
- ☐ 06 Fewer than 100 Employees

⑦ DURING THE NEXT 12 MONTHS, HOW MUCH DO YOU ANTICIPATE YOUR ORGANIZATION WILL SPEND ON COMPUTER HARDWARE, SOFTWARE, PERIPHERALS, AND SERVICES FOR YOUR LOCATION? (check one only)

- ☐ 01 Less than $10,000
- ☐ 02 $10,000 to $49,999
- ☐ 03 $50,000 to $99,999
- ☐ 04 $100,000 to $499,999
- ☐ 05 $500,000 to $999,999
- ☐ 06 $1,000,000 and Over

⑧ WHAT IS YOUR COMPANY'S YEARLY SALES REVENUE? (check one only)

- ☐ 01 $500, 000, 000 and above
- ☐ 02 $100, 000, 000 to $500, 000, 000
- ☐ 03 $50, 000, 000 to $100, 000, 000
- ☐ 04 $5, 000, 000 to $50, 000, 000
- ☐ 05 $1, 000, 000 to $5, 000, 000

⑨ WHAT LANGUAGES AND FRAMEWORKS DO YOU USE? (check all that apply)

- ☐ 01 Ajax
- ☐ 02 C
- ☐ 03 C++
- ☐ 04 C#
- ☐ 05 Hibernate
- ☐ 06 J++/J#
- ☐ 07 Java
- ☐ 08 JSP
- ☐ 09 .NET
- ☐ 10 Perl
- ☐ 11 PHP
- ☐ 12 PL/SQL
- ☐ 13 Python
- ☐ 14 Ruby/Rails
- ☐ 15 Spring
- ☐ 16 Struts
- ☐ 17 SQL
- ☐ 18 Visual Basic
- ☐ 98 Other

⑩ WHAT ORACLE PRODUCTS ARE IN USE AT YO SITE? (check all that apply)

ORACLE DATABASE
- ☐ 01 Oracle Database 11*g*
- ☐ 02 Oracle Database 10*g*
- ☐ 03 Oracle9*i* Database
- ☐ 04 Oracle Embedded Database (Oracle Lite, Times Ten, Berkeley DB)
- ☐ 05 Other Oracle Database Release

ORACLE FUSION MIDDLEWARE
- ☐ 06 Oracle Application Server
- ☐ 07 Oracle Portal
- ☐ 08 Oracle Enterprise Manager
- ☐ 09 Oracle BPEL Process Manager
- ☐ 10 Oracle Identity Management
- ☐ 11 Oracle SOA Suite
- ☐ 12 Oracle Data Hubs

ORACLE DEVELOPMENT TOOLS
- ☐ 13 Oracle JDeveloper
- ☐ 14 Oracle Forms
- ☐ 15 Oracle Reports
- ☐ 16 Oracle Designer
- ☐ 17 Oracle Discoverer
- ☐ 18 Oracle BI Beans
- ☐ 19 Oracle Warehouse Builder
- ☐ 20 Oracle WebCenter
- ☐ 21 Oracle Application Express

ORACLE APPLICATIONS
- ☐ 22 Oracle E-Business Suite
- ☐ 23 PeopleSoft Enterprise
- ☐ 24 JD Edwards EnterpriseOne
- ☐ 25 JD Edwards World
- ☐ 26 Oracle Fusion
- ☐ 27 Hyperion
- ☐ 28 Siebel CRM

ORACLE SERVICES
- ☐ 28 Oracle E-Business Suite On Demand
- ☐ 29 Oracle Technology On Demand
- ☐ 30 Siebel CRM On Demand
- ☐ 31 Oracle Consulting
- ☐ 32 Oracle Education
- ☐ 33 Oracle Support
- ☐ 98 Other
- ☐ 99 None of the Above

08014004